T0180228

Lecture Notes in Computer Science 12552

More information about this subseries at http://www.springer.com/series/7410

Rafael Pass · Krzysztof Pietrzak (Eds.)

Theory
of Cryptography

18th International Conference, TCC 2020
Durham, NC, USA, November 16–19, 2020
Proceedings, Part III

 Springer

Editors
Rafael Pass
Cornell Tech
New York, NY, USA

Krzysztof Pietrzak
Institute of Science and Technology Austria
Klosterneuburg, Austria

ISSN 0302-9743   ISSN 1611-3349   (electronic)
Lecture Notes in Computer Science
ISBN 978-3-030 64380-5   ISBN 978-3-030-64381-2   (eBook)
https://doi.org/10.1007/978-3-030-64381-2

LNCS Sublibrary: SL4 – Security and Cryptology

This Springer imprint is published by the registered company Springer Nature Switzerland AG
The registered company address is: Gewerbestrasse 11, 6330 Cham, Switzerland

Preface

The 18th Theory of Cryptography Conference (TCC 2020) was held virtually during November 16–19, 2020. It was sponsored by the International Association for Cryptologic Research (IACR). The general chair of the conference was Alessandra Scafuro.

TCC 2020 was originally planned to be co-located with FOCS 2020 in Durham, North Carolina, USA. Due to the COVID-19 pandemic both events were converted into virtual events, and were held on the same day at the same time. The authors uploaded videos of roughly 20 minutes prior to the conference, and at the conference had a 10-minute window to present a summary of their work and answer questions. The virtual event would not have been possible without the generous help of Kevin and Kay McCurley, and we would like to thank them wholeheartedly.

The conference received 167 submissions, of which the Program Committee (PC) selected 71 for presentation. Each submission was reviewed by at least four PC members. The 39 PC members (including PC chairs), all top researchers in the field, were helped by 226 external reviewers, who were consulted when appropriate. These proceedings consist of the revised version of the 71 accepted papers. The revisions were not reviewed, and the authors bear full responsibility for the content of their papers.

As in previous years, we used Shai Halevi's excellent Web-review software, and are extremely grateful to him for writing it, and for providing fast and reliable technical support whenever we had any questions.

This was the 7th year that TCC presented the Test of Time Award to an outstanding paper that was published at TCC at least eight years ago, making a significant contribution to the theory of cryptography, preferably with influence also in other areas of cryptography, theory, and beyond. This year the Test of Time Award Committee selected the following paper, published at TCC 2008: "Perfectly-Secure MPC with Linear Communication Complexity" by Zuzana Trubini and Martin Hirt. The Award Committee recognized this paper "for introducing hyper-invertible matrices to perfectly secure multiparty computation, thus enabling significant efficiency improvements and, eventually, constructions with minimal communication complexity."

We are greatly indebted to many people who were involved in making TCC 2020 a success. A big thanks to the authors who submitted their papers and to the PC members and external reviewers for their hard work, dedication, and diligence in reviewing the papers, verifying the correctness, and in-depth discussions. A special thanks goes to the general chair Alessandra Scafuro and the TCC Steering Committee.

October 2020

Rafael Pass
Krzysztof Pietrzak

Organization

General Chair

Alessandra Scafuro   North Carolina State University, USA

Program Chairs

Rafael Pass   Cornell Tech, USA
Krzysztof Pietrzak   IST Austria, Austria

Program Committee

Prabhanjan Ananth	University of California, Santa Barbara, USA
Marshall Ball	Columbia University, USA
Sonia Belaïd	CryptoExperts, France
Jeremiah Blocki	Purdue University, USA
Andrej Bogdanov	The Chinese University of Hong Kong, Hong Kong
Chris Brzuszka	Aalto University, Finland
Ignacio Cascudo	IMDEA Software Institute, Spain
Kai-Min Chung	Academia Sinica, Taiwan
Aloni Cohen	Boston University, USA
Ran Cohen	Northeastern University, USA
Nico Dottling	CISPA - Helmholtz Center for Information Security, Germany
Stefan Dziembowski	University of Warsaw, Poland
Oriol Farràs	Universitat Rovira i Virgili, Spain
Georg Fuchsbauer	TU Wien, Austria
Niv Gilboa	Ben-Gurion University of the Negev, Israel
Vipul Goyal	Carnegie Mellon University, USA
Mohammad Hajiabadi	University of California, Berkeley, USA
Justin Holmgren	NTT Research, USA
Zahra Jafargholi	Aarhus University, Denmark
Yael Tauman Kalai	Microsoft Research and MIT, USA
Seny Kamara	Brown University, USA
Dakshita Khurana	University of Illinois Urbana-Champaign, USA
Markulf Kohlweiss	The University of Edinburgh, UK
Ilan Komargodski	NTT Research, USA
Huijia Lin	University of Washington, USA
Mohammad Mahmoody	University of Virginia, USA
Jesper Buus Nielsen	Aarhus University, Denmark
Emmanuela Orsini	KU Leuven, Belgium
Sunoo Park	MIT and Harvard University, USA

Anat Paskin-Cherniavsky	Ariel University, Israel
Oxana Poburinnaya	Simons Institute for the Theory of Computing, USA
Silas Richelson	University of California, Riverside, USA
Alon Rosen	IDC Herzliya, Israel
Abhi Shelat	Northeastern University, USA
Nicholas Spooner	University of California, Berkeley, USA
Uri Stemmer	Ben-Gurion University of the Negev, Israel
Justin Thaler	Georgetown University, USA
Daniel Wichs	Northeastern University and NTT Research, USA
Eylon Yogev	Boston University, USA, and Tel Aviv University, Israel

External Reviewers

Hamza Abusalah	Yilei Chen	Rex Fernando
Amit Agarwal	Ilaria Chillotti	Ben Fisch
Archita Agarwal	Arka Rai Choudhuri	Cody Freitag
Divesh Aggarwal	Hao Chung	Shiuan Fu
Navid Alamati	Michele Ciampi	Tommaso Gagliardoni
Younes Talibi Alaoui	Katriel Cohn-Gordon	Chaya Ganesh
Bar Alon	Sandro Coretti	Sanjam Garg
Joel Alwen	Sandro Coretti-Drayton	Romain Gay
Joël Alwen	Henry Corrigan-Gibbs	Marilyn George
Miguel Ambrona	Geoffroy Couteau	Marios Georgiou
Ghous Amjad	Dana Dachman-Soled	Essam Ghadafi
Christian Badertscher	Hila Dahari	Alexandru Gheorghiu
Saikrishna Badrinarayanan	Jost Daniel	Satrajit Ghosh
	Pratish Datta	Aarushi Goel
James Bartusek	Bernardo David	Sasha Golovnev
Balthazar Bauer	Bernardo Machado David	Junqing Gong
Carsten Baum	Gareth Davies	Rishab Goyal
Alex Block	Akshay Degwekar	Daniel Grier
Alexander Block	Jack Doerner	Alex Grilo
Jonathan Bootle	Rafael Dowsley	Siyao Guo
Adam Bouland	Betul Durak	Iftach Haitner
Elette Boyle	Betül Durak	Britta Hale
Zvika Brakerski	Naomi Ephraim	Ariel Hamlin
Pedro Branco	Daniel Escudero	Adam Blatchley Hansen
Benedikt Bünz	Grzegorz Fabianski	Alexander Hartl
Alper Cakan	Islam Faisal	Carmit Hazay
Matteo Campanelli	Xiong Fan	Javier Herranz
Wouter Castryck	Song Fang	Kyle Hogan
Hubert Chan	Antonio Faonio	Thibaut Horel
Lijie Chen	Prastudy Fauzi	Yao-Ching Hsieh
Yanlin Chen	Serge Fehr	James Hulett

Shih-Han Hung
Rawane Issa
Håkon Jacobsen
Aayush Jain
Abhishek Jain
Ruta Jawale
Zhengzhong Jin
Fatih Kaleoglu
Chethan Kamath
Simon Holmgaard Kamp
Pihla Karanko
Shuichi Katsumata
Tomasz Kazana
Thomas Kerber
Fuyuki Kitagawa
Susumu Kiyoshima
Michael Klooß
Dima Kogan
Dmitry Kogan
Lisa Kohl
Yash Kondi
Yashvanth Kondi
Venkata Koppula
Ashutosh Kumar
Po-Chun Kuo
Thijs Laarhoven
Fabien Laguillaumie
Kasper Green Larsen
Eysa Lee
Seunghoon Lee
Yi Lee
Tancrède Lepoint
Xiao Liang
Chengyu Lin
Wei-Kai Lin
Yao-Ting Lin
Quanquan Liu
Tianren Liu
Alex Lombardi
Sébastien Lord
Julian Loss
George Lu
Ji Luo
Fermi Ma
Yi-Hsin Ma
Urmila Mahadev

Saeed Mahloujifar
Christian Majenz
Nikolaos Makriyannis
Giulio Malavolta
Mary Maller
Easwar Mangipudi
Nathan Manohar
Jeremias Mechler
Pierre Meyer
Tarik Moataz
Tomoyuki Morimae
Tamer Mour
Marta Mularczyk
Jörn Müller-Quade
Ryo Nishimaki
Olga Nissenbaum
Adam O'Neill
Maciej Obremski
Michele Orrù
Elena Pagnin
Georgios Panagiotakos
Omer Paneth
Alain Passelègue
Sikhar Patranabis
Alice Pellet–Mary
Rafael Del Pino
Rolando La Placa
Antoine Plouviez
Antigoni Polychroniadou
Sihang Pu
Chen Qian
Luowen Qian
Willy Quach
Jordi Ribes-González
Thomas Ricosset
Schuyler Rosefield
Dragos Rotaru
Lior Rotem
Sylvain Ruhault
Alexander Russell
Paul Rösler
Pratik Sarkar
Or Sattath
Sarah Scheffler
Adam Sealfon
Gil Segev

Ido Shahaf
Sina Shiehian
Omri Shmueli
Jad Silbak
Mark Simkin
Luisa Siniscalchi
Marjan Skrobot
Fang Song
Pratik Soni
Akshayaram Srinivasan
Ron Steinfeld
Patrick Struck
Marika Swanberg
Akira Takahashi
Aravind Thyagarajan
Rotem Tsabary
Yiannis Tselekounis
Prashant Vasudevan
Muthuramakrishnan
    Venkitasubramaniam
Daniele Venturi
Mikhail Volkhov
Philip Wadler
Hendrik Waldner
Mingyuan Wang
Tianhao Wang
Rachit Garg and
    Brent Waters
Hoeteck Wee
Weiqiang Wen
Jeroen van Wier
David Wu
Sophia Yakoubov
Takashi Yamakawa
Lisa Yang
Kevin Yeo
Michal Zajac
Mark Zhandry
Bingsheng Zhang
Chen-Da Liu Zhang
Hong-Sheng Zhou
Jiadong Zhu
Vassilis Zikas
Georgios Zirdelis

Contents – Part III

Universal Composition with Global Subroutines: Capturing Global Setup Within Plain UC

Christian Badertscher[1]($\boxtimes$) (iD), Ran Canetti[2], Julia Hesse[3], Björn Tackmann[4], and Vassilis Zikas[5]

[1] IOHK, Zurich, Switzerland
christian.badertscher@iohk.io
[2] Boston University, Boston, MA, USA
canetti@bu.edu
[3] IBM Research, Zurich, Switzerland
jhs@zurich.ibm.com
[4] DFINITY, Zurich, Switzerland
bjoern@dfinity.org
[5] University of Edinburgh, Edinburgh, UK
vzikas@inf.ed.ac.uk

Abstract. The Global and Externalized UC frameworks [Canetti-Dodis-Pass-Walfish, TCC 07] extend the plain UC framework to additionally handle protocols that use a "global setup", namely a mechanism that is also used by entities outside the protocol. These frameworks have broad applicability: Examples include public-key infrastructures, common reference strings, shared synchronization mechanisms, global blockchains, or even abstractions such as the random oracle. However, the need to work in a specialized framework has been a source of confusion, incompatibility, and an impediment to broader use.

We show how security in the presence of a global setup can be captured within the plain UC framework, thus significantly simplifying the treatment. This is done as follows:

- We extend UC-emulation to the case where both the emulating protocol π and the emulated protocol ϕ make subroutine calls to protocol γ that is accessible also outside π and ϕ. As usual, this notion considers only a single instance of ϕ or π (alongside γ).
- We extend the UC theorem to hold even with respect to the new notion of UC emulation. That is, we show that if π UC-emulates ϕ in the presence of γ, then $\rho^{\phi \to \pi}$ UC-emulates ρ for any protocol ρ, even when ρ uses γ directly, and in addition calls many instances of ϕ, all

C. Badertscher—Work done while author was at the University of Edinburgh, Scotland.
R. Canetti—Member of the CPIIS. Supported by NSF Awards 1931714, 1801564, 1414119, and the DARPA DEVE program.
B. Tackmann—Work partly done while author was at IBM Research – Zurich, supported in part by the European Union's Horizon 2020 research and innovation programme under grant agreement No. 780477 PRIViLEDGE.

R. Pass and K. Pietrzak (Eds.): TCC 2020, LNCS 12552, pp. 1–30, 2020.
https://doi.org/10.1007/978-3-030-64381-2_1

of which use the same instance of γ. We prove this extension using the existing UC theorem as a black box, thus further simplifying the treatment.

We also exemplify how our treatment can be used to streamline, within the plain UC model, proofs of security of systems that involve global set-up, thus providing greater simplicity and flexibility.

1 Introduction

Modular security analysis of cryptographic protocols calls for an iterative process, where in each iteration the analyst first partitions the given system into basic functional components, then separately specifies the security properties of each component, then demonstrates how the security of the overall system follows from the security of the components, and then proceeds to further partition each component. The key attraction here is the potential ability to analyze the security of each component once, in a simplified "in vitro" setting, and then re-use the asserted security guarantees in the various contexts in which this component is used.

A number of analytical frameworks have been devised over the years with this goal in mind, e.g. [MR91, Bea91, HM97, Can00, PW00, Can01, BPW04, Mau11, KMT20, HS16, CKKR19]. These frameworks allow representing protocols, tasks, and attacks, and also offer various composition operations and associated security-preserving composition theorems that substantiate the above analytical process. The overarching goal here is to have an analytical framework that is as expressive as possible, and at the same time allows for a nimble and effective de-compositional analytical process.

Modularity in these frameworks is obtained as follows. (We use here the terminology of the UC framework [Can01], but so far the discussion applies to all these frameworks.) We first define when a protocol π "emulates" another protocol ϕ. Ideally, this definition should consider a setting with only a single instance of π (or ϕ) and no other protocols. A general composition theorem then guarantees that if π *emulates* protocol ϕ, then for *any* protocol ρ, that makes "subroutine calls" to potentially multiple instances of ϕ, the protocol $\rho^{\phi \to \pi}$ emulates ρ, where $\rho^{\phi \to \pi}$ is the protocol that is essentially identical to ρ except that each subroutine call to an instance of ϕ is replaced with a subroutine call to an instance of π.

This composition theorem is indeed a powerful tool: It allows analyzing a protocol in a highly simplified setting that involves only a single instance of the protocol and no other components, and then deducing security in general multi-component systems. However, the general composition theorem can only be applied when protocols π and ϕ do not share any "module" with the calling protocol, ρ. That is, the theorem applies only when there is no module, or protocol, γ, such that γ is a subroutine of π or ϕ, and at the same time γ is used directly as a subroutine of ρ. Furthermore, when ρ calls multiple instances of ϕ, no module γ can be a subroutine of two different instances of ϕ.

This limitation has proven to be a considerable impediment when coming to analyze realistic systems, and in particular when trying to de-compose such system to smaller components as per the above methodology. Indeed, realistic systems often include some basic components that require trust in external entities or are expensive to operate. It then makes sense to minimize the number of such components and have them shared by as many other components as possible. Examples for such shared components include public-key infrastructure, long-lived signing modules, shared synchronization and timing mechanisms, common reference strings, and even more complex constructs such as blockchains and public repositories.

Overcoming this limitation turns out to take quite different forms, depending on the underlying model of computation. When the model of computation is static, namely the identities, programs, and connectivity graph of computing elements are fixed throughout the computation, extending the basic composition theorem to account for shared (or, "global") subroutines is relatively straightforward. (Examples include the restricted model of [Can20, Section 2], as well as [BPW07,KMT20].) However, restricting ourselves to a static model greatly limits the applicability of the framework, and more importantly the power of the composition theorem. Indeed, static models are not conducive to capturing prevalent situations where multiple instances of a simple protocol are invoked concurrently and dynamically, and where all sessions share some global infrastructure; examples include secure communication sessions, payment protocols, cryptocurrencies, automated contracts.

In order to be able to benefit from compositional analysis with shared modules even when the analyzed protocols are dynamic in nature, new composition theorems and frameworks were formulated, such as the Joint-State UC (JUC) theorem [CR03] and later the Generalized UC (GUC) and Extended UC (EUC) models [CDPW07].

However the GUC modeling is significantly more complex than the plain UC model. Furthermore, the extended model needs to be used throughout the analysis, even in parts that are unrelated to the global subroutine. In particular, working in the GUC model requires directly analyzing a protocol in a setting where it runs alongside other protocols. This stands in contrast to the plain UC model of protocol execution, which consists only of a single instance of the analyzed protocol, and no other "moving parts." Additionally, while the basic UC framework has been updated and expanded several times in recent years, the GUC model has not been updated since its inception. Furthermore, the claimed relationship between statements made in the EUC framework and statements made in the GUC framework has some apparent inaccuracies.[1]

Our Contribution. We simplify the treatment of universal composition with global subroutines for fully dynamic protocols. Specifically, We show how to

---

[1] Indeed, there is at the moment no completely consistent composition theorem for EUC protocols. For instance, the notion of a challenge protocol is not sufficiently well specified. Also the treatment of external identities is lacking. This is discussed further in [BCH+20].

capture GUC-emulation with respect to global subroutines, and provide a theorem akin to the GUC theorem, all within the plain UC modeling. This theorem, which we call the Universal Composition with Global Subroutines (UCGS) theorem, allows for fully reaping all the (de-)compositional benefits of the GUC modeling, while keeping the model simple, minimizing the formalism, and enabling smooth transition between components.

We present our results in two steps. First, we present the modeling and theorem within the restricted model of computation of [Can20, Section 2]. Indeed, here the GUC and UCGS modeling is significantly less expressive - but it introduces the basic approach, and is almost trivial to formulate and prove. Next we explain the challenges involved in applying this approach to the full-fledged UC framework, and describe how we handle them. This is where most of the difficulty - and benefit - of this work lies.

Let us first briefly recall UC security within that restricted model. The model postulates a static system where the basic computing elements (called *machines*) send information to each other via fixed channels (or, ports). That is, machines have unique identities, and each machine has a set of machine identities with which it can communicate. Within each machine, each channel is labeled as either *input* or *output*. A system is a collection of machines where the communication sets are globally consistent, namely if machine M can send information to machine M' with channel labeled input (resp., output) then the system contains a machine M' that can send information labeled output (resp., input) to M. In this case we say that M' is a subroutine (resp., caller) of M.

A protocol is a set π of machines with consistent labeling as above, except that some machines in π may have output channels to machines which are not part of π. These channels are the *external channels* of π. The machines in π that have external channels are called the *top level machines* of π.

An execution of a protocol π with an environment machine $\mathcal{Z}$ and an adversary machine $\mathcal{A}$ is an execution of the system that consists of $(\pi \cup \{\mathcal{Z}, \mathcal{A}\})$, where the external channels of π are connected to $\mathcal{Z}$, and $\mathcal{A}$ is connected to all machines in the system via a channel (port) named *backdoor*. The execution starts with an activation of $\mathcal{Z}$ and continues via a sequence of activations until $\mathcal{Z}$ halts with some binary decision value. Let $\text{EXEC}_{\pi,\mathcal{A},\mathcal{Z}}$ denote the random variable describing the decision bit of $\mathcal{Z}$ following an execution with π and $\mathcal{A}$. We say that protocol π UC-emulates protocol ϕ if for any polytime adversary $\mathcal{A}$ there exists a polytime adversary $\mathcal{S}$ such that for any polytime $\mathcal{Z}$ we have $\text{EXEC}_{\pi,\mathcal{A},\mathcal{Z}} \approx \text{EXEC}_{\phi,\mathcal{S},\mathcal{Z}}$.

The universal composition operation in this model is a simple machine replacement operation: Let ρ be a protocol, let ϕ be a subset of the machines in ρ that is a protocol in and of itself, and let π be a protocol that has the same set of external identities as ϕ, and where π and $\rho \setminus \phi$ are *identity-disjoint*, i.e. the identities of the machines in π are disjoint from the identities of the machines in $\rho \setminus \phi$. Then the composed protocol $\rho^{\phi \to \pi}$ is defined as $(\rho \setminus \phi) \cup \pi$. The UC theorem states that if π UC-emulates ϕ, then for any ρ such that π and $\rho \setminus \phi$ are identity-disjoint we have that $\rho^{\phi \to \pi}$ UC-emulates ρ. (Notice that here the

UC operation replaces only a single "protocol instance". Indeed, here there is no natural concept of "multiple instances" of a protocol.)

In this restricted model, protocol γ is a global subroutine of a protocol π' if γ is a subroutine of π', and at the same time some of the top level machines of π' are actually in γ. Said otherwise, π' consists of two parts, γ and $\pi = \pi' \setminus \gamma$, where both π and γ include machines that take inputs directly from outside π', and in addition some machines in γ take inputs also from machines in π. Observe that this structure allows γ to be a subroutine also of protocols other than π.

The Universal Composition with Global Subroutines (UCGS) theorem for such protocols takes the following form: Let ρ, π, ϕ and γ be such that $\pi' = \pi \cup \gamma$ and $\phi' = \phi \cup \gamma$ are protocols where π' UC-emulates ϕ' (and in addition π and $\rho \setminus \phi$ are identity-disjoint). Then the protocol $((\rho \setminus \phi') \cup \pi')$ UC-emulates ρ. Observe, however, that in this model the UCGS theorem follows immediately from the standard UC theorem: Indeed, $(\rho \setminus \phi') \cup \pi' = (\rho \setminus \phi) \cup \pi = \rho^{\phi \to \pi}$. See illustration in Fig. 1.

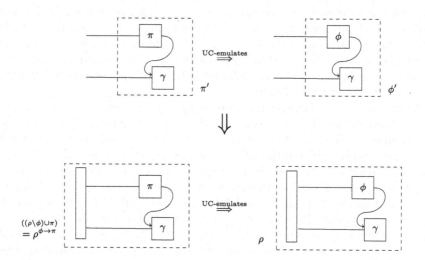

Fig. 1. UC with Global Subroutines (UCGS) in the restricted setting of [Can20, Section 2]: Protocol γ is a global subroutine of protocol π' if γ takes input from $\pi = \pi' \setminus \gamma$ and also from outside π'. Then plain UC theorem already guarantees that if π' UC-realizes protocol ϕ', where $\phi' = \phi \cup \gamma$, then for any ρ that calls ϕ and γ, the protocol $((\rho \setminus \phi) \cup \pi) = \rho^{\phi \to \pi}$ UC-emulates ρ.

Extending the Treatment to the Full-Fledged UC Framework. While formulating UC with global subroutines within the above basic model is indeed simple, it is also of limited applicability: While it is in principle possible to use security in this model to infer security in systems that involve multiple instances of the analyzed protocol, inference is still limited to static systems where all identities and connectivity is fixed beforehand. The formalism breaks down when attempting to express systems where connectivity is more dynamic in nature, as prevalent in reality. In order to handle such situations, the full-fledged UC framework has a very different underlying model of distributed computation, allowing machines to form communication patterns and generate other machines in a dynamic way throughout the computation. Crucially, even in dynamic and evolving systems, the framework allows delineating those sets of processes that make up "protocol instances," and then allows using single-instance-security of protocols to deduce security of the entire system.

To gain this level of expressiveness, the framework introduces a number of constructs. One such construct is the introduction of the session identifier (SID) field, that allows identifying the machines (processes) in a protocol instance. Specifically, an *instance* (or, *session*) of a protocol π with SID s, at a given point during an execution of a system is the set of machines that have program π and SID s. The *extended session* of π with SID s consists of the machines of this session, their subroutines, and the transitive closure of all the machines that were created by the these subroutines during the execution so far. Another added construct is the concept of *subroutine respecting protocols*. Informally, protocol π is subroutine respecting if, in any extended session s of π, the only machines, that provide output to, or responds to inputs from, machines outside this extended instance, are the actual "main" machines of this instance (namely the machines with code π and SID s). Machines in the extended session, which are not the main machines, only take input from and provide output to other machines of this extended instance.

While the SIDs and the restriction to subroutine respecting protocols are key to the ability of the UC framework to model prevalent dynamic situations, they appear to get in the way of the ability to prove UC with global subroutines. In particular, simply applying the UC theorem as in the basic model is no longer possible. Indeed (referring to Fig. 1), neither π nor ϕ are subroutine respecting, and the constructs π' and ϕ', which were legitimate protocols in the basic model, are not legitimate protocols in the full-fledged model, since they don't have the same program or SID. Note that this is not just a technicality: In a dynamically evolving system with multiple instances of π and γ there can be many possible ways of delineating protocol instances, and so the composition theorem may not even be well-defined!

We get around this barrier by providing a mechanism for encapsulating an instance of ϕ and one (or more) instances of γ within a single "transparent envelope protocol" $M[\phi, \gamma]$ such that a single instance of $M[\phi, \gamma]$ has the same effect as the union of the instance of ϕ and the instances of γ used by this instance of ϕ. To accomplish that, we extend the shell and body mechanism that's already used in the UC framework to enforce subroutine respecting behavior and to implement the UC operation. A similar encapsulation is done for π and γ. Furthermore, the transformation guarantees that both $M[\phi, \gamma]$ and $M[\pi, \gamma]$ are now subroutine respecting, even though neither ϕ nor π are. This enables us to invoke the UC theorem (this time in the full-fledged UC model) to obtain our main result:

Main Theorem (Informal). *Assume π, ϕ, γ are such that $\mathsf{M}[\pi, \gamma]$ UC-emulates $\mathsf{M}[\phi, \gamma]$. Then for (essentially) any protocol ρ we have that $\rho^{\phi \to \pi}$ UC-emulates ρ.*

Our result follows the spirit of the UC theorem: It allows using the security of a single instance of π (in the presence of γ) to deduce security of a system that involves multiple instances of π (again, in the presence of γ). Said otherwise, the theorem allows dissecting a complex, dynamic, multi-instance system into simple, individual components, analyze the security of a single instance of a component, and deduce security of the overall system - even in the prevalent cases where multiple (or even all) of the individual components are using the same global subroutines. See depiction in Fig. 2.

We prove the new composition theorem in a modular way. That is, our proof makes black-box use of the plain UC theorem, thus avoiding the need to re-prove it from scratch, as in the GUC and EUC modeling.

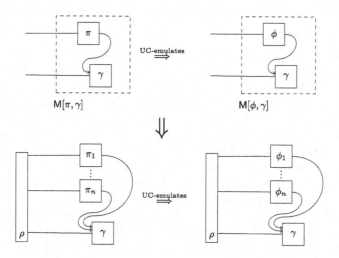

Fig. 2. UC with global subroutines in the full-fledged UC framework: We encapsulate a single instance of π plus one or more instances of γ within a single instance of a protocol $\mathsf{M}[\pi, \gamma]$ that remains transparent to π and γ and is in addition subroutine respecting. We then show that if $\mathsf{M}[\pi, \gamma]$ UC-emulates $\mathsf{M}[\pi, \phi]$ then the protocol $\rho^{\phi \to \pi}$ UC-emulates ρ for essentially any ρ—even when ρ and all the instances of ϕ (resp., π) use the same global instances of γ.

Demonstrating the Use of Our Treatment. We showcase our UCGS theorem in two settings. A first setting is that of analyzing the security of signature-based authentication and key exchange protocols in a setting where the signature module is global and in particular shared by multiple instances of the authentication module, as well as by arbitrary other protocols. This setting was studied in [CSV16] within the GUC framework. We demonstrate how our formalism and results can be used to cast the treatment of [CSV16] within the plain UC framework. The resulting treatment is clearer, simpler, and more general. For instance, in our treatment, the Generalized Functionality Composition theorem from [CSV16] turns out to be a direct implication of the standard UC composition theorem.

The other setting is that of composable analysis of blockchains, where assuming global subroutines is essential and permeates all the works in the literature. In a nutshell, in [BMTZ17], a generic ledger was described which, as proved there, is GUC-emulated by (a GUC version of) the Bitcoin backbone protocol [GKL15] in the presence of a global clock functionality used to allow the parties to remain synchronized. This ledger was, in turn, used within another protocol, also having access to the global clock, in order to implement a cryptocurrency-style ledger, which, for example, prevents double spending. [BMTZ17] then argues that using the GUC composition theorem one can replace, in the latter construction, the generic ledger by the backbone protocol. As we demonstrate here, such a generic replacement faces several issues due to inaccuracies in GUC. Instead, we show how to apply our theorem to directly derive the above statement in the UC framework.

Composition with Global Subroutines in Other General Frameworks. Several other general frameworks for defining security of protocols use a static machine model akin to the restricted variant of the UC model described above, where machines communicate only via connections ("ports") that are fixed ahead of time, and the only way to compose systems is by way of connecting them using a pre-defined set of ports. (Examples include the reactive simulatability of [PW00, BPW07], the IITM framework of Küsters and Thuengertal [KMT20], the abstract cryptography of Maurer and Renner [MR11], the iUC framework of Camenisch et al. [CKKR19].) In these frameworks, the single-instance global-state composition theorem immediately follows from plain secure composition, in very much the same way as the single-instance UCGS theorem follows immediately from the plain UC theorem in the restricted UC model (see Fig. 1).

However, these frameworks do not provide mechanisms for modular analysis of systems where the de-composition of the system to individual modules is determined dynamically during the course of the computation. In particular, composition with global state in these frameworks does not address this important case either. In contrast, as described above, this fully dynamic, multi-instance case is the focus of this work. So far, this case has been addressed only in the GUC and EUC frameworks, as well as in the work of Hofheinz and Shoup [HS16] which proposes an extension of their model to accommodate certain specific ideal functionalities as distinguished machines.

We note that the IITM framework of Küsters and Thuengertal [KMT20] (as well as the recent iUC model [CKKR19] that builds on top of the IITM framework) does contain an additional construct that allows machines to interact in a somewhat dynamically determined way: While each machine has a fixed set of other machines that it can interact with, and protocols are defined as fixed sets of machines that have globally consistent "communication sets", the framework additionally allows unboundedly many instances of each machine, where all instances have the same identity, code, and "communication set". Furthermore, if the communication sets of machines M, M' allows them to communicate, then each instance of M can communicate with each instance of M'. Indeed, this additional feature enables the IITM framework to express systems where the communication is arbitrarily dynamic.

However, this extra feature appears to fall short of enabling fully modular analysis of such dynamic systems. Indeed, the IITM framework still can only compose systems along the static, a-priori fixed boundaries of machine ports. This means that systems that include multiple instances of some protocol, where the boundaries of the individual instances are dynamically determined, cannot be analyzed in a modular way—rather, the framework only allows for direct analysis of all protocol instances at once, en bloc. This of course holds even in the presence of global subroutines. Example of such systems include secure pairwise communication systems where the communicating parties are determined dynamically, block-chain applications where different quorums of participants join to make decisions at different times, etc. See e.g.. [BCL+11, CSV16, GHM+17].

In contrast, the goal of this work is to allow de-composing such systems to individual instances, deducing the security of the overall composite system from the security of an individual instance—and carrying this through even when many (or all) instances use the same global subroutines (see Fig. 2).

A related work by Camenisch et al. [CDT19] introduces a new UC variant that they call multi-protocol UC (MUC) and that allows the environment to instantiate multiple challenge protocols that can interact with each other. It is an interesting future research direction to formulate this more general type of UC execution following the approach taken in this work, i.e., to model it following standard UC and making black-box use of the UC composition theorem to derive a composition theorem for this type of protocol.

2   Formulating and Proving the UCGS Theorem

In this section, we formulate and prove the main result of this work. In Sect. 2.1 we present the transformation that takes protocols π and γ and constructs a single, transparent encapsulation protocol $\mathsf{M}[\pi, \gamma]$ that behaves like a single instance of π along with one (or more) instances of a "global subroutine protocol" γ. We formulate UC emulation with Global Subroutines in Sect. 2.2, state the Universal Composition theorem with Global Subroutines composition in Sect. 2.3 and conclude with remarks in Sect. 2.4. We also provide a proof sketch. See [BCH+20] for the full proof.

2.1   Treating Multiple Protocols as a Single Protocol

We start by defining the transformation that takes two protocols π and γ and combines them into a single protocol $\mu = \mathsf{M}[\pi, \gamma]$, such that one instance of μ behaves like one instance of π and one or more instances of γ, and where the instances of γ take inputs both from the instance of π within μ, and from outside μ. We refer to μ as the *management protocol*.

The goal of the construction is to ensure that an instance of protocol μ presents the exact same behavior as one instance of π alongside one (or more) instances of γ, while at the same time making sure that, from the point of view of the basic UC framework, μ remains a subroutine-respecting protocol. This will mean that incoming communication to μ specifies a session ID for μ, plus a session identifier for either the instance of π or an instance of γ. The input is then forwarded internally either to the instance of π or to the appropriate instance of γ. Outgoing communication is handled similarly. Note that it is important to make sure that the (virtual) instances of π and γ receive communication that is formatted exactly as it would be, were it the case that π and γ are independent machines. (This is needed so that the behavior of π and γ will remain unchanged.) See depiction in Fig. 3.

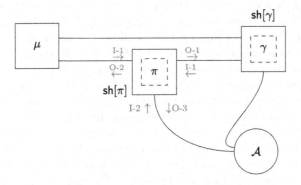

Fig. 3. The three main components of our management protocol $\mu = \mathsf{M}[\pi, \gamma]$ handling access to π and γ, both equipped with shells $\mathsf{sh}[\cdot]$. For $\mathsf{sh}[\pi]$, different types of incoming and outgoing messages are indicated in gray.

In order to allow black-box use of the UC composition theorem in the proof of our new composition theorem, we need to make sure that an instance of μ mimics the execution of a *single* instance of π (alongside one or more instances of γ). That is, μ must make sure that the various machines of an instance of μ maintain a single, consistent virtual instance of π. To maintain the necessary information about the execution, we allow the management protocol μ to make use of a *directory ITI* similar to the one used to ensure the subroutine-exposing property. That is, we embed a special ITI called *execution graph directory* in the operation of the management protocol (and shells) that acts as a central accumulator of knowledge.[2]

---

[2] While there are alternative solutions such as an extra shell propagating information about the execution graph, the directory appears to be a technically simple solution for our transformation. Our transformation is a proof technique, and as such the transformed protocol is not meant to be deployed in reality (where one may argue that such a central entity is unrealistic).

We now detail the execution graph directory for the structured protocol μ. The following generic shell mechanism—implemented by an additional, outermost shell of μ and all its subroutines—makes sure that this outermost shell layer maintains information about the induced execution graph as well as additional auxiliary information extracted from the underlying protocol (i.e. the body in the view of this additional shell). Let $\mathsf{pid}_{\mathrm{egDIR}}$ be an exclusive identifier, i.e., an identifier that never appears in any execution of the base protocol. Assume the session identifier is sid.

- The ITI with special identifier $(\mu, \mathsf{sid} \| \mathsf{pid}_{\mathrm{egDIR}})$ never activates its body and the shell processes three types of requests: first, when activated with input (REGISTER, aux) from an ITI M, it stores the entry (M, aux) in an ordered list (initially empty) unless M is already recorded in the list. Second, when activated with input (INVOKE, M', aux) from an already registered ITI M and ITI M' is not yet registered, then record $(M \rightarrow M')$. Also, record (M', aux) unless M' is already registered. The return value to M in both cases is the trivial output ok. The party allows any registered ITI M to query the stored list and ignores any message on the backdoor tape.
- For any other ITI running in this instance, when activated for the first time, the shell sends (REGISTER, aux) to ITI $(\mu, \mathsf{sid} \| \mathsf{pid}_{\mathrm{egDIR}})$ where aux can denote any auxiliary information. (Note that reveal-sender id and forced-write flags are set). When receiving ok it resumes processing its first activation by activating its body (which in structured protocols might be another shell oblivious of the above interaction).
- For any other ITI running in this instance, when the shell processes an external write request from its body to an ITI M, it sends (INVOKE, M, aux) to ITI $(\mu, \mathsf{sid} \| \mathsf{pid}_{\mathrm{egDIR}})$ where aux can denote any auxiliary information, before resuming with processing the external write request.

By exclusivity of $\mathsf{pid}_{\mathrm{egDIR}}$, the shell operates in an oblivious fashion from the point of view of the body. Since the shell only talks to $\mathsf{pid}_{\mathrm{egDIR}}$, this in turn is even oblivious to the environment and the adversary.

In fact, this is not entirely obvious: while no interaction via the backdoor tape indeed means that the adversary can neither corrupt nor extract information from the directory, another corrupted ITI in the system might get information from $\mathsf{pid}_{\mathrm{egDIR}}$ via a normal query and give the result to the adversary. This, however, is not possible: in UC, model-related instructions are organized in shell layers, where each shell is unaware of the outer shells, and treats the inner shells as part of the body. Now, the shell layer describing the model-related instructions to communicate with directories is outside of the shell implementing the corruption layer and therefore, the corruption layer is unaware of the directory. For more details, see [Can20, Section 5.1]. We note that this observation is already crucial for the standard UC composition theorem and not novel for our work, because corruptions must not invalidate the subroutine-exposing property of a protocol and hence corruptions should not interfere with the subroutine-exposing shell (or the shell introduced by the UC operator).

To conclude, the above mechanism is used by $M[\pi, \gamma]$ and its subsidiaries $sh[\cdot]$ in the following way: first, whenever a new machine with code $M[\cdot]$ is about to spawn an instance of π, it registers with the directory and defines as auxiliary input the extended identity of the instance of π it is going to spawn (and can also halt if it sees that another session already started). Second, the machines running code $sh[\cdot]$ use the INVOKE calls and put as auxiliary input the information $eid_{src} \to eid_{dest}$ of the virtual ITIs of $sh[\cdot]$ to additionally store the invocation graph of the main instance of π which in particular allows to infer what the (virtual) main instance of π is (see below for why this is important). In particular, all ITIs in the extended session of $M[\pi, \gamma]$ use the same execution graph directory ITI. To see that we get all properties we need from this, we refer to Proposition 1.

We now give a formal definition of $M[\pi, \gamma]$. The construction uses the body and shell formalism from [Can20].

The Management Protocol. In a nutshell, $M[\pi, \gamma]$ is a standard UC protocol that works as follows:

- $M[\pi, \gamma]$ exposes its subroutine structure to a directory ITI (which the environment can access) and its invocation graph to an additional execution graph directory ITI as discussed above to ensure that $M[\pi, \gamma]$ is subroutine respecting.
- $M[\pi, \gamma]$ can be invoked with an arbitrary session identifier. It allows the environment to invoke exactly one (top-level) instance of π with a freely chosen session identifier (note that addressing this "challenge protocol" is done in an abstract manner by using an identifier MAIN). Additionally, arbitrarily many instances of γ (again with arbitrary session identifiers) can be invoked (again the addressing is done in an abstract fashion using identifier GLOBAL).
- When an ITI running $M[\pi, \gamma]$, say with party ID pid, provides input to π in session s, then it wraps this input and invokes the ITI with code $sh[\pi]$, party id pid, and a session ID that encodes s. This ITI unwraps the received content and provides it to the main party pid of π in session s. A similar mechanism happens between any two machines to ensure that this instance of π is oblivious of this overlay.
- The machines running $sh[\pi]$ (resp. $sh[\gamma]$) detect, using the execution graph directory, when a "main party of π (resp. γ)" provides subroutine output to an external party, and can then provide this output to the correct main party $M[\pi, \gamma]$ which delivers it to the environment. Note that when $M[\pi, \gamma]$ delivers such outputs to the environment, it only reveals the party ID and session ID, and whether the source was the global subroutine (using identifier GLOBAL) or the single invoked instance (using identifier MAIN). Recall that the UC control function plays a similar role. We note in passing that $M[\pi, \gamma]$ can ensure that at most one session of π is invoked by the concept of the execution graph directory and block any attempt to create a new session of π if one exists already.
- $M[\pi, \gamma]$ refuses to communicate with the adversary, i.e., it does not communicate over the backdoor tape and is hence also incorruptible.

In order to map this to a program, we quickly recall the message passing mechanism in UC. UC uses the external-write mechanism via which a machine can instruct the control function to invoke a machine with a given input on one of three tapes. Messages are either written on the input tape (e.g., when a party calls a subsidiary), or on the subroutine-output tape (e.g., when a subsidiary returns an output to a caller), or on the backdoor tape (which only models the interaction with the adversary). Therefore, our transformation has to take care to route all the messages of the "wrapped" instance of π to the correct machines by taking care of inputs, subroutine outputs, and backdoor messages.

Code of Transformation. The formal description of the management protocol $M[\pi, \gamma]$, which is parameterized by two ITMs π and γ, as well as the code of the associated shell of the transformation, denoted sh[code] that takes as parameters the ITM code and is a structured protocol that runs code as its body, are provided in Appendix A.

Runtime Considerations as a Standard UC Protocol. The protocols generated by $M[\cdot]$ are standard UC protocols executed by an environment $\mathcal{Z}$. The run-time of $M[\cdot]$ and sh$[\cdot]$ deserves further discussion. Recall that in a parameterized system, each ITI only starts executing after receiving import at least k—where k is the security parameter. That means when $M[\cdot]$ is first invoked it requires import k to before executing, the execution graph directory requires additional import k, and the sub-protocol sh$[\pi]$ or sh$[\gamma]$ to which the message is directed also requires import k before executing. We define $M[\cdot]$ such that it begins executing only after receiving import at least $3k$; this ensures that the initial operation has sufficient import to complete. The further operations performed by $M[\cdot]$ and the shell sh of π and γ are only administrative such as copying and routing messages between ITIs, which means that they can be accounted for by slightly increasing the involved polynomials.

An Alternative Management Protocol. We note that defining $M[\pi, \gamma]$ so that the main parties of an instance of $M[\pi, \gamma]$ consist of ITIs that run exclusively shell code, and where the ITIs that have body π or γ are subroutines of these main parties of $M[\pi, \gamma]$, is a design choice that was made mainly for clarity of exposition and to clearly delineate the various parts of the management protocol. Alternatively, one can define a different management protocol, $M[\pi, \gamma]'$, where the code of the main ITIs of $M[\pi, \gamma]$ becomes part of the shell code of the ITIs whose body runs either π or γ. That is, the main parties of an instance of $M[\pi, \gamma]'$ will be the union of the main parties of the relevant top-level instance of π, along with the main parties of the relevant top-level instances of γ. One advantage of this formalism is that there are no additional management-only ITIs, and so the runtime issues mentioned in the previous paragraph do not come up. In addition, we believe that the restriction to regular setups can be relaxed. Additional details are provided in [BCH+20].

2.2   UC Emulation with Global Subroutines

We now define a variant of UC emulation that intends to capture, within the plain UC model, the notion of EUC-emulation from [CDPW07]. Namely, we say what it means for a protocol π to UC-emulate another protocol ϕ, in the case where either π or ϕ or both are using another protocol γ as subroutine, where γ can be accessed as subroutine of other protocols, i.e., is "global" or "shared".

Definition 1. (UC emulation with global subroutines). *Let π, ϕ and γ be protocols. We say that π ξ-UC-emulates ϕ in the presence of γ if protocol $M[\pi, \gamma]$ ξ-UC-emulates protocol $M[\phi, \gamma]$.*

Note that in the above, ξ can be any identity bound as of standard UC. Recall that it is a tool to get more fine-grained security statements and technically restricts the environment to interact with the protocol instances π and γ in a certain way.

Our definition of UC-emulation in the presence of a global subroutine is very general, and we need further terminology in preparation for the conditions under which the composition theorem applies. Consider the case where we want to analyze security of multiple instances of a protocol π which individually are subroutine respecting except that they all call a global subroutine γ. In the terminology of [CDPW07], such protocols are called *γ-subroutine respecting*. We generalize their definition and allow for more than one instance of γ.

Definition 2 (γ-subroutine respecting). *A protocol π is called γ-subroutine respecting if the four conditions of the standard subroutine respecting property required from any (sub-)party of some instance of π are relaxed as follows:*

- *the conditions do not apply to those sub-parties of instance s that also belong to some extended session s' of protocol γ;*
- *(sub-)parties of s may pass input to machines that belong to some extended session s' of protocol γ, even if those machines are not yet part of the extended instance of s.*

While the definition above allows π to violate subroutine respecting through subroutines with a code that is also used by γ, we are only interested in protocols π where subsidiaries only communicate with outside protocols if they belong to the subroutine γ. To this end, we will only consider γ-subroutine-respecting protocols π where γ is itself subroutine respecting.

For our composition theorem to hold, we must impose a light technical condition on the shared subroutine. The condition states that (a) a shared subroutine does not spawn new ITIs by providing subroutine output to them, and (b) the shared subroutine may not invoke the outside protocol as a subroutine. On a high level, this prevents that the shared subroutine itself spawns new higher-level sessions. On a technical level, the composition theorem relies on a hybrid argument that would not work if the shared subroutine spawns, for example, new sessions for which it is not decidable in a dynamic fashion whether or not they actually belong to the main instance of the protocol under consideration. To our knowledge, all global setups used in the literature satisfy these restrictions. For example, a global CRS does not output the reference string to parties who never asked for it, a global ledger requires parties to register before participating in the protocol, and a global clock only tells the time on demand. An example of a hypothetical functionality that violates this condition is a global channel functionality that outputs a message to a receiver whose extended identity can be freely chosen by the sender.

Definition 3 (Regular setup). *Let ϕ, γ be protocols. We say that γ is a ϕ-regular setup if, in any execution, the main parties of an instance of γ do not invoke a new ITI of ϕ via a message destined for the subroutine output tape, and do not have an ITI with code ϕ as subsidiary.*

As will become clear in Proposition 1, when considering a protocol ϕ that is γ-subroutine respecting, where γ itself is ϕ-regular and subroutine respecting, then we naturally have a clean interaction between ϕ and "a global subroutine" γ without any unexpected artifacts. For example, γ does not initiate new ITIs with code ϕ, neither as new protocol sessions "outside of γ" nor as proper subroutines of γ itself.

We next state the useful proposition that our transformation is by default subroutine respecting and preserves the behavior of the involved protocols in the following sense: Let π, γ be as before, and let α be a protocol that invokes at most one session of π. Let $\widehat{\alpha}$ be the protocol that executes α as a virtual ITI within a shell. Let sid_M be an otherwise unused SID.

- When α provides input m to ITI eid_{dest} with code $\text{code} \in \{\pi, \gamma\}$, then $\widehat{\alpha}$ instead provides input $((m, \text{eid}_{\text{src}}), \text{eid}'_{\text{dest}})$ to $M[\pi, \gamma]$ with SID sid_M, where eid_{src} is the extended identity of the virtual instance of α and $\text{eid}'_{\text{dest}}$ equals eid_{dest} except that its code-field code' is set to MAIN if $\text{code} = \pi$ and to GLOBAL if $\text{code} = \gamma$ (and results in the same subroutine being invoked as α does).
- When $\widehat{\alpha}$ obtains subroutine output $((m, \text{eid}_{\text{src}}), \text{eid}_{\text{dest}})$ from $M[\pi, \gamma]$ with SID sid_M, where eid_{dest} is the extended identity of the virtual instance of α, then $\widehat{\alpha}$ emulates subroutine output m from eid_{src} to α, overwriting code MAIN of eid_{src} with π and code GLOBAL with γ.

Proposition 1 ($M[\pi, \gamma]$ is subroutine respecting and preserves behavior). *Let γ be subroutine respecting and π be γ-subroutine respecting. Then the protocol $M[\pi, \gamma]$ is subroutine respecting. In addition, let γ be π-regular, and let α be a protocol that invokes at most one subroutine with code π. Denote by $\widehat{\alpha}$ the transformed protocol described above. Then the transcript established by the set of virtual ITIs in an execution of some environment with $\widehat{\alpha}$ is identical to the transcript established by the set of ITIs induced by the environment that has the same random tape but interacts with α.*

The proof is deferred to [BCH+20].

2.3 Universal Composition with Global Subroutines

We are now ready to state a composition theorem that lets us replace protocol instances in the presence of a global setup. See Fig. 4 for a graphical depiction.

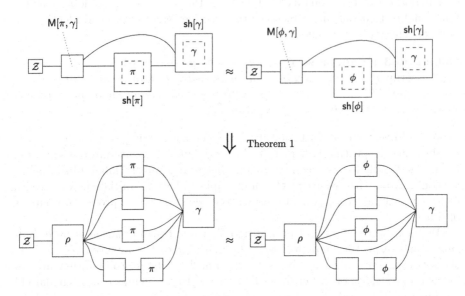

Fig. 4. A graphical depiction of our composition theorem in the presence of global setups. **Top:** π UC-emulates ϕ (Definition 1). **Bottom:** Replacement of ϕ by π in some context protocol ρ. See Theorem 1 for the assumptions made on ρ, π and γ for replacement to go through. Empty boxes indicate subroutines of ρ that are not π or ϕ.

Theorem 1 (Universal Composition with Global Subroutines – UCGS Theorem). *Let ρ, ϕ, π, γ be subroutine-exposing protocols, where γ is a ϕ-regular setup and subroutine respecting, ϕ, π are γ-subroutine respecting and ρ is (π, ϕ, ξ)-compliant and $(\pi, \mathsf{M}[\mathsf{code}, \gamma], \xi)$-compliant for $\mathsf{code} \in \{\phi, \pi\}$. Assume π ξ-UC-emulates ϕ in the presence of γ, then $\rho^{\phi \to \pi}$ UC-emulates ρ.*

In line with the run-time discussion for $\mathsf{M}[\cdot]$, protocol ρ only starts executing after receiving import at least $4k$. This ensures that, during the execution, the modified version of ρ (which we refer to as ϑ in the proof) has a sufficient run-time budget to accommodate the creation of the additional ITI $\mathsf{M}[\mathsf{code}, \gamma]$, its execution graph directory, as well as an additional directory introduced by the proof technique in this theorem.

Proof (outline). In the spirit of our overall approach, we aim at applying the UC composition theorem instead of reproving composition from scratch. Thus, we choose the following high level structure of the proof. We modify each invocation of ϕ within ρ separately. For each $i = 1, \ldots, n$, we first rewrite ρ such that the management protocol $M[\phi, \gamma]$ is invoked instead of the i-th ϕ. Then, we replace ϕ with π within this instance of the management protocol. This is done by invoking the UC composition theorem. Afterwards, we remove the management protocol instance again and let ρ instead call π directly. All modifications are oblivious from the perspective of the environment. The full proof can be found in [BCH+20]. □

We point out that our composition proof makes it explicit that no changes to the concrete interaction between ϕ (resp. π) and the instances of the global subroutine γ are needed. This is important point to consider, since often all instances of ϕ (resp.π) within ρ would share the same instance (or a fixed number of instances) of γ and hence our theorem shows that this behavior is preserved. Such specific cases (where a bounded number of instances of γ can be assumed to exist) follow as a special case of our treatment.

2.4   On Existing Global UC Statements and Proofs

In general, statements found in the literature work in the externalized UC (EUC) subspace of GUC. Although we argue in [BCH+20] that EUC as a framework has some subtle issues, most known protocols do look fine in a meaningful context (which should be made explicit). First, most global setups in the literature are easily seen to be regular, i.e., only provide output to the requesting ITI (examples include a clock, random oracle, ledger functionality). Next, proofs typically assume a sort of domain separation between claimed identities by the environment and real ITIs in the system. (Note that this is not given by the model: even if the environment cannot claim external identities in the same session as the test session, the test session does not have to exist when first accessing the global setup.) In UC 2020 [Can20], one can define ξ as a condition on allowed identities in the system. Two typical restrictions are found in the literature such as in [BMTZ17]:

(a) ξ is satisfied if (i) any eid of an ITI in the system is not declared by the environment as an external source eid in a request to γ. This is typically a minimal requirement, as otherwise, whatever the global setup provides to a protocol, this information could be first claimed by the environment (for the entire test session) even before spawning the test session. This is problematic unless we have very simple setups such as a common-reference string or a plain global random oracle [BGK+18].

(b) As a further restriction, one could enforce that γ provides *per session guarantees*: ξ is satisfied if whenever (additionally to above) eid $= (\mu, \text{sid}||\text{pid})$ and eid$' = (\mu', \text{sid}||\text{pid}')$ are the source extended identities in an input to γ, then $\mu = \mu'$ has to hold. This technically does not allow any other instance to access the shared information, but still the information is formally accessible by the environment claiming an external identity of this session. This model is useful when certain elements of the setup need to be programmed by a simulator, while keeping the overall model of execution close to standard UC.

If proofs conducted in EUC have the above restrictions assumed when proving indistinguishability of the simulation, then it is conceivable that these proofs are transferable into our new model to satisfy precondition of Theorem 1 and thus composition is again established. We discuss such "EUC statements" in the next section. In particular, Sect. 3.2 recovers an EUC example in detail, where we also show how our model can capture various forms of "shared subroutines" ranging from subroutines fully accessible by the environment to subroutines shared only by the challenge protocol (which captures joint-state UC (JUC)).

3   Applications of the UCGS Theorem

We provide two examples to showcase how to prove emulation statements in the UC model in the presence of global subroutines and to verify that the preconditions of the UCGS Theorem are satisfied. The first example is global public-key infrastructure (specifically, adapting the treatment of [CSV16]). The second example is a global clock (adapting the treatment of [BMTZ17]).

These examples bring forth two additional technical aspects of universal composition with global subroutines within the UC framework: The first has to do with the mechanics of having one ideal functionality call another ideal functionality as a subroutine, and the second has to do with the need to find a judicious way to define the external-identities predicate ξ for the management protocol so as to make the best use of the UCGS theorem. (Indeed, these aspects of UC with global subroutines have been lacking in the treatment of [CDPW07].)

Section 3.1 introduces the formalism for having an ideal functionality call another ideal functionality as subroutine. Section 3.2 presents the application to modeling global public-key infrastructure. Section 3.3 presents the application to modeling global clock in the context of blockchains.

3.1   Interaction Between Ideal Functionality and Shared Subroutine

The UCGS theorem essentially state that if protocol π UC-emulates protocol ϕ in the presence of γ, and both π and ϕ are γ-subroutine respecting, then $\rho^{\phi \to \pi}$ UC-emulates ρ for any ρ. A natural use-case of the theorem is when the emulated protocol, ϕ, is an ideal protocol for some ideal functionality $\mathcal{F}$, and γ is an ideal protocol for some ideal functionality $\mathcal{G}$. This means that to make meaningful use of the theorem, $\mathcal{F}$ should make subroutine calls to γ, which in this case means that $\mathcal{F}$ should call dummy parties for $\mathcal{G}$.

A simplistic way to do that would be to simply have $\mathcal{F}$ directly call (and thus create) dummy parties for $\mathcal{G}$. However, in this case, by the definition of dummy parties as per the UC framework [Can20], the PID of the created dummy party will be the identity of $\mathcal{F}$. This may be overly restrictive, since the emulating protocol, π might have other ITIs call $\mathcal{G}$. So, instead, we define a mechanism whereby $\mathcal{F}$ does not directly call a dummy party for $\mathcal{G}$. Instead, $\mathcal{F}$ creates a new "intermediate dummy party," which serves as a relay of inputs and outputs between $\mathcal{F}$ and the dummy party of $\mathcal{G}$. The identity (specifically the PID) of the intermediate dummy party is determined (by $\mathcal{F}$) so as to enable realization of ϕ by protocols π where the PIDs of the parties that use $\mathcal{G}$ are meaningful for the overall security. (This mechanism can be viewed as a way to make rigorous informal statements such as "provide input x to $\mathcal{G}$ on behalf of [sender] S" [CSV16].) Details follow.

Definition 4 (Intermediary dummy party). *Let $\mathcal{F}$ be an ideal functionality and γ some protocol. We define the operation of an intermediary dummy party with code $\mathrm{IM}_{\mathcal{F},\gamma}$ as below. Let (p, s) be the party and session id indicated on the identity tape, and let CIM (code of intermediary) be an exclusive syntactic delimiter ending the description of the code $\mathrm{IM}_{\mathcal{F},\gamma}$.*

- *When activated with input $(\textsc{call}, (s', p'), v)$ from an ITI with code $\mathcal{F}$ and sid s: the party only acts if the content of the identity tape matches $(\cdot||\mathsf{CIM}, \cdot||\cdot)$ and the reveal-sender-id flag is set. Then, provide input v to the ITI $\mathrm{eid}_t :=$ $(\gamma, s'||p')$ (with reveal-sender identity and forced-write flags set).*
- *Upon receiving a value v' on the subroutine output from an ITI with identity $\mathrm{eid} = (\gamma, s'||p')$ (for some s', p'): the party only acts if the content of the identity tape matches $(\cdot||\mathsf{CIM}, \cdot||\cdot)$ and the reveal-sender-id flag is set. Then, provide subroutine output $(\textsc{return}, (s', p'), v')$ to the ITI with identity $\mathrm{eid}_t :=$ $(\mathcal{F}, s||\perp)$ (with reveal-sender identity and forced-write flags set).*
- *Any other message on any tape that is not matching to some case above is ignored.*

A functionality $\mathcal{F}$ can now contain general instructions of the form "provide input x on behalf of P in session s to an instance of γ running in session s' and PID P'" and is understood as the following operation: the ITI running code $\mathcal{F}$ in some session sid provides input $(\textsc{call}, (s', P'), x)$ to intermediary dummy party with identity (s, P) and code $\mathrm{IM}_{\mathcal{F},\gamma}$. Now, P (in session s) will appear as the PID of the ITI invoking γ. $\mathcal{F}$ can process the answers when obtaining the returned values from the intermediary dummy party on its subroutine output tape.

Often it is clear from the context—and standard for EUC-like statements— that only one session of γ with a predefined session identifier $\tilde{\mathrm{sid}}$ is expected to be running, and that each main party (with PID) P of the challenge session s can participate in the shared process γ (i.e. by invoking ITI with identity $(\tilde{s}, P)$ and code γ). In such cases, the statement "output x on behalf of P to γ" by an ideal functionality $\mathcal{F}$ in (challenge) session s is understood as providing input $(\textsc{call}, (\tilde{s}, P), x)$ to the intermediary dummy party with identity (s, P) (and code $\mathrm{IM}_{\mathcal{F},\gamma}$) with exactly the desired effect that the ITI with code γ, PID P and sid $\tilde{\mathrm{sid}}$ is invoked, and where P in session s appears as the official caller.

Clearly, the intermediary is a modeling tool that no environment should tamper with. Hence, for the sake of clarity, when we speak of UC realization of an ideal functionality interacting with a global subroutine, we mean the following:

Definition 5 (Realization with interaction with shared subroutine).
We say that π UC-realizes $\mathcal{F}$ in the presence of γ w.r.t. ξ-identity bounded environments, if Definition 1 holds for the particular choice of $\phi :=$ IDEAL$_\mathcal{F}$ and with respect to the identity bound ξ' that equals ξ augmented with the restriction that no eid specified by the environment (source or destination) can specify code with delimiter CIM.

The intermediary dummy party provides a guaranteed interaction channel and formalizes what was implicitly assumed in prior work when a functionality interacts with, e.g., a global setup such as an certification functionality in the name of a party.

3.2   Example 1: Authentication with Global Certification

Authentication with respect to a global certification functionality (often called PKI) aims at formalizing the fact that if a certified verification key for a digital signature is globally available, then any signature generated with respect to that key can be verified globally, by anyone, even if the signature was generated in the context of a specific protocol. This in particular mean that protocols that employ certified digital signatures might have global "side effects". For example, if Alice signs a message in a particular session, using a signing key for which there is a globally accessible certificate, then *anyone* can cross-check that it was Alice who signed the message. In particular, this might mean that Alice can incur further liabilities.

[CSV16] provides a treatment of this situation within the GUC framework of [CDPW07]. We use the UCGS theorem provide an alternative (and arguably simpler) treatment within the plain UC framework.

The Global Certification Functionality. The shared subroutine is $\gamma =$ IDEAL$_{\mathcal{G}_{cert}^{pid}}$. Note that the functionality is parameterized by a party identity pid. We assume that the functionality is following the standard PID-wise corruption mechanism as specified in [Can20]: this means that the functionality manages corruption messages for party identifiers that are main parties in the execution of IDEAL$_\mathcal{F}$, and marks those party identifiers as corrupted for which it received a corruption message on the backdoor tape.[3]

Functionality $\mathcal{G}_{cert}^{pid}$

Variable: $pk \leftarrow \perp$.

Adversarial key registration: Upon receiving (REGISTER, sid, v) on the backdoor tape and if pid is corrupted and $pk = \perp$ then update $pk \leftarrow v$.

---

[3] The functionality is also expected to provide this list upon a special request from dummy party with PID $\mathscr{A}$ such that the corruption sets can be verified by the environment to be identical in both the ideal and real worlds.

Signature Generation: Upon receiving a value (SIGN, sid, m) from a party with PID pid (via input to the dummy party with SID sid and PID pid):

(a) If this is the first request then do:
  1. If pid is not corrupted then output (KEYGEN) to the adversary (via the backdoor tape). Upon receiving (VERIFICATION KEY, v) from the adversary (on the backdoor tape) and if pid is still not corrupted store $pk \leftarrow v$ internally.
  2. Check at this point that $pk \neq \perp$. If not, then ignore the request.
(b) Output (SIGN, m) to the adversary (via the backdoor tape). Upon receiving (SIGNATURE, m, σ) from the adversary (on the backdoor tape), verify that no entry $(m, \sigma, 0)$ is recorded. If it is, then output $\perp$ to the caller. Else, output (SIGNATURE, m, σ) to the calling party and record the entry $(m, \sigma, 1)$.

Signature Verification: Upon receiving a value (VERIFY, sid, m, σ) from party P (including the adversary) do the following: first, if $pk = \perp$ then output (VERIFIED, $m, 0$) to P. Else, output (VERIFY, m, σ) to the adversary (via backdoor tape). Upon receiving (VERIFIED, m, f, ϕ) from the adversary (on the backdoor tape) do:

(a) If (m, σ, b') is recorded then set $f = b'$.
(b) Else, if the signer is not corrupted, and no entry $(m, \sigma', 1)$ for any σ' is recorded, then set $f = 0$ and record the entry $(m, \sigma, 0)$.
(c) Else set $f = \phi$, and record the entry (m, σ, f).
(d) Output (VERIFIED, m, f) to P.

The Protocol. The protocol ϕ_{auth}^A works as follows, where the shared subroutine is $\gamma = \mathrm{IDEAL}_{\mathcal{G}_{\mathrm{cert}}^A}$, where A is part of the code. Note that we use the eid of the caller as the PID of the sender (to prevent that arbitrary machines can send messages in the name of A), and also simply choose the session-id $\mathrm{sid}_0 = A$ for the shared subroutine. We further assume an unprotected medium to *send* messages, which as specified in [Can20] can be modeled by simply letting the shell forward sent messages to the adversary (via the backdoor tape) and interpret specific inputs on the backdoor tape as received messages.

(a) Upon receiving an input (SEND, sid, B, m) from party A[4], verify that this machine's eid is $(\phi_{\mathrm{auth}}^A, \mathrm{sid}\|A)$; otherwise, ignore the request. Then, set $\mathrm{sid}_0 = A$ and $m' = (m; \mathrm{sid}; B)$, send (SIGN, m') to $\mathcal{G}_{\mathrm{cert}}^A$ (i.e., the input is given to the ITI running code γ in session sid_0 with pid $= A$) to obtain the response (SIGNATURE, $\mathrm{sid}_0, m', \sigma$), send (sid; $A; m; \sigma$) to ITI $(\phi_{\mathrm{auth}}^A, \mathrm{sid}\|B)$ (via the unprotected communication medium).
(b) Upon receiving message (sid$'$; $A; m; \sigma$) from the unprotected communication medium, this party, denote its eid by $(\phi_{\mathrm{auth}}^A, \mathrm{sid}\|B)$, sets $\mathrm{sid}_0 = A$, sets

---

[4] Let us emphasize that party (i.e., machine) A is not a participant of the protocol ϕ_{auth}^A (i.e., does not run the code ϕ_{auth}^A), but is the ITI which invokes the (sender's part of the) protocol ϕ_{auth}^A (with PID A).

$m' = (m; \mathsf{sid}; B)$, sends $(\textsc{Verify}, \mathsf{sid}_0, m', \sigma)$ to $\mathcal{G}^A_{\mathsf{cert}}$ (i.e., the input is given to the ITI running code γ in session sid_0 with $\mathsf{pid} = B$), and obtains a response $(\textsc{Verified}, m', f)$. If $f = 1$ then B outputs $(\textsc{Sent}, \mathsf{sid}, A, B, m)$ (with target eid $\mathsf{eid}_t = B$) and halts. Else B halts with no output.

We also assume here standard byzantine corruption of protocol ITIs as defined in [Can20]: for a structured protocol, this involves interaction with a special *corruption aggregation ITI* that aggregates all corruption information (provided by the shell of the protocols). The goal of this is that the environment receives "genuine" information about the corruption sets during the execution. The corruption aggregation is identified by a special PID $\mathscr{A}$.

The Realized Functionality. The realized functionality provides authenticated message exchange between a sender A and a chosen receiver. Note that the adversarial ability to obtain legitimate signatures on messages allows to produce a publicly verifiable trail of the message transmission between A and B (which is referred to by the term non-deniable in [CSV16]). As above, we follow the standard PID-wise corruption model for functionalities [Can20].

Functionality $\mathcal{F}^A_{\mathsf{cert\text{-}auth}}$

(a) Upon receiving an input $(\textsc{Send}, \mathsf{sid}, B, m)$ from party A, first verify that the calling (dummy) party (running $\text{IDEAL}_{\mathcal{F}^A_{\mathsf{cert\text{-}auth}}}$ in session sid by definition) encodes the PID A. Ignore the request if this is not the case. Then, generate public delayed-output to B, i.e., first output $(\textsc{Sent}, \mathsf{sid}, A, B, m)$ to the adversary on the backdoor tape. Once delivery is granted by the adversary, output $(\textsc{Sent}, \mathsf{sid}, A, B, m)$ to B.[a]

(b) Upon receiving $(\textsc{External-info}, \mathsf{sid}, A, B, m')$ from the adversary, if an output was not yet delivered to B, then set $\mathsf{sid}_0 = A$ and output $(\textsc{Sign}, \mathsf{sid}_0, (m', \mathsf{sid}, B))$ on behalf of A to $\text{IDEAL}_{\mathcal{G}^A_{\mathsf{cert}}}$ (in session sid_0) and forward the response to the adversary.

(c) Upon receiving a value $(\textsc{Corrupt-send}, \mathsf{sid}, B', m')$ from the adversary[b]: if A is marked as corrupted and an output was not yet delivered to B', then output $(\textsc{Sent}, A, B', \mathsf{sid}; m')$ to B'.

(d) Upon receiving $(\textsc{Report})$, from a party P via dummy party with pid $\mathscr{A}$, first set $\mathsf{sid}_0 = A$ and output $(\textsc{Report})$ on behalf of $\mathscr{A}$ to $\text{IDEAL}_{\mathcal{G}^A_{\mathsf{cert}}}$ (in session sid_0). Upon receiving the set of corrupted parties, add the PIDs of the marked corrupted parties of this functionality and output the list to P (via dummy party $\mathscr{A}$).

---

[a] It is instructive to recall what "output m to B" means if no explicit dummy party is mentioned via which this output is delivered [Can20, Section 7.3]: it means that the functionality produces output to a main party running the dummy protocol with session sid and $\mathsf{pid} = B$ and this dummy party produces the output towards the machine with $\mathsf{eid} = B$.

[b] This is an additional adversarial capability beyond what is minimally provided by the standard PID-wise corruption model.

The Identity Bound on the Environment. In order to show in which contexts the protocol is secure, we have to specify an identity bound. For the result to be broadly applicable, we have to find the least restrictive conditions on the allowed interaction between the environment and the challenge protocol (and γ) such that the realization statement holds.

In our specific case, we can give the following guarantee which basically says that the environment cannot claim the extended identity of the signer: more precisely, we mean that the environment is not allowed to claim source eid eid in requests to π running in a session s if eid has been already used as the PID to sign a value $(m, s, \cdot)$ and PID is not marked as corrupted. Conversely, the environment is not allowed to invoke γ to sign a value $(m, s, \cdot)$ using as PID an extended id eid which has been used before as the caller of π running in session s and which is not marked as corrupted. Furthermore, it is not allowed that the environment provides input to the ITI $(\gamma, \cdot \| \mathscr{A})$ (where "not allowed" means that the input provided by the environment is formally rejected if the condition is satisfied by the state of the system at the moment of providing the input. See more details in [Can20]). All other invocations are allowed.

Implications of the Above Identity Bound. Recall that any non-trivial bound ξ restricts the class of context protocols ρ for which the UCGS theorem applies: Essentially the theorem applies only to those protocols ρ which manage to guarantee that the bound ξ remains valid for any combination of ϕ and γ as subroutines within ρ, and similarly for any combination of π and γ as subroutines of $\rho^{\phi \to \pi}$. In the above case, this means that authenticity of the sender identity is guaranteed as long as the context protocol ρ makes sure that the global certification module γ only takes signature requests from entities that correctly represent their identity. Since the underlying model guarantees that the caller identity is correctly represented, except for the case of inputs provided by the environment, this means that authenticity is guaranteed as long as ρ makes sure that γ does not take inputs directly from the environment.

We note that the restriction also touches the corruption model in order to ensure PID-wise corruption. We force the environment to obtain the system's corruption information only through one corruption aggregation machine, which in our case is the functionality (resp. challenge protocol) that provides the entire system's view to $\mathcal{Z}$. Note that this is in accordance with the approach that there is exactly one machine in an execution that provides this information to the environment. We thus have:

Lemma 1. *Let I be an extended identity, and let $\xi_{\bar{I}}$ be the predicate that allows all extended identities other than I as described above. Protocol ϕ^I_{auth} UC-realizes $\mathcal{F}^I_{\mathrm{cert\text{-}auth}}$ in the presence of $\gamma = \mathrm{IDEAL}_{\mathcal{G}^I_{\mathrm{cert}}}$ with respect to the identity bound $\xi_{\bar{I}}$.*

The proof is deferred to [BCH+20].

3.3 Example 2: Composable Blockchains with a Global Clock

Motivation. We next showcase the shared-setups composition theorem by demonstrating how it can be applied to obtain composition (i.e., subroutine replacement) in a context in which global (shared) setups have recently become the norm, namely that of composable blockchains. Concretely, a number of recent works [BGK+18, BGM+18, KKKZ18, BMTZ17] analyze the backbone protocol (intuitively corresponding to the the consensus layer) of mainstream cryptocurrencies, such as Bitcoin and Ouroboros assuming a *global (shared) clock* functionality which is used for enforcing synchrony.

In a nutshell these works prove that by providing access to a global clock $\mathcal{G}_{clock}$ (along with some additional local or global setups) the underlying backbone implements a functionality $\mathcal{F}_{Ledger}$ that abstract a transaction ledger with eventual consistency guarantees (more concretely, a ledger enforcing the so-called common-prefix, liveness, and chain quality property, cf. [GKL15, PSS17].

Let us focus on [BMTZ17]. This work proved that inducing a special way (discussed below) in which the global (shared) clock functionality is used— i.e., a special registration/deregistration mechanism—there exists a simulator in the $\{\mathcal{F}_{Ledger}, \mathcal{G}_{clock}\}$-hybrid world that emulates the behavior of any adversary attacking the Bitcoin backbone protocol in the $\{\mathcal{G}_{clock}, \mathcal{F}_{RO}, \mathcal{F}_{net}\}$-hybrid world, where $\mathcal{F}_{RO}$ and $\mathcal{F}_{net}$ are standard (local to the protocol) UC functionalities. The goal of this modeling is to enable abstracting the internals of the ledger protocol, designing protocols that have access to the ledger functionality (and the global clock), and then using the GUC theorem to argue that any protocol which is proved security assuming access to this local ledger functionality will remain secure when the functionality is replaced by the Bitcoin backbone protocol. Assuming existence of such a composition theorem, [BMTZ17] proceeded in proposing a construction of a *cryptocurrency ledger*—namely a ledger functionality that also checks signatures of parties—assuming a ledger as above and a signatures functionality. However, as discussed, the GUC modeling does not provide sufficiently detailed treatment of external identities so as to make the above approach go through.

We show how the UCGS Theorem can be used by arguing that the preconditions of Theorem 1 are satisfied for the involved components.

Context Restrictions. First we need to fix the (identity bound) predicate ξ used to define the applicable context. Recall, that ξ is intended to restrict the set (or rather the sequence) of extended identities that the environment can claim when contacting protocols. Let us first consider what happens if we do not impose any restriction. We argue that any such unrestricted access makes the global clock functionality behave in a way that no longer ensures synchrony.

To this direction let us recall the basic idea behind clock $\mathcal{G}_{clock}$. For clarity, we show a concrete clock functionality formulated in our model in Fig. 5. The functionality $\mathcal{G}_{clock}$ stores a monotonically increasing counter τ_{sid} (corresponding to the current time or global round) which any party can request by issuing a special CLOCK-READ command. Furthermore, any honest party can send a message CLOCK-UPDATE to the clock which records it and once all honest parties have sent such a request while the time was τ_{sid}, the clock increases its time, i.e., sets $\tau_{\mathsf{sid}} := \tau_{\mathsf{sid}} + 1$.

The above clock was used as follows to ensure synchrony—i.e., that no party starts its round $\rho + 1$ before every party has finished round ρ—which was a property necessary for the security proof in the above blockchain protocols: In each round, as soon as a party has completed all its actions (sent and received all its messages) for the current round, it signals this to the clock by sending a CLOCK-UPDATE command; from that point on this party keeps asking the clock for the time whenever activated and proceeds to the next round only once it observes that this counter advances. As the latter event requires everyone to signal that they are done with the current round, this gives us the desired synchrony guarantee. Notably, by design of the setup, any $\mathcal{G}_{\mathrm{clock}}$-ideal protocol γ is trivially regular (according to Definition 3). This is true because the clock has a special registration mechanism which forces it to only talk to ITIs which have already registered with it and therefore never spawns new ITIs as required by that definition.

So what happens to the above, when ξ is overly liberal? If the environment is allowed to impersonate the protocol session of a party towards the clock (by issuing an external write request with the source-ID being the session of that party) then the environment is able to make the clock advance without waiting for this party, thus entirely destroys the above round structure. This points to the following natural ξ: The environment is not able to issue any request to the clock which has source ID the ID of a party that already exists in the system, or to spawn any ITI for which it already claimed an external identity before in an interaction with the clock. This corresponds to item (a) in the last paragraph of Sect. 2.4.[5] This requirement is assumed and shown to be sufficient in [BMTZ17] and therefore implies that the environment cannot make the clock ignore existing honest parties playing the protocol, hence the clock will enable the above synchronous rounds structure. In the following we will use this ξ to apply Theorem 1; for clarity we denote it as ξ_{sync}.

Applying the Composition Theorem. Assume now that we want to prove that in the aforementioned construction of the cryptocurrency ledger from the simpler (backbone) ledger $\mathcal{F}_{\mathrm{Ledger}}$ from [BMTZ17] we can replace the simpler ledger $\mathcal{F}_{\mathrm{Ledger}}$ by the backbone protocol. This corresponds to proving Theorem 1 for γ being the $\mathcal{G}_{\mathrm{clock}}$-ideal protocol, π being the backbone protocol, ϕ being the $\mathcal{F}_{\mathrm{Ledger}}$-ideal protocol, and ρ being the construction of the cryptocurrency ledger with access to ϕ. All protocols, π, ϕ, ρ can access protocol γ. First, by inspection of these protocols, we can verify that ρ, ϕ, π, γ are subroutine respecting. Note that although the protocols logic is involved, the subroutine structure is quite simple (i.e., subroutine calls only go to ideal protocols that formalize either local

---

[5] Clearly, if we assume again PID-wise corruption like previous paragraphs, we need to further restrict the environment to access only the corruption aggregation machine of the ledger protocol to obtain the natural interpretation of "PID-wise corruption".

Functionality $\mathcal{G}_{\text{clock}}$

The functionality manages the set $\mathcal{P}$ of registered machines (identified by extended identities), i.e., a machine is added to $\mathcal{P}$ when receiving input REGISTER (and removes a machine from $\mathcal{P}$ when receiving DE-REGISTER. The requests give activation back to the calling machine).

For each identity $P \in \mathcal{P}$ it manages a variable d_P. For each session identifier sid specified in an extended identity $P \in \mathcal{P}$, the clock manages a variable τ_{sid} (all these integer variables are initially 0).

Synchronization:

- Upon receiving (CLOCK-UPDATE, sid_C) from $P \in \mathcal{P}$, first verify that the calling (dummy) party encodes P as its PID; otherwise ignore the request. Set $d_P := 1$; execute *Round-Update* and forward (CLOCK-UPDATE, sid_C, P) to $\mathcal{A}$.
- Upon receiving (CLOCK-READ, sid_C) from any ITI P, execute *Round-Update*, and then return (CLOCK-READ, $\text{sid}_C, \tau_{\text{sid}}$) to the requestor, where sid corresponds to the session identifier encoded in P.

Procedure Round-Update: For each managed session sid do: If $d_P = 1$ for all uncorrupted $P = (\cdot, \text{sid}\|\cdot) \in \mathcal{P}$, then set $\tau_{\text{sid}} := \tau_{\text{sid}} + 1$ and reset $d_P := 0$ for all identities $P = (\cdot, \text{sid}\|\cdot) \in \mathcal{P}$.

Fig. 5. A global clock functionality. We remark that due to the clean definition of shared subroutines in our model, the depicted global clock has a simpler structure than the clock in the original version of [BMTZ17]. Still, the clock offers the same functionality towards calling ITIs.

or global setups). In particular, although not directly claimed in the original version of in [BMTZ17], it is possible to convert both ϕ and π into subroutine-exposing protocols by applying the exposing mechanism (by equipping the protocols with the respective subroutine-exposing shell). Finally, both π and ϕ are by design subroutine respecting except with calls to γ (note that this is due to the fact that a similar concept exists in EUC). Finally, restricting the environment via ξ_{sync} ensures that the use of γ (i.e., the clock) will induce the desired synchronous structure specified for the simulation proof from [BMTZ17]. Given all of this, the UC-realization proof of [BMTZ17] can be translated to this model (the overhead is identical to the overhead in the previous example) to conclude that π UC-emulate ϕ in the presence of γ when the environment is ξ_{sync}-identity-bounded. Thus we can apply Theorem 1 to prove that $\rho^{\phi \to \pi}$ UC-emulates ρ whenever the context protocol calls the subroutine (to be replaced) in the legal way as defined by ξ_{sync} and obtain the desired statement.

Acknowledgments. We thank the anonymous reviewers of Eurocrypt and TCC 2020 for their corrections and suggestions to improve this work.

A   The Code of the Transformation

Protocol $M[\pi, \gamma]$

Let $\text{eid}_M = (\text{code}_M, \text{sid}_M \| \text{pid}_M)$ be code, SID, and PID of this ITI as written on the identity tape. Initialize $\text{sid}_\pi := \varepsilon$ as the empty string and $H[.]$ as an empty map. Set $\text{eid}_{\text{egDIR}} := (\text{code}_M, \text{sid}_M \| \text{pid}_{\text{egDIR}})$.

Subroutine exposing. Machine $M[\cdot]$ follows the subroutine-exposing instructions, i.e., it registers itself and all invoked subroutines in the directory ITI.

Incoming messages on the input tape.

- Upon receiving an input $\text{in} := (m, \text{eid}')$, where eid' is an extended identity, parse $m := ((m', \text{eid}_{\text{src}}), \text{eid}_{\text{dest}})$ where $\text{eid}_{\text{dest}} = (\text{code}, \text{sid}_{\text{dest}} \| \text{pid}_{\text{dest}})$ is an extended identity. If $\text{code} = \text{MAIN}$ overwrite (within eid_{dest}) $\text{code} \leftarrow \pi$, in case of GLOBAL overwrite $\text{code} \leftarrow \gamma$. Otherwise, overwrite $\text{code} \leftarrow \bot$. Additionally, store the source machine as $H[\text{eid}_{\text{src}}] \leftarrow \text{eid}'$. //*Unwrap the real message, set the correct code, and remember the source machine.*

- If $\text{sid}_\pi = \varepsilon$ then query the execution graph directory $\text{eid}_{\text{egDIR}}$. If there is some entry (M, sid) where M is an ITI with code π, then set $\text{sid}_\pi := \text{sid}$ for the first such entry. Discard and give up activation if $\text{code} \notin \{\pi, \gamma\}$ or if $\text{pid}_{\text{dest}} \neq \text{pid}_M$ or if $\text{code} = \pi \wedge \text{sid}_\pi \neq \varepsilon \wedge \text{sid}_{\text{dest}} \neq \text{sid}_\pi$. //*Only talk to one instance of π, or to γ*

- If $\text{code} = \pi$ then set $\text{sid}_\pi := \text{sid}_{\text{dest}}$. Define $\text{eid} := (\text{sh}[\text{code}], (\text{sid}_{\text{dest}}, \text{sid}_M) \| \text{pid}_M)$. Send $(\text{REGISTER}, \text{sid}_{\text{dest}})$ to $\text{eid}_{\text{egDIR}}$. Issue the external-write request $(f := 1, \text{eid}, t, r := 1, \text{eid}_M, (m', \text{eid}_{\text{src}}))$, where t denotes the input tape. //*Send message to corresponding shell*

Incoming messages on the subroutine-output tape.

- Upon receiving a subroutine output $\text{sub-out} := (m, \text{eid})$, where $\text{eid} = (\text{code}, \text{sid} \| \text{pid})$ is an extended identity, parse $\text{code} = (\text{sh}[\text{code}'], (\text{sid}', \text{sid}'') \| \text{pid})$ and $m := ((m', \text{eid}_{\text{src}}), \text{eid}_{\text{dest}})$.

- If $\text{sid}_\pi = \varepsilon$ then query $\text{eid}_{\text{egDIR}}$ for the list of registered ITIs, and if some entry (M, sid) exists, where M has code π, set $\text{sid}_\pi := \text{sid}$ for the first such entry. Discard and give up activation if $\text{code}' \notin \{\pi, \gamma\}$ or if $\text{code} = \pi \wedge \text{sid}_\pi = \varepsilon$ or if $\text{code}' = \pi$ but $\text{eid} \neq (\text{sh}[\pi], (\text{sid}_\pi, \text{sid}_M) \| \text{pid}_M)$. //*Only talk to one instance of π, or to γ*

- If $\text{eid}_{\text{src}} = (\pi, \text{sid} \| \text{pid})$ (for some pid, sid) then set $\text{eid}'_{\text{src}} := (\text{MAIN}, \text{sid} \| \text{pid})$, if $\text{eid}_{\text{src}} = (\gamma, \text{sid} \| \text{pid})$ (for some pid, sid) then set $\text{eid}'_{\text{src}} := (\text{GLOBAL}, \text{sid} \| \text{pid})$. Overwrite $m := (m', \text{eid}'_{\text{src}})$. //*Hide source of message from calling ITI*

- Issue an external-write request: If $H[\text{eid}_{\text{dest}}] \neq \bot$, then issue $(f' = 1, H[\text{eid}_{\text{dest}}], t, r' = 1, \text{eid}_M, m)$, and otherwise, issue $(f' = 1, \text{eid}_{\text{dest}}, t, r' = 1, \text{eid}_M, m)$ where t denotes in both cases the subroutine-output tape.

Incoming messages for the backdoor tape. This protocol ignores messages to the backdoor tapes (and does not write to the backdoor tape of any other machine).

Shell sh[code]

Let eid_{sh} denote the contents on the identity tape and let pid_{sh} and $\mathsf{sid}_{sh} =: (\mathsf{sid}_{loc}, \mathsf{sid}_M)$ denote the PID and SID, respectively. Set $\mathsf{eid}_{egDIR} := (\mathsf{code}_M, \mathsf{sid}_M \| \mathsf{pid}_{egDIR})$ (where pid_{egDIR} is a publicly known special PID and code_M can be extracted from the extended identity of the sender on the input tape upon first invocation).

Incoming messages.
//*Relay message to virtual ITI*
I-1: Upon receiving an input or subroutine output (m, eid), where $\mathsf{eid} = (\psi, \mathsf{sid} \| \mathsf{pid})$ is an extended identity, parse m as (m', eid_{src}). Query eid_{egDIR} for the list of the registered ITIs. If eid is not contained in the list, or sid is not either sid_M or of the form $(*, \mathsf{sid}_M)$, then ignore the message. Otherwise, do:
- If the virtual ITI $M' = (\mathsf{code}, \mathsf{sid}_{loc} \| \mathsf{pid}_{sh})$ already exists, then message m' and eid_{src} are written to the corresponding tape of M'. Virtual ITI M' is then activated.
- If the virtual ITI $M' = (\mathsf{code}, \mathsf{sid}_{loc} \| \mathsf{pid}_{sh})$ does not exist yet, then a new one is created, i.e., a new configuration for program code with the corresponding identity is created and the request is executed as above.

//*Corruption handling: only existing virtual ITIs can be corrupted, shells are incorruptible*
I-2: Upon receiving m on the backdoor tape, sh parses it as $(m', \mathsf{eid}_{dest})$, where eid_{dest} is an extended identity. If $\mathsf{eid}_{dest} \neq (\mathsf{code}, \mathsf{sid}_{loc} \| \mathsf{pid}_{sh})$ then discard the input and give up activation (i.e., ITIs running $\mathsf{sh}[\cdot]$ are not corrupted).
   1: If the virtual ITM $M' = \mathsf{eid}_{dest}$ does not exist yet, then give up activation.
   2: If the virtual ITM $M' = \mathsf{eid}_{dest}$ exists, m' is written on its backdoor tape and M' is activated.

Outgoing messages.
//*Shell can give input to any subsidiary of* M[]
O-1: If the virtual ITI of the body issues an external-write instruction $(f, \mathsf{eid}_{dest}, t, r, \mathsf{eid}_{src}, m)$ where t denotes the input tape, then:
   (*) Parse $\mathsf{eid}_{dest} =: (\mathsf{code}_{dest}, (\mathsf{sid}_{dest} \| \mathsf{pid}_{dest}))$. Send (INVOKE, $\mathsf{sh}[\mathsf{code}_{dest}], \mathsf{eid}_{src} \to \mathsf{eid}_{dest})$ to eid_{egDIR}. Issue an external-write instruction $(f, (\mathsf{sh}[\mathsf{code}_{dest}], (\mathsf{sid}_{dest}, \mathsf{sid}_M) \| \mathsf{pid}_{dest}), t, r, \mathsf{eid}_{sh}, m')$ where $m' = (m, \mathsf{eid}_{src})$.
//*Subroutine output either goes to* M[] *or to another shell*
O-2: If the virtual ITI of the body issues an external-write instruction $(f, \mathsf{eid}_{dest}, t, r, \mathsf{eid}_{src}, m)$ where t denotes the subroutine-output tape, query eid_{egDIR} to obtain the list of registered ITIs and the execution graph structure of the virtual ITIs.
   - //*Detecting the sessions of* π *and* γ *that produce output to the environment/context protocol.*
     If the obtained execution graph reveals that (1) this ITI with $\mathsf{sid}_{sh} = (\mathsf{sid}_{loc}, \mathsf{sid}_M)$ is a main party of the test session of π (i.e., the one invoked by $\mathsf{M}[\pi, \gamma]$) and eid_{dest} is not part of this extended test session *or* (2) eid_{dest} is not part of the extended test session and this ITI runs a virtual ITI with code γ: then issue an external-write instruction $(f, \mathsf{eid}_M, t, r, (\mathsf{sh}[\mathsf{code}], \mathsf{sid}_{sh} \| \mathsf{pid}_{sh}), m')$, where $m' = ((m, \mathsf{eid}_{src}), \mathsf{eid}_{dest})$,

eid_M denotes the unique identity from the list of registered devices running code $code_M$ with identity $(sid_M \| pid_{sh})$.

- *//Otherwise, the subroutine output goes to a ITI which must be part of this extended instance.* Else, proceed as in O-1 position (∗) and use the subroutine relation $eid_{dest} \to eid_{src}$ when talking to eid_{egDIR}.

//Enable communication with adversary

O-3: If the virtual ITI sends backdoor message m' to the adversary, then define the message $m := (m', (code, sid_{loc} \| pid_{sh}))$ and execute the external-write request $(f' = 0, (\bot, \bot), t, r' = 1, (sh[code], sid_{loc} \| pid_{sh}), m')$ destined for the adversary ITI.

References

[BCH+20] Badertscher, C., Canetti, R., Hesse, J., Tackmann, B., Zikas, V.: Universal composition with global subroutines: Capturing global setup within plain UC. Cryptology ePrint Archive (2020)

[BCL+11] Barak, B., Canetti, R., Lindell, Y., Pass, R., Rabin, T.: Secure computation without authentication. J. Cryptol. **24**(4), 720–760 (2010). https://doi.org/10.1007/s00145-010-9075-9

[Bea91] Beaver, D.: Secure multiparty protocols and zero-knowledge proof systems tolerating a faulty minority. J. Cryptol. **4**(2), 75–122 (1991). https://doi.org/10.1007/BF00196771

[BGK+18] Badertscher, C., Gaži, P., Kiayias, A., Russell, A., Zikas, V.: Ouroboros genesis: composable proof-of-stake blockchains with dynamic availability. In: ACM CCS, pp. 913–930 (2018)

[BGM+18] Badertscher, C., Garay, J., Maurer, U., Tschudi, D., Zikas, V.: But why does it work? A rational protocol design treatment of bitcoin. In: Nielsen, J.B., Rijmen, V. (eds.) EUROCRYPT 2018. LNCS, vol. 10821, pp. 34–65. Springer, Cham (2018). https://doi.org/10.1007/978-3-319-78375-8_2

[BMTZ17] Badertscher, C., Maurer, U., Tschudi, D., Zikas, V.: Bitcoin as a transaction ledger: a composable treatment. In: Katz, J., Shacham, H. (eds.) CRYPTO 2017. LNCS, vol. 10401, pp. 324–356. Springer, Cham (2017). https://doi.org/10.1007/978-3-319-63688-7_11

[BPW04] Backes, M., Pfitzmann, B., Waidner, M.: A general composition theorem for secure reactive systems. In: Naor, M. (ed.) TCC 2004. LNCS, vol. 2951, pp. 336–354. Springer, Heidelberg (2004). https://doi.org/10.1007/978-3-540-24638-1_19

[BPW07] Backes, M., Pfitzmann, B., Waidner, M.: The reactive simulatability (RSIM) framework for asynchronous systems. Inf. Comput. **205**(12), 1685–1720 (2007)

[Can00] Canetti, R.: Security and composition of multi-party cryptographic protocols. J. Cryptol. **13**(1), 143–202 (2000). https://doi.org/10.1007/s001459910006

[Can01] Canetti, R.: Universally composable security: a new paradigm for cryptographic protocols. In: FOCS, FOCS 2001, Washington, DC, USA, pp. 136–145. IEEE Computer Society (2001)

[Can20] Canetti, R.: Universally composable security. J. ACM **67**(5), 1–94 (2020)

[CDPW07] Canetti, R., Dodis, Y., Pass, R., Walfish, S.: Universally composable security with global setup. In: Vadhan, S.P. (ed.) TCC 2007. LNCS, vol. 4392, pp. 61–85. Springer, Heidelberg (2007). https://doi.org/10.1007/978-3-540-70936-7_4

[CDT19] Camenisch, J., Drijvers, M., Tackmann, B.: Multi-protocol UC and its use for building modular and efficient protocols. Cryptology ePrint Archive, report 2019/065, January 2019

[CKKR19] Camenisch, J., Krenn, S., Küsters, R., Rausch, D.: iUC: flexible universal composability made simple. In: Galbraith, S.D., Moriai, S. (eds.) ASIACRYPT 2019. LNCS, vol. 11923, pp. 191–221. Springer, Cham (2019). https://doi.org/10.1007/978-3-030-34618-8_7

[CR03] Canetti, R., Rabin, T.: Universal composition with joint state. In: Boneh, D. (ed.) CRYPTO 2003. LNCS, vol. 2729, pp. 265–281. Springer, Heidelberg (2003). https://doi.org/10.1007/978-3-540-45146-4_16

[CSV16] Canetti, R., Shahaf, D., Vald, M.: Universally composable authentication and key-exchange with global PKI. In: Cheng, C.-M., Chung, K.-M., Persiano, G., Yang, B.-Y. (eds.) PKC 2016. LNCS, vol. 9615, pp. 265–296. Springer, Heidelberg (2016). https://doi.org/10.1007/978-3-662-49387-8_11

[GHM+17] Gilad, Y., Hemo, R., Micali, S., Vlachos, G., Zeldovich, N.: Algorand: scaling byzantine agreements for cryptocurrencies. In: Proceedings of the 26th Symposium on Operating Systems Principles, SOSP 2017, New York, NY, USA, pp. 51–68. Association for Computing Machinery (2017)

[GKL15] Garay, J., Kiayias, A., Leonardos, N.: The bitcoin backbone protocol: analysis and applications. In: Oswald, E., Fischlin, M. (eds.) EUROCRYPT 2015. LNCS, vol. 9057, pp. 281–310. Springer, Heidelberg (2015). https://doi.org/10.1007/978-3-662-46803-6_10

[HM97] Hirt, M., Maurer, U.: Complete characterization of adversaries tolerable in secure multi-party computation. In: ACM PODC, pp. 25–34. ACM (1997)

[HS16] Hofheinz, D., Shoup, V.: GNUC: a new universal composability framework. J. Cryptol. 28(3), 423–508 (2016)

[KKKZ18] Kerber, T., Kohlweiss, M., Kiayias, A., Zikas, V.: Ouroboros crypsinous: Privacy-preserving proof-of-stake. IACR Cryptology ePrint Archive, 2018:1132 (2018). To appear at IEEE S&P 2019

[KMT20] Küsters, R., Tuengerthal, M., Rausch, D.: The IITM model: a simple and expressive model for universal composability. J. Cryptol. 33(4), 1461–1584 (2020). https://doi.org/10.1007/s00145-020-09352-1

[Mau11] Maurer, U.: Constructive cryptography – a new paradigm for security definitions and proofs. In: Mödersheim, S., Palamidessi, C. (eds.) TOSCA 2011. LNCS, vol. 6993, pp. 33–56. Springer, Heidelberg (2012). https://doi.org/10.1007/978-3-642-27375-9_3

[MR91] Micali, S., Rogaway, P.: Secure computation. In: Feigenbaum, J. (ed.) CRYPTO 1991. LNCS, vol. 576, pp. 392–404. Springer, Heidelberg (1992). https://doi.org/10.1007/3-540-46766-1_32

[MR11] Maurer, U., Renner, R.: Abstract cryptography. In: Innovations in Computer Science (2011)

[PSS17] Pass, R., Seeman, L., Shelat, A.: Analysis of the blockchain protocol in asynchronous networks. In: Coron, J.-S., Nielsen, J.B. (eds.) EUROCRYPT 2017. LNCS, vol. 10211, pp. 643–673. Springer, Cham (2017). https://doi.org/10.1007/978-3-319-56614-6_22

[PW00] Pfitzmann, B., Waidner, M.: Composition and integrity preservation of secure reactive systems. In: ACM CCS, pp. 245–254 (2000)

Security Analysis of *SPAKE2+*

Victor Shoup[(✉)]

New York University, New York, USA
shoup@cs.nyu.edu

Abstract. We show that a slight variant of Protocol *SPAKE2+*, which was presented but not analyzed in [17], is a secure *asymmetric* password-authenticated key exchange protocol (PAKE), meaning that the protocol still provides good security guarantees even if a server is compromised and the password file stored on the server is leaked to an adversary. The analysis is done in the UC framework (i.e., a simulation-based security model), under the computational Diffie-Hellman (CDH) assumption, and modeling certain hash functions as random oracles. The main difference between our variant and the original Protocol *SPAKE2+* is that our variant includes standard key confirmation flows; also, adding these flows allows some slight simplification to the remainder of the protocol. Along the way, we also (i) provide the first proof (under the same assumptions) that a slight variant of Protocol *SPAKE2* from [5] is a secure *symmetric* PAKE in the UC framework (previous security proofs were all in the weaker BPR framework [7]); (ii) provide a proof (under very similar assumptions) that a variant of Protocol *SPAKE2+* that is currently being standardized is also a secure asymmetric PAKE; (iii) repair several problems in earlier UC formulations of secure symmetric and asymmetric PAKE.

1 Introduction

A **password-authenticated key exchange (PAKE)** protocol allows two users who share nothing but a password to securely establish a session key. Ideally, such a protocol prevents an adversary, even one who actively participates in the protocol (as opposed to an eavesdropping adversary), to mount an *offline dictionary attack*. PAKE protocols were proposed initially by Bellovin and Merrit [9], and have been the subject of intensive research ever since.

A formal model of security for PAKE protocols was first proposed by Bellare, Pointcheval, and Rogaway [7]. We call this the **BPR framework for PAKE security**. The BPR framework is a "game based" security definition, as opposed to a "simulation based" security definition. A simulation-based security definition for PAKE was later given in [14]. We shall refer to this and similar simulation-based security definitions as the **UC framework for PAKE security**. Here, UC is short for "Universal Composability", as the definitions in [14] are couched in terms of the more general Universal Composability framework of [12]. As shown in [14], PAKE security in the UC framework implies PAKE

© International Association for Cryptologic Research 2020
R. Pass and K. Pietrzak (Eds.): TCC 2020, LNCS 12552, pp. 31–60, 2020.
https://doi.org/10.1007/978-3-030-64381-2_2

security in the BPR framework. In fact, the UC framework for PAKE security is stronger than the BPR framework in a number of ways that we will discuss further below.

Abdalla and Pointcheval [5] present Protocol *SPAKE2*, which itself is a variant of a protocol originally presented in [9] and analyzed in [7]. Protocol *SPAKE2* is a simple and efficient PAKE protocol, and was shown in [5] to be secure in the BPR security framework. Their proof of security is in the random oracle model [8] under the **computational Diffie-Hellman (CDH) assumption**.[1] The protocol also makes use of a *common reference string* consisting of two random group elements.

Protocol *SPAKE2* has never been proven secure in the UC framework. As we argue below, it seems very unlikely that it can be. One of our results is to show that by adding standard *key confirmation flows* to (a simplified version of) Protocol *SPAKE2* (which is anyway considered to be good security practice), the resulting protocol, which we call Protocol *KC-SPAKE2*, is secure in the UC framework (under the same assumptions).

Protocols *SPAKE2* and *KC-SPAKE2* are *symmetric* PAKE protocols, meaning that both parties must know the password when running the protocol. In the typical setting where one party is a client and the other a server, while the client may memorize their password, the server stores the password in some type of "password file". If this password file itself is ever leaked, then the client's password is totally compromised. From a practical security point of view, this vulnerability possibly negates any perceived benefits of using a PAKE protocol instead of a more traditional password-based protocol layered on top of a one-sided authenticated key exchange (which is still the overwhelming practice today).

In order to address this security concern, the notion of an **asymmetric PAKE** was studied in [19], where the UC framework of [14] is extended to capture the notion that after a password file is leaked, an adversary must still carry out an *offline dictionary attack* to retrieve a client's password. The paper also gives a general mechanism for transforming a secure PAKE into a secure asymmetric PAKE.[2]

In [17], a variant of Protocol *SPAKE2*, called Protocol *SPAKE2+*, is introduced. This protocol is meant to be a secure asymmetric PAKE, while being simpler and more efficient than what would be obtained by directly applying the transformation in [19] to Protocol *SPAKE2* or *KC-SPAKE2*. However, the security of Protocol *SPAKE2+* was never formally analyzed.

In this paper, we propose adding standard key confirmation flows to (a simplified version of) Protocol *SPAKE2+*, obtaining a protocol called Protocol *KC-SPAKE2+*, which we prove is a secure asymmetric PAKE in the UC framework (under the CDH assumption, in the random oracle model, and with

---

[1] The CDH assumption, in a group $\mathbb{G}$ of prime order q generated by $g \in \mathbb{G}$, asserts that given g^α, g^β, for random $\alpha, \beta \in \mathbb{Z}_q$, it is hard to compute $g^{\alpha\beta}$.

[2] The paper [19] was certainly not the first to study asymmetric PAKE protocols, nor is it the first to propose a formal security definition for such protocols.

a common reference string). This is our main result. We also present and justify various design choices in both the details of the protocol and the ideal functionality used in its security analysis. As we discuss below, some changes in the ideal functionality in [19] were necessary in order to obtain meaningful results. Since some changes were necessary, we also made other changes in the name of making things simpler.

Comparison to OPAQUE. In [23], a stronger notion of asymmetric PAKE security is introduced, wherein the adversary cannot initiate an offline dictionary attack until *after* the password file is leaked. None of the protocols analyzed here are secure in this stronger sense. Nevertheless, the protocols we analyze here may still be of interest. First, while an offline dictionary attack may be initiated before the password file is leaked, such a dictionary attack must be directed at a particular client. Second, the protocols we analyze here are quite simple and efficient, and unlike the *OPAQUE* protocol in [23], they do not require hashing a password to a group element. Third, the protocols we analyze here are proved secure under the CDH assumption, while the *OPAQUE* protocol is proved secure under the stronger "one-more Diffie-Hellman assumption".

In Defense of Programmable Random Oracles. Our main results are proofs of security in the UC framework using programmable random oracles. The same is true for many other results in this area (including [23]), and results in [20] suggest that secure asymmetric PAKE protocols may only be possible with programmable random oracles.

Recently, results that use programmable random oracles in the UC framework have come to be viewed with some skepticism (see, for example, [11,15]). We wish to argue (briefly) that such skepticism is a bit overblown (perhaps to sell a new "brand" of security) and that such results are still of considerable value.

Besides the fact that in any security analysis the random oracle model is at best a heuristic device (see, for example, [13]), there is a concern that in the UC framework, essential composability properties may be lost. (In fact, this composability concern applies to any type of "programmable" set-up assumption, such as a *common reference string*, and not just to random oracles.)

While composability with random oracles is a concern, in most applications, it is not an insurmountable problem. First, the ideal functionalities we define in this paper will all be explicitly in a multi-user/multi-instance setting where a single random oracle is used for all users and user instances. Second, even if one wants to use the *same* random oracle in this and other protocols, that is not a problem, *so long as all of the protocols involved coordinate on how their inputs are presented to the random oracle.* Specifically, as long as all protocols present their inputs to the random oracle using some convention that partitions the oracle's input space (say, by prefixing some kind of "protocol ID" and/or "protocol instance ID"), there will be no unwanted interactions, and it will be "as if" each different protocol (or protocol instance) is using its own, independent random oracle. In the UC framework, this is all quite easily justified using the

public system parameters: random $a, b \in \mathbb{G}$
shared secret password: π

P Q

$\alpha \xleftarrow{\text{R}} \mathbb{Z}_q, u \leftarrow g^\alpha a^\pi$ $\beta \xleftarrow{\text{R}} \mathbb{Z}_q, v \leftarrow g^\beta b^\pi$

$$\xrightarrow{\hspace{2cm} u \hspace{2cm}}$$

$$\xleftarrow{\hspace{2cm} v \hspace{2cm}}$$

$w \leftarrow (v/b^\pi)^\alpha$ $w \leftarrow (u/a^\pi)^\beta$
$k \leftarrow H(\pi, id_P, id_Q, u, v, w)$ $k \leftarrow H(\pi, id_P, id_Q, u, v, w)$

session key: k

Fig. 1. Protocol *SPAKE2*

JUC theorem [16]. Granted, such coordination among protocols in a protocol stack may be a bit inconvenient, but is not the end of the world.

Full Version of the Paper. Because of space limitations, a number of details have been omitted from this extended abstract. We refer the reader to the full version of the paper [25] for these details.

2 Overview

We start by considering Protocol *SPAKE2*, which is shown in Fig. 1, and which was first presented and analyzed in [5]. Here, $\mathbb{G}$ is a group of prime order q, generated by $g \in \mathbb{G}$, and H is a hash function that outputs elements of the set $\mathcal{K}$ of all possible session keys. Passwords are viewed as elements of $\mathbb{Z}_q$. The protocol also assumes public system parameters $a, b \in \mathbb{G}$, which are assumed to be random elements of $\mathbb{G}$ that are generated securely, so that no party knows their discrete logarithms.

This protocol is perfectly symmetric and can be implemented with the two flows sent in any order or even concurrently. In [5], it was shown to be secure in the BPR framework, under the CDH assumption, and modeling H as a random oracle.

Their security analysis, however, did not take corruption queries (which leak passwords to the adversary) into account, which must be done in order to prove *forward security* in the BPR framework. Later, [1] show that Protocol *SPAKE2* does indeed provide forward security in the BPR framework,[3] also in the random oracle model, but under the stronger *Gap CDH assumption.*[4]

---

[3] The security theorem in [1] only applies to so-called "weak" corruptions in the BPR framework, in which corrupting a party reveals to the adversary only its password, and not the internal state of any corresponding protocol instance.

[4] The Gap CDH assumption asserts that the problem of computing $g^{\alpha\beta}$, given g^α, g^β for random $\alpha, \beta \in \mathbb{Z}_q$, is hard even if the attacker has access to a *DDH oracle*. Such

> public system parameters: random $a, b \in \mathbb{G}$
> password: π, $(\phi_0, \phi_1) := F(\pi, id_P, id_Q)$
>
> P $\qquad\qquad\qquad\qquad\qquad\qquad$ Q
>
> secret: ϕ_0, ϕ_1 $\qquad\qquad\qquad\qquad$ secret: $\phi_0, c := g^{\phi_1}$
>
> $\alpha \xleftarrow{\text{R}} \mathbb{Z}_q, u \leftarrow g^\alpha a^{\phi_0}$ $\qquad\qquad\qquad$ $\beta \xleftarrow{\text{R}} \mathbb{Z}_q, v \leftarrow g^\beta b^{\phi_0}$
>
> $\xrightarrow{\quad u \quad}$
>
> $\xleftarrow{\quad v \quad}$
>
> $w \leftarrow (v/b^{\phi_0})^\alpha, d \leftarrow (v/b^{\phi_0})^{\phi_1}$ $\qquad$ $w \leftarrow (u/a^{\phi_0})^\beta, d \leftarrow c^\beta$
> $k \leftarrow H(\phi_0, id_P, id_Q, u, v, w, d)$ $\qquad$ $k \leftarrow H(\phi_0, id_P, id_Q, u, v, w, d)$
>
> session key: k

Fig. 2. Protocol *SPAKE2+*

A major drawback of Protocol *SPAKE2* is that if one of the two parties represents a server, and if the server's password file is leaked to the adversary, then the adversary immediately learns the user's password. The initial goal of this research was to analyze the security of Protocol *SPAKE2+*, shown in Fig. 2, which was designed to mitigate against such password file leakage. Protocol *SPAKE2+* was presented in [17], but only some intuition of security was given, rather than a proof. The claim in [17] was that it is secure under the CDH assumption in the random oracle model, but even the security model for this claim was not specified.

The goal is to analyze such a protocol in the model where the password file may be leaked. In the case of such a leakage, the basic security goal is that the adversary cannot log into the server unless it succeeds in an *offline* dictionary attack (note that the adversary can certainly impersonate the server to a client).

In terms of formal models for this setting, probably the best available model is the UC framework for asymmetric PAKE security in [19], which builds on the UC framework for ordinary (i.e., symmetric) PAKE security in [14]. Even without password file leakage, the UC framework is stronger than, and preferable to, the BPR framework in a number of important aspects.

- The UC framework models *arbitrary* password selection, where some passwords may be related, and where the choice of password can be arbitrary, rather than chosen from some assumed distribution. In contrast, the BPR framework assumes that all passwords are independently drawn from some specific distribution.

---

an oracle is given triples (g^μ, g^ν, g^κ), and returns "yes" if $\kappa = \mu\nu$ and "no" otherwise. This is not a *falsifiable* assumption (as defined in [24]). This is in contrast to the weaker *interactive CDH assumption*, in which it is required that $g^\mu = g^\alpha$. This is the same assumption used to analyze the well-known DHIES and ECIES schemes (which are essentially just "hashed" ElGamal schemes) in the random oracle model. See [3], where is called the *Strong Diffie-Hellman* assumption.

- In the BPR framework, when the adversary guesses any one password, the game is over and the adversary wins. This means that in a system of 1,000,000 users, if the adversary guesses any one user's password in an online dictionary attack, there are no security guarantees at all for the remaining 999,999 users. In contrast, in the UC framework, guessing one password has no effect on the security of other passwords (to the extent, of course, that those other passwords are independent of the guessed password).
- It is not clear what the security implications of the BPR framework are for secure-channel protocols that are built on top of a secure PAKE protocol. (We will discuss this in more detail in the following paragraphs.) In contrast, PAKE security in the UC framework implies simulation-based security of any secure-channel protocol built on top of the PAKE protocol.

For these reasons, we prefer to get a proof of security in the UC framework. However, Protocol *SPAKE2* itself does not appear to be secure in UC framework for symmetric PAKE (as defined in [14]), and for the same reason, Protocol *SPAKE2+* is not secure in UC framework for asymmetric PAKE (as defined in [19]). One way to see this is as follows. Suppose that in Protocol *SPAKE2* an adversary interacts with Q, and runs the protocol honestly, making a guess that the correct password is π'. Now, at the time the adversary delivers the random group element u to Q, no simulator can have any idea as to the adversary's guess π' (even if it is allowed to see the adversary's queries to the random oracle H), and Q will respond with some v, and from Q's perspective, the key exchange protocol is over, and Q may start using the established session key k in some higher-level secure-channel protocol. For example, at some later time, the adversary might see a message together with a MAC on that message using a key derived from k. At this later time, the adversary can then query H at the appropriate input to determine whether its guess π' was correct or not. However, in the ideal functionality presented in [14], making a guess at a password after the key is established is not allowed. On a practical level, good security practice dictates that any reasonable ideal functionality should not allow this, as any failed online dictionary attack should be detectable by the key exchange protocol. On a more fundamental level, in any reasonable UC formulation, the simulator (or the simulator together with ideal functionality) must decide immediately, at the time a session key is established, whether it is a "fresh" key, a copy of a "fresh" key, or a "compromised" key (one that may be known to the adversary). In the above example, the simulator cannot possibly classify Q's key at the time that the key is established, because it has no way of knowing if the password π' that the adversary has in mind (but which at that time is completely unknown to the simulator) is correct or not. Because it *might* be correct, that would suggest we *must* classify the key as "compromised", even though it may not be. However, if the ideal functionality allowed for that, this would be an unacceptably weak notion of security, as then *every* interaction with the adversary would result in a "compromised" session key.

The obvious way to solve the problem noted above is to enhance Protocol *SPAKE2* with extra *key confirmation flows*. This is anyway considered good security practice, and the IETF draft specification [26] already envisions such an enhancement.

Note that [1] shows that Protocol *SPAKE2* provides forward security in the BPR framework. This suggests that the notion of forward security defined in [7] is not really very strong; in particular, it does not seem strong enough to prove a meaningful simulation-based notion of security for a channel built on top of a PAKE protocol.

In concurrent and independent work, [2] show that Protocol *SPAKE2* is secure in the UC framework, but with respect to a weak ideal functionality (which, again, does not seem strong enough to prove a meaningful simulation-based notion of security for a channel built on top of a PAKE protocol). They also show that Protocol *SPAKE2* with additional key confirmation flows is secure in the UC framework, with respect to an ideal functionality very similar to that considered here. We note that all of their security proofs make use of the very strong *Gap* CDH assumption, mentioned above, whereas all of our results only make use of the *standard* CDH assumption.

2.1 Outline

In Sect. 3, we introduce Protocol *KC-SPAKE2*, which is a variation of Protocol *SPAKE2* that includes key confirmation. In Sect. 4 we give a fairly self-contained overview of the general UC framework, and in Sect. 4.2, we specify the symmetric PAKE ideal functionality that we will use to analyze Protocol *KC-SPAKE2* in the UC framework (discussing why we made certain changes to the UC formulation in [14]). In Sect. 5, we introduce Protocol *KC-SPAKE2+*, which is to Protocol *KC-SPAKE2* as Protocol *SPAKE2+* is to Protocol *SPAKE2*. In Sect. 6, we specify the *asymmetric* PAKE ideal functionality that we will use to analyze Protocol *KC-SPAKE2+* in the UC framework, and we discuss why we made certain changes to the UC formulation in [19]. Section 7 describes Protocol *IETF-SPAKE2+*, which is a variant of Protocol *KC-SPAKE2+* that generalizes the protocol described in the IETF draft specification [26]. Section 8 gives formal statements of our security theorems. All of our security proofs are in the random oracle model under the CDH assumption (with some additional, standard assumptions on some symmetric primitives for Protocol *IETF-SPAKE2+*). Although we do not have space in this extended abstract to present proofs of these theorems (but which are presented in the full version of the paper [25]), in Sect. 9 we present a very brief sketch of some of the main ideas.

3 Protocol *KC-SPAKE2*

We begin by presenting a protocol, *KC-SPAKE2*, which is a simplified version of Protocol *SPAKE2* with key confirmation flows. This protocol is essentially Protocol *PFS-SPAKE2* presented in the paper [6]. In that paper, this protocol was shown to provide perfect forward secrecy in the BPR framework [7] (under the

$$\boxed{\begin{array}{l}
\qquad\qquad\text{public system parameter: random } a \in \mathbb{G} \\
\qquad\qquad\qquad \text{shared secret password: } \pi \\[2mm]
P \qquad\qquad\qquad\qquad\qquad\qquad\qquad Q \\[2mm]
\alpha \xleftarrow{\text{R}} \mathbb{Z}_q, u \leftarrow g^\alpha a^\pi \qquad\xrightarrow{\quad u \quad}\quad \beta \xleftarrow{\text{R}} \mathbb{Z}_q, v \leftarrow g^\beta \\
\qquad\qquad\qquad\qquad\qquad\qquad\qquad w \leftarrow (u/a^\pi)^\beta \\
\qquad\qquad\qquad\qquad\qquad\qquad\qquad (k, k_1, k_2) \leftarrow H(\pi, id_P, id_Q, u, v, w) \\[1mm]
\qquad\qquad\qquad\qquad\qquad\quad\xleftarrow{\;v, k_1\;} \\
w \leftarrow v^\alpha \\
(k, k_1, k_2) \leftarrow H(\pi, id_P, id_Q, u, v, w) \\
\text{validate } k_1 \\[2mm]
\qquad\qquad\qquad\qquad\quad\xrightarrow{\quad k_2 \quad}\quad \text{validate } k_2 \\[2mm]
\qquad\qquad\qquad\qquad\text{session key: } k
\end{array}}$$

Fig. 3. Protocol *KC-SPAKE2*

CDH assumption in the random oracle model). Our goal here is to analyze Protocol *KC-SPAKE2* in the UC model, and then to augment Protocol *KC-SPAKE2* so that it is secure against server compromise in the UC framework. Note that in the paper [4], a protocol that is very similar to Protocol *KC-SPAKE2* was also shown to provide perfect forward secrecy in the BPR framework (also under the CDH assumption in the random oracle model).

Protocol *KC-SPAKE2* makes use of a cyclic group $\mathbb{G}$ of prime order q generated by $g \in G$. It also makes use of a hash function H, which we model as a random oracle, and which outputs elements of the set $\mathcal{K} \times \mathcal{K}_{\text{auth}} \times \mathcal{K}_{\text{auth}}$, where $\mathcal{K}$ is the set of all possible session keys, and $\mathcal{K}_{\text{auth}}$ is an arbitrary set of super-polynomial size, used for explicit key confirmation. The protocol has a public system parameter $a \in \mathbb{G}$, which is assumed to be a random element of $\mathbb{G}$ that is generated securely, so that no party knows its discrete logarithm. Furthermore, passwords are viewed as elements of $\mathbb{Z}_q$. Protocol *KC-SPAKE2* is described in Fig. 3. Both users compute the value $w = g^{\alpha\beta}$, and then compute $(k, k_1, k_2) \leftarrow H(\pi, id_P, id_Q, u, v, w)$. Note that P "blinds" the value g^α by multiplying it by a^π, while Q does not perform a corresponding blinding. Also, P checks that the authentication key k_1' it receives is equal to the authentication key k_1 that it computed; otherwise, P aborts *without sending* k_2. Likewise, Q checks that the authentication key k_2' it receives is equal to the authentication key k_2 that it computed; otherwise, Q aborts. The value k is the session key.

In this protocol, it is essential that the P first sends the flow u, and then Q responds with v, k_1, and only then (if k_1 is valid) does P respond with k_2. Also, in this protocol, as well as Protocol *KC-SPAKE2+* (in Sect. 5), it is essential that P validates that $v \in \mathbb{G}$ and Q validates that $u \in \mathbb{G}$.

It is useful to think of P as the client and Q as the server. From a practical point of view, this is a very natural way to assign roles: the client presumably initiates any session with the server, and the first flow of Protocol *KC-SPAKE2* can piggyback on that initial message. In addition, as we transition from Protocol *KC-SPAKE2* to Protocol *KC-SPAKE2+*, we will also assign P the role of client and Q the role of server.

Detecting Failed Online Dictionary Attacks. From a practical perspective, it is desirable to be able to detect a failed online dictionary attack and to take preventive action. In Protocol *KC-SPAKE2*, a client P can detect a (potential) failed online dictionary attack when it receives an invalid authentication key k_1 (of course, the authentication key could be invalid for other, possibly benign, reasons, such as a transmission error). Moreover, the adversary can only learn if its password guess was correct by seeing how P responds. Indeed, the adversary learns nothing at all if it does not send the second flow to P. Now consider how a server Q may detect a (potential) failed online dictionary attack. After the server sends out k_1, the adversary can already check if its guess was correct. If its guess was incorrect, it cannot feasibly respond with a valid k_2, and such an adversary would presumably not even bother sending k_2. Thus, if Q times out waiting for k_2, then to be on the safe side, Q must consider such a time-out to be a potential online dictionary attack. If, from a security perspective, it is viewed that online dictionary attacks against the server are more likely, it might be advantageous to flip the roles of P and Q, so that it is the client that sends the first authentication key. Unfortunately, in the typical setting where the client sends the first flow, this will increase the number of flows from 3 to 4. Although we do not analyze this variant or its asymmetric secure "+" variant, it should be straightforward to modify the proofs presented here to cover these variants as well. Finally, as we already mentioned above, in the original Protocol *SPAKE2*, which provides no explicit key confirmation, it is impossible to detect a failed online dictionary attack in the key exchange protocol itself.

4   Simulation-Based Definition of Secure PAKE

Protocol *KC-SPAKE2* was already analyzed in the BPR framework. Our goal is to analyze Protocol *KC-SPAKE2* in the UC framework. The main motivation for doing so is that we eventually want to analyze the asymmetric Protocol *KC-SPAKE2+* in the UC framework.

We give a fairly self-contained definition of a secure PAKE. Our definition is a simulation-based definition that is essentially in the UC framework of [12]. We do not strictly adhere to all of the low-level mechanics and conventions given in [12]. Indeed, it is not really possible to do so, for a couple of reasons. First, between the time of its original appearance on the eprint archive and the time of this writing, the paper [12] has been revised a total of 14 times, with some of those revisions being quite substantial. So it is not clear what "the" definition of the UC framework is. Second, as pointed out in [22] and [21], the definitions in the contemporaneous versions of [12] were mathematically inconsistent. While there are more recent versions of [12], we have not yet been able to independently validate that these newer versions actually correct the problems identified in [22]

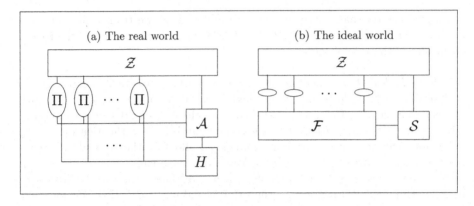

Fig. 4. The real and ideal worlds in the UC framework

and [21], while not introducing new problems. Our point of view, however, is that even though it is extremely difficult to get all of the details right, the core of the UC framework is robust enough so as to give meaningful security guarantees even if some of the low-level mechanics are vaguely or even inconsistently specified, and that these security guarantees are mainly independent of small changes to these low-level mechanics. In fact, it is fair to say that most papers that purport to prove results in the UC framework are written without any serious regard toward, or even knowledge of, most of these low-level mechanics.

Our definitions of security for PAKE differ from that presented in [14], which was the first paper to formally define secure PAKE in the UC framework. Some of these differences are due to the fact that we eventually will modify this functionality to deal with server corruptions, and so we will already modify the definition to be more compatible with this. While the paper [19] builds on [14] to model asymmetric PAKE, the paper [20] identifies several flaws in the model of [19]. Thus, we have taken it upon ourselves to correct these flaws in a reasonable way.

4.1   Review of the UC Framework

We begin with a very brief, high-level review of the UC framework. Figure 4a shows a picture of the "real world" execution of a Protocol Π. The oval shapes represent individual machines that are faithfully executing the protocol Π. The environment $\mathcal{Z}$ represents higher-level protocols that use Π as a sub-protocol, as well as any adversary that is attacking those higher-level protocols. However, all of these details are abstracted away, and $\mathcal{Z}$ can be quite arbitrary. The adversary $\mathcal{A}$ represents an adversary attacking Protocol Π. Adversary $\mathcal{A}$ communicates continuously with $\mathcal{Z}$, so as to coordinate its attack on Π with any ongoing attack on a higher-level protocol. The protocol machines receive their inputs from $\mathcal{Z}$ and send their outputs to $\mathcal{Z}$. Normally, one would think of these inputs as coming from and going to a higher-level protocol. The protocol machines also send and receive messages from $\mathcal{A}$, but not with each other. Indeed, among other things, the adversary $\mathcal{A}$ essentially models a completely insecure network, effectively dropping, injecting, and modifying protocol messages at will. Figure 4a also shows a box labeled H. In our analysis of Protocol *KC-SPAKE2*, we model H a random oracle. This means that in the "real world", the protocol machines and the adversary $\mathcal{A}$ may directly query the random oracle H. The environment $\mathcal{Z}$ does not have direct access to H; however, it can access H indirectly via $\mathcal{A}$.

Figure 4b shows a picture of the "ideal world" execution. The environment $\mathcal{Z}$ is exactly the same as before. The box labeled $\mathcal{F}$ is an *ideal functionality* that is essentially a trusted third party that we *wish* we could use to run the protocol for us. The small oval shapes also represent protocol machines, but now these protocol machines are just simple "repeaters" that pass their inputs directly from $\mathcal{Z}$ to $\mathcal{F}$, and their outputs directly from $\mathcal{F}$ to $\mathcal{Z}$. The box labeled $\mathcal{S}$ is called a *simulator*, but really it is just an adversary that happens to operate in the "ideal world". The simulator $\mathcal{S}$ can converse with $\mathcal{Z}$, just as $\mathcal{A}$ did in the "real world". The simulator $\mathcal{S}$ can also interact with $\mathcal{F}$, but its influence on $\mathcal{F}$ will typically be limited: the precise influence that $\mathcal{S}$ can exert on $\mathcal{F}$ is determined by the specification of $\mathcal{F}$ itself. Typically, while $\mathcal{S}$ cannot cause any "bad events" that would violate security, it can still determine the order in which various events occur.

Roughly speaking, we say that Protocol Π *securely emulates* ideal functionality $\mathcal{F}$ if for every efficient adversary $\mathcal{A}$, there exists an efficient simulator $\mathcal{S}$, such that no efficient environment $\mathcal{Z}$ can effectively distinguish between the "real world" execution and the "ideal world" execution. The precise meaning of "efficient" here is a variant of polynomial time that adequately deals with a complex, multi-party system. We suggest the definitions in [21,22], but other definitions are possible as well. In the UC framework, saying that Protocol Π is "secure" means that it securely emulates $\mathcal{F}$. Of course, what "secure" means depends on the specification of $\mathcal{F}$.

4.2   An Ideal Functionality for PAKE

We now give our ideal functionality for PAKE. As mentioned above, the functionality we present here is a bit different from that in [14], and some of the low-level mechanics (relating to things like "session identifiers") is a bit different from those in [12].

- Party P inputs: ($\texttt{init-client}, rid, \pi$)
  Intuition: This models the initialization of a client and its relationship to a particular server, including the shared password π.
  ○ We say that P is *initialized as a client*, where rid is its *relationship ID* and π is its *password*.
  ○ Assumes (i) that P has not been previously initialized as either a client or server, and (ii) that no other client has been initialized with the same relation ID.[5]

---

[5] As we describe it, the ideal functionality imposes various pre-conditions on the inputs it receives. The reader may assume that if these are not met, an "error message" back to whoever sent the input. However, see Remark 1 below.

    ○ The simulator is sent $(\texttt{init-client}, P, rid)$.

    ○ Note that rid is a relationship ID that corresponds to a single client/server pair. In practice (and in the protocols analyzed here), such a relationship ID is a pair $rid = (id_P, id_Q)$.

- Party Q inputs: $(\texttt{init-server}, rid, \pi)$

  Intuition: This models the initialization of a server and its relationship to a particular client, including the shared password π.

      ○ We say that Q is *initialized as a server*, where rid is its *relationship ID* and π is its *password*.

      ○ Assumes (i) that Q has not been previously initialized at either a client or server, and (ii) that no other server has been initialized with the same relationship ID.

      ○ Assumes that if a client and server are both initialized with the same relationship ID rid, then they are both initialized with the same password π.

      ○ The simulator is sent $(\texttt{init-server}, Q, rid)$.

      ○ Note: for any relationship ID, there can be at most one client and one server with that ID, and we call this client and server *partners*.

- Party P inputs: $(\texttt{init-client-instance}, iid_P, \pi^*)$

  Intuition: This models the initialization of a client instance, which corresponds to a single execution of the key exchange protocol by the client, using possibly mistyped or misremembered password π^*.

      ○ Party P must have been previously initialized as a client.

      ○ The value iid_P is an *instance ID*, and must be unique among all instances of P.

      ○ The simulator is sent $(\texttt{init-client-instance}, P, iid_P, type)$, where $type := 1$ if $\pi^* = \pi$, and otherwise $type := 0$, and where π is P's password.

      ○ We call this instance (P, iid_P), and the ideal functionality sets the state of the instance to *original*.

      ○ We call π^* the *password of this instance*, and we say that this instance is *good* if $\pi^* = \pi$, and *bad* otherwise.

      ○ Note: a *bad* client instance is meant to model the situation in the actual, physical world where the human client mistypes or misremembers their password associated with the server.

- Party Q inputs: $(\texttt{init-server-instance}, iid_Q)$

  Intuition: This models the initialization of a server instance, which corresponds to a single execution of the key exchange protocol by the server.

      ○ Party Q must have been previously initialized as a server.

      ○ The value iid_Q is an *instance ID*, and must be unique among all instances of Q.

      ○ The simulator is sent $(\texttt{init-server-instance}, Q, iid_Q)$.

      ○ We call this instance (Q, iid_Q), and the ideal functionality sets the state of the instance to *original*.

○ If π is Q's password, we also define $\pi^* := \pi$ to be the *password of this instance*. Unlike client instances, server instances are always considered *good*.

- Simulator inputs: $(\mathtt{test\text{-}pwd}, X, iid_X, \pi')$
  Intuition: This models an *on-line* dictionary attack, whereby an attacker makes a *single* guess at a password by interacting with a particular client/server instance.
  ○ Assumes (i) that there is an instance (X, iid_X), where X is either a client or server, (ii) that this is the first $\mathtt{test\text{-}pwd}$ for (X, iid_X), and (iii) that the state of (X, iid_X) is either *original* or *abort*.
  ○ The ideal functionality tests if π' is equal to the password π^* of instance (X, iid_X):
  - if $\pi' = \pi^*$, then the ideal functionality does the following: (i) if the state of the instance is *original*, it changes the state to *correct-guess*, and (ii) sends the message $(\mathtt{correct})$ to the simulator.
  - if $\pi' \neq \pi^*$, then the ideal functionality does the following: (i) if the state of the instance is *original*, it changes the state to *incorrect-guess*, and (ii) sends the message $(\mathtt{incorrect})$ to the simulator.
  ○ Note: if X is a server or (X, iid_X) is a *good* client instance, then $\pi^* = \pi$, where π is X's password.

- Simulator inputs: $(\mathtt{fresh\text{-}key}, X, iid_X, sid)$
  Intuition: This models the successful termination of a protocol instance that returns to the corresponding client or server a *fresh* key, i.e., a key that is completely random and independent of all other keys and of the attacker's view, along with the given *session ID sid*. This is *not* allowed if a password guess was made against this instance.
  ○ Note: if X is a server or (X, iid_X) is a *good* client instance, then $\pi^* = \pi$, where π is X's password. The value *sid* is a *session ID* that is to be assigned to the instance (X, iid_X).
  ○ Assumes (i) that (X, iid_X) is an *original, good* instance, where X is either a client or a server, (ii) that there is no other instance (X, iid'_X) that has been assigned the same session ID *sid*, (iii) that X has a partner Y, and (iv) that there is no instance (Y, iid_Y) that has been assigned the same session ID *sid*.
  ○ The ideal functionality does the following: (i) assigns the session ID *sid* to the instance (X, iid_X), (ii) generates a random session key k, (iii) changes the state of the instance (X, iid_X) to *fresh-key*, and (iv) sends the output $(\mathtt{key}, iid_X, sid, k)$ to X.

- Simulator inputs: $(\mathtt{copy\text{-}key}, X, iid_X, sid)$
  Intuition: This models the successful termination of a protocol instance that returns to the corresponding client or server a *copy* of a fresh key, along with the given *session ID sid*. Note that a fresh key can be copied only once and only from an appropriate partner instance with a matching session ID. This is *not* allowed if a password guess was made against this instance.

○ Assumes (i) that (X, iid_X) is an *original, good* instance, where X is either a client or server, (ii) that there is no other instance (X, iid'_X) that has been assigned the same session ID *sid*, (iii) that X has a partner Y, (iv) that there is a unique instance (Y, iid_Y) that has been assigned the same session ID *sid*, and (v) the state of (Y, iid_Y) is *fresh-key*.

○ The ideal functionality does the following: (i) assigns the session ID *sid* to the instance (X, iid_X), (ii) changes the state of the instance (X, iid_X) to *copy-key*, and (iii) sends the output (key, iid_X, sid, k) to X, where k is the key that was previously generated for the instance (Y, iid_Y).

- Simulator inputs: (corrupt-key, X, iid_X, sid, k)
  Intuition: This models the successful termination of a protocol instance that returns to the corresponding client or server a *corrupt* key, i.e., a key that is known to the adversary, along with the given *session ID sid*. This is *only* allowed if a corresponding password guess against this *particular* instance was successful.

  ○ Assumes (i) that (X, iid_X) is a *correct-guess* instance, where X is either a client or server, (ii) that there is no other instance (X, iid'_X) that has been assigned the same session ID *sid*, and (iii) that if X has a partner Y, there is no instance (Y, iid_Y) that has been assigned the same session ID *sid*.

  ○ The ideal functionality does the following: (i) assigns the session ID *sid* to the instance (X, iid_X), (ii) changes the state of the instance (X, iid_X) to *corrupt-key*, and (iii) sends the output (key, iid_X, sid, k) to X.

- Simulator inputs: (abort, X, iid_X)
  Intuition: This models the unsuccessful termination of a protocol instance. Note that an incorrect password guess against an instance can only lead to its unsuccessful termination.

  ○ Assumes that (X, iid_X) is either an *original, correct-guess*, or *incorrect-guess* instance, where X is either a client or server.

  ○ The ideal functionality does the following: (i) changes the state of the instance (X, iid_X) to *abort*, and (ii) sends the output (abort, iid_X) to X.

4.3   Well-Behaved Environments

In the above specification of our ideal functionality, certain pre-conditions must be met on inputs received from the environment (via the parties representing clients and servers). To this end, we impose certain restrictions on the environment itself.

We say that an environment $\mathcal{Z}$ is **well behaved** if the inputs from clients and servers (which come from $\mathcal{Z}$) do not violate any of the stated preconditions. Specifically, this means that for the init-client and init-server inputs: (i) no two clients are initialized with same relationship ID, (ii) no two servers are initialized with the same relationship ID, and (iii) if a client and server are initialized with the same relationship ID, then they are initialized with the same password; moreover, for the init-client-instance and init-server inputs

(iv) no two instances of a given client or server are initialized with the same instance ID.

In formulating the notion that a concrete protocol "securely emulates" the ideal functionality, one restricts the quantification over all environments to all such *well-behaved* environments. It is easy to verify that all of the standard UC theorems, including dummy-adversary completeness, transitivity, and composition, hold when restricted to *well-behaved* environments.

Remark 1. In describing our ideal functionality, in processing an input from a client, server, or simulator, we impose pre-conditions on that input. In all cases, these pre-conditions can be efficiently verified by the ideal functionality, and one may assume that if these pre-conditions are not satisfied, then the ideal functionality sends an "error message" back to whoever sent it the input.

However, it is worth making two observations. First, for inputs from a client or server, these pre-conditions cannot be "locally" validated by the given client or server; however, the assumption that the environment is well-behaved guarantees that the corresponding pre-conditions will always be satisfied (see Remark 2 below for further discussion). Second, for inputs from simulator, the simulator itself has enough information to validate these pre-conditions, and so without loss of generality, we can also assume that the simulator does not bother submitting invalid inputs to the ideal functionality.

4.4 Liveness

In general, UC security by itself does not ensure any notion of protocol "liveness". For a PAKE protocol, it is natural to define such a notion of liveness as follows. In the real world, if the adversary faithfully delivers all messages between a *good* instance I of a client P and an instance J of P's partner server Q, then I and J will both output a session key and their session IDs will match. All of the protocols we examine here satisfy this notion of liveness.

With our PAKE ideal functionality, UC security implies that if an instance I of a client P and an instance J of P's partner server Q both output a session key, and their session IDs match, then one of them will hold a "fresh" session key, while the other will hold a copy of that "fresh" key.

If we also assume liveness, then UC security implies the following. Suppose that the adversary faithfully delivers all messages between a *good* instance I of a client P and an instance J of P's partner server Q. Then I and J will both output a session key, their session IDs will match, and one of them will hold a "fresh" session key, while the other will hold a copy of that "fresh" key. Moreover, by the logic of our ideal functionality, this implies that in the ideal world, the simulator did not make a guess at the password. See further discussion in Remark 7 below.

4.5 Further Discussion

Remark 2. As in [14], our ideal functionality does not specify how passwords are chosen or how a given clients/server pair come to agree upon a shared password.

All of these details are relegated to the environment. Our "matching password restriction", which says that in any well-behaved environment (Sect. 4.3), a client and server that share the same relationship ID must be initialized with the same password, really means this: *whatever the mechanism used for a client and server to agree upon a shared password, the agreed-upon password should be known to the client (resp., server) before the client (resp., server) actually runs an instance of the protocol.*

This "matching password restriction" seems perfectly reasonable and making it greatly simplifies both the logic of the ideal functionality and the simulators in our proofs.

Note that the fact that client inputs this shared password to the ideal functionality during client initialization is not meant to imply that in a real protocol the client actually stores this password anywhere. Indeed, in the actual, physical world, we expect that a human client may memorize their password and not store it anywhere (except during the execution of an instance of the protocol). Our model definitely allows for this.

Also note that whatever mechanisms are used to choose a password and share it between a client and server, as well as to choose relationship IDs and instance IDs, these mechanisms must satisfy the requirements of a well-behaved environment. These requirements are quite reasonable and easy to satisfy with well-known techniques under reasonable assumptions.

Remark 3. Our formalism allows us to model the situation in the actual, physical world where a human client mistypes or misremembers their password. This is the point of having the client pass in the password π^* when it initializes a client instance. The "matching password restriction" (see Remark 2) makes it easy for the ideal functionality to immediately classify a client as *good* or *bad*, according to whether or not $\pi^* = \pi$, where π is the password actually shared with the corresponding server.[6] The logic of our ideal functionality implies that the only thing that can happen to a *bad* instance is that either: (a) the instance aborts, or (b) the adversary makes one guess at π^*, and if that guess is correct, the adversary makes that instance accept a "compromised" key. In particular, no instance of the corresponding server will ever share a session ID or session key with a *bad* client instance.

Mistyped or misremembered passwords are also modeled in [14] and subsequent works (such as [19] and [20]). All of these works insist on "hiding" from the adversary, to some degree or other, whether or not the client instance is *bad*. It is not clear what the motivation for this really is. Indeed, in [14], they observe that "we are not aware of any application where this is needed". Moreover, in the typical situation where a client is running a secure-channels protocol on top of a PAKE protocol, an adversary will almost inevitably find out that a client

---

[6] Otherwise, if the corresponding server had not yet been initialized with a password π at the time this client instance had been initialized with a password π^*, the ideal functionality could not determine (or inform the simulator) whether or not $\pi^* = \pi$ at that time. This would lead to rather esoteric complications in the logic of the ideal functionality and the simulators in our proofs.

instance is *bad*, because it will most likely abort without a session key (or possibly, as required in [14], will end up with a session key that is not shared with any server instance).

So to keep things simple, and since there seems little motivation to do otherwise, our ideal simply notifies the simulator if a client instance is *good* or *bad*, and it does so immediately when the client instance is initialized. Indeed, as pointed out in [20], the mechanism [19] for dealing with mistyped or misremembered passwords was flawed. In [20], another mechanism is proposed, but our mechanism is much simpler and more direct.

Remark 4. One might ask: why is it necessary to explicitly model mistyped or misremembered passwords at all? Why not simply absorb *bad* client instances into the adversary. Indeed, from the point of view of preventing such a *bad* client from logging into a server, this is sufficient. However, it would not adequately model security for the client: if, say, a human client enters a password that is nearly identical to the correct password, this should not compromise the client's password in any way; however, we cannot afford to model this situation by giving this nearly-identical password to the adversary.

Note that the BPR framework [7] does not model mistyped or misremembered passwords at all. We are not aware of any protocols that are secure in the BPR framework that become blatantly insecure if a client enters a closely related but incorrect password.

Remark 5. In our formalism, in the real world, all instances of a given client are executed by a single client machine. This is an abstraction, and should not be taken too literally. In the real, physical world, a human client may choose to run instances of the protocol on different devices. Logically, there is nothing preventing us from mapping those different devices onto the same client machine in our formalism.

Remark 6. In our formalism, in the real world, a server instance must be initialized (by the environment) before a protocol message can be delivered (from the adversary) to that instance. This is an abstraction, and should not be taken too literally. In practice, a client could initiate a run of the protocol by sending an initial message over the network to the server, who would then initialize an instance of the protocol and then effectively let the adversary deliver the initial message to that instance.

Remark 7. As in all UC formulations of PAKE, the simulator (i.e., ideal-world adversary) gets to make at most one password guess per protocol instance, which is the best possible, since in the real world, an adversary may always try to log in with a password guess. Moreover, as discussed above in Sect. 4.4, then assuming the protocol provides liveness, the simulator does not get to make any password guesses for protocol executions in which the adversary only eavesdrops. This corresponds to the "Execute" queries in the BPR framework, in which an adversary passively eavesdrops on protocol executions, and which do not increase the odds of guessing a password. Unlike the formulation in [14], where this property requires a proof, this property is explicitly built in to the definition.

Remark 8. Our ideal functionality is explicitly a "multi-session" functionality: it models all of the parties in the system and all runs of the protocol.

Formally, for every client/server pair (P, Q) that share a relationship ID rid, this ID will typically be of he form $rid = (id_P, id_Q)$, where id_P is a client-ID and id_Q is a server-ID. This is how relationship IDs will be presented Protocol *KC-SPAKE2*, but it is not essential. In practice, the same client-ID may be associated with one user in relation to one server, and with a different user in relation to another server.

For a given party X, which may either be a client P or server Q, it will have associated with it several *instances*, each of which has an *instance ID iid_X*. Note that in the formal model, identifiers like P and Q denote some kind of formal identifier, although these are never intended to be used in any real protocols. Similarly, instance IDs are also not intended to be used in any real protocols. These are all just "indices" used in the formalism to identify various participants. It is the relationship IDs and session IDs that are meant to be used by and have meaning in higher-level protocols. Looking ahead, the session IDs for *KC-SPAKE2* will be the partial conversations (u, v).

Also note that every instance of a server Q in our formal model establishes sessions with instances of the same client P. In practice, of course, a "server" establishes sessions with many clients. One maps this onto our model by modeling such a "server" as a collection of several of our servers.

Remark 9. What we call a *relationship ID* corresponds to what is called a "session ID" in the classical UC framework [12]. Our ideal functionality explicitly models many "UC sessions"—this is necessary, as we eventually need to consider several such "UC sessions" since all of the protocols we analyze make use of common reference string and random oracles shared across many such "UC sessions". What we call a *session ID* actually corresponds most closely what is called a "subsession ID" in [14] (in the "multi-session extension" of their PAKE functionality). Note that [14], a client and server instance have to agree in advance on a "subsession ID". This is actually quite impractical, as it forces an extra round of communication just to establish such a "subsession ID". In contrast, our *session IDs* are computed as part of the protocol itself (which more closely aligns with the notion of a "session ID" in the BPR framework [7]).

In our model, after a session key is established, a higher-level protocol would likely use a string composed of the *relationship ID*, the *session ID*, and perhaps other elements, as a "session ID" in the sense of [12].

Remark 10. Our ideal functionality models explicit authentication in a fairly strict sense. Note that [14] does not model explicit authentication at all. Furthermore, as pointed out in [20], the formulation of explicit authentication in [19] is flawed. Our ideal functionality is quite natural in that when an adversary makes an unsuccessful password guess on a protocol instance, then when that instance terminates, the corresponding party will receive an abort message. Our formulation of explicit authentication is similar to that in [20], but is simpler because (as discussed above in Remark 3) we do not try to hide the fact that a client instance is *bad*. Another difference is that in our formulation, the simulator may first force an abort and then only later make its one password guess—this behavior does not appear to be allowed in the ideal functionality in [20]. This difference is essential to be able to analyze *KC-SPAKE2*, since an adversary may start a session with a server, running the protocol with a guessed password, but after the server sends the message v, k_1, the adversary can send the server some garbage, forcing an abort, and then at a later time, the adversary may evaluate the random oracle at the relevant point to see if its password guess was correct.

Remark 11. We do not explicitly model corrupt parties, or corruptions of any kind for that matter (although this will change somewhat when we model server compromise in the asymmetric PAKE model in Sect. 6). In particular, all client and server instances in the real world are assumed to faithfully follow their prescribed protocols. This may seem surprising, but it is not a real restriction. First of all, anything a statically corrupt party could do could be done directly by the adversary, as there are no authenticated channels in our real world. In addition, because the environment manages passwords, our formulation models adaptively exposing passwords, which corresponds to the "weak corruption model" of the BPR framework [7]. Moreover, just like the security model in [14], our security model implies security in the "weak corruption model" of the BPR framework.[7] The proof is essentially the same as that in [14]. However, just like in [14] (as well as in [19] and [20]), our framework does not model adaptive corruptions in which an adversary may obtain the internal state of a running protocol instance.[8]

5 Protocol *KC-SPAKE2+*

We present Protocol *KC-SPAKE2+* in Fig. 5. Given a password π, a client derives a pair $(\phi_0, \phi_1) \in \mathbb{Z}_q^2$ using a hash function F, which we model as a random oracle. The server, on the other hand, just stores the pair (ϕ_0, c), where $c := g^{\phi_1} \in \mathbb{G}$. Note that unlike Protocol *KC-SPAKE2*, in Protocol *KC-SPAKE2+*, a password π need not be an element of $\mathbb{Z}_q$, as it first gets passed through the hash function F.

6 An Ideal Functionality for Asymmetric PAKE

First, as we already noted, the attempt to formulate an asymmetric PAKE functionality in [19] was fundamentally flawed, as was demonstrated in [20]. One major problem identified in [20] was that after a server is compromised, we need

---

[7] Actually, our framework does not model the notion in [7] that allows password information stored on the server to be changed. That said, we are ultimately interested asymmetric PAKE, and we are not aware of any asymmetric PAKE functionality in the literature that models this notion.

[8] This type of corruption would correspond to the "strong corruption model" of the BPR framework [7]. Note that the protocol analyzed in [7] is itself only proven secure in the "weak corruption model".

---

public system parameter: random $a \in \mathbb{G}$

password: π, $(\phi_0, \phi_1) := F(\pi, id_P, id_Q)$

P Q

secret: ϕ_0, ϕ_1 secret: $\phi_0, c := g^{\phi_1}$

$\alpha \xleftarrow{\text{R}} \mathbb{Z}_q, u \leftarrow g^\alpha a^{\phi_0}$ $\xrightarrow{\quad u \quad}$ $\beta \xleftarrow{\text{R}} \mathbb{Z}_q, v \leftarrow g^\beta$

$w \leftarrow (u/a^{\phi_0})^\beta, d \leftarrow c^\beta$

$(k, k_1, k_2) \leftarrow$

$H(\phi_0, id_P, id_Q, u, v, w, d)$

$w \leftarrow v^\alpha, d \leftarrow v^{\phi_1}$ $\xleftarrow{\quad v, k_1 \quad}$

$(k, k_1, k_2) \leftarrow$

$H(\phi_0, id_P, id_Q, u, v, w, d)$

validate k_1

$\xrightarrow{\quad k_2 \quad}$ validate k_2

session key: k

Fig. 5. Protocol *KC-SPAKE2+*

a good way to bound the number of "offline test" queries in the ideal world in terms of the number of "random oracle" queries in the real world. The paper [20] points out that the ideal functionality suggested in [19] cannot actually be realized by *any* protocol (including the protocol presented in [19]) for which the "password file record" stored on the server is efficiently and deterministically computable from the password. However, the "fix" proposed in [20] relies in an essential way on the notion of polynomial running time in the UC framework as formulated in [12], and as pointed out in [22], this notion of running time is itself flawed (and may or may not have been repaired in later versions of [12]). Moreover, ignoring these technical problems, the "fix" in [20] is not very satisfactory, as it does not yield a *strict* bound on the number of "offline test" queries in terms of the number "random oracle" queries. Rather, it only guarantees that the simulator runs in time bounded by some polynomial in the number of bits passed to the adversary from the environment.

We propose a simple and direct way of dealing with this issue. It is a somewhat protocol-specific solution, but it gets the job done, and is hopefully of more general utility. We assume that the protocol in question makes use of a hash function F, which we model as a random oracle, and that inputs to F are of the form (π, rid), where rid is a relationship ID, and π is a password. However, the ideal functionality for accessing this random oracle is a bit non-standard. Specifically, in the real world, the *adversary* is not allowed direct access to this random oracle. Rather, for the adversary to obtain the output value of the random oracle at some input, the *environment* must specifically instruct the random oracle functionality to give this output value to the adversary. More precisely, the environment may send an input message (`oracle-query`, π, rid) to the random oracle functionality, who responds by sending the message $(\texttt{oracle-query}, \pi, rid, F(\pi, rid))$ to the adversary.[9] Note that machines representing clients and servers may access F directly.

Now, in our ideal functionality for asymmetric PAKE, when the environment sends an input $(\texttt{oracle-query}, \pi, rid)$, this is sent to the asymmetric PAKE functionality, who simply forwards the message $(\texttt{oracle-query}, \pi, rid)$ to the simulator.[10] *Moreover*, when the simulator makes an "offline test" query to the ideal functionality, the ideal functionality will only allow such a query if there was already a corresponding $\texttt{oracle-query}$. This simple mechanism restricts the number of "offline line" test queries made against a particular rid in the ideal world strictly in terms of the number of "random oracle" queries made with the same rid in the real world.

In addition to supporting the $\texttt{oracle-query}$ interface discussed above, the following changes are made to the ideal functionality in Sect. 4.2. There is a new interface:

- Server Q inputs: $(\texttt{compromise-server})$
    - ○ The simulator is sent $(\texttt{compromise-server}, Q)$.
    - ○ We say that Q is *compromised*.

Note that in the real world, upon receiving $(\texttt{compromise-server})$, server Q sends to the adversary its "password file record" for this particular client/server pair (for Protocol *KC-SPAKE2+*, this would be the pair (ϕ_0, c)).[11] However, the server Q otherwise continues to faithfully execute its protocol as normal. There is a second new interface, which allows for "offline test" queries:

- Simulator inputs: $(\texttt{offline-test-pwd}, Q, \pi')$
    - ○ Assumes (i) that Q is a compromised server, and (ii) that the environment has already submitted the query $(\texttt{oracle-query}, rid, \pi')$ to the ideal functionality, where rid is Q's relationship ID.
    - ○ The simulator is sent $(\texttt{correct})$ if $\pi' = \pi$, and $(\texttt{incorrect})$ if $\pi' \neq \pi$.

Finally, to model the fact that once a server Q is corrupted, the simulator is always able to impersonate the server to its partner P, we modify the $\texttt{corrupt-key}$ interface as follows. Specifically, condition (i), which states:

(i) that (X, iid_X) is a *correct-guess* instance, where X is either a client or server

is replaced by the following:

(i) that either: (a) (X, iid_X) is a *correct-guess* instance, where X is either a client or server, or (b) (X, iid_X) is an *original, good* instance and X's partner is a compromised server

7   Protocol *IETF-SPAKE2+*

---

[9] Note that in the specific UC framework of [12], the environment sends this message to the random oracle functionality via a special "dummy" party.

[10] This allows the simulator to "program" the random oracle.

[11] As in [21], we model this type of compromise simply by a message sent from the environment, rather than the more indirect mechanism in [12].

$$\boxed{\begin{array}{c}
\text{public system parameters: random } a, b \in \mathbb{G} \\
\text{password: } \pi, \quad (\phi_0, \phi_1) := F(\pi, id_P, id_Q) \\[4pt]
\text{associated data: } D
\end{array}}$$

P Q

secret: ϕ_0, ϕ_1 secret: $\phi_0, c := g^{\phi_1}$

$\alpha \stackrel{\text{R}}{\leftarrow} \mathbb{Z}_q, u \leftarrow g^\alpha a^{\phi_0}$ $\xrightarrow{\quad u \quad}$ $\beta \stackrel{\text{R}}{\leftarrow} \mathbb{Z}_q,\ v \leftarrow g^\beta b^{\phi_0}$

           $w \leftarrow (u^\ell/a^{\lambda\phi_0})^\beta,\ d \leftarrow c^{\lambda\beta}$

           $(k, k_1, k_2) \leftarrow$

             $H(\phi_0, id_P, id_Q, u, v, w, d, D)$

$w \leftarrow (v^\ell/b^{\lambda\phi_0})^\alpha,\ d \leftarrow (v^\ell/b^{\lambda\phi_0})^{\phi_1}$ $\xleftarrow{\quad v, k_1 \quad}$

$(k, k_1, k_2) \leftarrow$

   $H(\phi_0, id_P, id_Q, u, v, w, d, D)$

validate k_1

        $\xrightarrow{\quad k_2 \quad}$ validate k_2

         session key: k

Fig. 6. Protocol *IETF-SPAKE2+*

Here we describe Protocol *IETF-SPAKE2+*, which is generalization of the protocol called *SPAKE2+* in the IETF draft specification [26]. The protocol is presented in Fig. 6. Unlike the previous PAKE protocols we have presented, both client and server take as input **associated data** D, and the session key is computed as (u, v, D). We will discuss below in detail the semantic significance of this associated data.

Unlike in Protocol *KC-SPAKE2+*, group elements received by a party may lie in some larger group $\overline{\mathbb{G}}$ containing $\mathbb{G}$ as a subgroup. It is assumed that parties validate membership in $\overline{\mathbb{G}}$ (which is generally cheaper than validating membership in $\mathbb{G}$). Specifically, P should validate that $v \in \overline{\mathbb{G}}$ and Q should validate that $u \in \overline{\mathbb{G}}$. We also assume that the index of $\mathbb{G}$ in $\overline{\mathbb{G}}$ is ℓ, where ℓ is not divisible by q. Note that for all $x \in \overline{\mathbb{G}}$, we have $x^\ell \in \mathbb{G}$.

We shall denote by λ the image of ℓ in $\mathbb{Z}_q$. Note that $\lambda \neq 0$. We will be rather careful in our notation involving exponents on group elements. Namely, on elements in $\mathbb{G}$, exponents will always be elements of $\mathbb{Z}_q$. On elements that lie in $\overline{\mathbb{G}}$ but not necessarily in $\mathbb{G}$, the only exponent that will be used is the index ℓ.

Unlike in Protocol *KC-SPAKE2+*, the functions F and H in Protocol *IETF-SPAKE2+* are not modeled as random oracles; rather, they are defined as follows:

$$F(\pi, id_P, id_Q) := (\phi_0, \phi_1) \tag{1}$$
$$\text{where} \quad (\phi_0, \phi_1) := F_1(f) \quad \text{and} \quad f := F_0(\pi, id_P, id_Q).$$

and

$$H(\phi_0, id_P, id_Q, u, v, w, d, D) := (k, k_1, k_2),$$
$$\text{where} \quad k_1 := H_1(h; 1, u, D), \quad k_2 := H_1(h; 2, v, D) \tag{2}$$
$$\text{and} \quad (k, h) := H_0(\phi_0, id_P, id_Q, u, v, w, d).$$

Here, the functions F_0, F_1, H_0, H_1 are modeled as follows:

- F_0 is modeled as a random oracle producing an output $f \in \mathcal{F}$, where $\mathcal{F}$ is some large finite set.
- F_1 is modeled as a pseudorandom generator (PRG) with seed space $\mathcal{F}$ and output space $\mathbb{Z}_q \times \mathbb{Z}_q$.
- H_0 is modeled as a random oracle producing an output $(k, h) \in \mathcal{K} \times \mathcal{H}$, where $\mathcal{H}$ is some large finite set.
- H_1 is modeled as a pseudorandom function (PRF) with key space $\mathcal{H}$, input space $\{1, 2\} \times \overline{\mathbb{G}} \times \mathcal{D}$, and output space $\mathcal{K}_{\text{auth}}$. As before, we assume that the size of $\mathcal{K}_{\text{auth}}$ is super-polynomial.

Remark 12. We can actually prove security under significantly weaker assumptions on F_1 and H_1. See the full version of the paper [25] for details.

Remark 13. The second public parameter $b \in \mathbb{G}$ is not necessary, and all of our proofs of security hold even if the discrete log of b is fixed and/or known to the adversary. In particular, one can set $b = 1$.

Remark 14. In the IETF draft specification [26], the function F_0 is defined to be *PBKFD*, which outputs two bit strings p_0 and p_1, and $F_1(p_0, p_1) = (\phi_0, \phi_1) = (p_0 \bmod q, p_1 \bmod q)$, where p_0 and p_1 are viewed as the binary representations of integers. Here, *PBKFD* is a *password-based key derivation function* designed to slow down brute-force attackers. Examples are *Scrypt* [RFC7914] and *Argon2* [10]. The inputs to *PBKFD* are encoded using a prefix-free encoding scheme. The lengths of p_0 and p_1 should be significantly longer than the bit length of q to ensure that ϕ_0 and ϕ_1 have distributions that are statistically close to uniform on $\mathbb{Z}_q$. In order to minimize the reliance on random oracles, it is also possible to incorporate the final stage of *PBKFD* in the function F_1.

Remark 15. In the IETF draft specification, the function H_0 is defined to be a *hash function Hash*, which may be *SHA256* or *SHA512* [RFC6234]. The inputs to *Hash* are encoded using a prefix-free encoding scheme. The output of *Hash* is a bit string $h \parallel k$. The computation of the function $H_1(h; i, x, D)$, where $i \in \{1, 2\}$, $x \in \overline{\mathbb{G}}$, and $D \in \mathcal{D}$, is defined as follows. First, we compute

$$(h_2 \parallel h_1) = KDF(nil, h, \texttt{"ConfirmationKeys"} \parallel D).$$

Here, *KDF* is a key derivation function such as *HKDF* [RFC5869], which takes as input a salt (here, *nil*), intermediate keying material (here, h), info string (here, $\texttt{"ConfirmationKeys"} \parallel D$), as well as a derived-key-length parameter (not shown here). The output of H_1 is $MAC(h_i, x)$, where *MAC* is a *message authentication code*, such as *HMAC* [RFC2104] or *CMAC-AES-128* [RFC4493], which takes as input a key (here, h_i) and a message (here, x). In the modes of operation used here, it is reasonable to view *KDF* as a PRF (with key h), and to view *MAC* (with key h_i) as a PRF. Assuming both of these are PRFs implies that H_1 itself is a PRF.

Remark 16. We model the above implementations of H_0 and F_0 as independent random oracles. Ideally, this would be verified by carrying out a complete analysis in the indifferentiability framework [18]. As proved in [18], the implementation of H_0 as a standard hash function, like *SHA256* or *SHA512*, with prefix-free input encoding, is indeed a random oracle in the indifferentiability framework, under appropriate assumptions on the underlying compression function. We are not aware of an analogous analysis for the implementation of F_0 as a standard password-based key derivation function, like *Scrypt*, or of any possible interactions between the hash functions used in both (which may be the same). Also, for H_0, it would be preferable that its inputs were prefixed with some sort of protocol ID, and that higher-level protocols that use the same hash function similarly prefix their inputs with an appropriate protocol ID. (which includes the system parameters a and b). This would ensure that there are no unwanted interactions between random oracles used in different protocols. Similarly, it would be preferable if F_0 were implemented by first hashing its input using the same hash function used for H_0, but prefixed with a different protocol ID (and which includes the system parameters a and b). This would ensure no unwanted interactions between these two random oracles. Despite these recommendations, it seems highly unlikely that the current IETF draft specification [26] has any real weaknesses.

Remark 17. The IETF draft specification allows id_P and/or id_Q to be omitted as inputs to H_0 and F_0 under certain circumstances. Our analysis does not cover this.

Remark 18. The IETF draft specification allows the parties to negotiate a ciphersuite. Our analysis does not cover this. We assume a fixed ciphersuite is used by all parties throughout the lifetime of the protocol.

Remark 19. Including u and v as inputs to H_1 is superfluous, and could have been omitted without any loss in security. Equivalently, in the IETF draft specification discussed above in Remark 15, we could just set $(k_1, k_2) := (h_1, h_2)$, and forgo the *MAC* entirely.

Remark 20. The IETF draft specification insists that the client checks that $v^\ell \neq 1$ and that the server checks that $u^\ell \neq 1$. This is superfluous. We will ignore this. Indeed, one can easily show that a protocol that makes these checks securely emulates one that does not. Note, however, that by making these checks, the "liveness property" (see Sect. 4.4) only holds with overwhelming probability (rather than with probability 1).

Remark 21. The IETF draft specification allows the server to send v and k_1 as separate messages. We will ignore this. Indeed, one can easily show that a protocol that sends these as separate messages securely emulates one that does not. This is based on the fact that in the IETF draft specification, even if v and k_1 are sent by the server as separate messages, they are sent by the server only after it receives u, and the client does nothing until it receives both v and k_1.

7.1   Extending the Ideal Functionality to Handle Associated Data

The only change required to deal with associated data are the `init-client-instance` and `init-client-instance` interfaces. In both cases, the associated data D is passed along as an additional input to the ideal functionality, which in turn passes it along immediately as an additional output to the simulator.

Remark 22. In practice, the value of D is determined outside of the protocol by some unspecified mechanism. The fact that D is passed as an input to `init-client-instance` and `init-server-instance` means that D must be fixed for that instance before the protocol starts. The fact that the value is sent to the simulator means that the protocol does not treat D as private data.

Remark 23. Our ideal functionality for PAKE allows a client instance and a server instance to share a session key only if their session IDs are equal. For Protocol *IETF-SPAKE2+*, since the session ID is computed as (u, v, D), the ideal functionality will allow a client instance and a server instance to share a session key only if their associated data values are equal. In fact, as will be evident from our proof of security, in Protocol *IETF-SPAKE2+*, if an adversary faithfully delivers messages between a client instance and a server instance, but their associated data values do not match, then neither the client nor the server instance will accept any session key at all. Our ideal functionality does not model this stronger security property.

8   Statement of Main Results

Our main results are the following:

Theorem 1. *Under the CDH assumption for $\mathbb{G}$, and modeling H as a random oracle, Protocol KC-SPAKE2 securely emulates the ideal functionality in Sect. 4.2 (with respect to all well-behaved environments as in Sect. 4.3).*

Theorem 2. *Under the CDH assumption for $\mathbb{G}$, and modeling H and F as random oracles, Protocol KC-SPAKE2+ securely emulates the ideal functionality in Sect. 6 (with respect to all well-behaved environments as in Sect. 4.3).*

Theorem 3. *Under the CDH assumption for $\mathbb{G}$, assuming F_1 is a PRG, assuming H_1 is a PRF, and modeling H_0 and F_0 as random oracles, Protocol IETF-SPAKE2+ securely emulates the ideal functionality in Sect. 6 (with respect to all well-behaved environments as in Sect. 4.3, and with associated data modeled as in Sect. 7.1).*

Because of space limitations, we refer the reader to the full version of the paper [25] for proofs of these theorems. In the full version of the paper, we also briefly discuss alternative proofs under an the interactive CDH assumption, which yield tighter reductions.

9   Sketch of Proof Ideas

Although we do not have space to provide detailed proofs, we can give a sketch of some of the main ideas.

Protocol *KC-SPAKE2*. We start by giving an informal argument that Protocol *KC-SPAKE2* is a secure symmetric PAKE under the CDH assumption, and modeling H as a random oracle. We make use of a "Diffie-Hellman operator", defined as follows: for $\alpha, \beta \in \mathbb{Z}_q$, define

$$[g^\alpha, g^\beta] = g^{\alpha\beta}. \tag{3}$$

We first make some simple observations about this operator. For all $x, y, z \in \mathbb{G}$ and all $\mu, \nu \in \mathbb{Z}_q$, we have

$$[x, y] = [y, x], \quad [xy, z] = [x, z][y, z], \quad \text{and} \quad [x^\mu, y^\nu] = [x, y]^{\mu\nu}.$$

Also, note that $[x, g^\mu] = x^\mu$, so given any two group elements x and y, if we know the discrete logarithm of either one, we can efficiently compute $[x, y]$.

Using this notation, the CDH assumption can be stated as follows: given random $s, t \in \mathbb{G}$, it is hard to compute $[s, t]$.

First, consider a passive adversary that eavesdrops on a run of the protocol between an instance of P and an instance of Q. He obtains a conversation (u, v, k_1, k_2). The session key and authentication values are computed by P and Q is

$$(k, k_1, k_2) = H(\pi, id_P, id_Q, u, v, [u/a^\pi, v]). \tag{4}$$

Intuitively, to mount an offline dictionary attack, the adversary's goal is to query the random oracle H at as many *relevant* points as possible, where here, a relevant point is one of the form

$$(\pi', id_P, id_Q, u, v, [u/a^{\pi'}, v]), \tag{5}$$

where $\pi' \in \mathbb{Z}_q$. By evaluating H at relevant points, and comparing the outputs to the values k_1, k_2 (as well as values derived from k), the adversary can tell whether or not $\pi' = \pi$.

The following lemma shows that under the CDH assumption, he is unable to make even a single relevant query:

Lemma 1. *Under the CDH assumption, the following problem is hard: given random $a, u, v \in \mathbb{G}$, compute $\gamma \in \mathbb{Z}_q$ and $w \in \mathbb{G}$ such that $w = [u/a^\gamma, v]$.*

Proof. Suppose we have an adversary that can efficiently solve the problem in the statement of the lemma with non-negligible probability. We show how to use this adversary to solve the CDH problem with non-negligible probability. Given a challenge instance (s, t) for the CDH problem, we compute

$$\mu \xleftarrow{\text{R}} \mathbb{Z}_q, \quad a \leftarrow g^\mu,$$

and then we give the adversary

$$a, \quad u := s, \quad v := t.$$

Suppose now that the adversary computes for us $\gamma \in \mathbb{Z}_q$ and $w \in \mathbb{G}$ such that $w = [u/a^\gamma, v]$. Then we have

$$w = [u, v][a, v]^{-\gamma} \tag{6}$$

Since we know the discrete log of a, we can compute $[a, v]$, and therefore, we can compute $[u, v] = [s, t]$

$\square$

Next, consider an active adversary that engages in the protocol with an instance of server Q.

Now, in the adversary's attack, he submits the first message u to Q. Next, Q chooses v at random and sends this to the adversary. Server Q also computes k, k_1, k_2 as in (4) and also sends k_1 to the adversary. Again, the adversary's goal is to evaluate the random oracle H at as many relevant points, as in (5), as possible. Of course, an adversary that simply follows the protocol using some guess π' for the password can always make one relevant query. What we want to show is that it is infeasible to make more than one relevant query. This is implied by the following lemma:

Lemma 2. *Under the CDH assumption, the following problem is hard: given random $a, v \in \mathbb{G}$, compute $\gamma_1, \gamma_2 \in \mathbb{Z}_q$ and $u, w_1, w_2 \in \mathbb{Z}_q$ such that $\gamma_1 \neq \gamma_2$ and $w_i = [u/a^{\gamma_i}, v]$ for $i = 1, 2$.*

Proof. Suppose that we are given an instance (s, t) of the CDH problem. We give the adversary

$$a := s, \quad v := t.$$

The adversary computes for us γ_1, γ_2 and w_1, w_2 such that $\gamma_1 \neq \gamma_2$, and

$$w_i = [u/a^{\gamma_i}, v] = [u, v][a, v]^{-\gamma_i} \quad (i = 1, 2).$$

Then we have

$$w_2/w_1 = [a, v]^{\gamma_1 - \gamma_2}. \tag{7}$$

This allows us to compute $[a, v] = [s, t]$. $\square$

Note that if an adversary tries to mount a dictionary attack by interacting with an instance of a client P, by design, the adversary gets only one guess at the password: the only random oracle query that matters is the one that yields the value k_1 that the adversary sends to the client instance.

Protocol _KC-SPAKE2+_. It is not hard to argue that Protocol _KC-SPAKE2+_ offers the same level of security as protocol _KC-SPAKE2_ under normal conditions, when the server is not compromised. However, consider what happens if the server Q is compromised in protocol _KC-SPAKE2+_, and the adversary obtains ϕ_0 and c. At this point, the adversary could attempt an offline dictionary attack, as follows: evaluate F at points (π', id_P, id_Q) for various passwords π', trying to find π' such that $F(\pi', id_P, id_Q) = (\phi_0, \cdot)$. If this succeeds, then with high probability, $\pi' = \pi$, and the adversary can easily impersonate the client P.

The key property we want to prove is the following: if the above dictionary attack fails, then under the CDH assumption, the adversary cannot impersonate the client.

To prove this property, first suppose that an adversary compromises the server, then attempts a dictionary attack, and finally, attempts to log in to the server. Compromising the server means that the adversary obtains ϕ_0 and $c = g^{\phi_1}$. Now suppose the dictionary attack fails, which means that the adversary has not evaluated F at the point (π, id_P, id_Q). The value ϕ_1 is completely random, and the adversary has no other information about ϕ_1, other than the fact that $c = g^{\phi_1}$. When he attempts to log in, he sends the server Q some group element u', and the server responds with $v := g^{\beta}$ for random $\beta \in \mathbb{Z}_q$. To successfully impersonate the client, he must explicitly query the random oracle H at the point $(\phi_0, id_P, id_Q, u', v, [u'/a^{\phi_0}, v], [c, v])$, which means, in particular, he has to compute $[c, v]$. But since, from the adversary's point of view, c and v are random group elements, computing $[c, v]$ is tantamount to solving the CDH problem.

The complication we have not addressed in this argument is that the adversary may also interact with the client P at some point, giving some arbitrary message (v', k_1') to an instance of P, and in the above algorithm for solving the CDH, we have to figure out how the CDH solver should respond to this message. Assuming that (v', k_1') did not come from an instance of Q, the only way that P will not abort is if k_1' is the output of a query to H explicitly made by the adversary; moreover, this query must have been $(\phi_0, id_P, id_P, u, v', [u/a^{\phi_0}, v'], [c, v'])$, where u is the random group element generated by this instance of P. Now, with overwhelming probability, there is at most one query to H that outputs k_1'; however, we have to determine if it is of the required form. We may assume that our CDH solver knows $\log_g a$ (in addition to ϕ_0), and so our CDH solver needs to be able to determine, given adversarially chosen $v', w', d' \in \mathbb{G}$, whether or not $w' = [u, v']$ and $d' = [c, v']$. Since it does not know $\log_g c$, our CDH solver would appear to need an oracle to answer such queries. Without the additional condition $w' = [u, v']$, we would require the interactive CDH assumption; however, with this additional condition, we can use the "Twin Diffie-Hellman Trapdoor

Test" from [17] to efficiently implement this oracle, and so we only need the *standard* CDH assumption.

References

1. Abdalla, M., Barbosa, M.: Perfect forward security of SPAKE2. Cryptology ePrint Archive, Report 2019/1194 (2019). https://eprint.iacr.org/2019/1194
2. Abdalla, M., Barbosa, M., Bradley, T., Jarecki, S., Katz, J., Xu, J.: Universally composable relaxed password authenticated key exchange. Cryptology ePrint Archive, Report 2020/320 (2020). https://eprint.iacr.org/2020/320
3. Abdalla, M., Bellare, M., Rogaway, P.: The Oracle Diffie-Hellman assumptions and an analysis of DHIES. In: Naccache, D. (ed.) CT-RSA 2001. LNCS, vol. 2020, pp. 143–158. Springer, Heidelberg (2001). https://doi.org/10.1007/3-540-45353-9_12
4. Abdalla, M., Bresson, E., Chevassut, O., Möller, B., Pointcheval, D.: Provably secure password-based authentication in TLS. In: Proceedings of the 2006 ACM Symposium on Information, Computer and Communications Security, ASIACCS 2006, pp. 35–45 (2006). https://doi.org/10.1145/1128817.1128827
5. Abdalla, M., Pointcheval, D.: Simple password-based encrypted key exchange protocols. CT-RSA **2005**, 191–208 (2005)
6. Becerra, J., Ostrev, D., Skrobot, M.: Forward secrecy of spake2. Cryptology ePrint Archive, Report 2019/351 (2019). https://eprint.iacr.org/2019/351
7. Bellare, M., Pointcheval, D., Rogaway, P.: Authenticated key exchange secure against dictionary attacks. Cryptology ePrint Archive, Report 2000/014 (2000). https://eprint.iacr.org/2000/014
8. Bellare, M., Rogaway, P.: Random oracles are practical: a paradigm for designing efficient protocols. In: CCS 1993, Proceedings of the 1st ACM Conference on Computer and Communications Security, Fairfax, Virginia, USA, 3–5 November 1993, pp. 62–73. ACM (1993). https://doi.org/10.1145/168588.168596
9. Bellovin, S.M., Merritt, M.: Encrypted key exchange: password-based protocols secure against dictionary attacks. In: 1992 IEEE Computer Society Symposium on Research in Security and Privacy, Oakland, CA, USA, 4–6 May 1992, pp. 72–84 (1992)
10. Biryukov, A., Dinu, D., Khovratovich, D.: Argon2: the memory-hard function for password hashing and other applications (2017). https://github.com/P-H-C/phc-winner-argon2/blob/master/argon2-specs.pdf
11. Camenisch, J., Drijvers, M., Gagliardoni, T., Lehmann, A., Neven, G.: The wonderful world of global random oracles. In: Nielsen, J.B., Rijmen, V. (eds.) EUROCRYPT 2018. LNCS, vol. 10820, pp. 280–312. Springer, Cham (2018). https://doi.org/10.1007/978-3-319-78381-9_11
12. Canetti, R.: Universally composable security: A new paradigm for cryptographic protocols. Cryptology ePrint Archive, Report 2000/067 (2000). https://eprint.iacr.org/2000/067
13. Canetti, R., Goldreich, O., Halevi, S.: The random oracle methodology, revisited. J. ACM **51**(4), 557–594 (2004)
14. Canetti, R., Halevi, S., Katz, J., Lindell, Y., MacKenzie, P.: Universally composable password-based key exchange. Cryptology ePrint Archive, Report 2005/196 (2005). https://eprint.iacr.org/2005/196

15. Canetti, R., Jain, A., Scafuro, A.: Practical UC security with a global random oracle. In: Proceedings of the 2014 ACM SIGSAC Conference on Computer and Communications Security, Scottsdale, AZ, USA, 3–7 November 2014, pp. 597–608 (2014)
16. Canetti, R., Rabin, T.: Universal composition with joint state. In: Boneh, D. (ed.) CRYPTO 2003. LNCS, vol. 2729, pp. 265–281. Springer, Heidelberg (2003). https://doi.org/10.1007/978-3-540-45146-4_16
17. Cash, D., Kiltz, E., Shoup, V.: The twin Diffie-Hellman problem and applications. Cryptology ePrint Archive, Report 2008/067 (2008). https://eprint.iacr.org/2008/067
18. Coron, J.-S., Dodis, Y., Malinaud, C., Puniya, P.: Merkle-Damgård revisited: how to construct a hash function. In: Shoup, V. (ed.) CRYPTO 2005. LNCS, vol. 3621, pp. 430–448. Springer, Heidelberg (2005). https://doi.org/10.1007/11535218_26
19. Gentry, C., MacKenzie, P., Ramzan, Z.: A method for making password-based key exchange resilient to server compromise. In: Dwork, C. (ed.) CRYPTO 2006. LNCS, vol. 4117, pp. 142–159. Springer, Heidelberg (2006). https://doi.org/10.1007/11818175_9
20. Hesse, J.: Separating standard and asymmetric password-authenticated key exchange. Cryptology ePrint Archive, Report 2019/1064 (2019). https://eprint.iacr.org/2019/1064
21. Hofheinz, D., Shoup, V.: GNUC: a new universal composability framework. J. Cryptol. **28**(3), 423–508 (2015). https://doi.org/10.1007/s00145-013-9160-y
22. Hofheinz, D., Unruh, D., Müller-Quade, J.: Polynomial runtime and composability. Cryptology ePrint Archive, Report 2009/023 (2009). https://eprint.iacr.org/2009/023
23. Jarecki, S., Krawczyk, H., Xu, J.: OPAQUE: an asymmetric PAKE protocol secure against pre-computation attacks. In: Nielsen, J.B., Rijmen, V. (eds.) EURO-CRYPT 2018. LNCS, vol. 10822, pp. 456–486. Springer, Cham (2018). https://doi.org/10.1007/978-3-319-78372-7_15
24. Naor, M.: On cryptographic assumptions and challenges. In: Boneh, D. (ed.) CRYPTO 2003. LNCS, vol. 2729, pp. 96–109. Springer, Heidelberg (2003). https://doi.org/10.1007/978-3-540-45146-4_6
25. Shoup, V.: Security analysis of SPAKE2+. Cryptology ePrint Archive, Report 2020/313 (2020). https://eprint.iacr.org/2020/313
26. Taubert, T., Wood, C.A.: SPAKE2+, an Augmented PAKE. Internet-Draft draft-bar-cfrg-spake2plus-00, Internet Engineering Task Force, March 2020. https://datatracker.ietf.org/doc/draft-bar-cfrg-spake2plus/

Schrödinger's Pirate: How to Trace a Quantum Decoder

Mark Zhandry[✉]

Princeton University, USA & NTT Research, Princeton, USA
mzhandry@gmail.com

Abstract. We explore the problem of traitor tracing where the pirate decoder can contain a quantum state. Our main results include:

- We show how to overcome numerous definitional challenges to give a meaningful notion of tracing for quantum decoders
- We give negative results, demonstrating barriers to adapting classical tracing algorithms to the quantum decoder setting.
- On the other hand, we show how to trace quantum decoders in the setting of (public key) private linear broadcast encryption, capturing a common approach to traitor tracing.

1 Introduction

Quantum computers pose a looming threat to cryptography. By an unfortunate coincidence, the enhanced computational power of quantum computers allows for solving the exact mathematical problems, such as factoring and discrete log, underlying the bulk of public-key cryptography used today [Sho94]. The good news is that "quantum-safe" mathematical tools—such as lattices, multivariate equations, or isogenies—exist that can be used as a drop-in replacement in many setting. Nevertheless, many challenges remain. For example, using a quantum-safe drop-in replacement does not always guarantee the security of the overall protocol, as many of the classical proof techniques fail to carry over to the quantum setting [VDG98, ARU14, BDF+11]. It may also be that quantum attackers may get "superposition access" to the honest parties, opening up new avenues of attack [KM10, Zha12a, DFNS14, KLLN16].

In this work, we consider an entirely different threat from quantum computers, which to our knowledge has not been identified before: quantum piracy!

Traitor Tracing. The focus of this work will be the setting of traitor tracing, one of the fundamental goals in cryptography. Originally defined by Chor, Fiat and Naor [CFN94], traitor tracing helps protect content distributors from piracy. In such a system, every legitimate user has their own secret decryption key which can decrypt ciphertexts. The content distributor is worried about a user distributing their key to unauthorized users. Of course, little can be done to stop a user from distributing their key. Instead, in the event that the distributor discovers an unauthorized decryption key, the distributor would like to identify the

© International Association for Cryptologic Research 2020
R. Pass and K. Pietrzak (Eds.): TCC 2020, LNCS 12552, pp. 61–91, 2020.
https://doi.org/10.1007/978-3-030-64381-2_3

source of the key, so that the user (deemed a "traitor") can be prosecuted or have their credentials revoked. This "tracing" should be possible even if the user tries to hide their identity, say, by embedding their key in an obfuscated pirate decoder program. What's more, tracing should still succeed even if many malicious users pool their keys into a single decoder. As sketched in [CFN94], classical tracing can readily be build from generic public key encryption, albeit with large ciphertexts. Therefore, the goal is typically to devise traitor tracing with small ciphertexts. Numerous number-theoretic [BSW06, GGH+13, BZ14, GKW18] and combinatorial schemes [CFN94, BN08] have been shown, with various trade-offs between system parameters and the computational assumptions needed for security.

Most of cryptography concerns several honest parties communicating with each other, while an adversary eavesdrops or manipulates the communication between them. Traitor tracing is in some sense the opposite: several *dis*honest parties (namely, the traitor(s) and the receiver of the pirate decoder) communicate, while the *honest* party (the content distributor) is intercepting this communication (the decoder). This role reversal makes traitor tracing a fascinating problem, as the very cryptographic techniques employed to help secure communication between honest partiescan be employed by the dishonest parties in an attempt to hide their identity and protect themselves from being traced.

Traitor Tracing Meets Quantum Attackers. The aforementioned role reversal also has interesting consequences once quantum computers are involved, as we now highlight. Certainly, the underlying mathematical tools now need to be quantum resistant; for example, post-quantum obfuscation [BGMZ18] or LWE-based traitor tracing [GKW18] can be used. The proofs of security must also work for quantum attackers; existing traitor tracing schemes satisfy this as well. What is obtained is the following: if a *classical* pirate decoder is intercepted from a quantum traitor, that traitor can be identified.

But now suppose the traitor has a quantum computer and is sending its decoder to a quantum recipient. Just as a classical traitor can attempt to use classical cryptographic techniques to evade detection, this quantum traitor could now try to leverage *quantum cryptography*. Quantum cryptography uses the unusual features of quantum physics such as no-cloning to achieve never-before-possible applications, such as information-theoretic key agreement [BB87], unforgeable currency [Wie83, AC12], unclonable programs [Aar09], certifiable randomness [BCM+18], and secret keys that self-destruct after use [AGKZ20].

Therefore, we can imagine the traitors creating and sending a decoder comprising a *quantum* state. We stress that the entire system remains classical under normal operation: keys, ciphertexts, encryption, and decryption are all entirely classical and can be run on classical computers and classical networks. The attacker only ever receives classical communication from the honest parties. Even so, the quantum attackers can use a communication channel outside of the system: they can meet in person to exchange the decoder, or perhaps send the decoder over an outside quantum-enabled network. Nothing the content distributor does can prevent the traitor from sending a quantum decoding device.

Existing traitor tracing results *do not* handle such quantum decoders. In more detail, essentially all classical tracing algorithms work by testing a decoder on a variety of different ciphertexts and examining the outputs. When moving to quantum decoders, the measurement principle in quantum mechanics means that extracting information from a quantum state may irreversibly alter it. This means, after potentially the first ciphertext is decrypted, the decoder's state may be irreversibly altered into a state that is no longer capable of decrypting, essentially self-destructing. Now, a useful pirate decoder would likely *not* self-destruct on valid ciphertexts. However, a decoder that eventually self-destructs but evades tracing may be a worthwhile compromise for a traitor. Moreover, all classical tracing algorithms will also run the decoder on many *invalid* ciphertexts, and the utility of the decoder does not require it to decrypt such ciphertexts.

The above discussion means even the most basic of classical traitor tracing results—for example, the aforementioned generic scheme from public key encryption—may no longer work in the setting of quantum decoders. In fact, it turns out that even *defining* tracing in this setting is non-trivial, for reasons discussed in Sect. 1.2 below.

We note that similar issues may arise any time there is adversarial communication that the *honest* party is trying to learn information from. In such cases, the adversary may benefit from using quantum communication, even if the cryptosystem itself entirely classical. Software watermarking [BGI+01, CHN+16] is another example of where such issues may arise. In such cases, classical security proofs should be revisited, and new techniques are likely needed. In this work, we focus exclusively on the case of traitor tracing, but we expect the tools we develop to be useful for other similar settings.

1.1 Our Results

Definition. Our first result is a new definition for what it means to be a secure tracing scheme in the presence of quantum decoders. As we will see, the obvious "quantumization" of the classical definition leads to a nonsensical definition. We must therefore carefully devise a correct quantum definition of traitor tracing, which requires developing new ideas.

Negative Result. One could have hoped that the tracing algorithm could be entirely classical, except for the part where it runs the decoder. We show barriers to such classical tracing algorithms, in particular showing that such algorithms cannot trace according to our security notion. Thus, any tracing algorithm satisfying our definition must be inherently quantum.

Positive Result. Finally, we develop a quantum tracing algorithm. Our tracing algorithm works on any private linear broadcast encryption (PLBE) scheme satisfying certain requirements. This in particular captures the constructions from generic public key encryption and from obfuscation, simply replacing the classical tracing algorithm with ours. As demonstrated by our negative result, our tracing requires new inherently quantum ideas. In particular, we employ a technique of [MW04], which was previously used in the entirely different setting of quantum Arthur-Merlin games.

1.2   Technical Overview

Live Quantum Decoders. For simplicity in the following discussion, we will assume the message space is just a single bit. Classically, the definition of security for a traitor tracing system is roughly as follows: define a "good" pirate decoder as one that can guess the message with probability noticeably larger than $1/2$. Then security requires that any good pirate decoder can be traced with almost certainty to some user identity controlled by the adversary.

First, we will change terminology slightly. For a classical decoder, whether the decoder is good or bad is a fixed and immutable property. However, quantumly, whether the decoder can decrypt or not is potentially in flux as we disrupt the decoder by interrogating it. Therefore, we prefer the terms "live" and "dead" to "good" and "bad": a live decoder is one that, in its current state, would successfully decrypt a random ciphertext. Unlike the classical case, a live decoder may become dead after such decryption.

We now describe several examples which illustrate the difficulties in defining liveness of quantum decoders.

Example 1. We will consider two simple attacks. In both cases, the adversary controls a single secret key sk_i for user i. It creates two programs, D_0 which has sk_i hard-coded and decrypts according to the honest decryption procedure, and D_1 which simply outputs a random bit.

The first adversary, A, chooses a random bit b, and outputs the decoder D_b. A is entirely classical, and any reasonable notion of liveness would assign D_0 to be live and D_1 to be dead, so A outputs a live decoder with probability $1/2$.

The second adversary, B, chooses a random bit b, and outputs the decoder

$$|\text{☠}_b\rangle = \frac{1}{\sqrt{2}}|D_0\rangle + \frac{(-1)^b}{\sqrt{2}}|D_1\rangle \ .$$

Here, $|\text{☠}_b\rangle$ is a quantum superposition of the two decoders D_0, D_1, with a "phase" that depends on b. To run the decoders, simply run in superposition to get the superposition of outputs of the decoders, finally measuring and outputting the result. The question is then: with what probability does B output a live decoder?

On one hand, we might be tempted to assign both decoders $|\text{☠}_0\rangle, |\text{☠}_1\rangle$ to be live, since both decoders can readily be verified to have a probability $3/4 > 1/2$ of decrypting. In any case, the phase does not fundamentally change the nature of the decoders, so any reasonable notion of liveness should assign $|\text{☠}_0\rangle$ and $|\text{☠}_1\rangle$ either both live or both dead. In this case, B's output is deterministically either live or dead. In particular, A and B have different distributions of liveness.

On the other hand, consider the *density matrices* of the outputs of A and B. For a quantum process outputting state $|\psi_i\rangle$ with probability p_i, the density matrix is $\sum_i p_i |\psi_i\rangle\langle\psi_i|$. According to the postulates of quantum mechanics, no physical operation (even computationally unbounded) can distinguish states with identical density matrices. But a routine calculation shows that the density matrices of A and B are in fact identical, meaning that the notion of liveness must be non-physical! Such a non-physical security definition cannot possibly reflect real-world security goals. We note that this example can be readily generalized to any non-trivial[1] way to assign liveness to quantum states.

Idea 1: Measuring the Decoder. We observe that $|\text{☠}_b\rangle$ in the above example are really just simple quantum versions of probability distributions: the decoders $|\text{☠}_b\rangle$ can be roughly thought of as being D_0 with probability $1/2$ and D_1 with probability $1/2$. For classical pirate decoders, similar issues arise if we try to apply the notion of "live" to the entire probability distribution over decoders. Instead, classically we would only consider the goodness of actual concrete pirate decoder produced by the adversary. The only thing quantum about our example is that it turned a probability distribution—which models uncertainty in the outcome, and is therefore non-physical—into a well-defined physical object.

Motivated by the role of measurements in quantum mechanics, the natural solution to the above example is to consider $|\text{☠}_b\rangle$ as being a superposition over live and dead decoders[2]. The security definition and challenger will then *measure* whether the decoder is live or dead, rather than try to assign liveness to the overall quantum state. In the example above, this is done by simply measuring $|\text{☠}_b\rangle$, obtaining a random choice of D_0, D_1, and then performing the classical test for liveness. If the decoder measures to be live, then we require the decoder to actually be live, and moreover we require tracing to succeed. This easily resolves the above example, since measuring live vs dead will simply collapse the quantum decoder to a classical probability distribution.

More abstractly, a decoder has some actual probability $\hat{p}$ of decrypting random ciphertexts; in our $|\text{☠}_b\rangle$ example, $\hat{p} = 3/4$. However, this probability is hidden inside the quantum state and cannot be accessed in a physically meaningful way. The solution is instead to *measure* or *observe* the success probability, resulting in a measured success probability p. For $|\text{☠}_b\rangle$ as given above, when we observe p, we find that it can be either $1/2$ or 1, each with 50% probability.

Example 2. In the case of more general decoders, however, defining the procedure to measure success probabilities is non-trivial. We cannot in general simply perform the standard measurement as above, as doing so might break the decoder. As a simple example, the decoder's state could be the quantum Fourier transform applied to $|\text{☠}_b\rangle$ from the example above. Evaluation simply applies the inverse transform, recovering $|\text{☠}_b\rangle$, and then running the decoder as above. If we try to observe p by performing a standard measurement on this "encoded" decoder, the measurement will result in garbage. The observed p will therefore be $1/2$, despite the actual overall success probability of the decoder still being $3/4$.

---

[1] By non-trivial, we mean there is at least one live state and one dead state.

[2] In much the same way that Schrödinger's cat is neither live nor dead, but is rather a superposition over live and dead cats.

In Example 2, we could of course define our measurement for p as: perform the inverse Fourier transform, and then perform the standard measurement. While this works for this particular case, the example illustrates that care is needed in determining how to measure liveness, and that the exact way we measure p will depend on the decoder itself. We need an automated way to determine the appropriate measurement that works, regardless of how $|\skull\rangle$ operates.

Example 3. In the classical setting, the goodness or liveness of a decoder is determined by deciding whether the probability that the decoder correctly decrypts is above a given threshold. However, the exact probability cannot be computed efficiently: it amounts to determining the precise number of accepting inputs of a circuit, which is NP-hard. Therefore, most definitions of classical tracing are actually inefficient, in the sense that determining whether or not an adversary broke the security experiment cannot be determined in polynomial time.

Now, one could imagine *estimating* the success probability by simply running the decoder on several random ciphertexts. This gives rise to a definition of liveness that actually *can* be meaningfully translated to the quantum setting: namely, to measure liveness, run the decoder on several random ciphertexts in sequence, compute the fraction of ciphertexts that were correctly decrypted, and finally outputting "live" if the fraction exceeded a given threshold.

On the other hand, this notion of liveness has some limitations. First, suppose the measurement used q ciphertexts. Then the decoder could potentially decrypt q ciphertexts correctly and self-destruct. The decoder would measure as live, but actually result in a dead decoder, which would subsequently be untraceable.

Another issue is that this attempted notion of liveness is rather weak. A decoder may start off with a very high probability of decryption, and then reverse to a high probability of failure, so that overall the decoder appears dead to this test. Defining security relative to this notion of liveness would not guarantee any traceability for such decoders. Yet, such decoders would reasonably be considered useful, and would ideally be traced.

Motivated by the above discussion, we now give a "wish list" of features a liveness measurement should posses:

- It should collapse to the classical notion of goodness for a classical decoder.
- It should be "encoding independent". That is, if we apply some quantum transformation to the decoder's state (that gets undone when running the decoder), this should not affect the goodness of the decoder.
- If the same measurement is applied twice in a row (without any operations in between), it should return the same outcome both times. In other words, if a decoder is measured to be live, the resulting decoder should still be live.
- It should label decoders that start off with a high probability of decryption live, even if the decoder starts failing later.

Idea 2: Projective Implementations. In order to describe our solution, we recall some basic quantum measurement theory. A quantum state is simply a complex unit vector $|\psi\rangle$ of dimension d. For example, if the state consists of k qubits, d will be 2^k, with the components of $|\psi\rangle$ specifying weights for each of the d possible k-bit strings.

Any quantum measurement can be described as a positive operator valued measure (POVM). Such a measurement $\mathcal{M}$ is described by n Hermitian positive semi-definite matrices $M_1, \ldots, M_n$ such that $\sum_i M_i = \mathbf{I}$. When applying $\mathcal{M}$ to $|\psi\rangle$, the measurement results in outcome i with probability $p_i = \langle\psi|M_i|\psi\rangle$. The normalization on $|\psi\rangle$ and $\mathcal{M}$ ensures that this is a valid probability distribution. We stress that the matrices M_i and the weights in the vector $|\psi\rangle$ are not explicitly written out, but are implicitly defined by the measurement apparatus and the procedure that generates $|\psi\rangle$.

In our setting, we have the following POVM measurement: encrypt a random message bit m, run the pirate decoder on the resulting ciphertext, and then output 1 or 0 depending on whether the decoder correctly decrypts or not.

While the POVM formalism describes the probability distribution of the measurement, it does not describe the post-measurement quantum state. Indeed, many measurement apparatus could yield the same POVM, but result in different post-measurement states. A *general quantum measurement*, in contrast, determines both the measurement outcomes and the post-measurement states.

Our goal, given a POVM $\mathcal{M}$ and a state $|\psi\rangle$, is to learn the probability distribution from applying $\mathcal{M}$ to $|\psi\rangle$. The discussion above demonstrates that the actual probability distribution is information-theoretically hidden and inaccessible. Instead, we want a measurement $\mathcal{M}'$ that *measures* the distribution, such that $|\psi\rangle$ is a superposition over states with "well-defined" output distributions.

We interpret the above as the following. For a POVM $\mathcal{M}$ over outputs $\{1, \ldots, n\}$, we want a measurement $\mathcal{M}'$ which outputs a distribution (as in, it outputs a probability vector) over $\{1, \ldots, n\}$ such that $\mathcal{M}$ generates the same distribution of outputs as the following procedure:

- First, measure $\mathcal{M}'$ to obtain an observed distribution D
- Then sample a random value in $\{1, \ldots, n\}$ according to D.

Additionally, we want that subsequently applying $\mathcal{M}$ to the post-measurement state will yield exactly the distribution D, corresponding to measuring a decoder as live actually yielding a live decoder. We will call $\mathcal{M}'$ the *projective implementation* of $\mathcal{M}$ [3]. See Sect. 3 for a precise definition.

For general $\mathcal{M}$, there is no way to come up with a projective implementation $\mathcal{M}'$. In fact, we show that the existence of $\mathcal{M}'$ is equivalent to the matrices $M_1, \ldots, M_n$ in $\mathcal{M}$ all commuting, and when it exists $\mathcal{M}'$ is unique. Concretely, $\mathcal{M}'$ is the projective measurement in the simultaneous eigenbasis of the $M_1, \ldots, M_n$.

In our case, $\mathcal{M}$ has two outcomes, either correct or incorrect decryption, and normalization ($M_0 + M_1 = \mathbf{I}$) implies that M_0 and $M_1 = \mathbf{I} - M_0$ always commute. Therefore, $\mathcal{M}'$ must exist. Our test of liveness, essentially, will perform

---

[3] This terminology comes from the fact that we will ultimately set $\mathcal{M}'$ to be a "projective" measurement.

the measurement $\mathcal{M}'$ to get a distribution over $\{0, 1\}$—which is equivalent to measuring a success probability p—and then output "live" if p is sufficiently large; otherwise it outputs "dead".

We note that this liveness measurement satisfies all of our "wish list" items. In the case of classical decoders, M_0, M_1 are diagonal matrices whose entries are the success probabilities of the various classical decoders. As such, our projective implementation reduces to the classical goodness notion. Applying any encoding to the decoder state simply rotates the eigenbases of (M_0, M_1), but our notion automatically adjusts to such a rotation. The measurement is projective, implying that applying it twice will always yield the same answer. Finally, the notion captures the success probability of decrypting the very first ciphertext, and is not dependent on any subsequent decrypting abilities.

Our Quantum Tracing Model. With a notion of liveness in hand, we now turn to our tracing model. Even in the classical case there are potentially multiple tracing models. The most permissive for the tracing algorithm is to give the tracer the entire code of the decoder. This tracing model captures the setting where the decoder is an actual piece of software that the tracer has access to. Analogously, in the quantum setting we could give the tracer the actual quantum state representing the decoder, corresponding to a quantum software model.

On the other hand, over twenty-plus years of work on classical traitor tracing, the community has largely settled on a weaker "black box" model where the tracer can only query the decoder on ciphertexts and see the responses, but otherwise cannot observe how the decoder works. This is motivated in part due to the possibility of the decoder being *obfuscated* [BGI+01, GGH+13]—which informally hides everything about a program except for its input/output behavior—meaning the tracing algorithm does not gain much by inspecting the decoder's code. Moreover, in many cases it is desirable to trace an actually physical decoder box constructed by the traitors. In this case, various hardware security measures might be in place to prevent inspecting the decoder's operation.

In the black box setting, however, it is trivial to devise untraceable decoders: the decoder simply maintains a counter and ceases to function after a certain number of decryptions. If the number of ciphertexts the decoder decrypts is set small enough, tracing will become impossible. Such decoders are clearly less useful to pirates, but nonetheless represent a way for traitors to evade tracing.

The classical solution is to restrict attention to *stateless* decoders. The implicit assumption in this model is that the tracer has some way to reset or rewind the decoder to its original state. In the software setting, such resets are trivial. Such resets may also be plausible—perhaps a hard reboot or cutting power will cause the counter to reset—depending on the hardware employed by the traitors.

Motivated by the years of development leading to the classical black box stateless decoder model, we would like to develop an analogous model for quantum decoders. However, we immediately face a definitional issue: for a general quantum decoder, it may be information-theoretically impossible to rewind the decoder to its initial state. This holds true even if we consider the software setting where the tracer has complete unfettered access to the decoder.

Our Solution. We now describe our solution. Recall that, outside of measurements, quantum operations are indeed reversible. Therefore, we can imagine running the decoder until the measurement that produces the decrypted value. Then, we assume the ability to run all the operations, save for the final measurement, in reverse. This rewinding cannot possibly recover the initial state of the decoder, but in some sense it represents the closest we can get to a full rewinding. For example, in this model, the decoder's operation is "projective," which implies that a second decryption of the *same* ciphertext immediately following the first actually will *not* further alter the decoder's state, and moreover is guaranteed to give the same output. Analogous to the gentle measurement lemma [Aar04], if a particular decoder output occurs with overwhelming probability, a projective measurement will only negligibly affect the decoder's state. In particular, such projections collapse to the notion of stateless decoders in the classical setting.

Our black box decoder model therefore assumes that the decoder's operation is a projective measurement. Our precise formalization of a quantum black box model is somewhat delicate; see Sect. 4 for details. At a high level, what gets measured is not the adversary's output itself, but rather the single bit indicating whether the decoder was correct. This is done partly to accommodate relaxed decoder models from the classical literature [GKW18], and also motivated by the level of access that our ultimate tracing algorithm will need.

Our black box quantum decoder model is a natural generalization of the classical stateless decoder model. However, it remains to be seen whether it actually represents a realistic model of quantum hardware devices. Nevertheless, we emphasize that in the setting of quantum *software* decoders, it is always possible to perform the rewinding to implement a projective decoder. As a result, our model at least captures what is possible in the software setting.

Negative Result for Classical Black Box Tracing. One may hope that existing classical tracing algorithms for stateless decoders might also work for projective decoders, or at least that alternate classical tracing[4] could be devised. We show, unfortunately, that such classical tracing is unlikely. Concretely, for any $0 < \epsilon < 1/2$, we devise a quantum projective black box pirate decoder such that:

- The decoder starts out with decryption probability at least $1/2 + \epsilon$.
- For any polynomial-length sequence of classical ciphertext queries, there is a non-negligible probability that the decoder will respond to all queries with 0.

If the decoder outputs zero on all queries, it is clearly impossible to trace. The usual classical notions of tracing require that the tracing algorithm identifies

---

[4] By classical tracing, we mean that the tracer only queries the decoder on classical ciphertexts, and then uses the classical outputs in some way to accuse a user.

a traitor with overwhelming probability by making $q = \mathsf{poly}(1/\epsilon)$ queries. Our counterexample would invalidate this definition.

We note that the definition of tracing could be relaxed to allow for some inverse polynomial probability τ that tracing fails, and then allow the number of queries by the tracer to be $q = \mathsf{poly}(1/\epsilon, 1/\tau)$. Our counterexample does not rule out such a weaker tracing notion. Nevertheless, our counter example shows that the existing guarantees of classical tracing algorithms do not carry over to the quantum projective decoder setting. Additionally, it shows that if one wants to achieve the strong tracing guarantees analogous to tracing classical decoders, the tracing algorithm should make *quantum* queries to the decoder. Thus, our model of black box decoders will allow for such quantum queries. Again, such queries are always possible for software decoders.

Our Quantum Tracing Algorithm. We now turn to our tracing algorithm. We observe that essentially all classical traitor tracing solutions work abstractly as follows: the tracer generates ciphertexts from invalid distributions D_S for various subsets S of users, where decryption is possible only for users in S. An additional guarantee is typically that only users in the symmetric difference of S and T can distinguish D_S from D_T. The tracer estimates the probabilities $\hat{p}_S$ that the pirate decoder decrypts D_S by testing the decoder on various samples from D_S. Typically, the first S is the set of all users, corresponding to D_S being all valid ciphertexts. Subsequently, additional sets S are considered. Large gaps between the $\hat{p}_S$ then give information about the identities of the traitor(s).

This framework is very broad, encompassing essentially the entire body of traitor tracing literature. For example, it encompasses the private linear broadcast encryption (PLBE) approach of [BSW06], which is the backbone of most of the various algebraic traitor tracing constructions [BSW06, GGH+13, BZ14, GKW18]. Here, the sets S have the form $[i] = \{1, 2, \ldots, i\}$ for various i. This framework also encompasses combinatorial schemes such as [CFN94, BN08]. For example, the most basic scheme of [CFN94] uses the bit-fixing sets $S_{i,b} = \{x \in \{0, 1\}^k : x_i = b\}$. The fingerprinting code-based construction of [BN08] uses a set structure that is actually kept secret, except to the tracer.

Our goal will be to upgrade classical tracing algorithms to work with quantum decoders. As we will see, there are numerous problems that must be overcome.

Approximating $\mathcal{M}'$ Efficiently. We first aim to build a quantum analog of this classical probability estimation. For exactly the same reasons encountered when defining traitor tracing, the actual success probabilities $\hat{p}_S$ cannot be accessed in any physical way for a quantum decoder. As in the discussion leading to our tracing definition, the most natural alternative is to instead *measure* the success probability, obtaining a measurement p_S. In the case of S being all users, this means the tracing algorithm would need to implement the measurement $\mathcal{M}'$ from above, and for other S analogous measurements will be needed.

However, while a projective implementation $\mathcal{M}'$ is guaranteed to exist, we have not guaranteed that it is computationally efficient. In fact, it *cannot* be computationally efficient, even classically. This is simply because, even classically, we cannot efficiently learn the exact output distribution of a program[5]. Classically, this is resolved by having the tracer *estimate* the success probability of the decoder, and demonstrating that an estimate is good enough for tracing.

We would therefore like to develop a procedure that approximates the measurement $\mathcal{M}'$. Yet the matrices M_i are exponentially-large, being only implicitly defined by the measurement apparatus of the decoder. Therefore, eigendecomposition would be intractable. Our negative result also means cannot use classical estimation techniques, since those work by running the decoder on classical ciphertexts.

Instead, we devise an operation on the quantum pirate decoder that tries ciphertexts *in superposition*; our operation will still work in the black box projection model for pirate decoders, which allows for such quantum queries. Our algorithm makes use of the fact that $\mathcal{M}'$ is *projective*. More precisely, if $\mathcal{M}_c = (M_{c,0}, M_{c,1})$ is the measurement which tests if the decoder correctly decrypts c, then $\mathcal{M}_c$ is guaranteed to be projective by our decoder model. The overall measurement POVM $\mathcal{M}_c = (M_0, M_1)$ for testing correctness on a random ciphertext is then the *average* or *mixture* of the $\mathcal{M}_c$:

$$M_b = \sum_c \Pr[c] M_{c,b} \ .$$

Our black box decoder model allows us to evaluate the projective $\mathcal{M}_c$ for any ciphertext c, or even evaluate the $\mathcal{M}_c$ for *superpositions* of c values. We demonstrate how to use this ability to compute an approximation of $\mathcal{M}'$.

To do so, we employ a technique of Watrous and Marriott [MW04], which was originally used for decreasing error in quantum Arthur-Merlin games. We show that their algorithm, with some small modifications, works in our setting to achieve a reasonable approximation of $\mathcal{M}'$. At a very high level, the algorithm runs $\mathcal{M}_c$ over a superposition of c, and getting a measurement outcome b_1. Then we apply a particular measurement to the superposition of c, obtaining measurement d_1. We interleave and repeat both measurements a number of times, obtaining a sequence $d_0 = 0, b_1, d_1, b_2, d_2 \dots$. The output is p' where $1 - p'$ is the fraction of bit flips in the sequence.

Following the analysis from [MW04], we show that the output of this measurement indeed approximates the distribution of $\mathcal{M}'$. One wrinkle is that [MW04] did not care about the post-measurement state of the decoder, whereas we want the post-measurement states for $\mathcal{M}'$ and the approximation to be "close" in some sense. We show that, by being careful about exactly when the sequence of measurements is terminated, we can guarantee the necessary closeness.

On Computational Indistinguishability. Recall that, in addition to estimating probabilities p_S, classical tracing algorithms typically rely on p_S and p_T being

---

[5] This means that the security experiment is inefficient. However, the same is true of classical traitor tracing experiments for essentially the same reason.

close for different sets S, T, as long as the adversary controls no users in the symmetric difference between S, T. Classically, such closeness follows readily from the indistinguishability between (many samples of) D_S, D_T. Indeed, if p_S, p_T were far, a distinguisher could use the samples to compute an estimate of the success probability, and then guess which distribution the samples came from.

Quantumly, such closeness is non-obvious. Since the POVMs corresponding to D_S, D_T simply run the decoder on a single classical ciphertext, we know that the probability the decoder is correct on the two distributions must be close. This implies that the *means* of the distributions on p_S and p_T must be close. But this alone is insufficient. For example, for a given decoder, p_S might be always measure to be $3/4$, whereas p_T measures to be $1/2$ or 1 with equal probability. Both distributions have the same mean, but are nevertheless far apart.

Now, our algorithm for approximating the projective implementation allows us to efficiently estimate p_S or p_T, which would therefore allow us to distinguish the two cases above. However, our algorithm runs the decoder on *quantum superpositions* of exponentially-many ciphertexts, and this quantumness is somewhat inherent, per our negative result. But perhaps such superpositions are actually distinguishable, even if the individual ciphertext samples are not? For example, [GKZ19] shows that superpositions over LWE samples can be distinguished, despite individual samples being presumably indistinguishable.

We show that, nonetheless, if polynomially-many samples of D_S and D_T are computationally indistinguishable, then the distributions over measured p_S and p_T must be close, in some sense[6]. We show this by a careful application of the small-range distributions of Zhandry [Zha12a]. These distributions allow us to approximate the measurements of p_S or p_T using only a polynomial number of classical samples from either ciphertext distribution.

Handling Non-simultaneous Measurements. Based on the above indistinguishability result, we know, for a given decoder state, that p_S and p_T being far means the attacker must in fact control a user in the symmetric difference between S and T. As in the classical case, we would therefore like to use this information to narrow down our list of suspected traitors. Unfortunately, we cannot actually simultaneously measure p_S and p_T for the same state: once we measure one of them, say p_S, the decoder state is potentially irreversibly altered. If we then measure p_T, we will get a result, but p_T and p_S will be measurements from different states, and it is not obvious what comparing p_S and p_T yields.

Nevertheless, we show that if p_S and p_T are measured in succession, and if the underlying distributions D_S and D_T are indistinguishable (for polynomially many samples), then p_S and p_T will in fact be close. Supposing we applied the actual projective implementation corresponding to D_S, we know that the resulting decoder $|\text{⚔}s\rangle$ is an eigenstate of the measurement. Thus, if we applied the projective implementation a second time to $|\text{⚔}s\rangle$, obtaining a second measurement p'_S of $\hat{p}_S$, then $p_S = p'_S$. We show that if we relax to using our approxima-

---

[6] Statistical closeness is too-strong a requirement, which is also true classically. Instead, we consider a weaker notion of distance based on the Euclidean distance.

tion algorithm, then $p'_S \approx p_S$. If we replace this second measurement on $|\text{☠}_S\rangle$ with our approximation of p_T, then by our computational indistinguishability guarantee, $p_T \approx p'_S \approx p_S$ (notice that p'_S is never actually computed; it is just used in the analysis). Thus, if p_S and p_T are far, the adversary must control a user in the symmetric difference between S and T, as desired.

How to Trace PLBE. Up until this point, our discussion has applied broadly to most tracing algorithms and one may hope to simply swap out the probability estimation steps of classical tracing algorithms with our approximate projective implementation algorithm. Unfortunately, this does not appear to work in general. To see the issue, consider a tracing algorithm which first computes (an estimate of) p_S. We know that the decoder is live, so $p_{[N]}$ (the success probability for valid ciphertexts) must be noticeably higher than $1/2$; let's say $p_{[N]} = 1$. Suppose p_S is measured to be $1/2 \ll p_{[N]}$. We therefore know that the adversary must control a user in $[N] \setminus S$. However, this might not be sufficient for accusing a user: perhaps S only contains $N/2$ users, in which case we have only narrowed the attacker down to half the users. Tracing must then proceed to compute p_T for a different set T. But at this point, perhaps the decoder has actually collapsed to a dead decoder and we can no longer learn any information from it.

The takeaway is: the very first time any gap is found, the decoder could potentially now be dead, and we should therefore be ready to accuse a user. In the example above, if S contained all but one user, say user N, we could then immediately accuse user N. We would then satisfy the desired tracing guarantee, despite having a now-useless decoder. If on the other hand p_S were measured to be greater than $1/2$, we can continue to measure p_T. The same issue occurs if there is more than one user in $S \setminus T$, so we would want to have T contain all users in S except a single user, say user $N - 1$.

What is needed, therefore, is a linear set structure, where it is possible to encrypt to subsets $[j]$ of users, $j = N, N - 1, \ldots, 0$, where users $i \leq j$ can decrypt, users $i > j$ cannot, and it is impossible to distinguish $[j]$ from $[j - 1]$ unless the adversary controls user j. In other words, we need *private linear broadcast encryption* (PLBE) as defined by [BSW06]. Based on the above, we show that any PLBE with the right properties (elaborated below) can be traced. Our tracing algorithm proceeds essentially as the classical tracing algorithm given in [BSW06], except that we use our quantum approximation algorithm to compute the various probabilities $p_{[j]}$. We also must compute the $p_{[j]}$ in a particular order, namely in order of *decreasing* j, whereas the order does not matter in [BSW06].

Applications and Limitations. Fortunately, PLBE is the most common approach to building traitor tracing, and therefore our tracing algorithm is broadly applicable. For example, sufficiently strong PLBE can be instantiated from

- Generic public key encryption, resulting in ciphertexts and public keys that grow linearly with the number of users.
- From post-quantum obfuscation [BGMZ18], following [GGH+13,BZ14], resulting in constant-sized ciphertexts.

– In the setting of bounded collusions, we can use bounded-collusion secure functional encryption, which can be instantiated from generic public key encryption [AV19]. The resulting scheme has ciphertexts growing linearly in the collusion bound (but independent of the total number of users).

We note that PLBE can also be constructed from pairings [BSW06], though this instantiation is not useful in our context since pairings are insecure against quantum attackers.

Unfortunately, our analysis does not seem to extend to a variant of PLBE that was recently constructed from LWE by Goyal, Koppula, and Waters [GKW18] for subtle reasons. Indeed, their version of PLBE has encryptions to sets $[j]$ for $j < N$ requiring a *secret encryption key*, and indistinguishability of $D_{[j]}$ and $D_{[j-1]}$ only holds for those who do not know the secret encryption key. The implication is that tracing can only be carried out by the holder of the secret key. The fact that tracing requires a secret key is itself not a problem for us, as we can similarly consider a secret key version of tracing. The issue is that, when we prove $p_{[j]}$ is close to $p_{[j-1]}$, we need indistinguishability between $[j]$ and $[j-1]$ to hold for polynomially ciphertexts. On the other hand, [GKW18] only remains secure for a constant number of ciphertexts, and the natural ways of extending [GKW18] to handle more ciphertexts will blow up the ciphertext too much. We therefore leave tracing quantum decoders for [GKW18] as an important open problem.

We also note that our approach does not appear to extend to combinatorial traitor tracing schemes, such as [CFN94, BN08]. In these schemes, the sets S do not have the needed linear structure. As discussed above, this means that the decoder could fail on the first distribution D_S for $S \neq [N]$, and no longer work for *any* other distribution. Since $[N] \setminus S$ contains more than 1 identity, there is no way to accuse a user using our approach. We leave as an interesting open question developing a tracing algorithm for these combinatorial constructions, or alternatively demonstrating a quantum pirate decoder that cannot be traced.

1.3 Paper Outline

Section 2 gives a basic background in quantum notation and operations. In Sect. 3, we develop our notion of projective implementations, which will be used in Sect. 4 to define traitor tracing for pirate decoders. In Sect. 5, we demonstrate that quantum access to a quantum decoder is necessary for tracing. In Sect. 6, we develop our algorithm for estimating the success probability of a pirate decoder, which is then used in our tracing algorithm in Sect. 7.

2 Quantum Preliminaries

In this work, we will make use of two formalisms for quantum measurements. The first, a *positive operator valued measure* (POVM), is a general form of quantum measurement. A POVM $\mathcal{M}$ is specified by a finite index set $\mathcal{I}$ and a set $\{M_i\}_{i \in \mathcal{I}}$

of hermitian positive semidefinite matrices M_i with the normalization requirement $\sum_{i \in \mathcal{I}} M_i = \mathbf{I}$. The matrices M_i are called *items* of the POVM. When applying a POVM $\mathcal{M}$ to a quantum state $|\psi\rangle$, the result of the measurement is i with probability $p_i = \langle\psi|M_i|\psi\rangle$. The normalization requirements for $\mathcal{M}$ and $|\psi\rangle$ imply that $\sum_i p_i = 1$, and therefore this is indeed a probability distribution. We denote by $\mathcal{M}(|\psi\rangle)$ the distribution obtained by applying $\mathcal{M}$ to $|\psi\rangle$.

The POVM formalism describes the probabilities of various outcomes, but it does not specify how $|\psi\rangle$ is affected by measurement. Indeed, there will be many possible implementations of a measurement giving rise to the same probability distribution of outcomes, but resulting in different post-measurement states.

To account for this, the second formalism we will use is simply called a *quantum measurement*. Here, a quantum measurement $\mathcal{E}$ is specified by a finite index set $\mathcal{I}$ and a set $\{E_i\}_{i \in \mathcal{I}}$ of matrices E_i (not necessarily hermitian nor positive) such that $\sum_{i \in \mathcal{I}} E_i^\dagger E_i = \mathbf{I}$. The matrices E_i are called *measurement operators*. When applying a quantum measurement $\mathcal{E}$ to a quantum state $|\psi\rangle$, the result of the measurement is i with probability $p_i = \langle\psi|E_i^\dagger E_i|\psi\rangle = \|E_i|\psi\rangle\|^2$. Conditioned on the outcome being i, the post-measurement state is $E_i|\psi\rangle/\sqrt{p_i}$, where the factor $\sqrt{p_i}$ is to ensure that the state is normalized.

We note that any quantum measurement $\mathcal{E}$ is associated with a POVM $\mathcal{M} = \mathsf{POVM}(\mathcal{E})$ with $M_i = E_i^\dagger E_i$. We will call $\mathcal{E}$ an *implementation* of $\mathcal{M}$. We note that while each quantum measurement implements exactly one POVM, each POVM may be implemented by many possible quantum measurements.

A *projective measurement* is a quantum measurement where the E_i are projections: E_i are hermitian and satisfy $E_i^2 = E_i$. We note that $\sum_i E_i = \sum_i E_i^\dagger E_i = \mathbf{I}$ implies that $E_i E_j = 0$ for $i \neq j$.

A *projective POVM* is a POVM where M_i are projections. We note that the POVM associated with a projective measurement is projective. However, a projective POVM may be implemented by non-projective measurements. As with quantum measurements, a projective POVM will satisfy $M_i M_j = 0$ for $i \neq j$.

3   Commutative POVMs and Projective Implementations

In this section, we give some additional definitions for quantum measurements and POVMs, as well as some basic results. In Sect. 4, we use these definitions and results to define our notion of traitor tracing for pirate decoders.

Definition 1. *A POVM* $\mathcal{M} = \{M_i\}_{i \in \mathcal{I}}$ *is* commutative *if* $M_i M_j = M_j M_i \forall i, j$.

Let $\mathcal{I}$ be an index set, and let $\mathcal{D}$ be a finite set of distributions over $\mathcal{I}$. Let $\mathcal{E} = \{E_D\}_{D \in \mathcal{D}}$ be a projective measurement with index set $\mathcal{D}$. Consider the POVM $\mathcal{M} = \{M_i\}_{i \in \mathcal{I}}$ where $M_i = \sum_{D \in \mathcal{D}} E_D \Pr[D = i]$. Then $\mathcal{M}$ is equivalent to the following measurement process:

- First apply the measurement $\mathcal{E}$ to obtain a distribution D
- Then choose a random sample i according to D

Definition 2. *For $\mathcal{E}, \mathcal{M}$ be as above, $\mathcal{E}$ is the* projective implementation *of $\mathcal{M}$.*

Lemma 1. *A POVM $\mathcal{M} = \{M_i\}_{i \in \mathcal{I}}$ is commutative if and only if it has a projective implementation; the projective implementation is unique.*

Proof. The proof is given in the Full Version [Zha20]. The basic idea is that a projective implementation corresponds to an eigenbasis for the simultaneous diagonalization of the M_i; such simultaneous diagonalization is possible if and only if the M_i commute.

Therefore, for a commutative POVM $\mathcal{M}$, we will let $\mathsf{ProjImp}(\mathcal{M})$ denote the unique projective measurement.

4 Defining Tracing of Quantum Pirates

4.1 Traitor Tracing Syntax

Here, we give the syntax for public key traitor tracing with public traceability. Variants with secret key encryption and/or secret key tracing are defined analogously. A traitor tracing system is a tuple of four algorithms (Gen, Enc, Dec, Trace) defined as follows:

- $\mathsf{Gen}(1^\lambda, 1^N)$ is a classical probabilistic polynomial time (PPT) algorithm that takes as input the security parameter and a number N of users, and samples a public key pk, and N secret keys $\mathsf{sk}_1, \ldots, \mathsf{sk}_N$.
- $\mathsf{Enc}(\mathsf{pk}, m)$ is a classical PPT algorithm that takes as input the public key pk and a message m, and outputs a ciphertext c.
- $\mathsf{Dec}(\mathsf{sk}_i, c)$ is a classical deterministic algorithm that takes as input a secret key sk_i for user i and a ciphertext, and outputs a message m'.
- $\mathsf{Trace}^{|\text{☠}\rangle}(\mathsf{pk}, m_0, m_1, \epsilon)$ takes as input the public key pk, two messages m_0, m_1, and a parameter ϵ. It makes queries to a pirate decoder $|\text{☠}\rangle$. It ultimately outputs a subset of $[N]$, which are the accused users.

4.2 Decoder Models

We now specify $|\text{☠}\rangle$ and what a query to $|\text{☠}\rangle$ does. $|\text{☠}\rangle$ consists of a collection of qubits $|\psi\rangle$ and the description of an efficient procedure U. U maps a ciphertext c to an efficiently computable unitary operation $U(c)$ which acts on $|\psi\rangle$.

The assumed operation of the decoder in this model, denoted $\mathsf{Eval}^{|\text{☠}\rangle}(c)$, is the following: on input a ciphertext c, compute $U(c)$. Then apply $U(c)$ to $|\psi\rangle$. Finally, measure the first qubit of $U(c)|\psi\rangle$, and output the result.

In the classical setting, various levels of access to the decoder may be possible. For example, the decoder may be a digital program, and the tracer actually obtains the program code. Alternatively, the decoder may be an actually physical piece of hardware, and the tracer has only access to the input/output behavior. In the quantum setting, one can imagine analogous scenarios. Below, we describe decoder models to capture some scenarios in the quantum decoder setting.

Software Decoder Model. The Software Decoder model will be the quantum analog of the classical setting where the decoder is a software program. In this model, a query to $|\skull\rangle$ consists of the empty string ϵ, and in response the Trace receives the entire state $|\skull\rangle$ (including U). In this sense, Trace has complete access to the entire decoder. Next, we will consider decoder models where Trace has limited access. Such models will be potential useful in hardware settings.

The Black Box Projection Model. We now develop a black box model of quantum decoders, which hopefully generalizes the classical notion of stateless decoders. Of course, some limitations of the decoder are necessary, to prevent simple counterexamples like self-destructing after a counter reaches a certain value. Our goal is to identify the minimal type of query access needed to allow tracing. The result is our *Black Box Projection* model. In our model, a query to $|\skull\rangle$ has the form $\sum_{\mathsf{aux},c,b} \alpha_{\mathsf{aux},c,b}|\mathsf{aux}, c, b\rangle$, where c ranges over ciphertexts, b over bits, and aux over an arbitrary domain. In response to the query, $|\skull\rangle$ does the following:

1. First, it performs the following action on basis states:

$$|\mathsf{aux}, c, b\rangle \otimes |\psi\rangle \mapsto |\mathsf{aux}, c, b\rangle \otimes U(c)|\psi\rangle .$$

2. Apply a controlled NOT (CNOT) to the b register, where the control bit is the first qubit of the decoder's state.
3. Next, it applies the inverse of Step 1:

$$|\mathsf{aux}, c, b\rangle \otimes |\psi\rangle \mapsto |\mathsf{aux}, c, b\rangle \otimes U^\dagger(c)|\psi\rangle .$$

4. Finally, it measures the b register, and then returns the result b as well as whatever remains in the aux, c registers.

Note that the query is a projective measurement on $|\psi\rangle$. Recall that applying a projective measurement twice in a row will always result in identical outcomes. This is similar to how a classical stateless (deterministic) decoder will always produce the same outcome on repeated ciphertexts. Thus projective measurements are a generalization of stateless decoders, though other generalizations are possible.

Lemma 2. *Let $A^{|\skull\rangle}(\cdot)$ be any quantum polynomial-time algorithm that takes as input x and makes queries to $|\skull\rangle$ in the Black Box Projection model. Then there exists another quantum polynomial-time algorithm $B^{|\skull\rangle}(\cdot)$ in the Software Decoder model such that, for any x, y, $\Pr[A^{|\skull\rangle}(x) = y] = \Pr[B^{|\skull\rangle}(x) = y]$.*

Since the Black Box Projection model is the weakest model we consider, ability to trace in this model gives the strongest guarantees. We now discuss some of the choice made in our Black Box Projection model.

Superposition Queries. Our model allows queries on superpositions of ciphertexts. We could have instead required classical queries. Unfortunately, such a model seems untraceable, evidenced by our negative result in Sect. 5.

Returning the Ciphertext Registers. One could alternatively only return b' and not the ciphertext (the aux registers being held privately by Trace). This is equivalent to measuring the ciphertext, resulting in effectively a classical query model.

The Role of b. An alternative is to measure the first qubit of the decoder's state directly (that is, the intended output of the decoder), instead of measuring the result of XORing with b. We have two reasons for our modeling choice:

– The standard query model for quantum operations has the query response XORed into some registers provided as part of the query. Our modeling mimics this query behavior. We thus have the measurement applied to only the output of the decoder in the XOR query model, rather than having the measurement applied to the private state of the decoder.
– If we initialize the b registers to initially contain the correct answer expected from the decoder, the result of the query measurement will tell us whether the decoder answered correctly or incorrectly, as opposed to telling us the actual answer. This turns out to be crucial for our tracing algorithm. Indeed, as we will see in Sect. 6, the given Black Box Projection model will allow us to measure the success probability of the decoder. On the other hand, if the measurement were applied directly to the decoder state, we would be able to measure either of the probabilities p_r that the decoder outputs 1 on a random encryption of the bit r. To to get the success probability, we would need to know both p_0 and p_1. But in the quantum case it may not be possible to learn both values simultaneously if the measurements are "incompatible."

4.3   Correctness and Security

Definition 3. *A traitor tracing system is* correct *if, for all messages m and functions $N = N(\lambda), i = i(\lambda)$,*

$$\Pr[\mathsf{Dec}(\mathsf{sk}_i, \mathsf{Enc}(\mathsf{pk}, m)) = m : (\mathsf{pk}, \mathsf{sk}_1, \dots, \mathsf{sk}_N) \leftarrow \mathsf{Gen}(\lambda, N)] \geq 1 - \mathsf{negl}(\lambda)$$

For brevity, we omit the semantic security requirement and focus on tracing. Our definition is inspired by that of [GKW18], adapted to use our decoder model. For a decoder $|\text{🧟}\rangle = (U, |\psi\rangle)$, two messages m_0, m_1, consider the operation on $|\psi\rangle$:

– Choose a random bit $b \leftarrow \{0, 1\}$
– Run $c \leftarrow \mathsf{Enc}(\mathsf{pk}, m_b)$ to get a random encryption of m_b.
– Run $b' \leftarrow \mathsf{Eval}^{|\text{🧟}\rangle}(c)$.
– Output 1 if and only if $b = b'$; otherwise output 0.

Let $\mathcal{M} = (M_0, M_1)$ be the POVM given by this operation, which we call the *associated POVM* to the decoder. Note that M_0 and $M_1 = \mathbf{I} - M_0$ commute, so $\mathcal{M}$ has a projective implementation $\mathcal{M}' = \mathsf{ProjImp}(\mathcal{M}) = \{M'_p\}_p$, where each M'_p corresponds to the probability distribution on $\{0, 1\}$ that is 1 with probability p.

Tracing Experiment. For an adversary A, function $\epsilon(\cdot)$, and security parameter λ, we consider the following experiment on A:

- A gets λ, and replies with a number N. Both λ, N are represented in unary.
- Run $(\mathsf{pk}, \mathsf{sk}_1, \ldots, \mathsf{sk}_N) \leftarrow \mathsf{Gen}(1^\lambda, 1^N)$, and send pk to A.
- A then makes an arbitrary number of classical queries on identities $i \in [N]$; in response it receives sk_i. Let S be the set of i queried by A.
- Next, A outputs $(|\skull\rangle, m_0, m_1)$ for decoder $|\skull\rangle$ and messages m_0, m_1.

Now consider two possible operations on $|\skull\rangle$:

- $S' \leftarrow \mathsf{Trace}^{|\skull\rangle}(\mathsf{pk}, m_0, m_1, \epsilon)$. Let $\mathsf{BadTrace}$ as the event that $S \setminus S' \neq \emptyset$. We define the event $\mathsf{GoodTrace}$ as the event that $S' \neq \emptyset$
- Apply the measurement $\mathcal{M}'$ to $|\skull\rangle$, obtaining a probability p. Let Live be the event that $p \geq 1/2 + \epsilon$.

Definition 4. *A tracing system is* quantum traceable *if for all quantum polynomial time adversaries A and for every inverse polynomial ϵ, there is a negligible* negl *such that* $\Pr[\mathsf{BadTrace}] < \mathsf{negl}(\lambda)$ *and* $\Pr[\mathsf{GoodTrace}] \geq \Pr[\mathsf{Live}] - \mathsf{negl}(\lambda)$.

5   On the Necessity of Quantum Queries

We consider a variant of our Black Box Projection model where queries to the decoder are only on *classical* ciphertexts c. Concretely, when a query is made to $|\skull\rangle$, the c registers are additionally measured, to ensure that only a classical ciphertext is input. We call this the Classical Black Box Projection model.

Theorem 1. *Any traitor tracing scheme which operates in the Classical Black Box Projection model is* not *quantum traceable according to Definition 4.*

Proof. We construct an adversary A which chooses an arbitrary polynomial N, a random $j \in [N]$, and queries for secret key sk_j. It then chooses two arbitrary distinct messages m_0, m_1 and constructs the following decoder $|\skull\rangle$. First let

$$\mathsf{Dec}'(c) := \begin{cases} b & \text{if } \mathsf{Dec}(\mathsf{sk}_j, c) = m_b \\ 0 & \text{otherwise} \end{cases}$$

Let $\mathcal{H}$ have basis $\{|c\rangle\}_c \cup \{|\perp\rangle\}$, where c ranges over all possible ciphertexts. The decoder's initial state is $|\perp\rangle \otimes |0\rangle |m_0, m_1, \mathsf{sk}_j\rangle$. That is, the decoder's state consists of the system $\mathcal{H}$ initialized to $|\perp\rangle$, a qubit $\mathcal{H}_2$ initialized to $|0\rangle$, as well as the messages m_0, m_1 and the secret key sk_j. Define the vectors $|\phi_c\rangle \in \mathcal{H}$ as $|\phi_c\rangle = \sqrt{2\epsilon}|\perp\rangle + \sqrt{1 - 2\epsilon}|c\rangle$. Let $U(c)$ be the unitary over $\mathcal{H}_2 \otimes \mathcal{H}$:

$$U(c) = (|1 - \mathsf{Dec}'(c)\rangle\langle 1| + |\mathsf{Dec}'(c)\rangle\langle 0|) \otimes |\phi_c\rangle\langle\phi_c| + \mathbf{I} \otimes (\mathbf{I} - |\phi_c\rangle\langle\phi_c|)$$

The output register for $|\skull\rangle$ is set to $\mathcal{H}_2$. Informally, $U(c)$ applies the projective measurement $(P_c, Q_c = \mathbf{I} - P_c)$, where $P_c := |\phi_c\rangle\langle\phi_c|$. Then conditioned on the measurement output being 1, it XORs $\mathsf{Dec}'(c)$ into the output register.

In the Full Version [Zha20], we demonstrate that $|\overset{\text{☠}}{\smile}\rangle$ will almost certainly measure to be live for parameter ϵ; that is, $\Pr[\mathsf{Live}] \geq 1 - \mathsf{negl}$. On the other hand, we show that $\Pr[\mathsf{GoodTrace}] < 1 - \delta$, for some inverse polynomial δ that depends on the number of queries made by the tracing algorithm. This is proved by showing that there is some inverse polynomial probability that all tracing queries are answered with 0, in which case tracing is impossible.   □

6   On Mixtures of Projective Measurements

We now develop some additional tools that will be used in our quantum tracing algorithm in Section 7. We will explore efficient approximations of projective implementations, as well as questions of computational indistinguishability.

We consider the following abstract setup. We have a collection $\mathcal{P} = \{\mathcal{P}_i\}_{i \in \mathcal{I}}$ of binary outcome projective measurements $\mathcal{P}_i = (P_i, Q_i)$ over the same Hilbert space $\mathcal{H}$. Here, P_i corresponds to output 0, and Q_i corresponds to output 1. We will assume we can efficiently measure the $\mathcal{P}_i$ for superpositions of i, meaning we can efficiently perform the following projective measurement over $\mathcal{I} \otimes \mathcal{H}$:

$$\left(\sum_i |i\rangle\langle i| \otimes P_i , \sum_i |i\rangle\langle i| \otimes Q_i \right) \tag{1}$$

Here, we call $\mathcal{P}$ a *collection of projective measurements*, and call $\mathcal{I}$ the *control*. For a distribution D over $\mathcal{I}$, let $\mathcal{P}_D$ be the POVM which samples a random $i \leftarrow D$, applies the measurement $\mathcal{P}_i$, and outputs the resulting bit. We call $\mathcal{P}_D$ a *mixture of projective measurements*. The POVM is given by the matrices (P_D, Q_D) where

$$P = \sum_{i \in \mathcal{I}} \Pr[i \leftarrow D] P_i \quad \text{and} \quad Q = \sum_{i \in \mathcal{I}} \Pr[i \leftarrow D] Q_i$$

In this section, we will address two questions:

- Since $\mathcal{P}_D$ has a binary outcome, there exists a projective implementation $\mathcal{M} = \mathsf{ProjImp}(\mathcal{P}_D)$. Can we efficiently approximate the measurement?
- If D_0, D_1 are computationally indistinguishable, what does that say about the outcomes of $\mathcal{M}_0 = \mathsf{ProjImp}(\mathcal{P}_{D_0})$ and $\mathcal{M}_1 = \mathsf{ProjImp}(\mathcal{P}_{D_1})$?

6.1   Additional Definitions

Shift Distance. For $a \in \mathbb{R}$ and interval $[b, c] \subseteq \mathbb{R}$, denote the distance between a and $[b, c]$ as $|a - [b, c]| := \min_{x \in [b,c]} |a - x|$. For $a \in [b, c]$, the distance is 0 and for $a \notin [b, c]$, the distance is $\max(a - c, b - a)$. Let D_0, D_1 be two distributions over $\mathbb{R}$, with cumulative density functions f_0, f_1, respectively. Let $\epsilon \in \mathbb{R}$. The Shift distance with parameter ϵ is defined as:

$$\Delta_{\mathsf{Shift}}^\epsilon(D_0, D_1) := \sup_{x \in \mathbb{R}} \left| f_0(x) - [f_1(x - \epsilon), f_1(x + \epsilon)] \right|$$

Note that small shift distance does *not* imply small statistical difference, as distributions with disjoint supports can have small shift distance. Also note the triangle-like inequality $\Delta_{\mathsf{Shift}}^{\epsilon_1 + \epsilon_2}(D_0, D_2) \leq \Delta_{\mathsf{Shift}}^{\epsilon_1}(D_0, D_1) + \Delta_{\mathsf{Shift}}^{\epsilon_2}(D_1, D_2)$.

Shift Distance for Measurements. Let $\mathcal{M} = (M_i)_{i \in \mathcal{I}}$ and $\mathcal{N} = (N_j)_{j \in \mathcal{J}}$ be real-valued quantum measurements over the same quantum system $\mathcal{H}$. The shift distance between $\mathcal{M}, \mathcal{N}$, denoted $\Delta^\epsilon_{\mathsf{Shift}}(\mathcal{M}, \mathcal{N})$ is defined as

$$\Delta^\epsilon_{\mathsf{Shift}}(\mathcal{M}, \mathcal{N}) := \sup_{|\psi\rangle} \Delta^\epsilon_{\mathsf{Shift}}(\, \mathcal{M}(|\psi\rangle) \, , \, \mathcal{N}(|\psi\rangle) \,)$$

Almost Projective Measurements. We define "almost" projectivity, based on the fact that repeated consecutive projective measurements yield the same output.

Definition 5. *A real-valued quantum measurement $\mathcal{M} = (M_i)_{i \in \mathcal{I}}$ is (ϵ, δ)-almost projective if the following is true: for any quantum state $|\psi\rangle$, apply $\mathcal{M}$ twice in a row to $|\psi\rangle$, obtaining measurement outcomes x, y. Then $\Pr[|x - y| \leq \epsilon] \geq 1 - \delta$.*

6.2   Approximating Projective Implementations

We now address the question of efficiently approximating the projective implementation $\mathcal{M} = \mathsf{ProjImp}(\mathcal{P}_D)$ of a mixture of projective measurements $\mathcal{P}_D$. We note that exact measurement is computationally infeasible, as it captures computing acceptance probabilities of circuits. Instead, we employ techniques from [MW04] to develop an algorithm API which efficiently *approximates* the projective implementation of $\mathcal{P}_D$. We first define two subroutines.

Controlled Projection. Let $\mathcal{P} = \{\mathcal{P}_i = (P_i, Q_i)\}_{i \in \mathcal{I}}$ be a collection of projective measurements over $\mathcal{H}$. Let D a distribution with random coin set $\mathcal{R}$. We will abuse notation and let $\mathcal{R}$ also denote the $|\mathcal{R}|$-dimensional Hilbert space. The *controlled projection* is the measurement $\mathsf{CProj}_{\mathcal{P},D} = (\mathsf{CProj}^0_{\mathcal{P},D}, \mathsf{CProj}^1_{\mathcal{P},D})$ where

$$\mathsf{CProj}^0_{\mathcal{P},D} = \sum_{r \in \mathcal{R}} |r\rangle\langle r| \otimes P_{D(r)} \quad , \quad \mathsf{CProj}^1_{\mathcal{P},D} = \sum_{r \in \mathcal{R}} |r\rangle\langle r| \otimes Q_{D(r)} \; .$$

$\mathsf{CProj}_{\mathcal{P},D}$ is readily implemented using the measurement in Eq. 1. First, initialize control registers $\mathcal{I}$ to 0. Then perform the map $|r\rangle|i\rangle \mapsto |r\rangle|i \oplus D(r)\rangle$ to the $\mathcal{R} \times \mathcal{I}$ registers. Next, apply the mixture of projective measurements assumed in Eq. 1. Finally, perform the map $|r\rangle|i\rangle \mapsto |r\rangle|i \oplus D(r)\rangle$ again to un-compute the control registers, and discard the control registers.

Uniform Test. Define $\mathsf{IsUniform}_{\mathcal{R}} = (|\mathbb{1}_{\mathcal{R}}\rangle\langle\mathbb{1}_{\mathcal{R}}|, \mathbf{I} - |\mathbb{1}_{\mathcal{R}}\rangle\langle\mathbb{1}_{\mathcal{R}}|)$ where

$$|\mathbb{1}_{\mathcal{R}}\rangle = \frac{1}{\sqrt{|\mathcal{R}|}} \sum_{r \in \mathcal{R}} |r\rangle \; .$$

The Algorithm API. Our algorithm is parameterized by a distribution D, collection of projective measurements $\mathcal{P}$, and real values $0 < \epsilon, \delta \leq 1$, and is denoted as $\mathsf{API}_{\mathcal{P},D}^{\epsilon,\delta}$. On input a quantum state $|\psi\rangle$ over Hilbert space $\mathcal{H}$, it works as follows:

1. Initialize a new register $\mathcal{R}$ to the state $|\mathbb{1}_{\mathcal{R}}\rangle$.
2. Initialize a classical list $L = (0)$.
3. Repeat the following "main loop" a total of $T = \lceil \ln(4/\delta)/\epsilon^2 \rceil$ times:
   (a) Apply the controlled projection $\mathsf{CProj}_{\mathcal{P},D}$ over the joint system $\mathcal{R} \otimes \mathcal{H}$, resulting in measurement outcome b_{2i-1}. Append b_{2i-1} to the end of L.
   (b) Apply the Uniform Test $\mathsf{IsUniform}_{\mathcal{R}}$ to the system $\mathcal{R}$, resulting in measurement outcome b_{2i}. Append b_{2i} to the end of L.
4. Let t be the number of bit flips in the sequence $L = (0, b_1, b_2, \ldots, b_{2T})$, and let $\tilde{p} = t/2T$ be the fraction of bit flips
5. If in the last iteration of the "main loop" $b_{2T} = 1$, repeat the "main loop" until the first time $b_{2i} = 0$.
6. Discard the $\mathcal{R}$ registers, and output $\tilde{p}$.

Theorem 2. *For any $\epsilon, \delta, \mathcal{P}, D$, we have that:*

- $\Delta_{\mathsf{Shift}}^{\epsilon}(\mathsf{API}_{\mathcal{P},D}^{\epsilon,\delta}, \mathsf{ProjImp}(\mathcal{P}_D)) \leq \delta$. *That is,* API *approximates the projective implementation* $\mathsf{ProjImp}(\mathcal{P}_D)$.
- $\mathsf{API}_{\mathcal{P},D}^{\epsilon,\delta}$ *is* (ϵ, δ)-*almost projective.*
- *The expected run time of* $\mathsf{API}_{\mathcal{P},D}^{\epsilon,\delta}$ *is* $X \times \mathsf{poly}(1/\epsilon, \log(1/\delta))$, *where* X *is the combined run time of* D, *the procedure mapping* i *to the measurement* (P_i, Q_i), *and the run-time of the measurement* (P_i, Q_i).

Proof. Let $|\psi\rangle$ be an arbitrary state. Write $|\psi\rangle = \sum_p \alpha_p |\psi_p\rangle$ where $|\psi_p\rangle$ are eigenvectors of $\mathcal{P}_D$ with eigenvalue p^7. In other words, $Q_D |\psi_p\rangle = p |\psi_p\rangle$. Define the following states:

- $|u_p^0\rangle = \frac{1}{\sqrt{(1-p)|\mathcal{R}|}} \sum_r |r\rangle P_{D(r)} |\psi_p\rangle$. Notice that

$$\langle u_p^0 | u_p^0 \rangle = \frac{1}{(1-p)|\mathcal{R}|} \left(\sum_r \langle r | \langle \psi_p | P_{D(r)} \right) \left(\sum_s |s\rangle P_{D(s)} |\psi_p\rangle \right)$$

$$= \frac{1}{(1-p)} \langle \psi_p | \left(\frac{1}{|\mathcal{R}|} \sum_r P_{D(r)} \right) |\psi_p\rangle = \frac{1}{1-p} \langle \psi_p | P_D |\psi_p\rangle = 1 \ .$$

Also, notice that $\mathsf{CProj}_{\mathcal{P},D}^0 |u_p^0\rangle = |u_p^0\rangle$ whereas $\mathsf{CProj}_{\mathcal{P},D}^1 |u_p^0\rangle = 0$.

- $|u_p^1\rangle = \frac{1}{\sqrt{p|\mathcal{R}|}} \sum_r |r\rangle Q_{D(r)} |\psi_p\rangle$. By an analogous calculation for $|u_p^0\rangle$, we have that $\langle u_p^1 | u_p^1 \rangle = 1$. Since different eigenvectors of $\mathcal{P}_D$ are orthogonal, we also have that $\langle u_p^1 | u_{p'}^1 \rangle = 0$ for $p \neq p'$. Since $P_i Q_i = 0$, we have $\langle u_p^1 | u_{p'}^0 \rangle = 0$ for any p, p' (not necessarily distinct). This means $B = \{|u_p^b\rangle\}_{b,p}$ is orthonormal. Also, notice that $\mathsf{CProj}_{\mathcal{P},D}^0 |u_p^1\rangle = 0$ whereas $\mathsf{CProj}_{\mathcal{P},D}^1 |u_p^1\rangle = |u_p^1\rangle$.

---

[7] Note that there may be repeated eigenvalues. The $|\psi_p\rangle$ are therefore the projections of $|\psi\rangle$ onto the eigenspaces.

- $|v_p^0\rangle = |\mathbb{1}_\mathcal{R}\rangle \otimes |\psi_p\rangle$. Notice that $|v_p^0\rangle = \sqrt{1-p}|u_p^0\rangle + \sqrt{p}|u_p^1\rangle$. Also notice that $\mathsf{IsUniform}_\mathcal{R}^0 \otimes \mathbf{I}|v_p^0\rangle = |v_p^0\rangle$ and $\mathsf{IsUniform}_\mathcal{R}^1 \otimes \mathbf{I}|v_p^0\rangle = 0$
- $|v_p^1\rangle = -\sqrt{p}|u_p^0\rangle + \sqrt{1-p}|u_p^1\rangle$. Notice that $\langle v_p^b|v_{p'}^{b'}\rangle$ is 1 if $b = b' \wedge p = p'$ and 0 otherwise. This means $B' = \{|v_p^b\rangle\}$ is orthonormal, spanning the same space as B. Finally, notice that $\mathsf{IsUniform}_\mathcal{R}^0 \otimes \mathbf{I}|v_p^1\rangle = 0$ and $\mathsf{IsUniform}_\mathcal{R}^1 \otimes \mathbf{I}|v_p^1\rangle = |v_p^1\rangle$.

At the beginning of the first run of the "main loop" (Step 3), the state of the system is $|\psi_0\rangle := |\mathbb{1}_\mathcal{R}\rangle \otimes |\psi\rangle$. Writing this state in the basis B', we have

$$|\mathbb{1}_\mathcal{R}\rangle \otimes |\psi\rangle = \sum_p \alpha_p |v_p^0\rangle \ .$$

Let $|\psi_L\rangle$ for $L \in \{0,1\}^z$ denote the *unnormalized* state of the system after the first z measurements, if the sequence of measurement outcomes is L. Let $t(L)$ denote the number of bit flips in the sequence $0, L_1, L_2, \ldots, L_z$.

Claim. $|\psi_L\rangle = \theta_L \sum_p \alpha_p (\sqrt{p})^{t(L)} (\sqrt{1-p})^{z-t(L)} \begin{cases} |v_p^{L_z}\rangle & \text{if } z \bmod 2 = 0 \\ |u_p^{L_z}\rangle & \text{if } z \bmod 2 = 1 \end{cases}$ where θ_L is a global phase factor, $|\theta_L| = 1$.

Proof. We prove by induction. The base case $z = 0$ is true. Now assume that the claim is true for $z - 1$. We prove the odd z case, the even case being essentially identical. Let L' be L but with the last entry removed. By induction we have

$$|\psi_{L'}\rangle = \theta_{L'} \sum_p \alpha_p (\sqrt{p})^{t(L')} (\sqrt{1-p})^{z-1-t(L')} |v_p^{L_z}\rangle \ .$$

Observe that $|v_p^b\rangle = \sqrt{1-p}|u_p^b\rangle - (-1)^b|u_b^{1-b}\rangle$. We apply $\mathsf{CProj}_{\mathcal{P},D}$; if the outcome is b, this projects onto $\{|u_p^b\rangle\}_p$. If $L_z = L'_{z-1} \oplus c$, then $t(L) = t(L') + c$, and

$$|\psi_L\rangle = \theta_{L'}(-1)^{cL_z} \sum_p \alpha_p (\sqrt{p})^{t(L')+c} (\sqrt{1-p})^{z-t(L')-c} |u_p^{L_z}\rangle$$

Setting θ_L appropriately gives the desired outcome.   □

At Step 4, the unnormalized state is $|\psi_L\rangle$ as defined above, where L contains the results of measurements. The probability of obtaining a particular L is

$$\langle \psi_L | \psi_L \rangle = \sum_p |\alpha_p|^2 (p)^{t(L)} (1-p)^{2T-t(L)} \ .$$

L is therefore distributed according to the following distribution:

- First apply $\mathsf{ProjImp}(\mathcal{P}_D)$ to $|\psi\rangle$ to obtain a value p
- Let K be a list of $2T$ independent coin flips with expected value p.
- Set L_i to be the parity of the first i bits of K.

Then $2T\tilde{p} = t(L)$ is just the number 1s in K. Hoeffding's inequality then gives

$$\Pr[|\tilde{p} - p| \geq \epsilon/2] \leq 2e^{-2(2T)(\epsilon/2)^2} \leq \delta/2 < \delta \ ,$$

for $T \geq \ln(4/\delta)/\epsilon^2$. This implies that $\Delta^\epsilon_{\mathsf{Shift}}(p, \tilde{p}) \leq \Delta^{\epsilon/2}_{\mathsf{Shift}}(p, \tilde{p}) \leq \delta/2 \leq \delta$.

We now analyze the run-time, which is dominated by the number of iterations of the main loop, including Step 5. Note that Step 5 terminates once the number of bit flips in L is even. The number of iterations is identically distributed to:

– Sample p by running $\mathsf{ProjImp}(\mathcal{P}_D)$.
– Flip $2T$ biased random coins whose probability of outputting 1 is p.
– Flip an even number of additional coins until the overall parity is 0.
– Output the total number of coin tosses, divided by 2.

We can simplify this experiment by pairing off the coin tosses, and only looking at the parity of each pair, which itself is a biased coin with expectation $q = 2p(1 - p)$:

– Sample p by running $\mathsf{ProjImp}(\mathcal{P}_D)$.
– Flip T biased random coins whose probability of outputting 1 is $q = 2p(1-p)$.
– Flip additional coins until the overall parity is 0.
– Output the total number of coin tosses.

Let $T'(q)$ be the expected number of additional coins for a given q; note that $q \in [0, 1/2]$. Note that $T'(0) = 0$, since the parity is always even. For $q > 0$, if the parity is even after T steps, no additional flips are needed. Assuming T is even, a routine calculation shows that the probability the parity is odd after the first T steps is $(1 - (1 - 2q)^{2T})/2$, in which case an expected $1/q$ additional flips are needed. Thus $T'(q) := (1 - (1 - 2q)^{2T})/2q$ for $q > 0$. For $q \in (0, 1/2]$, T' is monotonically decreasing, and $\lim_{q \to 0} T'(q) = 2T$. Therefore, for any fixed q, we can upper bound the total expected number of coin tosses to $T + 2T = 3T$. By linearity of expectation, this also holds over any distribution over q. Thus, the expected number of runs of the main loop is at most $3T$.

Finally, we consider applying API twice to the same state. Notice that, since the first run of API is guaranteed to stop when the last bit of L is 0, this corresponds to $\mathcal{R}$ containing a uniform superposition. But this means that when we start the second run of API, the state going into the main loop will actually be identical to the state at the end of the first run. We can therefore view the two runs of API as a single run, but with a larger value of T. The overall list K produced by both runs, but stopping at Step 4 in the second run, is then distributed according to:

– Sample p by running $\mathsf{ProjImp}(\mathcal{P}_D)$.
– Flip $2T$ biased random coins whose probability of outputting 1 is p.
– Flip an even number of additional random coins, until a 0 is found.
– Then flip $2T$ more biased random coins.
– Let K be the overall list of coin flips.

The first output, $\tilde{p}_1$, is then just the fraction of 1's in the first $2T$ bits of K, whereas the second output, $\tilde{p}_2$, is the fraction of 1's in the last $2T$ bits of K. These fractions are independent. Recalling that

$$\Pr[|\tilde{p} - p| \geq \epsilon/2] \leq \delta/2,$$

we have that $\Pr[|\tilde{p}_1 - \tilde{p}_2| \geq \epsilon] \leq \delta$. Thus API is (ϵ, δ)-almost projective.   □

6.3   On Computational Indistinguishability

Here, we show that if the underlying distributions D_0, D_1 are computationally indistinguishable, then the resulting projective implementations $\mathcal{M}_0 = \mathsf{ProjImp}(\mathcal{P}_{D_0})$ and $\mathcal{M}_1 = \mathsf{ProjImp}(\mathcal{P}_{D_1})$ are close.

Theorem 3. *Let ρ be an efficiently constructible mixed state, and D_0, D_1 efficiently sampleable, computationally indistinguishable distributions. For any inverse polynomial ϵ, there exists a negligible δ such that $\Delta^\epsilon_{\mathsf{Shift}}(\mathcal{M}_0(\rho), \mathcal{M}_1(\rho)) \leq \delta$.*

Proof. The rough idea is that we will switch from the projective implementation $\mathcal{M}_b$ to our approximation API. Since API is efficient, we argue that the results of API must be close. The difficulty is that API makes queries on a *superposition* of exponentially-many samples from the respective D_b distribution, whose indistinguishability does not follow from the indistinguishability of single samples. We nevertheless show that the outputs of API under the two distributions must be close by using the small-range distributions of Zhandry [Zha12a].

Consider an adversary A producing a mixture ρ. Let $\mathcal{R}$ be the space of random coins for D_0, D_1; we can assume wlog that they share the same random coin space. We now define the following sequence of hybrid distributions:

Hybrid 0. The distribution is $p_0 \leftarrow \mathcal{M}_0(\rho)$ where ρ is generated by A.

Hybrid 1. Here, we choose a random permutation Π on $\mathcal{R}$. Let $D_0^\Pi(r) = D_0(\Pi(r))$. Run $p_1 \leftarrow \mathsf{ProjImp}(\mathcal{P}_{D_0^\Pi})$. Since D_0 and D_0^Π are identical distributions, the measurements $\mathcal{P}_{D_0}$ and $\mathcal{P}_{D_0^\Pi}$ are identical, and therefore so are their projective implementations. Thus, p_0 and p_1 are identically distributed.

Hybrid 2. Here, we will generate $p_2 \leftarrow \mathsf{API}^{\epsilon', \delta'}_{\mathcal{P}, D_0^\Pi}(\rho)$, for a function δ' and an inverse polynomial ϵ' to be chosen later. By Theorem 2, we have that $\Delta^{\epsilon'}_{\mathsf{Shift}}(p_1, p_2) \leq \delta'$.

Hybrid 3. Now we change Π to be the small-range functions $\Sigma = G \circ F$ of Zhandry [Zha12a], where $F : \mathcal{R} \to [s]$ and $G : [s] \to \mathcal{R}$ are random functions, and s is a parameter. Let $p_3 \leftarrow \mathsf{API}^{\epsilon', \delta'}_{\mathcal{P}, D_0^\Sigma}(\rho)$. Let Φ be the distribution of random *functions* on $\mathcal{R}$. Yuen and Zhandry show the following:

Theorem 4 ([Yue14, Zha15]). *For any quantum algorithm B making Q quantum queries to Π or Φ, $|\Pr[B^\Pi() = 1] - \Pr[B^\Phi() = 1]| \leq O(Q^3/|\mathcal{R}|)$.*

Theorem 5 ([Zha12a]). *For any quantum algorithm B making Q quantum queries to Φ or Σ, $|\Pr[B^\Phi() = 1] - \Pr[B^\Sigma() = 1]| \leq O(Q^3/|\mathcal{R}|)$.*

Theorems 4 and 5 in particular means that $\Delta^0_{\mathsf{Shift}}(p_2, p_3) \leq O(Q^3/s + Q^3/|\mathcal{R}|)$.

Hybrid 4. This is the same as Hybrid 3, except that we change F to be a $2Q$-wise independent function E. Let $p_4 \leftarrow \mathsf{API}^{\epsilon', \delta'}_{\mathcal{P}, D^{G \circ E}_0}(\rho)$. Since API only makes Q queries to F or E, the following theorem implies that p_3 and p_4 are identically distributed:

Theorem 6 ([Zha12b]). *For any quantum algorithm B making Q quantum queries to F or E, $\Pr[B^F() = 1] = \Pr[B^E() = 1]$.*

Assume $|\mathcal{R}| > s$, adding random coins to $\mathcal{R}$ that are ignored by D_0, D_1 if necessary. Then $\Delta^{\epsilon'}_{\mathsf{Shift}}(p_0, p_4) \leq O(Q^3/s) + \delta'$.

Hybrid 5. Next, we switch to using the distribution $D^{G \circ E}_1(r) = D_1(G(E(r)))$. Let $p_5 \leftarrow \mathsf{API}^{\epsilon', \delta'}_{\mathcal{P}, D^{G \circ E}_1}(\rho)$. Note that $D_b(G(\cdot))$ can be interpreted as a list of s samples from D_b, which the input selecting which sample to use. Since D_0 and D_1 are computationally indistinguishable, so are s samples. Notice that the entire experiment in Hybrids 4/5 are efficient. Therefore, by a straightforward argument, we have that $\Delta^0_{\mathsf{Shift}}(p_5, p_6) \leq \gamma$ where γ is negligible.

Hybrids 6–9. **Hybrid** $6 + g$ is identical to **Hybrid** $5 - g$ except for replacing D_0 with D_1. In **Hybrid 9**, the output is exactly $\mathcal{M}_1(\rho)$. Putting everything together, we have that $\Delta^{2\epsilon'}_{\mathsf{Shift}}(\mathcal{M}_0(\rho), \mathcal{M}_1(\rho)) \leq O(Q^3/s) + 2\delta' + \gamma$.

Let ϵ be an inverse polynomial, and suppose $\delta := \Delta^{\epsilon}_{\mathsf{Shift}}(\mathcal{M}_0(\rho), \mathcal{M}_1(\rho))$ is non-negligible, lower bounded by an inverse-polynomial w infinitely often. Set $\epsilon' = \epsilon/2$ and $\delta' = w/4$. Then $\log(1/\delta')$ is logarithmic. Recall $Q = O(\log(1/\delta')^3/(\epsilon')^2)$. For the infinitely-many values of the security parameter where $\delta \geq w$, we have that $w \leq \delta \leq O(Q^3/s) + w/2 + \gamma$, which re-arranges to $w \leq O(\log(1/w)^3/\epsilon^6 s) + 2\gamma$. But now choose $s = 2 \times O(\ (1/\epsilon)^6 (1/w) \log(1/w)^3\ )$, a polynomial. This gives $w \leq w/2 + 2\gamma$, or $w \leq 4\gamma$, which can only happen for finitely many security parameters since γ is negligible, a contradiction. Thus δ must be negligible. $\qquad\qquad\qquad\qquad\qquad\qquad\qquad\qquad\qquad\qquad\qquad\qquad\qquad\quad\square$

Corollary 1. *Let ρ be an efficiently constructible, potentially mixed state, and let D_0, D_1 be two computationally indistinguishable distributions. Then for any inverse polynomial ϵ and any function δ, there exists a negligible* negl *such that $\Delta^{3\epsilon}_{\mathsf{Shift}}(\mathsf{API}^{\epsilon, \delta}_{\mathcal{P}, D_0}, \mathsf{API}^{\epsilon, \delta}_{\mathcal{P}, D_1}) \leq 2\delta +$ negl.*

7 Tracing PLBE

7.1 Private Linear Broadcast Encryption

Our construction will use the Private Linear Broadcast Encryption (PLBE) framework of Boneh, Sahai, and Waters [BSW06]. A PLBE scheme is a triple of probabilistic *classical* polynomial time algorithms $(\mathsf{Gen'}, \mathsf{Enc'}, \mathsf{Dec'})$ where:

- $\mathsf{Gen'}(1^N, 1^\lambda)$ takes as input a number of users N and a security parameter λ. It outputs a public key pk, plus N user secret keys sk_i for $i \in [N]$.
- $\mathsf{Enc'}(\mathsf{pk}, j, m)$ takes as input the public key, an index $j \in [0, N]$, and a message m. It outputs a ciphertext c.
- $\mathsf{Dec'}(\mathsf{sk}_i, c)$ takes as input a secret key sk_i for user i and a ciphertext, and outputs a message m' or a special abort symbol $\perp$.

Correctness. For correctness, we require that user i can decrypt ciphertexts with index j, so long as $i \leq j$. That is there exists a negligible function $\mathsf{negl}(\lambda)$ such that for every λ and $N \leq 2^\lambda$, for every $i \in [N]$ and $j \geq i$, we have that

$$\Pr[\mathsf{Dec'}(\mathsf{sk}_i, \mathsf{Enc'}(\mathsf{pk}, j, m)) = m : (\mathsf{pk}, \{\mathsf{sk}_i\}_{i \in [N]}) \leftarrow \mathsf{Gen'}(N, \lambda)] > 1 - \mathsf{negl}(\lambda) .$$

Security. We need two security requirements. The first is *indistinguishability security*, which requires semantic security for encryptions to $j = 0$:

Definition 6. *A PLBE scheme* $(\mathsf{Gen'}, \mathsf{Enc'}, \mathsf{Dec'})$ *is* indistinguishable secure *if for all quantum polynomial time adversaries A, there exists a negligible* negl *such that the probability A wins in the following game is at most $1/2 + \mathsf{negl}(\lambda)$:*

- *A gets λ as input, and sends a number N represented in unary.*
- *Run $(\mathsf{pk}, \mathsf{sk}_1, \ldots, \mathsf{sk}_N) \leftarrow \mathsf{Gen'}(\lambda, N)$, and send pk to A.*
- *A then makes an arbitrary number of classical queries on identities $i \in [N]$; in response it receives sk_i.*
- *Next, A outputs a pair of messages (m_0, m_1). In response, choose a random bit b and send A the ciphertext $c \leftarrow \mathsf{Enc'}(\mathsf{pk}, j = 0, m_b)$.*
- *A makes more queries for sk_i.*
- *Finally, A outputs a guess b' for b. Output "win" if and only if $b' = b$.*

Second, we need *index hiding security* which says that encrypts to $j - 1$ and j are only distinguishable to an adversary that has the secret key for user j.

Definition 7. *A PLBE scheme* $(\mathsf{Gen'}, \mathsf{Enc'}, \mathsf{Dec'})$ *is* index hiding secure *if for all quantum polynomial time adversaries A, there exists a negligible function negl such that the probabilities A wins in the following game is at most $1/2 + \mathsf{negl}(\lambda)$:*

- *A gets λ as input, and sends a number N represented in unary.*
- *Run $(\mathsf{pk}, \mathsf{sk}_1, \ldots, \mathsf{sk}_N) \leftarrow \mathsf{Gen'}(\lambda, N)$, and send pk to A.*
- *A then makes an arbitrary number of classical queries on identities $i \in [N]$; in response it receives sk_i. Let S be the set of i queried by A.*
- *Next, A outputs a pair of (j, m) for $j \in [N]$ such that $j \notin S$. Choose a random bit b and send A the ciphertext $c \leftarrow \mathsf{Enc'}(\mathsf{pk}, j - b, m)$ to index $j - b$*
- *A is allowed to make more queries on identities $i \in [N] \backslash j$, to which it receives sk_i in response.*
- *Finally, A outputs a guess b' for b. Output "win" if and only if $b' = b$.*

From PLBE to Traitor Tracing. Following [BSW06], the first three algorithms of our traitor tracing construction $(\mathsf{Gen}, \mathsf{Enc}, \mathsf{Dec}, \mathsf{Trace})$ we be immediately derived from the PLBE scheme: $\mathsf{Gen} = \mathsf{Gen}'$, $\mathsf{Enc}(\mathsf{pk}, m) = \mathsf{Enc}'(\mathsf{pk}, j = N, m)$, and $\mathsf{Dec} = \mathsf{Dec}'$. Correctness is immediate. In the following, we describe Trace.

7.2   The Quantum Algorithm Trace

Where we depart from [BSW06] is in our tracing algorithm, which we now need to trace quantum pirates. First, we briefly explain how to implement API using Black Box Projection queries.

Concretely, let $|\text{💀}'\rangle$ be $|\text{💀}\rangle$, except that we augment the decoder with a qubit $\mathcal{H}_2$ originally set to $|0\rangle$. Let $\mathcal{H}_2' \times \mathcal{C}$ be control registers, where $\mathcal{H}_2'$ is another qubit and $\mathcal{C}$ is a ciphertext register. Consider the following measurement process on registers $\mathcal{H}_2' \otimes \mathcal{C} \otimes \mathcal{H}_2 \otimes \mathcal{H}$:

- Perform the map $|b'\rangle|b\rangle \to |b'\rangle|b \oplus b'\rangle$ on the $\mathcal{H}_2' \otimes \mathcal{H}_2$ registers
- Make a Black Box Projection query using the registers $\mathcal{C} \otimes \mathcal{H}_2$ as the query registers. Let o be the result.
- Perform the map $|b'\rangle|b\rangle \to |b'\rangle|b \oplus b'\rangle$ on the $\mathcal{H}_2' \otimes \mathcal{H}_2$ registers
- Output $1 - o$.

This measurement process has exactly the form of a collection of projective measurements $\mathcal{P}$ in Eq. 1. For a decoder in its initial state (meaning $\mathcal{H}_2$ is initialized to $|0\rangle$) and for a given bit/ciphertext pair (b, c), the corresponding measurement $\mathcal{P}_{(b,c)}$ outputs 1 exactly when the decoder would output b. Thus, we can run the algorithm API on $|\text{💀}'\rangle$.

We now give our algorithm $\mathsf{Trace}^{|\text{💀}\rangle}(\mathsf{pk}, m_0, m_1, \epsilon)$:

1. Let $\epsilon' = \epsilon/4(N+1)$ and $\delta' = 2^{-\lambda}$.
2. Run $\tilde{p}_N \leftarrow \mathsf{API}_{\mathcal{P}, D_N}^{\epsilon', \delta'}(|\text{💀}'\rangle)$, where D_j is the following distribution:
   - Run $b \leftarrow \{0, 1\}$
   - Compute $c \leftarrow \mathsf{Enc}'(\mathsf{pk}, j, m_b)$
   - Output (b, c).
3. If $\tilde{p}_N < 1/2 + \epsilon - \epsilon'$, abort and output the empty set $\{\}$.
4. Otherwise, initialize $S' = \{\}$. Then for $j = N$ to $j = 1$,
   - Compute $\tilde{p}_{j-1} \leftarrow \mathsf{API}_{\mathcal{P}, D_{j-1}}^{\epsilon', \delta'}(|\text{💀}'\rangle)$
   - If $\tilde{p}_{j-1} < \tilde{p}_j - 4\epsilon'$, add j to S'.
   Finally, output S'.

Theorem 7. *If* $(\mathsf{Gen}', \mathsf{Enc}', \mathsf{Dec}')$ *is indistinguishable secure and index hiding secure for quantum adversaries, then* $(\mathsf{Gen}, \mathsf{Enc}, \mathsf{Dec}, \mathsf{Trace})$ *is quantum traceable.*

Proof. Consider an adversary A which has secret keys for identities in S, and produces a pirate decoder $|\text{💀}\rangle$. Let ϵ be an inverse polynomial. Define the events $\mathsf{GoodTrace}, \mathsf{BadTrace}, \mathsf{Live}$ as in Definition 4.

We first argue that $\Pr[\mathsf{BadTrace}]$ is negligible. Suppose that there is a non-negligible probability s that $\mathsf{BadTrace}$ happens. Then for a random choice of j, it is the case that with (non-negligible) probability at least s/N, both (1) A never queries j, and (2) $\tilde{p}_{j-1} < \tilde{p}_j - 4\epsilon'$.

Let ρ be the state produced by the following process:

- Choose a random j, and run the tracing experiment
- If A ever makes a query on j, abort and output an arbitrary quantum state.
- Next run Trace, stopping immediately after $\tilde{p}_j$ is computed.
- Output the state $|\skull'\rangle$.

Consider running Trace for one more iteration, applying $\mathsf{API}^{\epsilon',\delta'}_{\mathcal{P},D_{j-1}}$ to ρ to obtain a measurement $\tilde{p}_{j-1}$. By assumption, we have that $\tilde{p}_{j-1} \geq \tilde{p}_j - 4\epsilon'$ with non-negligible probability s/N.

Now consider instead stopping Trace at iteration j to obtain ρ, but then applying $\mathsf{API}^{\epsilon',\delta'}_{\mathcal{P},D_j}$ to ρ a second time, obtaining a second measurement $\tilde{p}'_j$ of p_j. We stress that in this case, we do *not* compute $\tilde{p}_{j-1}$. Since API is (ϵ',δ') projective, we know that $|\tilde{p}_j - \tilde{p}'_j| \leq \epsilon'$ except with probability at most δ'.

Since j was never queried, encryptions to index j and $j-1$ are indistinguishable. By Corollary 1, this means the distributions on $\tilde{p}'_j$ and $\tilde{p}_{j-1}$ satisfy $\Delta^{3\epsilon'}_{\mathsf{Shift}}(\tilde{p}'_j, \tilde{p}_{j-1}) \leq \mathsf{negl}$. But by our triangle-like inequality, this means that $\tilde{p}_{j-1} \geq \tilde{p}_j - 4\epsilon'$ except with negligible probability, a contradiction.

We now argue that $\Pr[\mathsf{GoodTrace}] \geq \Pr[\mathsf{Live}] - \mathsf{negl}(\lambda)$. First, let Abort be the event that tracing aborts in Step 3. Let p_N be the probability obtained from applying $\mathcal{M}'$ to the decoder outputted by A. Note that Live is the event that $p_N > 1/2 + \epsilon$. We then have that $\Delta^{\epsilon'}_{\mathsf{Shift}}(p_N, \tilde{p}_N) \leq \delta'$. Therefore, $\Pr[\neg\mathsf{Abort}] \geq \Pr[\mathsf{Live}] - \delta'$

Next, let Fail be the event that $\tilde{p}_0 \geq 1/2 + 4\epsilon'$. Let ρ be the state right before measuring $\tilde{p}_0$. Let p_0 be the random variable corresponding to applying $\mathcal{P}_{D_0}$ to ρ. Recall that for $j = 0$, encryptions of m_0 and m_1 are computationally indistinguishable. This means that $p_0 \leq 1/2 + \mathsf{negl}$. By Corollary 1, this means $\Pr[\mathsf{Fail}] < \mathsf{negl}$. Thus, $\Pr[\neg\mathsf{Abort} \wedge \neg\mathsf{Fail}] \geq \Pr[\mathsf{Live}] - \mathsf{negl}$.

Finally, we note that if neither of Fail or Abort happen, then $\tilde{p}_N - \tilde{p}_0 > \epsilon - 4\epsilon' = 4N\epsilon'$. But then it must have been some j such that $\tilde{p}_j - \tilde{p}_{j-1} > 4\epsilon'$, meaning S' is non-empty and therefore $\mathsf{GoodTrace}$ happens. Thus $\Pr[\mathsf{GoodTrace}] \geq \Pr[\neg\mathsf{Abort} \wedge \neg\mathsf{Fail}] \geq \Pr[\mathsf{Live}] - \mathsf{negl}$, as desired. $\qquad\square$

References

[Aar04] Aaronson, S.: Limitations of quantum advice and one-way communication. In: Proceedings 19th IEEE Annual Conference on Computational Complexity, 2004, pp. 320–332. IEEE (2004)

[Aar09] Aaronson, S.: Quantum copy-protection and quantum money. In: 2009 24th Annual IEEE Conference on Computational Complexity, pp. 229–242 (2009)

[AC12] Aaronson, S., Christiano, P.: Quantum money from hidden subspaces. In: Howard, J.K., Pitassi, T. (eds.) 44th ACM STOC, pp. 41–60. ACM Press (2012)

[AGKZ20] Amos, R., Georgiou, M., Kiayias, A., Zhandry, M.: One-shot signatures and applications to hybrid quantum/classical authentication. In: Makarychev, K., Makarychev, Y., Tulsiani, M., Kamath, G., Chuzhoy, J. (eds.) 52nd ACM STOC, pp. 255–268. ACM Press (2020)

[ARU14] Ambainis, A., Rosmanis, A., Unruh, D.: Quantum attacks on classical proof systems: the hardness of quantum rewinding. In: 55th FOCS, pp. 474–483. IEEE Computer Society Press (2014)

[AV19] Ananth, P., Vaikuntanathan, V.: Optimal bounded-collusion secure functional encryption. In: Hofheinz, D., Rosen, A. (eds.) TCC 2019. LNCS, vol. 11891, pp. 174–198. Springer, Cham (2019). https://doi.org/10.1007/978-3-030-36030-6_8

[BB87] Bennett, C.H., Brassard, G.: Quantum public key distribution reinvented. SIGACT News 18(4), 51–53 (1987)

[BCM+18] Brakerski, Z., Christiano, P., Mahadev, U., Vazirani, U.V., Vidick, T.: A cryptographic test of quantumness and certifiable randomness from a single quantum device. In: Thorup, M. (ed.) 59th FOCS, pp. 320–331. IEEE Computer Society Press (2018)

[BDF+11] Boneh, D., Dagdelen, Ö., Fischlin, M., Lehmann, A., Schaffner, C., Zhandry, M.: Random oracles in a quantum world. In: Lee, D.H., Wang, X. (eds.) ASIACRYPT 2011. LNCS, vol. 7073, pp. 41–69. Springer, Heidelberg (2011). https://doi.org/10.1007/978-3-642-25385-0_3

[BGI+01] Barak, B., et al.: On the (Im)possibility of obfuscating programs. In: Kilian, J. (ed.) CRYPTO 2001. LNCS, vol. 2139, pp. 1–18. Springer, Heidelberg (2001). https://doi.org/10.1007/3-540-44647-8_1

[BGMZ18] Bartusek, J., Guan, J., Ma, F., Zhandry, M.: Return of GGH15: provable security against zeroizing attacks. In: Beimel, A., Dziembowski, S. (eds.) TCC 2018. LNCS, vol. 11240, pp. 544–574. Springer, Cham (2018). https://doi.org/10.1007/978-3-030-03810-6_20

[BN08] Boneh, D., Naor, M.: Traitor tracing with constant size ciphertext. In: Ning, P., Syverson, P.F., Jha, S. (eds.) ACM CCS 2008, pp. 501–510. ACM Press (2008)

[BSW06] Boneh, D., Sahai, A., Waters, B.: Fully collusion resistant traitor tracing with short ciphertexts and private keys. In: Vaudenay, S. (ed.) EUROCRYPT 2006. LNCS, vol. 4004, pp. 573–592. Springer, Heidelberg (2006). https://doi.org/10.1007/11761679_34

[BZ14] Boneh, D., Zhandry, M.: Multiparty key exchange, efficient traitor tracing, and more from indistinguishability obfuscation. In: Garay, J.A., Gennaro, R. (eds.) CRYPTO 2014. LNCS, vol. 8616, pp. 480–499. Springer, Heidelberg (2014). https://doi.org/10.1007/978-3-662-44371-2_27

[CFN94] Chor, B., Fiat, A., Naor, M.: Tracing traitors. In: Desmedt, Y.G. (ed.) CRYPTO 1994. LNCS, vol. 839, pp. 257–270. Springer, Heidelberg (1994). https://doi.org/10.1007/3-540-48658-5_25

[CHN+16] Cohen, A., Holmgren, J., Nishimaki, R., Vaikuntanathan, V., Wichs, D.: Watermarking cryptographic capabilities. In: Wichs, D., Mansour, Y. (eds.) 48th ACM STOC, pp. 1115–1127. ACM Press (2016)

[DFNS14] Damgård, I., Funder, J., Nielsen, J.B., Salvail, L.: Superposition attacks on cryptographic protocols. In: Padró, C. (ed.) ICITS 2013. LNCS, vol.

8317, pp. 142–161. Springer, Cham (2014). https://doi.org/10.1007/978-3-319-04268-8_9

[GGH+13] Garg, S., Gentry, C., Halevi, S., Raykova, M., Sahai, A., Waters, B.: Candidate indistinguishability obfuscation and functional encryption for all circuits. In: 54th FOCS, pp. 40–49. IEEE Computer Society Press (2013)

[GKW18] Goyal, R., Koppula, V., Waters, B.: Collusion resistant traitor tracing from learning with errors. In: Diakonikolas, I., Kempe, D., Henzinger, M. (eds.) 50th ACM STOC, pp. 660–670. ACM Press (2018)

[GKZ19] Grilo, A.B., Kerenidis, I., Zijlstra, T.: Learning-with-errors problem is easy with quantum samples. Phys. Rev. A **99**, 032314 (2019)

[KLLN16] Kaplan, M., Leurent, G., Leverrier, A., Naya-Plasencia, M.: Breaking symmetric cryptosystems using quantum period finding. In: Robshaw, M., Katz, J. (eds.) CRYPTO 2016. Part II, volume 9815 of LNCS, pp. 207–237. Springer, Heidelberg (2016). https://doi.org/10.1007/978-3-662-53008-5_8

[KM10] Kuwakado, H., Morii, M.: Quantum distinguisher between the 3-round feistel cipher and the random permutation. In: 2010 IEEE International Symposium on Information Theory, pp. 2682–2685. IEEE (2010)

[MW04] Marriott, C., Watrous, J.: Quantum arthur-merlin games. In: Proceedings 19th IEEE Annual Conference on Computational Complexity, 2004, pp. 275–285 (2004)

[Sho94] Shor, P.W.: Algorithms for quantum computation: discrete logarithms and factoring. In: 35th FOCS, pp. 124–134. IEEE Computer Society Press (1994)

[VDG98] Van De Graaf, J.: Towards a formal definition of security for quantum protocols (1998)

[Wie83] Wiesner, S.: Conjugate coding. SIGACT News **15**(1), 78–88 (1983)

[Yue14] Yuen, H.: A quantum lower bound for distinguishing random functions from random permutations. Quant. Inf. Comput. **14**(13–14), 1089–1097 (2014)

[Zha12a] Zhandry, M.: How to construct quantum random functions. In: 53rd FOCS, pp. 679–687. IEEE Computer Society Press (2012)

[Zha12b] Zhandry, M.: Secure identity-based encryption in the quantum random oracle model. In: Safavi-Naini, R., Canetti, R. (eds.) CRYPTO 2012. LNCS, vol. 7417, pp. 758–775. Springer, Heidelberg (2012). https://doi.org/10.1007/978-3-642-32009-5_44

[Zha15] Zhandry, M.: A note on the quantum collision and set equality problems. Quant. Inf. Comput. **15**(7& 8) (2015)

[Zha20] Zhandry, M.: Schrödinger's pirate: How to trace a quantum decoder (full version) (2020)

Quantum Encryption with Certified Deletion

Anne Broadbent[(✉)] and Rabib Islam

Department of Mathematics and Statistics,
University of Ottawa, Ottawa, ON, Canada
{abroadbe,risla028}@uottawa.ca

Abstract. Given a ciphertext, is it possible to prove the *deletion* of the underlying plaintext? Since classical ciphertexts can be copied, clearly such a feat is impossible using classical information alone. In stark contrast to this, we show that quantum encodings enable *certified deletion*. More precisely, we show that it is possible to encrypt classical data into a quantum ciphertext such that the recipient of the ciphertext can produce a *classical* string which proves to the originator that the recipient has relinquished any chance of recovering the plaintext should the key be revealed. Our scheme is feasible with current quantum technology: the honest parties only require quantum devices for single-qubit preparation and measurements; the scheme is also robust against noise in these devices. Furthermore, we provide an analysis that is suitable in the finite-key regime.

1 Introduction

Consider the following scenario: Alice sends a ciphertext to Bob, but in addition, she wants to encode the data in a way such that Bob can prove to her that he *deleted* the information contained in the ciphertext. Such a deletion should prevent Bob from retrieving any information on the encoded plaintext once the key is revealed. We call this *certified deletion.*

Informally, this functionality stipulates that Bob should not be able to do the following two things simultaneously: (1) Convince Alice that he has deleted the ciphertext; and (2) Given the key, recover information about the encrypted message. To better understand this concept, consider an analogy to certified deletion in the physical world: "encryption" would correspond to locking information into a keyed safe, the "ciphertext" comprising of the locked safe. In this case, "deletion" may simply involve returning the safe in its original state. This "deletion" is intrinsically certified since, without the safe (and having never had access to the key and the safe at the same time), Bob is relinquishing the possibility of gaining access to the information (even in the future when the key may be revealed) by returning the safe. However, in the case that encryption is digital, Bob may retain a copy of the ciphertext; there is therefore no meaningful way for him to certify "deletion" of the underlying information, since clearly a

R. Pass and K. Pietrzak (Eds.): TCC 2020, LNCS 12552, pp. 92–122, 2020.
https://doi.org/10.1007/978-3-030-64381-2_4

copy of the ciphertext is just as good as the original ciphertext, when it comes time to use the key to decrypt the data.

Quantum information, on the other hand, is known for its no-cloning principle [8,19,36], which states that quantum states cannot, in general, be copied. This quantum feature has been explored in many cryptographic applications, including unforgeable money [35], quantum key distribution (QKD) [2], and more (for a survey, see [4]).

1.1 Summary of Contributions

In this work, we add to the repertoire of functionalities that are classically impossible but are achievable with unconditional security using quantum information. We give a formal definition of certified deletion encryption and certified deletion security. Moreover, we construct an encryption scheme which, as we demonstrate, satisfies these notions (in addition, our proofs are applicable in the finite-key regime). Furthermore, our scheme is technologically simple since it can be implemented by honest parties who have access to rudimentary quantum devices (that is, they only need to prepare single-qubit quantum states, and perform single-qubit measurements); we also show that our scheme is robust against noise in these devices. We now elaborate on these contributions.

Definitions. In order to define our notion of encryption, we build on the *quantum encryption of classical messages* (QECM) framework [3][1] (for simplicity, our work is restricted to the single-use, private-key setting). To the QECM, we add a *delete* circuit which is used by Bob if he wishes to delete his ciphertext and generate a corresponding verification state, and a *verify* circuit which uses the key and is used by Alice to determine whether Bob really deleted the ciphertext.

Next, we define the notion of certified deletion security for a QECM scheme (See Fig. 1 and Definition 13). Our definition is inspired by elements of the definition in [33]. The starting point for this definition is the well-known indistinguishability experiment, this time played between an adversary $\mathcal{A} = (\mathcal{A}_0, \mathcal{A}_1, \mathcal{A}_2)$ and a challenger. After running the Key Generation procedure, the adversary $\mathcal{A}_0$ submits an n-bit plaintext msg_0 to the challenger. Depending on a random bit b, the challenger either encrypts msg_0 or a dummy plaintext 0^n, and sends the ciphertext to $\mathcal{A}_1$. The adversary $\mathcal{A}_1$ then produces a candidate classical "deletion certificate", y. Next, the key is sent to the adversary $\mathcal{A}_2$ who produces an output bit $b' \in \{0,1\}$.[2] A scheme is deemed *secure* if the choice of b does not change the probability of the following event: "$b' = 1$ *and* the deletion certificate y is accepted". We note that it would be incorrect to formulate a definition

---

[1] Apart from sharing this basic definition, our work differs significantly from [3]. For instance, the adversarial models are fundamentally different, since we consider here a single adversary, while [3] is secure against *two* separate adversaries.

[2] The key is leaked *after* y is produced; this is required because otherwise, with access to the ciphertext and the key, the adversary could (via purification), retrieve the plaintext without affecting the ciphertext, and therefore could decrypt while simultaneously producing a convincing proof of deletion.

that conditions on y being accepted (see discussion in [33]). We note that certified deletion security does not necessarily imply ciphertext indistinguishability; hence these two properties are defined and proven separately.

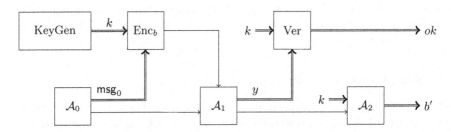

Fig. 1. Schematic representation of the security notion for certified deletion security. The game is parametrized by $b \in \{0, 1\}$ and Enc_0 outputs an encryption of 0^n while Enc_1 encrypts its input, msg_0. Security holds if for each adversary $\mathcal{A} = (\mathcal{A}_0, \mathcal{A}_1, \mathcal{A}_2)$, the probability of $(b' = 1 \ and \ ok = 1)$ is essentially the same, regardless of the value of b.

Scheme. In Sect. 4, we present our scheme. Our encoding is based on the well-known Wiesner encoding [35]. Informally, the message is encoded by first generating m random Wiesner states, $|r\rangle^\theta$ $(r, \theta \in \{0, 1\}^m)$ (for notation, see Sect. 2.1). We let $r|_{\mathcal{I}}$ be the substring of r where qubits are encoded in the computational basis, and we let $r|_{\bar{\mathcal{I}}}$ be the remaining substring of r (where qubits are encoded in the Hadamard basis). Then, in order to create a classical *proof of deletion*, Bob measures the entire ciphertext in the Hadamard basis. The result is a classical string, and Alice accepts the deletion if all the bits corresponding to positions encoded in the Hadamard basis are correct according to $r|_{\bar{\mathcal{I}}}$. As for the message msg, it is encoded into $x' = \mathsf{msg} \oplus H(r|_{\mathcal{I}}) \oplus u$, where H is a two-universal hash function and u is a fresh, random string. Intuitively speaking, the use of the hash function is required in order to prevent that *partial* information retained by Bob could be useful in distinguishing the plaintext, while the random u is used to guarantee security in terms of an encryption scheme. Robustness of the protocol is achieved by using an error correcting code and including an encrypted version of the error syndrome. We note that while our definitions do not require it, our scheme provides a further desirable property, namely that the proof of deletion is a classical string only.

Proof. In Sect. 5, we present the security analysis of our scheme and give concrete security parameters (Theorem 3 and its proof). First, the fact that the scheme is an encryption scheme is relatively straightforward; it follows via a generalization of the quantum one-time pad (see Sect. 5.1). Next, correctness and robustness (Sect. 5.2) follow from the properties of the encoding and of the error correcting mechanism.

Next, the proof of security for certified deletion has a number of key steps. First, we apply the security notion of certified deletion (Definition 13) to our concrete scheme (Scheme 1). This yields a "prepare-and-measure" security game (see Game 1). However, for the purposes of the analysis, it is convenient to consider instead an entanglement-based game (this is a common proof technique for quantum protocols that include the preparation of random states [17,25]). In this game (Game 2), the adversary, Bob, creates an initial entangled state, from which Alice derives (via measurements in a random basis θ of her choosing) the value of $r \in \{0,1\}^m$. We show that, without loss of generality, Bob can produce the proof of deletion, y, *before* he receives any information from Alice (this is due, essentially, to the fact that the ciphertext is uniformly random from Bob's point of view). Averaging over Alice's choice of basis θ, we arrive at a very powerful intuition: in order for Bob's probability of creating an acceptable proof of deletion y (*i.e.* he produces a string where the positions corresponding to $\theta = 1$ match with $r|_{\bar{\mathcal{I}}}$) to be high, he must unavoidably have a low probability of correctly guessing $r|_{\mathcal{I}}$. The above phenomenon is embodied in the following *entropic uncertainty relation* for smooth entropies [30,31]. We consider the scenario of Eve preparing a tripartite state ρ_{ABE} with Alice, Bob, and Eve receiving the A, B and E systems, respectively (here, A and B contain n qubits). Next, Alice either measures all of her qubits in the computational basis to obtain string X, or she measures all of her qubits in the Hadamard basis to obtain string Z; meanwhile, Bob measures his qubits in the Hadamard basis to obtain Z'. We then have the relation:

$$H^{\epsilon}_{\min}(X \mid E) + H^{\epsilon}_{\max}(Z \mid Z') \geq n, \qquad (1)$$

In the above, $\epsilon \leq 0$ is a smoothing parameter which represents a probability of failure, and the smooth min-entropy $H^{\epsilon}_{\min}(X \mid E)$ characterizes the average probability that Eve guesses X correctly using her optimal strategy and given her quantum register E, while the smooth max-entropy $H^{\epsilon}_{\max}(Z \mid Z')$ corresponds to the number of bits that are needed in order to reconstruct Z from Z' up to a failure probability ϵ (for details, see Sect. 2.4).

Our proof technique thus consists in formally analysing the entanglement-based game and applying the appropriate uncertainty relation in the spirit of the one above. Finally, we combine the bound on Bob's min-entropy with a universal$_2$ hash function and the Leftover Hashing Lemma of [21] to prove indistinguishability between the cases $b = 0$ and $b = 1$ after Alice has been convinced of deletion.

1.2   Related Work

To the best of our knowledge, the first use of a quantum encoding to certify that a ciphertext is completely "returned" was developed by Unruh [33] in the context of *revocable timed-release encryption*[3]: in this case, the revocation process is fully quantum. Our main security definition (Definition 13) is closely related

---

[3] Revocable time-release encryption can equivalently be thought of as a revocable time-lock puzzle [23], which does not satisfy standard cryptographic security (since the plaintexts are recoverable, by design, in polynomial time). In contrast, here we achieve a semantic-security-type security definition.

to the security definitions from this work. On the technical side, our work differs significantly since [33] uses techniques related to CSS codes and quantum random oracles, whereas we use privacy amplification and uncertainty relations. Our work also considers the concept of "revocation" outside the context of timed-release encryption, and it is also a conceptual and technical improvement since it shows that a proof of deletion can be classical. Fu and Miller [11] gave the first evidence that quantum information could be used to prove *deletion* of information and that this could be verified using classical interaction only: they showed that, via a two-party nonlocality game (involving classical interaction), Alice can become convinced that Bob has *deleted* a single-bit ciphertext (in the sense that the deleted state is unreadable even if Bob were to learn the key). Their results are cast in the device-independent setting (meaning that security holds against arbitrarily malicious quantum devices). Further related work (that is independent from ours) by Coiteux-Roy and Wolf [7] touches on the question of provable deletion using quantum encodings. However, their work is not concerned with encryption schemes, and therefore does not consider leaking of the key. By contrast, we are explicitly concerned with what it would mean to delete a quantum ciphertext. We note, however, that there are similarities between our scheme and the proposed scheme in [7], namely the use of conjugate coding, with the message encoded in one basis and its conjugate basis, to prove deletion.

Relationship with Quantum Key Distribution. It can be instructive to compare our results to the ones obtained in the analysis of QKD [29]. Firstly, our adversarial model appears different since in certified deletion, we have one honest party (Alice, the sender) and one cheating party (Bob, the receiver), whereas QKD involves two honest parties (Alice and Bob) and one adversary (Eve). Next, the interaction model is different since certified deletion is almost non-interactive, whereas QKD involves various rounds of interaction between Alice and Bob. However, the procedures and proof techniques for certified deletion are close to the ones used in QKD: we use similar encodings into Wiesner states, similar privacy amplification and error correction, and the analysis via an entanglement-based game uses similar entropic uncertainty relations, leading to a security parameter that is very similar to the one in [29]. While we are not aware of any direct reduction from the security of a QKD scheme to certified deletion, we note that, as part of our proof technique, we manage to essentially map the adversarial model for certified deletion to one similar to the QKD model since we *split* the behaviour of our adversarial Bob into multiple phases: preparation of the joint state ρ_{ABE}, measurement of a register B in a determined basis, and finally bounding the advantage that the adversary has in *simultaneously* making Alice accept the outcome of the measurement performed on B *and* predicting some measurement outcome on register A given quantum side-information E. This scenario is similar to QKD, although we note that the measurement bases are not chosen randomly but are instead consistently in the Hadamard basis (for Bob's measurement) and that Eve's challenge is to predict Alice's measurement in the computational basis only (this situation is reminiscent of the *single-basis parameter estimation* technique [20,29]).

1.3   Applications and Open Questions

While the main focus of this work is on the foundations of certified deletion, we can nevertheless envisage potential applications which we briefly discuss below (we leave the formal analyses for future work).

Protection Against Key Leakage. Almost all encryption schemes suffer from the drawback that, eventually (given enough computational time and power), keys are leaked. Here, certified deletion could be used to mitigate this risk. For instance, using certified deletion, a sender using a storage server for encrypted data could at any time (and in particular, as soon as the sender has doubts that the keys are about to be leaked) request a proof of deletion of the data. This could give some reassurance on the secrecy of the data; in contrast, classical solutions clearly are inadequate.

Protection Against Data Retention. In 2016, the European Union adopted a regulation on the processing and free movement of personal data [26]. Included is a clause on the "right to be forgotten": a person should be able to have their data erased whenever its retention is no longer necessary. See also [12]. Certified deletion encryption might help facilitate this scenario in the following way: if a party were to provide their data to an organization via a certified deletion encryption, the organization would be able to certify deletion of the data using the deletion circuit included in the scheme. Future work could develop a type of homomorphic encryption with certified deletion so that the ciphertexts could be useful to some extent while a level of security, in terms of deletion, is maintained. Also useful would be a type of "public verifiability" which would enable parties other than the originator to verify deletion certificates. Contact tracing [5] is another relevant scenario where individual data could be safeguarded against data retention by using certified deletion.

Encryption with Classical Revocation. The concept of *ciphertext revocation* allows a recipient to provably *return* a ciphertext (in the sense that the sender can confirm that the ciphertext is returned and that the recipient will *not* be able to decrypt, even if the key is leaked in the future); such a functionality is unachievable with classical information alone, but it is known to be achievable using quantum ciphertexts [33]. In a sense, our contribution is an extension of revocation since from the point of view of the recipient, whether quantum information is deleted or returned, the end result is similar: the recipient is unable to decrypt even given the key. Our scheme, however, has the advantage of using classical information only for the deletion.

  As a use case for classical revocation, consider a situation where Bob loans Alice an amount of money. Alice agrees to pay back the full amount in time T plus 15 % interest if Bob does not recall the loan within that time. To implement this scheme, Alice uses a certified deletion encryption scheme to send Bob an encrypted cheque and schedules her computer to send Bob the key at time T. If Bob wishes to recall the loan within time T, he sends Alice the deletion string.

Another possible application is *timed-release encryption* [33], where the key is included in the ciphertext, but with the ciphertext encoded in a classical timed-release encryption.

Composable and Everlasting Security. We leave as an open question the composability of our scheme (as well as security beyond the one-time case). We note that through a combination of composability with our quantum encoding, it may be possible to transform a long-term computational assumption into a temporary one. That is, a computational assumption would need to be broken *during* a protocol, or else the security would be information-theoretically secure as soon as the protocol ends. This is called *everlasting security* [32].

For example, consider the situation encountered in a zero-knowledge proof system for a Σ-protocol (for instance, for graph 3-colouring [14]): the prover commits to an encoding of an NP-witness using a statistically binding and computationally concealing commitment scheme. The verifier then randomly chooses which commitments to open, and the prover provides the information required to open the commitment. If, in addition, we could encode the commitments with a scheme that provides composable certified deletion, then the verifier could also prove that the unopened commitments are effectively *deleted*. This has the potential of ensuring that the zero-knowledge property becomes *statistical* as long as the computational assumption is not broken *during* the execution of the proof system. This description assumes an extension of our certified deletion encoding to the computational setting and also somehow assumes that the verifier would collaborate in its deletion actions (we leave for future work the formal statement and analysis). Nevertheless, since zero-knowledge proofs are building blocks for a host of cryptographic protocols, certified deletion has the potential to unleash everlasting security; this is highly desirable given steady progress in both algorithms and quantum computers. Another potential application would be proving erasure (in the context where there is no encryption) [7].

Outline. The remainder of this paper is structured as follows. Section 2 is an introduction to concepts and notation used in the rest of this work. Section 3 lays out the novel security definitions which appear in this paper. Section 4 is an exposition of our main scheme, while Sect. 5 provides a security analysis.

2 Preliminaries

In this section, we outline certain concepts and notational conventions which are used throughout the article. We assume that the reader has a basic familiarity with quantum computation and quantum information. We refer to [18] for further background.

2.1 Notation

We make use of the following notation: for a function $f \colon X \to \mathbb{R}$, we denote

$$\mathbb{E}_x f(x) = \frac{1}{|X|} \sum_{x \in X} f(x). \tag{2}$$

We represent the Hamming weight of strings as the output of a Hamming weight function $\omega\colon \{0,1\}^* \to \mathbb{N}$. If $x_1, \ldots, x_n$ are strings, then we define $(x_1, \ldots, x_n)$ to be the concatenation of these strings. Let $[n]$ denote the set $\{1, 2, \ldots, n\}$. Then, for any string $x = (x_1, \ldots, x_n)$ and any subset $\mathcal{I} \subseteq [n]$, we use $x|_{\mathcal{I}}$ to denote the string x restricted to the bits indexed by $\mathcal{I}$. We call a function $\eta\colon \mathbb{N} \to \mathbb{R}_{\geq 0}$ *negligible* if for every positive polynomial p, there exists an integer N such that, for all integers $n > N$, it is true that $\eta(n) < \frac{1}{p(n)}$.

We let $\mathcal{Q} := \mathbb{C}^2$ denote the state space of a single qubit, and we use the notation $\mathcal{Q}(n) := \mathcal{Q}^{\otimes n}$ for any $n \in \mathbb{N}$. Let $\mathcal{H}$ be a Hilbert space. The group of unitary operators on $\mathcal{H}$ is denoted by $\mathcal{U}(\mathcal{H})$, and the set of density operators on $\mathcal{H}$ is denoted by $\mathcal{D}(\mathcal{H})$. Through density operators, a Hilbert space may correspond to a *quantum system*, which we represent by capital letters. The set of diagonal density operators on $\mathcal{H}$ is denoted by $\mathfrak{D}(\mathcal{H})$—the elements of this set represent classical states. Discrete random variables are thus modeled as finite-dimensional quantum systems, called *registers*. A register X takes values in $\mathcal{X}$. A density operator $|x\rangle\langle x|$ will be denoted as $\Gamma(x)$. We employ the operator norm, which we define for a linear operator $A\colon \mathcal{H} \to \mathcal{H}'$ between finite-dimensional Hilbert spaces $\mathcal{H}$ and $\mathcal{H}'$ as $\|A\| = \sup\{\|Av\| \mid v \in \mathcal{H}, \|v\| = 1\}$. Moreover, for two density operators $\rho, \sigma \in \mathcal{D}(\mathcal{H})$, we use the notation $\rho \leq \sigma$ to say that $\sigma - \rho$ is positive semi-definite.

In order to illustrate correlations between a classical register X and a quantum state A, we use the formalism of a *classical-quantum* state:

$$\rho_{XA} = \sum_{x \in \mathcal{X}} P_X(x)\Gamma(x)_X \otimes \rho_{A|X=x}, \tag{3}$$

where $P_X(x) := \Pr[X = x]_\rho = \mathrm{Tr}[\Gamma(x)_X \rho_{XA}]$ and $\rho_{A|X=x}$ is the state of A conditioned on the event that $X = x$.

Let $\Gamma(x_i) \in \mathfrak{D}(\mathcal{H})$ be classical states for integers i such that $1 \leq i \leq n$. Then we use the notation $\Gamma(x_1, x_2, \ldots, x_n) := \Gamma(x_1) \otimes \Gamma(x_2) \otimes \cdots \otimes \Gamma(x_n)$.

Let $\mathsf{H} \in \mathcal{U}(\mathcal{Q})$ denote the Hadamard operator, which is defined by $|0\rangle \mapsto \frac{|0\rangle + |1\rangle}{\sqrt{2}}$, $|1\rangle \mapsto \frac{|0\rangle - |1\rangle}{\sqrt{2}}$. For any strings $x, \theta \in \{0,1\}^n$, we define $|x^\theta\rangle = \mathsf{H}^\theta |x\rangle = \mathsf{H}^{\theta_1} |x_1\rangle \otimes \mathsf{H}^{\theta_2} |x_2\rangle \otimes \cdots \otimes \mathsf{H}^{\theta_n} |x_n\rangle$. States of the form $|x^\theta\rangle$ are here called *Wiesner states* in recognition of their first use in [35].

We make use of the Einstein-Podolsky-Rosen (EPR) state [10], defined as $|\mathrm{EPR}\rangle = \frac{1}{\sqrt{2}}(|0\rangle \otimes |0\rangle + |1\rangle \otimes |1\rangle)$.

We use $x \xleftarrow{\$} X$ to denote sampling an element $x \in X$ uniformly at random from a set X. This uniform randomness is represented in terms of registers in the fully mixed state which is, given a d-dimensional Hilbert space $\mathcal{H}$, defined as $\frac{1}{d}\mathbb{1}_d$, where $\mathbb{1}_d$ denotes the identity matrix with d rows.

For two quantum states $\rho, \sigma \in \mathcal{D}(\mathcal{H})$, we define the *trace distance* $\|\rho - \sigma\|_{\mathrm{Tr}} := \frac{1}{2}\|\rho - \sigma\|$. Note also an alternative formula for the trace distance: $\|\rho - \sigma\|_{\mathrm{Tr}} = \max_P \mathrm{Tr}[P(\rho - \sigma)]$, where $P \leq \mathbb{1}_d$ is a positive operator. Hence, in terms of a physical interpretation, the trace distance is the upper bound for the difference in probabilities with respect to the states ρ and σ that a measurement outcome P may occur on the state.

We define purified distance, which is a metric on quantum states.

Definition 1. (Purified Distance). *Let A be a quantum system. For two (sub-normalized) states ρ_A, σ_A, we define the* generalized fidelity,

$$F(\rho_A, \sigma_A) := \left(\mathrm{Tr} \left[\sqrt{\sqrt{\rho_A} \sigma_A \sqrt{\rho_A}} \right] + \sqrt{1 - \mathrm{Tr}[\rho_A]} \sqrt{1 - \mathrm{Tr}[\sigma_A]} \right)^2, \quad (4)$$

and the purified distance,

$$P(\rho_A, \sigma_A) := \sqrt{1 - F(\rho_A, \sigma_A)}. \quad (5)$$

2.2 Hash Functions and Error Correction

We make use of universal$_2$ hash functions, first introduced by Carter and Wegman [6].

Definition 2. (Universal$_2$ Hashing). *Let $\mathfrak{H} = \{H \colon \mathcal{X} \to \mathcal{Z}\}$ be a family of functions. We say that $\mathfrak{H}$ is* universal$_2$ *if $\Pr[H(x) = H(x')] \leq \frac{1}{|\mathcal{Z}|}$ for any two distinct elements $x, x' \in \mathcal{X}$, when H is chosen uniformly at random from $\mathfrak{H}$.*

Such families exist if $|\mathcal{Z}|$ is a power of two (see [6]). Moreover, there exist universal$_2$ families of hash functions which take strings of length n as input and which contain $2^{O(n)}$ hash functions; therefore it takes $O(n)$ bits to specify a hash function from such a family [34]. Thus, when we discuss communication of hash functions, we assume that both the sender and the recipient are aware of the family from which a hash function has been chosen, and that the transmitted data consists of $O(n)$ bits used to specify the hash function from the known family.

In the context of error correction, we note that linear error correcting codes can generate syndromes, and that corrections to a message can be made when given the syndrome of the correct message. This is called syndrome decoding. Therefore, we implicitly refer to syndrome decoding of an $[n, n - s]$-linear code which handles codewords of length n and generates syndromes of length $s < n$ when we use functions synd: $\{0,1\}^n \to \{0,1\}^s$ and corr: $\{0,1\}^n \times \{0,1\}^s \to \{0,1\}^n$, where synd is a syndrome-generating function and corr is a string-correcting function. We also make reference to the distance of an error correcting code, which is the minimum distance between distinct codewords.

2.3 Quantum Channels and Measurements

Let A and B be two quantum systems, and let X be a classical register. A *quantum channel* $\Phi \colon A \to B$ is a completely positive trace-preserving (CPTP) map. A *generalized measurement* on A is a set of linear operators $\{M_A^x\}_{x \in \mathcal{X}}$, where $x \in \mathcal{X}$ are potential classical outcomes, such that

$$\sum_{x \in \mathcal{X}} (M_A^x)^\dagger (M_A^x) = 1_A. \tag{6}$$

A *positive-operator valued measure* (POVM) on A is a set of Hermitian positive semidefinite operators $\{M_A^x\}_{x \in \mathcal{X}}$, where $x \in \mathcal{X}$ are potential classical outcomes, such that

$$\sum_{x \in \mathcal{X}} (M_A^x) = 1_A. \tag{7}$$

We also represent measurements with CPTP maps such as $\mathcal{M}_{A \to X}$, which map quantum states in system A to classical states in register X using POVMs.

For two registers X and Y, if we have a function, $f \colon \mathcal{X} \to \mathcal{Y}$ then we denote by $\mathcal{E}_f \colon X \to XY$ the CPTP map

$$\mathcal{E}_f[\cdot] := \sum_{x \in X} |f(x)\rangle_Y \Gamma(x)_X \cdot \Gamma(x)_X \langle f(x)|_Y. \tag{8}$$

In this work, measurement of a qubit in our scheme will always occur in one of two bases: the computational basis $(\{|0\rangle, |1\rangle\})$ or the Hadamard basis $(\{|+\rangle, |-\rangle\})$. Thus, for a quantum system A, we notate these measurements as $\{M_A^{\theta,x}\}_{x \in \{0,1\}}$, where $x \in \{0,1\}$ ranges over the possible outcomes, and where $\theta \in \{0,1\}$ determines the basis of measurement ($\theta = 0$ indicates computational basis and $\theta = 1$ indicates Hadamard basis).

Let $\{M_A^x\}_x$ and $\{N_A^y\}_y$ be two POVMs acting on a quantum system A. We define the overlap

$$c(\{M_A^x\}_x, \{N_B^y\}_y) := \max_{x,y} \left\| \sqrt{M_A^x} \sqrt{N_A^y} \right\|_\infty^2. \tag{9}$$

wherever dealing with an m-qubit quantum system A, we define, for all $i = 1, \ldots, m$,

$$c_i := c\left(\{M_{A_i}^{0,x}\}_x, \{M_{A_i}^{1,y}\}_y\right). \tag{10}$$

We assume our measurements are ideal, so $c_i = 1/2$.

2.4   Entropic Uncertainty Relations

The purpose of entropy is to quantify the amount of uncertainty an observer has concerning the outcome of a random variable. Since the uncertainty of random variables can be understood in different ways, there exist different kinds of entropy. Key to our work are min- and max-entropy, first introduced by Renner and König [15,21], as a generalization of conditional Rényi entropies [22] to the quantum setting. Min-entropy, for instance, quantifies the degree of uniformity of the distribution of a random variable.

Definition 3. (Min-entropy). *Let A and B be two quantum systems. For any bipartite state ρ_{AB}, we define*

$$H_{\min}(A \mid B)_\rho := \sup\{\xi \in \mathbb{R} \mid \exists \text{ state } \sigma_B \text{ such that } \rho_{AB} \leq 2^{-\xi} 1_A \otimes \sigma_B\}. \quad (11)$$

Max-entropy quantifies the size of the support of a random variable, and is here defined by its dual relation to min-entropy.

Definition 4. (Max-entropy). *Let A and B be two quantum systems. For any bipartite state ρ_{AB}, we define*

$$H_{\max}(A \mid B)_\rho := -H_{\min}(A \mid C)_\rho, \quad (12)$$

where ρ_{ABC} is any pure state with $\mathrm{Tr}_C[\rho_{ABC}] = \rho_{AB}$, for some quantum system C.

In order to deal with finite-size effects, it is necessary to generalize min- and max-entropy to their smooth variants.

Definition 5. (Smooth Entropies). *Let A and B be two quantum systems. For any bipartite state ρ_{AB}, and $\epsilon \in \left[0, \sqrt{\mathrm{Tr}[\rho_{AB}]}\right)$, we define*

$$H_{\min}^\epsilon(A \mid B)_\rho := \sup_{\substack{\tilde{\rho}_{AB} \\ P(\tilde{\rho}_{AB}, \rho_{AB}) \leq \epsilon}} H_{\min}(A \mid B)_{\tilde{\rho}}, \quad (13)$$

$$H_{\max}^\epsilon(A \mid B)_\rho := \inf_{\substack{\tilde{\rho}_{AB} \\ P(\tilde{\rho}_{AB}, \rho_{AB}) \leq \epsilon}} H_{\max}(A \mid B)_{\tilde{\rho}}. \quad (14)$$

It is of note that smooth entropies satisfy the following inequality, commonly referred to as the data-processing inequality [28].

Proposition 1. *Let $\epsilon \geq 0$, ρ_{AB} be a quantum state, and $\mathcal{E} \colon \mathcal{D}(\mathcal{H}_A) \to \mathcal{D}(\mathcal{H}_C)$ be a CPTP map. Define $\sigma_{AC} := (1_{\mathcal{D}(\mathcal{H}_A)} \otimes \mathcal{E})(\rho_{AB})$. Then,*

$$H_{\min}^\epsilon(A \mid B)_\rho \leq H_{\min}^\epsilon(A \mid C)_\sigma \quad \text{and} \quad H_{\max}^\epsilon(A \mid B)_\rho \leq H_{\max}^\epsilon(A \mid C)_\sigma. \quad (15)$$

We use one half of the generalized uncertainty relation theorem found in [27], the precursor of which was introduced by Tomamichel and Renner [31]. The original uncertainty relation was understood in terms of its application to QKD, and was used to prove the secrecy of the key in a finite-key analysis of QKD [30].

Proposition 2. *Let $\epsilon \geq 0$, let ρ_{ACE} be a tripartite quantum state, let $\{M_A^x\}_{x \in \mathcal{X}}$ and $\{N_A^z\}_{z \in \mathcal{Z}}$ be two POVMs acting on A, and let $\{P_A^k\}_{k \in \mathcal{K}}$ be a projective measurement acting on A. Then the post-measurement states*

$$\rho_{XKC} = \sum_{x,k} \langle x|x\rangle \otimes \langle k|k\rangle \otimes \mathrm{Tr}_{AE}\left[\sqrt{M_A^x} P_A^k \rho_{ACE} P_A^k \sqrt{M_A^x}\right] \quad (16)$$

and

$$\rho_{YKE} = \sum_{y,k} \langle y|y\rangle \otimes \langle k|k\rangle \otimes \mathrm{Tr}_{AC}\left[\sqrt{N_A^y}P_A^k\rho_{ACE}P_A^k\sqrt{N_A^y}\right] \qquad (17)$$

satisfy

$$H_{\min}^{\epsilon}(X \mid KC)_\rho + H_{\max}^{\epsilon}(Y \mid KE)_\rho \geq \log\frac{1}{c_{\mathcal{K}}} \qquad (18)$$

where $c_{\mathcal{K}} = \max_{k,x,y}\left\|\sqrt{M_A^x}P^k\sqrt{N_A^y}\right\|_{\infty}$.

We also use the Leftover Hashing Lemma, introduced by Renner [21]. It is typically understood in relation to the privacy amplification step of QKD. We state it in the form given in [29].

Proposition 3. *Let* $\epsilon \geq 0$ *and* σ_{AX} *be a classical-quantum state, with* X *a classical register which takes values on* $\mathcal{X} = \{0,1\}^s$. *Let* $\mathfrak{H}$ *be a universal$_2$ family of hash functions from* $\mathcal{X}$ *to* $\mathcal{Y} = \{0,1\}^n$. *Let* $\chi_Y = \frac{1}{2^n}\mathbb{1}_{\mathcal{D}(\mathcal{Y})}$ *be the fully mixed state,* $\rho_{SH} = \frac{1}{|\mathfrak{H}|}\sum_{H\in\mathfrak{H}}\Gamma(H)_{SH}$ *and* $\zeta_{AYSH} = \mathrm{Tr}_X[\mathcal{E}_f(\sigma_{AX}\otimes\rho_{SH})]$ *for the function* $f\colon (x,H) \mapsto H(x)$ *be the post-hashing state. Then,*

$$\|\zeta_{AYSH} - \chi_Y \otimes \zeta_{ASH}\|_{\mathrm{Tr}} \leq \frac{1}{2}2^{-\frac{1}{2}(H_{\min}^{\epsilon}(X|A)_\sigma - n)} + 2\epsilon. \qquad (19)$$

2.5 Statistical Lemmas

The following lemmas are required to bound a specific max-entropy quantity. They are both proven in [29] as part of a security proof of finite-key QKD, and this line of thinking originated in [30].

The following lemma is a consequence of Serfling's bound [24].

Lemma 1. *Let* $Z_1,\ldots Z_m$ *be random variables taking values in* $\{0,1\}$. *Let* $m = s+k$. *Let* $\mathcal{I}$ *be an independent and uniformly chosen subset of* $[m]$ *with* s *elements. Then, for* $\nu \in [0,1]$ *and* $\delta \in (0,1)$,

$$\Pr\left[\sum_{i\in\mathcal{I}} Z_i \leq k\delta \wedge \sum_{i\in\bar{\mathcal{I}}} Z_i \geq s(\delta + \nu)\right] \leq \exp\left(\frac{-2\nu^2 sk^2}{m(k+1)}\right). \qquad (20)$$

It will also be useful to condition a quantum state on future events. The following lemma from [29] states that, given a classical-quantum state, there may exist a nearby state on which a certain event does not occur.

Lemma 2. *Let* ρ_{AX} *be a classical-quantum state with* X *a classical register, and* $\Omega\colon \mathcal{X} \to \{0,1\}$ *be an event with* $\Pr[\Omega]_\rho = \epsilon < \mathrm{Tr}[\rho_{AX}]$. *Then there exists a classical-quantum state* $\tilde{\rho}_{AX}$ *with* $\Pr[\Omega]_{\tilde{\rho}} = 0$ *and* $P(\rho_{AX}, \tilde{\rho}_{AX}) \leq \sqrt{\epsilon}$.

2.6   Quantum Encryption and Security

Whenever an adversary $\mathcal{A}$ is mentioned, it is assumed to be quantum and to have unbounded computational power, and we allow it to perform generalized measurements.

Considering that the scheme introduced in this paper is an encryption scheme with a quantum ciphertext, we rely on the "quantum encryption of classical messages" framework developed by Broadbent and Lord [3]. This framework describes an encryption scheme as a set of parameterized CPTP maps which satisfy certain conditions.

Definition 6. (Quantum Encryption of Classical Messages). *Let n be an integer. An n-quantum encryption of classical messages (n-QECM) is a tuple of uniform efficient quantum circuits $\mathcal{S} = (\mathsf{key}, \mathsf{enc}, \mathsf{dec})$ implementing CPTP maps of the form*

- $\Phi_\lambda^{\mathsf{key}} \colon \mathcal{D}(\mathbb{C}) \to \mathcal{D}(\mathcal{H}_{K,\lambda})$,
- $\Phi_\lambda^{\mathsf{enc}} \colon \mathcal{D}(\mathcal{H}_{K,\lambda} \otimes \mathcal{H}_M) \to \mathcal{D}(\mathcal{H}_{T,\lambda})$, *and*
- $\Phi_\lambda^{\mathsf{dec}} \colon \mathcal{D}(\mathcal{H}_{K,\lambda} \otimes \mathcal{H}_{T,\lambda}) \to \mathcal{D}(\mathcal{H}_M)$,

where $\mathcal{H}_M = \mathcal{Q}(n)$ is the plaintext space, $\mathcal{H}_{T,\lambda} = \mathcal{Q}(\ell(\lambda))$ is the ciphertext space, and $\mathcal{H}_{K,\lambda} = \mathcal{Q}(\kappa(\lambda))$ is the key space for functions $\ell, \kappa \colon \mathbb{N}^+ \to \mathbb{N}^+$.

For all $\lambda \in \mathbb{N}^+, k \in \{0,1\}^{\kappa(\lambda)}$, and $m \in \{0,1\}^n$, the maps must satisfy

$$\mathrm{Tr}[\Gamma(k)\Phi^{\mathsf{key}}(1)] > 0 \Rightarrow \mathrm{Tr}[\Gamma(m)\Phi_k^{\mathsf{dec}} \circ \Phi_k^{\mathsf{enc}}\Gamma(m)] = 1, \qquad (21)$$

where λ is implicit, Φ_k^{enc} is the CPTP map defined by $\rho \mapsto \Phi^{\mathsf{enc}}(\Gamma(k) \otimes \rho)$, and we define Φ_k^{dec} analogously. We also define the CPTP map $\Phi_{k,0}^{\mathsf{enc}} \colon \mathcal{D}(\mathcal{H}_M) \to \mathcal{D}(\mathcal{H}_{T,\lambda})$ by

$$\rho \mapsto \Phi_k^{\mathsf{enc}}(\Gamma(\mathbf{0})) \qquad (22)$$

where $\mathbf{0} \in \{0,1\}^n$ is the all-zero bit string, and the CPTP map $\Phi_{k,1}^{\mathsf{enc}} \colon \mathcal{D}(\mathcal{H}_M) \to \mathcal{D}(\mathcal{H}_{T,\lambda})$ by

$$\rho \mapsto \sum_{m \in \{0,1\}^n} \mathrm{Tr}[\Gamma(m)\rho] \cdot \Phi_k^{\mathsf{enc}}(\Gamma(m)). \qquad (23)$$

As part of the security of our scheme, we wish to ensure that should an adversary obtain a copy of the ciphertext and were to know that the original message is one of two hypotheses, she would not be able to distinguish between the hypotheses. We refer to this notion of security as ciphertext indistinguishability (called indistinguishable security in [3]). It is best understood in terms of a scheme's resilience to an adversary performing what we refer to as a distinguishing attack.

Definition 7. (Distinguishing Attack). *Let $\mathcal{S} = (\mathsf{key}, \mathsf{enc}, \mathsf{dec})$ be an n-QECM. A distinguishing attack is a quantum adversary $\mathcal{A} = (\mathcal{A}_0, \mathcal{A}_1)$ implementing CPTP maps of the form*

- $\mathcal{A}_{0,\lambda} \colon \mathcal{D}(\mathbb{C}) \to \mathcal{D}(\mathcal{H}_M \otimes \mathcal{H}_{S,\lambda})$ *and*

$$- \mathcal{A}_{1,\lambda} \colon \mathcal{D}(\mathcal{H}_{T,\lambda} \otimes \mathcal{H}_{S,\lambda}) \to \mathcal{D}(\mathcal{Q})$$

where $\mathcal{H}_{S,\lambda} = \mathcal{Q}(s(\lambda))$ for a function $s \colon \mathbb{N}^+ \to \mathbb{N}^+$.

Definition 8. (Ciphertext Indistinguishability). *Let $\mathcal{S} = (\text{key}, \text{enc}, \text{dec})$ be an n-QECM. Then we say that $\mathcal{S}$ has* ciphertext indistinguishability *if for all distinguishing attacks $\mathcal{A}$ there exists a negligible function η such that*

$$\underset{b}{\mathbb{E}} \underset{k \leftarrow \mathcal{K}}{\mathbb{E}} \operatorname{Tr}[\Gamma(b)\mathcal{A}_{1,\lambda} \circ (\Phi^{enc}_{k,b} \otimes \mathbb{1}_S) \circ \mathcal{A}_{0,\lambda}(1)] \leq \frac{1}{2} + \eta(\lambda) \tag{24}$$

where λ is implicit on the left-hand side, $b \in \{0,1\}$, and $\mathcal{K}_\lambda$ is the random variable distributed on $\{0,1\}^{\kappa(\lambda)}$ such that

$$\Pr[\mathcal{K}_\lambda = k] = \operatorname{Tr}[\Gamma(k)\Phi^{key}_\lambda(1)]. \tag{25}$$

3 Security Definitions

In this section, we introduce a new description of the certified deletion security notion. First, however, we must augment our QECM framework to allow it to detect errors on decryption.

Definition 9. (Augmented Quantum Encryption of Classical Messages). *Let n be an integer. Let $\mathcal{S} = (\text{key}, \text{enc}, \text{dec})$ be an n-QECM. An n-augmented quantum encryption of classical messages (n-AQECM) is a tuple of uniform efficient quantum circuits $\hat{\mathcal{S}} = (\text{key}, \text{enc}, \widehat{\text{dec}})$, where $\widehat{\text{dec}}$ implements a CPTP map of the form*

$$\Phi^{\widehat{dec}}_\lambda \colon \mathcal{D}(\mathcal{H}_{K,\lambda} \otimes \mathcal{H}_{T,\lambda}) \to \mathcal{D}(\mathcal{H}_M \otimes \mathcal{Q}). \tag{26}$$

For all $\lambda \in \mathbb{N}^+, k \in \{0,1\}^{\kappa(\lambda)}$, and $m \in \{0,1\}^n$, the maps corresponding to the circuits must satisfy

$$\operatorname{Tr}[\Gamma(k)\Phi^{key}(1)] > 0 \Rightarrow \operatorname{Tr}[\Gamma(m) \otimes \Gamma(1)\Phi^{\widehat{dec}}_k \circ \Phi^{enc}_k \Gamma(m)] = 1, \tag{27}$$

where λ is implicit, Φ^{enc}_k is the CPTP map defined by $\rho \mapsto \Phi^{enc}(\Gamma(k) \otimes \rho)$, and we define Φ^{dec}_k analogously.

The extra qubit (which will be referred to as a flag), though by itself without any apparent use, may serve as a way to indicate that the decryption process did not proceed as expected in any given run. In the case of decryption without error, the circuit should output $\Gamma(1)$, and in the case of decryption error, the circuit should output $\Gamma(0)$. This allows us to define a criterion by which an AQECM might be robust against a certain amount of noise.

Since the original QECM framework will no longer be used for the rest of this paper, we henceforth note that all further references to the QECM framework are in fact references to the AQECM framework.

Definition 10. (Robust Quantum Encryption of Classical Messages).
Let $S = (\text{key}, \text{enc}, \text{dec})$ be an n-QECM. We say that S is ϵ-robust if, for all adversaries A implementing CPTP maps of the form

$$A \colon \mathcal{D}(\mathcal{H}_{T,\lambda}) \to \mathcal{D}(\mathcal{H}_{T,\lambda}), \tag{28}$$

and for two distinct messages $m, m' \in \mathcal{H}_M$, we have that

$$\mathop{\mathbb{E}}_{k \leftarrow \mathcal{K}} \text{Tr}[\Gamma(m') \otimes \Gamma(1)\Phi_k^{\text{dec}} \circ A \circ \Phi_k^{\text{enc}}\Gamma(m)] \leq \epsilon. \tag{29}$$

In other words, a QECM is ϵ-robust if, under interference by an adversary, the event that decryption yields a different message than was encrypted and that the decryption circuit approves of the outcome is less than or equal to ϵ. This is functionally equivalent to a one-time quantum authentication scheme, where messages are classical (see *e.g.* [1,9,13]).

Our description takes the form of an augmentation of the QECM framework described in Definition 9. Given a QECM with key k and encrypting message m, the certified deletion property should guarantee that the recipient, Bob, cannot do the following two things simultaneously: (1) Make Alice, the sender, accept his certificate of deletion; and (2) Given k, recover information about m.

Definition 11. (Certified Deletion Encryption). *Let $S = (\text{key}, \text{enc}, \text{dec})$ be an n-QECM. Let* del *and* ver *be efficient quantum circuits implemented by CPTP maps of the form*

- $\Phi_\lambda^{\text{del}} \colon \mathcal{D}(\mathcal{H}_{T,\lambda}) \to \mathcal{D}(\mathcal{H}_{D,\lambda})$
- $\Phi_\lambda^{\text{ver}} \colon \mathcal{D}(\mathcal{H}_{K,\lambda} \otimes \mathcal{H}_{D,\lambda}) \to \mathcal{D}(\mathcal{Q})$

where $\mathcal{H}_{D,\lambda} = \mathcal{Q}(d(\lambda))$ for a function $d \colon \mathbb{N}^+ \to \mathbb{N}^+$.
For all $\lambda \in \mathbb{N}^+$, $k \in \{0,1\}^{\kappa(\lambda)}$, and $m \in \{0,1\}^n$, the maps must satisfy

$$\text{Tr}[\Gamma(k)\Phi^{\text{key}}(1)] > 0 \implies \text{Tr}[\Gamma(1)\Phi^{\text{ver}} \circ (\Gamma(k) \otimes (\Phi^{\text{del}} \circ \Phi_k^{\text{enc}}\Gamma(m)))] = 1 \tag{30}$$

where λ is implicit.
We call the tuple $S' = (\text{key}, \text{enc}, \text{dec}, \text{del}, \text{ver})$ an n-certified deletion encryption (n-CDE).

Definition 12. (Certified Deletion Attack). *Let $S = (\text{key}, \text{enc}, \text{dec}, \text{del}, \text{ver})$ be an n-CDE. A* certified deletion attack *is a quantum adversary $A = (A_0, A_1, A_2)$ implementing CPTP maps of the form*

- $A_{0,\lambda} \colon \mathcal{D}(\mathbb{C}) \to \mathcal{D}(\mathcal{H}_M \otimes \mathcal{H}_{S,\lambda})$,
- $A_{1,\lambda} \colon \mathcal{D}(\mathcal{H}_{T,\lambda} \otimes \mathcal{H}_{S,\lambda}) \to \mathcal{D}(\mathcal{H}_{D,\lambda} \otimes \mathcal{H}_{S,\lambda} \otimes \mathcal{H}_{T',\lambda})$, *and*
- $A_{2,\lambda} \colon \mathcal{D}(\mathcal{H}_{K,\lambda} \otimes \mathcal{H}_{S,\lambda} \otimes \mathcal{H}_{T',\lambda}) \to \mathcal{D}(\mathcal{Q})$

where $\mathcal{H}_{S,\lambda} = \mathcal{Q}(s(\lambda))$ and $\mathcal{H}_{T',\lambda} = \mathcal{Q}(\ell'(\lambda))$ for functions $s, \ell' \colon \mathbb{N}^+ \to \mathbb{N}^+$.

We are now ready to define our notion of certified deletion security. We refer the reader to Sect. 1.1 for an informal explanation of the definition, and we recall that notation $\Phi_{k,b}^{\text{enc}}$ is defined in Eq. (22).

Definition 13. (Certified Deletion Security). *Let* $\mathcal{S} = (\mathsf{key}, \mathsf{enc}, \mathsf{dec}, \mathsf{del}, \mathsf{ver})$ *be an* n-CDE. *For any fixed and implicit* $\lambda \in \mathbb{N}^+$, *we define the CPTP map* $\Phi_k^{\mathsf{ver}} : \mathcal{D}(\mathcal{H}_{K,\lambda} \otimes \mathcal{H}_{D,\lambda}) \to \mathcal{D}(\mathcal{Q} \otimes \mathcal{H}_{K,\lambda})$ *by*

$$\rho \mapsto \Phi^{\mathsf{ver}}(\Gamma(k) \otimes \rho) \otimes \Gamma(k). \tag{31}$$

Let $b \in \{0,1\}$, *let* $\mathcal{A}$ *be a certified deletion attack, and let*

$$p_b = [\,\mathbb{E}_{k \leftarrow \mathcal{K}} \operatorname{Tr}[(\Gamma(1,1))(\mathbb{1} \otimes \mathcal{A}_2) \circ (\Phi_k^{\mathsf{ver}} \otimes \mathbb{1}_{ST'}) \circ \mathcal{A}_1 \circ (\Phi_{k,b}^{\mathsf{enc}} \otimes \mathbb{1}_S) \circ \mathcal{A}_0(1)], \tag{32}$$

where λ *is implicit, and where* $\mathcal{K}_\lambda$ *is the random variable distributed on* $\{0,1\}^{\kappa(\lambda)}$ *such that*

$$\Pr[\mathcal{K}_\lambda = k] = \operatorname{Tr}[\Gamma(k)\Phi_\lambda^{\mathsf{key}}(1)]. \tag{33}$$

Then we say that $\mathcal{S}$ *is* η-*certified deletion secure if, for all certified deletion attacks* $\mathcal{A}$, *there exists a negligible function* η *such that*

$$|p_0 - p_1| \leq \eta(\lambda). \tag{34}$$

4   Constructing an Encryption Scheme with Certified Deletion

Scheme 1 aims to exhibit a noise-tolerant prepare-and-measure n-CDE with ciphertext indistinguishability and certified deletion security.

Table 1. Overview of nomenclature used in Sect. 4 and Sect. 5

$M_A^{\theta,x}$	Measurement operator acting on system A with setting θ and outcome x
$\mathcal{M}_{A \to X \mid S^\Theta}^{\mathcal{I}}$	Measurement map applied on the qubits of system A indexed by $\mathcal{I}$, with setting S^Θ, and outcome stored in register X
λ	Security parameter
n	Length, in bits, of the message
$m = \kappa(\lambda)$	Total number of qubits sent from encrypting party to decrypting party
k	Length, in bits, of the string used for verification of deletion
$s = m - k$	Length, in bits, of the string used for extracting randomness
$\tau = \tau(\lambda)$	Length, in bits, of error correction hash
$\mu = \mu(\lambda)$	Length, in bits, of error syndrome
θ	Basis in which the encrypting party prepares her quantum state
δ	Threshold error rate for the verification test

(*continued*)

Table 1. (*continued*)

Θ	Set of possible bases from which θ is chosen
$\mathfrak{H}_{pa}$	Universal$_2$ family of hash functions used in the privacy amplification scheme
$\mathfrak{H}_{ec}$	Universal$_2$ family of hash functions used in the error correction scheme
H_{pa}	Hash function used in the privacy amplification scheme
H_{ec}	Hash function used in the error correction scheme
S^{Θ}	Seed for the choice of θ
$S^{H_{pa}}$	Seed for the choice of the hash function used in the error correction scheme
$S^{H_{ec}}$	Seed for the choice of the hash function used in the privacy amplification scheme
synd	Function that computes the error syndrome
corr	Function that computes the corrected string

Scheme 1. (Prepare-and-Measure Certified Deletion) Let $n, \lambda, \tau, \mu, m = s + k$ be integers. Let $\Theta = \{\theta \in \{0,1\}^m \mid \omega(\theta) = k\}$. Let both $\mathfrak{H}_{ec} := \{h \colon \{0,1\}^s \to \{0,1\}^{\tau}\}$ and $\mathfrak{H}_{pa} := \{h \colon \{0,1\}^s \to \{0,1\}^n\}$ be universal$_2$ families of hash functions. Let synd: $\{0,1\}^n \to \{0,1\}^{\mu}$ be an error syndrome function, let corr: $\{0,1\}^n \times \{0,1\}^{\mu} \to \{0,1\}^n$ be the corresponding function used to calculate the corrected string, and let $\delta \in [0,1]$ be a tolerated error rate for verification. We define a *noise-tolerant prepare-and-measure n-CDE* by Circuits 1–5. This scheme satisfies both Eq. (21) and Eq. (30). It is therefore an n-CDE.

5   Security Analysis

In this section, we present the security analysis for Scheme 1: in Sect. 5.1, we show the security of the scheme in terms of an encryption scheme, then, in Sect. 5.2, we show that the scheme is correct and robust. Finally in Sect. 5.3, we show that the scheme is a certified deletion scheme.

5.1   Ciphertext Indistinguishability

In considering whether Scheme 1 has ciphertext indistinguishability (Definition 8), one need only verify that an adversary, given a ciphertext, would not be able to discern whether a known message was encrypted.

Circuit 1: The key generation circuit key.

Input : None.

Output: A key state $\rho \in \mathcal{D}(\mathcal{Q}(k + m + n + \mu + \tau) \otimes \mathfrak{H}_{\mathrm{pa}} \otimes \mathfrak{H}_{\mathrm{ec}}))$.

1 Sample $\theta \xleftarrow{\$} \Theta$.

2 Sample $r|_{\bar{\mathcal{I}}} \xleftarrow{\$} \{0,1\}^k$ where $\bar{\mathcal{I}} = \{i \in [m] \mid \theta_i = 1\}$.

3 Sample $u \xleftarrow{\$} \{0,1\}^n$.

4 Sample $d \xleftarrow{\$} \{0,1\}^\mu$.

5 Sample $e \xleftarrow{\$} \{0,1\}^\tau$.

6 Sample $H_{\mathrm{pa}} \xleftarrow{\$} \mathfrak{H}_{\mathrm{pa}}$.

7 Sample $H_{\mathrm{ec}} \xleftarrow{\$} \mathfrak{H}_{\mathrm{ec}}$.

8 Output $\rho = \Gamma(r|_{\bar{\mathcal{I}}}, \theta, u, d, e, H_{\mathrm{pa}}, H_{\mathrm{ec}})$.

Circuit 2: The encryption circuit enc.

Input : A plaintext state $\Gamma(\mathsf{msg}) \in \mathcal{D}(\mathcal{Q}(n))$ and a key state
$\Gamma(r|_{\bar{\mathcal{I}}}, \theta, u, d, e, H_{\mathrm{pa}}, H_{\mathrm{ec}}) \in \mathcal{D}(\mathcal{Q}(k + m + n + \mu + \tau) \otimes \mathfrak{H}_{\mathrm{pa}} \otimes \mathfrak{H}_{\mathrm{ec}})$.

Output: A ciphertext state $\rho \in \mathcal{D}(\mathcal{Q}(m + n + \tau + \mu))$.

1 Sample $r|_{\mathcal{I}} \xleftarrow{\$} \{0,1\}^s$ where $\mathcal{I} = \{i \in [m] \mid \theta_i = 0\}$.

2 Compute $x = H_{\mathrm{pa}}(r|_{\mathcal{I}})$ where $\mathcal{I} = \{i \in [m] \mid \theta_i = 0\}$.

3 Compute $p = H_{\mathrm{ec}}(r|_{\mathcal{I}}) \oplus d$.

4 Compute $q = \mathrm{synd}(r|_{\mathcal{I}}) \oplus e$.

5 Output $\rho = \Gamma(r^\theta) \otimes \Gamma(\mathsf{msg} \oplus x \oplus u, p, q)$.

Circuit 3: The decryption circuit dec.

Input : A key state
$\Gamma(r|_{\bar{\mathcal{I}}}, \theta, u, d, e, H_{\mathrm{pa}}, H_{\mathrm{ec}}) \in \mathcal{D}(\mathcal{Q}(k + m + n + \mu + \tau) \otimes \mathfrak{H}_{\mathrm{pa}} \otimes \mathfrak{H}_{\mathrm{ec}})$
and a ciphertext $\rho \otimes \Gamma(c, p, q) \in \mathcal{D}(\mathcal{Q}(m + n + \mu + \tau))$.

Output: A plaintext state $\sigma \in \mathcal{D}(\mathcal{Q}(n))$ and an error flag $\gamma \in \mathcal{D}(\mathcal{Q})$.

1 Compute $\rho' = \mathsf{H}^\theta \rho \mathsf{H}^\theta$.

2 Measure ρ' in the computational basis. Call the result r.

3 Compute $r' = \mathrm{corr}(r|_{\mathcal{I}}, q \oplus e)$ where $\mathcal{I} = \{i \in [m] \mid \theta_i = 0\}$.

4 Compute $p' = H_{\mathrm{ec}}(r') \oplus d$.

5 If $p \neq p'$, then set $\gamma = \Gamma(0)$. Else, set $\gamma = \Gamma(1)$.

6 Compute $x' = H_{\mathrm{pa}}(r')$.

7 Output $\sigma \otimes \gamma = \Gamma(c \oplus x' \oplus u) \otimes \gamma$.

Circuit 4: The deletion circuit del.

Input : A ciphertext $\rho \otimes \Gamma(c, p, q) \in \mathcal{D}(\mathcal{Q}(m + n + \mu + \tau))$.

Output: A certificate string state $\sigma \in \mathcal{D}(\mathcal{Q}(m))$.

1 Measure ρ in the Hadamard basis. Call the output y.

2 Output $\sigma = \Gamma(y)$.

Circuit 5: The verification circuit ver.

    Input : A key state
$$\Gamma(r|_{\bar{\mathcal{I}}}, \theta, u, d, e, H_{\mathrm{pa}}, H_{\mathrm{ec}}) \in \mathcal{D}(\mathcal{Q}(k + m + n + \mu + \tau) \otimes \mathfrak{H}_{\mathrm{pa}} \otimes \mathfrak{H}_{\mathrm{ec}})$$
          and a certificate string state $\Gamma(y) \in \mathcal{D}(\mathcal{Q}(m))$.

    Output: A bit.

1 Compute $\hat{y}' = \hat{y}|_{\bar{\mathcal{I}}}$ where $\bar{\mathcal{I}} = \{i \in [m] \mid \theta_i = 1\}$.

2 Compute $q = r|_{\bar{\mathcal{I}}}$.

3 If $\omega(q \oplus \hat{y}') < k\delta$, output 1. Else, output 0.

Theorem 1. *Scheme 1 has ciphertext indistinguishability.*

Proof. For any distinguishing attack $\mathcal{A} = (\mathcal{A}_0, \mathcal{A}_1)$, any state $\rho = \rho_S \otimes \Gamma(\mathsf{msg}) \in \mathcal{D}(\mathcal{H}_S \otimes \mathcal{Q}(n))$, and where $k = (r|_{\bar{\mathcal{I}}}, \theta, u, d, e, H_{\mathrm{pa}}, H_{\mathrm{ec}}) \in \{0,1\}^{k+m+n+\mu+\tau} \times \mathfrak{H}_{\mathrm{pa}} \times \mathfrak{H}_{\mathrm{ec}}$ is a key, we have that

$$\mathop{\mathbb{E}}_{k} \left(\mathbb{1}_S \otimes \Phi_{k,1}^{\mathrm{enc}} \right)(\rho) = \frac{1}{2^{m+n+\mu+\tau}|\mathfrak{H}_{\mathrm{pa}}||\mathfrak{H}_{\mathrm{ec}}|} \sum_k \rho_S \otimes \Gamma(r^\theta) \otimes \Gamma(\mathsf{msg} \oplus x \oplus u, p, q)$$

$$= \frac{1}{2^{m+n+\mu+\tau}|\mathfrak{H}_{\mathrm{pa}}||\mathfrak{H}_{\mathrm{ec}}|} \sum_k \rho_S \otimes \Gamma(r^\theta) \otimes \Gamma(x \oplus u, p, q)$$

$$= \mathop{\mathbb{E}}_{k} \left(\mathbb{1}_S \otimes \Phi_{k,0}^{\mathrm{enc}} \right)(\rho),$$

where the second equality is due to the uniform distribution of both $\mathsf{msg} \oplus x \oplus u$ and u. Therefore, an adversary can do no better than guess b correctly half of the time in a distinguishing attack. This implies perfect ciphertext indistinguishability with $\eta = 0$. $\qquad\square$

5.2 Correctness

Thanks to the syndrome and correction functions included in the scheme, the decryption circuit is robust against a certain amount of noise; that is, below such a level of noise, the decryption circuit outputs Alice's original message with high probability. This noise threshold is determined by the distance of the linear code used. In particular, where Δ is the distance of the code, decryption should proceed normally as long as fewer than $\lfloor \frac{\Delta-1}{2} \rfloor$ errors occur to the quantum encoding of $r|_{\mathcal{I}}$ during transmission through the quantum channel.

    To account for greater levels of noise (such as may occur in the presence of an adversary), we show that the error correction measures implemented in Scheme 1 ensure that errors in decryption are detected with high probability. In other words, we show that the scheme is ϵ_{rob}-robust, where $\epsilon_{\mathrm{rob}} := \frac{1}{2^\tau}$.

    Recall that τ is the length of the error correction hash, and that μ is the length of the error correction syndrome. Consider that Bob has received a ciphertext state $\rho_B \otimes \Gamma(c, p, q) \in \mathcal{D}(\mathcal{Q}(m+n+\mu+\tau))$ and a key $(r|_{\bar{\mathcal{I}}}, \theta, u, d, e, H_{\mathrm{pa}}, H_{\mathrm{ec}}) \in \Theta \times \{0,1\}^{n+\mu+\tau} \times \mathfrak{H}_{\mathrm{pa}} \times \mathfrak{H}_{\mathrm{ec}}$. Given θ, Bob learns $\mathcal{I}$. This allows him to perform the following measurement on ρ_B:

$$\mathcal{M}_{B \to Y}^{\mathcal{I}}(\cdot) = \sum_{y \in \{0,1\}^s} |y\rangle_Y \left(M_{B_{\mathcal{I}}}^{0,y}\right) \cdot \left(M_{B_{\mathcal{I}}}^{0,y}\right)^\dagger \langle y|_Y \tag{35}$$

The new register Y contains a hypothesis of the random string Alice used in generating c. Since ρ_B was necessarily transmitted through a quantum channel, it may have been altered due to noise. Bob calculates a corrected estimate: $\hat{x} = \mathrm{corr}(y, q \oplus e)$. Finally, he compares a hash of the estimate with $p \oplus d$, which is the hash of Alice's corresponding randomness. This procedure is represented by a function $\mathrm{ec} \colon \{0,1\}^s \times \{0,1\}^\mu \times \mathfrak{H}_{\mathrm{ec}} \to \{0,1\}$ defined by

$$\mathrm{ec}(x, y) = \begin{cases} 0 & \text{if } H_{\mathrm{ec}}(x) \neq y \\ 1 & \text{else.} \end{cases} \tag{36}$$

To record the value of this test, we use a flag $F^{\mathrm{ec}} := \mathrm{ec}(\hat{x}, p \oplus d)$. It is very unlikely that both $F^{\mathrm{ec}} = 1$ and the outcome of Bob's decryption procedure is not equal to Alice's originally intended message. This is shown in the following proposition, the proof of which follows that of an analogous theorem in [29].

Theorem 2. *If* $r|_{\mathcal{I}} \in \{0,1\}^s$ *is the random string Alice samples in encryption, and* $\hat{x} = \mathrm{corr}(y, q \oplus e)$, *then*

$$\Pr[H_{pa}(r|_{\mathcal{I}}) \neq H_{pa}(\hat{x}) \wedge F^{\mathrm{ec}} = 1] \leq \frac{1}{2^\tau}. \tag{37}$$

Proof.

$$\Pr[H_{\mathrm{pa}}(r|_{\mathcal{I}}) \neq H_{\mathrm{pa}}(\hat{x}) \wedge F^{\mathrm{ec}} = 1] \tag{38}$$
$$= \Pr[H_{\mathrm{pa}}(r|_{\mathcal{I}}) \neq H_{\mathrm{pa}}(\hat{x}) \wedge H_{\mathrm{ec}}(p \oplus d) = H_{\mathrm{ec}}(\hat{x})]$$
$$= \Pr[H_{\mathrm{pa}}(r|_{\mathcal{I}}) \neq H_{\mathrm{pa}}(\hat{x}) \wedge H_{\mathrm{ec}}(r|_{\mathcal{I}}) = H_{\mathrm{ec}}(\hat{x})] \tag{39}$$
$$\leq \Pr[r|_{\mathcal{I}} \neq \hat{x} \wedge H_{\mathrm{ec}}(r|_{\mathcal{I}}) = H_{\mathrm{ec}}(\hat{x})] \tag{40}$$
$$= \Pr[r|_{\mathcal{I}} \neq \hat{x}] \Pr[H_{\mathrm{ec}}(r|_{\mathcal{I}}) = H_{\mathrm{ec}}(\hat{x})] \tag{41}$$
$$\leq \Pr[H_{\mathrm{ec}}(r|_{\mathcal{I}}) = H_{\mathrm{ec}}(\hat{x}) \mid r|_{\mathcal{I}} \neq \hat{x}] \tag{42}$$
$$\leq \frac{1}{\|\mathfrak{H}_{\mathrm{ec}}\|} = \frac{1}{2^\tau}. \tag{43}$$

$\square$

5.3 Certified Deletion Security

We now prove certified deletion security of Scheme 1. Our technique consists in formalizing a game (Game 1) that corresponds to the security definition (Definition 13) applied to Scheme 1. Next, we develop an entanglement-based sequence of interactions (Game 2) which accomplish the same task as in the previous Game. We analyze this game and, afterwards, we show formally that the aforementioned analysis, via its relation to Game 1, implies the certified deletion security of Scheme 1. To begin, we describe a game which exhibits a certified deletion attack on Scheme 1, and which thus allows us to examine whether the scheme has certified deletion security. In what follows, the challenger represents the party who would normally encrypt and send the message (Alice), and the adversary $\mathcal{A}$ represents the recipient (Bob). The adversary sends the challenger a candidate message $\mathsf{msg}_0 \in \{0, 1\}^n$ and Alice chooses, with uniform randomness, whether to encrypt 0^n or msg_0; security holds if, for any adversary, the probabilities of the following two events are negligibly close:

- verification passes *and* Bob outputs 1, in the case that Alice encrypted 0^n;
- verification passes *and* Bob output 1, in the case that Alice encrypted msg_0.

Game 1. (Prepare-and-Measure Game). Let $\mathcal{S} = (\mathsf{key}, \mathsf{enc}, \mathsf{dec}, \mathsf{del}, \mathsf{ver})$ be an n-CDE with λ implicit, and with circuits defined as in Scheme 1. Let $\mathcal{A} = (\mathcal{A}_0, \mathcal{A}_1, \mathcal{A}_2)$ be a certified deletion attack. The game is parametric in $b \xleftarrow{\$} \{0, 1\}$ and is called Game 1(b).

1. Run $\Gamma(\mathsf{msg}_0)_M \otimes \rho_S \leftarrow \mathcal{A}_0(1)$. Generate

$$\Gamma(\theta, u, d, e, H_{\mathrm{pa}}, H_{\mathrm{ec}}, r|_{\bar{\mathcal{I}}})_K \leftarrow \Phi^{\mathsf{key}}. \tag{44}$$

Denote

$$\mathsf{msg} := \begin{cases} 0^n & \text{if } b = 0 \\ \mathsf{msg}_0 & \text{if } b = 1. \end{cases} \tag{45}$$

Compute

$$\begin{aligned} \Gamma(r^\theta)_T &\otimes \Gamma(\mathsf{msg} \oplus x \oplus u, p, q)_T \\ &\leftarrow \Phi^{\mathsf{enc}}(\Gamma(\theta, u, d, e, H_{\mathrm{pa}}, H_{\mathrm{ec}}, r|_{\bar{\mathcal{I}}})_K \otimes \Gamma(\mathsf{msg})_M). \end{aligned} \tag{46}$$

2. Run

$$\Gamma(y)_D \otimes \rho'_S \otimes \rho_{T'} \leftarrow \mathcal{A}_1(\Gamma(r^\theta)_T \otimes \Gamma(\mathsf{msg} \oplus x \oplus u, p, q)_T \otimes \rho_S). \tag{47}$$

Compute

$$\Gamma(ok) \leftarrow \Phi^{\mathsf{ver}}(\Gamma(\theta, u, d, e, H_{\mathrm{pa}}, H_{\mathrm{ec}}, r|_{\bar{\mathcal{I}}})_K \otimes \Gamma(y)_D). \tag{48}$$

3. If $ok = 1$, run

$$\Gamma(b') \leftarrow \mathcal{A}_2(\Gamma(r|_{\bar{\mathcal{I}}}, \theta, u, d, e, H_{\mathrm{pa}}, H_{\mathrm{ec}})_{K'} \otimes \rho'_S \otimes \rho_{T'}); \tag{49}$$

else, $b' := 0$.

Let p_b be the probability that the output of Game 1(b) is 1. Comparing Game 1 with Definition 13, we note that the former runs the adversary to the end only in the case that $ok = 1$, while the latter runs the adversary to the end in both cases. However, the obtained distribution for p_b is the same, since in Game 1, $p_b = 1$ whenever the adversary outputs 1 *and* $ok = 1$. Hence we wish to bound $|p_0 - p_1|$ in Game 1. Instead of directly analyzing Game 1, we analyze a game wherein the parties use entanglement; this allows us to express the game in a format that is conducive for the analysis that follows.

Game 2. (EPR Game). Alice is the sender, and Bob is the recipient and adversary. The game is parametric in $b \xleftarrow{\$} \{0,1\}$ and is called Game 2(b).

1. Bob selects a string $\mathsf{msg}_0 \in \{0,1\}^n$ and sends msg_0 to Alice. Bob prepares a tripartite state $\rho_{ABB'} \in \mathcal{D}(\mathcal{Q}(3m))$ where each system contains m qubits. Bob sends the A system to Alice and keeps the systems B and B'. Bob measures the B system in the Hadamard basis and obtains a string $y \in \{0,1\}^m$. Bob sends y to Alice.

2. Alice samples $\theta \xleftarrow{\$} \Theta$, $u \xleftarrow{\$} \{0,1\}^n$, $d \xleftarrow{\$} \{0,1\}^\mu$, $e \xleftarrow{\$} \{0,1\}^\tau$, $H_{\mathrm{pa}} \xleftarrow{\$} \mathfrak{H}_{\mathrm{pa}}$, and $H_{\mathrm{ec}} \xleftarrow{\$} \mathfrak{H}_{\mathrm{ec}}$. She applies a CPTP map to system A which measures A_i according to the computational basis if $\theta_i = 0$ and the Hadamard basis if $\theta_i = 1$. Call the result r. Let $\mathcal{I} = \{i \in [m] \mid \theta_i = 0\}$. Alice computes $x = H_{\mathrm{pa}}(r|_{\mathcal{I}})$, $p = H_{\mathrm{ec}}(r|_{\mathcal{I}}) \oplus d$, and $q = \mathrm{synd}(r|_{\mathcal{I}}) \oplus e$. Alice selects a message:

$$\mathsf{msg} := \begin{cases} 0^n & \text{if } b = 0 \\ \mathsf{msg}_0 & \text{if } b = 1. \end{cases} \tag{50}$$

If $\omega(y \oplus r|_{\bar{\mathcal{I}}}) < k\delta$, $ok := 1$ and Alice sends

$$(\mathsf{msg} \oplus x \oplus u, r|_{\bar{\mathcal{I}}}, \theta, u, d, e, p, q, H_{\mathrm{pa}}, H_{\mathrm{ec}}) \tag{51}$$

to Bob. Else, $ok := 0$ and $b := 0$.

3. If $ok = 1$, Bob computes

$$\begin{aligned} \Gamma(b') &\leftarrow \mathcal{E}(\rho_{B'} \otimes \\ &\Gamma(\mathsf{msg} \oplus x \oplus u, \mathsf{msg}_0, r_{\bar{\mathcal{I}}}, \theta, u, d, e, p, q, H_{\mathrm{pa}}, H_{\mathrm{ec}})) \end{aligned} \tag{52}$$

for some CPTP map $\mathcal{E}$; else $b' := 0$.

Game 2 is intended to model a purified version of Game 1. Note that Bob's measurememement of B in the Hadamard basis is meant to mimic the del circuit of Scheme 1. Although it may seem strange that we impose a limitation of measurement basis on Bob here, it is in fact no limitation at all; indeed, since Bob prepares $\rho_{ABB'}$, he is in total control of the state that gets measured, and hence may assume an arbitrary degree of control over the measurement outcome. Therefore, the assumption that he measures in the Hadamard basis is made without loss of generality.

It may also appear that the adversary in Game 1 has more information when producing the deletion string than Bob in Game 2. This, however, is not true, as the adversary in Game 1 has only received information from Alice that appears to him to be uniformly random (as mentioned, the statement is formalized later, in Sect. 5.4). In order to further the analysis, we assign more precise notation for the maps described in Game 2.

Bob's Measurements. Measurement of Bob's system B of m qubits in Step 1 is represented using two CPTP maps: one acting on the systems in $\mathcal{I}$, with outcome recorded in register Y; and one acting on the systems in $\bar{\mathcal{I}}$, with outcome recorded in W. Note, however, that Bob has no access to θ, and therefore has no way of determining $\mathcal{I}$. The formal separation of registers Y and W is simply for future ease of specifying the qubits to which we refer.

Recall the definition of the measurements $M_B^{x,y}$ from Sect. 2.3.

The first measurement, where the outcome is stored in register Y, is defined by

$$\mathcal{M}_{B \to Y}^{\mathcal{I}}(\cdot) = \sum_{y \in \{0,1\}^s} |y\rangle_Y \left(M_{B_{\mathcal{I}}}^{1,y}\right) \cdot \left(M_{B_{\mathcal{I}}}^{1,y}\right)^\dagger \langle y|_Y \tag{53}$$

and the second, where the outcome is stored in register W, is defined by

$$\mathcal{M}_{B \to W}^{\bar{\mathcal{I}}}(\cdot) = \sum_{w \in \{0,1\}^k} |w\rangle_W \left(M_{B_{\bar{\mathcal{I}}}}^{1,w}\right) \cdot \left(M_{B_{\bar{\mathcal{I}}}}^{1,w}\right)^\dagger \langle w|_W, \tag{54}$$

where $M_{B_{\mathcal{I}}}^{1,y} := \bigotimes_{i \in \mathcal{I}} M_{B_i}^{1,y_i}$, and the definition of $M_{B_{\bar{\mathcal{I}}}}^{1,w}$ is analogous.

Alice's Measurements. We represent the randomness of Alice's sampling using seed registers. Thus, the randomness used for Alice's choice of basis is represented as

$$\rho_{S^\Theta} = \frac{1}{\binom{m}{k}} \sum_{\theta \in \Theta} \Gamma(\theta)_{S^\Theta}. \tag{55}$$

Similarly, Alice's randomness for choice of a hash function for privacy amplification is represented as

$$\rho_{S^{H_{\mathrm{pa}}}} = \frac{1}{|\mathfrak{H}_{\mathrm{pa}}|} \sum_{h \in \mathfrak{H}_{\mathrm{pa}}} \Gamma(h)_{S^{H_{\mathrm{pa}}}}. \tag{56}$$

Recall that $m = s + k$, where k is the weight of all strings in Θ. Measurement of Alice's system A of m qubits in Step 2 is represented using two CPTP maps: one acting on the systems in $\mathcal{I}$, with outcome recorded in register X (by definition, these qubits are measured in the computational basis); and one acting on the systems in $\bar{\mathcal{I}}$, with outcome recorded in register V (by definition, these qubits are measured in the Hadamard basis).

$$\mathcal{M}_{A \to X|S^\Theta}^{\mathcal{I}}(\cdot) = \sum_{\theta \in \Theta} \sum_{x \in \{0,1\}^s} |x\rangle_X \left(M_{A_{\mathcal{I}}}^{0,x} \otimes \Gamma(\theta)_{S^\Theta}\right) \cdot \left(M_{A_{\mathcal{I}}}^{0,x} \otimes \Gamma(\theta)_{S^\Theta}\right)^\dagger \langle x|_X;$$

and the second measurement, where the outcome is stored in register V, is defined by

$$\mathcal{M}_{A \to V|S^\Theta}^{\bar{\mathcal{I}}}(\cdot) = \sum_{\theta \in \Theta} \sum_{v \in \{0,1\}^k} |v\rangle_V \left(M_{A_{\bar{\mathcal{I}}}}^{1,v} \otimes \Gamma(\theta)_{S^\Theta}\right) \cdot \left(M_{A_{\bar{\mathcal{I}}}}^{1,v} \otimes \Gamma(\theta)_{S^\Theta}\right)^\dagger \langle v|_V,$$

where $M_{A_{\mathcal{I}}}^{0,x} := \bigotimes_{i \in \mathcal{I}} M_{A_i}^{0,x_i}$ and the definition of $M_{A_{\bar{\mathcal{I}}}}^{1,v}$ is analogous.

We also introduce a hypothetical measurement for the sake of the security analysis. Consider the case where Alice measures all of her qubits in the Hadamard basis. In this case, instead of $\mathcal{M}^{\mathcal{I}}_{A \to X|S^\Theta}$, Alice would use the measurement

$$\mathcal{M}^{\mathcal{I}}_{A \to Z|S^\Theta}(\cdot) = \sum_{\theta \in \Theta} \sum_{z \in \{0,1\}^s} |z\rangle_Z \left(M^{1,z}_{A_{\mathcal{I}}} \otimes \Gamma(\theta)_{S^\Theta} \right) \cdot \left(M^{1,z}_{A_{\mathcal{I}}} \otimes \Gamma(\theta)_{S^\Theta} \right)^{\dagger} \langle z|_Z.$$

Each of Alice's and Bob's measurements commute with each other as they all act on distinct quantum systems. We can thus define the total measurement map

$$\mathcal{M}_{AB \to VWXY|S^\Theta} = \mathcal{M}^{\mathcal{I}}_{A \to X|S^\Theta} \circ \mathcal{M}^{\bar{\mathcal{I}}}_{A \to V|S^\Theta} \circ \mathcal{M}^{\mathcal{I}}_{B \to Y} \circ \mathcal{M}^{\bar{\mathcal{I}}}_{B \to W}. \tag{57}$$

The overall post-measurement state (i.e. the joint state held by Alice and Bob after both their measurements) is denoted σ_{VWXYS^Θ}. We analogously define the hypothetical post-measurement state $\hat{\sigma}_{VWZYS^\Theta}$ (which is the joint state of Alice and Bob given Alice has used $\mathcal{M}_{A \to Z|S^\Theta}$).

Alice's Verification: Alice completes the verification procedure by comparing the V register to the W register. If they differ in less than $k\delta$ bits, then the test is passed. The test is represented by a function comp: $\{0,1\}^k \times \{0,1\}^k \to \{0,1\}$ defined by

$$\text{comp}(v,w) = \begin{cases} 0 & \text{if } \omega(v \oplus w) \geq k\delta \\ 1 & \text{else.} \end{cases} \tag{58}$$

To record the value of this test, we use a flag $F^{\text{comp}} := \text{comp}(v,w)$.

The import of the outcome of this comparison test is that if Bob is good at guessing Alice's information in the Hadamard basis, it is unlikely that he is good at guessing Alice's information in the computational basis. This trade-off is represented in the uncertainty relation of Proposition 2.

Note that we can define the post-comparison test state, since $A|_{\mathcal{I}}$ is disjoint from $A|_{\bar{\mathcal{I}}}$ and $B|_{\mathcal{I}}$ is disjoint from $B|_{\bar{\mathcal{I}}}$. The state is denoted $\tau_{ABVWS^\Theta|F^{\text{comp}}=1}$.

The following proposition shows that in order to ensure that Bob's knowledge of X is limited after a successful comparison test, and receiving the key, his knowledge about Alice's hypothetical Hadamard measurement outcome must be bounded below.

Proposition 4. *Let $\epsilon \geq 0$. Then*

$$H^\epsilon_{\min}(X \wedge F^{\text{comp}} = 1|VWS^\Theta B')_\sigma + H^\epsilon_{\max}(Z \wedge F^{\text{comp}} = 1|Y)_\sigma \geq s. \tag{59}$$

Proof. We apply Proposition 2 to the state $\tau_{ABVWS^\Theta|F^{\text{comp}}=1}$. To do this, we equate $C = VWS^\Theta B'$ and $E = S^\Theta B$. Using the measurement maps $\mathcal{M}_{A \to X|S^\Theta}$ and $\mathcal{M}_{A \to Z|S^\Theta}$ as the POVMS and using $\{\langle\theta|\theta\rangle\}$ as the projective measurement, applying Proposition 2 yields

$$H^\epsilon_{\min}(X \wedge F^{\text{comp}} = 1|VWS^\Theta B')_\sigma + H^\epsilon_{\max}(Z \wedge F^{\text{comp}} = 1|S^\Theta B)_\tau \geq s. \tag{60}$$

We then apply the measurement map $\mathcal{M}_{B \to Y | S^\ominus}$ and discard $S^\ominus$. Finally, by Proposition 1, we note that

$$H_{\max}^\epsilon(Z \wedge F^{\text{comp}} = 1 \mid S^\ominus B)_\tau \leq H_{\max}^\epsilon(Z \wedge F^{\text{comp}} = 1 \mid Y)_{\hat{\sigma}}, \tag{61}$$

which concludes the proof. $\square$

In the spirit of [29], we provide an upper bound for the max-entropy quantity, thus establishing a lower bound for the min-entropy quantity.

Proposition 5. *Letting $\nu \in (0, 1)$, we define*

$$\epsilon(\nu) := \exp\left(\frac{-sk^2\nu^2}{m(k+1)}\right). \tag{62}$$

Then, for any $\nu \in (0, \frac{1}{2} - \delta]$ such that $\epsilon(\nu)^2 < \Pr[F^{\text{comp}} = 1]_\sigma = \Pr[F^{\text{comp}} = 1]_{\hat{\sigma}}$,

$$H_{\max}^{\epsilon(\nu)}(Z \wedge F^{\text{comp}} = 1 \mid Y)_{\hat{\sigma}} \leq s \cdot h(\delta + \nu) \tag{63}$$

where

$$h(x) := -x \log x - (1 - x) \log(1 - x). \tag{64}$$

Proof. Define the event

$$\Omega := \begin{cases} 1 & \text{if } \omega(Z \oplus Y) \geq s(\delta + \nu) \\ 0 & \text{else.} \end{cases} \tag{65}$$

Using Lemma 1, we get that

$$\Pr\left[F^{\text{comp}} = 1 \wedge \Omega\right]_{\hat{\sigma}} = \Pr\left[\omega(V \oplus W) \leq k\delta \wedge \omega(Z \oplus Y) \geq s(\delta + \nu)\right]_\sigma \tag{66}$$

$$\leq \epsilon(\nu)^2. \tag{67}$$

Given the state $\hat{\sigma}_{ZYF^{\text{comp}}=1}$, we use Lemma 2 to get the state $\tilde{\sigma}_{ZYF^{\text{comp}}}$ with $\Pr[\Omega]_{\tilde{\sigma}} = 0$ and

$$P(\hat{\sigma}_{ZYF^{\text{comp}}=1}, \tilde{\sigma}_{ZYF^{\text{comp}}}) \leq \epsilon(\nu). \tag{68}$$

Since $\Pr[F^{\text{comp}} = 1]_{\tilde{\sigma}} = 1$, we get that

$$H_{\max}^{\epsilon(\nu)}(Z \wedge F^{\text{comp}} = 1 \mid Y)_{\hat{\sigma}} \leq H_{\max}(Z \wedge F^{\text{comp}} = 1 \mid Y)_{\tilde{\sigma}} = H_{\max}(Z \mid Y)_{\tilde{\sigma}}. \tag{69}$$

Expanding this conditional max-entropy [27, Sect. 4.3.2], we obtain

$$H_{\max}(Z \mid Y)_{\tilde{\sigma}} = \log\left(\sum_{y \in \{0,1\}^s} \Pr[Y = y]_{\tilde{\sigma}} 2^{H_{\max}(Z|Y)_{\tilde{\sigma}}}\right) \tag{70}$$

$$\leq \max_{\substack{y \in \{0,1\}^s \\ \Pr[Y=y]_{\tilde{\sigma}} > 0}} H_{\max}(Z \mid Y = y)_{\tilde{\sigma}} \tag{71}$$

$$\leq \max_{\substack{y \in \{0,1\}^s \\ \Pr[Y=y]_{\tilde{\sigma}} > 0}} \log |\{z \in \{0,1\}^s : \Pr[Z = z \mid Y = y]_{\tilde{\sigma}} > 0\}| \tag{72}$$

$$= \max_{y \in \{0,1\}^s} \log |\{z \in \{0,1\}^s : \Pr[Z = z \wedge Y = y]_{\tilde{\sigma}} > 0\}|. \tag{73}$$

Since $\Pr[\Omega]_{\tilde{\sigma}} = 0$, we have

$$|\{z \in \{0,1\}^s : \Pr[Z = z \wedge Y = y]_{\tilde{\sigma}} > 0\}|$$
$$\leq |\{z \in \{0,1\}^s : \omega(z \oplus y) < s(\delta + \nu)\}| \tag{74}$$

$$= \sum_{\gamma=0}^{\lfloor s(\delta+\nu) \rfloor} \binom{s}{\gamma}. \tag{75}$$

When $\delta + \nu \leq 1/2$ (see [16, Sect. 1.4]), we have that $\sum_{\gamma=0}^{\lfloor s(\delta=\nu) \rfloor} \binom{s}{\gamma} \leq 2^{s \cdot h(\delta+\nu)}$. $\qquad\square$

At this point, we use Proposition 3, the Leftover Hashing Lemma, to turn the min-entropy bound into a statement about how close to uniformly random the string $\tilde{X} = H_{\mathrm{pa}}(X)$ is from Bob's perspective. We name this final state $\zeta_{\tilde{X}SF^{\mathrm{comp}}E \wedge F^{\mathrm{comp}}=1} = \mathrm{Tr}_X[\mathcal{E}_f(\sigma_{XS^{\ominus}SH_{\mathrm{ec}}F^{\mathrm{comp}}} \otimes \rho_{SH_{\mathrm{pa}}})]$ for the function $f : (X, H_{\mathrm{pa}}) \mapsto H_{\mathrm{pa}}(X)$. We compare this to the state $\chi_{\tilde{X}} \otimes \zeta_{SF^{\mathrm{comp}}E \wedge F^{\mathrm{comp}}=1}$ where $\chi_{\tilde{X}}$ is the fully mixed state on $\tilde{X}$.

Proposition 6. *Let $\epsilon(\nu)$ be as defined in (62). Then for any $\nu \in (0, \frac{1}{2} - \delta]$ such that $\epsilon(\nu)^2 < \Pr[F^{\mathrm{comp}} = 1]_\sigma$, we have*

$$\|\zeta_{\tilde{X}SF^{\mathrm{comp}}E \wedge F^{\mathrm{comp}}=1} - \chi_{\tilde{X}} \otimes \zeta_{SF^{\mathrm{comp}}E \wedge F^{\mathrm{comp}}=1}\|_{\mathrm{Tr}} \leq \frac{1}{2} 2^{-\frac{1}{2}g(\nu)} + 2\epsilon(\nu), \tag{76}$$

where $g(\nu) := s(1 - h(\delta + \nu)) - n$.

Proof. By Proposition 5, we see that

$$H_{\max}^{\epsilon(\nu)}(Z \wedge F^{\mathrm{comp}} = 1 \mid Y)_\sigma \leq s \cdot h(\delta + \nu). \tag{77}$$

Together, with Proposition 4, and taking $q = 1 - h(\delta + \nu)$, we get:

$$H_{\min}^\epsilon(X \wedge F^{\mathrm{comp}} = 1 | VWS^{\ominus}B')_\sigma \geq sq. \tag{78}$$

Finally, applying Proposition 3, we obtain the desired inequality. $\qquad\square$

For the case where $\epsilon(\nu)^2 \geq \Pr[F^{\mathrm{comp}} = 1]_\sigma$, we note that the trace distance $\|\zeta_{\tilde{X}SF^{\mathrm{comp}}E \wedge F^{\mathrm{comp}}=1} - \chi_{\tilde{X}} \otimes \zeta_{SF^{\mathrm{comp}}E \wedge F^{\mathrm{comp}}=1}\|_{\mathrm{Tr}}$ is upper bounded by $\Pr[F^{\mathrm{comp}} = 1]_\zeta$. Hence, considering the inequality $\Pr[F^{\mathrm{comp}} = 1]_\zeta \leq \epsilon(\nu)^2 \leq \epsilon(\nu)$ results in the proof of the following corollary.

Corollary 1. *For any $\nu \in (0, \frac{1}{2} - \delta]$, the following holds:*

$$\|\zeta_{\tilde{X}SF^{\mathrm{comp}}E \wedge F^{\mathrm{comp}}=1} - \chi_{\tilde{X}} \otimes \zeta_{SF^{\mathrm{comp}}E \wedge F^{\mathrm{comp}}=1}\|_{\mathrm{Tr}} \tag{79}$$

$$\leq \frac{1}{2} \sqrt{2^{-s(1-h(\delta+\nu))+n}} + 2\epsilon(\nu). \tag{80}$$

Finally, we would like to translate this into a statement about $|p_0 - p_1|$ in Game 2.

Corollary 2. *The difference of probabilities*

$$|\Pr[b' = 1 \wedge ok = 1 \mid Game\ 2(0)] - \Pr[b' = 1 \wedge ok = 1 \mid Game\ 2(1)]| \qquad (81)$$

is negligible.

Proof. Let $\zeta^b_{\tilde{X}SF^{\mathrm{comp}}E \wedge F^{\mathrm{comp}}=1}$ be the state of $\zeta_{\tilde{X}SF^{\mathrm{comp}}E \wedge F^{\mathrm{comp}}=1}$ in the case that $b \in \{0,1\}$ was selected at the beginning of Game 2. Note that the following trace distance is bounded above by a negligible function:

$$\left\| \zeta^0_{\tilde{X}SF^{\mathrm{comp}}E \wedge F^{\mathrm{comp}}=1} - \zeta^1_{\tilde{X}SF^{\mathrm{comp}}E \wedge F^{\mathrm{comp}}=1} \right\|_{\mathrm{Tr}} \qquad (82)$$

$$\leq \left\| \zeta^0_{\tilde{X}SF^{\mathrm{comp}}E \wedge F^{\mathrm{comp}}=1} - \chi_{\tilde{X}} \otimes \zeta_{SF^{\mathrm{comp}}E \wedge F^{\mathrm{comp}}=1} \right\|_{\mathrm{Tr}}$$
$$+ \left\| \zeta^1_{\tilde{X}SF^{\mathrm{comp}}E \wedge F^{\mathrm{comp}}=1} - \chi_{\tilde{X}} \otimes \zeta_{SF^{\mathrm{comp}}E \wedge F^{\mathrm{comp}}=1} \right\|_{\mathrm{Tr}} \qquad (83)$$

$$\leq 2 \left(\frac{1}{2} \sqrt{2^{-s(1-h(\delta+\nu))+n}} + 2\epsilon(\nu) \right). \qquad (84)$$

Next, note the following equality:

$$\Pr[b' = 1 \wedge ok = 1 \mid Game\ 2(b)] \qquad (85)$$

$$= \sum_{\zeta} \mathrm{Tr}[\zeta_{\tilde{X}SF^{\mathrm{comp}}E \wedge F^{\mathrm{comp}}=1}] \Pr[b' = 1 \mid Game\ 2(b)] \qquad (86)$$

Hence,

$$|\Pr[b' = 1 \wedge ok = 1 \mid Game\ 2(0)] - \Pr[b' = 1 \wedge ok = 1 \mid Game\ 2(1)]| \qquad (87)$$

$$\leq \sum_{\zeta} \mathrm{Tr}[\zeta_{\tilde{X}SF^{\mathrm{comp}}E \wedge F^{\mathrm{comp}}=1}] \left\| \zeta^0_{\tilde{X}SF^{\mathrm{comp}}E \wedge F^{\mathrm{comp}}=1} - \zeta^1_{\tilde{X}SF^{\mathrm{comp}}E \wedge F^{\mathrm{comp}}=1} \right\|_{\mathrm{Tr}}$$

$$\qquad (88)$$

$$\leq \sum_{\zeta} 2\, \mathrm{Tr}[\zeta_{\tilde{X}SF^{\mathrm{comp}}E \wedge F^{\mathrm{comp}}=1}] \left(\frac{1}{2} \sqrt{2^{-s(1-h(\delta+\nu))+n}} + 2\epsilon(\nu) \right) \qquad (89)$$

$$= 2 \left(\frac{1}{2} \sqrt{2^{-s(1-h(\delta+\nu))+n}} + 2\epsilon(\nu) \right). \qquad (90)$$

The conclusion follows from convexity and the physical interpretation of the trace distance (see Sect. 2). In particular, the difference in probabilities of obtaining the measurement outcome $b' = 1$ given states ζ^0 and ζ^1 is bounded above by the aforementioned trace distance. □

5.4   Security Reduction

We now show that the security of Game 1 can be reduced to that of Game 2. In order to do so, we construct a sequence of games starting at Game 1 and ending at Game 2, and show that each transformation can only increase the advantage in distinguishing the case $b = 0$ from $b = 1$. For a game G, let $\mathsf{Adv}(G) = |p_0 - p_1|$ be the *advantage*, as defined in Eq. (34).

Proposition 7. $\mathsf{Adv}(Game\ 1) \leq \mathsf{Adv}(Game\ 2)$.

Proof. We show a sequence of games, transforming Game 1 to Game 2, such that each successive transformation either has no effect on, or can potentially increase the advantage.

Let G be a game like Game 1 except that in G, we run

$$\mathcal{A}_1(\Gamma(r^\theta)_T \otimes \Gamma(\alpha_1, \alpha_2, \alpha_3)_T \otimes \rho_S),\qquad(91)$$

where $\alpha_1, \alpha_2, \alpha_3$ are uniformly random bit strings of the appropriate length. Verification is performed as usual, and if $ok = 1$, we run

$$\mathcal{A}_2(\Gamma(r|_{\bar{\mathcal{I}}}, \theta, \mathsf{msg} \oplus x \oplus \alpha_1, H_{\mathrm{ec}}(r|_{\mathcal{I}}) \oplus \alpha_2, \mathrm{synd}(r|_{\mathcal{I}}) \oplus \alpha_3, H_{\mathrm{pa}}, H_{\mathrm{ec}})_{K'} \otimes \rho_S' \otimes \rho_{T'}).\qquad(92)$$

By a change of variable, $\mathsf{Adv}(Game\ 1) = \mathsf{Adv}(G)$.

Next, we obtain G' from G by defining a new adversary $\mathcal{A}_1'$ which is like $\mathcal{A}_1'$, but only receives part of register T. Thus we run

$$\mathcal{A}_1'(\Gamma(r^\theta)_T \otimes \rho_S),\qquad(93)$$

and to compensate, we directly give $\mathcal{A}_2$ the information that was previously hidden by the α values:

$$\mathcal{A}_2'(\Gamma(r|_{\bar{\mathcal{I}}}, \theta, \mathsf{msg} \oplus x, H_{\mathrm{ec}}(r|_{\mathcal{I}}), \mathrm{synd}(r|_{\mathcal{I}}), H_{\mathrm{pa}}, H_{\mathrm{ec}})_{K'} \otimes \rho_S' \otimes \rho_{T'})\qquad(94)$$

Then $\mathsf{Adv}(G) \leq \mathsf{Adv}(G')$, since an adversary $\mathcal{A}'$ for G' can simulate any adversary $\mathcal{A}$ in G, and win with the same advantage. To do this, $\mathcal{A}'$ simply creates its own randomness for α_1, α_2 and α_3, and adjusts the input to $\mathcal{A}_2$ based on its own knowledge of $\mathsf{msg} \oplus x$, $H_{\mathrm{ec}}(r|_{\mathcal{I}})$ and $\mathrm{synd}(r|_{\mathcal{I}})$.

Let G'' be a game like G' except that, in G'', instead of $\mathcal{A}_1'$ being given $\Gamma(r^\theta)$, m EPR pairs are prepared, yielding quantum systems A and B, of which the adversary $\mathcal{A}_1'$ is given B. System A is measured in basis θ yielding a string r, and $\mathcal{A}_1'$ then computes

$$\Gamma(y)_D \otimes \rho_S' \otimes \rho_{T'} \leftarrow A_1'(\rho_B \otimes \rho_S).\qquad(95)$$

We show that, due to the measurement of system A, adversary $\mathcal{A}_1'$ receives $\Gamma(r^\theta)$, where r is uniformly random. The post-measurement state, conditioned on the measurement of system A yielding outcome r, will be equivalent to

$$|\psi_r\rangle = \left(\mathsf{H}^\theta\, \Gamma(r)\, \mathsf{H}^\theta \otimes 1_m\right)|\mathrm{EPR}^m\rangle\qquad(96)$$

$$= \left(\mathsf{H}^\theta \otimes 1_m\right)(\Gamma(r) \otimes 1_m)\left(1_m \otimes \mathsf{H}^\theta\right)|\mathrm{EPR}^m\rangle\qquad(97)$$

$$= \sum_{\tilde{r} \in \{0,1\}^m} \frac{1}{2^{m/2}}\left(\mathsf{H}^\theta\, \Gamma(r)|\tilde{r}\rangle\right)\left(\mathsf{H}^\theta\, |\tilde{r}\rangle\right)\qquad(98)$$

$$= \frac{1}{2^{m/2}}\left(\mathsf{H}^\theta\, |r\rangle\right)\left(\mathsf{H}^\theta\, |r\rangle\right)\qquad(99)$$

$$= \frac{1}{2^{m/2}}|r^\theta\rangle \otimes |r^\theta\rangle,\qquad(100)$$

which occurs with probability $\||\psi_r\rangle\|^2 = \frac{1}{2^m}$. Therefore, the advantage in G' is the same as the advantage in G''.

Let G''' be a game like G'' except that, in G''', instead of system A being measured before running $\mathcal{A}'_1$, system A is measured after running $\mathcal{A}'_1$. Then the advantage is unchanged because the measurement and $\mathcal{A}_1$ act on distinct systems, and therefore commute.

We note that G''' is like Game 2 except that, in the latter game, Bob is the party that prepares the state. Since allowing Bob to select the initial state can only increase the advantage, we get that $\mathsf{Adv}(G''') \leq \mathsf{Adv}(Game\ 2)$. This concludes the proof. □

Theorem 3. *Scheme 1 is certified deletion secure.*

Proof. Through a combination of Corollary 2 and Proposition 7, we arrive at the following inequality:

$$|\Pr[b' = 1 \wedge ok = 1 \mid Game\ 2(0)] - \Pr[b' = 1 \wedge ok = 1 \mid Game\ 1(1)]| \quad (101)$$

$$\leq 2\left(\frac{1}{2}\sqrt{2^{-s(1-h(\delta+\nu))+n}} + 2\epsilon(\nu)\right). \quad (102)$$

Since Game 1 is a certified deletion attack for Scheme 1, we see that Scheme 1 is η-certified deletion secure for

$$\eta(\lambda) = 2\left(\frac{1}{2}\sqrt{2^{-(s(\lambda))(1-h(\delta+\nu))+n}} + 2\exp\left(\frac{-(s(\lambda))(k(\lambda))^2\nu^2}{(m(\lambda))((k(\lambda))+1)}\right)\right), \quad (103)$$

which is negligible for large enough functions s, k. □

Acknowledgments. We would like to thank Carl Miller for related discussions. We are grateful to the anonymous reviewers for help in improving this work. This work was supported by the U.S. Air Force Office of Scientific Research under award number FA9550- 17-1-0083, Canada's NSERC, an Ontario ERA, and the University of Ottawa's Research Chairs program.

References

1. Barnum, H., Crépeau, C., Gottesman, D., Smith, A., Tapp, A.: Authentication of quantum messages. In: FOCS 2002, pp. 449–485 (2002). https://doi.org/10.1109/SFCS.2002.1181969
2. Bennett, C.H., Brassard, G.: Quantum cryptography: public key distribution and coin tossing. In: International Conference on Computers, Systems and Signal Processing, pp. 175–179 (1984)
3. Broadbent, A., Lord, S.: Uncloneable quantum encryption via oracles. In: TQC 2020, pp. 4:1–4:22 (2020). https://doi.org/10.4230/LIPIcs.TQC.2020.4
4. Broadbent, A., Schaffner, C.: Quantum cryptography beyond quantum key distribution. Des. Codes Crypt. **78**(1), 351–382 (2015). https://doi.org/10.1007/s10623-015-0157-4

5. Canetti, R., Trachtenberg, A., Varia, M.: Anonymous collocation discovery: harnessing privacy to tame the coronavirus (2020). https://arxiv.org/abs/2003.13670
6. Carter, J.L., Wegman, M.N.: Universal classes of hash functions. J. Comp. Syst. Sci. **18**(2), 143–154 (1979). https://doi.org/10.1016/0022-0000(79)90044-8
7. Coiteux-Roy, X., Wolf, S.: Proving erasure. In: IEEE International Symposium on Information Theory, ISIT 2019 (2019). https://doi.org/10.1109/ISIT.2019.8849661
8. Dieks, D.: Communication by EPR devices. Phys. Lett. A **92**(6), 271–272 (1982). https://doi.org/10.1016/0375-9601(82)90084-6
9. Dupuis, F., Nielsen, J.B., Salvail, L.: Actively secure two-party evaluation of any quantum operation. In: CRYPTO 2012, pp. 794–811 (2012). https://doi.org/10. 1007/978-3-642-32009-5_46
10. Einstein, A., Podolsky, B., Rosen, N.: Can quantum-mechanical description of physical reality be considered complete? Phys. Rev. Lett. **47**(10), 777–780 (1935). https://doi.org/10.1103/physrev.47.777
11. Fu, H., Miller, C.A.: Local randomness: examples and application. Phys. Rev. A **97**(3), 032324 (2018). https://doi.org/10.1103/PhysRevA.97.032324
12. Garg, S., Goldwasser, S., Vasudevan, P.N.: Formalizing data deletion in the context of the right to be forgotten. CRYPTO 2020 (2020)
13. Garg, S., Yuen, H., Zhandry, M.: New security notions and feasibility results for authentication of quantum data. In: CRYPTO 2017, vol. 2, pp. 342–371 (2017). https://doi.org/10.1007/978-3-319-63715-0_12
14. Goldreich, O., Micali, S., Wigderson, A.: Proofs that yield nothing but their validity for all languages in NP have zero-knowledge proof systems. J. ACM **38**(3), 690–728 (1991). https://doi.org/10.1145/116825.116852
15. König, R., Renner, R., Schaffner, C.: The operational meaning of min-and max-entropy. IEEE Trans. Inform. Theo. **55**(9), 4337–4347 (2009). https://doi.org/10. 1109/TIT.2009.2025545
16. van Lint, J.H., van der Geer, G.: Introduction to Coding Theory and Algebraic Geometry. Birkhäuser, Basel (2012). https://doi.org/10.1007/978-3-0348-9286-5
17. Lo, H.K., Chau, H.F.: Unconditional security of quantum key distribution over arbitrarily long distances. Sci. **283**(5410), 2050–2056 (1999). https://doi.org/10. 1126/science.283.5410.2050
18. Nielsen, M.A., Chuang, I.L.: Quantum Computation and Quantum Information. Cambridge University Press, Cambridge (2000)
19. Park, J.L.: The concept of transition in quantum mechanics. Found. Phys. **1**(1), 23–33 (1970). https://doi.org/10.1007/BF00708652
20. Pfister, C., Lütkenhaus, N., Wehner, S., Coles, P.J.: Sifting attacks in finite-size quantum key distribution. N. J. Phys. **18**(5), 053001 (2016). https://doi.org/10. 1088/1367-2630/18/5/053001
21. Renner, R.: Security of quantum key distribution. Int. J. Quantum Inf. **06**(01), 1–127 (2005). https://doi.org/10.1142/S0219749908003256
22. Rényi, A.: On measures of entropy and information. In: Proceedings of the Fourth Berkeley Symposium on Mathematical Statistics and Probability, vol. 1, pp. 547–561 (1961)
23. Rivest, R.L., Shamir, A., Wagner, D.A.: Time-lock puzzles and timed-release crypto. Technical report, Massachusetts Institute of Technology (1996)
24. Serfling, R.J.: Probability inequalities for the sum in sampling without replacement. Ann. Statist. **2**(1), 39–48 (1974). https://doi.org/10.1214/aos/1176342611
25. Shor, P.W., Preskill, J.: Simple proof of security of the BB84 quantum key distribution protocol. Phys. Rev. Lett. **85**(2), 441–444 (2000). https://doi.org/10.1103/ physrevlett.85.441

26. The European parliament and the council of the European union: regulation (EU) 2016/679. Official J. Eur. Union L **119**, 1–88 (2016). https://eur-lex.europa.eu/eli/reg/2016/679/oj

27. Tomamichel, M.: A framework for non-asymptotic quantum information theory. Ph. D. thesis, ETH Zurich (2012). https://doi.org/10.3929/ethz-a-7356080

28. Tomamichel, M., Colbeck, R., Renner, R.: Duality between smooth min-and max-entropies. IEEE Trans. Inform. Theo. **56**(9), 4674–4681 (2010). https://doi.org/10.1109/TIT.2010.2054130

29. Tomamichel, M., Leverrier, A.: A largely self-contained and complete security proof for quantum key distribution. Quantum **1**, 14 (2017). https://doi.org/10.22331/q-2017-07-14-14

30. Tomamichel, M., Lim, C.C.W., Gisin, N., Renner, R.: Tight finite-key analysis for quantum cryptography. Nat. Comm. **3**, 634 (2012). https://doi.org/10.1038/ncomms1631

31. Tomamichel, M., Renner, R.: Uncertainty relation for smooth entropies. Phys. Rev. Lett. **106**(11) (2011). https://doi.org/10.1103/PhysRevLett.106.110506

32. Unruh, D.: Everlasting multi-party computation. In: CRYPTO 2013, pp. 380–397 (2013). https://doi.org/10.1007/978-3-642-40084-1_22

33. Unruh, D.: Revocable quantum timed-release encryption. In: EUROCRYPT 2014, pp. 129–146 (2014). https://doi.org/10.1007/978-3-642-55220-5_8

34. Wegman, M.N., Carter, J.L.: New hash functions and their use in authentication and set equality. J. Comp. Syst. Sci. **22**(3), 265–279 (1981). https://doi.org/10.1016/0022-0000(81)90033-7

35. Wiesner, S.: Conjugate coding. ACM SIGACT News **15**(1), 78–88 (1983). https://doi.org/10.1145/1008908.1008920

36. Wootters, W.K., Zurek, W.H.: A single quantum cannot be cloned. Nature **299**, 802–803 (1982). https://doi.org/10.1038/299802a0

Secure Quantum Extraction Protocols

Prabhanjan Ananth[1][✉] and Rolando L. La Placa[2]

[1] University of California, Santa Barbara, USA
prabhanjan@cs.ucsb.edu
[2] MIT, Cambridge, USA
rlaplaca@mit.edu

Abstract. Knowledge extraction, typically studied in the classical setting, is at the heart of several cryptographic protocols. The prospect of quantum computers forces us to revisit the concept of knowledge extraction in the presence of quantum adversaries.

We introduce the notion of secure quantum extraction protocols. A secure quantum extraction protocol for an NP relation $\mathcal{R}$ is a classical interactive protocol between a sender and a receiver, where the sender gets as input the instance $\mathbf{y}$ and witness $\mathbf{w}$ while the receiver only gets the instance $\mathbf{y}$ as input. There are two properties associated with a secure quantum extraction protocol: (a) *Extractability*: for any efficient quantum polynomial-time (QPT) adversarial sender, there exists a QPT extractor that can extract a witness $\mathbf{w}'$ such that $(\mathbf{y}, \mathbf{w}') \in \mathcal{R}$ and, (b) *Zero-Knowledge*: a malicious receiver, interacting with the sender, should not be able to learn any information about $\mathbf{w}$.

We study and construct two flavors of secure quantum extraction protocols.
- **Security against QPT malicious receivers**: First we consider the setting when the malicious receiver is a QPT adversary. In this setting, we construct a secure quantum extraction protocol for NP assuming the existence of quantum fully homomorphic encryption satisfying some mild properties (already satisfied by existing constructions [Mahadev, FOCS'18, Brakerski CRYPTO'18]) and quantum hardness of learning with errors. The novelty of our construction is a new non-black-box technique in the quantum setting. All previous extraction techniques in the quantum setting were solely based on quantum rewinding.
- **Security against classical PPT malicious receivers**: We also consider the setting when the malicious receiver is a classical probabilistic polynomial time (PPT) adversary. In this setting, we construct a secure quantum extraction protocol for NP solely based on the quantum hardness of learning with errors. Furthermore, our construction satisfies *quantum-lasting security*: a malicious receiver cannot later, long after the protocol has been executed, use a quantum computer to extract a valid witness from the transcript of the protocol.

Both the above extraction protocols are *constant round* protocols.

We present an application of secure quantum extraction protocols to zero-knowledge (ZK). Assuming quantum hardness of learning with

© International Association for Cryptologic Research 2020
R. Pass and K. Pietrzak (Eds.): TCC 2020, LNCS 12552, pp. 123–152, 2020.
https://doi.org/10.1007/978-3-030-64381-2_5

errors, we present the first construction of ZK argument systems for NP in constant rounds based on the quantum hardness of learning with errors with: (a) zero-knowledge against QPT malicious verifiers and, (b) soundness against classical PPT adversaries. Moreover, our construction satisfies the stronger (quantum) auxiliary-input zero knowledge property and thus can be composed with other protocols secure against quantum adversaries.

1   Introduction

Knowledge extraction is a quintessential concept employed to argue the security of classical zero-knowledge systems and secure two-party and multi-party computation protocols. The seminal work of Feige, Lapidot and Shamir [19] shows how to leverage knowledge extraction to construct zero-knowledge protocols. The ideal world-real world paradigm necessarily requires the simulator to be able to extract the inputs of the adversaries to argue the security of secure computation protocols.

Typically, knowledge extraction is formalized by defining a knowledge extractor that given access to the adversarial machine, outputs the input of the adversary. The prototypical extraction technique employed in several cryptographic protocols is rewinding. In the rewinding technique, the extractor, with oracle access to the adversary, rewinds the adversary to a previous state to obtain more than one protocol transcript which in turn gives the ability to the extractor to extract from the adversary. While rewinding has proven to be quite powerful, it has several limitations [22]. Over the years, cryptographers have proposed novel extraction techniques to circumvent the barriers of rewinding. Each time a new extraction technique was invented, it has advanced the field of zero-knowledge and secure computation. As an example, the breakthrough work of Barak [7] proposed a non-black-box extraction technique – where the extractor crucially uses the code of the verifier for extraction – and used this to obtain the first feasibility result on constant-round public-coin zero-knowledge argument system for NP. Another example is the work of Pass [35] who introduced the technique of super-polynomial time extraction and presented the first feasibility result on 2-round concurrent ZK argument system albeit under a weaker simulation definition.

Extracting from Quantum Adversaries. The prospect of quantum computers introduces new challenges in the design of zero-knowledge and secure computation protocols. As a starting step towards designing these protocols, we need to address the challenge of knowledge extraction against quantum adversaries. So far, the only technique used to extract from quantum adversaries is quantum rewinding [42], which has already been studied by a few works [3,27,38,40,42] in the context of quantum zero-knowledge protocols.

Rewinding a quantum adversary, unlike its classical counterpart, turns out to be tricky due to two reasons, as stated in Watrous [42]: firstly, intermediate quantum states of the adversary cannot be copied (due to the universal no-cloning theorem) and secondly, if the adversary performs some measurements then this adversary cannot be rewound since measurements in general are irreversible processes. As a result, the existing quantum rewinding techniques tend to be "oblivious" [38], to rewind the adversary back to an earlier point, the extraction should necessarily forget all the information it has learnt from that point onwards. As a result of these subtle issues, the analysis of quantum rewinding turns out to be quite involved making it difficult to use it in the security proofs. Moreover, existing quantum rewinding techniques [38,42] pose a bottleneck towards achieving a constant round extraction technique; we will touch upon this later.

In order to advance the progress of constructing quantum-secure (or post-quantum) cryptographic protocols, it is necessary that we look beyond quantum rewinding and explore new quantum extraction techniques.

1.1 Results

We introduce and study new techniques that enable us to extract from quantum adversaries.

Our Notion: Secure Quantum Extraction Protocols. We formalize this by first introducing the notion of secure quantum extraction protocols. This is a classical interactive protocol between a sender and a receiver and is associated with a NP relation. The sender has an NP instance and a witness while the receiver only gets the NP instance. In terms of properties, we require the following to hold:

- *Extractability:* An extractor, implemented as a quantum polynomial time algorithm, can extract a valid witness from an adversarial sender. We model the adversarial sender as a quantum polynomial time algorithm that follows the protocol but is allowed to choose its randomness; in the classical setting, this is termed as *semi-malicious* and we call this semi-malicious quantum adversaries[1].

  We also require *indistinguishability of extraction:* that is, the adversarial sender cannot distinguish whether it's interacting with the honest receiver or an extractor. In applications, this property is used to argue that the adversary cannot distinguish whether it's interacting with the honest party or the simulator.
- *Zero-Knowledge:* A malicious receiver should not be able to extract a valid witness after interacting with the sender. The malicious receiver can either be a classical probabilistic polynomial time algorithm or a quantum polynomial time algorithm. Correspondingly, there are two notions of quantum extraction protocols we study: quantum extraction protocols secure against quantum adversarial receivers (qQEXT) and quantum extraction protocols secure against classical adversarial receivers (cQEXT).

---

[1] In the literature, this type of semi-malicious adversaries are also referred to as *explainable* adveraries.

There are two reasons why we only study extraction against semi-malicious adversaries, instead of malicious adversaries (who can arbitrarily deviate from the protocol): first, even extracting from semi-malicious adversaries turns out to be challenging and we view this as a first step towards extraction from malicious adversaries and second, in the classical setting, there are works that show how to leverage extraction from semi-malicious adversaries to achieve zero-knowledge protocols [9,11] or secure two-party computation protocols [4].

Quantum extraction protocols are interesting even if we only consider classical adversaries, as they present a new method for proving zero-knowledge. For instance, to demonstrate zero-knowledge, we need to demonstrate a simulator that has a computational capability that a malicious prover doesn't have. Allowing quantum simulators in the classical setting [28] is another way to achieve this asymmetry between the power of the simulator and the adversary besides the few mentioned before (rewinding, superpolynomial, or non-black-box). Furthermore, quantum simulators capture the notion of knowledge that could be learnt if a malicious verifier had access to a quantum computer.

Quantum-Lasting Security. A potential concern regarding the security of cQEXT protocols is that the classical malicious receiver participating in the cQEXT protocol could later, long after the protocol has been executed, use a quantum computer to learn the witness of the sender from the transcript of the protocol and its own private state. For instance, the transcript could contain an ElGamal encryption of the witness of the sender; while a malicious classical receiver cannot break it, after the protocol is completed, it could later use a quantum computer to learn the witness. This is especially interesting in the event (full-fledged) quantum computers might become available in the future. First introduced by Unruh [39], we study the concept of quantum-lasting security; any quantum polynomial time (QPT) adversary given the transcript and the private state of the malicious receiver, should not be able to learn the witness of the sender. Our construction will satisfy this security notion and thus our protocol is resilient against the possibility of quantum computers being accessible in the future.

Result #1: Constant Round qQEXT protocols. We show the following result.

Theorem 1 (Informal). *Assuming quantum hardness of learning with errors and a quantum fully homomorphic encryption scheme (for arbitrary poly-time computations)[2], satisfying, (1) perfect correctness for classical messages and, (2) ciphertexts of poly-sized classical messages have a poly-sized classical description, there exists a constant round quantum extraction protocol secure against quantum poly-time receivers.*

We clarify what we mean by perfect correctness. For every public key, every valid fresh ciphertext of a classical message can always be decrypted correctly. Moreover, we require that for every valid fresh ciphertext, of a classical message, the evaluated ciphertext can be decrypted correctly with probability negligibly

---

[2] As against leveled quantum FHE, which can be based on quantum hardness of LWE.

close to 1. We note that the works of [14,31] give candidates for quantum fully homomorphic encryption schemes satisfying both the above properties.

En route to proving the above theorem, we introduce a new non black extraction technique in the quantum setting building upon a *classical* non-black extraction technique of [11]. We view identifying the appropriate classical non-black-box technique to also be a contribution of our work. A priori it should not be clear whether classical non-black-box techniques are useful in constructing their quantum analogues. For instance, it is unclear how to utilize the well known non-black-box technique of Barak [7]; at a high level, the idea of Barak [7] is to commit to the code of the verifier and then prove using a succinct argument system that either the instance is in the language or it has the code of the verifier. In our setting, the verifier is a quantum circuit which means that we would require succinct arguments for quantum computations which we currently don't know how to achieve.

Non-black-box extraction overcomes the disadvantage quantum rewinding poses in achieving constant round extraction; the quantum rewinding employed by [42] requires polynomially many rounds (due to sequential repetition) or constant rounds with non-negligible gap between extraction and verification error [38].

This technique was concurrently developed by Bitansky and Shmueli [12] (see "Comparison with [12]" paragraph) and they critically relied upon this to construct a constant-round zero-knowledge argument system for NP and QMA, thus resolving a long-standing open problem in the round complexity of quantum zero-knowledge.

Subsequent Work. Many followup works have used the non-black-box extraction technique we introduce in this work to resolve other open problems in quantum cryptography. For instance, our technique was adopted to prove that quantum copy-protection is impossible [6]; resolving a problem that was open for more than a decade. It was also used to prove that quantum VBB for classical circuits is impossible [2,6]. In yet another exciting follow up work, this technique was developed further to achieve the first constant round post-quantum secure MPC protocol [1].

Result #2: Constant Round cQEXT protocols. We also present a construction of quantum extraction protocols secure against classical adversaries (cQEXT). This result is incomparable to the above result; on one hand, it is a weaker setting but on the other hand, the security of this construction can solely be based on the hardness of learning with errors.

Theorem 2 (Informal). *Assuming quantum hardness of learning with errors, there exists a constant round quantum extraction protocol secure against classical PPT adversaries and satisfying quantum-lasting security.*

Our main insight is to turn the "test of quantumness" protocol introduced in [15] into a quantum extraction protocol using cryptographic tools. In fact, our techniques are general enough that they might be useful to turn any protocol that can verify a quantum computer versus a classical computer into a quantum extraction protocol secure against classical adversaries; the transformation additionally assumes quantum hardness of learning with errors. Our work presents a new avenue for using "test of quantumness" protocols beyond using them just to test whether the server is quantum or not.

We note that it is conceivable to construct "test of quantumness" protocols from DDH (or any other quantum-insecure assumption). The security of the resulting extraction protocol would then be based on DDH and quantum hardness of learning with errors – the latter needed to argue quantum-lasting security. However, the security of our protocol is solely based on the quantum hardness of learning with errors.

Result #3: Constant Round QZK for NP with Classical Soundness. As an application, we show how to construct constant quantum zero-knowledge argument systems secure against quantum verifiers based on quantum hardness of learning with errors; however, the soundness is still against classical PPT adversaries.

Moreover, our protocol satisfies zero-knowledge against quantum verifiers with arbitrary quantum auxiliary state. Such protocols are also called auxiliary-input zero-knowledge protocols [24] and are necessary for composition. Specifically, our ZK protocol can be composed with other protocols to yield new protocols satisfying quantum security.

Theorem 3 (Constant Round Quantum ZK with Classical Soundness; Informal). *Assuming quantum hardness of learning with errors, there exists a constant round black box quantum zero-knowledge system with negligible soundness against classical PPT algorithms. Moreover, our protocol satisfies (quantum) auxiliary-input zero-knowledge property.*

A desirable property from a QZK protocol is if the verifier is classical then the simulator is also classical. While our protocol doesn't immediately satisfy this property, we show, nonetheless, that there is a simple transformation that converts into another QZK protocol that has this desirable property.

Application: Authorization with Quantum Cloud. Suppose Eva wants to convince the cloud services offered by some company that she has the authorization to access a document residing in the cloud. Since the authorization information could leak sensitive information about Eva, she would rather use a zero-knowlede protocol to prove to the cloud that she has the appropriate authorization. While we currently don't have scalable implementations of quantum computers, this could change in the future when organizations (e.g. governments, IBM, Microsoft, etc.) could be the first ones to develop a quantum computer. They could in principle then use this to break the zero-knowledge property of Eva's protocol and learn sensitive information about her. In this case, it suffices to use a QZK protocol but only requiring soundness against malicious classical users; in the nearby future, it is reasonable to assume that even if organizations with enough resources get to develop full-fledged quantum computers, it'll take a while before everyday users will have access to one.

1.2 Related Work

Quantum Rewinding. Watrous [42] introduced the quantum analogue of the rewinding technique. Later, Unruh [38] introduced yet another notion of quantum rewinding with the purpose of constructing quantum zero-knowledge proofs of knowledge. Unruh's rewinding does have extractability, but it requires that the underlying protocol to satisfy *strict soundness*. Furthermore, the probability that the extractor succeeds is not negligibly close to 1. The work of [3] shows that relative to an oracle, many classical zero-knowledge protocols are quantum insecure, and that the strict soundness condition from [38] is necessary in order for a sigma protocol to be a quantum proofs of knowledge.

Quantum and Classical Zero-Knowledge. Zero-knowledge against quantum adversaries was first studied by Watrous [42]. He showed how the GMW protocol [23] for graph 3-colorability is still zero-knowledge against quantum verifiers. Other works [18,26,27,29,33,38] have extended the study of classical protocols that are quantum zero-knowledge, and more recently, Broadbent et al. [17] extended the notion of zero-knowledge to QMA languages. By using ideas from [32] to classically verify quantum computation, the protocol in [17] was adapted to obtained classical argument systems for quantum computation in [41]. All known protocols, with non-negligible soundness error, take non-constant rounds.

On the other hand, zero knowledge proof and argument systems have been extensively studied in classical cryptography. In particular, a series of recent works [8–11] resolved the round complexity of zero knowledge argument systems.

Comparison with [12]. In a recent exciting work, [12] construct a constant round QZK with soundness against quantum adversaries for NP and QMA.

- The non-black-box techniques used in their work was concurrently developed and are similar to the techniques used in our QEXT protocol secure against quantum receivers[3].
- Subsequent to their posting, using completely different techniques, we developed QEXT secure against classical receivers and used it to build a constant round QZK system with classical soundness. There are a few crucial differences between our QZK argument system and theirs:
  1. Our result is based on quantum hardness of learning with errors while their result is based on the existence of quantum fully homomorphic encryption for arbitrary polynomial computations and quantum hardness of learning with errors.
  2. The soundness of their argument system is against quantum polynomial time algorithms while ours is only against classical PPT adversaries.

---

[3] A copy of our QEXT protocol secure against quantum receivers was privately communicated to the authors of [12] on the day of their public posting and our paper was posted online in about two weeks from then [5].

1.3   Quantum Extraction with Security Against Classical Receivers: Overview

We start with the overview of quantum extraction protocols with security against classical receivers.

Starting Point: Noisy Trapdoor Claw-Free Functions. Our main idea is to turn the "test of quantumness" from [15] into an extraction protocol. Our starting point is a noisy trapdoor claw-free function (NTCF) family [15,31,32], parameterized by key space $\mathcal{K}$, input domain $\mathcal{X}$ and output domain $\mathcal{Y}$. Using a key $\mathbf{k} \in \mathcal{K}$, NTCFs allows for computing the functions, denoted by $f_{\mathbf{k},0}(x) \in \mathcal{Y}$ and $f_{\mathbf{k},1}(x) \in \mathcal{Y}$ [4], where $x \in \mathcal{X}$. Using a trapdoor td associated with a key $\mathbf{k}$, any y in the support of $f_{\mathbf{k},b}(x)$, can be efficiently inverted to obtain x. Moreover, there are "claw" pairs (x_0, x_1) such that $f_{\mathbf{k},0}(x_0) = f_{\mathbf{k},1}(x_1)$. Roughly speaking, the security property states that it is computationally hard even for a quantum computer to simultaneously produce $y \in \mathcal{Y}$, values (b, x_b) and (d, u) such that $f_{\mathbf{k},b}(x_b) = y$ and $\langle d, J(x_0) \oplus J(x_1) \rangle = u$, where $J(\cdot)$ is an efficienctly computable injective function mapping $\mathcal{X}$ into bit strings. What makes this primitive interesting is its quantum capability that we will discuss when we recall below the test of [15].

Test of Quantumness [15]. Using NTCFs, [15] devised the following test [5]:

– The classical client, who wants to test whether the server it's interacting with is quantum or classical, first generates a key $\mathbf{k}$ along with a trapdoor td associated with a noisy trapdoor claw-free function (NTCF) family. It sends $\mathbf{k}$ to the server.
– The server responds back with $y \in \mathcal{Y}$.
– The classical client then sends a **challenge** bit $\mathbf{a}$ to the server.
– If $\mathbf{a} = 0$, the server sends a pre-image x_b along with bit b such that $f_{\mathbf{k},b}(x_b) = y$. If $\mathbf{a} = 1$, the server sends a vector d along with a bit u satisfying the condition $\langle d, J(x_0) \oplus J(x_1) \rangle = u$, where x_0, x_1 are such that $f_{\mathbf{k},0}(x_0) = f_{\mathbf{k},1}(x_1) = y$.

The client can check if the message sent by the server is either a valid pre-image or a valid d that is correlated with respect to both the pre-images.

Intuitively, since the (classical) server does not know, at the point when it sends y, whether it will be queried for (b, x_b) or (d, u), by the security of NTCFs, it can only answer one of the queries. While the quantum capability of NTCFs allows for a quantum server to maintain a superposition of a claw at the time it sent y and depending on the query made by the verifier it can then perform the appropriate quantum operations to answer the client; thus it will always pass the test.

---

[4] The efficient implementation of f only approximately computes f and we denote this by f'. We ignore this detail for now.

[5] As written, this test doesn't have negligible soundness but we can achieve negligible soundness by parallel repetition.

From Test of Quantumness to Extraction. A natural attempt to achieve extraction is the following: the sender takes the role of the client and the receiver takes the role of the server and if the test passes, the sender sends the witness to the receiver. We sketch this attempt below.

- Sender on input instance-witness pair $(\mathbf{y}, \mathbf{w})$ and receiver on input instance $\mathbf{y}$ run a "test of quantumness" protocol where the receiver (taking the role of the server) needs to convince the sender (taking the role of the classical client) that it is a quantum computer.
- If the receiver succeeds in the "test of quantumness" protocol then the sender $\mathbf{w}$, else it aborts.

Note that a quantum extractor can indeed succeed in the test of quantumness protocol and hence, it would receive $\mathbf{w}$ while a malicious classical adversary will not.

However, the above solution is not good enough for us. It does not satisfy indistinguishability of extraction: the sender can detect whether it's interacting with a quantum extractor or an honest receiver.

Achieving Indistinguishability of Extraction. To ensure indistinguishability of extraction, we rely upon a tool called secure function evaluation [9,21] that satisfies quantum security. A secure function evaluation (SFE) allows for two parties P_1 and P_2 to securely compute a function on their inputs in a such a way that only one of the parties, say P_2, receives the output of the function. In terms of security, we require that: (i) P_2 doesn't get information about P_1's input beyond the output of the function and, (ii) P_1 doesn't get any information about P_2's input (in fact, even the output of the protocol is hidden from P_1).

The hope is that by combining SFE and test of quantumness protocol, we can guarantee that a quantum extractor can still recover the witness by passing the test of quantumness as before but the sender doesn't even know whether the receiver passed or not. To implement this, we assume a structural property from the underlying test of quantumness protocol: until the final message of the protocol, the client cannot distinguish whether it's talking to a quantum server or a classical server. This structural property is satisfied by the test of quantumness protocol [15] sketched above.

Using this structural property and SFE, here is another attempt to construct a quantum extraction protocol: let the test of quantumness protocol be a k-round protocol.

- Sender on input instance-witness pair $(\mathbf{y}, \mathbf{w})$ and receiver on input instance $\mathbf{y}$ run the first $(k - 1)$ rounds of the test of quantumness protocol where the receiver (taking the role of the server) needs to convince the sender (taking the role of the receiver) that it can perform quantum computations.

- Sender and receiver then run a SFE protocol for the following functionality G: it takes as input $\mathbf{w}$ and the first $(k-1)$ rounds of the test of quantumness protocol from the sender, the kth round message from the receiver[6] and outputs $\mathbf{w}$ if indeed the test passed, otherwise output $\perp$. Sender will take the role of P_1 and the receiver will take the role of P_2 and thus, only the receiver will receive the output of G.

Note that the security of SFE guarantees that the output of the protocol is hidden from the sender and moreover, the first $(k-1)$ messages of the test of quantumness protocol doesn't reveal the information about whether the receiver is a quantum computer or not. These two properties ensure the sender doesn't know whether the receiver passed the test or not. Furthermore, the quantum extractor still succeeds in extracting the witness $\mathbf{w}$ since it passes the test.

The only remaining property to prove is zero-knowledge.

Challenges in Proving Zero-Knowledge. How do we ensure that a malicious classical receiver was not able to extract the witness? The hope would be to invoke the soundness of the test of quantumness protocol to argue this. However, to do this, we need all the k messages of the test of quantumness protocol.

To understand this better, let us recall how the soundness of the test of quantumness works: the client sends a challenge bit $\mathbf{a} = 0$ to the server who responds back with (b, x_b), then the client rewinds the server and instead sends the challenge bit $\mathbf{a} = 1$ and it receives (d, u): this contradicts the security of NTCFs since a classical PPT adversary cannot simultaneously produce both a valid pre-image (b, x_b) and a valid correlation vector along with the prediction bit (d, u).

Since the last message is fed into the secure function evaluation protocol and inaccessible to the simulator, we cannot use this rewinding strategy to prove the zero-knowledge of the extraction protocol.

Final Template: Zero-Knowledge via Extractable Commitments [36,37]. To overcome this barrier, we force the receiver to commit, using an extractable commitment scheme, to the kth round of the test of quantumness protocol before the SFE protocol begins. An extractable commitment scheme is one where there is an extractor who can extract an input x being committed from the party committing to x. Armed with this tool, we give an overview of our construction below.

- Sender on input instance-witness pair $(\mathbf{y}, \mathbf{w})$ and receiver on input instance $\mathbf{y}$ run the first $(k-1)$ rounds of the test of quantumness protocol where the receiver (taking the role of the server) needs to convince the sender (taking the role of the receiver) that it can perform quantum computations.

---

[6] It follows without loss of generality that the server (and thus, the receiver of the quantum extraction protocol) computes the final message of the test of quantumness protocol.

- The kth round of the test of quantumness protocol is then committed by the receiver, call it **c**, using the extractable commitment scheme[7].
- Finally, the sender and the receiver then run a SFE protocol for the following functionality G: it takes as input **w** and the first $(k-1)$ rounds of the test of quantumness protocol from the sender, the decommitment of **c** from the receiver and outputs **w** if indeed the test passed, otherwise output $\perp$. Sender will take the role of P_1 and the receiver will take the role of P_2 and thus, only the receiver will receive the output of G.

Let us remark about zero-knowledge since we have already touched upon the other properties earlier. To argue zero-knowledge, construct a simulator that interacts honestly with the malicious receiver until the point the extraction protocol is run. Then, the simulator runs the extractor of the commitment scheme to extract the final message of the test of quantumness protocol. It then rewinds the test of quantumness protocol to the point where the simulator sends a different challenge bit (see the informal description of [15] given before) and then runs the extractor of the commitment scheme once again to extract the kth round message of the test of quantumness protocol. Recall that having final round messages corresponding to two different challenge bits is sufficient to break the security of NTCFs; the zero-knowledge property then follows.

A couple of remarks about our simulator. Firstly, the reason why our simulator is able to rewind the adversary is because the adversary is a classical PPT algorithm. Secondly, our simulator performs *double rewinding* – not only does the extractor of the commitment scheme perform rewinding but also the test of quantumness protocol is rewound.

1.4 Constant Round QZK Argument Systems with Classical Soundness

We show how to use the above quantum extraction protocol secure against classical receivers (cQEXT) to construct an interactive argument system satisfying classical soundness and quantum ZK.

From Quantum Extraction to Quantum Zero-Knowledge. As a starting point, we consider the quantum analogue of the seminal FLS technique [19] to transform a quantum extraction protocol into a quantum ZK protocol. A first attempt to construct quantum ZK is as follows: let the input to the prover be instance **y** and witness **w** while the input to the verifier is **y**.

- The verifier commits to some trapdoor td. Call the commitment **c** and the corresponding decommitment **d**.
- The prover and verifier then execute a quantum extraction protocol with the verifier playing the role of the sender, on input $(\mathbf{c}, \mathbf{d})$, while the prover plays the role of the receiver on input **c**.

---

[7] In the technical sections, we use a specific construction of extractable commitment scheme by [36,37] since we additionally require security against quantum adversaries.

- The prover and the verifier then run a witness-indistinguishable protocol where the prover convinces the verifier that either y belongs to the language or it knows td.

At first sight, it might seem that the above template should already give us the result we want; unfortunately, the above template is insufficient. The verifier could behave maliciously in the quantum extraction protocol but the quantum extraction protocol only guarantees security against semi-malicious senders. Hence, we need an additional mechanism to protect against malicious receivers. Of course, we require witness-indistinguishability to hold against quantum verifiers and we do know candidates satisfying this assuming quantum hardness of learning with errors [13,30].

Handling Malicious Behavior in QEXT. To check that the verifier behaved honestly in the quantum extraction protocol, we ask the verifier to reveal the inputs and random coins used in the quantum extraction protocol. At this point, the prover can check if the verifier behaved honestly or not. Of course, this would then violate soundness: the malicious prover upon receiving the random coins from the verifier can then recover td and then use this to falsely convince the verifier to accept its proof. We overcome this by forcing the prover to commit (we again use the extractable commitment scheme of [36]) to some string td' just before the verifier reveals the inputs and random coins used in the quantum extraction protocol. Then we force the prover to use the committed td' in the witness-indistinguishable protocol; the prover does not gain any advantage upon seeing the coins of the verifier and thus, ensuring soundness.

One aspect we didn't address so far is the aborting issue of the verifier: if the verifier aborts in the quantum extraction protocol, the simulator still needs to produce a transcript indistinguishable from that of the honest prover. Luckily for us, the quantum extraction protocol we constructed before already allows for simulatability of aborting adversaries.

To summarise, our ZK protocol consists of the following steps: (i) first, the prover and the verifier run the quantum extraction protocol, (ii) next the prover commits to a string td' using [36], (iii) the verifier then reveals the random coins used in the extraction protocol and, (iv) finally, the prover and the verifier run a quantum WI protocol where the prover convinces the verifier that it either knows a trapdoor td' or that y is a YES instance.

1.5   Quantum Extraction with Security Against Quantum Receivers: Overview

We show how to construct extraction protocols where we prove security against quantum receivers. At first sight, it might seem that quantum extraction and quantum zero-knowledge properties are contradictory since the extractor has the same computational resources as the malicious receiver. However, we provide more power to the extractor by giving the extractor non-black-box access to the semi-malicious sender. There is a rich literature on non-black-box techniques in the classical setting starting with the work of [7].

Quantum Extraction via Circular **In***security of QFHE.* The main tool we employ in our protocol is a fully homomorphic encryption qFHE scheme[8] that allows for public homomorphic evaluation of quantum circuits. Typically, we require a fully homomorphic encryption scheme to satisfy semantic security. However, for the current discussion, we require that qFHE to satisfy a stronger security property called 2-circular **in**security:

> Given qFHE.Enc(PK$_1$, SK_2) (i.e., encryption of SK_2 under PK$_1$), qFHE.Enc(PK_2, SK$_1$), where (PK$_1$, SK$_1$) and (PK_2, SK_2) are independently generated public key-secret key pairs, we can efficiently recover SK$_1$ and SK_2.

Later, we show how to get rid of 2-circular **in**security property by using lockable obfuscation [25,43]. Here is our first attempt to construct the extraction protocol:

- The sender, on input instance **y** and witness **w**, sends three ciphertexts: CT$_1$ ← qFHE.Enc(PK$_1$, td), CT$_2$ ← qFHE.Enc(PK$_1$, **w**) and CT$_3$ ← qFHE.Enc(PK_2, SK$_1$).
- The receiver sends td$'$.
- If td$'$ = td then the sender sends SK_2.

A quantum extractor with non-black-box access to the private (quantum) state of the semi-malicious sender S does the following:

- It first encrypts the private (quantum) state of S under public key PK$_1$.
- Here is our main insight: the extractor can homomorphically evaluate the next message function of S on CT$_1$ and the encrypted state of S. The result is CT$_1^*$ = qFHE.Enc(PK$_1$, S(td)). But note that S(td) is nothing but SK_2; note that S upon receiving td$'$ = td outputs SK_2. Thus, we have CT$_1^*$ = qFHE.Enc(PK$_1$, SK_2).
- Now, the extractor has both CT$_3$ = qFHE.Enc(PK_2, SK$_1$) and CT$_1^*$ = qFHE.Enc(PK$_1$, SK_2). It can then use the circular **in**security of qFHE to recover SK$_1$, SK_2.
- Finally, it decrypts CT$_2$ to obtain the witness **w**!

The correctness of extraction alone is not sufficient; we need to argue that the sender cannot distinguish whether it's interacting with the honest receiver or the extractor. This is not true in our protocol since the extractor will always compute the next message function of S on td$'$ = td whereas an honest receiver will send td$'$ = td only with negligible probability.

Indistinguishability of Extraction: SFE Strikes Again. We already encountered a similar issue when we were designing extraction protocols with security against classical receivers and the tool we used to solve that issue was secure function evaluation (SFE); we will use the same tool here as well.

Using SFE, we make another attempt at designing the quantum extraction protocol.

---

[8] Recall that a classical FHE scheme [16,20] allows for publicly evaluating an encryption of a message x using a circuit C to obtain an encryption of $C(x)$.

- The sender, on input instance $\mathbf{y}$ and witness $\mathbf{w}$, sends three ciphertexts: $\mathsf{CT}_1 \leftarrow \mathsf{qFHE.Enc}(\mathsf{PK}_1, \mathsf{td})$, $\mathsf{CT}_2 \leftarrow \mathsf{qFHE.Enc}(\mathsf{PK}_1, \mathbf{w})$ and $\mathsf{CT}_3 \leftarrow \mathsf{qFHE.Enc}(PK_2, \mathsf{SK}_1)$.
- The sender and the receiver executes a secure two-party computation protocol, where the receiver feeds td' and the sender feeds in $(\mathsf{td}, \mathbf{w})$. After the protocol finishes, the receiver recovers $\mathbf{w}$ if $\mathsf{td}' = \mathsf{td}$, else it recovers $\bot$. The sender doesn't receive any output.

The above template guarantees indistinguishability of extraction property[9].

We next focus on zero-knowledge. To do this, we need to argue that the td' input by the malicious receiver can never be equal to td. One might falsely conclude that the semantic security of qFHE would imply that td is hidden from the sender and hence the argument follows. This is not necessarily true; the malicious receiver might be able to "maul" the ciphertext CT_1 into the messages of the secure function evaluation protocol in such a way that the implicit input committed by the receiver is td'. We need to devise a mechanism to prevent against such mauling attacks.

Preventing Mauling Attacks. We prevent the mauling attacks by forcing the receiver to commit to random strings $(r_1, \ldots, r_\ell)$ in the first round, where $|\mathsf{td}| = \ell$, even before it receives the ciphertexts $(\mathsf{CT}_1, \mathsf{CT}_2, \mathsf{CT}_3)$ from the sender. Once it receives the ciphertexts, the receiver is supposed to commit to every bit of the trapdoor using the randomness $r_1, \ldots, r_\ell$; that is, the ith bit of td is committed using r_i.

Using this mechanism, we can then provably show that if the receiver was able to successfully maul the qFHE ciphertext then it violates the semantic security of qFHE using a non-uniform adversary.

Replacing Circular Insecurity with Lockable Obfuscation [25,43]. While the above protocol is a candidate for quantum extraction protocol secure against quantum receivers; it is still unsatisfactory since we assume a quantum FHE scheme satisfying 2-circular insecurity. We show how to replace 2-circular insecure QFHE with *any* QFHE scheme (satisfying some mild properties already satisfied by existing candidates) and lockable obfuscation for classical circuits. A lockable obfuscation scheme is an obfuscation scheme for a specific class of functionalities called compute-and-compare functionalities; a compute-and-compare functionality is parameterized by C, α (lock), β such that on input x, it outputs β if $C(x) = \alpha$. As long as α is sampled uniformly at random and independently of C, lockable obfuscation completely hides the circuit C, α and β. The idea to replace 2-circular insecure QFHE with lockable obfuscation[10] is as follows:

---

[9] There is a subtle point here that we didn't address: the transcript generated by the extractor is encrypted under qFHE. But after recovering the secret keys, the extractor could decrypt the encrypted transcript.

[10] It shouldn't be too surprising that lockable obfuscation can be used to replace circular insecurity since one of the applications [25,43] of lockable obfuscation was to demonstrate counter-examples for circular security.

obfuscate the circuit, with secret key SK_2, ciphertext qFHE.Enc(SK_2, r) hard-wired, that takes as input qFHE.Enc(PK_1, SK_2), decrypts it to obtain SK_2', then decrypts qFHE.Enc(SK_2, r) to obtain r' and outputs SK_1 if $r' = r$. If the adversary does not obtain qFHE.Enc(PK_1, SK_2) then we can first invoke the security of lockable obfuscation to remove SK_1 from the obfuscated circuit and then it can replace qFHE.Enc($PK_1, \mathbf{w}$) with qFHE.Enc($PK_1, \perp$). The idea of using fully homomorphic encryption along with lockable obfuscation to achieve non-black-box extraction was first introduced, in the classical setting, by [11].

Unlike our cQEXT construction, the non-black-box technique used for qQEXT does not directly give us a constant round quantum zero-knowledge protocol for NP. This is because an adversarial verifier that aborts can distinguish between the extractor or the honest prover (receiver in qQEXT). The main issue is that the extractor runs the verifier homomorphically, so it cannot detect if the verifier aborted at any point in the protocol without decrypting. But if the verifier aborted, the extractor wouldn't be able to decrypt in the first place – it could attempt to rewind but then this would destroy the initial quantum auxiliary state.

2   Preliminaries

We denote the security parameter by λ. We denote (classical) computational indistiguishability of two distributions $\mathcal{D}_0$ and $\mathcal{D}_1$ by $\mathcal{D}_0 \approx_{c,\varepsilon} \mathcal{D}_1$. In the case when ε is negligible, we drop ε from this notation.

Languages and Relations. A language $\mathcal{L}$ is a subset of $\{0,1\}^*$. A relation $\mathcal{R}$ is a subset of $\{0,1\}^* \times \{0,1\}^*$. We use the following notation:

- Suppose $\mathcal{R}$ is a relation. We define $\mathcal{R}$ to be *efficiently decidable* if there exists an algorithm A and fixed polynomial p such that $(x, w) \in \mathcal{R}$ if and only if $A(x, w) = 1$ and the running time of A is upper bounded by $p(|x|, |w|)$.
- Suppose $\mathcal{R}$ is an efficiently decidable relation. We say that $\mathcal{R}$ is a NP relation if $\mathcal{L}(\mathcal{R})$ is a NP language, where $\mathcal{L}(\mathcal{R})$ is defined as follows: $x \in \mathcal{L}(R)$ if and only if there exists w such that $(x, w) \in \mathcal{R}$ and $|w| \leq p(|x|)$ for some fixed polynomial p.

2.1   Learning with Errors

In this work, we are interested in the decisional learning with errors (LWE) problem. This problem, parameterized by n, m, q, χ, where $n, m, q \in \mathbb{N}$, and for a distribution χ supported over $\mathbb{Z}$ is to distinguish between the distributions $(\mathbf{A}, \mathbf{As} + \mathbf{e})$ and $(\mathbf{A}, \mathbf{u})$, where $\mathbf{A} \xleftarrow{\$} \mathbb{Z}_q^{m \times n}, \mathbf{s} \xleftarrow{\$} \mathbb{Z}_q^{n \times 1}, \mathbf{e} \xleftarrow{\$} \chi^{m \times 1}$ and $\mathbf{u} \leftarrow \mathbb{Z}_q^{m \times 1}$. Typical setting of m is $n \log(q)$, but we also consider $m = \text{poly}(n \log(q))$.

We base the security of our constructions on the quantum hardness of learning with errors problem.

2.2   Notation and General Definitions

For completeness, we present some of the basic quantum definitions, for more details see [34].

Quantum States and Channels. Let $\mathcal{H}$ be any finite Hilbert space, and let $L(\mathcal{H}) := \{\mathcal{E} : \mathcal{H} \to \mathcal{H}\}$ be the set of all linear operators from $\mathcal{H}$ to itself (or endomorphism). Quantum states over $\mathcal{H}$ are the positive semidefinite operators in $L(\mathcal{H})$ that have unit trace. Quantum channels or quantum operations acting on quantum states over $\mathcal{H}$ are completely positive trace preserving (CPTP) linear maps from $L(\mathcal{H})$ to $L(\mathcal{H}')$ where $\mathcal{H}'$ is any other finite dimensional Hilbert space.

A state over $\mathcal{H} = \mathbb{C}^2$ is called a qubit. For any $n \in \mathbb{N}$, we refer to the quantum states over $\mathcal{H} = (\mathbb{C}^2)^{\otimes n}$ as n-qubit quantum states. To perform a standard basis measurement on a qubit means projecting the qubit into $\{|0\rangle, |1\rangle\}$. A quantum register is a collection of qubits. A classical register is a quantum register that is only able to store qubits in the computational basis.

A unitary quantum circuit is a sequence of unitary operations (unitary gates) acting on a fixed number of qubits. Measurements in the standard basis can be performed at the end of the unitary circuit. A (general) quantum circuit is a unitary quantum circuit with 2 additional operations: (1) a gate that adds an ancilla qubit to the system, and (2) a gate that discards (trace-out) a qubit from the system. A quantum polynomial-time algorithm (QPT) is a uniform collection of quantum circuits $\{C_n\}_{n \in \mathbb{N}}$.

Quantum Computational Indistinguishability. When we talk about quantum distinguishers, we need the following definitions, which we take from [42].

Definition 1 (Indistinguishable collections of states). *Let I be an infinite subset $I \subset \{0,1\}^*$, let $p : \mathbb{N} \to \mathbb{N}$ be a polynomially bounded function, and let ρ_x and σ_x be $p(|x|)$-qubit states. We say that $\{\rho_x\}_{x \in I}$ and $\{\sigma_x\}_{x \in I}$ are **quantum computationally indistinguishable collections of quantum states** if for every QPT $\mathcal{E}$ that outputs a single bit, any polynomially bounded $q : \mathbb{N} \to \mathbb{N}$, and any auxiliary $q(|x|)$-qubits state ν, and for all $x \in I$, we have that*

$$|\Pr[\mathcal{E}(\rho_x \otimes \nu) = 1] - \Pr[\mathcal{E}(\sigma_x \otimes \nu) = 1]| \leq \epsilon(|x|)$$

for some negligible function $\epsilon : \mathbb{N} \to [0, 1]$. We use the following notation

$$\rho_x \approx_{Q,\epsilon} \sigma_x$$

and we ignore the ϵ when it is understood that it is a negligible function.

Definition 2 (Indistinguishability of channels). *Let I be an infinite subset $I \subset \{0,1\}^*$, let $p, q : \mathbb{N} \to \mathbb{N}$ be polynomially bounded functions, and let $\mathcal{D}_x, \mathcal{F}_x$ be quantum channels mapping $p(|x|)$-qubit states to $q(|x|)$-qubit states. We say that $\{\mathcal{D}_x\}_{x \in I}$ and $\{\mathcal{F}_x\}_{x \in I}$ are **quantum computationally indistinguishable***

collection of channels *if for every QPT $\mathcal{E}$ that outputs a single bit, any polynomially bounded $t : \mathbb{N} \to \mathbb{N}$, any $p(|x|) + t(|x|)$-qubit quantum state ρ, and for all $x \in I$, we have that*

$$\left| \Pr\left[\mathcal{E}\left((\mathcal{D}_x \otimes \mathsf{Id})(\rho) \right) = 1 \right] - \Pr\left[\mathcal{E}\left((\mathcal{F}_x \otimes \mathsf{Id})(\rho) \right) = 1 \right] \right| \leq \epsilon(|x|)$$

for some negligible function $\epsilon : \mathbb{N} \to [0,1]$. We will use the following notation

$$\mathcal{D}_x(\cdot) \approx_{Q,\epsilon} \mathcal{F}_x(\cdot)$$

and we ignore the ϵ when it is understood that it is a negligible function.

Interactive Models. We model an interactive protocol between a prover, Prover, and a verifier, Verifier, as follows. There are 2 registers $\mathsf{R}_{\mathsf{Prover}}$ and $\mathsf{R}_{\mathsf{Verifier}}$ corresponding to the prover's and the verifier's private registers, as well as a message register, R_M, which is used by both Prover and Verifier to send messages. In other words, both prover and verifier have access to the message register. We denote the size of a register R by $|\mathsf{R}|$ – this is the number of bits or qubits that the register can store. We will have 2 different notions of interactive computation. Our honest parties will perform classical protocols, but the adversaries will be allowed to perform quantum protocols with classical messages.

1. **Classical protocol:** An interactive protocol is classical if $\mathsf{R}_{\mathsf{Prover}}$, $\mathsf{R}_{\mathsf{Verifier}}$, and R_M are classical, and Prover and Verifier can only perform classical computation.
2. **Quantum protocol with classical messages:** An interactive protocol is quantum with classical messages if either one of $\mathsf{R}_{\mathsf{Prover}}$ or $\mathsf{R}_{\mathsf{Verifier}}$ is a quantum register, and R_M is classical. Prover and Verifier can perform quantum computations if their respective private register is quantum, but they can only send classical messages.

When a protocol has classical messages, we can assume that the adversarial party will also send classical messages. This is without loss of generality, because the honest party can enforce this condition by always measuring the message register in the computational basis before proceeding with its computations.

Non-Black-Box Access. Let S be a QPT party (e.g. either prover or verifier in the above descriptions) involved in specific quantum protocol. In particular, S can be seen as a collection of QPTs, $S = (S_1, ..., S_\ell)$, where ℓ is the number of rounds of the protocol, and S_i is the quantum operation that S performs on the ith round of the protocol.

We say that a QPT Q has *non-black-box access* to S, if Q has access to an efficient classical description for the operations that S performs in each round, $(S_1, ..., S_\ell)$, as well as access to the initial auxiliary inputs of S.

Interaction Channel. For a particular protocol (Prover, Verifier), the interaction between Prover and Verifier on input $\mathbf{y}$ induces a quantum channel $\mathcal{E}_{\mathbf{y}}$ acting on their private input states, ρ_{Prover} and σ_{Verifier}. We denote the view of Verifier when interacting with Prover by

$$\text{View}_{\text{Verifier}}\left(\langle\text{Prover}\left(\mathbf{y}, \rho_{\text{Prover}}\right), \text{Verifier}\left(\mathbf{y}, \sigma_{\text{Verifier}}\right)\rangle\right),$$

and this view is defined as the verifiers output. Specifically,

$$\text{View}_{\text{Verifier}}\left(\langle\text{Prover}\left(\mathbf{y}, \rho_{\text{Prover}}\right), \text{Verifier}\left(\mathbf{y}, \sigma_{\text{Verifier}}\right)\rangle\right) := \text{Tr}_{R_{\text{Prover}}}\left[\mathcal{E}_{\mathbf{y}}\left(\rho_{\text{Prover}} \otimes \sigma_{\text{Verifier}}\right)\right].$$

From the verifier's point of view, the interaction induces the channel $\mathcal{E}_{\mathbf{y},V}(\sigma) = \mathcal{E}_{\mathbf{y}}(\sigma \otimes \rho_{\text{Prover}})$ on its private input state.

3 Secure Quantum Extraction Protocols

We define the notion of quantum extraction protocols below. An extraction protocol, associated with an NP relation, is a *classical* interactive protocol between a sender and a receiver. The sender has an NP instance and a witness; the receiver only has the NP instance.

In terms of properties, we require the property that there is a QPT extractor that can extract the witness from a semi-malicious sender (i.e., follows the protocol but is allowed to choose its own randomness) even if the sender is a QPT algorithm. Moreover, the semi-malicious sender should not be able to distinguish whether it's interacting with the extractor or the honest receiver.

In addition, we require the following property (zero-knowledge): the interaction of any malicious receiver with the sender should be simulatable without the knowledge of the witness. The malicious receiver can either be classical or quantum and thus, we have two notions of quantum extraction protocols corresponding to both of these cases.

In terms of properties required, this notion closely resembles the concept of zero-knowledge argument of knowledge (ZKAoK) systems. There are two important differences:

- Firstly, we do not impose any completeness requirement on our extraction protocol.
- In ZKAoK systems, the prover can behave maliciously (i.e., deviates from the protocol) and the argument of knowledge property states that the probability with which the extractor can extract is negligibly close to the probability with which the prover can convince the verifier. In our definition, there is no guarantee of extraction if the sender behaves maliciously.

Definition 3 (Quantum extraction protocols secure against quantum adversaries). *A **quantum extraction protocol secure against quantum adversaries**, denoted by qQEXT is a classical protocol between two classical PPT algorithms, sender S and a receiver R and is associated with an NP relation $\mathcal{R}$. The input to both the parties is an instance $\mathbf{y} \in \mathcal{L}(\mathcal{R})$. In addition, the sender also gets as input the witness $\mathbf{w}$ such that $(\mathbf{y}, \mathbf{w}) \in \mathcal{R}$. At the end of the protocol, the receiver gets the output $\mathbf{w}'$. The following properties are satisfied by qQEXT:*

- **Quantum Zero-Knowledge:** *Let* $p : \mathbb{N} \to \mathbb{N}$ *be any polynomially bounded function. For every* $(\mathbf{y}, \mathbf{w}) \in \mathcal{R}$, *for any QPT algorithm* R^* *with private quantum register of size* $|\mathsf{R}_{\mathsf{R}^*}| = p(\lambda)$, *for any large enough security parameter* $\lambda \in \mathbb{N}$, *there exists a QPT simulator* Sim *such that,*

$$\mathsf{View}_{\mathsf{R}^*} \left(\langle \mathsf{S}(1^\lambda, \mathbf{y}, \mathbf{w}), \mathsf{R}^*(1^\lambda, \mathbf{y}, \cdot) \rangle \right) \approx_Q \mathsf{Sim}(1^\lambda, \mathsf{R}^*, \mathbf{y}, \cdot).$$

- **Semi-Malicious Extractability:** *Let* $p : \mathbb{N} \to \mathbb{N}$ *be any polynomially bounded function. For any large enough security parameter* $\lambda \in \mathbb{N}$, *for every* $(\mathbf{y}, \mathbf{w}) \in \mathcal{L}(\mathcal{R})$, *for every semi-malicious[11] QPT* S^* *with private quantum register of size* $|\mathsf{R}_{\mathsf{S}^*}| = p(\lambda)$, *there exists a QPT extractor* $\mathsf{Ext} = (\mathsf{Ext}_1, \mathsf{Ext}_2)$ *(possibly using the code of* S^* *in a non-black box manner), the following holds:*
  - **Indistinguishability of Extraction:** $\mathsf{View}_{\mathsf{S}^*} \left(\langle \mathsf{S}^*(1^\lambda, \mathbf{y}, \mathbf{w}, \cdot), \mathsf{R}(1^\lambda, \mathbf{y}) \rangle \right)$ $\approx_Q \mathsf{Ext}_1 \left(1^\lambda, \mathsf{S}^*, \mathbf{y}, \cdot \right)$
  - *The probability that* Ext_2 *outputs* $\mathbf{w}'$ *such that* $(\mathbf{y}, \mathbf{w}') \in \mathcal{R}$ *is negligibly close to 1.*

Definition 4 (Quantum extraction protocols secure against classical adversaries). *A* ***quantum extraction protocol secure against classical adversaries*** *cQEXT is defined the same way as in Definition 3 except that instead of quantum zero-knowledge, cQEXT satisfies classical zero-knowledge property defined below:*

- **Classical Zero-Knowledge:** *Let* $p : \mathbb{N} \to \mathbb{N}$ *be any polynomially bounded function. For any large enough security parameter* $\lambda \in \mathbb{N}$, *for every* $(\mathbf{y}, \mathbf{w}) \in \mathcal{R}$, *for any classical PPT algorithm* R^* *with auxiliary information* $\mathsf{aux} \in \{0, 1\}^{\mathrm{poly}(\lambda)}$, *there exists a classical PPT simulator* Sim *such that*

$$\mathsf{View}_{\mathsf{R}^*} \left(\langle \mathsf{S}(1^\lambda, \mathbf{y}, \mathbf{w}), \mathsf{R}^*(1^\lambda, \mathbf{y}, \mathsf{aux}) \rangle \right) \approx_c \mathsf{Sim}(1^\lambda, \mathsf{R}^*, \mathbf{y}, \mathsf{aux}).$$

Quantum-Lasting Security. A desirable property of cQEXT protocols is that a classical malicious receiver, long after the protocol has been executed cannot use a quantum computer to learn the witness of the sender from the transcript of the protocol along with its own private state. We call this property *quantum-lasting security*, first introduced by Unruh [39]. We formally define quantum-lasting security below.

Definition 5 (Quantum-Lasting Security). *A cQEXT protocol is said to be* **quantum-lasting secure** *if the following holds: for any large enough security parameter* $\lambda \in \mathbb{N}$, *for any classical PPT* R^*, *for any QPT adversary* $\mathcal{A}^*$, *for any auxiliary information* $\mathsf{aux} \in \{0, 1\}^{\mathrm{poly}(\lambda)}$, *for any auxiliary state of polynomially many qubits,* ρ, *there exist a QPT simulator* Sim^* *such that:*

$$\mathcal{A}^* \left(\mathsf{View}_{\mathsf{R}^*} \left\langle \mathsf{S}(1^\lambda, \mathbf{y}, \mathbf{w}), \mathsf{R}^*(1^\lambda, \mathbf{y}, \mathsf{aux}) \right\rangle, \rho \right) \approx_Q \mathsf{Sim}^*(1^\lambda, \mathbf{y}, \mathsf{aux}, \rho)$$

---

[11] A QPT algorithm is said to be semi-malicious in the quantum extraction protocol if it follows the protocol but is allowed to choose the randomness for the protocol.

4   QEXT Secure Against Classical Receivers

In this section, we show how to construct quantum extraction protocols secure against classical adversaries based solely on the quantum hardness of learning with errors.

Tools

- Quantum-secure computationally-hiding and perfectly-binding non-interactive commitments, Comm.

  We instantiate the underlying commitment scheme in [36] using Comm to obtain a quantum-secure extractable commitment scheme. Instead of presenting a definition of quantum-secure extractable commitment scheme and then instantiating it, we directly incorporate the construction of [36] in the construction of the extraction protocol.
- Noisy trapdoor claw-free functions $\{f_{\mathbf{k},b} : \mathcal{X} \to D_{\mathcal{Y}}\}_{\mathbf{k} \in \mathcal{K}, b \in \{0,1\}}$.
- Quantum-secure secure function evaluation protocol $\mathsf{SFE} = (\mathsf{SFE.S}, \mathsf{SFE.R})$.

Construction. We present the construction of the quantum extraction protocol (S, R) in Fig. 2 for an NP language $\mathcal{L}$.

We prove the following lemma in the full version.

Lemma 1. *Assuming the quantum security of* Comm, SFE *and NTCFs, the protocol* (S, R) *is a quantum extraction protocol secure against classical adversaries for NP. Moreover,* (S, R) *satisfies quantum-lasting security.*

5   Application: Classical ZK Arguments Secure Against Quantum Verifiers

In this section, we show how to construct a quantum zero-knowledge, classical prover, argument system for NP secure against quantum verifiers; that is, the protocol is classical, the malicious prover is also a classical adversary but the malicious verifier can be a polynomial time quantum algorithm. To formally define this notion, consider the following definition.

Definition 6 (Classical arguments for NP). *A classical interactive protocol* (Prover, Verifier) *is a* **classical ZK argument system** *for an NP language* $\mathcal{L}$, *associated with an NP relation* $\mathcal{L}(\mathcal{R})$, *if the following holds:*

- **Completeness:** *For any* $(\mathbf{y}, \mathbf{w}) \in \mathcal{L}(\mathcal{R})$, *we have that* $\Pr[\langle \mathsf{Prover}(1^\lambda, \mathbf{y}, \mathbf{w}), \mathsf{Verifier}(1^\lambda, \mathbf{y})\rangle = 1] \geq 1 - \mathsf{negl}(\lambda)$, *for some negligible function* negl.
- **Soundness:** *For any* $\mathbf{y} \notin \mathcal{L}$, *any classical PPT adversary* Prover*, and any polynomial-sized auxiliary information* aux, *we have that* $\Pr[\langle \mathsf{Prover}^*(1^\lambda, \mathbf{y}, \mathsf{aux}), \mathsf{Verifier}(1^\lambda, \mathbf{y})\rangle = 1] \leq \mathsf{negl}(\lambda)$, *for some negligible function* negl.

F

Input of sender: $\left(\left\{\mathbf{c}_{i,0}^{(j)}, \mathbf{c}_{i,1}^{(j)}, (sh_{i,w_i}^{(j)})', (\mathbf{d}_{i,w_i}^{(j)})', \mathsf{td}_i, \mathbf{k}_i, y_i, v_i, w_i^{(j)}\right\}_{i,j\in[k]}, \mathbf{w}\right)$

Input of receiver: $\left(\left\{sh_{i,\overline{w_i}}^{(j)}, \mathbf{d}_{i,\overline{w_i}}^{(j)}\right\}_{i,j\in[k]}\right)$

- If for any $i, j \in [k]$, $\mathbf{c}_{i,w_i}^{(j)} \neq \mathsf{Comm}\left(1^\lambda, (sh_{i,w_i}^{(j)})'; (\mathbf{d}_{i,w_i}^{(j)})'\right)$ or $\mathbf{c}_{i,\overline{w_i}}^{(j)} \neq$
  $\mathsf{Comm}\left(1^\lambda, sh_{i,\overline{w_i}}^{(j)}; \mathbf{d}_{i,\overline{w_i}}^{(j)}\right)$, output $\perp$.

- For every $i \in [k]$, let $(x_{i,0}, x_{i,1}) \leftarrow \mathsf{Inv}(\mathbf{k}_i, \mathsf{td}_i, y_i)$.
  - *Check if the commitments commit to the same message*: Output $\perp$ if the
    following does not hold: for every $j, j' \in [k]$, we have $\left(sh_{i,w_i}^{(j)}\right)' \oplus sh_{i,w_i}^{(j)} =$
    $\left(sh_{i,w_i}^{(j')}\right)' \oplus sh_{i,w_i}^{(j')}$.

  - If $v_i = 0$: let $(b_i, J(x'_{i,b_i})) = (sh_{i,w_i}^{(j)})' \oplus sh_{i,\overline{w_i}}^{(j)}$, where $J(\cdot)$ is the injection in
    the definition of NTCF. Since $J(\cdot)$ can be efficiently inverted, recover x'_{i,b_i}.
    If $x'_{i,b_i} \neq x_{i,b_i}$, output $\perp$.

  - If $v_i = 1$: let $(u_i, d_i) = \left(sh_{i,w_i}^{(j)}\right)' \oplus sh_{i,\overline{w_i}}^{(j)}$. If $\langle d_i, J(x_{i,0}) \oplus J(x_{i,1})\rangle \neq u_i$, or if
    $d_i \notin G_{\mathbf{k}_i,0,x_{i,0}} \cap G_{\mathbf{k}_i,1,x_{i,1}}$ output $\perp$.

- Otherwise, output $\mathbf{w}$.

Fig. 1. Description of the function **F** associated with the SFE.

We say that a classical argument system for NP is a QZK (quantum zero-knowledge) classical argument system for NP if in addition to the above properties, a classical interactive protocol satisfies zero-knowledge against malicious receivers.

Definition 7 (QZK classical argument system for NP). *A classical interactive protocol* (Prover, Verifier) *is a **quantum zero-knowledge classical argument system** for a language $\mathcal{L}$, associated with an NP relation $\mathcal{L}(\mathcal{R})$ if both of the following hold.*

- (Prover, Verifier) *is a classical argument for $\mathcal{L}$ (Definition 6).*
- **Quantum Zero-Knowledge**: *Let $p : \mathbb{N} \to \mathbb{N}$ be any polynomially bounded function. For any QPT* Verifier* *that on instance $\mathbf{y} \in \mathcal{L}$ has private register of size $|\mathsf{R}_{\mathsf{Verifier}^*}| = p(|\mathbf{y}|)$, there exist a QPT* Sim *such that the following two collections of quantum channels are quantum computationally indistinguishable,*

Input of sender: $(\mathbf{y}, \mathbf{w})$.
Input of receiver: $\mathbf{y}$

- S: Compute $\forall i \in [k], (\mathbf{k}_i, \mathsf{td}_i) \leftarrow \mathsf{Gen}(1^\lambda; r_i)$, where $k = \lambda$. Send $(\{\mathbf{k}_i\}_{i \in [k]})$.

- R: For every $i \in [k]$, choose a random bit $b_i \in \{0,1\}$ and sample a random $y_i \leftarrow f'_{\mathbf{k}_i, b_i}(x_{i, b_i})$, where $x_{i, b_i} \xleftarrow{\$} \mathcal{X}$. Send $\{y_i\}_{i \in [k]}$. (Recall that $f'_{\mathbf{k}, b}(x)$ is a distribution over $\mathcal{Y}$.)

- S: Send bits $(v_1, \ldots, v_k)$, where $v_i \xleftarrow{\$} \{0,1\}$ for $i \in [k]$.

- R: For every $i, j \in [k]$, compute the commitments $\mathbf{c}_{i,0}^{(j)} \leftarrow \mathsf{Comm}(1^\lambda, sh_{i,0}^{(j)}; \mathbf{d}_{i,0}^{(j)})$ and $\mathbf{c}_{i,1}^{(j)} \leftarrow \mathsf{Comm}(1^\lambda, sh_{i,1}^{(j)}; \mathbf{d}_{i,1}^{(j)})$, where $sh_{i,0}^{(j)}, sh_{i,1}^{(j)} \xleftarrow{\$} \{0,1\}^{\mathsf{poly}(\lambda)}$ for $i, j \in [k]$. Send $\left(\left\{\mathbf{c}_{i,0}^{(j)}, \mathbf{c}_{i,1}^{(j)}\right\}_{i,j \in [k]}\right)$.

  Note: The reason why we have k^2 commitments above is because we repeat (in parallel) the test of quantumness protocol k times and for each repetition, the response of the receiver is committed using k commitments; the latter is due to [36].

- S: For every $i, j \in [k]$, send random bits $w_i^{(j)} \in \{0,1\}$.

- R: Send $\left(\left\{(sh_{i,w_i}^{(j)})', (\mathbf{d}_{i,w_i}^{(j)})'\right\}_{i,j \in [k]}\right)$.

- S and R run SFE, associated with the two-party functionality $\mathbf{F}$ defined in Figure 1; S takes the role of SFE.S and R takes the role of SFE.R. The input to SFE.S is $\left(\left\{\mathbf{c}_{i,0}^{(j)}, \mathbf{c}_{i,1}^{(j)}, (sh_{i,w_i}^{(j)})', (\mathbf{d}_{i,w_i}^{(j)})', \mathsf{td}_i, \mathbf{k}_i, y_i, v_i, w_i^{(j)}\right\}_{i,j \in [k]}, \mathbf{w}\right)$ and the input to SFE.R is $\left(\left\{sh_{i,\overline{w_i}}^{(j)}, \mathbf{d}_{i,\overline{w_i}}^{(j)}\right\}_{i,j \in [k]}\right)$.

Fig. 2. Quantum extraction protocol (S, R) secure against classical receivers.

- $\{\mathsf{Sim}(\mathbf{y}, \mathsf{Verifier}^*, \cdot)\}_{\mathbf{y} \in \mathcal{L}}$
- $\{\mathsf{View}_{\mathsf{Verifier}^*}(\langle \mathsf{Prover}(\mathbf{y}, \mathsf{aux}_1), \mathsf{Verifier}^*(\mathbf{y}, \cdot)\rangle)\}_{\mathbf{y} \in \mathcal{L}}$.

In other words, that for every $\mathbf{y} \in \mathcal{L}$, for any bounded polynomial $q : \mathbb{N} \to \mathbb{N}$, for any QPT distinguisher $\mathcal{D}$ that outputs a single bit, and any $p(|\mathbf{y}|) + q(|\mathbf{y}|)$-qubits quantum state ρ,

$$\big| \Pr\left[\mathcal{D}\left(\mathsf{Sim}(\mathbf{y}, \mathsf{Verifier}^*, \cdot) \otimes I\right)(\rho)) = 1\right]$$

$$- \Pr\left[\mathcal{D}\left((\mathsf{View}_{\mathsf{Verifier}^*}(\langle \mathsf{Prover}(\mathbf{y}, \mathsf{aux}_1), \mathsf{Verifier}^*(\mathbf{y}, \cdot)\rangle) \otimes I)(\rho)) = 1\right] \big| \leq \epsilon(|\mathbf{y}|)$$

Witness-Indistinguishability Against Quantum Verifiers. As a building block, we also consider witness indistinguishable (WI) argument systems for NP languages secure against quantum verifiers. We define this formally below.

Definition 8 (Quantum WI for an $\mathcal{L} \in$ NP). *A classical protocol* (Prover, Verifier) *is a **quantum witness indistinguishable argument system** for an NP language $\mathcal{L}$ if both of the following hold.*

- (Prover, Verifier) *is a classical argument for $\mathcal{L}$ (Definition 6).*
- **Quantum WI**: *Let $p : \mathbb{N} \to \mathbb{N}$ be any polynomially bounded function. For every $\mathbf{y} \in \mathcal{L}$, for any two valid witnesses $\mathbf{w}_1$ and $\mathbf{w}_2$, for any QPT* Verifier* *that on instance $\mathbf{y}$ has private quantum register of size $|\mathsf{R}_{\mathsf{Verifier}^*}| = p(|\mathbf{y}|)$, we require that*

$$\mathsf{View}_{\mathsf{Verifier}^*}\left(\langle\mathsf{Prover}(\mathbf{y}, \mathbf{w}_1), \mathsf{Verifier}^*(\mathbf{y}, \cdot)\rangle\right) \approx_Q \mathsf{View}_{\mathsf{Verifier}^*}\left(\langle\mathsf{Prover}(\mathbf{y}, \mathbf{w}_2), \mathsf{Verifier}^*(\mathbf{y}, \cdot)\rangle\right).$$

If (Prover, Verifier) *is a quantum proof system (sound against unbounded provers), we say that* (Prover, Verifier) *is a **quantum witness indistinguishable proof system** for $\mathcal{L}$.*

Instantiation. By suitably instantiating the constant round WI argument system of Blum [13] with perfectly binding quantum computational hiding commitments, we achieve a constant round quantum WI classical argument system assuming quantum hardness of learning with errors.

Construction. We present a construction of constant round quantum zero-knowledge classical argument system for NP.

Tools

- Perfectly-binding and quantum-computational hiding non-interactive commitments Comm.
- Quantum extraction protocol secure against classical adversaries cQEXT = (S, R) associated with the relation $\mathcal{R}_{\mathrm{EXT}}$ as constructed in Sect. 6.
- Quantum witness indistinguishable classical argument system Π_{WI} = (Π_{WI}.Prover, Π_{WI}.Verifier) (Definition 8) for the relation $\mathcal{R}_{\mathsf{wi}}$ (Fig. 3).

Construction. Let $\mathcal{L}$ be an NP language. We describe a classical interactive protocol (Prover, Verifier) for $\mathcal{L}$ in Fig. 4.

We prove following lemma in the full version.

Lemma 2. *Assuming the security of* Comm, cQEXT *and* Π_{WI}, *the classical interactive protocol* (Prover, Verifier) *is a quantum zero-knowledge classical argument system for NP.*

Instance: $\left(\mathbf{y}, \mathsf{td}, \left\{ (\mathbf{c}_0^{(j)})^*, (\mathbf{c}_1^{(j)})^* \right\}_{j \in [k]} \right)$

Witness: $\left(\mathbf{w}, \left\{ (sh_0^{(j)}, \mathbf{d}_0^{(j)}, sh_1^{(j)}, \mathbf{d}_1^{(j)}) \right\}_{j \in [k]} \right)$

NP verification: Accept if one of the following two conditions are satisfied:

- $(\mathbf{y}, \mathbf{w}) \in \mathcal{R}$.
- If for every $j \in [k]$, it holds that
  - $(\mathbf{c}_0^{(j)})^* = \mathsf{Comm}(1^\lambda, sh_0^{(j)}; \mathbf{d}_0^{(j)})$
  - $(\mathbf{c}_1^{(j)})^* = \mathsf{Comm}(1^\lambda, sh_1^{(j)}; \mathbf{d}_1^{(j)})$
  - $\mathsf{td} = sh_0^{(j)} \oplus sh_1^{(j)}$

Fig. 3. Relation $\mathcal{R}_{\mathsf{wi}}$ associated with Π_{WI}.

6 QEXT Secure Against Quantum Adversaries

6.1 Construction of QEXT

We present a construction of quantum extraction protocols secure against quantum adversaries, denoted by qQEXT. First, we describe the tools used in this construction.

- Quantum-secure
  computationally-hiding and perfectly-binding non-interactive commitments Comm.
- Quantum fully homomorphic encryption scheme with some desired properties, (qFHE.Gen, qFHE.Enc, qFHE.Dec, qFHE.Eval).
  - It admits homomorphic evaluation of arbitrary computations,
  - It admits perfect correctness,
  - The ciphertext of a classical message is also classical.
  We show in the full version that there are qFHE schemes satisfying the above properties.
- Quantum-secure two-party secure computation SFE with the following properties:
  - Only one party receives the output. We designate the party receiving the output as the receiver SFE.R and the other party to be SFE.S.
  - Security against quantum passive senders.
  - IND-Security against quantum malicious receivers.

- **Trapdoor Committment by Verifier**: Verifier: sample $\mathsf{td} \leftarrow \{0,1\}^\lambda$. Compute $\mathbf{c} \leftarrow \mathsf{Comm}(1^\lambda, \mathsf{td}; \mathbf{d})$, where $\mathbf{d} \leftarrow \{0,1\}^{\mathrm{poly}(\lambda)}$ is the randomness used in the commitment. Send $\mathbf{c}$ to Prover.

- **Trapdoor Extraction Phase**: Prover and Verifier run the quantum extraction protocol cQEXT with Verifier taking the role of the sender cQEXT.S and Prover taking the role of the receiver cQEXT.R. The input of cQEXT.S is $(1^\lambda, \mathbf{c}, \mathbf{d}; \mathbf{r}_{\mathrm{qext}})$ and the input of cQEXT.R is $(1^\lambda, \mathbf{c})$, where $\mathbf{r}_{\mathrm{qext}}$ is the randomness used by the sender in cQEXT. Let the transcript generated during the execution of cQEXT be $\mathcal{T}_{\mathsf{Verifier} \to \mathsf{Prover}}$.
  Note: The trapdoor extraction phase will be used by the simulator, while proving zero-knowledge, to extract the trapdoor from the malicious verifier.

- **Trapdoor Commitment by Prover**:
  - Let $k = \lambda$. For every $j \in [k]$, Prover sends $(\mathbf{c}_0^{(j)})^* = \mathsf{Comm}(1^\lambda, sh_0^{(j)}; \mathbf{d}_0^{(j)})$ and $(\mathbf{c}_1^{(j)})^* = \mathsf{Comm}(1^\lambda, sh_1^{(j)}; \mathbf{d}_1^{(j)})$, where $sh_0^{(j)}, sh_1^{(j)} \xleftarrow{\$} \{0,1\}^{\mathrm{poly}(\lambda)}$.

  - For every $j \in [k]$, Verifier sends bit $b^{(j)} \xleftarrow{\$} \{0,1\}$ to Prover.

  - Prover sends $\left\{ \left(sh_{b^{(j)}}^{(j)}, \mathbf{d}_{b^{(j)}}^{(j)}\right) \right\}_{j \in [k]}$ to Verifier.

- **Check if Verifier cheated in Trapdoor Extraction Phase**: Verifier sends $\mathbf{r}_{\mathrm{qext}}, \mathbf{d}, \mathsf{td}$ to Prover. Then Prover checks the following:
  - Let $\mathcal{T}_{\mathsf{Verifier} \to \mathsf{Prover}}$ be $(m_1^S, m_1^R, \ldots, m_{t'}^S, m_{t'}^R)$, where the message m_i^R (resp., m_i^S) is the message sent by the receiver (resp., sender) in the ith round and t' is the number of rounds of cQEXT. Let the message produced by $\mathsf{S}\left(1^\lambda, \mathbf{c}, \mathbf{d}; \mathbf{r}_{\mathrm{qext}}\right)$ in the ith round be $\widetilde{m}_i^S$.

  - If for any $i \in [t']$, $\widetilde{m}_i^S \neq m_i^S$ then Prover aborts. If $\mathbf{c} \neq \mathsf{Comm}(1^\lambda, \mathsf{td}; \mathbf{d})$ then Prover aborts.

- **Quantum WI**: Prover and Verifier run Π_{WI} with Prover taking the role of Π_{WI} prover Π_{WI}.Prover and Verifier taking the role of Π_{WI} verifier Π_{WI}.Verifier. The input to Π_{WI}.Prover is the security parameter 1^λ, instance $\left(\mathbf{y}, \mathsf{td}, \left\{(\mathbf{c}_0^{(j)})^*, (\mathbf{c}_1^{(j)})^*\right\}_{j \in [k]}\right)$ and witness $(\mathbf{w}, \perp)$. The input to Π_{WI}.Verifier is the security parameter 1^λ and instance $\left(\mathbf{y}, \mathsf{td}, \left\{(\mathbf{c}_0^{(j)})^*, (\mathbf{c}_1^{(j)})^*\right\}_{j \in [k]}\right)$.

- **Decision step**: Verifier computes the decision step of Π_{WI}.Verifier.

Fig. 4. (Classical Prover) Quantum zero-knowledge argument systems for NP.

C

Input: CT
Hardwired values: $\mathbf{r}$ (lock), $\mathbf{k}, \mathsf{SK}_1, \mathsf{CT}^*$.

- $\mathsf{SK}_2' \leftarrow \mathsf{qFHE.Dec}(\mathsf{SK}_1, \mathsf{CT})$

- $\mathbf{r}' \leftarrow \mathsf{qFHE.Dec}(\mathsf{SK}_2', \mathsf{CT}^*)$

- If $\mathbf{r}' = \mathbf{r}$, output $\mathbf{k}$. Else, output $\perp$.

Fig. 5. Circuits used in the lockable obfuscation

---

f

Input of sender: $(\mathsf{td}, \mathbf{c}, \mathbf{c}_1^*, \ldots, \mathbf{c}_\ell^*, \mathsf{SK}_2)$
Input of receiver: $(\mathbf{d}, r_1, \ldots, r_\ell)$

- If $\left(\mathbf{c} \leftarrow \mathsf{Comm}\left(1^\lambda, (r_1, \ldots, r_\ell); \mathbf{d}\right)\right) \bigwedge \left(\forall i \in [\ell], \mathbf{c}_i^* \leftarrow \mathsf{Comm}\left(1^\lambda, \mathsf{td}_i; r_i\right)\right)$, output SK_2. Here, td_i denotes the ith bit of td.

- Otherwise, output $\perp$.

Fig. 6. Description of the function f associated with the SFE.

- Quantum-secure lockable obfuscation $\mathbf{LObf} = (\mathsf{Obf}, \mathsf{ObfEval})$ for $\mathcal{C}$, where every circuit $\mathbf{C}$, parameterized by $(\mathbf{r}, \mathbf{k}, \mathsf{SK}_1, \mathsf{CT}^*)$, in $\mathcal{C}$ is defined in Fig. 5. Note that $\mathcal{C}$ is a compute-and-compare functionality.

Construction. We construct a protocol (S, R) in Fig. 7 for a NP language $\mathcal{L}$, and the following lemma shows that (S, R) is a quantum extraction protocol.

We prove the following lemma in the full version.

Lemma 3. *Assuming the quantum security of* Comm, SFE, qFHE *and* **LObf**, (S, R) *is a quantum extraction protocol for* $\mathcal{L}$ *secure against quantum adversaries.*

Input of sender: $(\mathbf{y}, \mathbf{w})$.
Input of receiver: $\mathbf{y}$

- R: sample $(r_1, \ldots, r_\ell) \xleftarrow{\$} \{0,1\}^{\ell \cdot \text{poly}(\lambda)}$. Compute $\mathbf{c} \leftarrow \text{Comm}\left(1^\lambda, (r_1, \ldots, r_\ell); \mathbf{d}\right)$, where $\ell = \lambda$ and $\mathbf{d}$ is the randomness used to compute $\mathbf{c}$. Send $\mathbf{c}$ to S.

- S:
  - Compute the qFHE.Setup twice; $(\text{PK}_i, \text{SK}_i) \leftarrow \text{qFHE.Setup}(1^\lambda)$ for $i \in \{1, 2\}$.

  - Compute $\text{CT}_1 \leftarrow \text{qFHE.Enc}(\text{PK}_1, (\text{td}\|\mathbf{w}))$, where $\text{td} \xleftarrow{\$} \{0,1\}^\lambda$.

  - Compute $\widetilde{\mathbf{C}} \leftarrow \text{Obf}(1^\lambda, \mathbf{C}[\mathbf{r}, \mathbf{k}, \text{SK}_1, \text{CT}^*])$, where $\mathbf{r} \xleftarrow{\$} \{0,1\}^\lambda$ and $\mathbf{k} \xleftarrow{\$} \{0,1\}^\lambda$, CT^* is defined below and $\mathbf{C}[\mathbf{r}, \mathbf{k}, \text{SK}_1, \text{CT}^*]$ is defined in Figure 5.
    * $\text{CT}^* \leftarrow \text{qFHE.Enc}(\text{PK}_2, \mathbf{r})$

  Send $\text{msg}_1 = \left(\text{CT}_1, \widetilde{\mathbf{C}}, \text{otp} := \mathbf{k} \oplus \text{SK}_1\right)$.

- R: compute $\mathbf{c}_i^* \leftarrow \text{Comm}\left(1^\lambda, 0; r_i\right)$ for $i \in [\ell]$. Send $(\mathbf{c}_1^*, \ldots, \mathbf{c}_\ell^*)$ to S.

- S and R run SFE, associated with the two-party functionality f defined in Figure 6; S takes the role of SFE.S and R takes the role of SFE.R. The input to SFE.S is $(\text{td}, \mathbf{c}, \mathbf{c}_1^*, \ldots, \mathbf{c}_\ell^*, \text{SK}_2)$ and the input to SFE.R is $(\mathbf{d}, r_1, \ldots, r_\ell)$.

Fig. 7. Quantum extraction protocol (S, R)

Acknowledgements. We are grateful to Kai-Min Chung for many clarifications regarding quantum zero-knowledge proof and argument systems. We thank Thomas Vidick and Urmila Mahadev for answering questions about noisy trapdoor claw-free functions. We thank Abhishek Jain for helpful discussions and pointing us to the relevant references.

References

1. Agarwal, A., Bartusek, J., Goyal, V., Khurana, D., Malavolta, G.: Post-quantum multi-party computation in constant rounds (2020)
2. Alagic, G., Brakerski, Z., Dulek, Y., Schaffner, C.: Impossibility of quantum virtual black-box obfuscation of classical circuits (2020)
3. Ambainis, A., Rosmanis, A., Unruh, D.: Quantum attacks on classical proof systems: the hardness of quantum rewinding. In: FOCS (2014)
4. Ananth, P., Jain, A.: On secure two-party computation in three rounds. In: Kalai, Y., Reyzin, L. (eds.) TCC 2017. LNCS, vol. 10677, pp. 612–644. Springer, Cham (2017). https://doi.org/10.1007/978-3-319-70500-2_21

5. Ananth, P., La Placa, R.L.: Secure quantum extraction protocols. arXiv preprint arXiv:1911.07672 (2019)
6. Ananth, P., La Placa, R.L.: Secure software leasing. arXiv preprint arXiv:2005.05289 (2020)
7. Barak, B.: How to go beyond the black-box simulation barrier. In: Proceedings 42nd IEEE Symposium on Foundations of Computer Science, pp. 106–115. IEEE (2001)
8. Bitansky, N., Brakerski, Z., Kalai, Y., Paneth, O., Vaikuntanathan, V.: 3-message zero knowledge against human ignorance. In: Hirt, M., Smith, A. (eds.) TCC 2016. LNCS, vol. 9985, pp. 57–83. Springer, Heidelberg (2016). https://doi.org/10.1007/978-3-662-53641-4_3
9. Bitansky, N., Canetti, R., Paneth, O., Rosen, A.: On the existence of extractable one-way functions. SIAM J. Comput. 45(5), 1910–1952 (2016)
10. Bitansky, N., Kalai, Y.T., Paneth, O.: Multi-collision resistance: a paradigm for keyless hash functions. In: Proceedings of the 50th Annual ACM SIGACT Symposium on Theory of Computing, pp. 671–684. ACM (2018)
11. Bitansky, N., Khurana, D., Paneth, O.: Weak zero-knowledge beyond the black-box barrier. In: Proceedings of the 51st Annual ACM SIGACT Symposium on Theory of Computing, pp. 1091–1102. ACM (2019)
12. Bitansky, N., Shmueli, O.: Post-quantum zero knowledge in constant rounds. In: STOC (2020)
13. Blum, M.: How to prove a theorem so no one else can claim it. In: Proceedings of the International Congress of Mathematicians, vol. 1, p. 2. Citeseer (1986)
14. Brakerski, Z.: Quantum FHE (almost) as secure as classical. In: Shacham, H., Boldyreva, A. (eds.) CRYPTO 2018. LNCS, vol. 10993, pp. 67–95. Springer, Cham (2018). https://doi.org/10.1007/978-3-319-96878-0_3
15. Brakerski, Z., Christiano, P., Mahadev, U., Vazirani, U., Vidick, T.: A cryptographic test of quantumness and certifiable randomness from a single quantum device. In: 2018 IEEE 59th Annual Symposium on Foundations of Computer Science (FOCS), pp. 320–331. IEEE (2018)
16. Brakerski, Z., Vaikuntanathan, V.: Efficient fully homomorphic encryption from (standard) LWE. SIAM J. Comput. 43(2), 831–871 (2014)
17. Broadbent, A., Ji, Z., Song, F., Watrous, J.: Zero-knowledge proof systems for QMA. In: 2016 IEEE 57th Annual Symposium on Foundations of Computer Science (FOCS), pp. 31–40. IEEE (2016)
18. Chailloux, A., Ciocan, D.F., Kerenidis, I., Vadhan, S.: Interactive and noninteractive zero knowledge are equivalent in the help model. In: Canetti, R. (ed.) TCC 2008. LNCS, vol. 4948, pp. 501–534. Springer, Heidelberg (2008). https://doi.org/10.1007/978-3-540-78524-8_28
19. Feige, U., Lapidot, D., Shamir, A.: Multiple noninteractive zero knowledge proofs under general assumptions. SIAM J. Comput. 29(1), 1–28 (1999)
20. Gentry, C., et al.: Fully homomorphic encryption using ideal lattices. In: STOC, vol. 9, pp. 169–178 (2009)
21. Gentry, C., Halevi, S., Vaikuntanathan, V.: i-hop homomorphic encryption and rerandomizable yao circuits. In: Rabin, T. (ed.) CRYPTO 2010. LNCS, vol. 6223, pp. 155–172. Springer, Heidelberg (2010). https://doi.org/10.1007/978-3-642-14623-7_9
22. Goldreich, O., Krawczyk, H.: On the composition of zero-knowledge proof systems. SIAM J. Comput. 25(1), 169–192 (1996)

23. Goldreich, O., Micali, S., Wigderson, A.: Proofs that yield nothing but their validity and a methodology of cryptographic protocol design. In: 27th Annual Symposium on Foundations of Computer Science, 1986, pp. 174–187. IEEE (1986)
24. Goldreich, O., Oren, Y.: Definitions and properties of zero-knowledge proof systems. J. Cryptol. **7**(1), 1–32 (1994). https://doi.org/10.1007/BF00195207
25. Goyal, R., Koppula, V., Waters, B.: Lockable obfuscation. In: 2017 IEEE 58th Annual Symposium on Foundations of Computer Science (FOCS), pp. 612–621. IEEE (2017)
26. Hallgren, S., Kolla, A., Sen, P., Zhang, S.: Making classical honest verifier zero knowledge protocols secure against quantum attacks. In: Aceto, L., Damgård, I., Goldberg, L.A., Halldórsson, M.M., Ingólfsdóttir, A., Walukiewicz, I. (eds.) ICALP 2008. LNCS, vol. 5126, pp. 592–603. Springer, Heidelberg (2008). https://doi.org/10.1007/978-3-540-70583-3_48
27. Jain, R., Kolla, A., Midrijanis, G., Reichardt, B.W.: On parallel composition of zero-knowledge proofs with black-box quantum simulators. arXiv preprint quant-ph/0607211 (2006)
28. Kalai, Y.T., Khurana, D.: Non-interactive non-malleability from quantum supremacy. In: Boldyreva, A., Micciancio, D. (eds.) CRYPTO 2019. LNCS, vol. 11694, pp. 552–582. Springer, Cham (2019). https://doi.org/10.1007/978-3-030-26954-8_18
29. Kobayashi, H.: General properties of quantum zero-knowledge proofs. In: Canetti, R. (ed.) TCC 2008. LNCS, vol. 4948, pp. 107–124. Springer, Heidelberg (2008). https://doi.org/10.1007/978-3-540-78524-8_7
30. Lombardi, A., Schaeffer, L.: A note on key agreement and non-interactive commitments. IACR Cryptol. ePrint Arch. **2019**, 279 (2019)
31. Mahadev, U.: Classical homomorphic encryption for quantum circuits. In: 2018 IEEE 59th Annual Symposium on Foundations of Computer Science (FOCS), pp. 332–338. IEEE (2018)
32. Mahadev, U.: Classical verification of quantum computations. In: 2018 IEEE 59th Annual Symposium on Foundations of Computer Science (FOCS), pp. 259–267. IEEE (2018)
33. Matsumoto, K.: A simpler proof of zero-knowledge against quantum attacks using Grover's amplitude amplification. arXiv preprint quant-ph/0602186 (2006)
34. Nielsen, M.A., Chuang, I.: Quantum computation and quantum information (2002)
35. Pass, R.: Simulation in quasi-polynomial time, and its application to protocol composition. In: Biham, E. (ed.) EUROCRYPT 2003. LNCS, vol. 2656, pp. 160–176. Springer, Heidelberg (2003). https://doi.org/10.1007/3-540-39200-9_10
36. Pass, R., Wee, H.: Black-box constructions of two-party protocols from one-way functions. In: Reingold, O. (ed.) TCC 2009. LNCS, vol. 5444, pp. 403–418. Springer, Heidelberg (2009). https://doi.org/10.1007/978-3-642-00457-5_24
37. Prabhakaran, M., Rosen, A., Sahai, A.: Concurrent zero knowledge with logarithmic round-complexity. In: FOCS (2002)
38. Unruh, D.: Quantum proofs of knowledge. In: Pointcheval, D., Johansson, T. (eds.) EUROCRYPT 2012. LNCS, vol. 7237, pp. 135–152. Springer, Heidelberg (2012). https://doi.org/10.1007/978-3-642-29011-4_10
39. Unruh, D.: Everlasting multi-party computation. In: Canetti, R., Garay, J.A. (eds.) CRYPTO 2013. LNCS, vol. 8043, pp. 380–397. Springer, Heidelberg (2013). https://doi.org/10.1007/978-3-642-40084-1_22
40. Unruh, D.: Computationally binding quantum commitments. In: Fischlin, M., Coron, J.-S. (eds.) EUROCRYPT 2016. LNCS, vol. 9666, pp. 497–527. Springer, Heidelberg (2016). https://doi.org/10.1007/978-3-662-49896-5_18

41. Vidick, T., Zhang, T.: Classical zero-knowledge arguments for quantum computations. arXiv preprint arXiv:1902.05217 (2019)
42. Watrous, J.: Zero-knowledge against quantum attacks. SIAM J. Comput. **39**(1), 25–58 (2009)
43. Wichs , D., Zirdelis, G.: Obfuscating compute-and-compare programs under LWE. In: 2017 IEEE 58th Annual Symposium on Foundations of Computer Science (FOCS), pp. 600–611. IEEE (2017)

Non-interactive Classical Verification of Quantum Computation

Gorjan Alagic[1,2], Andrew M. Childs[2], Alex B. Grilo[3], and Shih-Han Hung[2(✉)]

[1] National Institute of Standards and Technology,
Gaithersburg, Maryland, USA
[2] Department of Computer Science, UMIACS, and QuICS,
University of Maryland, College Park, Maryland, USA
shung@umd.edu
[3] Sorbonne Université, CNRS and LIP6, Paris, France

Abstract. In a recent breakthrough, Mahadev constructed an interactive protocol that enables a purely classical party to delegate any quantum computation to an untrusted quantum prover. We show that this same task can in fact be performed *non-interactively* (with setup) and in *zero-knowledge*.

Our protocols result from a sequence of significant improvements to the original four-message protocol of Mahadev. We begin by making the first message instance-independent and moving it to an offline setup phase. We then establish a parallel repetition theorem for the resulting three-message protocol, with an asymptotically optimal rate. This, in turn, enables an application of the Fiat-Shamir heuristic, eliminating the second message and giving a non-interactive protocol. Finally, we employ classical non-interactive zero-knowledge (NIZK) arguments and classical fully homomorphic encryption (FHE) to give a zero-knowledge variant of this construction. This yields the first purely classical NIZK argument system for QMA, a quantum analogue of NP.

We establish the security of our protocols under standard assumptions in quantum-secure cryptography. Specifically, our protocols are secure in the Quantum Random Oracle Model, under the assumption that Learning with Errors is quantumly hard. The NIZK construction also requires circuit-private FHE.

1 Introduction

Quantum computing devices are expected to solve problems that are infeasible for classical computers. However, as significant progress is made toward constructing quantum computers, it is challenging to verify that they work correctly, particularly when devices reach scales where classical simulation is infeasible. This problem has been considered in various models, such as with multiple entangled quantum provers [18,24,25,27,30,35,37,42] or with verifiers who have limited quantum resources [2,13,14,36]. Such solutions are not ideal since they require assumptions about the ability of the provers to communicate or require the verifier to have some quantum abilities.

© International Association for Cryptologic Research 2020
R. Pass and K. Pietrzak (Eds.): TCC 2020, LNCS 12552, pp. 153–180, 2020.
https://doi.org/10.1007/978-3-030-64381-2_6

In a major breakthrough, Mahadev recently described the first secure protocol enabling a purely classical verifier to certify the quantum computations of a single untrusted quantum prover [34]. The Mahadev protocol uses a quantum-secure cryptographic assumption to give the classical verifier leverage over the quantum prover. The protocol is sound under the assumption that Learning with Errors (LWE) does not admit a polynomial-time quantum algorithm. This assumption is widely accepted, and underlies some of the most promising candidates for quantum-secure cryptography [3].

The Mahadev Protocol. Mahadev's result settled a major open question concerning the power of *quantum-prover interactive arguments* (QPIAs). In a QPIA, two computationally-bounded parties (a quantum prover $\mathcal{P}$ and a classical verifier $\mathcal{V}$) interact with the goal of solving a decision problem. Mahadev's result showed that there is a four-round[1] QPIA for BQP with negligible completeness error and constant soundness error $\delta \approx 3/4$. The goal of the protocol is for the verifier to decide whether an input Hamiltonian H from a certain class (which is BQP-complete) has a ground state energy that is low (YES) or high (NO).

The protocol has a high-level structure analogous to classical Σ-protocols [21]:

1. $\mathcal{V}$ generates a private-public key pair (pk, sk) and sends pk to $\mathcal{P}$;
2. $\mathcal{P}$ prepares the ground state of H and then coherently evaluates a certain classical function f_{pk}. This yields a state of the form $\sum_x \alpha_x |x\rangle_X |f_{pk}(x)\rangle_Y$, where the ground state is in a subregister of X. $\mathcal{P}$ measures Y and sends the result y to $\mathcal{V}$. $\mathcal{P}$ holds a superposition over the preimages of y.
3. $\mathcal{V}$ replies with a uniformly random *challenge* bit $c \in \{0, 1\}$.
4. If $c = 0$ ("test round"), $\mathcal{P}$ measures X in the computational basis and sends the outcome. If $c = 1$ ("Hadamard round"), $\mathcal{P}$ measures X in the Hadamard basis and sends the outcome.

After the four message rounds above are completed, the verifier uses their knowledge of H and the secret key sk to either accept or reject the instance H.

Our Results. In this work, we show that the Mahadev protocol can be transformed into protocols with significantly more favorable parameters, and with additional properties of interest. Specifically, we show how to build non-interactive protocols (with setup) for the same task, with negligible completeness and soundness errors. One of our protocols enables a verifier to publish a single public "setup" string and then receive arbitrarily many proofs from different provers, each for a different instance. We also construct a non-interactive protocol that satisfies the zero-knowledge property [10].

In principle, one could ask for slightly less interaction: the prover and the verifier receive the instance from a third party, and then the prover simply sends a proof to the verifier, with no setup. While we cannot rule such a protocol out,

---

[1] We take one round to mean a single one-way message from the prover to the verifier, or vice-versa. The Mahadev protocol involves four such messages.

constructing it seems like a major challenge (and may even be impossible). Such a proof must be independent of the secret randomness of the verifier, making it difficult to apply Mahadev's "cryptographic leash." Without cryptographic assumptions, such a protocol would imply BQP $\subseteq$ MA [1], which is unlikely.

All of our results are conditioned on the hardness of the LWE problem for quantum computers; we call this *the LWE assumption*. This assumption is inherited from the Mahadev protocol. For the zero-knowledge protocol, we also require fully-homomorphic encryption (FHE) with circuit privacy [38]. Our security proofs hold in the Quantum Random Oracle Model (QROM) [11]. For simplicity, we assume that the relevant security parameters are polynomial in the input BQP instance size n, so that efficient algorithms run in time poly(n) and errors are (ideally) negligible in n.

Transforming the Mahadev Protocol. We apply several transformations to the Mahadev protocol:

1. making the first message instance-independent (i.e., moving it to an offline setup phase);
2. applying parallel repetition, via a new parallel repetition theorem;
3. adding zero-knowledge, by means of classical NIZKs and classical FHE; and
4. applying Fiat-Shamir (in the QROM [11]).

Establishing that these transformations satisfy desirable properties is challenging. For instance, since cheating provers can now be quantum, classical parallel repetition theorems do not apply.

Instance-Independent Setup. Our first transformation is relatively simple, at a high level. Instead of setting the basis choice depending on the 2-local term of that we want to measure, we can just pick the basis uniformly at random and the choice is correct with probability $\frac{1}{4}$. When we consider multiple copies of the ground state, and each copy is assigned both a random choice of basis and a 2-local terms, then about $\frac{1}{4}$ of the copies get a consistent assignment. Thus, we can make the initial message instance-independent (and move it to an offline setup phase) by increasing the number of parallel measurements by a constant factor. We explain this transformation in more detail in Sect. 3. We refer to the resulting protocol as "the three-round Mahadev protocol," denoted by $\mathfrak{M}$.

Parallel Repetition. Parallel repetition of a protocol is a very desirable property since it decreases the soundness error exponentially, without increasing the number of rounds of interaction (as in serial repetition). Given the importance of the Mahadev protocol, parallel repetition could be a useful tool for applying it in practice. However, several complications arise when attempting to show this. First, the Mahadev protocol is clearly private-coin, which is precisely the category of protocol that is challenging even in the classical setting [6,29]. Second, classical proofs of parallel repetition typically involve constructing a single-copy prover that uses many rounds of nested rejection sampling. The quantum analogue of such a procedure, quantum rewinding, can only be applied in special circumstances [5,45] and seems difficult to apply to parallel repetition.

We establish our new parallel repetition theorem with alternative techniques, suited specifically for the Mahadev protocol. We show that, for NO instances, the accepting paths of the verifier for the two different challenges ($c = 0$ and $c = 1$) correspond to two nearly (computationally) orthogonal projectors. We also show that this persists in k-fold parallel repetition, meaning that each pair of distinct challenge strings $\mathbf{c}, \mathbf{c}' \in \{0,1\}^k$ corresponds to nearly orthogonal projectors. From there, a straightforward argument shows that the prover cannot succeed on a non-negligible fraction of challenge strings. We show that k-fold parallel repetition yields the same optimal soundness error δ^k as sequential repetition.

Taken together with the first transformation, the result is a three-round QPIA (with offline setup) for verifying BQP. We denote the k-fold parallel repetition of $\mathfrak{M}$ by $\mathfrak{M}^k$.

Theorem 1.1. *Under the* LWE *assumption, $\mathfrak{M}^k$ is a three-round protocol (with offline setup) for verifying* BQP *with completeness $1 - \mathrm{negl}(n)$ and soundness error $2^{-k} + \mathrm{negl}(n)$.*

Zero-Knowledge. Zero-knowledge is a very useful cryptographic property of proof systems. Roughly, a protocol is zero-knowledge if the verifier "learns nothing" from the interaction with the honest prover, except that they have a "yes" instance. This notion is formalized by requiring an efficient simulator whose output distribution is indistinguishable from the distribution of the protocol outcomes.

In our next result, we show how to modify the protocol $\mathfrak{M}^k$ of Theorem 1.1 to achieve zero-knowledge against arbitrary classical verifiers. Our approach is similar to that of [19], but uses a purely classical verifier. Instead of the prover providing the outcomes of the measurements to be checked by the verifier (as in $\mathfrak{M}^k$), a classical non-interactive zero-knowledge proof (NIZK) is provided. However, the NP statement "the measurements will pass verification" depends on the inversion trapdoor of the verifier, which must remain secret from the prover. To overcome this obstacle, we use classical fully homomorphic encryption (FHE). In the setup phase, an encryption of the verifier's secret keys is provided to the prover, enabling the prover to later compute the NIZK homomorphically. To establish the zero-knowledge property, we require the FHE scheme to have circuit privacy, which means that the verifier cannot learn the evaluated circuit *from the ciphertext* provided by the prover. To prove the zero-knowledge property, we also need the extra assumption that the setup phase is performed by a trusted third party, since we cannot rely on the verifier to perform it honestly anymore.

In classical zero-knowledge arguments, it is common to consider efficient provers who are provided an NP-witness of the statement to prove. In the quantum setting, if we assume that the quantum polynomial-time prover has access to a quantum proof of a QMA statement,[2] we achieve the following.

---

[2] QMA is a quantum analogue of NP. In QMA, an untrusted quantum proof is given to a quantum poly-time verifier.

Theorem 1.2 (Informal). *Under the* LWE *assumption, if circuit-private FHE exists, then there exists a three-round zero-knowledge argument for* QMA *(with trusted setup) with negligible completeness and soundness error.*

Fiat-Shamir Transformation. In the above protocols (both $\mathfrak{M}^k$ and its ZK-variant), the second message of the verifier is a uniformly random $\mathbf{c} \in \{0,1\}^k$. In the final transformation, we eliminate this "challenge" round via the well-known Fiat-Shamir transform [23]: the prover generates the challenge bits $\mathbf{c} \in \{0,1\}^k$ themselves by evaluating a public hash function $\mathcal{H}$ on the transcript of the protocol thus far. In our case, this means that the prover selects[3] $\mathbf{c} := \mathcal{H}(H, pk, y)$. Of course, the verifier also needs to adapt their actions at the verdict stage, using $\mathbf{c} = \mathcal{H}(H, pk, y)$ when deciding acceptance/rejection. The resulting protocols now only have a setup phase and a single message from the prover to the verifier.

Fiat-Shamir (FS) is typically used to establish security in the Random Oracle Model, in the sense that FS preserves soundness up to negligible loss provided $\mathcal{H}$ has superpolynomially large range [7,40]. It is straightforward to see that this last condition is required; it is also the reason we applied parallel repetition prior to FS. A well-known complication in the quantum setting is that quantum computers can evaluate any public classical function $\mathcal{H}$ in superposition via the unitary operator $U_\mathcal{H} \colon |x\rangle|y\rangle \mapsto |x\rangle|y \oplus \mathcal{H}(x)\rangle$. This means we must use the Quantum Random Oracle Model (QROM) [11], which grants all parties oracle access to $U_\mathcal{H}$. Proving the security of transformations like FS in the QROM is the subject of recent research, and newly developed techniques have largely shown that FS in the QROM preserves soundness for so-called Σ-protocols [22,33]. Extending those results to our protocols is relatively straightforward. Applying FS to $\mathfrak{M}^k$ then yields the following.

Theorem 1.3. *Let* $k = \omega(\log n)$, *and let* FS($\mathfrak{M}^k$) *denote the protocol resulting from applying Fiat-Shamir to the k-fold parallel repetition of the three-round Mahadev protocol. Under the* LWE *assumption, in the QROM,* FS($\mathfrak{M}^k$) *is a non-interactive protocol (with offline setup) for verifying* BQP *with negligible completeness and soundness errors.*

If we instead apply the Fiat-Shamir transform to the zero-knowledge protocol from Theorem 1.2, we achieve the following.[4]

Theorem 1.4 (Informal). *Under the* LWE *assumption, in the QROM, there exists a classical non-interactive zero-knowledge argument (with trusted offline setup) for* QMA, *with negligible completeness and soundness errors.*

Related Results. After an initial version of our work was made public, showing how the Mahadev protocol can be reduced to four rounds using parallel repetition and the Fiat-Shamir transform, Chia, Chung, and Yamakawa posted a

---

[3] Here pk and y are k-tuples since we are transforming parallel-repeated protocols.

[4] Note that FS($\mathfrak{M}^k$) in Theorem 1.3 is also a protocol for verifying QMA with negligible error if the prover is given a quantum witness.

preprint [17] describing the same result, with an alternative proof of parallel repetition. They also showed how to make the verifier run in polylog time using indistinguishability obfuscation. Our work was performed independently, and we subsequently improved our result to make the protocol non-interactive with setup and zero-knowledge.

Radian and Sattath [41] recently established what they call "a parallel repetition theorem for NTCFs," which are the aforementioned classical functions f_{pk}. However, the context of [41] is very different from ours and their parallel repetition theorem follows from a purely classical result.

Broadbent, Ji, Song, and Watrous [16] presented the first quantum zero-knowledge proofs for QMA with efficient provers. Vidick and Zhang [44] combined this protocol with the Mahadev protocol [34] to make the communication classical. Broadbent and Grilo [15] showed a "quantum Σ" zero-knowledge proof for QMA (with a quantum verifier). In the non-interactive setting, Coladangelo, Vidick, and Zhang [19] constructed a non-interactive zero-knowledge argument with quantum setup and Broadbent and Grilo [15] showed a quantum statistical zero-knowledge proof in the secret parameter model.

Open Problems. This work raises several natural open questions. First, is it possible to prove the soundness of our protocol when the oracle $\mathcal{H}$ is instantiated with a concrete (e.g., correlation-intractable [39]) hash function? Our current analysis only applies in an idealized model.

Another natural line of work is studying parallel repetition for other QPIAs such as [12,26,44], perhaps including small modifications such as "random termination" as needed in purely classical private-coin protocols [8,29,31].

Finally, a similar classical NIZK protocol can also be achieved using the techniques of locally simulatable proofs [15,28]. We leave as an open problem understanding whether such a protocol could give us extra useful properties.

2   Preliminaries and Notation

Most algorithms we consider are efficient, meaning that they run in time polynomial in both the input size (typically n) and the security parameter (typically λ). We assume that n and λ are polynomially-related. The two main classes of algorithms of interest are PPT (probabilistic poly-time) and QPT (quantum poly-time). We say that $f = \text{negl}(n)$ if $f = o(n^{-c})$ for every constant c. We denote by U_f the efficient map that coherently implements a classical function $f\colon \{0,1\}^n \to \{0,1\}^m$, i.e., $U_f|x\rangle|y\rangle = |x\rangle|y \oplus f(x)\rangle$, when there exists an efficient deterministic circuit that computes f.

2.1   The Local Hamiltonian Problem and Verification for BQP

Any promise problem $L = (L_{\text{yes}}, L_{\text{no}}) \in$ QMA can be reduced to the local Hamiltonian problem such that for $x \in L_{\text{yes}}$, the Hamiltonian H_x has a low-energy ground state $|\psi_x\rangle$, and for $x \in L_{\text{no}}$, all quantum states have large energy [32].

While the quantum witness $|\psi_x\rangle$ may be hard to prepare for general $L \in$ QMA, it can be prepared efficiently if $L \in$ BQP. Furthermore, the problem remains QMA-complete even with a Hamiltonian that can be measured by performing standard (Z) and Hadamard (X) basis measurements [9,20,36].

Problem 2.1. The 2-local ZX-Hamiltonian promise problem $\text{ZX}_{a,b} = (\text{ZX}_{\text{yes}},$ $\text{ZX}_{\text{no}})$, with parameters $a, b \in \mathbb{R}$, $b > a$ and gap $b - a > \text{poly}(n)^{-1}$, is defined as follows. An instance is a local Hamiltonian $H = \sum_{i<j} J_{ij}(X_i X_j + Z_i Z_j)$, where $J_{ij} \in \mathbb{R}$ with $2\sum_{i<j}|J_{ij}| = 1$ and each X_i (resp. Z_i) is a Pauli X (resp. Pauli Z) gate acting on the ith qubit. For $H \in \text{ZX}_{\text{yes}}$, the smallest eigenvalue of H is at most a, while if $H \in \text{ZX}_{\text{no}}$, the smallest eigenvalue of H is at least b.

Note that given the normalization factors, we can see that each term $(X_i X_j$ or $Z_i Z_j)$ is associated with the probability $p_{ij} = |J_{ij}|$. When working with Hamiltonian terms S, we overload the notation for convenience. First, we write S_j to denote the Pauli operator assigned by S to qubit j, so that $S = \bigotimes_j S_j$. Second, we write $i \in S$ to indicate that i is a qubit index for which S does not act as the identity, i.e., $S_i \neq \mathbb{1}$. We let $p_S := p_{ij}$ for $i, j \in S$ and $m_S \in \{\pm 1\}$ be the sign of J_{ij}.

Morimae and Fitzsimons present a protocol (the "MF protocol") with a quantum prover $\mathcal{P}$ and a limited verifier $\mathcal{V}$ who only needs to perform single-qubit X and Z basis measurements [36]. $\mathcal{P}$ prepares the ground state of the Hamiltonian and sends it to $\mathcal{V}$, who then samples a term S with probability p_S and performs the corresponding measurement $\{M_{\pm 1} = \frac{1 \pm S}{2}\}$. Notice that Z or X basis measurements suffice to estimate the energy of S. The success probability with input state ρ is $\sum_S p_S \text{tr}(M_{-m_S}\rho) = \frac{1}{2} - \frac{1}{2}\text{tr}(H\rho)$, and negligible error can be achieved with parallel repetition.[5]

In the following discussion, we encode S by an n-bit string $h(S)$: for each $i \in S$, set $h_i = 0$ (resp. 1) for a Z (resp. X) basis measurement. For other qubits, the choice is irrelevant but we set $h_i = 0$ for concreteness. We let $\alpha_{h,\rho} := \text{tr}(M_{-m_S}\rho)$ denote the success probability of the MF protocol described above with the state ρ, conditioned on the event that $h = h(S)$ is sampled. Thus the success probability with ρ is $\mathbb{E}_h[\alpha_{h,\rho}]$.

2.2   The Mahadev Protocol for BQP Verification

The Mahadev protocol relies crucially on two special classes of functions: Noisy Trapdoor Claw-free Functions (NTCFs) $\mathcal{F}$ and Noisy Trapdoor Injective Functions (NTIFs) $\mathcal{G}$. Both can be constructed based on the LWE assumption [12,34] and come with four polynomial-time algorithms ($\text{Gen}_{\mathcal{F}}, \text{Chk}_{\mathcal{F}}, \text{Inv}_{\mathcal{F}}, \text{Samp}_{\mathcal{F}}$) and ($\text{Gen}_{\mathcal{G}}, \text{Chk}_{\mathcal{G}}, \text{Inv}_{\mathcal{G}}, \text{Samp}_{\mathcal{G}}$). For complete details, and for the LWE construction, see [12,34].

---

[5] $\mathcal{V}$ receives T copies of the ground state of H and performs an independent test on each copy. By accepting if at least $(2-a-b)T/4$ copies accept, both the completeness and soundness errors are suppressed to negligible with polynomial $T(|x|)$ (cf. [34, Theorem 8.4]). See [43, Sect. 3] for details.

The Mahadev protocol [34] for BQP verification allows V to request an X or Z basis measurement outcome without revealing the basis to P. The aim of the protocol is to verify that the prover's response, when appropriately decoded, is close to the measurement outcomes of some n-qubit quantum state ρ. Crucially, this guarantee holds simultaneously for all basis choices $h \in \{0,1\}^n$, where 0 (resp. 1) denotes a Z (resp. X) basis measurement. With this guarantee, the verifier can then apply the verification procedure of the MF protocol to the decoded responses of the prover in order to decide acceptance or rejection.

In the following protocol, for each qubit, if Z (resp. X) basis measurement is desired, then an NTIF (resp. NTCF) key is sent. Since $\mathsf{Chk}_{\mathcal{F}}$ and $\mathsf{Chk}_{\mathcal{G}}$ (resp. $\mathsf{Samp}_{\mathcal{F}}$ and $\mathsf{Samp}_{\mathcal{G}}$) are identical [34], we denote them by Chk (resp. Samp). We let $\mathsf{Gen}(1^\lambda, h)$ for $h \in \{0,1\}^*$ denote the following key generation algorithm: for every bit i of h, run $(pk_i, sk_i) \leftarrow \mathsf{Gen}_{\mathcal{G}}(1^\lambda)$ if $h_i = 0$ and $(pk_i, sk_i) \leftarrow \mathsf{Gen}_{\mathcal{F}}(1^\lambda)$ if $h_i = 1$. Set $pk = (pk_i)_i$ and $sk = (sk_i)_i$ and output the key pairs (pk, sk).

Protocol 1 (Mahadev Protocol).

Setup *Choose a security parameter $\lambda \geq n$. Both P and V receive an instance of Problem 2.1, namely $H = \sum_S p_S \frac{1 + m_S S}{2}$.*

Round V_1. *V samples r terms $S = (S_1, \ldots, S_r)$ and computes $h = h(S)$, the concatenation of $h(S_1), \ldots, h(S_r)$. V generates the key pair $(pk, sk) \leftarrow \mathsf{Gen}(1^\lambda, h)$ and sends pk to P.*

Round P_1. *P prepares $|\phi\rangle^{\otimes r} = \sum_{b \in \{0,1\}^{nr}} \phi_b |b\rangle_W$, r copies of the n-qubit ground state of H. For $j \in [r], \ell \in [n]$ and each qubit $W_{j\ell}$ in W, P performs Samp on input the key $pk_{j\ell}$ coherently and yields a state negligibly close to $\frac{1}{|\mathcal{X}|^{n/2}} \sum_{x \in \mathcal{X}^n} \sum_{b \in \{0,1\}^{nr}} \phi_b |b\rangle_W |x\rangle_X |\psi_{f_{pk}(b,x)}\rangle_Y$, where $|\psi_{f_{pk}(b,x)}\rangle :=$ $\bigotimes_{j \in [r], \ell \in [n]} |\psi_{f_{pk_{j\ell}}(b_{j\ell}, x_{j\ell})}\rangle$. Next, P measures Y and sends the outcome y to V.*

Round V_2. *V responds with a uniformly random "challenge" bit $c \in \{0,1\}$. We call $c = 0 =: \mathfrak{t}$ a "test round" and $c = 1 =: \mathfrak{h}$ a "Hadamard round."*

Round P_2. *If $c = \mathfrak{t}$, P measures WX in the computational basis. If $c = \mathfrak{h}$, P measures WX in the Hadamard basis. In either case, P sends the measurement outcome (w, t) to V.*

Verdict *If $c = \mathfrak{t}$, V accepts if $\bigwedge_{j \in [r], \ell \in [n]} \mathsf{Chk}(pk_{j\ell}, w_{j\ell}, t_{j\ell}, y_{j\ell}) = 1$.*

If $c = \mathfrak{h}$, V performs the following: for each copy j and qubit $\ell \in [n]$,

1. *if $h_{j\ell} = 0$, run $(e_{j\ell}, x_{b_{j\ell}, y_{j\ell}}) \leftarrow \mathsf{Inv}_{\mathcal{G}}(sk_{j\ell}, y_{j\ell})$. If $h_{j\ell} = 1$, run $x_{0, y_{j\ell}} \leftarrow \mathsf{Inv}_{\mathcal{F}}(sk_{j\ell}, 0, y_{j\ell})$ and $x_{1, y_{j\ell}} \leftarrow \mathsf{Inv}_{\mathcal{F}}(sk_{j\ell}, 1, y_{j\ell})$ to get both preimages. Then compute $e_{j\ell} = t_{j\ell} \cdot (x_{0, y_{j\ell}} \oplus x_{1, y_{j\ell}}) \oplus w_{j\ell}$.*

   If any of the above the algorithms returns reject for any j, ℓ, or $t_{j\ell}$ is trivial (e.g., 0^n, see [12]), reject. Otherwise store $e = (e_{j\ell})_{j \in [r], \ell \in [n]}$ as the witness to the next check.

2. *V sets $v_j = 1$ if the witness $(e_{j\ell})_{\ell \in S_j}$ satisfies $M_{-m_{S_j}}$ (defined in Section 2.1).[6]*

Finally, V accepts if $\sum_{j \in [r]} v_j \geq (2 - a - b)r/4$.

---

[6] A string e satisfies a projector M if $\langle e|M|e\rangle = 1$, i.e., $|e\rangle$ lies in the support of M.

Theorem 2.1 (Theorems 1.1 and 8.6 in [34]). *Under the* LWE *assumption, Protocol 1 is a four-message quantum-prover interactive argument for the class* BQP *with completeness error* $\mathrm{negl}(n)$ *and soundness error* $3/4 + \mathrm{negl}(n)$.

3 Instance-Independent Key Generation

We now show how to generate the keys in the Mahadev protocol before the parties receive the input Hamiltonian, in an offline setup phase. To that end, we modify the MF protocol so the sampling of the Hamiltonian term is independent of the performed measurements. In our variant, for some $r = \mathrm{poly}(n)$, $\mathcal{V}$ samples n-bit strings $h_1, \ldots, h_r$ uniformly and independent 2-local terms $S_1, \ldots, S_r$ according to distribution π (in which S is sampled with the probability p_S from Sect. 2.1). We say the bases h_i and the terms S_i are *consistent* if, when the observable for the jth qubit in S_i is Z (resp., X) then the jth bit of h_i is 0 (resp., 1). Since h_i is uniformly sampled and S_i is 2-local, they are consistent with probability at least $\frac{1}{4}$.

In an r-copy protocol, we let $A := \{i \in [r] : h_i \text{ and } S_i \text{ are consistent}\}$ and denote $t = |A|$. For each $i \in A$, $\mathcal{V}_i$ decides as in the MF protocol: if $i \notin A$, then $\mathcal{V}_i$ accepts. Thus we consider the following protocol.

Protocol 2 (A Modified Parallel-Repeated MF Protocol for $\mathrm{zx}_{a,b}$)

Setup. $\mathcal{V}$ samples the bases $h_1, \ldots, h_r \leftarrow \{0,1\}^n$ *uniformly.*
Round 1. $\mathcal{P}$ *sends the witness state ρ (r copies of the ground state).*
Round 2. $\mathcal{V}$ *measures the quantum state ρ in the bases $h_1, \ldots, h_r$. For each copy $i \in [r]$, $\mathcal{V}$ samples terms $S_1, \ldots, S_r \leftarrow \pi$. $\mathcal{V}$ records the subset $A \subseteq [r]$ of consistent copies. For each copy $i \in A$, $\mathcal{V}$ sets $v_i = 1$ if the outcome satisfies M_{-ms} and 0 otherwise. $\mathcal{V}$ accepts if $\sum_{i \in A} v_i \geq (2 - a - b)|A|/4$.*

For sufficiently large r, with high probability, there are around $r/4$ consistent copies. Thus to achieve the same completeness and soundness, it suffices to increase the number of copies by a constant factor. We thus have the following fact.

Lemma 3.1. *The completeness error and soundness error of Protocol 2 are negligible, provided $r = \omega\left(\frac{\log n}{(b-a)^2}\right)$ copies are used.*

Proof. First we observe that for each copy, with probability $1/4$, $\mathcal{V}$ measures the quantum state with a term sampled from the distribution π; otherwise $\mathcal{V}$ accepts. Thus for an instance H, the effective Hamiltonian to verify is $\tilde{H}^{\otimes r}$ where $\tilde{H} = \frac{31+H}{4}$. Following the standard parallel repetition theorem for QMA, we know that $\mathcal{P}$'s optimal strategy is to present the ground state of $\tilde{H}$, which is also the ground state of H.

With probability $\binom{r}{t}(\frac{1}{4})^t(\frac{3}{4})^{r-t}$, there are t consistent copies. Now for $i \in A$, we let X_i be a binary random variable corresponding to the decision of $\mathcal{V}_i$. For soundness, by Hoeffding's inequality[7] the success probability for A such that $|A| = t$ is

$$\Pr[\text{accept}|A] = \Pr\left[\frac{1}{t}\sum_{i\in A}X_i \geq \frac{c+s}{2}\right]$$

$$\leq \Pr\left[\frac{1}{t}\sum_{i\in A}X_i - s \geq \frac{c-s}{2}\right] \leq 2e^{-\frac{tg^2}{2}},$$

where $g = c - s$ is the promise gap. Then the overall success probability is

$$\Pr[\text{accept}] = 2 \cdot 4^{-r}\sum_{t=0}^{r}\binom{r}{t}3^{r-t}e^{-tg^2/2} \tag{1}$$

$$= 2\left(\frac{e^{-g^2/2}+3}{4}\right)^r \leq 2(1 - g^2/16)^r \leq 2e^{-rg^2/16}$$

since $1 - x/2 \geq e^{-x}$ for $x \in [0,1]$ and $1 - x \leq e^{-x}$ for $x \geq 0$. Thus $r = \omega(g^{-2}\log n)$ suffices to suppress the soundness error to $n^{-\omega(1)}$. Since $g^{-1} = \text{poly}(n)$, polynomially many copies suffice to achieve negligible soundness error.

For completeness, again by Hoeffding's inequality,

$$\Pr[\text{reject}|A] = \Pr\left[\frac{1}{t}\sum_{i\in A}X_i < \frac{c+s}{2}\right]$$

$$\leq \Pr\left[c - \frac{1}{t}\sum_{i\in A}X_i > \frac{c-s}{2}\right] \leq 2e^{-\frac{tg^2}{2}}.$$

By the same calculation as in (1), the completeness error is negligible if we set $r = \omega(g^{-2}\log n)$. $\qquad\square$

Remark 3.1. The terms S_i are sampled *independently* of the interaction in the protocol. We let $\text{term}(H, s)$ denote the deterministic algorithm that outputs a term from H according to distribution π when provided the randomness $s \in \{0,1\}^p$ for sufficiently large polynomial p. For bases $h \in \{0,1\}^{nr}$ and $s \in \{0,1\}^p$, $\alpha_{h,s,\rho}$ denotes the success probability when $\mathcal{P}$ sends the quantum state ρ.

The modifications to the MF protocol which resulted in Protocol 2 above can also be made (with minor adjustments) to the Mahadev protocol (Protocol 1). These changes are as follows:

1. In **Round** $\mathcal{V}_1$, the measurement bases h are sampled uniformly at random and S is not sampled.
2. In the **Verdict** stage for a Hadamard round ($c = 1$), $\mathcal{V}$ computes the measurement outcomes, as in check 1. Then $\mathcal{V}$ samples terms $S_1, \ldots, S_r \leftarrow \pi$ and for the consistent copies, $\mathcal{V}$ performs the check in 2.

We refer to this variant of Protocol 1 as "the three-round Mahadev protocol", and denote it by $\mathfrak{M}$.

---

[7] $\Pr[\frac{1}{n}\sum_i X_i - \mu \geq \delta] \leq e^{-2t\delta^2}$ for i.i.d. $X_1, \ldots, X_n \in [0,1]$.

4 A Parallel Repetition Theorem for the Mahadev Protocol

In a k-fold parallel repetition of $\mathfrak{M}$, an honest prover runs the honest single-fold prover independently for each copy of the protocol. Meanwhile, the honest verifier runs the single-fold verifier independently for each copy, accepting if and only if all k verifiers accept. The completeness error clearly remains negligible. To control soundness error, we establish a parallel repetition theorem.

In preparation, we fix the following notation related to the Verdict stage of $\mathfrak{M}$. We refer frequently to the notation from our description of Protocol 1 above, which applies to $\mathfrak{M}$ as well. First, the check $\bigwedge_{j \in [r], \ell \in [n]} \mathsf{Chk}(pk_{j\ell}, w_{j\ell}, t_{j\ell}, y_{j\ell}) = 1$ in a test round is represented by a projection $\Pi_{sk,\mathsf{t}}$ acting on registers WXY. Specifically, this is the projector whose image is spanned by all inputs (w, t, y) that are accepted by the verifier in the Verdict stage. Note that running Chk does not require the trapdoor sk, but the relation implicitly depends on it. For notational convenience, we also denote $\Pi_{sk,\mathsf{t}}$ as $\Pi_{s,sk,\mathsf{t}}$, though the projector does not depend on s (defined in Remark 3.1). Second, the two Hadamard round checks 1 and 2 of the Verdict stage are represented by a projector $\Pi_{s,sk,\mathfrak{h}}$.

4.1 A Lemma for the Single-Copy Protocol

We begin by showing an important fact about the single-copy protocol: the verifier's accepting paths associated to the two challenges correspond to nearly orthogonal[8] projectors. Moreover, in a certain sense this property holds even for input states that are adaptively manipulated by a dishonest prover after they have learned which challenge will take place. This fact is essential in our analysis of the parallel repetition of many copies in the following sections.

The Setup. As discussed in [34], any prover $\mathcal{P}$ can be characterized as follows. First, pick a state family $|\Psi_{pk}\rangle$; this state is prepared on registers $WXYE$ after receiving pk. Here Y is the register that will be measured in Round $\mathcal{P}_1$, W and X are the registers that will be measured in Round $\mathcal{P}_2$, and E is the private workspace of $\mathcal{P}$. Then, choose two unitaries U_{t} and $U_{\mathfrak{h}}$ to describe the Round $\mathcal{P}_2$ actions of $\mathcal{P}$ before any measurements, in the test round and Hadamard round, respectively. Both U_{t} and $U_{\mathfrak{h}}$ act on $WXYE$, but can only be classically controlled on Y, as they must be implemented after $\mathcal{P}$ has measured Y and sent the result to the verifier. (Of course, a cheating prover is not constrained to follow the honest protocol, but we can nevertheless designate a fixed subsystem Y that carries their message.) We will write $\mathcal{P} = (|\Psi_{pk}\rangle, U_{\mathsf{t}}, U_{\mathfrak{h}})$, where it is implicit that $|\Psi_{pk}\rangle$ is a family of states parameterized by pk.

At the end of the protocol, the registers WXY are measured and given to the verifier. Recall that we can view the final actions of the verifier as applying one of two measurements: a test-round measurement or a Hadamard-round

---

[8] Strictly speaking, the projectors are only nearly orthogonal when applied to states prepared by efficient provers.

measurement. Let $\Pi_{s,sk,\mathfrak{t}}$ and $\Pi_{s,sk,\mathfrak{h}}$ denote the "accept" projectors for those measurements, respectively. For a given prover $\mathcal{P}$, we additionally define

$$\Pi_{s,sk,\mathfrak{t}}^{U_{\mathfrak{t}}} := U_{\mathfrak{t}}^{\dagger}(\Pi_{s,sk,\mathfrak{t}} \otimes \mathbb{1}_E)U_{\mathfrak{t}}, \quad \Pi_{s,sk,\mathfrak{h}}^{U_{\mathfrak{h}}} := U_{\mathfrak{h}}^{\dagger}(H_{WX}\Pi_{s,sk,\mathfrak{h}}H_{WX} \otimes \mathbb{1}_E)U_{\mathfrak{h}},$$

where H_{WX} denotes the Hadamard transform on registers WX, i.e., the Hadamard gate applied to every qubit in those registers. These projectors have a natural interpretation: they describe the action of the two accepting projectors of the verifier on the initial state $|\Psi_{pk}\rangle$ of the prover, taking into account the (adaptive) attacks the prover makes in Round $\mathcal{P}_2$.

A Key Lemma. We now prove a fact about the single-copy protocol. The proof is largely a matter of making some observations about the results from [34], and then combining them in the right way.

Recall that, after the setup phase, for any instance H of the ZX-Hamiltonian problem (Problem 2.1), $\mathfrak{M}$ begins with the verifier $\mathcal{V}$ making a measurement basis choice $h \in \{0,1\}^{nr}$ for all the qubits. After interacting with a prover $\mathcal{P}$, the verifier either rejects or produces a candidate measurement outcome, which is then tested as in Protocol 2. We let $D_{\mathcal{P},h}$ denote the distribution of this candidate measurement outcome for a prover $\mathcal{P}$ and basis choice h, averaged over all measurements and randomness of $\mathcal{P}$ and $\mathcal{V}$. It is useful to compare $D_{\mathcal{P},h}$ with an "ideal" distribution $D_{\rho,h}$ obtained by simply measuring some (nr)-qubit quantum state ρ (i.e., a candidate ground state) according to the basis choices specified by h, with no protocol involved. Formally, we state the following lemma.

Lemma 4.1. *Let* $\mathcal{P} = (|\Psi_{pk}\rangle, U_{\mathfrak{t}}, U_{\mathfrak{h}})$ *be a prover in* $\mathfrak{M}$ *such that, for every* $h \in \{0,1\}^{nr}$ *and* $s \in \{0,1\}^p$,

$$\mathop{\mathbb{E}}_{(pk,sk)\leftarrow\mathsf{Gen}(1^\lambda,h)}[\langle\Psi_{pk}|\Pi_{s,sk,\mathfrak{t}}^{U_{\mathfrak{t}}}|\Psi_{pk}\rangle] \geq 1 - \mathrm{negl}(n). \tag{2}$$

Then there exists an (nr)-*qubit quantum state* ρ *such that, for every* h, s,

$$\mathbb{E}_{(pk,sk)\leftarrow\mathsf{Gen}(1^\lambda,h)}[\langle\Psi_{pk}|\Pi_{s,sk,\mathfrak{h}}^{U_{\mathfrak{h}}}|\Psi_{pk}\rangle] \leq \alpha_{h,s,\rho} + \mathrm{negl}(n),$$

where $\alpha_{h,s,\rho}$ *(see Remark 3.1) is the success probability in the MF protocol with basis choice* h *and quantum state* ρ.

Proof. Up to negligible terms, (2) means that $\mathcal{P}$ is what Mahadev calls a *perfect prover*. She establishes two results ([34, Claim 7.3] and [34, Claim 5.7]) which, when taken together, directly imply the following fact about perfect provers. For every perfect prover $\mathcal{P}$, there exists an efficiently preparable quantum state ρ such that $D_{\mathcal{P},h}$ is computationally indistinguishable from $D_{\rho,h}$ for all basis choices $h \in \{0,1\}^{nr}$. In particular, the proof is obtained in two steps. First, for every perfect prover, there exists a nearby "trivial prover" whose attack in a Hadamard round commutes with standard basis measurement on the committed state [34, Claim 5.7]. Second, for every trivial prover, the distribution is computationally indistinguishable from measuring a consistent quantum state ρ in any basis h [34, Claim 7.3]. Mahadev shows this for exactly perfect provers, but the proofs can be easily adapted to our "negligibly-far-from-perfect" case.

Now consider two ways of producing a final accept/reject output of the verifier. In the first case, an output is sampled from the distribution $D_{\mathcal{P},h}$ and the verifier applies the final checks in $\mathfrak{M}$. In this case, the final outcome is obtained by performing the measurement $\{\Pi_{s,sk,\mathfrak{h}}^{U_\mathfrak{h}}, \mathbb{1} - \Pi_{s,sk,\mathfrak{h}}^{U_\mathfrak{h}}\}$ on the state $|\Psi_{pk}\rangle$, and accepting if the first outcome is observed. In the second case, an output is sampled from the distribution $D_{\rho,h}$ and the verifier applies the final checks in the MF protocol. In this case, the acceptance probability is $\alpha_{h,s,\rho}$ simply by definition. The result then follows directly. $\qquad\square$

Notice that for the soundness case, there is no state that succeeds non-negligibly in the MF protocol. In this case, Lemma 4.1 implies that for perfect provers the averaged projection

$$\underset{(pk,sk)\leftarrow\mathsf{Gen}(1^\lambda,h),h,s}{\mathbb{E}}[\langle\Psi_{pk}|\Pi_{s,sk,\mathfrak{h}}^{U_\mathfrak{h}}|\Psi_{pk}\rangle]$$

is negligible. In other words, provers who succeed almost perfectly in the test round must almost certainly fail in the Hadamard round. We emphasize that this is the case even though the prover can adaptively change their state (by applying $U_\mathfrak{t}$ or $U_\mathfrak{h}$) after learning which round will take place. This formalizes the intuitive claim we made at the beginning of the section about "adaptive orthogonality" of the two acceptance projectors corresponding to the two round types.

4.2 The Parallel Repetition Theorem

Characterization of a Prover in the k-Fold Protocol. We now discuss the behavior of a general prover in a k-fold protocol. We redefine some notation, and let $\mathcal{V}$ be the verifier and $\mathcal{P}$ an arbitrary prover in the k-fold protocol.

In the Setup phase, the key pairs $(pk_1, sk_1), \ldots, (pk_k, sk_k)$ are sampled according to the correct NTCF/NTIF distribution.[9] The secret keys $sk = (sk_1, \ldots, sk_k)$[10] are given to $\mathcal{V}$, whereas $pk = (pk_1, \ldots, pk_k)$ is given to $\mathcal{P}$.

In Round $\mathcal{P}_1$, without loss of generality, the action of $\mathcal{P}$ prior to measurement is to apply a unitary $U_{0,pk}$ on the zero state $|0\rangle_{WXYE}$, producing the state $|\Psi_{pk}\rangle_{WXYE} := U_{0,pk}|0\rangle_{WXYE}$. Each of W, X, Y is now a k-tuple of registers, and E is the prover's workspace. To generate the "commitment" message to $\mathcal{V}$, $\mathcal{P}$ performs standard basis measurement on Y. We write $|\Psi_{pk}\rangle_{WXYE} = \sum_y \beta_y |\Psi_{pk,y}\rangle_{WXE}|y\rangle_Y$. When the measurement outcome is y, the side state $\mathcal{P}$ holds is then $|\Psi_{pk,y}\rangle_{WXE}$. In the following analysis of the success

---

[9] Recall that the keys are sampled by choosing uniform bases h and running $\mathsf{Gen}(1^\lambda, h)$.

[10] The verifier can learn the corresponding bases h from sk; see [34] for details.

probability of $\mathcal{P}$, we consider the superposition $|\Psi_{pk}\rangle_{WXYE}$ instead of a classical mixture of the states $|\Psi_{pk,y}\rangle_{WXE}$ using the principle of deferred measurement.

In Round $\mathcal{P}_2$, without loss of generality, the action of $\mathcal{P}$ consists of a general operation (that can depend on c), followed by the honest action. The general operation is some efficient unitary U_c on $WXYE$. The honest action is measurement in the right basis, i.e., for each i, W_iX_i is measured in the standard basis (if $c_i = 0$) or the Hadamard basis (if $c_i = 1$). Equivalently, the honest action is (i.) apply $\mathfrak{H}_{WX}^c := \bigotimes_{i=1}^k (H^{c_i})_{W_iX_i}$, i.e., for each $\{i : c_i = 1\}$ apply a Hadamard to every qubit of W_iX_i, and then (ii.) apply standard basis measurement.

In the Verdict stage, $\mathcal{V}$ first applies for each i the two-outcome measurement corresponding to the Π_{s_i,sk_i,c_i} from the single-copy protocol. The overall decision is then to accept if the measurements accept for all i. We let

$$(\Pi_{s,sk,c})_{WXY} := \bigotimes_{i=1}^k (\Pi_{s_i,sk_i,c_i})_{W_iX_iY_i} \tag{3}$$

denote the corresponding acceptance projector for the entire k-copy protocol. The effective measurement on $|\Psi_{pk}\rangle_{WXYE}$ is then described by the projection

$$\left(\Pi_{s,sk,c}^{U_c}\right)_{WXYE} := (U_c^\dagger)_{WXYE}(\mathfrak{H}^c\Pi_{s,sk,c,y}\mathfrak{H}^c \otimes \mathbb{1}_E)(U_c)_{WXYE} .$$

The success probability of $\mathcal{P}$, which is characterized by the state $|\Psi_{pk}\rangle$ and family of unitaries $\{U_c\}_{c\in\{0,1\}^n}$, is thus $\displaystyle\mathop{\mathbb{E}}_{(pk,sk)\leftarrow\mathsf{Gen}(1^\lambda,h),h,s,c}\left[\langle\Psi_{pk}|\Pi_{s,sk,c}^{U_c}|\Psi_{pk}\rangle\right]$.

The Proof of Parallel Repetition. Recall that Lemma 4.1 states that the projectors corresponding to the two challenges in $\mathfrak{M}$ are nearly orthogonal, even when one takes into account the prover's adaptively applied unitaries. We show that this property persists in the k-copy protocol. Specifically, we show that all 2^k challenges are nearly orthogonal (in the same sense as in Lemma 4.1) with respect to any state $|\Psi_{pk}\rangle$ and any post-commitment unitaries U_c of the prover.

This can be explained informally as follows. For any two distinct challenges $c \neq c'$, there exists a coordinate i such that $c_i \neq c_i'$, meaning that one enters a test round in that coordinate while the other enters a Hadamard round. In coordinate i, by the single-copy result (Lemma 4.1), the prover who succeeds with one challenge should fail with the other. A complication is that, since we are dealing with an interactive argument, we must show that a violation of this claim leads to an *efficient* single-copy prover that violates the single-copy result. Once we have shown this, we can then apply it to any distinct challenge pairs $c \neq c'$. It then follows that we may (approximately) decompose $|\Psi_{pk}\rangle$ into components accepted in each challenge, each of which occurs with probability 2^{-k}. We can then use this decomposition to express the overall success probability of $\mathcal{P}$ in terms of this decomposition. As $|\Psi_{pk}\rangle$ is of course a normalized state, it will follow that the overall soundness error is negligibly close to 2^{-k}.

The "adaptive orthogonality" discussed above is formalized in Lemma 4.2. Recall that any prover in the k-fold parallel repetition of $\mathfrak{M}$ can be characterized by a state family $\{|\Psi_{pk}\rangle\}_{pk}$ that is prepared in Round $\mathcal{P}_1$ and a family of unitaries $\{U_c\}_{c\in\{0,1\}^k}$ that are applied in Round $\mathcal{P}_2$.

Lemma 4.2. *Let $\mathcal{P}$ be a prover in the k-fold parallel repetition of $\mathfrak{M}$ that prepares $|\Psi_{pk}\rangle$ in Round $\mathcal{P}_1$ and performs U_c in Round $\mathcal{P}_2$. Let $a, b \in \{0,1\}^k$ such that $a \neq b$ and choose i such that $a_i \neq b_i$. Then there is an (nr)-qubit quantum state ρ such that for every basis choice h and randomness s,*

$$\mathop{\mathbb{E}}_{(pk,sk)\leftarrow\mathsf{Gen}(1^\lambda,h)}\left[\langle\Psi_{pk}|\Pi^{U_b}_{s,sk,b}\Pi^{U_a}_{s,sk,a} + \Pi^{U_a}_{s,sk,a}\Pi^{U_b}_{s,sk,b}|\Psi_{pk}\rangle\right] \leq 2\alpha^{1/2}_{h_i,s_i,\rho} + \mathrm{negl}(n),$$

where $\alpha_{h_i,s_i,\rho}$ (see Remark 3.1) is the success probability with ρ conditioned on the event that h_i is sampled.

Proof. Since we are proving an upper bound for a quantity that is symmetric under the interchange of b and a, we can assume that $b_i = 0$ and $a_i = 1$ without loss of generality.

We first claim that there exists a quantum state ρ such that

$$\mathop{\mathbb{E}}_{(pk,sk)\leftarrow\mathsf{Gen}(1^\lambda,h)}\left[\langle\Psi_{pk}|\Pi^{U_b}_{s,sk,b}\Pi^{U_a}_{s,sk,a}\Pi^{U_b}_{s,sk,b}|\Psi_{pk}\rangle\right] \leq \alpha_{h_i,s_i,\rho} + \mathrm{negl}(n) \qquad (4)$$

for all basis choices h and randomness s. For a contradiction, suppose that is not the case. Then there exists a basis choice h^* and s^* and a polynomial η such that for every state ρ,

$$\mathop{\mathbb{E}}_{(pk,sk)\leftarrow\mathsf{Gen}(1^\lambda,h^*)}\left[\langle\Psi_{pk}|\Pi^{U_b}_{s^*,sk,b}\Pi^{U_a}_{s^*,sk,a}\Pi^{U_b}_{s^*,sk,b}|\Psi_{pk}\rangle\right] > \alpha_{h^*_i,s^*_i,\rho} + 1/\eta(n).$$

We show that this implies the existence of an efficient prover $\mathcal{P}^*$ for the single-copy three-round Mahadev protocol $\mathfrak{M}$ who violates Lemma 4.1. Define the following projector on $WXYE$:

$$\Sigma_a := U^\dagger_a(H^a \otimes \mathbb{1}_E)((\mathbb{1} \otimes \cdots \otimes \mathbb{1} \otimes \Pi \otimes \mathbb{1} \otimes \cdots \otimes \mathbb{1}) \otimes \mathbb{1}_E)(H^a \otimes \mathbb{1}_E)U_a.$$

Here Π denotes the single-copy protocol acceptance projector for the Hadamard round, with key sk_i and basis choice h^*_i, s^*_i. In the above, Π acts on the ith set of registers, i.e., $W_iX_iY_i$. The projector Σ_a corresponds to performing the appropriate Hadamard test in the ith protocol copy, and simply accepting all other copies unconditionally. It follows that $\Pi^{U_a}_{s,sk,a} \preceq \Sigma_a$, and we thus have

$$\mathop{\mathbb{E}}_{(pk,sk)\leftarrow\mathsf{Gen}(1^\lambda,h^*)}\left[\langle\Psi_{pk}|\Pi^{U_b}_{s^*,sk,b}\Sigma_a\Pi^{U_b}_{s^*,sk,b}|\Psi_{pk}\rangle\right]$$
$$\geq \mathop{\mathbb{E}}_{(pk,sk)\leftarrow\mathsf{Gen}(1^\lambda,h^*)}\left[\langle\Psi_{pk}|\Pi^{U_b}_{s^*,sk,b}\Pi^{U_a}_{s^*,sk,a}\Pi^{U_b}_{s^*,sk,b}|\Psi_{pk}\rangle\right]$$
$$> \alpha_{h^*_i,s^*_i,\rho} + 1/\eta. \qquad (5)$$

The single-copy prover $\mathcal{P}^*$ interacts with the single-copy verifier $\mathcal{V}^*$ as follows.

- In the Setup phase, after receiving the public key pk^*, initialize $k-1$ internally simulated verifiers, and set pk to be the list of their keys, with pk^* inserted in the ith position. Let $h = (h_1, \ldots, h_k)$ be the basis choices, and note that all but h_i are known to $\mathcal{P}^*$.
- Using the algorithms of $\mathcal{P}$, perform the following repeat-until-success (RUS) procedure for at most $q = \eta^4$ steps.
    1. Prepare the state $|\Psi_{pk}\rangle$ on registers $WXYE$, and then apply the unitary U_b.
    2. Apply the measurement determined by $\Pi_{s,sk,b}$ (defined in (3)); for index i we can use pk^* because $b_i = 0$; for the rest we know the secret keys.
    3. If the measurement rejects, go to step (1.), and otherwise apply $U_b^\dagger$ and output the state.
  If the RUS procedure does not terminate within q steps, then $\mathcal{P}^*$ prepares a state[11] $|\Phi_{pk}^*\rangle$ by performing Samp coherently on $|0^n\rangle_W$ (see Round 2 of Protocol 1).
  Note that if $\mathcal{P}^*$ terminates within q steps, the resulting state is

$$|\Phi_{pk}\rangle := \frac{\Pi_{s^*,sk,b}^{U_b}|\Psi_{pk}\rangle}{\|\Pi_{s^*,sk,b}^{U_b}|\Psi_{pk}\rangle\|} \, ;$$

  otherwise $|\Phi_{pk}^*\rangle$ is prepared.
- For the Round $\mathcal{P}_1$ message, measure the Y_i register of $|\Phi_{pk}\rangle$ and send the result to $\mathcal{V}^*$.
- When $\mathcal{V}^*$ returns the challenge bit w in Round 3, if $w = b_i = 0$, apply U_b (resp. $\mathbb{1}$) to $|\Phi_{pk}\rangle$ (resp. $|\Phi_{pk}^*\rangle$), and otherwise apply U_a. Then behave honestly, i.e., measure $W_i X_i$ in computational or Hadamard bases as determined by w, and send the outcomes.

By the RUS construction and the fact that $b_i = 0$, the state $|\Phi_{pk}\rangle$ or $|\Phi_{pk}^*\rangle$ is in the image of the test-round acceptance projector in the ith coordinate. This means that, when $\mathcal{V}^*$ enters a test round, i.e., $w = 0 = b_i$, $\mathcal{P}^*$ is accepted perfectly. In other words, $\mathcal{P}^*$ is a perfect prover[12] and thus satisfies the hypotheses of Lemma 4.1.

Now consider the case when $\mathcal{V}^*$ enters a Hadamard round, i.e., $w = 1$. Let

$$\Omega := \{(pk, sk) : \langle \Psi_{pk}|\Pi_{s^*,sk,b}^{U_b}|\Psi_{pk}\rangle > q^{-1/2}\}$$

denote the set of "good" keys. For $(pk, sk) \in \Omega$, the probability of not terminating within $q = \text{poly}(n)$ steps is at most $(1 - q^{-1/2})^q \leq e^{-\sqrt{q}}$. Therefore, the success probability of RUS for the good keys is $1 - \text{negl}(n)$. Thus we have

$$\mathop{\mathbb{E}}_{sk|\Omega} \left[\langle \Phi_{pk}|\Sigma_a|\Phi_{pk}\rangle\right] \Pr[\Omega] \leq \alpha_{h_i^*,s_i^*,\rho} + \text{negl}(n)$$

---

[11] To pass the test round, any efficiently preparable state suffices.

[12] While we used $\Pi_{h^*,sk,b}$ in the RUS procedure, and h_i^* is (almost always) not equal to the h_i selected by $\mathcal{V}^*$, the result is still a perfect prover state. This is because, as described in Protocol 1, the acceptance test in the test round is independent of the basis choice.

where we let $\mathop{\mathbb{E}}\limits_{X|E}[f(X)] := \frac{1}{\Pr[E]}\sum_{x \in E} p(x)f(x)$ denote the expectation value of $f(X)$ conditioned on event E for random variable X over finite set $\mathcal{X}$ with distribution p and function $f \colon \mathcal{X} \to [0,1]$. Now we divide (5) into two terms and find

$$
\begin{aligned}
\alpha_{h_i^*,s_i^*,\rho} + \eta^{-1} &< \mathop{\mathbb{E}}_{(pk,sk)}\left[\langle\Psi_{pk}|\Pi^{U_b}_{s^*,sk,b}\Sigma_a\Pi^{U_b}_{s^*,sk,b}|\Psi_{pk}\rangle\right] \\
&= \Pr[\Omega]\mathop{\mathbb{E}}_{(pk,sk)|\Omega}\left[\langle\Psi_{pk}|\Pi^{U_b}_{s^*,sk,b}\Sigma_a\Pi^{U_b}_{s^*,sk,b}|\Psi_{pk}\rangle\right] \\
&\quad + \Pr[\overline{\Omega}]\mathop{\mathbb{E}}_{(pk,sk)|\overline{\Omega}}\left[\langle\Psi_{pk}|\Pi^{U_b}_{s^*,sk,b}\Sigma_a\Pi^{U_b}_{s^*,sk,b}|\Psi_{pk}\rangle\right] \\
&\leq \Pr[\Omega]\mathop{\mathbb{E}}_{(pk,sk)|\Omega}\left[\langle\Psi_{pk}|\Pi^{U_b}_{s^*,sk,b}\Sigma_a\Pi^{U_b}_{s^*,sk,b}|\Psi_{pk}\rangle\right] + q^{-1/2} \\
&\leq \alpha_{h_i^*,\rho} + \mathrm{negl}(n) + q^{-1/2}.
\end{aligned}
$$

Since $q = \eta^4$, this is a contradiction. Therefore (4) holds for every h, s, i.e.,

$$
\mathop{\mathbb{E}}_{(pk,sk)\leftarrow\mathsf{Gen}(1^\lambda,h)}[\langle\Psi_{pk}|\Pi^{U_b}_{s,sk,b}\Pi^{U_a}_{s,sk,a}\Pi^{U_b}_{s,sk,b}|\Psi_{pk}\rangle] \leq \alpha_{h_i,s_i,\rho} + \mathrm{negl}(n).
$$

It then follows that

$$
\begin{aligned}
&\mathop{\mathbb{E}}_{(pk,sk)\leftarrow\mathsf{Gen}(1^\lambda,h)}\left[\langle\Psi_{pk}|\Pi^{U_b}_{h,sk,b}\Pi^{U_a}_{h,sk,a} + \Pi^{U_a}_{h,sk,a}\Pi^{U_b}_{h,sk,b}|\Psi_{pk}\rangle\right] \\
&= 2\mathop{\mathbb{E}}_{(pk,sk)\leftarrow\mathsf{Gen}(1^\lambda,h)}\left[\mathrm{Re}(\langle\Psi_{pk}|\Pi^{U_b}_{h,sk,b}\Pi^{U_a}_{h,sk,a}|\Psi_{pk}\rangle)\right] \\
&\leq 2\mathop{\mathbb{E}}_{(pk,sk)\leftarrow\mathsf{Gen}(1^\lambda,h)}\left[|\langle\Psi_{pk}|\Pi^{U_b}_{h,sk,b}\Pi^{U_a}_{h,sk,a}|\Psi_{pk}\rangle|\right] \\
&\leq 2\mathop{\mathbb{E}}_{(pk,sk)\leftarrow\mathsf{Gen}(1^\lambda,h)}\left[\langle\Psi_{pk}|\Pi^{U_b}_{h,sk,b}\Pi^{U_a}_{h,sk,a}\Pi^{U_b}_{h,sk,b}|\Psi_{pk}\rangle^{1/2}\right] \\
&\leq 2\mathop{\mathbb{E}}_{(pk,sk)\leftarrow\mathsf{Gen}(1^\lambda,h)}\left[\langle\Psi_{pk}|\Pi^{U_b}_{h,sk,b}\Pi^{U_a}_{h,sk,a}\Pi^{U_b}_{h,sk,b}|\Psi_{pk}\rangle\right]^{1/2} \leq 2\alpha_{h_i,s_i,\rho}^{1/2} + \mathrm{negl}(n)
\end{aligned}
$$

as claimed.   □

We remark that this adaptive orthogonality is guaranteed under a computational assumption. Assuming that no efficient quantum adversary can break the underlying security properties based on plain LWE, the projections are pairwise orthogonal in the sense of averaging over the key pairs (pk, sk) and with respect to any quantum state $|\Psi_{pk}\rangle$ prepared by an efficient quantum circuit.

We also emphasize that, in Lemma 4.2, for each pair $a \neq b$ the left-hand side is upper-bounded by the acceptance probability of measuring some state ρ in the basis h_i, and the quantum state ρ may be different among distinct choices of (a, b) and i. This implies that if $\mathcal{P}$ succeeds with one particular challenge perfectly[13] when we average over h and s, Lemma 4.2 and standard amplification techniques

---

[13] More concretely, if for some fixed a, $\Pi_{s,sk,a}|\Psi_{pk}\rangle = |\Psi_{pk}\rangle$.

(see Sect. 3) imply that it succeeds on challenge $b \neq a$ with probability at most
$$\mathop{\mathbb{E}}_{(pk,sk)\leftarrow\mathsf{Gen}(1^\lambda)} \langle \Psi_{pk}|\Pi_{s,sk,b}|\Psi_{pk}\rangle \leq \mathrm{negl}(n).$$ We note that this strategy leads to acceptance probability at most $2^{-k} + \mathrm{negl}(n)$.

Since pairwise orthogonality holds with respect to *any* efficiently preparable quantum state by Lemma 4.2, our parallel repetition theorem follows.

First, we state a key technical lemma.

Lemma 4.3. *Let $A_1, \ldots, A_m$ be projectors and $|\psi\rangle$ be a quantum state. Suppose there are real numbers $\delta_{ij} \in [0,2]$ such that $\langle\psi|A_iA_j+A_jA_i|\psi\rangle \leq \delta_{ij}$ for all $i \neq j$. Then $\langle\psi|A_1 + \cdots + A_m|\psi\rangle \leq 1 + \left(\sum_{i<j}\delta_{ij}\right)^{1/2}$.*

Proof. Let $\alpha := \langle\psi|A_1 + \ldots + A_m|\psi\rangle$. We have

$$
\begin{aligned}
\alpha^2 &\leq \langle\psi|(A_1 + \cdots + A_m)^2|\psi\rangle \\
&= \alpha + \sum_{i<j}\langle\psi|A_iA_j + A_jA_i|\psi\rangle \\
&\leq \alpha + \sum_{i<j}\delta_{ij}
\end{aligned}
\tag{6}
$$

The first inequality holds since $|\psi\rangle\langle\psi| \preceq \mathbb{1}$, and thus

$$\langle\psi|(A_1 + \cdots + A_m)|\psi\rangle\langle\psi|(A_1 + \cdots + A_m)|\psi\rangle \leq \langle\psi|(A_1 + \cdots + A_m)^2|\psi\rangle.$$

The equality (6) holds since each A_i is idempotent, and thus

$$
\begin{aligned}
\langle\psi|(A_1 + \cdots + A_m)^2|\psi\rangle &= \langle\psi|A_1^2 + \cdots + A_m^2|\psi\rangle + \sum_{i<j}\langle\psi|A_iA_j + A_jA_i|\psi\rangle \\
&= \langle\psi|A_1 + \cdots + A_m|\psi\rangle + \sum_{i<j}\langle\psi|A_iA_j + A_jA_i|\psi\rangle.
\end{aligned}
$$

Now observe that for $\beta > 0$, $x^2 \leq x + \beta$ implies $x \leq \frac{1}{2}(1 + \sqrt{1+4\beta}) \leq \frac{1}{2}(1 + (1 + 2\sqrt{\beta})) = 1 + \sqrt{\beta}$. Thus $\alpha \leq 1 + \sqrt{\sum_{i<j}\delta_{ij}}$ as claimed. $\qquad\square$

Observe that when the projectors are mutually orthogonal, we have $A_1 + \cdots + A_m \preceq \mathbb{1}$ and the bound clearly holds. Lemma 4.3 describes a relaxed version of this fact. In our application, the projectors and the state are parameterized by the key pair, and we use this bound to show that the average of pairwise overlaps is small. We are now ready to establish our parallel repetition theorem.

Lemma 4.4. *Let k be a positive integer and let $\{U_c\}_{c\in\{0,1\}^k}$ be any set of unitaries that may be implemented by $\mathcal{P}$ after the challenge coins are sent. Let $|\Psi_{pk}\rangle$ be any state $\mathcal{P}$ holds in the commitment round, and suppose $\mathcal{P}$ applies U_c followed by honest measurements when the coins are c. Then there exists a negligible function ϵ such that $\mathcal{V}_1, \ldots, \mathcal{V}_k$ accept $\mathcal{P}$ with probability at most $2^{-k} + \epsilon(n)$.*

Proof. The success probability of any prover in the k-fold protocol is

$$\Pr[\text{success}] = 2^{-k} \mathop{\mathbb{E}}_{(pk,sk)\leftarrow\mathsf{Gen}(1^\lambda,h),h,s} [\langle\Psi_{pk}| \sum_c \Pi^{U_c}_{s,sk,c} |\Psi_{pk}\rangle]$$

where h,s are drawn from uniform distributions.

Define a total ordering on $\{0,1\}^k$ such that $a < b$ if $a_i < b_i$ for the smallest index i such that $a_i \neq b_i$. Then by Lemma 4.3, we have

$$\Pr[\text{success}] \leq 2^{-k} + 2^{-k} \mathop{\mathbb{E}}_{h,s} \left[\sum_{a<b} \mathop{\mathbb{E}}_{(pk,sk)\leftarrow\mathsf{Gen}(1^\lambda,h)} [\langle\Psi_{pk}| \Pi^{U_a}_{s,sk,a}\Pi^{U_b}_{s,sk,b} + \Pi^{U_b}_{s,sk,b}\Pi^{U_a}_{s,sk,a} |\Psi_{pk}\rangle] \right]^{1/2}.$$

By Lemma 4.2, there exists a negligible function δ such that

$$\mathop{\mathbb{E}}_{(pk,sk)\leftarrow\mathsf{Gen}(1^\lambda,h)} [\langle\Psi_{pk}| \Pi^{U_a}_{s,sk,a}\Pi^{U_b}_{s,sk,b} + \Pi^{U_b}_{s,sk,b}\Pi^{U_a}_{s,sk,a} |\Psi_{pk}\rangle] \leq 2\alpha^{1/2}_{h_{i(a,b)},\rho_{ab}} + \delta$$

for every pair (a,b). Here $i(a,b)$ is the smallest index i such that $a_i \neq b_i$ and ρ_{ab} is the reduced quantum state associated with a,b, as guaranteed by Lemma 4.2. Let μ be the soundness error of the MF protocol. We have

$$\Pr[\text{success}] \leq 2^{-k} + 2^{-k} \mathop{\mathbb{E}}_{h,s} \left[\sum_{a<b} \left(2\alpha^{1/2}_{h_{i(a,b)},s_{i(a,b)},\rho_{ab}} + \delta \right) \right]^{1/2}$$

$$\leq 2^{-k} + 2^{-k} \mathop{\mathbb{E}}_{h,s} \left[\sum_{a<b} 2\alpha^{1/2}_{h_{i(a,b)},s_{i(a,b)},\rho_{ab}} \right]^{1/2} + 2^{-k} \sqrt{\binom{2^k}{2}} \delta^{1/2}$$

$$\leq 2^{-k} + 2^{-k} \left[\sum_{a<b} 2 \left(\mathop{\mathbb{E}}_{h,s} [\alpha_{h_{i(a,b)},s_{i(a,b)},\rho_{ab}}] \right)^{1/2} \right]^{1/2} + \delta^{1/2}$$

$$\leq 2^{-k} + 2^{-k} \left[\sum_{a<b} 2\mu^{1/2} \right]^{1/2} + \delta^{1/2}$$

$$\leq 2^{-k} + 2^{-k} \left[2^k(2^k - 1)\mu^{1/2} \right]^{1/2} + \delta^{1/2}$$

$$\leq 2^{-k} + \mu^{1/4} + \delta^{1/2}$$

where the second and third inequalities hold by Jensen's inequality. Amplifying the soundness of the MF protocol, μ is negligible using polynomially many copies by Lemma 3.1. Thus the soundness error is negligibly close to 2^{-k}. □

We note that Mahadev shows the soundness error for a single-copy protocol is negligibly close to $3/4$ [34], whereas Lemma 4.4 implies the error can be upper bounded by $1/2 + \mathrm{negl}(n)$. Mahadev obtains soundness error $3/4 + \mathrm{negl}(n)$ by considering a general prover $\mathcal{P}$ who, for each basis h, succeeds in the test round (characterized by $\Pi_{h,sk,t}$) with probability $1 - p_{h,t}$, in the first stage of the Hadamard round with probability $1 - p_{h,\mathfrak{h}}$, and in the second stage of the Hadamard round with probability at most $\sqrt{p_{h,\mathfrak{t}}} + p_{h,\mathfrak{h}} + \alpha_{h,\rho} + \text{negl}(n)$ for some state ρ [34, Claim 7.1]. These contributions are combined by applying the triangle inequality for trace distance. This analysis is loose since the two stages are both classical, and $\mathcal{P}$ must pass both stages to win the Hadamard round.

Finally, Lemma 4.4 immediately implies the following theorem.

Theorem 4.1. *Let $\mathfrak{M}^k$ be the k-fold parallel repetition of the three-round Mahadev protocol $\mathfrak{M}$. Under the LWE assumption, the soundness error of $\mathfrak{M}^k$ is at most $2^{-k} + \text{negl}(n)$.*

For completeness, we present the three-round protocol $\mathfrak{M}^k$.

Protocol 3 (Verification with instance-independent setup).

Setup $\mathcal{V}$ *samples random bases $h \in \{0,1\}^{nrk}$ and runs the key generation algorithm $(pk, sk) \leftarrow \text{Gen}(1^\lambda, h)$. $\mathcal{V}$ samples a string $s \in \{0,1\}^{prk}$ uniformly. $\mathcal{V}$ sends the public keys pk to $\mathcal{P}$.*

Round $\mathcal{P}_1$. $\mathcal{P}$ *queries* Samp *coherently on the witness state $|\psi\rangle^{\otimes rk}$, followed by a standard basis measurement on register Y. The outcome is sent to $\mathcal{V}$.*

Round $\mathcal{V}_2$. $\mathcal{V}$ *samples $c_1, \dots, c_k \leftarrow \{0,1\}$ and sends $c = (c_1, \dots, c_k)$ to $\mathcal{P}$.*

Round $\mathcal{P}_2$. *For each $i \in [k]$, $j \in [r]$, $\ell \in [n]$,*

1. *if $c_i = 0$, $\mathcal{P}$ performs a standard basis measurement and gets $u_{ij\ell} = (w_{ij\ell}, t_{ij\ell})$;*
2. *if $c_i = 1$, $\mathcal{P}$ performs a Hadamard basis measurment and gets $u_{ij\ell} = (w_{ij\ell}, t_{ij\ell})$.*

$\mathcal{P}$ *sends u to $\mathcal{V}$.*

Verdict *For each $i \in [k]$,*

1. *If $c_i = 0$, $\mathcal{V}$ accepts iff $\bigwedge_{j,\ell} \text{Chk}(pk_{j\ell}, w_{j\ell}, t_{j\ell}, y_{j\ell}) = 1$.*
2. *If $c_i = 1$, $\mathcal{V}$ records the set $A_i \subseteq [r]$ of consistent copies. For each $j \in A_i$ and $\ell \in [n]$:*
   (a) *If $h_{ij\ell} = 0$, run $(b_{ij}, x_{b_{ij}, y_{ij}}) \leftarrow \text{Inv}_{\mathcal{G}}(sk_{ij}, y_{ij})$. Set $e_{ij\ell} = b_{ij\ell}$; if $h_{ij} = 1$, compute $x_{0, y_{ij\ell}}, x_{1, y_{ij\ell}}$ and $e_{ij\ell} = t_{ij\ell} \cdot (x_{0, y_{ij\ell}} \oplus x_{1, y_{ij\ell}}) \oplus w_{ij}$. If any of the algorithms rejects or any of $t_{ij\ell}$ is trivial (e.g., $t_{ij\ell} = 0$, see [34]), $\mathcal{V}$ sets $v_{ij} = 0$; otherwise enters the next step.*
   (b) *$\mathcal{V}$ computes the terms $S_{ij} = \text{term}(H, s_{ij})$ for each $i \in [k], j \in [r]$. Set $v_{ij} = 1$ if $(e_{ij\ell})_{\ell \in S_{ij}}$ satisfies $M_{-m_{S_{ij}}}$ and $v_{ij} = 0$ otherwise.*
   Then $\mathcal{V}$ sets $v_i = 1$ if $\sum_{j \in A_i} v_{ij} \geq (2 - a - b)|A_i|/4$ and 0 otherwise.

$\mathcal{V}$ *accepts iff $v_i = 1$ for every $i \in [k]$.*

The verdict function is $\text{verdict}(H, s, sk, y, c, u) := \bigwedge_{i=1}^{k} v_i$.

Theorem 4.2. *For $r = \omega(\frac{\log n}{(b-a)^2})$ and $k = \omega(\log n)$, Protocol 3 is a quantum prover interactive argument for $\text{zX}_{a,b}$ with negligible completeness error and soundness error.*

5   A Classical Zero-Knowledge Argument for QMA

To turn $\mathfrak{M}^k$ into a zero-knowledge protocol, we first consider an intermediate protocol in which $\mathcal{P}$ first encrypts the witness state $|\psi\rangle^{\otimes rk}$ with a quantum one-time pad. Then in Round $\mathcal{P}_2$, $\mathcal{P}$ sends the one-time pad key β, γ along with the response u. In the verdict stage, $\mathcal{V}$ uses the keys to decrypt the response. We denote the verdict function as

$$\mathsf{verdict}'(H, s, sk, y, c, \beta, \gamma, u) := \mathsf{verdict}(H_{\beta,\gamma}, s, sk, y, c, u) \tag{7}$$

where $H_{\beta,\gamma} := X^\beta Z^\gamma H Z^\gamma X^\beta$ is the instance conjugated by the one-time pad.

Obviously, this is not zero-knowledge yet, as the verifier can easily recover the original measurement outcomes on the witness state. To address this issue, we take the approach of [16,19] and invoke a NIZK protocol for NP languages. The language $\mathcal{L}$ that we consider is defined as follows:

$$\begin{aligned}
\mathcal{L} := \{(H, s, sk, \xi, y, c, \chi) : \; &\exists \, \tau = (\beta, \gamma, u, r_1, r_2), \\
&\xi = \mathsf{commit}(u; r_1) \wedge \chi = \mathsf{commit}(\beta, \gamma; r_2) \\
&\wedge \mathsf{verdict}'(H, s, sk, y, c, \beta, \gamma, u) = 1\},
\end{aligned}$$

where r_1, r_2 are the randomness for a computationally secure bit commitment scheme. However, this alone is insufficient since, to agree on an instance without introducing more message exchanges, $\mathcal{V}$ must reveal sk, s before $\mathcal{P}$ sends a NIZK proof. Revealing sk, s enables a simple attack on soundness: $\mathcal{P}$ can ensure the verifier accepts all instances by using the secret key to forge a valid response u, committing to it, and computing the NIZK proof.

The solution is to invoke a quantum-secure classical FHE scheme and to let $\mathcal{P}$ homomorphically compute a NIZK proof. This requires $\mathcal{P}$ to only use an encrypted instance. In the setup phase, $\mathcal{P}$ is given the ciphertexts $csk = \mathsf{FHE.Enc}_{hpk}(sk)$ and $cs = \mathsf{FHE.Enc}_{hpk}(s)$. Next, in Round $\mathcal{P}_2$, $\mathcal{P}$ computes $cx = \mathsf{FHE.Enc}_{hpk}(x)$ where $x := (H, s, sk, \xi, y, c, \chi)$ since the partial transcript (y, c, ξ, χ) has already been fixed. $\mathcal{P}$ then computes

$$ce = \mathsf{FHE.Eval}_{hpk}(\mathsf{NIZK.P}, cc, cx, c\tau) = \mathsf{FHE.Enc}_{hpk}(\mathsf{NIZK.P}(\mathsf{crs}, x, \tau)),$$

where $c\tau = \mathsf{FHE.Enc}_{hpk}(\tau)$, and sends ce to $\mathcal{V}$. Finally, $\mathcal{V}$ decrypts the encrypted NIZK proof ce and outputs $\mathsf{NIZK.V}(\mathsf{crs}, x, e)$. The above transformation yields a three-message zero-knowledge protocol for quantum computation with trusted setup from a third party, described as follows.

Protocol 4 (Setup phase $\mathsf{setup}(\lambda, N, M)$**).** *The algorithm* setup *takes two integers* N, M *as input, and outputs two strings* $\mathsf{st}_\mathcal{V}, \mathsf{st}_\mathcal{P}$ *with the following steps.*

1. *Run* $\mathsf{crs} \leftarrow \mathsf{NIZK.Setup}(1^\lambda)$.
2. *Sample uniform bases* $h \leftarrow \{0,1\}^N$ *and run* $(pk, sk) \leftarrow \mathsf{Gen}(1^\lambda, h)$.
3. *Run the FHE key generation algorithm* $(hpk, hsk) \leftarrow \mathsf{FHE.Gen}(1^\lambda)$.
4. *Run encryption on the secret key* $csk \leftarrow \mathsf{FHE.Enc}_{hpk}(sk)$.

5. *Choose keys* (β, γ) *and randomness* r_1 *uniformly and compute* $\xi =$ $\mathsf{commit}(\beta, \gamma; r_1)$.
6. *Sample a random string* $s_1, \ldots, s_M \in \{0,1\}^p$ *(see Remark 3.1) uniformly and compute its encryption* $cs = \mathsf{FHE.Enc}_{hpk}(s)$.

Output $\mathsf{st}_\mathcal{V} = (\mathsf{crs}, sk, hsk, hpk, \xi)$ *and* $\mathsf{st}_\mathcal{P} = (\mathsf{crs}, pk, hpk, csk, cs, \beta, \gamma, r_1)$.

Protocol 5 (An interactive protocol).

Setup *Run* $\mathsf{st}_\mathcal{V}, \mathsf{st}_\mathcal{P} \leftarrow \mathsf{setup}(\lambda, nrk, rk)$. *Send* $\mathsf{st}_\mathcal{V} = (\mathsf{crs}, sk, hsk, hpk, \xi)$ *to* $\mathcal{V}$ *and* $\mathsf{st}_\mathcal{P} = (\mathsf{crs}, pk, hpk, csk, cs, \beta, \gamma, r_1)$ *to* $\mathcal{P}$.
Round $\mathcal{P}_1$. $\mathcal{P}$ *aborts if* pk *is invalid.* $\mathcal{P}$ *queries* Samp *coherently on the witness state* $X^\beta Z^\gamma |\psi\rangle^{\otimes rk}$.
Round $\mathcal{V}_2$. $\mathcal{V}$ *samples* $c_1, \ldots, c_k \leftarrow \{0,1\}$ *and sends* $c = (c_1, \ldots, c_k)$ *to* $\mathcal{P}$.
Round $\mathcal{P}_2$. *For each* $i \in [k]$, $j \in [r]$, $\ell \in [n]$,
  1. *if* $c_i = 0$, $\mathcal{P}$ *performs a standard basis measurement and gets* $u_{ij\ell} = (w_{ij\ell}, t_{ij\ell})$.
  2. *if* $c_i = 1$, $\mathcal{P}$ *performs a Hadamard basis measurement and gets* $u_{ij\ell} = (w_{ij\ell}, t_{ij\ell})$.

$\mathcal{P}$ *sends* $\chi := \mathsf{commit}(u; r_2)$ *and*

$$ce := \mathsf{FHE.Eval}_{hpk}(\mathsf{NIZK.P}, cc, cx, c\tau),$$

where cc, cx *and* $c\tau$ *are the encryptions of* crs, x *and* τ *respectively.*
Verdict. $\mathcal{V}$ *accepts if* $\mathsf{NIZK.V}(\mathsf{crs}, x, \mathsf{FHE.Dec}_{hsk}(ce)) = 1$.

We show Protocol 5 is complete, sound, and zero-knowledge. For the detailed proofs, see the full version [4].

Theorem 5.1. *Protocol 5 has negligible completeness and soundness errors.*

Theorem 5.2. *Assuming the existence of a non-interactive bit commitment scheme with perfect binding and computational hiding, Protocol 5 is zero-knowledge.*

6 Round Reduction by Fiat-Shamir Transformation

In this section we show that the Fiat-Shamir transformation can be used make the k-fold parallel three-round Mahadev protocol $\mathfrak{M}$ non-interactive with a setup phase, while keeping both the completeness and the soundness errors negligible. This will also be the case for the zero-knowledge variant of the same, i.e., Protocol 5.

6.1 Fiat-Shamir for Σ-protocols in the QROM

The Fiat-Shamir (FS) transformation turns any public-coin three-message inter-active argument, also called a Σ-protocol, into a single-message protocol in the random oracle model (ROM). In the standard approach, one proves that the Fiat-Shamir transformation preserves soundness in the ROM. In this idealized cryptographic model, all parties receive oracle access to a uniformly random function $\mathcal{H}$. Against quantum adversaries, there is a well-known complication: a quantum computer can easily evaluate any actual instantiation of $\mathcal{H}$ (with a concrete public classical function) in superposition via

$$U_{\mathcal{H}} : |x, y\rangle |z\rangle \mapsto |x, y\rangle |z \oplus \mathcal{H}(x, y)\rangle .$$

We thus work in the Quantum Random Oracle Model (QROM), in which all parties receive quantum oracle access to $U_{\mathcal{H}}$.

We make use of the following theorem of [22]; we describe the underlying reduction in the full version [4].

Theorem 6.1. (Quantum Security of Fiat-Shamir [22, Theorem 2]). *For every QPT prover $\mathcal{A}^{\mathcal{H}}$ in the transformed protocol, there exists a QPT prover $\mathcal{S}$ for the underlying Σ-protocol such that*

$$\Pr_{\Theta}[V(x, y, \Theta, m) = 1 : (y, m) \leftarrow \langle \mathcal{S}^{\mathcal{A}}, \Theta \rangle]$$

$$\geq \frac{1}{2(2q+1)(2q+3)} \Pr_{\mathcal{H}}[V(x, y, \mathcal{H}(x, y), m) = 1, \ (y, m) \leftarrow \mathcal{A}^{\mathcal{H}}(x)] - \frac{1}{(2q+1)|\mathcal{Y}|}.$$

In the above, $(y, m) \leftarrow \langle \mathcal{S}^{\mathcal{A}}, \Theta \rangle$ indicates that y and m are the first-round and third-round (respectively) messages of $\mathcal{S}^{\mathcal{A}}$, when it is given the random challenge Θ in the second round.

6.2 Extension to Generalized Σ-protocols

In this section, we show that Fiat-Shamir also preserves soundness for a more general family of protocols, which we call "generalized Σ-protocols." In such a protocol, $\mathcal{V}$ can begin the protocol by sending an initial message to $\mathcal{P}$.

Protocol 6 (Generalized Σ-protocol). *Select a public function $f : \mathcal{R} \times L \to \mathcal{W}$, a finite set $\mathcal{C}$, and a distribution D over $\mathcal{R}$. The protocol begins with $\mathcal{P}$ and $\mathcal{V}$ receiving an input x.*

Round 1. *$\mathcal{V}$ samples randomness $r \in \mathcal{R}$ from distribution D and computes message $w = f(r, x)$, which is sent to $\mathcal{P}$.*
Round 2. *$\mathcal{P}$ sends a message y to $\mathcal{V}$.*
Round 3. *$\mathcal{V}$ responds with a uniformly random classical challenge $c \in \mathcal{C}$.*
Round 4. *$\mathcal{P}$ sends a response m to $\mathcal{V}$.*
Verdict. *$\mathcal{V}$ outputs a bit computed by a Boolean function $V(r, x, y, c, m)$.*

Notice that the original Mahadev protocol [34] is a generalized Σ-protocol: the distribution D describes the distribution for the secret key, and f computes the public key. Similarly, the k-fold parallel repetition of our instance-independent protocol is also a generalized Σ-protocol since our trusted setup phase can be seen as a message from the verifier.

Fiat-Shamir for generalized Σ protocols. The FS transformation for generalized Σ-protocols is similar to standard ones: in the Verdict stage, $\mathcal{V}$ computes $c = \mathcal{H}(x, w, y)$ and accepts if and only if $V(r, x, y, c, m) = 1$.

Protocol 7. (FS-transformed generalized Σ protocol). *Select a public function $f : \mathcal{R} \times L \to \mathcal{W}$, a finite set $\mathcal{C}$, and a distribution D over $\mathcal{R}$. $\mathcal{P}$ and $\mathcal{V}$ receive an input x and are given access to a random oracle $\mathcal{H}$.*

Round 1. *$\mathcal{V}$ samples randomness $r \in \mathcal{R}$ from distribution D, and computes message $w = f(r, x)$, which is sent to $\mathcal{P}$.*

Round 2. *$\mathcal{P}$ sends a message (y, m) to $\mathcal{V}$.*

Verdict. *$\mathcal{V}$ computes $c = \mathcal{H}(x, w, y)$ and then outputs a bit computed by a Boolean function $V(r, x, y, c, m)$.*

To show that generalized Σ-protocols remain secure under the FS transformation, similarly to the idea for Σ-protocols, we give a reduction. Conditioned on any randomness r, the prover is $\mathcal{A}_r^{\mathcal{H}}(x) := \mathcal{A}^{\mathcal{H}}(x, f(r, x))$.[14] The prover $\mathcal{B}$ in the Σ-protocol runs $\mathcal{S}^{\mathcal{A}_r}$ and outputs its decision. Given the success probability of $\mathcal{A}$, we establish a lower bound on that of $\mathcal{B}$, as follows. For the proof, see the full version [4].

Lemma 6.1 (Fiat-Shamir Transformation for generalized Σ protocol). *Suppose that*

$$\Pr_{r, \mathcal{H}}[V(r, x, y, \mathcal{H}(x, f(r, x), y), m) = 1 : (y, m) \leftarrow \mathcal{A}^{\mathcal{H}}(x, f(r, x))] = \epsilon.$$

Then

$$\Pr_{r, \Theta}[V(r, x, y, \Theta, m) = 1 : (y, m) \leftarrow \langle \mathcal{B}, \Theta \rangle] \geq \frac{\epsilon}{2(2q+1)(2q+3)} - \frac{1}{(2q+1)|\mathcal{Y}|}.$$

Lemma 6.1 immediately gives the following theorem.

Theorem 6.2. *If a language L admits a generalized Σ-protocol with soundness error s, then after the Fiat-Shamir transformation, the soundness error against provers who make up to q queries to a random oracle is $O(sq^2 + q|\mathcal{Y}|^{-1})$.*

Proof. Suppose there is a prover who succeeds in the transformed protocol with success probability ϵ. Then by Lemma 6.1, we may construct a prover who succeeds with probability at least $\frac{\epsilon}{O(q^2)} - O\left(\frac{1}{q|\mathcal{Y}|}\right)$. By the soundness guarantee, we have $\frac{\epsilon}{O(q^2)} - O\left(\frac{1}{q|\mathcal{Y}|}\right) \leq s$ and thus $\epsilon \leq O(q^2 s + q|\mathcal{Y}|^{-1})$.   □

---

[14] Though the prover does not learn the private randomness r, its action depends on r implicitly.

By Theorem 6.2, if both s and $|\mathcal{Y}|^{-1}$ are negligible in security parameter λ, the soundness error of the transformed protocols remains negligible against an efficient prover who makes $q = \mathrm{poly}(\lambda)$ queries. Theorem 1.3 follows directly from Theorem 6.2.

6.3 Non-interactive Zero-Knowledge for QMA

We now show that, using the Fiat-Shamir transformation, our three-round protocol proposed in Protocol 5 can be converted into a non-interactive zero-knowledge argument (with trusted setup) for QMA in the Quantum Random Oracle model. The resulting protocol is defined exactly as Protocol 5, with two modifications: (i.) instead of Round $\mathcal{V}_2$, the prover $\mathcal{P}$ computes the coins c by evaluating the random oracle $\mathcal{H}$ on the protocol transcript thus far, and (ii.) the NIZK instance x is appropriately redefined using these coins.

We remark that since the setup in this protocol is trusted, it follows from Theorem 6.2 that the compressed protocol is complete and sound, and therefore we just need to argue about the zero-knowledge property.

Theorem 6.3. *The Fiat-Shamir transformation of Protocol 5 is zero-knowledge.*

Proof. The simulator $\mathcal{S}^{\mathcal{V}_2^*}$ can sample the trapdoor keys for NTCF/NTIF functions and private keys for the FHE scheme, enabling simulation of the transcript for every challenge sent by the verifier. In particular, one can run the same proof with the variant $\mathcal{S}^{\mathcal{H}}$ that queries the random oracle $\mathcal{H}$ for the challenges instead of receiving it from a malicious verifier $\mathcal{V}^*$.   □

Acknowledgments. We thank Kai-Min Chung, Andrea Coladangelo, Bill Fefferman, Serge Fehr, Christian Majenz, Christian Schaffner, Umesh Vazirani, and Thomas Vidick for helpful discussions.

AMC and SHH acknowledge support from NSF grant CCF-1813814 and from the U.S. Department of Energy, Office of Science, Office of Advanced Scientific Computing Research, Quantum Testbed Pathfinder program under Award Number DE-SC0019040. GA acknowledges support from the NSF under grant CCF-1763736, from the U.S. Army Research Office under Grant Number W911NF-20-1-0015, and from the U.S. Department of Energy under Award Number DE-SC0020312. Part of this work was completed while GA was supported by the Dutch Research Council (NWO) through travel grant 040.11.708. Part of this work was completed while AG was visiting the Joint Center for Quantum Information and Computer Science, University of Maryland and the Simons Institute for the Theory of Computing.

References

1. Aaronson, S.: BQP and the polynomial hierarchy. In: STOC 2010, pp. 141–150 (2010). arXiv:0910.4698
2. Aharonov, D., Ben-Or, M., Eban, E., Mahadev, U.: Interactive proofs for quantum computations. (2017). arXiv:1704.04487
3. Alagic, G., et al.: Status report on the first round of the NIST post-quantum cryptography standardization process (2019)
4. Alagic, G., Childs, A.M., Grilo, A.B., Hung, S.-H.: Non-interactive classical verification of quantum computation (2019). arXiv:1911.08101
5. Ambainis, A., Rosmanis, A., Unruh, D.: Quantum attacks on classical proof systems: the hardness of quantum rewinding. In: FOCS 2014, pp. 474–483 (2014). https://eprint.iacr.org/2014/296 Cryptology ePrint Archive Report 2014/296
6. Bellare, M., Impagliazzo, R., Naor, M.: Does parallel repetition lower the error in computationally sound protocols? FOCS **1997**, 374–383 (1997)
7. Bellare, M., Rogaway, P.: Random oracles are practical: a paradigm for designing efficient protocols. CCS **1993**, 62–73 (1993)
8. Berman, I., Haitner, I., Tsfadia, E.: A tight parallel-repetition theorem for random-terminating interactive arguments (2019). https://eprint.iacr.org/2019/393 Cryptology ePrint Archive, Report 2019/393
9. Biamonte, J.D., Love, P.J.: Realizable Hamiltonians for universal adiabatic quantum computers. Phys. Rev. A **78**(1), 012352 (2008). arXiv:0704.1287
10. Blum, M., Feldman, P., Micali, S.: Non-interactive zero-knowledge and its applications. In: STOC 1988, pp. 103–112 (1988)
11. Boneh, D., Dagdelen, Ö., Fischlin, M., Lehmann, A., Schaffner, C., Zhandry, M.: Random oracles in a quantum world. In: Lee, D.H., Wang, X. (eds.) ASIACRYPT 2011. LNCS, vol. 7073, pp. 41–69. Springer, Heidelberg (2011). https://doi.org/10.1007/978-3-642-25385-0_3
12. Brakerski, Z., Christiano, P., Mahadev, U., Vazirani, U., Vidick, T.: A cryptographic test of quantumness and certifiable randomness from a single quantum device. In: FOCS 2018, pp. 320–331 (2018). arXiv:1804.00640
13. Broadbent, A.: How to verify a quantum computation. Theory Comput. **14**(11), 1–37 (2018). arXiv:1509.09180
14. Broadbent, A., Fitzsimons, J., Kashefi, E.: Universal blind quantum computation. In: FOCS 2009, pp. 517–526 (2009). arXiv:0807.4154
15. Broadbent, A., Grilo, A.B.: Zero-knowledge for QMA from locally simulatable proofs (2019). arXiv:1911.07782
16. Broadbent, A., Ji, Z., Song, F., Watrous, J.: Zero-knowledge proof systems for QMA. In: FOCS 2016, pp. 31–40 (2016). arXiv:1604.02804
17. Chia, N.-H., Chung, K.-M., Yamakawa, T.: Classical verification of quantum computations with efficient verifier (2019). arXiv:1912.00990
18. Coladangelo, A., Grilo, A.B., Jeffery, S., Vidick, T.: Verifier-on-a-leash: new schemes for verifiable delegated quantum computation, with quasilinear resources. In: Ishai, Y., Rijmen, V. (eds.) EUROCRYPT 2019. LNCS, vol. 11478, pp. 247–277. Springer, Cham (2019). https://doi.org/10.1007/978-3-030-17659-4_9
19. Coladangelo, A., Vidick, T., Zhang, T.: Non-interactive zero-knowledge arguments for QMA, with preprocessing (2019). arXiv:1911.07546
20. Cubitt, T., Montanaro, A.: Complexity classification of local Hamiltonian problems. SIAM J. Comput. **45**(2), 268–316 (2016). arXiv:1311.3161

21. Damgård, I.: On Σ-protocols. University of Aarhus, Department for Computer Science. Lecture Notes (2002)

22. Don, J., Fehr, S., Majenz, C., Schaffner, C.: Security of the Fiat-Shamir transformation in the quantum random-oracle model. In: Boldyreva, A., Micciancio, D. (eds.) CRYPTO 2019. LNCS, vol. 11693, pp. 356–383. Springer, Cham (2019). https://doi.org/10.1007/978-3-030-26951-7_13

23. Fiat, A., Shamir, A.: How to prove yourself: practical solutions to identification and signature problems. In: Odlyzko, A.M. (ed.) CRYPTO 1986. LNCS, vol. 263, pp. 186–194. Springer, Heidelberg (1987). https://doi.org/10.1007/3-540-47721-7_12

24. Fitzsimons, J.F., Hajdušek, M.: Post hoc verification of quantum computation (2015). arXiv:1512.04375

25. Gheorghiu, A., Kashefi, E., Wallden, P.: Robustness and device independence of verifiable blind quantum computing. New J. Phys. **17**(8), 083040 (2015). arXiv:1502.02571

26. Gheorghiu, A., Vidick, T.: Computationally-secure and composable remote state preparation (2019). arXiv:1904.06320

27. Grilo, A.B.: A simple protocol for verifiable delegation of quantum computation in one round. In: ICALP 2019, pp. 28:1–28:13 (2019)

28. Grilo, A.B., Slofstra, W., Yuen, H.: Perfect zero knowledge for quantum multi-prover interactive proofs. In: FOCS 2019, pp. 611–635 (2019). arXiv:1905.11280

29. Haitner, I.: A parallel repetition theorem for any interactive argument. FOCS **2009**, 241–250 (2009)

30. Hajdušek, M., Pérez-Delgado, C.A., Fitzsimons, J.F.: Device-independent verifiable blind quantum computation (2015). arXiv:1502.02563

31. Håstad, J., Pass, R., Wikström, D., Pietrzak, K.: An efficient parallel repetition theorem. In: Micciancio, D. (ed.) TCC 2010. LNCS, vol. 5978, pp. 1–18. Springer, Heidelberg (2010). https://doi.org/10.1007/978-3-642-11799-2_1

32. Kitaev, A.Y., Shen, A.H., Vyalyi, M.N.: Classical and quantum computation. American Mathematical Society, Providence (2002)

33. Liu, Q., Zhandry, M.: Revisiting post-quantum Fiat-Shamir. In: Boldyreva, A., Micciancio, D. (eds.) CRYPTO 2019. LNCS, vol. 11693, pp. 326–355. Springer, Cham (2019). https://doi.org/10.1007/978-3-030-26951-7_12

34. Mahadev, U.: Classical verification of quantum computations. In: FOCS 2018, pp. 259–267 (2018). arXiv:1804.01082

35. McKague, M.: Interactive proofs for BQP via self-tested graph states. Theory Comput. **12**(3), 1–42 (2016). arXiv:1309.5675

36. Morimae, T., Fitzsimons, J.F.: Post hoc verification with a single prover (2016). arXiv:1603.06046

37. Natarajan, A., Vidick, T.: A quantum linearity test for robustly verifying entanglement. In: STOC 2017, pp. 1003–1015 (2017). arXiv:1610.03574

38. Ostrovsky, R., Paskin-Cherniavsky, A., Paskin-Cherniavsky, B.: Maliciously circuit-private FHE. In: Garay, J.A., Gennaro, R. (eds.) CRYPTO 2014. LNCS, vol. 8616, pp. 536–553. Springer, Heidelberg (2014). https://doi.org/10.1007/978-3-662-44371-2_30

39. Peikert, C., Shiehian, S.: Noninteractive zero knowledge for NP from (plain) learning with errors. Cryptology ePrint Archive, Report 2019/158 (2019). https://eprint.iacr.org/2019/158

40. Pointcheval, D., Stern, J.: Security arguments for digital signatures and blind signatures. J. Cryptol. **13**(3), 361–396 (2000)

41. Radian, R., Sattath, O.: Semi-quantum money (2019). arXiv:1908.08889

42. Reichardt, B.W., Unger, F., Vazirani, U.: Classical command of quantum systems. Nature **496**(7446), 456–460 (2013). arXiv:1209.0448
43. Vidick, T., Watrous, J.: Quantum proofs. Found. Trends Theor. Comput. Sci. **11**(1–2), 1–215 (2016). arXiv:1610.01664
44. Vidick, T., Zhang, T.: Classical zero-knowledge arguments for quantum computations (2019). arXiv:1902.05217
45. Watrous, J.: Zero-knowledge against quantum attacks. SIAM J. Comput. **39**(1), 25–58 (2009). arXiv:quant-ph/0511020

Classical Verification of Quantum Computations with Efficient Verifier

Nai-Hui Chia[1,2], Kai-Min Chung[3], and Takashi Yamakawa[4(✉)]

[1] Joint Center for Quantum Information and Computer Science,
University of Maryland, College Park, USA
nchia@umd.edu

[2] Department of Computer Science, University of Texas at Austin, Austin, USA

[3] Institute of Information Science, Academia Sinica, Taipei, Taiwan
kmchung@iis.sinica.edu.tw

[4] NTT Secure Platform Laboratories, Tokyo, Japan
takashi.yamakawa.ga@hco.ntt.co.jp

Abstract. In this paper, we extend the protocol of classical verification of quantum computations (CVQC) recently proposed by Mahadev to make the verification efficient. Our result is obtained in the following three steps:

- We show that parallel repetition of Mahadev's protocol has negligible soundness error. This gives the first constant round CVQC protocol with negligible soundness error. In this part, we only assume the quantum hardness of the learning with error (LWE) problem similar to Mahadev's work.
- We construct a two-round CVQC protocol in the quantum random oracle model (QROM) where a cryptographic hash function is idealized to be a random function. This is obtained by applying the Fiat-Shamir transform to the parallel repetition version of Mahadev's protocol.
- We construct a two-round CVQC protocol with an efficient verifier in the CRS+QRO model where both prover and verifier can access a (classical) common reference string generated by a trusted third party in addition to quantum access to QRO. Specifically, the verifier can verify a $\mathsf{QTIME}(T)$ computation in time $\mathsf{poly}(n, \log T)$ where n is the security parameter. For proving soundness, we assume that a standard model instantiation of our two-round protocol with a concrete hash function (say, SHA-3) is sound and the existence of post-quantum indistinguishability obfuscation and post-quantum fully homomorphic encryption in addition to the quantum hardness of the LWE problem.

1 Introduction

Quantum computers that outperform classical supercomputers have been realized recently [7] and may play a role similar to the super clusters in the foreseeable future. Indeed, this is happening now—IBM has provided an online platform

© International Association for Cryptologic Research 2020
R. Pass and K. Pietrzak (Eds.): TCC 2020, LNCS 12552, pp. 181–206, 2020.
https://doi.org/10.1007/978-3-030-64381-2_7

for public users to run their computational tasks on IBM's quantum computing server [1]. Since quantum computers would be accessed by clients with only classical devices, verifying quantum computation by a classical computer has become a major issue in this setting. To address this problem, there are several works toward reducing the verifier's quantum resource for verifying quantum computation [5,15,21,35]. However, it was unknown if the verifier could be purely classical until Mahadev [32] finally gave an affirmative solution. Specifically, she constructed an interactive protocol between an efficient classical verifier (a BPP machine) and an efficient quantum prover (a BQP machine) where the verifier can verify the result of the BQP computation. (In the following, we call such a protocol a CVQC protocol.[1]) Soundness of her protocol relies on a computational assumption that the learning with error (LWE) problem [40] is hard for an efficient quantum algorithm, which has been widely used in the field of cryptography. We refer to the extensive survey by Peikert [38] for details about LWE and its cryptographic applications.

Although the verifier in Mahadev's protocol is purely classical, it is not "efficient". In the classical cryptographic literature of delegating (classical) computation, efficient verifier that can verify a delegated time T computation in $o(T)$ time is a necessary requirement (as otherwise, the verifier performs the computation on its own). Indeed, many previous works suggested that the verifier's runtime can be $\mathsf{poly}\log(T)$ in the classical setting [9,14,16,25–30,34,42]. In contrast, in the literature of delegating quantum computation, the focus is mainly on reducing the required quantum power for the verifier, and all existing protocols with a single prover (e.g., in blind quantum computation [15] and Mahadev's protocol [32]) inherently requires the verifier to run in $poly(T)$ time to verify the delegated computation, even for verifiers with weak quantum power.

Therefore, whether a CVQC protocol with an efficient verifier (i.e., with runtime $o(T)$) exists is a natural and fundamental theoretical question. Also, from a technical perspective, classical efficient verifier protocols are closely related to PCP proofs, where many protocols are constructed based on PCP proofs, and a partial converse result is proven by Rothblum and Vadhan [43]. On the other hand, whether a quantum version of the PCP theorem holds is still an open question in quantum complexity theory [4]. Thus, the challenge of constructing a protocol with an efficient verifier is potentially related to the challenge of constructing quantum PCP proofs. While our construction relies on several strong and non-standard assumptions, our protocol provides the first feasibility result (in any reasonable models) that answers this question of efficient verifier CVQC protocol affirmatively.

1.1   Our Results

In this paper, our main result is a CVQC protocol with an efficient verifier, and we have also reached two milestones on the path to the final result. We summarize them as follows:

---

[1] "CVQC" stands for "Classical Verification of Quantum Computations".

Parallel Repetition of Mahadev's Protocol. We first show that parallel repetition version of Mahadev's protocol has negligible soundness error. Note that Mahadev's protocol has soundness error $3/4$, which means that a cheating prover may convince the verifier even if it does not correctly computes the BQP computation with probability at most $3/4$. Though we can exponentially reduce the soundness error by sequential repetition, we need super-constant rounds to reduce the soundness error to be negligible. If parallel repetition works to reduce the soundness error, then we need not increase the number of round. However, parallel repetition may not reduce soundness error for computationally sound protocols in general [11,39]. Thus, it was open to construct constant round protocol with negligible soundness error. We manage to answer this question by giving the first constant round CVQC protocol with negligible soundness error.

Two-Round CVQC Protocol. Based on the parallel repetition version of Mahadev's protocol with negligible soundness, we then construct a two-round CVQC protocol in the quantum random oracle model (QROM) [12] where a cryptographic hash function is idealized to be a random function that is only accessible as a quantum oracle. This is obtained by applying the Fiat-Shamir transform [19,20,31] to the parallel repetition version of Mahadev's protocol.

CVQC Protocol with an Efficient Verifier. Finally, we construct a two-round CVQC protocol with logarithmic-time verifier in the CRS+QRO model where both prover and verifier can access to a (classical) common reference string generated by a trusted third party in addition to quantum access to QRO. For proving soundness, we assume that a standard model instantiation of our two-round protocol with a concrete hash function (say, SHA-3) is sound and the existence of post-quantum indistinguishability obfuscation [10,22] and (post-quantum) fully homomorphic encryption (FHE) [23] in addition to the quantum hardness of the LWE problem.

1.2   Technical Overview

Overview of Mahadev's Protocol. First, we recall the high-level structure of Mahadev's 4-round CVQC protocol.[2] On input a common input x, a quantum prover and classical verifier proceeds as below to prove and verify that x belongs to a BQP language L.

First Message: The verifier generates a pair of "key" k and a "trapdoor" td, sends k to the prover, and keeps td as its internal state.

Second Message: The prover is given the key k, generates a classical "commitment" y along with a quantum state $|st_P\rangle$, sends y to the verifier, and keeps $|st_P\rangle$ as its internal state.

Third Message: The verifier randomly picks a "challenge" $c \xleftarrow{\$} \{0,1\}$ and sends c to the prover. Following the terminology in [32], we call the case of $c = 0$ the "test round" and the case of $c = 1$ the "Hadamard round".

---

[2] See Sect. 3.1 for more details.

Fourth Message: The prover is given a challenge c, generates a classical "answer" a by using the state $|st_P\rangle$, and sends a to the verifier.

Final Verification: Finally, the verifier returns $\top$ indicating acceptance or $\bot$ indicating rejection. In case $c = 0$, the verification can be done publicly, that is, the final verification algorithm need not use td.

Mahadev showed that the protocol achieves negligible completeness error and constant soundness error against computationally bounded cheating provers. More precisely, she showed that if $x \in L$, then the verifier accepts with probability $1 - \mathsf{negl}(n)$ where n is the security parameter, and if $x \notin L$, then any quantum polynomial time cheating prover can let the verifier accept with probability at most $3/4$. For proving this, she first showed the following lemma:[3]

Lemma 1 (informal). *For any $x \notin L$, if a quantum polynomial time cheating prover passes the test round with probability $1 - \mathsf{negl}(n)$, then it passes the Hadamard with probability $\mathsf{negl}(n)$ assuming the quantum hardness of the LWE problem.*

Given the above lemma, it is easy to prove the soundness of the protocol. Roughly speaking, we consider a decomposition of the Hilbert space $\mathcal{H}_P$ for the prover's internal state $|\psi_P\rangle$ into two subspaces S_0 and S_1 so that S_0 (resp. S_1) consists of quantum states that lead to rejection (resp. acceptance) in the test round. That is, we define these subspaces so that if the cheating prover's internal state after sending the second message is $|s_0\rangle \in S_0$ (resp. $|s_1\rangle \in S_1$), then the verifier returns rejection (acceptance) in the test round (i.e., the case of $c = 0$). Here, we note that the decomposition is well-defined since we can assume that a cheating prover just applies a fixed unitary on its internal space and measures some registers for generating the fourth message in the test round without loss of generality. Let Π_b be the projection onto S_b and $|\psi_b\rangle := \Pi_b|\psi_P\rangle$ for $b \in \{0, 1\}$. Then $|\psi_0\rangle$ leads to rejection in the test round (with probability 1), so if the verifier uniformly chooses $c \xleftarrow{\$} \{0, 1\}$, then $|\psi_0\rangle$ leads to acceptance with probability at most $1/2$. On the other hand, since $|\psi_1\rangle$ leads to the acceptance in the test round (with probability 1), by Lemma 1, $|\psi_1\rangle$ leads to the acceptance in the Hadamard round with only negligible probability. Therefore, the verifier uniformly chooses $c \xleftarrow{\$} \{0, 1\}$, then $|\psi_1\rangle$ leads to acceptance with probability at most $1/2 + \mathsf{negl}(n)$. Therefore, intuitively speaking, $|\psi_P\rangle = |\psi_0\rangle + |\psi_1\rangle$ leads to acceptance with probability at most $1/2 + \mathsf{negl}(n)$, which completes the proof of soundness. We remark that here is a small gap since measurements are not linear and thus we cannot simply conclude that $|\psi_P\rangle$ leads to acceptance with probability at most $1/2 + \mathsf{negl}(n)$ even though the same property holds for both $|\psi_0\rangle$ and $|\psi_1\rangle$. Indeed, Mahadev just showed that the soundness error is at most

---

[3] Strictly speaking, she just proved a similar property for what is called a "measurement protocol" instead of CVQC protocol. But this easily implies a similar statement for CVQC protocol since CVQC protocol can be obtained by combining a measurement protocol and the (amplified version of) Morimae-Fitzsimons protocol [35] without affecting the soundness error as is done in [32, Section 8].

3/4 instead of $1/2 + \mathsf{negl}(n)$ to deal with this issue. A concurrent work by Alagic et al. [6] proved that the Mahadev's protocol actually achieves soundness error $1/2 + \mathsf{negl}(n)$ with more careful analysis.

Parallel Repetition. Now, we turn our attention to parallel repetition version of Mahadev's protocol. Our goal is to prove that the probability that the verifier accepts on $x \notin L$ is negligible if the verifier and prover run the Mahadev's protocol m-times parallelly for sufficiently large m and the verifier accepts if and only if it accepts on the all coordinates.

Our first step is to consider a decomposition of the prover's space $\mathcal{H}_P$ into two subspaces $S_{i,0}$ and $S_{i,1}$ for each $i \in [m]$ similarly to the stand-alone case. Specifically, we want to define these subspaces so that $S_{i,0}$ (resp. $S_{i,1}$) consists of quantum states that lead to rejection (resp. acceptance) in the test round on the i-th coordinate. However, such subspaces are not well-defined since a cheating prover's behavior in the fourth round depends on challenges $c = c_1....c_m \in \{0,1\}^m$ on all coordinates. Thus, even if we focus on the test round on the i-th coordinate, all other challenges $c_{-i} = c_1...c_{i-1}c_{i+1}...c_m$ still have flexibility, and a different choice of c_{-i} leads to a different prover's behavior. In other words, the prover's strategy should be described as a unitary over $\mathcal{H}_C \otimes \mathcal{H}_P$ where $\mathcal{H}_C$ is a Hilbert space to store a challenge. Therefore $S_{i,0}$ and $S_{i,1}$ cannot be well-defined as a decomposition of $\mathcal{H}_P$ if we define them as above.

Therefore, we need to define these subspaces in a little different way. Specifically, our idea is to define them as subspaces that "know" and "do not know" an answer for the test round on i-th coordinate. More precisely, for any fixed noticeable "threshold" $\gamma = 1/\mathsf{poly}(n)$, we ideally require the followings:

1. ($S_{i,0}$ **"does not know" an answer.**) If the fourth message generation algorithm of the cheating prover runs with an internal state $|\psi_{i,0}\rangle \in S_{i,0}$, then it passes the test round on i-th coordinate with probability at most γ when the challenge c is uniformly chosen from $\{0,1\}^m$ such that $c_i = 0$.
2. ($S_{i,1}$ **"knows" an answer.**) There is an efficient algorithm that is given any $|\psi_{i,1}\rangle \in S_{i,1}$ as input and outputs an accepting answer for the test round on i-th coordinate with overwhelming probability.
3. (**Efficient projection.**) A measurement described by $\{\Pi_{S_{i,0}}, \Pi_{S_{i,1}}\}$ can be performed efficiently where $\Pi_{S_{i,0}}$ and $\Pi_{S_{i,1}}$ denote projections to $S_{i,0}$ and $S_{i,1}$, respectively.

Unfortunately, we do not know how to achieve these requirements in the above clean form. Nonetheless, we can show that a "noisy" version of the above requirements can be achieved by using the techniques taken from works on an amplification theorem for QMA [33,36]. We will explain this in more detail in the next paragraph since this is the technical core of our proof. In the rest of this paragraph, we explain how to prove the soundness of the parallel repetition version of Mahadev's protocol assuming that the above requirements are satisfied in the clean form as above for simplicity. Here, we observe that for any $i \in [m]$ and $b \in \{0,1\}$, any efficiently generated $|\psi_{i,b}\rangle \in S_{i,b}$ leads to acceptance in the verification on i-th coordinate for any fixed c such that $c_i = b$ with probability at most $2^{m-1}\gamma + \mathsf{negl}(n)$. This can be seen by a similar argument to the stand-alone case: The case of $b = 0$ follows from the above requirement 1 considering that the number of $c \in \{0,1\}^m$ such that $c_i = 0$ is 2^{m-1}. The case of $b = 1$ follows from the above requirement 2 combined with Lemma 1 assuming the quantum hardness of LWE.

Our next step is to sequentially apply projections onto $S_{i,0}$ and $S_{i,1}$ for $i = 1, ..., m$ to further decompose the prover's state $|\psi_P\rangle$. More precisely, for any fixed $c = c_1...c_m \in \{0,1\}^m$, we define

$$|\psi_0\rangle := \Pi_{S_{1,0}}|\psi_P\rangle, \qquad |\psi_1\rangle := \Pi_{S_{1,1}}|\psi_P\rangle$$

and

$$|\psi_{\bar{c}_1,...,\bar{c}_{i-1},0}\rangle := \Pi_{S_{i,0}}|\psi_{\bar{c}_1,...,\bar{c}_{i-1}}\rangle, \qquad |\psi_{\bar{c}_1,...,\bar{c}_{i-1},1}\rangle := \Pi_{S_{i,1}}|\psi_{\bar{c}_1,...,\bar{c}_{i-1}}\rangle$$

for $i = 2, ..., m$ where $\bar{c}_i$ denotes $1 - c_i$. Then we have

$$|\psi\rangle = |\psi_{c_1}\rangle + |\psi_{\bar{c}_1,c_2}\rangle + \cdots + |\psi_{\bar{c}_1,...,\bar{c}_{m-1},c_m}\rangle + |\psi_{\bar{c}_1,...,\bar{c}_m}\rangle.$$

Here, for each $i \in [m]$, we have $|\psi_{\bar{c}_1,...,\bar{c}_{i-1},c_i}\rangle \in S_{i,c_i}$ by definition. Therefore, $|\psi_{\bar{c}_1,...,\bar{c}_{i-1},c_i}\rangle$ leads to acceptance on the verification on i-th coordinate with probability at most $2^{m-1}\gamma + \mathsf{negl}(n)$ when the challenge is c. Moreover, if we consider the above decomposition for a randomly chosen c, then we have $E_{c \xleftarrow{\$} \{0,1\}^m}[\||\psi_{\bar{c}_1,...,\bar{c}_m}\rangle\|] \leq 2^{-m}$ since an expected norm is halved whenever we apply either of projections onto $S_{i,0}$ or $S_{i,1}$ randomly. Therefore, we can conclude that the verifier accepts on the all coordinates with probability at most $2^{m-1}\gamma + 2^{-m} + \mathsf{negl}(n)$. This is not negligible since we need to assume that γ is noticeable due to a technical reason. However, we can make $2^{m-1}\gamma + 2^{-m} + \mathsf{negl}(n)$ as small as any noticeable function by appropriately setting $m = O(\log n)$ and $\gamma = 1/\mathsf{poly}(n)$. This implies that a cheating adversary's winning probability is $\mathsf{negl}(n)$ if we set $m = \omega(\log n)$.

How to Define $S_{i,0}$ and $S_{i,1}$. In this paragraph, we explain how to define subspaces $S_{i,0}$ and $S_{i,1}$ and achieve a noisy version of the requirements in the previous paragraph. For defining these subspaces, we borrow a lemma from [36], which was originally used for proving an amplification theorem for QMA. Since their lemma is a little complicated to state in a general form, we only explain what is ensured by their lemma in our context. In our context, their lemma ensures that there is an efficient operator Q over $\mathcal{H}_C \times \mathcal{H}_P$ where $\mathcal{H}_C$ is a register for storing a challenge $c \in \{0,1\}^m$ such that

1. (Eigenvectors span $\mathcal{H}_P$.) there is a orthonormal basis $\{|\hat{\alpha}_j\rangle\}_j$ of $\mathcal{H}_P$ such that $|0^m\rangle_C|\hat{\alpha}_j\rangle_P$ is an eigenvector of Q with eigenvalue $e^{i\theta_j}$ for some θ_j,
2. (Eigenvalue corresponds to success probability.) if the fourth message generation algorithm of the cheating prover runs with an internal state $|\hat{\alpha}_j\rangle$, then it passes the test round on i-th coordinate with probability $p_j := \cos^2(\theta_j/2)$ when the challenge c is uniformly chosen from $\{0,1\}^m$ such that $c_i = 0$, and

3. (Extractable) there is an extraction algorithm that is given a state $|\hat{\alpha}_j\rangle$ and outputs an accepting answer for the test round on i-th coordinate with overwhelming probability in time $\mathsf{poly}(n, p_j^{-1})$.

Given this lemma, our rough idea is to define $S_{i,0}$ (resp. $S_{i,1}$) as a subspace spanned by $|\hat{\alpha}_j\rangle$ such that $p_j \leq \gamma$ (resp. $p_j > \gamma$). Then, it is easy to see that $S_{i,0}$ and $S_{i,1}$ satisfy the requirements 1 and 2 (i.e., $S_{i,0}$ "does not know" an answer and $S_{i,1}$ "knows" an answer). However, we do not know how to efficiently perform a projection onto $S_{i,0}$ or $S_{i,1}$ since there is no known efficient algorithm for phase estimation without an approximation error. On the other hand, we can efficiently approximate a phase with an approximation error $1/\mathsf{poly}(n)$ [36]. Then, our next idea is to introduce an inverse polynomial gap between thresholds for $S_{i,0}$ and $S_{i,1}$, i.e., we define $S_{i,0}$ (resp. $S_{i,1}$) as a subspace spanned by $|\hat{\alpha}_j\rangle$ such that $p_j \leq \gamma$ (resp. $p_j \geq \gamma + 1/\mathsf{poly}(n)$). Then, we can efficiently perform a projection to $S_{i,0}$ or $S_{i,1}$ by using the phase estimation algorithm with an approximation error $1/\mathsf{poly}(n)$ if the original state does not have a "grey area", which is a space spanned by $|\hat{\alpha}_j\rangle$ such that $p_j \in (\gamma, \gamma + 1/\mathsf{poly}(n))$. However, it may be the case that the original state is dominated by the grey area. To resolve this issue, we randomly set the threshold γ from T possible choices so that we can upper bound the expected norm of the grey area component by $O(1/T)$. In the main body, we formalize this "noisy" version of the decomposition and show that this suffices for proving the soundness of parallel repetition version of Mahadev's protocol.

Remark 1. We remark that parallel repetition of Mahadev's protocol is also analyzed in a concurrent work of Alagic et al. [6], who gave an elegant analysis. Their analysis starts from the same observation (Lemma 1) but is interestingly different from ours (see Sect. 1.3 for further discussion). An advantage of our analysis is that it is more constructive. Namely, we show that the ("noisy" version of) projection to $S_{i,0}$ and $S_{i,1}$ can be constructed efficiently. This is a useful feature that has found application in the work of [18], who constructed CVQC protocols for quantum sampling problems. They used the technique developed here to analyze parallel repetition of their protocol (while the analysis of [6] does not seem to generalize).

Two-Round Protocol via Fiat-Shamir Transform. Here, we explain how to convert the parallel repetition version of Mahadev's protocol to a two-round protocol in the QROM. First, we observe that the third message of the Mahadev's protocol is public-coin, and thus the parallel repetition version also satisfies this property. Then by using the Fiat-Shamir transform [20], we can replace the third message with hash value of the transcript up to the second round. Though the Fiat-Shamir transform was originally proven sound only in the classical ROM, recent works [19,31] showed that it is also sound in the QROM. This enables us to apply the Fiat-Shamir transform to the parallel repetition version of Mahadev's protocol to obtain a two-round protocol in the QROM.

Making Verification Efficient. Finally, we explain how to make the verification efficient. Our idea is to delegate the verification procedure itself to the prover by using delegation algorithm for classical computation. Since the verification is classical, this seems to work at first glance. However, there are the following two problems:

1. There is not a succinct description of the verification procedure since the verification procedure is specified by the whole transcript whose size is $\mathsf{poly}(T)$ when verifying a language in $\mathsf{QTIME}(T)$. Then the verifier cannot specify the verification procedure to delegate within time $O(\log(T))$.
2. Since the CVQC protocol is not publicly verifiable (i.e., verification requires a secret information that is not given to the prover), the prover cannot know the description of the verification procedure, which is supposed to be delegated to the prover.

We solve the first problem by using a succinct randomized encoding, which enables one to generate a succinct encoding of a Turing machine M and an input x so that the encoding only reveals the information about $M(x)$ and not M or x. Then our idea is that instead of sending the original first message, the verifier just sends a succinct encoding of (V_1, s) where V_1 denotes the Turing machine that takes s as input and works as the first-message-generation algorithm of the CVQC protocol with randomness $PRG(s)$ where PRG is a pseudorandom number generator. This enables us to make the transcript of the protocol succinct (i.e., the description size is logarithmic in T) so that the verifier can specify the verification procedure succinctly. To be more precise, we have to use a strong output-compressing randomized encoding [8], where the encoding size is independent of the output length of the Turing machine. They construct a strong output-compressing randomized encoding based on iO and other mild assumptions in the common reference string. Therefore our CVQC protocol also needs the common reference string.

We solve the second problem by using FHE. Namely, the verifier sends an encryption of the trapdoor td by FHE, and the prover performs the verification procedure over the ciphertext and provides a proof that it honestly applied the homomorphic evaluation by SNARK. Then the verifier decrypts the resulting FHE ciphertext and accepts if the decryption result is "accept" and the SNARK proof is valid.

In the following, we describe (a simplified version of) our construction. Suppose that we have a 2-round CVQC that works as follows:

First message: Given an instance x, the verifier generates a pair (k, td) of a "key" and "trapdoor", sends k to P, and keeps td as its internal state.

Second message: Given x and k, the prover generates a response e and sends it to the verifier.

Verification: Given x, k, td, e, the verifier returns $\top$ indicating acceptance or $\bot$ indicating rejection.

Then we construct a CVQC protocol with efficient verification as follows.

Setup: It generates a CRS for a strong output-compressing randomized encoding.

First Message: Given a CRS and an instance x, the verifier picks a seed s for PRG and a public and secret keys $(\mathsf{pk}_\mathsf{fhe}, \mathsf{sk}_\mathsf{fhe})$ of FHE, computes $\mathsf{ct} \xleftarrow{\$}$ $\mathsf{FHE.Enc}(\mathsf{pk}_\mathsf{fhe}, s)$ and generates a succinct encoding $\widehat{M_\mathsf{inp}}$ of $M(s)$ where M is a classical Turing machine that works as follows:

$M(s)$: Given a seed s for PRG, it generates (k, td) as in the building block CVQC protocol by using a randomness $PRG(s)$ and outputs k.

Then the verifier sends $(\widehat{M_\mathsf{inp}}, \mathsf{pk}_\mathsf{fhe}, \mathsf{ct})$ to the prover and keeps sk_fhe as its internal state.

Second Message: The prover obtains k by decoding $\widehat{M_\mathsf{inp}}$, computes e as in the building block CVQC protocol, and homomorphically evaluates a classical circuit $C[x, e]$ on ct to generate ct' where $C[x, e]$ is a circuit that works as follows:

$C[x, e](s)$: Given a seed s for PRG, it generates (k, td) as in the building block CVQC protocol by using a randomness $PRG(s)$ and returns 1 if and only if e is an accepting answer in the building block CVQC w.r.t. x and (k, td).

Then the prover generates a SNARK proof π_snark that proves that there exists e' such that ct' is a result of a homomorphic evaluation of the circuit $C[x, e]$ on ct. Then it sends $(\mathsf{ct}', \pi_\mathsf{snark})$ to the verifier

Verification: The verifier accepts if the decryption result of ct' is 1 and π_snark passes the verification of SNARK.

Intuitively, the soundness of the above protocol can be proven by considering the following hybrids. In the first hybrid, the verifier extracts the witness e' from π_snark by using the extractability of SNARK and runs the original verification of the building block CVQC on the second message e' instead of checking if the decryption result of ct' is 1. This decreases the cheating prover's success probability by a factor of $\mathsf{poly}(n)$ since the extraction succeeds with probability $1/\mathsf{poly}(n)$ and if the extraction succeeds, the verifier's output should be the same. In the next hybrid, we change ct to an encryption of $0^{|s|}$ instead of s. Since the verifier no longer uses sk_fhe, this hybrid is indistinguishable from the previous one by the CPA security of FHE. In the next hybrid, we generate $\widehat{M_\mathsf{inp}}$ by a simulation algorithm of the strong output-compressing randomized encoding from $M(s) = k$. This hybrid is indistinguishable from the previous one by the security of the strong output-compressing randomized encoding. In the next hybrid, we replace k that is used as an input of the simulation algorithm of the strong output-compressing randomized encoding with a one generated with a true randomness instead of $PRG(s)$. This hybrid is indistinguishable from the previous one by the security of PRG noting that s is no longer used for generating ct. In this final hybrid, a cheating prover is essentially only given k and has no information about td, and it wins if and only if the extraction algorithm of SNARK extracts an accepting second message e' of the building block CVQC. Thus, the winning probability in the final hybrid is negligible due to the soundness of the building block CVQC. Therefore the above efficient verification version is also sound.

Though the above proof sketch can be made rigorous if we assume adaptive extractability for SNARK, we want to instantiate SNARK in the QROM [17], which is only proven to have non-adaptive extractability. Specifically, it only ensures the extractability in the setting where the statement is chosen before making any query to the random oracle. To deal with this issue, we first expand the protocol to the four-round protocol where the verifier randomly sends a "salt" z, which is a random string of a certain length, in the third round and the prover uses the "salted" random oracle $H(z, \cdot)$ for generating the SNARK proof. Since the statement to be proven by SNARK is determined up to the second round, and the salting essentially makes the random oracle "fresh", we can argue the soundness of the CVQC protocol even with the non-adaptive extractability of the SNARK. At this point, we obtain four-round CVQC protocol with efficient verification. Here, we observe that the third message is just a salt z, which is public-coin. Therefore we can just apply the Fiat-Shamir transform again to make the protocol two-round.

1.3 Related Works

Verification of Quantum Computation. There is a long line of researches on verification of quantum computation. Except for solutions relying on computational assumptions, there are two type of settings where verification of quantum computation is known to be possible. In the first setting, instead of considering purely classical verifier, we assume that a verifier can perform a certain kind of weak quantum computations [5,15,21,35]. In the second setting, we assume that a prover is splitted into two remote servers that share entanglement but do not communicate [41]. Though these works do not give a CVQC protocol in our sense, the advantage is that we need not assume any computational assumption for the proof of soundness, and thus they are incomparable to Mahadev's result and ours.

Subsequent to Mahadev's breakthrough result, Gheorghiu and Vidick [24] gave a CVQC protocol that also satisfies blindness, which ensures that a prover cannot learn what computation is delegated. We note that their protocol requires polynomial number of rounds.

Post-quantum Indistinguishability Obfuscation. There are several candidates of post-quantum indistniguishability obfuscation [2,3,13,44]. Especially, the recent work by Brakerski et al. [13] gave a construction of indistniguishability obfuscation based on the LWE assumption and a certain type of circular security of LWE-based encryption schemes against subexponential time adversaries.

Concurrent Work. In a concurrent and independent work, Alagic et al. [6] also shows similar results to our first and second results, parallel repetition theorem for the Madadev's protocol and a two-round CVQC protocol by the Fiat-Shamir transform. We note that our third result, a two-round CVQC protocol with efficient verification, is unique in this paper. On the other hand, they also give a construction of non-interactive zero-knowledge arguments for QMA, which is not given in this paper.

We mention that we have learned the problem of parallel repetition for Mahadev's protocol from the authors of [6] on March 2019, but investigated the problem independently later as a stepping stone toward making the verifier efficient. Interestingly, the analyses of parallel repetition in the two works are quite different. Briefly, the analysis in [6] relies on the observation that for any two different challenges $c_1 \neq c_2 \in \{0,1\}^m$, the projections of an efficient-generated prover's state on the accepting subspaces corresponding to c_1 and c_2 are almost orthogonal, which leads to an elegant proof of the parallel repetition theorem.

As mentioned, we additionally show that the projections can be approximated "efficiently" by constructing an efficient quantum procedure (Lemma 4). This is the main technical step in our proof, where we combine several tools such as Jordan's lemma, phase estimation, and random thresholding to construct the efficient projector. We then use this efficient projector iteratively to bound the success probability of the prover. Our construction of the efficient projection has found applications in a related context in [18].

2 Preliminaries

Notations. For a bit $b \in \{0,1\}$, $\bar{b}$ denotes $1 - b$. For a finite set $\mathcal{X}$, $x \xleftarrow{\$} \mathcal{X}$ means that x is uniformly chosen from $\mathcal{X}$. For finite sets $\mathcal{X}$ and $\mathcal{Y}$, $\mathsf{Func}(\mathcal{X}, \mathcal{Y})$ denotes the set of all functions with domain $\mathcal{X}$ and range $\mathcal{Y}$. A function $f : \mathbb{N} \to [0, 1]$ is said to be negligible if for all polynomial p and sufficiently large $n \in \mathbb{N}$, we have $f(n) < 1/p(n)$ and said to be overwhelming if $1 - f$ is negligible. We denote by poly an unspecified polynomial and by negl an unspecified negligible function. We say that a classical (resp. quantum) algorithm is efficient if it runs in probabilistic polynomial-time (resp. quantum polynominal time). For a quantum or randomized algorithm $\mathcal{A}$, $y \xleftarrow{\$} \mathcal{A}(x)$ means that $\mathcal{A}$ is run on input x and outputs y and $y := \mathcal{A}(x; r)$ means that $\mathcal{A}$ is run on input x and randomness r and outputs y. For an interactive protocol between a "prover" P and "verifier" V, $y \xleftarrow{\$} \langle P(x_P), V(x_V) \rangle \rangle(x)$ means an interaction between them with prover's private input x_P verifier's private input x_V, and common input x outputs y. For a quantum state $|\psi\rangle$, $M_{\mathbf{X}} \circ |\psi\rangle$ means a measurement in the computational basis on the register $\mathbf{X}$ of $|\psi\rangle$. We denote by $\mathsf{QTIME}(T)$ a class of languages decided by a quantum algorithm whose running time is at most T. We use n to denote the security parameter throughout the paper.

2.1 Learning with Error Problem

Roughly speaking, the learning with error (LWE) is a problem to solve system of noisy linear equations. Regev [40] proved that the hardness of LWE can be reduced to hardness of certain worst-case lattice problems via quantum reductions. We do not give a definition of LWE in this paper since we use the hardness of LWE only for ensuring the soundness of the Mahadev's protocol (Lemma 3), which is used as a black-box manner in the rest of the paper. Therefore, we use exactly the same assumption as that used in [32], to which we refer for detailed definitions and parameter settings for LWE.

2.2   Quantum Random Oracle Model

The quantum random oracle model (QROM) [12] is an idealized model where a real-world hash function is modeled as a quantum oracle that computes a random function. More precisely, in the QROM, a random function $H : \mathcal{X} \to \mathcal{Y}$ of a certain domain $\mathcal{X}$ and range $\mathcal{Y}$ is uniformly chosen from $\mathsf{Func}(\mathcal{X}, \mathcal{Y})$ at the beginning, and every party (including an adversary) can access to a quantum oracle O_H that maps $|x\rangle|y\rangle$ to $|x\rangle|y \oplus H(x)\rangle$. We often abuse notation to denote $\mathcal{A}^H$ to mean a quantum algorithm $\mathcal{A}$ is given oracle O_H.

2.3   Lemma

Here, we give a simple lemma, which is used in the proof of soundness of parallel repetition version of the Mahadev's protocol in Sect. 3.3.

Lemma 2. *Let $|\psi\rangle = \sum_{i=1}^{m} |\psi_i\rangle$ be a quantum state and M be a projective measurement. Then we have*

$$\Pr[M \circ |\psi\rangle = 1] \leq m \sum_{i=1}^{m} \||\psi_i\rangle\|^2 \Pr\left[M \circ \frac{|\psi_i\rangle}{\||\psi_i\rangle\|} = 1\right]$$

A proof can be found in the full version.

3   Parallel Repetition of Mahadev's Protocol

3.1   Overview of Mahadev's Protocol

Here, we recall Mahadev's protocol [32]. We only give a high-level description of the protocol and properties of it and omit the details since they are not needed to show our result.

The protocol is run between a quantum prover P and a classical verifier V on a common input x. The aim of the protocol is to enable a verifier to classically verify $x \in L$ for a BQP language L with the help of interactions with a quantum prover. The protocol is a 4-round protocol where the first message is sent from V to P. We denote the i-th message generation algorithm by V_i for $i \in \{1,3\}$ or P_i for $i \in \{2,4\}$ and denote the verifier's final decision algorithm by V_{out}. Then a high-level description of the protocol is given below.

V_1: On input the security parameter 1^n and x, it generates a pair (k, td) of a "key" and "trapdoor", sends k to P, and keeps td as its internal state.

P_2: On input x and k, it generates a classical "commitment" y along with a quantum state $|\mathsf{st}_P\rangle$, sends y to P, and keeps $|\mathsf{st}_P\rangle$ as its internal state.

V_3: It randomly picks a "challenge" $c \xleftarrow{\$} \{0,1\}$ and sends c to P.[4] Following the terminology in [32], we call the case of $c = 0$ the "test round" and the case of $c = 1$ the "Hadamard round".

P_4: On input $|st_P\rangle$ and c, it generates a classical "answer" a and sends a to P.

V_{out}: On input k, td, y, c, and a, it returns $\top$ indicating acceptance or $\bot$ indicating rejection. In case $c = 0$, the verification can be done publicly, that is, V_{out} need not take td as input.

For the protocol, we have the following properties:

Completeness: For all $x \in L$, we have $\Pr[\langle P, V \rangle(x)] = \bot] = \mathsf{negl}(n)$.

Soundness: If the LWE problem is hard for quantum polynomial-time algorithms, then for any $x \notin L$ and a quantum polynomial-time cheating prover P^*, we have $\Pr[\langle P^*, V \rangle(x)] = \bot] \leq 3/4$.

We need a slightly different form of soundness implicitly shown in [32], which roughly says that if a cheating prover can pass the "test round" (i.e., the case of $c = 0$) with overwhelming probability, then it can pass the "Hadamard round" (i.e., the case of $c = 1$) only with a negligible probability.

Lemma 3 (implicit in [32]). *If the LWE problem is hard for quantum polynomial-time algorithms, then for any $x \notin L$ and a quantum polynomial-time cheating prover P^* such that $\Pr[\langle P^*, V \rangle(x)] = \bot \mid c = 0] = \mathsf{negl}(n)$, we have $\Pr[\langle P^*, V \rangle(x)] = \top \mid c = 1] = \mathsf{negl}(n)$.*

We will also use the following simple fact:

Fact 1 *There exists an efficient prover that passes the test round with probability 1 (but passes the Hadamard round with probability 0) even if $x \notin L$.*

3.2 Parallel Repetition

Here, we prove that the parallel repetition of Mahadev's protocol decrease the soundness bound to be negligible. Let P^m and V^m be m-parallel repetitions of the honest prover P and verifier V in Mahadev's protocol. Then we have the following:

Theorem 1 (Completeness). *For all $m = \Omega(\log^2(n))$, for all $x \in L$, we have $\Pr[\langle P^m, V^m \rangle(x)] = \bot] = \mathsf{negl}(n)$.*

Theorem 2 (Soundness). *For all $m = \Omega(\log^2(n))$, if the LWE problem is hard for quantum polynomial-time algorithms, then for any $x \notin L$ and a quantum polynomial-time cheating prover P^*, we have $\Pr[\langle P^*, V^m \rangle(x)] = \top] \leq \mathsf{negl}(n)$.*

The completeness (Theorem 1) easily follows from the completeness of Mahadev's protocol. In the next subsection, we prove the soundness (Theorem 2).

---

[4] The third message is just a public-coin, and does not depend on the transcript so far or x.

3.3   Proof of Soundness

First, we remark that it suffices to show that for any $\mu = 1/\mathrm{poly}(n)$, there exists $m = O(\log(n))$ such that the success probability of the cheating prover is at most μ. This is because we are considering $\omega(\log(n))$-parallel repetition, in which case the number of repetitions is larger than any $m = O(\log(n))$ for sufficiently large n, and thus we can just focus on the first m coordinates ignoring the rest of the coordinates. Thus, we prove the above claim in this section.

Characterization of Cheating Prover. Any cheating prover can be characterized by a tuple (U_0, U) of unitaries over Hilbert space $\mathcal{H}_\mathbf{C} \otimes \mathcal{H}_\mathbf{X} \otimes \mathcal{H}_\mathbf{Z} \otimes \mathcal{H}_\mathbf{Y} \otimes \mathcal{H}_\mathbf{K}.$[5] A prover characterized by (U_0, U) works as follows.[6]

Second Message: Upon receiving $k = (k_1, ..., k_m)$, it applies U_0 to the state $|0\rangle_\mathbf{X} \otimes |0\rangle_\mathbf{Z} \otimes |0\rangle_\mathbf{Y} \otimes |k\rangle_\mathbf{K}$, and then measures the Y register to obtain $y = (y_1, ..., y_m)$. Then it sends $\mathbf{y}$ to V and keeps the resulting state $|\psi(k, y)\rangle_{\mathbf{X},\mathbf{Z}}$ over $\mathcal{H}_{\mathbf{X},\mathbf{Z}}$.

fourth Message: Upon receiving $c \in \{0, 1\}^m$, it applies U to $|c\rangle_\mathbf{C}|\psi(k, y)\rangle_{\mathbf{X},\mathbf{Z}}$ and then measures the $\mathbf{X}$ register in computational basis to obtain $a = (a_1, ..., a_m)$. We denote the designated register for a_i by $\mathbf{X}_i$.

For each $i \in [m]$, we denote by Acc_{k_i,y_i} the set of a_i such that the verifier accepts a_i in the test round on the i-th coordinate when the first and second messages are k_i and y_i, respectively. Note that one can efficiently check if $a_i \in \mathsf{Acc}_{k_i,y_i}$ without knowing the trapdoor behind k_i since verification in the test round can be done publicly as explained in Sect. 3.1.

We first give ideas about Lemma 4 that is the main lemma for this section. For each coordinate $i \in [m]$, we would like to decompose the space $\mathcal{H}_{\mathbf{X},\mathbf{Z}}$ into a subspace $S_{i,0}$ that "does not know" $a_i \in \mathsf{Acc}_{k_i,y_i}$ and a subspace $S_{i,1}$ that "knows" $a_i \in \mathsf{Acc}_{k_i,y_i}$. Ideally, we want to prove the following statement: For any $i \in [m]$ and $|\psi\rangle \in \mathcal{H}_{\mathbf{X},\mathbf{Z}}$, if we decompose it as

$$|\psi\rangle = |\psi_0\rangle + |\psi_1\rangle$$

where $|\psi_0\rangle \in S_{i,0}$ and $|\psi_1\rangle \in S_{i,1}$, then we have the followings:[7]

1. ($|\psi_0\rangle$ **"does not know"** $a_i \in \mathsf{Acc}_{k_i,y_i}$.) If we apply U to $|c\rangle_\mathbf{C}|\psi_0\rangle_{\mathbf{X},\mathbf{Z}}$ for $c \xleftarrow{\$} \{0, 1\}^m$ such that $c_i = 0$ and measures the $\mathbf{X}_i$ register in computational basis to obtain a_i, then $a_i \in \mathsf{Acc}_{k_i,y_i}$ with "small" probability.[8]
2. ($|\psi_1\rangle$ **"knows"** $a_i \in \mathsf{Acc}_{k_i,y_i}$.) There is an efficient algorithm that is given $|\psi_1\rangle$ as input and outputs $a_i \in \mathsf{Acc}_{k_i,y_i}$ with overwhelming probability.

---

[5] $\mathcal{H}_\mathbf{X} \otimes \mathcal{H}_\mathbf{Z}$ corresponds to $\mathcal{H}_P$ in Sect. 1.2.

[6] Here, we hardwire into the cheating prover the instance $x \notin L$ on which it will cheat instead of giving it as an input.

[7] $|\psi_0\rangle$ and $|\psi_1\rangle$ correspond to $|\psi_{i,0}\rangle$ and $|\psi_{i,1}\rangle$ in Sect. 1.2, respectively.

[8] The threshold for "small" can be set to be any noticeable function.

3. (**Efficient projection.**) A measurement described by $\{\Pi_{S_{i,0}}, \Pi_{S_{i,1}}\}$ can be performed efficiently where $\Pi_{S_{i,0}}$ and $\Pi_{S_{i,1}}$ denote projections to $S_{i,0}$ and $S_{i,1}$, respectively.

If this is true, then the rest of the proof would be easy following the outline described in Sect. 1.2. However, we do not know how to prove it in the above clean form. Therefore we prove a noisy version of the above claim where

1. the way of decomposition is randomized,
2. there is an error term, i.e., we decompose $|\psi\rangle$ as

$$|\psi\rangle = |\psi_0\rangle + |\psi_1\rangle + |\psi_{err}\rangle$$

by using a state $|\psi_{err}\rangle$ whose norm is "small" on average, and
3. we have $\||\psi_0\rangle\|^2 + \||\psi_1\rangle\|^2 \le \||\psi\rangle\|^2$. We note that this condition automatically follows if $|\psi_0\rangle$ and $|\psi_1\rangle$ are orthogonal as in the above clean version, but they may not be orthogonal in our case.

Specifically, our lemma is stated as follows:

Lemma 4. *Let (U_0, U) be any prover's strategy. Let $m = O(\log n)$, $i \in [m]$, $\gamma_0 \in [0,1]$, and $T \in \mathbb{N}$ such that $\frac{\gamma_0}{T} = 1/\mathsf{poly}(n)$. Let γ be sampled uniformly randomly from $[\frac{\gamma_0}{T}, \frac{2\gamma_0}{T}, \ldots, \frac{T\gamma_0}{T}]$. Then, there exists an efficient quantum procedure $G_{i,\gamma}$ such that for any (possibly sub-normalized) quantum state $|\psi\rangle_{\mathbf{X},\mathbf{Z}}$,*

$$G_{i,\gamma}|0^m\rangle_{\mathbf{C}}|\psi\rangle_{\mathbf{X},\mathbf{Z}}|0^t\rangle_{ph}|0\rangle_{th}|0\rangle_{in} = z_0|0^m\rangle_{\mathbf{C}}|\psi_0\rangle_{\mathbf{X},\mathbf{Z}}|0^t 01\rangle_{ph,th,in}$$
$$+ z_1|0^m\rangle_{\mathbf{C}}|\psi_1\rangle_{\mathbf{X},\mathbf{Z}}|0^t 11\rangle_{ph,th,in} + |\psi'_{err}\rangle$$

where t is the number of qubits in the register ph, $z_0, z_1 \in \mathbb{C}$ such that $|z_0| = |z_1| = 1$, and $z_0, z_1, |\psi_0\rangle_{\mathbf{X},\mathbf{Z}}, |\psi_1\rangle_{\mathbf{X},\mathbf{Z}}$, and $|\psi'_{err}\rangle$ may depend on γ.
Furthermore, the following properties are satisfied.

1. (***Error is Small.***) *If we define $|\psi_{err}\rangle_{\mathbf{X},\mathbf{Z}} := |\psi\rangle_{\mathbf{X},\mathbf{Z}} - |\psi_0\rangle_{\mathbf{X},\mathbf{Z}} - |\psi_1\rangle_{\mathbf{X},\mathbf{Z}}$, then we have $E_\gamma[\||\psi_{err}\rangle_{\mathbf{X},\mathbf{Z}}\|^2] \le \frac{6}{T} + \mathsf{negl}(n)$.*
2. (***Efficient projection.***) *For any fixed γ, $\Pr[M_{ph,th,in} \circ |\psi'_{err}\rangle \in \{0^t 01, 0^t 11\}] = 0$. This implies that if we apply the measurement $M_{ph,th,in}$ on $\frac{G_{i,\gamma}|0^m\rangle_{\mathbf{C}}|\psi\rangle_{\mathbf{X},\mathbf{Z}}|0^t\rangle_{ph}|0\rangle_{th}|0\rangle_{in}}{\||\psi\rangle_{\mathbf{X},\mathbf{Z}}\|}$, then the outcome is $0^t b 1$ with probability $\||\psi_b\rangle_{\mathbf{X},\mathbf{Z}}\|^2$ and the resulting state in the register $(\mathbf{X}, \mathbf{Z})$ is $\frac{|\psi_b\rangle_{\mathbf{X},\mathbf{Z}}}{\||\psi_b\rangle_{\mathbf{X},\mathbf{Z}}\|}$ ignoring a global phase factor.*
3. (***Projection halves the squared norm.***) *For any fixed γ, $E_{b\in\{0,1\}}[\||\psi_b\rangle_{\mathbf{X},\mathbf{Z}}\|^2] \le \frac{1}{2}\||\psi\rangle_{\mathbf{X},\mathbf{Z}}\|^2$.*
4. ($|\psi_0\rangle$ "***does not know***" $a_i \in \mathsf{Acc}_{k_i,y_i}$.) *For any fixed γ and $c \in \{0,1\}^m$ such that $c_i = 0$, we have*

$$\Pr\left[M_{\mathbf{X}_i} \circ U\frac{|c\rangle_{\mathbf{C}}|\psi_0\rangle_{\mathbf{X},\mathbf{Z}}}{\||\psi_0\rangle_{\mathbf{X},\mathbf{Z}}\|} \in \mathsf{Acc}_{k_i,y_i}\right] \le 2^{m-1}\gamma + \mathsf{negl}(n).$$

Procedure 1 $G_{i,\gamma}$

---

1. Do quantum phase estimation U_{est} on $Q = (2\Pi_{in} - I)(2\Pi_{i,out} - I)$ with input state $|0^m\rangle_{\mathbf{C}} |\psi\rangle_{\mathbf{X,Z}}$ and τ-bit precision and failure probability 2^{-n} where the parameter τ will be specified later, i.e.,

$$U_{est} |u\rangle_{\mathbf{C,X,Z}} |0^t\rangle_{ph} \rightarrow \sum_{\theta \in (-\pi, \pi]} \alpha_\theta |u\rangle_{\mathbf{C,X,Z}} |\theta\rangle_{ph}.$$

such that $\sum_{\theta \notin \tilde{\theta} \pm 2^{-\tau}} |\alpha_\theta|^2 \leq 2^{-n}$ for any eigenvector $|u\rangle_{\mathbf{C,X,Z}}$ of Q with eigenvalue $e^{i\tilde{\theta}}$.

2. Apply $U_{th} : |u\rangle_{\mathbf{C,X,Z}} |\theta\rangle_{ph} |0\rangle_{th} \xrightarrow{U_{th}} |u\rangle_{\mathbf{C,X,Z}} |\theta\rangle_{ph} |b\rangle_{th}$, where $b = 1$ if $\cos^2(\theta/2) \geq \gamma - \delta$.

3. Apply $U_{est}^\dagger$.

4. Apply $U_{in} : |c\rangle_{\mathbf{C}} |0\rangle_{in} \xrightarrow{U_{in}} |c\rangle_{\mathbf{C}} |b'\rangle_{in}$, where $b' = 1$ if $c = 0^m$.

---

5. ($|\psi_1\rangle$ **"knows"** $a_i \in \mathsf{Acc}_{k_i, y_i}$.) For any fixed γ, there exists an efficient quantum algorithm Ext_i such that

$$\Pr\left[\mathsf{Ext}_i\left(\frac{|0^m\rangle_{\mathbf{C}}|\psi_1\rangle_{\mathbf{X,Z}}}{\||\psi_1\rangle_{\mathbf{X,Z}}\|}\right) \in \mathsf{Acc}_{k_i, y_i}\right] = 1 - \mathsf{negl}(n).$$

We prove that the algorithm $G_{i,\gamma}$ given in Fig. 1 satisfies the above conditions. The proof is based on a lemma about two projectors shown by Nagaj, Wocjan, and Zhang [36], which in turn is based on the Jordan's lemma. See the full version for a proof.

In Lemma 4, we showed that by fixing any $i \in [m]$, we can partition any prover's state $|\psi\rangle_{\mathbf{X,Z}}$ into $|\psi_0\rangle_{\mathbf{X,Z}}$, $|\psi_1\rangle_{\mathbf{X,Z}}$, and $|\psi_{err}\rangle_{\mathbf{X,Z}}$ with certain properties. In the following, we sequentially apply Lemma 4 for each $i \in [m]$ to further decompose the prover's state.

Lemma 5. *Let m, γ_0, T be as in Lemma 4, and let $\gamma_i \xleftarrow{\$} [\frac{\gamma_0}{T}, \frac{2\gamma_0}{T}, \ldots, \frac{T\gamma_0}{T}]$ for each $i \in [m]$. For any $c \in \{0,1\}^m$, a state $|\psi\rangle_{\mathbf{X,Z}}$ can be partitioned as follows.*

$$|\psi\rangle_{\mathbf{X,Z}} = |\psi_{c_1}\rangle_{\mathbf{X,Z}} + |\psi_{\bar{c}_1, c_2}\rangle_{\mathbf{X,Z}} + \cdots + |\psi_{\bar{c}_1, \ldots, \bar{c}_{m-1}, c_m}\rangle_{\mathbf{X,Z}} + |\psi_{\bar{c}_1, \ldots, \bar{c}_m}\rangle_{\mathbf{X,Z}} + |\psi_{err}\rangle_{\mathbf{X,Z}}$$

where the way of partition may depend on the choice of $\hat{\gamma} = \gamma_1 \ldots \gamma_m$. Further, the following properties are satisfied.

1. *For any fixed $\hat{\gamma}$ and any c, $i \in [m]$ such that $c_i = 0$, we have*

$$\Pr\left[M_{\mathbf{X}_i} \circ U \frac{|0^m\rangle_{\mathbf{C}}|\psi_{\bar{c}_1, \ldots, \bar{c}_{i-1}, 0}\rangle_{\mathbf{X,Z}}}{\||\psi_{\bar{c}_1, \ldots, \bar{c}_{i-1}, 0}\rangle_{\mathbf{X,Z}}|} \in \mathsf{Acc}_{k_i, y_i}\right] \leq 2^{m-1}\gamma_0 + \mathsf{negl}(n).$$

2. *For any fixed $\hat{\gamma}$ and any c, $i \in [m]$ such that $c_i = 1$, there exists an efficient algorithm Ext_i such that*

$$\Pr\left[\mathsf{Ext}_i\left(\frac{|0^m\rangle_{\mathbf{C}}|\psi_{\bar{c}_1, \ldots, \bar{c}_{i-1}, 1}\rangle_{\mathbf{X,Z}}}{\||\psi_{\bar{c}_1, \ldots, \bar{c}_{i-1}, 1}\rangle_{\mathbf{X,Z}}\|}\right) \in \mathsf{Acc}_{k_i, y_i}\right] = 1 - \mathsf{negl}(n).$$

3. *For any fixed $\hat{\gamma}$, we have $E_c[\| |\psi_{\bar{c}_1,...,\bar{c}_m}\rangle_{\mathbf{X},\mathbf{Z}}\|^2] \leq 2^{-m}$.*
4. *For any fixed c, we have $E_{\hat{\gamma}}[\| |\psi_{err}\rangle_{\mathbf{X},\mathbf{Z}}\|^2] \leq \frac{6m^2}{T} + \mathsf{negl}(n)$.*
5. *For any fixed $\hat{\gamma}$ and c there exists an efficient quantum algorithm $H_{\hat{\gamma},c}$ that is given $|\psi\rangle_{\mathbf{X},\mathbf{Z}}$ as input and produces $\frac{|\psi_{\bar{c}_1,...,\bar{c}_{i-1},c_i}\rangle_{\mathbf{X},\mathbf{Z}}}{\| |\psi_{\bar{c}_1,...,\bar{c}_{i-1},c_i}\rangle_{\mathbf{X},\mathbf{Z}}\|}$ with probability $\| |\psi_{\bar{c}_1,...,\bar{c}_{i-1},c_i}\rangle_{\mathbf{X},\mathbf{Z}}\|^2$ ignoring a global phase factor.*

Proof. We inductively define $|\psi_{c_1}\rangle_{\mathbf{X},\mathbf{Z}},...,|\psi_{\bar{c}_1,...,\bar{c}_m}\rangle_{\mathbf{X},\mathbf{Z}}$ as follows.

First, we apply Lemma 4 for the state $|\psi\rangle_{\mathbf{X},\mathbf{Z}}$ with $\gamma = \gamma_1$ to give a decomposition

$$|\psi\rangle_{\mathbf{X},\mathbf{Z}} = |\psi_0\rangle_{\mathbf{X},\mathbf{Z}} + |\psi_1\rangle_{\mathbf{X},\mathbf{Z}} + |\psi_{err,1}\rangle_{\mathbf{X},\mathbf{Z}}$$

where $|\psi_{err,1}\rangle_{\mathbf{X},\mathbf{Z}}$ corresponds to $|\psi_{err}\rangle_{\mathbf{X},\mathbf{Z}}$ in Lemma 4.

For each $i = 2,...,m$, we apply Lemma 4 for the state $|\psi_{\bar{c}_1,...,\bar{c}_{i-1}}\rangle_{\mathbf{X},\mathbf{Z}}$ with $\gamma = \gamma_i$ to give a decomposition

$$|\psi_{\bar{c}_1,...,\bar{c}_{i-1}}\rangle_{\mathbf{X},\mathbf{Z}} = |\psi_{\bar{c}_1,...,\bar{c}_{i-1},0}\rangle_{\mathbf{X},\mathbf{Z}} + |\psi_{\bar{c}_1,...,\bar{c}_{i-1},1}\rangle_{\mathbf{X},\mathbf{Z}} + |\psi_{err,i}\rangle_{\mathbf{X},\mathbf{Z}}$$

where $|\psi_{\bar{c}_1,...,\bar{c}_{i-1},0}\rangle_{\mathbf{X},\mathbf{Z}}$, $|\psi_{\bar{c}_1,...,\bar{c}_{i-1},1}\rangle_{\mathbf{X},\mathbf{Z}}$, and $|\psi_{err,i}\rangle_{\mathbf{X},\mathbf{Z}}$ corresponds to $|\psi_0\rangle_{\mathbf{X},\mathbf{Z}}$, $|\psi_1\rangle_{\mathbf{X},\mathbf{Z}}$, and $|\psi_{err}\rangle_{\mathbf{X},\mathbf{Z}}$ in Lemma 4, respectively.

Then it is easy to see that we have

$$|\psi\rangle_{\mathbf{X},\mathbf{Z}} = |\psi_{c_1}\rangle_{\mathbf{X},\mathbf{Z}} + |\psi_{\bar{c}_1,c_2}\rangle_{\mathbf{X},\mathbf{Z}} + \cdots + |\psi_{\bar{c}_1,...,\bar{c}_{m-1},c_m}\rangle_{\mathbf{X},\mathbf{Z}} + |\psi_{\bar{c}_1,...,\bar{c}_m}\rangle_{\mathbf{X},\mathbf{Z}} + |\psi_{err}\rangle_{\mathbf{X},\mathbf{Z}}$$

where we define $|\psi_{err}\rangle_{\mathbf{X},\mathbf{Z}} := \sum_{i=1}^{m} |\psi_{err,i}\rangle_{\mathbf{X},\mathbf{Z}}$.

The first and second claims immediately follow from the fourth and fifth claims of Lemma 4 and $\gamma_i \leq \gamma_0$ for each $i \in [m]$.

By the third claim of Lemma 4, we have $E_{c_1...c_i}[\| |\psi_{\bar{c}_1,...,\bar{c}_i}\rangle_{\mathbf{X},\mathbf{Z}}\|] \leq \frac{1}{2}E_{c_1...c_{i-1}}[\| |\psi_{\bar{c}_1,...,\bar{c}_{i-1}}\rangle_{\mathbf{X},\mathbf{Z}}\|]$. This implies the third claim.

By the first claim of Lemma 4, we have $E_{\gamma_i}[\| |\psi_{err,i}\rangle_{\mathbf{X},\mathbf{Z}}\|^2] \leq \frac{6}{T} + \mathsf{negl}(n)$. The fourth claim follows from this and the Cauchy-Schwarz inequality.

Finally, for proving the fifth claim, we define the procedure $H_{\hat{\gamma},c}$ as described in Procedure 2 We can easily see that $H_{\hat{\gamma},c}$ satisfies the desired property by the second claim of Lemma 4.

Given Lemma 5, we can start proving Theorem 2.

Proof (Proof of Theorem 2).
First, we recall how a cheating prover characterized by (U_0, U) works. When the first message k is given, it first applies

$$U_0|0\rangle_{\mathbf{X},\mathbf{Z}}|0\rangle_{\mathbf{Y}}|k\rangle_{\mathbf{K}} \xrightarrow{\text{measure } \mathbf{Y}} |\psi(k,y)\rangle_{\mathbf{X},\mathbf{Z}}|k\rangle_{\mathbf{K}}.$$

to generate the second message y and $|\psi(k,y)\rangle_{\mathbf{X},\mathbf{Z}}$. Then after receiving the third message c, it applies U on $|c\rangle_{\mathbf{C}}|\psi(k,y)\rangle_{\mathbf{X},\mathbf{Z}}$ and measures the register $\mathbf{X}$ in the computational basis to obtain the fourth message a. In the following, we just write $|\psi\rangle_{\mathbf{X},\mathbf{Z}}$ to mean $|\psi(k,y)\rangle_{\mathbf{X},\mathbf{Z}}$ for notational simplicity. Let $M_{i,k_i,\mathsf{td}_i,y_i,c_i}$ be

Procedure 2 $H_{\hat{\gamma},c}$

On input $|\psi\rangle_{\mathbf{X},\mathbf{Z}}$, it works as follows:
For each $i = 1, ..., m$, it applies
1. Prepare registers $\mathbf{C}$, (ph_1, th_1, in_1),..., (ph_m, th_m, in_m) all of which are initialized to be $|0\rangle$.
2. For each $i = 1, ..., m$, do the following:
    1. Apply G_{i,γ_i} on the quantum state in the registers $(\mathbf{C}, \mathbf{X}, \mathbf{Z}, ph_i, th_i, in_i)$.
    2. Measure the registers (ph_i, th_i, in_i) in the computational basis.
    3. If the outcome is $0^t c_i 1$, then it halts and returns the state in the register $(\mathbf{X}, \mathbf{Z})$. If the outcome is $0^t \bar{c}_i 1$, continue to run. Otherwise, immediately halt and abort.

the measurement that outputs the verification result of the value in the register $\mathbf{X}_i$ w.r.t. $k_i, \mathsf{td}_i, y_i, c_i$, and let $M_{k,\mathsf{td},y,c}$ be the measurement that returns $\top$ if and only if $M_{i,k_i,\mathsf{td}_i,y_i,c_i}$ returns $\top$ for all $i \in [m]$ where $k = (k_1, ..., k_m)$, $\mathsf{td} = (\mathsf{td}_1, ..., \mathsf{td}_m)$, $y = (y_1, ..., y_m)$ and $c = (c_1, ..., c_m)$. With this notation, a cheating prover's success probability can be written as

$$\Pr_{k,\mathsf{td},y,c}[M_{k,\mathsf{td},y,c} \circ U|c\rangle_{\mathbf{C}}|\psi\rangle_{\mathbf{X},\mathbf{Z}} = \top].$$

Let γ_0, $\hat{\gamma}$, and T be as in Lemma 5. According to Lemma 5, for any fixed $\hat{\gamma}$ and $c \in \{0,1\}^m$, we can decompose $|\psi\rangle_{\mathbf{X},\mathbf{Z}}$ as

$$|\psi\rangle_{\mathbf{X},\mathbf{Z}} = |\psi_{c_1}\rangle_{\mathbf{X},\mathbf{Z}} + |\psi_{\bar{c}_1,c_2}\rangle_{\mathbf{X},\mathbf{Z}} + \cdots + |\psi_{\bar{c}_1,...,\bar{c}_{m-1},c_m}\rangle_{\mathbf{X},\mathbf{Z}} + |\psi_{\bar{c}_1,...,\bar{c}_{m-1},\bar{c}_m}\rangle_{\mathbf{X},\mathbf{Z}} + |\psi_{err}\rangle_{\mathbf{X},\mathbf{Z}}.$$

To prove the theorem, we show the following two inequalities. First, for any fixed $\hat{\gamma}$, $i \in [m]$, $c \in \{0,1\}^m$ such that $c_i = 0$, k_i, td_i, and y_i, we have

$$\Pr\left[M_{i,k_i,\mathsf{td}_i,y_i,0} \circ \frac{U|c\rangle_{\mathbf{C}}|\psi_{\bar{c}_1,...,\bar{c}_{i-1},0}\rangle_{\mathbf{X},\mathbf{Z}}}{\||\psi_{\bar{c}_1,...,\bar{c}_{i-1},0}\rangle_{\mathbf{X},\mathbf{Z}}\|} = \top\right] \le 2^{m-1}\gamma_0 + \mathsf{negl}(n). \quad (1)$$

This easily follows from the first claim of Lemma 5
    Second, for any fixed $\hat{\gamma}$, $i \in [m]$, and $c \in \{0,1\}^m$ such that $c_i = 1$, we have

$$\underset{k,\mathsf{td},y}{E}\left[\||\psi_{\bar{c}_1,...,\bar{c}_{i-1},1}\rangle_{\mathbf{X},\mathbf{Z}}\|^2 \Pr\left[M_{i,k_i,\mathsf{td}_i,y_i,1} \circ U\frac{|c\rangle_{\mathbf{C}}|\psi_{\bar{c}_1,...,\bar{c}_{i-1},1}\rangle_{\mathbf{X},\mathbf{Z}}}{\||\psi_{\bar{c}_1,...,\bar{c}_{i-1},1}\rangle_{\mathbf{X},\mathbf{Z}}\|} = \top\right]\right] = \mathsf{negl}(n)$$

$$(2)$$

assuming the quantum hardness of LWE problem.
    For proving Eq. 2, we consider a cheating prover against the original Mahadev's protocol on the i-th coordinate described below:

1. Given k_i, it picks $k_{-i} = k_1...k_{i-1}, k_{i+1}, ..., k_m$ as in the protocol and computes $U_0|0\rangle_{\mathbf{X},\mathbf{Z}}|0\rangle_{\mathbf{Y}}|k\rangle_{\mathbf{K}}$ and measure the register $\mathbf{Y}$ to obtain $y = (y_1, ..., y_m)$ along with the corresponding state $|\psi\rangle_{\mathbf{X},\mathbf{Z}} = |\psi(k,y)\rangle_{\mathbf{X},\mathbf{Z}}$.

2. Apply $H_{\hat{\gamma},c}$ (which is defined in the fifth claim of Lemma 5) to generate the state $\frac{|\psi_{\bar{c}_1,\ldots,\bar{c}_{i-1},1}\rangle_{\mathbf{X},\mathbf{Z}}}{\||\psi_{\bar{c}_1,\ldots,\bar{c}_{i-1},1}\rangle_{\mathbf{X},\mathbf{Z}}\|}$, which succeeds with probability $\||\psi_{\bar{c}_1,\ldots,\bar{c}_{i-1},1}\rangle_{\mathbf{X},\mathbf{Z}}\|^2$ (ignoring a global phase factor). We denote by Succ the event that it succeeds in generating the state. If it fails to generate the state, then it overrides y_i by picking it in a way such that it can pass the test round with probability 1, which can be done according to Fact 1. Then it sends y_i to the verifier.

3. Given a challenge c'_i, it works as follows:
   - When $c'_i = 0$ (i.e., Test round), if Succ occurred, then it runs Ext_i in the second claim of Lemma 5 on input $\frac{|0^m\rangle_\mathbf{C}|\psi_{\bar{c}_1,\ldots,\bar{c}_{i-1},1}\rangle_{\mathbf{X},\mathbf{Z}}}{\||\psi_{\bar{c}_1,\ldots,\bar{c}_{i-1},1}\rangle_{\mathbf{X},\mathbf{Z}}\|}$ to generate a fourth message accepted with probability $1 - \mathsf{negl}(n)$. If Succ did not occur, then it returns a fourth message accepted with probability 1, which is possible by Fact 1.
   - When $c'_i = 1$ (i.e., Hadamard round), if Succ occurred, then it computes $U\frac{|c\rangle_\mathbf{C}|\psi_{\bar{c}_1,\ldots,\bar{c}_{i-1},1}\rangle_{\mathbf{X},\mathbf{Z}}}{\||\psi_{\bar{c}_1,\ldots,\bar{c}_{i-1},1}\rangle_{\mathbf{X},\mathbf{Z}}\|}$ and measure the register $\mathbf{X}_i$ to obtain the fourth message a_i. If Succ did not occur, it just aborts.

Then we can see that this cheating adversary passes the test round with overwhelming probability and passes the Hadamard round with the probability equal to the LHS of Eq. 2. Therefore, Eq. 2 follows from Lemma 3 assuming the quantum hardness of LWE problem.

Now, we are ready to prove the soundness of the parallel repetition version of Mahadev's protocol (Theorem 2). As remarked at the beginning of Sect. 3.3, it suffices to show that for any $\mu = 1/\mathsf{poly}(n)$, there exists $m = O(\log(n))$ such that the success probability of the cheating prover is at most μ. Here we set $m = \log\frac{1}{\mu^2}$, $\gamma_0 = 2^{-2m}$, and $T = 2^m$. Note that this parameter setting satisfies the requirement for Lemma 5 since $m = \log\frac{1}{\mu^2} = \log(\mathsf{poly}(n)) = O(\log n)$ and $\frac{\gamma_0}{T} = 2^{-3m} = \mu^6 = 1/\mathsf{poly}(n)$. Then we have

$$\Pr_{k,\mathsf{td},y,c}\left[M_{k,\mathsf{td},y,c} \circ U|c\rangle_\mathbf{C}|\psi\rangle_{\mathbf{X},\mathbf{Z}} = \top\right]$$

$$= \Pr_{k,\mathsf{td},y,c,\hat{\gamma}}\left[M_{k,\mathsf{td},y,c} \circ U|c\rangle_\mathbf{C}\left(\sum_{i=1}^{m}|\psi_{\bar{c}_1,\ldots,\bar{c}_{i-1},c_i}\rangle_{\mathbf{X},\mathbf{Z}} + |\psi_{\bar{c}_1,\ldots,\bar{c}_m}\rangle_{\mathbf{X},\mathbf{Z}} + |\psi_{err}\rangle_{\mathbf{X},\mathbf{Z}}\right) = \top\right]$$

$$\leq (m+2)\mathop{E}_{k,\mathsf{td},y,c,\hat{\gamma}}\left[\sum_{i=1}^{m}\||\psi_{\bar{c}_1,\ldots,\bar{c}_{i-1},c_i}\rangle_{\mathbf{X},\mathbf{Z}}\|^2 \Pr\left[M_{k,\mathsf{td},y,c} \circ U\frac{|c\rangle_\mathbf{C}|\psi_{\bar{c}_1,\ldots,\bar{c}_{i-1},c_i}\rangle_{\mathbf{X},\mathbf{Z}}}{\||\psi_{\bar{c}_1,\ldots,\bar{c}_{i-1},c_i}\rangle_{\mathbf{X},\mathbf{Z}}\|} = \top\right]\right.$$

$$\left. + \||\psi_{\bar{c}_1,\ldots,\bar{c}_m}\rangle_{\mathbf{X},\mathbf{Z}}\|^2 \Pr\left[M_{k,\mathsf{td},y,c} \circ U\frac{|c\rangle_\mathbf{C}|\psi_{\bar{c}_1,\ldots,\bar{c}_m}\rangle_{\mathbf{X},\mathbf{Z}}}{\||\psi_{\bar{c}_1,\ldots,\bar{c}_m}\rangle_{\mathbf{X},\mathbf{Z}}\|} = \top\right]\right.$$

$$\left. + \||\psi_{err}\rangle_{\mathbf{X},\mathbf{Z}}\|^2 \Pr\left[M_{k,\mathsf{td},y,c} \circ U\frac{|c\rangle_\mathbf{C}|\psi_{err}\rangle_{\mathbf{X},\mathbf{Z}}}{\||\psi_{err}\rangle_{\mathbf{X},\mathbf{Z}}\|} = \top\right]\right]$$

$$\leq (m+2)\mathop{E}_{k,\mathsf{td},y,c,\hat{\gamma}}\left[\sum_{i=1}^{m}\||\psi_{\bar{c}_1,\ldots,\bar{c}_{i-1},c_i}\rangle_{\mathbf{X},\mathbf{Z}}\|^2 \Pr\left[M_{i,k_i,\mathsf{td}_i,y_i,c_i} \circ U\frac{|c\rangle_\mathbf{C}|\psi_{\bar{c}_1,\ldots,\bar{c}_{i-1},c_i}\rangle_{\mathbf{X},\mathbf{Z}}}{\||\psi_{\bar{c}_1,\ldots,\bar{c}_{i-1},c_i}\rangle_{\mathbf{X},\mathbf{Z}}\|} = \top\right]\right.$$

$$\left. + \||\psi_{\bar{c}_1,\ldots,\bar{c}_m}\rangle_{\mathbf{X},\mathbf{Z}}\|^2 + \||\psi_{err}\rangle_{\mathbf{X},\mathbf{Z}}\|^2\right]$$

$$\leq (m+2)(m(2^{m-1}\gamma_0 + \mathsf{negl}(n)) + 2^{-m} + \frac{6m^2}{T} + \mathsf{negl}(n))$$

$$\leq \mathsf{poly}(\log\mu^{-1})\mu^2 + \mathsf{negl}(n).$$

The first equation follows from Lemma 5. The first inequality follows from Lemma 2. The second inequality holds since considering the verification on a particular coordinate just increases the acceptance probability and probabilities are at most 1. The third inequality follows from Eq. 1 and 2, which give an upper bound of the first term and Lemma 5, which gives upper bounds of the second and third terms. The last inequality follows from our choices of γ_0, T, and m. For sufficiently large n, this can be upper bounded by μ. Since $\Pr_{k,\mathsf{td},y,c}[M_{k,\mathsf{td},y,c} \circ U|c\rangle_{\mathbf{C}}|\psi\rangle_{\mathbf{X},\mathbf{Z}} = \top]$ is the success probability of a cheating prover, the above inequality means that for any $\mu = 1/\mathsf{poly}(n)$, there exists $m = O(\log(n))$ such that the success probability of the cheating prover is at most μ. As remarked at the beginning of Sect. 3.3, this suffices for proving that a chearing prover's success probability is negligible when $m = \omega(\log n)$.

4   Two-Round Protocol via Fiat-Shamir Transform

In this section, we show that if we apply the Fiat-Shamir transform to m-parallel version of the Mahadev's protocol, then we obtain two-round protocol in the QROM. That is, we prove the following theorem.

Theorem 3. *Assuming LWE assumption, there exists a two-round CVQC protocol with overwhelming completeness and negligible soundness error in the QROM.*

Proof. Let $m > n$ be a sufficiently large integer so that m-parallel version of the Mahadev's protocol has negligible soundness. For notational simplicity, we abuse the notation to simply use V_i, P_i, and V_{out} to mean the m-parallel repetitions of them. Let $H : \mathcal{Y} \to \{0,1\}^m$ be a hash function idealized as a quantum random oracle where $\mathcal{X}$ is the space of the second message y and $\mathcal{Y} = \{0,1\}^m$. Our two-round protocol is described below:

First Message: The verifier runs V_1 to generate (k, td). Then it sends k to the prover and keeps td as its state.

Second Message: The prover runs P_2 on input k to generate y along with the prover's state $|\mathsf{st}_P\rangle$. Then set $c := H(y)$, and runs P_4 on input $|\mathsf{st}_P\rangle$ and y to generate a. Finally, it returns (y, a) to the verifier.

Verification: The verifier computes $c = H(y)$, runs $V_{\mathsf{out}}(k, \mathsf{td}, y, c, a)$, and outputs as V_{out} outputs.

It is clear that the completeness is preserved given that H is a random oracle. We can reduce the soundness of this protocol to the soundness of m-parallel version of the Mahadev's protocol by using the result of [19], which shows that Fiat-Shamir transform preserves soundness in the QROM. See the full version for details.

5   Making Verifier Efficient

In this section, we construct a CVQC protocol with efficient verification in the CRS+QRO model where a classical common reference string is available for both prover and verifier in addition to quantum access to QRO. Our main theorem in this section is stated as follows:

Theorem 4. *Assuming LWE assumption and existence of post-quantum iO, post-quantum FHE, and two-round CVQC protocol in the standard model, there exists a two-round CVQC protocol for* QTIME(T) *with verification complexity* poly($n, \log T$) *in the CRS+QRO model.*

Remark 2. One may think that the underlying two-round CVQC protocol can be in the QROM instead of in the standard model since we rely on the QROM anyway. However, this is not the case since we need to use the underlying two-round CVQC in a non-black box way, which cannot be done if that is in the QROM. Since our two-round protocol given in Sect. 4 is only proven secure in the QROM, we do not know any two-round CVQC protocol provably secure in the standard model. On the other hand, it is widely used heuristic in cryptography that a scheme proven secure in the QROM is also secure in the standard model if the QRO is instantiated by a well-designed cryptographic hash function. For example, many candidates for the NIST post-quantum standardization [37] give security proofs in the QROM and claim their security in the real world. Therefore, we believe that it is reasonable to assume that a standard model instantiation of the scheme in Sect. 4 with a concrete hash function is sound.

Remark 3. One may think we need not assume CRS in addition to QRO since CRS may be replaced with an output of QRO. This can be done if CRS is just a uniformly random string. However, in our construction, CRS is non-uniform and has a certain structure. Therefore we cannot implement CRS by QRO.

5.1   Four-Round Protocol

First, we construct a four-round scheme with efficient verification, which is transformed into two-round protocol in the next subsection. Our construction is based on the following building blocks. Definitions of them can be found in the full version.

- A two-round CVQC protocol $\Pi = (P = P_2, V = (V_1, V_{\mathsf{out}}))$ in the standard model, which works as follows:

  V_1: On input the security parameter 1^n and x, it generates a pair (k, td) of a"key" and "trapdoor", sends k to P, and keeps td as its internal state.

  P_2: On input x and k, it generates a response e and sends it to V.

  V_{out}: On input x, k, td, e, it returns $\top$ indicating acceptance or $\bot$ indicating rejection.

- A post-quantum PRG PRG : $\{0,1\}^{\ell_s} \rightarrow \{0,1\}^{\ell_r}$ where ℓ_r is the length of randomness for V_1.

- An FHE scheme $\Pi_{\mathsf{FHE}} = (\mathsf{FHE.KeyGen}, \mathsf{FHE.Enc}, \mathsf{FHE.Eval}, \mathsf{FHE.Dec})$ with post-quantum CPA security.
- A strong output compressing randomized encoding scheme $\Pi_{\mathsf{RE}} = (\mathsf{RE.Setup}, \mathsf{RE.Enc}, \mathsf{RE.Dec})$ with post-quantum security. We denote the simulator for Π_{RE} by $\mathcal{S}_{\mathsf{re}}$.
- A SNARK $\Pi_{\mathsf{SNARK}} = (P_{\mathsf{snark}}, V_{\mathsf{snark}})$ in the QROM for an NP language L_{snark} defined below:

  We have $(x, \mathsf{pk}_{\mathsf{fhe}}, \mathsf{ct}, \mathsf{ct}') \in L_{\mathsf{snark}}$ if and only if there exists e such that $\mathsf{ct}' = \mathsf{FHE.Eval}(\mathsf{pk}_{\mathsf{fhe}}, C[x, e], \mathsf{ct})$ where $C[x, e]$ is a circuit that works as follows:

  $C[x, e](s)$: Given input s, it computes $(k, \mathsf{td}) \xleftarrow{\$} V_1(1^n, x; PRG(s))$, and returns 1 if and only if $V_{\mathsf{out}}(x, k, \mathsf{td}, e) = \top$ and 0 otherwise.

Let L be a BPP language decided by a quantum Turing machine QTM (i.e., for any $x \in \{0,1\}^*$, $x \in L$ if and only if QTM accepts x), and for any T, L_T denotes the set consisting of $x \in L$ such that QTM accepts x in T steps. Then we construct a 4-round CVQC protocol $(\mathsf{Setup}_{\mathsf{eff}}, P_{\mathsf{eff}} = (P_{\mathsf{eff},2}, P_{\mathsf{eff},4}), V_{\mathsf{eff}} = (V_{\mathsf{eff},1}, V_{\mathsf{eff},3}, V_{\mathsf{eff,out}}))$ for L_T in the CRS+QRO model where the verifier's efficiency only logarithmically depends on T. Let $H : \{0,1\}^{2n} \times \{0,1\}^{2n} \to \{0,1\}^n$ be a quantum random oracle.

$\mathsf{Setup}_{\mathsf{eff}}(1^n)$: The setup algorithm takes the security parameter 1^n as input, generates $\mathsf{crs}_{\mathsf{re}} \xleftarrow{\$} \{0,1\}^\ell$ and computes $\mathsf{ek}_{\mathsf{re}} \xleftarrow{\$} \mathsf{RE.Setup}(1^n, 1^\ell, \mathsf{crs}_{\mathsf{re}})$ where ℓ is a parameter specified later. Then it outputs a CRS for verifier $\mathsf{crs}_{V_{\mathsf{eff}}} := \mathsf{ek}_{\mathsf{re}}$ and a CRS for prover $\mathsf{crs}_{P_{\mathsf{eff}}} := \mathsf{crs}_{\mathsf{re}}.$[9]

$V_{\mathsf{eff},1}^H$: Given $\mathsf{crs}_{V_{\mathsf{eff}}} = \mathsf{ek}_{\mathsf{re}}$ and x, it generates $s \xleftarrow{\$} \{0,1\}^{\ell_s}$ and $(\mathsf{pk}_{\mathsf{fhe}}, \mathsf{sk}_{\mathsf{fhe}}) \xleftarrow{\$} \mathsf{FHE.KeyGen}(1^n)$, computes $\mathsf{ct} \xleftarrow{\$} \mathsf{FHE.Enc}(\mathsf{pk}_{\mathsf{fhe}}, s)$ and $\widehat{M_{\mathsf{inp}}} \xleftarrow{\$} \mathsf{RE.Enc}(\mathsf{ek}_{\mathsf{re}}, M, s, T')$ where M is a Turing machine that works as follows:

  $M(s)$: Given an input $s \in \{0,1\}^{\ell_s}$, it computes $(k, \mathsf{td}) \xleftarrow{\$} V_1(1^n, x; PRG(s))$ and outputs k

  and T' is specified later. Then it sends $(\widehat{M_{\mathsf{inp}}}, \mathsf{pk}_{\mathsf{fhe}}, \mathsf{ct})$ to P_{eff} and keeps $\mathsf{sk}_{\mathsf{fhe}}$ as its internal state.

$P_{\mathsf{eff},2}^H$: Given $\mathsf{crs}_{P_{\mathsf{eff}}} = \mathsf{crs}_{\mathsf{re}}$, x and the message $(\widehat{M_{\mathsf{inp}}}, \mathsf{pk}_{\mathsf{fhe}}, \mathsf{ct})$ from the verifier, it computes $k \leftarrow \mathsf{RE.Dec}(\mathsf{crs}_{\mathsf{re}}, \widehat{M_{\mathsf{inp}}})$, $e \xleftarrow{\$} P_2(x, k)$, and $\mathsf{ct}' \leftarrow \mathsf{FHE.Eval}(\mathsf{pk}_{\mathsf{fhe}}, C[x, e], \mathsf{ct})$ where $C[x, e]$ is a classical circuit defined above. Then it sends ct' to V_{eff} and keeps $(\mathsf{pk}_{\mathsf{fhe}}, \mathsf{ct}, \mathsf{ct}', e)$ as its state.

$V_{\mathsf{eff},3}^H$ Upon receiving ct', it randomly picks $z \xleftarrow{\$} \{0,1\}^{2n}$ and sends z to P_{eff}.

$P_{\mathsf{eff},4}^H$ Upon receiving z, it computes $\pi_{\mathsf{snark}} \xleftarrow{\$} P_{\mathsf{snark}}^{H(z,\cdot)}((x, \mathsf{pk}_{\mathsf{fhe}}, \mathsf{ct}, \mathsf{ct}'), e)$ and sends π_{snark} to V_{eff}.

$V_{\mathsf{eff,out}}^H$: It returns $\top$ if $V_{\mathsf{snark}}^{H(z,\cdot)}((x, \mathsf{pk}_{\mathsf{fhe}}, \mathsf{ct}, \mathsf{ct}'), \pi_{\mathsf{snark}}) = \top$ and $1 \leftarrow \mathsf{FHE.Dec}(\mathsf{sk}_{\mathsf{fhe}}, \mathsf{ct}')$ and $\bot$ otherwise.

---

[9] We note that we divide the CRS into $\mathsf{crs}_{V_{\mathsf{eff}}}$ and $\mathsf{crs}_{P_{\mathsf{eff}}}$ just for the verifier efficiency and soundness still holds even if a cheating prover sees $\mathsf{crs}_{V_{\mathsf{eff}}}$.

Choice of Parameters.

- We set ℓ to be an upper bound of the length of k where $(k, \mathrm{td}) \xleftarrow{\$} V_1(1^n, x)$ for $x \in L_T$. We note that we have $\ell = \mathrm{poly}(n, T)$.
- We set T' to be an upperbound of the running time of M on input $s \in \{0,1\}^{\ell_s}$ when $x \in L_T$. We note that we have $T' = \mathrm{poly}(n, T)$.

Verification Efficiency. By encoding efficiency of Π_{RE} and verification efficiency of Π_{SNARK}, V_{eff} runs in time $\mathrm{poly}(n, |x|, \log T)$.

Remark 4. We note that the running time of the setup algorithm is $\mathrm{poly}(T)$. This can be done by a trusted party that has a strong (classical) computational power. Alternatively, as in the classical delegating computation literature, we can consider an offline/online setting where the verifier can spend a one-time cost of $\mathrm{poly}(T)$ to setup the CRS in the offline stage, and use it to delegate multiple quantum computation efficiently in the online stage.

Theorem 5 (Completeness). *For any* $x \in L_T$,

$$\Pr\left[\langle P_{\mathrm{eff}}^H(\mathrm{crs}_{P_{\mathrm{eff}}}), V_{\mathrm{eff}}^H(\mathrm{crs}_{V_{\mathrm{eff}}})\rangle(x) = \bot\right] = \mathsf{negl}(n)$$

where $(\mathrm{crs}_{P_{\mathrm{eff}}}, \mathrm{crs}_{V_{\mathrm{eff}}}) \xleftarrow{\$} \mathsf{Setup}_{\mathrm{eff}}(1^n)$.

Proof. This easily follows from completeness and correctness of the underlying primitives.

Theorem 6 (Soundness). *For any* $x \notin L_T$ *any efficient quantum cheating prover* $\mathcal{A}$,

$$\Pr\left[\langle \mathcal{A}^H(\mathrm{crs}_{P_{\mathrm{eff}}}, \mathrm{crs}_{V_{\mathrm{eff}}}), V_{\mathrm{eff}}^H(\mathrm{crs}_{V_{\mathrm{eff}}})\rangle(x) = \top\right] = \mathsf{negl}(n)$$

where $(\mathrm{crs}_{P_{\mathrm{eff}}}, \mathrm{crs}_{V_{\mathrm{eff}}}) \xleftarrow{\$} \mathsf{Setup}_{\mathrm{eff}}(1^n)$.

A proof can be found in the full version.

5.2 Reducing to Two-Round via Fiat-Shamir

Since the third message is public-coin in the four-round protocol in the previous section, we can apply the Fiat-Shamir transform similarly to Sect. 4. Then we obtain the two-round CVQC protocol in the QROM, which completes the proof of Theorem 4. Details can be found in the full version.

Acknowledgement. Kai-Min Chung is partially supported by the Academia Sinica Career Development Award under Grant no. 23-17, and MOST QC project under Grant no. MOST 108-2627-E-002-001-.

Nai-Hui Chia were supported by Scott Aaronson's Vannevar Bush Faculty Fellowship.

References

1. IBM quantum experience. https://quantum-computing.ibm.com/docs/. Accessed 22 May 2020
2. Agrawal, S.: Indistinguishability obfuscation without multilinear maps: new methods for bootstrapping and instantiation. In: Ishai, Y., Rijmen, V. (eds.) EUROCRYPT 2019. LNCS, vol. 11476, pp. 191–225. Springer, Cham (2019). https://doi.org/10.1007/978-3-030-17653-2_7
3. Agrawal, S., Pellet-Mary, A.: Indistinguishability obfuscation without maps: attacks and fixes for noisy linear FE. In: Canteaut, A., Ishai, Y. (eds.) EUROCRYPT 2020. LNCS, vol. 12105, pp. 110–140. Springer, Cham (2020). https://doi.org/10.1007/978-3-030-45721-1_5
4. Aharonov, D., Arad, I., Vidick, T.: Guest column: the quantum PCP conjecture. SIGACT News **44**(2), 47–79 (2013)
5. Aharonov, D., Ben-Or, M., Eban, E., Mahadev, U.: Interactive proofs for quantum computations. arXiv:1704.04487 (2017)
6. Alagic, G., Childs, A.M., Grilo, A.B., Hung, S.-H.: Non-interactive classical verification of quantum computation. In: TCC 2020 (2020, to appear)
7. Arute, F., et al.: Quantum supremacy using a programmable superconducting processor. Nature **574**(7779), 505–510 (2019)
8. Badrinarayanan, S., Fernando, R., Koppula, V., Sahai, A., Waters, B.: Output compression, MPC, and iO for turing machines. In: Galbraith, S.D., Moriai, S. (eds.) ASIACRYPT 2019. LNCS, vol. 11921, pp. 342–370. Springer, Cham (2019). https://doi.org/10.1007/978-3-030-34578-5_13
9. Badrinarayanan, S., Kalai, Y.T., Khurana, D., Sahai, A., Wichs, D.: Succinct delegation for low-space non-deterministic computation. In: Diakonikolas, I., Kempe, D., Henzinger, M. (eds.) 50th ACM STOC, pp. 709–721. ACM Press, June 2018
10. Barak, B., et al.: On the (im)possibility of obfuscating programs. J. ACM **59**(2), 6:1–6:48 (2012)
11. Bellare, M., Impagliazzo, R., Naor, M.: Does parallel repetition lower the error in computationally sound protocols? In: 38th FOCS, pp. 374–383. IEEE Computer Society Press, October 1997
12. Boneh, D., Dagdelen, Ö., Fischlin, M., Lehmann, A., Schaffner, C., Zhandry, M.: Random oracles in a quantum world. In: Lee, D.H., Wang, X. (eds.) ASIACRYPT 2011. LNCS, vol. 7073, pp. 41–69. Springer, Heidelberg (2011). https://doi.org/10.1007/978-3-642-25385-0_3
13. Brakerski, Z., Döttling, N., Garg, S., Malavolta, G.: Factoring and pairings are not necessary for iO: Circular-secure LWE suffices. IACR Cryptol. ePrint Arch., 2020:1024 (2020)
14. Brakerski, Z., Holmgren, J., Kalai, Y.T.: Non-interactive delegation and batch NP verification from standard computational assumptions. In: Hatami, H., McKenzie, P., King, V. (eds.) 49th ACM STOC, pp. 474–482. ACM Press, June 2017
15. Broadbent, A., Fitzsimons, J., Kashefi, E.: Universal blind quantum computation. In: 50th FOCS, pp. 517–526. IEEE Computer Society Press, October 2009
16. Canetti, R., et al.: Fiat-Shamir: from practice to theory. In: Charikar, M., Cohen, E. (eds.) 51st ACM STOC, pp. 1082–1090. ACM Press, June 2019
17. Chiesa, A., Manohar, P., Spooner, N.: Succinct arguments in the quantum random oracle model. In: Hofheinz, D., Rosen, A. (eds.) TCC 2019. LNCS, vol. 11892, pp. 1–29. Springer, Cham (2019). https://doi.org/10.1007/978-3-030-36033-7_1

18. Chung, K.-M., Lee, Y., Lin, H.-H., Wu, X.: Constant-round blind classical verification of quantum sampling (2020, in submission)
19. Don, J., Fehr, S., Majenz, C., Schaffner, C.: Security of the Fiat-Shamir transformation in the quantum random-oracle model. In: Boldyreva, A., Micciancio, D. (eds.) CRYPTO 2019. LNCS, vol. 11693, pp. 356–383. Springer, Cham (2019). https://doi.org/10.1007/978-3-030-26951-7_13
20. Fiat, A., Shamir, A.: How to prove yourself: practical solutions to identification and signature problems. In: Odlyzko, A.M. (ed.) CRYPTO 1986. LNCS, vol. 263, pp. 186–194. Springer, Heidelberg (1987). https://doi.org/10.1007/3-540-47721-7_12
21. Fitzsimons, J.F., Kashef, E.: Unconditionally verifiable blind quantum computation. Phys. Rev. A $96(1)$, 012303 (2017)
22. Garg, S., Gentry, C., Halevi, S., Raykova, M., Sahai, A., Waters, B.: Candidate indistinguishability obfuscation and functional encryption for all circuits. SIAM J. Comput. $45(3)$, 882–929 (2016)
23. Gentry, C.: Fully homomorphic encryption using ideal lattices. In: Mitzenmacher, M. (ed.) 41st ACM STOC, pp. 169–178. ACM Press, May/June 2009
24. Gheorghiu, A., Vidick, T.: Computationally-secure and composable remote state preparation. In: 60th FOCS, pp. 1024–1033. IEEE Computer Society Press (2019)
25. Goldwasser, S., Kalai, Y.T., Rothblum, G.N.: Delegating computation: interactive proofs for muggles. J. ACM $62(4)$, 27:1–27:64 (2015)
26. Holmgren, J., Rothblum, R.: Delegating computations with (almost) minimal time and space overhead. In: Thorup, M. (ed.) 59th FOCS, pp. 124–135. IEEE Computer Society Press, October 2018
27. Kalai, Y.T., Paneth, O., Yang, L.: How to delegate computations publicly. In: Charikar, M., Cohen, E. (eds.) 51st ACM STOC, pp. 1115–1124. ACM Press, June 2019
28. Kalai, Y.T., Raz, R., Rothblum, R.D.: Delegation for bounded space. In: Boneh, D., Roughgarden, T., Feigenbaum, J. (eds.) 45th ACM STOC, pp. 565–574. ACM Press, June 2013
29. Kalai, Y.T., Raz, R., Rothblum, R.D.: How to delegate computations: the power of no-signaling proofs. In: Shmoys, D.B. (ed.) 46th ACM STOC, pp. 485–494. ACM Press, May/June 2014
30. Kilian, J.: A note on efficient zero-knowledge proofs and arguments (extended abstract). In: 24th ACM STOC, pp. 723–732. ACM Press, May 1992
31. Liu, Q., Zhandry, M.: Revisiting post-quantum Fiat-Shamir. In: Boldyreva, A., Micciancio, D. (eds.) CRYPTO 2019. LNCS, vol. 11693, pp. 326–355. Springer, Cham (2019). https://doi.org/10.1007/978-3-030-26951-7_12
32. Mahadev, U.: Classical verification of quantum computations. In: Thorup, M. (ed.) 59th FOCS, pp. 259–267. IEEE Computer Society Press, October 2018
33. Marriott, C., Watrous, J.: Quantum Arthur–Merlin games. Comput. Complex. $14(2)$, 122–152 (2005). https://doi.org/10.1007/s00037-005-0194-x
34. Micali, S.: Computationally sound proofs. SIAM J. Comput. $30(4)$, 1253–1298 (2000)
35. Morimae, T., Fitzsimons, J.F.: Post hoc verification with a single prover. Phys. Rev. Lett. 120, 040501 (2018)
36. Nagaj, D., Wocjan, P., Zhang, Y.: Fast amplification of QMA. arXiv:0904.1549 (2009)
37. NIST: Post-quantum cryptography standardization. https://csrc.nist.gov/Projects/Post-Quantum-Cryptography. Accessed 21 Sep 2020
38. Peikert, C.: A decade of lattice cryptography. Found. Trends Theor. Comput. Sci. $10(4)$, 283–424 (2016)

39. Pietrzak, K., Wikström, D.: Parallel repetition of computationally sound protocols revisited. In: Vadhan, S.P. (ed.) TCC 2007. LNCS, vol. 4392, pp. 86–102. Springer, Heidelberg (2007). https://doi.org/10.1007/978-3-540-70936-7_5
40. Regev, O.: On lattices, learning with errors, random linear codes, and cryptography. J. ACM **56**(6), 34:1–34:40 (2009)
41. Reichardt, B.W., Unger, F., Vazirani, U.: Classical command of quantum systems. Nature **496**(7746), 456 (2013)
42. Reingold, O., Rothblum, G.N., Rothblum, R.D.: Constant-round interactive proofs for delegating computation. In: Wichs, D., Mansour, Y. (eds.) 48th ACM STOC, pp. 49–62. ACM Press, June 2016
43. Rothblum, G.N., Vadhan, S.P.: Are PCPs inherent in efficient arguments? Comput. Complex. **19**(2), 265–304 (2010)
44. Wee, H., Wichs, D.: Candidate obfuscation via oblivious LWE sampling. IACR Cryptol. ePrint Arch., 2020:1042 (2020)

Coupling of Random Systems

David Lanzenberger$^{(\boxtimes)}$ and Ueli Maurer

Department of Computer Science, ETH Zurich, 8092 Zurich, Switzerland
{landavid,maurer}@inf.ethz.ch

Abstract. This paper makes three contributions. First, we present a simple theory of random systems. The main idea is to think of a probabilistic system as an equivalence class of distributions over deterministic systems. Second, we demonstrate how in this new theory, the optimal information-theoretic distinguishing advantage between two systems can be characterized merely in terms of the statistical distance of probability distributions, providing a more elementary understanding of the distance of systems. In particular, two systems that are ϵ-close in terms of the best distinguishing advantage can be understood as being equal with probability $1 - \epsilon$, a property that holds statically, without even considering a distinguisher, let alone its interaction with the systems. Finally, we exploit this new characterization of the distinguishing advantage to prove that any threshold combiner is an amplifier for indistinguishability in the information-theoretic setting, generalizing and simplifying results from Maurer, Pietrzak, and Renner (CRYPTO 2007).

1 Introduction

1.1 Random Systems

A *random system* is an object of general interest in computer science and in particular in cryptography. Informally, a random system is an abstract object which operates in rounds. In the i-th round, an input (or query) X_i is answered with a random output Y_i, and each round may (probabilistically) depend on the previous rounds. In previous work [9,12], a random system $\mathbf{S}$ is defined by a sequence of conditional probability distributions $\mathrm{p}^{\mathbf{S}}_{Y_i|X^iY^{i-1}}$ (or $\mathrm{p}^{\mathbf{S}}_{Y^i|X^i}$) for $i \geq 1$. This captures exactly the input-output behavior of a probabilistic system, as it gives the probability distribution of any output Y_i, conditioned on the previous inputs $X^i = (X_1, \ldots, X_i)$ and outputs $Y^{i-1} = (Y_1, \ldots, Y_{i-1})$.

For example, a uniform random function (URF) from $\mathcal{X}$ to $\mathcal{Y}$ is a random system $\mathbf{R}$ corresponding to the following behavior: Every new input $x_i \in \mathcal{X}$ is answered with an independent uniform random value $y_i \in \mathcal{Y}$ and every input that was given before is answered consistently. Similarly, a uniform random permutation is a random system $\mathbf{P}$ (different from $\mathbf{R}$).

Many statements appearing in the cryptographic literature are about random systems (even though they are usually expressed in a specific language, for example using pseudo-code). For example, the optimal distinguishing advantage $\mathrm{Adv}^{\mathcal{D}}(\mathbf{S}, \mathbf{T})$ of a distinguisher class $\mathcal{D}$ between two systems $\mathbf{S}$ and $\mathbf{T}$ only

© International Association for Cryptologic Research 2020
R. Pass and K. Pietrzak (Eds.): TCC 2020, LNCS 12552, pp. 207–240, 2020.
https://doi.org/10.1007/978-3-030-64381-2_8

depends on the behavior of **S** and **T**. In particular, it is independent of how **S** is implemented (in program code), whether it is a Turing Machine, or how efficient it is. For example, the well-known URP-URF switching lemma [3,10] is a statement about the optimal information-theoretic distinguishing advantage between the two random systems **R** and **P** (see above). Clearly, the switching lemma holds irrespective of the concrete implementations of the systems **R** or **P**, e.g., whether they employ eager or lazy sampling.

1.2   Random Systems as Equivalence Classes

An abstract object can (usually) be represented as an equivalence class of objects from a lower abstraction layer. Perhaps surprisingly, this can give new insight about the object and also be technically useful. As an example, assume our (abstract) objects are pairs (X, Y) of probability distributions over the same set. If we let $[(\mathsf{X}, \mathsf{Y})]$ denote the equivalence class of all random experiments $\mathcal{E}$ with two arbitrarily correlated random variables X and Y distributed according to X and Y, we can express the statistical distance as follows (also known as *Coupling Lemma* [1]):

$$\delta(\mathsf{X}, \mathsf{Y}) = \inf_{\mathcal{E} \in [(\mathsf{X}, \mathsf{Y})]} \Pr^{\mathcal{E}}(X \neq Y).$$

Note that the statistical distance $\delta(\mathsf{X}, \mathsf{Y})$ is defined at the level of probability distributions, and thus does not require any joint distribution between X and Y (let alone a random experiment with accordingly distributed random variables). Nevertheless, the coupling interpretation provides a very intuitive and elementary understanding of the statistical distance. Moreover, it is a powerful technique that can be used to show the closeness (in statistical distance) of two probability distributions X and Y: one exhibits *any* random experiment $\mathcal{E}$ with cleverly correlated random variables X and Y (distributed according to X and Y) such that $\Pr^{\mathcal{E}}(X = Y)$ is close to 1. This coupling technique has been used extensively for example to prove that certain Markov chains are rapidly mixing, i.e., they converge quickly to their stationary distribution (see for example [1]).

The gist of such reasoning is to lower the level of abstraction in order to define or interpret a property, or to prove a statement in a more elementary and intuitive manner.

In this paper, we apply the outlined way of thinking to random systems. We explore a lower level of abstraction which we call *probabilistic discrete systems*. A probabilistic discrete system (PDS) is defined as a (probability) distribution over deterministic discrete systems (DDS). Loosely speaking, this captures the fact that for any implementation of a random system we can fix the randomness (say, the "random tape") to obtain a deterministic system. We then observe that there exist different PDS that are observationally equivalent, i.e., their input-output behavior is equal, implying that they correspond to the same random system. Thus, we propose to think of a random system **S** as an *equivalence class* of PDS and write S ∈ **S** for a PDS S that behaves like **S** (i.e., it is an element of the equivalence class $\mathbf{S}$). For example, a uniform random function $\mathbf{R}$ can be implemented by a PDS R that initially samples the complete function table and by a PDS R′ that employs lazy sampling. These are two different PDS (R ≠ R′), but they are behaviorally equivalent and thus correspond to the same random system, i.e., R ∈ $\mathbf{R}$ and R′ ∈ $\mathbf{R}$ (see also the later Example 5).

Many interesting properties of random systems depend on what interaction is allowed with the system. Usually, this is formalized based on the notion of *environments* and, in cryptography, the notion of *distinguishers*. Such environments are complex objects (similar to random systems) which maintain state and can ask adaptive queries. This can pose a significant challenge for example when proving indistinguishability bounds, and naturally leads to the following question:

> Is it possible to express properties which classically involve environments equivalently as natural intrinsic properties of the systems *themselves*, i.e., without the explicit concept of an environment?

We answer this question in the positive. The key idea is to exploit the equivalence classes: we prove that the optimal information-theoretic distinguishing advantage $\mathrm{Adv}(\mathbf{S}, \mathbf{T})$ is equal to $\Delta(\mathbf{S}, \mathbf{T})$, the infimum statistical distance $\delta(\mathsf{S}, \mathsf{T})$ for PDS $\mathsf{S} \in \mathbf{S}$ and $\mathsf{T} \in \mathbf{T}$. By combining this result with the above coupling interpretation of the statistical distance, we can think of the distinguishing advantage $\mathrm{Adv}(\mathbf{R}, \mathbf{I})$ between a real system $\mathbf{R}$ and an ideal system $\mathbf{I}$ as a *failure probability* of $\mathbf{R}$, i.e., the probability that $\mathbf{R}$ is not equal to $\mathbf{I}$. This is quite surprising since being equal is a purely *static* property, whereas the traditional distinguishing advantage appears to be inherently dynamic.

The coupling theorem for random systems is not only of conceptual interest. It also represents a novel technique to prove indistinguishability bounds in an elementary fashion: in the core of such a proof, one only needs to bound the statistical distance of probability distributions over deterministic systems (for example by using the Coupling Method mentioned above). Usually, the fact that the distribution is over systems will be irrelevant. In particular, the interaction with the systems and the complexity of (adaptive) environments is completely avoided.

1.3   Security and Indistinguishability Amplification

Security amplification is a central theme of cryptography. Turning weak objects into strong objects is useful as it allows to weaken the required assumptions. Indistinguishability amplification is a special kind of security amplification, where the quantity of interest is the closeness (in terms of adaptive indistinguishability) to some idealized system. Most of the well-known constructions achieving indistinguishability amplification do this by combining many moderately close systems into a single system that is very close to its ideal form.

In this paper, we take a more general approach to indistinguishability amplification and present results that allow (for example) to combine many moderately close systems into *multiple* systems that are jointly very close to independent instances of their ideal form. This is useful, since many cryptographic protocols need several independent instantiations of a scheme, for example a (pseudo-)random permutation.

1.4   Motivating Examples for Indistinguishability Amplification

As a first motivating example, consider the following construction $\mathbf{C}$ that combines three independent random[1] permutations[2] π_1, π_2, and π_3 into two random permutations by cascading (composing) them as follows:

$$\mathbf{C}(\pi_1, \pi_2, \pi_3) = (\pi_1 \circ \pi_3, \pi_2 \circ \pi_3).$$

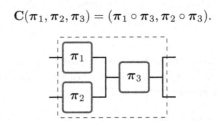

If, say, the second constructed permutation is (forward-)queried with x, the value x is input to π_2 and the output $x' = \pi_2(x)$ is forwarded to π_3. The output of $\pi_3(x')$ is the response to the query x.

Clearly, if *any two* of the three random permutations π_i are a (perfect) uniform random permutation $\mathbf{P}$, then $(\pi_1 \circ \pi_3, \pi_2 \circ \pi_3)$ behaves exactly as if all three random permutations π_i are perfect uniform random permutations (i.e., it behaves as two independent uniform random permutations $(\mathbf{P}, \mathbf{P}')$). Thus, we call $\mathbf{C}$ a $(2, 3)$-*combiner* for the pairs $(\pi_1, \mathbf{P}), (\pi_2, \mathbf{P}), (\pi_3, \mathbf{P})$.

What, however, can we say when the π_i are only ϵ_i-close[3] to a uniform random permutation? A straightforward hybrid argument shows that

$$\mathrm{Adv}((\pi_1 \circ \pi_3, \pi_2 \circ \pi_3), (\mathbf{P}, \mathbf{P}')) \leq \min(\epsilon_1 + \epsilon_2, \epsilon_1 + \epsilon_3, \epsilon_2 + \epsilon_3),$$

where $\mathrm{Adv}(\cdot, \cdot)$ denotes the optimal distinguishing advantage over all adaptive (computationally unbounded) distinguishers. Intuitively though, one might hope that if *all* ϵ_i (as opposed to only two of them) are small, a better bound is achievable. Ideally, this bound should be smaller than the individual ϵ_i, i.e., we want to obtain indistinguishability amplification. A consequence of one of our results (Theorem 3) is that this is indeed possible. We have

$$\mathrm{Adv}((\pi_1 \circ \pi_3, \pi_2 \circ \pi_3), (\mathbf{P}, \mathbf{P}')) \leq 2(\epsilon_1\epsilon_2 + \epsilon_1\epsilon_3 + \epsilon_2\epsilon_3) - 3\epsilon_1\epsilon_2\epsilon_3.$$

---

[1] Throughout this paper, we use the word *random* as in *random variable*, i.e., not implying uniformity of a distribution.

[2] We assume the permutations to be stateless and both-sided (though all claims remain true if the permutations are all one-sided). A both-sided permutation is a permutation that allows forward- and backward-queries, i.e., queries to π and π^{-1}.

[3] By ϵ-close we mean that any adaptive (computationally unbounded) distinguisher has distinguishing advantage at most ϵ.

More generally, it is natural to ask the following question[4]:

> How many independent random permutations that are ϵ'-close to a uniform random permutation need to be combined to obtain m random permutations that are (jointly) ϵ-close (for $\epsilon \ll \epsilon'$) to m independent uniform random permutations?

This question has been studied for the special case $m = 1$ (see for example [12,18,19]), and it is known that the cascade of n independent random permutations (each ϵ-close to a uniform random permutation) is $\frac{1}{2}(2\epsilon)^n$-close to a uniform random permutation. Of course, there is a straightforward way to use such a construction for $m = 1$ multiple times in order to obtain a basic indistinguishability result for $m > 1$: one simply partitions the n independent random permutations $\pi_1, \ldots, \pi_n$ into sets of equal size and cascades the permutations in each set.

Example 1. We can construct four random permutations from 20 random permutations as follows:

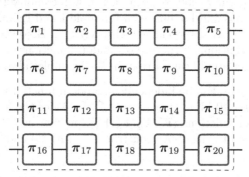

If the π_i are independent and all ϵ-close (say, 2^{-10}-close) to a uniform random permutation, Theorem 1 of [12] implies that the construction above yields four random permutations that are jointly $64\epsilon^5$-close (($2.3\epsilon)^5$-close, $2^{-44.0}$-close) to four independent uniform random permutations.

Naturally, one might ask whether it is possible to construct four random permutations to get stronger amplification (i.e., a larger exponent) without using more random permutations. This is indeed possible, as the following example illustrates.

Example 2. Consider the following construction of four random permutations:

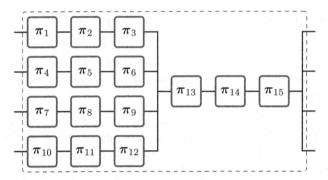

The main advantage of this construction is that it makes use of only 15 (instead of 20) random permutations. Our results imply that if the π_i are independent and ϵ-close (say, 2^{-10}-close) to a uniform random permutation, then the constructed four random permutations are *jointly* $320\epsilon^6$-close ($(2.7\epsilon)^6$-close, $2^{-51.6}$-close) to four *independent* uniform random permutations.

Instead of random permutations one can just as well combine random functions: the same constructions and bounds as in Example 1 and Example 2 apply if we replace the cascade $\circ$ with the elementwise XOR $\oplus$. However, in this setting, we show that the additional structure of random functions can be exploited to achieve even stronger amplification than in the examples above.

Example 3. Let $\mathbf{F}_1, \ldots, \mathbf{F}_{10}$ be independent random functions over a finite field $\mathbb{F}$, and let A be a 4×10 MDS[5] matrix over $\mathbb{F}$. Consider the following construction of four random functions $(\mathbf{F}'_1, \mathbf{F}'_2, \mathbf{F}'_3, \mathbf{F}'_4)$, making use of only 10 random functions (as opposed to the above constructions with 20 and 15, respectively):

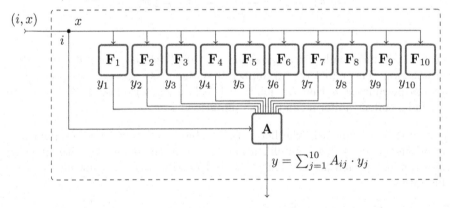

On input x to the i-th constructed function $\mathbf{F}'_i$ (for $i \in \{1, 2, 3, 4\}$), all random functions $\mathbf{F}_1, \ldots, \mathbf{F}_{10}$ are queried with x, and the answers $y_1, \ldots, y_{10}$ are combined to the result $y = \sum_{j=1}^{10} A_{ij} \cdot y_j$.

---

[5] An MDS (maximum distance separable) matrix [8,16] is a matrix over a finite field for which every square submatrix is non-singular.

Our results imply that if the $\mathbf{F}_i$ are independent and ϵ-close (say, 2^{-10}-close) to a uniform random function, the four random functions $(\mathbf{F}'_1, \mathbf{F}'_2, \mathbf{F}'_3, \mathbf{F}'_4)$ are jointly $7680\epsilon^7$-close $((3.6\epsilon)^7$-close, $2^{-57.0}$-close) to four independent uniform random functions.

1.5 Contributions and Outline

We briefly state our main contributions in a simplified manner. In Sect. 3, we define deterministic discrete systems and probabilistic discrete systems together with an equivalence relation capturing the input-output behavior. Moreover, we argue that we can characterize a random system by an equivalence class of PDS.

In Sect. 4, we define the distance Δ for random systems as

$$\Delta(\mathbf{S}, \mathbf{T}) := \inf_{\substack{\mathsf{S} \in \mathbf{S} \\ \mathsf{T} \in \mathbf{T}}} \delta(\mathsf{S}, \mathsf{T}).$$

We then present Theorem 1, stating that for any two random systems[6] $\mathbf{S}$ and $\mathbf{T}$ we have

$$\Delta(\mathbf{S}, \mathbf{T}) = \mathrm{Adv}(\mathbf{S}, \mathbf{T}),$$

and there exist PDS $\mathsf{S} \in \mathbf{S}$ and $\mathsf{T} \in \mathbf{T}$ such that $\delta(\mathsf{S}, \mathsf{T}) = \Delta(\mathbf{S}, \mathbf{T})$. By combining this result with the coupling interpretation of the statistical distance (see above), we can think in a mathematically precise sense of the distinguishing advantage $\mathrm{Adv}(\mathbf{R}, \mathbf{I})$ between a real system $\mathbf{R}$ and an ideal system $\mathbf{I}$ as the probability of a failure event, i.e., the probability of the event that $\mathbf{R}$ and $\mathbf{I}$ are not equal. More specifically, we phrase a coupling theorem for random systems (Theorem 2), stating that for any two random systems $\mathbf{S}$ and $\mathbf{T}$ there exist PDS $\mathsf{S} \in \mathbf{S}$ and $\mathsf{T} \in \mathbf{T}$ with a joint distribution (or coupling) such that

$$\mathrm{Adv}(\mathbf{S}, \mathbf{T}) = \Pr(\mathsf{S} \neq \mathsf{T}).$$

The coupling theorem also represents a novel technique to prove indistinguishability bounds in an elementary fashion: in the core of such a proof, one only needs to bound the statistical distance of probability distributions over deterministic systems (for example by using the Coupling Method mentioned above). Often, the fact that the distribution is over systems will be irrelevant. In particular, the interaction with the systems and the complexity of (adaptive) environments is completely avoided, as the potential failure event can be thought of as being triggered *before* the interaction started.

Finally, in Sect. 5, we demonstrate how our coupling theorem can be used to prove indistinguishability bounds. We present Theorem 3, stating that any (k, n)-combiner is an amplifier for indistinguishability. A simplified variant of

---

[6] Recall that a random system is an *equivalence class* of probabilistic discrete systems with the same input-output behavior.

the bound can be expressed as follows (see Corollary 1): If C is a (k, n)-combiner for $(\mathsf{F}_1, \mathsf{I}_1), \ldots, (\mathsf{F}_n, \mathsf{I}_n)$ and $\mathrm{Adv}(\mathsf{F}_i, \mathsf{I}_i) \leq \epsilon$ for all $i \in [n]$, then

$$\mathrm{Adv}(\mathsf{C}(\mathsf{F}_1, \ldots, \mathsf{F}_n), \mathsf{C}(\mathsf{I}_1, \ldots, \mathsf{I}_n)) \leq \frac{1}{2}\binom{n}{k-1} \cdot (2\epsilon)^{n-k+1}.$$

The indistinguishability amplification results of [12] are a special case of this corollary (for $k = 1$ and $n = 2$).

Moreover, we demonstrate how these indistinguishability results can be instantiated by combiners transforming n independent random functions (random permutations) into $m < n$ random functions (random permutations), obtaining indistinguishability amplification.

1.6 Related Work

There exists a vast amount of literature on information-theoretic indistinguishability of various constructions, in particular for the analysis of symmetric key cryptography. Prominent examples are constructions transforming uniform random functions into uniform random permutations or vice-versa: the Luby-Rackoff construction [6] (or Feistel construction), similar constructions by Naor and Reingold [14], the truncation of a random permutation [5], and the XOR of random permutations [2,7].

Random Systems. The characterization of random systems by their input-output behavior in the form of a sequence of conditional distributions $\mathsf{p}_{Y_i|X^iY^{i-1}}$ (or $\mathsf{p}_{Y^i|X^i}$) was first described in [9].

Indistinguishability Proof Techniques. There exist various techniques for proving information-theoretic indistinguishability bounds. A prominent approach is to define a failure condition such that two systems are equivalent before said condition is satisfied (see also [9]). Maurer, Pietrzak, and Renner proved in [12] that there always exists such a failure condition that is optimal, showing that this technique allows to prove perfectly tight indistinguishability bounds. At first glance, the lemma of [12] seems to be similar to our coupling theorem. While both statements are tight characterizations of the distinguishing advantage, the crucial advantage of our result is that it allows to remove the complexity of the adaptive interaction when reasoning about indistinguishability of random systems. This enables reasoning at the level of probability distributions: one can think of a failure event occurring or not before the interaction even begins. The interactive hard-core lemma shown by Tessaro [17] in the computational setting allows this kind of reasoning as well, though it only holds for so-called "cc-stateless systems".

More involved proof techniques include directly bounding the statistical distance of the transcript distributions, such as Patarin's H-coefficient method [15], and most recently, the Chi-squared method [4].

Indistinguishability Amplification. Examples of previous indistinguishability amplification results are the various computational XOR lemmas, Vaudenay's product theorem for random permutations [18,19], as well as the more abstract product theorem for (stateful) random systems [12] (and so-called *neutralizing constructions*). In [13], some of the results of [12] have been proved in the computational setting.

A different type of indistinguishability amplification is shown in [11,12], where the amplification is with respect to the distinguisher class, lifting non-adaptive indistinguishability to adaptive indistinguishability.

2 Preliminaries

Notation. For $n \in \mathbb{N}$, we let $[n]$ denote the set $\{1, \ldots, n\}$ with the convention $[0] = \emptyset$. The set of sequences (or strings) of length n over the alphabet $\mathcal{A}$ is denoted by $\mathcal{A}^n$. An element of $\mathcal{A}^n$ is denoted by $a^n = (a_1, \ldots, a_n)$ for $a_i \in \mathcal{A}$. The empty sequence is denoted by ϵ. The set of finite sequences over alphabet $\mathcal{A}$ is denoted by $\mathcal{A}^* := \cup_{i \in \mathbb{N}} \mathcal{A}^i$ and the set of non-empty finite sequences is denoted by $\mathcal{A}^+ := \mathcal{A}^* - \{\epsilon\}$. A set $A \subseteq \mathcal{A}^*$ is *prefix-closed* if $(a_1, a_2, \ldots, a_i) \in A$ implies $(a_1, a_2, \ldots, a_j) \in A$ for any $j \leq i$. For two sequences $x^i \in \mathcal{X}^i$ and $\hat{x}^j \in \mathcal{X}^j$, the concatenation $x^i | \hat{x}^j$ is the sequence $(x_1, \ldots, x_i, \hat{x}_1, \ldots, \hat{x}_j) \in \mathcal{X}^{i+j}$.

A (total) function from X to Y is a binary relation $f \subseteq X \times Y$ such that for every $x \in X$ there exists a unique $y \in Y$ with $(x, y) \in f$. A *partial function* from X to Y is a total function from X' to Y for a subset $X' \subseteq X$. The *domain* of a function f is denoted by $\mathsf{dom}(f)$. The *support* of a function $f : X \to Y$ with $0 \in Y$, for example a distribution, is defined by $\mathsf{supp}(f) := \{x \mid x \in X, f(x) \neq 0\}$.

A multiset over $\mathcal{A}$ is a function $M : \mathcal{A} \to \mathbb{N}$. We represent multisets in set notation, e.g., $M = \{(a, 2), (b, 7)\}$ denotes the multiset M with domain $\{a, b\}$, $M(a) = 2$, and $M(b) = 7$. The cardinality $|M|$ of a multiset is $\sum_{a \in \mathsf{dom}(M)} M(a)$. The union $\cup$, intersection $\cap$, sum $+$, and difference $-$ of two multisets is defined by the pointwise maximum, minimum, sum, and difference, respectively. Finally, the symmetric difference $M \triangle M'$ of two multisets is defined by $M \cup M' - M \cap M'$.

Throughout this paper, we use the following notion of a (finite) *distribution*.

Definition 1. *A distribution (or measure) over $\mathcal{A}$ is a function $\mathsf{X} : \mathcal{A} \to \mathbb{R}_{\geq 0}$ with finite support. The* weight *of a distribution is defined by*

$$|\mathsf{X}| := \sum_{a \in \mathcal{A}} \mathsf{X}(a).$$

A probability distribution is a distribution X with weight 1 (i.e., $|\mathsf{X}| = 1$). Moreover, overloading the notation, we define for a distribution X over $\mathcal{A}$ and $A \subseteq \mathcal{A}$

$$\mathsf{X}(A) := \sum_{a \in A} \mathsf{X}(a).$$

In the following, we do *not* demand that a distribution has weight 1, i.e., we do not assume probability distributions (unless stated explicitly). This is important, as the proof of one of our main results (Theorem 1) relies on distributions of arbitrary weight.

Definition 2. *The* marginal distribution X_i *of a distribution* X *over* $\mathcal{A}_1 \times \cdots \times \mathcal{A}_n$ *is defined as*

$$X_i(a_i) = \sum_{a' \in \mathcal{A}_1 \times \cdots \times \mathcal{A}_n, a'_i = a_i} X(a').$$

Lemma 1. *Let* $X_1, \ldots, X_n$ *be distributions over* $\mathcal{A}_1, \ldots, \mathcal{A}_n$, *respectively, such that all* X_i *have the same weight* $p \in \mathbb{R}_{\geq 0}$. *Then, there exists a (joint) distribution* X *over* $\mathcal{A}_1 \times \cdots \times \mathcal{A}_n$ *with weight* p *and marginals* X_i.

Proof. A possible choice is $X(a_1, \ldots, a_n) := p^{-(n-1)} \prod_{i \in [n]} X_i(a_i)$.

Definition 3. *The* statistical distance *of two distributions* $X : \mathcal{A} \to \mathbb{R}_{\geq 0}$ *and* $Y : \mathcal{A} \to \mathbb{R}_{\geq 0}$ *is*

$$\delta(X, Y) := \sum_{a \in \mathcal{A}} \max(0, X(a) - Y(a)) = |X| - \sum_{a \in \mathcal{A}} \min(X(a), Y(a)).$$

Note that for distributions X and Y of different weight, i.e., $|X| \neq |Y|$, the statistical distance is not symmetric ($\delta(X, Y) \neq \delta(Y, X)$). Moreover, for distributions of the same weight, i.e., $|X| = |Y|$, we have $\delta(X, Y) = \frac{1}{2} \sum_{a \in \mathcal{A}} |X(a) - Y(a)|$.

The following lemma, proved in Appendix A, is an immediate consequence of the definition of the statistical distance.

Lemma 2. *Let* $\langle \mathcal{A}_i \rangle_{i \in [n]}$ *be a partition of a set* $\mathcal{A}$, *and let* $X_1, \ldots, X_n$ *as well as* $Y_1, \ldots, Y_n$ *be distributions over* $\mathcal{A}$ *such that* $\mathsf{supp}(X_i) \subseteq \mathcal{A}_i$ *and* $\mathsf{supp}(Y_i) \subseteq \mathcal{A}_i$ *for all* $i \in [n]$. *For* $X := \sum_{i \in [n]} X_i$ *and* $Y := \sum_{i \in [n]} Y_i$ *we have*

$$\delta(X, Y) = \sum_{i \in [n]} \delta(X_i, Y_i).$$

Definition 4. *For a distribution* $X : \mathcal{A} \to \mathbb{R}_{\geq 0}$ *and a function* $f : \mathcal{A} \to \mathcal{B}$, *the* f-transformation *of* X, *denoted by* $f(X)$, *is the distribution over* $\mathcal{B}$ *defined by*[7]

$$f(X) := X \circ f^{-1}.$$

The following lemma states that the statistical distance of two distributions cannot increase if a function f is applied (to both distributions). This is well-known for the case in which X and Y are probability distributions. We prove the claim in Appendix A.

---

[7] In the expression $X \circ f^{-1}$, the function X is such that $X(A) = \sum_{a \in A} X(a)$ for $A \subseteq \mathcal{A}$. Moreover, f^{-1} denotes the preimage of f, i.e., $f^{-1}(b) := \{a \mid a \in \mathcal{A}, f(a) = b\}$.

Lemma 3. *For two distributions* X *and* Y *over* $\mathcal{A}$ *and any total function* $f :$ $\mathcal{A} \to \mathcal{B}$ *we have*

$$\delta(X, Y) \geq \delta(f(X), f(Y)).$$

Lemma 4. (Coupling Lemma, Lemma 3.6 of [1]). *Let* X, Y *be probability distributions over the same set.*

1. *For any joint distribution of* X *and* Y *we have*

$$\delta(X, Y) \leq \Pr(X \neq Y).$$

2. *There exists a joint distribution of* X *and* Y *such that*

$$\delta(X, Y) = \Pr(X \neq Y).$$

3 Discrete Random Systems

3.1 Deterministic Discrete Systems

A deterministic discrete $(\mathcal{X}, \mathcal{Y})$-system is a system with input alphabet $\mathcal{X}$ and output alphabet $\mathcal{Y}$. The system's first output (or response) $y_1 \in \mathcal{Y}$ is a function of the first input (or query) $x_1 \in \mathcal{X}$. The second output y_2 is a priori a function of the first two inputs x_1, x_2 *and* the first output y_1. However, since y_1 is already a function of x_1, it is more minimal to define y_2 as a function of the first two inputs $x^2 = (x_1, x_2) \in \mathcal{X}^2$. In general, the i-th output $y_i \in \mathcal{Y}$ is a function of the first i inputs $x^i \in \mathcal{X}^i$.

Definition 5. *A deterministic discrete* $(\mathcal{X}, \mathcal{Y})$-*system (or* $(\mathcal{X}, \mathcal{Y})$-*DDS) is a partial function*

$$s : \mathcal{X}^+ \to \mathcal{Y}$$

with prefix-closed domain. An $(\mathcal{X}, \mathcal{Y})$-*DDS* s *is* finite *if* $\mathcal{X}$ *is finite and* $\mathsf{dom}(s) \subseteq$ $\cup_{i \leq n} \mathcal{X}^i$ *for some* $n \in \mathbb{N}$. *Moreover, we let* $\mathsf{dom}_1(s)$ *denote the input alphabet for the first query, i.e.,* $\mathsf{dom}_1(s) = \mathsf{dom}(s) \cap \mathcal{X}^1$.

A DDS is an abstraction capturing exactly the input-output behavior of a deterministic system. Thus, it is independent of any implementation details that describe how the outputs are produced. One can therefore think of a DDS as an equivalence class of more explicit implementations. For example, different programs (or Turing machines) can correspond to the same DDS. Moreover, the fact that there is state is captured canonically by letting each output depend on the previous sequence of inputs, as opposed to introducing an explicit state space.

In this paper, we restrict ourselves to finite systems. We note that the definitions and claims can be generalized to infinite systems. Alternatively, one can often interpret an infinite system as a parametrized family of finite systems.

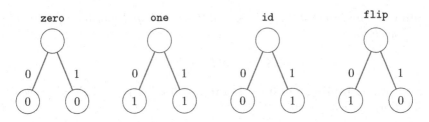

Fig. 1. The four single-query ($\{0,1\},\{0,1\}$)-DDS zero, one, id, flip.

Example 4. Figure 1 depicts the four single-query ($\{0,1\},\{0,1\}$)-DDS zero, one, id, and flip, i.e., all total functions from $\{0,1\}$ to $\{0,1\}$

$$\texttt{zero}(x) := 0, \quad \texttt{one}(x) := 1, \quad \texttt{id}(x) := x, \quad \texttt{flip}(x) := 1 - x.$$

An environment is an object (similar to a DDS) that interacts with a system s by producing the inputs x_i for s and receiving the corresponding outputs y_i. Environments are adaptive and stateful, i.e., a produced input x_i is a function of all the previous outputs $y^{i-1} = (y_1, \ldots, y_{i-1})$. Moreover, we allow an environment to stop at any time.

Definition 6. *A deterministic discrete environment for an* ($\mathcal{X},\mathcal{Y}$)-*DDS (or* ($\mathcal{Y},\mathcal{X}$)-*DDE) is a partial function*

$$e : \mathcal{Y}^* \to \mathcal{X}$$

with prefix-closed domain.

Definition 7. *The* transcript *of a system s in environment e, denoted by* $\mathrm{tr}(s,e)$, *is the sequence of pairs* $(x_1, y_1), (x_2, y_2), \ldots, (x_l, y_l)$, *defined for $i \geq 1$ by*

$$x_i = e(y_1, \ldots, y_{i-1}) \quad \text{and} \quad y_i = s(x_1, \ldots, x_i).$$

We require the environment e to be compatible *with s, i.e., the environment must not query s outside of the system's domain. Formally, this means that $y_i = s(x_1, \ldots, x_i)$ is defined whenever $x_i = e(y_1, \ldots, y_{i-1})$ is defined. If $e(y_1, \ldots, y_{i-1})$ is undefined (the environment stops), the transcript ends and has length $l = i-1$.*

3.2 Probabilistic Discrete Systems

We define probabilistic systems (environments) as *distributions* over deterministic systems (environments). Note that even though we use the term *probabilistic*, we do not assume that the corresponding distributions are probability distributions (i.e., they do not need to sum up to 1, unless explicitly stated).

Definition 8. *A probabilistic discrete* ($\mathcal{X},\mathcal{Y}$)-*system S (or* ($\mathcal{X},\mathcal{Y}$)-*PDS) is a distribution over* ($\mathcal{X},\mathcal{Y}$)-*DDS such that all DDS in the support of S have the* *same domain, denoted[8] by* dom(S). *We always assume that* S *is* finite, *i.e.,* $\mathcal{X}$ *is finite and* dom(S) $\subseteq \cup_{i \leq n} \mathcal{X}^i$ *for some* $n \in \mathbb{N}$.

Definition 9. *A* probabilistic discrete environment *for an* $(\mathcal{X}, \mathcal{Y})$-*PDS (or* $(\mathcal{Y}, \mathcal{X})$-*PDE) is a distribution over* $(\mathcal{Y}, \mathcal{X})$-*DDE.*

Observe that a PDS contains all information for a system that can be executed arbitrarily many times, i.e., a system that can be rewound and then queried again on the same randomness. We consider the standard setting in which a system can only be executed once (see Definition 7). In this setting, there exist different PDS that behave identically from the perspective of any environment, i.e., they exhibit the same behavior. The following example demonstrates this.

Example 5. Let V be the uniform probability distribution over the set of all single-query $(\{0,1\}, \{0,1\})$-DDS $\{\texttt{zero}, \texttt{one}, \texttt{id}, \texttt{flip}\}$ (see Fig. 1), i.e.,

$$V := \{(\texttt{zero}, 1/4), (\texttt{one}, 1/4), (\texttt{id}, 1/4), (\texttt{flip}, 1/4)\}.$$

For any input $x \in \{0,1\}$, the system V outputs a uniform random bit. Formally, the transcript distribution $\text{tr}(V, e_x)$ for an environment e_x that inputs $x \in \{0,1\}$ (i.e., $e_x(\epsilon) = x$) is

$$\text{tr}(V, e_x) = \{((x, 0), 1/2), ((x, 1), 1/2)\}.$$

The PDS V represents a system that samples the answers for both possible inputs $x \in \{0,1\}$ independently (even though only one query is answered). Clearly, the exact same behavior can be implemented by sampling a uniform bit and using it for whatever query is asked, resulting in the PDS

$$V' := \{(\texttt{zero}, 1/2), (\texttt{one}, 1/2), (\texttt{id}, 0), (\texttt{flip}, 0)\}.$$

It is easy to verify that for any $\alpha \in [0, 1/2]$, the following PDS V_α has the same behavior as V:

$$V_\alpha := \{(\texttt{zero}, \alpha), (\texttt{one}, \alpha), (\texttt{id}, 1/2 - \alpha), (\texttt{flip}, 1/2 - \alpha)\}.$$

Actually, it is not difficult to show that *every* PDS with the behavior of V is of the form V_α. Thus, we can think of the random system **V** (that responds for every input $x \in \{0, 1\}$ with a uniform random bit) as the *equivalence class*

$$[V] = \{V_\alpha \mid \alpha \in [0, 1/2]\}.$$

More generally, we define two PDS to be equivalent if their transcript distributions are the same in all environments. It is easy to see that considering only deterministic environments results in the same equivalence notion that is obtained when considering probabilistic environments.

---

[8] Note that we are overloading the notation of dom($\cdot$), as S is a function from deterministic systems to $\mathbb{R}_{\geq 0}$.

Definition 10. *Two $(\mathcal{X}, \mathcal{Y})$-PDS* S *and* T *are equivalent, denoted by* S ≡ T, *if they have the same domain and*[9]

$$\mathrm{tr}(\mathsf{S}, e) = \mathrm{tr}(\mathsf{T}, e) \quad \textit{for all compatible } (\mathcal{Y}, \mathcal{X})\textit{-DDE } e.$$

The equivalence class of a PDS S *is denoted by* [S] := {S' | S', S ≡ S'}.

The following lemma, proved in Appendix A, states that for S and T to be equivalent it suffices that the transcript distribution $\mathrm{tr}(\mathsf{S}, e)$ is equal to $\mathrm{tr}(\mathsf{T}, e)$ for all *non-adaptive*[10] deterministic environments e.

Lemma 5. *For any two $(\mathcal{X}, \mathcal{Y})$-PDS* S *and* T *with the same domain we have* S ≡ T *if and only if*

$$\mathrm{tr}(\mathsf{S}, e) = \mathrm{tr}(\mathsf{T}, e) \quad \textit{for all compatible non-adaptive } (\mathcal{Y}, \mathcal{X})\textit{-DDE } e.$$

Stated differently, an equivalence class [S] of PDS can be characterized by the transcript distributions for all non-adaptive deterministic environments. Since a non-adaptive deterministic environment is uniquely described by a sequence $x^k \in \mathcal{X}^k$ of inputs and the corresponding transcript distribution $\mathrm{tr}(\mathsf{S}, e)$ is essentially the distribution of observed outputs under the input sequence x^k, it follows immediately that an equivalence class of PDS describes exactly a random system as introduced in [9] (where a characterization in the form of a sequence of conditional distributions $\mathrm{p}_{Y_i | X^i Y^{i-1}}$ or $\mathrm{p}_{Y^i | X^i}$ was used).

Notation 1. We use bold-face font **S** to denote a *random system*, an equivalence class of PDS. Since the transcript distribution $\mathrm{tr}(\mathsf{S}, e)$ does (by definition) only depend on the random system **S** and not on the concrete element S ∈ **S** of the equivalence class, we write

$$\mathrm{tr}(\mathbf{S}, e)$$

to denote the transcript distribution of the random system **S** in environment e.

4   Coupling Theorem for Discrete Systems

4.1   Distance of Equivalence Classes and the Coupling Theorem

The optimal distinguishing advantage is widely-used in the (cryptographic) literature to quantify the distance between random systems. It can be defined as the supremum statistical distance of the transcripts under all compatible $(\mathcal{Y}, \mathcal{X})$-DDE. In the information-theoretic setting, this is equivalent to the classical definition as the supremum difference of the probability that a (probabilistic) distinguisher outputs 1 when interacting with each system.

---

[9] $\mathrm{tr}(\mathsf{S}, e)$ denotes the $\mathrm{tr}(\cdot, e)$-transformation of the distribution S (see Definition 4).

[10] A non-adaptive environment must choose every query x_i independently of the previous outputs $y_1, \ldots, y_{i-1}$. Formally, $e(y^i)$ only depends on the length i of the sequence y^i, i.e., we have $e(y^i) = e(\hat{y}^i)$ for any $i \in \mathbb{N}$ and $y^i, \hat{y}^i \in \mathcal{Y}^i$.

Definition 11. *For two random* $(\mathcal{X}, \mathcal{Y})$-*systems* **S** *and* **T** *with the same domain, the* optimal distinguishing advantage $\mathrm{Adv}(\mathbf{S}, \mathbf{T})$ *is defined by*

$$\mathrm{Adv}(\mathbf{S}, \mathbf{T}) := \sup_{e} \delta(\mathrm{tr}(\mathbf{S}, e), \mathrm{tr}(\mathbf{T}, e)),$$

where the supremum is over all compatible $(\mathcal{Y}, \mathcal{X})$-*DDE.*

Understanding a random system as an equivalence class of probabilistic discrete systems gives rise to the following distance notion Δ:

Definition 12. *For two random* $(\mathcal{X}, \mathcal{Y})$-*systems* **S** *and* **T** *with the same domain we define*

$$\Delta(\mathbf{S}, \mathbf{T}) := \inf_{\substack{\mathsf{S} \in \mathbf{S} \\ \mathsf{T} \in \mathbf{T}}} \delta(\mathsf{S}, \mathsf{T}).$$

Note that since there exist PDS S and S' that are equivalent ($\mathsf{S} \equiv \mathsf{S}'$) even though $\delta(\mathsf{S}, \mathsf{S}') = 1$ (for example V_0 and $\mathsf{V}_{1/2}$ from Example 5), taking the infimum seems to be necessary to quantify the distance of random systems in a meaningful way. We can now state the first theorem.

Theorem 1. *For any two random* $(\mathcal{X}, \mathcal{Y})$-*systems* **S** *and* **T** *with the same domain we have*

$$\Delta(\mathbf{S}, \mathbf{T}) = \mathrm{Adv}(\mathbf{S}, \mathbf{T}),$$

and there exist PDS $\mathsf{S} \in \mathbf{S}$ *and* $\mathsf{T} \in \mathbf{T}$ *such that* $\delta(\mathsf{S}, \mathsf{T}) = \Delta(\mathbf{S}, \mathbf{T})$.

The coupling theorem for random systems is an immediate consequence of Theorem 1 and the classical Coupling Lemma (Lemma 4).

Theorem 2 (Coupling Theorem for Random Systems). *For any two random systems* **S** *and* **T** *there exist PDS* $\mathsf{S} \in \mathbf{S}$ *and* $\mathsf{T} \in \mathbf{T}$ *with a joint distribution (or coupling) such that*

$$\mathrm{Adv}(\mathbf{S}, \mathbf{T}) = \Pr(\mathsf{S} \neq \mathsf{T}).$$

4.2   Proof of Theorem 1

The Single-Query Case. We start by proving Theorem 1 for single-query random systems. Let **S** and **T** be two single-query $(\mathcal{X}, \mathcal{Y})$-systems, represented by the two $(\mathcal{X}, \mathcal{Y})$-PDS $\mathsf{S} \in \mathbf{S}$ and $\mathsf{T} \in \mathbf{T}$. Observe that a single-query $(\mathcal{X}, \mathcal{Y})$-DDS s is a function from $\mathcal{X}$ to $\mathcal{Y}$, and can thus be represented by a tuple

$$(y_{x_1}, y_{x_2}, \ldots, y_{x_n}) \in \mathcal{Y}^n, \text{ where } \mathcal{X} = \{x_1, \ldots, x_n\} \text{ and } s(x_i) = y_{x_i}.$$

Hence, we can represent **S** and **T** as distributions over $\mathcal{Y}^n$ for $n = |\mathcal{X}|$. If S_i and T_i are the marginal distributions of the i-th index of **S** and **T**, respectively, then an environment that inputs the value $x_i \in \mathcal{X}$ will observe either S_i or T_i. From

Definition 11 it follows that an optimal environment chooses i such that $\delta(\mathsf{S}_i, \mathsf{T}_i)$ is maximized, so we have

$$\mathrm{Adv}(\mathbf{S}, \mathbf{T}) = \max_{i \in [n]} \delta(\mathsf{S}_i, \mathsf{T}_i).$$

The following lemma directly implies that there exist PDS $\mathsf{S}' \in \mathbf{S}$ and $\mathsf{T}' \in \mathbf{T}$ such that $\delta(\mathsf{S}', \mathsf{T}') = \mathrm{Adv}(\mathbf{S}, \mathbf{T})$. This proves Theorem 1 for single-query systems.

Lemma 6. *For each $i \in [n]$, let X_i and Y_i be distributions over $\mathcal{A}_i$, such that all X_i have the same weight $p_\mathsf{X} \in \mathbb{R}_{\geq 0}$ and all Y_i have the same weight $p_\mathsf{Y} \in \mathbb{R}_{\geq 0}$. Then there exist (joint) distributions X and Y over $\mathcal{A}_1 \times \cdots \times \mathcal{A}_n$ with marginals X_i and Y_i, respectively, such that*

$$\delta(\mathsf{X}, \mathsf{Y}) = \max_{i \in [n]} \delta(\mathsf{X}_i, \mathsf{Y}_i).$$

Proof. As $\delta(\mathsf{X}_i, \mathsf{Y}_i) = p_\mathsf{X} - \sum_{a \in \mathcal{A}_i} \min(\mathsf{X}_i(a), \mathsf{Y}_i(a))$, we have

$$\max_{i \in [n]} \delta(\mathsf{X}_i, \mathsf{Y}_i) = p_\mathsf{X} - \min_{i \in [n]} \sum_{a \in \mathcal{A}_i} \min(\mathsf{X}_i(a), \mathsf{Y}_i(a)).$$

Let $\tau := \min_{i \in [n]} \sum_{a \in \mathcal{A}_i} \min(\mathsf{X}_i(a), \mathsf{Y}_i(a))$. Clearly, for every $i \in [n]$, there exist distributions $\mathsf{E}_i, \mathsf{X}'_i$, and Y'_i such that E_i has weight τ (i.e., $|\mathsf{E}_i| = \tau$) and

$$\mathsf{X}_i = \mathsf{E}_i + \mathsf{X}'_i \text{ and } \mathsf{Y}_i = \mathsf{E}_i + \mathsf{Y}'_i.$$

By invoking Lemma 1 three times, we obtain the joint distributions E, X', and Y' of all $\mathsf{E}_i, \mathsf{X}'_i$, and Y'_i, respectively. We let $\mathsf{X} := \mathsf{E} + \mathsf{X}'$ and $\mathsf{Y} := \mathsf{E} + \mathsf{Y}'$. It is easy to verify that X has the marginals X_i and Y has the marginals Y_i. Moreover,

$$\sum_{v \in \mathcal{A}_1 \times \cdots \times \mathcal{A}_n} \min(\mathsf{X}(v), \mathsf{Y}(v)) \geq \sum_{v \in \mathcal{A}_1 \times \cdots \times \mathcal{A}_n} \mathsf{E}(v) = |\mathsf{E}| = \tau,$$

which implies $\delta(\mathsf{X}, \mathsf{Y}) \leq p_\mathsf{X} - \tau = \max_{i \in [n]} \delta(\mathsf{X}_i, \mathsf{Y}_i)$.

Finally, we have $\delta(\mathsf{X}, \mathsf{Y}) \geq \delta(\mathsf{X}_i, \mathsf{Y}_i)$ for all $i \in [n]$ due to Lemma 3 and thus $\delta(\mathsf{X}, \mathsf{Y}) \geq \max_{i \in [n]} \delta(\mathsf{X}_i, \mathsf{Y}_i)$, concluding the proof. $\square$

The General Case. Before proving the general case of Theorem 1, we introduce the following notion of a successor system.

Notation 2. For an $(\mathcal{X}, \mathcal{Y})$-DDS s and any first query $x \in \mathrm{dom}_1(s)$, we let $s^{\uparrow x}$ denote the $(\mathcal{X}, \mathcal{Y})$-DDS that behaves like s after the first query x has been input. That is, if s answers at most q queries, $s^{\uparrow x}$ answers at most $(q - 1)$ queries. Formally,

$$s^{\uparrow x}(\hat{x}^i) := s(x | \hat{x}^i).$$

Analogously, we define for a $(\mathcal{Y}, \mathcal{X})$-DDE e the successor $e^{\uparrow y}(\hat{y}^i) := e(y | \hat{y}^i)$. Finally, for an $(\mathcal{X}, \mathcal{Y})$-PDS S, we let $\mathsf{S}^{\uparrow x \downarrow y}$ denote the transformation of S with the partial function $s \mapsto s^{\uparrow x \downarrow y}$ (see Definition 4), where $s^{\uparrow x \downarrow y}$ is equal to $s^{\uparrow x}$ if $s(x) = y$ and undefined otherwise.

We stress that if S is a probability distribution (i.e., it sums to 1), $S^{\uparrow x \downarrow y}$ is in general not a probability distribution anymore: the weight $|S^{\uparrow x \downarrow y}|$ is the probability that S responds with y to the query x.

Proof. *(of Theorem 1).* We prove the theorem using (arbitrary) representatives S and T of the equivalence classes, i.e., **S** and **T** correspond to [S] and [T], respectively. First, observe that $\Delta(\mathbf{S}, \mathbf{T}) \geq \mathrm{Adv}(\mathbf{S}, \mathbf{T})$, since we have for any environment e and any $S' \in [S]$ and $T' \in [T]$

$$\delta(S', T') \geq \delta(\mathrm{tr}(S', e), \mathrm{tr}(T', e)) = \delta(\mathrm{tr}(S, e), \mathrm{tr}(T, e)).$$

The inequality is due to Lemma 3 and the equality is due to Definition 10. Thus, it only remains to prove that for all q-query PDS S and T with the same domain there exist $S' \in [S]$ and $T' \in [T]$ such that

$$\delta(S', T') = \sup_{e} \delta(\mathrm{tr}(S, e), \mathrm{tr}(T, e)). \tag{1}$$

The proof of (1) is by induction over the maximal number of answered queries $q \in \mathbb{N}$. If $q = 0$, the claim follows immediately. Otherwise ($q \geq 1$), let $\mathcal{X}' \subseteq \mathcal{X}$ be the input alphabet for the first query, i.e., $\mathcal{X}' = \mathrm{dom}_1(S) = \mathrm{dom}_1(T)$. We have

$$\sup_{e} \delta(\mathrm{tr}(S, e), \mathrm{tr}(T, e)) = \max_{x \in \mathcal{X}'} \sup_{\substack{e \\ e(\epsilon) = x}} \delta(\mathrm{tr}(S, e), \mathrm{tr}(T, e))$$

$$= \max_{x \in \mathcal{X}'} \sup_{\substack{e \\ e(\epsilon) = x}} \sum_{y \in \mathcal{Y}} \delta(\mathrm{tr}(S^{\uparrow x \downarrow y}, e^{\uparrow y}), \mathrm{tr}(T^{\uparrow x \downarrow y}, e^{\uparrow y}))$$

$$= \max_{x \in \mathcal{X}'} \sum_{y \in \mathcal{Y}} \sup_{e'} \delta(\mathrm{tr}(S^{\uparrow x \downarrow y}, e'), \mathrm{tr}(T^{\uparrow x \downarrow y}, e')).$$

The second step is due to Lemma 2. In the last step, we used that the environment is adaptive: for each possible value $y \in \mathcal{Y}$, the subsequent query strategy may be chosen separately.

As $S^{\uparrow x \downarrow y}$ and $T^{\uparrow x \downarrow y}$ are systems answering at most $q - 1$ queries, we can invoke the induction hypothesis to obtain $S_{xy} \in [S^{\uparrow x \downarrow y}]$ and $T_{xy} \in [T^{\uparrow x \downarrow y}]$ for each $(x, y) \in \mathcal{X}' \times \mathcal{Y}$ such that

$$\sup_{e'} \delta(\mathrm{tr}(S^{\uparrow x \downarrow y}, e'), \mathrm{tr}(T^{\uparrow x \downarrow y}, e')) = \delta(S_{xy}, T_{xy}).$$

For each $(x, y) \in \mathcal{X}' \times \mathcal{Y}$, we prepend an initial query to the deterministic systems in the support of S_{xy} to obtain the q-query PDS S'_{xy} that answers the first query x (deterministically) with y, that is undefined for all $x' \neq x$ as first query, and $S'^{\uparrow x \downarrow y}_{xy} = S_{xy}$. T'_{xy} is defined analogously. This does not change the statistical distance: we have for every $(x, y) \in \mathcal{X}' \times \mathcal{Y}$

$$\delta(S_{xy}, T_{xy}) = \delta(S'_{xy}, T'_{xy}).$$

Next, we define the PDS $S'_x := \sum_{y \in \mathcal{Y}} S'_{xy}$ and $T'_x := \sum_{y \in \mathcal{Y}} T'_{xy}$. We obtain via Lemma 2 that

$$\sum_{y \in \mathcal{Y}} \delta(S'_{xy}, T'_{xy}) = \delta(S'_x, T'_x).$$

By Lemma 6, there exists a joint distribution[11] S' of all S'_x and a joint distribution T' of all T'_x such that

$$\max_{x \in \mathcal{X}'} \delta(S'_x, T'_x) = \delta(S', T').$$

Finally, observe that $S' \in [S]$ and $T' \in [T]$, which concludes the proof.   □

5   Indistinguishability Amplification from Combiners

The goal of indistinguishability amplification is to construct an object which is ϵ-close to its ideal from objects which are only ϵ'-close to their ideal for ϵ much smaller than ϵ'. The most basic type of this construction is to XOR two independent bits B_1 and B_2. It is easy to verify that if B_1 and B_2 are ϵ_1- and ϵ_2-close (in statistical distance) to the uniform bit U, respectively, then $B_1 \oplus B_2$ will be $2\epsilon_1\epsilon_2$-close to the uniform bit. The crucial property of the XOR construction is the following: if at least *one* of the bits B_1 or B_2 is perfectly uniform, then their XOR is perfectly uniform as well. This property is satisfied not only for single bits, but actually also for bitstrings (with bitwise XOR) and even for any quasigroup. Interestingly, it was shown in [12] that an analogous indistinguishability amplification result to the XOR of two bits holds for constructions based on (stateful) random systems, and it is sufficient to assume only such a combiner property of a construction.

In this section, we prove that indistinguishability amplification is obtained from more general combiners. All of the above examples are special cases of such a combiner. In particular, Theorem 1 of [12] is a simple corollary to our Theorem 3.

5.1   Constructions and Combiners

Usually (see for example [12]), an n-ary construction C is defined as a system communicating with component systems $S_1, \ldots, S_n$ and providing an outer communication interface. This means that $C(S_1, \ldots, S_n)$ is a system for any (compatible) component systems $S_1, \ldots, S_n$. In this paper, we use a more abstract notion of a construction, ignoring the details of the interfaces and messages. The

---

[11] It is easy to see that a DDS s which is defined for first inputs from the set $\{x_1, \ldots, x_q\}$ can be represented equivalently as a tuple $(s_{x_1}, \ldots, s_{x_q})$, where s_{x_i} is a DDS which is only defined for x_i as first input. Analogously, a probabilistic discrete system can be understood as a joint distribution of PDS S_{x_i}. Clearly, such a representation does not influence the statistical distance.

amplification statements we make are independent of these details, and thereby simpler and stronger. Nevertheless, it may be easier for the reader to simply think of a construction C as a random system.

Definition 13. *Let $\mathcal{S}_1, \ldots, \mathcal{S}_n, \mathcal{S}_{n+1}$ be sets of $(\mathcal{X}, \mathcal{Y})$-DDS such that for all $i \in [n+1]$, the elements of $\mathcal{S}_i$ have the same domain. An n-ary construction C is a probability distribution over functions from $\mathcal{S}_1 \times \cdots \times \mathcal{S}_n$ to $\mathcal{S}_{n+1}$ such that for any probability distributions S_i and S_i' over $\mathcal{S}_i$ with $\mathsf{S}_i \equiv \mathsf{S}_i'$ we have*[12]

$$\mathsf{C}(\mathsf{S}_1, \ldots, \mathsf{S}_n) \equiv \mathsf{C}(\mathsf{S}_1', \ldots, \mathsf{S}_n').$$

In many settings (especially in cryptography), we have a pair of random systems (F, I), where F is the *real* system, and I is the *ideal* system. A *combiner* is a construction that combines component systems $\mathsf{S}_1, \ldots, \mathsf{S}_n$ such that only some of the component systems S_i need to be ideal for the whole resulting system $\mathsf{C}(\mathsf{S}_1, \ldots, \mathsf{S}_n)$ to behave as if all component systems were ideal. The following definition makes this rigorous.

Definition 14. *Let $\mathcal{A} \subseteq \{0,1\}^n$ be a monotone*[13] *set. An n-ary construction C is an $\mathcal{A}$-combiner for $(\mathsf{F}_1, \mathsf{I}_1), \ldots, (\mathsf{F}_n, \mathsf{I}_n)$ if for any choice of bits $b^n \in \mathcal{A}$ we have*

$$\mathsf{C}(\langle \mathsf{F}_1/\mathsf{I}_1, \ldots, \mathsf{F}_n/\mathsf{I}_n \rangle_{b^n}) \equiv \mathsf{C}(\mathsf{I}_1, \ldots, \mathsf{I}_n),$$

where $\langle x_1/y_1, \ldots, x_n/y_n \rangle_{b^n} = (z_1, \ldots, z_n)$ where $z_i = x_i$ if $b_i = 0$ and $z_i = y_i$ otherwise.

A special case of an $\mathcal{A}$-combiner is a threshold construction where the whole system behaves as if all component systems were ideal if only k (arbitrary) component systems are ideal. We call such a construction a (k, n)-*combiner*.

Definition 15. *An $\mathcal{A}$-combiner C is a (k, n)-combiner for $(\mathsf{F}_1, \mathsf{I}_1), \ldots, (\mathsf{F}_n, \mathsf{I}_n)$ if $\{b^n \mid b^n \in \{0,1\}^n, \sum_i b_i \geq k\} \subseteq \mathcal{A}$.*

For example, it is easy to see that for any two random functions[14] F_1 and F_2 and the *uniform*[15] random functions R and R' on n-bit strings, we have

$$\mathsf{F}_1 \oplus \mathsf{R}' \equiv \mathsf{R} \oplus \mathsf{F}_2 \equiv \mathsf{R} \oplus \mathsf{R}' \equiv \mathsf{R},$$

---

[12] In the following, all distributions are *probability* distributions (i.e., all distributions sum up to 1). Moreover, certain expressions involving multiple distributions make only sense if a joint distribution is defined. For all such expressions, we mean the *independent* joint distribution.

[13] A set $\mathcal{A} \subseteq \{0,1\}^n$ is monotone if for every $b^n \in \mathcal{A}$ we have $\hat{b}^n \in \mathcal{A}$ for every $\hat{b}^n \in \{0,1\}^n$ with $\hat{b}_i \geq b_i$.

[14] A random function from $\mathcal{X}$ to $\mathcal{Y}$ is a system that answers queries consistently, i.e., if a query $x_i \in \mathcal{X}$ is answered with $y_i \in \mathcal{Y}$, the system answers any subsequent query $x_j = x_i$ again with the same value $y_j = y_i$.

[15] A uniform random function from $\mathcal{X}$ to $\mathcal{Y}$ is a random function that answers every query x_i that has not been asked before with an independent uniform response $y_i \in \mathcal{Y}$.

where $\oplus$ is the binary construction that forwards every query x_i to both component systems and returns the bitwise XOR of both answers. Thus, $\oplus$ is a (deterministic) $(1,2)$-combiner for (F_1, R) and (F_2, R'). Note that in [12], a $(1,2)$-combiner is called "neutralizing construction".

5.2   Proving Indistinguishability Amplification Results

Due to the coupling theorem for random systems, we can think of the distinguishing advantage $\mathrm{Adv}(F_i, I_i)$ as a failure probability of F_i, i.e., the probability that F_i is not equal to I_i. Since an $\mathcal{A}$-combiner behaves as if all component systems were ideal if the component systems described by any $a \in \mathcal{A}$ are ideal, one might (naively) hope that the failure probability of $C(F_1, \ldots, F_n)$ was at most the probability that certain component systems fail, i.e.,

$$\mathrm{Adv}(C(F_1, \ldots, F_n), C(I_1, \ldots, I_n)) \stackrel{?}{\leq} \Pr(X \notin \mathcal{A}), \qquad (2)$$

where $X = (X_1, \ldots, X_n)$ for independent Bernoulli random variables X_i with $\Pr(X_i = 0) = \mathrm{Adv}(F_i, I_i)$. However, the reasoning behind this is unsound because it assumes the real system F_i to behave ideally (as I_i) with probability $1 - \mathrm{Adv}(F_i, I_i)$. This is too strong (and not true): when we condition on the event (with probability $1 - \mathrm{Adv}(F_i, I_i)$) in which the real and ideal systems are equal, we also condition the ideal system, changing its original behavior.

Not only is the above reasoning unsound, the bound (2) simply does not hold, since it would for example imply that

$$\delta(B_1 \oplus \cdots \oplus B_n, U) \stackrel{?}{\leq} \prod_{i=1}^{n} \delta(B_i, U)$$

for independent bits B_i and the uniform bit U. However, it is easy to verify that $\delta(B_1 \oplus \cdots \oplus B_n, U) = 2^{n-1} \prod_{i=1}^{n} \delta(B_i, U)$, i.e., there is an extra factor 2^{n-1}.

The following technical lemma describes a general proof technique and can be used as a tool to prove indistinguishability amplification results for any $\mathcal{A}$-combiner. The key idea is to consider distributions B and B' over $\mathcal{A} \cup \{0^n\}$, inducing distributions $C(\langle F_1/I_1, \ldots, F_n/I_n \rangle_B)$ and $C(\langle F_1/I_1, \ldots, F_n/I_n \rangle_{B'})$ (recall Definition 14 for the notation). We then use Theorem 1 to exhibit a coupling in which systems F_i and I_i are equal with probability $1 - \mathrm{Adv}(F_i, I_i)$ and argue that the two constructions are equal (in the coupling) unless for one of the indices $i \in [n]$ where $F_i \neq I_i$ we have $B_i \neq B'_i$. The proof of Theorem 3 shows how to instantiate this lemma, choosing suitable distributions B and B'.

Lemma 7. *Let C be an $\mathcal{A}$-combiner for $(F_1, I_1), \ldots, (F_n, I_n)$ and let B, B' be any probability distributions over $\mathcal{A} \cup \{0^n\}$ such that $B(0^n) > 0$ and $B'(0^n) = 0$. Then,*

$$\mathrm{Adv}(C(F_1, \ldots, F_n), C(I_1, \ldots, I_n))$$
$$\leq B(0^n)^{-1} \cdot \sum_{e \in \{0,1\}^n} \delta(\mathrm{blind}(B, e), \mathrm{blind}(B', e)) \cdot \Pr(E = e),$$

where $\mathrm{blind}(x, m)$ *is the tuple derived from* x *by removing all elements at the indices at which* $m_i = 0$*, and* $E = (E_1, \ldots, E_n)$ *for independent Bernoulli random variables* E_i *with* $\Pr(E_i = 1) = \mathrm{Adv}(\mathsf{F}_i, \mathsf{l}_i)$*.*

Proof. By Lemma 9 (see Appendix A) we have for probability distribution B'' over $\{0, 1\}$ with $\mathsf{B}''(0) = \mathsf{B}(0^n)$

$$\mathrm{Adv}(\mathsf{C}(\mathsf{F}_1, \ldots, \mathsf{F}_n), \mathsf{C}(\mathsf{l}_1, \ldots, \mathsf{l}_n))$$
$$= \mathsf{B}(0^n)^{-1} \cdot \mathrm{Adv}(\langle \mathsf{C}(\mathsf{F}_1, \ldots, \mathsf{F}_n)/\mathsf{C}(\mathsf{l}_1, \ldots, \mathsf{l}_n)\rangle_{\mathsf{B}''}, \mathsf{C}(\mathsf{l}_1, \ldots, \mathsf{l}_n)).$$

Observe that we have $\langle \mathsf{C}(\mathsf{F}_1, \ldots, \mathsf{F}_n)/\mathsf{C}(\mathsf{l}_1, \ldots, \mathsf{l}_n)\rangle_{\mathsf{B}''} \equiv \mathsf{C}(\langle \mathsf{F}_1/\mathsf{l}_1, \ldots, \mathsf{F}_n/\mathsf{l}_n\rangle_{\mathsf{B}})$ and $\mathsf{C}(\mathsf{l}_1, \ldots, \mathsf{l}_n) \equiv \mathsf{C}(\langle \mathsf{F}_1/\mathsf{l}_1, \ldots, \mathsf{F}_n/\mathsf{l}_n\rangle_{\mathsf{B}'})$, since C is an $\mathcal{A}$-combiner. Thus,

$$\mathrm{Adv}(\langle \mathsf{C}(\mathsf{F}_1, \ldots, \mathsf{F}_n)/\mathsf{C}(\mathsf{l}_1, \ldots, \mathsf{l}_n)\rangle_{\mathsf{B}''}, \mathsf{C}(\mathsf{l}_1, \ldots, \mathsf{l}_n))$$
$$= \mathrm{Adv}(\mathsf{C}(\langle \mathsf{F}_1/\mathsf{l}_1, \ldots, \mathsf{F}_n/\mathsf{l}_n\rangle_{\mathsf{B}}), \mathsf{C}(\langle \mathsf{F}_1/\mathsf{l}_1, \ldots, \mathsf{F}_n/\mathsf{l}_n\rangle_{\mathsf{B}'})).$$

According to Theorem 1 there exist $(\mathsf{F}_i', \mathsf{l}_i') \in [\mathsf{F}_i] \times [\mathsf{l}_i]$ for every $i \in [n]$ such that $\delta(\mathsf{F}_i', \mathsf{l}_i') = \mathrm{Adv}(\mathsf{F}_i, \mathsf{l}_i)$. Thus,

$$\mathrm{Adv}(\mathsf{C}(\langle \mathsf{F}_1/\mathsf{l}_1, \ldots, \mathsf{F}_n/\mathsf{l}_n\rangle_{\mathsf{B}}), \mathsf{C}(\langle \mathsf{F}_1/\mathsf{l}_1, \ldots, \mathsf{F}_n/\mathsf{l}_n\rangle_{\mathsf{B}'}))$$
$$= \mathrm{Adv}(\mathsf{C}(\langle \mathsf{F}_1'/\mathsf{l}_1', \ldots, \mathsf{F}_n'/\mathsf{l}_n'\rangle_{\mathsf{B}}), \mathsf{C}(\langle \mathsf{F}_1'/\mathsf{l}_1', \ldots, \mathsf{F}_n'/\mathsf{l}_n'\rangle_{\mathsf{B}'}))$$
$$\leq \delta(\mathsf{C}(\langle \mathsf{F}_1'/\mathsf{l}_1', \ldots, \mathsf{F}_n'/\mathsf{l}_n'\rangle_{\mathsf{B}}), \mathsf{C}(\langle \mathsf{F}_1'/\mathsf{l}_1', \ldots, \mathsf{F}_n'/\mathsf{l}_n'\rangle_{\mathsf{B}'}))$$
$$\leq \delta(\langle \mathsf{F}_1'/\mathsf{l}_1', \ldots, \mathsf{F}_n'/\mathsf{l}_n'\rangle_{\mathsf{B}}, \langle \mathsf{F}_1'/\mathsf{l}_1', \ldots, \mathsf{F}_n'/\mathsf{l}_n'\rangle_{\mathsf{B}'}),$$

where the last step is due to Lemma 3.

We exhibit a random experiment $\mathcal{E}$ with random variables[16] $F_i' \sim \mathsf{F}_i'$, $I_i' \sim \mathsf{l}_i'$, $B \sim \mathsf{B}$, and $B' \sim \mathsf{B}'$, such that $L := \langle F_1'/I_1', \ldots, F_n'/I_n'\rangle_B \sim \langle \mathsf{F}_1'/\mathsf{l}_1', \ldots, \mathsf{F}_n'/\mathsf{l}_n'\rangle_{\mathsf{B}}$ and $R := \langle F_1'/I_1', \ldots, F_n'/I_n'\rangle_{B'} \sim \langle \mathsf{F}_1'/\mathsf{l}_1', \ldots, \mathsf{F}_n'/\mathsf{l}_n'\rangle_{\mathsf{B}'}$. Define $E_i := [F_i' \neq I_i']$ and $E := (E_1, \ldots, E_n)$.

Observe that the joint distribution of F_i' and I_i' as well as B and B' can be chosen arbitrary (as long as the marginal distributions are respected). Let $\mathcal{C}_\delta(\cdot, \cdot)$ denote the joint distribution described in Lemma 4, and let the joint distribution of F_i' and I_i' be $\mathcal{C}_\delta(\mathsf{F}_i', \mathsf{l}_i')$. Moreover, the joint distribution of B and B' is chosen such that[17]

$$\Pr^{\mathcal{E}}(\mathrm{blind}(B, e) = b, \mathrm{blind}(B', e) = b', E = e)$$
$$= \mathcal{C}_\delta(\mathrm{blind}(\mathsf{B}, e), \mathrm{blind}(\mathsf{B}', e))(b, b') \cdot \Pr^{\mathcal{E}}(E = e).$$

---

[16] We write $X \sim \mathsf{X}$ to denote that the random variable X is distributed according to the distribution X.

[17] Note that even though the joint distribution of B and B' depends on E, the random variable B is still independent of $((F_1', I_1'), \ldots, (F_n', I_n'))$.

Thus we have by Lemma 4

$$
\begin{aligned}
\delta(\langle \mathsf{F}'_1/\mathsf{I}'_1, \ldots, \mathsf{F}'_n/\mathsf{I}'_n \rangle_{\mathsf{B}}, & \langle \mathsf{F}'_1/\mathsf{I}'_1, \ldots, \mathsf{F}'_n/\mathsf{I}'_n \rangle_{\mathsf{B}'}) \\
& \leq \Pr^{\mathcal{E}}(L \neq R) \\
& = \sum_{e \in \{0,1\}^n} \Pr^{\mathcal{E}}(L \neq R, E = e) \\
& = \sum_{e \in \{0,1\}^n} \Pr^{\mathcal{E}}(\text{blind}(B, e) \neq \text{blind}(B', e), E = e) \\
& = \sum_{e \in \{0,1\}^n} \delta(\text{blind}(\mathsf{B}, e), \text{blind}(\mathsf{B}', e)) \cdot \Pr^{\mathcal{E}}(E = e),
\end{aligned}
$$

which concludes the proof.   □

Observe that Lemma 7 by itself does not imply indistinguishability amplification for any combiner. In particular, one needs to prove the existence of suitable distributions B and B' such that the distance $\delta(\text{blind}(\mathsf{B}, e), \text{blind}(\mathsf{B}', e))$ is small for many $e \in \{0,1\}^n$ (ideally it is zero for all $\bar{e} \notin \mathcal{A}$, where $\bar{e}$ is the bitwise complement of e). We show the following indistinguishability amplification theorem for all (k, n)-combiners.

Theorem 3. *If* C *is a* (k, n)*-combiner for* $(\mathsf{F}_1, \mathsf{I}_1), \ldots, (\mathsf{F}_n, \mathsf{I}_n)$, *then*

$$
\mathrm{Adv}(\mathsf{C}(\mathsf{F}_1, \ldots, \mathsf{F}_n), \mathsf{C}(\mathsf{I}_1, \ldots, \mathsf{I}_n)) \leq \sum_{i=n-k+1}^{n} \xi_{i-(n-k),i} \cdot \Pr\left(\sum_{j \in [n]} E_j = n - k + 1 \right),
$$

where

$$
\xi_{l,m} := \frac{1}{2} \cdot \left(1 + \sum_{j=l}^{m} \binom{m}{j} \cdot \binom{j-1}{l-1} \right),
$$

and the E_i *are jointly independent Bernoulli random variables with* $\Pr(E_i = 1) = \mathrm{Adv}(\mathsf{F}_i, \mathsf{I}_i)$.

As discussed before, one might (naively) hope for threshold combiners to achieve the indistinguishability bound

$$
\mathrm{Adv}(\mathsf{C}(\mathsf{F}_1, \ldots, \mathsf{F}_n), \mathsf{C}(\mathsf{I}_1, \ldots, \mathsf{I}_n)) \overset{?}{\leq} \Pr\left(\sum_{j \in [n]} E_j \geq n - k + 1 \right).
$$

This bound does not hold and thus correction factors as in Theorem 3 (i.e., the factors $\xi_{i-(n-k),i}$) are in general unavoidable. As we have $\xi_{1,2} = 2$, Theorem 1 of [12] is an immediate corollary of Theorem 3 (for $k = 1$ and $n = 2$). More generally we have $\xi_{1,n} = 2^{n-1}$, which is tight due to the above discussed example.

Proof (of Theorem 3). For $k \geq 1$ and $n \geq k$ we represent distributions $\mathsf{B}_{k,n}, \mathsf{B}'_{k,n}$ using multisets $A_{k,n}, A'_{k,n}$ over $\mathcal{A} \cup \{0^n\}$, with the natural understanding that $\mathsf{B}_{k,n}$ $(\mathsf{B}'_{k,n})$ is the probability distribution with $\mathsf{B}_{k,n}(a) = A_{k,n}(a)/|A_{k,n}|$. Let

$$A'_{k,n} := \bigcup_{j \in \{k,k+2,\dots,n\}} \left\{ \left(b, \binom{j-1}{k-1}\right) \;\middle|\; b \in \{0,1\}^n, \sum_{i \in [n]} b_i = j \right\} \quad \text{and}$$

$$A_{k,n} := \{(0^n, 1)\} \cup \bigcup_{j \in \{k+1,k+3,\dots,n\}} \left\{ \left(b, \binom{j-1}{k-1}\right) \;\middle|\; b \in \{0,1\}^n, \sum_{i \in [n]} b_i = j \right\}.$$

For a multiset M over $\{0,1\}^n$, let $\mathrm{blind}_m(M)$ be the multiset over $\{0,1\}^{n-m}$ derived from M by removing the bits at m fixed positions, say the first m bits, for every element. We only consider multisets for which $\mathrm{blind}_m(M)$ is well-defined, i.e., it does not matter at which m positions the bits are removed. We prove below the following statement:

$$\forall k \geq 1, \forall n \geq k: \quad |A_{k,n}| = |A'_{k,n}| = \xi_{k,n}$$
$$\wedge \, \forall j \geq k : \mathrm{blind}_j(A_{k,n}) = \mathrm{blind}_j(A'_{k,n}) \tag{3}$$
$$\wedge \, \forall j < k : |\mathrm{blind}_j(A_{k,n}) \,\triangle\, \mathrm{blind}_j(A'_{k,n})| = 2\xi_{k-j,n-j}.$$

This implies the claim via Lemma 7, since we have

$$\mathrm{Adv}(\mathsf{C}(\mathsf{F}_1,\dots,\mathsf{F}_n), \mathsf{C}(\mathsf{I}_1,\dots,\mathsf{I}_n))$$
$$\leq \mathsf{B}_{k,n}(0^n)^{-1} \cdot \sum_{e \in \{0,1\}^n} \delta(\mathrm{blind}(\mathsf{B}_{k,n},e), \mathrm{blind}(\mathsf{B}'_{k,n},e)) \cdot \Pr(E = e)$$
$$= |A_{k,n}| \cdot \sum_{i=0}^{n} \frac{|\mathrm{blind}_{n-i}(A_{k,n}) \,\triangle\, \mathrm{blind}_{n-i}(A'_{k,n})|}{2|A_{k,n}|} \cdot \Pr\left(\sum_{j \in [n]} E_j = i\right)$$
$$= \sum_{i=n-k+1}^{n} \xi_{i-(n-k),i} \cdot \Pr\left(\sum_{j \in [n]} E_j = i\right).$$

In the second step we have used that for any two multisets M, M' representing probability distributions M, M' we have $\delta(\mathsf{M}, \mathsf{M}') = |M \,\triangle\, M'|/(2|M|)$ if $|M| = |M'|$.

We prove (3) by induction over n. Observe that

$$\mathrm{blind}_1(A'_{k,n}) = \bigcup_{j \in \{k,k+2,\dots,n-1\}} \left\{ \left(b, \binom{j-1}{k-1}\right) \;\middle|\; b \in \{0,1\}^{n-1}, \sum_{i \in [n]} b_i = j \right\}$$
$$\cup \bigcup_{j \in \{k-1,k+1,\dots,n-1\}} \left\{ \left(b, \binom{j}{k-1}\right) \;\middle|\; b \in \{0,1\}^{n-1}, \sum_{i \in [n]} b_i = j \right\}.$$

Similarly, we see that

$$\mathrm{blind}_1(A_{k,n}) = \{(0^{n-1}, 1)\}$$

$$\cup \bigcup_{j \in \{k+1, k+3, \ldots, n-1\}} \left\{ \left(b, \binom{j-1}{k-1} \right) \,\middle|\, b \in \{0,1\}^{n-1}, \sum_{i \in [n]} b_i = j \right\}$$

$$\cup \bigcup_{j \in \{k, k+2, \ldots, n-1\}} \left\{ \left(b, \binom{j}{k-1} \right) \,\middle|\, b \in \{0,1\}^{n-1}, \sum_{i \in [n]} b_i = j \right\}.$$

If $k = 1$, it is easy to see that $|A_{k,n}| = |A'_{k,n}| = \xi_{k,n}$, as well as $\mathrm{blind}_1(A'_{k,n}) = \mathrm{blind}_1(A_{k,n})$ and $|\mathrm{blind}_0(A_{k,n}) \triangle \mathrm{blind}_0(A'_{k,n})| = 2\xi_{k,n}$ (since $A_{k,n}$ and $A'_{k,n}$ are disjoint). Otherwise ($k \geq 2$), we use the identity $\binom{j}{k-1} - \binom{j-1}{k-1} = \binom{j-1}{k-2}$ to obtain

$$\mathrm{blind}_1(A'_{k,n}) - \mathrm{blind}_1(A_{k,n}) \cap \mathrm{blind}_1(A'_{k,n})$$

$$= \bigcup_{j \in \{k-1, k+1, \ldots, n-1\}} \left\{ \left(b, \binom{j-1}{k-2} \right) \,\middle|\, b \in \{0,1\}^{n-1}, \sum_{i \in [n]} b_i = j \right\}$$

$$= A'_{k-1, n-1}.$$

Analogously, we see that

$$\mathrm{blind}_1(A_{k,n}) - \mathrm{blind}_1(A_{k,n}) \cap \mathrm{blind}_1(A'_{k,n})$$

$$= \{(0^{n-1}, 1)\} \cup \bigcup_{j \in \{k, k+2, \ldots, n-1\}} \left\{ \left(b, \binom{j-1}{k-2} \right) \,\middle|\, b \in \{0,1\}^{n-1}, \sum_{i \in [n]} b_i = j \right\}$$

$$= A_{k-1, n-1}.$$

As by induction hypothesis $\mathrm{blind}_{k-1}(A_{k-1,n-1}) = \mathrm{blind}_{k-1}(A'_{k-1,n-1})$, we have $\mathrm{blind}_k(A_{k,n}) = \mathrm{blind}_k(A'_{k,n})$. Since blinding does not change the cardinality of a multiset, it follows $|A_{k,n}| = |A'_{k,n}| = \xi_{k,n}$. Moreover, as $A_{k,n}$ and $A'_{k,n}$ are disjoint we have $|\mathrm{blind}_0(A_{k,n}) \triangle \mathrm{blind}_0(A'_{k,n})| = 2\xi_{k,n}$. Finally, for $j \geq 1$ and $j < k$ we have

$$|\mathrm{blind}_j(A_{k,n}) \triangle \mathrm{blind}_j(A'_{k,n})| = |\mathrm{blind}_{j-1}(A_{k-1,n-1}) \triangle \mathrm{blind}_{j-1}(A'_{k-1,n-1})|$$

$$\overset{\text{(I.H.)}}{=} 2\xi_{(k-1)-(j-1),(n-1)-(j-1)} = 2\xi_{k-j,n-j},$$

which concludes the proof. □

The following corollary to Theorem 3 provides simpler (but worse) bounds.

Corollary 1. *If* C *is a* (k, n)-*combiner for* $(\mathsf{F}_1, \mathsf{I}_1), \ldots, (\mathsf{F}_n, \mathsf{I}_n)$, *then*

(i)

$$\mathrm{Adv}(\mathsf{C}(\mathsf{F}_1, \ldots, \mathsf{F}_n), \mathsf{C}(\mathsf{I}_1, \ldots, \mathsf{I}_n)) \leq$$

$$2^{n-k} \sum_{j=n-k+1}^{n} \binom{j-1}{n-k} \cdot \mathrm{Pr}\left(\sum_{i \in [n]} E_i = j \right),$$

where the E_i are jointly independent Bernoulli random variables with
$\Pr(E_i = 1) = \mathrm{Adv}(\mathsf{F}_i, \mathsf{I}_i)$.

(ii) if $\mathrm{Adv}(\mathsf{F}_i, \mathsf{I}_i) \leq \epsilon$ for all $i \in [n]$ we have

$$\mathrm{Adv}(\mathsf{C}(\mathsf{F}_1, \ldots, \mathsf{F}_n), \mathsf{C}(\mathsf{I}_1, \ldots, \mathsf{I}_n)) \leq \frac{1}{2}\binom{n}{k-1} \cdot (2\epsilon)^{n-k+1}.$$

(iii) if $\mathrm{Adv}(\mathsf{F}_i, \mathsf{I}_i) \leq \epsilon$ for all $i \in [n]$ we have

$$\mathrm{Adv}(\mathsf{C}(\mathsf{F}_1, \ldots, \mathsf{F}_n), \mathsf{C}(\mathsf{I}_1, \ldots, \mathsf{I}_n)) \leq \left(2e\frac{n}{n-k+1} \cdot \epsilon\right)^{n-k+1}.$$

Proof. Lemma 10 in Appendix A states that $\xi_{l,m} \leq 2^{m-l}\binom{m-1}{l-1}$. This immediately implies the bound (i) via Theorem 3.
We use bound (i) to obtain the bound (ii) as follows

$$\mathrm{Adv}(\mathsf{C}(\mathsf{F}_1, \ldots, \mathsf{F}_n), \mathsf{C}(\mathsf{I}_1, \ldots, \mathsf{I}_n)) \leq 2^{n-k} \sum_{j=n-k+1}^{n} \binom{j-1}{n-k} \cdot \Pr\left(\sum_{i \in [n]} E_i = j\right)$$

$$\leq 2^{n-k} \sum_{j=n-k+1}^{n} \binom{j-1}{n-k} \cdot \binom{n}{j} \epsilon^j (1-\epsilon)^{n-j}$$

$$\leq 2^{n-k} \sum_{j=n-k+1}^{n} \binom{j}{n-k+1} \cdot \binom{n}{j} \epsilon^j (1-\epsilon)^{n-j}$$

$$= 2^{n-k} \binom{n}{n-k+1} \epsilon^{n-k+1}$$

$$= \frac{1}{2}\binom{n}{k-1} \cdot (2\epsilon)^{n-k+1}.$$

The first *equality* is due to the identity $\sum_{j=m}^{n} \binom{j}{m}\binom{n}{j}\epsilon^j(1-\epsilon)^{n-j} = \binom{n}{m}\epsilon^m$. An easy proof of the identity is by considering n independent Bernoulli random variables X_i with $\Pr(X_i = 1) = \epsilon$ and their sum $X := X_1 + \cdots + X_n$. The left-hand expression of the identity is simply the expected value

$$\mathbb{E}\left[\binom{X}{m}\right] = \mathbb{E}\left[\sum_{\substack{I \subseteq [n] \\ |I|=m}} \left[\bigwedge_{i \in I}(X_i = 1)\right]\right] = \sum_{\substack{I \subseteq [n] \\ |I|=m}} \Pr\left(\bigwedge_{i \in I}(X_i = 1)\right) = \binom{n}{m}\epsilon^m.$$

Finally, bound (iii) is derived from bound (ii) via the well-known inequality $\binom{n}{k} \leq (2en/k)^k$. □

The bound

$$\mathrm{Adv}(\mathsf{C}(\mathsf{F}_1, \ldots, \mathsf{F}_n), \mathsf{C}(\mathsf{I}_1, \ldots, \mathsf{I}_n)) \leq \left(2e\frac{n}{n-k+1} \cdot \epsilon\right)^{n-k+1}$$

from Corollary 1 (iii) is perhaps suited best (even though it is the loosest) in order to intuitively understand the behavior of the obtained indistinguishability amplification.

On the Number of Queries. Many indistinguishability bounds are presented with a dependency on the number of queries q the adversary is allowed to ask. For reasons of simplicity, we understand the number of queries as a property of a discrete system, i.e., the number of queries that a system answers. This is only a conceptual difference, and all of our results can still be used with the former perspective. For example, this means that if the indistinguishability of the component systems is for distinguishers asking up to q queries, our results can be applied to the corresponding systems that *answer* only q queries. Usually, if the component systems $F_1, \ldots, F_n$ answer only q queries, then the overall constructed system $C(F_1, \ldots, F_n)$ will answer only up to q' queries, for some q' depending on q. As a consequence, the resulting indistinguishability bound $\mathrm{Adv}(C(F_1, \ldots, F_n), C(I_1, \ldots, I_n))$ holds for any distinguisher asking up to q' queries.

5.3   A Simple (k, n)-Combiner for Random Functions

We present a simple (k, n)-combiner for arbitrary k and $n \geq k$. For a finite field $\mathbb{F}$, let $A \in \mathbb{F}^{k \times n}$ be a $(k \times n)$-matrix with $k \leq n$, and let $\mathcal{A} \subseteq \{0, 1\}^n$ be the (monotone) set containing all $v \in \{0, 1\}^n$ with $v_{i_1} = \cdots = v_{i_k} = 1$ for k distinct indices, such that the columns $i_1, \ldots, i_k$ of A are linearly independent. Consider the deterministic n-ary construction $C : \mathbb{F}^n \to \mathbb{F}^k$ defined by[18]

$$C(x_1, \ldots, x_n) := A \cdot (x_1, \ldots, x_n)^{\mathsf{T}}.$$

It is easy to see that C is an $\mathcal{A}$-combiner for $(X_1, U), \ldots, (X_n, U)$, where X_i are arbitrary probability distributions over $\mathbb{F}$ and U is the uniform distribution over $\mathbb{F}$. Moreover, if A is an MDS matrix[19], it is straightforward to verify using basic linear algebra that C is a (k, n)-combiner. Assuming the field $\mathbb{F}$ has sufficiently many elements ($|\mathbb{F}| \geq k + n$) such a matrix is easy to construct (for example, one can take a Vandermonde matrix or a Cauchy matrix [8]).

The above construction can be generalized to a (k, n)-combiner C' which combines n independent random functions $F_1, \ldots, F_n$ (from $\mathcal{X}$ to $\mathbb{F}$) to k random functions $F'_1, \ldots, F'_k$ as depicted in Fig. 2. By the argument above, C' is a (k, n)-combiner for $(F_1, R), \ldots, (F_n, R)$, where the F_i are arbitrary random functions and R is a uniform random function (assuming A is an MDS matrix).

Assuming $\mathrm{Adv}(F_i, R) \leq \epsilon$, Corollary 1 implies that

$$\mathrm{Adv}((F'_1, \ldots, F'_k), R^k) \leq \frac{1}{2} \binom{n}{k-1} (2\epsilon)^{n-k+1},$$

where R^k are k independent parallel uniform random functions.

---

[18] One can think of an element of $\mathbb{F}^l$ as a single-query DDS with unary input alphabet $\{\diamond\}$ and output alphabet $\mathbb{F}^l$.

[19] Recall that an MDS (maximum distance separable) matrix [8,16] is a matrix over a finite field for which every square submatrix is non-singular.

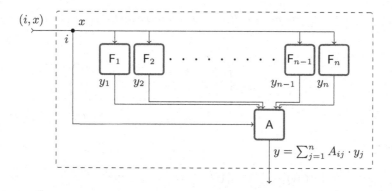

Fig. 2. Construction C' transforms the n random functions $F_1, \ldots, F_n$ to k random functions, where k is the number of rows of the matrix A. For an input $x \in \mathbb{F}$ to the i-th constructed function F'_i, the output is the dot product $\sum_{j=1}^{n} A_{ij} \cdot y_j$, where $y_i = F_i(x)$.

5.4   Combining Systems Forming a Quasi-Group

We consider the setting of combining random systems forming a quasigroup[20] with some construction $\odot$. Examples of such systems include one- or both-sided stateless random permutations with the cascade $\circ$, or (possibly stateful) random functions with the elementwise XOR $\oplus$. Given n independent such systems, the goal is to obtain $m < n$ systems that are (jointly) close to m independent uniform systems. The known results from [12] lead to the following straightforward construction: we partition the n systems into m sets of size n/m, and then use the $(1, n/m)$-combiner $\odot$ to combine each set into one system (see Example 1). Assuming that each component system is ϵ-close to uniform, this will yield an indistinguishability bound of[21]

$$\frac{m}{2}(2\epsilon)^{n/m}.$$

In the following, we show that by sharing a few systems among the m combined sets, much stronger indistinguishability amplification is obtained, roughly squaring the above bound. As a result, only about half as many systems need to be combined in order to obtain the same indistinguishability as with the straightforward construction.

Lemma 8. *Assume a set of deterministic discrete systems $\mathcal{Q}$ forming a quasigroup with the construction $\odot$. Let $Q_1, \ldots, Q_n$ be PDS over $\mathcal{Q}$ with $\mathrm{Adv}(Q_i, U) \leq \epsilon$, where U is the uniform distribution over $\mathcal{Q}$. Let $\langle S_i \rangle_{i \in [m+1]}$ be a partition of*

---

[20] A quasigroup is a set $\mathcal{X}$ with a binary operation $\odot \colon \mathcal{X}^2 \to \mathcal{X}$ such that for any $a, b \in \mathcal{X}$ there exist unique $x, y \in \mathcal{X}$ such that $a \odot x = b$ and $y \odot a = b$.

[21] The factor m accounts for the *joint* indistinguishability of the m systems.

$[n]$ with $|S_i| = \frac{n}{m+1}$ for all[22] i. Then, the deterministic construction C defined by[23]

$$\mathsf{C}(q_1,\ldots,q_n) := \begin{pmatrix} (\odot_{j\in S_1} q_j) \odot \odot_{j\in S_{m+1}} q_j \\ (\odot_{j\in S_2} q_j) \odot \odot_{j\in S_{m+1}} q_j \\ \cdots \\ (\odot_{j\in S_m} q_j) \odot \odot_{j\in S_{m+1}} q_j \end{pmatrix}$$

satisfies

$$\mathrm{Adv}(\mathsf{C}(\mathsf{Q}_1,\ldots,\mathsf{Q}_n),\mathsf{U}^n) \le \frac{m(m+1)}{4}(2\epsilon)^{2n/(m+1)},$$

where U^n are n independent parallel instances of U.

Proof. We rewrite C as the application of multiple combiners

$$\mathsf{C}(\mathsf{Q}_1,\ldots,\mathsf{Q}_n) = \mathsf{C}'_{m,m+1}\Big(\bigodot_{j\in S_1} \mathsf{Q}_j,\ldots,\bigodot_{j\in S_{m+1}} \mathsf{Q}_j\Big), \qquad (4)$$

where $\mathsf{C}'_{m,m+1}$ is the $(m,m+1)$-combiner defined by

$$\mathsf{C}'_{m,m+1}(q_1,\ldots,q_{m+1}) := (q_1 \odot q_{m+1},\ldots,q_m \odot q_{m+1}).$$

Since each inner argument $(\odot_{j\in S_i} \cdot)$ to the construction $\mathsf{C}'_{m,m+1}$ in (4) is a $(1,n/(m+1))$-combiner, we have by Corollary 1 for any $i \in [m+1]$

$$\mathrm{Adv}\Big(\bigodot_{j\in S_i} \mathsf{Q}_j,\mathsf{U}\Big) \le \frac{1}{2}(2\epsilon)^{n/(m+1)}.$$

Again invoking Corollary 1 for $c'_{m,m+1}$ yields

$$\mathrm{Adv}(\mathsf{C}(\mathsf{Q}_1,\ldots,\mathsf{Q}_n),\mathsf{U}^n) \le 2 \cdot \binom{m+1}{2}\Big(\max_{i\in[m+1]} \mathrm{Adv}\Big(\bigodot_{j\in S_i} \mathsf{Q}_j,\mathsf{U}\Big)\Big)^2$$

$$\le \frac{m(m+1)}{4}(2\epsilon)^{2n/(m+1)}.$$

$\square$

6   Conclusions and Open Problems

We presented a simple systems theory of random systems. The key insight was to interpret a random system as probability distribution over deterministic systems, and to consider *equivalence classes* of probabilistic systems induced by the

---

[22] This requires n to be divisible by $m + 1$.

[23] Since a quasigroup operation may be non-commutative and non-associative, we assume a fixed combination tree to be defined with each set S_i.

behavior equivalence relation. We demonstrated how this perspective on random systems provides an elementary characterization of the classical distinguishing advantage and is also a useful tool to prove indistinguishability bounds.

Finally, we have shown a general indistinguishability amplification theorem for any (k, n)-combiner. We demonstrated how the theorem can be instantiated to combine n stateless random permutations (one- or both-sided), which are only moderately close to uniform random permutations, into $m < n$ random permutations that are jointly very close to uniform random permutations. For random functions, we have shown that even stronger indistinguishability amplification can be obtained. Several open questions remain:

(i) Any $\mathcal{A}$-combiner is also a (k, n)-combiner for sufficiently large k. In this sense, the bound of Theorem 3 applies also to any $\mathcal{A}$-combiner. A natural question is whether significantly better indistinguishability amplification is possible for general (non-threshold) $\mathcal{A}$-combiners. In particular, can the presented technique (Lemma 7) be used to prove such a bound? It seems that a new idea is necessary to prove such a bound, considering that the current proof strongly relies on the symmetry in the threshold case.

(ii) It is easy to see that the proved indistinguishability bound for (k, n)-combiners is perfectly tight for the case $k = 1$. Is it also tight for general k? For special cases, such as $(k, n) = (2, 3)$, it is not too difficult to show that the presented bound is very close to tight.

(iii) We have shown how MDS matrices allow to combine n independent random functions over a field to m random functions. However, the same technique does not immediately apply to random permutations. The bounds shown in Lemma 8 are the first non-trivial ones in the more general setting of combining systems forming a quasigroup. It may be possible to improve substantially over said bounds, possibly also by making stronger assumptions (e.g., explicitly assuming permutations). In particular, one might hope to improve the exponent $2n/(m + 1)$.

(iv) Our treatment is in the information-theoretic setting. A natural question is whether our results can be extended to the computational setting. Under certain assumptions on the component systems, the special case of a $(1, n)$-combiner was shown to provide computational indistinguishability amplification in [13].

(v) Can the coupling theorem be used to prove amplification results that strengthen the distinguisher class? For example, can we get more general lifting of non-adaptive indistinguishability to adaptive indistinguishability than what is shown in [11,12]?

Appendix

A Proofs of Basic Lemmas

Proof. (of Lemma 2). By the definition of the statistical distance we have

$$\delta(X, Y) = \sum_{a \in \mathcal{A}} \max(0, X(a) - Y(a))$$

$$= \sum_{i \in [k]} \sum_{a \in \mathcal{A}_i} \max(0, X(a) - Y(a))$$

$$= \sum_{i \in [k]} \sum_{a \in \mathcal{A}_i} \max(0, X_i(a) - Y_i(a))$$

$$= \sum_{i \in [k]} \delta(X_i, Y_i).$$

$\square$

Proof. (of Lemma 3). We have

$$\delta(f(X), f(Y)) = \sum_{b \in \mathcal{B}} \max(0, f(X)(b) - f(Y)(b))$$

$$= \sum_{b \in \mathcal{B}} \max(0, \sum_{a \in f^{-1}(b)} X(a) - Y(a))$$

$$\leq \sum_{b \in \mathcal{B}} \sum_{a \in f^{-1}(b)} \max(0, X(a) - Y(a))$$

$$= \sum_{a \in \mathcal{A}} \max(0, X(a) - Y(a))$$

$$= \delta(X, Y).$$

In the fourth step, we used that f is a total function from $\mathcal{A}$ to $\mathcal{B}$. $\square$

Proof. (of Lemma 5). It suffices to show that if we have

$$\text{tr}(S, e) = \text{tr}(T, e) \text{ for all compatible non-adaptive } (\mathcal{Y}, \mathcal{X})\text{-DDE } e,$$

then the same is true for *all* compatible $(\mathcal{Y}, \mathcal{X})$-DDE e (even adaptive ones). Assume there exists an adaptive $(\mathcal{Y}, \mathcal{X})$-DDE e such that

$$\text{tr}(S, e) \neq \text{tr}(T, e),$$

implying that there exists a transcript $\hat{t} = (\hat{x}_1, \hat{y}_1), (\hat{x}_2, \hat{y}_2), \ldots, (\hat{x}_l, \hat{y}_l)$ such that[24] $\text{tr}(S, e)(\hat{t}) \neq \text{tr}(T, e)(\hat{t})$. Let e' be the environment which queries the

---

[24] Recall that $\text{tr}(S, e)$ denotes the transcript distribution of the interaction between S and e, so $\text{tr}(S, e)(\hat{t})$ is the probability of transcript $\hat{t}$ in this interaction.

inputs of $\hat{t}$, i.e., $(\hat{x}_1, \hat{x}_2, \ldots, \hat{x}_l)$. Clearly, e' is non-adaptive and deterministic. Observe moreover that for any $(\mathcal{X}, \mathcal{Y})$-DDS s and any compatible $(\mathcal{Y}, \mathcal{X})$-DDE $\tilde{e}$, the transcript $\text{tr}(s, \tilde{e})$ is $\hat{t}$ if and only if $s(\hat{x}^i) = \hat{y}_i$ and $\tilde{e}(\hat{y}^{i-1}) = \hat{x}_i$ for all $i \in [l]$. Since we have $e(\hat{y}^{i-1}) = e'(\hat{y}^{i-1}) = \hat{x}_i$ for all $i \in [l]$, we obtain

$$\text{tr}(\mathsf{S}, e')(\hat{t}) = \mathsf{S}(\{s \mid s \in \text{dom}(\mathsf{S}), \forall i \in [l] : s(\hat{x}^i) = \hat{y}_i\}) = \text{tr}(\mathsf{S}, e)(\hat{t}) \text{ and}$$
$$\text{tr}(\mathsf{T}, e')(\hat{t}) = \mathsf{T}(\{s \mid s \in \text{dom}(\mathsf{T}), \forall i \in [l] : s(\hat{x}^i) = \hat{y}_i\}) = \text{tr}(\mathsf{T}, e)(\hat{t}).$$

Hence, $\text{tr}(\mathsf{S}, e')(\hat{t}) \neq \text{tr}(\mathsf{T}, e')(\hat{t})$ and therefore $\text{tr}(\mathsf{S}, e') \neq \text{tr}(\mathsf{T}, e')$, concluding the proof. □

Lemma 9. (cf. Lemma 3 of [12]). *For any two compatible PDS S, T and any probability distribution B over $\{0, 1\}$*

$$\text{Adv}(\langle \mathsf{S}/\mathsf{T} \rangle_\mathsf{B}, \mathsf{T}) = \mathsf{B}(0) \cdot \text{Adv}(\mathsf{S}, \mathsf{T}).$$

Proof. Observe that

$$\begin{aligned}
\text{Adv}^\mathsf{D}(\langle \mathsf{S}/\mathsf{T} \rangle_\mathsf{B}, \mathsf{T}) &= \text{Pr}^{\mathsf{DT}}(Z = 1) - \text{Pr}^{\mathsf{D}\langle \mathsf{S}/\mathsf{T} \rangle_\mathsf{B}}(Z = 1) \\
&= \mathsf{B}(0) \cdot \left(\text{Pr}^{\mathsf{DT}}(Z = 1) - \text{Pr}^{\mathsf{DS}}(Z = 1) \right) \\
&\quad + \mathsf{B}(1) \cdot \left(\text{Pr}^{\mathsf{DT}}(Z = 1) - \text{Pr}^{\mathsf{DT}}(Z = 1) \right) \\
&= \mathsf{B}(0) \cdot \left(\text{Pr}^{\mathsf{DT}}(Z = 1) - \text{Pr}^{\mathsf{DS}}(Z = 1) \right) \\
&= \mathsf{B}(0) \cdot \text{Adv}^\mathsf{D}(\mathsf{S}, \mathsf{T}).
\end{aligned}$$

□

Lemma 10. *Let $\xi_{l,m}$ for $l, m \in \mathbb{N} \setminus \{0\}$ be defined by*

$$\xi_{l,m} := \frac{1}{2} \cdot \left(1 + \sum_{j=l}^{m} \binom{m}{j} \cdot \binom{j-1}{l-1} \right).$$

Then,

(i)

$$\xi_{l,m} = 2 \cdot \xi_{l,m-1} + \xi_{l-1,m-1} - 1$$

(ii)

$$2^{m-l} \cdot \binom{m-1}{l-1} \in [\xi_{l,m}, 2\xi_{l,m} - 1].$$

Proof. Consider the expression $t_{l,m} := \sum_{j=l}^{m} \binom{m}{j} \binom{j-1}{l-1}$. Observe that $t_{l,m}$ is the number of possibilities to select a first subset of $[m]$ with size at least l and then selecting exactly $l - 1$ elements (but never the smallest one) of the first subset for a second subset. Consider the element $m \in [m]$. There are $t_{l-1,m-1}$ possibilities for it to be in the second subset (and thus also in the first), and $2t_{l,m-1}$ possibilities for it not to be in the second subset (either it is in the first subset or not). Thus, we have $t_{l,m} = 2t_{l,m-1} + t_{l-1,m-1}$.

We have $\xi_{l,m} = \frac{1}{2}(1 + t_{l,m})$, and therefore

$$
\begin{aligned}
2 \cdot \xi_{l,m-1} + \xi_{l-1,m-1} - 1 &= (1 + t_{l,m-1}) + \frac{1}{2}(1 + t_{l-1,m-1}) - 1 \\
&= \frac{1}{2}(1 + 2t_{l,m-1} + t_{l-1,m-1}) \\
&= \frac{1}{2}(1 + t_{l,m}) \\
&= \xi_{l,m}.
\end{aligned}
$$

The bound (iii) can be proved by induction over m. For $m = 1$ or $m = l$, the claim trivially holds. For $m > 1$ and $l < m$ we have (using (i))

$$
\begin{aligned}
\xi_{l,m} &= 2\xi_{l,m-1} + \xi_{l-1,m-1} - 1 \\
&\leq 2 \cdot 2^{m-1-l}\binom{m-2}{l-1} + 2^{m-l}\binom{m-2}{l-2} \\
&= 2^{m-l} \cdot \left(\binom{m-2}{l-1} + \binom{m-2}{l-2}\right) \\
&= 2^{m-l}\binom{m-1}{l-1}.
\end{aligned}
$$

Moreover,

$$
\begin{aligned}
2\xi_{l,m} - 1 &= 2\left(2\xi_{l,m-1} + \xi_{l-1,m-1} - 1\right) - 1 \\
&= 2(2\xi_{l,m-1} - 1) + (2\xi_{l-1,m-1} - 1) \\
&\geq 2 \cdot 2^{m-1-l}\binom{m-2}{l-1} + 2^{m-l}\binom{m-2}{l-2} \\
&= 2^{m-l} \cdot \left(\binom{m-2}{l-1} + \binom{m-2}{l-2}\right) \\
&= 2^{m-l}\binom{m-1}{l-1}.
\end{aligned}
$$

This concludes the proof.   □

References

1. Aldous, D.: Random walks on finite groups and rapidly mixing markov chains. In: Azéma, J., Yor, M. (eds.) Séminaire de Probabilités XVII 1981/82. LNM, vol. 986, pp. 243–297. Springer, Heidelberg (1983). https://doi.org/10.1007/BFb0068322
2. Bellare, M., Impagliazzo, R.: A tool for obtaining tighter security analyses of pseudorandom function based constructions, with applications to PRP to PRF conversion. IACR Crypt. ePrint Arch., 24 (1999). http://eprint.iacr.org/1999/024

3. Bellare, M., Rogaway, P.: The security of triple encryption and a framework for code-based game-playing proofs. In: Vaudenay, S. (ed.) EUROCRYPT 2006. LNCS, vol. 4004, pp. 409–426. Springer, Heidelberg (2006). https://doi.org/10.1007/11761679_25

4. Dai, W., Hoang, V.T., Tessaro, S.: Information-theoretic indistinguishability via the chi-squared method. In: Katz, J., Shacham, H. (eds.) CRYPTO 2017. LNCS, vol. 10403, pp. 497–523. Springer, Cham (2017). https://doi.org/10.1007/978-3-319-63697-9_17

5. Hall, C., Wagner, D., Kelsey, J., Schneier, B.: Building PRFs from PRPs. In: Krawczyk, H. (ed.) CRYPTO 1998. LNCS, vol. 1462, pp. 370–389. Springer, Heidelberg (1998). https://doi.org/10.1007/BFb0055742

6. Luby, M., Rackoff, C.: How to construct pseudorandom permutations from pseudorandom functions. SIAM J. Comput. $17(2)$, 373–386 (1988)

7. Lucks, S.: The sum of PRPs Is a secure PRF. In: Preneel, B. (ed.) EUROCRYPT 2000. LNCS, vol. 1807, pp. 470–484. Springer, Heidelberg (2000). https://doi.org/10.1007/3-540-45539-6_34

8. MacWilliams, F.J., Sloane, N.J.A.: The Theory of Error-Correcting Codes. No. 16 in North-Holland Mathematical Library, North-Holland Pub. Co. (1977)

9. Maurer, U.: Indistinguishability of random systems. In: Knudsen, L.R. (ed.) EUROCRYPT 2002. LNCS, vol. 2332, pp. 110–132. Springer, Heidelberg (2002). https://doi.org/10.1007/3-540-46035-7_8

10. Maurer, U.: Conditional equivalence of random systems and indistinguishability proofs. In: 2013 IEEE International Symposium on Information Theory Proceedings (ISIT), pp. 3150–3154, July 2013

11. Maurer, U., Pietrzak, K.: Composition of random systems: when two weak make one strong. In: Naor, M. (ed.) Theory of Cryptography, pp. 410–427. Springer, Heidelberg (2004). https://doi.org/10.1007/978-3-540-24638-1_23

12. Maurer, U., Pietrzak, K., Renner, R.: Indistinguishability amplification. In: Menezes, A. (ed.) CRYPTO 2007. LNCS, vol. 4622, pp. 130–149. Springer, Heidelberg (2007). https://doi.org/10.1007/978-3-540-74143-5_8

13. Maurer, U., Tessaro, S.: Computational indistinguishability amplification: tight product theorems for system composition. In: Halevi, S. (ed.) CRYPTO 2009. LNCS, vol. 5677, pp. 355–373. Springer, Heidelberg (2009). https://doi.org/10.1007/978-3-642-03356-8_21

14. Naor, M., Reingold, O.: On the construction of pseudo-random permutations: luby-rackoff revisited (extended abstract). In: Proceedings of the Twenty-Ninth Annual ACM Symposium on Theory of Computing, pp. 189–199. STOC 1997, Association for Computing Machinery, New York (1997). https://doi.org/10.1145/258533.258581

15. Patarin, J.: The "coefficients h" technique. In: Avanzi, R.M., Keliher, L., Sica, F. (eds.) Selected Areas in Cryptography, pp. 328–345. Springer, Heidelberg (2009). https://doi.org/10.1007/978-3-642-04159-4_21

16. Singleton, R.: Maximum distance q-nary codes. IEEE Trans. Inf. Theory $10(2)$, 116–118 (1964). https://doi.org/10.1109/TIT.1964.1053661

17. Tessaro, S.: Security amplification for the cascade of arbitrarily weak PRPs: tight bounds via the interactive hardcore lemma. In: Ishai, Y. (ed.) Theory of Cryptography, pp. 37–54. Springer, Heidelberg (2011). https://doi.org/10.1007/978-3-642-19571-6_3

18. Vaudenay, S.: Provable security for block ciphers by decorrelation. In: Morvan, M., Meinel, C., Krob, D. (eds.) STACS 1998. LNCS, vol. 1373, pp. 249–275. Springer, Heidelberg (1998). https://doi.org/10.1007/BFb0028566

19. Vaudenay, S.: Adaptive-attack norm for decorrelation and super-pseudorandomness. In: Heys, H., Adams, C. (eds.) SAC 1999. LNCS, vol. 1758, pp. 49–61. Springer, Heidelberg (2000). https://doi.org/10.1007/3-540-46513-8_4. http://dl.acm.org/citation.cfm?id=646555.694585

Towards Defeating Backdoored Random Oracles: Indifferentiability with Bounded Adaptivity

Yevgeniy Dodis[1], Pooya Farshim[2(✉)], Sogol Mazaheri[3], and Stefano Tessaro[4]

[1] New York University, New York, USA
dodis@cs.nyu.edu
[2] University of York, York, UK
pooya.farshim@gmail.com
[3] Technische Universität Darmstadt, Darmstadt, Germany
sogol.mazaheri@cryptoplexity.de
[4] University of Washington, Seattle, USA
tessaro@cs.washington.edu

Abstract. In the backdoored random-oracle (BRO) model, besides access to a random function H, adversaries are provided with a backdoor oracle that can compute arbitrary leakage functions f of the function table of H. Thus, an adversary would be able to invert points, find collisions, test for membership in certain sets, and more. This model was introduced in the work of Bauer, Farshim, and Mazaheri (Crypto 2018) and extends the auxiliary-input idealized models of Unruh (Crypto 2007), Dodis, Guo, and Katz (Eurocrypt 2017), Coretti et al. (Eurocrypt 2018), and Coretti, Dodis, and Guo (Crypto 2018). It was shown that certain security properties, such as one-wayness, pseudorandomness, and collision resistance can be re-established by combining two independent BROs, even if the adversary has access to both backdoor oracles.

In this work we further develop the technique of combining two or more independent BROs to render their backdoors useless in a more general sense. More precisely, we study the question of building an *indifferentiable* and backdoor-free random function by combining multiple BROs. Achieving full indifferentiability in this model seems very challenging at the moment. We however make progress by showing that the xor combiner goes well beyond security against preprocessing attacks and offers indifferentiability as long as the adaptivity of queries to different backdoor oracles remains logarithmic in the input size of the BROs. We even show that an extractor-based combiner of three BROs can achieve indifferentiability with respect to a linear adaptivity of backdoor queries. Furthermore, a natural restriction of our definition gives rise to a notion of *indifferentiability with auxiliary input*, for which we give two positive feasibility results.

To prove these results we build on and refine techniques by Göös et al. (STOC 2015) and Kothari et al. (STOC 2017) for decomposing distributions with high entropy into distributions with more structure and show how they can be applied in the more involved adaptive settings.

© International Association for Cryptologic Research 2020
R. Pass and K. Pietrzak (Eds.): TCC 2020, LNCS 12552, pp. 241–273, 2020.
https://doi.org/10.1007/978-3-030-64381-2_9

Keywords: Hash functions · Indifferentiability · Backdoors · Auxiliary input · Communication complexity

1   Introduction

Hash functions are one of the most fundamental building blocks in protocol design. For this reason, both the cryptanalysis and provable security of hash functions have been active areas of research in recent years. The first known instances of collisions and chosen-prefix collisions in SHA-1 were recently demonstrated by Stevens et al. [26] and Leurent and Peyrin [20], respectively. Furthermore, feasibility of built-in adversarial weaknesses (aka. backdoors) in efficient hash functions have been demonstrated by Fischlin, Janson, and Mazaheri [13]. A practical way to provide safeguards against similar failures of hash functions is to *combine* a number of independent hash functions so that the resulting function is at least as secure as their strongest. Most works in this area have focused attention on a setting where at least one of the hash functions is secure, although positive results when *all* underlying hash functions have weaknesses have also been demonstrated [15,22].

In this work we are interested in protecting hash functions against a variety of attacks that may arise due to backdoors, cryptanalytic advances, or preprocessing attacks. We carry out our study in the recent backdoored random-oracle (BRO) model, which uniformly treats these settings and also permits strong adversarial settings where all hash functions may be weak.

1.1   The BRO Model

Bauer, Farshim, and Mazaheri (BFM) [3] at Crypto 2018 formulated a new model for the analysis of hash functions that substantially weakens the traditional random-oracle (RO) model. Here an adversary, on top of direct access to the random oracle, is able to obtain arbitrary functions of the function table of the random oracle.[1] The implications of this weakening are manifold. To start with, positive results in this model imply positive results in the traditional setting where all but one of the hash functions is weak. Second, this model captures arbitrary preprocessing attacks on hash functions, another highly active area of research [6,7,10,27]. Finally, it allows to model unrestricted adversarial capabilities, which can adaptively depend on input instances, and thus captures built-in as well as inadvertent weaknesses that may or may not be discovered in course of time.

BFM studied three natural combiners in this setting: those of concatenation, cascade, and xor combiners:

$$\mathsf{C}_\mathsf{|}^{\mathsf{H}_1,\mathsf{H}_2}(x) := \mathsf{H}_1(x)|\mathsf{H}_2(x) \qquad\qquad \mathsf{C}_\mathsf{o}^{\mathsf{H}_1,\mathsf{H}_2}(x) := \mathsf{H}_2(\mathsf{H}_1(x))$$

---

[1] The model allows for a parameterization of the class of functions that can be computed. Both BFM and we here work with respect to the full set of functions.

$$\mathsf{C}_\oplus^{\mathsf{H}_1,\mathsf{H}_2}(x) := \mathsf{H}_1(x) \oplus \mathsf{H}_2(x) .$$

They showed, using new types of reductions to problems with high communication complexity, that central cryptographic security properties, such as one-way security, pseudorandomness, and collision resistance are indeed achievable by these combiners.

The reductions to communication complexity problems are at times tedious and very specific to the combiner. Moreover, the hardness of the communication complexity problem underlying collision resistance is conjectural and still remains to be proven. Furthermore, a number of deployed protocols have only been shown to be secure in the random-oracle model, and thus may rely on properties beyond one-wayness, pseudorandomness, or collision resistance.

This raises the question whether or not other cryptographic properties expected from a good hash function are also met by these combiners. In other words: *Can combining two or more backdoored random oracles render access to independent but adaptive auxiliary information useless?* We formalize and study this question in the indifferentiability framework, which has been immensely successful in justifying the soundness of hash-function designs.

1.2   Indifferentiability

A common paradigm in the design of hash functions is to start with some underlying primitive, and through some construction build a more complex one. The provable security of such constructions have been analyzed through two main approaches. One formulates specific goals (such as collision resistance) and goes on to show that the construction satisfies them if its underlying primitives satisfy their own specific security properties. Another is a general approach, whose goal is to show that a (wide) class of security goals are simultaneously met.

The latter has been formalized in a number of frameworks, notably in the UC framework of Canetti [5], the reactive systems framework of Pfitzmann and Waidner [24], and the indifferentiability framework of Maurer, Renner, and Holenstein [23]. The latter is by now a standard methodology to study the soundness of cryptographic constructions, particularly symmetric ones such as hash functions [4,8] and block-ciphers [1,9,12,16] in idealized models of computation.

In the MRH framework, a public primitive H is available and the goal is to build another primitive, say a random oracle RO, from H through a construction C^H. Indifferentiability formalizes a set of necessary and sufficient conditions for the construction C^H to securely replace its ideal counterpart RO in a wide range of environments: for a *simulator* Sim, the systems $(\mathsf{C}^\mathsf{H}, \mathsf{H})$ and $(\mathsf{RO}, \mathsf{Sim}^\mathsf{RO})$ should be indistinguishable. The composition theorem proved by MRH states that, if C^H is indifferentiable from RO, then C^H can securely replace RO in arbitrary single-stage contexts. A central corollary of this composition theorem is that indifferentiability implies any single-stage security goal, which includes among others, one-wayness, collision resistance, PRG/PRF security, and more.

1.3 Contributions

With the above terminology in hand, the central question tackled in this work is whether or not combiners that are *indifferentiable* from a conventional (backdoor-free) random oracle exist, when the underlying primitives are two (or more) backdoored random oracles.

Let us consider the concatenation combiner $H_1(x)|H_2(x)$, where H_1 and H_2 are both backdoored. This construction was shown to be one-way, collision resistant, and PRG secure if both underlying functions are highly compressing. Despite this, the concatenation combiner cannot be indifferentiable from a random oracle: using the backdoor oracle for H_1 an attacker can compute two inputs x and x' such that $H_1(x) = H_1(x')$, query them to the construction and return 1 iff the left sides of the outputs match. However, any simulator attempting to find such a pair with respect to a backdoor-free random oracle must place an exponentially large number of queries. Attacks on the cascade combiner $H_2(H_1(x))$ were also given in [3, Section D.2] for a wider range of parameter regimes, leaving only the expand-then-compress case as potentially indifferentiable. Finally, the xor combiner $H_1(x) \oplus H_2(x)$, which is simpler, more efficient, and one of the most common ways to combine hash functions, resists these.[2]

DECOMPOSITION OF DISTRIBUTIONS. When proving results in the presence of auxiliary input, Uhruh [27] observed that pre-computation (or leakage) on a random oracle can reveal a significant amount of information only on restricted parts of its support. The problem of dealing with auxiliary input was later revised in a number of works [6,7,10]. In particular Coretti et al. [7], building on work in communication complexity, employed a *pre-sampling technique* to prove a number of positive results in the RO model with auxiliary input with tighter bounds. At a high level, this method permits writing a high min-entropy distribution (here, over a set of functions) as the convex combination of a (large) number of distributions which are fixed on a certain number (p) of points and highly unpredictable on the rest, the so-called $(p, 1 - \delta)$-dense distributions. This technique was originally introduced in the work of Göös et al. [14].

THE SIMULATOR. Our simulator for the xor combiner builds on this technique to decompose distributions into a convex combination of $(p, 1 - \delta)$-dense distributions. Simulation of backdoor oracles is arguably quite natural and proceeds as follows. Starting with uniform random oracles H_1 and H_2, on each backdoor query f for H_1 the simulator computes $z = f(H_1)$ and updates the distribution of the random oracle H_1 to be uniform conditioned on the output of f being z. This distribution is then decomposed into a convex combination of $(p, 1 - \delta)$-dense distributions, from which one function is sampled. For all of the p fixed points, the simulator sets the value of H_2 consistently with the random oracle and the distribution of H_2 is updated accordingly. An analogous procedure is implemented as the simulator for the second backdoored random oracle.

---

[2] Further, an indifferentiability proof of the expand-then-compress cascade combiner would closely follow that of the xor combiner and thus we focus on the latter here.

TECHNICAL ANALYSIS. The first technical contribution of our work is a refinement of the decomposition technique which can be used to *adaptively* decompose distributions after backdoor queries. We show that this refinement is sufficiently powerful to allow proving indifferentiability up to a logarithmic (in the input size of the BROs) number of switches between the backdoor queries. We prove this via a sequence of games which are carefully designed so as to be compatible with the decomposition technique. A key observation is that in contrast to previous works in the AI-RO model, we do not replace the dense (intuitively, unpredictable) part of the distribution of random oracles with uniform: backdoor functions "see" the entire table of the random oracle and this replacement would result in a noticeable change. Second, we modify the number of fixed points in the (partially) dense distributions so that progressively smaller sets of points are fixed. Even though each leakage corresponds to fixing a large number of points, it is proportionally smaller than the previous number of fixed points. Thus the overall bound remains small.

SIMULATOR EFFICIENCY. Our simulator runs in doubly exponential time in the bit-length of the random oracle and thus is of use in information-theoretic settings. These include the vast majority of symmetric constructions. Protocols based on computational assumptions (such as public-key encryption) escape this treatment: the overall adversary obtained via the composition would run the decomposition algorithm and hence will not be poly-time. This observation, however, also applies to the BRO model as the backdoor oracles also allow for non-polynomial time computation, trivially breaking any computational assumption if unrestricted. Despite this, in a setting where the computational assumption holds relative to the backdoor oracles, positive results may hold. We can for example restrict the backdoor capability to achieve this. Another promising avenue is to rely on an independent idealized model such as the generic-group model (GGM) and for instance, prove IND-CCA security of Hashed ElGamal in the BRO and (backdoor-free) GGM models. We leave exploring these solutions to future work.

AN EXTRACTOR-BASED COMBINER WITH IMPROVED SECURITY. We apply the above proof technique to the analysis of an alternative combiner for three independent backdoored random oracles, which relies on 2-out-of-3-source extractors that output good randomness as long as two out of the three of the inputs have sufficient min-entropy. Given such an extractor Ext, our combiner is

$$\mathsf{C}_{3\mathsf{ext}}^{\mathsf{H}_1,\mathsf{H}_2,\mathsf{H}_3}(x) := \mathsf{Ext}\big(\mathsf{H}_1(x),\mathsf{H}_2(x),\mathsf{H}_3(x)\big) .$$

As mentioned above, our simulator for the xor combiner programs H_2 on the fixed points for H_1 (and vice versa) using the random oracle. This results in a loss since dense values are replaced with uniform values. In contrast, here the extractor ensures that image values are closer to uniform and thus the overall loss is lower. We show that a 2-out-of-3-source extractor can tolerate even a number of switches between the backdoor oracles which is slightly sub-linear in the size of the BRO inputs. This gives us more hope for unbounded adaptivity, in case improved decomposition techniques are found.

COMPOSITION. Let c denote the number of times the adversary switches between one backdoor oracle to the other. Regarding the query complexities of our simulators, each query to the backdoor oracle translates to roughly $N^{1-2^{-c}}$ queries to the random oracle for the xor combiner and roughly $N^{1-3/(c+1)}/\log M$ queries to the random oracle for the extractor combiner. This in particular means that, for a wide range of parameters, composition is only meaningful with respect to security notions whereby the random oracle can tolerate a large number of queries. This, for example, would be the case for one-way, PRG, and PRF security notions where the security bounds are of the form $\mathcal{O}(q/N)$. However, with respect to a smaller number of switches (as well as in the auxiliary-input setting with no adaptivity), collision resistance can still be achieved.

INDIFFERENTIABILITY WITH AUXILIARY INPUT. When our definition of indifferentiability is restricted so that only a single backdoor query to each hash function at the onset is allowed, we obtain a notion that formalizes *indifferentiability with auxiliary input*. This definition is interesting as it is sufficiently strong to allow for the generic replacement of random oracles with iterative constructions even in the presence of preprocessing attacks. Accordingly, our positive results in the BRO model when considered with no adaptivity translate to indifferentiability with independent preprocessing attacks. To complement this picture, we also discuss the case of auxiliary-input indifferentiability with a single BRO and show, as expected, that a salted indifferentiable construction is also indifferentiable with auxiliary input.

OPEN PROBLEMS. In order to overcome the bounded adaptivity restriction and prove full indifferentiability, one would require an improved decomposition technique which fixes considerably less points after each leakage. This, at the moment, seems (very) challenging and is left as an open question. In particular, such a result would simultaneously give new proofs of known communication complexity lower bounds for a host of problems, such as set-disjointness and intersection, potentially a proof of the conjecturally hard problem stated in [3], and many others. (We note that improved decomposition techniques can potentially also translate to improved bounds.) Indeed the xor combiner may achieve security well beyond what we establish here (and indeed the original work of BFM does so for specific games). Finally, as the extractor combiner suggests, the form of the combiner and the number of underlying BROs can also affect the overall bounds.

2   Preliminaries

Throughout the paper, when we write $[N]$ for any uppercase letter N, we use the convention that N is an integer and a power of two, i.e., $N = 2^n$ for some $n \in \mathbb{N}$. Let $[N] := \{0, \ldots, N-1\}$ denote the set of all n-bit strings. We use $[M]^N$ to denote the set of all bit-strings of length $N \cdot \log M$, which corresponds to the set of all functions $\mathsf{F} : [N] \to [M]$. We denote the uniform distribution over an arbitrary finite set S by $\mathcal{U}_S$.

For $\mathsf{F} \in [M]^N$ and $I \subseteq [N]$ we denote by F_I the projection of F onto the points in I. Let μ be a probability density function over $[M]^N$. We define $\mu(D) := \Pr_{\mathsf{F} \sim \mu}[\mathsf{F} \in D]$ as the probability that a sample randomly drawn from μ falls into the domain $D \subseteq [M]^N$. By $\mu|_D$ we denote the density μ conditioned on the domain D. For a function $f : [M]^N \rightarrow \{0,1\}^\ell$ and $z \in \{0,1\}^\ell$, by $\mu|_{f(\cdot)=z}$ we denote μ conditioned on $f(\mathsf{F}) = z$ for all $\mathsf{F} \sim \mu|_{f(\cdot)=z}$.

For a set of assignments $A \subseteq \{(a,b) : (a,b) \in [N] \times [M]\}$, by $\mu|_A$ we denote μ conditioned on $\mathsf{F}_{\{a\}} = b$ for all $(a,b) \in A$ and all $\mathsf{F} \sim \mu|_A$. We further let $A_{.1} \subseteq [N]$ (resp. $A_{.2} \subseteq [M]$) denote the set containing the first (resp. second) coordinates of all elements in A.

For an algorithm Alg we denote by $\mathsf{Alg}[param](input)$ a call of the algorithm with (constant) parameters $param$ and variable inputs $input$. This is to increase clarity among multiple calls to the algorithm about the main input, while the parameters remain unchanged.

2.1 Backdoored Random Oracles

We recall the definition of the backdoored random-oracle model from [3]. The $\mathsf{BRO}(N_1, M_1, \ldots, N_k, M_k)$ model (for some $k \in \mathbb{N}$) defines a setting where all parties have access to k functions $\mathsf{H}_1, \ldots, \mathsf{H}_k$, where H_i's are chosen uniformly and independently at random from $[M_i]^{N_i}$, while the adversarial parties also have access to the corresponding backdoor oracles BD_i's. A backdoor oracle BD_i can be queried on functions f and return $f(\mathsf{H}_i)$. If for all $i \in [k]$ we have $N_i = N$ and $M_i = M$, we simply refer to this model as $k\text{-}\mathsf{BRO}(N, M)$ and when N and M are clear from the context, we simply use $k\text{-}\mathsf{BRO}$.

These models may be weakened by restricting the adversary to query BD_i only on functions f in some capability class $\mathcal{F}_i$. However our results as well as those in [3] hold for arbitrary backdoor capabilities. In other words an adversary can (adaptively) query arbitrary functions f to any of the backdoor oracles.

2.2 Indifferentiability in the BRO Model

We follow the indifferentiability framework of Maurer, Renner, and Holenstein (MRH) [23]. Here the underlying honest interfaces are k random oracles H_i and respective adversarial interfaces BD_i. We define the advantage of a differentiator $\mathcal{D}$ with respect to a construction $\mathsf{C}^{\mathsf{H}_i}$ and a simulator $\mathsf{Sim}^{\mathsf{RO}} := (\mathsf{SimH}_i^{\mathsf{RO}}, \mathsf{SimBD}_i^{\mathsf{RO}})$ as

$$\mathsf{Adv}_{\mathsf{C}^{\mathsf{H}_i}, \mathsf{Sim}}^{\mathrm{indiff}}(\mathcal{D}) := \left| \Pr\left[\mathcal{D}^{\mathsf{C}^{\mathsf{H}_i}, \mathsf{H}_i, \mathrm{BD}_i}\right] - \Pr\left[\mathcal{D}^{\mathsf{RO}, \mathsf{SimH}_i^{\mathsf{RO}}, \mathsf{SimBD}_i^{\mathsf{RO}}}\right] \right|,$$

where RO is a random oracle whose domain and co-domain match those of C.

We emphasize that the simulators do not get access to any backdoor oracles. This ensures that any attack against a construction with backdoors translates to one against the underlying random oracles *without* any backdoors.

2.3   Randomness Extractors

Let X be a random variable. The min-entropy of X is defined as $\mathbf{H}_\infty(X) := -\log \max_x \Pr[X = x]$. The random variable X is called a (weak) k-source if $\mathbf{H}_\infty(X) \geq k$, i.e., $\Pr[X = x] \leq 2^{-k}$. The min-entropy of a distribution typically determines how many bits can be extracted from it which are close to uniform. The notion of closeness is formalized by the statistical distance. For two random variables X and Y over a common support D, their statistical distance is defined as $\mathrm{SD}(X, Y) := \frac{1}{2} \sum_{z \in D} |\Pr[X = z] - \Pr[Y = z]|$.

In this paper we are interested in extractors that do not require seeds but rather rely on multiple weak sources.

Definition 1 (Multi-source extractors). *An efficient function* $\mathsf{Ext} : [N_1] \times \ldots \times [N_t] \to [M]$ *is a* $(k_1, \ldots, k_t, \varepsilon)$-*extractor if for all weak* k_i-*sources* X_i *over domains* $[N_i]$, *we have:*

$$\mathrm{SD}\big(\mathsf{Ext}(X_1, \ldots, X_t), \mathcal{U}_{[M]}\big) \leq \varepsilon \ ,$$

where ε *is usually defined as a function of* $k_1, \ldots, k_t$. *We call* Ext *an* s-*out-of-*t $(k_1, \ldots, k_t, \varepsilon)$-*extractor if* $\mathsf{Ext}(X_1, \ldots, X_t)$ *is* ε-*close to uniform even if only* s *sources fulfill the min-entropy condition.*

Below we define useful classes of distributions, the so-called (partially) dense distributions, resp. dense probability density functions. Intuitively, bit strings from a dense distribution are unpredictable not only as a whole but also in any of their substrings and any combination of those substrings.

Definition 2 (Dense distributions). *Let* μ *be a probability density function over* $[M]^N$. *Then*

- μ *is called* $(1 - \delta)$-*dense if for* $\mathsf{F} \sim \mu$, *it holds that for every subset* $I \subseteq [N]$ *we have* $\mathbf{H}_\infty(\mathsf{F}_I) \geq (1 - \delta) \cdot |I| \cdot \log M$.
- μ *is called* $(p, 1 - \delta)$-*dense if for* $\mathsf{F} \sim \mu$ *there exists a set* $I \subseteq [N]$ *of size* $|I| \leq p$ *such that* $\mathbf{H}_\infty(\mathsf{F}_I) = 0$, *while for every subset* $J \subseteq [N] \setminus I$ *we have* $\mathbf{H}_\infty(\mathsf{F}_J) \geq (1 - \delta) \cdot |J| \cdot \log M$. *That is,* μ *is fixed on at most* p *coordinates and* $(1 - \delta)$-*dense on the rest.*

We call a distribution dense, if the corresponding density function is dense.

3   Decomposition of High Min-Entropy Distributions

Any high min-entropy distribution can be written as a convex combination of distributions that are fixed on a number of points and dense on the rest (i.e., $(p, 1 - \delta)$-dense distributions for some p and $\delta > 0$).[3] The decomposition technique introduced by Göös et al. [14] has its origins in communication complexity

---

[3] A convex combination of distributions $\mu_1, \ldots, \mu_n$ is a distribution that can be written as $\alpha_1 \cdot \mu_1 + \ldots + \alpha_n \cdot \mu_n$, where $\alpha_1, \ldots, \alpha_n$ are non-negative real numbers that sum up to 1.

theory. We generalize this technique, with a terminology closer to that of Kothari et al. [18], in order to allow for adaptive leakage. The original lemma, also used by Coretti et al. [7], can be easily derived as a special case of our lemma. For this, one assumes that the starting distribution before the leakage was uniform, in other words $(0, 1)$-dense.

When proving results in the auxiliary-input random-oracle (AI-RO) model, Uhruh [27] observed that pre-computation (or leakage) on a random oracle can cause a significant decrease of its min-entropy only on restricted parts of its support (i.e., on p points), causing that part to become practically fixed, while the rest remains indistinguishable from random to a bounded-query distinguisher. This means that after fixing p coordinates of the random oracle, the rest can be lazily sampled from a uniform distribution. Coretti et al. [7] recently gave a different and tighter proof consisting of two main steps. First, the decomposition technique is used to show that the distribution of a random oracle given some leakage is *statistically* close to a $(p, 1 - \delta)$-dense distribution. Second, they prove that no *bounded-query* algorithm can distinguish a $(p, 1 - \delta)$-dense distribution from one that is fixed on the same p points and is otherwise uniform (a so-called p-bit-fixing distribution), as suggested by Unruh [27].

Since in the BRO model adaptive queries are allowed, a function queried to the backdoor oracle is able to "see" the entire random oracle, rather than a restricted part of it. Hence, when analyzing the distribution of a random oracle after adaptive leakage, it is crucial that we keep the distributions *statistically close*. In other words we use $(p, 1 - \delta)$-dense distributions instead of p-bit-fixing.

In the k-BRO model, we are concerned with multiple queries to the backdoor oracles, i.e., continuous and adaptive leakage that can depend on previously leaked information about both hash functions. Intuitively, since the leakage function can be arbitrary, it can in particular depend on the previously leaked values. We still need to argue that the distribution obtained after leakage about a $(p_{\mathrm{prv}}, 1 - \delta_{\mathrm{prv}})$ distribution, which is not necessarily uniform, is also close to a convex combination of $(p, 1 - \delta)$ distributions. Naturally, we have $\delta \geq \delta_{\mathrm{prv}}$, since min-entropy decreases after new leakage, and $p \geq p_{\mathrm{prv}}$, since additional points are fixed. Looking ahead, in the indifferentiability proofs, this refined decomposition lemma allows us to simply fix a new portion p_{frsh} of the simulated hash function after each leakage (i.e., backdoor query) and not to worry about the rest, which still has high entropy and can be lazily sampled (from a dense distribution) upon receiving the next query.

Lemma 1 (Refined decomposition after leakage). *Let μ be a $(p_{\mathrm{prv}}, 1 - \delta_{\mathrm{prv}})$-dense density function over $[M]^N$ for some $p_{\mathrm{prv}}, \delta_{\mathrm{prv}} \geq 0$. Let $f : [M]^N \to \{0, 1\}^\ell$ be an arbitrary function and $z \in \{0, 1\}^\ell$ be a bit string. Then for any $p_{\mathrm{frsh}}, \gamma > 0$, the density function conditioned on the leakage $\mu|_{f(\cdot)=z}$ is γ-close to a convex combination of finitely many $(p, 1 - \delta)$-dense density functions for some p and δ such that*

$$p_{\mathrm{prv}} \leq p \leq p_{\mathrm{prv}} + p_{\mathrm{frsh}} \quad and \quad \delta_{\mathrm{prv}} \leq \delta \leq \frac{\delta_{\mathrm{prv}} \cdot \log M \cdot (N - p_{\mathrm{prv}}) + \ell_z + \log \gamma^{-1}}{p_{\mathrm{frsh}} \cdot \log M},$$

where $\ell_z := \mathbf{H}_\infty(\mathsf{G}) - \mathbf{H}_\infty(\mathsf{F})$ *is the min-entropy deficiency of* $\mathsf{F} \sim \mu|_{f(\cdot)=z}$ *compared to* $\mathsf{G} \sim \mu$.

Proof. This refined decomposition lemma differs from the original lemma in that the starting density function μ is $(p_{\mathrm{prv}}, 1 - \delta_{\mathrm{prv}})$-dense. As a first step, we modify the original decomposition algorithm from [14,18] so that it additionally gets the set of p_{prv} indices $I_{\mathrm{prv}} \subseteq [N]$ that are already fixed in μ from the start.

Our refined decomposition algorithm RefinedDecomp, given below, recursively decomposes the domain $[M]^N$, according to the density function after leakage $\mu_z := \mu|_{f(\cdot)=z}$, into $d + 1$ partitions $D_1, \ldots, D_d, D_{\mathrm{err}} \subseteq [M]^N$ such that $\left(\bigcup_{i=1}^d D_i \right) \cup D_{\mathrm{err}} = [M]^N$, where err stands for erroneous. For all i with $1 \le i \le d$ the partition D_i defines a $(p, 1 - \delta)$-dense density function $\mu_z|_{D_i}$.

Each recursive call on a domain D to RefinedDecomp (other than the call leading to D_{err}, which we will discuss shortly) returns a pair (D_i, I_i), where D_i represents a subset of $[M]^N$, where the images of all points in the set $I_i \subset [N]$ are fixed to the same values under all functions $\mathsf{H} \in D_i$. In other words, we have $\mathsf{H}_{I_i} = \alpha_i$ for some $\alpha_i \in [M]^{|I_i|}$. The algorithm finds such a pair (D_i, I_i) by considering the biggest set I_i (excluding those points fixed from the start, i.e., I_{prv}) such that the min-entropy of F_{I_i} (for $\mathsf{F} \sim \mu_z|_D$) is too small (as determined by the rate δ) and then finding some α_i which is a very likely value of F_{I_i}. Then I_i is returned with some D_i as the partition that contains all H with $\mathsf{H}_{I_i} = \alpha_i$. The next recursive call will exclude D_i from the considered domain.

Decomposition halts either if the probability of a sample falling into the current domain is smaller than γ (i.e., $\mu_z(D) \le \gamma$) or the current distribution is already $(p_{\mathrm{prv}}, 1 - \delta)$-dense. In both cases the algorithm returns the current domain D together with an empty set. In the former case the returned domain is marked as an erroneous domain $D_{\mathrm{err}} := D$, since it may not define a $(p, 1 - \delta)$-dense distribution. Let us without loss of generality assume that μ_z is not $(p_{\mathrm{prv}} + p_{\mathrm{frsh}}, 1 - \delta)$-dense, as otherwise the claim holds trivially.

The formal definition of the algorithm RefinedDecomp is given below. We initialize the desired density rate as $\delta := \frac{\delta_{\mathrm{prv}} \cdot \log M \cdot (N - p_{\mathrm{prv}}) + \ell_z + \log \gamma^{-1}}{p_{\mathrm{frsh}} \cdot \log M}$ before calling RefinedDecomp.

RefinedDecomp$[\mu_z, \delta, \gamma, I_{\mathrm{prv}}](D)$

if $\mu_z(D) \le \gamma$ **then return** $(D_{\mathrm{err}} \leftarrow D, \emptyset)$

if $\mu_z|_D$ is $(|I_{\mathrm{prv}}|, 1 - \delta)$-dense **then return** $(D, \emptyset)$

for $\mathsf{F} \sim \mu_z|_D$ let $I \subseteq [N]$ be a maximal set such that
$$\mathbf{H}_\infty(\mathsf{F}_I) < (1 - \delta) \cdot |I| \cdot \log M \quad \text{and} \quad I \cap I_{\mathrm{prv}} = \emptyset.$$

let $\alpha \in [M]^{|I|}$ be such that $\Pr[\mathsf{F}_I = \alpha] > 2^{-(1-\delta) \cdot |I| \cdot \log M}$.

$D_\alpha \leftarrow D \cap \{\mathsf{F} \in [M]^N \mid \mathsf{F}_I = \alpha\}$

$D_{\ne \alpha} \leftarrow D \cap \{\mathsf{F} \in [M]^N \mid \mathsf{F}_I \ne \alpha\}$

return $((D_\alpha, I), \mathsf{RefinedDecomp}[\mu_z, \delta, \gamma, I_{\mathrm{prv}}](D_{\ne \alpha}))$

Now we turn our attention to proving that every partition D_i (other than D_{err}) returned by the above decomposition algorithm defines a density function $\mu_z|_{D_i}$ which is $(p, 1 - \delta)$-dense.

Claim 1. *For all values of i with $1 \leq i \leq d$ it holds that the density function $\mu_z|_{D_i}$ is $(p, 1 - \frac{\delta_{\mathrm{prv}} \cdot \log M \cdot (N - p_{\mathrm{prv}}) + \ell_z + \log \gamma^{-1}}{p_{\mathrm{frsh}} \cdot \log M})$-dense, where $p_{\mathrm{prv}} \leq p \leq p_{\mathrm{prv}} + p_{\mathrm{frsh}}$.*

Proof. Let $\delta := \frac{\delta_{\mathrm{prv}} \cdot \log M \cdot (N - p_{\mathrm{prv}}) + \ell_z + \log \gamma^{-1}}{p_{\mathrm{frsh}} \cdot \log M}$. Let I be the set of freshly fixed points in $\mu_z|_{D_i}$ and $\overline{I \cup I_{\mathrm{prv}}} := [N] \setminus (I \cup I_{\mathrm{prv}})$. Let $\alpha_{\cup} \in [N]^{|I \cup I_{\mathrm{prv}}|}$ be such that $\mathsf{F}_{I \cup I_{\mathrm{prv}}} = \alpha_{\cup}$ for $\mathsf{F} \sim \mu_z|_{D_i}$. We first argue for the $(1 - \delta)$-density of $\mu_z|_{D_i}$ on values projected to $\overline{I \cup I_{\mathrm{prv}}}$ and afterwards bound the size of I.

1. Suppose $\mu_z|_{D_i}$ is not $(1 - \delta)$-dense on $\overline{I \cup I_{\mathrm{prv}}}$. Then there exists a non-empty set which violates the density property. That is, there exists a non-empty set $J \subseteq \overline{I \cup I_{\mathrm{prv}}}$ and some $\beta \in [N]^{|J|}$ such that, with the probability taken over $\mathsf{F} \sim \mu_z|_{D_i}$, we have:

$$\Pr[\mathsf{F}_J = \beta] > 2^{-(1-\delta) \cdot |J| \cdot \log M}.$$

Now the union of the three sets $I^* := I \cup I_{\mathrm{prv}} \cup J$ forms a new set such that for some $\beta^* \in [N]^{|I \cup I_{\mathrm{prv}} \cup J|}$ we have

$$\begin{aligned}
\Pr[\mathsf{F}_{I^*} = \beta^*] &= \Pr[\mathsf{F}_{I \cup I_{\mathrm{prv}}} = \alpha_{\cup} \wedge \mathsf{F}_J = \beta] \\
&= \Pr[\mathsf{F}_{I \cup I_{\mathrm{prv}}} = \alpha_{\cup}] \cdot \Pr[\mathsf{F}_J = \beta | \mathsf{F}_{I \cup I_{\mathrm{prv}}} = \alpha_{\cup}] \\
&> 2^{-(1-\delta) \cdot |I \cup I_{\mathrm{prv}}| \cdot \log M} \cdot 2^{-(1-\delta) \cdot |J| \cdot \log M} \\
&= 2^{-(1-\delta) \cdot |I \cup I_{\mathrm{prv}} \cup J| \cdot \log M}.
\end{aligned}$$

Since J was assumed to be non-empty and disjoint from $I \cup I_{\mathrm{prv}}$ (and in particular with I), its existence violates the maximality of I. Therefore, $\mathsf{F}_{\overline{I \cup I_{\mathrm{prv}}}}$ is $(1 - \delta)$ dense.

2. We now bound the size of I, given that $\delta = \frac{\delta_{\mathrm{prv}} \cdot \log M \cdot (N - p_{\mathrm{prv}}) + \ell_z + \log \gamma^{-1}}{p_{\mathrm{frsh}} \cdot \log M}$. Let $\mathsf{F} \sim \mu_z$ and $\mathsf{G} \sim \mu$. We have $\mathbf{H}_\infty(\mathsf{F}) = \mathbf{H}_\infty(\mathsf{G}) - \ell_z \geq (1 - \delta_{\mathrm{prv}}) \cdot (N - p_{\mathrm{prv}}) \cdot \log M - \ell_z$, where the inequality holds, since μ is $(1 - \delta_{\mathrm{prv}})$-dense in $N - p_{\mathrm{prv}}$ rows. Let $\beta \in [M]^{|I|}$. Then we have:

$$\begin{aligned}
\Pr_{\mu_z|_{D_i}}[\mathsf{F}_I = \beta] &\leq \Pr_{\mu_z}[\mathsf{F}_I = \beta]/\mu_z(D_i) \\
&\leq \Pr_{\mu_z}[\mathsf{F}_I = \beta]/\gamma \\
&= \sum_{\beta' \in [M]^{N-|I|-|I_{\mathrm{prv}}|}} \Pr_{\mu_z}[\mathsf{F}_I = \beta \wedge \mathsf{F}_{[N] \setminus (I \cup I_{\mathrm{prv}})} = \beta']/\gamma \\
&\leq 2^{(N-|I|-p_{\mathrm{prv}}) \cdot \log M} \cdot 2^{-\mathbf{H}_\infty(\mathsf{F})}/\gamma \\
&\leq 2^{(N-|I|-p_{\mathrm{prv}}) \cdot \log M} \cdot 2^{-((1-\delta_{\mathrm{prv}}) \cdot (N-p_{\mathrm{prv}}) \cdot \log M - \ell_z)}/\gamma \\
&= 2^{\delta_{\mathrm{prv}} \cdot N \cdot \log M - \delta_{\mathrm{prv}} \cdot p_{\mathrm{prv}} \cdot \log M - |I| \cdot \log M + \ell_z}/\gamma \\
&= 2^{\delta_{\mathrm{prv}} \cdot \log M \cdot (N - p_{\mathrm{prv}}) - |I| \cdot \log M + \ell_z + \log \gamma^{-1}}.
\end{aligned}$$

Since by definition of the decomposition algorithm, there exists an $\alpha \in [M]^I$ such that $\mathrm{Pr}_{\mu_z|D_i}[\mathsf{F}_I = \alpha] > 2^{-(1-\delta)\cdot|I|\cdot\log M}$, we obtain

$$|I| \leq \frac{\delta_{\mathrm{prv}} \cdot \log M \cdot (N - p_{\mathrm{prv}}) + \ell_z + \log \gamma^{-1}}{\delta \cdot \log M}.$$

Substituting δ by $\frac{\delta_{\mathrm{prv}}\cdot\log M\cdot(N-p_{\mathrm{prv}})+\ell_z+\log\gamma^{-1}}{p_{\mathrm{frsh}}\cdot\log M}$, we obtain $|I| \leq p_{\mathrm{frsh}}$ and therefore, for the total number of fixed points $p := |I \cup I_{\mathrm{prv}}|$ we get $p_{\mathrm{prv}} \leq p \leq p_{\mathrm{prv}} + p_{\mathrm{frsh}}$, as stated in the claim.

□

Therefore, μ_z can be written as a convex combination of $\mu_z|D_1, \ldots, \mu_z|D_d$ and $\mu_z|D_{\mathrm{err}}$, i.e., $\mu_z = \sum_{i=1}^d \mu_z(D_i) \cdot \mu_z|D_i + \mu_z(D_{\mathrm{err}}) \cdot \mu_z|D_{\mathrm{err}}$. Since $\mu_z(D_{\mathrm{err}}) \leq \gamma$ when the algorithm RefinedDecomp terminates, the distribution μ_z is γ-close to a convex combination of $(p, 1 - \delta)$ distributions. □

A special case of the above lemma for a uniform (i.e., $(0, 1)$-dense) starting distribution μ, where $p_{\mathrm{prv}} = 0$ and $\delta_{\mathrm{prv}} = 0$, implies the bound $\delta \leq (\ell_z + \log \gamma^{-1})/(p_{\mathrm{frsh}} \cdot \log M)$ used by Coretti et al. [7].

REMARK. Note that the coefficient of δ_{prv} in the right hand side of the inequality established in the lemma is of the order $\mathcal{O}(N/p_{\mathrm{frsh}})$. Looking ahead (see discussions on parameter estimation) this results in an increase in the number of points that the simulator needs to set. Thus any improvement in the bound established in this lemma would translate to tolerating a higher level of adaptivity and/or obtaining an improved bound.

Below we show that the expected min-entropy deficiency after leaking ℓ bits of information can be upper-bounded by ℓ bits.

Lemma 2. *Let F be a random variable over $[M]^N$ and $f : [M]^N \rightarrow \{0, 1\}^\ell$ be an arbitrary function. Let $\ell_z := \mathbf{H}_\infty(\mathsf{F}) - \mathbf{H}_\infty(\mathsf{F}|f(\mathsf{F}) = z)$ be the min-entropy deficiency of $\mathsf{F}|f(\mathsf{F}) = z$. Then, we have $\mathbb{E}_{z \in f(\mathrm{supp}(\mathsf{F}))}[\ell_z] \leq \ell$.*

Proof. Recall that $\widetilde{\mathbf{H}}_\infty(A|B) := -\log\left(\mathbb{E}_b[\max_a \mathrm{Pr}[A = a|B = b]]\right)$ defines the average min-entropy of A, given B.

$$\begin{aligned}
\mathbb{E}_{z \in f(\mathrm{supp}(\mathsf{F}))}[\ell_z] &= \mathbf{H}_\infty(\mathsf{F}) - \mathbb{E}_{z \in f(\mathrm{supp}(\mathsf{F}))}[\mathbf{H}_\infty(\mathsf{F}|f(\mathsf{F}) = z)] \\
&\leq \mathbf{H}_\infty(\mathsf{F}) - \widetilde{\mathbf{H}}_\infty(\mathsf{F}|f(\mathsf{F}) = z) \\
&\leq \mathbf{H}_\infty(\mathsf{F}) - \mathbf{H}_\infty(\mathsf{F}) + \log|f(\mathrm{supp}(\mathsf{F}))| \leq \ell,
\end{aligned}$$

where for deriving the second line we have used Jensen's inequality and for the third line we have used [11, Lemma 2.2.b].[4] □

---

[4] The lemma is as follows. Let A, B be random variables. Then we have $\widetilde{\mathbf{H}}_\infty(A|B) \geq \mathbf{H}_\infty(A, B) - n \geq \mathbf{H}_\infty(A) - n$, where B has at most 2^n possible values.

4   The Xor Combiner

In this section, we study the indifferentiability of the xor combiner $C_{\oplus}^{H_1,H_2}(x) :=$ $H_1(x) \oplus H_2(x)$ in the 2-BRO model from a random oracle RO. We show indifferentiability against adversaries that switch between the two backdoor oracles BD_1 and BD_2 only a logarithmic number of times, while arbitrarily interleaving queries to the underlying BROs H_1 and H_2, as well as to the random oracle RO.

To prove indifferentiability we need to show that there exists a simulator $Sim := (SimH_1^{RO}, SimH_2^{RO}, SimBD_1^{RO}, SimBD_2^{RO})$ such that no distinguisher placing a "reasonable" number of queries can distinguish

$$(C_{\oplus}^{H_1,H_2}, H_1, H_2, BD_1, BD_2) \quad \text{and} \quad (RO, SimH_1^{RO}, SimH_2^{RO}, SimBD_1^{RO}, SimBD_2^{RO}).$$

Such a simulator is described in Fig. 1. Simulating the evaluation queries to H_1 and H_2 is straightforward. In simulating the backdoor queries, we take advantage of the decomposition technique (discussed in Sect. 3) for transforming high min-entropy distributions into distributions that have a number of fixed points and are dense otherwise. The backdoor simulator $SimBD_1$ (resp. $SimBD_2$) computes the queried function f on the truth table of H_1 (resp. H_2), where H_1 and H_2 are initialized by picking two functions uniformly at random. For the sake of simplicity, we consider an adversary that makes Q consecutive queries, ignoring evaluation and RO-queries in between, to one backdoor oracle before moving to the other. After the i-th sequence of Q queries to one of the backdoor oracles, the leaked backdoor information is translated into fixing p_i rows of the hash function such that the rest is dense and the resulting distribution is statistically close to the true one. In other words, the distribution conditioned on the leakage is γ-close (for some $\gamma > 0$) to a convex combination of $(p, 1 - \delta)$-dense distributions obtained after decomposition.

Regarding the density rates δ_i's, we use odd values of i for the distributions obtained after backdoor queries on H_1 and even values of i for distributions of H_2. Note that is crucial for the statistical distance of these two distributions on the entire table to remain small, since the distinguisher can adaptively query a backdoor oracle which sees and can depend on the *entire* hash function table (as opposed to a limited number of rows).

Finding a distribution, which is partly fixed and partly dense, is performed by the FixRows algorithm from Fig. 1. On input of a distribution μ_z, integer $p \in \mathbb{N}$, and a set $I_{prv} \in [N]$, the algorithm FixRows returns a new distribution which is fixed on points in a set I of size at most $p + |I_{prv}|$ and is for some δ, $(1 - \delta)$-dense on the rest, together with a set of assignments A for elements in I according to the output distribution. The FixRows algorithm internally calls the refined decomposition algorithm, whose existence is guaranteed by Lemma 1 and its output distribution is one of the distributions in the convex combination returned by RefinedDecomp.

Upon fixing rows of one simulated BRO, the same rows in the other simulated BRO have to be fixed in a way that consistency with RO is assured. More precisely, for any x if $H_1(x)$ is fixed, the simulator $SimBD_1$ will immediately

---

RO(x)

---

if $\exists y \in [M]$ s.t. $(x, y) \in \mathsf{hst}_{\mathsf{RO}}$ **then return** y
$y \twoheadleftarrow [M]$
$\mathsf{hst}_{\mathsf{RO}} \leftarrow \mathsf{hst}_{\mathsf{RO}} \cup \{(x, y)\}$
return y

SimH$_1^{\mathsf{RO}}$(x)

$y_1 \leftarrow H_1(x)$
$\mathsf{hst}_1 \leftarrow \mathsf{hst}_1 \cup \{(x, y_1)\}$
$\mathsf{hst}_2 \leftarrow \mathsf{hst}_2 \cup \{(x, \mathsf{RO}(x) \oplus y_1)\}$
$\mu_1 \leftarrow \mu_1|_{\mathsf{hst}_1}$; $\mu_2 \leftarrow \mu_2|_{\mathsf{hst}_2}$
$H_2 \twoheadleftarrow \mu_2$
return y_1

SimH$_2^{\mathsf{RO}}$(x)

$y_2 \leftarrow H_2(x)$
$\mathsf{hst}_2 \leftarrow \mathsf{hst}_2 \cup \{(x, y_2)\}$
$\mathsf{hst}_1 \leftarrow \mathsf{hst}_1 \cup \{(x, \mathsf{RO}(x) \oplus y_2)\}$
$\mu_2 \leftarrow \mu_2|_{\mathsf{hst}_2}$; $\mu_1 \leftarrow \mu_1|_{\mathsf{hst}_1}$
$H_1 \twoheadleftarrow \mu_1$
return y_2

SimBD$_1^{\mathsf{RO}}[\bar{p}, \gamma](f)$

$q \leftarrow q + 1$
$z \leftarrow f(H_1)$
$\mu_1 \leftarrow \mu_1|_{f(\cdot) = z}$
if $q = Q$ **do**
  $(\mu_1, A_1) \twoheadleftarrow \mathsf{FixRows}[\gamma](\mu_1, p_{2s+1}, \mathsf{hst}_{1.1})$
  $H_1 \twoheadleftarrow \mu_1$
  $\mathsf{hst}_1 \leftarrow \mathsf{hst}_1 \cup A_1$
  for $(x, y_1) \in A_1$ **do**
    $\mathsf{hst}_2 \leftarrow \mathsf{hst}_2 \cup \{(x, \mathsf{RO}(x) \oplus y_1)\}$
  $\mu_2 \leftarrow \mu_2|_{\mathsf{hst}_2}$
  $H_2 \twoheadleftarrow \mu_2$
  $q \leftarrow 0$
return z

SimBD$_2^{\mathsf{RO}}[\bar{p}, \gamma](f)$

$q \leftarrow q + 1$
$z \leftarrow f(H_2)$
$\mu_2 \leftarrow \mu_2|_{f(\cdot) = z}$
if $q = Q$ **then**
  $(\mu_2, A_2) \twoheadleftarrow \mathsf{FixRows}[\gamma](\mu_2, p_{2s+2}, \mathsf{hst}_{2.1})$
  $H_2 \twoheadleftarrow \mu_2$
  $\mathsf{hst}_2 \leftarrow \mathsf{hst}_2 \cup A_2$
  for $(x, y_2) \in A_2$ **do**
    $\mathsf{hst}_1 \leftarrow \mathsf{hst}_1 \cup \{(x, \mathsf{RO}(x) \oplus y_2)\}$
  $\mu_1 \leftarrow \mu_1|_{\mathsf{hst}_1}$
  $H_1 \twoheadleftarrow \mu_1$
  $q \leftarrow 0$
  $s \leftarrow s + 1$
return z

FixRows$[\gamma](\mu_z, p, I_{\mathsf{prv}})$

$((D_1, I_1), \ldots, (D_d, I_d), (D_{\mathsf{err}}, I_{\mathsf{err}})) \twoheadleftarrow \mathsf{RefinedDecomp}[\mu_z, p, \gamma, I_{\mathsf{prv}}]([M]^N)$
$D_{\mathsf{err}} \leftarrow [M]^N$
$(D_i, I_i) \twoheadleftarrow \{(D_1, I_1), \ldots, (D_d, I_d), (D_{\mathsf{err}}, I_{\mathsf{err}})\}$ with probability $\mu_z(D_i)$, where $i \in \{1, \ldots, d, \mathsf{err}\}$
$A \leftarrow \emptyset$; $F \twoheadleftarrow D_i$
for $x \in I_i$ **do** $A \leftarrow A \cup \{(x, F(x))\}$
return $(\mu|_{D_i}, A)$

Fig. 1. Indifferentiability simulator for the xor combiner. We assume initial values $\mathsf{hst}_1 = \mathsf{hst}_2 = \mathsf{hst}_{\mathsf{RO}} := \emptyset$, $\mu_1 = \mu_2 := \mathcal{U}_{[M]^N}$, $H_1, H_2 \twoheadleftarrow \mathcal{U}_{[M]^N}$, $q := 0$, and $s := 0$.

set $H_2(x) := \mathsf{RO}(x) \oplus H_1(x)$ (and, analogously, so does SimBD_2). The simulator specifies the number of points that it can afford to fix (since every such query requires a call to RO) and the statistical distance that it wants. Such a strategy to assure consistency with RO is also followed by evaluation simulators SimH_1 and SimH_2, where only one coordinate of each BRO is fixed.

Note that the simulator SimBD_1 programs values of H_2, which were supposed to be dense (after a first SimBD_2 query), to values that are uniform instead. Hence, we need to argue later that the statistical distance between a uniform and a dense distribution is small for the number of points that are being treated this way. This is formalized in Claim 2, below. Looking ahead, the need to keep the advantage of the differentiator small is the reason why the simulator adapts the number of fixed points with a differentiator's switch to the other backdoor oracle. Finally, via a hybrid argument we can upper bound the total number of random oracle queries by the simulator and the advantage of the differentiator.

Claim 2. *Let $\mathcal{U}$ be the uniform distribution and $\mathcal{V}$ be a $(1-\delta)$-dense distribution, both over the domain $[M]^t$. Then we have $\mathrm{SD}(\mathcal{U}, \mathcal{V}) \leq t \cdot \delta \cdot \log M$.*

Proof. This proof follows that of [7, Claim 3]. Let V_+ be the set of all values $z \in [M]^t$ for which $\Pr[\mathcal{V} = z] > 0$ holds. We can write the statistical distance between $\mathcal{U}$ and $\mathcal{V}$ as:

$$\mathrm{SD}(\mathcal{U}, \mathcal{V}) = \sum_{z \in [M]^t} \max\left\{0, \Pr[\mathcal{V} = z] - \Pr[\mathcal{U} = z]\right\}$$

$$= \sum_{z \in V_+} \max\left\{0, \Pr[\mathcal{V} = z] - \Pr[\mathcal{U} = z]\right\}$$

$$= \sum_{z \in V_+} \Pr[\mathcal{V} = z] \cdot \max\left\{0, 1 - \frac{\Pr[\mathcal{U} = z]}{\Pr[\mathcal{V} = z]}\right\} .$$

Now, observe that for any value $z \in [M]^t$, we have $\Pr[\mathcal{V} = z] \leq M^{-(1-\delta)\cdot t}$ and $\Pr[\mathcal{U} = z] = M^{-t}$. Hence we have:

$$\mathrm{SD}(\mathcal{U}, \mathcal{V}) \leq 1 - M^{-\delta \cdot t} \leq t \cdot \delta \cdot \log M ,$$

where the last inequality uses the fact that for all $x \geq 0$, it holds that $2^{-x} \geq 1-x$ (and hence, $x \geq 1 - 2^{-x}$). $\qquad\square$

The following theorem states our indifferentiability result for xor.

Theorem 1 (Indifferentiability of xor in 2-BRO with bounded adaptivity). *Consider the xor combiner $\mathsf{C}_\oplus^{\mathsf{H}_1,\mathsf{H}_2}(x) := \mathsf{H}_1(x) \oplus \mathsf{H}_2(x)$ in the 2-BRO model with backdoored hash functions $\mathsf{H}_1, \mathsf{H}_2 \in [M]^N$. It holds that for any $\bar{p} := (p_1, \ldots, p_{c+1}) \in \mathbb{N}^{c+1}$, $0 < \gamma < 1$, and an integer $c \geq 0$, there exists a simulator $\mathsf{Sim}[\bar{p}, \gamma] := (\mathsf{SimH}_1^{\mathsf{RO}}, \mathsf{SimH}_2^{\mathsf{RO}}, \mathsf{SimBD}_1^{\mathsf{RO}}[\bar{p}, \gamma], \mathsf{SimBD}_2^{\mathsf{RO}}[\bar{p}, \gamma])$ such that for any differentiator $\mathcal{D}$ that always makes Q queries to a backdoor oracle (starting from BD_1 and always receiving an ℓ-bit response) before switching to the other, with a total number of c switches, while being allowed to arbitrarily interleave up to q_H primitive queries as well as q_C construction queries, we have*

$$\mathsf{Adv}_{\mathsf{C}_\oplus^{\mathsf{H}_1,\mathsf{H}_2}, \mathsf{Sim}[\bar{p}, \gamma]}^{\mathrm{indiff}}(\mathcal{D}) \leq (c+1) \cdot \gamma$$

$$+ \log M \cdot \left(\sum_{i=1}^{c} p_i \cdot \delta_{i-1} + q_\mathsf{H} \cdot \delta_{c+1} + q_\mathsf{C} \cdot (\delta_c + \delta_{c+1})\right) ,$$

where $\delta_{-1} := \delta_0 := 0$ *and the density rate after the i-th sequence of Q-many backdoor queries is* $\delta_i := \left(\delta_{i-2} \cdot (N - \sum_{j=1}^{i-2} p_j) \cdot \log M + Q \cdot \ell + \log \gamma^{-1} \right) / \left(p_i \cdot \log M \right)$. *The simulator places at most* $q_{\mathsf{Sim}} \leq q_{\mathsf{H}} + \sum_{i=1}^{c+1} p_i$ *queries to the random oracle* RO.

Proof. We prove indifferentiability by (1) defining a simulator, (2) upper bounding the advantage of any differentiator in distinguishing the real and the simulated worlds, and (3) upper bounding the number of queries that the simulator makes to the random oracle.

Simulator. All four sub-algorithms of the simulator are described in Fig. 1. They share state, in particular, variables to keep track of the fixed history and the current distribution of the hash functions. Two sets $\mathsf{hst}_1, \mathsf{hst}_2$ are used to keep track of the fixed coordinates of the simulated hash functions H_1 and H_2, respectively. The density functions, from which the simulated backdoored hash functions will be sampled, are denoted by μ_1 and μ_2. Furthermore, the simulator uses a counter s to recognize switches from one backdoor oracle to the other in order to use the appropriate number of points to fix from the list $\bar{p}$. It also maintains a counter q for counting the number of consecutive queries to a backdoor oracle in order to decompose, i.e., substitute the current distribution with a partially fixed and partially dense distribution, only when necessary which is the case after each set of Q backdoor queries. We assume the initial values $\mu_1 = \mu_2 := \mathcal{U}_{[M]^N}$, $H_1, H_2 \leftarrow \mathcal{U}_{[M]^N}$, $\mathsf{hst}_1 = \mathsf{hst}_2 = \mathsf{hst}_{\mathsf{RO}} := \emptyset$, $q := 0$, and $s := 0$.

Security Analysis. Here we analyze the indifferentiability of the xor combiner using a sequence of eight games $\mathsf{Game}_0, \ldots, \mathsf{Game}_7$, where Game_0 and Game_7 are the real and ideal indifferentiability games, respectively. In the following we use the shorthand notation $\Pr[\mathcal{D}^{\mathsf{Game}_i}] := \Pr[\mathcal{D}^{\mathsf{Game}_i} = 1]$, where $\mathcal{D}^{\mathsf{Game}_i}$ indicates the interaction of an adversary $\mathcal{D}$ with a game Game_i. We define the intermediate games Game_1 through Game_6 by gradually modifying the oracles and highlighting the changes in each step. Unchanged oracles are omitted in games and correspond to those from their direct predecessor. We bound the advantage of differentiators in distinguishing every two consecutive games.

$\mathsf{Game}_0 : C_{\oplus}^{H_1, H_2}(x)$

$y_1 \leftarrow H_1(x); \; y_2 \leftarrow H_2(x)$
$y \leftarrow y_1 \oplus y_2$
return y

$\mathsf{Game}_0 : H_1(x)$	$\mathsf{Game}_0 : H_2(x)$	$\mathsf{Game}_0 : \mathrm{BD}_1(f)$	$\mathsf{Game}_0 : \mathrm{BD}_2(f)$
$y_1 \leftarrow H_1(x)$	$y_2 \leftarrow H_2(x)$	$z \leftarrow f(H_1)$	$z \leftarrow f(H_2)$
return y_1	**return** y_2	**return** z	**return** z

Game_1. We next update the distributions of hash functions based on past evaluation queries, backdoor queries, and the history of coordinates that are fixed through construction queries. The distributions μ_i are conditioned on these updates, but are never actually used (i.e., sampled from) in the game. Hence it is easy to see that these two games are identical, i.e., $\text{SD}(\text{Game}_0, \text{Game}_1) = 0$.

$\text{Game}_1 : C_\oplus^{H_1,H_2}(x)$

$y_1 \leftarrow H_1(x); \; y_2 \leftarrow H_2(x)$
$\text{hst}_1 \leftarrow \text{hst}_1 \cup \{(x, y_1)\}; \; \text{hst}_2 \leftarrow \text{hst}_2 \cup \{(x, y_2)\}$
$\mu_1 \leftarrow \mu_1|_{\text{hst}_1}; \; \mu_2 \leftarrow \mu_2|_{\text{hst}_2}$
$y \leftarrow y_1 \oplus y_2$
return y

$\text{Game}_1 : H_1(x)$	**$\text{Game}_1 : H_2(x)$**	**$\text{Game}_1 : \text{BD}_1(f)$**	**$\text{Game}_1 : \text{BD}_2(f)$**
$y_1 \leftarrow H_1(x)$	$y_2 \leftarrow H_2(x)$	$z \leftarrow f(H_1)$	$z \leftarrow f(H_2)$
$\text{hst}_1 \leftarrow \text{hst}_1 \cup \{(x, y_1)\}$	$\text{hst}_2 \leftarrow \text{hst}_2 \cup \{(x, y_2)\}$	$\mu_1 \leftarrow \mu_1|_{f(\cdot)=z}$	$\mu_2 \leftarrow \mu_2|_{f(\cdot)=z}$
$\mu_1 \leftarrow \mu_1|_{\text{hst}_1}$	$\mu_2 \leftarrow \mu_2|_{\text{hst}_2}$	**return** z	**return** z
return y_1	**return** y_2		

Game$_2$. Here, after each sequence of Q queries to a backdoor oracle, i.e., right before a switch, a $(p, 1-\delta)$-dense distribution μ_i' is obtained using the algorithm FixRows by decomposing the distribution of the corresponding hash function after responding to the last query (i.e., $\mu_i|_{f(\cdot)=z}$). However, since the new distributions μ_i' are never actually used elsewhere, Game$_2$ remains identical to Game$_1$, i.e., $\text{SD}(\text{Game}_1, \text{Game}_2) = 0$.

$\text{Game}_2 : \text{BD}_1(f)$	**$\text{Game}_2 : \text{BD}_2(f)$**
$q \leftarrow q + 1$	$q \leftarrow q + 1$
$z \leftarrow f(H_1); \; \mu_1 \leftarrow \mu_1|_{f(\cdot)=z}$	$z \leftarrow f(H_2); \; \mu_2 \leftarrow \mu_2|_{f(\cdot)=z}$
if $q = Q$ **then**	**if** $q = Q$ **then**
$\quad (\mu_1', A_1) \leftarrow \text{FixRows}[\gamma](\mu_1, p_{2s+1}, \text{hst}_{1.1})$	$\quad (\mu_2', A_2) \leftarrow \text{FixRows}[\gamma](\mu_2, p_{2s+2}, \text{hst}_{2.1})$
$\quad q \leftarrow 0$	$\quad q \leftarrow 0$
return z	$\quad s \leftarrow s + 1$
	return z

Game$_3$. In this game, evaluation queries on a value x, fix the image of both functions, i.e., to $H_1(x)$ and $H_2(x)$. Similarly, in backdoor simulation the rows in the assignments A_1 (resp. A_2) are fixed for the other hash function H_2 (resp. H_1) according to its current distribution. In both games, the oracles' responses are at all times consistent with their past responses (and the construction) and we still do not sample from the updated distributions. Hence, it does not matter, if more or less of the hash function tables are fixed in each query and therefore the two games are identical, i.e., $\text{SD}(\text{Game}_2, \text{Game}_3) = 0$.

$\text{Game}_3 : H_1(x)$	$\text{Game}_3 : H_2(x)$
$y_1 \leftarrow H_1(x)$	$y_2 \leftarrow H_2(x)$
$\text{hst}_1 \leftarrow \text{hst}_1 \cup \{(x, y_1)\}$	$\text{hst}_2 \leftarrow \text{hst}_2 \cup \{(x, y_2)\}$
$\text{hst}_2 \leftarrow \text{hst}_2 \cup \{(x, H_2(x))\}$	$\text{hst}_1 \leftarrow \text{hst}_1 \cup \{(x, H_1(x))\}$
$\mu_1 \leftarrow \mu_1\|_{\text{hst}_1} ; \; \mu_2 \leftarrow \mu_2\|_{\text{hst}_2}$	$\mu_2 \leftarrow \mu_2\|_{\text{hst}_2} ; \; \mu_1 \leftarrow \mu_1\|_{\text{hst}_1}$
return y_1	**return** y_2

$\text{Game}_3 : \text{BD}_1(f)$	$\text{Game}_3 : \text{BD}_2(f)$
$q \leftarrow q + 1$	$q \leftarrow q + 1$
$z \leftarrow f(H_1); \; \mu_1 \leftarrow \mu_1\|_{f(\cdot)=z}$	$z \leftarrow f(H_2); \; \mu_2 \leftarrow \mu_2\|_{f(\cdot)=z}$
if $q = Q$ **then**	**if** $q = Q$ **then**
$\quad (\mu_1', A_1) \twoheadleftarrow \text{FixRows}[\gamma](\mu_1, p_{2s+1}, \text{hst}_{1.1})$	$\quad (\mu_2', A_2) \twoheadleftarrow \text{FixRows}[\gamma](\mu_2, p_{2s+2}, \text{hst}_{2.1})$
$\quad$ **for** $x \in A_{1.1}$ **do**	$\quad$ **for** $x \in A_{2.1}$ **do**
$\quad\quad \text{hst}_2 \leftarrow \text{hst}_2 \cup \{(x, H_2(x))\}$	$\quad\quad \text{hst}_1 \leftarrow \text{hst}_1 \cup \{(x, H_1(x))\}$
$\quad \mu_2 \leftarrow \mu_2\|_{\text{hst}_2}$	$\quad \mu_1 \leftarrow \mu_1\|_{\text{hst}_1}$
$\quad q \leftarrow 0$	$\quad q \leftarrow 0$
return z	$\quad s \leftarrow s + 1$
	return z

Game$_4$. In this game the distributions obtained by decomposition actually replace the distributions conditioned on leakage. Hence, the histories are also updated and a new hash function H_i is later sampled for potential usage in the construction. According to Lemma 1, there is a convex combination of $(p, 1 - \delta)$-dense distributions which is γ-close to the real distribution, one of such distributions being the one returned by FixRows. Hence, the distinguishing advantage can increase by γ for every Q sequence of backdoor queries. I.e., $\left| \Pr[\mathcal{D}^{\text{Game}_3}] - \Pr[\mathcal{D}^{\text{Game}_4}] \right| \leq (c+1) \cdot \gamma$.

$\text{Game}_4 : \text{BD}_1(f)$	$\text{Game}_4 : \text{BD}_2(f)$
$q \leftarrow q + 1$	$q \leftarrow q + 1$
$z \leftarrow f(H_1); \; \mu_1 \leftarrow \mu_1\|_{f(\cdot)=z}$	$z \leftarrow f(H_2); \; \mu_2 \leftarrow \mu_2\|_{f(\cdot)=z}$
if $q = Q$ **then**	**if** $q = Q$ **then**
$\quad (\mu_1, A_1) \twoheadleftarrow \text{FixRows}[\gamma](\mu_1, p_{2s+1}, \text{hst}_{1.1})$	$\quad (\mu_2, A_2) \twoheadleftarrow \text{FixRows}[\gamma](\mu_2, p_{2s+2}, \text{hst}_{2.1})$
$\quad \text{hst}_1 \leftarrow \text{hst}_1 \cup A_1$	$\quad \text{hst}_2 \leftarrow \text{hst}_2 \cup A_2$
$\quad H_1 \twoheadleftarrow \mu_1$	$\quad H_2 \twoheadleftarrow \mu_2$
$\quad$ **for** $x \in A_{1.1}$ **do**	$\quad$ **for** $x \in A_{2.1}$ **do**
$\quad\quad \text{hst}_2 \leftarrow \text{hst}_2 \cup \{(x, H_2(x))\}$	$\quad\quad \text{hst}_1 \leftarrow \text{hst}_1 \cup \{(x, H_1(x))\}$
$\quad \mu_2 \leftarrow \mu_2\|_{\text{hst}_2}$	$\quad \mu_1 \leftarrow \mu_1\|_{\text{hst}_1}$
$\quad q \leftarrow 0$	$\quad q \leftarrow 0$
return z	$\quad s \leftarrow s + 1$
	return z

Game$_5$. This game behaves exactly as Game$_4$ except when fixing the same rows for the distribution of the other BRO. It fixes those points by calling $C_\oplus$ (rather than directly) and then redundantly updates the history with e.g.., some $(x, H_1(x) \oplus C_\oplus(x))$ and samples a new BRO from the updated distribution. However, since the construction $C_\oplus$ itself calls the BROs, Game_5 is only taking a detour and the two games are perfectly indistinguishable. Hence $\mathsf{SD}(\mathsf{Game}_4, \mathsf{Game}_5) = 0$.

$\underline{\mathsf{Game}_5 : H_1(x)}$

$y_1 \leftarrow H_1(x)$
$\mathsf{hst}_1 \leftarrow \mathsf{hst}_1 \cup \{(x, y_1)\}$
$\mathsf{hst}_2 \leftarrow \mathsf{hst}_2 \cup \{(x, C_\oplus(x) \oplus y_1)\}$
$\mu_1 \leftarrow \mu_1|_{\mathsf{hst}_1}; \; \mu_2 \leftarrow \mu_2|_{\mathsf{hst}_2}$
$H_2 \twoheadleftarrow \mu_2$
return y_1

$\underline{\mathsf{Game}_5 : \mathrm{BD}_1(f)}$

$q \leftarrow q + 1$
$z \leftarrow f(H_1); \; \mu_1 \leftarrow \mu_1|_{f(\cdot)=z}$
if $q = Q$ **then**
$\quad (\mu_1, A_1) \twoheadleftarrow \mathsf{FixRows}[\gamma](\mu_1, p_{2s+1}, \mathsf{hst}_{1.1})$
$\quad \mathsf{hst}_1 \leftarrow \mathsf{hst}_1 \cup A_1$
$\quad H_1 \twoheadleftarrow \mu_1$
$\quad$**for** $(x, y_1) \in A_1$ **do**
$\quad\quad \mathsf{hst}_2 \leftarrow \mathsf{hst}_2 \cup \{(x, C_\oplus(x) \oplus y_1)\}$
$\quad \mu_2 \leftarrow \mu_2|_{\mathsf{hst}_2}$
$\quad H_2 \twoheadleftarrow \mu_2$
$\quad q \leftarrow 0$
return z

$\underline{\mathsf{Game}_5 : H_2(x)}$

$y_2 \leftarrow H_2(x)$
$\mathsf{hst}_2 \leftarrow \mathsf{hst}_2 \cup \{(x, y_2)\}$
$\mathsf{hst}_1 \leftarrow \mathsf{hst}_1 \cup \{(x, C_\oplus(x) \oplus y_2)\}$
$\mu_2 \leftarrow \mu_2|_{\mathsf{hst}_2}; \; \mu_1 \leftarrow \mu_1|_{\mathsf{hst}_1}$
$H_1 \twoheadleftarrow \mu_1$
return y_2

$\underline{\mathsf{Game}_5 : \mathrm{BD}_2(f)}$

$q \leftarrow q + 1$
$z \leftarrow f(H_2); \; \mu_2 \leftarrow \mu_2|_{f(\cdot)=z}$
if $q = Q$ **then**
$\quad (\mu_2, A_2) \twoheadleftarrow \mathsf{FixRows}[\gamma](\mu_2, p_{2s+2}, \mathsf{hst}_{2.1})$
$\quad \mathsf{hst}_2 \leftarrow \mathsf{hst}_2 \cup A_2$
$\quad H_2 \twoheadleftarrow \mu_2$
$\quad$**for** $(x, y_2) \in A_2$ **do**
$\quad\quad \mathsf{hst}_1 \leftarrow \mathsf{hst}_1 \cup \{(x, C_\oplus(x) \oplus y_2)\}$
$\quad \mu_1 \leftarrow \mu_1|_{\mathsf{hst}_1}$
$\quad H_1 \twoheadleftarrow \mu_1$
$\quad q \leftarrow 0$
$\quad s \leftarrow s + 1$
return z

Game_6. We now modify $C_\oplus$ to start to resemble a lazily sampled random oracle. In the new construction oracle, a query is stored together with its image in the history $\mathsf{hst}_{\mathsf{RO}}$. In case a query is repeated, its stored image is simply returned. Otherwise, there are three cases to consider: the corresponding row to the current query x is fixed in both hash functions, in one of them, or in neither one. In the first case the output of the construction is computed by xoring the individual images stored in hst_1 and hst_2. In the second case, a uniformly random value is chosen (and later stored in $\mathsf{hst}_{\mathsf{RO}}$). In the final case, Game_6 behaves exactly as Game_5. So, the distinguishing advantage is bounded by distinguishing uniform points (set to uniform when xoring with the returned uniform value of $C_\oplus$) from dense points. In fact, according to Claim 2, for each evaluation query it adds at most $\delta_{c+1} \cdot \log M$, since δ_i's are increasing. Further, for all points that are fixed upon a backdoor query this adds $p_i \cdot \delta_{i-1} \cdot \log M$, except for the last one, since there will be no backdoor query after that which can see the entire p_{c+1} points.

$$\left| \Pr[\mathcal{D}^{\mathsf{Game}_5}] - \Pr[\mathcal{D}^{\mathsf{Game}_6}] \right| \leq \log M \cdot \left(\sum_{i=1}^{c} p_i \cdot \delta_{i-1} + q_H \cdot \delta_{c+1} \right)$$

$$\boxed{\begin{array}{l}
\text{Game}_6 : \mathsf{C}_{\oplus}^{\mathsf{H}_1,\mathsf{H}_2}(x) \\
\hline
\textbf{if } \exists y \in [M] \text{ s.t. } (x,y) \in \mathsf{hst}_{\mathsf{RO}} \textbf{ then return } y \\
\textbf{if } \exists y_1, y_2 \in [M] \text{ s.t. } (x,y_1) \in \mathsf{hst}_1 \wedge (x,y_2) \in \mathsf{hst}_2 \textbf{ then return } y_1 \oplus y_2 \\
\textbf{if } \exists y' \in [M] \text{ s.t. } (x,y') \in \mathsf{hst}_1 \vee (x,y') \in \mathsf{hst}_2 \textbf{ then} \\
\quad y \leftarrow [M] \\
\textbf{else} \\
\quad y_1 \leftarrow \mathsf{H}_1(x);\; y_2 \leftarrow \mathsf{H}_2(x) \\
\quad \mathsf{hst}_1 \leftarrow \mathsf{hst}_1 \cup \{(x,y_1)\};\; \mathsf{hst}_2 \leftarrow \mathsf{hst}_2 \cup \{(x,y_2)\} \\
\quad \mu_1 \leftarrow \mu_1|_{\mathsf{hst}_1};\; \mu_2 \leftarrow \mu_2|_{\mathsf{hst}_2} \\
\quad y \leftarrow y_1 \oplus y_2 \\
\quad \mathsf{hst}_{\mathsf{RO}} \leftarrow \mathsf{hst}_{\mathsf{RO}} \cup \{(x,y)\} \\
\textbf{return } y
\end{array}}$$

Game_7. The construction oracle in this game differs from Game_6 in that it never evaluates the individual hash functions anymore. Here, we can safely remove the second case distinction, where x is in both hst_1 and hst_2, since this case is covered by the first case where x has been queried to the construction itself. It remains to bound the distinguisher's advantage in distinguishing the two games while making queries x to the construction that are prior to the query fixed for neither hash function.

Claim. Let X and Y be two independent $(1-\delta)$ and $(1-\delta')$-dense distributions over a domain $[M]^N$. Then the xor distribution $X \oplus Y$ is $(1-(\delta+\delta'))$-dense over the same domain $[M]^N$.

Proof. Let $I \subseteq [N]$ and $z \in [M]^{|I|}$ be arbitrary. Then we have:

$$\Pr[X_I \oplus Y_I = z] = \sum_x \Pr[X_I = x \wedge Y_I = x \oplus z] = \sum_x \Pr[X_I = x] \cdot \Pr[Y_I = x \oplus z]$$
$$\leq 2^{|I| \cdot \log M} \cdot 2^{-(1-\delta) \cdot |I| \cdot \log M} \cdot 2^{-(1-\delta') \cdot |I| \cdot \log M}$$
$$= 2^{-(1-(\delta+\delta')) \cdot |I| \cdot \log M}.$$

$\square$

We can now bound the distinguisher's advantage by computing the distance between the sum of two dense distributions from uniform, given that only q_{C} queries to $\mathsf{C}_{\oplus}$ are allowed. Below, in the second line, we use the fact that according to Lemma 1, δ's should increase.

$$\left| \Pr[\mathcal{D}^{\text{Game}_6}] - \Pr[\mathcal{D}^{\text{Game}_7}] \right| \leq q_{\mathsf{C}} \cdot \log M \cdot \max_{0 \leq i \leq c} \{\delta_i + \delta_{i+1}\} = q_{\mathsf{C}} \cdot \log M \cdot (\delta_c + \delta_{c+1}).$$

$\mathsf{Game}_7 : \mathsf{C}_{\oplus}^{\mathsf{H}_1,\mathsf{H}_2}(x)$

---

if $\exists y \in [M]$ s.t. $(x,y) \in \mathsf{hst_{RO}}$ **then return** y

~~**if** $\exists y_1, y_2 \in [M]$ s.t. $(x,y_1) \in \mathsf{hst}_1 \wedge (x,y_2) \in \mathsf{hst}_2$ **then return** $y_1 \oplus y_2$~~

~~**if** $\exists y' \in [M]$ s.t. $(x,y') \in \mathsf{hst}_1 \vee (x,y') \in \mathsf{hst}_2$ **then**~~

    ~~$y \leftarrow [M]$~~

~~**else**~~

    ~~$y_1 \leftarrow \mathsf{H}_1(x); \; y_2 \leftarrow \mathsf{H}_2(x)$~~

    ~~$\mathsf{hst}_1 \leftarrow \mathsf{hst}_1 \cup \{(x,y_1)\}; \; \mathsf{hst}_2 \leftarrow \mathsf{hst}_2 \cup \{(x,y_2)\}$~~

    ~~$\mu_1 \leftarrow \mu_1|_{\mathsf{hst}_1}; \; \mu_2 \leftarrow \mu_2|_{\mathsf{hst}_2}$~~

    ~~$y \leftarrow y_1 \oplus y_2$~~

$\mathsf{hst_{RO}} \leftarrow \mathsf{hst_{RO}} \cup \{(x,y)\}$

return y

The last game Game_7 is identical to the simulated world. Therefore, the overall advantage of $\mathcal{D}$ is as stated in the theorem.

Query Complexity. The queries made by the simulator to RO consist of those made when simulating evaluation queries and those made when simulating backdoor queries. Responding to each evaluation query requires exactly one query to RO, which makes a total of q_{H} queries. Right after the Q-th consecutive backdoor query (i.e., right before a switch), the simulator fixes some rows of the other BRO, where for each fixed row one query to the random oracle RO is made. The maximum number of rows that should be fixed after each sequence of Q queries to BD_1 (resp. BD_2) is predetermined by the simulator's parameter $\bar{p}$. Hence we obtain the claimed query complexity $q_{\mathsf{H}} + \sum_{i=1}^{c+1} p_i$. $\qquad\square$

We now provide estimates for the involved parameters.

Corollary 1. *Let the number of switches be $c \geq 1$. Then for any $\alpha_1 > 1 - 1/F_{c+1}$, where F_i are the Fibonacci numbers, there is an indifferentiability simulator* Sim *for the $\mathsf{C}_{\oplus}$ construction in the 2-BRO model which has query complexity $q_{\mathsf{H}} + (c+1) \cdot N^{\alpha_1}$ for any distinguisher with q_{H} queries to the underlying BROs. Furthermore, any such distinguisher which places q_{C} construction queries and Q consecutive queries to the same backdoor oracle before switching has advantage at most*

$$(c+1) \cdot \gamma + \log M \cdot (c^2 B + 2q_{\mathsf{H}} + 2q_{\mathsf{C}}) \cdot N^{(1-\alpha_1) \cdot F_{c+1}/F_{c+2} - 1/F_{c+2}} \,,$$

against the simulator. Asymptotically in the query complexity is $q_{\mathsf{H}} + \mathcal{O}(N^{1-1/F_{c+2}})$ and the advantage $\mathcal{O}((q_{\mathsf{H}} + q_{\mathsf{C}}) \cdot Q \cdot \ell / N^{0.38/F_{c+2}})$.

Proof. From Lemma 1 we have that

$$\delta_i \leq (\delta_{i-2} \cdot A + B)/p_i \,,$$

where $A = N$ and $B = (Q\ell + \log \gamma^{-1})/\log M$. Recursively applying the equation we get for odd i

$$\delta_i \leq \frac{B}{p_i} + \frac{AB}{p_i p_{i-2}} + \cdots + \frac{A^{(i-1)/2}B}{p_i p_{i-2} \cdots p_1}$$

Using $p_i < A$, the terms progressively get larger. Thus, in general

$$\delta_i \leq \frac{c \cdot N^{(i-2+i \bmod 2)/2} B}{p_i p_{i-2} \cdots p_{1+(i+1) \bmod 2}} .$$

For the indifferentiability advantage to be small, we would need to minimize

$$\sum_{i=1}^{c} p_i \cdot \delta_{i-1} + (q_H + q_C)(\delta_c + \delta_{c+1}).$$

Let's assume $p_i = N^{\alpha_i}$ for some $\alpha_i \in [0, 1)$. Then the i-th summand for $i > 1$ is

$$c \cdot B \cdot N^{\alpha_i - \alpha_{i-1} - \alpha_{i-3} - \cdots - \alpha_{1+i \bmod 2} + (i-3+(i-1) \bmod 2)/2} .$$

To minimize, we set al.l terms equal to a common value $c \cdot B \cdot N^{\theta}$. We obtain

$$\alpha_i - \alpha_{i-1} - \ldots - \alpha_{1+i \bmod 2} + (i - 3 + (i - 1) \bmod 2)/2 = \theta ,$$

Solving this system of linear equations gives

$$\alpha_i = F_i \cdot \theta + F_{i-1} \cdot (\alpha_1 - 1) + 1 ,$$

where F_i are the Fibonacci numbers with $F_0 = 0$ and $F_1 = 1$.

We may arrange the terms so that $(\delta_c + \delta_{c+1}) = 2 \cdot N^{\theta}$ (not including the $(q_H + q_C)$ factor). To this end, we set $\alpha_{c+2} = 0$ so that $\delta_{c+1} = N^{\theta}/p_{c+2} = N^{\theta}$ and $\delta_c = N^{\theta}/p_{c+1} \leq N^{\theta}/p_{c+2} = N^{\theta}$. Thus we set $\alpha_{c+2} = 0$. This gives $\theta = (1-\alpha_1) \cdot F_{c+1}/F_{c+2} - 1/F_{c+2}$. Now for $\theta < 0$ we would need that $\alpha_1 > 1 - 1/F_{c+1}$. This means that the query complexity of the simulator is $q_H + (c+1) \cdot N^{\alpha_1}$ and its advantage is

$$(c + 1) \cdot \gamma + \log M \cdot (c^2 B + 2q_H + 2q_C) \cdot N^{(1-\alpha_1) \cdot F_{c+1}/F_{c+2} - 1/F_{c+2}} .$$

We obtain the bound stated in the asymptotic part of the corollary by setting $\alpha_1 := 1 - 1/F_{c+2} > 1 - 1/F_{c+1}$.   □

We note that in the special case where $c = 1$, we must have that $\alpha_1 > 1 - 1/F_2 = 0$. In particular we can set $\alpha_1 := 1/4$ to obtain a simulator that places $N^{\alpha_1} = N^{1/4} \leq \sqrt{N}$ queries. Thus in this case we obtain collision resistance. Note, however, that as soon as $c \geq 2$ we would need to have that $\alpha_1 > 1 - 1/F_3 = 1/2$, which means the simulator places at least $\sqrt{N}$ queries, and we do not get collision resistance.

The above corollary shows that the xor combiner can only tolerate a logarithmic number of switches in $\log N$, which we think of as the security parameter. This is due to the fact that the simulator complexity needs to be less than $N/2$ for it to be non-trivial. Although our bounds are arguably weak, they are still meaningful, and we conjecture that much better bounds in reality hold.

5   An Extractor-Based Combiner

In this section we study the indifferentiability of extractor-based combiners and show that they can give better security parameters compared to the xor combiner of Sect. 4. Recall that in the k-BRO model one considers adversaries that have access to all k backdoor oracles. A query to the backdoor oracle BD_i reveals some information about the underlying BRO H_i. The resulting distribution conditioned on the leakage can, using the decomposition technique, be translated into a distribution with a number of fixed coordinates, while the distribution of the rest remains dense. An indifferentiability simulator then fixes the same rows of the other BRO(s) in a way that consistency with the random oracle (which is to be indistinguishable from the construction) is ensured.

We demonstrated this idea for the xor combiner, where, before a switch to the other backdoor oracle, the simulator substituted p images of that BRO by uniformly random values, i.e., the result of the random oracle values xored with the ones just fixed. This causes a security loss of $p \cdot \delta \cdot \log M$ per switch, which corresponds to the advantage of an adversary distinguishing p uniform values from $(1 - \delta)$-dense ones. Now consider a multi-source $(k_1, \ldots, k_t, \varepsilon)$-extractor as the combiner in t-BRO. The hope would be that as long as the images of the BROs have high min-entropy, the output of the extractor is ε-close to uniform. This makes it possible for us to express the loss described above in terms of a negligible ε and forgo the requirement on δ to be negligible.

In this section we focus on 2-out-of-3-source extractors as combiners, i.e., extractors that only require a minimal amount of min-entropy from two of the sources. More formally, let $\mathsf{Ext} : [M]^3 \to [2]$ be a 2-out-of-3-source $(k_1, k_2, k_3, \varepsilon)$-extractor. For three functions $\mathsf{H}_1, \mathsf{H}_2, \mathsf{H}_3 : [N] \to [M]$, the combiner $\mathsf{C}_{3\mathrm{ext}}^{\mathsf{H}_1, \mathsf{H}_2, \mathsf{H}_3} :$ $[N] \to [2]$ is defined as $\mathsf{C}_{3\mathrm{ext}}^{\mathsf{H}_1, \mathsf{H}_2, \mathsf{H}_3}(x) := \mathsf{Ext}\big(\mathsf{H}_1(x), \mathsf{H}_2(x), \mathsf{H}_3(x)\big)$. Here we show that in the 3-BRO model the construction $\mathsf{C}_{3\mathrm{ext}}^{\mathsf{H}_1, \mathsf{H}_2, \mathsf{H}_3}$ is indifferentiable from a random oracle.

WHY NOT A TWO-SOURCE EXTRACTOR? Note that we cannot guarantee that images which are being fixed by the simulator in some H_i as a result of a BD_i-query have *any* min-entropy whatsoever. To understand why, simply consider an adversary that makes a backdoor query to BD_1 requesting a preimage of the zero-string $y^* := 0^{\log M}$ under H_1. Suppose BD_1 responds to this query with $x^* \in [N]$. In this case $\mathsf{H}_1(x^*)$ has no min-entropy, since $y^* = \mathsf{H}_1(x^*)$ was chosen by the adversary and is, therefore, completely predictable. Hence, $\mathsf{H}_1(x^*)$ cannot be used in a (k_1, k_2, ε)-two-source extractor, i.e., $\mathsf{Ext}(\mathsf{H}_1(x^*), \mathsf{H}_2(x^*))$, which relies on min-entropy from both sources for its output to be ε-close to uniform. Overall, using a two-source extractor does not seem to have any advantage over the xor combiner in the 2-BRO model. On the contrary, when using a 2-out-of-3-source extractor, assuming that the rows under consideration are not already fixed in the function tables of all three BROs due to some previous query, there will be two images with high min-entropy, from which we can extract a value ε-close to uniform. We give a proof of the following theorem, which is relatively similar to the one for xor, in the full version of the paper.

Theorem 2 (Indifferentiability of 2-out-of-3-source extractors in the 3-BRO model with bounded adaptivity). *Let* $\mathsf{Ext} : [M]^3 \to [2]$ *be a* $(k_1, k_2, k_3, \varepsilon)$-*2-out-of-3-source randomness extractor, where ε is a function of* k_1, k_2, k_3. *Consider the combiner* $\mathsf{C}_{3\mathsf{ext}}^{\mathsf{H}_1, \mathsf{H}_2, \mathsf{H}_3}(x) := \mathsf{Ext}(\mathsf{H}_1(x), \mathsf{H}_2(x), \mathsf{H}_3(x))$ *in the 3-BRO model with backdoored hash functions* $\mathsf{H}_1, \mathsf{H}_2, \mathsf{H}_3 \in [M]^N$. *It holds that for all values of* $\bar{p} := (p_1, \ldots, p_{c+1}) \in \mathbb{N}^{c+1}$, $0 < \gamma < 1$, *and an integer* $c \geq 0$, *there exists a simulator* $\mathsf{Sim}[\bar{p}, \gamma] := (\mathsf{SimH}_1^{\mathsf{RO}}, \mathsf{SimH}_2^{\mathsf{RO}}, \mathsf{SimH}_3^{\mathsf{RO}}, \mathsf{SimBD}_1^{\mathsf{RO}}[\bar{p}, \gamma]$, $\mathsf{SimBD}_2^{\mathsf{RO}}[\bar{p}, \gamma], \mathsf{SimBD}_3^{\mathsf{RO}}[\bar{p}, \gamma])$ *such that for any differentiator $\mathcal{D}$ that always makes Q queries to one backdoor oracle (always receiving an ℓ-bit response) before switching to the next, with a total number of c switches, while arbitrarily interleaving up to q_H primitive queries and q_C construction queries, we have*

$$\mathsf{Adv}_{\mathsf{C}_{3\mathsf{ext}}^{\mathsf{H}_1, \mathsf{H}_2, \mathsf{H}_3}, \mathsf{Sim}[\bar{p}, \gamma]}^{\mathsf{indiff}}(\mathcal{D}) \leq (c + 1) \cdot \gamma$$

$$+ \sum_{i=1}^{c} \mathsf{SD}\big(E_1 | \cdots | E_{p_i}, \mathcal{U}_{[2]^{p_i}}\big) + q_\mathsf{H} \cdot \mathsf{SD}\big(E_1, \mathcal{U}_{[2]}\big)$$

$$+ q_\mathsf{C} \cdot \varepsilon\big((1 - \delta_{c-1}) \cdot \log M, (1 - \delta_c) \cdot \log M, (1 - \delta_{c+1}) \cdot \log M\big),$$

where for all $n \in \mathbb{N}$, we define $E_n := \mathsf{Ext}(X, Y, Z)$ for some random variables X, Y, Z over $[M]$ such that at least 2 of them have min-entropy $(1 - \delta_c) \cdot \log M$. Furthermore, we let $\delta_{-2} := \delta_{-1} := \delta_0 := 0$ and for other values of $i \leq c + 1$ let $\delta_i := \big(\delta_{i-3} \cdot (N - \sum_{j=1}^{i-3} p_j) \cdot \log M + Q \cdot \ell + \log \gamma^{-1}\big) / (p_i \cdot \log M)$ be the density rate after the i-th sequence of Q-many backdoor queries. The simulator places at most $q_\mathsf{Sim} \leq q_\mathsf{H} + \sum_{i=1}^{c+1} p_i$ queries to the random oracle RO.

We include the proof of the above theorem in the full version of the paper.

5.1   Instantiation with the Pairwise Inner-Product Extractor

Next we investigate a concrete instantiation of such a 2-out-of-3-source extractor. General multi-source extractors such as those from [2, 21, 25] which require a minimal amount of min-entropy from *every* source are inapplicable in our setting. We can, however, use the pairwise inner-product extractor as introduced by Lee et al. [19], which roughly speaking needs the sum of min-entropies to be sufficient. Formally a pairwise inner-product extractor $\mathsf{Ext}_{\mathsf{pip}} : [M]^t \to [2]$ is defined as:

$$\mathsf{Ext}_{\mathsf{pip}}(x_1, \ldots, x_t) := \sum_{1 \leq i < j \leq t} x_i \cdot x_j \ .$$

This extractor is proven ([19], Corollary 1) to be a $(k_1, \ldots, k_t, \varepsilon)$-extractor with $\varepsilon = 2^{-(k+k' - \log M + 1)/2}$, where k and k' are the two largest values among $k_1, \ldots, k_t$. Hence, $\mathsf{Ext}_{\mathsf{pip}}$ is also a 2-out-of-t extractor.

We obtain the following corollary for the indifferentiability of the pairwise-inner-product, which we prove in the full version of the paper.

Corollary 2. *Let* $\mathsf{Ext}_{\mathrm{pip}} : [M]^t \to [2]$ *be a pairwise inner-product extractor. Then the construction* $\mathsf{C}_{\mathrm{pip}}^{\mathsf{H}_1,\mathsf{H}_2,\mathsf{H}_3}(x) := \mathsf{Ext}_{\mathrm{pip}}(\mathsf{H}_1(x), \mathsf{H}_2(x), \mathsf{H}_3(x))$ *in the 3-BRO model is indifferentiable from a random oracle, where*

$$\mathsf{Adv}^{\mathrm{indiff}}_{\mathsf{C}^{\mathsf{H}_1,\mathsf{H}_2,\mathsf{H}_3}_{3\mathrm{ext}},\mathsf{Sim}[p,\gamma]}(\mathcal{D}) \leq (c+1) \cdot \gamma$$

$$+ c \cdot \sqrt{(e^{p \cdot M^{-(1-2\delta_c)}} - 1)/2}$$

$$+ (q_{\mathsf{H}} + q_{\mathsf{C}}) \cdot 2^{-((1-2\delta_{c+1}) \cdot \log M + 1)/2},$$

while the simulator makes up to $q_{\mathsf{Sim}} \leq q_{\mathsf{H}} + (c+1) \cdot p$ *queries to* RO.

We now provide estimates for the involved parameters.

Corollary 3. *Let the number of switches be* $c \geq 1$ *and assume the range size of the three random oracles are* $M \geq N^9$. *Then there is an indifferentiability simulator* Sim *for the* $\mathsf{C}_{\mathrm{pip}}$ *construction in the 3-BRO model that places at most*

$$q_{\mathsf{H}} + (c+1) \cdot \left(\frac{6Q\ell}{\log M}\right)^{1/\alpha(c)} \cdot N^{1-1/\alpha(c)}$$

queries to RO, *where* $\alpha(c) := \lfloor \frac{c}{3} \rfloor + 1$, *against any distinguisher with* q_{H} *queries to the underlying BROs. Further, any such distinguisher with* q_{C} *construction queries and* Q *consecutive queries to the same backdoor oracle before switching, has advantage at most* $(c+1) \cdot \gamma + (c + q_{\mathsf{H}} + q_{\mathsf{C}})/N$ *against this simulator.*

Proof. The recurrence relations for δ_i in the statement of Theorem 2 can be written as

$$\delta_i \leq A \cdot \delta_{i-3} + B ,$$

where $A := N/p$ and $B := (Q\ell + \log \gamma^{-}1)/p \log M$. Solving this recurrence relation we get

$$\delta_i \leq \frac{A^{\lfloor \frac{i-1}{3} \rfloor + 1} - 1}{A - 1} \cdot B .$$

We set $\delta_{c+1} \leq 1/3$ so that the term $1 - 2\delta_{c+1}$ is positive. To this end, it is sufficient to have that

$$\frac{A^{\lfloor \frac{c}{3} \rfloor + 1} - 1}{A - 1} \cdot B \leq \frac{1}{3} .$$

Substituting A and B and removing the -1 in the numerator we need to have that

$$\left(\frac{N}{p}\right)^{\lfloor \frac{c}{3} \rfloor + 1} \leq \frac{A - 1}{3B} = \frac{(N/p - 1)p \log M}{3Q\ell} = \frac{N \log M - p \log M}{3Q\ell} \leq \frac{N \log M}{6Q\ell} ,$$

where for the last inequality we have assumed that $p \leq N/2$. Thus,

$$p \geq \left(\frac{6Q\ell}{\log M}\right)^{1/\alpha(c)} \cdot N^{1-1/\alpha(c)} ,$$

where $\alpha(c) := \lfloor \frac{c}{3} \rfloor + 1$. For sufficiently large c, the factor above is at most 2. The advantage stated in Corollary 2 is

$$(c+1) \cdot \gamma + c \cdot \sqrt{p/M^{1-2\delta_c}} + (q_H + q_C) \cdot \sqrt{1/M^{1-2\delta_{c+1}}} \ .$$

Since $1 - 2\delta_{c+1} \le 1 - 2/3 = 1/3$, $\delta_c \le \delta_{c+1}$, $p \le N$ and $M \ge N^9$, the advantage is upper-bounded by $(c+1) \cdot \gamma + (c + q_H + q_C)/N$.   □

Note that for $c = 1, 2$ the query complexity of the simulator does not involve the $N^{1-1/\alpha(c)}$ factor, and hence we obtain collision resistance. For $c \ge 3$, however there is a factor of at least $N^{1/2}$.

The above corollary shows that the extractor combiner can tolerate a *linear* number of switches in $\log N$ (which can be thought of as the security parameter) for the simulator query complexity to be less than $N/2$. As for the xor combiner we conjecture that (much) better bounds for the extractor combiner are possible.

6   Indifferentiability with Auxiliary Input

In this section we discuss indifferentiability in a setting where there is no adaptivity and the backdoor oracles are called only once at the onset. Although this may seem overly restrictive, the resulting definition is sufficiently strong to model indifferentiability in the presence of auxiliary input, whereby we would like to securely replace random oracles in generic applications even in the presence of auxiliary input.

In this setting we can view an indifferentiability simulator as operating in two stages: An off-line stage which responds to the single backdoor queries for each BRO, and an on-line stage which simulates direct evaluation calls to the underlying BROs. As defined, the off-line phase of the simulator can pass an arbitrary state to its on-line phase. Further, both stages have access to the reference object oracles (although the query complexities of both stages need to be small). More precisely, this definition in the 2-BRO requires that for any $(\mathcal{D}_{0,1}, \mathcal{D}_{0,2}, \mathcal{D}_1)$ in the real world with two BROs H_1 and H_2 with

$$z_1 \twoheadleftarrow \mathcal{D}_{0,1}(H_1); \ z_2 \twoheadleftarrow \mathcal{D}_{0,2}(H_2, z_1); \ b \twoheadleftarrow \mathcal{D}_1^{C^{H_1,H_2},H_1,H_2}(z_1, z_2) \ ,$$

there exists some $(\mathsf{Sim}_{0,1}^{\mathsf{RO}}, \mathsf{Sim}_{0,2}^{\mathsf{RO}}, \mathsf{Sim}_{1,1}^{\mathsf{RO}}, \mathsf{Sim}_{1,2}^{\mathsf{RO}})$ in the ideal (simulated) world

$$(z_1, st) \twoheadleftarrow \mathsf{Sim}_{0,1}^{\mathsf{RO}}(); \ (z_2, st) \twoheadleftarrow \mathsf{Sim}_{0,2}^{\mathsf{RO}}(st); \ b \twoheadleftarrow \mathcal{D}_1^{\mathsf{RO},\mathsf{Sim}_{1,1}^{\mathsf{RO}}[st],\mathsf{Sim}_{1,2}^{\mathsf{RO}}[st]}(z_1, z_2) \ ,$$

with indistinguishable outputs b. The on-line simulators can also share state.

Let us now take a step back and define indifferentiability with auxiliary input driven by a composition theorem: for any game $\mathcal{G}$ and any attacker $\mathcal{A}_1$ in this game against C^{H_1,H_2} which receives auxiliary input on H_1 and H_2, there is an attacker $\mathcal{B}_1$ on RO in the same game $\mathcal{G}$ but now *without* auxiliary input. More explicitly, the real world

$$z \twoheadleftarrow \mathcal{A}_0(\mathsf{H}_1, \mathsf{H}_2); \; b \twoheadleftarrow \mathcal{G}^{\mathsf{C}^{\mathsf{H}_1, \mathsf{H}_2}, \mathcal{A}_1^{\mathsf{H}_1, \mathsf{H}_2}}(z)$$

and the ideal world

$$(z, st) \twoheadleftarrow \mathcal{B}_0^{\mathsf{RO}}(); \; b \twoheadleftarrow \mathcal{G}^{\mathsf{RO}, \mathcal{B}_1^{\mathsf{RO}}}(z, st)$$

are indistinguishable. Once again the query complexity of $\mathcal{B}_0$ should be small (or even zero) to obtain a definition which meaningfully formalizes indifferentiability from random oracles without auxiliary input. This definition, however, turns out to be unachievable: $\mathcal{A}_0$ can simply encode a pair of collisions for the construction, which $\mathcal{B}_0$ will not be able to match (with respect to RO) without an exponentially large number of queries to RO.[5]

There are two natural ways to overcome this: (1) restrict the interface of the construction; or (2) restrict the form of preprocessing. The former is motivated by use of salting as a means to defeat preprocessing, and the latter by independence of preprocessing for BROs.

A final question arises here: is it possible to simplify this definition further by removing the quantification over $\mathcal{A}_1$ (as done for standard indifferentiability)? This could be done in the standard way by absorbing $\mathcal{A}_1$ into $\mathcal{G}$ to form a differentiator $\mathcal{D}$. However, this means that $\mathcal{D}$ must receive the auxiliary information z. The resulting notion is stronger and models composition with respect to *games* that also depend on preprocessing. Thus, due to its simplicity, strength, and the fact that we can establish positive results for it, we focus on this definitional approach. We now make the two definitions arising from (1) and (2) explicit.

SALTED AI-INDIFFERENTIABILITY. We call a construction C^{H} *salted* if the construction takes a salt $hk \in \{0,1\}^k$ as input and prepends all calls to H with hk. We define salted AI-indifferentiability from a random oracle by requiring that for any $(\mathcal{D}_0, \mathcal{D}_1)$ in the real world

$$z \twoheadleftarrow \mathcal{D}_0(\mathsf{H}); \; hk \twoheadleftarrow \{0,1\}^k; \; b \twoheadleftarrow \mathcal{D}_1^{\mathsf{C}^{\mathsf{H}(hk, \cdot)}(hk, \cdot), \mathsf{H}}(hk, z)$$

there is a simulator $(\mathsf{Sim}_0^{\mathsf{RO}}, \mathsf{Sim}_1^{\mathsf{RO}})$ in the ideal world

$$(z, st) \twoheadleftarrow \mathsf{Sim}_0^{\mathsf{RO}}(); \; hk \twoheadleftarrow \{0,1\}^k; \; b \twoheadleftarrow \mathcal{D}_1^{\mathsf{RO}(hk, \cdot), \mathsf{Sim}_1^{\mathsf{RO}}[st]}(hk, z)$$

---

[5] One can formulate an intermediate notion of indifferentiability from random oracle *with* auxiliary input. Without salting, this notion would not be of great help. Consider, for example, the case of domain extension via an iterative hashing mode. Due to Joux's multi-collision attack [17] one can encode exponentially many collisions for the construction in a small auxiliary input, whereas this would not be possible for the random oracle.

resulting in indistinguishable outputs b. We denote the advantage of $\mathcal{D}$ in the salted AI-indifferentiability game with simulator Sim for a construction C^H by $\mathsf{Adv}^{\mathsf{s\text{-}ai\text{-}indiff}}_{C^H,\mathsf{Sim}}(\mathcal{D})$. Notice that in the above definition, the distinguisher gets access to a *salted* RO. A different definition arises when the distinguisher gets access to an unsalted RO instead. However, since the simulated auxiliary information is computed given access to an unsalted RO (which can be interpreted as having implicit access to the salt), such a definition calls for the existence of a more powerful simulator. In particular, such Sim_0 and $\mathcal{D}_1$ can easily call RO on common points. The practical implications of such a definition are unclear to us, and moreover, it is strictly weaker than our definition.

AI-INDIFFERENTIABILITY WITH INDEPENDENT PREPROCESSING. We define AI-indifferentiability with independent preprocessing by requiring that for any adversary $(\mathcal{D}_{0,1}, \mathcal{D}_{0,2}, \mathcal{D}_1)$ in the real world

$$z_1 \twoheadleftarrow \mathcal{D}_{0,1}(\mathsf{H}_1); \; z_2 \twoheadleftarrow \mathcal{D}_{0,2}(\mathsf{H}_2); \; b \twoheadleftarrow \mathcal{D}_1^{C^{\mathsf{H}_1,\mathsf{H}_2},\mathsf{H}_1,\mathsf{H}_2}(z_1, z_2)$$

there is a simulator $(\mathsf{Sim}_{0,1}^{\mathsf{RO}}, \mathsf{Sim}_{0,2}^{\mathsf{RO}}, \mathsf{Sim}_{1,1}^{\mathsf{RO}}, \mathsf{Sim}_{1,2}^{\mathsf{RO}})$ in the ideal world

$$(z_1, st) \twoheadleftarrow \mathsf{Sim}_{0,1}^{\mathsf{RO}}(); \; (z_2, st) \twoheadleftarrow \mathsf{Sim}_{0,2}^{\mathsf{RO}}(st); \; b \twoheadleftarrow \mathcal{D}_1^{\mathsf{RO},\mathsf{Sim}_{1,1}^{\mathsf{RO}}[st],\mathsf{Sim}_{1,2}^{\mathsf{RO}}[st]}(z_1, z_2)$$

resulting in indistinguishable outputs b. Note that this is slightly weaker than the definition of indifferentiability in 2-BRO since z_2 is fully independent of z_1, whereas BRO indifferentiability allows for a limited amount of dependence. We denote by $\mathsf{Adv}^{\mathsf{ai\text{-}indiff}}_{C^H,\mathsf{Sim}}(\mathcal{D})$ the advantage of $\mathcal{D}$ in the AI-indifferentiability game with independent preprocessing with respect to a simulator Sim and a construction $C^{\mathsf{H}_1,\mathsf{H}_2}$ in the 2-BRO model.

We are now ready to prove our feasibility results for AI-indifferentiability.

Theorem 3. (AI-Indifferentiability). *Any construction* $C^{\mathsf{H}_1,\mathsf{H}_2}$ *that is indifferentiable with backdoors from a random oracle with no adaptive backdoor queries is also AI-indifferentiable from a random oracle with respect to independent preprocessing attacks. More precisely, for any auxiliary-input differentiator* $\mathcal{D} := (\mathcal{D}_{0,1}, \mathcal{D}_{0,2}, \mathcal{D}_1)$ *with independent preprocessing for two random oracles there is a 2-BRO differentiator* $\tilde{\mathcal{D}}$ *with one-time non-adaptive access to each backdoor oracle such that for any 2-BRO indifferentiability simulator* $\tilde{\mathsf{Sim}}$ *there is an auxiliary-input simulator* $\mathsf{Sim} := (\mathsf{Sim}_{0,1}, \mathsf{Sim}_{0,2}, \mathsf{Sim}_{1,1}, \mathsf{Sim}_{1,2})$ *such that*

$$\mathsf{Adv}^{\mathsf{ai\text{-}indiff}}_{C^{\mathsf{H}_1,\mathsf{H}_2},\mathsf{Sim}}(\mathcal{D}) = \mathsf{Adv}^{\mathsf{indiff}}_{C^{\mathsf{H}_1,\mathsf{H}_2},\tilde{\mathsf{Sim}}}(\tilde{\mathcal{D}}) \;.$$

Further, any salted construction C^H *that is indifferentiable (in the standard sense) from a random oracle is also salted AI-indifferentiable from a random oracle. More precisely, for any auxiliary-input differentiator* $\mathcal{D} := (\mathcal{D}_0, \mathcal{D}_1)$, *with an auxiliary input of size* ℓ, *there is a (standard) differentiator* $\tilde{\mathcal{D}}$ *such that for any indifferentiability simulator* $\tilde{\mathsf{Sim}}$ *there is an auxiliary-input simulator* $\mathsf{Sim} := (\mathsf{Sim}_0, \mathsf{Sim}_1)$ *such that for any* $p \in \mathbb{N}$ *and any* $\gamma > 0$

$$\mathsf{Adv}^{\text{s-ai-indiff}}_{\mathsf{C}^{\mathsf{H}}, \mathsf{Sim}}(\mathcal{D}) \le \mathsf{Adv}^{\text{indiff}}_{\mathsf{C}^{\mathsf{H}}, \tilde{\mathsf{Sim}}}(\tilde{\mathcal{D}}) + \frac{\ell + \log \gamma^{-1}}{p} + \frac{p}{2^k} + \gamma .$$

Proof. The first part of the theorem follows directly from the discussion above that indifferentiability with backdoors and no adaptivity is stronger than indifferentiability with auxiliary input for independent preprocessing.

We now prove the second part of the theorem.

Game_0:. We start with the real game in the salted AI-indifferentiability game:

$$z \twoheadleftarrow \mathcal{D}_0(\mathsf{H}); \; hk \twoheadleftarrow \{0,1\}^k; \; b \twoheadleftarrow \mathcal{D}_1^{\mathsf{C}^{\mathsf{H}(hk,\cdot)}(hk,\cdot),\mathsf{H}}(hk, z) .$$

Game_1:. We now move to the bit-fixing RO model

$$(z, A) \twoheadleftarrow \tilde{\mathcal{D}}_0(); \; hk \twoheadleftarrow \{0,1\}^k; \; b \twoheadleftarrow \mathcal{D}_1^{\mathsf{C}^{\mathsf{H}[A](hk,\cdot)}(hk,\cdot),\mathsf{H}[A]}(hk, z) .$$

Here $\tilde{\mathcal{D}}_0$ runs $\mathcal{D}_0$ by simulating an H for it and then runs the decomposition algorithm to get a set of assignments A for p fixed points (for any $p \in \mathbb{N}$). We may now apply [7, Theorem 5] to deduce that for any $\gamma > 0$,

$$\Pr[\mathsf{Game}_1] - \Pr[\mathsf{Game}_0] \le \frac{\ell + \log \gamma^{-1}}{p} + \gamma ,$$

where ℓ is the size of auxiliary information.

Game_2:. We now move to a setting where C uses H rather than $\mathsf{H}[A]$

$$(z, A) \twoheadleftarrow \tilde{\mathcal{D}}_0(); \; hk \twoheadleftarrow \{0,1\}^k; \; b \twoheadleftarrow \mathcal{D}_1^{\mathsf{C}^{\mathsf{H}(hk,\cdot)}(hk,\cdot),\mathsf{H}[A]}(hk, z) .$$

This modification is justified by the fact that the probability that a uniform hk is (the prefix of the first component of some point) in A is at most $p/2^k$. We have that $\Pr[\mathsf{Game}_2] - \Pr[\mathsf{Game}_1] \le p/2^k$.

Game_3: We now move to a world where $\mathcal{D}_1$ is replaced by a differentiator $\tilde{\mathcal{D}}_1$ that gets the list A and does not query H on points in A:

$$(z, A) \twoheadleftarrow \tilde{\mathcal{D}}_0(); \; hk \twoheadleftarrow \{0,1\}^k; \; b \twoheadleftarrow \tilde{\mathcal{D}}_1^{\mathsf{C}^{\mathsf{H}(hk,\cdot)}(hk,\cdot),\mathsf{H}}(hk, z, A) .$$

Here $\tilde{\mathcal{D}}_1(hk, z, A)$ runs $\mathcal{D}_1(hk, z)$ relaying its queries to the first oracle to its own first oracle and the second oracle queries to its own second oracle except when a queried point appears as a prefix of the first component of an entry in A in which case $\tilde{\mathcal{D}}_1$ uses A to answer the query. We have that $\Pr[\mathsf{Game}_3] - \Pr[\mathsf{Game}_2] = 0$.

Game$_4$:. We now absorb $\tilde{\mathcal{D}}_0$ and $\tilde{\mathcal{D}}_1$ into a single differentiator $\tilde{\mathcal{D}}$:

$$b \leftarrow \tilde{\mathcal{D}}^{\mathsf{C}^{\mathsf{H}(hk,\cdot)}(hk,\cdot),\mathsf{H}} \ .$$

Here $\tilde{\mathcal{D}}$ simply runs $\tilde{\mathcal{D}}_0$, followed by picking $hk \leftarrow \{0,1\}^k$, and then running $\tilde{\mathcal{D}}_1$. We have that $\Pr[\mathsf{Game}_4] - \Pr[\mathsf{Game}_3] = 0$.

Game$_5$:. We now use the standard indifferentiability of the construction to move to the world

$$b \leftarrow \tilde{\mathcal{D}}^{\mathsf{RO}(hk,\cdot),\tilde{\mathsf{Sim}}^{\mathsf{RO}}} \ ,$$

where $\tilde{\mathsf{Sim}}$ is an indifferentiability simulator. We have that $\Pr[\mathsf{Game}_3] - \Pr[\mathsf{Game}_2] \leq \mathsf{Adv}^{\mathrm{indiff}}_{\mathsf{C}^{\mathsf{H}},\tilde{\mathsf{Sim}}}(\tilde{\mathcal{D}})$.

Game$_6$:. We now syntactically unroll $\tilde{\mathcal{D}}$ into $(\tilde{\mathcal{D}}_0, \tilde{\mathcal{D}}_1)$:

$$(z, A) \leftarrow \tilde{\mathcal{D}}_0(); \ hk \leftarrow \{0,1\}^k; \ b \leftarrow \tilde{\mathcal{D}}_1^{\mathsf{RO}(hk,\cdot),\tilde{\mathsf{Sim}}^{\mathsf{RO}}}(hk, z, A) \ .$$

We have that $\Pr[\mathsf{Game}_6] - \Pr[\mathsf{Game}_5] = 0$.

Game$_7$:. We further unroll $\tilde{\mathcal{D}}_1$ into $\mathcal{D}_1$ and define $\mathsf{Sim}_1[A]$ to be $\tilde{\mathsf{Sim}}$ except that it uses A to answers queries in A:

$$(z, A) \leftarrow \tilde{\mathcal{D}}_0(); \ hk \leftarrow \{0,1\}^k; \ b \leftarrow \mathcal{D}_1^{\mathsf{RO}(hk,\cdot),\mathsf{Sim}_1^{\mathsf{RO}}[A]}(hk, z) \ .$$

We have that $\Pr[\mathsf{Game}_7] - \Pr[\mathsf{Game}_6] = 0$.

Game$_8$:. Finally we define $\mathsf{Sim}_0 := \tilde{\mathcal{D}}_0$ and arrive at the simulated world

$$(z, A) \leftarrow \mathsf{Sim}_0(); \ hk \leftarrow \{0,1\}^k; \ b \leftarrow \mathcal{D}_1^{\mathsf{RO}(hk,\cdot),\mathsf{Sim}_1^{\mathsf{RO}}[A]}(hk, z) \ .$$

We have that $\Pr[\mathsf{Game}_8] - \Pr[\mathsf{Game}_7] = 0$.

The second part of theorem follows by summing the (in)equalities established above; that is for any $p \in \mathbb{N}$ and any $\gamma > 0$ we get that

$$\mathsf{Adv}^{\mathrm{s\text{-}ai\text{-}indiff}}_{\mathsf{C}^{\mathsf{H}},(\mathsf{Sim}_0,\mathsf{Sim}_1)}(\mathcal{D}_0, \mathcal{D}_1) = \Pr[\mathsf{Game}_0] - \Pr[\mathsf{Game}_8]$$

$$\leq \mathsf{Adv}^{\mathrm{indiff}}_{\mathsf{C}^{\mathsf{H}},\tilde{\mathsf{Sim}}}(\tilde{\mathcal{D}}) + \frac{\ell + \log \gamma^{-1}}{p} + \frac{p}{2^k} + \gamma \ .$$

$\square$

We may instantiate the first part of the theorem with the xor combiner and an indifferentiability simulator for it given in Sect. 4. In this case the off-line phase of the simulator makes no queries to the RO (and outputs simulated auxiliary inputs by picking hash functions for the queried backdoor functions to BD_1 and BD_2). This off-line phase also outputs two sets of p_1 and p_2 preset points as its state, which will be shared with the on-line phase of simulation. The second phase of the simulator is a simple xor indifferentiability simulator which ensures consistency with the preset points. Here our simulator fixes p_1 points for H_1 and p_2 points for H_2. This results in simulator query complexity of $q_H + p_1 + p_2$. The corresponding advantage bound is at most $2\gamma + q_H \cdot \log M \cdot \delta_2 + q_C \cdot \log M (\delta_1 + \delta_2)$ which is of order $\mathcal{O}(q_H \ell/p_2 + q_C(\ell/p_1 + \ell/p_2))$. Setting $p_1 = p_2 = p$ we get a simulator with $\mathcal{O}(q_H + p)$ queries for an advantage $\mathcal{O}((q_H + 2q_C)\ell/p)$. For $p = o(\sqrt{N})$ we get a bound that is meaningful for collision resistance.

As a result, we get that the xor combiner is collision resistant in the presence of independent auxiliary input (with no-salting). We note that the xor construction comes with added advantage that its security goes beyond AI-indifferentiability, and is also more domain efficient. Strictly speaking, however, the two settings are incomparable as the form of auxiliary information changes.

Acknowledgments. Dodis was partially supported by gifts from VMware Labs, Facebook and Google, and NSF grants 1314568, 1619158, 1815546. Mazaheri was supported by the German Federal Ministry of Education and Research (BMBF) and by the Hessian State Ministry for Higher Education, Research and the Arts, within ATHENE. Tessaro was partially supported by NSF grants CNS-1930117 (CAREER), CNS-1926324, CNS-2026774, a Sloan Research Fellowship, and a JP Morgan Faculty Award.

References

1. Andreeva, E., Bogdanov, A., Dodis, Y., Mennink, B., Steinberger, J.P.: On the indifferentiability of key-alternating ciphers. In: Canetti, R., Garay, J.A. (eds.) CRYPTO 2013. LNCS, vol. 8042, pp. 531–550. Springer, Heidelberg (2013). https://doi.org/10.1007/978-3-642-40041-4_29
2. Barak, B., Kindler, G., Shaltiel, R., Sudakov, B., Wigderson, A.: Simulating independence: new constructions of condensers, ramsey graphs, dispersers, and extractors. In: 37th ACM STOC, pp. 1–10 (2005)
3. Bauer, B., Farshim, P., Mazaheri, S.: Combiners for backdoored random Oracles. In: Shacham, H., Boldyreva, A. (eds.) CRYPTO 2018. LNCS, vol. 10992, pp. 272–302. Springer, Cham (2018). https://doi.org/10.1007/978-3-319-96881-0_10
4. Bertoni, G., Daemen, J., Peeters, M., Van Assche, G.: On the indifferentiability of the sponge construction. In: Smart, N. (ed.) EUROCRYPT 2008. LNCS, vol. 4965, pp. 181–197. Springer, Heidelberg (2008). https://doi.org/10.1007/978-3-540-78967-3_11
5. Canetti, R.: Universally composable security: a new paradigm for cryptographic protocols. In: 42nd FOCS, pp. 136–145 (2001)
6. Coretti, S., Dodis, Y., Guo, S.: Non-uniform bounds in the random-permutation, ideal-cipher, and generic-group models. In: Shacham, H., Boldyreva, A. (eds.) CRYPTO 2018. LNCS, vol. 10991, pp. 693–721. Springer, Cham (2018). https://doi.org/10.1007/978-3-319-96884-1_23
7. Coretti, S., Dodis, Y., Guo, S., Steinberger, J.: Random Oracles and non-uniformity. In: Nielsen, J.B., Rijmen, V. (eds.) EUROCRYPT 2018. LNCS, vol. 10820, pp. 227–258. Springer, Cham (2018). https://doi.org/10.1007/978-3-319-78381-9_9

8. Coron, J.-S., Dodis, Y., Malinaud, C., Puniya, P.: Merkle-Damgård revisited: how to construct a hash function. In: Shoup, V. (ed.) CRYPTO 2005. LNCS, vol. 3621, pp. 430–448. Springer, Heidelberg (2005). https://doi.org/10.1007/11535218_26

9. Coron, J.-S., Patarin, J., Seurin, Y.: The Random Oracle Model and the Ideal Cipher Model Are Equivalent. In: Wagner, D. (ed.) CRYPTO 2008. LNCS, vol. 5157, pp. 1–20. Springer, Heidelberg (2008). https://doi.org/10.1007/978-3-540-85174-5_1

10. Dodis, Y., Guo, S., Katz, J.: Fixing cracks in the concrete: random oracles with auxiliary input, revisited. In: Coron, J.-S., Nielsen, J.B. (eds.) EUROCRYPT 2017. LNCS, vol. 10211, pp. 473–495. Springer, Cham (2017). https://doi.org/10.1007/978-3-319-56614-6_16

11. Dodis, Y., Reyzin, L., Smith, A.: Fuzzy extractors: how to generate strong keys from biometrics and other noisy data. In: Cachin, C., Camenisch, J.L. (eds.) EUROCRYPT 2004. LNCS, vol. 3027, pp. 523–540. Springer, Heidelberg (2004). https://doi.org/10.1007/978-3-540-24676-3_31

12. Dodis, Y., Stam, M., Steinberger, J., Liu, T.: Indifferentiability of confusion-diffusion networks. In: Fischlin, M., Coron, J.-S. (eds.) EUROCRYPT 2016. LNCS, vol. 9666, pp. 679–704. Springer, Heidelberg (2016). https://doi.org/10.1007/978-3-662-49896-5_24

13. Fischlin, M., Janson, C., Mazaheri, S.: Backdoored hash functions: Immunizing HMAC and HKDF. CSF **2018**, 105–118 (2018)

14. Göös, M., Lovett, S., Meka, R., Watson, T., Zuckerman, D.: Rectangles are non-negative juntas. In: 47th ACM STOC, pp. 257–266 (2015)

15. Hoch, J.J., Shamir, A.: On the strength of the concatenated hash combiner when all the hash functions are weak. In: Aceto, L., Damgård, I., Goldberg, L.A., Halldórsson, M.M., Ingólfsdóttir, A., Walukiewicz, I. (eds.) ICALP 2008. LNCS, vol. 5126, pp. 616–630. Springer, Heidelberg (2008). https://doi.org/10.1007/978-3-540-70583-3_50

16. Holenstein, T., Künzler, R., Tessaro, S.: The equivalence of the random oracle model and the ideal cipher model, revisited. In: 43rd ACM STOC, pp. 89–98 (2011)

17. Joux, A.: Multicollisions in iterated hash functions. Application to cascaded constructions. In: Franklin, M. (ed.) CRYPTO 2004. LNCS, vol. 3152, pp. 306–316. Springer, Heidelberg (2004). https://doi.org/10.1007/978-3-540-28628-8_19

18. Kothari, P.K., Meka, R., Raghavendra, P.: Approximating rectangles by juntas and weakly-exponential lower bounds for LP relaxations of CSPs. In: 49th ACM STOC, pp. 590–603 (2017)

19. Lee, C., Lu, C., Tsai, S., Tzeng, W.: Extracting randomness from multiple independent sources. IEEE Trans. Inf. Theory **51**(6), 2224–2227 (2005)

20. Leurent, G., Peyrin, T.: From collisions to chosen-prefix collisions application to full SHA-1. In: Ishai, Y., Rijmen, V. (eds.) EUROCRYPT 2019. LNCS, vol. 11478, pp. 527–555. Springer, Cham (2019). https://doi.org/10.1007/978-3-030-17659-4_18

21. Li, X.: Three-source extractors for polylogarithmic min-entropy. In: 56th FOCS, pp. 863–882 (2015)

22. Liskov, M.: Constructing an ideal hash function from weak ideal compression functions. In: Biham, E., Youssef, A.M. (eds.) SAC 2006. LNCS, vol. 4356, pp. 358–375. Springer, Heidelberg (2007). https://doi.org/10.1007/978-3-540-74462-7_25

23. Maurer, U., Renner, R., Holenstein, C.: Indifferentiability, impossibility results on reductions, and applications to the random Oracle methodology. In: Naor, M. (ed.) TCC 2004. LNCS, vol. 2951, pp. 21–39. Springer, Heidelberg (2004). https://doi.org/10.1007/978-3-540-24638-1_2

24. Pfitzmann, B., Waidner, M.: A model for asynchronous reactive systems and its application to secure message transmission. In: 2001 IEEE Symposium on Security and Privacy, pp. 184–200 (2001)

25. Raz, R.: Extractors with weak random seeds. In: 37th ACM STOC, pp. 11–20 (2005)

26. Stevens, M., Bursztein, E., Karpman, P., Albertini, A., Markov, Y.: The first collision for full SHA-1. In: Katz, J., Shacham, H. (eds.) CRYPTO 2017. LNCS, vol. 10401, pp. 570–596. Springer, Cham (2017). https://doi.org/10.1007/978-3-319-63688-7_19

27. Unruh, D.: Random Oracles and auxiliary input. In: Menezes, A. (ed.) CRYPTO 2007. LNCS, vol. 4622, pp. 205–223. Springer, Heidelberg (2007). https://doi.org/10.1007/978-3-540-74143-5_12

Zero-Communication Reductions

Varun Narayanan[1(✉)], Manoj Prabhakaran[2], and Vinod M. Prabhakaran[1]

[1] TIFR, Mumbai, India
{varun.narayanan,vinodmp}@tifr.res.in
[2] IIT, Bombay, Mumbai, India
mp@cse.iitb.ac.in

Abstract. We introduce a new primitive in information-theoretic cryptography, namely *zero-communication reductions* (ZCR), with different levels of security. We relate ZCR to several other important primitives, and obtain new results on upper and lower bounds.

In particular, we obtain new upper bounds for PSM, CDS and OT complexity of functions, which are exponential in the information complexity of the functions. These upper bounds complement the results of Beimel et al. [BIKK14] which broke the circuit-complexity barrier for "high complexity" functions; our results break the barrier of input size for "low complexity" functions.

We also show that lower bounds on secure ZCR can be used to establish lower bounds for OT-complexity. We recover the known (linear) lower bounds on OT-complexity [BM04] via this new route. We also formulate the lower bound problem for secure ZCR in purely linear-algebraic terms, by defining the *invertible rank* of a matrix.

We present an **Invertible Rank Conjecture**, proving which will establish super-linear lower bounds for OT-complexity (and if accompanied by an explicit construction, will provide explicit functions with super-linear circuit lower bounds).

1 Introduction

Modern cryptography has developed a remarkable suite of information-theoretic primitives, like secret-sharing and its many variants, secure multi-party computation (MPC) in a variety of information-theoretic settings, (multi-server) private information retrieval (PIR), randomness extractors, randomized encoding, private simultaneous messages (PSM) protocols, conditional disclosure of secrets (CDS), and non-malleable codes, to name a few. Even computationally secure primitives are often built using these powerful tools. Further, a rich web of connections tie these primitives together.

Even as these primitives are often simple to define, and even as a large body of literature has investigated them over the years, many open questions remain. For instance, the efficiency of secret-sharing, communication complexity in MPC, PIR, and CDS, characterization of functions that admit MPC (without honest majority or setups) all pose major open problems. Interestingly, recent progress in some of these questions have arisen from surprising new connections

© International Association for Cryptologic Research 2020
R. Pass and K. Pietrzak (Eds.): TCC 2020, LNCS 12552, pp. 274–304, 2020.
https://doi.org/10.1007/978-3-030-64381-2_10

across primitives (e.g., MPC from PIR [BIKK14], CDS from PIR [LVW17], and secret-sharing from CDS [LVW18, AA18]).

In this work, we introduce a novel information-theoretic primitive called *Zero-Communication Reductions* (ZCR) that fits right into this toolkit, and provides a bridge to information theoretic tools which were so far not brought to bear on cryptographic applications. The goal of a ZCR scheme is to let two parties compute a function on their joint inputs, without communicating with each other! Instead, in a ZCR from a function f to a *predicate* ϕ, each party locally produces an output candidate *along with an input to the predicate*. The correctness requirement is that when the predicate outputs 1 ("accepts"), then the output candidates produced by the two parties should be correct; when the predicate outputs 0, correctness is not guaranteed. The non-triviality requirement places a (typically exponentially small) lower bound on the acceptance probability. We also define a natural security notion for ZCR, resulting in a primitive that is challenging to realize, and requires predicates with cryptographic structure.

Thanks to its minimalistic nature, ZCR emerges as a fundamental primitive. In this work we develop a theory that connects it with other fundamental cryptographic and information-theoretic notions. We highlight two classes of important applications of ZCR to central questions in information-theoretic cryptography – one for upper bounds and one for lower bounds. On the former front, we derive new upper bounds for communication in PSM and CDS protocols and for "OT-complexity" of a function – i.e., the number of OTs needed by an information-theoretically secure 2-Party Computation (2PC) protocol for the function – in terms of (internal) *information complexity*, a fundamental complexity measure of a 2-party function closely related to its communication complexity. On the other hand, we present a new potential route for strong lower bounds for OT-complexity, via Secure ZCR (SZCR), which has a much simpler combinatorial and linear algebraic structure compared to 2PC protocols.

Barriers: Avoiding and Confronting. One of the key questions that motivates our work is that of lower bounds for "cryptographic complexity" of 2-party functions – i.e., the number of accesses to oblivious transfer (or any other finite complete functionality) needed to securely evaluate the function (say, against honest-but-curious adversaries). Proving such lower bounds would imply lower bounds on representations that can be used to construct protocols. Specifically, small circuits and efficient private information retrieval (PIR) schemes imply low cryptographic complexity. As such, establishing strong lower bounds for cryptographic complexity will entail showing breakthrough results on circuit complexity and also on PIR lower bounds (which in turn has implications to Locally Decodable Codes).

Nevertheless, there is room to pursue cryptographic complexity lower bound questions without necessarily breaking these barriers. Firstly, there are existential questions of cryptographic complexity lower bounds that remain open, while the corresponding questions for circuit lower bounds are easy and pose no barrier by themselves. Secondly, when perfect correctness is required, the cryptographic lower bound questions are interesting and remain open for *randomized func-*

tions with very fine-grained probability values. In these cases, since the input (or index) must be long enough to encode the random choice, the corresponding circuit lower bounds and PIR lower bounds are already implied.

Finally, cryptographic complexity provides a non-traditional route—though still difficult—to attack these barriers. In fact, this work could be seen as providing a step along this path. We formulate SZCR lower bounds as a linear algebraic question of lower bounding what we call the *invertible rank*, which in turn implies cryptographic complexity and hence circuit complexity and PIR lower bounds. We conjecture that there exist matrices (representing the truth table of functions) that have a high invertible rank. Attacking the circuit complexity lower bound question translates to finding such matrices explicitly.

1.1   Our Results

We summarize our main contributions, and elaborate on them below.

- **New Primitives.** We define zero-communication reductions with different levels of security (ZCR, WZCR, and SZCR). We kick-start a theory of zero-communication reductions with several basic feasibility and efficiency results.
- **New Upper Bounds via Information Complexity.** Building on results of [BW16, KLL+15] which related information complexity of functions to communication complexity and "partition" complexity, we obtain constructions of ZCR whose complexity is upper bounded by the information complexity of the function. This in turn lets us obtain new upper bounds for statistically secure PSM, CDS, and OT complexity, which are exponential in the information complexity of the functions. As a concrete illustration of our upper bounds based on information complexity, for the "*bursting noise function*" of Ganor, Kol and Raz [GKR15], we obtain an *exponential improvement* over all existing constructions.
- **A New Route to Lower Bounds.** We show that an upper bound on OT-complexity of a function f implies an upper bound on the complexity of a SZCR from f to a predicate corresponding to OT. Hence lower bounding the latter would provide a potential route to lower bounding OT-complexity.
- We motivate the feasibility of this new route in a couple of ways:
  - We recover the known (linear) lower bounds on OT-complexity [BM04] via this new route by providing lower bounds on SZCR complexity.
  - We formulate the lower bound problem for SZCR in purely linear-algebraic terms, by defining the *invertible rank* of a matrix. We present our **Invertible Rank Conjecture**, proving which will establish super-linear lower bounds for OT-complexity (and if accompanied by an explicit construction, will provide explicit functions with super-linear circuit lower bounds).

Defining ZCR and SZCR. Our first contribution is definitional. The zero-communication model that we introduce is a powerful framework that, on the one hand, is convenient to analyze and, on the other hand, has close connections to a range of cryptographic primitives. Our definition builds on a line of work that used zero-communication protocols for studying communication and information complexity, in classical and quantum settings (see, e.g., [KLL+15] and references therein), but we extend the model significantly to enable the cryptographic connections we seek. In Sect. 2, we define three variants – ZCR, WZCR, and SZCR– with three levels of security (none, weak, and standard or strong). All these reductions relate a function f to a predicate ϕ, and, optionally, a correlation ψ, with the primary complexity measure being "non-triviality" or "acceptance probability" of the reduction: A μ-ZCR (or μ-WZCR, or μ-SZCR) needs to *accept* the outputs produced by the non-communicating parties with probability at least $2^{-\mu}$, and may abort otherwise.

(In)Feasibility Results. We follow up on the definitions with several basic positive and negative results about SZCR, presented in Sect. 4. In particular, we show that every function f has a non-trivial SZCR to some predicate ϕ_f (using no correlation); also every function f has a SZCR to the AND predicate, using some correlation ψ_f. Complementing these results, we show that for many natural choices of the predicate (AND, OR, or XOR), there are functions f which *do not* have a SZCR to the predicate, if no correlation is used. In fact, we *completely characterize* all functions that have a SZCR to these predicates.

On the other hand, there are predicates which are *complete* in the sense that any function f has a SZCR to it (possibly using a common random string). In a dual manner, a correlation ψ can be considered complete if any function f can be reduced to a constant-sized predicate like AND using ψ. Our results (discussed below) show that the predicate $\phi_{\mathsf{supp(OT+)}}$– which checks if its inputs are in the support of one or more instances of the oblivious transfer (OT) correlation – is a complete predicate (Theorem 3) and OT is a complete correlation (Theorem 12). These results rely on OT being complete for secure 2-party computation and having a "regularity" structure.

We also consider reducing *randomized functionalities without inputs* to *randomized predicates*; in this case, we characterize the optimal non-triviality achievable (Theorem 9).

Upper Bounds. Our upper bounds for CDS, PSM and 2PC for a function f are obtained by first constructing a ZCR (or WZCR) from f to a simple predicate. We offer two sets of results – perfectly secure constructions with complexity exponential in the communication complexity of f, and statistically secure constructions with complexity exponential in the information complexity.

The first set of results presented in Sect. 6.1, may be informally stated as follows.

Theorem 1 (Informal). *For a deterministic function* $f : \mathcal{X} \times \mathcal{Y} \to \{0,1\}$, *with communication complexity* ℓ, *there exist perfectly secure protocols for CDS, PSM and 2PC using OTs, all with communication complexity* $O(2^{\ell})$. *Further, the 2PC protocol uses* $O(2^{\ell})$ *invocations of OT.*

They follow from a sequence of connections illustrated below:

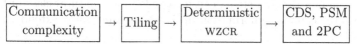

Here tiling refers to partitioning the function's domain $\mathcal{X} \times \mathcal{Y}$ into *monochromatic rectangles* – i.e., sets $\mathcal{X}' \times \mathcal{Y}'$ on which the function's value remains constant.

We significantly improve on these results (while sacrificing perfect security) in our second set of constructions presented in Sect. 6.2. They follow the outline below.

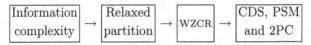

Note that now, instead of a tiling of f, we only require a (relaxed) *partition* of f [JK10,KLL+15], which allows overlapping monochromatic rectangles with fractional weights. The connection between information complexity and relaxed partition is a non-trivial result of Kerenidis et al. [KLL+15], that builds on [BW16]. We then construct a WZCR from a relaxed partition, and finally show how a WZCR (in fact, a ZCR) can be turned into a CDS, PSM or 2PC protocol. This leads us to the following theorem, stated in terms of the information complexity of f, $\mathsf{IC}_\epsilon(f)$, and statistical PSM, CDS and 2PC.

Theorem 2 (Informal). *Let $f : \mathcal{X} \times \mathcal{Y} \to \{0,1\}$ be a deterministic function. For any constant $\epsilon > 0$, the communication complexity of ϵ-PSM of f, communication complexity of ϵ-CDS for predicate f, and OT and communication complexity of ϵ-secure 2PC of f are upperbounded by $2^{O\left(\mathsf{IC}_{\epsilon/8}(f)\right)}$.*

This result is all the more interesting because it is known that information complexity can be exponentially smaller than communication complexity. In particular, Ganor, Kol and Raz described an explicit (partial) function in [GKR15], called the "bursting noise function," which on inputs of size n, have a communication complexity lower bound of $\Omega(\log \log n)$ and an information complexity upper bound of $O(\log \log \log n)$. Note that the existing general 2PC techniques do not achieve sub-linear OT-complexity. Theorem 1 would allow $O(\log n)$ OT-complexity, whereas Theorem 2 brings it down to $O(\log \log n)$.

Our results can be seen as complementing [BIKK14] which offered improvements over the circuit size for "very high complexity" functions. We offer the best known protocols, improving over the input size, and even the communication complexity, for "very low complexity" functions.

Constructions of SZCR and Connection to Lower Bounds. We show that for a function f with OT-complexity m, there is a μ-SZCR from f to the constant-depth predicate $\phi_{\mathsf{supp}(\mathsf{OT}+)}$ (which checks if its inputs are in the support of oblivious transfer (OT) correlations), where μ is roughly m:

Theorem 3 (Informal). *If a deterministic functionality f with domain $\{0,1\}^n \times \{0,1\}^n$ and has OT-complexity m, then there exists an $(m+O(n))$-SZCR from f to $\phi_{\mathsf{supp}(\mathsf{OT}^{m+1})}$, possibly using a common random string.*

This result is proved more generally in Theorem 11, where it is also shown that the common random string can be avoided for a natural class of functions f (which are "common-information-free"). The results also extend to a "dual version" where the reduction is to a simple AND predicate, but uses a *correlation* that provides m copies of OT (Theorem 12).

A consequence of Theorem 3 is that it can recover the best known lower bound for OT-complexity in terms of one-way communication complexity [BM04]. We show

$$\begin{matrix} \text{One-way communication} \\ \text{complexity} \end{matrix} \quad \leq \quad \begin{matrix} \text{Predicate-domain} \\ \text{complexity of SZCR} \end{matrix} \quad \leq \quad \text{OT-complexity}$$

where the first bound is shown using a simple support based argument (Lemma 2), and the second one follows from the upper bound on the *domain size of the predicate* $\phi_{\mathsf{supp}(\mathsf{OT}^k)}$ in Theorem 3. This is formally stated and proved as Corollary 2.

Invertible Rank. Theorem 3 provides a new potential route for lower bounding OT-complexity of f, by lower bounding μ or k in a μ-SZCR from f to $\phi_{\mathsf{supp}(\mathsf{OT}^k)}$. In turn, this problem can be formulated as a *purely linear-algebraic question* of what we term "invertible rank" (Sect. 5.1). Compared to previous paths for lower bounding OT-complexity [BM04, PP14], this new route is not known to be capped at linear bounds, and could even be seen as a stepping stone towards a fresh line of attack on circuit complexity lower bounds (as they are implied by OT-complexity lower bounds).

Invertible rank characterizes the best complexity – in terms of non-triviality *and* predicate-domain complexity – achievable by a SZCR from f to ϕ^+ (conjunction of one or more instances of ϕ). Specifically, for a matrix M_f encoding a function f and a matrix P_ϕ encoding a predicate, we have:

Theorem 4 (Informal). *If a function f has a perfect μ-SZCR to ϕ^k then the invertible rank of M_f w.r.t. P_ϕ is at most $\mu + k$.*

This characterization, combined with Theorem 3 implies that if a deterministic n-bit input functionality f has OT-complexity m, then its invertible rank w.r.t. P_{OT} is $O(m + n)$. Hence, a super-linear lower bound on invertible rank w.r.t. P_{OT} would imply super-linear OT-complexity, and consequently, super-linear circuit complexity for f. We conjecture the existence of function families f with super-linear invertible rank, and leave it as an important open problem to resolve it.

1.2   Related Work

As mentioned above, zero-communication protocols have been used to study communication and information complexity, in classical and quantum settings. The model can be traced back to the work of Gisin and Gisin [GG99], who proposed it as a local-hidden variable model (i.e., no quantum effects) that could explain apparent violation of the Bell inequality, when there is a significant probability of abort (i.e., missed detection) built into the system. More recently,

Kerenidis et al. [KLL+15], using a compression lemma by Braverman and Weinstein [BW16], presented a zero-communication protocol with non-abort probability of at least $2^{-O(IC)}$, given a protocol for computing f with information complexity IC.

OT-complexity was explicitly introduced as a fundamental measure of complexity of a function f by Beimel and Malkin [BM04], who also presented a lower bound for f's OT-complexity in terms of the one-way communication complexity of f. In [PP14] an information-theoretic measure called tension was developed, and was shown to imply lower bounds for OT-complexity, among other things. Unfortunately, both these techniques can yield lower bounds on OT-complexity that are at most the length of the inputs. On the other hand, the best known feasibility result for OT-complexity, achieved via connections to PIR, by Beimel et al. [BIKK14], is sub-exponential (a.k.a. weakly exponential) in the input length. Closing this gap, even existentially, is an open problem.

In the PSM model, all functions are computable [FKN94] and efficient protocols are known when the function has small non-deterministic branching programs [FKN94,IK97]. Upper bounds on communication complexity were studied by Beimel et al. [BIKK14]. See [AHMS18] and references therein for lower bounds. In CDS, protocols have been constructed with communication complexity linear in the formula size [GIKM00]. Efficient protocols were later developed for branching programs [KN97] and arithmetic span programs [AR17]. Liu et al. [LVW17] obtained an upper bound of $2^{O(\sqrt{k \log k})}$ for arbitrary predicates with domain $\{0,1\}^k \times \{0,1\}^k$. Applebaum et al. [AA18] showed that amortized complexity over very long secrets can be brought down to a constant.

1.3 Technical Overview

We discuss some of the technical aspects of a few of our contributions mentioned above.

A New Model of Secure Computation. ZCR and its secure variants present a fundamentally new cryptographic primitive, highlighting aspects of secure computation common to many seemingly disparate notions like PSM, CDS and secure 2PC using correlated randomness.

Recall that in a ZCR from a function f to a predicate ϕ, each party locally produces an output candidate along with an input to the predicate. The output candidates produced by the two parties should be correct when the predicate outputs 1. Instances of zero-communication models have appeared in the communication complexity literature (see [KLL+15]), but they typically prescribed a specific predicate as part of the model (e.g.., the equality predicate). By allowing an arbitrary predicate rather than one that is fixed as part of the model, we view our protocols as *reductions* from 2-party functionalities to predicates. This generalization is key to obtaining the various connections we develop.

Secondly, we add security requirements to the model. One may expect that a zero-communication protocol is naturally secure, as neither party receives *any* information about the other party's input or output. While that is the case for honest parties, we shall allow the adversary to learn the outcome of the predicate as well. This is the "right" definition, in that it allows interpreting a zero-communication protocol as a standard secure computation protocol when the predicate is implemented by a trusted party, who announces its result to the two parties. The secure version of ZCR – called SZCR – admits stronger lower bounds (and even impossibility results), as discussed below.

We further generalize the notion of zero-communication reduction to allow the two parties access to a correlation ψ, rather than just common randomness as in the original models in the literature.

In Fig. 1, we illustrate a zero communication reduction from a functionality $f = (f_A, f_B)$ to a predicate ϕ, using a correlation ψ.

The reduction is specified as a pair of randomized algorithms $(\mathfrak{A}, \mathfrak{B})$ executed by two parties, Alice and Bob. Alice, given input x and her part of the correlation R, samples $(A, U) \leftarrow \mathfrak{A}(x, R)$, where A is her proposed output for the functionality f, and U is her input to ϕ. Similarly, Bob computes $(B, V) \leftarrow \mathfrak{B}(y, S)$. The non-triviality guarantee is that $\phi(U, V) = 1$ with a positive probability $2^{-\mu}$, and correctness guarantee is that conditioned on $\phi(U, V) = 1$, the outputs of Alice and Bob are (almost always) correct.

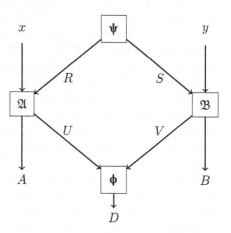

Fig. 1. The random variables involved in a ZCR.

The security definitions we attach to WZCR and SZCR could be seen as based on the standard simulation paradigm. However, when defining statistical (rather than perfect) security in the case of SZCR, a novel aspect emerges for us. Note that a μ-SZCR needs to accept an execution with probability only $2^{-\mu}$, which can be negligible. As such, allowing a negligible statistical error in security would allow one to have no security guarantees at all whenever the execution is not aborting, and would render SZCR no different from WZCR. The "right" security definition of SZCR with statistical security is to require security to hold *conditioned on acceptance* (as well as over all).

PSM, CDS, and 2PC from ZCR. Due to its minimalistic nature, a ZCR can be used as a reduction in the context of PSM, CDS, and 2PC. At a high-level, a ZCR from f to a predicated ϕ could be thought of as involving a "trusted party" which implements ϕ. Since the reduction itself involves no communication, it can easily be turned into a PSM, CDS or 2PC scheme for the function f, if we can "securely implement" a trusted party for ϕ in the respective model. One complication however, is that a ZCR can abort with a high probability. This is handled by repeating the execution several times (inversely proportional to the acceptance probability), and using the answer produced in an execution that is accepted.

While it may appear at first that ZCR with a security guarantee will be needed here, we can avoid it. This is done by designing the secure component (PSM, CDS, or 2PC) to not implement the predicate ϕ directly, but to implement a *selector function* as described below. Recall that in an execution of the ZCR protocol, Alice and Bob will generate candidate outputs (a, b) as well as inputs (u, v) for ϕ. The parties will now carry out this protocol n times in parallel, to generate (a_i, b_i) and (u_i, v_i), for $i = 1$ to n. The selector function accepts all (a_i, b_i, u_i, v_i) as inputs and outputs a pair (a_i, b_i) such that $\phi(u_i, v_i) = 1$, without revealing i itself (we choose n sufficiently large as to guarantee that there will be at least one such instance, except with negligible probability; if multiple such i exist, then, say, the largest index is selected).

The overall communication complexity of the resulting protocol is exactly determined by the PSM, CDS, or 2PC protocol for the selector function (as the ZCR itself adds no communication overhead). By instantiating our results for the predicate ϕ_{AND}, the selector function has a small *formula complexity*, and hence efficient PSM, CDS, and 2PC protocols.

ZCR and Information Complexity. WZCR and the notion of relaxed partition [JK10, KLL+15] are intimately connected to each other. A relaxed partition of a 2-input function f could be seen as a tiling of the function table with fractionally weighted tiles such that each cell in the table is covered by (almost) 1 unit worth of tiles, (almost) all of them having the same color (i.e., output value) as the cell itself. The goal of a partition is to use as few tiles as possible – or more precisely, to minimize the total weight of all the tiles used. In Lemma 4, we show that a relaxed partition can be turned into a WZCR of f to the predicate ϕ_{AND}, with acceptance probability roughly equal to the reciprocal of the total weights of the tile. (In fact, if no error were to be allowed, a WZCR with maximum acceptance probability exactly corresponds to a partition with minimum total weight.) A result of [KLL+15] can then be used to relate this acceptance probability to the information complexity of f.

Thus, via ZCR, we can upper bound PSM, CDS, and OT-complexity of functions by a quantity exponential in their information complexity. While this upper bound is rather loose in the worst case, in general, it appears incomparable to all other known upper bounds.

SZCR from 2PC. Any boolean function f has a SZCR to a predicate ϕ_f with acceptance probability of at least $1/4$ (Theorem 5). However, the computational complexity (measured in size or depth) of ϕ_f is as much as that of f. An important question is whether – and how well can – a function be reduced to a *universal, constant-depth* predicate.

We show that if the predicate is ϕ_{AND}, and no correlations are used (except possibly common randomness), then only *simple* functions have a SZCR to the predicate. (Simple functions are those that are not complete [MPR13].)

On the other hand, there is a *universal* constant-depth predicate $\phi_{\text{supp}(OT+)}$, which simply checks if its inputs are in the support of several copies of oblivious transfer correlations, such that every function f has a SZCR to it. In fact, we show that f has a μ-SZCR (i.e., a SZCR with acceptance probability $2^{-\mu}$) to $\phi_{\mathsf{supp}(\mathsf{OT+})}$ where μ is at most the OT complexity of f. (Corollary 1). (In this result, OT can be replaced by a general class of correlations, called "regular correlations.")

The idea is to transform a 2-party protocol Π^{OT} that (against passive corruption) perfectly securely realizes f using OT correlations, into a SZCR from f to $\phi_{\mathsf{supp}(\mathsf{OT+})}$. The transformation relies on the fact that any protocol admits *transcript factorization*: i.e., the probability of a transcript q occurring in an execution of Π^{OT}, given inputs (x, y) and OT correlation (u, v) to the two parties respectively, can be written as

$$\Pr_{\Pi^{\mathsf{OT}}}(q|x, y, u, v) = \rho(x, u, q) \cdot \sigma(y, v, q),$$

for some functions ρ and σ. This could be exploited by the parties to non-interactively sample an instance of the protocol execution, and derive their outputs from it. One issue here is that since the parties have access to OTs, the product structure on the transcript distribution applies only conditioned on their respective views from the OT. Thus, it is in fact the views in the OT, u and v that the two parties sample locally, conditioned on their own inputs and a transcript q that is determined by a common random string.[1] $\phi_{\mathsf{supp}(\mathsf{OT+})}$ is used to check if the two views of the OT correlations sampled thus are compatible with each other.

Several technical complications arise in the above plan. In particular, ensuring that the abort event does not reveal any information beyond the input and output to each party, requires a careful choice of probabilities with which each party selects its view of the OT correlations; also, each party unilaterally forces an abort with some probability (implemented using a couple of extra OTs included in the input to $\phi_{\mathsf{supp}(\mathsf{OT+})}$). For simplicity, here we summarize the scheme for a common-information-free function f. In this case, there will be no common random string. We fix an arbitrary transcript q^* (which has a non-zero probability of occurring), and define

$$\rho^{\dagger} := \max_x \sum_u \rho(x, u, q^*), \qquad \sigma^{\dagger} := \max_y \sum_v \sigma(y, v, q^*). \qquad (1)$$

Recall that a SZCR is given by a pair of algorithms $(\mathfrak{A}, \mathfrak{B})$ which, respectively, take x and y as inputs, and output (U, A) and (V, B) (Fig. 1). We define these algorithms below. In addition to the quantities mentioned above, we also refer to the algorithms Π_A^{out} and Π_B^{out} which are the output computation algorithms of the protocol Π.

$\mathfrak{A}(x)$: For each $u \in \mathcal{U}$, let $(U, A) = (u, \Pi_A^{\mathsf{out}}(x, u, q^*))$ with probability $\frac{\rho(x, u, q^*)}{\rho^{\dagger}}$, and $(\bot, \bot)$ with remaining probability (if any).

$\mathfrak{B}(y)$: For each $u \in \mathcal{U}$, let $(V, B) = (v, \Pi_B^{\mathsf{out}}(y, v, q^*))$ with probability $\frac{\sigma(y, v, q^*)}{\sigma^{\dagger}}$, and $(\bot, \bot)$ with remaining probability (if any).

---

[1] For secure protocols for common-information-free functions, a transcript can be fixed, avoiding the need for a common random string.

Note that for x which maximizes the expression defining $\rho^\dagger$, $\mathfrak{A}(x)$ does not set $(u, a) = (\bot, \bot)$, but in general, this costs the SZCR in terms of non-triviality. This sacrifice in acceptance probability is needed for Alice to even out the acceptance probability across her different inputs, so that Bob's view combined with the acceptance event, does not reveal information about x (beyond $f(x, y)$). Nevertheless, we can show that the probability of acceptance is lower bounded by $2^{-(m+n)}$, where m is the number of OTs (so u, v are each $2m$-bit strings) and the combined input of f is n bits long.

The construction is somewhat more delicate when f admits common-information. This means that there is some common information that Alice and Bob could agree on if they are given $(x, f_A(x, y))$ and $(y, f_B(x, y))$ respectively. For such functions, the SZCR construction above is modified so that a candidate value for the common information is given as a common random string; it is arranged that the execution is rejected by the predicate if the common information in the common random string is not correct. Also, in this case, we can no more choose an arbitrary transcript (even after fixing the common information); instead we argue that there is a "good" transcript for each value of common information, that would let us still obtain a similar non-triviality guarantee as in the case of common-information-free f.

We give an analogous result for SZCR to ϕ_{AND}, but *using* OT correlations. Here, each party locally checks if their input is consistent with a given transcript (determined by common randomness) and their share of OT correlations. Here also, for the sake of security, even if it is consistent, the party aborts with a carefully calibrated probability.

In both the above transformations from a secure 2PC protocol Π for f to a SZCR, an important consideration is the probability of not aborting. To establish our connection with OT-complexity, we need a μ-SZCR where μ is directly related to the number of OTs used in Π, and *not the length of the transcripts*. One element in establishing such a SZCR is an analysis of the given 2PC protocol when it is run with correlations drawn using a wrong distribution. We refer the reader to Theorem 11 and its proof for further details.

Invertible Rank. The conditions of a SZCR (from a possibly randomized function to a possible randomized predicate) without correlations can be captured purely in linear algebraic terms, leading to the definition of a new linear-algebraic complexity measure for functions.

The correctness condition for μ-SZCR of f to ϕ has the form $A^\mathsf{T} P B = 2^{-\mu} M$, where M and P are matrices that encode the function f and the predicate ϕ in a natural way. If P were to be replaced with the identity matrix, and μ by 0, the smallest possible size of P would correspond to the rank of M. In defining invertible rank with respect to a finite matrix P_ϕ, we let $P = P_\phi^{\otimes k}$ and ask for the smallest k possible, for a given μ (thus the invertible rank is analogous to *log-rank*). Also, A, B are required to satisfy natural stochasticity properties so that they correspond to valid probabilistic actions.

In addition to the correctness guarantees, we also incorporate the security guarantees of SZCR into our complexity measure. This takes the form of the existence of simulators, which are again captured using linear transformations. The "invertibility" in the term invertible rank refers to the existence of such simulators.

We remark that linear-algebraic complexity measures have been prevalent in studying the computational or communication complexity of functions – matrix rigidity [Val77], sign rank [PS86], the "rank measure" of Razborov [Raz90], approximate rank [ALSV13] and probabilistic rank [AW17] have all led to important advances in our understanding of functions. In particular, Razborov's rank measure was instrumental in establishing exponential lower bounds for linear secret-sharing schemes [RPRC16, PR17]. Invertible rank provides a new linear-algebraic complexity measure that is closely related to *secure two-party computation*, via our results on SZCR; this is in contrast with the prior measures which were motivated by computational complexity, (insecure) two-party communication complexity, or secret-sharing (which does not address the issues of secure two-party computation),

Organization of the Rest of the Paper

We present the formal definitions of ZCR, WZCR and SZCR in Sect. 2. Before continuing to our results, we summarize relevant background information in Sect. 3. The basic feasibility results in our model are presented in Sect. 4. The connections with lower bounds are given in Sect. 5, and the upper bounds on CDS, PSM and 2PC are given in Sect. 6. Several proof details are given in in the full version [NPP20].

2   Defining Zero-Communication Secure Reductions

We refer the reader to Fig. 1, which illustrates the random variables involved in a zero communication reduction from a functionality $f = (f_A, f_B)$ to a predicate ϕ, using a correlation ψ. The reduction is specified as a pair of randomized algorithms $(\mathfrak{A}, \mathfrak{B})$ executed by two parties, Alice and Bob. Alice, given input x and her part of the correlation R, samples $(A, U) \leftarrow \mathfrak{A}(x, R)$, where A is her proposed output for the functionality f, and U is her input to ϕ. Similarly, Bob computes $(B, V) \leftarrow \mathfrak{B}(y, S)$. The non-triviality guarantee is that $\phi(U, V) = 1$ with a positive probability $2^{-\mu}$, and correctness guarantee is that conditioned on $\phi(U, V) = 1$, the outputs of Alice and Bob are almost always correct.

We shall define three notions of such a reduction (ZCR, WZCR and SZCR) depending on the level of security implied (no security, weak security and standard security).

Notation: Below, $\mathfrak{p}(R)$ denotes the distribution of a random variable R, $\mathsf{Pr}(r, s)$ stands for $\mathsf{Pr}(R = r, S = s)$, where R, S are random variables, and $\mathsf{Pr}_{\mathfrak{A}}(\alpha|\beta)$ denotes the probability that a probabilistic process $\mathfrak{A}$ outputs α on input β. $|D_1 - D_2|$ denotes the statistical difference between two distributions D_1, D_2. (Further notes on notation are given in Sect. 3.)

Definition 1. *Let* $f : \mathcal{X} \times \mathcal{Y} \to \mathcal{A} \times \mathcal{B}$ *and* $\phi : \mathcal{U} \times \mathcal{V} \to \{0,1\}$ *be randomized functions, and let* ψ *be a distribution over* $\mathcal{R} \times \mathcal{S}$. *For any* $\mu, \epsilon \geq 0$, *a* (μ, ϵ)-*zero-communication reduction (*ZCR*) from* f *to the predicate* ϕ *using* ψ *is a pair of probabilistic algorithms* $\mathfrak{A} : \mathcal{X} \times \mathcal{R} \to \mathcal{U} \times \mathcal{A}$ *and* $\mathfrak{B} : \mathcal{Y} \times \mathcal{S} \to \mathcal{V} \times \mathcal{B}$ *such that the following holds.*

Define jointly distributed random variables (R, S, U, V, A, B, D), *conditioned on each* $(x, y) \in \mathcal{X} \times \mathcal{Y}$, *as*

$$\Pr(r, s, u, v, a, b, d | x, y) = \Pr_{\psi}(r, s) \cdot \Pr_{\mathfrak{A}}(u, a | x, r) \cdot \Pr_{\mathfrak{B}}(v, b | y, s) \cdot \Pr_{\phi}(d | u, v).$$

- **Non-Triviality:** $\forall (x, y) \in \mathcal{X} \times \mathcal{Y}$, $\Pr(D = 1 | x, y) \geq 2^{-\mu}$.
- **Correctness:** $\forall (x, y) \in \mathcal{X} \times \mathcal{Y}$, $|\mathfrak{p}((A, B) | x, y, D = 1) - f(x, y)| \leq \epsilon$.

In other words, in a ZCR, Alice and Bob compute "candidate outputs" a and b, as well as two messages u and v, respectively, such that correctness (i.e., $f(x, y) = (a, b)$) is required only when ϕ "accepts" (u, v). We allow Alice and Bob to coordinate their actions using the output of ψ. We also allow a small error probability of ϵ. To be non-trivial, we require a lower bound $2^{-\mu}$ on the probability of ϕ accepting. Note that as μ increases from 0 to ∞, the non-triviality constraint gets relaxed.

Next, we add a weak security condition to ZCR as follows: Consider an "eavesdropper" who gets to observe whether the predicate ϕ accepts or not. We require that this reveals (almost) no information about the inputs (x, y) to the eavesdropper. Technically, we require the probability of accepting to remain within a multiplicative factor of $(1 - \epsilon)^{\pm 1}$ as the inputs are changed.

Definition 2. *For any* $\mu \geq 0$, $\epsilon \geq 0$, *a* (μ, ϵ)-*ZCR* $(\mathfrak{A}, \mathfrak{B})$ *from* f *to* ϕ *using* ψ *is a* (μ, ϵ)-*weakly secure zero-communication reduction (*WZCR*) if the following condition holds.*

- **Weak Security:** $\forall (x, y), (x', y') \in \mathcal{X} \times \mathcal{Y}$,

$$\Pr(D = 1 | x, y) \geq (1 - \epsilon) \Pr(D = 1 | x', y'),$$

where D *is the random variable corresponding to the output of* ϕ, *as defined in Definition 1.*

Finally, we present our strongest notion of security, SZCR. The definition corresponds to security against passive corruption of one of Alice and Bob in a secure computation protocol (using ϕ and ψ as trusted parties) that realizes the following functionality $f_{\mu'}$ (for some $\mu' \leq \mu$): After computing $(a, b) \leftarrow f(x, y)$, with probability $2^{-\mu'}$ the functionality sends the respective outputs to the two parties ("accepting" case); with the remaining probability, it sends the output only to the corrupt party. The definition of SZCR involves a refinement not present in (statistical) security of secure computation: We require that even *conditioned on* the execution "accepting" – which could occur with a negligible probability – security holds. The formal definition of SZCR includes the correctness and (weak) security properties of a WZCR, and further requires the existence of two simulators $\hat{S}_A$ (for corrupt Alice) and $\hat{S}_B$ (for corrupt Bob), with separate conditions for the accepting and non-accepting cases. We formalize these conditions below.

Definition 3. *For any* $\mu \geq 0$, $\epsilon \geq 0$, *a* (μ, ϵ)-WZCR $(\mathfrak{A}, \mathfrak{B})$ *from* f *to* ϕ *using* ψ *is a* (μ, ϵ)-secure zero-communication reduction *(SZCR) if the following conditions hold.*

- **Security:** $\forall x \in \mathcal{X}, y \in \mathcal{Y}$, and a, b s.t. $\mathsf{Pr}_f(a, b | x, y) > 0$

$$\left| \mathfrak{p}\left(R, U | x, y, a, b, D = 1 \right) - \hat{S}_A(x, a, 1) \right| \leq \epsilon, \tag{2}$$

$$\left| \mathfrak{p}\left(S, V | x, y, a, b, D = 1 \right) - \hat{S}_B(y, b, 1) \right| \leq \epsilon, \tag{3}$$

$$\left| \mathfrak{p}\left(R, U | x, y, D = 0 \right) - \hat{S}_A(x, f_A(x, y), 0) \right| \leq \epsilon, \tag{4}$$

$$\left| \mathfrak{p}\left(S, V | x, y, D = 0 \right) - \hat{S}_B(y, f_B(x, y), 0) \right| \leq \epsilon. \tag{5}$$

where the random variables R, S, U, V, D *are as defined in Definition 1, and* $\hat{S}_A : \mathcal{X} \times \mathcal{A} \times \mathcal{D} \to \mathcal{R} \times \mathcal{U}$ *and* $\hat{S}_B : \mathcal{Y} \times \mathcal{B} \times \mathcal{D} \to \mathcal{S} \times \mathcal{V}$ *are randomized functions.*

Above, (2) and (4) correspond to corrupting Alice, with the first one being the accepting case. (The other two equations correspond to corrupting Bob.) Note that in these cases the adversary's view consists of (R, U), in addition to the input x and the boolean variable D (accepting or not), which are given to the environment as well. In the accepting case, the environment also observes the outputs (a, b). In either case, $\hat{S}_A$ is given $(x, f_A(x, y), D)$ as inputs; in the accepting case, we naturally require that the simulated view has the same output a as $f_A(x, y)$ given to $\hat{S}_A$.

Special Cases. A few special cases of the above definitions will be of interest, and we use specialized notation for them. A perfect reduction guarantees *perfect* correctness and security, wherein $\epsilon = 0$. In this case instead of $(\mu, 0)$-ZCR (WZCR, SZCR), we simply say μ-ZCR (WZCR, SZCR).

For deterministic f, when $\epsilon = 0$, the security conditions (2)–(5) in Definition 3 can be replaced with the following equivalent conditions: $\forall x, y, r, s, u, v, d$,

$$\mathsf{Pr}(r, u, d | x, y_1) = \mathsf{Pr}(r, u, d | x, y_2), \text{ if } f_A(x, y_1) = f_A(x, y_2), \tag{6}$$

$$\mathsf{Pr}(s, v, d | x_1, y) = \mathsf{Pr}(s, v, d | x_2, y), \text{ if } f_B(x_1, y) = f_B(x_2, y). \tag{7}$$

A formal proof of this equivalence is provided in the full version [NPP20].

We would consider perfect SZCR of a functionality f to a predicate ϕ using no correlation. This notion of reduction still suffices for many of our connections (e.g., to lower bounds on OT complexity), while being simpler to analyze. A correlation ψ which only offers a common random string to the two parties is denoted as ψ^{CRS}. Indeed, for ZCR and WZCR, ψ^{CRS} is the only non-trivial correlation one may consider.

3 Preliminaries for the Remainder

Before proceeding further, we present background material and some notation needed for the remainder of the paper.

Probability Notation. The probability assigned by a distribution D (or a probabilistic process D) to a value x is denoted as $\mathsf{Pr}_D(x)$, or simply $\mathsf{Pr}(x)$, when the distribution is understood. We write $x \leftarrow D$ to denote sampling a value according to the distribution D. Given two distributions D_1, D_2, we write $|D_1 - D_2|$ to denote the statistical difference (a.k.a. total variation distance) between the two.

For a random variable X, we write $\mathfrak{p}(X)$ to denote the probability distribution associated with it. We write $\mathfrak{p}(X|Y = y)$ (or simply $\mathfrak{p}(X|y)$, letting the lower case y signify that it is the value of the random variable Y), to denote the distribution of a random variable X, conditioned on the value y for a random variable Y that is jointly distributed with X.

Functionalities. We denote a 2-party functionality as $f : \mathcal{X} \times \mathcal{Y} \to \mathcal{A} \times \mathcal{B}$, to indicate that the functionality accepts an input $x \in \mathcal{X}$ from Alice and $y \in \mathcal{Y}$ from Bob, computes $(a, b) = f(x, y)$, and sends a to Alice and b to Bob. We allow f to be a randomized function too, in which case $f(x, y)$ stands for a probability distribution over $\mathcal{A} \times \mathcal{B}$, for each $(x, y) \in \mathcal{X} \times \mathcal{Y}$; for readability, we write $\mathsf{Pr}_f(a, b|x, y)$ instead of $\mathsf{Pr}_{f(x,y)}(a, b)$ to denote the probability of $f(x, y)$ outputting (a, b). We write $f = (f_A, f_B)$, where $f_A : \mathcal{X} \times \mathcal{Y} \to \mathcal{A}$ and $f_B : \mathcal{X} \times \mathcal{Y} \to \mathcal{B}$ are such that (making the randomness ξ used by f explicit), $f(x, y; \xi) = (f_A(x, y; \xi), f_B(x, y; \xi))$. If f_B is a constant function, we identify f with f_A and refer to it as a *one-sided functionality*. Similarly, if $f_A = f_B$, then we may use f to refer to either of these functions; in this case, we refer to f as a *symmetric functionality*.

Correlations. A correlation ψ over a domain $\mathcal{R} \times \mathcal{S}$ is the same as a 2-party randomized functionality $\psi : \{\bot\} \times \{\bot\} \to \mathcal{R} \times \mathcal{S}$ (i.e., a functionality with no inputs). $\mathsf{supp}(\psi) = \{(r, s)|\mathsf{Pr}_\psi(r, s) > 0\}$ is the support of ψ. We say that a correlation is *regular* if (1) $\forall (r, s) \in \mathsf{supp}(\psi)$, $\mathsf{Pr}_\psi(r, s) = \frac{1}{|\mathsf{supp}(\psi)|}$, (2) $\forall r \in \mathcal{R}$, $\sum_{s \in \mathcal{S}} \mathsf{Pr}_\psi(r, s) = \frac{1}{|\mathcal{R}|}$, and (3) $\forall s \in \mathcal{S}$, $\sum_{r \in \mathcal{R}} \mathsf{Pr}_\psi(r, s) = \frac{1}{|\mathcal{S}|}$. Common examples of regular correlations are those corresponding to Oblivious Transfer (OT) and Oblivious Linear Function Evaluation (OLE), and their n-fold repetitions. Another regular correlation of interest is the common randomness correlation ψ^{CRS}, in which $(r, s) \in \mathsf{supp}(\psi^{\mathsf{CRS}})$ if only if $r = s$.

We denote t independent copies of a correlation ψ by ψ^t. It will be convenient to denote ψ^t for an unspecified t by ψ^+.

Predicates. We shall also refer to predicates of the form $\phi : \mathcal{U} \times \mathcal{V} \to \{0, 1\}$. Again, as in the case of functionalities above, a predicate could be randomized. Given a correlation ψ over $\mathcal{U} \times \mathcal{V}$, we define the predicate $\phi_{\mathsf{supp}(\psi)}$ so that $\phi_{\mathsf{supp}(\psi)}(u, v) = 1$ iff $(u, v) \in \mathsf{supp}(\psi)$. The predicate $\phi_{\mathsf{supp}^*(\psi)}$ is defined identically, except that we allow the domain of $\phi_{\mathsf{supp}^*(\psi)}$ to be $(\mathcal{U} \cup \{\bot\}) \times (\mathcal{V} \cup \{\bot\})$ where $\bot$ is a symbol not in $\mathcal{U} \cup \mathcal{V}$.

It will also be convenient to define $\mathsf{supp}(\boldsymbol{\psi}^+) := \bigcup_{t=1}^{\infty} \mathsf{supp}(\boldsymbol{\psi}^t)$.

Evaluation Graph G_f. For a functionality f, it is useful to define a bipartite graph G_f [MPR13].

Definition 4. *For a randomized functionality $f : \mathcal{X} \times \mathcal{Y} \rightarrow \mathcal{A} \times \mathcal{B}$, the weighted graph G_f is defined as the bipartite graph on vertices $(\mathcal{X} \times \mathcal{A}) \cup (\mathcal{Y} \times \mathcal{B})$ with weight on edge $((x,a),(y,b)) = \mathsf{Pr}_f(a,b|x,y)$.*

Note that for deterministic f, the graph G_f is unweighted (all edges have weight 1 or 0). If f is a correlation, with no inputs, the nodes in the graph G_f can be identified with $\mathcal{A} \cup \mathcal{B}$.

Definition 5. *In an evaluation graph G_f, a* connected component *is a set of edges that form a connected component in the unweighted graph consisting only of edges in G_f with positive weight. A function f is said to be* common-information-free *if all the edges in G_f belong to the same connected component.*

For each connected component C in G_f, we define $\mathcal{X}_C \subseteq \mathcal{X}$ as the set $\{x | \exists y, a, b \text{ s.t. } ((x,a),(y,b)) \in C\}$; $\mathcal{Y}_C \subseteq \mathcal{Y}$ is defined analogously. Also, we define $C|_{\mathcal{X} \times \mathcal{Y}} := \{(x,y) | \exists (a,b) \text{ s.t. } ((x,a),(y,b)) \in C\}$.

For a correlation $\boldsymbol{\psi}$, we will denote by $\boldsymbol{\psi}|_C$ the restriction of $\boldsymbol{\psi}$ to the connected component C. That is, $\mathsf{Pr}_{\boldsymbol{\psi}|_C}(a,b) \propto \mathsf{Pr}_{\boldsymbol{\psi}}(a,b)$ for $(a,b) \in C$ and 0 otherwise.

A simple functionality [MPR12, MPR13] is one whose graph G_f consists of connected components that are all *product graphs*. For deterministic functionalities, it can be defined as follows:

Definition 6. *A deterministic functionality $f = (f_A, f_B)$ with domain $\mathcal{X} \times \mathcal{Y}$ is a* simple functionality *if there exist no $x, x' \in \mathcal{X}$ and $y, y' \in \mathcal{Y}$ such that $f_A(x,y) = f_A(x,y')$ and $f_B(x,y) = f_B(x',y)$ but either $f_A(x',y) \neq f_A(x',y')$ or $f_B(x,y') \neq f_B(x',y')$.*

Simple functionalities satisfy the following (see [MPR12]).

Lemma 1. *If (f_A, f_B) is a simple deterministic functionality, then there exists a partition $\mathcal{X} \times \mathcal{Y}$ into k rectangles $(A_i \times B_i)_{i \in [k]}$ for some number k such that the following properties are satisfied.*

1. *For each $i \in [k]$, for any $x \in A_i$, whenever $y, y' \in B_i$, $f_A(x,y) = f_A(x,y')$. Similarly, for each $y \in B_i$ whenever $x, x' \in A_i$, $f_B(x,y) = f_B(x',y)$.*
2. *For distinct $i, j \in [k]$, if $A_i \cap A_j \neq \emptyset$ (in this case B_i and B_j are disjoint), if $x \in A_i \cap A_j$ and $y \in B_i$ and $y' \in B_j$ then $f_A(x,y) \neq f_A(x,y')$.*
3. *For distinct $i, j \in [k]$, if $B_i \cap B_j \neq \emptyset$, if $y \in B_i \cap B_j$ and $x \in A_i$ and $x' \in A_j$ then $f_B(x,y) \neq f_B(x',y)$.*

Secure Protocols and OT Complexity. A standard (interactive) 2-party protocol using a correlation $\boldsymbol{\psi}$, denoted as $\Pi^{\boldsymbol{\psi}}$, consists of a pair of computationally unbounded randomized parties Alice and Bob. We write $(r, s, q, a, b) \leftarrow \Pi^{\boldsymbol{\psi}}(x, y)$

to denote the outcome of an execution of Π^{Ψ} on inputs (x, y), as follows: Sample $(r, s) \leftarrow \Psi$, and give r to Alice and s to Bob. Then they exchange messages to (probabilistically) generate a transcript q. Finally, Alice samples a based on her view (x, r, q) and outputs it; similarly, Bob outputs b based on (y, s, q).

We are interested in *passive secure* protocols for computing a 2-party function $f : \mathcal{X} \times \mathcal{Y} \to \mathcal{A} \times \mathcal{B}$, possibly with a statistical error. See the full version [NPP20] for a formal definition of secure 2-party computation protocols that use correlations.

It is well-known that there are correlations – like *randomized oblivious transfer (OT) correlation* – that can be used to perfectly securely compute any function f using its circuit representation (see [Gol04]) or sometimes more efficiently using its truth table [BIKK14]. The *OT-complexity* of a functionality f is the smallest number of independent instances of OT-correlations needed by a perfectly secure 2-party protocol that securely realizes f against passive adversaries.

Transcript Factorization. An important and well-known property (e.g.., [CK91]) of a protocol Π^{Ψ} is that the probability of generating the transcript, as a function of (x, y, r, s), can be factorized into separate functions of (x, r) and (y, s). More formally, there exist *transcript factorization functions* $\rho : \mathcal{X} \times \mathcal{R} \times \mathcal{Q} \to [0, 1]$ and $\sigma : \mathcal{Y} \times \mathcal{S} \times \mathcal{Q} \to [0, 1]$, such that

$$\Pr_{\Pi^{\Psi}}(q | x, y, r, s) = \rho(x, r, q) \cdot \sigma(y, s, q). \tag{8}$$

To see this, note that a transcript $q = (m_1, \ldots, m_N)$ is generated by $\Pi^{\Psi}(x, y)$, given (r, s) from Ψ, if Alice produces the message m_1 given (x, r), and then Bob produces m_2 given (y, s) as well as m_1, and so forth. That is,

$$\Pr_{\Pi^{\Psi}}(m_1, \ldots, m_N | x, y, r, s) = \Pr(m_1 | x, r) \cdot \Pr(m_2 | y, s, m_1) \cdot \Pr(m_3 | x, r, m_1, m_2) \cdot \ldots.$$

We get (8) by collecting the products of odd factors and of even factors separately as $\rho(x, r, m_1, \ldots, m_N)$ and $\sigma(y, s, m_1, \ldots, m_N)$.

We remark that the only property regarding the nature of a protocol we shall need in our results is the transcript factorization property. As such, our results stated for protocols in Theorems 11 and 12 are applicable more broadly to "pseudo protocols" which are distributions over transcripts satisfying (8), without necessarily being realizable using protocols [PP16].

The following claim about protocols (which holds for pseudo protocols as well) would be useful in our proofs. The proof for the same is provided in the full version [NPP20].

Claim 1. *Let Π^{Ψ} be a perfectly secure protocol for computing a deterministic functionality f. For any two edges $((x_1, a_1), (y_1, b_1))$ and $((x_2, a_2), (y_2, b_2))$ in the same connected component of G_f, for all transcripts $q \in \mathcal{Q}$, it holds that $\Pr_{\Pi^{\Psi}}(q | x_1, y_1, a_1, b_1) = \Pr_{\Pi^{\Psi}}(q | x_2, y_2, a_2, b_2)$.*

Private Simultaneous Messages & Conditional Disclosure of Secrets. We refer to the full version [NPP20] for a detailed description of private simultaneous messages (PSM) and conditional disclosure of secrets (CDS). In this paper, we use statistically secure variants of both these models of secure computation. An ϵ-secure PSM protocol (represented as ϵ-PSM) guarantees that for every input (x, y), Carol recovers $f(x, y)$ with at least $1 - \epsilon$ probability and that whenever f evaluates to the same value for two different inputs, Carol's view for these inputs are at most ϵ far in statistical distance. An ϵ-secure CDS protocol (represented as ϵ-CDS) is defined similarly.

4   Feasibility Results

In this section, we present several feasibility and infeasibility results for our various models. For want of space, we defer the proofs of these results to the full version [NPP20]. Note that all our feasibility results are backward compatible and all the impossibility results are forward compatible. That is, a SZCR implies a WZCR which in turn implies a ZCR, whereas, impossibility of a ZCR implies impossibility of WZCR which implies impossibility of SZCR. We define a simple predicate of interest, $\phi_{\mathsf{AND}} : \{0, 1\} \times \{0, 1\} \to \{0, 1\}$, which refers to the AND predicate. The following show that any functionality has a SZCR with $\epsilon = 0$, i.e., perfect correctness and security, to appropriate predicates using no correlation.

Theorem 5. *For every (possibly randomized) functionality $f : \mathcal{X} \times \mathcal{Y} \to \mathcal{A} \times \mathcal{B}$, there exists a predicate ϕ_f such that f has a perfect $\log(|\mathcal{A}||\mathcal{B}|)$-SZCR to ϕ_f using no correlation.*

Following theorem establishes that any functionality has a perfect SZCR to ϕ_{AND} using an appropriate correlation.

Theorem 6. *For every deterministic functionality $f : \mathcal{X} \times \mathcal{Y} \to \mathcal{A} \times \mathcal{B}$, there exists a correlation ψ_f such that f has a perfect $\log(|\mathcal{X}||\mathcal{Y}|)$-SZCR to ϕ_{AND} using ψ_f.*

We next look at the computational power of the predicate ϕ_{AND} in the context of reductions using common randomness (ψ^{CRS}). As we shall see in Lemma 3, every deterministic functionality has a perfect WZCR to ϕ_{AND}. In contrast, the next theorem shows that only simple functionalities have perfect SZCR to ϕ_{AND} using common randomness.

Theorem 7. *A deterministic functionality f has a perfect μ-SZCR to ϕ_{AND} using ψ^{CRS}, for some $\mu < \infty$, if and only if it is simple.*

An even simpler predicate $\phi_{\mathsf{XOR}} : \{0, 1\} \times \{0, 1\} \to \{0, 1\}$ refers to the XOR predicate. The following theorem shows that it has very limited power and even the AND function does not have a reduction to ϕ_{XOR}.

Theorem 8. *A deterministic functionality $f = (f_A, f_B)$ has a perfect μ-SZCR to ϕ_{XOR} using ψ^{CRS}, for some $\mu < \infty$, if and only if there exists sets $A \subseteq \mathcal{X}$ and $B \subseteq \mathcal{Y}$ such that,*

1. *For all $x \in \mathcal{X}$, $f_A(x, y) = f_A(x, y')$ if and only if $y, y' \in B$ or $y, y' \in \bar{B}$.*
2. *For all $y \in \mathcal{Y}$, $f_B(x, y) = f_B(x', y)$ if and only if $x, x' \in A$ or $x, x' \in \bar{A}$.*

Finally, we consider reducing a randomized functionality without inputs (i.e., a correlation) to a randomized predicate. To state our result, we define a measure of "productness" of a correlation ψ over $\mathcal{R} \times \mathcal{S}$:

$$K(\psi) = \max_{(\lambda_1, \lambda_2)} \min_{r \in \mathcal{R}, s \in \mathcal{S}} \frac{\mathsf{Pr}_{\lambda_1}(r)\mathsf{Pr}_{\lambda_1}(s)}{\mathsf{Pr}_{\psi}(r,s)}, \tag{9}$$

where the maximum[2] is taken over all pairs of distributions λ_1, λ_2 over $\mathcal{R}$ and $\mathcal{S}$ respectively.

Theorem 9. *For any correlation ψ there exists a predicate ϕ_ψ such that ψ has a perfect μ-SZCR to ϕ_ψ using no correlation, where $\mu = -\log(K(\psi))$. Further, if ψ has a perfect μ'-SZCR to any predicate ϕ using no correlation, then $\mu' \geq \mu$.*

5   Lower Bounds via SZCR

SZCR provides a new route for approaching lower bound proofs. The high-level approach, for showing a lower bound for a certain complexity measure is in two parts:

- First show that an upper bound on that complexity measure implies an upper bound on a complexity measure related to SZCR.
- Then showing a lower bound for SZCR implies the desired lower bound.

The complexity measure related to SZCR that we use is what we call the invertible rank of a matrix associated with the function. In Sect. 5.2, we upper bound invertible rank by OT complexity. While invertible rank of a matrix (with respect to another matrix) is easy to define, establishing super-linear lower bounds for it is presumably difficult (circuit complexity lower bounds being a barrier). But currently, even showing the existence of functions whose matrices have super-linear invertible rank remains open. One may wonder if invertible rank would turn out to not have interesting lower bounds at all. In Sect. 5.3, we present some evidence that invertible rank has non-trivial lower bounds, as it is an upper bound on communication complexity, and use it to recover the best known lower bounds on OT complexity.

5.1   Linear Algebraic Characterization of SZCR

Conditions for SZCR naturally yield a linear algebraic characterization. In this section, we focus on perfect SZCR using no correlation (i.e., $(\mu, 0)$-SZCR).

A brief introduction to invertible rank was given in Sect. 1.3. Below, we shall formally define this quantity. But first, we set up some notation. It will be convenient to consider matrices as having elements indexed by pairs of elements $(a, b) \in \mathcal{A} \times \mathcal{B}$ for arbitrary finite sets $\mathcal{A}$ and $\mathcal{B}$. Below, for clarity, we write $M(a, b)$

---

[2] The supremum is achieved since we are maximizing a continuous function over a compact set.

instead of $M_{a,b}$ to denote the element indexed by (a,b) in the matrix M. For a matrix M indexed by $\mathcal{A} \times \mathcal{B}$, $[M]_\triangleright$ be the matrix indexed by $\mathcal{A} \times (\mathcal{B} \times \mathcal{A})$ and $[M]_\triangleleft$ be the matrix indexed by $\mathcal{A} \times (\mathcal{A} \times \mathcal{B})$ defined as follows: For all $a, a' \in \mathcal{A}$ and $b \in \mathcal{B}$,

$$[M]_\triangleright(a, (b, a')) = [M]_\triangleleft(a, (a', b)) = \begin{cases} M(a,b) & \text{if } a = a', \\ 0 & \text{otherwise.} \end{cases}$$

A matrix M with non-negative entries indexed by $\mathcal{A} \times \mathcal{B}$, is said to be *stochastic* if $\forall a \in \mathcal{A}$, $\sum_{b \in \mathcal{B}} M(a, b) = 1$. A matrix M indexed by $\mathcal{A} \times (\mathcal{B} \times \mathcal{C})$, is said to be $\mathcal{B}$-*block stochastic* if $\forall b \in \mathcal{B}$, $\displaystyle\sum_{a \in \mathcal{A}, c \in \mathcal{C}} M(a, (b, c)) = 1$.

Though we shall define invertible rank generally for a matrix (w.r.t. another matrix), our motivation is to use it as a complexity measure of a possibly randomized function (w.r.t. a predicate). Towards this, we represent a function f using a matrix M_f, and also define a 0–1 matrix P_ϕ for a predicate ϕ.

Definition 7. *For a (possibly randomized) function* $f : \mathcal{X} \times \mathcal{Y} \to \mathcal{A} \times \mathcal{B}$, M_f *is the matrix indexed by* $(\mathcal{X} \times \mathcal{A}) \times (\mathcal{Y} \times \mathcal{B})$, *defined as follows: For all* $(x, a) \in \mathcal{X} \times \mathcal{A}$ *and* $(y, b) \in \mathcal{Y} \times \mathcal{B}$,

$$M_f((x, a), (y, b)) = \mathsf{Pr}_f(a, b | x, y).$$

For a predicate $\phi : \mathcal{U} \times \mathcal{V} \to \{0, 1\}$, *the matrix* P_ϕ *indexed by* $\mathcal{U} \times \mathcal{V}$ *is defined as follows. For all* $(u, v) \in \mathcal{U} \times \mathcal{V}$,

$$P_\phi(u, v) = \phi(u, v)$$

Given a matrix P indexed by $\mathcal{U} \times \mathcal{V}$, the tensor-power $P^{\otimes k}$ is a matrix indexed by $\mathcal{U}^k \times \mathcal{V}^k$, where $P^{\otimes k}((u_1, \ldots, u_k), (v_1, \ldots, v_k)) = \prod_{i=1}^{k} P(u_i, v_i)$. We note that for the k-fold conjunction ϕ^k of a predicate ϕ, we have $P_{\phi^k} = P_\phi^{\otimes k}$.

Now, we are ready to define the invertible rank of a matrix M w.r.t. a matrix P. To motivate the definition, consider M to be of the form M_f for a function $f : \mathcal{X} \times \mathcal{Y} \to \mathcal{A} \times \mathcal{B}$, and P to be of the form P_ϕ for some predicate $\phi : \mathcal{U} \times \mathcal{V} \to \{0, 1\}$. Suppose $(\mathfrak{A}, \mathfrak{B})$ is a (perfect) μ-ZCR from f to ϕ. Consider a $\mathcal{U} \times (\mathcal{X} \times \mathcal{A})$ dimensional matrix A and a $\mathcal{V} \times (\mathcal{Y} \times \mathcal{B})$ dimensional matrix B corresponding to $\mathfrak{A}$ and $\mathfrak{B}$, respectively, as follows:

$$A(u, (x, a)) = \mathsf{Pr}_{\mathfrak{A}}(u, a | x) \qquad B(v, (y, b)) = \mathsf{Pr}_{\mathfrak{B}}(v, b | y).$$

Note that A is $\mathcal{X}$-block stochastic and B is $\mathcal{Y}$-block stochastic. Given a 0-1 matrix Q indexed by $\mathcal{U} \times \mathcal{V}$, with $Q(u, v) = \phi(u, v)$ for a predicate ϕ, we can write the function implemented by the ZCR as a matrix $W = A^\mathsf{T} Q B$, indexed by $(\mathcal{X} \times \mathcal{A}) \times (\mathcal{Y} \times \mathcal{B})$. The probability of the ZCR accepting, given input (x, y), is $\sum_{a,b} W((x, a), (y, b))$. If $(\mathfrak{A}, \mathfrak{B})$ is a (perfect) μ-WZCR from f to ϕ, then we have $W = 2^{-\mu'} M_f$ for some $\mu' \le \mu$. This corresponds to the condition (10) below. Now, if $(\mathfrak{A}, \mathfrak{B})$ is a SZCR, we also have a security guarantee when either party is corrupt. Note that when both parties are honest, the *environment's* view of the protocol, consisting of (x, y, a, b), is specified by the matrix W above. But when Bob, say, is corrupt, the view also includes the message v that Bob sends to ϕ, and hence it would be specified by a matrix indexed by $(\mathcal{X} \times \mathcal{A}) \times (\mathcal{Y} \times \mathcal{B} \times \mathcal{V})$. This matrix can be written as $A^\mathsf{T} \cdot Q \cdot [B]_\rhd$ (where $[B]_\rhd$ "copies" the row index information of B to the column index, corresponding to v becoming visible outside the protocol). On the other hand, the security condition says that this view can be simulated by having $\hat{S}_B$ sample v given (y, b); $\hat{S}_B$ can be encoded in a stochastic matrix H indexed by $(\mathcal{Y} \times \mathcal{B}) \times \mathcal{V}$. The view of the environment in the simulated execution, taking into account the fact that it aborts with probability $1 - 2^{-\mu}$, can be written as $2^{-\mu} M_f \cdot [H]_\lhd$ (where $[H]_\lhd$ is derived from H by adding the row index information (y, b) to the column index v). This aspect of SZCR is reflected in (12) in the definition below. Similarly, (11) corresponds to security against corruption of Alice.

Thus the linear algebraic conditions in the definition below correspond to the existence of a μ-SZCR from f to ϕ^k. The invertible rank of M_f w.r.t. P_ϕ corresponds to minimizing μ and k simultaneously (or more concretely, their sum).

Definition 8. *Given a matrix M indexed by $(\mathcal{X} \times \mathcal{A}) \times (\mathcal{Y} \times \mathcal{B})$ and matrix P indexed by $\mathcal{U} \times \mathcal{V}$, the μ^*-invertible rank of M w.r.t. P is defined as*

$$\mathsf{IR}_P^{(\mu^*)}(M) = \min_{A, B, G, H, \mu} k$$

subject to $\mu \leq \mu^*$ and

$$A^\mathsf{T} \cdot P^{\otimes k} \cdot B = 2^{-\mu} M, \tag{10}$$

$$[A]_\rhd^\mathsf{T} \cdot P^{\otimes k} \cdot B = 2^{-\mu} [G]_\lhd^\mathsf{T} \cdot M, \tag{11}$$

$$A^\mathsf{T} \cdot P^{\otimes k} \cdot [B]_\rhd = 2^{-\mu} M \cdot [H]_\lhd, \tag{12}$$

where A is a $\mathcal{X}$-block stochastic matrix indexed by $\mathcal{U}^k \times (\mathcal{X} \times \mathcal{A})$, B is a $\mathcal{Y}$-block stochastic matrix indexed by $\mathcal{V}^k \times (\mathcal{Y} \times \mathcal{B})$, G is a stochastic matrix indexed by $(\mathcal{X} \times \mathcal{A}) \times \mathcal{U}^k$, and H is a stochastic matrix indexed by $(\mathcal{Y} \times \mathcal{B}) \times \mathcal{V}^k$.

The invertible rank *of M w.r.t. P is defined as*

$$\mathsf{IR}_P(M) = \min_\mu \mathsf{IR}_P^{(\mu)}(M) + \mu.$$

As discussed above, a $(\mu, 0)$-SZCR from f to ϕ^k (using no correlation) corresponds to the existence of matrices A, B, G, H that satisfy the conditions (10)–(12). Then the invertible rank of M_f w.r.t. P_ϕ would be upper bounded by $\mu + k$. This is captured in the following theorem (proven in the full version [NPP20].

Theorem 10. *For a (possibly randomized) functionality $f : \mathcal{X} \times \mathcal{Y} \rightarrow \mathcal{A} \times \mathcal{B}$ and a predicate $\phi : \mathcal{U} \times \mathcal{V} \rightarrow \{0, 1\}$, f has a perfect μ-SZCR to ϕ using no correlation if and only if $\mathsf{IR}_{P_\phi}^{(\mu)}(M_f) \leq 1$. Further, if f has a perfect μ-SZCR to ϕ^k using no correlation then $\mathsf{IR}_{P_\phi}(M_f) \leq \mu + k$.*

Invertible Rank w.r.t. OT. Let P_{OT} denote the matrix that corresponds to the predicate $\phi_{\mathsf{supp}(\mathsf{OT})}$.[3] It can be written as the following circulant matrix:

$$P_{\mathsf{OT}} = \begin{bmatrix} 1 & 0 & 0 & 1 \\ 1 & 1 & 0 & 0 \\ 0 & 1 & 1 & 0 \\ 0 & 0 & 1 & 1 \end{bmatrix}$$

We present a conjecture on the existence of functions f which have super-linear invertible ranks with respect to P_{OT}.

Conjecture 1 (**Invertible Rank Conjecture**). There exists a family of functions $f_n : \{0,1\}^n \times \{0,1\}^n \to \{0,1\} \times \{0,1\}$ such that $\mathsf{IR}_{P_{\mathsf{OT}}}(M_{f_n}) = \omega(n)$.

Proving this conjecture, for a family of common-information-free functions, would imply super-linear lower bounds for OT complexity, thanks to Corollary 1 in the sequel. Finding such an explicit family f_n would be a major breakthrough, as it would give a function family with super-linear circuit complexity.

On the other hand, a weakly exponential upper bound of $2^{\tilde{O}(\sqrt{n})}$ exists on invertible rank of n-bit input functions, as implied by an upper bound on OT-complexity [BIKK14], re-instantiated using the 2-server PIR protocols of [DG16].

The following corollary of Theorems 10 and 3 gives a purely linear algebraic problem – namely, lower bounding invertible rank – that can yield OT complexity lower bounds.

Corollary 1. *If a deterministic common-information-free functionality $f : \{0,1\}^n \times \{0,1\}^n \to \mathcal{A} \times \mathcal{B}$ has OT-complexity m, then $\mathsf{IR}_{P_{\mathsf{OT}}}(M_f) = O(m+n)$.*

Proof: Recall that by Theorem 3, there exists a μ-SZCR from f to $\phi_{\mathsf{supp}(\mathsf{OT}^{m+1})}$, where $\mu = m + O(n)$. We will use the further guarantee that, since f is common-information-free, this SZCR does not use any correlation. Then, by Theorem 10, we have $\mathsf{IR}_{P_{\mathsf{OT}}}(M_f) \leq (m+1) + \mu = O(m+n)$.[4] $\square$

5.2 SZCR vs. OT Complexity

In this section we prove Theorem 3 and its extensions, that show that SZCR lower bounds translate to lower bounds for OT-complexity, or more generally, 2PC complexity w.r.t. any *regular* correlation ψ (see Sect. 3). Our main result in this section is Theorem 11, where we transform a perfectly secure 2PC protocol for a general deterministic functionality f using a regular correlation ψ, into a SZCR from f to the predicate $\phi_{\mathsf{supp}^*(\psi)}$. (Recall from Sect. 3 that $\phi_{\mathsf{supp}^*(\psi)}$ is a predicate that evaluates to 1 on inputs $(u,v) \in \mathsf{supp}(\psi)$; it allows u or v to be the symbol $\bot$, in which case it evaluates to 0.) Theorem 3 follows from this result when ψ is taken as OT^m.

---

[3] More generally, for a correlation ψ, the 0-1 matrix corresponding to the associated predicate $\phi_{\mathsf{supp}(\psi)}$ will be denoted as P_ψ.

[4] Using the sharper statement from Theorem 11, we would have $\mu = m + 2n$, and hence we have $\mathsf{IR}_{P_{\mathsf{OT}}}(M_f) \leq 2(m+n) + 1$.

Theorem 11. *If protocol Π^ψ using regular correlation ψ distributed over $\mathcal{U} \times \mathcal{V}$ computes a deterministic functionality $f : \mathcal{X} \times \mathcal{Y} \rightarrow \mathcal{A} \times \mathcal{B}$ with perfect security, then f has a μ-SZCR to $\phi_{\mathsf{supp}^*(\psi)}$ using ψ^{CRS}, where $\mu = \log \frac{|\mathcal{U}| \, |\mathcal{V}| |\mathcal{X}|^2 |\mathcal{Y}|^2}{|\mathsf{supp}(\psi)|}$.*

Additionally, if f is common-information-free, then f has a μ'-SZCR to $\phi_{\mathsf{supp}^*(\psi)}$ using no correlation, where $\mu' = \log \frac{|\mathcal{U}| \, |\mathcal{V}| |\mathcal{X}| |\mathcal{Y}|}{|\mathsf{supp}(\psi)|}$.

A proof of this theorem is provided in the full version [NPP20]. Theorem 3 is obtained by specializing the above result to the correlation of OT.

Proof: [Proof of Theorem 3] A single instance of OT is a regular correlation with its support being a $1/2$ fraction of its entire domain (see the matrix P_{OT}). Hence m independent OTs form a regular correlation OT^m distributed over $\mathcal{U} \times \mathcal{V} = \{0,1\}^{2m} \times \{0,1\}^{2m}$ such that $\frac{|\mathsf{supp}(\mathsf{OT}^m)|}{|\mathcal{U}||\mathcal{V}|} = \frac{1}{2^m}$. Invoking Theorem 11 for $|\mathcal{X}| = |\mathcal{Y}| = 2^n$, we get a μ-SZCR from f to $\phi_{\mathsf{supp}^*(\mathsf{OT}^m)}$ using ψ^{CRS}, where $\mu = \log \frac{|\mathcal{U}||\mathcal{V}||\mathcal{X}|^2|\mathcal{Y}|^2}{|\mathsf{supp}(\mathsf{OT}^m)|} = m + 4n$. (If f is common-information-free, i.e., it has a single connected component in G_f, then ψ^{CRS} is not needed and $\mu = m + 2n$.)

Recall that the domain of $\phi_{\mathsf{supp}^*(\mathsf{OT}^m)}$ contains a special symbol $\bot$, in addition to $2m$ bit long strings that are in the support of OT^m. It is not hard to see that we can implement the functionality of this symbol $\bot$ using an additional instance of OT. That is, every (u, v) in the domain of $\phi_{\mathsf{supp}^*(\mathsf{OT}^m)}$ can be encoded as $(\hat{u}, \hat{v})$ in the domain of $\phi_{\mathsf{supp}(\mathsf{OT}^{m+1})}$ so that $\phi_{\mathsf{supp}^*(\mathsf{OT}^m)}(u, v) = \phi_{\mathsf{supp}(\mathsf{OT}^{m+1})}(\hat{u}, \hat{v})$. Hence, f has a μ-SZCR to $\phi_{\mathsf{supp}(\mathsf{OT}^{m+1})}$ using a ψ^{CRS} (or, if f is common-information-free, using no correlation). □

We also prove Theorem 12, which is a "dual version" of Theorem 11: Here, when the protocol Π^ψ is transformed into a SZCR, instead of ψ transforming into the predicate, it remains a correlation that is used by the reduction; this reduction is to the constant-sized predicate ϕ_{AND}.

Theorem 12. *Suppose Π^ψ is a perfectly secure protocol for a deterministic functionality $f : \mathcal{X} \times \mathcal{Y} \rightarrow \mathcal{A} \times \mathcal{B}$, that uses a regular correlation ψ over $\mathcal{R} \times \mathcal{S}$. Then f has a μ-SZCR to ϕ_{AND} using ψ, where $\mu = \log |\mathcal{X}||\mathcal{Y}||\mathcal{R}||\mathcal{S}|$.*

The reduction and its analysis is similar to that in Theorem 11. A detailed proof is provided in the full version [NPP20].

5.3 Communication Complexity vs. SZCR

In this section, we lower bound the domain size of a predicate ϕ to which a functionality has a non-trivial SZCR. In combination with Theorem 11, which provides an upper bound on the domain size of the predicate in terms of OT complexity, we obtain a lower bound on OT complexity in terms of (one-way) communication complexity, reproducing a result of [BM04].

More precisely, the connection between the domain size of ϕ and the communication complexity of f is captured below. To be able to base the lower bound on the *one-way communication complexity* of f, we consider a one-sided functionality f.

Lemma 2. *Let $f : \mathcal{X} \times \mathcal{Y} \to \mathcal{A} \times \{\perp\}$ be a deterministic one-sided functionality such that for all y, y' there exists some x such that $f_A(x, y) \neq f_A(x, y')$. For any predicate $\phi : \mathcal{U} \times \mathcal{V} \to \{0, 1\}$, and $\mu > 0$, f has a perfect μ-SZCR to ϕ using no correlation only if $|\mathcal{V}| \geq |\mathcal{Y}|$.*

Proof: We will show that if f has a perfect μ-SZCR to ϕ using no correlation, then there exists a one-way communication protocol for computing f_A, where the message is an element of the set $\mathcal{V}$. By our assumption, no two inputs of Bob are equivalent w.r.t. f_A. Hence in a one-way communication protocol for f_A, Bob must communicate his exact input to Alice. This implies that $|\mathcal{V}| \geq |\mathcal{Y}|$.

Suppose $(\mathfrak{A}, \mathfrak{B})$ is a μ-SZCR from f to the predicate ϕ using no correlation. Consider the jointly distributed random variables (U, A, V, D) (as described in Fig. 1), conditioned on input (x, y). Since $f_B(x, y) = \perp$ for all (x, y), the security condition (3) (for $\epsilon = 0$) guarantees that $\Pr(v|x, y, D = 1) = \Pr(\hat{S}_B(y, \perp, 1) = v)$, for all x, y, v.

The one-way communication protocol for computing f when Alice and Bob have inputs x and y, respectively can be described as follows. Bob picks a v in the support of the distribution $\hat{S}_B(y, \perp, 1)$, and sends it to Alice. Alice, chooses $(u, a) \in \mathcal{U} \times \mathcal{A}$ such that $\Pr_{\mathfrak{A}}(u, a|x) > 0$ and $\phi(u, v) = 1$, and outputs a. Existence of such a pair (u, a) is argued as follows. By non-triviality of the SZCR, $\Pr(D = 1|x, y) > 0$ and since v is in the support of $\hat{S}_B(y, \perp, 1)$,

$$\Pr(v|x, y, D = 1) = \Pr(\hat{S}_B(y, \perp, 1) = v) > 0.$$

Hence, $\Pr(D = 1|x, y, v) > 0$. This implies that there exists (u, a) such that $\Pr(a, u, v, D = 1|x, y) > 0$. The new one-way communication protocol is correct since the perfect correctness of $(\mathfrak{A}, \mathfrak{B})$ implies that $a = f_A(x, y)$. $\square$

Corollary 2. *If f is a deterministic functionality with one-sided output, such that for all y, y' there exists some x such that $f_A(x, y) \neq f_A(x, y')$, then its OT complexity is lower bounded by its one-way computation complexity.*

Proof: Since f is a one-sided (hence common-information-free) functionality, by Theorem 11 f has a perfect non-trivial SZCR to $\phi_{\mathsf{supp}(\mathsf{OT}^{m+1})}$ using no correlation if the OT complexity of f is m. Since f is one-sided, by Lemma 2, 2^{m+1} is at least the size of the domain of the non-computing user. This proves the claim. $\square$

6   Upper Bounds

In this section, we show that ZCR provides a new path to protocols in different secure computation models. In Sect. 6.1, we obtain upper bounds on CDS, PSM and 2PC, in terms of the *communication complexity* of the functions being computed, followed by improved upper bounds in Sect. 6.2 which leverage ZCR and its connections to information complexity.

6.1   Upper Bounds Using Communication Complexity

In this section, we follow the outline below to prove Theorem 1.

For a deterministic function $f : \mathcal{X} \times \mathcal{Y} \to \mathcal{Z}$, a k-tiling is the partition of $\mathcal{X} \times \mathcal{Y}$ into k monochromatic rectangles – i.e., sets $R_1, \ldots, R_k$ such that $R_i = \mathcal{X}_i \times \mathcal{Y}_i$ and $\exists z_i \in \mathcal{Z}$ s.t., $\forall (x,y) \in R_i$, $f(x,y) = z_i$. (Then, abusing the notation, we write $f(R_i)$ to denote z_i.) We refer to the smallest number k such that f has a k-tiling, as the tiling number of f. The first step above is standard: Communication complexity of ℓ implies a protocol with at most 2^ℓ transcripts, and the inputs consistent with each transcript corresponds to a monochromatic tile.

The last step requires a (non-trivial) perfect deterministic WZCR from f to (say) ϕ_{AND} using ψ^{CRS}. If ℓ is the length of the common random string supplied by ψ^{CRS}, the resulting CDS, PSM or 2PC (in the OT-hybrid model) protocols for f, will have $O(2^\ell)$ communication complexity (as well as OT complexity, in the case of 2PC). Further, we show that such a WZCR can be readily constructed from a tiling for f, with 2^ℓ tiles. Lemma 3 summarizes the upperbounds we obtain using such constructions under different secure computation models. The detailed construction of all the protocols are relegated to the full version [NPP20].

Lemma 3. *For a deterministic function $f : \mathcal{X} \times \mathcal{Y} \to \mathcal{Z}$, if f admits a k-tiling, then the following exist.*

1. *A perfectly secure CDS for predicate f (when $\mathcal{Z} = \{0,1\}$) with $O(k)$ communication.*
2. *A perfectly secure PSM for f with $O(k \log |\mathcal{Z}|)$ communication.*
3. *A perfectly secure 2-party symmetric secure function evaluation protocol for f, against passive corruption, with $O(k \log |\mathcal{Z}|)$ communication and OT invocations.*

Remark 1. In our proof of the above lemma, we show a $(\mu, 0)$-WZCR for *any* deterministic functionality $g : \mathcal{X} \times \mathcal{Y} \to \mathcal{A} \times \mathcal{B}$ to ϕ_{AND} (with $\mu = \log(k_1 \cdot k_2)$ where k_1 and k_2 are the tiling numbers of g_A and g_B, respectively). This is in contrast with Theorem 7 where we showed that only simple functions have a $(\mu, 0)$-SZCR to ϕ_{AND} for any $\mu > 0$.

Lemma 3, combined with the fact that a communication complexity of ℓ implies a tiling with at most 2^ℓ tiles, proves Theorem 1.

6.2   Upper Bounds Using Information Complexity

In this section we follow the outline below to prove Theorem 2.

Information complexity	$\to$	Relaxed partition	$\to$	WZCR	$\to$	CDS, PSM and 2PC

In Sect. 6.2.1, we present the definitions as well as the first step from [KLL+15], and show how a relaxed partition of f can be turned into a WZCR for f. Then, in Sect. 6.2.2, we show how a WZCR (in fact, a ZCR) can be transformed into (statistically secure) PSM, CDS, and 2PC protocols. A detailed form of the final result is presented in Theorem 13 (from which Theorem 2 follows).

6.2.1 Information Complexity and Relaxed Partition

First, we define information complexity and relaxed partition bound.

Information Complexity. Consider a deterministic function $f : \mathcal{X} \times \mathcal{Y} \to \mathcal{Z}$ and a possibly randomized non-secure protocol Π for computing f. When Π is executed with $x \in \mathcal{X}$ and $y \in \mathcal{Y}$, respectively, as inputs of Alice and Bob, let $\Pi(x, y)$ be the random variable for the transcript of the protocol, and let A and B denote the outputs of Alice and Bob, respectively. For jointly distributed random variables (X, Y) over $\mathcal{X} \times \mathcal{Y}$, the error of the protocol $\mathrm{error}_{X,Y}^{f}(\Pi) = \Pr[A \neq f(X, Y) \text{ or } B \neq f(X, Y)]$. For $\epsilon \geq 0$, information complexity of a function is defined as

$$\mathsf{IC}_\epsilon(f) = \max_{\mathsf{p}(X,Y)} \min_{\Pi : \mathrm{error}_{X,Y}^{f}(\Pi) \leq \epsilon} I(X; \Pi(X, Y)|Y) + I(Y; \Pi(X, Y)|X).$$

Relaxed Partition. Relaxed partition bound was originally defined in [KLL+15], extending partition bound defined in [JK10]. Here we provide an equivalent definition of the relaxed partition bound that makes the connection with WZCR clearer.

Definition 9 (Relaxed partition bound). *Consider a deterministic function* $f : \mathcal{X} \times \mathcal{Y} \to \mathcal{Z}$. *For every rectangle* $R \in 2^{\mathcal{X}} \times 2^{\mathcal{Y}}$ *and* $z \in \mathcal{Z}$, *let* $w(R, z) \in [0, 1]$. *The relaxed partition bound for* $\epsilon \geq 0$, *denoted by* $\bar{\mathsf{prt}}_\epsilon(f)$, *is defined as* $\min \frac{1}{\eta}$ *subject to:* $\sum_{R,z} w(R, z) = 1$,

$$\sum_{R:(x,y)\in R} w(R, f(x, y)) \geq \eta(1 - \epsilon), \qquad \forall(x, y) \in \mathcal{X} \times \mathcal{Y}$$

$$\sum_{R:(x,y)\in R} \sum_{z \in \mathcal{Z}} w(R, z) \leq \eta, \qquad \forall(x, y) \in \mathcal{X} \times \mathcal{Y}$$

$$w(R, z) \geq 0. \qquad \forall R \in 2^{\mathcal{X}} \times 2^{\mathcal{Y}}, z \in \mathcal{Z}$$

The following proposition restates a theorem due to Kerenidis et al. [KLL+15] that gives a connection between relaxed partition bound and information complexity. The statement has been modified for our purposes.

Proposition 1 (Theorem 1.1 in *[KLL+15]*). *There is a positive constant* C *such that for every function* $f : \mathcal{X} \times \mathcal{Y} \to \mathcal{Z}$ *and* $\epsilon > 0$,

$$\log \bar{\mathsf{prt}}_{2\epsilon}(f) \leq \left(\frac{9C \cdot \mathsf{IC}_\epsilon(f)}{\epsilon^2} + \frac{3C}{\epsilon} + \log |\mathcal{Z}| \right).$$

See the full version [NPP20] for details on the modification of [KLL+15, Theorem 1.1] which gives the above form. Interestingly, this result is established in [KLL+15] via a notion of *zero communication protocols*, which is similar to (albeit more restricted than) our notion of ZCR. This is not surprising given the close connection between relaxed partition bound and WZCR that we establish below. The following lemma is proved in the full version [NPP20].

Lemma 4. *For any $f : \mathcal{X} \times \mathcal{Y} \to \mathcal{Z}$, functionality (f, f) has a (μ, ϵ)-WZCR to Φ_{AND} using ψ^{CRS}, where $\mu = \log \frac{\bar{\text{prt}}_\epsilon(f)}{1 - \epsilon}$.*

6.2.2 From ZCR to Secure Computation

In this section we use ZCR to construct protocols for statistically secure PSM, CDS and secure 2PC. To accomplish this, the parties carry out the ZCR protocol n times, for n sufficiently large as to guarantee (except with negligible probability) that there will be at least one instance which would accept. Amongst these n executions, a selector function selects the candidate outputs corresponding to a reduction in which the predicate is accepted, without revealing the execution itself. For this we use the notion of selector functions, which we next define. We conclude this section with Theorem 13, which formally states and proves the claim in Theorem 2.

Definition 10. *For a predicate $\phi : \mathcal{U} \times \mathcal{V} \to \{0, 1\}$, finite set $\mathcal{Z}$ and $t \in \mathbb{N}$, we define selector function $\text{Sel}^{\phi, \mathcal{Z}, t} : \mathcal{U}^t \times \mathcal{Z}^t \times \mathcal{V}^t \to \mathcal{Z}$ as follows. For $u^t := (u_1, \ldots, u_t) \in \mathcal{U}^t, v^t := (v_1, \ldots, v_t) \in \mathcal{V}^t$ and $z^t := (z_1, \ldots, z_t) \in \mathcal{Z}^t$,*

$$\text{Sel}^{\phi, \mathcal{Z}, t}(u^t, v^t, z^t) = \begin{cases} z_i \text{ if } \exists i \text{ s.t. } \phi(u_i, v_i) = 1, \forall j > i, \phi(u_j, v_j) = 0, \\ z^* \text{ otherwise.} \end{cases}$$

Here, z^* is a fixed arbitrary member of $\mathcal{Z}$. For the specific case where $\mathcal{Z} = \{0, 1\}$, we will set $z^* = 0$.

Selector function for the predicate ϕ_{AND} is of special interest. The following lemma shows that for $t \in \mathbb{N}$ and finite set $\mathcal{Z}$, there is an efficient PSM protocol and a secure 2-party protocol that compute $\text{Sel}^{\phi_{\text{AND}}, \mathcal{Z}, t}$, when Alice and Bob get inputs $(u^t, z^t) \in \mathcal{U}^t \times \mathcal{Z}^t$ and $v^t \in \mathcal{V}^t$, respectively. When $\mathcal{Z} = \{0, 1\}$, there is an efficient protocol for CDS with predicate $\text{Sel}^{\phi_{\text{AND}}, \mathcal{Z}, t}$. We use this to show upper bounds for communication complexity of statistically secure PSM and CDS protocols, and for OT complexity and communication complexity of statistically secure 2PC.

Lemma 5. *The following statements hold for the predicate ϕ_{AND}, $t \in \mathbb{N}$ and a finite set $\mathcal{Z}$.*

    (i). $\text{Sel}^{\phi_{\text{AND}}, \mathcal{Z}, t} : (\mathcal{U}^t \times \mathcal{Z}^t) \times \mathcal{V}^t \to \mathcal{Z}$ has perfect PSM with communication complexity $O(t^2 \cdot \log |\mathcal{Z}|)$.

    (ii). CDS for the predicate $\text{Sel}^{\phi_{\text{AND}}, \{0,1\}, t} : (\mathcal{U}^t \times \{0, 1\}^t) \times \mathcal{V}^t \to \{0, 1\}$ and domain $\{0, 1\}$ has communication complexity $O(t)$.

(iii). The functionality $\left(\mathsf{Sel}^{\phi_{\mathsf{AND}},\mathcal{Z},t}, \mathsf{Sel}^{\phi_{\mathsf{AND}},\mathcal{Z},t},\right) : (\mathcal{U}^t \times \mathcal{Z}^t) \times \mathcal{V}^t \to \mathcal{Z} \times \mathcal{Z}$ *has a perfectly secure 2PC protocol with communication complexity and OT complexity* $O(t \cdot \log |\mathcal{Z}|)$.

Since there are efficient PSM protocols for branching programs, the first statement is shown by providing a small branching program for $\mathsf{Sel}^{\phi_{\mathsf{AND}},\mathcal{Z},t}$. Statements (ii) and (iii) are proved by showing that $\mathsf{Sel}^{\phi_{\mathsf{AND}},\{0,1\},t}$ and $\mathsf{Sel}^{\phi_{\mathsf{AND}},\mathcal{Z},t}$, respectively, have small formulas [FKN94], [IK97]. The detailed proof is provided in the full version [NPP20].

We now proceed to give constructions for *statistically secure* PSM, CDS and 2PC using ZCR. All the three constructions follow the same framework. We start with ZCR of a functionality f to predicate ϕ. The ZCR is executed (independently) sufficiently many times to guarantee that at least one of the executions satisfy the predicate but with negligible probability. The output of a reduction in which the predicate was accepted is securely chosen using the selector function for the predicate. Following lemma summarizes the upper bounds we obtain for statistically secure PSM, CDS and 2PC *via.* constructions using ZCR. Detailed proof of the lemma is provided in the full version [NPP20].

Lemma 6. *Let* $f : \mathcal{X} \times \mathcal{Y} \to \mathcal{Z}$ *be a deterministic function and* $\perp$ *be a constant function with the same domain If* $(f, \perp)$ *has a* (μ, ϵ)-*ZCR to* ϕ *using* ψ^{CRS}, *then for* $t = 2^\mu \ln \frac{1}{\epsilon}$, *we obtain the following upper bound.*

1. *The* 4ϵ-*PSM complexity of* f *is at most the PSM complexity of the selector function* $\mathsf{Sel}^{\phi,\mathcal{Z},t} : (\mathcal{U}^t \times \mathcal{Z}^t) \times \mathcal{V}^t \to \mathcal{Z}$.
2. *The communication complexity of* 4ϵ-*CDS for predicate* f *(when* $\mathcal{Z} = \{0,1\}$*) is at most that of CDS for predicate* $\mathsf{Sel}^{\phi,\mathcal{Z},t} : (\mathcal{U}^t \times \mathcal{Z}^t) \times \mathcal{V}^t \to \mathcal{Z}$.
3. *The communication complexity (respectively, OT complexity) of* 4ϵ-*secure computation of the functionality* (f, f) *is at most the communication complexity (respectively, OT complexity) of perfectly secure computation of the symmetric functionality* $\left(\mathsf{Sel}^{\phi,\mathcal{Z},t}, \mathsf{Sel}^{\phi,\mathcal{Z},t}\right) : (\mathcal{U}^t \times \mathcal{Z}^t) \times \mathcal{V}^t \to \mathcal{Z} \times \mathcal{Z}$.

Theorem 13. *Let* $f : \mathcal{X} \times \mathcal{Y} \to \mathcal{Z}$ *be a deterministic function and* $\epsilon > 0$. *There exists a positive constant* C *such that for*

$$K = 2^{\left(\frac{9C \cdot \mathsf{IC}_\epsilon(f)}{\epsilon^2} + \frac{3C}{\epsilon} + \log |\mathcal{Z}|\right)} \cdot \left(\frac{\ln(1/2\epsilon)}{1 - 2\epsilon}\right),$$

1. *The communication complexity of* 8ϵ-*PSM of* f *is* $O\left(K^2 \log |\mathcal{Z}|\right)$.
2. *The communication complexity of* 8ϵ-*CDS for predicate* f *(when* $\mathcal{Z} = \{0,1\}$*) and domain* $\{0,1\}$ *is* $O(K)$.
3. *The OT complexity and communication complexity of* 8ϵ-*secure computation of* f *is* $O\left(K \log |\mathcal{Z}|\right)$.

Proof: The statistically secure protocols described in the above lemma taken together with the connection between WZCR and information complexity allow us to prove our upper bounds on complexities in terms of information complexity for these models. Specifically, it follows from Proposition 1 and Lemma 4 that (f, f) (hence $(f, \perp)$) has a $(\mu, 2\epsilon)$-ZCR to ϕ_{AND} using ψ^{CRS}, where

$$\mu \leq \log \frac{1}{1 - 2\epsilon} \cdot \left(\frac{9C \cdot \mathsf{IC}_\epsilon(f)}{\epsilon^2} + \frac{3C}{\epsilon} + \log |\mathcal{Z}| \right).$$

Using the statement 1 in Lemma 6 along with Lemma 5, we can now show that there exists an 8ϵ-PSM protocol for f with communication complexity $O\left(\left(2^\mu \cdot \log \frac{1}{2\epsilon} \right)^2 \cdot \log |\mathcal{Z}| \right)$. Similarly, using statement 2 in Lemmas 6 and 5, we can show that there is an 8ϵ-CDS protocol for predicate f with communication complexity $O\left(2^\mu \cdot \log \frac{1}{2\epsilon} \cdot \log |\{0,1\}| \right)$. And using statement 3 in Lemmas 6 and 5, we can show that there is an 8ϵ-secure 2-party protocol for f with communication complexity $O\left(2^\mu \cdot \log \frac{1}{2\epsilon} \cdot \log |\mathcal{Z}| \right)$. This proves the theorem. □

Acknowledgement. This research was supported by Ministry of Science and Technology, Israel and Department of Science and Technology, Government of India, under Joint Indo-Israel Project DST/INT/ISR/P-16/2017. V. Narayanan and V. Prabhakaran were supported by the Department of Atomic Energy, Government of India, under project no. RTI4001; M. Prabhakaran was supported by the Dept. of Science and Technology, India via the Ramanujan Fellowship; V. Narayanan acknowledges the discussions with Tulasi Mohan Molli on various topics in communication complexity.

References

[AA18] Applebaum, B., Arkis, B.: On the power of amortization in secret sharing: d-uniform secret sharing and CDS with constant information rate. In: Beimel, A., Dziembowski, S. (eds.) TCC 2018. LNCS, vol. 11239, pp. 317–344. Springer, Cham (2018). https://doi.org/10.1007/978-3-030-03807-6_12

[AHMS18] Applebaum, B., Holenstein, T., Mishra, M., Shayevitz, O.: The communication complexity of private simultaneous messages, revisited. In: Nielsen, J.B., Rijmen, V. (eds.) EUROCRYPT 2018. LNCS, vol. 10821, pp. 261–286. Springer, Cham (2018). https://doi.org/10.1007/978-3-319-78375-8_9

[ALSV13] Alon, N., Lee, T., Shraibman, A., Vempala, S.S.: The approximate rank of a matrix and its algorithmic applications. In: STOC, pp. 675–684 (2013)

[AR17] Applebaum, B., Raykov, P.: From private simultaneous messages to zero-information arthur-merlin protocols and back. J. Cryptology **30**, 961–988 (2017)

[AW17] Alman, J., Williams, R.R.: Probabilistic rank and matrix rigidity. In: STOC, pp. 641–652 (2017)

[BIKK14] Beimel, A., Ishai, Y., Kumaresan, R., Kushilevitz, E.: On the cryptographic complexity of the worst functions. In: Lindell, Y. (ed.) TCC 2014. LNCS, vol. 8349, pp. 317–342. Springer, Heidelberg (2014). https://doi.org/10.1007/978-3-642-54242-8_14

[BM04] Beimel, A., Malkin, T.: A quantitative approach to reductions in secure computation. In: Naor, M. (ed.) TCC 2004. LNCS, vol. 2951, pp. 238–257. Springer, Heidelberg (2004). https://doi.org/10.1007/978-3-540-24638-1_14

[BW16]   Braverman, M., Weinstein, O.: A discrepancy lower bound for information complexity. Algorithmica, pp. 846–864 (2016)

[CK91]   Chor, B., Kushilevitz, E.: A zero-one law for boolean privacy. SIAM J. Discrete Math. **4**(1), 36–47 (1991)

[DG16]   Dvir , Z., Gopi, S.: 2-server PIR with subpolynomial communication. J. ACM **63**(4), 39:1–39:15 (2016)

[FKN94] Feige, U., Kilian, J., Naor, M.: A minimal model for secure computation (extended abstract). In: STOC, pp. 554–563 (1994)

[GG99]   Gisin, N., Gisin, B.: A local hidden variable model of quantum correlation exploiting the detection loophole. Phys. Lett. A **260**(5), 323–327 (1999)

[GIKM00] Gertner, Y., Ishai, Y., Kushilevitz, E., Malkin, T.: Protecting data privacy in private information retrieval schemes. J. Comput. Syst. Sci. **60**(3), 592–629 (2000)

[GKR15] Ganor, A., Kol, G., Raz, R.: Exponential separation of information and communication for boolean functions. In: STOC, pp. 557–566 (2015)

[Gol04] Goldreich, O.: Foundations of Cryptography: Basic Applications. Cambridge University Press, New York (2004)

[IK97]   Ishai, Y., Kushilevitz, E.: Private simultaneous messages protocols with applications. In: ISTCS, pp. 174–184 (1997)

[JK10]   Jain, R., Klauck, H.: The partition bound for classical communication complexity and query complexity. In: CCC, pp. 247–258 (2010)

[KLL+15] Kerenidis, I., Laplante, S., Lerays, V., Roland, J., Xiao, D.: Lower bounds on information complexity via zero-communication protocols and applications. SIAM J. Comput. **44**(5), 1550–1572 (2015)

[KN97]   Kushilevitz, E., Nisan, N.: Communication Complexity. Cambridge University Press, New York (1997)

[LVW17] Liu, T., Vaikuntanathan, V., Wee, H.: Conditional disclosure of secrets via non-linear reconstruction. In: Katz, J., Shacham, H. (eds.) CRYPTO 2017. LNCS, vol. 10401, pp. 758–790. Springer, Cham (2017). https://doi.org/10.1007/978-3-319-63688-7_25

[LVW18] Liu, T., Vaikuntanathan, V., Wee, H.: Towards breaking the exponential barrier for general secret sharing. In: Nielsen, J.B., Rijmen, V. (eds.) EUROCRYPT 2018. LNCS, vol. 10820, pp. 567–596. Springer, Cham (2018). https://doi.org/10.1007/978-3-319-78381-9_21

[MPR12] Maji, H.K., Prabhakaran, M., Rosulek, M.: A unified characterization of completeness and triviality for secure function evaluation. In: Galbraith, S., Nandi, M. (eds.) INDOCRYPT 2012. LNCS, vol. 7668, pp. 40–59. Springer, Heidelberg (2012). https://doi.org/10.1007/978-3-642-34931-7_4

[MPR13] Maji, H., Prabhakaran, M., Rosulek, M.: Complexity of Multi-Party Computation Functionalities. Cryptology and Information Security Series, vol. 10, pp. 249–283. IOS Press, Amsterdam (2013)

[NPP20] Narayanan, V., Prabhakaran, M., Prabhakaran, V.: Zero-communication reductions. In: Cryptology ePrint Archive (2020)

[PP14]   Prabhakaran, V., Prabhakaran, M.: Assisted common information with an application to secure two-party sampling. IEEE Trans. Inf. Theory **60**(6), 3413–3434 (2014)

[PP16]   Prabhakaran, M.M., Prabhakaran, V.M.: Rényi information complexity and an information theoretic characterization of the partition bound. In: ICALP, pp. 88:1–88:14 (2016)

[PR17]   Pitassi, T., Robere, R.: Strongly exponential lower bounds for monotone computation. In: STOC, pp. 1246–1255 (2017)

[PS86]   Paturi, R., Simon, J.: Probabilistic communication complexity. J. Comput. Syst. Sci. **33**(1), 106–123 (1986)

[Raz90]   Razborov, A.A.: Applications of matrix methods to the theory of lower bounds in computational complexity. Combinatorica **10**(1), 81–93 (1990)

[RPRC16] Robere, R., Pitassi, T., Rossman, B., Cook, S.A.: Exponential lower bounds for monotone span programs. In: FOCS, pp. 406–415 (2016)

[Val77]   Valiant, L.G.: Graph-theoretic arguments in low-level complexity. In: Mathematical Foundations of Computer Science, pp. 162–176 (1977)

Lower Bounds on the Time/Memory Tradeoff of Function Inversion

Dror Chawin$^{(\boxtimes)}$, Iftach Haitner, and Noam Mazor

School of Computer Science, Tel Aviv University, Tel Aviv, Israel
quefumas@gmail.com, iftachh@cs.tau.ac.il, noammaz@gmail.com

Abstract. We study time/memory tradeoffs of *function inversion*: an algorithm, i.e., an *inverter*, equipped with an s-bit advice on a randomly chosen function $f \colon [n] \mapsto [n]$ and using q oracle queries to f, tries to invert a randomly chosen output y of f, i.e., to find $x \in f^{-1}(y)$. Much progress was done regarding *adaptive* function inversion—the inverter is allowed to make *adaptive* oracle queries. Hellman [IEEE transactions on Information Theory '80] presented an adaptive inverter that inverts with high probability a random f. Fiat and Naor [SICOMP '00] proved that for any s, q with $s^3 q = n^3$ (ignoring low-order terms), an s-advice, q-query variant of Hellman's algorithm inverts a constant fraction of the image points of *any* function. Yao [STOC '90] proved a lower bound of $sq \geq n$ for this problem. Closing the gap between the above lower and upper bounds is a long-standing open question.

Very little is known of the *non-adaptive* variant of the question—the inverter chooses its queries *in advance*. The only known upper bounds, i.e., inverters, are the *trivial* ones (with $s + q = n$), and the only lower bound is the above bound of Yao. In a recent work, Corrigan-Gibbs and Kogan [TCC '19] partially justified the difficulty of finding lower bounds on non-adaptive inverters, showing that a lower bound on the time/memory tradeoff of non-adaptive inverters implies a lower bound on low-depth Boolean circuits. Bounds that, for a strong enough choice of parameters, are notoriously hard to prove.

We make progress on the above intriguing question, both for the adaptive and the non-adaptive case, proving the following lower bounds on restricted families of inverters:

Linear-advice (adaptive inverter). If the advice string is a linear function of f (e.g., $A \times f$, for some matrix A, viewing f as a vector in $[n]^n$), then $s + q \in \Omega(n)$. The bound generalizes to the case where the advice string of $f_1 + f_2$, i.e., the coordinate-wise addition of the truth tables of f_1 and f_2, can be computed from the description of f_1 and f_2 by a *low* communication protocol.

Affine non-adaptive decoders. If the non-adaptive inverter has an *affine decoder*—it outputs a linear function, determined by the advice string and the element to invert, of the query answers—then $s \in \Omega(n)$ (regardless of q).

I. Haitner—Member of the Check Point Institute for Information Security.

N. Mazor et al.—Research supported by ERC starting grant 638121 and Israel Science Foundation grant 666/19.

© International Association for Cryptologic Research 2020
R. Pass and K. Pietrzak (Eds.): TCC 2020, LNCS 12552, pp. 305–334, 2020.
https://doi.org/10.1007/978-3-030-64381-2_11

> **Affine non-adaptive decision trees.** If the non-adaptive inversion algorithm is a d-depth *affine decision tree*—it outputs the evaluation of a decision tree whose nodes compute a linear function of the answers to the queries—and $q < cn$ for some universal $c > 0$, then $s \in \Omega(n/d \log n)$.

Keywords: Function inverters · Random functions · Time/memory tradeoff

1 Introduction

In the *function-inversion* problem, an algorithm, *inverter*, attempts to find a preimage for a randomly chosen $y \in [n]$ of a random function $f: [n] \to [n]$. The inverter is equipped with an s-bit advice on f, and may make q oracle queries to f. Since s lowerbounds the inverter space complexity and q lowerbounds the inverter time complexity, it is common to refer to the relation between s and q as the inverter's *time/memory tradeoff*. The function-inversion problem is central to both theoretical and practical cryptography. On the theoretical end, the security of many systems relies on the existence of one-way functions. While the task of inverting one-way functions is very different from that of inverting random functions, understanding the latter task is critical towards developing lower bounds on the possible (black-box) implications of one-way functions, e.g., Impagliazzo and Rudich [18], Gennaro et al. [14]. But advances on this problem (at least on the positive side, i.e., inverters) are likely to find practical applications. Indeed, algorithms for function inversion are used to expose weaknesses in existing cryptosystems.

Much progress was done regarding *adaptive* function inversion—the inverter may choose its queries adaptively (i.e., based on answers for previous queries). Hellman [17] presented an adaptive inverter that inverts with high probability a random f. Fiat and Naor [12] proved that for any s, q with $s^3 q = n^3$ (ignoring low-order terms), an s-advice q-query variant of Hellman's algorithm inverts a constant fraction of the image points of *any* function. Yao [27] proved a lower bound of $s \cdot q \geq n$ for this problem. Closing the gap between the above lower and upper bounds is a long-standing open question. In contrast, very little is known about the non-adaptive variant of this problem—the inverter performs all queries at once. This variant is interesting since such inverter is likely be highly parallelizable, making it significantly more tractable for real world applications. The only known upper bounds for this variant, i.e., inverters, are the *trivial* ones (i.e., $s + q = n$), and the only known lower bound is the above bound of Yao [27]. In a recent work, Corrigan-Gibbs and Kogan [9] have partially justified the difficulty of finding lower bounds on this seemingly easier to tackle problem, showing that lower bounds on non-adaptive inversion imply circuit lower bounds that, for strong enough parameters, are notoriously hard (see further details in Sect. 1.1).

1.1   Our Results

We make progress on this intriguing question, proving lower bounds on restricted families of inverters. To state our results, we use the following formalization to capture inverters with a preprocessing phase: such inverters have two parts, the *preprocessing* algorithm that gets as input the function to invert f and outputs an advice string a, and the *decoding* algorithm that takes as input the element to invert y, the advice string a, and using restricted query access to f tries to find a preimage of y. We start with describing our bound for the time/memory tradeoff of linear-advice (adaptive) inverters, and then present our lower bounds for non-adaptive inverters. In the following, fix $n \in \mathbb{N}$ and let $\mathcal{F}$ be the set of all functions from $[n]$ to $[n]$.

Linear-Advice Inverters. We start with a more formal description of adaptive function inverters.

Definition 1.1. (Adaptive inverters, informal). *An s-advice, q-query adaptive inverter is a deterministic algorithm pair* $C := (C_{pre}, C_{dec})$, *where* $C_{pre} : \mathcal{F} \rightarrow \{0,1\}^s$, *and* $C_{dec}^{(\cdot)} : [n] \times \{0,1\}^s \rightarrow [n]$ *is a q-query algorithm. We say that* C *inverts* $\mathcal{F}$ *with high probability if*

$$\Pr_{\substack{f \leftarrow \mathcal{F} \\ a := C_{pre}(f)}} \left[\Pr_{\substack{x \leftarrow [n] \\ y := f(x)}} \left[C_{dec}^f(y, a) \in f^{-1}(y) \right] \geq 1/2 \right] \geq 1/2.$$

It is common to refer to a ($:= C_{pre}(f)$) as the *advice string*. In *linear-advice* inverters, the preprocessing algorithm C_{pre} is restricted to output a linear function of f. That is, $C_{pre}(f_1) + C_{pre}(f_2) = C_{pre}(f_1 + f_2)$, where the addition $f_1 + f_2$ is coordinate-wise with respect to an arbitrary group over $[n]$, and the addition $C_{pre}(f_1) + C_{pre}(f_2)$ is over an arbitrary group that contains the image of C_{pre}. An example of such a preprocessing algorithm is $C_{pre}(f) := A \times f$, for $A \in \{0,1\}^{s \times n}$, viewing $f \in \mathcal{F}$ as a vector in $[n]^n$. For such inverters, we present the following bound.

Theorem 1.2. (Bound on linear-advice inverters). *Assume there exists an s-advice q-query inverter with linear preprocessing that inverts $\mathcal{F}$ with high probability. Then $s + q \cdot \log n \in \Omega(n)$.*

We prove Theorem 1.2 via a reduction from *set disjointness*, a classical problem in the study of two-party communication complexity. The above result generalizes to the following bound that replaces the restriction on the decoder (e.g., linear and short output) with the ability to compute the advice string of $f_1 + f_2$ by a low-communication protocol over the inputs f_1 and f_2.

Theorem 1.3. (Bound on additive-advice inverters, informal). *Assume there exists a q-query inverter $C := (C_{pre}, \cdot)$ and an s-bit communication two-party protocol (P_1, P_2) such that for every $f_1, f_2 \in \mathcal{F}$, the output of P_1 in $(P_1(f_1), P_2(f_2))$ equals with constant probability to $C_{pre}(f_1 + f_2)$. Then $s + q \cdot \log n \in \Omega(n)$.*

The above bound indeed generalizes Theorem 1.2: a preprocessing algorithm of the type required by Theorem 1.2 immediately implies a two-party party protocol of the type required by Theorem 1.3.

Non-adaptive Inverters. In the non-adaptive setting, the decoding algorithm has two phases: the *query selection* algorithm that chooses the queries as a function of the advice and the element to invert y, and the actual decoder that receives the answers to these queries along with the advice string and y.

Definition 1.4. (Non-adaptive inverters, informal). *An s-advice, q-query non-adaptive inverter is a deterministic algorithm triplet of the form* $\mathsf{C} := (\mathsf{C_{pre}}, \mathsf{C_{qry}}, \mathsf{C_{dec}})$, *where* $\mathsf{C_{pre}} \colon \mathcal{F} \rightarrow \{0,1\}^s$, $\mathsf{C_{qry}} \colon [n] \times \{0,1\}^s \rightarrow [n]^q$ *and* $\mathsf{C_{dec}} \colon [n] \times \{0,1\}^s \times [n]^q \rightarrow [n]$. *We say that* C *inverts* $\mathcal{F}$ *with high probability if*

$$
\Pr_{\substack{f \leftarrow \mathcal{F} \\ a = \mathsf{C_{pre}}(f)}} \left[\Pr_{\substack{x \leftarrow [n] \\ y = f(x) \\ v = \mathsf{C_{qry}}(y,a)}} \left[\mathsf{C_{dec}}(y, a, f(v)) \in f^{-1}(y) \right] \geq 1/2 \right] \geq 1/2.
$$

Note that the query vector v is of length q, so the answer vector $f(v)$ contains q answers. Assuming there exists a field $\mathbb{F}$ of size n (see Remark 1.7), we provide two lower bounds for such inverters.

Affine Decoders. The first bound regards inverters with *affine decoders*. A decoder algorithm $\mathsf{C_{dec}}$ is *affine* if it computes an affine function of f's answers. That is, for every image $y \in [n]$ and advice $a \in \{0,1\}^s$, there exists a q-sparse vector $\alpha_y^a \in \mathbb{F}^n$ and a field element $\beta_y^a \in \mathbb{F}$ such that $\mathsf{C_{dec}}(y, a, f(\mathsf{C_{qry}}(y,a))) = \langle \alpha_y^a, f \rangle + \beta_y^a$ for every $f \in \mathcal{F}$. For this type of inverters, we present the following lower bound.

Theorem 1.5. (Bound on non-adaptive inverters with affine decoders, informal). *Assume there exists an s-advice non-adaptive function inverter with an affine decoder, that inverts $\mathcal{F}$ with high probability. Then $s \in \Omega(n)$.*

Note that the above bound on s holds even if the inverter queries f on all inputs. While Theorem 1.5 is not very insightful for its own sake, as we cannot expect a non-adaptive inverter to have such a limiting structure, it is important since it can be generalized to *affine decision trees*, a much richer family of non-adaptive inverters defined below. In addition, the result should be contrasted with the question of *black-box function computation*, see Sect. 1.2, for which linear algorithm are *optimal*. Thus, Theorem 1.5 highlights the differences between these two related problems.

Affine Decision Trees. The second bound regards inverters whose decoders are *affine decision trees*. An *affine decision tree* is a decision tree whose nodes compute an *affine* function, over $\mathbb{F}$, of the input vector. A decoder algorithm

C_{dec} is an *affine decision tree*, if for every image $y \in [n]$, advice $a \in \{0,1\}^s$ and queries $v = C_{\text{qry}}(y, a)$, there exists an affine decision tree $T^{y,a}$ such that $C_{\text{dec}}(y, a, f(v)) = T^{y,a}(f)$ (i.e., the output of $T^{y,a}$ on input f) for every $f \in \mathcal{F}$. For such inverters, we present the following bound.

Theorem 1.6. (Bounds on non-adaptive inverters with affine decision-tree decoders). *Assume there exists an s-advice q-query non-adaptive function inverter with a d-depth affine decision-tree decoder, that inverts $\mathcal{F}$ with high probability. Then the following hold:*

- *$q < cn$, for some universal constant c, $\implies s \in \Omega(n/d \log n)$.*
- *$q \in n^{1-\Theta(1)} \implies s \in \Omega(n/d)$.*

That is, we pay a factor of $1/d$ comparing to the affine decoder bound, and the bound on s only holds for not too large q. Affine decision trees are much stronger than affine decoders, since the choice of the affine operations it computes can be *adaptively dependent* on the results of previous affine operations. For example, a depth d affine decision tree can compute *any* function on d linear combinations of the inputs. In particular, multiplication of function values, e.g., $f(1) \cdot f(2)$, which cannot be computed by an affine decoder, can be computed by a depth two decision tree. We note that an affine decision tree of depth q can compute *any* function of its q queries. Unfortunately, for $d = q$, our bound only reproduces (up to log factors) the lower bound of Yao [27].

Remark 1.7. (Field size). In Theorems 1.5 and 1.6, the field size is assumed to be exactly n (the domain of the function to invert). Decoders over fields smaller than n are not particularly useful, since their output cannot cover all possible preimages of f. Our proof breaks down for fields of size larger than n, since we cannot use linear equations to represent the constraint that the decoder's output must be contained in the smaller set $[n]$.

Applications to Valiant's Common-Bit Model. Corrigan-Gibbs and Kogan [9] showed that a lower bound on the time/memory tradeoff of *strongly non-adaptive* function inverters—the queries may not depend on the advice—implies a lower bound on circuit size in *Valiant's common-bit model* [23,24]. Applying the reduction of [9] with Theorem 1.6 yields the following bound: for every $n \in \mathbb{N}$ for which there exists an n-size field $\mathbb{F}$, there is an explicit function $f : \mathbb{F}^n \mapsto \mathbb{F}^n$ that cannot be computed by a three-layer circuit of the following structure:

1. It has $o(n/d \log n)$ middle layer gates.
2. Each output gate is connected to $n^{1-\Theta(1)}$ inputs gates (and to an arbitrary number of middle-layer gates).
3. Each output gate computes a function which is computable by a d-depth linear decision tree in the inputs (and depends arbitrarily on the middle layer).

In fact, our bound yields that such circuits cannot even approximate f so that every output gate outputs the right value with probability larger than $1/2$, over the inputs.

1.2   Additional Related Work

Adaptive Inverters

Upper Bounds. The main result in this setting is the s-advice, q-query inverter of Hellman [17], Fiat and Naor [12] that inverts a constant fraction of the image of any function, for any s, q such that $s^3q = n^3$ (ignoring low-order terms). When used for random *permutations*, a variant on the same idea implies an optimum inverter with $s \cdot q = n$. The inverter of Hellman, Fiat and Naor has found application to practical cryptanalysis, e.g., Biryukov and Shamir [5], Biryukov et al. [6], Oechslin [20].

Lower Bounds. A long line of research (Gennaro et al. [14], Dodis et al. [11], Abusalah et al. [1], Unruh [22], Coretti et al. [8], De et al. [10]) provides lower bounds for various variations on the classical setting, such as that of randomized inversion algorithms that succeed on a sub-constant fraction of functions. None of these lower bounds, however, manage to improve on Yao's lower bound of $s \cdot q = n$, leaving a large gap between this lower bound and Hellman, Fiat and Naor's inverter.

Non-adaptive Inverters

Upper Bounds. In contrast with the adaptive case, it is not clear how to exploit non-adaptive queries in a non trivial way. Indeed, the only known inverters are the trivial ones (roughly, the advice is the function description, or the inverter queries the function on all inputs).

Lower Bounds. Somewhat surprisingly, the only known lower bound for non-adaptive inverters is Yao's, mentioned above. This defies the basic intuition that this task should be easier than the adaptive case, due to the extreme limitations under which non-adaptive inverters operate. This difficulty was partially justi-fied by the recent reduction of Corrigan-Gibbs and Kogan [9] (see Sect. 1.1) that implies that a strong enough lower bound on even strongly non-adaptive invert-ers, would yield a lower bound on low-depth Boolean circuits that is notoriously hard to prove.

Relation to Data Structures. The problem of function inversion with advice may also be phrased as a problem in data structures, where the advice string serves as a succinct data structure for answering questions about f. In particular, it bears strong similarity to the *substring search* problem using the cell-probe model [25]. This is the task of ascertaining the existence of a certain element within a large, unsorted database, using as few queries to the database and as little preprocessing as possible. Upper and lower bounds easily carry over between the two problems, a connection which was made in Corrigan-Gibbs and Kogan [9], where it was used to obtain previously unknown upper bounds on substring search.

Index Coding and Black-Box Function Computation. A syntactically related problem to function inversion is the so-called *black-box function computation*: an algorithm tries to compute $f(x)$, for a randomly chosen x, using an advice of length s on f, and by querying f on q inputs other than x. Yao [26] proved that $s \cdot q \geq n$, and presented a linear, non-adaptive algorithm that matches this lower bound.

A much-researched special case of this problem is known as the *index coding* problem [4], originally inspired by information distribution over networks. In this setting, a single party is in possession of a vector f, and broadcasts a short message a such that n different recipients may each recover a particular value of f, using the broadcast message and knowledge of certain other values of f, as determined by a *knowledge graph*. The analogy to non-adaptive black-box function computation is obvious when considering a as the advice string, and the access to various values of f as queries. While Yao's bound on the time/memory tradeoff also holds for the index coding problem, other lower bounds, some of which consider "linear" algorithms [3,4,15,16,19], do not seem to be relevant for the function inversion problem.

Open Questions

The main challenge remains to gain a better understanding on the power of adaptive and non-adaptive function inverters. A more specific challenge is to generalize our bound on affine decoders and decision trees to affine operations over arbitrary (large) fields.

Paper Organization

A rather detailed description of our proof technique is given in Sect. 2. Basic notations, definitions and facts are given in Sect. 3, where we also prove several basic claims regarding random function inversion. The bound on linear-advice inverters is given in Sect. 4, and the bounds on non-adaptive inverters are given in Sect. 5.

2 Our Technique

In this section we provide a rather elaborate description of our proof technique. We start with the bound on linear-advice inverters in Sect. 2.1, and then in Sect. 2.2 describe the bounds for non-adaptive inverters.

2.1 Linear-Advice Inverters

Our lower bound for inverters with linear advice (and its immediate generalization to additive-advice inverters) is proved via a reduction from *set disjointness*, a classical problem in the study of two-party communication complexity. In the set disjointness problem, two parties, Alice and Bob, receive two subsets, $\mathcal{X}$

and $\mathcal{Y} \subseteq [n]$, respectively, and by communicating with each other try to determine whether $\mathcal{X} \cap \mathcal{Y} = \emptyset$. The question is how many bits the parties have to exchange in order to output the right answer with high probability. Given an inverter with linear advice, we use it to construct a protocol that solves the set disjointness problem on *all* inputs in $\mathcal{Q} := \{\mathcal{X}, \mathcal{Y} \subseteq [n] : |\mathcal{X} \cap \mathcal{Y}| \leq 1\}$ by exchanging $s + q \cdot \log n$ bits. Razborov [21] proved that to answer with constant success probability on all input pairs in $\mathcal{Q}$, the parties have to exchange $\Omega(n)$ bits. Hence, the above reduction implies the desired lower bound on the time/memory tradeoff of such inverters.

Fix a q-query s-advice inverter $\mathsf{C} := (\mathsf{C}_{\mathsf{pre}}, \mathsf{C}_{\mathsf{dec}})$ with linear advice, and assume for simplicity that C's success probability is one. The following observation immediately follows by definition: let $a_f := \mathsf{C}_{\mathsf{pre}}(f)$ and $a_g := \mathsf{C}_{\mathsf{pre}}(g)$ be the advice strings for some functions f and $g \in \mathcal{F}$, respectively. The linearity of $\mathsf{C}_{\mathsf{pre}}$ yields that $a := a_f + a_g = \mathsf{C}_{\mathsf{pre}}(f + g)$. That is, a is the advice for the function $f + g$ (all additions are over the appropriate groups). Given this observation, we use C to solve set disjointness as follows: Alice and Bob (locally) convert their input sets $\mathcal{X}$ and $\mathcal{Y}$ to functions f_A and f_B respectively, such that for any $x \in \mathcal{X} \cap \mathcal{Y}$ it holds that $f(x) := (f_\mathsf{A} + f_\mathsf{B})(x) = 0$, and $f(x)$ is *uniform* for $x \notin \mathcal{X} \cap \mathcal{Y}$. Alice then sends $a_\mathsf{A} := \mathsf{C}_{\mathsf{pre}}(f_\mathsf{A})$ to Bob who uses it to compute $a := \mathsf{C}_{\mathsf{pre}}(f) = a_\mathsf{A} + \mathsf{C}_{\mathsf{pre}}(f_\mathsf{B})$. Equipped with the advice a and the help of Alice, Bob then emulates $\mathsf{C}_{\mathsf{dec}}(0, a)$ and finds $x \in f^{-1}(0)$, if such exists. Since f is unlikely to map many elements outside of $\mathcal{X} \cap \mathcal{Y}$ to 0, finding such x is highly correlated with $\mathcal{X} \cap \mathcal{Y} \neq \emptyset$. In more details, the set disjointness protocol is defined as follows.

Protocol 2.1. (Set disjointness protocol $\Pi = (\mathsf{A}(\mathcal{X}), \mathsf{B}(\mathcal{Y}))$)

1. *A samples $f_\mathsf{A} \in \mathcal{F}$ by letting $f_\mathsf{A}(i) := \begin{cases} 0 & i \in \mathcal{X} \\ \sim [n] & otherwise. \end{cases}$*

2. *B samples $f_\mathsf{B} \in \mathcal{F}$ analogously, with respect to $\mathcal{Y}$.*
   - *Let $f := f_\mathsf{A} + f_\mathsf{B}$.*

3. *A sends $a_\mathsf{A} := \mathsf{C}_{\mathsf{pre}}(f_\mathsf{A})$ to B, and B sets $a := a_\mathsf{A} + \mathsf{C}_{\mathsf{pre}}(f_\mathsf{B})$.[1]*

4. *B emulates $\mathsf{C}_{\mathsf{dec}}^f(0, a)$ while answering each query r that $\mathsf{C}_{\mathsf{dec}}$ makes to f as follows:*
   (a) *B sends r to A.*
   (b) *A sends $w_\mathsf{A} := f_\mathsf{A}(r)$ back to B.*
   (c) *B replies $w := w_\mathsf{A} + f_\mathsf{B}(r)$ to $\mathsf{C}_{\mathsf{dec}}$ (as the value of $f(r)$).*
   - *Let x be $\mathsf{C}_{\mathsf{dec}}$'s answer at the end of the above emulation.*

5. *The parties reject if $x \in \mathcal{X} \cap \mathcal{Y}$ (using an additional $\Theta(\log n)$ bits to find it out), and accept otherwise.*

---

[1] If the inverter is only assumed to have additive advice, this step is replaced with the parties interacting in the guaranteed protocol for computing the advice for f from the descriptions of f_A and f_B.

The communication complexity of Π is essentially $s + q \cdot \log n$. It is also clear that the parties accept if $\mathcal{X} \cap \mathcal{Y} = \emptyset$. For the complementary case, by construction, the intersection point of $\mathcal{X} \cap \mathcal{Y}$ is in $f^{-1}(0)$. Furthermore, since $f(i)$ is a random value for all $i \notin \mathcal{X} \cap \mathcal{Y}$, with constant probability *only* the intersection point is in $f^{-1}(0)$. Therefore, the protocol is likely to answer correctly also in the case that $|\mathcal{X} \cap \mathcal{Y}| = 1$.

2.2   Non-adaptive Inverters

We focus on inverters with an affine decoder, and discuss the extension to affine decision tree decoders in Sect. 2.2. The proof follows by bounding the success probability of *zero-advice* inverters—the preprocessing algorithm outputs an empty string. In particular, we prove that the success probability of such inverters is at most $2^{-\Omega(n)}$. Thus, by a union bound over all advice strings, in order to invert $\mathcal{F}$ with high probability, the advice string of a general (non-zero-advice) inverter has to be of length $\Omega(n)$.[2] Let $\mathsf{C} := (\mathsf{C}_{\mathsf{qry}}, \mathsf{C}_{\mathsf{dec}})$ be a zero-advice q-query non-adaptive inverter with an affine decoder. Let F be a random element of $\mathcal{F}$, and for $i \in [n]$, let Y_i be a randomly and independently selected element of $[n]$. Let $X_i := \mathsf{C}_{\mathsf{dec}}(Y_i, F(\mathsf{C}_{\mathsf{qry}}(Y_i)))$, i.e., C's answer on challenge Y_i, and let Z_i be the indicator for $\{F(X_j) = Y_j\}$ for all $j \in [i]$, i.e., the event that C answers the first i challenges correctly. We prove the bound by showing that for some $m \in \Theta(n)$ it holds that

$$\Pr[Z_m] \in 2^{-\Omega(m)} \tag{1}$$

Note that Eq. (1) bounds the probability that C inverts m random elements drawn from $[n]$ (where some of them might have no preimage at all), whereas we are interested in bounding the probability that C inverts a *random output* of F. Yet, since F is a random function, its image covers with very high probability a constant fraction of $[n]$, and thus Eq. (1) can be easily manipulated to derive that

$$\Pr_{f \leftarrow \mathcal{F}} \left[\Pr_{\substack{x \leftarrow [n] \\ y = f(x) \\ v = \mathsf{C}_{\mathsf{qry}}(f,y)}} \left[\mathsf{C}_{\mathsf{dec}}(y, f(v)) \in f^{-1}(y) \right] \geq 1/2 \right] < 2^{-\Omega(m)} = 2^{-\Omega(n)} \tag{2}$$

Hence, in order to invert a random function with high probability, a non-zero-advice inverter has to use advice of length $\Omega(n)$.

We prove Eq. (1) by showing that for every $i \in [m]$ it holds that

$$\Pr[Z_i \mid Z_{i-1}] < 3/5 \tag{3}$$

That is, for small enough i, the algorithm C is likely to fail on inverting the ith challenge, even when conditioned on the successful inversion of the first $i - 1$

---

[2] This first part of the proof is rather standard, cf., Akshima et al. [2].

challenges. We note that it is easy to bound $\Pr[Z_i \mid Z_{i-1}]$ for *zero*-query inverters. The conditioning on Z_{i-1} roughly gives $\Theta(i)$ bits of information about F. Thus, this conditioning gives at most one bit of information about $F^{-1}(Y_i)$, and the inverter does not have enough information to invert Y_i. When moving to non-zero-queries inverters, however, the situation gets much more complicated. By making the right queries, that may depend on Y_i, the inverter can exploit this "small" amount of information to find the preimage of Y_i. This is what happens, for instance, in the adaptive inverter of Hellman [17]. Hence, for bounding $\Pr[Z_i \mid Z_{i-1}]$, we critically exploit the assumption that C is non-adaptive and has an affine decoder. In particular, we bound $\Pr[Z_i \mid Z_{i-1}]$ by translating the event Z_i into an affine system of equations and then use a few observations about the structure of the above system to derive the desired bound. These equations will have the form $M \times F = V$, viewing F as a random vector in $[n]^n$, for

$$\mathbf{M} := \begin{pmatrix} \mathbf{M}^{i-1} \\ \mathbf{M}^i \end{pmatrix} \text{ and } V := \begin{pmatrix} V^{i-1} \\ V^i \end{pmatrix}, \text{ such that:}$$

1. $\mathbf{M}^{i-1}$ is a deterministic function of $(X_{<i}, Y_{<i})$ and $\mathbf{M}^i$ is a deterministic function of Y_i, letting $X_{<i}$ stand for $(X_1, \ldots, X_{i-1})$ and likewise for $Y_{<i}$.
2. The event $M^{i-1} \times F' = V^{i-1}$ is the event $\bigwedge_{j<i} \{(F'(X_j) = Y_j) \wedge (\mathsf{C}_{\mathsf{dec}}(Y_j, F'(\mathsf{C}_{\mathsf{qry}}(Y_j))) = X_j)\}$, for F' being a uniform, and independent, element of $\mathcal{F}$.
   (In particular, $M^{i-1} \times F = V^{i-1}$ implies that Z_{i-1} holds, and binds the value of $(X_{<i}, Y_{<i})$ to V^{i-1}.)
3. The event $M^i \times F' = V^i$ is the event $\{\mathsf{C}_{\mathsf{dec}}(Y_i, F'(\mathsf{C}_{\mathsf{qry}}(Y_i))) = X_i\}$.
   (In particular, $M^i \times F = V^i$ binds the value of X_i to V^i.)

The above $\mathbf{M}$ and V are defined as follows: assume for ease of notation that C has a *linear*, and not affine, decoder. That is, for every $y \in [n]$ there exists a (q-sparse) vector $\alpha_y \in \mathbb{F}^n$ such that $\langle \alpha_y, F \rangle = X_y$. By definition, for every $j < i$:

1. $\langle \alpha_{Y_j}, F \rangle = X_j$.

Conditioning on Z_{i-1} further implies that for every $j < i$:

2. $F(X_j) = Y_j$.

Let $\ell := 2i - 2$, and let $\mathbf{M}^{i-1} \in \mathbb{F}^{\ell \times n}$ be the (random) matrix defined by $\mathbf{M}^{i-1}_{2k-1} := \alpha_{Y_k}$ and $\mathbf{M}^{i-1}_{2k} := e_{X_k}$, letting e_j being the *unit vector* $(0^{j-1}, 1, 0^{n-j})$. Let $V^{i-1} \in \mathbb{F}^\ell$ be the (random) vector defined by $V^{i-1}_{2k-1} := X_k$ and $V^{i-1}_{2k} = Y_k$. By definition, the event Z_{i-1} is equivalent to the event $\mathbf{M}^{i-1} \times F = V^{i-1}$. The computation C makes on input Y_i can also be described by the linear equation $\langle \alpha_{Y_i}, F \rangle = X_i$. Let $\mathbf{M} := \begin{pmatrix} \mathbf{M}^{i-1} \\ \alpha_{Y_i} \end{pmatrix}$ and $V := \begin{pmatrix} V^{i-1} \\ X_i \end{pmatrix}$. We make use of the following claims (see proofs in Sect. 3.2).

Definition 2.2. (Spanned unit vectors). *For a matrix $A \in \mathbb{F}^{a \times n}$, let $\mathcal{E}(A) := \{j \in [n] : e_j \in \mathrm{Span}(A)\}$, for $\mathrm{Span}(A)$ being the (linear) span of A's rows.*

That is, $\mathcal{E}(\mathbf{A})$ is the set of indices of all unit vectors spanned by $\mathbf{A}$. It is clear that $|\mathcal{E}(\mathbf{A})| \leq \mathrm{rank}(\mathbf{A}) \leq \min\{a, n\}$. The following claim states that for $j \notin \mathcal{E}(\mathbf{A})$, knowing the value of $\mathbf{A} \times F$ gives no information about F_j.

Claim 2.3. *Let $\mathbf{A} \in \mathbb{F}^{a \times n}$ and $v \in \mathrm{Im}(\mathbf{A})$. Then for every $j \in [n] \setminus \mathcal{E}(\mathbf{A})$ and $y \in [n]$, it holds that $\Pr_{f \leftarrow [n]^n}[f_j = y \mid \mathbf{A} \times f = v] = 1/n$.*

The second claim roughly states that by concatenating a c-row matrix to a given matrix $\mathbf{A}$, one does not increase the spanned unit set of $\mathbf{A}$ by more than c elements.

Claim 2.4. *For every $\mathbf{A} \in \mathbb{F}^{\ell \times n}$ there exists an ℓ-size set $\mathcal{S}_A \subseteq [n]$ such that the following holds: for every $\mathbf{B} \in \mathbb{F}^{c \times n}$ there exists a c-size set $\mathcal{S}_B \subseteq [n]$ such that $\mathcal{E}\begin{pmatrix} \mathbf{A} \\ \mathbf{B} \end{pmatrix} \subseteq \mathcal{S}_A \cup \mathcal{S}_B$.*

For bounding $\Pr[Z_i \mid Z_{i-1}]$ using the above observations, we write

$$\Pr[Z_i \mid Z_{i-1}] = \Pr[Z_i \wedge X_i \in \mathcal{E}(\mathbf{M}) \mid Z_{i-1}] + \Pr[Z_i \wedge X_i \notin \mathcal{E}(\mathbf{M}) \mid Z_{i-1}] \quad (4)$$

and finish the proof by separately bounding the two terms of the above equation. Let $H := (X_i, Y_{\leq i}, \mathbf{M}, V)$. We first note that

$$
\begin{aligned}
\Pr[Z_i \wedge X_i \notin \mathcal{E}(\mathbf{M}) \mid Z_{i-1}] &\leq \Pr[Z_i \mid X_i \notin \mathcal{E}(\mathbf{M}), Z_{i-1}] \\
&= \mathop{\mathrm{E}}_{(x_i, y_{\leq i}, m, v) \leftarrow H \mid X_i \notin \mathcal{E}(\mathbf{M}), Z_{i-1}}[\Pr[F(x_i) = y_i \mid m \times F = v, Y_{\leq i} = y_{\leq i}]] \\
&= \mathop{\mathrm{E}}_{(x_i, y_{\leq i}, m, v) \leftarrow H \mid X_i \notin \mathcal{E}(\mathbf{M}), Z_{i-1}}[\Pr[F(x_i) = y_i \mid m \times F = v]] \\
&= 1/n. \quad (5)
\end{aligned}
$$

The first equality holds by definition of Z_{i-1}, the second equality since F is independent of Y, and the last one follows by Claim 2.3. For bounding the left-hand term of Eq. (4), let $\mathcal{S}$ and T be the ℓ-size set and the index guaranteed by Claim 2.4 for the matrices $\mathbf{M}^{i-1}$ and vector α_{Y_i}, respectively. Compute,

$$
\begin{aligned}
\Pr[Z_i \wedge X_i \in \mathcal{E}(\mathbf{M}) \mid Z_{i-1}] &\leq \Pr[Y_i \in F(\mathcal{E}(\mathbf{M})) \mid Z_{i-1}] \\
&\leq \Pr[Y_i \in F(\mathcal{S} \cup \{T\}) \mid Z_{i-1}] \\
&\leq \Pr[Y_i \in F(\mathcal{S}) \mid Z_{i-1}] + \Pr[Y_i = F(T) \mid Z_{i-1}]. \quad (6)
\end{aligned}
$$

The second inequality is by Claim 2.4. Since $F(\mathcal{S})$ is independent of Y_i, it holds that

$$\Pr[Y_i \in F(\mathcal{S}) \mid Z_{i-1}] \leq |\mathcal{S}|/n = \ell/n \quad (7)$$

Bounding $\Pr[Y_i = F(T) \mid Z_{i-1}]$ is more involved since T might depend on Y_i.[3] Yet since f is a random function, a simple counting argument yields that for any

---

[3] Indeed, this dependency between the queries to f and the value to invert is exactly what makes (efficient) inversion by adaptive inverters possible.

(fixed and independent of f) function g:

$$\Pr_{f \leftarrow \mathcal{F}} \left[\Pr_{y \leftarrow [n]} [y = f(g(y))] \geq 1/2 \right] \leq n^{-n/3} \tag{8}$$

Let $H := (X_{<i}, Y_{<i})$, and for $h = (x_{<i}, y_{<i}) \in \text{Supp}(H)$ compute

$$\Pr_{f \leftarrow F | Z_{i-1}, H=h} [\Pr [Y_i = f(T) \mid H = h] \geq 1/2]$$

$$\leq \frac{1}{\Pr [H = h, Z_{i-1} \mid Y_{<i} = y_{<i}]} \cdot \Pr_{f \leftarrow F | Y_{<i} = y_{<i}} [\Pr [Y_i = F(T) \mid H = h] \geq 1/2]$$

$$= \frac{1}{\Pr [H = h, Z_{i-1} \mid Y_{<i} = y_{<i}]} \cdot \Pr_{f \leftarrow F} [\Pr [Y_i = F(T) \mid H = h] \geq 1/2]$$

$$\leq \frac{1}{\Pr [H = h, Z_{i-1} \mid Y_{<i} = y_{<i}]} \cdot n^{-n/3}$$

$$\leq n^{n/4} \cdot n^{-n/3} \in o(1). \tag{9}$$

The first equality holds since F is independent of Y. The second inequality holds by Eq. (8), noting that under the conditioning on $H = h$, the value of T is a deterministic function of Y_i. The third inequality holds since for not too big i, $\Pr [H = h, Z_{i-1} \mid Y_{<i} = y_{<i}] \geq n^{-n/4}$, since this probabilistic event is essentially a system of linear equations over a randomly selected vector. Since the above holds for any h, we conclude that $\Pr [Y_i = F(T) \mid Z_{i-1}] \leq 1/2 + o(1)$. Putting it all together, yields that $\Pr [Z_i \mid Z_{i-1}] < 1/n + \ell/n + 1/2 + o(1) < 3/5$, for not too large i.

Affine Decision Trees. Similarly to the affine decoder case, we prove the theorem by bounding $\Pr [Z_i \mid Z_{i-1}]$ for all "not too large i". Also in this case, we bound this probability by translating the conditioning on Z_{i-1} into a system of affine equations. In particular, we would like to find proper definitions for the matrix $\mathbf{M} = \begin{pmatrix} \mathbf{M}^{i-1} \\ \mathbf{M}^i \end{pmatrix}$ and vector $V = \begin{pmatrix} V^{i-1} \\ V^i \end{pmatrix}$, functions of $(X_{\leq i}, Y_{\leq i})$, such that conditions 1–3 mentioned in the affine decoder case hold.

We achieve these conditions by adding for each $j < i$ an equation for each of the linear computations done in the decision tree that computes X_j from Y_j. The price is that rather than having $\Theta(i)$ equations, we now have $\Theta(d \cdot i)$, for d being the depth of the decision tree. In order to have $\mathbf{M}^i$ a deterministic function of Y_i alone, we cannot simply make $\mathbf{M}^i$ reflect the d linear computations performed by the decoder, since each of these may depend on the results of previous computations, and thus depend on F. So rather, we have to add a row (i.e., an equation) for each of the q queries the decoder might use (queries that span all possible computations), which by definition also imply the dependency on q. Taking these additional rows into account yields the desired bound.

3   Preliminaries

3.1   Notation

All logarithms considered here are in base two. We use calligraphic letters to denote sets, uppercase for random variables and probabilistic events, lowercase for functions and fixed values, and bold uppercase for matrices. Let $[n] := \{1, \ldots, n\}$. Given a vector $v \in \Sigma^n$, let v_i denote its ith entry, let $v_{<i} := v_{1,\ldots,i-1}$ and let $v_{\leq i} := v_{1,\ldots,i}$. Let $\binom{[n]}{k}$ denote the set of all subsets of $[n]$ of size k. The vector v is q-*sparse* if it has no more than q non-zero entries.

Functions. We naturally view functions from $[n]$ to $[m]$ as vectors in $[m]^n$, by letting $f_i = f(i)$. For a finite ordered set $\mathcal{S} := \{s_1, \ldots, s_k\}$, let $f(\mathcal{S}) := \{f(s_1), f(s_2), \ldots, f(s_k)\}$. Let $f^{-1}(y) := \{x \in [n] \colon f(x) = y\}$ and let $\text{Im}(f) = \{f(x) \colon x \in [n]\}$. A function $f \colon \mathbb{F}^n \to \mathbb{F}$, for a field $\mathbb{F}$ and $n \in \mathbb{N}$, is *affine* if there exist a vector $v \in \mathbb{F}^n$ and a constant $\beta \in \mathbb{F}$ such that $f(x) = \langle v, x \rangle + \beta$ for every $x \in \mathbb{F}^n$, letting $\langle v, x \rangle := \sum v_i \cdot x_i$ (all operations are over $\mathbb{F}$).

Distributions and Random Variables. The support of a distribution P over a finite set $\mathcal{S}$ is defined by $\text{Supp}(P) := \{x \in \mathcal{S} : P(x) > 0\}$. For a set $\mathcal{S}$, let $s \leftarrow \mathcal{S}$ denote that s is uniformly drawn from $\mathcal{S}$. For $\delta \in [0,1]$, let $h(\delta) := -\delta \log \delta - (1 - \delta) \log(1 - \delta)$, i.e., the binary entropy function.

3.2   Matrices and Linear Spaces

We identify the elements of a finite field of size n with the elements of the set $[n]$, using some arbitrary, fixed, mapping. Let e_i denote the ith unit vector $e_j = (0^{j-1}, 1, 0^{n-j})$.

For a matrix $\mathbf{A} \in \mathbb{F}^{a \times b}$, let $\mathbf{A}_i$ denote the ith row of $\mathbf{A}$. The span of $\mathbf{A}$'s rows is defined by $\text{Span}(\mathbf{A}) := \{v \in \mathbb{F}^b \colon \exists \delta_1, \ldots, \delta_a \in \mathbb{F} \colon v = \sum_{i=1}^a \delta_i \mathbf{A}_i\}$. Let $\text{Im}(\mathbf{A}) = \{v \in \mathbb{F}^a \colon \exists w \in \mathbb{F}^b \ \colon \ \mathbf{A} \times w = v\}$, or equivalently, the image set of the function $f_{\mathbf{A}}(w) := \mathbf{A} \times w$. We use the following well-known fact:

Fact 3.1. *Let $\mathbb{F}$ be a finite field of size n, let $\mathbf{A} \in \mathbb{F}^{a \times b}$, let $v \in \text{Im}(\mathbf{A})$, and let $\mathcal{F} \subseteq \mathbb{F}^b$ be the solution set of the system of equations $\mathbf{A} \times F = v$. Then $|\mathcal{F}| = n^{b - \text{rank}(\mathbf{A})}$.*

We also make use of the following less standard notion.

Definition 3.2. (Spanned unit vectors). *For a matrix $\mathbf{A} \in \mathbb{F}^{a \times b}$, let $\mathcal{E}(\mathbf{A}) := \{j \in [b] \colon e_j \in \text{Span}(\mathbf{A})\}$.*

That is, $\mathcal{E}(\mathbf{A})$ is the indices of all unit vectors spanned by $\mathbf{A}$. It is clear that $|\mathcal{E}(\mathbf{A})| \leq \text{rank}(\mathbf{A}) \leq \min\{a, b\}$. It is also easy to see that for any $v \in \text{Im}(\mathbf{A})$, $\mathcal{E}(\mathbf{A})$ holds those entries that are *common to all solutions w of the system* $\mathbf{A} \times w = v$.[4] The following claim states that for $i \notin \mathcal{E}(\mathbf{A})$, the number of solutions w of the system $\mathbf{A} \times w = v$ with $w_i = y$, is the same for every y.

---

[4] That is, for every $i \in \mathcal{E}(\mathbf{A})$, w_i can be described as a linear combination of the entries of v, and thus w_i is fixed by v.

Claim 3.3. *Let $\mathbb{F}$ be a finite field of size n, let $\boldsymbol{A} \in \mathbb{F}^{a \times b}$ and $v \in \mathrm{Im}(\boldsymbol{A})$. Then for every $i \in [n] \setminus \mathcal{E}(\boldsymbol{A})$ and $y \in [n]$, it holds that $\mathrm{Pr}_{f \leftarrow [n]^b} [f_i = y \mid \boldsymbol{A} \times f = v] = 1/n$.*

Proof. Let $\mathcal{F}_{\boldsymbol{A},v} := \{f \in [n]^b : \boldsymbol{A} \times f = v\}$ be the set of solutions for the equation $\boldsymbol{A} \times F = v$. Since, by assumption, $\boldsymbol{A} \times F = v$ has a solution, by Fact 3.1 it holds that $|\mathcal{F}_{\boldsymbol{A},v}| = n^{b - \mathrm{rank}(\boldsymbol{A})}$. Next, let $\boldsymbol{A}' := \begin{pmatrix} \boldsymbol{A} \\ e_i \end{pmatrix}, v' := \begin{pmatrix} v \\ y \end{pmatrix}$, and
$\mathcal{F}_{\boldsymbol{A},v,i,y} := \{f \in [n]^b : \boldsymbol{A}' \times f = v'\}$ (i.e., $\mathcal{F}_{\boldsymbol{A},v,i,y}$ is the set of solutions for $\boldsymbol{A}' \times F = v'$). Since, by assumption, $e_i \notin \mathrm{Span}(\boldsymbol{A})$, it holds that $\boldsymbol{A}' \times F = v'$ has a solution and $|\mathcal{F}_{\boldsymbol{A},v,i,y}| = n^{b - \mathrm{rank}(\boldsymbol{A}')} = n^{b - \mathrm{rank}(\boldsymbol{A}) - 1}$. We conclude that $\mathrm{Pr}_{f \leftarrow [n]^b} [f_i = y \mid \boldsymbol{A} \times f = v] = \frac{|\mathcal{F}_{\boldsymbol{A},v,i,y}|}{|\mathcal{F}_{\boldsymbol{A},v}|} = 1/n$.

The following claim states that adding a small number of rows to a given matrix $\boldsymbol{A}$ does not increase the set $\mathcal{E}(\boldsymbol{A})$ by much.

Claim 3.4. *For every $\boldsymbol{A} \in \mathbb{F}^{\ell \times n}$ there exists an ℓ-size set $\mathcal{S}_A \subseteq [n]$ such that the following holds: for any $\boldsymbol{B} \in \mathbb{F}^{c \times n}$ there exists a c-size set $\mathcal{S}_B \subseteq [n]$ for which*

$$\mathcal{E} \begin{pmatrix} \boldsymbol{A} \\ \boldsymbol{B} \end{pmatrix} \subseteq \mathcal{S}_A \cup \mathcal{S}_B.$$

Proof. Standard row operations performed on a matrix $\boldsymbol{M}$ do not affect $\mathrm{Span}(\boldsymbol{M})$, and thus do not affect $\mathcal{E}(\boldsymbol{M})$. Therefore, we may assume that both $\boldsymbol{A}$ and $\boldsymbol{B}$ are in row canonical form.[5] For a matrix $\boldsymbol{M}$ in row canonical form, let $\mathcal{L}(\boldsymbol{M}) := \{i \in [n] : \text{ the } i^{\text{th}} \text{ column of } \boldsymbol{M} \text{ contains a leading 1} \}$. Let $\mathcal{S}_A := \mathcal{L}(\boldsymbol{A})$ and note that $|\mathcal{S}_A| = \mathrm{rank}(\boldsymbol{A}) \leq \ell$. Perform Gaussian elimination on $\begin{pmatrix} \boldsymbol{A} \\ \boldsymbol{B} \end{pmatrix}$ to yield a matrix $\boldsymbol{E}$ in row canonical form, and let $\mathcal{S}_E := \mathcal{L}(\boldsymbol{E})$. Note that $\mathcal{S}_A \subseteq \mathcal{S}_E$, since adding rows to a matrix may only expand the set of leading ones. Furthermore, $|\mathcal{S}_E| = \mathrm{rank}(\boldsymbol{E}) \leq \mathrm{rank}(\boldsymbol{A}) + c$. Clearly, $\mathcal{E}(\boldsymbol{E}) \subseteq \mathcal{S}_E$, and we can write $\mathcal{S}_E = \mathcal{S}_A \cup \mathcal{S}_B$, for $\mathcal{S}_B := (\mathcal{S}_E \setminus \mathcal{S}_A)$. Finally, $|\mathcal{S}_B| = |\mathcal{S}_E| - |\mathcal{S}_A| \leq \mathrm{rank}(\boldsymbol{A}) + c - \mathrm{rank}(\boldsymbol{A}) = c$, and the proof follows.

3.3 Random Functions

Let $\mathcal{F}_n$ be the set of all functions from $[n]$ to $[n]$. We make the following observations.

Claim 3.5. *Let $S_1, \ldots, S_n \subseteq [n]$ be c-size sets, and for $f \in \mathcal{F}_n$ let $\mathcal{K}_f := \{y \in [n] : y \in f(S_y)\}$. Then for any $\mu \in [0, \frac{1}{2}]$:*

$$\Pr_{f \leftarrow \mathcal{F}_n} [|\mathcal{K}_f| \geq \mu n] \leq 2^{2 \lceil \mu n \rceil \log(1/\mu) + \lceil \mu n \rceil \log(c/n)}.$$

---

[5] (1) all zero rows are at the bottom (2) the first non-zero entry in each row is equal to 1 (known as the "leading 1") (3) the leading 1 in each row appears strictly to the right of the leading 1 in all the rows above it (4) a column that contains a leading 1 is zero in all other entries. It is a well-known fact that a matrix can be reduced to row canonical form using Gaussian elimination, and the set of columns containing a leading 1 is unique.

Proof. For $\mathcal{T} := \{t_1, \ldots, t_{\lceil \mu n \rceil}\} \subseteq [n]$, let $\mathcal{F}_{\mathcal{T}} := \{f \in \mathcal{F}_n : \mathcal{T} \subseteq \mathcal{K}_f\}$. We make a rough over-counting for the size of $\mathcal{F}_{\mathcal{T}}$: one can describe $f \in \mathcal{F}_{\mathcal{T}}$ by choosing $x_i \in [n]$ for each set $\mathcal{S}_{t_i}$, and require that $f(x_i) = t_i$ (to ensure $t_i \in f(\mathcal{S}_{t_i})$). There are at most $c^{\lceil \mu n \rceil}$ ways to perform these choices. There are no constraints on the remaining $n - \lceil \mu n \rceil$ values of f. Therefore $|\mathcal{F}_{\mathcal{T}}| \leq c^{\lceil \mu n \rceil} \cdot n^{n - \lceil \mu n \rceil}$. This immediately implies that $\Pr_{f \leftarrow \mathcal{F}_n, \mathcal{T} \leftarrow \binom{[n]}{\lceil \mu n \rceil}} [\mathcal{T} \subseteq \mathcal{K}_f] \leq \left(\frac{c}{n}\right)^{\lceil \mu n \rceil}$. We conclude that

$$\Pr_{f \leftarrow \mathcal{F}_n} [|\mathcal{K}_f| \geq \mu n] = \Pr[\exists \mathcal{T} \subseteq \mathcal{K}_f : |\mathcal{T}| = \lceil \mu n \rceil]$$

$$\leq \sum_{\mathcal{T} \in \binom{[n]}{\lceil \mu n \rceil}} \Pr_{f \leftarrow \mathcal{F}_n} [\mathcal{T} \subseteq \mathcal{K}_f] \leq \binom{n}{\lceil \mu n \rceil} \cdot \left(\frac{c}{n}\right)^{\lceil \mu n \rceil} \leq 2^{2\lceil \mu n \rceil \log(1/\mu) + \lceil \mu n \rceil \log(c/n)}.$$

The last inequality follows from Facts 3.11 and 3.10, and the fact that $\log(1/\mu) \geq \log(n/\lceil \mu n \rceil)$.

Claim 3.6. *Let $n \in \mathbb{N}$, let $F \leftarrow \mathcal{F}_n$ and let W be an event (jointly distributed with F) of probability at least p. Let $Y \leftarrow [n]$ be independent of F and W. Then for every c-size sets $\mathcal{S}_1, \ldots, \mathcal{S}_n \subseteq [n]$ and $\gamma \in [0, \frac{1}{2}]$, it holds that*

$$\Pr[Y \in F(\mathcal{S}_Y) \mid W] \leq \gamma + 2^{2\lceil \gamma n \rceil \log(1/\gamma) + \lceil \gamma n \rceil \log(c/n) + \log(1/p)}.$$

Proof. Let $\mathcal{K}_f := \{y \in [n] : y \in f(\mathcal{S}_y)\}$. For $\gamma \in [0, 1]$, compute:

$$\Pr[Y \in F(\mathcal{S}_Y) \mid W] = \Pr[Y \in \mathcal{K}_F \mid W]$$

$$\leq \Pr[|\mathcal{K}_F| \geq \gamma n \mid W] \cdot \Pr[Y \in \mathcal{K}_F \mid W, |\mathcal{K}_F| \geq \gamma n]$$

$$+ \Pr[|\mathcal{K}_F| < \gamma n \mid W] \cdot \Pr[Y \in \mathcal{K}_F \mid W, |\mathcal{K}_F| < \gamma n]$$

$$\leq \Pr[|\mathcal{K}_F| \geq \gamma n \mid W] + \gamma. \tag{10}$$

The last inequality holds since Y is independent of W and F. Since $\Pr[W] \geq p$, it holds that:

$$\Pr[|\mathcal{K}_F| \geq \gamma n \mid W] \leq \frac{\Pr[|\mathcal{K}_F| \geq \gamma n]}{\Pr[W]} \leq 2^{2\lceil \gamma n \rceil \log(1/\gamma) + \lceil \gamma n \rceil \log(c/n) + \log(1/p)} \tag{11}$$

The second inequality is by Claim 3.5. We conclude that:

$$\Pr[Y \in F(\mathcal{S}_Y) \mid W] \leq \gamma + 2^{2\lceil \gamma n \rceil \log(1/\gamma) + \lceil \gamma n \rceil \log(c/n) + \log(1/p)}.$$

The next claim bounds the probability that a random function compresses an image set.

Claim 3.7. *For any $n \in \mathbb{N}$ and $\tau, \delta \in [0, \frac{1}{2}]$, it holds that*
$$\alpha_{\tau, \delta} := \Pr_{f \leftarrow \mathcal{F}_n} [\exists \mathcal{X} \subseteq [n] : |\mathcal{X}| \geq \tau n \wedge |f(\mathcal{X})| \leq \delta n] \leq 2^{n(h(\tau) + h(\delta)) + \lfloor \tau n \rfloor \log \delta}.$$

Proof. Compute:

$$\alpha_{\tau,\delta} = \Pr_{f \leftarrow \mathcal{F}_n} \left[\exists \mathcal{X}, \mathcal{Y} \subseteq [n] : |\mathcal{X}| \geq \tau n \wedge |\mathcal{Y}| \leq \delta n \wedge f(\mathcal{X}) \subseteq \mathcal{Y} \right]$$

$$\leq \Pr_{f \leftarrow \mathcal{F}_n} \left[\exists \mathcal{X}, \mathcal{Y} \subseteq [n] : |\mathcal{X}| = \lfloor \tau n \rfloor \wedge |\mathcal{Y}| = \lfloor \delta n \rfloor \wedge f(\mathcal{X}) \subseteq \mathcal{Y} \right]$$

$$\leq \sum_{\mathcal{Y} \in \binom{[n]}{\lfloor \delta n \rfloor}} \sum_{\mathcal{X} \in \binom{[n]}{\lfloor \tau n \rfloor}} \Pr \left[f(\mathcal{X}) \subseteq \mathcal{Y} \right] \leq \binom{n}{\lfloor \delta n \rfloor} \binom{n}{\lfloor \tau n \rfloor} \cdot \delta^{\lfloor \tau n \rfloor}$$

$$\leq 2^{n(h(\tau)+h(\delta))+\lfloor \tau n \rfloor \log \delta}.$$

The last inequality follows from Fact 3.11, and since h is monotone in $[0, \frac{1}{2}]$.

The last claim states that an algorithm that inverts $f(x)$ with good probability, is likely to return x itself.

Claim 3.8. *Let* C *be a function from* $\mathcal{F}_n \times [n]$ *to* $[n]$ *such that* $\Pr_{\substack{f \leftarrow \mathcal{F}_n \\ x \leftarrow [n]}} \left[\mathsf{C}(f, f(x)) \in f^{-1}(f(x)) \right] \geq \alpha.$ *Then,* $\Pr_{\substack{f \leftarrow \mathcal{F}_n \\ x \leftarrow [n]}} \left[\mathsf{C}(f, f(x)) = x \right] \geq \frac{\alpha^2}{8}.$

Proof. For $f \in \mathcal{F}_n$ let $\mathcal{P}_f(x) := f^{-1}(f(x)) \setminus \{x\}$. We would like to provide a bound on the size of this set to ensure that x is output with high probability. Compute

$$\Pr_{\substack{f \leftarrow \mathcal{F}_n \\ x \leftarrow [n]}} \left[\mathsf{C}(f, f(x)) = x \right] = \Pr \left[\mathsf{C}(f, f(x)) = x \wedge \mathsf{C}(f, f(x)) \in f^{-1}(f(x)) \right]$$

$$\geq \Pr \left[\mathsf{C}(f, f(x)) = x \mid \mathsf{C}(f, f(x)) \in f^{-1}(f(x)) \right] \cdot \alpha. \quad (12)$$

We now provide a lower bound for the left-hand term. For $d \geq 1$ compute

$$\Pr_{\substack{f \leftarrow \mathcal{F}_n \\ x \leftarrow [n]}} \left[\mathsf{C}(f, f(x)) = x \mid \mathsf{C}(f, f(x)) \in f^{-1}(f(x)) \right]$$

$$\geq \Pr \left[\mathsf{C}(f, f(x)) = x \wedge |\mathcal{P}_f(x)| \leq d \mid \mathsf{C}(f, f(x)) \in f^{-1}(f(x)) \right]$$

$$= \Pr \left[\mathsf{C}(f, f(x)) = x \mid |\mathcal{P}_f(x)| \leq d, \mathsf{C}(f, f(x)) \in f^{-1}(f(x)) \right]$$

$$\cdot \Pr \left[|\mathcal{P}_f(x)| \leq d \mid \mathsf{C}(f, f(x)) \in f^{-1}(f(x)) \right]$$

$$\geq \frac{1}{d+1} \cdot \Pr \left[|\mathcal{P}_f(x)| \leq d \mid \mathsf{C}(f, f(x)) \in f^{-1}(f(x)) \right]$$

$$= \frac{1}{d+1} \left(1 - \Pr \left[|\mathcal{P}_f(x)| > d \mid \mathsf{C}(f, f(x)) \in f^{-1}(f(x)) \right] \right). \quad (13)$$

By linearity of expectation, $\mathbb{E}_{f \leftarrow \mathcal{F}_n} [|\mathcal{P}_f(x)|] = \frac{n-1}{n} < 1$. Hence by Markov's inequality, $\Pr_{\substack{f \leftarrow \mathcal{F}_n \\ x \leftarrow [n]}} [|\mathcal{P}_f(x)| > d] < 1/d$. It follows that

$$\Pr_{\substack{f \leftarrow \mathcal{F}_n \\ x \leftarrow [n]}} \left[|\mathcal{P}_f(x)| > d \mid \mathsf{C}(f, f(x)) \in f^{-1}(f(x)) \right] \leq \frac{\Pr \left[|\mathcal{P}_f(x)| > d \right]}{\Pr \left[\mathsf{C}(f, f(x)) \in f^{-1}(f(x)) \right]} \leq \frac{1}{d\alpha}$$

$$(14)$$

Combining Eqs. (13) and (14) yields that

$$\Pr_{\substack{f \leftarrow \mathcal{F}_n \\ x \leftarrow [n]}} [\mathsf{C}(f, f(x)) = x \mid \mathsf{C}(f, f(x)) \in f^{-1}(f(x))] \geq \frac{1}{d+1}\left(1 - \frac{1}{d\alpha}\right) \quad (15)$$

Finally, by Eqs. (12) and (15) we conclude that

$$\Pr_{\substack{f \leftarrow \mathcal{F}_n \\ x \leftarrow [n]}} [\mathsf{C}(f, f(x)) = x] \geq \frac{\alpha}{d+1}\left(1 - \frac{1}{d\alpha}\right) \geq \frac{\alpha}{2d}\left(1 - \frac{1}{d\alpha}\right) = \frac{\alpha}{2d} - \frac{1}{2d^2}.$$

Setting $d = \frac{2}{\alpha}$ yields that $\Pr_{\substack{f \leftarrow \mathcal{F}_n \\ x \leftarrow [n]}} [\mathsf{C}(f, f(x)) = x] \geq \frac{\alpha^2}{4} - \frac{\alpha^2}{8} = \frac{\alpha^2}{8}$.

3.4 Additional Inequalities

We use the following easily-verifiable facts:

Fact 3.9. *For $x \geq 1$: $\log x \geq 1 - 1/x$.*

Fact 3.10. *For $\delta \leq 1/2$: $h(\delta) \leq -2\delta \log \delta$.*

We also use the following bound:

Fact 3.11. *([13]) $\binom{n}{k} \leq 2^{nh(\frac{k}{n})}$.*

4 Linear-Advice Inverters

In this section we present lower bounds on the time/memory tradeoff of adaptive function inverters with linear advice. The extension to additive-advice inverters is given in Sect. 4.1.

To simplify notation, the following definitions and results are stated with respect to a fixed $n \in \mathbb{N}$. Let $\mathcal{F}$ be the set of all functions from $[n]$ to $[n]$. All asymptotic notations (e.g., Θ) hide constant terms that are independent of n. We start by formally defining adaptive function inverters.

Definition 4.1. (Adaptive inverters). *An s-advice, q-query adaptive inverter is a deterministic algorithm pair $\mathsf{C} := (\mathsf{C}_{\mathsf{pre}}, \mathsf{C}_{\mathsf{dec}})$, where $\mathsf{C}_{\mathsf{pre}} : \mathcal{F} \to \{0,1\}^s$, and $\mathsf{C}_{\mathsf{dec}}^{(\cdot)} : [n] \times \{0,1\}^s \to [n]$ makes up to q oracle queries. For $f \in \mathcal{F}$ and $y \in [n]$, let*

$$\mathsf{C}(y; f) := \mathsf{C}_{\mathsf{dec}}^f(y, \mathsf{C}_{\mathsf{pre}}(f)).$$

That is, $\mathsf{C}_{\mathsf{pre}}$ is the *preprocessing* algorithm that takes as input the function description and outputs a string of length s that we refer to as the *advice* string. The oracle-aided $\mathsf{C}_{\mathsf{dec}}$ is the *decoder* algorithm that performs the actual inversion action. It receives the element to invert y and the advice string, and using q (possibly adaptive) queries to f, attempts to output a preimage of y. Finally, $\mathsf{C}(y; f)$ is the candidate preimage the algorithms of C produce for the element to invert y given the (restricted) access to f. We define adaptive inverters with linear advice as follows, recalling that we may view $f \in \mathcal{F}$ as a vector $\in [n]^n$.

Definition 4.2. (Linear preprocessing). *A deterministic algorithm* $\mathsf{C}_{\mathsf{pre}}$: $\mathcal{F} \to \{0,1\}^s$ *is linear if there exist an additive group* $\mathcal{G} \subseteq \{0,1\}^s$ *that contains* $\mathsf{C}_{\mathsf{pre}}(\mathcal{F})$, *and an additive group* $\mathcal{K}$ *of size* n *such that for every* $f_1, f_2 \in \mathcal{F}$ *it holds that* $\mathsf{C}_{\mathsf{pre}}(f_1 +_{\mathcal{K}} f_2) = \mathsf{C}_{\mathsf{pre}}(f_1) +_{\mathcal{G}} \mathsf{C}_{\mathsf{pre}}(f_2)$, *letting* $f_1 +_{\mathcal{K}} f_2 := ((f_1)_1 +_{\mathcal{K}} (f_2)_1, \ldots, (f_1)_n +_{\mathcal{K}} (f_2)_n)$.

Below we omit the subscripts from $+_{\mathcal{G}}$ and $+_{\mathcal{K}}$ when clear from the context.

We prove the bound for inverters with linear preprocessing by presenting a reduction from the well-known *set disjointness* problem.

Definition 4.3. (Set disjointness). *A protocol* $\Pi = (\mathsf{A}, \mathsf{B})$ *solves set disjointness with error* ε *over all inputs in* $\mathcal{Q} \subseteq \{(\mathcal{X}, \mathcal{Y}): \mathcal{X}, \mathcal{Y} \subseteq [\mathbb{N}]\}$, *if for every* $(\mathcal{X}, \mathcal{Y}) \in \mathcal{Q}$

$$\Pr_{\substack{r_{\mathsf{A}} \leftarrow \{0,1\}^*, r_{\mathsf{B}} \leftarrow \{0,1\}^* \\ r_p \leftarrow \{0,1\}^*}} [(\mathsf{A}(\mathcal{X}; r_{\mathsf{A}}), \mathsf{B}(\mathcal{Y}; r_{\mathsf{B}}))(r_p) = (\delta_{\mathcal{X}, \mathcal{Y}}, \delta_{\mathcal{X}, \mathcal{Y}})] \geq 1 - \varepsilon$$

for $\delta_{\mathcal{X}, \mathcal{Y}}$ *being the indicator for* $\mathcal{X} \cap \mathcal{Y} = \emptyset$.

Namely, except with probability ε over their private and public randomness, the two parties find out whether their input sets intersect. Set disjointness is known to require large communication over the following set of inputs.

Definition 4.4. (Communication complexity). *The* communication complexity *of a protocol* $\Pi = (\mathsf{A}, \mathsf{B})$, *denoted* $CC(\Pi)$, *is the maximal number of bits the parties exchange in an execution (over all possible inputs and randomness).*

Theorem 4.5. (Hardness set disjointness, Razborov [21]). *Exists* $\varepsilon > 0$ *such that for every protocol* Π *that solves set disjointness over* all *inputs in* $\mathcal{Q} := \{\mathcal{X}, \mathcal{Y} \subseteq [n]: |\mathcal{X} \cap \mathcal{Y}| \leq 1\}$ *with error* ε, *it holds that* $CC(\Pi) \geq \Omega(n)$.[6]

Our main result is the following reduction from set disjointness to function inversion.

Theorem 4.6. (From set disjointness to function inversion). *Assume exists an* s-advice, q-query *linear-advice inversion algorithm with* $\Pr_{\substack{f \leftarrow \mathcal{F} \\ x \leftarrow [n]}} [\mathsf{C}(f(x); f) \in f^{-1}(f(x))] \geq \alpha$, *and let* $\mathcal{Q} := \{\mathcal{X}, \mathcal{Y} \subseteq [n]: |\mathcal{X} \cap \mathcal{Y}| \leq 1\}$. *Then for every* $\varepsilon > 0$ *there exists a protocol that solves set disjointness with (one-sided) error* ε *and communication* $O\left(\frac{\log(\varepsilon)}{\log(1 - \alpha^2/8)} \cdot (s + q \log n)\right)$, *on all inputs in* $\mathcal{Q}$.

Combining Theorems 4.5 and 4.6 yields the following bound on linear-advice inverters.

---

[6] [21] proved a stronger result: there exists a distribution that fails all low communication protocols. For the sake of our argument, however, it is easier to work with the weaker statement of Theorem 4.5.

Corollary 4.7. (Theorem 1.2, **restated).** *Let* $\mathsf{C} = (\mathsf{C}_{\mathsf{pre}}, \mathsf{C}_{\mathsf{dec}})$ *be an s-advice q-query inversion algorithm with linear preprocessing such that* $\Pr_{\substack{f \leftarrow \mathcal{F} \\ x \leftarrow [n]}} \left[\mathsf{C}(f(x); f) \in f^{-1}(f(x)) \right] \geq \alpha$. *Then* $s + q \log n \in \Omega(\alpha^2 \cdot n)$.

Proof. (Proof of Corollary 4.7). By Theorem 4.6, the existence of an s-advice, q-query linear-advice inverter C with success probability $\geq \alpha$ implies that set disjointness can be solved over $\mathcal{Q}$, with error $\varepsilon > 0$ and communication complexity $O\left(\frac{\log(\varepsilon)}{\log(1-\alpha^2/8)} \cdot (s + q \log n) \right)$. Thus, Theorem 4.5 yields that $\frac{\log(\varepsilon)}{\log(1-\alpha^2/8)} \cdot (s + q \log n) \in \Omega(n)$. Since $\frac{\log(\varepsilon)}{\log(1-\alpha^2/8)} = \log(1/\varepsilon) \cdot \frac{1}{\log(1/(1-\alpha^2/8))}$, and since, by Fact 3.9, it holds that $\log(1/(1-\alpha^2/8)) \geq \alpha^2/8$, it follows that $s + q \log n \in \Omega(\alpha^2 \cdot n)$.

The rest of this section is devoted to proving Theorem 4.6. Fix an s-advice, q-query inverter $\mathsf{C} = (\mathsf{C}_{\mathsf{pre}}, \mathsf{C}_{\mathsf{dec}})$ with linear preprocessing. We use C in Protocol 4.8 to solve set disjointness. In the protocol below we identify a vector $v \in \{0,1\}^n$ with the set $\{i : v_i = 1\}$.

Protocol 4.8. $(\Pi = (\mathsf{A}, \mathsf{B}))$

A*'s input: $a \in \{0,1\}^n$.*
B*'s input: $b \in \{0,1\}^n$.*
Public randomness: $d \in [n]$.
Operation:
1. B *chooses* $y \leftarrow [n]$.
2. A *constructs a function* $f_{\mathsf{A}} : [n] \to [n]$ *as follows:*
   - *for i such that $a_i = 0$, it samples $f_{\mathsf{A}}(i + d \mod n)$ uniformly at random.*
   - *for i such that $a_i = 1$, it sets $f_{\mathsf{A}}(i + d \mod n) = 0$.*
3. B *constructs a function* $f_{\mathsf{B}} : [n] \to [n]$ *as follows:*
   - *for i such that $b_i = 0$, it samples $f_{\mathsf{B}}(i + d \mod n)$ uniformly at random.*
   - *for i such that $b_i = 1$, it sets $f_{\mathsf{B}}(i + d \mod n) = y$.*
   - *Let $f := f_{\mathsf{A}} + f_{\mathsf{B}}$.*
4. A *sends* $\mathsf{C}_{\mathsf{pre}}(f_{\mathsf{A}})$ *to* B.
5. B *sets* $c := \mathsf{C}_{\mathsf{pre}}(f_{\mathsf{A}}) +_{\mathcal{G}} \mathsf{C}_{\mathsf{pre}}(f_{\mathsf{B}}) = \mathsf{C}_{\mathsf{pre}}(f)$.
6. B *emulates* $\mathsf{C}_{\mathsf{dec}}^f(y, c)$: *whenever $\mathsf{C}_{\mathsf{dec}}$ sends a query r to f, algorithm B forwards it to A, and feeds $f_{\mathsf{A}}(r) + f_{\mathsf{B}}(r)$ back into $\mathsf{C}_{\mathsf{dec}}$.*
   - *Let x be $\mathsf{C}_{\mathsf{dec}}$'s output in the above emulation, and let $i = x - d \mod n$.*
7. B *sends* (i, b_i) *to* A. *If $a_i = b_i = 1$, algorithm A outputs False and informs B.*
8. *Otherwise, both parties output True.*

In the following we analyze the communication complexity and success probability of Π.

Claim 4.9. *(Π's communication complexity).* *It holds that* $CC(\Pi) \leq s + 2q(\log n + 1) + \log n + 3$.

Proof. 1. In Step 4, party A sends $C_{pre}(f_A)$ to B.

2. In Step 6, the parties exchange at most $2\log n + 2$ bits for every query C_{dec} makes.

3. In Step 7, the parties exchange at most $\log n + 3$ bits.

Thus, the total communication is bounded by $s + 2q(\log n + 1) + \log n + 3$.

Claim 4.10. *(Π's success probability).*

1. $\Pr[(A(a), B(b)) = (True, True)] = 1$
   for every $(a, b) \in \mathcal{Q}^0 := \{\mathcal{X}, \mathcal{Y} \subseteq [n] : |\mathcal{X} \cap \mathcal{Y}| = 0\}$.
2. $\Pr[(A(a), B(b)) = (False, False)] \geq \frac{\alpha^2}{8}$
   for every $(a, b) \in \mathcal{Q}^1 := \{\mathcal{X}, \mathcal{Y} \subseteq [n] : |\mathcal{X} \cap \mathcal{Y}| = 1\}$.

Proof. By construction, it is clear that Π always accepts (the parties output True) on inputs $(a, b) \in \mathcal{Q}^0$. Fix $(a, b) \in \mathcal{Q}^1$, and let Y, D, F, F_A, F_B and I be the values of y, d, f, f_A, f_B and i respectively, in a random execution of $(A(a), B(b))$. By construction, $F(j) = F_A(j) + F_B(j)$ for all $j \in [n]$. For j not in the intersection, either $F_A(j)$ or $F_B(j)$ is chosen uniformly at random by one of the parties, and therefore $F(j)$ is uniformly distributed and independent of all other outputs. For the intersection element w, it holds that $F(w) = y$, which is uniform, and since there is exactly one intersection, is independent from all other outputs.

Let $W := w + D \mod n$. Note that W is uniformly distributed over $[n]$ and is independent of F. Also note that, by construction, $Y = F(W)$. Therefore, (F, W, Y) is distributed exactly as $(F, X, F(X))$ for $X \leftarrow [n]$. Hence, the assumption on C yields that

$$\Pr[C(Y; F) \in F^{-1}(Y)] \geq \alpha$$

and by Claim 3.8,

$$\Pr[C(Y; F) = W] \geq \alpha^2/8.$$

Therefore, both parties output False with probability at least $\alpha^2/8$.

Proving Theorem 4.6. We now use Claims 4.9 and 4.10 to prove Theorem 4.6.

Proof. (Proof of Theorem 4.6). Let $t = \left\lceil \frac{\log(\varepsilon)}{\log(1 - \alpha^2/8)} \right\rceil$, and consider the protocol Π^t, in which on input (a, b) the parties interact in protocol Π for t times, and accept only if they do so in *all* iterations. By Claims 4.9 and 4.10, the communication complexity and success probability of Π^t in solving set disjointness over $\mathcal{Q}$ match the theorem statement.

4.1   Additive-Advice Inverters

The following result generalizes Corollary 4.7 by replacing the restriction on the decoder (e.g., linear and short output) with the ability to compute the advice string of $f_1 + f_2$ by a low-communication protocol over the inputs f_1 and f_2.

Theorem 4.11. (Bound on additive-advice inverters). *Let* $C = (C_{pre}, C_{dec})$ *be an* q-*query inversion algorithm such that* $\Pr_{\substack{f \leftarrow \mathcal{F} \\ x \leftarrow [n]}} [C(f(x); f) \in f^{-1}(f(x))] \geq$ α. *Assume exists a two-party protocol* (P_1, P_2) *with communication complexity* k *such that for every* $f_1, f_2 \in \mathcal{F}$, *the output of* P_2 *in* $(P_1(f_1), P_2(f_2))$ *equals to* $C_{pre}(f_1 + f_2)$ *with probability at least* $1 - \gamma$ *for some* $\gamma \geq 0$, *letting* $f_1 + f_2$ *be according to Definition 4.2. Then* $k + q \log n \in \Omega(\alpha^2(1 - \gamma) \cdot n)$.

Proof. The proof follows almost the exact same lines as that of Theorem 4.6, with the following changes: first, steps 4. and 5. in Protocol 4.8 are replaced by the parties A and B interacting in $(P_1(f_A), P_2(f_B))$, resulting in B outputting $C_{pre}(f_A + f_B)$ (thus, transmitting a total of $k + 2q(\log n + 1) + \log n + 3 \in O(k + q \log n)$ bits over the entire execution of the protocol). Second, note that due to the constant failure probability of (P_1, P_2) in computing $C_{pre}(f_A + f_B)$, the success probability of each execution of the protocol is now lowered by a constant factor $(1 - \gamma)$. This means that the rate of success when $\mathcal{X} \cap \mathcal{Y} \neq \emptyset$ is now bounded from below by only $\alpha^2(1 - \gamma)/8$ (rather than $\alpha^2/8$). The rest of the analysis is identical to that of Theorem 4.6.

5   Non-adaptive Inverters

In this section we present lower bounds on the time/memory tradeoff of non-adaptive function inverters. In Section 5.1, we present a bound for non-adaptive affine decoders, and in Section 5.2 we extend this bound to non-adaptive affine decision trees. To simplify notation, the following definitions and results are stated with respect to some fixed $n \in \mathbb{N}$, for which there exists a finite field of size n which we denote by $\mathbb{F}$. Let $\mathcal{F}$ be the set of all functions from $[n]$ to $[n]$. All asymptotic notations (e.g., Θ) hide constant terms that are independent of n. We start by formally defining non-adaptive function inverters.

Definition 5.1. (Non-adaptive inverters). *An* s-*advice* q-*query non-adaptive inverter is a deterministic algorithm triplet of the form* $C := (C_{pre}, C_{qry}, C_{dec})$, *where* $C_{pre} \colon \mathcal{F} \to \{0, 1\}^s$, $C_{qry} \colon [n] \times \{0, 1\}^s \to [n]^q$, *and* $C_{dec} \colon [n] \times \{0, 1\}^s \times [n]^q \to [n]$. *For* $f \in \mathcal{F}$ *and* $y \in [n]$, *let*

$$C(y; f) := C_{dec}\left(y, C_{pre}(f), f\left(C_{qry}(y, C_{pre}(f))\right)\right).$$

That is, C_{pre} is the *preprocessing* algorithm. It takes the function description as input and outputs a string of length s, to which we refer as the *advice* string. In the case that $s = 0$, we say that C has *zero-advice*, and omit C_{pre} from the notation. Algorithm C_{qry} is the *query selection* algorithm. It chooses the queries according to the element to invert y and the advice string, and outputs q indices, to which we refer as the *queries*. Algorithm C_{dec} is the *decoder* algorithm that performs the actual inversion. It receives the element y, the advice string and the function's answers to the (non-adaptive) queries selected by C_{qry} (the query indices themselves may be deduced from y and the advice), and attempts to output a preimage of y. Finally, $C(y; f)$ is the candidate preimage of y produced by the algorithms of C given the (restricted) access to f.

5.1 Affine Decoders

In this section we present our bound for non-adaptive affine decoders, defined as follows:

Definition 5.2. (Affine decoder). *A non-adaptive inverter* $C :=$ $(C_{pre}, C_{qry}, C_{dec})$ *has an* affine decoder, *if for every* $y \in [n]$ *and* $a \in \{0,1\}^s$ *there exists a q-sparse vector* $\alpha_y^a \in \mathbb{F}^n$ *and a field element* $\beta_y^a \in \mathbb{F}$, *such that for every* $f \in \mathcal{F}$: $C_{dec}(y, a, f(C_{qry}(y, a))) = \langle \alpha_y^a, f \rangle + \beta_y^a$.

The following theorem bounds the probability, over a random function f, that a non-adaptive inverter with an affine decoder inverts a random output of f with probability τ.

Theorem 5.3. *Let* $C = (C_{pre}, C_{qry}, C_{dec})$ *be an* s-*advice non-adaptive inverter with an affine decoder and let* $\tau \in [0, 1]$. *Then for every* $\delta \in [0, 1]$ *and* $m \leq n/16$, *it holds that*

$$\Pr_{f \leftarrow \mathcal{F}}\left[\Pr_{\substack{x \leftarrow [n] \\ y = f(x)}} [C(y; f) \in f^{-1}(y)] \geq \tau \right] \leq \alpha_{\tau,\delta} + 2^s \delta^{-m} \prod_{j=1}^{m} \left(\frac{2j}{n} + \max\left\{ \frac{1}{\sqrt[4]{n}}, \frac{4j}{n} \right\} \right)$$

for $\alpha_{\tau,\delta} := \Pr_{f \leftarrow \mathcal{F}}[\exists \tau n\text{-}size\ set\ \mathcal{X} \subset [n]: |f(\mathcal{X})| \leq \delta n]$.

While it is not easy to see what is the best choice, per τ, of the parameters δ and m above, the following corollary (proven in the full version) exemplifies the usability of Theorem 5.3 by considering the consequences of such a choice.

Corollary 5.4. (Theorem 1.5, **restated).** *Let* C *be as in Theorem 5.3, let* $\tau \geq 2 \cdot n^{-1/8}$ *and assume*

$$\Pr_{f \leftarrow \mathcal{F}}\left[\Pr_{\substack{x \leftarrow [n] \\ y = f(x)}} [C(y; f) \in f^{-1}(y)] \geq \tau \right] \geq 1/2, \text{ then } s \in \Omega(\tau^2 \cdot n).[7]$$

Our key step towards proving Theorem 5.3 is showing that even when conditioned on the (unlikely) event that a zero-advice inverter successfully inverts $i - 1$ random elements, the probability the inverter successfully inverts the next element is still low. To formulate the above statement, we define the following jointly distributed random variables: let F be uniformly distributed over $\mathcal{F}$ and let $Y = (Y_1, ..., Y_n)$ be a uniform vector over $[n]^n$. For a zero-advice inverter, we define the following random variables (jointly distributed with F and Y).

---

[7] The constant $1/2$ lowerbounding the probability is arbitrary.

Notation 5.5. *For a zero-advice inverter* D, *let* $X_i^{\mathsf{D}} := \mathsf{D}(Y_i; F)$, *let* Z_i^{D} *be the event* $\bigwedge_{j \in [i]} \{F(X_j^{\mathsf{D}}) = Y_j\}$, *and let* $X^{\mathsf{D}} = (X_1^{\mathsf{D}}, \ldots, X_n^{\mathsf{D}})$.

That is, X_i^{D} is D's answers to the challenges Y_i, and Z_i^{D} indicates whether D successfully answered each of the first i challenges. Given the above notation, our main lemma is stated as follows:

Lemma 5.6. *Let* D *be a zero-advice, non-adaptive inverter with affine decoder and let* Z^{D} *be as in Notation 5.5. Then for every* $i \in [n]$ *and* $\mu \in [0, \frac{1}{2}]$:

$$\Pr\left[Z_i^{\mathsf{D}} \mid Z_{i-1}^{\mathsf{D}}\right] \leq \frac{2i - 1}{n} + \mu + 2^{2\lceil \mu n \rceil \log(1/\mu) - \lceil \mu n \rceil \log(n) + (2i - 2)\log n}.$$

We prove Lemma 5.6 below, but first use it to prove Theorem 5.3.

Proving Theorem 5.3. Lemma 5.6 immediately yields a bound on the probability that D, *a zero-advice inverter, successfully inverts the first* i *elements of* Y. For proving Theorem 5.3, however, we need to bound the probability that D, and later on, an inverter with non-zero advice, finds a preimage of a *random output* of f. Yet, the conversion between these two measurements is rather straightforward. Hereafter we assume $n \geq 16$, as otherwise Theorem 5.3 is trivial, as $m = 0$.

Proof. (Proof of Theorem 5.3.). Let $\mathsf{C} = (\mathsf{C}_{\mathsf{pre}}, \mathsf{C}_{\mathsf{qry}}, \mathsf{C}_{\mathsf{dec}})$, $\tau \in [0, 1]$, $\delta \in [0, 1]$ and m be as in the theorem statement. Fix an advice string $a \in \{0, 1\}^s$, and let $\mathsf{C}^a = (\mathsf{C}_{\mathsf{qry}}^a, \mathsf{C}_{\mathsf{dec}}^a)$ denote the *zero-advice* inverter obtained by hardcoding a as the advice of C (i.e., $\mathsf{C}_{\mathsf{pre}}^a(f) = a$ for every f). For $j \in [n]$, let $Z_j = Z_j^{\mathsf{C}^a}$ and let $\mu_j := \max\left\{\sqrt[4]{1/n}, \frac{4j}{n}\right\}$. We start by showing that for every $j \leq n/16$ it holds that

$$\Pr\left[Z_j \mid Z_{j-1}\right] \leq \frac{2j}{n} + \mu_j \tag{16}$$

Indeed, by Lemma 5.6

$$\Pr\left[Z_j \mid Z_{j-1}\right] \leq \frac{2j - 1}{n} + \mu_j + 2^{\overbrace{2\lceil \mu_j n \rceil \log(1/\mu_j) - \lceil \mu_j n \rceil \log n + (2j - 2)\log n}^{\beta}} \tag{17}$$

We write,

$$\beta = \underbrace{2\lceil \mu_j n \rceil \log(1/\mu_j) - \frac{\lceil \mu_j n \rceil}{2}\log n}_{\beta_1} + \underbrace{\left(-\frac{\lceil \mu_j n \rceil}{2}\right)\log n + (2j - 2)\log n}_{\beta_2} \tag{18}$$

Since

$$\beta_1 \leq \lceil \mu_j n \rceil \left(\log \frac{1}{\mu_j^2} - \log \sqrt{n}\right) = \lceil \mu_j n \rceil \left(\log \frac{1}{\mu_j^2 \sqrt{n}}\right) \leq 0$$

and

$$\beta_2 = \frac{-\lceil \mu_j n \rceil}{2} \log n + 2j \log n - 2 \log n \le \frac{-2j}{n} n \log n + 2j \log n - 2 \log n \le -2 \log n,$$

we conclude that $\Pr\left[Z_j \mid Z_{j-1}\right] \le \frac{2j-1}{n} + \mu_j + 2^{-2\log n} \le \frac{2j}{n} + \mu_j$, proving Eq. (16).
Eq. (16) immediately yields that

$$\Pr\left[Z_m\right] = \prod_{j=1}^{m} \Pr\left[Z_j \mid Z_{j-1}\right] \le \prod_{j=1}^{m} \left(\frac{2j}{n} + \mu_j\right) \tag{19}$$

We use the above to produce a bound on the number of elements that C^a successfully inverts. Let $\mathcal{G}_{\mathcal{Y}}^a(f) := \{y \in [n] : C^a(y; f) \in f^{-1}(y)\}$, and compute:

$$\Pr\left[Z_m\right] = \Pr_{f \leftarrow \mathcal{F}}\left[\forall j \in [m] : Y_j \in \mathcal{G}_{\mathcal{Y}}^a(f)\right]$$

$$\ge \Pr_{f \leftarrow \mathcal{F}}\left[\forall j \in [m] : Y_j \in \mathcal{G}_{\mathcal{Y}}^a(f) \bigwedge |\mathcal{G}_{\mathcal{Y}}^a(f)| \ge \delta n\right]$$

$$= \Pr_{f \leftarrow \mathcal{F}}\left[\forall j \in [m] : Y_j \in \mathcal{G}_{\mathcal{Y}}^a(f) \mid |\mathcal{G}_{\mathcal{Y}}^a(f)| \ge \delta n\right] \cdot \Pr_{f \leftarrow \mathcal{F}}\left[|\mathcal{G}_{\mathcal{Y}}^a(f)| \ge \delta n\right]$$

$$\ge \delta^m \cdot \Pr_{f \leftarrow \mathcal{F}}\left[|\mathcal{G}_{\mathcal{Y}}^a(f)| \ge \delta n\right]. \tag{20}$$

Combining Eqs. (19) and (20) yields the following bound on the number of images C^a successfully inverts:

$$\Pr\left[|\mathcal{G}_{\mathcal{Y}}^a(f)| \ge \delta n\right] \le \delta^{-m} \cdot \prod_{j=1}^{m} \left(\frac{2j}{n} + \mu_j\right) \tag{21}$$

We now adapt the above bound to (the non zero-advice) C. Let $\mathcal{G}_{\mathcal{Y}}(f) := \{y \in [n] : C(y; f) \in f^{-1}(y)\}$ and let $\mathcal{G}_{\mathcal{X}}(f) = f^{-1}(\mathcal{G}_{\mathcal{Y}}(f))$. By Eq. (21) and a union bound,

$$\Pr_{f \leftarrow \mathcal{F}}\left[|\mathcal{G}_{\mathcal{Y}}(f)| \ge \delta n\right] \le 2^s \cdot \delta^{-m} \cdot \prod_{j=1}^{m} \left(\frac{2j}{n} + \mu_j\right) \tag{22}$$

We conclude that

$$\Pr_{f \leftarrow \mathcal{F}}\left[\Pr_{\substack{x \leftarrow [n] \\ y = f(x)}}\left[C(y; f) \in f^{-1}(y)\right] \ge \tau\right] = \Pr_{f \leftarrow \mathcal{F}}\left[|\mathcal{G}_{\mathcal{X}}(f)| \ge \tau n\right]$$

$$= \Pr_{f \leftarrow \mathcal{F}}\left[|\mathcal{G}_{\mathcal{X}}(f)| \ge \tau n \bigwedge |\mathcal{G}_{\mathcal{Y}}(f)| < \delta n\right] + \Pr_{f \leftarrow \mathcal{F}}\left[|\mathcal{G}_{\mathcal{X}}(f)| \ge \tau n \bigwedge |\mathcal{G}_{\mathcal{Y}}(f)| \ge \delta n\right]$$

$$\le \Pr_{f \leftarrow \mathcal{F}}\left[|\mathcal{G}_{\mathcal{X}}(f)| \ge \tau n \bigwedge |\mathcal{G}_{\mathcal{Y}}(f)| < \delta n\right] + \Pr_{f \leftarrow \mathcal{F}}\left[|\mathcal{G}_{\mathcal{Y}}(f)| \ge \delta n\right]$$

$$\le \alpha_{\tau,\delta} + 2^s \cdot \delta^{-m} \cdot \prod_{j=1}^{m} \left(\frac{2j}{n} + \mu_j\right).$$

The second inequality follows by the definition of $\alpha_{\tau,\delta}$ and Eq. (22).

Proving Lemma 5.6 In the rest of this section we prove Lemma 5.6. Fix a zero-advice non-adaptive inverter with an affine decoder $\mathsf{D} = (\mathsf{D}_{\mathsf{qry}}, \mathsf{D}_{\mathsf{dec}})$, $i \in [n]$ and $\mu \in [0, \frac{1}{2}]$. Let $X := X^{\mathsf{D}}$ and, for $j \in [n]$ let $Z_j := Z_j^{\mathsf{D}}$. We start by proving the following claim that bounds the probability in hand, assuming X_i, the inverter's answer, is coming from a small linear space. (Recall, from Definition 3.2, that $\mathcal{E}(\mathbf{M}) = \{j \in [m]: e_j \in \mathrm{Span}(\mathbf{M})\}$, where e_j is the jth unit vector in $\mathbb{F}^n$.)

Claim 5.7. Let $\mathbf{A} \in \mathbb{F}^{\ell \times n}$, let $v \in \mathrm{Im}(\mathbf{A})$, let $\mathbf{B}^1, \ldots, \mathbf{B}^n \in \mathbb{F}^{t \times n}$, and, for $y \in [n]$, let $\mathbf{A}^y := \begin{pmatrix} \mathbf{A} \\ \mathbf{B}^y \end{pmatrix}$. Then

$$\Pr\left[Y_i \in F(\mathcal{E}(\mathbf{A}^{Y_i})) \mid \mathbf{A} \times F = v\right] \leq \left(\frac{\ell}{n} + \mu\right) + 2^{2\lceil \mu n \rceil \log(1/\mu) + \lceil \mu n \rceil \log(t/n) + \ell \log n}.$$

Proof. By Claim 3.4 there exist an ℓ-size set $\mathcal{S} := \mathcal{S}_{\mathbf{A}}$ and t-size sets $\{\mathcal{S}_k := \mathcal{S}_{\mathbf{B}^k}\}_{k \in [n]}$ such that

$$\mathcal{E}(\mathbf{A}^y) \subseteq \mathcal{S} \cup \mathcal{S}_y \tag{23}$$

for every $y \in [n]$. By Fact 3.1,

$$\Pr\left[\mathbf{A} \times F = v\right] = \frac{n^{n-\mathrm{rank}(\mathbf{A})}}{n^n} \geq n^{-\ell} \tag{24}$$

Compute,

$$\Pr\left[Y_i \in F(\mathcal{E}(\mathbf{A}^{Y_i})) \mid \mathbf{A} \times F = v\right] \leq \Pr\left[Y_i \in F(\mathcal{S} \cup \mathcal{S}_{Y_i}) \mid \mathbf{A} \times F = v\right]$$
$$\leq \Pr\left[Y_i \in F(\mathcal{S}) \mid \mathbf{A} \times F = v\right] + \Pr\left[Y_i \in F(\mathcal{S}_{Y_i}) \mid \mathbf{A} \times F = v\right]$$
$$\leq \frac{\ell}{n} + \Pr\left[Y_i \in F(\mathcal{S}_{Y_i}) \mid \mathbf{A} \times F = v\right]. \tag{25}$$

The first inequality holds since $\mathcal{E}(\mathbf{A}^{Y_i}) \subseteq \mathcal{S} \cup \mathcal{S}_{Y_i}$, and the last one since $|\mathcal{S}| \leq \ell$ and Y_i is independent of F. Applying Claim 3.6 with respect to $p := n^{-\ell}$, $\gamma := \mu$, $W := \{\mathbf{A} \times F = v\}$, $Y := Y_i$ and the sets $\mathcal{S}_1, \ldots \mathcal{S}_n$, yields that

$$\Pr\left[Y_i \in F(\mathcal{S}_{Y_i}) \mid \mathbf{A} \times F = v\right] \leq \mu + 2^{2\lceil \mu n \rceil \log(1/\mu) + \lceil \mu n \rceil \log(t/n) + \ell \log n} \tag{26}$$

We conclude that $\Pr[Y_i \in F(\mathcal{E}(\mathbf{A}(Y_i))) \mid \mathbf{A} \times F = v] \leq \frac{\ell}{n} + \mu + 2^{2\lceil \mu n \rceil \log(1/\mu) + \lceil \mu n \rceil \log(t/n) + \ell \log n}$.

Given the above claim, we prove Lemma 5.6 as follows.

Proof. (Proof of Lemma 5.6). Since D has an affine decoder, for every $y \in [n]$ and $X := \mathsf{D}(y; F)$ there exist a q-sparse vector $\alpha^y \in \mathbb{F}^n$ and a field element $\beta^y \in \mathbb{F}$ such that $\langle \alpha^y, F \rangle + \beta^y = X$. Therefore, for every $j < i$:

1. $\langle \alpha^{Y_j}, F \rangle = -\beta^{Y_j} + X_j$.

Conditioning on Z_{i-1} further implies that for every $j < i$:

2. $F(X_j) = Y_j$.

Let $\ell := 2i - 2$, and let $\mathbf{M}^{i-1} \in \mathbb{F}^{\ell \times n}$ be the (random) matrix defined, for every $j \in [i-1]$, by $\mathbf{M}^{i-1}_{2j-1} := \alpha^{Y_j}$ and $\mathbf{M}^{i-1}_{2j} := e_{X_j}$. Let $V^{i-1} \in \mathbb{F}^\ell$ be the (random) vector defined by $V^{i-1}_{2j-1} := -\beta^{Y_j} + X_j$ and $V^{i-1}_{2j} = Y_j$. By definition, conditioned on Z_{i-1} it holds that $\mathbf{M}^{i-1} \times F = V^{i-1}$. This incorporates in a single equation all that is known about F given Z_{i-1}. To take into account the knowledge gained from the queries made while attempting to invert Y_i, we combine the above with α^{Y_i} and $\langle \alpha^{Y_i}, F \rangle$, into the matrix $\mathbf{M} := \begin{pmatrix} \mathbf{M}^{i-1} \\ \alpha^{Y_i} \end{pmatrix}$ and vector $V := \begin{pmatrix} V^{i-1} \\ \langle \alpha^{Y_i}, F \rangle \end{pmatrix}$.
By definition, $\mathbf{M} \times F = V$. We write

$$\Pr[Z_i \mid Z_{i-1}] = \Pr[Z_i \wedge X_i \in \mathcal{E}(\mathbf{M}) \mid Z_{i-1}] + \Pr[Z_i \wedge X_i \notin \mathcal{E}(\mathbf{M}) \mid Z_{i-1}] \quad (27)$$

and prove the lemma by separately bounding the two terms of the above equation. Let $H := (Y_{<i}, \mathbf{M}^{i-1}, V^{i-1})$, and note that

$$\Pr[Z_i \wedge X_i \in \mathcal{E}(\mathbf{M}) \mid Z_{i-1}] \leq \Pr[Y_i \in F(\mathcal{E}(\mathbf{M})) \mid Z_{i-1}]$$
$$= \operatorname*{E}_{h \leftarrow H \mid Z_{i-1}} [\Pr[Y_i \in F(\mathcal{E}(\mathbf{M})) \mid H = h, Z_{i-1}]]$$
$$= \operatorname*{E}_{h = (y_{<i}, m^{i-1}, v^{i-1}) \leftarrow H \mid Z_{i-1}} \left[\Pr\left[Y_i \in F\left(\mathcal{E}\begin{pmatrix} m^{i-1} \\ \alpha^{Y_i} \end{pmatrix} \right) \mid H = h, m^{i-1} \times F = v^{i-1} \right] \right]$$
$$= \operatorname*{E}_{(y_{<i}, m^{i-1}, v^{i-1}) \leftarrow H \mid Z_{i-1}} \left[\Pr\left[Y_i \in F\left(\mathcal{E}\begin{pmatrix} m^{i-1} \\ \alpha^{Y_i} \end{pmatrix} \right) \mid Y_{<i} = y_{<i}, m^{i-1} \times F = v^{i-1} \right] \right]$$
$$= \operatorname*{E}_{(y_{<i}, m^{i-1}, v^{i-1}) \leftarrow H \mid Z_{i-1}} \left[\Pr\left[Y_i \in F\left(\mathcal{E}\begin{pmatrix} m^{i-1} \\ \alpha^{Y_i} \end{pmatrix} \right) \mid m^{i-1} \times F = v^{i-1} \right] \right]$$
$$\leq \left(\frac{2i-2}{n} + \mu \right) + 2^{2\lceil \mu n \rceil \log(1/\mu) + \lceil \mu n \rceil \log(1/n) + (2i-2)\log n}. \quad (28)$$

The first inequality holds by the definition of Z_i. The second equality holds by the definition of Z_{i-1}. The third equality holds since the event $\{Y_{<i} = y_{<i}, m^{i-1} \times F = v^{i-1}\}$ implies that $\{\mathbf{M}^{i-1} = m^{i-1}, V^{i-1} = v^{i-1}\}$. The last equality holds since F is independent of Y, and the last inequality follows by Claim 5.7 with respect to $\mathbf{A} := m^{i-1}, v := v^{i-1}$, and $(\mathbf{B}^1, \ldots, \mathbf{B}^n) := (\alpha^1, \ldots, \alpha^n)$ (viewing α^i as a matrix in $\mathbb{F}^{1 \times n}$).

For bounding the right-hand term of Eq. (27), let $H := (X_i, Y_{\leq i}, \mathbf{M}, V)$, and compute

$$\Pr[Z_i \wedge X_i \notin \mathcal{E}(\mathbf{M}) \mid Z_{i-1}] \leq \Pr[Z_i \mid X_i \notin \mathcal{E}(\mathbf{M}), Z_{i-1}]$$
$$= \operatorname*{E}_{h \leftarrow H \mid X_i \notin \mathcal{E}(\mathbf{M}), Z_{i-1}} [\Pr[Z_i \mid H = h, Z_{i-1}]]$$
$$= \operatorname*{E}_{h = (x_i, y_{\leq i}, m, v) \leftarrow H \mid X_i \notin \mathcal{E}(\mathbf{M}), Z_{i-1}} [\Pr[F(x_i) = y_i \mid H = h, m \times F = v]]$$
$$= \operatorname*{E}_{(x_i, y_{\leq i}, m, v) \leftarrow H \mid X_i \notin \mathcal{E}(\mathbf{M}), Z_{i-1}} [\Pr[F(x_i) = y_i \mid Y_{\leq i} = y_{\leq i}, m \times F = v]]$$

$$= \mathop{\mathrm{E}}_{(x_i, y_{\leq i}, m, v) \leftarrow H | X_i \notin \mathcal{E}(\mathbf{M}), Z_{i-1}} [\Pr[F(x_i) = y_i \mid m \times F = v]]$$

$$= 1/n. \tag{29}$$

The second equality holds by the definition of Z_{i-1}. The third equality holds since the event $\{Y_{\leq i} = y_{\leq i}, m \times F = v\}$ implies that $\{\mathbf{M} = m, V = v\}$, and X_i is a function of V. The fourth equality holds since F is independent from Y. The last inequality follows by Claim 3.3. Combining Eqs. (27) to (29), we conclude that

$$\Pr[Z_i \mid Z_{i-1}] \leq \left(\frac{2i-2}{n} + \mu \right) + 2^{2\lceil \mu n \rceil \log(1/\mu) + \lceil \mu n \rceil \log(1/n) + (2i-2)\log n} + 1/n$$

$$= \frac{2i-1}{n} + \mu + 2^{2\lceil \mu n \rceil \log(1/\mu) - \lceil \mu n \rceil \log(n) + (2i-2)\log n}.$$

5.2 Affine Decision Trees

In this section we present lower bounds for non-adaptive affine decision trees. These are formally defined as follows:

Definition 5.8. (Affine decision trees). *An n-input* affine decision tree *over $\mathbb{F}$ is a labeled, directed, degree $|\mathbb{F}|$ tree $\mathcal{T}$. Each internal node v of $\mathcal{T}$ has label $\alpha_v \in \mathbb{F}^n$, each leaf ℓ of $\mathcal{T}$ has label $o_\ell \in \mathbb{F}$, and the $|\mathbb{F}|$ outgoing edges of every internal node are labeled by the elements of $\mathbb{F}$. Let $\Gamma_{\mathcal{T}}(v, \gamma)$ denote the (direct) child of v connected via the edge labeled by γ. The* node path $p = (p_1, \ldots, p_{d+1})$ *of $\mathcal{T}$ on input $w \in \mathbb{F}^n$ is defined by:*

- *p_1 is the root of $\mathcal{T}$.*
- *$p_{i+1} = \Gamma_{\mathcal{T}}(p_i, \langle \alpha_{p_i}, w \rangle)$.*

The edge path *of $\mathcal{T}$ on w is defined by $(\langle \alpha_{p_1}, w \rangle, \cdots, \langle \alpha_{p_d}, w \rangle)$. Lastly, the* output *of $\mathcal{T}$ on w, denoted $\mathcal{T}(w)$, is the value of $o_{p_{d+1}}$.*

Note that the edge path determines the computation path and output. Given the above, affine decision tree decoders are defined as follows.

Definition 5.9. (Affine decision tree decoder). *An inversion algorithm $\mathsf{C} := (\mathsf{C}_{\mathsf{pre}}, \mathsf{C}_{\mathsf{qry}}, \mathsf{C}_{\mathsf{dec}})$ has a d-depth* affine decision tree decoder, *if for every $y \in [n]$, $a \in \{0,1\}^s$ and $v = \mathsf{C}_{\mathsf{qry}}(y, a)$, there exists an n-input, d-depth affine decision tree $\mathcal{T}^{y,a}$ such that $\mathsf{C}_{\mathsf{dec}}(y, a, f(v)) = \mathcal{T}^{y,a}(f)$.*

Note that such a decision tree may be of size $O(n^d)$. The following theorem bounds the probability, over a random function f, that a non-adaptive inverter with an affine decision tree decoder inverts a random output of f with probability τ.

Theorem 5.10. *Let* C *be an s-advice,* $(q \leq n/16)$-*query, non-adaptive inverter with a d-depth affine decision tree decoder, and let* $\tau \in [0,1]$. *Then for every* $\delta \in [0,1]$ *and* $m \leq \frac{n \log(n/q)}{4(d+1) \log n}$ *it holds that*

$$
\Pr_{\substack{f \leftarrow \mathcal{F}}} \left[\Pr_{\substack{x \leftarrow [n] \\ y = f(x)}} \left[\mathsf{C}(y;f) \in f^{-1}(y) \right] \geq \tau \right]
$$

$$
\leq \alpha_{\tau,\delta} + 2^s \cdot \delta^{-m} \prod_{j=1}^{m} \left(\frac{(d+1)j}{n} + \max\left\{ \sqrt[4]{q/n}, \frac{2(d+1)j \log n}{n \log(n/q)} \right\} \right)
$$

for $\alpha_{\tau,\delta} := \Pr_{f \leftarrow \mathcal{F}_n} [\exists \tau n\text{-size set } \mathcal{X} \subset [n]\colon |f(\mathcal{X})| \leq \delta n]$.

Comparing to the bound we derive on affine decoders (Theorem 5.3), we are paying above for the tree depth d, but also for the number of queries q. In particular, we essentially multiply each term of the above product by the tree depth d, and by $\frac{\log n}{\log(n/q)}$. In addition, the theorem only holds for smaller values of m. The following corollary exemplifies the usability of Theorem 5.10 by considering the consequences of two choices of parameters.

Corollary 5.11. (Theorem 1.6, restated). *Let* C *be as in Theorem 5.10 and assume*
$$
\Pr_{f \leftarrow \mathcal{F}} \left[\Pr_{\substack{x \leftarrow [n] \\ y = f(x)}} \left[\mathsf{C}(y;f) \in f^{-1}(y) \right] \geq \tau \right] \geq 1/2, \text{ then the following holds:}
$$

- *If* $q \leq n \cdot (\tau/2)^8$, *then* $s \in \Omega(n/d \cdot \tau^2/\log n)$.
- *If* $q \leq n^{1-\epsilon}$, *then* $s \in \Omega(n/d \cdot \tau^2 \epsilon)$.

Proof. Omitted, follows by Theorem 5.10 using very similar lines to those used to derive Corollary 5.4 from Theorem 5.3.

The proof of Theorem 5.10 is omitted and can be found in the full version of this paper.

Acknowledgments. We are thankful to Dmitry Kogan, Uri Meir and Alex Samorodnitsky for very useful discussions. We also thank the anonymous reviewers for their comments.

References

1. Abusalah, H., Alwen, J., Cohen, B., Khilko, D., Pietrzak, K., Reyzin, L.: Beyond hellman's time-memory trade-offs with applications to proofs of space. In: Takagi, T., Peyrin, T. (eds.) ASIACRYPT 2017. LNCS, vol. 10625, pp. 357–379. Springer, Cham (2017). https://doi.org/10.1007/978-3-319-70697-9_13
2. Akshima, D., Cash, A., Drucker, H., Wee, et al.: Time-space tradeoffs and short collisions in merkle-damgård hash functions. In: Annual International Cryptology Conference (CRYPTO), pp. 157–186 (2020)

3. Alon, N., Balla, I., Gishboliner, L., Mond, A., Mousset, F.: The minrank of random graphs over arbitrary fields. Isr. J. Math. **235**(1), 63–77 (2019). https://doi.org/10.1007/s11856-019-1945-8

4. Bar-Yossef, Z., Birk, Y., Jayram, T., Kol, T.: Index coding with side information. IEEE Trans. Inform. Theor. **57**(3), 1479–1494 (2011)

5. Biryukov, A., Shamir, A.: Cryptanalytic time/memory/data tradeoffs for stream ciphers. In: Okamoto, T. (ed.) ASIACRYPT 2000. LNCS, vol. 1976, pp. 1–13. Springer, Heidelberg (2000). https://doi.org/10.1007/3-540-44448-3_1

6. Biryukov, A., Shamir, A., Wagner, D.: Real time cryptanalysis of A5/1 on a PC. In: Goos, G., Hartmanis, J., van Leeuwen, J., Schneier, B. (eds.) FSE 2000. LNCS, vol. 1978, pp. 1–18. Springer, Heidelberg (2001). https://doi.org/10.1007/3-540-44706-7_1

7. Chawin, D., Haitner, I., Mazor, N.: Lower bounds on the time/memory tradeoff of function inversion. Technical report TR20-089, Electronic Colloquium on Computational Complexity (2020)

8. Coretti, S., Dodis, Y., Guo, S., Steinberger, J.: Random oracles and non-uniformity. In: Nielsen, J.B., Rijmen, V. (eds.) EUROCRYPT 2018. LNCS, vol. 10820, pp. 227–258. Springer, Cham (2018). https://doi.org/10.1007/978-3-319-78381-9_9

9. Corrigan-Gibbs, H., Kogan, D.: The function-inversion problem: barriers and opportunities. In: Hofheinz, D., Rosen, A. (eds.) TCC 2019. LNCS, vol. 11891, pp. 393–421. Springer, Cham (2019). https://doi.org/10.1007/978-3-030-36030-6_16

10. De, A., Trevisan, L., Tulsiani, M.: Time space tradeoffs for attacks against one-way functions and PRGs. In: Rabin, T. (ed.) CRYPTO 2010. LNCS, vol. 6223, pp. 649–665. Springer, Heidelberg (2010). https://doi.org/10.1007/978-3-642-14623-7_35

11. Dodis, Y., Guo, S., Katz, J.: Fixing cracks in the concrete: random oracles with auxiliary input, revisited. In: Coron, J., Nielsen, J.B. (eds.) EUROCRYPT 2017. LNCS, vol. 10211, pp. 473–495. Springer, Cham (2017). https://doi.org/10.1007/978-3-319-56614-6_16

12. Fiat, A., Naor, M.: Rigorous time-space trade-offs for inverting functions. SIAM J. Comput. **29**(3), 790–803 (2000)

13. Galvin, D.: Three tutorial lectures on entropy and counting. Technical report 1406.7872, arXiv (2014)

14. Gennaro, R., Gertner, Y., Katz, J., Trevisan, L.: Bounds on the efficiency of generic cryptographic constructions. SIAM J. Comput. **35**(1), 217–246 (2005)

15. Golovnev, A., Regev, O., Weinstein, O.: The minrank of random graphs. IEEE Trans. Inform. Theor. **64**(11), 6990–6995 (2018)

16. Haviv, I., Langberg, M.: On linear index coding for random graphs. In: 2012 IEEE International Symposium on Information Theory Proceedings, pp. 2231–2235. IEEE (2012)

17. Hellman, M.: A cryptanalytic time-memory trade-off. IEEE Trans. Inform. Theor. **26**(4), 401–406 (1980)

18. Impagliazzo, R., Rudich, S.: Limits on the provable consequences of one-way permutations. In: Annual ACM Symposium on Theory of Computing (STOC), pp. 44–61 (1989)

19. Lubetzky, E., Stav, U.: Nonlinear index coding outperforming the linear optimum. IEEE Trans. Inform. Theor. **55**(8), 3544–3551 (2009)

20. Oechslin, P.: Making a faster cryptanalytic time-memory trade-Off. In: Boneh, D. (ed.) CRYPTO 2003. LNCS, vol. 2729, pp. 617–630. Springer, Heidelberg (2003). https://doi.org/10.1007/978-3-540-45146-4_36

21. Razborov, A.A.: On the distributional complexity of disjointness. Theor. Comput. Sci. **106**(2), 385–390 (1992)

22. Unruh, D.: Random oracles and auxiliary input. In: Menezes, A. (ed.) CRYPTO 2007. LNCS, vol. 4622, pp. 205–223. Springer, Heidelberg (2007). https://doi.org/10.1007/978-3-540-74143-5_12

23. Valiant, L.G.: Graph-theoretic arguments in low-level complexity. In: Gruska, J. (ed.) MFCS 1977. LNCS, vol. 53, pp. 162–176. Springer, Heidelberg (1977). https://doi.org/10.1007/3-540-08353-7_135

24. Valiant, L.G.: Why is boolean complexity theory difficult. Boolean Funct. Complex. **169**, 84–94 (1992)

25. Yao, A.C.: Should tables be sorted? J. ACM **28**(3), 615–628 (1981)

26. Yao, A.C.: Protocols for secure computations. In: Annual Symposium on Foundations of Computer Science (FOCS), pp. 160–164 (1982)

27. Yao, A.C.: Coherent functions and program checkers. In: Annual ACM Symposium on Theory of Computing (STOC), pp. 84–94 (1990)

Super-Linear Time-Memory Trade-Offs
for Symmetric Encryption

Wei Dai[1], Stefano Tessaro[2], and Xihu Zhang[2(✉)]

[1] University of California, San Diego, La Jolla, USA
weidai@eng.ucsd.edu
[2] University of Washington, Seattle, USA
{tessaro,xihu}@cs.washington.edu

Abstract. We build symmetric encryption schemes from a pseudorandom function/permutation with domain size N which have very high
security – in terms of the amount of messages q they can securely encrypt
– assuming the adversary has $S < N$ bits of memory. We aim to *minimize*
the number of calls k we make to the underlying primitive to achieve a
certain q, or equivalently, to *maximize* the achievable q for a given k. We
target in particular $q \gg N$, in contrast to recent works (Jaeger and Tessaro, EUROCRYPT '19; Dinur, EUROCRYPT '20) which aim to beat
the birthday barrier with *one* call when $S < \sqrt{N}$.

Our first result gives new and explicit bounds for the Sample-then-
Extract paradigm by Tessaro and Thiruvengadam (TCC '18). We show
instantiations for which $q = \Omega\left((N/S)^k\right)$. If $S < N^{1-\alpha}$, Thiruvengadam
and Tessaro's weaker bounds only guarantee $q > N$ when $k = \Omega(\log N)$.
In contrast, here, we show this is true already for $k = \Theta(1/\alpha)$.

We also consider a scheme by Bellare, Goldreich and Krawczyk
(CRYPTO '99) which evaluates the primitive on k independent random
inputs, and masks the message with the XOR of the outputs. Here, we
show $q = \Omega\left((N/S)^{k/2}\right)$, using new combinatorial bounds on the list-
decodability of XOR codes which are of independent interest. We also
study best-possible attacks against this construction.

1   Introduction

A number of very recent works [2,19,20,28,29,39,45,48] extend the concrete
security treatment of provable security to account for the *memory complexity* of an adversary. For symmetric encryption, Jaeger and Tessaro [39] showed
for example that randomized counter-mode encryption (CTR) is secure against
attackers encrypting $q = \Theta(N/S)$ messages, where S is the memory complexity
of the adversary and $N = 2^n$ is the domain size of the underlying PRF/PRP,
which is assumed to be sufficiently secure. This is a *linear* time-memory trade-off
– reducing S by a multiplicative factor $\varepsilon < 1$ allows us to increase by a factor
$1/\varepsilon$ the tolerable data complexity of the attack.

W. Dai—Work done in part while visiting the University of Washington.

R. Pass and K. Pietrzak (Eds.): TCC 2020, LNCS 12552, pp. 335–365, 2020.
https://doi.org/10.1007/978-3-030-64381-2_12

The benefit of such a trade-off is that *if $S < \sqrt{N}$*, one can tolerate $q > \sqrt{N}$, which *is* beyond the so-called "birthday barrier." Building schemes with beyond-birthday security is a prime line of research in symmetric cryptography, but constructions are generally less efficient without imposing any memory restrictions on the adversary.

OUR CONTRIBUTIONS: SUPER-LINEAR TRADE-OFFS. The trade-off for CTR relies on a thin margin: For $N = 2^{128}$, we only improve upon memory-unbounded analyses if $S \ll 2^{64}$. While 2^{64} bits is a large amount of memory, it is not *unreasonably* large. One should therefore ask whether we can do better – either take advantage of a weaker memory limitation or be able to encrypt a much larger number of messages. More broadly, we want to paint a full picture of what security is attainable under a given memory restriction – complementing our understanding of the landscape *without* memory constraints.

More concretely, we consider constructions which make k calls to a given block cipher[1] with domain size N, and ask the following question:

If the adversary is bounded to $S < N$ bits of memory, what is the highest security we can achieve (in terms of allowable encryptions q) by a construction making k calls?

Tessaro and Thiruvengadam [45] showed that one can achieve security for $q \gg N$ encrypted messages at the cost of $k = \Omega(\log N)$, whereas here we do much better by giving schemes that can do so already for $k = O(1)$: They can in particular encrypt up to $q = \Theta((N/S)^{c(k)})$ messages, for $c(k) > 1$. (This is what we refer to as a *super-linear* trade-off.) For one of our two constructions (in fact, the same construction as [45], but with a much better analysis), we get $c(k) = k - 1$ for messages of length n, and $c(k) = k$ for bit messages. These trade-offs appear best-possible (or close to best-possible), but proving optimality for now seems to be out of reach – we move first steps by studying attacks against one of our constructions.

These schemes can securely encrypt $q \gg N$ messages as long as $S < N$. It is important to appreciate that *without* the restriction, $q < N$ is an inherent barrier for current proof techniques (cf. [45] for a discussion).

ON PRACTICE AND THEORY. We stress that our approach is *foundational*. Even for $k \geqslant 2$, practitioners may find the resulting constructions not viable. Still, security beyond $q > N$ may be interesting in practice – we may want to implement a block cipher with smaller block length (e.g., $N = 2^{80}$) and then be able to still show security against $q = 2^{128}$ encryptions, as long as $S < 2^{80}$, which is a reasonable assumption.

We also stress that the question we consider here is natural in its own right, and is a cryptographic analogue and a scaled-up version of the line of works initiated by Raz [43], with a stronger focus on precise bounds and thus different techniques. (We discuss the connection further in Sect. 1.4 below.)

---

[1] Assumed to be a secure PRP/PRF.

1.1   Our Contributions

We start with a detailed overview of our contributions. (A technical overview is deferred to the next two sections.) Our constructions make k calls to a function $\mathsf{F}_K : \{0,1\}^n \to \{0,1\}^n$ keyed with a key K – this is generally obtained from a block cipher like AES (in which case, $n = 128$). We will use the shorthand $N = 2^n$. For the presentation of our results in this introduction, it is helpful to assume F_K behaves as a random function or a random permutation – this can be made formal via suitable PRF/PRP assumptions, and we discuss this at the end of this section in more detail.

THE SAMPLE-THEN-EXTRACT CONSTRUCTION. The first part of this paper revisits the *Sample-then-Extract (StE)* construction of [45]. StE depends on a parameter $k \geqslant 1$ as well as a (strong) randomness extractor[2] $\mathsf{Ext} : (\{0,1\}^n)^k \times \{0,1\}^s \to \{0,1\}^\ell$. The encryption of a message $M \in \{0,1\}^\ell$ under key K is then

$$C = (R_1, \ldots, R_k, \mathsf{sd}, \mathsf{Ext}(\mathsf{F}_K(0 \parallel R_1) \parallel \cdots \parallel \mathsf{F}_K(k-1 \parallel R_k), \mathsf{sd}) \oplus M) , \quad (1)$$

where $\mathsf{sd} \in \{0,1\}^s$ and $R_1, \ldots, R_k \in \{0,1\}^{n-\log k}$ are chosen afresh upon each encryption. We also extend StE to encrypt arbitrary-length messages (which can have variable length), amortizing the cost of including $\mathsf{sd}, R_1, \ldots, R_k$, in the ciphertext. (For this introduction, however, we only deal with fixed-length messages for ease of exposition.)

   Prior work only gives a sub-optimal analysis: For $k = \Theta(\log N) = \Theta(n)$, Tessaro and Thiruvengadam [45] show security against $q = N^{1.5}$ encryptions whenever $S = N^{1-\alpha}$ for a constant $\alpha > 0$. Here, we prove a much better bound. For example, for $\ell = n$, and a suitable choice of Ext, we show security up to

$$q = \Theta((N/S)^{k-1})$$

encryptions. This is improved to $q = \Theta((N/S)^k)$ for bit messages. Therefore, if $S < N^{1-\alpha}$, we can achieve security up to $q = N^{1.5}$ encryptions with $k = 1 + \frac{1.5}{\alpha}$, which is constant if α is constant.

THE k-XOR CONSTRUCTION. Our second result considers a generalization of randomized counter-mode encryption, introduced by Bellare, Goldreich, and Krawczyk [7], which we refer to as the *k-XOR construction*. For even $k \geqslant 1$, to encrypt $M \in \{0,1\}^n$, we pick random $R_1, \ldots, R_k \in \{0,1\}^n$, and output

$$C = (R_1, \ldots, R_k, \mathsf{F}_K(R_1) \oplus \cdots \oplus \mathsf{F}_K(R_k) \oplus M) . \quad (2)$$

Alternatively, k-XOR can be viewed as an instance of StE with a seedless Ext. For this construction, we prove security up to $q = \Theta((N/S)^{k/2})$ encryptions. We note that in [7], a memory-independent bound of $q = \Theta(N/k)$ was proved for the case where $q \leqslant N$. The two results are complementary. The bound from [7] does not tell us anything for $q > N$, in contrast to our bound, but can beat (in

---

[2] Recall that this means that $(\mathsf{Ext}(X, \mathsf{sd}), \mathsf{sd})$ and (U, sd) are (statistically) indistinguishable for $\mathsf{sd} \xleftarrow{\$} \{0,1\}^s$, $U \xleftarrow{\$} \{0,1\}^\ell$, whenever X has sufficient min-entropy.

concrete terms) our bound for $q < N/k$. Different from our results on StE, our proof only works if we assume that F_K is a random *function*. We note however that this is consistent with the fact that even for the memory-unbounded setting, no bound based on a random permutation is known. We however discuss how to instantiate F_K from a PRP, and this will result in a construction similar to the above, just with a high number of calls to F.

It is also clear that we cannot expect to prove any better bound, unless we change the sampling of the indices $R_1, \ldots, R_k$. This is because after $q = N^{k/2}$ queries we will see, with very high probability, an encryption with $R_{2i-1} = R_{2i}$ for all $i = 1, \ldots, k/2$. This attack only requires $S = O(k \log N)$. However, it is not clear whether this attack extends to leverage larger values of S. Further discussion of attacks can be found in the full version.

Our proof relies on new *tight* combinatorial bounds on the list-decodability of XOR codes which are of independent interest and improve upon earlier works. Indeed, using existing best-possible bounds in our proof would result in a weaker bound with exponent $k/4$ (More details in the full version).

REDUCING THE CIPHERTEXT SIZE. In the above constructions, the ciphertext size grows with k. An interesting question is whether we can avoid this – in the full version we do so for the case $S = \Omega(N)$. For this setting, our StE analysis gives $k = \Omega(n)$, and thus, the ciphertext has $\Omega(n^2)$ extra random bits in addition to the masked plaintext. In contrast, we present a variant of the StE construction where the number of extra bits in the ciphertext is reduced to $O(n)$. To this end, we use techniques from randomness extraction and randomness-efficient sampling to instantiate our construction.

INSTANTIATING F_K. We instantiate F_K from a keyed function/permutation which we assume to be a pseudorandom function (PRF) or permutation (PRP). The catch is that if we aim for security against $q > N$ queries, we *need* F_K to be secure for adversaries that also run with time complexity larger than $t > q > N$.

This assumption is not unreasonable, as already discussed in [45] – one necessary condition is that the key is longer than $\log q$ bits to prevent a memory-less key-recovery distinguisher (e.g., one would use AES-256 instead of AES-128).[3] This is also easily seen to be sufficient in the ideal-cipher model, where PRP security *only* depends on the key length. Furthermore, our reductions give adversaries using memory $S < N$, and it is plausible that non-trivial attacks against block ciphers may use large amounts of memory. And finally, key-extension techniques [9,26,27,33] can give ciphers with security beyond N.

1.2 Our Techniques – Sample-Then-Extract

We discuss both constructions, StE and k-XOR, in separate sections, starting with the former.

TIGHTER HYBRIDS. Our proof follows a paradigm (first introduced explicitly in [16], and then adapted in [39] to the memory-bounded setting) developing

---

[3] The best non-trivial attack against AES-256 uses time approximately 2^{254} [12].

hybrid-arguments in terms of Shannon-type metrics. This results in bounds of the form $\sqrt{q \cdot \varepsilon}$, whereas a classical hybrid arguments would give us bounds of the form $q\sqrt{\varepsilon}$. We do not know whether the square root *can* be removed – Dinur [19] shows how to do so in the Switching Lemma of [39], but it is unclear whether his techniques apply here.[4]

The core of our approach relies on understanding the distance from the uniform distribution for a sample with form

$$Y(\mathsf{F}) = (R_1, \ldots, R_k, \mathsf{sd}, \mathsf{Ext}(\mathsf{F}(0 \,\|\, R_1) \,\|\, \cdots \,\|\, \mathsf{F}(k-1 \,\|\, R_k), \mathsf{sd})) \,,$$

for a randomly chosen function $\mathsf{F} : \{0,1\}^n \to \{0,1\}^n$, given additionally access to (arbitrary) S bits of leakage $\mathcal{L}(\mathsf{F})$. We will measure this distance in terms of KL divergence, by lower bounding the conditional Shannon entropy $\mathsf{H}(Y(\mathsf{F})|\mathcal{L}(\mathsf{F}))$. Giving a bound which is as large as possible will require the use of a number of tools in novel ways.

DECOMPOSITION LEMMA. For starters, we will crucially rely on the decomposition lemma of Göös et al. [32]: It shows that F_z – which is defined as F conditioned on $\mathcal{L}(\mathsf{F}) = z$ – is statistically γ-close to a convex combination of $(P, 1-\delta_z)$-dense random variable. A $(P, 1-\delta)$-dense random variable, in this context, is distributed over functions $\mathsf{F}' : \{0,1\}^n \to \{0,1\}^n$ and is such that there exists a set $\mathcal{P} \subseteq \{0,1\}^n$ of size P with the property that: (1) the outputs $\mathsf{F}'(x)$ are *fixed* for all $x \in \mathcal{P}$, whereas (2) for any subset $I \subseteq \{0,1\}^n \setminus \mathcal{P}$, the outputs $\{\mathsf{F}'(x)\}_{x \in I}$ have jointly min-entropy at least $|I| \cdot (1-\delta)n$. It is important to notice that there is a trade-off between γ, δ, and P, in that $\delta_z = (S_z + \log(1/\gamma))/(Pn)$, where $S_z = n2^n - \mathsf{H}_\infty(\mathsf{F}_z)$.

EXTRACTION FROM VARYING AMOUNTS OF MIN-ENTROPY. Our analysis will choose the parameters δ and P carefully – the key point, however, is that when we replace F_z with a $(P, 1-\delta)$-dense function F', the total min-entropy of $\mathsf{F}'(0 \,\|\, R_1) \,\|\, \cdots \,\|\, \mathsf{F}'(k-1 \,\|\, R_k)$ grows with the number of probes R_i such that $(i \,\|\, R_i) \notin \mathcal{P}$, i.e., the set of "good" probes which land on an input for which the output is *not* fixed. To get some intuition, if one ignores the pre-pended probe index i, the number of good probes $g \in \{0, 1, \ldots, k\}$ would follow a binomial distribution with parameter $|\mathcal{P}|/N$, and overall min-entropy is $g \cdot (1-\delta)n$.

Therefore, the extractor is now applied to a random variable which has variable amount of min-entropy, which depends on g. Here, it is useful to use an extractor based on a 2-universal hash function: Indeed, the Leftover-Hash Lemma (LHL) [38] guarantees a very useful property, namely that while the extractor itself is *fixed*, the entropy of its output increases as the entropy of its input increases. Specifically, the entropy of the ℓ-bit output becomes $\ell - \min\{\ell, 2^{\ell+1-h}\}$ when the input has min-entropy $h \approx g(1-\delta)n$.

Our approach is dual to the smoothed min-entropy approach of Vadhan [47], which is used to build locally-computable extractors in a way that resembles

---

[4] This improvement is irrelevant as long as we only infer the resources needed for constant advantage, which is the standard angle on tightness in symmetric cryptography. However, as pointed out e.g. in [33], exact bounds also often matter.

ours. In our language, but with different techniques, he shows that with good probability, $g = \Theta(k)$, where $k = \Theta(\lambda)$. This does not work well for us (we care mostly about $k = O(1)$), and thus we take a more fine-grained approach geared towards understanding the behavior of g.

THE ADVANTAGE OF SHANNON ENTROPY. It is crucial for the quality of the established trade-off to adopt a Shannon-entropy version of the LHL. The more common version bounds the statistical distance as $2^{(\ell+1-h)/2}$, and following this path would *only* give us a lower bound on q which is (roughly) the square root of what we prove. We note that a Shannon-theoretic version of the LHL was already proved by Bennet, Brassard, Crépeau, and Maurer [10], and the fact that a different distance metric can reduce the entropy loss is implicit in [4].[5]

EXTRA REMARKS. A few more remarks are in order. Our approach is similar, but also different from that of Coretti et al. [14,15]. They use the decomposition lemma in a similar way to transition to (what they refer to as) the *bit-fixing random oracle* (BF-RO), i.e., a model where F is fixed on P positions, and *completely random* on the remaining ones (as opposed to being just $(1-\delta)$-dense, as in our case). Using the BF-RO abstraction yields very suboptimal bounds. Their generic approach would incur an additive factor of $(S + \log(1/\gamma))k/P$, which is too large.

1.3   Our Techniques - k-XOR

Our approach for StE given above does not yield usable results for k-XOR – namely, any choice of δ prevents us from proving that $F_z(0 \parallel R_1) \oplus \cdots \oplus F_z(k - 1 \parallel R_k)$ is very close to uniform, even if none of the probes lands in $\mathcal{P}$. A unifying treatment of both constructions appears to require finding a strengthening of the decomposition lemma. Instead, we follow a different path.

PREDICTING XORs. The core of our analysis bounds the ability of predicting $F(R_1) \oplus \cdots \oplus F(R_k)$ for a random function $F : \{0,1\}^n \to \{0,1\}$, given (arbitrary) S bits of leakage on F. We aim to upper bound the advantage $\Delta(N, S, k)$ which measures how much beyond probability $\frac{1}{2}$ an adversary can guess the XOR given the leakage and $R_1, \ldots, R_k$. The focus is on *single-bit* outputs – a bound for the multi-bit case will follow from a hybrid argument. Although this problem has been studied [17,22,35,37,46], both in the contexts of locally-computable extractors for the bounded-storage model and of randomness extraction, none of these techniques gives bounds which are tight enough for us. (We elaborate on this below.) Here, we shall prove that

$$\Delta(N, S, k) = O((S/N)^{k/2}) \,.$$

THE CODING CONNECTION. Our solution leverages a connection with the list-decoding of the *k-fold XOR code* (or k-XOR code, for short): This encodes F

---

[5] The benefits of reducing entropy loss by targeting Shannon-like metrics were also very recently studied by Agrawal [1] in a different context.

(which we think now as an N-bit string $F \in \{0,1\}^N$) as an N^k-dimensional bit-vector k-XOR$(F) \in \{0,1\}^{N^k}$ such that its component $(R_1, \ldots, R_k) \in [N]^k$ takes value $F(R_1) \oplus \cdots \oplus F(R_k)$. At the same time, a (deterministic) adversary $\mathcal{A}$ which on input $R_1, \ldots, R_k$ and the leakage $Z = L(F)$ attempts to predict $F(R_1) \oplus \cdots \oplus F(R_k)$ can be thought of as family of 2^S "noisy strings" $\{C_Z = \mathcal{A}(\cdot, Z)\}_{Z \in \{0,1\}^S}$.

Prior works (such as [17]) focused (directly or indirectly) on *approximate* list-decoding, as they give *reductions*, transforming $\mathcal{A}$ and L into some predictor for F, under some slightly larger leakage. (How much larger the leakage is depends on the approximate list size.) Here, instead, we follow a combinatorial blueprint inspired by [6,8], albeit very different in its execution. Concretely, we introduce a parameter $\varepsilon > 0$ (to be set to a more concrete value later), and for all $Z \in \{0,1\}^S$, let $\mathcal{B}_Z$ be the Hamming Ball of radius $(1/2-\varepsilon)N^k$ around C_Z. Now, when picking $F \xleftarrow{\$} \{0,1\}^N$, exactly one of two cases can arise:

(i) k-XOR$(F) \in \mathcal{B}_Z$ for some $Z \in \{0,1\}^S$, in which case the overlap between C_Z and k-XOR(F) is potentially very high.
(ii) $F \notin \bigcup_Z \mathcal{B}_Z$, in which case $\mathcal{A}$ will be able to predict $F(R_1) \oplus \cdots \oplus F(R_k)$ with probability at most $1/2 + \varepsilon$ over the random choice of $R_1, \ldots, R_k$ - *no matter* how $L(F)$ is defined!

Now, let L_ε^k be an upper bound on the number of codewords k-XOR(F) within any of the $\mathcal{B}_Z$. Then,

$$\Delta(N, S, k) \leqslant \varepsilon + 2^S \cdot L_\varepsilon^k / 2^N . \tag{3}$$

TIGHT BOUNDS ON LIST-DECODING SIZE. What remains to be done here is to find a bound on L_ε^k – we are not aware of any tight bounds in the literature, and we give such bounds here.

Our approach (and its challenges) are illustrated best in the case $k = 1$. Specifically, define random variables $T_1, \ldots, T_N$, where, for all $R \in [N]$, $T_R = 1$ if $C_Z(R) = F(R)$ and $T_R = 0$ else. When we pick F at random, the T_i's are independent, and a Chernoff bound tells us that

$$\Pr\left[\sum_{R=1}^N T_R \geqslant \left(\frac{1}{2} + \varepsilon\right) N\right] \leqslant 2^{-\Omega(\varepsilon^2 N)} ,$$

which in turn implies $L_\varepsilon^1 \leqslant 2^{N(1-\varepsilon^2)}$. Therefore, setting ε to be of order slightly larger than $\sqrt{S/N}$ gives us the right bound.

Our proof for $k > 1$ will follow a similar blueprint, except that this will require us to prove a (much harder!) concentration bound on a sum of N^k variables which are highly dependent. We will prove such concentration using the method of moments. The final bound will be of the form $L_\varepsilon^k \leqslant 2^{N(1-\varepsilon^{2/k})}$.

RELATIONSHIP TO PAST WORKS. We are not aware of any prior work address-ing the question of proving tight bounds for the XOR code *directly*, but prior techniques can non-trivially be combined to obtain non-trivial bounds. The best-possible bound we could derive is $(S/N)^{k/4}$. This can be obtained by combining the approach of De and Trevisan [17] with the *combinatorial* approximate list-decoding bounds of [37]. Alternatively, one could use the approximate list decoding bounds from [11]. The resulting indistinguishability bound is harder to evaluate, but it is inferior for small values of S (roughly, $S < N^{2/3}$). Further details are in the full version.

OPTIMALITY. We discuss attacks against k-XOR in the full version. In particular, one can easily see that if we want the bound to hold *for all* values of S, then it cannot be improved, as it is tight for small $S = O(k \log N)$. For a broader range of values of S, we give an attack which succeeds with $q = \Theta((N^k/S^{k-1})$ messages and for $k = 2$ we provide an attack that succeeds with $q = \Theta((N/S)^2)$ – it is a good question whether our bound can be improved for larger values of S, or in the case where the $R_1, \ldots, R_k$ are *distinct*. (This would preclude our small-memory attack.)

Our general attack that works for any S and k, stores all linear equations that have all variables fall in $x_1, \ldots, x_S$ and checks consistency. It is expected that a linear dependent equation would appear within $q = O(N^k/S^{k-1})$ queries. Our next attack addresses the case where $k = 2$. By modeling each variable as a vertex and representing each equation as an edge in the graph, the attack exploits the tree structure formed by linear independent equations and succeeds within $q = O((N/S)^2)$ queries. However, for $k \geqslant 3$, similar analysis no longer applies as the hypergraph structure is hard to analyze.

1.4   Further Related Work

SPACE-TIME TRADE-OFFS FOR LEARNING PROBLEMS. A related line of works is that initiated by Raz [43] on space-time trade-offs for learning problems, which has by now seen several follow-ups [5,24,25,40,44]. In particular, Raz proposes a scheme encrypting each bit m_i as $(a_i, \langle a_i, s \rangle + m_i)$ where $s \xleftarrow{\$} \{0,1\}^n$ is a secret key, and $a_i \xleftarrow{\$} \{0,1\}^n$ is freshly sampled for each bit. This scheme allows to encrypt 2^n bits as long as the adversary's memory is at most n^2/c bits, for some (small) constant $c > 1$. We *can* scale up this setting to ours, by thinking of s as the exponentially large table of a random function, but the resulting scheme would also incur exponential complexity. Some follow-up works consider the cases where the a_i's are *sparse* [5,25], but they only study the problem of *recovering s*, and it does not seem possible to obtain (sufficiently sharp) indistinguishability bounds from these results.

Closest to our work on k-XOR is a recent concurrent paper [24] by Garg, Kothari and Raz, which studies the streaming indistinguishability of Goldreich's PRG [30] against memory bounded adversaries. Their target are bounds for arbitrary predicates for Goldreich's PRG, and they prove indistinguishability for up to $q = \Theta((N/S)^{k/9})$ output bits when the predicate is k-XOR. The setting of the analysis is almost identical to ours, with the difference being that we think of the PRG seed as being an exponentially large random table. Thus our techniques also yield a tighter bound in their setting for this special case,[6] and we believe they should also yield improved bounds for more general predicates.

On the flip side, it is an exciting open question whether the branching-program framework underlying all of these works can be adapted to obtain bounds as sharp as ours in the indistinguishability setting.

THE BOUNDED-STORAGE MODEL. In both cases, our proofs consider the intermediate setting where S bits of leakage $Z = \mathcal{L}(F)$ are given about F, and we want to show that the output of some locally computable function $g(F, R)$ is random enough given Z, where R is potentially public randomness. This is exactly what is considered in the *Bounded Storage Model* (BSM) [3,17,23,42,47] and in the *bounded-retrieval model* (BRM) [18,21]. Indeed, our StE construction can be traced back to the approach of locally-computable extractors [47], and the k-XOR construction resembles the constructions of [3,23,42]. A substantial difference, however, is that we are inherently concerned about the small-probe setting (i.e., $k = O(1)$) and the case where $S = N^{1-\alpha}$, whereas generally the BSM considers $S = O(N)$ and a *linear* number of probes. We also take a more concrete approach towards showing as-tight-as-possible bounds for a given target k. It would be beneficial to address whether our techniques can be used to improve existing BSM/BRM schemes.

Another difference is that our bounds are typically multiplied by the number of encryption queries. This can be done non-trivially, for example, by using Shannon entropy as a measure of randomness, and relying on the reduced entropy loss for extraction with respect to Shannon entropy, as we do for StE.

2 Definitions

Let $\mathbb{N} = \{0, 1, 2, \dots\}$. For $N \in \mathbb{N}$ let $[N] = \{1, 2, \dots, N\}$. If A and B are finite sets, then $\mathsf{Fcs}(A, B)$ denotes the set of all functions $F : A \to B$ and $\mathsf{Perm}(A)$ denotes the set of all permutations on the set A. The set of size k subsets of A is $\binom{A}{k}$. Picking an element uniformly at random from A and assigning it to s is denoted by $s \xleftarrow{\$} A$. The set of finite vectors with entries in A is $(A)^*$ or A^*. Thus $\{0, 1\}^*$ is the set of finite length strings.

If $M \in \{0, 1\}^*$ is a string, then $|M|$ denotes its bit length. If $m \in \mathbb{N}$ and $M \in (\{0, 1\}^m)^*$, then $|M|_m = |M|/m$ denote the block length of M and M_i denote the i-th m-bit block of M. When using the latter notation, m will be clear from context. The *Hamming weight* $\mathsf{hw}(x)$ of $x \in \{0, 1\}^n$ is defined as $\mathsf{hw}(x) = |\{i \in [n] \mid x_i \neq 0\}|$. The *Hamming ball* of radius r around $z \in \{0, 1\}^n$ is defined as $\mathcal{B}(z; r) = \{x \in \{0, 1\}^n \mid \mathsf{hw}(x \oplus z) \leqslant r\}$.

We say that a random variable X is a *convex combination* of random variables $X_1, \dots, X_t$ (with the same range as X) if there exists $\alpha_1, \dots, \alpha_t \geqslant 0$ such that $\sum_{i=1}^{t} \alpha_i = 1$ and for any x in the range of X, it holds that $\Pr[X = x] = \sum_{i=1}^{t} \alpha_i \Pr[X_i = x]$.

---

[6] There is a small formal difference, in that our analysis of k-XOR evaluates the given function on random indices, whereas in [24] these indices are distinct.

GAMES. Our cryptographic reductions will use pseudocode games (inspired by the code-based framework of [9]). See Fig. 1 for some example games. We let $\Pr[G]$ denote the probability that game G outputs true. It is to be understood that the model underlying this pseudocode is the formalism we now describe.

COMPUTATIONAL MODEL. Our algorithms are randomized when not specified otherwise. If $\mathcal{A}$ is an algorithm, then $y \leftarrow \mathcal{A}^{O_1, O_2, \cdots}(x_1, \ldots; r)$ denotes running $\mathcal{A}$ on inputs $x_1, \ldots$ and coins r with access to oracles $O_1, O_2, \ldots$ to produce output y. The notation $y \xleftarrow{\$} \mathcal{A}^{O_1, O_2, \cdots}(x_1, \ldots)$ denotes picking r at random then running $y \leftarrow \mathcal{A}^{O_1, O_2, \cdots}(x_1, \ldots; r)$. The set of all possible outputs of $\mathcal{A}$ when run with inputs $x_1, \ldots$ is $[\mathcal{A}(x_1, \ldots)]$. Adversaries and distinguishers are algorithms. The notation $y \leftarrow O(x_1, \ldots)$ is used for calling oracle O with inputs $x_1, \ldots$ and assigning its output to y (even if the value assigned to y is not deterministically chosen).

We say that an algorithm (or adversary) $\mathcal{A}$ runs in time t if its description size and running time are at most t. We say that adversary $\mathcal{A}$ is *S-bounded* if it uses at most S bits of memory during its execution, for any possible oracle it is given access to and any possible input.

INFORMATION THEORY. For a random variable X with probability distribution $P(x) = \Pr[X = x]$, the *Shannon entropy* $\mathsf{H}(X)$ and *collision entropy* $\mathsf{H}_2(X)$ are defined as $\mathsf{H}(X) = -\sum_x P(x) \log P(x)$ and $\mathsf{H}_2(X) = -\log\left(\sum_x P(x)^2\right)$. The min-entropy of X is $\mathsf{H}_\infty(X) = -\log \max_x P(x)$. For two random variables X, Y with joint distribution $Q(x, y) = \Pr[X = x, Y = y]$, the *conditional Shannon entropy* and *conditional min-entropy* are defined by $\mathsf{H}(Y|X) = \sum_{x,y} Q(x, y) \log \frac{Q(x)}{Q(x,y)}$ and $\mathsf{H}_\infty(Y|X) = -\log \sum_x \max_y Q(x, y)$, where $Q(x) = \sum_y Q(x, y)$ is the marginal distribution of X.

2.1 Streaming Indistinguishability

We review the streaming indistinguishability framework of Jaeger and Tessaro [39], which considers a setting where a sequence, $\mathbf{X}$, of random variables

$$X_1, X_2, \ldots, X_q$$

with range $[N]$ is given, one by one, to a (memory-bounded) distinguisher $\mathcal{A}$. The distinguisher will need to tell apart this setting from another one, where it is given $\mathbf{Y} = (Y_1, Y_2, \ldots, Y_q)$ instead.

THE STREAMING MODEL. More formally, in the i-th step (for $i \in [q]$), the distinguisher $\mathcal{A}$ has a state σ_{i-1} and stage number i. Then it receives $V_i \in \{X_i, Y_i\}$ based on which it updates its state to σ_i. We denote by $\sigma_i(\mathcal{A}(\mathbf{X}))$ and $\sigma_i(\mathcal{A}(\mathbf{Y}))$ the state after receiving X_i and Y_i when running $\mathcal{A}$ on streams $\mathbf{X}$ and $\mathbf{Y}$, respectively. We say here that $\mathcal{A}$ is *S-bounded* if all states have bit-length at most S.[7]

---

[7] Note, quite crucially, that this is different from the definition of S-bounded algorithms, in that we relax our notion of space-boundedness to only consider the states between stages. This is sufficient for our applications, although the model can be restricted.

Game $G_F^{fn}(\mathcal{A})$	Game $G_{SE,b}^{indr}(\mathcal{A})$
$K \xleftarrow{\$} F.Ks$	$K \xleftarrow{\$} SE.Ks$
$b \xleftarrow{\$} \mathcal{A}^{FN}$	$b' \xleftarrow{\$} \mathcal{A}^{ENC}$
Return $b = 1$	Return $b' = 1$
$FN(X)$	$ENC(M)$
$Y \leftarrow F(K, X)$	$C_1 \leftarrow SE.Enc(K, M)$
Return Y	$C_0 \xleftarrow{\$} \{0, 1\}^{|M|+SE.xl}$
	Return C_b

Fig. 1. Security games for PRF/PRP security of a family of functions (Left) and INDR security of an encryption scheme (Right).

We also assume that $\sigma_q \in \{0, 1\}$, and think of σ_q as the output of $\mathcal{A}$. We define the following streaming-distinguishing advantage

$$\mathsf{Adv}_{\mathbf{X},\mathbf{Y}}^{dist}(\mathcal{A}) = \Pr\left[\mathcal{A}(\mathbf{X}) \Rightarrow 1\right] - \Pr\left[\mathcal{A}(\mathbf{Y}) \Rightarrow 1\right] .$$

We shall use the following lemma by [39].

Lemma 1. *Let* $\mathbf{X} = (X_1, \ldots, X_q)$ *be independent and uniformly distributed over* $[N]$ *and let* $\mathbf{Y} = (Y_1, \ldots, Y_q)$ *be distributed over the same support as* $\mathbf{X}$*. Then,*

$$\mathsf{Adv}_{\mathbf{X},\mathbf{Y}}^{dist}(\mathcal{A}) \leq \frac{1}{\sqrt{2}}\sqrt{q \log N - \sum_{i=1}^{q} \mathsf{H}(Y_i \mid \sigma_{i-1}(\mathcal{A}(\mathbf{Y})))} .$$

2.2 Cryptographic Preliminaries

FAMILY OF FUNCTIONS. A function family F is a function of the form $F : F.Ks \times F.Dom \to F.Rng$. It is understood that there is some algorithm that samples from the set $F.Ks$, and that fixing $K \in F.Ks$, there is some algorithm that computes the function $F_K(\cdot) = F(K, \cdot)$. For our purposes, it suffices to restrict to function families where $F.Dom = \{0,1\}^n$ and $F.Rng = \{0,1\}^m$ for some n and m.

A blockcipher is a family of functions F for which $F.Dom = F.Rng$ and for all $K \in F.Ks$ the function $F(K, \cdot)$ is a permutation.

We let $RF_{n,m} : Fcs(\{0,1\}^n, \{0,1\}^m) \times \{0,1\}^n \to \{0,1\}^m$ be the function family of all functions mapping n-bits to m-bits, i.e. for any $F \in Fcs(\{0,1\}^n, \{0,1\}^m)$ and $x \in \{0,1\}^n$, we define $RF_{n,m}(F, x) = F(x)$. We let $RP_n : Perm(\{0,1\}^n) \times \{0,1\}^n \to \{0,1\}^n$ be the function family of all permutations on n bits. It is defined so that for any $P \in Perm(\{0,1\}^n)$ and $x \in \{0,1\}^n$, $RP_n(P, x) = P(x)$.

PSEUDORANDOMNESS SECURITY. For security we will consider both pseudorandom function (PRF) and pseudorandom permutation (PRP) security.

Let F be a function family with $F.Dom = \{0,1\}^n$ and $F.Rng = \{0,1\}^m$. PRF security asks F to be indistinguishable from $RF_{n,m}$. More formally, consider the function evaluation game $\mathsf{G}_\mathsf{F}^{\mathsf{fn}}(\mathcal{A})$, in which adversary simply gets access to an oracle evaluating F_K for a random and fixed key K. The PRF advantage of $\mathcal{A}$ against F is defined to be

$$\mathsf{Adv}_\mathsf{F}^{\mathsf{prf}}(\mathcal{A}) = \Pr[\mathsf{G}_\mathsf{F}^{\mathsf{fn}}(\mathcal{A})] - \Pr[\mathsf{G}_{\mathsf{RF}_{n,m}}^{\mathsf{fn}}(\mathcal{A})] .$$

Similarly, PRP security of a blockcipher F with $\mathsf{F.Dom} = \{0,1\}^n$ is defined to be

$$\mathsf{Adv}_\mathsf{F}^{\mathsf{prp}}(\mathcal{A}) = \Pr[\mathsf{G}_\mathsf{F}^{\mathsf{fn}}(\mathcal{A})] - \Pr[\mathsf{G}_{\mathsf{RP}_n}^{\mathsf{fn}}(\mathcal{A})] .$$

SYMMETRIC ENCRYPTION. A symmetric encryption scheme SE specifies key space $\mathsf{SE.Ks}$, and algorithms $\mathsf{SE.Enc}$, and $\mathsf{SE.Dec}$ (where the last of these is deterministic) as well as set $\mathsf{SE.M}$. Encryption algorithm $\mathsf{SE.Enc}$ takes as input key $K \in \mathsf{SE.Ks}$ and message $M \in \mathsf{SE.M}$ to output a ciphertext C. We assume there exists a constant expansion length $\mathsf{SE.xl} \in \mathbb{N}$ such that $|C| = |M| + \mathsf{SE.xl}$. Decryption algorithm $\mathsf{SE.Dec}$ takes as input ciphertext C to output $M \in \mathsf{SE.M} \cup \{\bot\}$. We write $K \xleftarrow{\$} \mathsf{SE.Ks}$, $C \xleftarrow{\$} \mathsf{SE.Enc}(K, M)$, and $M \leftarrow \mathsf{SE.Dec}(C)$.

Correctness requires for all $K \in \mathsf{SE.Ks}$ and all sequences of messages $\boldsymbol{M} \in (\mathsf{SE.M})^*$ that $\Pr[\forall i : \boldsymbol{M}_i = \boldsymbol{M}_i'] = 1$ where the probability is over the coins of encryption in the operations $C_i \xleftarrow{\$} \mathsf{SE.Enc}(K, \boldsymbol{M}_i)$ and $\boldsymbol{M}_i' \leftarrow \mathsf{SE.Dec}(K, C_i)$ for $i = 1, \ldots, |\boldsymbol{M}|$.

For security we will require the output of encryption to look like a random string. Consider the game $\mathsf{G}_{\mathsf{SE},b}^{\mathsf{indr}}(\mathcal{A})$ shown on the right side of Fig. 1. It is parameterized by a symmetric encryption scheme SE, adversary $\mathcal{A}$, and bit $b \in \{0,1\}$. The adversary is given access to an oracle ENC which, on input a message M, returns either the encryption of that message or a random string of the appropriate length according to the secret bit b. The advantage of $\mathcal{A}$ against SE is defined by $\mathsf{Adv}_{\mathsf{SE}}^{\mathsf{indr}}(\mathcal{A}) = \Pr[\mathsf{G}_{\mathsf{SE},1}^{\mathsf{indr}}(\mathcal{A})] - \Pr[\mathsf{G}_{\mathsf{SE},0}^{\mathsf{indr}}(\mathcal{A})]$.

3   Sample-Then-Extract

The $\mathsf{StE} = \mathsf{StE}[\mathsf{F}, k, \mathsf{Ext}]$ scheme is defined in Fig. 2: It was originally proposed by Tessaro and Thiruvengadam [45], and it is based on ideas from the context of locally-computable extractors [47]. The scheme is extended here to encrypt multiple blocks of message with the same randomness $R_1 \ldots, R_k$, and the same extractor seed sd. The scheme $\mathsf{StE}[\mathsf{F}, k, \mathsf{Ext}]$ uses a keyed function family F which maps $\{0,1\}^n$ to $\{0,1\}^n$, as well as an extractor $\mathsf{Ext} : \{0,1\}^{kn} \times \{0,1\}^s \rightarrow \{0,1\}^\ell$.

Below, we instantiate the extractor Ext with 2-universal hash function [13]. We recall that $\mathsf{h} : \{0,1\}^w \times \{0,1\}^s \rightarrow \{0,1\}^\ell$ is 2-universal if for all distinct $x, y \in \{0,1\}^w$, it holds that $\Pr[\mathsf{sd} \xleftarrow{\$} \{0,1\}^s : \mathsf{h}(x, \mathsf{sd}) = \mathsf{h}(y, \mathsf{sd})] = 2^{-\ell}$. For conciseness, we often write $\mathsf{h}_{\mathsf{sd}}(x) = \mathsf{h}(x, \mathsf{sd})$. If $\ell \leqslant s$, a construction with $w = s$ interprets both the input x and the seed sd as elements of the extension field $\mathbb{F}_{2^w}$, and $\mathsf{h}(x, \mathsf{sd})$ consists of the first ℓ bits of the product of x and sd.

Scheme StE[F, k, Ext]

Procedure Enc(K, M)

$B \leftarrow |M|_\ell$

$M_1, \ldots, M_B \leftarrow M$; $\mathsf{sd} \xleftarrow{\$} \{0,1\}^s$

$\mathbf{R} = (R_1, \ldots, R_k) \xleftarrow{\$} \left(\{0,1\}^{n - \lceil \log k \rceil} \right)^k$

For $i \in [B]$ do

    For $j \in [k]$ do

        $V_{i,j} \leftarrow \mathsf{F}(K, (j-1) \| (R_j + i - 1))$

For $i \in [B]$ do

    $C_i \leftarrow M_i \oplus \mathsf{Ext}(V_{i,1} \| \ldots \| V_{i,k}, \mathsf{sd})$

Return $(\mathsf{sd}, \mathbf{R}, C_1, \ldots, C_B)$

Procedure Dec(K, C)

$(\mathsf{sd}, \mathbf{R}, C_1, \ldots, C_B) \leftarrow C$

For $i \in [B]$ do

    For $j \in [k]$ do

        $V_{i,j} \leftarrow \mathsf{F}(K, (j-1) \| (R_j + i - 1))$

For $i \in [B]$ do

    $M_i \leftarrow C_i \oplus \mathsf{Ext}(V_{i,1} \| \cdots \| V_{i,k}, \mathsf{sd})$

Return $M_1 \| \cdots \| M_B$

Fig. 2. The sample-then-extract encryption scheme $\mathsf{SE} = \mathsf{StE}[\mathsf{F}, k, \mathsf{Ext}]$, with $\mathsf{F.Dom} = \{0,1\}^n$. All additions and subtractions are done under modulus $2^{n - \lceil \log k \rceil}$. The key space and message space of SE are $\mathsf{SE.Ks} = \mathsf{F.Ks}$ and $\mathsf{SE.M} = (\{0,1\}^\ell)^+$.

A SMALL-CIPHERTEXT VERSION OF StE. We also study a version of StE which produces small ciphertexts, using techniques from randomness efficient sampling. The proof resembles that for StE given below, and the details are deferred to the full version due to limited space.

3.1 Security of StE

The security of StE scheme is captured by the following theorem. We first consider the case where F is a PRF – which we prove below first. We will state a very similar theorem for the PRP case below.[8]

The proof of the main theorem is deferred to Sect. 3.2.

Theorem 1. (Security of StE). *Let $N = 2^n$, let $\mathsf{F} : \mathsf{F.Ks} \times \{0,1\}^n \rightarrow \{0,1\}^n$ be a keyed function family. Let Ext be a 2-universal hash function $h : \{0,1\}^{kn} \times \{0,1\}^{kn} \rightarrow \{0,1\}^\ell$. For any S-bounded q-query adversary $\mathcal{A}_{\mathsf{indr}}$, where each query consists of messages of at most B ℓ-bit blocks such that $B \leqslant N/k$, there exists an $(S + B\ell)$-bounded PRF adversary $\mathcal{A}_{\mathsf{prf}}$ (with similar time complexity as $\mathcal{A}_{\mathsf{indr}}$) that issues at most qkB queries to the oracle, such that*

$$\mathsf{Adv}^{\mathsf{indr}}_{\mathsf{StE}[\mathsf{F}, k, \mathsf{h}]}(\mathcal{A}_{\mathsf{indr}}) \leqslant \mathsf{Adv}^{\mathsf{prf}}_{\mathsf{F}}(\mathcal{A}_{\mathsf{prf}}) + \sqrt{\frac{1}{2} q B \varepsilon} \,,$$

where

$$\varepsilon = \frac{\ell}{N^k} + \sum_{t=0}^{k} \binom{k}{t} \left(\frac{(2S + 2kn)B}{N} \right)^t \cdot \min\{\ell, 2^{\ell+1} \cdot (2/N)^{k-t}\} \,.$$

---

[8] The PRP assumption leads to more straightforward instantiations via a block cipher. The PRF instantiation is trickier, as we need PRFs that are highly secure – these can be instantiated with a much higher cost from a good PRP.

INSTANTIATIONS AND INTERPRETATIONS. We discuss instantiations of the above theorem for specific parameter regimes. We consider two choices of ℓ, which result in different bounds. In fact, a subtle aspect of the bound is the appearance of a min: Depending on the choice of ℓ (relative to N), we will have different t^* such that $2^{\ell+1} \cdot (2/N)^{k-t} > \ell$ for all $t < t^*$, and the value t^* affects the bound.

We give two corollaries. The first one dispenses with any fine-tuning, and just upper bounds the min with $2^{\ell+1} \cdot (2/N)^{k-t}$. This bound however is enough to give us a strong trade-off of $q = \Omega(N^k/S^k)$ for $\ell = O(1)$. However, for another common target, $\ell = n$, this would give us $q = \Omega(N^{k-1}/S^k)$. Our second corollary will show how the setting t^* in that case will lead to a stronger lower bound of $q = \Omega(N^{k-1}/S^{k-1})$. (In both cases, we are stating this for $B = 1$.)

Corollary 1. *With the same setup as Theorem 1, we have*

$$\mathsf{Adv}^{\mathsf{indr}}_{\mathsf{StE}[\mathsf{F},k,\mathsf{h}]}(\mathcal{A}_{\mathsf{indr}}) \leqslant \mathsf{Adv}^{\mathsf{prf}}_{\mathsf{F}}(\mathcal{A}_{\mathsf{prf}}) + \sqrt{2^{\ell}qB\left(\frac{(2S+2kn)B+3}{N}\right)^k}.$$

Corollary 2. *With the same setup as Theorem 1, in addition to $n = \ell$, $n \geqslant 4$, and $k \geqslant 2$, we have*

$$\mathsf{Adv}^{\mathsf{indr}}_{\mathsf{StE}[\mathsf{F},k,\mathsf{h}]}(\mathcal{A}_{\mathsf{indr}}) \leqslant \mathsf{Adv}^{\mathsf{prf}}_{\mathsf{F}}(\mathcal{A}_{\mathsf{prf}}) + \sqrt{2qBk\left(\frac{(2S+2kn)B+4n}{N}\right)^{k-1}}.$$

We defer the proof of both corollaries to the full version.

We further provides an analysis over parameters of practical interests. Concretely, if we instantiate F by a PRF that maps 128-bit to 128-bit, that is, $N = 2^{128}$, and we let the block size $\ell = 128$ bit. Then for any adversary that uses at most $S = 2^{80}$ bit of memory and encrypts at most 1 GB message per query (i.e. $B = 2^{33-7} = 2^{26}$), by following the coarse analysis of Corollary 1 and letting $k = 15$, our scheme can tolerate roughly $q = 2^{(128-80-26-1)\cdot 15-128-26} = 2^{161}$ queries. However, we do not need such a large k to achieve $q > N$. Notice that $\ell = n = 128$, we can use Corollary 2 to improve the analysis. Then by setting $k = 9$, we have $q = 2^{(128-80-26-1)\cdot(k-1)-26-1} = 2^{21\cdot8-27} = 2^{141}$ queries encrypting 1GB message. Note that similar analysis can be obtained when adapting the following PRP instantiation.

PRP INSTANTIATION. The security of StE instantiated by a PRP is captured by the following theorem. Since the StE-PRP security proof is similar to StE-PRF proof (the latter is slightly easier to present), we provide a proof sketch for the PRP case in the full version, highlighting the modifications from the PRF case.

Theorem 2. (Security of StE in PRP). *Let $N = 2^n \geqslant 16$, let $\mathsf{F} : \mathsf{F.Ks} \times \{0,1\}^n \to \{0,1\}^n$ be a keyed permutation family. Let Ext be a 2-universal hash function $\mathsf{h} : \{0,1\}^{kn} \times \{0,1\}^{kn} \to \{0,1\}^{\ell}$. For any S-bounded q-query adversary $\mathcal{A}_{\mathsf{indr}}$, where each query consists of messages of at most B ℓ-bit blocks such that $(S + k(n+1))B \leqslant N/2$, there exists an $(S + B\ell)$-bounded PRP adversary $\mathcal{A}_{\mathsf{prp}}$*

(with similar time complexity as $\mathcal{A}_{\mathsf{indr}}$) that issues at most qkB queries to the oracle, such that

$$\mathsf{Adv}^{\mathsf{indr}}_{\mathsf{StE}[\mathsf{F},k,h]}(\mathcal{A}_{\mathsf{indr}}) \leqslant \mathsf{Adv}^{\mathsf{prp}}_{\mathsf{F}}(\mathcal{A}_{\mathsf{prp}}) + \sqrt{\frac{1}{2}qB\varepsilon} \ ,$$

where

$$\varepsilon = \frac{\ell}{N^k} + \sum_{t=0}^{k} \binom{k}{t} \left(\frac{(4S + 4kn)B}{N} \right)^t \cdot \min\{\ell, 2^{\ell+1} \cdot (16/N)^{k-t}\} \ .$$

3.2   Proof of Theorem 1

OUTLINE AND PRELIMINARIES. Most of the proof will consider the StE scheme with direct access to a random function $\mathsf{RF}_{n,n}$. It is immediate to derive a bound when the scheme is instantiated by F at the cost of an additive term $\mathsf{Adv}^{\mathsf{prf}}_{\mathsf{F}}(\mathcal{A}_{\mathsf{prf}})$.

We will be using Lemma 1, applied to a stream consisting of encryptions of the all-zero plaintext (padded to B blocks) or truly random ciphertexts, which we define more formally below. In particular, this will require upper bounding the difference in Shannon entropy (from uniform) of the output of the i-th query, given the adversary's state at that point. As in the proof of the k-XOR construction, we relax our requirements a little, and assume the adversary can generate *arbitrary* S bits of leakage of RF. We will then be using a version of the leftover-hash lemma for bounding Shannon entropy (Proposition 1) to prove the desired bound.

We would naturally need (at the very least) to understand the min-entropy of $V_{i,1}\| \cdots \|V_{i,k}$ conditioned on the state σ_i of stage i. In fact, we will use an even more fine-grained approach, and see $V_{i,1}\| \cdots \|V_{i,k}$ as the convex combination of variables with different levels of entropy. To this end, we will use an approach due to Göös et al. [32] which decomposes a random variable with high min-entropy (in this case, the random function table *conditioned* on σ_i) into a convex combination of (easier to work with) *dense variables*. We use here the definition from [15]:

Definition 1. *A random variable X with range $[M]^N$ is called:*

- $(1-\delta)$*-dense if for every subset $I \subseteq [N]$, the random variable X_I, which is X restricted on coordinates set I, satisfies*

$$\mathsf{H}_\infty(X_I) \geqslant (1-\delta) \cdot |I| \cdot \log M \ .$$

- $(P, 1-\delta)$*-dense if at most P coordinates of X is fixed and X is $(1-\delta)$-dense on the rest coordinates*

STREAMING SETUP. We first define some notations. We use bold-face to denote a vector $\mathbf{R} = (R_1, \ldots, R_k)$. Moreover, we define

$$\mathbf{R}^{\{j\}} = (R_1 + j - 1, R_2 + j - 1, ..., R_k + j - 1) \ ,$$

and $\mathbf{R}^{\{1:j\}} = (\mathbf{R}^{\{1\}}, \mathbf{R}^{\{2\}}, \ldots, \mathbf{R}^{\{j\}})$. For a function F with n-bit inputs, we can further define

$$F[\mathbf{R}^{\{j\}}] := F(0 \parallel R_1 + j - 1) \parallel \cdots \parallel F(k - 1 \parallel R_k + j - 1)) \, .$$

Naturally, we extend this to

$$F[\mathbf{R}^{\{1:j\}}] := (F[\mathbf{R}^{\{1\}}], F[\mathbf{R}^{\{2\}}], \ldots, F[\mathbf{R}^{\{j\}}])$$

Below, we first prove an upper bound for streaming indistinguishability and later upper bound $\mathsf{Adv}^{\mathrm{indr}}_{\mathsf{StE}[\mathsf{RF},k,h]}$ via the streaming distinguishing advantage. To this end, we define the following two sequences $\mathbf{X} = (X_1, \ldots, X_q)$ and $\mathbf{Y} = (Y_1, \ldots, Y_q)$ of random variables such that:

- $X_i = (W_i, \mathsf{sd}_i, \mathbf{R}_i)$, where $W_i \xleftarrow{\$} \{0,1\}^{B \cdot \ell}$,
- $Y_i = (\mathsf{h}_{\mathsf{sd}_i}(F[\mathbf{R}_i^{\{1\}}]), \ldots, \mathsf{h}_{\mathsf{sd}_i}(F[\mathbf{R}_i^{\{B\}}])), \mathsf{sd}_i, \mathbf{R}_i)$, where F is randomly chosen function from n bits to n bits. (Note that the *same* sampled function is used across all Y_i's.)

In both streams, $\mathsf{sd}_i \xleftarrow{\$} \{0,1\}^s$, and $\mathbf{R}_i = (R_{i,1}, \ldots, R_{i,k})$ is a vector of k random probes. We use L to denote the string length of the stream elements, i.e.,

$$L = |X_i| = |Y_i| = B\ell + s + k(n - \log k) \, .$$

MAIN LEMMA. We will use Lemma 1, and rely on the following lemma, which is the core of our analysis.

Lemma 2. *For any S-bounded adversary $\mathcal{A}$ and for all $i \in [q]$,*

$$\mathsf{H}(Y_i \mid \sigma_{i-1}(\mathcal{A}(\mathbf{Y}))) \geqslant L - B\varepsilon$$

where

$$\varepsilon = \frac{\ell}{N^k} + \sum_{t=0}^{k} \binom{k}{t} \left(\frac{(2S + 2kn)B}{N} \right)^t \cdot \min\left\{ \ell, 2^{\ell+1} \left(\frac{2}{N} \right)^{k-t} \right\} \, .$$

Proof (of Lemma 2). First, we point out that we can easily find a deterministic function $\mathcal{L}$ such that

$$\mathsf{H}(Y_i \mid \sigma_{i-1}(\mathcal{A}(\mathbf{Y}))) \geqslant \mathsf{H}(Y \mid \mathcal{L}(F)) \, .$$

The function $\mathcal{L}$ is first easily described in randomized form: given F, first simulates the first $i - 1$ steps of the interaction of $\mathcal{A}$ with the stream $(Y_1, \ldots, Y_{i-1})$ (by sampling $\mathsf{sd}_1, \ldots, \mathsf{sd}_{i-1}$, as well as $\mathbf{R}_1, \ldots, \mathbf{R}_{i-1}$ itself), and then outputs $\sigma_{i-1}(\mathcal{A}(\mathbf{Y}))$. Then, $\mathcal{L}$ can be made deterministic by fixing the randomness. Therefore, we will now lower bound $\mathsf{H}(Y \mid \mathcal{L}(F))$ for an arbitrary function $\mathcal{L}$.

We now want to better characterize the distribution of F conditioned on $\mathcal{L}(F)$. To this end, we use the following lemma, originally due to Göös *et al.* [32], here in a format stated in [14,15].

Lemma 3. *If Γ is a random variable with range $[N]^N$ with min-entropy deficiency $S_\Gamma = n \cdot N - \mathsf{H}_\infty(\Gamma)$, then for every $\delta > 0, \gamma > 0$, Γ can be represented as a convex combination of finitely many $(P, 1 - \delta)$-dense variables $\{\Lambda_1, \Lambda_2, ...\}$ for*

$$P = \frac{S_\Gamma + \log 1/\gamma}{\delta \cdot n}$$

and an additional random variable Λ_{end} whose weight is less than γ.

For every $z \in \{0,1\}^S$, we define F_z to be the random function F conditioned on $\mathcal{L}(F) = z$. We define accordingly its min-entropy deficiency $S_z = n \cdot N - \mathsf{H}_\infty(F_z)$. Also, we set $\delta_z = \frac{S_z + \log 1/\gamma}{P \cdot n}$, for some P to be chosen below. By applying Lemma 3, F_z is decomposed into finite number of $(P, 1 - \delta_z)$-dense variables $\{\Lambda_{z,1}, \Lambda_{z,2}, ...\}$, and an additional variable $\Lambda_{z,\mathsf{end}}$ with weight less than γ. We use α_i to denote the weight of each decomposed dense variable in the convex combination. It holds that $\sum_t \alpha_t \geqslant 1 - \gamma$. Also, by the concavity of conditional entropy over probability mass functions,

$$\mathsf{H}(\mathsf{h}_{\mathsf{sd}}(F_z[\mathbf{R}^{\{j\}}]) \mid \mathsf{sd}, \mathbf{R}, F_z[\mathbf{R}^{\{1:j-1\}}])$$
$$\geqslant \sum_t \alpha_t \cdot \mathsf{H}(\mathsf{h}_{\mathsf{sd}}(\Lambda_{z,t}[\mathbf{R}^{\{j\}}]) \mid \mathsf{sd}, \mathbf{R}, \Lambda_{z,t}[\mathbf{R}^{\{1:j-1\}}]) . \quad (4)$$

It will be sufficient now to give a single entropy lower bound for any variable Λ which is $(P, 1 - \delta_z)$-dense, and apply the bound to all $\{\Lambda_{z,1}, \Lambda_{z,2}, ...\}$. In particular, now note that

$$\mathsf{H}(\mathsf{h}_{\mathsf{sd}}(\Lambda[\mathbf{R}^{\{j\}}]) \mid \mathsf{sd}, \mathbf{R}, \Lambda[\mathbf{R}^{\{1:j-1\}}]) = \underset{r}{\mathbf{E}} \left[\mathsf{H}(\mathsf{h}_{\mathsf{sd}}(\Lambda[r^{\{j\}}]) \mid \mathsf{sd}, \Lambda[r^{\{1:j-1\}}]) \right]$$
$$\geqslant \ell - \underset{r}{\mathbf{E}} \left[\min \left\{ \ell, 2^{\ell+1} \cdot 2^{-\mathsf{H}_\infty(\Lambda[r^{\{j\}}] \mid \Lambda[r^{\{1:j-1\}}])} \right\} \right] . \quad (5)$$

The last inequality follows from the following version of the Leftover Hash Lemma for Shannon entropy. (We give a proof in the full version for completeness, but note that the proof is similar to that of [10].)

Proposition 1. *If $\mathsf{h} : \{0,1\}^w \times \{0,1\}^s \to \{0,1\}^\ell$ is a 2-universal hash function, then for any random variables $W \in \{0,1\}^w$ and Z, if seed $\mathsf{sd} \leftarrow \{0,1\}^s$*

$$\mathsf{H}(\mathsf{h}_{\mathsf{sd}}(W) \mid \mathsf{sd}, Z) \geqslant \ell - \min\{\ell, 2^{\ell+1} \cdot 2^{-\mathsf{H}_\infty(W|Z)}\} .$$

First off, note that

$$\mathsf{H}_\infty(\Lambda[r^{\{j\}}] \mid \Lambda[r^{\{1:j-1\}}]) = -\log \left(\sum_{V \in ([N]^k)^{j-1}} \max_{v \in [N]^k} \Pr \left[\Lambda[r^{\{1:j\}}] = V \| v \right] \right)$$

where V enumerates all possible outcome of $\Lambda[r^{\{1:j-1\}}] = (\Lambda[r^{\{1\}}], ..., \Lambda[r^{\{j-1\}}])$, and v iterates over all possible outcome of $\Lambda[r^{\{j\}}]$.

Now, suppose that exactly t probes of $\boldsymbol{r}^{\{j\}}$ hit the P fixed coordinates of Λ and assume that t_0 coordinates of $\boldsymbol{r}^{\{1:j-1\}}$ are fixed. Then, using the fact that Λ is $(1-\delta)$-dense on the remaining $jk - t - t_0$ coordinates, by the union bound, the following inequality holds (the details of calculation can be found in the full version).

$$\log\left(\sum_{V\in([N]^k)^{j-1}} \max_{v\in[N]^k} \Pr\left[\Lambda[\boldsymbol{r}^{\{1:j\}}] = V \parallel v\right]\right) \leqslant n\left[\delta k(j-1) - (1-\delta)(k-t)\right].$$

Therefore, if t probes of $\boldsymbol{r}^{\{j\}}$ hit the P fixed coordinates of Λ, we have

$$\mathsf{H}_\infty(\Lambda[\boldsymbol{r}^{\{j\}}] \mid \Lambda[\boldsymbol{r}^{\{1:j-1\}}]) \geqslant n\left[(1-\delta)(k-t) - \delta k(j-1)\right]. \tag{6}$$

Now, for $1 \leqslant t \leqslant k$, we let P_t to be the number of fixed coordinates in the domain of t-th probe – in particular, $0 \leqslant P_t \leqslant N/k$ and $\sum_t P_t = P$. Then, let

$$\mu := \mathbf{E}_{\boldsymbol{r}}\left[\min\{\ell, 2^{\ell+1} \cdot 2^{-\mathsf{H}_\infty(\Lambda[\boldsymbol{r}^{\{j\}}]|\Lambda[\boldsymbol{r}^{\{1:j-1\}}])}\}\right]$$

as in (5). Then,

$$\mu \leqslant \sum_{t=0}^{k} \sum_{U\in\binom{[k]}{t}} \left(\prod_{u\in U}\left(\frac{P_u}{N/k}\right)\prod_{v\notin U}\left(1 - \frac{P_v}{N/k}\right)\min\{\ell, 2^{\ell+1}N^{\delta(j-1)k+(\delta-1)(k-t)}\}\right)$$

$$\leqslant \sum_{t=0}^{k} \sum_{U\in\binom{[k]}{t}} \left(\prod_{u\in U}\left(\frac{P_u}{N/k}\right) \cdot \min\{\ell, 2^{\ell+1} \cdot N^{\delta(j-1)k+(\delta-1)(k-t)}\}\right).$$

The above expression is maximized when $P_u = P/k$ for all u. The proof can be found in the full version. Thus we have

$$\mu \leqslant \sum_{t=0}^{k} \binom{k}{t}\left(\frac{P}{N}\right)^t \cdot \min\{\ell, 2^{\ell+1} \cdot N^{\delta(j-1)k+(\delta-1)(k-t)}\}$$

$$= \sum_{t=0}^{k} \binom{k}{t}\left(\frac{P}{N}\right)^t \cdot \min\{\ell, 2^{\ell+1} \cdot 2^{\frac{(S_z+\log(1/\gamma))}{P}(jk-t)}\frac{1}{N^{k-t}}\} =: \nu.$$

Plugging this into (4) yields

$$\mathsf{H}(\mathsf{h}_{\mathsf{sd}}(F_z[\mathbf{R}^{\{j\}}]) \mid \mathsf{sd}, \mathbf{R}, F_z[\mathbf{R}^{\{1:j-1\}}]) \geqslant (1-\gamma) \cdot (\ell - \nu). \tag{7}$$

Next, we will need to take everything in expectation over the sampling of F (and hence of $z = \mathcal{L}(F)$). To this end, we use the following claim to compute $\mathbf{E}_z[\nu]$.

Claim. For any $0 \leqslant t \leqslant k$, $1 \leqslant j \leqslant B$, if $P \geqslant Bk - t$, then it holds that:

$$\mathbf{E}_z[2^{\frac{S_z(jk-t)}{P}}] \leqslant 2^{\frac{S(Bk-t)}{P}}.$$

We left the proof of claim to the full version, but note that the proof is similar to the one from [15]. Now, note that for any function f,

$$\mathbf{E}_z[\min\{\ell, f(z)\}] = \sum_z \Pr[z] \cdot \min\{\ell, f(z)\} \leqslant \min\{\ell, \mathbf{E}_z[f(z)]\}, \qquad (8)$$

because $\min\{a, b\} + \min\{c, d\} \leqslant \min\{a + c, b + d\}$ for any a, b, c, d. Using (8), combined with linearity of expectation and the above claim,

$$\mathbf{E}_z[\mu] \leqslant \sum_{t=0}^{k} \binom{k}{t} \left(\frac{P}{N}\right)^t \cdot \mathbf{E}_z\left[\min\left\{\ell, \frac{2^{\ell+1} \cdot 2^{\frac{(S_z+\log(1/\gamma))}{P}(jk-t)}}{N^{k-t}}\right\}\right]$$

$$\leqslant \sum_{t=0}^{k} \binom{k}{t} \left(\frac{P}{N}\right)^t \cdot \min\left\{\ell, 2^{\ell+1} \cdot \mathbf{E}_z\left[\frac{2^{\frac{(S_z+\log(1/\gamma))}{P}(jk-t)}}{N^{k-t}}\right]\right\}$$

$$\leqslant \sum_{t=0}^{k} \binom{k}{t} \left(\frac{P}{N}\right)^t \cdot \min\left\{\ell, \frac{2^{\ell+1} \cdot 2^{\frac{(S+\log(1/\gamma))}{P}(Bk-t)}}{N^{k-t}}\right\}.$$

Further, we will now finally set $\gamma = N^{-k}$ and $P = (S+kn)B \geqslant Bk$ and simplify this to

$$\mathbf{E}_z[\mu] \leqslant \sum_{t=0}^{k} \binom{k}{t} \left(\frac{(S+kn)B}{N}\right)^t \cdot \min\left\{\ell, \frac{2^{\ell+1} \cdot 2^k}{N^{k-t}}\right\}$$

$$= \sum_{t=0}^{k} \binom{k}{t} \left(\frac{2(S+kn)B}{N}\right)^t \cdot \min\left\{\ell, 2^{\ell+1} \cdot \left(\frac{2}{N}\right)^{k-t}\right\}, \qquad (9)$$

because $\frac{S+\log 1/\gamma}{P} \cdot (Bk - t) \leqslant \frac{1}{B}Bk \leqslant k$. Therefore, taking expectations of (7), and using (9), yields

$$\mathsf{H}(\mathsf{h}_{\mathsf{sd}}(F[\mathbf{R}^{\{j\}}]) \mid \mathsf{sd}, \mathbf{R}, F[\mathbf{R}^{\{1:j-1\}}], \mathcal{L}(F))$$

$$\geqslant \left(1 - \frac{1}{N^k}\right) \cdot \left(\ell - \sum_{t=0}^{k} \binom{k}{t} \left(\frac{2(S+kn)B}{N}\right)^t \cdot \min\left\{\ell, 2^{\ell+1} \cdot \left(\frac{2}{N}\right)^{k-t}\right\}\right)$$

$$\geqslant \ell - \sum_{t=0}^{k} \binom{k}{t} \left(\frac{2(S+kn)B}{N}\right)^t \cdot \min\left\{\ell, 2^{\ell+1} \cdot \left(\frac{2}{N}\right)^{k-t}\right\} - \frac{\ell}{N^k}.$$

The proof is concluded by applying chain rule of conditional entropy and obtain

$$\mathsf{H}(\mathsf{h}_{\mathsf{sd}}(F[\mathbf{R}^{\{1\}}]), ..., \mathsf{h}_{\mathsf{sd}}(F[\mathbf{R}^{\{B\}}]), \mathsf{sd}, \mathbf{R} \mid \mathcal{L}(F))$$

$$= \mathsf{H}(\mathsf{sd}, \mathbf{R} \mid \mathcal{L}(F)) + \mathsf{H}(\mathsf{h}_{\mathsf{sd}}(F[\mathbf{R}^{\{1\}}]), ..., \mathsf{h}_{\mathsf{sd}}(F[\mathbf{R}^{\{B\}}]) \mid \mathsf{sd}, \mathbf{R}, \mathcal{L}(F))$$

$$= L - B\ell + \sum_{j=1}^{B} \mathsf{H}(\mathsf{h}_{\mathsf{sd}}(F[\mathbf{R}^{\{j\}}]) \mid \mathsf{sd}, \mathbf{R}, \mathsf{h}_{\mathsf{sd}}(F[\mathbf{R}^{\{1\}}]), ..., \mathsf{h}_{\mathsf{sd}}(F[\mathbf{R}^{\{j-1\}}]), \mathcal{L}(F))$$

$$\geqslant L - B\left(\sum_{t=0}^{k} \left(\binom{k}{t} \left(\frac{(2S+2kn)B}{N}\right)^t \cdot \min\{\ell, 2^{\ell+1} \cdot (2/N)^{k-t}\}\right) + \frac{\ell}{N^k}\right).$$

$\square$

4 Time-Memory Trade-Off for the K-XOR Construction

In this section, we show that the k-XOR construction (given in Fig. 3), first analyzed by Bellare, Goldreich, and Krawczyk [7] in the memory-independent setting, is secure upto $q = (N/S)^{k/2}$ queries for S-bounded adversaries. For the rest of the section, we fix positive integers n and k (required to be even) and let $N = 2^n$.

Scheme $\mathsf{Xor}[\mathsf{F}, k]$

$\underline{\mathsf{Enc}(K, M)}$

For $i \in [k]$ do $R_i \stackrel{\$}{\leftarrow} \mathsf{F.Dom}$
$Y \leftarrow \bigoplus_{i \in [k]} \mathsf{F}(K, R_i)$
Return $(R_1, \ldots, R_k, Y \oplus M)$

$\underline{\mathsf{Dec}(K, C)}$

$(R_1, \ldots, R_k, Z) \leftarrow C$
$Y \leftarrow \bigoplus_{i \in [k]} \mathsf{F}(K, R_i)$
Return $Y \oplus Z$

Fig. 3. The k-XOR encryption scheme, $\mathsf{SE} = \mathsf{Xor}[\mathsf{F}, k]$. The key space and message space of SE are $\mathsf{SE.Ks} = \mathsf{F.Ks}$ and $\mathsf{SE.M} = \mathsf{F.Rng}$.

Theorem 3. *Let $\mathsf{F} : \mathsf{F.Ks} \times \{0,1\}^n \to \{0,1\}^m$ be a function family. Let $\mathsf{SE} = \mathsf{Xor}[\mathsf{F}, k]$ be the k-XOR encryption scheme for some positive integer k. Let $\mathcal{A}_{\mathsf{indr}}$ be an S-bounded INDR-adversary against SE that makes at most q queries to Enc. Then, an S-bounded PRF-adversary $\mathcal{A}_{\mathsf{prf}}$ can be constructed such that*

$$\mathsf{Adv}^{\mathsf{indr}}_{\mathsf{SE}}(\mathcal{A}_{\mathsf{indr}}) \leqslant \mathsf{Adv}^{\mathsf{prf}}_{\mathsf{F}}(\mathcal{A}_{\mathsf{prf}}) + 2mq \cdot \sqrt{\left(\frac{4(S + nk)}{N}\right)^k}. \tag{10}$$

Moreover, $\mathcal{A}_{\mathsf{prf}}$ makes at most $q \cdot k$ queries to its FN oracle and has running time about that of $\mathcal{A}_{\mathsf{indr}}$.

DISCUSSION OF BOUNDS. Our bound supports $q > N$ even with relative small k. Concretely, suppose $S = 2^{80}$ and $N = 2^{128}$. Then for $k = 6$, we can already support upto roughly $q = 2^{(128-80) \cdot (6/2) - 8} = 2^{136}$ queries. Note that it does not makes sense to set $q < S$ in our bound. This is because q queries can be stored with $O(q)$ memory. Furthermore, if $q < N/k$, then one can apply the memory independent bound of Bellare, Goldreich, and Krawczyk [7] which is of the form $O(q^2/N^k)$. Hence, our bound really shines when $q \geqslant N$. Lastly, we suspect that our bound is likely not tight in general (it is when $S = O(k \log N)$). In the full version, we show attacks for a broader range of values of S that achieve constant success advantage with $q = O(\left(\frac{N}{S}\right)^k)$.

The above theorem also requires F to be a good PRF – in the full version we discuss how to instantiate it from a block cipher.

Theorem 3 follows from standard hybrid arguments and the single-bit case under random functions, i.e. INDR security of $\mathsf{Xor}[\mathsf{RF}_{n,1}, k]$, which is captured by the following lemma.

Lemma 4. *Let* $\mathsf{SE} = \mathsf{Xor}[\mathsf{RF}_{n,1}, k]$ *be the k-XOR encryption scheme for some positive integer k. For any S-bounded adversary $\mathcal{A}_{\mathsf{indr}}$ that makes q queries to* ENC,

$$\mathsf{Adv}_{\mathsf{SE}}^{\mathsf{indr}}(\mathcal{A}_{\mathsf{indr}}) \leqslant 2q \cdot \sqrt{\left(\frac{4(S+nk)}{N}\right)^k}. \tag{11}$$

The proof of Theorem 3 from Lemma 4 consists of standard hybrid arguments (over switching PRF output to random, then over m-output bits to independently random). We shall first prove Lemma 4 and defer the hybrid arguments for later in this section.

BIT-DISTINGUISHING TO BIT-GUESSING. It shall be convenient to consider the following information theoretic quantity $\mathsf{Guess}(\cdot)$, defined for any bit-value random variable B as $\mathsf{Guess}(B) = |2 \cdot \Pr[B = 1] - 1|$. As usual, we extend this to conditioning via $\mathsf{Guess}(B \mid Z) = \mathbf{E}_z [\mathsf{Guess}(B \mid Z = z)]$. Intuitively, $\mathsf{Guess}(B \mid Z)$ denotes the best possible guessing advantage for bit B, which is also the best bit-distinguishing advantage. Note that if U is a uniform random bit that is independent of Z (B and Z could be correlated), then for any adversary $\mathcal{A}$,

$$\Pr[\mathcal{A}(B, Z) \Rightarrow 1] - \Pr[\mathcal{A}(U, Z) \Rightarrow 1] \leqslant \mathsf{Guess}(B \mid Z). \tag{12}$$

Proof of Lemma 4. Consider the INDR games $\mathsf{G}_{\mathsf{SE},0}^{\mathsf{indr}}$ and $\mathsf{G}_{\mathsf{SE},1}^{\mathsf{indr}}$. We would like to bound

$$\mathsf{Adv}_{\mathsf{SE}}^{\mathsf{indr}}(\mathcal{A}_{\mathsf{indr}}) = \Pr[\mathsf{G}_{\mathsf{SE},1}^{\mathsf{indr}}(\mathcal{A}_{\mathsf{indr}})] - \Pr[\mathsf{G}_{\mathsf{SE},0}^{\mathsf{indr}}(\mathcal{A}_{\mathsf{indr}})]$$

Towards this end, let us consider hybrid games $\mathsf{H}_0, \ldots, \mathsf{H}_q$ as follows.

Game H_i	$\mathrm{ENC}_i(M)$
$F \xleftarrow{\$} \mathsf{Fcs}(\{0,1\}^n, \{0,1\})$	$(R_1, \ldots, R_k) \xleftarrow{\$} (\{0,1\}^n)^k$
$j \leftarrow 0 \; ; \; b \xleftarrow{\$} \mathcal{A}_{\mathsf{indr}}^{\mathrm{ENC}_i}$	If $j \geqslant i$ then $Z \xleftarrow{\$} \{0,1\}$
Return $b = 1$	Else $Z \leftarrow F(R_1) \oplus \cdots \oplus F(R_k) \oplus M$
	$j \leftarrow j + 1 \; ; \; \text{Return } (R_1, \ldots, R_k, Z)$

Note that $\mathsf{H}_0 = \mathsf{G}_{\mathsf{SE},0}^{\mathsf{indr}}(\mathcal{A}_{\mathsf{indr}})$ (ideal) and $\mathsf{H}_q = \mathsf{G}_{\mathsf{SE},1}^{\mathsf{indr}}(\mathcal{A}_{\mathsf{indr}})$ (real). Fix some $i \in \{1, \ldots, q\}$. Let $B_i = F(R_{i,1}) \oplus \cdots \oplus F(R_{i,k})$. It holds (by (12)) that

$$\Pr[\mathsf{H}_i] - \Pr[\mathsf{H}_{i-1}] \leqslant \mathsf{Guess}(B_i \mid \sigma_{i-1}(\mathcal{A}_{\mathsf{indr}}), (R_{i,1}, \ldots, R_{i,k})), \tag{13}$$

where $\sigma_{i-1}(\mathcal{A}_{\mathsf{indr}})$ is the state of $\mathcal{A}_{\mathsf{indr}}$ right the point where it makes its i-th query to ENC_i (and we assume this query to contain M), and $R_{i,1}, \ldots, R_{i,k}$ are the random inputs generated in that query. Note that $|\sigma_{i-1}(\mathcal{A}_{\mathsf{indr}})| \leqslant S$ and σ_{i-1} is a (randomized-)function of the function table F. However, there must exist a deterministic function $\mathcal{L}_i : \{0,1\}^N \to \{0,1\}^S$, so that

$$\mathsf{Guess}(B_i \mid \sigma_{i-1}(\mathcal{A}_{\mathsf{indr}}), R_{i,1}, \ldots, R_{i,k}) \leqslant \mathsf{Guess}(B_i \mid \mathcal{L}_i(F), R_{i,1}, \ldots, R_{i,k}).$$

Hence, to prove Lemma 4, it suffices to show the following lemma.

Lemma 5. *Let* $\mathcal{L} : \{0,1\}^N \rightarrow \{0,1\}^S$ *be any function. Then, for* $F \xleftarrow{\$} \{0,1\}^N$, *and* $R_1, \ldots, R_k \xleftarrow{\$} [N]$,

$$\mathrm{Guess}(F[R_1] \oplus \cdots \oplus F[R_k] \mid \mathcal{L}(F), R_1, \ldots, R_k) \leqslant 2 \cdot \left(\frac{4(S+nk)}{N} \right)^{k/2} . \quad (14)$$

Assuming Lemma 5, we can derive that

$$\mathsf{Adv}^{\mathsf{indr}}_{\mathsf{SE}}(\mathcal{A}_{\mathsf{indr}}) = \sum_{i=0}^{q} \Pr[\mathsf{H}_i] - \Pr[\mathsf{H}_{i-1}]$$

$$\leqslant \sum_{i=1}^{q} \mathrm{Guess}(B_i \mid \sigma_{i-1}(\mathcal{A}_{\mathsf{indr}}), R_{i,1}, \ldots, R_{i,k}))$$

$$\leqslant \sum_{i=1}^{q} \mathrm{Guess}(B_i \mid \mathcal{L}_i(F), R_{i,1}, \ldots, R_{i,k}) \leqslant 2q \cdot \left(\frac{4(S+nk)}{N} \right)^{k/2} ,$$

which concludes the proof of Lemma 4.   □

CONNECTION TO LIST-DECODABILITY OF k-XOR CODE. Lemma 5 is the technical core of our result. Before we go into the details of the proof, we need to recall the definition of list-decoding. Consider the code $k\text{-XOR} : \{0,1\}^N \rightarrow \{0,1\}^{N^k}$, which is defined by

$$k\text{-XOR}(x)[I] = x[I_1] \oplus \cdots \oplus x[I_k] ,$$

for any $I = (I_1, \ldots, I_k) \in [N]^k$. We say that $k\text{-XOR} : \{0,1\}^N \rightarrow \{0,1\}^{N^k}$ is (ε, L)-list-decodable if for any $z \in \{0,1\}^{N^k}$, there exists at most L codewords within a Hamming ball of radius εN^k around z. The proof of Lemma 5 consists of two steps. First, we translate the left-hand side of (14) in terms of list-decoding properties of k-XOR code. Second, we apply a new list-decoding bound for k-XOR code to obtain (14). We now give some intuition on how Guess relates to list-decoding. First, we fix some deterministic guessing strategy g for $F[R_1] \oplus \cdots \oplus F[R_k]$ given leakage $\mathcal{L}(F)$ and indices $R_1, \ldots, R_k$, which is a function of the form $g : \{0,1\}^S \times [N]^k \rightarrow \{0,1\}$ (looking ahead, g shall be fixed to be the "best" one). Note that g can be interpreted as 2^S elements of $\{0,1\}^{N^k}$. In particular, let $g' : \{0,1\}^S \rightarrow \{0,1\}^{N^k}$ be the function defined to be

$$g'(x) = g(x, (0, \ldots, 0)) \| \cdots \| g(x, (1, \ldots, 1)) .$$

We let G be the set $\{g'(0^S), g'(0^{S-1}1), \ldots, g'(1^S)\}$. Our set G of 2^S guesses lie in the co-domain of the k-XOR code. We now consider a partition of the $\{0,1\}^N$ into sets **Good** and **Bad**, where

$$\mathbf{Good} = \left\{ F \in \{0,1\}^N \mid \not\exists z \in G : \mathsf{hw}(k\text{-XOR}(F), z) \leqslant \left(\frac{1}{2} - \varepsilon/2 \right) N^k \right\} ,$$

$$\mathbf{Bad} = \left\{ F \in \{0,1\}^N \mid \exists z \in G : \mathsf{hw}(k\text{-XOR}(F), z) \leqslant \left(\frac{1}{2} - \varepsilon/2 \right) N^k \right\} .$$

Note that conditioned on $F \in \mathbf{Good}$, then the guessing strategy g should not achieve advantage better than ε. Using Lemma 6 given below, whose proof shall be given in Sect. 4.1, we can upper-bound the total number of codewords in $\mathbf{Bad}$, as a function of ε.

Lemma 6. *The k-XOR code is $(\frac{1}{2} - \varepsilon/2, 2^{N - \epsilon^{2/k} N/4})$-list decodable, i.e. for any $z \in \{0,1\}^{N^k}$, there are at most $2^{N - \epsilon^{2/k} N/4}$ codewords that are within hamming distance $(\frac{1}{2} - \varepsilon/2) N^k$ of z.*

Finally, obtaining the right-hand size of (14) amounts to picking an ε to minimize $\Pr[F \in \mathbf{Bad}] + \varepsilon$. We proceed to the proof, which formalizes the above intuition.

Proof. (of Lemma 5). Consider the code $\mathsf{k\text{-}XOR} : \{0,1\}^N \to \{0,1\}^{N^k}$ defined by

$$\mathsf{k\text{-}XOR}(x)[I] = x[I_1] \oplus \cdots \oplus x[I_k] ,$$

for any $I \in [N]^k$. For notational convenience, let $B = F[R_1] \oplus \cdots \oplus F[R_k]$ and $Z = \mathcal{L}(F)$. Consider the following function $Q : \{0,1\}^S \times [N]^k \to [-1,1]$,

$$Q(z, I) = 2 \cdot \Pr[B = 1 \mid \mathcal{L}(F) = z, (R_1, \ldots, R_k) = I] - 1 , \quad (15)$$

where the probability is taken over F. By definition of Guess,

$$\mathrm{Guess}(B \mid \mathcal{L}(F), R_1, \ldots, R_k) = \mathbf{E}[|Q(Z, I)|] , \quad (16)$$

where $Z = \mathcal{L}(F)$ and $I \xleftarrow{\$} [N]^k$. Now, we would like to describe the best guessing strategy $g_z[I]$ for bit B given $\mathcal{L}(F) = z$ and indices I. For each $z \in \{0,1\}^S$, we define $g_z \in \{0,1\}^{N^k}$ as follows. For each $I \in [N]^k$ we let $g_z[I] = 1$ if $Q(z, I) \geqslant 0$ and set $g_z[I] = 0$ otherwise. Intuitively, $g_z[I]$ encodes the best guess for $B = F[I_1] \oplus \cdots F[I_k]$ given that $\mathcal{L}(F) = z$. Hence, for any z and I

$$\frac{1 - |Q(z, I)|}{2} = \Pr[B \neq g_{z,I} \mid \mathcal{L}(F) = z, (R_1, \ldots, R_k) = I] . \quad (17)$$

Taking expectation of both sides over $I \xleftarrow{\$} [N]^k$,

$$\frac{1 - \mathbf{E}[|Q(z, I)|]}{2} = \Pr[B \neq g_{z,I} \mid \mathcal{L}(F) = z] = \frac{\mathrm{hw}(\mathsf{k\text{-}XOR}(F) \oplus g_z)}{N^k} , \quad (18)$$

where, recall, $\mathrm{hw}(\cdot)$ denotes the hamming weight (number of 1's) of a given string. With slight abuse of notation, we define $Q(z)$ to be

$$Q(z) = \mathbf{E}_{I \xleftarrow{\$} [N]^k}[|Q(z, I)|] = 1 - 2 \cdot \frac{\mathrm{hw}(\mathsf{k\text{-}XOR}(F) \oplus g_z)}{N^k} . \quad (19)$$

$Q(z)$ encodes the best possible guessing advantage when $\mathcal{L}(F) = z$, i.e.

$$\mathrm{Guess}(B \mid \mathcal{L}(F), R_1, \ldots, R_k) = \mathbf{E}[Q(Z)] .$$

Define E to be the event that k-XOR(F) is of distance more than $(\frac{1}{2} - \varepsilon/2)N^k$ from $g_{\mathcal{L}(F)}$ for some ε to be determined later. Note that given E, then

$$\mathsf{hw}(\mathsf{k\text{-}XOR}(F) \oplus g_{\mathcal{L}(F)}) \geqslant \left(\frac{1}{2} - \varepsilon/2\right) N^k$$

which means that and $Q(\mathcal{L}(F)) \leqslant \varepsilon$. Hence,

$$\mathbf{E}\left[Q(Z)\right] = \Pr\left[E\right] \cdot \mathbf{E}\left[Q(Z) \mid E\right] + \Pr\left[\neg E\right] \cdot \mathbf{E}\left[Q(Z) \mid \neg E\right] \tag{20}$$

$$\leqslant \varepsilon + \Pr\left[\mathsf{hw}(\mathsf{k\text{-}XOR}(F) \oplus g_{\mathcal{L}(F)}) \leqslant \left(\frac{1}{2} - \varepsilon/2\right) N^k\right] \tag{21}$$

$$\leqslant \varepsilon + \Pr\left[\exists s \in \{0,1\}^S : \mathsf{hw}(\mathsf{k\text{-}XOR}(F) \oplus g_s) \leqslant \left(\frac{1}{2} - \varepsilon/2\right) N^k\right] \tag{22}$$

$$\leqslant \varepsilon + \sum_{s \in \{0,1\}^S} \Pr\left[\mathsf{hw}(\mathsf{k\text{-}XOR}(F) \oplus g_s) \leqslant \left(\frac{1}{2} - \varepsilon/2\right) N^k\right] \tag{23}$$

$$\leqslant \varepsilon + 2^S \cdot 2^{-\epsilon^{2/k} N/4}, \tag{24}$$

where the last equation is by the $((\frac{1}{2} - \varepsilon), 2^{-\epsilon^{2/k} N/4})$-list decodability of k-XOR-code (Lemma 6). We now set

$$\varepsilon = \sqrt{\left(\frac{4(S + nk)}{N}\right)^k},$$

which makes it so that $\mathbf{E}\left[Q(f(X))\right] \leqslant \varepsilon + 2^{-nk} \leqslant 2 \cdot \varepsilon$. Hence,

$$\mathrm{Guess}(Y \mid f(X), R_1, \ldots, R_k) \leqslant 2 \cdot \left(\frac{4(S + nk)}{N}\right)^{k/2}. \tag{25}$$

This justifies Lemma 5. □

4.1   List Decodability of K-XOR Codes

We relied on the list-decodability of k-XOR code in the proof of Lemma 5. Recall that $\mathsf{k\text{-}XOR} : \{0,1\}^N \to \{0,1\}^{N^k}$ is (ε, L)-list-decodable if for any $z \in \{0,1\}^{N^k}$, there exists at most L codewords within a Hamming ball of radius εN^k around z. The list-decoding property of XOR-code has been studied extensively in complexity theory in the context of hardness amplification. The connection between Yao's XOR Lemma (for a good survey, see [31]) and the list-decodability of XOR-code was first observed by Trevisan [46]. So proofs of hardness amplification results (e.g. [34,41]) using XOR in fact yields algorithmic list-decoding bounds for xor-codes. More recently, [36] has also given approximate list-decoding bounds for k-XOR. We discuss in the full version how the approximate list-decoding bound by [36] can be viewed as (non-approximate) list-decoding bound which lead to an inferior result for the k-XOR construction that promise security upto $q = (N/S)^{k/4}$ instead of $q = (N/S)^{k/2}$. Where as previous works on list-decoding of k-XOR-code focus on algorithmic list-decoding, we are interested in the setting of combinatorial list-decoding, and the best trade-off possible between error ε (especially when it is very close to $1/2$) and the list size L.

Before we begin, we first show the following moment bound on sum of $\{-1, 1\}$-valued random variables.

Lemma 7. *Let* $F_1, \ldots, F_N$ *be i.i.d random variables with* $F_i \xleftarrow{\$} \{-1, 1\}$. *Then, for any even* $m \in \mathbb{N}$

$$\mathbf{E}\left[\left(\sum_{i \in [N]} F_i\right)^m\right] \leqslant (mN)^{m/2} . \tag{26}$$

Proof. Let us first expand the expectation.

$$\mathbf{E}\left[\left(\sum_{i \in [N]} F_i\right)^m\right] = \sum_{I \in [N]^m} \mathbf{E}\left[\prod_{i \in I} F_i\right] .$$

We claim that the inside expectation, $\mathbf{E}\left[\prod_{i \in I} F_i\right]$, is either 0 or 1 depending on I. In particular, define I to be even if for every $i \in [N]$, the number of i contained in I is even. First, for any $i \in [N]$, since F_i takes value in $\{-1, 1\}$, it holds that $F_i \cdot F_i = 1$. Hence, observe that $\mathbf{E}\left[\prod_{i \in I} F_i\right]$ is 1 if I is even. Otherwise, if I is not even, we claim that expectation is 0. To see this, suppose i_0 appears an odd number of times in the vector I. We can expand the expectation by conditioning on the value of F_{i_0} being 1 or -1:

$$\mathbf{E}\left[\prod_{i \in I} F_i\right] = \mathbf{E}\left[F_{i_0} \cdot \prod_{i \neq i_0} F_i\right] = \mathbf{E}\left[\prod_{i \neq i_0} F_i\right] - \mathbf{E}\left[\prod_{i \neq i_0} F_i\right] = 0 .$$

Therefore,

$$\mathbf{E}\left[\left(\sum_{i \in [N]} F_i\right)^m\right] \leqslant |\{I \in [N]^m \mid I \text{ is even }\}| .$$

For an upper bound of number of even I's, consider the following way of generating even I's. First, we pick a perfect matching (recall that a perfect matching on the complete graph on m vertices is a subset of $m/2$-edges that uses all m vertices) on complete graph of m-vertices, K_m. Then, for each edge, $e = (v_0, v_1)$, in the matching, we assign a value $i \in [N]$ to nodes v_0 and v_1, i.e. $\ell(v_0) = \ell(v_1) = i$. Now, reading the labels off of each node (wlog we can assume the set of nodes is $[m]$), we obtain an $I = (\ell(0), \ldots, \ell(m-1)) \in [N]^m$ that is even. Note that any even I can be generated in such a way, since given any even I it is easy to find a perfect matching and labeling that results in I.

We move on to compute the number of ways the above can be done. Note that the number of perfect matching is $(m-1) \times (m-3) \times \cdots \times 1$. To see this, let us fix an order of vertices $[m]$, say $1, \ldots, m$. At each step, we shall assign an edge to the smallest vertex that does not yet have an edge. Note that at the i-th step (with i starting at 0), there are exactly $(m-2i-1)$ ways to pick the next edge. Hence, the number of perfect matchings on K_m is bounded above by

$$\frac{m!}{2^{m/2}(m/2)!} = \frac{\binom{m}{m/2}}{2^{m/2}} \cdot (m/2)! \leqslant \frac{2^m}{2^{m/2}} \cdot (m/2)^{m/2} \leqslant m^{m/2} .$$

Next, for each perfect matching, there are $N^{m/2}$ ways of assigning values to edges, since each one of the $m/2$ edges can be assigned any of the N-values. Hence,

$$\mathbf{E}\left[\left(\sum_{i \in [N]} F_i\right)^m\right] \leqslant (m)^{m/2} \cdot N^{m/2} = (mN)^{m/2} .$$

Equipped with Lemma 7, we proceed to prove Lemma 6.

Proof (of Lemma 6). We identify the sets $[N^k]$ with $[N]^k$. Fix some $z \in \{0, 1\}^{N^k}$. Let $Z = (Z_1, \ldots, Z_{N^k})$ be the N^k-vector such that $Z_I = (-1)^{z_I}$ for any $I \in [N]^k$. Let $F_1, \ldots, F_n \xleftarrow{\$} \{-1, 1\}$. For each $I \in [N]^k$, we define random variable $B_I = \prod_{i \in I} F_i$. Note that if we map B_I to $\{0, 1\}$, i.e. define b_I such that $B_I = (-1)^{b_I}$, then $(b_1, \ldots, b_{N^k})$ is just a uniformly random codeword in $\{0, 1\}^{N^k}$. We have now that for any $I \in [N^k]$, $(-1)^{b_I \oplus z_I} = Z_I \cdot B_I$. Fix some codeword $(b_1, \ldots, b_{N^k}) \in \{0, 1\}^{N^k}$. The hamming distance between it and z is the hamming weight of $s = (b_I \oplus z_I)_{I \in [N]^k}$. Now, note that $hw(s) \leqslant (1/2 - \varepsilon/2)N^k$ if and only if $\sum_I (-1)^{s_I} \geqslant \varepsilon N^k$. Hence, to show that there are at most $2^{N - \varepsilon^{2/k} N/4}$ codewords within radius $(1/2 - \varepsilon/2)N^k$ of z, it suffices to show the following bound,

$$\Pr\left[\sum_{I \in [N]^k} Z_I \cdot B_I \geqslant \varepsilon N^k\right] \leqslant 2^{-\varepsilon^{2/k} N/4} . \tag{27}$$

Let us compute the p-th moment of $\sum_{I \in [N]^k} Z_I \cdot B_I$ for some even p (we shall fix the particular value of p later).

$$\mathbf{E}\left[\left(\sum_{I \in [N]^k} Z_I \cdot B_I\right)^p\right] = \mathbf{E}\left[\sum_{I_1,\ldots,I_p} Z_{I_1} \cdots Z_{I_p} B_{I_1} \cdots B_{I_p}\right] \tag{28}$$

$$= \sum_{I_1,\ldots,I_p} (Z_{I_1} \cdots Z_{I_p}) \mathbf{E}\left[B_{I_1} \cdots B_{I_p}\right] \tag{29}$$

$$\leqslant \sum_{I_1,\ldots,I_p} \mathbf{E}\left[B_{I_1} \cdots B_{I_p}\right] \tag{30}$$

$$= \mathbf{E}\left[\left(\sum_{I \in [N]^k} B_I\right)^p\right] \tag{31}$$

$$= \mathbf{E}\left[\left(\sum_{i \in [N]} F_i\right)^{k \cdot p}\right] \tag{32}$$

$$\leqslant (kpN)^{kp/2}, \tag{33}$$

where (30) is because $\mathbf{E}\left[B_{I_1} \cdots B_{I_p}\right] \in \{0, 1\}$ and $Z_{I_1} \cdots Z_{I_p} \in \{-1, 1\}$. To see the former claim, compute that

$$\mathbf{E}\left[B_{I_1} \cdots B_{I_p}\right] = \mathbf{E}\left[\prod_{j \in [p]} \prod_{i \in I_j} F_i\right] = \sum_{i \in [N]} \mathbf{E}\left[F_i^{k_i}\right],$$

for some $k_1, \ldots, k_N$. Note that $\mathbf{E}\left[F_i^k\right] = 1$ for any even power k, and $\mathbf{E}\left[F_i^k\right] = 0$ for any odd power k. We note that after (30), the expression is *independent* of Z. This is the crucial fact that we rely on when computing the moments of $\sum_{I \in [N]^k} Z_I \cdot B_I$. Applying Markov's inequality to the p-th moment of $\sum_{I \in [N]^k} Z_I \cdot B_I$ and using (33) as well as Lemma 7, we get

$$\Pr\left[\sum_{I \in [N]^k} Z_I \cdot B_I \geqslant \varepsilon N^k\right] \leqslant \frac{(kpN)^{kp/2}}{\varepsilon^p N^{kp}} \leqslant \left(\frac{kp}{\varepsilon^{2/k} N}\right)^{kp/2}. \tag{34}$$

Now, we would be done if we could set p so that $\frac{kp}{\varepsilon^{2/k} N} = \frac{1}{2}$. We cannot do so directly since it only makes sense when p is an even integer. However, we can set $p = p_0$ to be the smallest even integer such that $2kp_0 \geqslant \varepsilon^{2/k} N$. In other words, we set $p = p_0 = 2 \cdot \lceil \frac{\varepsilon^{2/k} N}{4k} \rceil$. Note that the right hand side of (34) is minimized when $\frac{kp}{\varepsilon^{2/k} N} = \frac{1}{e}$ and increases as p deviates from this value. Hence, to derive the final bound, as long as $\frac{kp_0}{\varepsilon^{2/k} N} \geqslant \frac{1}{e}$ (which is easily checked), we can plug $p = p_1 = (\varepsilon^{2/k} N)/2k$ into the right-hand side of (34) to derive the final bound of $2^{-\varepsilon^{2/k} N/4}$. $\qquad\square$

Acknowledgments. Wei Dai was partially supported by grant NSF CNS-1717640. Stefano Tessaro and Xihu Zhang were partially supported by NSF grants CNS-1930117 (CAREER), CNS-1926324, a Sloan Research Fellowship, and a JP Morgan Faculty Award.

References

1. Agrawal, R.: Samplers and extractors for unbounded functions. In: Achlioptas, D., Végh, L.A. (eds.) Approximation, Randomization, and Combinatorial Optimization. Algorithms and Techniques (APPROX/RANDOM 2019), volume 145 of Leibniz International Proceedings in Informatics (LIPIcs), pp. 59:1–59:21, Dagstuhl, Germany (2019). Schloss Dagstuhl-Leibniz-Zentrum fuer Informatik

2. Auerbach, B., Cash, D., Fersch, M., Kiltz, E.: Memory-tight reductions. In: Katz, J., Shacham, H. (eds.) CRYPTO 2017. LNCS, vol. 10401, pp. 101–132. Springer, Cham (2017). https://doi.org/10.1007/978-3-319-63688-7_4

3. Aumann, Y., Rabin, M.O.: Information theoretically secure communication in the limited storage space model. In: Wiener, M. (ed.) CRYPTO 1999. LNCS, vol. 1666, pp. 65–79. Springer, Heidelberg (1999). https://doi.org/10.1007/3-540-48405-1_5

4. Barak, B., et al.: Leftover hash lemma, revisited. In: Rogaway, P. (ed.) CRYPTO 2011. LNCS, vol. 6841, pp. 1–20. Springer, Heidelberg (2011). https://doi.org/10.1007/978-3-642-22792-9_1

5. Beame, P., Gharan, S.O., Yang, X.: Time-space tradeoffs for learning finite functions from random evaluations, with applications to polynomials. In: Bubeck, S., Perchet, V., Rigollet, P. (eds.) Conference On Learning Theory, COLT 2018, volume 75 of Proceedings of Machine Learning Research, Stockholm, Sweden, 6–9 July 2018, pp. 843–856. PMLR (2018)

6. Bellare, M., Dai, W.: Defending against key exfiltration: efficiency improvements for big-key cryptography via large-alphabet subkey prediction. In: Thuraisingham, B.M., Evans, D., Malkin, T., Xu, D. (eds.) ACM CCS 2017, pp. 923–940. ACM Press, October/November 2017

7. Bellare, M., Goldreich, O., Krawczyk, H.: Stateless evaluation of pseudorandom functions: security beyond the birthday barrier. In: Wiener, M. (ed.) CRYPTO 1999. LNCS, vol. 1666, pp. 270–287. Springer, Heidelberg (1999). https://doi.org/10.1007/3-540-48405-1_17

8. Bellare, M., Kane, D., Rogaway, P.: Big-key symmetric encryption: resisting key exfiltration. In: Robshaw, M., Katz, J. (eds.) CRYPTO 2016. LNCS, vol. 9814, pp. 373–402. Springer, Heidelberg (2016). https://doi.org/10.1007/978-3-662-53018-4_14

9. Bellare, M., Rogaway, P.: The security of triple encryption and a framework for code-based game-playing proofs. In: Vaudenay, S. (ed.) EUROCRYPT 2006. LNCS, vol. 4004, pp. 409–426. Springer, Heidelberg (2006). https://doi.org/10.1007/11761679_25

10. Bennett, C.H., Brassard, G., Crepeau, C., Maurer, U.M.: Generalized privacy amplification. IEEE Trans. Inf. Theory **41**(6), 1915–1923 (1995)

11. Bogdanov, A., Sabin, M., Vasudevan, P.N.: XOR codes and sparse learning parity with noise. In: Chan, T.M. (ed.) 30th SODA, pp. 986–1004. ACM-SIAM, January 2019

12. Bogdanov, A., Khovratovich, D., Rechberger, C.: Biclique cryptanalysis of the full AES. In: Lee, D.H., Wang, X. (eds.) ASIACRYPT 2011. LNCS, vol. 7073, pp. 344–371. Springer, Heidelberg (2011). https://doi.org/10.1007/978-3-642-25385-0_19

13. Carter, L., Wegman, M.N.: Universal classes of hash functions. J. Comput. Syst. Sci. **18**(2), 143–154 (1979)

14. Coretti, S., Dodis, Y., Guo, S.: Non-uniform bounds in the random-permutation, ideal-cipher, and generic-group models. In: Shacham, H., Boldyreva, A. (eds.) CRYPTO 2018. LNCS, vol. 10991, pp. 693–721. Springer, Cham (2018). https://doi.org/10.1007/978-3-319-96884-1_23

15. Coretti, S., Dodis, Y., Guo, S., Steinberger, J.: Random oracles and non-uniformity. In: Nielsen, J.B., Rijmen, V. (eds.) EUROCRYPT 2018. LNCS, vol. 10820, pp. 227–258. Springer, Cham (2018). https://doi.org/10.1007/978-3-319-78381-9_9

16. Dai, W., Hoang, V.T., Tessaro, S.: Information-theoretic indistinguishability via the chi-squared method. In: Katz, J., Shacham, H. (eds.) CRYPTO 2017. LNCS, vol. 10403, pp. 497–523. Springer, Cham (2017). https://doi.org/10.1007/978-3-319-63697-9_17

17. De, A., Trevisan, L.: Extractors using hardness amplification. In: Dinur, I., Jansen, K., Naor, J., Rolim, J. (eds.) APPROX/RANDOM -2009. LNCS, vol. 5687, pp. 462–475. Springer, Heidelberg (2009). https://doi.org/10.1007/978-3-642-03685-9_35

18. Di Crescenzo, G., Lipton, R., Walfish, S.: Perfectly secure password protocols in the bounded retrieval model. In: Halevi, S., Rabin, T. (eds.) TCC 2006. LNCS, vol. 3876, pp. 225–244. Springer, Heidelberg (2006). https://doi.org/10.1007/11681878_12

19. Dinur, I.: On the streaming indistinguishability of a random permutation and a random function. In: Canteaut, A., Ishai, Y. (eds.) EUROCRYPT 2020. LNCS, vol. 12106, pp. 433–460. Springer, Cham (2020). https://doi.org/10.1007/978-3-030-45724-2_15

20. Dinur, I.: tight time-space lower bounds for finding multiple collision pairs and their applications. In: Canteaut, A., Ishai, Y. (eds.) EUROCRYPT 2020. LNCS, vol. 12105, pp. 405–434. Springer, Cham (2020). https://doi.org/10.1007/978-3-030-45721-1_15

21. Dziembowski, S.: Intrusion-resilience via the bounded-storage model. In: Halevi, S., Rabin, T. (eds.) TCC 2006. LNCS, vol. 3876, pp. 207–224. Springer, Heidelberg (2006). https://doi.org/10.1007/11681878_11

22. Dziembowski, S., Maurer, U.M.: Tight security proofs for the bounded-storage model. In: 34th ACM STOC, pp. 341–350. ACM Press, May 2002

23. Dziembowski, S., Maurer, U.M.: Optimal randomizer efficiency in the bounded-storage model. J. Cryptol. **17**(1), 5–26 (2004). https://doi.org/10.1007/s00145-003-0309-y

24. Garg, S., Kothari, P.K., Raz, R.: Time-space tradeoffs for distinguishing distributions and applications to security of Goldreich's PRG. CoRR, abs/2002.07235 (2020)

25. Garg, S., Raz, R., Tal, A.: Extractor-based time-space lower bounds for learning. In: Diakonikolas, I., Kempe, D., Henzinger, M. (eds.) Proceedings of the 50th Annual ACM SIGACT Symposium on Theory of Computing, STOC 2018, Los Angeles, CA, USA, 25–29 June 2018, pp. 990–1002. ACM (2018)

26. Gaži, P.: Plain versus randomized cascading-based key-length extension for block ciphers. In: Canetti, R., Garay, J.A. (eds.) CRYPTO 2013. LNCS, vol. 8042, pp. 551–570. Springer, Heidelberg (2013). https://doi.org/10.1007/978-3-642-40041-4_30

27. Gaži, P., Tessaro, S.: Efficient and optimally secure key-length extension for block ciphers via randomized cascading. In: Pointcheval, D., Johansson, T. (eds.) EURO-CRYPT 2012. LNCS, vol. 7237, pp. 63–80. Springer, Heidelberg (2012). https://doi.org/10.1007/978-3-642-29011-4_6

28. Ghoshal, A., Jaeger, J., Tessaro, S.: The memory-tightness of authenticated encryption. In: Micciancio, D., Ristenpart, T. (eds.) CRYPTO 2020. LNCS, vol. 12170, pp. 127–156. Springer, Cham (2020). https://doi.org/10.1007/978-3-030-56784-2_5

29. Ghoshal, A., Tessaro, S.: On the memory-tightness of hashed ElGamal. In: Canteaut, A., Ishai, Y. (eds.) EUROCRYPT 2020. LNCS, vol. 12106, pp. 33–62. Springer, Cham (2020). https://doi.org/10.1007/978-3-030-45724-2_2

30. Goldreich, O.: Candidate one-way functions based on expander graphs. Cryptology ePrint Archive, Report 2000/063 (2000). http://eprint.iacr.org/2000/063

31. Goldreich, O., Nisan, N., Wigderson, A.: On Yao's XOR-lemma. In: Goldreich, O. (ed.) Studies in Complexity and Cryptography. Miscellanea on the Interplay between Randomness and Computation. LNCS, vol. 6650, pp. 273–301. Springer, Heidelberg (2011). https://doi.org/10.1007/978-3-642-22670-0_23

32. Göös, M., Lovett, S., Meka, R., Watson, T., Zuckerman, D.: Rectangles are non-negative juntas. In: Servedio, R.A., Rubinfeld, R. (eds.) 47th ACM STOC, pp. 257–266. ACM Press, June 2015

33. Hoang, V.T., Tessaro, S.: Key-alternating ciphers and key-length extension: exact bounds and multi-user security. In: Robshaw, M., Katz, J. (eds.) CRYPTO 2016. LNCS, vol. 9814, pp. 3–32. Springer, Heidelberg (2016). https://doi.org/10.1007/978-3-662-53018-4_1

34. Impagliazzo, R.: Hard-core distributions for somewhat hard problems. In: 36th FOCS, pp. 538–545. IEEE Computer Society Press, October 1995

35. Impagliazzo, R., Jaiswal, R., Kabanets, V.: Approximately list-decoding direct product codes and uniform hardness amplification. In: 47th FOCS, pp. 187–196. IEEE Computer Society Press, October 2006

36. Impagliazzo, R., Jaiswal, R., Kabanets, V.: Approximate list-decoding of direct product codes and uniform hardness amplification. SIAM J. Comput. 39(2), 564–605 (2009)

37. Impagliazzo, R., Jaiswal, R., Kabanets, V., Wigderson, A.: Uniform direct product theorems: simplified, optimized, and derandomized. In: Ladner, R.E., Dwork, C. (eds.) 40th ACM STOC, pp. 579–588. ACM Press, May 2008

38. Impagliazzo, R., Levin, L.A., Luby, M.: Pseudo-random generation from one-way functions (extended abstracts). In: 21st ACM STOC, pp. 12–24. ACM Press, May 1989

39. Jaeger, J., Tessaro, S.: Tight time-memory trade-offs for symmetric encryption. In: Ishai, Y., Rijmen, V. (eds.) EUROCRYPT 2019. LNCS, vol. 11476, pp. 467–497. Springer, Cham (2019). https://doi.org/10.1007/978-3-030-17653-2_16

40. Kol, G., Raz, R., Tal, A.: Time-space hardness of learning sparse parities. In: Hatami, H., McKenzie, P., King, V. (eds.) 49th ACM STOC, pp. 1067–1080. ACM Press, June 2017

41. Levin, L.A.: One way functions and pseudorandom generators. Combinatorica 7(4), 357–363 (1987). https://doi.org/10.1007/BF02579323

42. Maurer, U.M.: Conditionally-perfect secrecy and a provably-secure randomized cipher. J. Cryptol. 5(1), 53–66 (1992). https://doi.org/10.1007/BF00191321

43. Raz, R.: Fast learning requires good memory: a time-space lower bound for parity learning. In: Dinur, I. (ed.) 57th FOCS, pp. 266–275. IEEE Computer Society Press, October 2016
44. Raz, R.: A time-space lower bound for a large class of learning problems. In: Umans, C. (ed.) 58th FOCS, pp. 732–742. IEEE Computer Society Press, October 2017
45. Tessaro, S., Thiruvengadam, A.: Provable time-memory trade-offs: symmetric cryptography against memory-bounded adversaries. In: Beimel, A., Dziembowski, S. (eds.) TCC 2018. LNCS, vol. 11239, pp. 3–32. Springer, Cham (2018). https://doi.org/10.1007/978-3-030-03807-6_1
46. Trevisan, L.: List-decoding using the XOR lemma. In: 44th FOCS, pp. 126–135. IEEE Computer Society Press, October 2003
47. Vadhan, S.P.: On constructing locally computable extractors and cryptosystems in the bounded storage model. In: Boneh, D. (ed.) CRYPTO 2003. LNCS, vol. 2729, pp. 61–77. Springer, Heidelberg (2003). https://doi.org/10.1007/978-3-540-45146-4_4
48. Wang, Y., Matsuda, T., Hanaoka, G., Tanaka, K.: Memory lower bounds of reductions revisited. In: Nielsen, J.B., Rijmen, V. (eds.) EUROCRYPT 2018. LNCS, vol. 10820, pp. 61–90. Springer, Cham (2018). https://doi.org/10.1007/978-3-319-78381-9_3

Algebraic Distinguishers: From Discrete Logarithms to Decisional Uber Assumptions

Lior Rotem[✉] and Gil Segev

School of Computer Science and Engineering, Hebrew University of Jerusalem,
Jerusalem 91904, Israel
{lior.rotem,segev}@cs.huji.ac.il

Abstract. The algebraic group model, introduced by Fuchsbauer, Kiltz and Loss (CRYPTO '18), is a substantial relaxation of the generic group model capturing algorithms that may exploit the representation of the underlying group. This idealized yet realistic model was shown useful for reasoning about cryptographic assumptions and security properties defined via *computational* problems. However, it does not generally capture assumptions and properties defined via *decisional* problems. As such problems play a key role in the foundations and applications of cryptography, this leaves a significant gap between the restrictive generic group model and the standard model.

We put forward the notion of *algebraic distinguishers*, strengthening the algebraic group model by enabling it to capture decisional problems. Within our framework we then reveal new insights on the algebraic interplay between a wide variety of decisional assumptions. These include the decisional Diffie-Hellman assumption, the family of Linear assumptions in multilinear groups, and the family of Uber assumptions in bilinear groups.

Our main technical results establish that, from an algebraic perspective, these decisional assumptions are in fact all polynomially equivalent to either the most basic discrete logarithm assumption or to its higher-order variant, the q-discrete logarithm assumption. On the one hand, these results increase the confidence in these strong decisional assumptions, while on the other hand, they enable to direct cryptanalytic efforts towards either extracting discrete logarithms or significantly deviating from standard algebraic techniques.

1 Introduction

One of the most successful and influential idealized models in cryptography is the generic group model [Nec94, BL96, Sho97, Mau05], most often used to analyze

L. Rotem and G. Segev—Supported by the European Union's Horizon 2020 Framework Program (H2020) via an ERC Grant (Grant No. 714253).
L. Rotem—Supported by the Adams Fellowship Program of the Israel Academy of Sciences and Humanities.

R. Pass and K. Pietrzak (Eds.): TCC 2020, LNCS 12552, pp. 366–389, 2020.
https://doi.org/10.1007/978-3-030-64381-2_13

the security of group-based cryptographic assumptions and constructions. The generic group model captures group-based computations that do not exploit any specific property of the representation of the underlying group, by withholding from algorithms the concrete representations of group elements. At a high level, the access of generic algorithms to group elements is mediated by an oracle, and is restricted to the abstract group operation and to checking equalities among group elements throughout the computation. On the one hand, the generic group model captures a wide and natural class of algorithms, and a proof of security in this model means that a successful adversary must step outside this class. This enables, in particular, to direct candidate constructions and cryptanalytic efforts away from generic impossibility or hardness results. On the other hand, however, the assumption that adversaries are completely oblivious to the representation of the group and its elements is often unrealistic to some extent (see for example [FKL18, JS13] and the discussion therein).

The Algebraic Group Model. With this gap in mind, Fuchsbauer, Kiltz and Loss [FKL18] elegantly introduced the algebraic group model, as an intermediary model between the generic group model and the standard model.[1] Roughly speaking, an algebraic algorithm may use the representation of group elements in any arbitrary manner, but whenever it outputs a group element, it must supply together with it an "algebraic explanation" for how it came up with this element. Informally, this explanation is a representation of the outputted element, in the basis of all group elements that the algorithm has received so far.

Fuchsbauer et al. showed that though a considerable weakening of the generic group model, the algebraic group model provides a very advantageous framework for proving security reductions which are unknown to hold in the standard model. For example, within the algebraic group model, they reduced the security of very useful cryptographic schemes such as the BLS signature scheme [BLS01] and Groth's zero-knowledge SNARK [Gro16], to the hardness of very simple variants of the discrete logarithm problem. Follow-up works have continued to exemplify the usefulness of the model, by providing security reductions from the hardness of a large class of computational Diffie-Hellman-like problems to the hardness of the discrete logarithm problem [MTT19]; and from the unforgeability of blind Schnorr signatures [Sch91, Sch01] and variants thereof to the hardness of simple computational problems in cyclic groups [FPS20]. Moreover, the recent work of Agrikola, Hofheinz and Kastner [AHK20] provided a standard-model implementation of (a relaxation of) the algebraic group model.

Computational vs. Decisional Problems. One commonality which is shared by all of the aforesaid results, is that they all deal with assumptions and security properties that are defined via *computational problems* (i.e., search problems in which an algorithm is required to output group elements). This should come as no surprise: Algorithms for decisional problems are challenged with outputting a decision *bit*, and do not, generally speaking, output any group elements. As

---

[1] Previous, extraction-based, definitions may be found in the earlier works of Boneh and Venkatesan [BV98] and of Paillier and Vergnaud [PV05].

Fuchsbauer et al. point out, this means that such algorithms (to which we refer as distinguishers) are vacuously algebraic, and that in principal, decisional problems are not captured within the algebraic group model. Fuchsbauer et al. posed the important open problem of whether or not their approach can be extended to capture decisional algebraic problems and algebraic distinguishers, as these play key roles in the foundations and applications of cryptography. Developing such a model will enable to analyze the security of indistinguishability-based cryptographic problems and constructions while enjoying the key advantages of the algebraic group model.

1.1   Our Contributions

Algebraic Distinguishers. We put forward a generalized framework that captures algebraic distinguishers within the algebraic group model. Following Fuchsbauer et al. [FKL18], our framework fits the intuition according to which the algebraic group model "lies in between the standard model and the generic group model". Concretely, our notion of algebraic distinguishers allows such algorithms to rely on the explicit representation of group elements in any arbitrary manner, while still requiring that they "explain" their decision via an "algebraic witness".

In our framework this witness corresponds to a non-trivial equality relation satisfied by a subset of the group elements which the algebraic distinguisher has received or has computed throughout its execution. We carefully formulate an additional requirement regarding this witness in order to guarantee its non-triviality and usefulness: Loosely speaking, we ask that whenever the algebraic distinguisher can tell two distributions apart, then this witness serves as a "good differentiator" between these two distributions. Our requirement is a rather mild one (much stronger requirements hold in the generic group model), and it is sufficient for proving highly non-trivial reductions, as discussed below. Our notion of algebraic distinguishers is formulated in a general manner, allowing for flexibility and versatility in its applications (e.g., it can be used to reason about the indistinguishability of hybrid distributions that are introduced within proofs of security and are not part of the original formulation of the problem under consideration – as we demonstrate, for example, in Sect. 5). We refer the reader to Sect. 1.2 for a high-level description of our framework.

From Discrete Logarithms to Decisional Uber Assumptions. Within our framework we reveal new insights on the algebraic interplay between a wide variety of decisional assumptions. These include the seemingly modest decisional Diffie-Hellman assumption and the family of Linear assumptions [Sha07], as well as the seemingly substantially stronger family of decisional Uber assumptions [BBG05, Boy08].

Our main technical results show that, from an algebraic perspective, these decisional assumptions are in fact all polynomially equivalent to either the most basic discrete logarithm assumption (in the case of the decisional Diffie-Hellman and Linear assumptions) or to its generalized higher-order variant, the q-discrete logarithm assumption (in the case of the entire family of decisional Uber assumptions). We refer the reader to Sect. 1.2 for a high-level description of our results and for informal theorem statements.

Interpreting Our Framework and Results. Prior to our work, these decisional assumptions that we consider were simply known to unconditionally hold in the generic group model, without any indication of a non-trivial interplay among them. Moreover, prior to our work, the algebraic group model enabled to reason only about computational problems, whereas our framework enables both to reason about decisional problems and to reduce their algebraic hardness to that of computational problems. In this light, the contributions of our framework and technical results can be interpreted in the following, somewhat equivalent, manners:

- From the perspective of designing cryptographic schemes, our equivalence between the algebraic hardness of extracting discrete logarithms and that of seemingly much stronger assumptions increases the confidence in such stronger assumptions.
- From the perspective of cryptanalytic efforts, the introduction of the family of Uber assumptions [BBG05,Boy08] enabled directing nearly all such efforts towards a specific and well-defined family of decisional assumptions. Our results show that these efforts either can be significantly further directed towards extracting discrete logarithms, or should deviate from all algebraic techniques that are captured within our framework.

1.2 Overview of Our Framework and Results

In this section we provide a high-level overview of our framework and technical results. We start by reviewing our definition of algebraic distinguishers, and the intuition behind it, in more detail. For a formal exposition and discussion of the definition, see Sect. 3.

A First Attempt. As a first attempt of defining algebraic distinguishers, consider demanding that whenever an algebraic distinguisher accepts (i.e., outputs 1), it should output a "decision" vector $\vec{w}$ such that $\prod_i g_i^{w_i} = 1$, where $g_1, g_2, \ldots$ are the group elements that the distinguisher has observed, and 1 is the unity of the group. This is inspired by the approach of Fuchsbauer et al. who adapted from the generic group model the restriction of producing new group elements only as combinations of previously observed elements. The above requirement couples this restriction with another constraint posed on algorithms in the generic group model: The fact that essentially the only useful information on which generic algorithms can base their decisions is the equality pattern among the group elements that they have observed. Put differently, the basic algebraic information which can lead a generic distinguisher to accept (or to reject), is a non-trivial equality relation among the group elements that it has observed. Thus, the vector $\vec{w}$ captures the zero test induced by this relation.

Of course, such a zero test can always be produced by setting $\vec{w}$ to be the all-zeros vector, and so we need to add some non-triviality requirement. A possible route is demanding that whenever an algebraic algorithm accepts, the vector $\vec{w}$ has to be non-zero (i.e., $\vec{w} \neq \vec{0}$). Such a demand, however, seems unrealistic since a distinguisher can always accept even without "having knowledge" of such a non-zero vector $\vec{w}$. Moreover, it is not enough to ask that $\vec{w} \neq \vec{0}$. Consider, for example, the decisional Diffie-Hellman problem in which the distinguisher is asked to distinguish between a tuple of the form $(g, g^x, g^y, g^{x \cdot y})$ and a tuple of the form (g, g^x, g^y, g^z) for a uniform choice of x, y and z. In this case, a vector $\vec{w}$ whose any of the last three entries is 0, cannot be used in order to distinguish between the distributions, since when projected onto the support of such a vector $\vec{w}$, the two distributions coincide.

Our Definition. In light of the above discussion, our definition of algebraic distinguishers is somewhat more subtle. Informally, it asks that if an algebraic distinguisher A runs in time t and distinguishes between two distributions D_0 and D_1 with advantage ϵ, then there exists some bit $b \in \{0,1\}$ such that the following holds: On input drawn from D_b, the distinguisher A outputs a "good" vector $\vec{w}$ with probability at least ϵ/t^2 (this is in addition to the requirement that $\prod_i g_i{}^{w_i} = 1$ with probability 1). We define a "good" vector $\vec{w}$ to be such that D_0 and D_1 remain distinct even when projected onto the support of $\vec{w}$. Informally, by projecting a distribution onto the support of $\vec{w}$, we mean "erasing" all group elements whose corresponding entry in $\vec{w}$ is 0 (See Sect. 3.2 for a formal definition of this operation). This requirement (and even stronger forms thereof) indeed holds in the generic group model (as we discuss in Sect. 3.3), implying that our definition of the algebraic group model in fact lies between the generic group model and the standard one. We remark that even stronger requirements might be justifiable, and refer the reader to Sect. 3.2.

In groups which are equipped with a k-linear map, a distinguisher has additional algebraic power: It can infer information from equalities in the target group as well. Whereas in the generic group model, equalities in the source group induce linear polynomials in the exponent, equalities in the target group induce polynomials of degree up to k. We capture this fact by allowing the distinguisher to output a "degree k zero test" as its algebraic witness, and refer the reader to Sect. 5.1 and to the full version of this paper [RS20] for the formal definition.

The Algebraic Hardness of the Decisional Uber Assumption in Bilinear Groups. In the setting of bilinear groups, Boneh, Boyen and Goh [BBG05] and Boyen [Boy08] introduced the Uber family of decisional assumptions. Each assumption in the family is parameterized by two tuples of m-variate polynomials $\vec{r} = (r_1, \ldots, r_t)$ and $\vec{s} = (s_1, \ldots, s_t)$ and an m-variate polynomial f. Roughly, the assumption states that given a generator g of the source group, and given the group elements $g^{r_1(x_1, \ldots, x_m)}, \ldots, g^{r_t(x_1, \ldots, x_m)}$ and $e(g, g)^{s_1(x_1, \ldots, x_m)}, \ldots, e(g, g)^{s_t(x_1, \ldots, x_m)}$, it is infeasible to distinguish between $e(g, g)^{f(x_1, \ldots, x_m)}$ and a uniformly-random element in the target group for a uniform choice of $x_1, \ldots, x_m$. Boneh et al. proved that as long as $\vec{r}, \vec{s}$ and f do not admit a trivial solution, the $(\vec{r}, \vec{s}, f)$-Uber problem is hard in the generic group model.

Within our framework, we reduce the hardness of the $(\vec{r}, \vec{s}, f)$-Uber problem to the hardness of the q-discrete logarithm problem in the source group, where in the q-discrete logarithm problem an adversary needs to retrieve a secret exponent x given $(g, g^x, \ldots, g^{x^q})$, and q is polynomial in the number of polynomials in $\vec{r}$ and in $\vec{s}$ and in the their degree.

Theorem 1.1 (Informal). *Let $(\vec{r}, \vec{s}, f)$ represent m-variate polynomials which do not admit a trivial solution to the $(\vec{r}, \vec{s}, f)$-Uber problem, and let A be an algebraic algorithm for the $(\vec{r}, \vec{s}, f)$-Uber problem relative to a source group $\mathbb{G}$ and a target group $\mathbb{G}_T$. Then, there exists an algorithm B for the q-Discrete Logarithm problem in $\mathbb{G}$, whose running time and success probability are polynomially-related to those of A.*

The proof of Theorem 1.1 consists of two parts. First, inspired by the work of Ghadafi and Groth [GG17], we consider an intermediate variant of the Uber assumption which is univariate, in the sense that it involves only a single secret exponent x (instead of m secret exponents $x_1, \ldots, x_m$). We observe that the work of Ghadafi and Groth immediately implies that for any triplet $(\vec{r}, \vec{s}, f)$, the existence of a successful *algebraic* distinguisher for the $(\vec{r}, \vec{s}, f)$-Uber assumption implies the existence of a successful *algebraic* distinguisher for the univariate variant as well.

In the second (and main) part of the proof, we reduce within our framework the hardness of this univariate variant to that of the q-discrete logarithm problem. Technical details omitted, the main idea is to embed the secret exponent x of the q-discrete logarithm challenge as the secret exponent used to generate the input in the univariate Uber assumption. This is where the parameter q comes into play; since the polynomials $(\vec{r}, \vec{s}, f)$ may be of high degree, generating the input to the univariate Uber assumption may require knowledge of group elements of the form g^{x^i} for different values of i. As discussed above, a successful algebraic distinguisher for univariate Uber assumption returns a zero test as an algebraic witness for its decision. We observe that if $(\vec{r}, \vec{s}, f)$ do not admit a trivial solution to the $(\vec{r}, \vec{s}, f)$-Uber problem, this witness induces a non-zero univariate polynomial with one of its roots being x. Consequently, we can retrieve x by finding the roots of this polynomial (for example, by using the Berlekamp-Rabin algorithm [Ber70, Rab80]) and searching for the root which is consistent with the input to the q-discrete logarithm problem.

The Algebraic Hardness of the Decisional k-Linear Problem in k-Linear Groups. In the Decisional k-Linear problem introduced by Shacham [Sha07], a distinguisher is given an input of the form $(g, g^{\alpha_1}, \ldots, g^{\alpha_k}, g^{\beta}, g^{\alpha_1 \cdot r_1}, \ldots, g^{\alpha_k \cdot r_k})$ and needs to distinguish between the group element $g^{\beta \cdot \sum_{i=1}^{k} r_i}$ and a uniformly random group element g^z. Observe that this family of assumptions generalizes the Decisional Diffie-Hellman assumption (which corresponds to $k = 1$) and the Decisional Linear assumption [BBS04] (which corresponds to $k = 2$). Seemingly, this family forms a hierarchy; for any k, the k-Linear assumption implies the $(k + 1)$-Linear assumption. As for the other direction, Shacham proved that in a generic group equipped with a $(k+1)$-linear map the $(k+1)$-Linear assumption holds, even though it is easy to break the k-Linear assumption. Within our algebraic framework, we prove a more refined relation among the different assumptions in the family: For k-linear groups, we show an equivalence between the k-Linear problem in the source group and the discrete logarithm in the source group.

Theorem 1.2 (Informal). *Let* A *be an algebraic algorithm for the k-Linear problem relative to a group* $\mathbb{G}$ *equipped with a k-linear map. Then, there exists an algorithm* B *for Discrete Logarithm assumption in* $\mathbb{G}$, *whose running time and success probability are polynomially-related to those of* A.

An immediate corollary of Theorem 1.2 is an equivalence (within our framework) between the Decisional Diffie-Hellman assumption and the discrete logarithm assumption in groups without a bilinear map (see Sect. 3.2 for our model which captures such groups); and an equivalence between the Decisional Linear assumption and the discrete logarithm assumption in bilinear groups (without a trilinear map – see Sect. 5.1 for definition of such groups in our model). We refer the reader to the full version of this paper [RS20] for the formal statement and proof of Theorem 1.2. For concreteness, we now provide a more detailed account of the proof outline for Theorem 1.2 for the simple case of $k = 1$.

Warm-Up: From Decisional Diffie-Hellman to Discrete Logarithms. Consider an algebraic distinguisher D which runs in time t and has advantage ϵ in breaking the Decisional Diffie-Hellman assumption in a group $\mathbb{G}$. As discussed above, this means that on input of the form $(g, g^x, g^y, g^{x \cdot y + b \cdot z})$ for some $b \in \{0, 1\}$ and a uniform choice of x, y and z, D outputs a vector $\vec{w} = (w_0, w_1, w_2, w_3)$ such that:

1. $g^{w_0} \cdot g^{w_1 \cdot x} \cdot g^{w_2 \cdot y} \cdot g^{w_3 \cdot (x \cdot y + b \cdot z)} = 1$; and
2. There exists $\sigma \in \{0, 1\}$ such that if $b = \sigma$, then with probability at least ϵ/t^2 it holds that w_1, w_2 and w_3 are all non-zero.

These facts can be used to construct an algorithm A breaking the discrete logarithm problem in $\mathbb{G}$. For concreteness and brevity, in this overview we focus on the case in which $\sigma = 0.$[2] The adversary A receives as input a group element $\mathbf{R} := g^r$ and embeds it as part of the input to D: With probability $1/2$, it embeds r instead of x by sampling y on its own and invoking D on $(g, \mathbf{R}, g^y, \mathbf{R}^y)$; and with probability $1/2$ it embeds r instead of y. Suppose that D returns a vector $\vec{w}$ for which $0 \notin \{w_1, w_2, w_3\}$ (which, according to condition 2 above, happens with probability at least ϵ/t^2). We can rewrite the first condition in additive notation to deduce the bilinear bivariate equation $w_0 + w_1 \cdot x + w_2 \cdot y + w_3 \cdot x \cdot y = 0$. If r was embedded to replace x then A, knowing y, can solve the equation for x and output the correct discrete logarithm r. This works as long as the coefficient of x in this equation is non-zero; i.e., as long as $w_1 + w_3 \cdot y \neq 0$. But whenever $0 \notin \{w_1, w_2, w_3\}$, this can only happen if $y = -w_1/w_3$. Hence, if r was embedded to replace y, A may simply return $-w_1/w_3$ in order to output the correct discrete logarithm r.

---

[2] In the full reduction (Sect. 4), we consider two attacks, one per each possible value of σ, and the adversary A chooses which one of them to execute uniformly at random.

1.3   Additional Related Work

Beullens and Wee [BW19] have put forth the Knowledge of Orthogonality Assumption (KOALA), which is similar in spirit to our extension of the algebraic group model. The assumption deals with the problem of distinguishing between vectors of group elements whose exponents are uniformly drawn from some *linear subspace V* and vectors of independently (and uniformly) sampled group elements. Roughly speaking, KOALA holds if for any probabilistic polynomial-time algorithm which can distinguish between the two afore-described distributions, there exists an extractor which outputs a vector from the orthogonal complement $V^\perp$. Though similar in spirit, our model significantly generalizes KOALA. First, our model supports interactive security games, whereas KOALA considers a non-interactive game. In interactive games, our model also accounts for the entire view of the adversary, which may extend beyond just vectors of group elements. Second, and more importantly, KOALA seems to be tailored to prove the security of concrete obfuscation schemes, and hence only deals with the pseudorandomness of very specific distributions. In contrast, even when restricted to non-interactive games, our model can be used to reason about the ability to distinguish between *any* two distributions over group elements.

More generally speaking, these aforesaid differences between our model and KOALA precisely exemplify the motivation of the our work. Over the years, various knowledge assumptions in cyclic groups have been introduced in order to reason about the security of different constructions. The algebraic group model provides a unified framework for capturing *computational* knowledge assumptions. The motivation behind the introduction of our model is to capture in a similar manner decisional knowledge assumptions, such as KOALA, as well.

In a recent and independent work, Bauer, Fuchsbauer and Loss [BFL20] have considered (among other things) the computational variant of the Uber problem of Boneh, Boyen and Goh [BBG05,Boy08] in bilinear groups. Concretely, Bauer et al. reduced this variant to the q-Discrete Logarithm problem within the algebraic group model of Fuchsbauer et al. [FKL18], where q is the maximum (total) degree of the challenge polynomials in the instance of the Uber problem. Our result regarding the Uber problem (Theorem 1.1) differs from theirs in that we consider the decisional variant of the Uber problem within our decisional algebraic group model. Both our work and theirs utilize a similar technique of embedding randomizations of the secret exponent of the q-Discrete Logarithm instance into the secret exponents of the Uber problem instance (the concrete randomizations, however, are different). This is in contrast to our proof of Theorem 1.2, which employs a different technique.

1.4   Paper Organization

The remainder of this paper is organized as follows. First, in Sect. 2 we review the basic notation and definitions underlying the algebraic group model. In Sect. 3 we present our generalized framework capturing algebraic distinguishers, and as a warm-up, Sect. 4 includes a proof of the equivalence within our framework of the decisional Diffie-Hellman problem and the discrete logarithm problem. In Sect. 5 we extend our framework to bilinear groups, and prove our hardness result for the Uber family of decisional problems in such groups. In the full version of this paper [RS20], we generalize our framework to multilinear groups, and prove our hardness result for the decisional k-Linear problem in k-linear groups.

2   Preliminaries

In this section we briefly review the basic notions and definitions underlying the algebraic-group model [FKL18]. Throughout this work, for a distribution X we denote by $x \leftarrow X$ the process of sampling a value x from the distribution X. Similarly, for a set $\mathcal{X}$ we denote by $x \leftarrow \mathcal{X}$ the process of sampling a value x from the uniform distribution over $\mathcal{X}$. For an integer $n \in \mathbb{N}$, we use the notation $[n]$ to denote the set $\{1, \ldots, n\}$.

Game-Based Security Definitions. Notions of security within the algebraic-group model are formalized using "security games", following the classic framework of Bellare and Rogaway [BR06]. A game $\mathbf{G}$ is parameterized by a set par of public parameters, and is comprised of an adversary A interacting with a challenger via oracle access. Such a game is described by a main procedure and possibly additional oracle procedures, which describe the manner in which the challenger replies to oracle queries issued by the adversary. We denote by $\mathbf{G}_{par}$ a game $\mathbf{G}$ with public parameters par, and we denote by $\mathbf{G}_{par}^{\mathsf{A}}$ the output of $\mathbf{G}_{par}$ when executed with an adversary A (note that $\mathbf{G}_{par}^{\mathsf{A}}$ is a random variable defined over the randomness of both A and the challenger). We denote by $\mathbf{Time}_{\mathsf{A}}^{\mathbf{G}_{par}}$ the worst-case running time of $\mathbf{G}_{par}$ when executed with an adversary A. An adversary A participating in a game $\mathbf{G}_{par}$ is said to win whenever $\mathbf{G}_{par}^{\mathsf{A}} = 1$, and the advantage of A in $\mathbf{G}_{par}$ is defined as $\mathbf{Adv}_{\mathsf{A}}^{\mathbf{G}_{par}} \stackrel{\text{def}}{=} \Pr\left[\mathbf{G}_{par}^{\mathsf{A}} = 1\right]$.

All security games in this paper are *algebraic*, which means that their public parameters consist of a description $\mathcal{G} = (\mathbb{G}, p, g)$ of a cyclic group $\mathbb{G}$ of prime order p generated by the generator g (generally speaking, one can consider definitions in which par may include additional parameters, but this will not be necessary for our purposes). In actual instantiation of cryptographic primitives that rely on cyclic groups, such a description $\mathcal{G}$ is usually generated via a group-generation algorithm $\mathsf{GroupGen}(1^\lambda)$, where $\lambda \in \mathbb{N}$ is the security parameter that determines the bit-length of the prime p. However, we will abstract this fact away in the paper, since our reductions hold for fixing of the security parameter or of the underlying group.

Similarly to Fuchsbauer et al. we use boldface upper-case letters (e.g., $\mathbf{Z}$) to denote elements of the group $\mathbb{G}$ in algebraic games, in order to distinguish them from other variables in the game. Figure 1 exemplifies the notion of an algebraic game by describing the games associated with the Discrete Logarithm problem and the q-Discrete Logarithm problem that we consider in Sects. 4 and 5, respectively.

$\mathbf{DLOG}_{\mathcal{G}}^{\mathsf{A}}$	$q\text{-}\mathbf{DLOG}_{\mathcal{G}}^{\mathsf{A}}$
1. $x \leftarrow \mathbb{Z}_p$	1. $x \leftarrow \mathbb{Z}_p$
2. $\mathbf{X} := g^x$	2. $\mathbf{X}_i := g^{x^i}$ for all $i \in [q]$
3. $x' \leftarrow \mathsf{A}(\mathbf{X})$	3. $x' \leftarrow \mathsf{A}(\mathbf{X}_1, \ldots, \mathbf{X}_q)$
4. If $x' = x$ output 1, and otherwise output 0	4. If $x' = x$ output 1, and otherwise output 0

Fig. 1. Examples of algebraic games relative to a cyclic group $\mathcal{G} = (\mathbb{G}, p, g)$ and an adversary A. The game $\mathbf{DLOG}_{\mathcal{G}}^{\mathsf{A}}$ (on the left) captures the Discrete Logarithm problem, and the game $q\text{-}\mathbf{DLOG}_{\mathcal{G}}^{\mathsf{A}}$ (on the right) captures the q-Discrete Logarithm problem (note that setting $q = 1$ corresponds to the Discrete Logarithm problem).

Algebraic Algorithms. Fuchsbauer et al. [FKL18] presented the following notion of *algebraic algorithms*. In order to differentiate their notion from our extension which captures algorithms in *decisional* security games as well, we will refer to algorithms that satisfy their definition as *computationally-algebraic* ones. Roughly speaking, an algorithm A is computationally algebraic if whenever it outputs a group element $\mathbf{Z}$, it also outputs a representation of this element in the basis comprised of all group elements A has observed so far.

Definition 2.1 ([FKL18]). *Let $\mathcal{G} = (\mathbb{G}, p, g)$ be a description of a cyclic group. An algorithm A participating in an algebraic game with parameters $\mathcal{G}$ is said to be* computationally algebraic *if whenever A outputs a group element $\mathbf{Z} \in \mathbb{G}$, it also outputs a vector $\vec{z} = (z_0, \ldots, z_k) \in \mathbb{Z}_p^{k+1}$ such that $\mathbf{Z} = \prod_{i=0}^k \mathbf{X}_i^{z_i}$, where $\mathbf{X}_1, \ldots, \mathbf{X}_k$ are the group elements that A has received so far in the game and $\mathbf{X}_0 = g$.*

3 Our Framework: Algebraic Distinguishers

In this section we present our framework, extending that of Fuchsbauer et al. [FKL18] to consider algebraic distinguishers. We start by defining decisional algebraic games; then move on to present and discuss our notion of (fully-)algebraic algorithms, which covers in particular algebraic distinguishers; and finally, we observe that every generic algorithm is also an algebraic one within our framework.

3.1 Decisional Algebraic Games

The game-based definitions presented in Sect. 2 are suitable for *computational* games, which are aimed at capturing the hardness of computational problems (e.g., the computational Diffie-Hellman problem) and computational security properties of cryptographic primitives (e.g., unforgeability of signature schemes).

Decisional games on the other hand are aimed at capturing decisional cryptographic problems (e.g., the decisional Diffie-Hellman problem) and indistinguishability based security properties of cryptographic primitives (e.g., semantic security of an encryption scheme). At the end of a decisional game, the adversary outputs either the acceptance symbol Acc, in which case the output of the game is 1, or the rejection symbol Rej, in which case the output of the game is 0. The advantage of an adversary A in distinguishing between two decisional games $\mathbf{G}_{par}$ and $\mathbf{G}'_{par'}$ is defined as

$$\mathbf{Adv}_{\mathsf{A}}^{\mathbf{G}_{par},\mathbf{G}'_{par'}} \stackrel{\text{def}}{=} \left| \Pr\left[\mathbf{G}_{par}^{\mathsf{A}} = 1\right] - \Pr\left[\mathbf{G}'^{\mathsf{A}}_{par'} = 1\right] \right|.$$

Typically, a decisional security definition will be obtained by a single decisional game $\mathbf{G}$ with an additional parameter bit b, where the adversary needs to distinguish between the cases $b = 0$ and $b = 1$. For brevity, we will refer to the advantage of an adversary A in distinguishing between $\mathbf{G}_{par,0}$ and $\mathbf{G}_{par,1}$ simply as the advantage of A in G_{par}, and we will use the notation $\mathbf{Adv}_{\mathsf{A}}^{\mathbf{G}_{par}} \stackrel{\text{def}}{=} \mathbf{Adv}_{\mathsf{A}}^{\mathbf{G}_{par,0},\mathbf{G}_{par,1}}$. The running time of $\mathbf{G}_{par}^{\mathsf{A}}$ is defined as the maximum of the running times of $\mathbf{G}_{par,0}^{\mathsf{A}}$ and of $\mathbf{G}_{par,1}^{\mathsf{A}}$.

Figure 2 exemplifies the notion of a decisional algebraic game by presenting the game associated with the Decisional Diffie-Hellman problem that we consider in Sect. 4. As discussed in Sect. 2, recall that we use boldface upper-case letters (e.g., $\mathbf{Z}$) to denote elements of the underlying group $\mathbb{G}$ in order to distinguish them from other variables in the game.

$\underline{\mathbf{DDH}_{\mathcal{G},b}^{\mathsf{A}}}$

1. $x,y,z \leftarrow \mathbb{Z}_p$
2. $\mathbf{X} := g^x, \mathbf{Y} := g^y, \mathbf{Z} := g^{xy+(1-b)z}$
3. $\mathsf{Sym} \leftarrow \mathsf{A}(\mathbf{X},\mathbf{Y},\mathbf{Z})$
4. If $\mathsf{Sym} = \mathsf{Acc}$ then output 1, and otherwise output 0

Fig. 2. An example of a decisional algebraic game relative to a cyclic group $\mathcal{G} = (\mathbb{G}, p, g)$ and an adversary A. The game $\mathbf{DDH}_{\mathcal{G},b}^{\mathsf{A}}$ captures the Decisional Diffie-Hellman problem.

3.2   Extending the Notion of Algebraic Algorithms

In order to define (fully-)algebraic algorithms, we first introduce some additional notation. For an algebraic game $\mathbf{G}$, a group description $\mathcal{G} = (\mathbb{G}, p, g)$ and an algorithm A, we use $\mathsf{View}_{\mathsf{A}}^{\mathbf{G}_{\mathcal{G}}}$ to denote the random variable which is the view of A in the game $\mathbf{G}_{\mathcal{G}}$. As is standard, the view of A consists of its randomness, its input, and all incoming messages that it receives throughout the game (if any such messages exist). Moreover, for an additional fixed vector $\vec{w}$ of elements in

$\mathbb{Z}_p$, we denote by $\left[\mathsf{View}_{\mathsf{A}}^{\mathbf{G}_{\mathcal{G}}}\right]_{supp(\vec{w})}$ the random variable obtained from $\mathsf{View}_{\mathsf{A}}^{\mathbf{G}_{\mathcal{G}}}$ by omitting all group elements whose corresponding entry in $\vec{w}$ is 0 (where the ith group element observed by A is naturally associated with the ith entry of $\vec{w}$). That is, for a fixed vector $\vec{w}$ of k group elements, the distribution associated with $\left[\mathsf{View}_{\mathsf{A}}^{\mathbf{G}_{\mathcal{G}}}\right]_{supp(\vec{w})}$ is defined by first sampling a view V according to $\mathsf{View}_{\mathsf{A}}^{\mathbf{G}_{\mathcal{G}}}$; and then for each $i \in [\min\{k, m\}]$ for which $w_i = 0$, replacing the ith group element in V with the unique erasure symbol $\perp$, where m is the number of group elements in V. Hence, fixing $\vec{w}$, the random variable $\left[\mathsf{View}_{\mathsf{A}}^{\mathbf{G}_{\mathcal{G}}}\right]_{supp(\vec{w})}$ is defined over the randomness of A and of the challenger in $\mathbf{G}_{\mathcal{G}}$. For two random variables X_1 and X_2, we use the notation $X_1 \not\equiv X_2$ to indicate that X_1 and X_2 are *not* identically distributed.

Definition 3.1. *Let $\mathcal{G} = (\mathbb{G}, p, g)$ be a description of a cyclic group. An algorithm A participating in an algebraic game with parameters $\mathcal{G}$ is said to be algebraic if it is computationally-algebraic (per Definition 2.1) and in addition, whenever A outputs either the Acc or the Rej symbols, it also outputs a vector $\vec{w}$ of elements in $\mathbb{Z}_p$ such that the following conditions hold:*

1. *$\prod_{i=0}^{k} \mathbf{X}_i^{w_i} = 1_{\mathbb{G}}$, where $\mathbf{X}_1, \dots, \mathbf{X}_k$ are the group elements that A has received so far in the game, $\mathbf{X}_0 = g$ and $1_{\mathbb{G}}$ is the identity element of $\mathbb{G}$.*
2. *For any two decisional algebraic games $\mathbf{G}$ and $\mathbf{G}'$, there exists $\mathbf{H} \in \{\mathbf{G}, \mathbf{G}'\}$ such that*

$$\Pr_{\vec{w}} \left[\left[\mathsf{View}_{\mathsf{A}}^{\mathbf{G}_{\mathcal{G}}}\right]_{supp(\vec{w})} \not\equiv \left[\mathsf{View}_{\mathsf{A}}^{\mathbf{G}'_{\mathcal{G}}}\right]_{supp(\vec{w})} \right] \geq \frac{\epsilon}{t^2},$$

where $\epsilon = \mathbf{Adv}_{\mathsf{A}}^{\mathbf{G}_{\mathcal{G}}, \mathbf{G}'_{\mathcal{G}}}$, $t = \mathbf{Time}_{\mathsf{A}}^{\mathbf{H}_{\mathcal{G}}}$ and the probability is taken over the choice of $\vec{w}$ induced by a random execution of $\mathbf{H}_{\mathcal{G}}$ with A.

We clarify that the probability in the second condition of Definition 3.1 is over the choice of vector $\vec{w}$ in a random execution of $\mathbf{H}_{\mathcal{G}}$ with A; meaning, it is taken over the randomness of A and of the challenger in $\mathbf{H}_{\mathcal{G}}$. The event inside the probability means that for the chosen $\vec{w}$, the random variable $\left[\mathsf{View}_{\mathsf{A}}^{\mathbf{G}_{\mathcal{G}}}\right]_{supp(\vec{w})}$ is distributed differently than the random variable $\left[\mathsf{View}_{\mathsf{A}}^{\mathbf{G}'_{\mathcal{G}}}\right]_{supp(\vec{w})}$.

Intuitively, whenever an algebraic algorithm accepts or rejects in an algebraic game, it also produces a zero test, defined by the vector $\vec{w}$, which is passed by the group elements that the algorithm has observed during the game. Of course, such a zero test can always be produced by simply setting the vector $\vec{w}$ to be the all zeros vector.

One possible way to mend this situation is by requiring that whenever an algebraic algorithm accepts (by outputting the symbol Acc), the vector $\vec{w}$ which it outputs has to be non-zero. Alas, this approach suffers from two caveats. Firstly, this requirement is unrealistic, as an algorithm can always accept even without "having knowledge" of such a non-zero vector $\vec{w}$. Concretely, following

Fuchsbauer et al. [FKL18], we aim to have a definition which distills some fundamental algebraic principle from many hardness results in the generic group model; while simultaneously getting rid of the unrealistic assumption that algorithms are oblivious to the concrete representation of group elements. Secondly, the intuition behind Definition 3.1 is that the vector $\vec{w}$ serves as a "witness" which explains the adversary's decision and differentiates between the two games (just like the vector $\vec{z}$ in the definition of Fuchsbauer et al. – Definition 2.1 – serves as a witness which explains how the algorithm has come up with the group element $\mathbf{Z}$). Therefore, it is not enough to ask that $\vec{w} \neq \vec{0}$, since even then it might be that the joint distribution of the group elements in the support of $\vec{w}$ is identical in both games, rendering the zero test associated with $\vec{w}$ *useless* in distinguishing between them.

The second condition in Definition 3.1 accommodates these two lines of reasoning. It is *descriptive* of generic group algorithms (see Sect. 3.3 for further details; this also sheds light as to where the term t^2 comes from), and it makes sure that the views of the adversary in both games remain different even when projected onto the support of $\vec{w}$. Theoretically speaking, it still might be the case that the zero test associated $\vec{w}$ passes with equal probabilities in both games,[3] but we are not aware of a natural construction or assumption for which this is the case, and in particular for the applications of the model presented in this paper the second condition of Definition 3.1 is sufficient. Hence, we opted not to strengthen our definition beyond that. We do believe however, that if one finds an application for which it is necessary to require that the zero test associated $\vec{w}$ passes with distinct probabilities in both games, then such a strengthening of the definition is justifiable.

3.3 Generic Algorithms Are Algebraic

Our definition of algebraic algorithms fits the intuition provided by Fuchsbauer et al. [FKL18] according to which the algebraic group model "lies in between the standard model and the generic group model". Informally, the generic group model captures algorithms that do not exploit the representation of the underlying group in any way, and as such, they should perform identically among all groups which are isomorphic to each other.

This intuition is typically formalized by withholding the group description from the generic algorithm and supplying it only with the group order p. The concrete representation of group elements is then replaced with some representation-independent handle (a random label in Shoup's model [Sho97] and an opaque

---

[3] Consider for example a decisional game $\mathbf{G}_{\mathcal{G},b}$ in which if $b = 0$, then the adversary A receives as input the tuple $(\mathbf{X}, \mathbf{X}^a, \mathbf{Y}, \mathbf{Y}^a)$ for some distinct fixed $\mathbf{X}$ and $\mathbf{Y}$ and a randomly chosen a, and if $b = 1$ then A receives as input the tuple $(\mathbf{Y}, \mathbf{Y}^a, \mathbf{X}, \mathbf{X}^a)$. On the one hand, the witness $\vec{w} = (a, -1, a, -1)$ satisfies both of the conditions of Definition 3.1. On the other hand, it is always the case that $\mathbf{X}^{w_1} \cdot (\mathbf{X}^a)^{w_2} \cdot \mathbf{Y}^{w_3} \cdot (\mathbf{Y}^a)^{w_4} = 1_{\mathbb{G}} = \mathbf{Y}^{w_1} \cdot (\mathbf{Y}^a)^{w_2} \cdot \mathbf{X}^{w_3} \cdot (\mathbf{X}^a)^{w_4}$, and hence the zero test induced by $\vec{w}$ is not actually helpful in distinguishing $\mathbf{G}_{\mathcal{G},0}$ from $\mathbf{G}_{\mathcal{G},1}$.

"pointer" in Maurer's model [Mau05]). Group operations are performed via queries to an oracle which curates the "true values" behind the handles.

Fuchsbauer et al. observed that any generic algorithm for a computational problem is an algebraic algorithm according to their framework (recall Sect. 2). Here, we show that our framework enables in addition to capture generic algorithms for decisional problems, thus providing a unified framework for relaxing the somewhat too-strict generic group model. This is captured by the following informal proposition.

Proposition 3.2. *Let* $\mathcal{G} = (\mathbb{G}, p, g)$ *be a description of cyclic group, and let* $\mathbf{G}_0$ *and* $\mathbf{G}_1$ *be decisional algebraic games. Let* $\mathsf{A}_{\mathsf{gen}}$ *be a generic algorithm that distinguishes between* $\mathbf{G}_0$ *and* $\mathbf{G}_1$ *with advantage* $\epsilon = \epsilon(p)$ *in time* $t = t(p)$. *Then, there exists an algebraic algorithm* $\mathsf{A}_{\mathsf{alg}}$ *such that* $\mathbf{Adv}_{\mathsf{A}_{\mathsf{Alg}}}^{\mathbf{G}_{0,\mathcal{G}},\mathbf{G}_{1,\mathcal{G}}} \approx \epsilon$ *and* $\mathsf{A}_{\mathsf{Alg}}$ *runs in time* $\approx t$.

The proof of Proposition 3.2 is based on the fact that the algebraic algorithm $\mathsf{A}_{\mathsf{alg}}$ can run the generic algorithm $\mathsf{A}_{\mathsf{gen}}$ and return the same output, while simulating the generic group oracle to $\mathsf{A}_{\mathsf{gen}}$. This simulation relies on the following two well-established observations resulting from the fact that $\mathsf{A}_{\mathsf{gen}}$ is a generic algorithm:

1. For any group element $\mathbf{Y}$ which $\mathsf{A}_{\mathsf{gen}}$ computes throughout the game, $\mathsf{A}_{\mathsf{alg}}$ can produce a representation of $\mathbf{Y}$ as $\prod_i \mathbf{X}_i^{v_i}$, where $\{\mathbf{X}_i\}_i$ are the group elements which $\mathsf{A}_{\mathsf{gen}}$ has observed so far and $\{v_i\}_i$ are values in $\mathbb{Z}_p$ *known to* $\mathsf{A}_{\mathsf{alg}}$.

2. Since the access that $\mathsf{A}_{\mathsf{gen}}$ has to the group is representation independent, the only useful information it acquires throughout the game is the equality pattern among the group elements that it receives or produces during the game. Hence, in order to distinguish between $\mathbf{G}_0$ and $\mathbf{G}_1$ with advantage ϵ, there must exist an equality relation which occurs in one game with probability which is greater by at least ϵ than the probability that this equality relation occurs in the other game. In particular, such an equality relation occurs with probability at least ϵ.

Once $\mathsf{A}_{\mathsf{gen}}$ terminates, $\mathsf{A}_{\mathsf{alg}}$ can choose at random one pair of elements out of all pairs of equal elements that arose throughout the computation, allowing repetition (that is, $\mathsf{A}_{\mathsf{alg}}$ may chose the same element twice, so there is always at least one pair of equal elements). Let the representation of these two equal elements be $\prod_i \mathbf{X}_i^{v_i}$ and $\prod_i \mathbf{X}_i^{v'_i}$. The vector $\vec{w}$ which $\mathsf{A}_{\mathsf{alg}}$ outputs together with its decision symbol is then defined by $w_i = v_i - v'_i$ for each i. The fact that the two group elements are equal guarantees that $\prod_i \mathbf{X}_i^{w_i} = 1_{\mathbb{G}}$ (this guarantees the first requirement of Definition 3.1). Moreover, there exists a bit $b \in \{0, 1\}$, such that with probability at least ϵ the list of elements produced by $\mathsf{A}_{\mathsf{gen}}$ in $\mathbf{G}_b$ includes a pair $\prod_i \mathbf{X}_i^{v_i}$ and $\prod_i \mathbf{X}_i^{v'_i}$ such that $\left[\mathsf{View}_{\mathsf{A}_{\mathsf{alg}}}^{\mathbf{G}_{0,\mathcal{G}}}\right]_{supp(\vec{w})} \neq \left[\mathsf{View}_{\mathsf{A}_{\mathsf{alg}}}^{\mathbf{G}_{1,\mathcal{G}}}\right]_{supp(\vec{w})}$ (for $\vec{w} = \vec{v} - \vec{v'}$). This is due to the fact that there exists $b \in \{0, 1\}$ for which some equality has to arise $\mathbf{G}_b$ with probability which is greater by ϵ than in $\mathbf{G}_{1-b}$. Finally, conditioned on such a pair being present in the list of elements produced by $\mathsf{A}_{\mathsf{gen}}$, the probability that $\mathsf{A}_{\mathsf{alg}}$ chooses it is at least $1/t^2$, since $\mathsf{A}_{\mathsf{gen}}$ produces at most t group elements; meaning there are at most t^2 pairs of elements (this guarantees the second requirement of Definition 3.1).

4   Warm-Up: The Algebraic Equivalence of DDH and DLog

As a first example for the usefulness of our new framework, we show that the hardness of the Decisional Diffie-Hellman problem with respect to algebraic distinguishers is implied by that of the Discrete Logarithm problem. Recall that the Discrete Logarithm and Decisional Diffie-Hellman problems are defined via the computational algebraic game $\mathbf{DLOG}_{\mathcal{G}}$ and the decisional algebraic game $\mathbf{DDH}_{\mathcal{G}}$ described in Figs. 1 and 2, respectively. We prove the following theorem:

Theorem 4.1. *Let $\mathcal{G} = (\mathbb{G}, p, g)$ be a description of a cyclic group. For any algebraic algorithm A there exists an algorithm B such that $\mathbf{Adv}_{\mathsf{B}}^{\mathrm{DLOG}_{\mathcal{G}}} \geq \epsilon/(4 \cdot t^2)$ and $\mathbf{Time}_{\mathsf{B}}^{\mathrm{DLOG}_{\mathcal{G}}} \leq t + \mathsf{poly}(\log p)$, where $\epsilon = \mathbf{Adv}_{\mathsf{A}}^{\mathrm{DDH}_{\mathcal{G}}}$ and $t = \mathbf{Time}_{\mathsf{A}}^{\mathrm{DDH}_{\mathcal{G}}}$.*

Note that Theorem 4.1 implies an equivalence between the algebraic hardness of the Decisional Diffie-Hellman problem and the hardness of the Discrete Logarithm problem. Informally, given as input (in addition to $\mathcal{G}$) a triplet of group elements $(\mathbf{X}, \mathbf{Y}, \mathbf{Z})$ and (black-box) access to an algorithm $\mathsf{A}_{\mathbf{DLOG}}$ breaking the Discrete Log problem, an algebraic distinguisher $\mathsf{A}_{\mathbf{DDH}}$ can be defined as follows. First, it invokes $\mathsf{A}_{\mathbf{DLOG}}$ on $\mathbf{X}$ to retrieve its potential discrete logarithm x, and then checks whether $\mathbf{Z} = \mathbf{Y}^x$. If so, it accepts and outputs the vector $\vec{w} = (x, -1, -x, 1)$, and if not (or if $\mathsf{A}_{\mathbf{DLOG}}$ fails), it rejects and outputs $\vec{w} = \vec{0}$. This straightforward algorithm satisfies our two requirements specified in Definition 3.1 (note that a similar algorithm that outputs the vector $\vec{w} = (0, 0, -x, 1)$ instead of the vector $\vec{w} = (x, -1, -x, 1)$ would satisfy our first requirement but not our second one).

Proof of Theorem 4.1. Let A be an algebraic algorithm participating in the game $\mathbf{DDH}_{\mathcal{G},b}$ for $b \in \{0, 1\}$. We construct an algorithm B participating in $\mathbf{DLOG}_{\mathcal{G}}$.

Algorithm B

Input: A group element $\mathbf{X}$ sampled uniformly at random by the challenger.

1. Sample $b \leftarrow \{0, 1\}$ and $y, z \leftarrow \mathbb{Z}_p$, and set $\mathbf{Y} := g^y$.
2. If $b = 0$:
   (a) Set $\mathbf{Z} := g^z$.
   (b) Invoke $\mathsf{A}(\mathbf{X}, \mathbf{Y}, \mathbf{Z})$ to obtain a decision symbol $\mathsf{Sym} \in \{\mathsf{Acc}, \mathsf{Rej}\}$ along with a vector $\vec{w} = (w_0, w_1, w_2, w_3) \in \mathbb{Z}_p^4$ such that $g^{w_0} \cdot \mathbf{X}^{w_1} \cdot \mathbf{Y}^{w_2} \cdot \mathbf{Z}^{w_3} = 1_{\mathbb{G}}$.
   (c) If $w_1 = 0$ then output $\perp$, and otherwise $x^* := -(w_0 + w_2 \cdot y + w_3 \cdot z)/w_1$.
3. If $b = 1$:

(a) Set $\mathbf{Z} := \mathbf{X}^y$.

(b) Sample $c \leftarrow \{0,1\}$ and set $\widetilde{\mathbf{X}} := \mathbf{X}^{1-c} \cdot \mathbf{Y}^c$ and $\widetilde{\mathbf{Y}} := \mathbf{X}^c \cdot \mathbf{Y}^{1-c}$.

(c) Invoke $\mathsf{A}(\widetilde{\mathbf{X}}, \widetilde{\mathbf{Y}}, \mathbf{Z})$ to obtain a decision symbol $\mathsf{Sym} \in \{\mathsf{Acc}, \mathsf{Rej}\}$ along with a vector $\vec{w} = (w_0, w_1, w_2, w_3) \in \mathbb{Z}_p^4$ such that $g^{w_0} \cdot \widetilde{\mathbf{X}}^{w_1} \cdot \widetilde{\mathbf{Y}}^{w_2} \cdot \mathbf{Z}^{w_3} = 1_{\mathbb{G}}$.

(d) If $c = 0$:
- If $w_1 + w_3 \cdot y = 0$ then output $\perp$, and otherwise output $x^* := -(w_0 + w_2 \cdot y)/(w_1 + w_3 \cdot y)$.

(e) If $c = 1$:
- If $w_3 = 0$ then output $\perp$, and otherwise output $x^* := -w_1/w_3$.

Let $\epsilon := \mathbf{Adv}_{\mathsf{A}}^{\mathbf{DDH}_{\mathcal{G}}}$ and $t := \mathbf{Time}_{\mathsf{A}}^{\mathbf{DDH}_{\mathcal{G}}}$. By our definition of an algebraic algorithm, there exists a bit $b^* \in \{0,1\}$ such that

$$\Pr_{\vec{w}} \left[\left[\mathsf{View}_{\mathsf{A}}^{\mathbf{DDH}_{\mathcal{G},0}} \right]_{supp(\vec{w})} \not\equiv \left[\mathsf{View}_{\mathsf{A}}^{\mathbf{DDH}_{\mathcal{G},1}} \right]_{supp(\vec{w})} \right] \geq \frac{\epsilon}{t^2},$$

where the probability is taken over the choice of $\vec{w}$ induced by a random execution of $\mathbf{DDH}_{\mathcal{G},b^*}$ with A. Say that the vector $\vec{w}$ outputted by A is *good* if $0 \notin \{w_1, w_2, w_3\}$, where w_1, w_2, w_3 are the entries of $\vec{w}$ which correspond to the three group elements that A receives as inputs. The predicate inside the probability is satisfied if and only if $\vec{w}$ is good; hence, $\Pr[\vec{w} \text{ is good}] \geq \epsilon/t^2$ over a random execution of $\mathbf{DDH}_{\mathcal{G},b^*}$ with A.

Denote by Hit the event in which the bit $b = b^*$, where b is the bit chosen by B in Step 1. Regardless of the value of b^*, it holds that $\Pr[\mathsf{Hit}] = 1/2$, and that $\Pr[\vec{w} \text{ is good}|\mathsf{Hit}] \geq \epsilon/t^2$ since conditioned on Hit, B perfectly simulates the game $\mathbf{DDH}_{\mathcal{G},b^*}$ to A. Consider two cases:

1. If $b^* = 0$: In this case, when $\vec{w}$ is good and Hit occurs, the linear equation $X \cdot w_1 + w_0 + w_2 \cdot y + w_3 \cdot z = 0$ in the indeterminate X has a unique solution $X = x^*$ and this is the output of B. Moreover, by the requirement $g^{w_0} \cdot \mathbf{X}^{w_1} \cdot \mathbf{Y}^{w_2} \cdot \mathbf{Z}^{w_3} = 1_{\mathbb{G}}$, it holds that $g^{x^*} = \mathbf{X}$. Therefore,

$$\begin{aligned}
\mathbf{Adv}_{\mathsf{B}}^{\mathbf{DLOG}_{\mathcal{G}}} &= \Pr\left[\mathbf{DLOG}_{\mathcal{G}}^{\mathsf{B}} = 1\right] \\
&\geq \Pr\left[\mathbf{DLOG}_{\mathcal{G}}^{\mathsf{B}} = 1 \middle| \vec{w} \text{ is good} \wedge \mathsf{Hit}\right] \cdot \Pr\left[\vec{w} \text{ is good} \wedge \mathsf{Hit}\right] \\
&= \frac{1}{2} \cdot \Pr\left[\vec{w} \text{ is good}|\mathsf{Hit}\right] \\
&\geq \frac{\epsilon}{2 \cdot t^2}.
\end{aligned}$$

2. If $b^* = 1$: Let C be the random variable describing the bit c sampled by B in Step 3(b), and let E denote the event in which $w_1 + w_3 \cdot \widetilde{y} = 0$ in an execution of $\mathbf{DDH}_{\mathcal{G},1}$ with A, where $g^{\widetilde{y}}$ is the group element given as the second input to A in the game. On the one hand, when $\vec{w}$ is good and $\overline{\mathsf{E}}$ and Hit occur, the linear equation $X \cdot (w_1 + w_3 \cdot \widetilde{y}) + w_0 + w_2 \cdot \widetilde{y} + w_3 \cdot z = 0$ in the indeterminate X has a unique solution $X = x^*$. Moreover, conditioned also on $C = 0$, this

is the output of B, and by the requirement $g^{w_0} \cdot \tilde{\mathbf{X}}^{w_1} \cdot \tilde{\mathbf{Y}}^{w_2} \cdot \mathbf{Z}^{w_3} = 1_{\mathbb{G}}$, it holds that $g^{x^*} = \mathbf{X}$. Hence,

$$
\Pr\left[\mathbf{DLOG}_{\mathcal{G}}^{\mathsf{B}} = 1 \middle| \vec{w} \text{ is good} \wedge \mathsf{Hit} \wedge \overline{\mathsf{E}}\right]
$$

$$
\geq \Pr\left[\mathbf{DLOG}_{\mathcal{G}}^{\mathsf{B}} = 1 \wedge C = 0 \middle| \vec{w} \text{ is good} \wedge \mathsf{Hit} \wedge \overline{\mathsf{E}}\right]
$$

$$
= \Pr\left[\mathbf{DLOG}_{\mathcal{G}}^{\mathsf{B}} = 1 \middle| \vec{w} \text{ is good} \wedge \mathsf{Hit} \wedge \overline{\mathsf{E}} \wedge C = 0\right] \cdot \Pr\left[C = 0\right] \quad (1)
$$

$$
= \frac{1}{2}, \tag{2}
$$

where (1) follows from the fact that the bits b and c that B samples are chosen independently, and since the view of A as invoked by B is independent of the bit c, and hence the events E and $\vec{w}$ is good are independent of the event $C = 0$.

On the other hand, when $\vec{w}$ is good, the linear equation $X \cdot w_3 + w_1 = 0$ in the indeterminate X has a unique solution $X = x^*$. Moreover, conditioned on Hit and on $C = 1$, this x^* is the output of B, and conditioned on E, it also holds that $g^{x^*} = \mathbf{X}$. It follows that,

$$
\Pr\left[\mathbf{DLOG}_{\mathcal{G}}^{\mathsf{B}} = 1 \middle| \vec{w} \text{ is good} \wedge \mathsf{Hit} \wedge \mathsf{E}\right]
$$

$$
\geq \Pr\left[\mathbf{DLOG}_{\mathcal{G}}^{\mathsf{B}} = 1 \wedge C = 1 \middle| \vec{w} \text{ is good} \wedge \mathsf{Hit} \wedge \mathsf{E}\right]
$$

$$
= \Pr\left[\mathbf{DLOG}_{\mathcal{G}}^{\mathsf{B}} = 1 \middle| \vec{w} \text{ is good} \wedge \mathsf{Hit} \wedge \mathsf{E} \wedge C = 1\right] \cdot \Pr\left[C = 1\right] \quad (3)
$$

$$
= \frac{1}{2}, \tag{4}
$$

where (3) holds for the same reasons as (1).

Putting (2) and (4) together,

$$
\mathbf{Adv}_{\mathsf{B}}^{\mathrm{DLOG}_{\mathcal{G}}}
$$

$$
= \Pr\left[\mathbf{DLOG}_{\mathcal{G}}^{\mathsf{B}} = 1\right]
$$

$$
\geq \Pr\left[\mathbf{DLOG}_{\mathcal{G}}^{\mathsf{B}} = 1 \middle| \vec{w} \text{ is good} \wedge \mathsf{Hit}\right] \cdot \Pr\left[\vec{w} \text{ is good} \wedge \mathsf{Hit}\right]
$$

$$
\geq \frac{\epsilon}{2 \cdot t^2} \cdot \left(\Pr\left[\mathbf{DLOG}_{\mathcal{G}}^{\mathsf{B}} = 1 \middle| \vec{w} \text{ is good} \wedge \mathsf{Hit} \wedge \mathsf{E}\right] \cdot \Pr\left[\mathsf{E}|\vec{w} \text{ is good} \wedge \mathsf{Hit}\right]\right.
$$

$$
\left. + \Pr\left[\mathbf{DLOG}_{\mathcal{G}}^{\mathsf{B}} = 1 \middle| \vec{w} \text{ is good} \wedge \mathsf{Hit} \wedge \overline{\mathsf{E}}\right] \cdot \Pr\left[\overline{\mathsf{E}}|\vec{w} \text{ is good} \wedge \mathsf{Hit}\right]\right)
$$

$$
\geq \frac{\epsilon}{4 \cdot t^2}.
$$

This concludes the proof of Theorem 4.1.

$\square$

5   The Algebraic Hardness of the Uber Family of Decisional Problems

In this section we prove that the hardness of the Uber family of decisional problems in bilinear groups [BBG05, Boy08] with respect to algebraic distinguishers is equivalent to that of the computational q-discrete logarithm problem, for an appropriate choice of q, in the source group (we formally define these assumptions in Sect. 5.2).

5.1   Algebraic Algorithms in Bilinear Groups

Before presenting our main theorem for this section, we first need to extend our framework to bilinear groups. We focus on *symmetric* bilinear groups for ease of presentation, but the definitions in this section easily generalize to capture asymmetric pairings as well. An algebraic game which is defined with respect to a symmetric bilinear group is parameterized by a group description of the form $\mathcal{G} = (\mathbb{G}, \mathbb{G}_T, p, g, e)$, where $\mathbb{G}$ and $\mathbb{G}_T$ are both cyclic groups of order p, g is a generator of $\mathbb{G}$, and $e : \mathbb{G} \times \mathbb{G} \to \mathbb{G}_T$ is a non-degenerate bilinear map. We will often use the notation $g_T := e(g, g)$.

Mizuide et al. [MTT19] extended the definition of Fuchsbauer et al. [FKL18] of computationally-algebraic algorithms to the setting of symmetric bilinear groups. We start by reviewing their definition (with slight notational modifications).

Definition 5.1. *Let $\mathcal{G} = (\mathbb{G}, \mathbb{G}_T, p, g, e)$ be a description of a symmetric bilinear group. An algorithm A participating in an algebraic game with parameters $\mathcal{G}$ is said to be* computationally-algebraic *if:*

1. *Whenever A outputs a group element $\mathbf{Z} \in \mathbb{G}$, it also outputs a vector $\vec{z}$ of elements in $\mathbb{Z}_p$ such that $\mathbf{Z} = \prod_{i=0}^{k} \mathbf{X}_i^{z_i}$, where $\mathbf{X}_1, \ldots, \mathbf{X}_k$ are the elements of $\mathbb{G}$ that A has received so far in the game and $\mathbf{X}_0 = g$.*
2. *Whenever A outputs a group element $\mathbf{V} \in \mathbb{G}_T$, it also outputs vectors $\vec{v}$ and $\vec{v'}$ of elements in $\mathbb{Z}_p$ such that $\mathbf{V} = \prod_{0 \le i \le j \le k} e(\mathbf{X}_i, \mathbf{X}_j)^{v_{k \cdot i + j}} \cdot \prod_{i=1}^{\ell} \mathbf{Y}_i^{v'_i}$, where $\mathbf{X}_1, \ldots, \mathbf{X}_k$ are the elements of $\mathbb{G}$ and $\mathbf{Y}_1, \ldots, \mathbf{Y}_\ell$ are the elements of $\mathbb{G}_T$ that A has received so far in the game and $\mathbf{X}_0 = g$.*

Before defining fully-algebraic algorithms in bilinear groups, we introduce some additional notation. The random variable $\mathsf{View}_{\mathsf{A}}^{\mathbf{G}_\mathcal{G}}$ is defined analogously to its definition in Sect. 3.2. For vectors $\vec{v}$ and $\vec{v'}$, we denote by $\left[\mathsf{View}_{\mathsf{A}}^{\mathbf{G}_\mathcal{G}} \right]_{supp(\vec{v}, \vec{v'})}$ the random variable obtained from $\mathsf{View}_{\mathsf{A}}^{\mathbf{G}_\mathcal{G}}$ by:

1. Omitting each element of $\mathbb{G}$ for which all of the corresponding entries in $\vec{v}$ are 0. That is, we omit the ith element of $\mathbb{G}$ that A observes if for all $j \ge i$ it holds that $v_{k \cdot i + j} = 0$ and for all $0 \le j < i$ it holds that $v_{k \cdot j + i} = 0$ (where k is the number of elements of $\mathbb{G}$ that A observes in the game).

2. Omitting all elements of $\mathbb{G}_T$ whose corresponding entry in $\vec{v'}$ is 0 (where the ith element of $\mathbb{G}_T$ observed by A is naturally associated with the ith entry of $\vec{v'}$).

Definition 5.2. *Let* $\mathcal{G} = (\mathbb{G}, \mathbb{G}_T, p, g, e)$ *be a description of a symmetric bilinear group. An algorithm* A *participating in an algebraic game with parameters* $\mathcal{G}$ *is said to be* algebraic *if it is computationally-algebraic (per Definition 5.1) and in addition, whenever* A *outputs either the* Acc *or the* Rej *symbols, it also outputs a pair* $(\vec{v}, \vec{v'})$ *of vectors of elements in* $\mathbb{Z}_p$ *such that the following conditions hold:*

1. $\prod_{0 \le i \le j \le k} e\left(\mathbf{X}_i, \mathbf{X}_j\right)^{v_{k \cdot i + j}} \cdot \prod_{i=1}^{\ell} \mathbf{Y}_i^{v_i'} = 1_{\mathbb{G}_T}$, *where* $\mathbf{X}_1, \ldots, \mathbf{X}_k$ *are the elements of* $\mathbb{G}$ *and* $\mathbf{Y}_1, \ldots, \mathbf{Y}_\ell$ *are the elements of* $\mathbb{G}_T$ *that* A *has received so far in the game, and* $1_{\mathbb{G}_T}$ *is the identity element in* $\mathbb{G}_T$.
2. *For any two decisional algebraic games* $\mathbf{G}$ *and* $\mathbf{G'}$, *there exists* $\mathbf{H} \in \{\mathbf{G}, \mathbf{G'}\}$ *such that*

$$\Pr_{(\vec{v}, \vec{v'})} \left[\left[\mathsf{View}_{\mathsf{A}}^{\mathbf{G}_\mathcal{G}} \right]_{supp(\vec{v}, \vec{v'})} \ne \left[\mathsf{View}_{\mathsf{A}}^{\mathbf{G'}_\mathcal{G}} \right]_{supp(\vec{v}, \vec{v'})} \right] \ge \frac{\epsilon}{t^2},$$

where $\epsilon = \mathbf{Adv}_{\mathsf{A}}^{\mathbf{G}_\mathcal{G}, \mathbf{G'}_\mathcal{G}}$, $t = \mathbf{Time}_{\mathsf{A}}^{\mathbf{H}_\mathcal{G}}$, *and the probability is taken over the choice of* $\left(\vec{v}, \vec{v'}\right)$ *induced by a random execution of* $\mathbf{H}_\mathcal{G}$ *with* A.

5.2   Algebraic Equivalence of the Uber and q-DLOG Problems

Before presenting the main reduction of this section, we first define the q-discrete logarithm problem and the Uber family of decisional problems [BBG05, Boy08]. The q-discrete logarithm problem is a parameterized generalization of the discrete logarithm problem, in which the adversary receives $\left(g^{x^i}\right)_{i \in \{0, \ldots, q\}}$ and needs to compute x. The "Uber assumption" is a family of decisional assumptions in bilinear maps: It is parameterized by two tuples of m-variate polynomials $\vec{r} = (r_1, \ldots, r_t)$ and $\vec{s} = (s_1, \ldots, s_t)$ and an m-variate polynomial f; each choice of $\vec{r}, \vec{s}$ and f yields a specific assumption. Roughly, the assumption states that given $g^{r_1(x_1, \ldots, x_m)}, \ldots, g^{r_t(x_1, \ldots, x_m)}$ and $g_T^{s_1(x_1, \ldots, x_m)}, \ldots, g_T^{s_t(x_1, \ldots, x_m)}$, it is difficult to distinguish between $g_T^{f(x_1, \ldots, x_m)}$ and a uniformly-random element in $\mathbb{G}_T$ for a uniform choice of $x_1, \ldots, x_m$ in $\mathbb{Z}_p$. Both assumptions are formally defined via the algebraic games q-**DLOG** and $(\vec{r}, \vec{s}, f)$-**UBER** in Fig. 3.

Note that there are choices of $\vec{r}, \vec{s}$ and f for which the $(\vec{r}, \vec{s}, f)$-**UBER** game can be easily won. If given access to $g^{\vec{r}(X_1, \ldots, X_m)}$ and to $g_T^{\vec{s}(X_1, \ldots, X_m)}$, one can obtain $g_T^{f(X_1, \ldots, X_m)}$ through a sequence of group operations and bilinear map operations (where X_i is a indeterminate replacing x_i), then one can distinguish between the case where $b = 0$ and the case where $b = 1$ by comparing $g_T^{f(X_1, \ldots, X_m)}$ to $\mathbf{Z}$. To rule out such trivial attacks, Boneh et al. introduced the following definition.

q-**DLOG**$_{\mathcal{G}}^{\mathsf{A}}$	$(\vec{r}, \vec{s}, f)$-**UBER**$_{\mathcal{G}, b}^{\mathsf{A}}$
1. $x \leftarrow \mathbb{Z}_p$ 2. For $i = 1, \ldots, q$: $\mathbf{X}_i := g^{x^i}$. 3. $x' \leftarrow \mathsf{A}(\mathbf{X}_1, \ldots, \mathbf{X}_q)$ 4. If $x' = x$ output 1, and otherwise output 0	1. $x_1, \ldots, x_m, z \leftarrow \mathbb{Z}_p$. 2. $\vec{\mathbf{X}} := g^{\vec{r}(x_1, \ldots, x_m)}$. 3. $\vec{\mathbf{Y}} := g_T^{\vec{s}(x_1, \ldots, x_m)}$. 4. $\mathbf{Z} := g_T^{f(x_1, \ldots, x_m) + (1-b)z}$. 5. $\mathsf{Sym} \leftarrow \mathsf{A}(\vec{\mathbf{X}}, \vec{\mathbf{Y}}, \mathbf{Z})$. 6. If $\mathsf{Sym} = \mathsf{Acc}$ output 1, and otherwise output 0

Fig. 3. The game q-**DLOG**$_{\mathcal{G}}^{\mathsf{A}}$ (on the left) captures the q-Discrete Logarithm assumption; and the game $(\vec{r}, \vec{s}, f)$-**UBER**$_{\mathcal{G}, b}^{\mathsf{A}}$ (on the right) defines the Uber assumption of Boneh, Boyen and Goh [BBG05] parameterized by a triplet $(\vec{r}, \vec{s}, f)$ where $\vec{r}$ and $\vec{s}$ are vectors of m-variate polynomials and f is an m-variate polynomial. The notation $\vec{\mathbf{X}} := g^{\vec{r}(x_1, \ldots, x_m)}$ is a shorthand for $\vec{\mathbf{X}} := (g^{r_1(x_1, \ldots, x_m)}, \ldots, g^{r_t(x_1, \ldots, x_m)})$ and the notation $\vec{\mathbf{Y}} := g_T^{\vec{s}(x_1, \ldots, x_m)}$ is defined similarly. Both games are defined relative to a bilinear group $\mathcal{G} = (\mathbb{G}, \mathbb{G}_T, p, g, e)$ and an adversary A. The q-**DLOG** game in bilinear groups is the same as the game defined in Sect. 2, when considering the discrete logarithm *to the source group*.

Definition 5.3. *Let $p \in \mathbb{N}$ be a prime, let $t, m \in \mathbb{N}$, let $\vec{r}, \vec{s} \in (\mathbb{F}_p[X_1, \ldots, X_m])^t$ be t-tuples of polynomials such that $r_1 = s_1 = 1$, and let $f \in \mathbb{F}[X_1, \ldots, X_m]$ be a polynomial. We say that f is* dependent *on $(\vec{r}, \vec{s})$ if there exist integers $\{\alpha_{i,j}\}_{0 \leq i \leq j \leq t}$ and $\{\beta_k\}_{k \in [t]}$ such that*

$$f = \sum_{0 \leq i \leq j \leq t} \alpha_{i,j} \cdot r_i \cdot r_j + \sum_{k \in [t]} \beta_k \cdot s_k.$$

If f is not dependent on $(\vec{r}, \vec{s})$, we say that it is independent *of $(\vec{r}, \vec{s})$.*

Observe, that we can only hope to reduce $(\vec{r}, \vec{s}, f)$-**UBER** to q-**DLOG** for triplets $(\vec{r}, \vec{s}, f)$ such that f is independent of $(\vec{r}, \vec{s})$. The following theorem, which is the main result of this section, states that such a reduction in fact applies to any such triplet $(\vec{r}, \vec{s}, f)$.

Theorem 5.4. *Let $\mathcal{G} = (\mathbb{G}, \mathbb{G}_T, p, g, e)$ be a description of a symmetric bilinear group, let $t, m \in \mathbb{N}$, let $\vec{r}, \vec{s} \in (\mathbb{F}_p[X_1, \ldots, X_m])^t$ be t-tuples of polynomials of degree at most d, and let $f \in \mathbb{F}[X_1, \ldots, X_m]$ be a polynomial of degree at most d which is independent of $(\vec{r}, \vec{s})$. Then, for any algebraic algorithm A there exists an algebraic algorithm B such that $\mathbf{Adv}_{\mathsf{B}}^{q\text{-}\mathbf{DLOG}_{\mathcal{G}}} \geq \epsilon / (4 \cdot T^2) - d \cdot (t^2 + t + 2)/(8 \cdot p)$ and $\mathbf{Time}_{\mathsf{B}}^{q\text{-}\mathbf{DLOG}_{\mathcal{G}}} \leq T + \mathsf{poly}(m, t, d, \log p)$, where $q = d \cdot (t^2 + t + 2)/2$, $\epsilon = \mathbf{Adv}_{\mathsf{A}}^{(\vec{r}, \vec{s}, f)\text{-}\mathbf{UBER}_{\mathcal{G}}}$ and $T = \mathbf{Time}_{\mathsf{A}}^{(\vec{r}, \vec{s}, f)\text{-}\mathbf{UBER}_{\mathcal{G}}}$.*

As a first step towards proving Theorem 5.4, we define an intermediate assumption which we call the "Randomized Univariate Uber Assumption". This assumption is obtained from $(\vec{r}, \vec{s}, f)$-**UBER** by the following modification:

$(\vec{r}, \vec{s}, f)\text{-}\mathbf{RUU}_{\mathcal{G},b}^{\mathsf{A}}$

1. $x, z \leftarrow \mathbb{Z}_p$.
2. $c_1, \ldots, c_m \leftarrow \{c \in \mathbb{Z}_p[X] \mid \deg(c) = (t^2 + t + 2)/2\}$
3. For $i = 1, \ldots, m$: $x_i := c_i(x)$.
4. $\vec{\mathbf{X}} := g^{\vec{r}(x_1, \ldots, x_m)}$.
5. $\vec{\mathbf{Y}} := g_T^{\vec{s}(x_1, \ldots, x_m)}$.
6. $\mathbf{Z} := g_T^{f(x_1, \ldots, x_m) + (1-b)z}$.
7. $\mathsf{Sym} \leftarrow \mathsf{A}(\vec{c}, \vec{\mathbf{X}}, \vec{\mathbf{Y}}, \mathbf{Z})$, where $\vec{c} = (c_1, \ldots, c_m)$.
8. If $\mathsf{Sym} = \mathsf{Acc}$ output 1, and otherwise output 0

Fig. 4. The game $(\vec{r}, \vec{s}, f)\text{-}\mathbf{RUU}_{\mathcal{G},b}^{\mathsf{A}}$ which captures our Randomized Univariate Uber assumption. The assumption is parameterized by a triplet $(\vec{r}, \vec{s}, f)$ where $\vec{r}$ and $\vec{s}$ are vectors of m-variate polynomials and f is an m-variate polynomial. The game is defined relative to a bilinear group $\mathcal{G} = (\mathbb{G}, \mathbb{G}_T, p, g, e)$ and an adversary A.

Instead of sampling $x_1, \ldots, x_m$ uniformly at random from $\mathbb{Z}_p$, the challenger samples a single $x \leftarrow \mathbb{Z}_p$ alongside m random polynomials $c_1, \ldots, c_m$, and sets $x_i := c_i(x)$. The Randomized Univariate Uber assumption is formalized via the game $(\vec{r}, \vec{s}, f)\text{-}\mathbf{RUU}$ described in Fig. 4.

The following lemma follows from the work of Ghadafi and Groth [GG17], and reduces the security of the Uber assumption to that of the Randomized Univariate Uber assumption.

Lemma 5.5. ([GG17]). *Let $\mathcal{G} = (\mathbb{G}, \mathbb{G}_T, p, g, e)$ be a description of a symmetric bilinear group, let $t, m \in \mathbb{N}$, let $\vec{r}, \vec{s} \in (\mathbb{F}_p[X_1, \ldots, X_m])^t$ be t-tuples of polynomials of degree at most d, and let $f \in \mathbb{F}[X_1, \ldots, X_m]$ be a polynomial which is independent of $(\vec{r}, \vec{s})$. Then, the following holds:*

1. *For any algebraic algorithm A there exists an algebraic algorithm B such that*

$$\mathbf{Adv}_{\mathsf{B}}^{(\vec{r}, \vec{s}, f)\text{-}\mathbf{RUU}_{\mathcal{G}}} = \mathbf{Adv}_{\mathsf{A}}^{(\vec{r}, \vec{s}, f)\text{-}\mathbf{UBER}_{\mathcal{G}}}$$

and

$$\mathbf{Time}_{\mathsf{B}}^{(\vec{r}, \vec{s}, f)\text{-}\mathbf{RUU}_{\mathcal{G}}} \leq \mathbf{Time}_{\mathsf{A}}^{(\vec{r}, \vec{s}, f)\text{-}\mathbf{UBER}_{\mathcal{G}}} + \mathsf{poly}(m, t, \log p).$$

2. *With probability at least $1 - d \cdot (t^2 + t + 2)/(2 \cdot p)$ over the choice of $c_1, \ldots, c_m$, the univariate polynomial $f(\vec{c}(X))$ is independent of $(\vec{r'}, \vec{s'})$, where $\vec{c}(X) = (c_1(X), \ldots, c_m(X))$, $\vec{r'} = (r_1(\vec{c}(X)), \ldots, r_t(\vec{c}(X)))$ and $\vec{s'} = (s_1(\vec{c}(X)), \ldots, s_t(\vec{c}(X)))$.*

We note that there are some small technical differences between the theorem proven by Ghadafi and Groth and Lemma 5.5. Ghadafi and Groth deal with a computational variant of the Uber assumption, in which the adversary can choose the polynomial f.[4] Additionally, they do not consider algebraic adversaries. We stress, however, that their reduction readily applies to imply Lemma 5.5.[5]

The main part of the proof of Theorem 5.4 is consists of the following lemma which reduces the security of the randomized univariate Uber assumption (against algebraic adversaries) to the security of the q-**DLOG** assumption. Together with Lemma 5.5, this immediately implies Theorem 5.4.

Lemma 5.6. *Let* $\mathcal{G} = (\mathbb{G}, \mathbb{G}_T, p, g, e)$ *be a description of a symmetric bilinear group, let* $t, m \in \mathbb{N}$, *let* $\vec{r}, \vec{s} \in (\mathbb{F}_p[X_1, \ldots, X_m])^t$ *be t-tuples of polynomials of degree at most d, and let* $f \in \mathbb{F}[X_1, \ldots, X_m]$ *be a polynomial of degree at most d which is independent of* $(\vec{r}, \vec{s})$. *Then, for any algebraic algorithm* A *there exists an algebraic algorithm* B *such that* $\mathbf{Adv}_B^{q\text{-}\mathbf{DLOG}_\mathcal{G}} \geq \epsilon/(4 \cdot T^2) - d \cdot (t^2 + t + 2)/(8 \cdot p)$ *and* $\mathbf{Time}_B^{q\text{-}\mathbf{DLOG}_\mathcal{G}} \leq T + \mathsf{poly}(d, t, \log p)$, *where* $q = d \cdot (t^2 + t + 2)/2$, $\epsilon = \mathbf{Adv}_B^{(\vec{r}, \vec{s}, f)\text{-}\mathbf{RUU}_\mathcal{G}}$ *and* $T = \mathbf{Time}_B^{(\vec{r}, \vec{s}, f)\text{-}\mathbf{RUU}_\mathcal{G}}$.

The proof of Lemma 5.6 can be found in the full version of this paper [RS20].

References

[AHK20] Agrikola, T., Hofheinz, D., Kastner, J.: On instantiating the algebraic group model from falsifiable assumptions. In: Canteaut, A., Ishai, Y. (eds.) EURO-CRYPT 2020. LNCS, vol. 12106, pp. 96–126. Springer, Cham (2020). https://doi.org/10.1007/978-3-030-45724-2_4

[BBG05] Boneh, D., Boyen, X., Goh, E.-J.: Hierarchical identity based encryption with constant size ciphertext. In: Cramer, R. (ed.) EUROCRYPT 2005. LNCS, vol. 3494, pp. 440–456. Springer, Heidelberg (2005). https://doi.org/10.1007/11426639_26

[BBS04] Boneh, D., Boyen, X., Shacham, H.: Short group signatures. In: Franklin, M. (ed.) CRYPTO 2004. LNCS, vol. 3152, pp. 41–55. Springer, Heidelberg (2004). https://doi.org/10.1007/978-3-540-28628-8_3

[Ber70] Berlekamp, E.R.: Factoring polynomials over large finite fields. Math. Comput. **24**(111), 713–735 (1970)

[BFL20] Bauer, B., Fuchsbauer, G., Loss, J.: A classification of computational assumptions in the algebraic group model. In: Micciancio, D., Ristenpart, T. (eds.) CRYPTO 2020. LNCS, vol. 12171, pp. 121–151. Springer, Cham (2020). https://doi.org/10.1007/978-3-030-56880-1_5

[BL96] Boneh, D., Lipton, R.J.: Algorithms for black-box fields and their application to cryptography. In: Koblitz, N. (ed.) CRYPTO 1996. LNCS, vol. 1109, pp. 283–297. Springer, Heidelberg (1996). https://doi.org/10.1007/3-540-68697-5_22

[BLS01] Boneh, D., Lynn, B., Shacham, H.: Short signatures from the weil pairing. In: Boyd, C. (ed.) ASIACRYPT 2001. LNCS, vol. 2248, pp. 514–532. Springer, Heidelberg (2001). https://doi.org/10.1007/3-540-45682-1_30

---

[4] In fact, in their work the adversary can choose a rational (partial) function instead of a polynomial.

[5] Concretely, in their proof the adversary B simply forwards its input to A (without the vector $\vec{c}$ of sampled polynomials); hence, B can simply output the same vector $\vec{w}$ that is returned by A.

[Boy08] Boyen, X.: The uber-assumption family – a unified complexity framework for bilinear groups. In: Galbraith, S.D., Paterson, K.G. (eds.) Pairing 2008. LNCS, vol. 5209, pp. 39–56. Springer, Heidelberg (2008). https://doi.org/10.1007/978-3-540-85538-5_3

[BR06] Bellare, M., Rogaway, P.: The security of triple encryption and a framework for code-based game-playing proofs. In: Vaudenay, S. (ed.) EUROCRYPT 2006. LNCS, vol. 4004, pp. 409–426. Springer, Heidelberg (2006). https://doi.org/10.1007/11761679_25

[BV98] Boneh, D., Venkatesan, R.: Breaking RSA may not be equivalent to factoring. In: Nyberg, K. (ed.) EUROCRYPT 1998. LNCS, vol. 1403, pp. 59–71. Springer, Heidelberg (1998). https://doi.org/10.1007/BFb0054117

[BW19] Beullens, W., Wee, H.: Obfuscating simple functionalities from knowledge assumptions. In: Lin, D., Sako, K. (eds.) PKC 2019. LNCS, vol. 11443, pp. 254–283. Springer, Cham (2019). https://doi.org/10.1007/978-3-030-17259-6_9

[FKL18] Fuchsbauer, G., Kiltz, E., Loss, J.: The algebraic group model and its applications. In: Shacham, H., Boldyreva, A. (eds.) CRYPTO 2018. LNCS, vol. 10992, pp. 33–62. Springer, Cham (2018). https://doi.org/10.1007/978-3-319-96881-0_2

[FPS20] Fuchsbauer, G., Plouviez, A., Seurin, Y.: Blind Schnorr signatures and signed ElGamal encryption in the algebraic group model. In: Canteaut, A., Ishai, Y. (eds.) EUROCRYPT 2020. LNCS, vol. 12106, pp. 63–95. Springer, Cham (2020). https://doi.org/10.1007/978-3-030-45724-2_3

[GG17] Ghadafi, E., Groth, J.: Towards a classification of non-interactive computational assumptions in cyclic groups. In: Takagi, T., Peyrin, T. (eds.) ASIACRYPT 2017. LNCS, vol. 10625, pp. 66–96. Springer, Cham (2017). https://doi.org/10.1007/978-3-319-70697-9_3

[Gro16] Groth, J.: On the size of pairing-based non-interactive arguments. In: Fischlin, M., Coron, J.-S. (eds.) EUROCRYPT 2016. LNCS, vol. 9666, pp. 305–326. Springer, Heidelberg (2016). https://doi.org/10.1007/978-3-662-49896-5_11

[JS13] Jager, T., Schwenk, J.: On the analysis of cryptographic assumptions in the generic ring model. J. Cryptol. **26**(2), 225–245 (2013). https://doi.org/10.1007/s00145-012-9120-y

[Mau05] Maurer, U.: Abstract models of computation in cryptography. In: Smart, N.P. (ed.) Cryptography and Coding 2005. LNCS, vol. 3796, pp. 1–12. Springer, Heidelberg (2005). https://doi.org/10.1007/11586821_1

[MTT19] Mizuide, T., Takayasu, A., Takagi, T.: Tight reductions for Diffie-Hellman variants in the algebraic group model. In: Matsui, M. (ed.) CT-RSA 2019. LNCS, vol. 11405, pp. 169–188. Springer, Cham (2019). https://doi.org/10.1007/978-3-030-12612-4_9

[Nec94] Nechaev, V.I.: Complexity of a determinate algorithm for the discrete logarithm. Math. Notes **55**(2), 91–101 (1994). https://doi.org/10.1007/BF02113297

[PV05] Paillier, P., Vergnaud, D.: Discrete-log-based signatures may not be equivalent to discrete log. In: Roy, B. (ed.) ASIACRYPT 2005. LNCS, vol. 3788, pp. 1–20. Springer, Heidelberg (2005). https://doi.org/10.1007/11593447_1

[Rab80] Rabin, M.O.: Probabilistic algorithms in finite fields. SIAM J. Comput. **9**(2), 273–280 (1980)

[RS20] Rotem, L., Segev, G.: Algebraic distinguishers: from discrete logarithms to decisional uber assumptions. Cryptology ePrint Archive, Report 2020/1144 (2020)

[Sch91] Schnorr, C.P.: Efficient signature generation by smart cards. J. Cryptol. **4**(3), 161–174 (1991). https://doi.org/10.1007/BF00196725

[Sch01] Schnorr, C.P.: Security of blind discrete log signatures against interactive attacks. In: Qing, S., Okamoto, T., Zhou, J. (eds.) ICICS 2001. LNCS, vol. 2229, pp. 1–12. Springer, Heidelberg (2001). https://doi.org/10.1007/3-540-45600-7_1

[Sha07] Shacham, H.: A Cramer-Shoup encryption scheme from the linear assumption and from progressively weaker linear variants. Cryptology ePrint Archive, Report 2007/074 (2007)

[Sho97] Shoup, V.: Lower bounds for discrete logarithms and related problems. In: Fumy, W. (ed.) EUROCRYPT 1997. LNCS, vol. 1233, pp. 256–266. Springer, Heidelberg (1997). https://doi.org/10.1007/3-540-69053-0_18

On the Security of Time-Lock Puzzles and Timed Commitments

Jonathan Katz[1], Julian Loss[1], and Jiayu Xu[2(✉)]

[1] University of Maryland, College Park, USA
[2] George Mason University, Fairfax, USA
jkatz2@gmail.com, lossjulian@gmail.com, jiayux@uci.edu

Abstract. Time-lock puzzles—problems whose solution requires some amount of *sequential* effort—have recently received increased interest (e.g., in the context of verifiable delay functions). Most constructions rely on the sequential-squaring conjecture that computing $g^{2^T} \bmod N$ for a uniform g requires at least T (sequential) steps. We study the security of time-lock primitives from two perspectives:

1. We give the first hardness result about the sequential-squaring conjecture in a non-generic model of computation. Namely, in a quantitative version of the algebraic group model (AGM) that we call the *strong* AGM, we show that any speed up of sequential squaring is as hard as factoring N.

2. We then focus on *timed commitments*, one of the most important primitives that can be obtained from time-lock puzzles. We extend existing security definitions to settings that may arise when using timed commitments in higher-level protocols, and give the first construction of *non-malleable* timed commitments. As a building block of independent interest, we also define (and give constructions for) a related primitive called *timed public-key encryption*.

1 Introduction

Time-lock puzzles, introduced by Rivest, Shamir, and Wagner [29], refer to a fascinating type of computational problem that requires a certain amount of sequential effort to solve. Time-lock puzzles can be used to construct timed commitments [7], which "encrypt a message m into the future" such that m remains computationally hidden for some time T, but can be recovered once this time has passed. Time-lock puzzles can be used to build various other primitives, including verifiable delay functions (VDFs) [5,6,28,33], zero-knowledge proofs [13], and non-malleable (standard) commitments [19], and have applications to fair coin tossing, e-voting, auctions, and contract signing [7,23]. In this work, we (1) provide the first formal evidence in support of the hardness of the most widely used time-lock puzzle [29] and (2) give new, stronger security definitions (and constructions) for timed commitments and related primitives. These contributions are explained in more detail next.

J. Katz—Portions of this work were done while at George Mason University.

© International Association for Cryptologic Research 2020
R. Pass and K. Pietrzak (Eds.): TCC 2020, LNCS 12552, pp. 390–413, 2020.
https://doi.org/10.1007/978-3-030-64381-2_14

Hardness in the (strong) AGM. The hardness assumption underlying the most popular time-lock puzzle [29] is that, given a random generator g in the group of quadratic residues[1] $\mathbb{QR}_N$ (where N is the product of two safe primes), it is hard to compute $g^{2^T} \bmod N$ in fewer than T sequential steps. We study this assumption in a new, strengthened version of the algebraic group model (AGM) [15] that we call the *strong AGM (SAGM)* that lies in between the generic group model (GGM) [24,32] and the AGM. Roughly, an algorithm $\mathcal{A}$ in the AGM is constrained as follows: for any group element x that $\mathcal{A}$ outputs, $\mathcal{A}$ must also output coefficients showing how x was computed from group elements previously given to $\mathcal{A}$ as input. The SAGM imposes the stronger constraint that $\mathcal{A}$ output the *entire path of its computation* (i.e., all intermediate group operations) that resulted in output x. We show that if $\mathbb{QR}_N$ is modeled as a strongly algebraic group, then computing $g^{2^T} \bmod N$ from g using fewer than T squarings is as hard as factoring N. Our result is the first formal argument supporting the sequential hardness of squaring in $\mathbb{QR}_N$, and immediately implies the security of Pietrzak's VDF [28] in the SAGM (assuming the hardness of factoring). Our technique deviates substantially from known proofs in the AGM, which use groups of (known) prime order. We also show that in the AGM, it is not possible to reduce the hardness of speeding up sequential squaring to factoring (assuming factoring is hard in the first place).

Non-malleable Timed Commitments. The second part of our paper is concerned with the security of *non-interactive timed commitments* (NITCs). A timed commitment differs from a regular one in that it additionally has a "forced decommit" routine that can be used to force open the commitment after a certain amount of time in case the committer refuses to open it. Moreover, a commitment comes with a proof that it can be forced open if needed. We introduce a strong notion of non-malleability for such schemes. To construct a non-malleable NITC, we formalize as a stepping stone a timed public-key analogue that we call *timed public-key encryption* (TPKE). We then show how to achieve an appropriate notion of CCA-security for TPKE. Finally, we show a generic transformation from CCA-secure TPKE to non-malleable NITC. Although our main purpose for introducing TPKE is to obtain a non-malleable NITC, we believe that TPKE is an independently interesting primitive worthy of further study.

1.1 Related Work

We highlight here additional works not already cited earlier. Mahmoody et al. [22] show constructions of time-lock puzzles in the random-oracle model, and Bitansky et al. [4] give constructions based on randomized encodings. In recent work, Malavolta and Thyagarajan [23] study a homomorphic variant of time-lock puzzles. Another line of work initiated by May [25] and later formalized by Rivest et al. [29] studies a model for timed message transmission between a sender and

---

[1] The problem was originally stated over the ring $\mathbb{Z}_N$. Subsequent works have studied it both over $\mathbb{QR}_N$ [28] and $\mathbb{J}_N$ (elements of $\mathbb{Z}_N^*$ with Jacobi symbol $+1$) [23].

receiver in the presence of a trusted server. Bellare and Goldwasser [3] considered a notion of "partial key escrow" in which a server can store keys in escrow and learn only some of them unless it expends significant computational effort; this model was subsequently studied by others [11,12] as well. Liu et al. [21] propose a time-released encryption scheme based on witness encryption in a model with a global clock.

Concurrent Work. In work concurrent with our own, Baum et al. [2] formalize time-lock puzzles and timed commitments in the framework of universal composability (UC) [9]; universally composable timed commitments are presumably also non-malleable. Baum et al. present constructions in the (programmable) random-oracle model that achieve their definitions, and show that their definitions are impossible to realize in the plain model. Ephraim et al. [14] also recently formalized a notion of non-malleable timed commitments that is somewhat different from our own. They do not distinguish between time-lock puzzles and timed commitments, which makes a direct comparison somewhat difficult. They also give a generic construction of a time-lock puzzle from a VDF in the random-oracle model. Finally, the work of Rotem and Segev [30] analyzes the hardness of speeding up sequential squaring and related functions over the ring $\mathbb{Z}_N$. Their analysis is in the *generic ring model* [1], where an algorithm can only perform additions and multiplications modulo N, but the algorithm does not get access to the actual representations of ring elements. This makes their analysis incomparable to our analysis in the strong AGM.

1.2   Overview of the Paper

We introduce notation and basic definitions in Sect. 2. In Sect. 3 we introduce the SAGM and state our hardness result about the sequential squaring assumption. We give definitions for TPKE and NITC in Sect. 2, and give a construction of CCA-secure TPKE in Sect. 4.2. In Sect. 4.3, we then show a simple, generic conversion from CCA-secure TPKE to non-malleable NITC.

2   Notation and Preliminaries

Notation. We use ":=" to denote a deterministic assignment, and "←" to denote assignment via a randomized process. In particular, "$x \leftarrow S$" denotes sampling a uniform element x from a set S. We denote the length of a bitstring x by $|x|$, and the length of the binary representation of an integer n by $||n||$. We denote the security parameter by κ. We write $\mathsf{Expt}^{\mathcal{A}}$ for the output of experiment Expt involving adversary $\mathcal{A}$.

Running Time. We consider running times of algorithms in some unspecified (but fixed) computational model, e.g., the Turing machine model. This is done both for simplicity of exposition and generality of our results. To simplify things further, we omit from our running-time analyses additive terms resulting from bitstring operations or passing arguments between algorithms, and we scale units so that multiplication in the group $\mathbb{QR}_N$ under consideration takes unit time. All algorithms are assumed to have arbitrary parallel computing resources.

The Quadratic Residue Group $\mathbb{QR}_N$. Let GenMod be an algorithm that, on input 1^κ, outputs (N, p, q) where $N = pq$ and $p \neq q$ are two safe primes (i.e., such that $\frac{p-1}{2}$ and $\frac{q-1}{2}$ are also prime) with $||p|| = ||q|| = \tau(\kappa)$; here, $\tau(\kappa)$ is defined such that the fastest factoring algorithm takes time 2^κ to factor N with probability $\frac{1}{2}$. GenMod may fail with negligible probability, but we ignore this from now on. It is well known that $\mathbb{QR}_N$ is cyclic with $|\mathbb{QR}_N| = \frac{\phi(N)}{4} = \frac{(p-1)(q-1)}{4}$.

For completeness, we define the factoring problem.

Definition 1. *For an algorithm $\mathcal{A}$, define experiment $\mathbf{FAC}^{\mathcal{A}}_{\mathsf{GenMod}}$ as follows:*

1. *Compute $(N, p, q) \leftarrow \mathsf{GenMod}(1^\kappa)$, and then run $\mathcal{A}$ on input N.*
2. *When $\mathcal{A}$ outputs integers $p', q' \notin \{1, N\}$, the experiment evaluates to 1 iff $N = p'q'$.*

The factoring problem is (t, ϵ)-hard relative to GenMod if for all $\mathcal{A}$ running in time t,

$$\Pr\left[\mathbf{FAC}^{\mathcal{A}}_{\mathsf{GenMod}} = 1\right] \leq \epsilon.$$

The Repeated Squaring Algorithm. Given an element $g \in \mathbb{QR}_N$, it is possible to compute $g^1, \ldots, g^{2^i}$ (all modulo N) in i steps: in step i, simply multiply each value $g^1, \ldots, g^{2^{i-1}}$ by $g^{2^{i-1}}$. (Recall that we allow unbounded parallelism.) In particular, it is possible to compute g^x for any positive integer x in $\lceil \log x \rceil$ steps. We denote by RepSqr the algorithm that on input (g, N, x) computes g^x in this manner.

Given a generator g of $\mathbb{QR}_N$, it is possible to sample a uniform element of $\mathbb{QR}_N$ by sampling $x \leftarrow \{0, \ldots, |\mathbb{QR}_N| - 1\}$ and running $\mathsf{RepSqr}(g, N, x)$. This assumes that $|\mathbb{QR}_N|$ (and hence factorization of N) is known; if this is not the case, one can instead sample $x \leftarrow \mathbb{Z}_{N^2}$, which results in a negligible statistical difference that we ignore for simplicity. Sampling a uniform element of $\mathbb{QR}_N$ in this way takes at most

$$\lceil \log x \rceil \leq \lceil \log N^2 \rceil \leq 4\tau(\kappa)$$

steps. We denote by $\theta(\kappa) = 4\tau(\kappa)$ the time to sample a uniform element of $\mathbb{QR}_N$.

The RSW Problem. We next formally define the repeated squaring problem in the presence of preprocessing. This problem was first proposed by Rivest, Shamir, and Wagner [29] and hence we refer to it as the *RSW problem*. We write elements of $\mathbb{G}$ (except for the fixed generator g) using bold, upper-case letters.

Definition 2. *For a stateful algorithm $\mathcal{A}$, define experiment $T\text{-}\mathbf{RSW}^{\mathcal{A}}_{\mathsf{GenMod}}$ as follows:*

1. *Compute $(N, p, q) \leftarrow \mathsf{GenMod}(1^\kappa)$.*

2. *Run $\mathcal{A}$ on input N in a preprocessing phase to obtain some intermediate state.*
3. *Sample $g \leftarrow \mathbb{QR}_N$ and run $\mathcal{A}$ on input g in the online phase.*
4. *When $\mathcal{A}$ outputs $\mathbf{X} \in \mathbb{QR}_N$, the experiment evaluates to 1 iff $\mathbf{X} = g^{2^T} \bmod N$.*

The T-RSW problem is (t_p, t_o, ϵ)-hard relative to GenMod *if for all algorithms $\mathcal{A}$ running in time t_p in the preprocessing phase and t_o in the online phase,*

$$\Pr\left[T\text{-}\mathbf{RSW}^{\mathcal{A}}_{\mathsf{GenMod}} = 1\right] \leq \epsilon.$$

Clearly, an adversary $\mathcal{A}$ can run $\mathsf{RepSqr}(g, N, 2^T)$ to compute $g^{2^T} \bmod N$ in T steps. This means there is a threshold $t^* \approx T$ such that the T-RSW problem is easy when $t_o \geq t^*$. In Sect. 3.1 we show that in the strong algebraic group model, when $t_o < t^*$ the T-RSW problem is (t_p, t_o, ϵ)-hard (for negligible ϵ) unless N can be factored in time roughly $t_p + t_o$. To put it another way, the fastest way to compute $g^{2^T} \bmod N$ (short of factoring N) is to run $\mathsf{RepSqr}(g, N, 2^T)$.

We also introduce a *decisional* variant of the RSW assumption where, roughly speaking, the problem is to distinguish $g^{2^T} \bmod N$ from a uniform element of $\mathbb{QR}_N$ in fewer than T steps.

Definition 3. *For a stateful algorithm $\mathcal{A}$, define experiment T-$\mathbf{DRSW}_{\mathsf{GenMod}}$ as follows:*

1. *Compute $(N, p, q) \leftarrow \mathsf{GenMod}(1^\kappa)$.*
2. *Run $\mathcal{A}$ on input N in a preprocessing phase to obtain some intermediate state.*
3. *Sample $g, \mathbf{X} \leftarrow \mathbb{QR}_N$ and a uniform bit $b \leftarrow \{0, 1\}$. If $b = 0$, run $\mathcal{A}$ on inputs $g, \mathbf{X}$; if $b = 1$, run $\mathcal{A}$ on inputs $g, g^{2^T} \bmod N$ in the online phase.*
4. *When $\mathcal{A}$ outputs a bit b', the experiment evaluates to 1 iff $b' = b$.*

The decisional T-RSW problem is (t_p, t_o, ϵ)-hard relative to GenMod *if for all algorithms $\mathcal{A}$ running in time t_p in the preprocessing phase and t_o in the online phase,*

$$\left| \Pr\left[T\text{-}\mathbf{DRSW}^{\mathcal{A}}_{\mathsf{GenMod}} = 1\right] - \frac{1}{2} \right| \leq \epsilon.$$

The decisional T-RSW problem is related to the generalized BBS (GBBS) assumption introduced by Boneh and Naor [7]; however, there are several differences. First, the adversary in the GBBS assumption is given the group elements $g, g^2, g^4, g^{16}, g^{256}, \ldots, g^{2^{2^k}}$ and then asked to distinguish $g^{2^{2^{k+1}}}$ from uniform. Second, the GBBS assumption does not account for any preprocessing. Our definition is also similar to the strong sequential squaring assumption [23] except that we do not give g to $\mathcal{A}$ in the preprocessing phase.

Non-interactive Zero-Knowledge. We recall the notion of a non-interactive zero-knowledge proof system, defined as follows.

Definition 4. *Let $\mathcal{L}_R$ be a language in NP defined by relation R. A $(t_p, t_v, t_{sgen}, t_{sp})$-non-interactive zero-knowledge proof (NIZK) system (for relation R) is a tuple of algorithms* NIZK = (GenZK, Prove, Vrfy, SimGen, SimProve) *with the following behavior:*

- *The randomized parameter generation algorithm* GenZK *takes as input the security parameter 1^κ and outputs a common reference string* crs.
- *The randomized prover algorithm* Prove *takes as input a string* crs, *an instance x, and a witness w. It outputs a proof π and runs in time at most t_p for all* crs, x *and w.*
- *The deterministic verifier algorithm* Vrfy *takes as input a string* crs, *an instance x, and a proof π. It outputs 1 (accept) or 0 (reject) and runs in time at most t_v for all* crs, x *and π.*
- *The randomized simulation parameter generation algorithm* SimGen *takes as input the security parameter 1^κ. It outputs a common reference string* crs *and a trapdoor td and runs in time at most t_{sgen}.*
- *The randomized simulation prover algorithm* SimProve *takes as input an instance x and a trapdoor td. It outputs a proof π and runs in time at most t_{sp}.*

We require perfect completeness: *For all* crs $\in \{$GenZK$(1^\kappa)\}$, *all $(x, w) \in R$, and all $\pi \in \{$Prove(crs, $x, w)\}$, it holds that* Vrfy(crs, $x, \pi) = 1$.

We next define zero-knowledge and soundness properties of a NIZK.

Definition 5. *Let* NIZK = (GenZK, Prove, Vrfy, SimGen, SimProve) *be a NIZK for relation R. For an algorithm $\mathcal{A}$, define experiment* $\mathbf{ZK}_{\mathsf{NIZK}}$ *as follows:*

1. *Compute* crs$_0$ $\leftarrow$ GenZK(1^κ) *and* crs$_1$ $\leftarrow$ SimGen(1^κ), *and choose a uniform bit $b \leftarrow \{0, 1\}$.*
2. *Run $\mathcal{A}$ on input* crs$_b$ *with access to a* prover oracle PROVE, *which behaves as follows: on input (x, w),* PROVE *returns $\bot$ if $(x, w) \notin R$; otherwise it generates $\pi_0 \leftarrow$* Prove(crs$_0$, x, w), $\pi_1 \leftarrow$ SimProve(crs$_1$, x, w) *and returns π_b.*
3. *When $\mathcal{A}$ outputs a bit b', the experiment evaluates to 1 iff $b' = b$.*

NIZK *is (t, ϵ)-zero-knowledge if for all adversaries $\mathcal{A}$ running in time t,*

$$\Pr\left[\mathbf{ZK}_{\mathsf{NIZK}}^{\mathcal{A}} = 1\right] \leq \frac{1}{2} + \epsilon.$$

Definition 6. *Let* NIZK = (GenZK, Prove, Vrfy, SimGen, SimProve) *be a NIZK for relation R. For an algorithm $\mathcal{A}$, define experiment* $\mathbf{SND}_{\mathsf{NIZK}}$ *as follows:*

1. *Compute* crs $\leftarrow$ GenZK(1^κ).
2. *Run $\mathcal{A}$ on input* crs.
3. *When $\mathcal{A}$ outputs (x, π), the experiment evaluates to 1 iff* Vrfy(crs, $x, \pi) = 1$ *and $x \notin \mathcal{L}_R$.*

NIZK *is (t, ϵ)-sound if for all adversaries $\mathcal{A}$ running in time t,*

$$\Pr\left[\mathbf{SND}_{\mathsf{NIZK}}^{\mathcal{A}} = 1\right] \leq \epsilon.$$

In our applications we also need the stronger notion of simulation soundness, which says that the adversary cannot produce a fake proof even if it has oracle access to the simulated prover algorithm.

Definition 7 (Simulation Soundness). *Let* NIZK = (GenZK, Prove, Vrfy, SimGen, SimProve) *be a NIZK for relation R. For an algorithm* $\mathcal{A}$, *define experiment* **SIMSND**$_{\mathsf{NIZK}}$ *as follows:*

1. *Compute* crs $\leftarrow$ SimGen(1^κ) *and initialize* $\mathcal{Q} := \varnothing$.
2. *Run* $\mathcal{A}$ *on input* crs *with access to a* simulated prover oracle SPROVE, *which behaves as follows: on input* (x, w), SPROVE *generates* $\pi \leftarrow$ SimProve(x, t), *sets* $\mathcal{Q} := \mathcal{Q} \cup \{x\}$, *and returns* π.
3. *When* $\mathcal{A}$ *outputs* (x, π), *the experiment evaluates to* 1 *iff* $x \notin \mathcal{Q}$, Vrfy(crs, x, π) = 1, *and* $x \notin \mathcal{L}_R$.

NIZK *is* (t, ϵ)-*simulation sound iff for all adversaries* $\mathcal{A}$ *running in time* t,

$$\Pr\left[\mathbf{SIMSND}^{\mathcal{A}}_{\mathsf{NIZK}} = 1\right] \leq \epsilon.$$

3   Algebraic Hardness of the RSW Problem

We briefly recall the AGM, and then introduce a refinement that we call the *strong AGM* (SAGM) that lies in between the GGM and the AGM. As the main result of this section, we show that the RSW assumption can be reduced to the factoring assumption in the strong AGM. (Unfortunately, it does not seem possible to extend this result to prove hardness of the decisional RSW assumption based on factoring in the same model.) For completeness, we also show that it is not possible to reduce hardness of RSW to hardness of factoring in the AGM (unless factoring is easy).

3.1   The Strong Algebraic Group Model

The *algebraic group model* (AGM), introduced by Fuchsbauer, Kiltz, and Loss [15], lies between the GGM and the standard model. As in the standard model, algorithms are given actual (bit-strings representing) group elements, rather than abstract handles for (or random encodings of) those elements as in the GGM. This means that AGM algorithms are strictly more powerful than GGM algorithms (e.g., when working in $\mathbb{Z}_N^*$ an AGM algorithm can compute Jacobi symbols), and in particular means that the computational difficulty of problems in the AGM depends on the group representation used. (In contrast, in the GGM all cyclic groups of the same order are not only isomorphic, but identical.) On the other hand, an algorithm in the AGM that outputs group elements must also output representations of those elements with respect to any inputs the algorithm has received; this restricts the algorithm in comparison to the standard model (which imposes no such restriction).

In the AGM all algorithms are *algebraic* [8,27]:

Definition 8 (Algebraic Algorithm). *An algorithm $\mathcal{A}$ over $\mathbb{G}$ is called* algebraic *if whenever $\mathcal{A}$ outputs a group element $\mathbf{X} \in \mathbb{G}$, it also outputs an integer vector $\boldsymbol{\lambda}$ with $\mathbf{X} = \prod_i L_i^{\lambda_i}$, where $\boldsymbol{L}$ denotes the (ordered) list of group elements that $\mathcal{A}$ has received as input up to that point.*

The original formulation of the AGM assumes that $\mathbb{G}$ is a group of (known) prime order but this is not essential and we do not make that assumption here.

The Strong AGM. The AGM does not directly provide a way to measure the number of (algebraic) steps taken by an algorithm. This makes it unsuitable for dealing with "fine-grained" assumptions like the hardness of the RSW problem. (This point is made more formal in Sect. 3.3. On the other hand, as we will see, from a "coarse" perspective any algebraic algorithm can be implemented using polylogarithmically many algebraic steps.) This motivates us to consider a refinement of the AGM that we call the *strong AGM (SAGM)*, which provides a way to directly measure the number of group operations performed by an algorithm.

In the AGM, whenever an algorithm outputs a group element $\mathbf{X}$ it is required to also provide an algebraic representation of $\mathbf{X}$ with respect to all the group elements the algorithm has received as input so far. In the SAGM we strengthen this, and require an algorithm to express any group element as either (1) a *product* of two previous group elements that it has either received as input or already computed in some intermediate step, or (2) an *inverse* of a previous group element. That is, we require algorithms to be *strongly algebraic*:

Definition 9 (Strongly Algebraic Algorithm). *An algorithm $\mathcal{A}$ over $\mathbb{G}$ is called* strongly algebraic *if in each (algebraic) step $\mathcal{A}$ does arbitrary local computation and then outputs[2] one or more tuples of the following form:*

1. *$(\mathbf{X}, \mathbf{X}_1, \mathbf{X}_2) \in \mathbb{G}^3$, where $\mathbf{X} = \mathbf{X}_1 \cdot \mathbf{X}_2$ and $\mathbf{X}_1, \mathbf{X}_2$ were either provided as input to $\mathcal{A}$ or were output by $\mathcal{A}$ in some previous step(s);*
2. *$(\mathbf{X}, \mathbf{X}_1) \in \mathbb{G}^2$, where $\mathbf{X} = \mathbf{X}_1^{-1}$ and $\mathbf{X}_1$ was either provided as input to $\mathcal{A}$ or was output by $\mathcal{A}$ in some previous step.*

Note that we allow arbitrary parallelism, since we allow strongly algebraic algorithms to output multiple tuples per step. As an example of a strongly algebraic algorithm, consider the following algorithm[3] $\widetilde{\mathsf{Mult}}$ computing the product of n input elements $\mathbf{X}_1, \ldots, \mathbf{X}_n$ in $\lceil \log n \rceil$ steps: If $n = 1$ then $\widetilde{\mathsf{Mult}}(\mathbf{X}_1)$ outputs $\mathbf{X}_1$; otherwise, $\widetilde{\mathsf{Mult}}(\mathbf{X}_1, \ldots, \mathbf{X}_n)$ runs $\mathbf{Y} := \widetilde{\mathsf{Mult}}(\mathbf{X}_1, \ldots, \mathbf{X}_{\lceil n/2 \rceil})$ and $\mathbf{Z} := \widetilde{\mathsf{Mult}}(\mathbf{X}_{\lceil n/2 \rceil + 1}, \ldots, \mathbf{X}_n)$ in parallel, and outputs $(\mathbf{YZ}, \mathbf{Y}, \mathbf{Z})$. It is also easy to see that the repeated squaring algorithm RepSqr described previously can be cast as a strongly algebraic algorithm $\widetilde{\mathsf{RepSqr}}$ such that $\widetilde{\mathsf{RepSqr}}(g, x)$ computes g^x in $\lceil \log x \rceil$ steps.

Any algebraic algorithm with polynomial-length output can be turned into a strongly algebraic algorithm that uses polylogarithmically many steps:

---

[2] Formally, we require $\mathcal{A}$ to output a flag in its final step to indicate its final output.

[3] In general we use $\tilde{\ }$ to indicate that an algorithm is strongly algebraic.

Theorem 1. *Let $\mathcal{A}$ be an algebraic algorithm over $\mathbb{G}$ taking as input n group elements $\mathbf{X}_1, \ldots, \mathbf{X}_n$ and outputting a group element $\mathbf{X}$ along with its algebraic representation $(\lambda_1, \ldots, \lambda_n)$ (so $\mathbf{X} = \mathbf{X}_1^{\lambda_1} \cdots \mathbf{X}_n^{\lambda_n}$), where $\lambda_i \leq 2^\kappa$. Then there is a strongly algebraic algorithm $\tilde{\mathcal{A}}$ over $\mathbb{G}$ running in $\kappa + \lceil \log n \rceil$ steps such that the final group element output by $\tilde{\mathcal{A}}$ is identically distributed.*

Proof. Consider the following strongly algebraic algorithm $\tilde{\mathcal{A}}(\mathbf{X}_1, \ldots, \mathbf{X}_n)$:

1. Run $\mathcal{A}(\mathbf{X}_1, \ldots, \mathbf{X}_n)$ and receive $\mathcal{A}$'s output $\mathbf{X}$ together with $(\lambda_1, \ldots, \lambda_n)$. (Note that this is not an algebraic step, since all computation is "internal" to $\tilde{\mathcal{A}}$ and no group element is being output by $\tilde{\mathcal{A}}$ here.)
2. Run $\mathbf{X}_1^{\lambda_1} := \widehat{\mathsf{RepSqr}}(\mathbf{X}_1, \lambda_1), \ldots, \mathbf{X}_n^{\lambda_n} := \widehat{\mathsf{RepSqr}}(\mathbf{X}_n, \lambda_n)$ in parallel.
3. Run $\widehat{\mathsf{Mult}}(\mathbf{X}_1^{\lambda_1}, \ldots, \mathbf{X}_n^{\lambda_n})$.

The theorem follows. ∎

Running Time in the SAGM. The SAGM directly allows us to count the number of algebraic steps used by an algorithm. So far, we have treated all steps in our discussion as algebraic steps. In some settings, however, we may also wish to account for other (non-group) computation that an algorithm does, measured in some underlying computational model (e.g., the Turing machine model). In this case we will express the running time of algorithms as a *pair* and say that a strongly algebraic algorithm runs in time (t_1, t_2) if it uses t_1 algebraic steps, and has running time t_2 in the underlying computational model.

3.2   Hardness of the RSW Problem in the Strong AGM

If the factorization of N (and hence $\phi(N)$) is known, then $g^{2^T} \bmod N$ can be computed in at most $\lceil \log \phi(N)/4 \rceil$ algebraic steps by first computing $z := 2^T \bmod \phi(N)/4$ and then computing $\widehat{\mathsf{RepSqr}}(g, z)$. Thus, informally, if the T-RSW problem is hard then factoring must be hard as well. Here we prove a converse in the SAGM, showing that the hardness of factoring implies the hardness of solving the T-RSW problem in fewer than T sequential steps for a strongly algebraic algorithm. We rely on a concrete version of the well-known result that N can be efficiently factored given any positive multiple of $\phi(N)$ (A proof follows by straightforward adaptation of the proof of [17, Theorem 8.50]):

Lemma 1. *Suppose $N \leftarrow \mathsf{GenMod}(1^\kappa)$ and $m = \alpha \cdot \phi(N)$ (where $\alpha \in \mathbb{Z}^+$). Then there exists an algorithm $\mathsf{Factor}(N, m)$ which runs in time at most $4 \lceil \log \alpha \cdot \tau(\kappa) + \tau(\kappa)^2 \rceil$ and outputs $p', q' \notin \{1, N\}$ such that $N = p'q'$ with probability at least $\frac{1}{2}$.*

We now show:

Theorem 2. *Assume that factoring is $(t_p + t_o + \theta(\kappa) + 4\lceil \log \alpha \cdot \tau(\kappa) + \tau(\kappa)^2 \rceil, \epsilon)$-hard relative to GenMod, and let T be any positive integer. Then the T-RSW problem is $\big((0, t_p), (T - 1, t_o), 2\epsilon\big)$-hard relative to GenMod in the SAGM.*

Proof. Let $\mathcal{A}$ be a strongly algebraic algorithm that runs in time t_p and uses no algebraic steps in the preprocessing phase, and runs in time t_o and uses at most $T - 1$ algebraic steps in the online phase. Let g be the generator given to $\mathcal{A}$ at the beginning of the online phase of $T\text{-}\mathbf{RSW}_{\mathsf{GenMod}}$. For any $\mathbf{X} \in \mathbb{QR}_N$ output by $\mathcal{A}$ as part of an algebraic step during the online phase of $T\text{-}\mathbf{RSW}_{\mathsf{GenMod}}$, we recursively define $\mathsf{DL}_{\mathcal{A}}(g, \mathbf{X}) \in \mathbb{Z}^+$ as:

- $\mathsf{DL}_{\mathcal{A}}(g, g) = 1$;
- If $\mathcal{A}$ outputs $(\mathbf{X}, \mathbf{X}_1, \mathbf{X}_2)$ in an algebraic step, then $\mathsf{DL}_{\mathcal{A}}(g, \mathbf{X}) = \mathsf{DL}_{\mathcal{A}}(g, \mathbf{X}_1) + \mathsf{DL}_{\mathcal{A}}(g, \mathbf{X}_2)$;
- If $\mathcal{A}$ outputs $(\mathbf{X}, \mathbf{X}_1)$ in an algebraic step, then $\mathsf{DL}_{\mathcal{A}}(g, \mathbf{X}) = -\mathsf{DL}_{\mathcal{A}}(g, \mathbf{X}_1)$.

Obviously, $g^{\mathsf{DL}_{\mathcal{A}}(g, \mathbf{X})} = \mathbf{X}$ for any $\mathbf{X} \in \mathbb{QR}_N$ output by $\mathcal{A}$. We have:

Claim. For any strongly algebraic algorithm $\mathcal{A}$ given only g as input and running in $s \geq 1$ algebraic steps, every $\mathbf{X} \in \mathbb{QR}_N$ output by $\mathcal{A}$ satisfies $|\mathsf{DL}_{\mathcal{A}}(g, \mathbf{X})| \leq 2^s$.

Proof. The proof is by induction on s. If $s = 1$, the only group elements $\mathcal{A}$ can output are g^{-1} or g^2, so the claim holds. Suppose the claim holds for $s - 1$. If $\mathcal{A}$ outputs $(\mathbf{X}, \mathbf{X}_1, \mathbf{X}_2)$ in step s, then $\mathbf{X}_1, \mathbf{X}_2$ must either be equal to g or have been output in a previous step. So the induction hypothesis tells us that $|\mathsf{DL}_{\mathcal{A}}(g, \mathbf{X}_1)|, |\mathsf{DL}_{\mathcal{A}}(g, \mathbf{X}_2)| \leq 2^{s-1}$. It follows that

$$|\mathsf{DL}_{\mathcal{A}}(g, \mathbf{X})| = |\mathsf{DL}_{\mathcal{A}}(g, \mathbf{X}_1) + \mathsf{DL}_{\mathcal{A}}(g, \mathbf{X}_2)| \leq |\mathsf{DL}_{\mathcal{A}}(g, \mathbf{X}_1)| + |\mathsf{DL}_{\mathcal{A}}(g, \mathbf{X}_2)| \leq 2^s.$$

Similarly, if $\mathcal{A}$ outputs $(\mathbf{X}, \mathbf{X}_1)$ in step s, then $|\mathsf{DL}_{\mathcal{A}}(g, \mathbf{X})| = |\mathsf{DL}_{\mathcal{A}}(g, \mathbf{X}_1)| \leq 2^{s-1}$. In either case, the claim holds for s as well.

We construct an algorithm $\mathcal{R}$ that factors N as follows. $\mathcal{R}$, on input N, runs the preprocessing phase of $\mathcal{A}(N)$, and then samples $g \leftarrow \mathbb{QR}_N$ and runs the online phase of $\mathcal{A}(g)$. When $\mathcal{A}$ produces its final output $\mathbf{X}$, then $\mathcal{R}$ (recursively) computes $x = \mathsf{DL}_{\mathcal{A}}(g, \mathbf{X})$. Finally, $\mathcal{R}$ sets $m := 4 \cdot (2^T - x)$ and outputs $\mathsf{Factor}(N, m)$.

When $\mathbf{X} = g^{2^T} \bmod N$ we have $x = 2^T \bmod \phi(N)/4$, i.e., $\phi(N)$ divides $m = 4 \cdot (2^T - x)$. Since, by the claim, $|x| < 2^T$, we have $m \neq 0$ and so m is a nontrivial (integer) multiple of $\phi(N)$ in that case. We thus see that $\mathcal{R}$ factors N with probability at least $\frac{1}{2} \cdot \Pr\left[T\text{-}\mathbf{RSW}^{\mathcal{A}}_{\mathsf{GenMod}} = 1\right]$. The running time of $\mathcal{R}$ is at most $t_p + t_o + \theta(\kappa) + 4\lceil \log \alpha \cdot \tau(\kappa) + \tau(\kappa)^2 \rceil$. This completes the proof.

3.3 The RSW Problem in the AGM

In the previous section we have shown that the hardness of the RSW problem can be reduced to the hardness of factoring in the *strong* AGM. Here, we show that a similar reduction in the (plain) AGM is impossible, unless factoring is easy. Specifically, we give a "meta-reduction" $\mathcal{M}$ that converts any such reduction $\mathcal{R}$ into an efficient algorithm for factoring. In the theorem that follows, we write $\mathcal{R}^{\mathcal{A}}$ to denote execution of $\mathcal{R}$ given (black-box) oracle access to another algorithm $\mathcal{A}$. When we speak of the running time of $\mathcal{R}$ we assign unit cost to its oracle calls.

Theorem 3. *Let $\mathcal{R}$ be a reduction running in time t_R and such that for any algebraic algorithm $\mathcal{A}$ with $\Pr\left[T\text{-}\mathbf{RSW}_{\mathsf{GenMod}}^{\mathcal{A}} = 1\right] = 1$, algorithm $\mathcal{B} = \mathcal{R}^{\mathcal{A}}$ satisfies $\Pr\left[\mathbf{FAC}_{\mathsf{GenMod}}^{\mathcal{B}} = 1\right] > \epsilon'$. Then there is an algorithm $\mathcal{M}$ running in time at most $t_R \cdot (T+1)$ with $\Pr\left[\mathbf{FAC}_{\mathsf{GenMod}}^{\mathcal{M}} = 1\right] > \epsilon'$.*

Proof. Let $\mathcal{R}$ be as described in the theorem statement. Intuitively, $\mathcal{M}$ simply runs $\mathcal{R}$, handling its oracle calls by simulating the behavior of an (algebraic) algorithm $\mathcal{A}$ that solves the RSW problem with probability 1. (Note that the running time of doing so is irrelevant insofar as analyzing the behavior of $\mathcal{R}$, since $\mathcal{R}$ cannot observe the running time of $\mathcal{A}$. For this reason, we also ignore the fact that $\mathcal{A}$ is allowed preprocessing, and simply consider an algorithm $\mathcal{A}$ for which $\mathcal{A}(N, g)$ outputs $(g^{2^T} \bmod N, 2^T)$.) Formally, $\mathcal{M}(N)$ runs $\mathcal{R}(N)$. When $\mathcal{R}$ makes an oracle query $\mathcal{A}(N', g)$, algorithm $\mathcal{M}$ answers the query by computing $\mathbf{X} = g^{2^T} \bmod N'$ (using RepSqr) and returning the answer $(\mathbf{X}, 2^T)$ to $\mathcal{R}$. Finally, $\mathcal{M}$ outputs the factors that are output by $\mathcal{R}$.

The assumptions of the theorem imply that $\mathcal{M}$ factors N with probability at least ϵ'. The running time of $\mathcal{M}$ is the running time of $\mathcal{R}$ plus the time to run RepSqr (i.e., T steps) each time $\mathcal{R}$ calls $\mathcal{A}$. $\square$

4   Non-malleable Timed Commitments

In this section we provide appropriate definitions for non-interactive (non-malleable) timed commitments (NITCs). As a building block toward our construction of NITCs, we introduce the notion of *time-released public-key encryption* (TPKE) and show how to construct CCA-secure TPKE.

4.1   Definitions

Timed commitments allow a committer to generate a commitment to a message m such that binding holds as usual, but hiding holds only until some designated time T; the receiver can "force open" the commitment by that time. Boneh and Naor [7] gave a (somewhat informal) description of the syntax of *interactive* timed-commitments and provided some specific constructions. We introduce the syntax of *non-interactive* timed commitments and then give appropriate security definitions.

Definition 10. *A $(t_{cm}, t_{cv}, t_{dv}, t_{fo})$-non-interactive timed commitment scheme (NITC) is a tuple of algorithms $\mathsf{TC} = (\mathsf{PGen}, \mathsf{Com}, \mathsf{ComVrfy}, \mathsf{DecomVrfy}, \mathsf{FDecom})$ with the following behavior:*

- *The randomized parameter generation algorithm PGen takes as input the security parameter 1^κ and outputs a common reference string crs.*
- *The randomized commit algorithm Com takes as input a string crs and a message m. It outputs a commitment C and proofs $\pi_{\mathsf{Com}}, \pi_{\mathsf{Decom}}$ in time at most t_{cm}.*

- *The deterministic* commitment verification algorithm ComVrfy *takes as input a string* crs, *a commitment* C, *and a proof* π_{Com}. *It outputs* 1 *(accept) or* 0 *(reject) in time at most* t_{cv}.
- *The deterministic* decommitment verification algorithm DecomVrfy *takes as input a string* crs, *a commitment* C, *a message* m, *and a proof* π_{Decom}. *It outputs* 1 *(accept) or* 0 *(reject) in time at most* t_{dv}.
- *The deterministic* forced decommit algorithm FDecom *takes as input a string* crs *and a commitment* C. *It outputs a message* m *or* $\perp$ *in time at least* t_{fo}.

We require that for all crs $\in \{\text{PGen}(1^\kappa)\}$, *all* $m \in \{0,1\}^\kappa$, *and all* $C, \pi_{\text{Com}}, \pi_{\text{Decom}}$ *output by* Com(crs, m), *it holds that*

$$\text{ComVrfy}(\text{crs}, C, \pi_{\text{Com}}) = \text{DecomVrfy}(\text{crs}, C, m, \pi_{\text{Decom}}) = 1$$

and FDecom(crs, C) = m.

To commit to message m, the committer runs Com to get C, π_{Com}, and π_{Decom}, and sends C and π_{Com} to a receiver. The receiver can run ComVrfy to check that C can be forcibly decommitted (if need be). To decommit, the committer sends m and π_{Decom} to the receiver, who can then run DecomVrfy to verify the claimed opening. If the committer refuses to decommit, C be opened using FDecom. NITCs are generally only interesting when $t_{fo} \gg t_{cv}, t_{dv}$, i.e., when forced opening of a commitment takes longer than the initial verification and decommitment verification.

NITCs must satisfy appropriate notions of both hiding and binding.

Hiding. For hiding, we introduce a notion of *non-malleability* for NITCs based on the CCA-security notion for (standard) commitments by Canetti et al. [10]. Specifically, we require hiding to hold even when the adversary is given access to an oracle that provides the (forced) openings of commitments of the adversary's choice. In the timed setting, the motivation behind providing the adversary with such an oracle is that (honest) parties may be running machines that can force open commitments at different speeds. As such, the adversary (as part of the higher-level protocol) could trick some party into opening commitments of the attacker's choice. Note that although the adversary could run the forced opening algorithm itself, doing so would incur a cost; in contrast, the adversary only incurs a cost of one time unit to make a query to the oracle.

Definition 11. *For an NITC scheme* TC *and algorithm* $\mathcal{A}$, *define experiment* **IND-CCA$_{\text{TC}}$** *as follows:*

1. *Compute* crs $\leftarrow$ PGen(1^κ).
2. *Run* $\mathcal{A}$ *on input* crs *with access to a decommit oracle* FDecom(crs, $\cdot$) *in a preprocessing phase.*
3. *When* $\mathcal{A}$ *outputs* (m_0, m_1), *choose a uniform bit* $b \leftarrow \{0,1\}$, *compute* $(C, \pi_{\text{Com}}, \star) \leftarrow$ Com(crs, m_b), *and run* $\mathcal{A}$ *on input* (C, π_{Com}) *in the online phase.* $\mathcal{A}$ *continues to have access to* FDecom(crs, $\cdot$), *except that* $\mathcal{A}$ *may not query this oracle on* C.

4. When $\mathcal{A}$ outputs a bit b', the experiment evaluates to 1 iff $b' = b$.

TC *is* (t_p, t_o, ϵ)-CCA-secure *if for all adversaries $\mathcal{A}$ running in preprocessing time t_p and online time t_o,*

$$\Pr\left[\textbf{IND-CCA}_{\textsf{TC}}^{\mathcal{A}} = 1\right] \leq \frac{1}{2} + \epsilon.$$

Binding. The binding property states that a commitment cannot be opened to two different messages. It also ensures that the receiver does not accept commitments that cannot be forced open to the correct message.

Definition 12 (BND-CCA Security for Commitments). *For a NITC scheme* TC *and algorithm $\mathcal{A}$, define experiment* $\textbf{BND-CCA}_{\textsf{TC}}$ *as follows:*

1. Compute $\textsf{crs} \leftarrow \textsf{PGen}(1^\kappa)$.
2. Run $\mathcal{A}$ on input $\textsf{crs}$ *with access to a decommit oracle* $\textsf{FDecom}(\textsf{crs}, \cdot)$.
3. When $\mathcal{A}$ outputs $(m, C, \pi_{\textsf{Com}}, \pi_{\textsf{Decom}}, m', \pi'_{\textsf{Decom}})$, *the experiment evaluates to 1 iff* $\textsf{ComVrfy}(\textsf{crs}, C, \pi_{\textsf{Com}}) = \textsf{DecomVrfy}(\textsf{crs}, C, m, \pi_{\textsf{Decom}}) = 1$ *and either of the following holds:*
   – $m' \neq m$ and $\textsf{DecomVrfy}(\textsf{crs}, C, m', \pi'_{\textsf{Decom}}) = 1$;
   – $\textsf{FDecom}(\textsf{crs}, C) \neq m$.

TC *is* (t, ϵ)-BND-CCA-secure *if for all adversaries $\mathcal{A}$ running in time t,*

$$\Pr\left[\textbf{BND-CCA}_{\textsf{TC}}^{\mathcal{A}} = 1\right] \leq \epsilon.$$

Time-Released Public-Key Encryption. TPKE can be thought of the counterpart of timed commitments for public-key encryption. As in the case of standard public-key encryption (PKE), a sender encrypts a message for a designated recipient using the recipient's public key; that recipient can decrypt and recover the message. *Timed* PKE additionally supports the ability for anyone (and not just the sender) to also recover the message, but only by investing more computational effort.

Definition 13. *A* (t_e, t_{fd}, t_{sd})-timed public-key encryption (TPKE) *scheme is a tuple of algorithms* $\textsf{TPKE} = (\textsf{KGen}, \textsf{Enc}, \textsf{Dec}_f, \textsf{Dec}_s)$ *with the following behavior:*

   – The randomized key-generation algorithm KGen *takes as input the security parameter 1^κ and outputs a pair of keys (pk, sk). We assume, for simplicity, that sk includes pk.*
   – The randomized encryption algorithm Enc *takes as input a public key pk and a message m, and outputs a ciphertext c. It runs in time at most t_e.*
   – The deterministic fast decryption algorithm $\textsf{Dec}_f$ *takes as input a secret key sk and a ciphertext c, and outputs a message m or $\perp$. It runs in time at most t_{fd}.*
   – The deterministic slow decryption algorithm $\textsf{Dec}_s$ *takes as input a public key pk and a ciphertext c, and outputs a message m or $\perp$. It runs in time* **at least** t_{sd}.

We require that for all (pk, sk) output by $\mathsf{KGen}(1^\kappa)$, all m, and all c output by $\mathsf{Enc}(pk, m)$, it holds that $\mathsf{Dec}_f(sk, c) = \mathsf{Dec}_s(pk, c) = m$.

Such schemes are only interesting when $t_{fd} \ll t_{sd}$, i.e., when fast decryption is much faster than slow decryption.

We consider security of TPKE against chosen-ciphertext attacks.

Definition 14. *For a TPKE scheme* TPKE *and algorithm* $\mathcal{A}$, *define experiment* $\mathbf{IND\text{-}CCA}^{\mathcal{A}}_{\mathsf{TPKE}}$ *as follows:*

1. *Compute* $(pk, sk) \leftarrow \mathsf{KGen}(1^\kappa)$.
2. *Run* $\mathcal{A}$ *on input* pk *with access to a decryption oracle* $\mathsf{Dec}_f(sk, \cdot)$ *in a pre-processing phase.*
3. *When* $\mathcal{A}$ *outputs* (m_0, m_1), *choose* $b \leftarrow \{0, 1\}$, *compute* $c \leftarrow \mathsf{Enc}(pk, m_b)$, *and run* $\mathcal{A}$ *on input* c *in the online phase.* $\mathcal{A}$ *continues to have access to* $\mathsf{Dec}_f(sk, \cdot)$, *except that* $\mathcal{A}$ *may not query this oracle on* c.
4. *When* $\mathcal{A}$ *outputs a bit* b', *the experiment evaluates to 1 iff* $b' = b$.

TPKE *is* (t_p, t_o, ϵ)-*CCA-secure iff for all* $\mathcal{A}$ *with preprocessing time* t_p *and online time* t_o,

$$\Pr\left[\mathbf{IND\text{-}CCA}^{\mathcal{A}}_{\mathsf{TPKE}} = 1\right] \le \frac{1}{2} + \epsilon.$$

We remark that in order for TPKE to be an independently interesting primitive, one might require that even for maliciously formed ciphertexts c, Dec_s and Dec_f always produce the same output (a property indeed enjoyed by our TPKE scheme in the next section). However, since our primary motivation is to obtain commitment schemes, we do not require this property and hence opt for a simpler definition that only requires correctness (i.e., of honestly generated ciphertexts).

4.2 CCA-Secure TPKE

Here we describe a construction of a TPKE scheme that is CCA-secure under the decisional RSW assumption. While our construction is in the standard model, it suffers from a slow encryption algorithm. In the full version of our paper, we describe a CCA-secure construction in the ROM in which encryption can be sped up, using the secret key.

The starting point of our construction is a CPA-secure TPKE scheme based on the decisional RSW assumption. In this scheme, the public key is a modulus N and a generator $g \in \mathbb{QR}_N$; the secret key contains $\phi(N)$. To encrypt a message $m \in \mathbf{Z}_N$ s.t. $\|m\| < \tau(\kappa) - 1$, the sender encodes m as $\mathbf{M} := m^2 \in \mathbb{QR}_N$. It then first computes a random generator $\mathbf{R}$ (by raising g to a random power modulo N), and then computes the ciphertext $(\mathbf{R}, \mathbf{R}^{2^T} \cdot \mathbf{M} \bmod N)$. This ciphertext can be decrypted quickly using $\phi(N)$, but can also be decrypted slowly without knowledge of the secret key. (To decode to the original m, one can just compute the square root over the integers, since $m^2 < N$.)

For any modulus N_1, N_2 and integer T, define the relation

$$R_{N_1,N_2,T} = \left\{ ((\mathbf{R}_1, \mathbf{R}_2, \mathbf{X}_1, \mathbf{X}_2), \mathbf{M}) \mid \bigwedge_{i=1,2} \mathbf{X}_i = \mathbf{R}_i^{2^T} \cdot \mathbf{M} \bmod N_i \right\}$$

Let (GenZK, Prove, Vrfy) be a $(t_{pr}, t_v, t_{sgen}, t_{sp})$-NIZK proof system for this relation. Define a TPKE scheme (parameterized by T) as follows:

- KGen(1^κ): For $i = 1, 2$ run $(N_i, p_i, q_i) \leftarrow$ GenMod(1^κ), compute $\phi_i :=$ $\phi(N_i) = (p_i - 1)(q_i - 1)$, set $z_i := 2^T \bmod \phi_i$. Choose $g_i \leftarrow \mathbb{QR}_{N_i}$ and run crs $\leftarrow$ GenZK(1^κ). Output $pk := (\text{crs}, N_1, N_2, g_1, g_2)$ and $sk :=$ $(\text{crs}, N_1, N_2, g_1, g_2, z_1, z_2)$.
- Enc$((\text{crs}, N_1, N_2, g_1, g_2), \mathbf{M})$: For $i = 1, 2$, choose $r_i \leftarrow \mathbb{Z}_{N_i^2}$ and compute

$$\mathbf{R}_i := g_i^{r_i} \bmod N_i, \quad \mathbf{Z}_i := \mathbf{R}_i^{2^T} \bmod N_i, \quad \mathbf{C}_i := \mathbf{Z}_i \cdot \mathbf{M} \bmod N_i,$$

  where the exponentiations are computed using RepSqr. Also compute $\pi \leftarrow$ Prove(crs, $(\mathbf{R}_1, \mathbf{R}_2, \mathbf{C}_1, \mathbf{C}_2), \mathbf{M}$). Output the ciphertext $(\mathbf{R}_1, \mathbf{R}_2, \mathbf{C}_1, \mathbf{C}_2, \pi)$.
- Dec$_f((\text{crs}, N_1, N_2, g_1, g_2, z_1, z_2), (\mathbf{R}_1, \mathbf{R}_2, \mathbf{C}_1, \mathbf{C}_2, \pi))$:   If Vrfy(crs, $(\mathbf{R}_1, \mathbf{R}_2, \mathbf{C}_1, \mathbf{C}_2), \pi) = 0$, then output $\perp$. Else compute $\mathbf{Z}_1 := \mathbf{R}_1^{z_1} \bmod N_1$ (using RepSqr) and $\mathbf{M} := \mathbf{C}_1 \mathbf{Z}_1^{-1} \bmod N$, and then output $\mathbf{M}$ if $||\mathbf{M}|| < \tau(\kappa)$ and $\perp$ otherwise.
- Dec$_s((\text{crs}, N_1, N_2, g_1, g_2), (\mathbf{R}_1, \mathbf{R}_2, \mathbf{C}_1, \mathbf{C}_2, \pi))$: If Vrfy(crs, $(\mathbf{R}_1, \mathbf{R}_2, \mathbf{C}_1, \mathbf{C}_2), \pi)$ $= 0$, then output $\perp$. Else compute $\mathbf{Z}_1 := \mathbf{R}_1^{2^T} \bmod N_1$ (using RepSqr) and $\mathbf{M} := \mathbf{C}_1 \mathbf{Z}_1^{-1} \bmod N_1$, and then output $\mathbf{M}$ if $||\mathbf{M}|| < \tau(\kappa)$ and $\perp$ otherwise..

Fig. 1. A CCA-secure TPKE scheme

We can obtain a CCA-secure TPKE scheme by suitably adapting the Naor-Yung paradigm [26,31] to the setting of timed encryption. The Naor-Yung approach constructs a CCA-secure encryption scheme by encrypting a message twice using independent instances of a CPA-secure encryption scheme accompanied by a simulation-sound NIZK proof of consistency between the two ciphertexts. In our setting, we need the NIZK proof system to also have "fast" verification and simulation (specifically, linear in the size of the input instance). We present the details of our construction in Fig. 1.

Subtleties in the Simulation. The proof of security in our context requires the ability to simulate both the challenge ciphertext and the decryption oracle using a "fast" decryption algorithm. The reason behind this is that if it were not possible to simulate decryption fast, then the reduction from the decisional RSW assumption would take too much time simulating the experiment for the adversary. Fast simulation is possible for two reasons. First, in the proof of the Naor-Yung construction, the simulator knows (at least) one of the secret keys at any time. Second, we use a NIZK with simulation soundness for which verification and proof simulation take linear time in the size of the instance (but not in the size of the circuit). Using these two components, the simulator can perform fast decryption on any correctly formed ciphertext. To reduce from decisional RSW, it embeds the decisional RSW challenge into the challenge ciphertext component for which the secret key is *not* known.

Concretely, for integers N s.t. $N = pq$ for primes p and q, let $\mathcal{C}$ be an arithmetic circuit over $\mathbb{Z}_N$, and let $\mathsf{SAT}_\mathcal{C}$ denote the set of all $(x, w) \in \{0, 1\}^*$ s.t. w is a satisfying assignment to $\mathcal{C}$ when $\mathcal{C}$'s wires are fixed according to the instance x. The works of Groth and Maller [16] as well as Lipmaa [20] show NIZK constructions for $\mathsf{SAT}_\mathcal{C}$ which have soundness and simulation soundness (with suitable parameters), perfect zero-knowledge, perfect correctness and are such that for all $\mathsf{crs} \in \{\mathsf{GenZK}(1^\kappa)\}$, $(\mathsf{crs}', td) \in \{\mathsf{SimGen}(1^\kappa)\}$, all $(x, w) \in \mathsf{SAT}_\mathcal{C}$ and all $x' \in \{0, 1\}^*$:

- For all $\pi \in \{\mathsf{Prove}(\mathsf{crs}, x, w)\}$, Vrfy runs within time $O(|x|)$ on input (crs, x, π).
- For all $\pi' \in \{\mathsf{SimProve}(x', td)\}$, Vrfy runs within time $O(|x'|)$ on input $(\mathsf{crs}', x', \pi')$.
- On input (x', td), $\mathsf{SimProve}$ runs in time $O(|x'|)$.

In other words, both Vrfy and $\mathsf{SimProve}$ run in a fast manner, i.e., linear in the scale of the input instance.

We remark that both of the above constructions work over $\mathbb{Z}_p$ for primes p only, but can be translated to circuits over $\mathbb{Z}_N$, where N is composite, with small overhead, as shown in [18]. The idea is very simple: any arithmetic operation over $\mathbb{Z}_N$ is emulated using multiple (smaller) values in $\mathbb{Z}_p$. The multiplicative overhead in this construction is roughly linear in the size difference between p and N and is ignored here for readability.

Theorem 4. *Suppose* NIZK *is* $(t_p + t_o, 2\epsilon_{ZK})$-*zero-knowledge and* $(t_p + t_o + \theta(\kappa), \epsilon_{SS})$-*simulation sound, and the decisional* T-*RSW problem is* $(t_p + T + t_{sg} + \theta(\kappa), t_o + t_{sp}, \epsilon_{DRSW})$-*hard relative to* GenMod. *Then the* $(t_{pr} + T, t_v + \theta(\kappa), T + \theta(\kappa))$-*TPKE scheme in Fig. 1 is* $(t_p, t_o, \epsilon_{ZK} + \epsilon_{SS} + 2\epsilon_{DRSW})$-*CCA-secure.*

Proof. Let $\mathcal{A}$ be an adversary with preprocessing time t_p and online time t_o. We define a sequence of experiments as follows.

Expt_0: This is the original CCA-security experiment **IND-CCA**$_{\mathsf{TPKE}}$. Denote $\mathcal{A}$'s challenge ciphertext by $(\mathbf{R}_1^*, \mathbf{R}_2^*, \mathbf{C}_1^*, \mathbf{C}_2^*, \pi^*)$.

Expt_1: Expt_1 is identical to Expt_0, except that crs and π^* are simulated. That is, in Gen run $(\mathsf{crs}, td) \leftarrow \mathsf{SimGen}(1^\kappa)$, and in the challenge ciphertext compute $\pi^* \leftarrow \mathsf{SimProve}((\mathbf{R}_1^*, \mathbf{R}_2^*, \mathbf{C}_1^*, \mathbf{C}_2^*), td)$.

We upper bound $|\Pr[\mathsf{Expt}_1^{\mathcal{A}} = 1] - \Pr[\mathsf{Expt}_0^{\mathcal{A}} = 1]|$ by constructing a reduction $\mathcal{R}_{ZK}$ to the zero-knowledge property of NIZK. $\mathcal{R}_{ZK}$ runs the code of Expt_0, except that it publishes the CRS from the zero-knowledge challenger, and uses the zero-knowledge proof from the zero-knowledge challenger as part of the challenge ciphertext. Concretely, $\mathcal{R}_{ZK}$ works as follows:

- Setup: $\mathcal{R}_{ZK}$, on input crs^*, for $i = 1, 2$ runs $(N_i, p_i, q_i) \leftarrow \mathsf{GenMod}(1^\kappa)$, computes $\phi_i := \phi(N_i) = (p_i - 1)(q_i - 1)$, sets $z_i := 2^T \bmod \phi_i$, and chooses

$g_i \leftarrow \mathbb{QR}_{N_i}$. Then $\mathcal{R}_{ZK}$ runs $\mathcal{A}(N, g, \mathsf{crs}^*)$.

$\mathcal{R}_{ZK}$ answers $\mathcal{A}$'s DEC queries using the fast decryption algorithm Dec_f. That is, on $\mathcal{A}$'s query $\mathsf{DEC}(\mathbf{R}_1, \mathbf{R}_2, \mathbf{C}_1, \mathbf{C}_2, \pi)$, $\mathcal{R}_{ZK}$ computes $\mathbf{Z}_1 := \mathsf{RepSqr}(\mathbf{R}_1, N_1, z_1)$ and $\mathbf{M} := \dfrac{\mathbf{C}_1}{\mathbf{Z}_1} \bmod N_1$; if $\mathsf{Vrfy}(\mathbf{R}_1, \mathbf{R}_2, \mathbf{C}_1, \mathbf{C}_2, \pi) = 1$ then $\mathcal{R}_{ZK}$ returns $\mathbf{M}$, otherwise $\mathcal{R}_{ZK}$ returns $\perp$.

- Online phase: When $\mathcal{A}$ makes its challenge query on $(\mathbf{M}_0, \mathbf{M}_1)$, $\mathcal{R}_{ZK}$ chooses $b \leftarrow \{0, 1\}$ and for $i = 1, 2$ chooses $r_1, r_2 \leftarrow \mathbb{Z}_{N^2}$, and computes

$$\mathbf{R}_i^* := \mathsf{RepSqr}(g_i, N_i, r_i), \quad \mathbf{Z}_i^* := \mathsf{RepSqr}(\mathbf{R}_i^*, N_i, z_i), \quad \mathbf{C}_i^* := \mathbf{Z}_i^* \cdot \mathbf{M} \bmod N_i,$$

$$\pi^* \leftarrow \mathsf{PROVE}((\mathbf{R}_1^*, \mathbf{R}_2^*, \mathbf{C}_1^*, \mathbf{C}_2^*), \mathbf{M}_b),$$

and outputs $(\mathbf{R}_1^*, \mathbf{R}_2^*, \mathbf{C}_1^*, \mathbf{C}_2^*, \pi^*)$. After that, $\mathcal{R}_{ZK}$ answers $\mathcal{A}$'s DEC queries just as in setup.

- Output: On $\mathcal{A}$'s output bit b', $\mathcal{R}_{ZK}$ outputs 1 if $b' = b$, and 0 otherwise.

$\mathcal{R}_{ZK}$ runs in time $t_p + t_o + 2\theta(\kappa)$ (t_p in the setup phase and $t_o + 2\theta(\kappa)$ in the online phase), and

$$|\Pr[\mathsf{Expt}_1^{\mathcal{A}} = 1] - \Pr[\mathsf{Expt}_0^{\mathcal{A}} = 1]| \le \epsilon_{ZK}.$$

Expt_2: Expt_2 is identical to Expt_1, except that $\mathbf{C}_2^*$ is computed as $\mathbf{U}_2 \cdot \mathbf{M}_b \bmod N_2$ (instead of $\mathbf{Z}_2^* \cdot \mathbf{M}_b \bmod N_2$), where $\mathbf{U}_2 := \mathsf{RepSqr}(g_2, N_2, u_2)$ and $u_2 \leftarrow \mathbb{Z}_{N_2^2}$.

We upper bound $|\Pr[\mathsf{Expt}_2^{\mathcal{A}} = 1] - \Pr[\mathsf{Expt}_1^{\mathcal{A}} = 1]|$ by constructing a reduction $\mathcal{R}_{DRSW}$ to the decisional T-RSW problem. $\mathcal{R}_{DRSW}$ runs the code of Expt_2, except that it does not know ϕ_2, and uses the group elements from the decisional T-RSW challenger as part of the challenge ciphertext. (Note that $\mathcal{A}$'s DEC queries can still be answered in a fast manner, since the decryption algorithm only uses $\mathbf{R}_1$, and $\mathcal{R}_{DRSW}$ knows ϕ_1.) Concretely, $\mathcal{R}_{DRSW}$ works as follows:

- Preprocessing phase: $\mathcal{R}_{DRSW}$, on input N, runs $(N_1, p_1, q_1) \leftarrow \mathsf{GenMod}(1^\kappa)$, computes $\phi_1 := \phi(N_1) = (p_1 - 1)(q_1 - 1)$, sets $z_1 := 2^T \bmod \phi_1$, and chooses $g_1 \leftarrow \mathbb{QR}_{N_1}$, $g \leftarrow \mathbb{QR}_N$; runs $(\mathsf{crs}, td) \leftarrow \mathsf{SimGen}(1^\kappa)$. Then $\mathcal{R}_{DRSW}$ runs $\mathcal{A}(\mathsf{crs}, N_1, N, g_1, g)$. $\mathcal{R}_{DRSW}$ answers $\mathcal{A}$'s DEC queries as described in Expt_1.

- Online phase: When $\mathcal{A}$ makes its challenge query on $(\mathbf{M}_0, \mathbf{M}_1)$, $\mathcal{R}_{DRSW}$ asks for $(g^*, \mathbf{X}^*)$ from the decisional RSW challenger, chooses $b \leftarrow \{0, 1\}$ and $r_1 \leftarrow \mathbb{Z}_{N_1^2}$, and computes

$$\mathbf{R}_1^* := \mathsf{RepSqr}(g_1, N_1, r_1), \quad \mathbf{Z}_1^* := \mathsf{RepSqr}(\mathbf{R}_1^*, N_1, z_1), \quad \mathbf{C}_1^* := \mathbf{Z}_1^* \cdot \mathbf{M}_b \bmod N_1,$$

$$\pi^* \leftarrow \mathsf{SimProve}((\mathbf{R}_1^*, g^*, \mathbf{C}_1^*, \mathbf{X}^* \cdot \mathbf{M}_b), td),$$

and returns $(\mathbf{R}_1^*, g^*, \mathbf{C}_1^*, \mathbf{X}^* \cdot \mathbf{M}_b, \pi^*)$. $\mathcal{R}$ answers $\mathcal{A}$'s DEC queries as described in Expt_1.

- Output: On $\mathcal{A}$'s output bit b', $\mathcal{R}_{DRSW}$ outputs 1 if $b' = b$, and 0 otherwise.

$\mathcal{R}_{DRSW}$ runs in time $t_p + t_{sgen}$ in the preprocessing phase, and time $t_o + t_{sprove}$ in the online phase, and

$$| \Pr[\mathsf{Expt}_2^{\mathcal{A}} = 1] - \Pr[\mathsf{Expt}_1^{\mathcal{A}} = 1]| \leq \epsilon_{DRSW}.$$

Expt_3: Expt_3 is identical to Expt_2, except that $\mathbf{C}_2^*$ is computed as $\mathbf{U}_2$ (instead of $\mathbf{U}_2 \cdot \mathbf{M}_b$). Since the distributions of $\mathbf{U}_2$ and $\mathbf{U}_2 \cdot \mathbf{M}_b$ are both uniform, this is merely a conceptual change, so

$$\Pr[\mathsf{Expt}_3^{\mathcal{A}} = 1] = \Pr[\mathsf{Expt}_2^{\mathcal{A}} = 1].$$

Expt_4: Expt_4 is identical to Expt_3, except that the DEC oracle uses $\mathbf{R}_2$ (instead of $\mathbf{R}_1$) to decrypt. That is, when $\mathcal{A}$ queries $\mathsf{DEC}(\mathbf{R}_1, \mathbf{R}_2, \mathbf{C}_1, \mathbf{C}_2, \pi)$, compute $\mathbf{Z}_2 := \mathsf{RepSqr}(\mathbf{R}_2, N_2, z_2)$ and $\mathbf{M} := \dfrac{\mathbf{C}_2}{\mathbf{Z}_2} \bmod N_2$.

Expt_4 and Expt_3 are identical unless $\mathcal{A}$ makes a query $\mathsf{DEC}(\mathbf{R}_1, \mathbf{R}_2, \mathbf{C}_1, \mathbf{C}_2, \pi)$ s.t. $\dfrac{\mathbf{C}_1}{\mathbf{R}_1^{2^T}} \bmod N_1 \neq \dfrac{\mathbf{C}_2}{\mathbf{R}_2^{2^T}} \bmod N_2$ (over $\mathbb{Z}$) but $\mathsf{Vrfy}(\mathbf{R}_1, \mathbf{R}_2, \mathbf{C}_1, \mathbf{C}_2, \pi) = 1$ (in which case $\mathcal{A}$ receives $\dfrac{\mathbf{C}_1}{\mathbf{R}_1^{2^T}} \bmod N_1$ in Expt_3 and $\dfrac{\mathbf{C}_2}{\mathbf{R}_2^{2^T}} \bmod N_2$ in Expt_4; in all other cases $\mathcal{A}$ receives either $\bot$ in both experiments, or $\dfrac{\mathbf{C}_1}{\mathbf{R}_1^{2^T}} \bmod N_1 = \dfrac{\mathbf{C}_2}{\mathbf{R}_2^{2^T}} \bmod N_2$ in both experiments). Denote this event Fake. We upper bound $\Pr[\mathsf{Fake}]$ by constructing a reduction $\mathcal{R}_{SS}$ to the simulation soundness of NIZK:

- Setup: $\mathcal{R}_{SS}$, on input crs, for $i = 1, 2$ runs $(N_i, p_i, q_i) \leftarrow \mathsf{GenMod}(1^\kappa)$, computes $\phi_i := \phi(N_i) = (p_i - 1)(q_i - 1)$, sets $z_i := 2^T \bmod \phi_i$, and chooses $g_i \leftarrow \mathbb{QR}_{N_i}$. Then $\mathcal{R}_{SS}$ runs $\mathcal{A}(N, g, \mathsf{crs})$.

  On $\mathcal{A}$'s query $\mathsf{DEC}(\mathbf{R}_1, \mathbf{R}_2, \mathbf{C}_1, \mathbf{C}_2, \pi)$, $\mathcal{R}_{SS}$ computes $\mathbf{Z}_1$ and $\mathbf{Z}_2$ as described in Expt_1. If $\mathsf{Vrfy}(\mathbf{R}_1, \mathbf{R}_2, \mathbf{C}_1, \mathbf{C}_2, \pi) = 0$, then $\mathcal{R}_{SS}$ returns $\bot$; otherwise $\mathcal{R}_{SS}$ checks if $\dfrac{\mathbf{C}_1}{\mathbf{R}_1^{2^T}} \bmod N_1 = \dfrac{\mathbf{C}_2}{\mathbf{R}_2^{2^T}} \bmod N_2$, and if so, it returns $\dfrac{\mathbf{C}_1}{\mathbf{R}_1^{2^T}} \bmod N_1$, otherwise it outputs $((\mathbf{R}_1, \mathbf{R}_2, \mathbf{C}_1, \mathbf{C}_2), \pi)$ to its challenger (and halts).
- Online phase: When $\mathcal{A}$ makes its challenge query on $(\mathbf{M}_0, \mathbf{M}_1)$, $\mathcal{R}_{SS}$ chooses $b \leftarrow \{0, 1\}$ and computes

$$\mathbf{R}_1^* := \mathsf{RepSqr}(g_1, N_1, r_1), \quad \mathbf{Z}_1^* := \mathsf{RepSqr}(\mathbf{R}_1^*, N_1, z_1), \quad \mathbf{C}_1^* := \mathbf{Z}_1^* \cdot \mathbf{M}_b \bmod N_1,$$

$$u_2 \leftarrow \mathbb{Z}_{N_2^2}, \mathbf{C}_2^* := \mathsf{RepSqr}(g_2, N_2, u_2),$$

$$\pi^* \leftarrow \mathsf{SPROVE}((\mathbf{R}_1^*, \mathbf{R}_2^*, \mathbf{C}_1^*, \mathbf{C}_2^*), td),$$

and outputs $(\mathbf{R}_1^*, \mathbf{R}_2^*, \mathbf{C}_1^*, \mathbf{C}_2^*, \pi^*)$. After that, $\mathcal{R}_{SS}$ answers $\mathcal{A}$'s $\mathsf{DEC}(\mathbf{R}_1, \mathbf{R}_2, \mathbf{C}_1, \mathbf{C}_2, \pi)$ query just as in setup.

$\mathcal{R}_{SS}$ runs in time at most $t_p + t_o + \theta(\kappa)$ (i.e., t_p in the setup phase and $t_o + \theta(\kappa)$ in the online phase). Up to the point that $\mathcal{R}_{SS}$ outputs, $\mathcal{R}_{SS}$ simulates Expt_4 perfectly. If Fake happens, then $\mathcal{R}_{SS}$ outputs $((\mathbf{R}_1, \mathbf{R}_2, \mathbf{C}_1, \mathbf{C}_2), \pi)$ s.t. $\dfrac{\mathbf{C}_1}{\mathbf{R}_1^{2^T}} \bmod N_1 \neq \dfrac{\mathbf{C}_2}{\mathbf{R}_2^{2^T}} \bmod N_2$ but $\mathsf{Vrfy}(\mathbf{R}_1, \mathbf{R}_2, \mathbf{C}_1, \mathbf{C}_2, \pi) = 1$, winning the simulation-soundness experiment. It follows that

$$| \Pr[\mathsf{Expt}_4^{\mathcal{A}} = 1] - \Pr[\mathsf{Expt}_3^{\mathcal{A}} = 1]| \leq \Pr[\mathsf{Fake}] \leq \Pr[\mathcal{R}_{SS} \text{ wins}] \leq \epsilon_{SS}.$$

Expt_5: Expt_5 is identical to Expt_4, except that $\mathbf{C}_1^*$ is computed as $\mathbf{U} \cdot \mathbf{M}_b \bmod N_1$ (instead of $\mathbf{Z}_1^* \cdot \mathbf{M}_b \bmod N_1$), where $\mathbf{U}_1 := \mathsf{RepSqr}(g_1, N_1, u_1)$ and $u_1 \leftarrow \mathbb{Z}_{N_1^2}$. The argument is symmetric to the one from Expt_1 to Expt_2; the reduction works because $\mathbf{R}_1$ is not used in DEC. We have

$$| \Pr[\mathsf{Expt}_5^{\mathcal{A}} = 1] - \Pr[\mathsf{Expt}_4^{\mathcal{A}} = 1]| \leq \epsilon_{DRSW}.$$

Expt_6: Expt_6 is identical to Expt_5, except that $\mathbf{C}_1^*$ is computed as $\mathbf{U}_1$ (instead of $\mathbf{U}_1 \cdot \mathbf{M}_b$). The argument is symmetric to the one from Expt_2 to Expt_3. We have

$$\Pr[\mathsf{Expt}_6^{\mathcal{A}} = 1] = \Pr[\mathsf{Expt}_5^{\mathcal{A}} = 1].$$

Furthermore, since b is independent of $\mathcal{A}$'s view in Expt_6, we have

$$\Pr[\mathsf{Expt}_6^{\mathcal{A}} = 1] = \frac{1}{2}.$$

Summing up the results above, we conclude that

$$\Pr\left[\mathbf{IND\text{-}CCA}_{\mathsf{TPKE}}^{\mathcal{A}} = 1\right] \leq \frac{1}{2} + \epsilon_{ZK} + \epsilon_{SS} + 2\epsilon_{DRSW},$$

which completes the proof.

4.3 Constructing Non-malleable Timed Commitments

In this section, we show how our notion of CCA-secure TPKE implies non-malleable timed commitments. The idea is very simple. At setup, the committer generates the parameters and keys for a TPKE TPKE and NIZKs $\mathsf{NIZK}_{\mathsf{Com}}$ and $\mathsf{NIZK}_{\mathsf{Decom}}$. To commit to a message m, the committer computes $c := \mathsf{Enc}(pk, m; r)$ (for some random coins r) and uses $\mathsf{NIZK}_{\mathsf{Com}}$ and $\mathsf{NIZK}_{\mathsf{Decom}}$ to prove that (1) it knows (m, r) s.t. $c = \mathsf{Enc}(pk, m; r)$. This proof will be used as π_{Com}, i.e., to prove that the commitment is well-formed; and (2) it knows r s.t. $c = \mathsf{Enc}(pk, m; r)$. This proof will be used as π_{Decom}, i.e., to prove (efficiently) that the opening to the commitment is the correct one. Our construction is presented in Fig. 2.

To be able to reduce from CCA-security of the underlying TPKE scheme for meaningful parameters, we require that proofs of the NIZK scheme can be simulated and verified (very) efficiently, i.e., take much less time than a forced decommit. This is satisfied when instantiating the TPKE scheme with our construction from the previous section, where this relation can be expressed via an arithmetic circuit. More generally, any scheme whose encryption algorithm can be expressed via an arithmetic circuit would satisfy our requirements.

Let $\mathsf{TPKE} = (\mathsf{KGen}, \mathsf{Enc}, \mathsf{Dec}_f, \mathsf{Dec}_s)$ be a (t_e, t_{fd}, t_{sd})-TPKE scheme, $\mathsf{NIZK_{Com}} = (\mathsf{GenZK_{Com}}, \mathsf{Prove_{Com}}, \mathsf{Vrfy_{Com}}, \mathsf{SimGen_{Com}}, \mathsf{SimProve_{Com}})$ be a $(t_{cp}, t_{cv}, t_{csgen}, t_{csp})$-NIZK for relation

$$R_{\mathsf{Com}} = \{(c, (m, r)) \mid c = \mathsf{Enc}(pk, m; r)\},$$

and $\mathsf{NIZK_{Decom}} = (\mathsf{GenZK_{Decom}}, \mathsf{Prove_{Decom}}, \mathsf{Vrfy_{Decom}}, \mathsf{SimGen_{Decom}}, \mathsf{SimProve_{Decom}})$ be a $(t_{dp}, t_{dv}, t_{dsgen}, t_{dsp})$-NIZK for relation

$$R_{\mathsf{Decom}} = \{((c, m), r) \mid c = \mathsf{Enc}(pk, m; r)\}.$$

Define an NITC scheme as follows:

- $\mathsf{PGen}(1^\kappa)$: Run $(pk, sk) \leftarrow \mathsf{KGen}(1^\kappa)$, $\mathsf{crs_{Com}} \leftarrow \mathsf{GenZK_{Com}}(1^\kappa)$, $\mathsf{crs_{Decom}} \leftarrow \mathsf{GenZK_{Decom}}(1^\kappa)$, and output $\mathsf{crs} := (pk, \mathsf{crs_{Com}}, \mathsf{crs_{Decom}})$.
- $\mathsf{Com}((pk, \mathsf{crs_{Com}}, \mathsf{crs_{Decom}}), m)$: Choose random coins r, compute $c := \mathsf{Enc}(pk, m; r)$, $\pi_{\mathsf{Com}} \leftarrow \mathsf{Prove}(\mathsf{crs_{Com}}, c, (m, r))$, $\pi_{\mathsf{Decom}} \leftarrow \mathsf{Prove}(\mathsf{crs_{Decom}}, (c, m), r)$, and output $(c, \pi_{\mathsf{Com}}, \pi_{\mathsf{Decom}})$.
- $\mathsf{ComVrfy}((pk, \mathsf{crs_{Com}}, \mathsf{crs_{Decom}}), c, \pi_{\mathsf{Com}})$: Output $\mathsf{Vrfy_{Com}}(\mathsf{crs_{Com}}, c, \pi_{\mathsf{Com}})$.
- $\mathsf{DecomVrfy}((pk, \mathsf{crs_{Com}}, \mathsf{crs_{Decom}}), c, m, \pi_{\mathsf{Decom}})$: Output $\mathsf{Vrfy_{Decom}}(\mathsf{crs_{Decom}}, (c, m), \pi_{\mathsf{Decom}})$.
- $\mathsf{FDecom}((pk, \mathsf{crs_{Com}}, \mathsf{crs_{Decom}}), c)$: Output $\mathsf{Dec}_s(pk, c)$.

Fig. 2. An NITC scheme.

Correctness of this scheme follows immediately from correctness of the underlying TPKE and NIZK schemes; we next show its CCA-security.

Theorem 5. *Suppose* TPKE *is* $(t_p + t_{csgen}, t_{csp}, \epsilon_{TPKE})$-*CCA-secure, and* $\mathsf{NIZK_{Com}}$ *is* $(t_p + t_o + t_e, \epsilon_{ZK})$-*zero-knowledge. Then the* $(t_e + \max\{t_{cp}, t_{dp}\}, t_{cv}, t_{dv}, t_{sd})$-*NITCS scheme in Fig. 2 is* $(t_p, t_o, \epsilon_{ZK} + \epsilon_{CCA})$-*CCA-secure.*

Proof. Let $\mathcal{A}$ be an adversary with preprocessing time t_p and online time t_o. Suppose $\mathcal{A}$'s challenge is (c^*, π^*). We define a sequence of experiments as follows.

Expt_0: This is the original CCA-security experiment **IND-CCA$_{\mathsf{TC}}$**.

Expt_1: Expt_1 is identical to Expt_0, except that $\mathsf{crs_{Com}}$ and π^* are simulated. That is, in the setup phase run $(\mathsf{crs_{Com}}, td) \leftarrow \mathsf{SimGen_{Com}}(1^\kappa)$, and in the challenge compute $\pi^* \leftarrow \mathsf{SimProve_{Com}}(c^*, td)$.

We upper bound $|\Pr[\mathsf{Expt}_1^{\mathcal{A}} = 1] - \Pr[\mathsf{Expt}_0^{\mathcal{A}} = 1]|$ by constructing a reduction $\mathcal{R}_{ZK}$ to the zero-knowledge property of $\mathsf{NIZK}_{\mathsf{Com}}$. $\mathcal{R}_{ZK}$ runs the code of Expt_1, except that it publishes the CRS from the zero-knowledge challenger, and uses the zero-knowledge proof from the zero-knowledge challenger as part of the challenge ciphertext; also, $\mathcal{R}_{ZK}$ simulates the decommit oracle DEC by running the fast decryption algorithm. Concretely, $\mathcal{R}_{ZK}$ works as follows:

- Setup: $\mathcal{R}_{ZK}$, on input crs^*, runs $P \leftarrow \mathsf{PGen}(1^\kappa)$, $(sk, pk) \leftarrow \mathsf{KGen}(P)$ and $\mathsf{crs}_{\mathsf{Decom}} \leftarrow \mathsf{GenZK}_{\mathsf{Decom}}(1^\kappa)$, sets $\mathsf{crs} := (pk, \mathsf{crs}^*, \mathsf{crs}_{\mathsf{Decom}})$, and runs $\mathcal{A}(\mathsf{crs})$. On $\mathcal{A}$'s query DEC(c), $\mathcal{R}_{ZK}$ returns $\mathsf{Dec}_s(sk, c)$.
- Online phase: When $\mathcal{A}$ makes its challenge query on (m_0, m_1), $\mathcal{R}_{ZK}$ chooses $b \leftarrow \{0,1\}$, computes $c^* \leftarrow \mathsf{Enc}(pk, m_b)$ and $\pi^* \leftarrow \mathsf{PROVE}(c^*, m_b)$, and outputs (c, π^*). After that, $\mathcal{R}$ answers $\mathcal{A}$'s DEC queries just as in setup.
- Output: On $\mathcal{A}$'s output bit b', $\mathcal{R}_{ZK}$ outputs 1 if $b' = b$, and 0 otherwise.

$\mathcal{R}_{ZK}$ runs in time $t_p + t_o + t_e$ (t_p in the setup phase and $t_o + t_e$ in the online phase), and

$$|\Pr[\mathsf{Expt}_1^{\mathcal{A}} = 1] - \Pr[\mathsf{Expt}_0^{\mathcal{A}} = 1]| \leq \epsilon_{ZK}.$$

Now we analyze $\mathcal{A}$'s advantage in Expt_1. Since the challenge is (c, π) where $c = \mathsf{Enc}(pk, m; r)$ and π is simulated without knowledge of m or r, and DEC simply runs Dec_s, $\mathcal{A}$'s advantage can be upper bounded directly by the CCA-security of TPKE. Formally, we upper bound $\mathcal{A}$'s advantage by constructing a reduction $\mathcal{R}_{CCA}$ to the CCA-security of TPKE (where $\mathcal{R}_{CCA}$'s decryption oracle is denoted $\mathsf{DEC}_{\mathsf{TPKE}}$):

- Preprocessing phase: $\mathcal{R}_{CCA}$, on input pk, computes $(\mathsf{crs}_{\mathsf{Com}}, td) \leftarrow \mathsf{SimGen}_{\mathsf{Com}}(1^\kappa)$, and runs $\mathcal{A}(\mathsf{crs}_{\mathsf{Com}})$. On $\mathcal{A}$'s query DEC(c), $\mathcal{R}_{CCA}$ queries $\mathsf{DEC}_{\mathsf{TPKE}}(c)$ and returns the result.
- Challenge query: When $\mathcal{A}$ outputs (m_0, m_1), $\mathcal{R}_{CCA}$ makes its challenge query on (m_0, m_1), and on its challenge ciphertext c^*, $\mathcal{R}_{CCA}$ computes $\pi^* \leftarrow \mathsf{SimProve}_{\mathsf{Com}}(c^*, td)$ and sends (c^*, π^*) to $\mathcal{A}$. After that, $\mathcal{R}$ answers $\mathcal{A}$'s DEC queries just as in preprocessing phase.
- Output: When $\mathcal{A}$ outputs a bit b', $\mathcal{R}_{CCA}$ also outputs b'.

$\mathcal{R}_{CCA}$ runs in time at most $t_p + t_{csgen}$ in the preprocessing phase, and time at most $t_o + t_{csp}$ in the online phase. $\mathcal{R}_{CCA}$ simulates Expt_1 perfectly, and wins if $\mathcal{A}$ wins. It follows that

$$\Pr[\mathsf{Expt}_1^{\mathcal{A}} = 1] = \Pr[\mathcal{R}_{CCA} \text{ wins}] \leq \frac{1}{2} + \epsilon_{CCA}.$$

Summing up all results above, we conclude that

$$\Pr\left[\mathbf{IND\text{-}CCA}_{\mathsf{TC}}^{\mathcal{A}} = 1\right] \leq \frac{1}{2} + \epsilon_{ZK} + \epsilon_{CCA},$$

which completes the proof.

We give a sketc.h of the argument of why our scheme satisfies our notion of binding. Recall that if $\mathcal{A}$ can win $\textbf{BND-CCA}_{\textsf{TC}}$, then it can produce a commitment c along with messages m, m' and proofs $\pi_{\textsf{Com}}, \pi_{\textsf{Decom}}$ s.t. $\textsf{ComVrfy}((pk, \textsf{crs}_{\textsf{Com}}, \textsf{crs}_{\textsf{Decom}}), c, \pi_{\textsf{Com}}) = \textsf{DecomVrfy}((pk, \textsf{crs}_{\textsf{Com}}, \textsf{crs}_{\textsf{Decom}}), c, m, \pi_{\textsf{Decom}}) = 1$, $m' \neq m$ and either

$$(1) : \textsf{FDecom}((pk, \textsf{crs}_{\textsf{Com}}, \textsf{crs}_{\textsf{Decom}}), c) = m'$$

or

$$(2) : \textsf{DecomVrfy}((pk, \textsf{crs}_{\textsf{Com}}, \textsf{crs}_{\textsf{Decom}}), c, m', \pi'_{\textsf{Decom}}) = 1.$$

Both (1) and (2) can be reduced from soundness of NIZK. For (1), unless $\mathcal{A}$ can come up with a fake proof $\pi_{\textsf{Com}}$, then $\textsf{ComVrfy}((pk, \textsf{crs}_{\textsf{Com}}, \textsf{crs}_{\textsf{Decom}}), c, \pi_{\textsf{Com}}) = 1$ implies that there exists m and r s.t. $\textsf{Enc}(pk, m; r) = c$. Now, correctness of TPKE implies that $\textsf{FDecom}((pk, \textsf{crs}_{\textsf{Com}}, \textsf{crs}_{\textsf{Decom}}), c) = \textsf{Dec}_s(pk, c) = \textsf{Dec}_f(sk, c) = m$. Similarly, for (2), unless $\mathcal{A}$ can come up with a fake proof $\pi_{\textsf{Decom}}$, then $\textsf{DecomVrfy}((pk, \textsf{crs}_{\textsf{Com}}, \textsf{crs}_{\textsf{Decom}}), c, m, \pi_{\textsf{Decom}}) = 1$ implies that there exists r s.t. $\textsf{Enc}(pk, m; r) = c$. In this case, correctness of TPKE asserts that $\textsf{Dec}_s(pk, c) = \textsf{Dec}_f(sk, c) = m \neq m'$. Hence the proof $\pi'_{\textsf{Decom}}$ must be fake, as otherwise, this would contradict correctness of TPKE with regard to m'.

References

1. Aggarwal, D., Maurer, U.: Breaking RSA generically is equivalent to factoring. In: Joux, A. (ed.) EUROCRYPT 2009. LNCS, vol. 5479, pp. 36–53. Springer, Heidelberg (2009). https://doi.org/10.1007/978-3-642-01001-9_2

2. Baum, C., David, B., Dowsley, R., Nielsen, J.B., Oechsner, S.: Tardis: time and relative delays in simulation. Cryptology ePrint Archive: report 2020/537 (2020)

3. Bellare, M., Goldwasser, S.: Verifiable partial key escrow. In: ACM Conference on Computer and Communications Security (CCS) 1997, pp. 78–91. ACM Press (1997)

4. Bitansky, N., Goldwasser, S., Jain, A., Paneth, O., Vaikuntanathan, V., Waters, B.: Time-lock puzzles from randomized encodings. In: Sudan, M., (ed.) ITCS 2016: 7th Conference on Innovations in Theoretical Computer Science, pp. 345–356, Cambridge, MA, USA, 14–16 Jan 2016. Association for Computing Machinery (2016)

5. Boneh, D., Bonneau, J., Bünz, B., Fisch, B.: Verifiable delay functions. In: Shacham, H., Boldyreva, A. (eds.) Advances in Cryptology-Crypto 2018, Part I. LNCS, vol. 10991, pp. 757–788. Springer, Cham (2018). https://doi.org/10.1007/978-3-319-96884-1_25

6. Boneh, D., Bünz, B., Fisch, B.: A survey of two verifiable delay functions. Cryptology ePrint Archive, report 2018/712 (2018). https://eprint.iacr.org/2018/712

7. Boneh, Dan, Naor, Moni: Timed commitments. In: Bellare, Mihir (ed.) CRYPTO 2000. LNCS, vol. 1880, pp. 236–254. Springer, Heidelberg (2000). https://doi.org/10.1007/3-540-44598-6_15

8. Boneh, D., Venkatesan, R.: Breaking RSA may not be equivalent to factoring. In: Nyberg, K. (ed.) EUROCRYPT 1998. LNCS, vol. 1403, pp. 59–71. Springer, Heidelberg (1998). https://doi.org/10.1007/BFb0054117

9. Canetti, R.: Universally composable security: a new paradigm for cryptographic protocols. In: 42nd Annual Symposium on Foundations of Computer Science (FOCS), pp. 136–145. IEEE (2001)

10. Canetti, R., Lin, H., Pass, R.: Adaptive hardness and composable security in the plain model from standard assumptions. In: 51st Annual Symposium on Foundations of Computer Science (FOCS), pp. 541–550. IEEE (2010)

11. Cathalo, J., Libert, B., Quisquater, J.-J.: Efficient and non-interactive timed-release encryption. In: Qing, S., Mao, W., López, J., Wang, G. (eds.) International Conference on Information and Communication Security (ICICS). LNCS, vol. 3783, pp. 291–303. Springer, Heidelberg (2005). https://doi.org/10.1007/11602897_25

12. Di Crescenzo, G., Ostrovsky, R., Rajagopalan, S.: Conditional oblivious transfer and timed-release encryption. In: Stern, J. (ed.) EUROCRYPT 1999. LNCS, vol. 1592, pp. 74–89. Springer, Heidelberg (1999). https://doi.org/10.1007/3-540-48910-X_6

13. Dwork, C., Naor, M.: Zaps and their applications. In: 41st Annual Symposium on Foundations of Computer Science (FOCS), pp. 283–293. IEEE (2000)

14. Ephraim, N., Freitag, C., Komargodski, I., Pass, R.: Non-malleable time-lock puzzles and applications. Cryptology ePrint Archive: report 2020/779 (2020)

15. Fuchsbauer, G., Kiltz, E., Loss, J.: The algebraic group model and its applications. In: Shacham, H., Boldyreva, A. (eds.) Advances in Cryptology-Crypto 2018, Part II. LNCS, vol. 10992, pp. 33–62. Springer, Cham (2018). https://doi.org/10.1007/978-3-319-96881-0_2

16. Groth, Jens, Maller, Mary: Snarky signatures: minimal signatures of knowledge from simulation-extractable SNARKs. In: Katz, Jonathan, Shacham, Hovav (eds.) CRYPTO 2017. LNCS, vol. 10402, pp. 581–612. Springer, Cham (2017). https://doi.org/10.1007/978-3-319-63715-0_20

17. Katz, J., Lindell, Y.: Introduction to Modern Cryptography, 2nd edn. Chapman & Hall/CRC Press, CRC Press, Boca Raton, London, New York (2014)

18. Kosba, A., et al.: How to use SNARKs in universally composable protocols. Cryptology ePrint Archive, report 2015/1093 (2015). http://eprint.iacr.org/2015/1093

19. Lin, H., Pass, R., Soni, P.: Two-round and non-interactive concurrent non-malleable commitments from time-lock puzzles. In: 58th Annual Symposium on Foundations of Computer Science (FOCS), pp. 576–587. IEEE (2017)

20. Lipmaa, H.: Simulation-extractable SNARKs revisited. Cryptology ePrint Archive, report 2019/612 (2019). https://eprint.iacr.org/2019/612

21. Liu, J., Jager, T., Kakvi, S.A., Warinschi, B.: How to build time-lock encryption. Des. Codes Crypt. **86**(11), 2549–2586 (2018). https://doi.org/10.1007/s10623-018-0461-x

22. Mahmoody, Mohammad, Moran, Tal, Vadhan, Salil: Time-lock puzzles in the random oracle model. In: Rogaway, Phillip (ed.) CRYPTO 2011. LNCS, vol. 6841, pp. 39–50. Springer, Heidelberg (2011). https://doi.org/10.1007/978-3-642-22792-9_3

23. Malavolta, Giulio, Thyagarajan, Sri Aravinda Krishnan: Homomorphic time-lock puzzles and applications. In: Boldyreva, Alexandra, Micciancio, Daniele (eds.) CRYPTO 2019. LNCS, vol. 11692, pp. 620–649. Springer, Cham (2019). https://doi.org/10.1007/978-3-030-26948-7_22

24. Maurer, Ueli: Abstract models of computation in cryptography. In: Smart, Nigel P. (ed.) Cryptography and Coding 2005. LNCS, vol. 3796, pp. 1–12. Springer, Heidelberg (2005). https://doi.org/10.1007/11586821_1

25. May, T.: Timed-release crypto (1993). http://cypherpunks.venona.com/date/1993/02/msg00129.html

26. Naor, M., Yung, M.: Public-key cryptosystems provably secure against chosen Ciphertext attacks. In: 22nd Annual ACM Symposium on Theory of Computing (STOC), pp. 427–437. ACM Press (1990)

27. Paillier, Pascal, Vergnaud, Damien: Discrete-log-based signatures may not be equivalent to discrete log. In: Roy, Bimal (ed.) ASIACRYPT 2005. LNCS, vol. 3788, pp. 1–20. Springer, Heidelberg (2005). https://doi.org/10.1007/11593447_1

28. Pietrzak, K.: Simple verifiable delay functions. In: Blum, A. (eds.) ITCS 2019: 10th Innovations in Theoretical Computer Science Conference, vol. 124, pp. 60:1–60:15, San Diego, CA, USA, 10–12 Jan 2019. Leibniz International Proceedings in Informatics (LIPIcs)

29. Rivest, R.L., Shamir, A., Wagner, D.A.: Time-lock puzzles and timed-release crypto. Technical report, MIT Laboratory for Computer Science (1996)

30. Rotem, Lior, Segev, Gil: Generically speeding-up repeated squaring is equivalent to factoring: sharp thresholds for all generic-ring delay functions. In: Micciancio, Daniele, Ristenpart, Thomas (eds.) CRYPTO 2020. LNCS, vol. 12172, pp. 481–509. Springer, Cham (2020). https://doi.org/10.1007/978-3-030-56877-1_17

31. Sahai, A.: Non-malleable non-interactive zero knowledge and adaptive chosen-ciphertext security. In: 40th Annual Symposium on Foundations of Computer Science (FOCS), pp. 543–553. IEEE (1999)

32. Shoup, V.: Lower bounds for discrete logarithms and related problems. In: Fumy, W. (ed.) EUROCRYPT 1997. LNCS, vol. 1233, pp. 256–266. Springer, Heidelberg (1997). https://doi.org/10.1007/3-540-69053-0_18

33. Wesolowski, B.: Efficient verifiable delay functions. In: Ishai, Y., Rijmen, V. (eds.) EUROCRYPT 2019. LNCS, vol. 11478, pp. 379–407. Springer, Cham (2019). https://doi.org/10.1007/978-3-030-17659-4_13

Expected-Time Cryptography: Generic Techniques and Applications to Concrete Soundness

Joseph Jaeger$^{(\boxtimes)}$ and Stefano Tessaro

Paul G. Allen School of Computer Science & Engineering,
University of Washington, Seattle, USA
{jsjaeger,tessaro}@cs.washington.edu

Abstract. This paper studies concrete security with respect to *expected-time* adversaries. Our first contribution is a set of generic tools to obtain tight bounds on the advantage of an adversary with expected-time guarantees. We apply these tools to derive bounds in the random-oracle and generic-group models, which we show to be tight.

As our second contribution, we use these results to derive concrete bounds on the soundness of public-coin proofs and arguments of knowledge. Under the lens of concrete security, we revisit a paradigm by Bootle et al. (EUROCRYPT '16) that proposes a general Forking Lemma for multi-round protocols which implements a rewinding strategy with expected-time guarantees. We give a tighter analysis, as well as a modular statement. We adopt this to obtain the first quantitative bounds on the soundness of Bulletproofs (Bünz et al., S&P 2018), which we instantiate with our expected-time generic-group analysis to surface inherent dependence between the concrete security and the statement to be proved.

Keywords: Concrete security · Proof systems

1 Introduction

Cryptography usually adopts a *worst-case* angle on complexity. For example, in the context of *concrete* security, a typical theorem shows that an adversary running for at most t steps succeeds with advantage at most ε. In this paper, we instead study the concrete security of cryptographic schemes and assumptions as a function of the *expected* running time of the adversary.

Expected-time complexity is a natural measure in its own right – e.g., it is very common in cryptanalysis, as it is often much easier to analyze. But it is also a useful technical tool – indeed, simulators and extractors are often expected time, sometimes inherently so [1]. To use these technical tools, we need assumptions to hold with respect to expected time.

The problem has been studied closely by Katz and Lindell [14], who also suggest expected-time adversaries as a natural model, which however also comes with several technical challenges. Either way, the resulting common wisdom is

© International Association for Cryptologic Research 2020
R. Pass and K. Pietrzak (Eds.): TCC 2020, LNCS 12552, pp. 414–443, 2020.
https://doi.org/10.1007/978-3-030-64381-2_15

that assumptions which are true with respect to (non-uniform) worst-case polynomial time are true for expected polynomial-time, and often more fine-grained statements are possible via Markov's inequality (see below). However, for concrete security, such generic argument fail to give tight bounds.

SUMMARY OF CONTRIBUTIONS. This paper makes progress on two fronts.

First, as our main technical contribution, we introduce general tools to give *tight* concrete security bounds in information-theoretic settings (e.g., in the random-oracle or generic-group models) for expected-time adversaries. Our tools can easily translate many existing proofs from the worst-case to the expected-time regime. We derive for example tight bounds for finding collisions in a random oracle, for the PRF security of random oracles, and for computing discrete logarithms in the generic-group model. We also obtain bounds for the security of key-alternating ciphers against expected-time adversaries.

Second, we study a "Forking Lemma" to prove soundness of *multi-round* public-coin proofs and arguments (of knowledge) satisfying a generalized notion of *special soundness*, enabling witness extraction from a suitable tree of accepting interactions. In particular, we follow a blueprint by Bootle et al. [6], which has also been adopted by follow-up works [7,8,24]. In contrast to prior works, we provide a concrete analysis of the resulting expected-time witness extraction strategy, and also give a modular treatment of the techniques which may be of independent interest.

We showcase these tools by deriving concrete bounds for the soundness of Bulletproofs [7] in terms of the expected-time hardness of solving the discrete logarithm problem. Instantiating the bound with our generic-group model analysis will in particular illustrate the dependence of soundness on group parameters and on the complexity of the statement to be proved. We are unaware of any such result having been proved, despite the practical appeal of these protocols.

The remainder of this introduction provides a detailed overview of our results.

1.1   Information-Theoretic Bounds for Expected-Time Adversaries

Our first contribution is a framework to prove tight bounds with respect to expected-time adversaries. We focus on *information-theoretic analyses*, such as those in the random oracle [3] and the generic group [18,22] models.

Our focus on tight bounds is what makes the problem hard. Indeed, one can usually obtain a non-tight bound using Markov's inequality. For example, the probability $\varepsilon(T, N)$ of a T-time adversary finding a collision in a random oracle with N outputs satisfies $\varepsilon(T, N) \leqslant T^2/2N$, and this bound is tight. If we instead aim to upper bound the probability $\varepsilon(\mu_T, N)$ of finding a collision for an adversary that runs in *expected* time $\mu_T = \mathsf{E}[T]$, Markov's inequality yields, for every $T^* > \mu_T$,

$$\varepsilon(\mu_T, N) \leqslant \Pr[T > T^*] + \frac{(T^*)^2}{2N} \leqslant \frac{\mu_T}{T^*} + \frac{(T^*)^2}{2N} \leqslant 2 \cdot \sqrt[3]{\frac{\mu_T^2}{2N}}, \qquad (1)$$

where the right-most inequality is the result of setting T^* such that $\frac{\mu_T}{T^*} = \frac{(T^*)^2}{2N}$. Here, we prove the better upper bound

$$\varepsilon(\mu_T, N) \leqslant \sqrt{\frac{\mu_T^2}{2N}}, \tag{2}$$

as a corollary of the techniques we introduce below. This bound is tight: To see this, take an adversary which initially flips a biased coin, which is heads with probability $\mu_T/\sqrt{N}$. If the coin is tails, it aborts, failing to find a collision. If the coin is heads, it makes $\sqrt{N}$ queries to find a collision with high probability. Then, this adversary succeeds with probability $\Omega(\mu_T/\sqrt{N}) = \Omega(\sqrt{\mu_T^2/N})$, and its expected run time is μ_T.

Both (1) and (2) show that $\mu_T \geqslant \Omega(\sqrt{N})$ must hold to find a collision *with probability one*. However, exact probability bounds are important in the regime $\mu_T = o(\sqrt{N})$. For example, say we are asked to find a collision in at least one out of u independent random oracles, and the expected number of queries to each is μ_T. Then, a hybrid argument bounds the probability by $u \cdot \varepsilon(\mu_T, N)$, making the difference between a square-root and a cube-root bound on $\varepsilon(\mu_T, N)$ important.

A GENERIC APPROACH FOR BAD-FLAG ANALYSES. We aim for a general approach to transform information-theoretic bounds for worst-case query complexity into bounds with respect to *expected* query complexity. If an existing analysis (with respect to worst-case complexity) follows a certain pattern, then we easily obtain an expected query complexity bound.

More concretely, many security proofs follow the "equivalent-until-bad" format (as formalized by Bellare and Rogaway [4], but equivalent formulations can be derived from the works of Maurer [17] and Shoup [23]). The goal here is to upper bound the advantage of an adversary $\mathcal{A}$ distinguishing two games G_0 and G_1, which behave *identically* until some bad flag bad is set. Then, the distinguishing advantage is upper bounded by the probability of setting bad to true – an event we denote as $\mathsf{BAD}^{\mathcal{A}}$. Typically, G_0 is the "real world" and G_1 is the "ideal world". Now, let Q_1 be the number of queries by an adversary $\mathcal{A}$ in G_1, which is a random variable. Then, we say that this game pair satisfies δ-*boundedness* if

$$\Pr\left[\mathsf{BAD}^{\mathcal{A}} \mid Q_1 = q\right] \leqslant \delta(q)$$

for all $q \geqslant 1$ and adversaries $\mathcal{A}$. This condition is not without loss of generality, but it can be ensured in all examples we verified.

Our first main theorem (Theorem 1) shows that if $\delta(q) = \Delta \cdot q^d/N$, then the probability of setting $\mathsf{BAD}^{\mathcal{A}}$ (in either of the two games), and hence the advantage of distinguishing G_0 and G_1, is upper bounded as

$$\Pr\left[\mathsf{BAD}^{\mathcal{A}}\right] \leqslant 5 \cdot \left(\frac{\Delta\mathsf{E}[Q_0]^d}{N}\right)^{1/d},$$

where (quite) crucially Q_0 is the number of queries of $\mathcal{A}$ in G_0. This asymmetry matters in applications - we typically measure complexity in the *real world*, but

δ-boundedness only holds in the ideal world.

PROOF IDEA. The key step behind the proof of Theorem 1 is the introduction of an *early-terminating* adversary $\mathcal{B}$, which behaves as $\mathcal{A}$ in attempting to set bad, but aborts early after $U = \left\lfloor \sqrt[d]{Nu/\Delta} \right\rfloor = \Theta(\sqrt[d]{N/\Delta})$ queries, where $u = 2^{-d}$. One can then show that (we can think of the following probabilities in G_0)

$$\Pr\left[\mathsf{BAD}^{\mathcal{A}}\right] \leqslant \Pr\left[\mathsf{BAD}^{\mathcal{B}}\right] + \Pr\left[Q_0 > U\right] ,$$

because $\Pr\left[\mathsf{BAD}^{\mathcal{A}} \wedge Q_0 \leqslant U\right] \leqslant \Pr\left[\mathsf{BAD}^{\mathcal{B}}\right]$. Markov's inequality then yields

$$\Pr\left[Q_0 > U\right] \leqslant \frac{\mathsf{E}\left[Q_0\right]}{U} = \Theta\left(\sqrt[d]{\Delta \mathsf{E}\left[Q_0\right]^d / N}\right) ,$$

which is of the right order.

Therefore, the core of the proof is to show $\Pr\left[\mathsf{BAD}^{\mathcal{B}}\right] = O\left(\sqrt[d]{\Delta \mathsf{E}\left[Q_0\right]^d / N}\right)$. This will require using δ-boundedness first, but a careful reader may observe that this will only upper bound the probability with respect to $\mathsf{E}\left[Q_1\right]$, and not $\mathsf{E}\left[Q_0\right]$. The bulk of the proof is then to switch between the two.

EXAMPLES. We apply the above framework to a few examples, to show its applicability. We show bounds on the hardness of discrete logarithms in the generic-group model [18,22], and on the collision-resistance and PRF security of random oracles. In particular, our framework also works for notions which are not indistinguishability based, such as collision-resistance of a random oracle, by introducing a suitable world G_1 where it is hard to win the game.

THE H-COEFFICIENT METHOD. Equivalent-until-bad analyses are not always the simplest way to prove security (despite the fact that in principle every analysis can be cast in this format, as shown in [19]). We also give a variant of the above approach tailored at proving security in a simpler version of the H-coefficient method [9,20] which considers what is referred to as *pointwise-proximity* in [12]. This amounts to using the standard H-coefficient method without bad transcripts. (To the best of our knowledge, this simpler version of the method is due to Bernstein [5].) This allows us to obtain expect-time versions of security bounds for the PRF/PRP switching lemma and for key-alternating ciphers, the latter building on top of work by Hoang and Tessaro [12]. We defer details on this to the full version of this paper [13].

1.2 Forking Lemmas and Concrete Soundness

One motivation for studying expected-time adversaries is as a *tool* to prove bounds for worst-case complexity, rather than as a goal on itself. We expose here one such application in the context of proving *soundness* bounds for public-coin proofs/arguments (of knowledge). In particular, soundness/proof-of-knowledge proofs for several protocols (like [6–8,24]) rely on generalizations of the Forking Lemma (originally proposed by Pointcheval and Stern [21] for three-round protocols) which adopt expected-time witness extraction strategies. These have only been analyzed in an asymptotic sense, and our goal is to give a concrete-security treatment. We propose here a modular treatment of these techniques, and instantiate our framework to provide concrete bounds on the soundness of Bulletproofs [7], a succinct proof system which has enjoyed wide popularity.

FORKING LEMMAS. Pointcheval and Stern's original "Forking Lemma" [21] deals with Σ-protocols that satisfy *special soundness* - these are three-round protocols, where a transcript takes the form (a, c, d), with c being the verifier's single *random* challenge. Here, given common input x, the prover P proves knowledge to V of a witness w for a relation R. The proof of knowledge property is proved by giving an *extractor* $\mathcal{B}$ which produces a witness for x given (black-box) access to a prover P* – if P* succeeds with probability ε, then $\mathcal{B}$ succeeds with probability (roughly) ε^2. Concretely, $\mathcal{B}$ simulates an execution of P* with a random challenge c, which results in a transcript (a, c, d), and then rewinds P* to just before obtaining c, and feeds a different challenge c' to obtain a transcript (a, c', d'). If both transcripts are accepting, and $c \neq c'$, a witness can be extracted via special soundness. Bellare and Neven [2] give alternative Forking Lemmas where $\mathcal{B}$'s success probability approaches ε, at the cost of a larger running time.

EXPECTED-TIME EXTRACTION. It is natural to expect that the success probability of $\mathcal{B}$ above degrades exponentially in the number of required accepting transcripts. Crucially, however, one can make the Forking Lemma tight with respect to probability if we relax $\mathcal{B}$ to have bounded *expected* running time. Now, $\mathcal{B}$ runs P* once with a random challenge c and, if it generates a valid transcript (a, c, d), we rewind P* to before receiving the challenge c, and keep re-running it from there with fresh challenges until we obtain a second valid transcript (a, c', d') for $c \neq c'$. The expected running time is only *twice* that of P*.

A GENERAL FORKING LEMMA. An extension of this idea underlies the analysis of recent succinct public-coin multi-round interactive arguments of knowledge [6–8,24], following a workflow introduced first by Bootle et al. (BCCGP) [6] which extracts a witness from a *tree* of multi-round executions obtained by clever rewinding of P*. In particular, since the number of generated accepted interactions is large (i.e., exponential in the number of rounds), the usage of an expected-time strategy is essential to extract with good enough probability.

These works in fact prove the stronger property of *witness-extended emulation* [11,16]. This means that with black-box access to a prover P*, an expected-time *emulator* E (1) generates a transcript with the same distribution as in an interaction between P* and the verifier V, *and* (2) if this transcript is accepting, then a valid witness is produced along with it. In the case of *arguments*, it is possible that (2) fails, but this would imply breaking an underlying assumption.

The BCCGP framework was refined in follow-up works [7,8,24], but these remain largely asymptotic. We give here a clean and modular treatment of the

BCCGP blueprint, which makes it amenable to a concrete security treatment. This will in particular require using our tools from the first part of the paper to analyze the probability that we generate a well-formed tree of transcripts from which a witness can be generated. We believe this to be of independent interest.

In the full version of this paper [13], we compare this expected-time forking lemma to one with strict running-time guarantees and confirm that the expected-time approach achieves a clear benefit in terms of tightness of the reduction.

APPLICATION TO BULLETPROOFS. Finally, we apply the above framework to obtain a bound on the *concrete soundness* for public-coin interactive argument systems, and focus on Bulletproofs [7][1]. We obtain a bound in terms of the expected-time hardness of the discrete logarithm problem, and we combine this with our generic-group analysis to get a bound on the soundness in the generic-group model[2]. Of independent interest, the result relies on a *tight* reduction of finding non-trivial discrete log relations to the plain discrete log problem – which we give in Lemma 3.

Our bound is in particular on the probability $\mathsf{Adv}_{\mathsf{PS},G}^{\mathsf{sound}}(\mathsf{P}^*)$ of a cheating prover P^* convincing a verifier V (from proof system PS) on input x generated by a (randomized) instance *generator* G, and we show that

$$\mathsf{Adv}_{\mathsf{PS},G}^{\mathsf{sound}}(\mathsf{P}^*) \leqslant \mathsf{Adv}_{\mathsf{PS},G}^{\mathsf{wit}}(\mathcal{B}) + O\left(\frac{q_{\mathsf{P}^*} \cdot LM^3 \log_2(M)}{\sqrt{|\mathbb{G}|}}\right),$$

where q_{P^*} measures the number of group operations by P^*, M is the number of multiplication gates for a circuit representing the relation R, L is a parameter of that circuit (which we assume is small for this discussion, but may be as large as $2M$), $\mathsf{Adv}_{\mathsf{PS},G}^{\mathsf{wit}}(\mathcal{B})$ is the probability of $\mathcal{B}$ extracting a witness w for an x sampled by G, where $\mathcal{B}$ is an extractor whose (expected) running time amounts to roughly M^3 that of P^*.

This bound is interesting because it highlights the dependence of the soundness probability on the group size $|\mathbb{G}|$ and on M. It in fact shows that for typical instantiations, where $|\mathbb{G}| \approx 2^{256}$, the guaranteed security level is fairly low for modest-sized circuits (say with $M = 2^{20}$). It is a good question whether this bound can be made tighter, in particular with respect to its dependence on M.

We also note that for specific instance generators G our tools may be helpful to estimate $\mathsf{Adv}_{\mathsf{PS},G}^{\mathsf{wit}}(\mathcal{B})$.

---

[1] Our focus is somewhat arbitrary, and motivated by the popularity of this proof system.

[2] This bound is helped by the fact that our casting of the generic-group model allows multi-exponentiations $(g_0, \ldots, g_n, a_0, \ldots, a_n \to \prod_{i=0}^{n} g_i^{a_i})$ as a unit operation. This does not change the derived bound in the generic-group model, while decreasing the number of generic-group queries made by the Bulletproofs verifier.

2 Preliminaries

Let $\mathbb{N} = \{0, 1, 2, \dots\}$ and $\mathbb{N}_{>0} = \mathbb{N} \setminus \{0\}$. For $N \in \mathbb{N}$, let $[N] = \{1, 2, \dots, N\}$. For $j > k$ we adopt the conventions that $\prod_{i=j}^{k} n_i = 1$ and $(m_j, m_{j+1}, \dots, m_k) = ()$. Equivalence mod p is denoted $\equiv_p$.

We let $\mathsf{Perm}(S)$ denote the set of all permutations on set S and $\mathsf{Fcs}(S, S')$ denote the set of all functions from S to S'. Sampling x uniformly from the set S is denoted $x \leftarrow_{\$} S$. The notation $S = S' \sqcup S''$ means that $S = S' \cup S''$ and $S' \cap S'' = \emptyset$, i.e., S' and S'' partition S. We let $\{0, 1\}^*$ denote the set of finite-length bitstrings and $\{0, 1\}^{\infty}$ denote the set of infinite-length bitstrings.

We let $y \leftarrow \mathcal{A}^{\mathrm{O}}(x_1, x_2, \dots; c)$ denote the execution of $\mathcal{A}$ on input $x_1, x_2, \dots$ and coins $c \in \{0, 1\}^{\infty}$ with access to oracle(s) O, producing output y. When c is chosen uniformly we write $y \leftarrow_{\$} \mathcal{A}^{\mathrm{O}}(x_1, x_2, \dots)$. For a stateful algorithm $\mathcal{A}$ with state s we use $y \leftarrow \mathcal{A}^{\mathrm{O}}(x_1, x_2, \dots : s; c)$ as shorthand for the expression $(y, s) \leftarrow A^{\mathrm{O}}(x_1, x_2, \dots, s; c)$. When some of an algorithm's output is not going to be used we will write $\cdot$ in place of giving it a variable name.

We use pseudocode games, inspired by the code-based game framework of Bellare and Rogaway [4]. See Fig. 1 for some example games. If H is a game, then $\Pr[\mathrm{H}]$ denotes the probability that it outputs true. We use $\wedge$, $\vee$, $\Leftrightarrow$, and $\neg$ for the logical operators "and", "or", "iff", and "not".

RUNNING-TIME CONVENTIONS. The most commonly used notion for the running time of an algorithm is worst-case. For this, one first fixes a computational model with an associated notion of computational steps. Then an algorithm $\mathcal{A}$ has worst-case running time t if for all choice of $x_1, x_2, \dots$ and c it performs at most t computation steps in the execution $\mathcal{A}^{\mathrm{O}}(x_1, x_2, \dots; c)$, no matter how O responds to any oracle queries $\mathcal{A}$ makes.

In this paper we are interested in proving bounds that instead depend on the expected number of computation steps that $\mathcal{A}$ performs. There may be randomness in how the inputs $x_1, x_2, \dots$ to $\mathcal{A}$ and the responses to O queries are chosen (in addition to the random selection of c).

There is more variation in how expected running time may be defined. We will provide our bounds in terms of the expected running time of adversaries interacting with the "real" world that they expect to interact with. Such a notion of expected runtime is brittle because the expected runtime of the adversary may vary greatly when executing in some other world; however, this notion is the strongest for the purposes of our results because it will guarantee the same bounds for notions of expected running time which restrict the allowed adversaries more. See [10,15] for interesting discussion of various ways to define expected polynomial time.

For many of the results of this paper, rather than directly measuring the runtime of the adversary we will look at the (worst-case or expected) number of oracle queries that it makes. The number of oracle queries can, of course, be upper bounded by the number of computational steps.

Game $\mathsf{H}_{\mathbb{G}}^{\mathsf{dl}}(\mathcal{A})$	Game $\mathsf{H}_{\mathbb{G},n}^{\mathsf{dl\text{-}rel}}(\mathcal{A})$	Adversary $\mathcal{C}(g,h)$
$g \leftarrow_\$ \mathbb{G}^*$	$\boldsymbol{g} \leftarrow (g_0,\dots,g_n) \leftarrow_\$ \mathbb{G}^n$	For $i = 0,\dots,n$
$h \leftarrow_\$ \mathbb{G}$	$(a_0,\dots,a_n) \leftarrow_\$ \mathcal{A}(\boldsymbol{g})$	$\quad x_i \leftarrow_\$ \mathbb{Z}_p;\ y_i \leftarrow_\$ \mathbb{Z}_p$
$a \leftarrow_\$ \mathcal{A}(g,h)$	If $\forall i, a_i \equiv_p 0$ then	$\quad g_i \leftarrow g^{x_i} \cdot h^{y_i}$
Return $(g^a = h)$	$\quad$ Return false	$(a_0,\dots,a_n) \leftarrow_\$ \mathcal{A}((g_0,\dots,g_n))$
	Return $(\prod_{i=0}^n g_i^{a_i} = 1_{\mathbb{G}})$	If $\sum_i a_i y_i \equiv_p 0$ then return 0
		Else return $-\sum_i a_i x_i / \sum_i a_i y_i$

Fig. 1. Left: Game defining discrete log security of group $\mathbb{G}$. **Middle:** Game defining discrete log relation security of group $\mathbb{G}$. **Right:** Reduction adversary for Lemma 3.

USEFUL LEMMAS. We will make use of Markov's inequality and the Schwartz-Zippel Lemma, which we reproduce here.

Lemma 1 (Markov's Inequality). *Let X be a non-negative random variable and $c > 0$ be a non-negative constant, then*

$$\Pr[X > c] \leqslant \Pr[X \geqslant c] \leqslant \mathsf{E}[X]/c.$$

Lemma 2 (Schwartz-Zippel Lemma). *Let $\mathbb{F}$ be a finite field and let $p \in \mathbb{F}[x_1, x_2, \dots x_n]$ be a non-zero polynomial with degree $d \geqslant 0$. Then*

$$\Pr[p(r_1, \dots, r_n) = 0] \leqslant d/|\mathbb{F}|$$

where the probability is over the choice of $r_1, \dots, r_n$ according to $r_i \leftarrow_\$ \mathbb{F}$.

DISCRETE LOGARITHM ASSUMPTIONS. Let $\mathbb{G}$ be a cyclic group of prime order p with identity $1_{\mathbb{G}}$ and $\mathbb{G}^* = \mathbb{G} \backslash \{1_{\mathbb{G}}\}$ be its set of generators. Let $(g_0, \dots, g_n) \in \mathbb{G}^n$ and $(a_0, \dots, a_n) \in \mathbb{Z}_p$. If $\prod_{i=0}^n g_i^{a_i} = 1_{\mathbb{G}}$ and a least one of the a_i are non-zero, this is said to be a non-trivial discrete log relation. It is believed to be hard to find non-trivial discrete log relations in cryptographic groups (when the g_i are chosen at random). We refer to computing $\prod_{i=0}^n g_i^{a_i}$ as a multi-exponentiation of size $n + 1$.

Discrete log relation security is defined by the game in the middle of Fig. 1. In it, the adversary $\mathcal{A}$ is given a vector $\boldsymbol{g} = (g_0, \dots, g_n)$ and attempts to find a non-trivial discrete log relation. We define $\mathsf{Adv}_{\mathbb{G},n}^{\mathsf{dl\text{-}rel}}(\mathcal{A}) = \Pr[\mathsf{H}_{\mathbb{G},n}^{\mathsf{dl\text{-}rel}}(\mathcal{A})]$. Normal discrete log security is defined by the game in the left panel of Fig. 1. In it, the adversary attempts to find the discrete log of $h \in \mathbb{G}$ with respect to a generator $g \in \mathbb{G}^*$. We define $\mathsf{Adv}_{\mathbb{G}}^{\mathsf{dl}}(\mathcal{A}) = \Pr[\mathsf{H}_{\mathbb{G}}^{\mathsf{dl}}(\mathcal{A})]$.

It is well known that discrete log relation security is asymptotically equivalent to discrete log security. The following lemma makes careful use of self-reducibility techniques to give a concrete bound showing that discrete log relation security is tightly implied by discrete log security.

Lemma 3. *Let $\mathbb{G}$ be a group of prime order p and $n \geqslant 1$ be an integer. For any $\mathcal{B}$, define $\mathcal{C}$ as shown in Fig. 1. Then*

$$\mathsf{Adv}_{\mathbb{G},n}^{\mathsf{dl\text{-}rel}}(\mathcal{B}) \leqslant \mathsf{Adv}_{\mathbb{G}}^{\mathsf{dl}}(\mathcal{C}) + 1/p.$$

Game $\mathsf{G}_b^{(G,G')}(\mathcal{A})$	$\text{ORAC}(x)$
$c_0 \leftarrow\!\!\$ \{0,1\}^\infty$	$t \leftarrow t + 1$
$c_1 \leftarrow\!\!\$ \{0,1\}^\infty$	If $\neg\mathsf{bad}$ then
$c_\mathcal{A} \leftarrow\!\!\$ \{0,1\}^\infty$	$\quad \mathsf{bad}_t \leftarrow G'(x : s'; c_0, c_1)$
$t \leftarrow 0$	$\quad$ If bad_t then $\mathsf{bad} \leftarrow \text{true}$
$\mathsf{bad} \leftarrow \text{false}$	If bad then $d \leftarrow b$
$s \leftarrow \varepsilon$	Else $d \leftarrow 1$
$s' \leftarrow \varepsilon$	$y \leftarrow G(d, x : s; c_1, c_d)$
Run $\mathcal{A}^{\text{ORAC}}(c_\mathcal{A})$	Return y

Fig. 2. Identical-until-bad games defined from game specification (G, G').

The runtime of $\mathcal{C}$ is that of $\mathcal{B}$ plus the time to perform $n+1$ multi-exponentiations of size 2 and some computations in the field $\mathbb{Z}_p$.

The proof of this theorem is deferred to the full version of the paper [13].

3   Bad Flag Analysis for Expected-Time Adversaries

In this section we show how to (somewhat) generically extend the standard techniques for analysis of "bad" flags from worst-case adversaries to expected-time adversaries. Such analysis is a fundamental tool for cryptographic proofs and has been formalized in various works [4,17,23]. Our results are tailored for the setting where the analysis of the bad flag is information theoretic (e.g., applications in ideal models), rather than reliant on computational assumptions.

We start by introducing our notation and model for identical-until-bad games in Sect. 3.1. Then in Sect. 3.2 we give the main theorem of this section which shows how to obtain bounds on the probability that an expected time adversary causes a bad flag to be set. Finally, in Sect. 3.3 we walk through some basic applications (collision-resistance and PRF security in the random oracle model and discrete log security in the generic group model) to show the analysis required for expected time adversaries follows from simple modifications of the techniques used for worst-case adversaries.

3.1   Notation and Experiments for Identical-Until-Bad Games

IDENTICAL-UNTIL-BAD GAMES. Consider Fig. 2 which defines a pair of games $\mathsf{G}_0^{(G,G')}$ and $\mathsf{G}_1^{(G,G')}$ from a *game specification* (G, G'). Here G and G' are stateful randomized algorithms. At the beginning of the game, coins c_0, c_1, and $c_\mathcal{A}$ are sampled uniformly at random[3]. The first two of these are used by G and G'

---

[3] In the measure-theoretic probability sense with each individual bit of the coins being sampled uniformly and independently.

while the last is used by $\mathcal{A}^4$. The counter t is initialized to 0, the flag bad is set to false, and states s and s' are initialized for use by G and G'.

During the execution of the game, the adversary $\mathcal{A}$ repeatedly makes queries to the oracle ORAC. The variable t counts how many queries $\mathcal{A}$ makes. As long as bad is still false (so ¬bad is true), for each query made by $\mathcal{A}$ the algorithm G' will be given this query to determine if bad should be set to true. When $b = 1$, the behavior of ORAC does not depend on whether bad is set because the output of the oracle is always determined by running $G(1, x : s; c_1, c_1)$. When $b = 0$, the output of the oracle is defined in the same way up until the point that bad is set to true. Once that occurs, the output is instead determined by running $G(0, x : s; c_1, c_0)$. Because these two games are identical except in the behavior of the code $d \leftarrow b$ which is only executed once bad = true, they are "identical-until-bad".

In this section, the goal of the adversary is to cause bad to be set to true. Bounding the probability that $\mathcal{A}$ succeeds in this can be used to analyze security notions in two different ways. For indistinguishability-based security notions (e.g., PRG or PRF security), the two games G_b would correspond to the two worlds the adversary is attempting to distinguish between. For other security notions (e.g., collision resistance or discrete log security), we think of one of the G_b as corresponding to the game the adversary is trying to win and the other as corresponding to a related "ideal" world in which the adversary's success probably can easily be bounded. In either case, the fundamental lemma of game playing [4] can be used to bound the advantage of the adversary using a bound on the probability that bad is set.

A COMBINED EXPERIMENT. For our coming analysis it will be useful to relate executions of $G_0^{(G,G')}(\mathcal{A})$ and $G_1^{(G,G')}(\mathcal{A})$ to each other. For this we can think of a single combined experiment in which we sample c_0, c_1, and $c_\mathcal{A}$ *once* and then run both games separately using these coins.

For $b \in \{0, 1\}$, we let $Q_b^\mathcal{A}$ be a random variable denoting how many oracle queries $\mathcal{A}$ makes in the execution of $G_b^{(G,G')}(\mathcal{A})$ during this experiment. We let $\mathsf{BAD}_t^\mathcal{A}[b]$ denote the event that G' sets bad_t to true in the execution of $G_b^{(G,G')}(\mathcal{A})$. Note that $\mathsf{BAD}_t^\mathcal{A}[0]$ will occur if and only if $\mathsf{BAD}_t^\mathcal{A}[1]$ occurs, because the behavior of both games are identical up until the first time that bad is set and G' is never again executed once bad is true. Hence we can simplify notation by defining $\mathsf{BAD}_t^\mathcal{A}$ to be identical to the event $\mathsf{BAD}_t^\mathcal{A}[0]$, while keeping in mind that we can equivalently think of this event as occurring in the execution of either game. We additionally define the event that bad is ever set $\mathsf{BAD}^\mathcal{A} = \bigvee_{i=1}^\infty \mathsf{BAD}_i^\mathcal{A}$, the event that bad is set by one of the first j queries the adversary makes $\mathsf{BAD}_{\leqslant j}^\mathcal{A} = \bigvee_{i=1}^j \mathsf{BAD}_j^\mathcal{A}$, and the event that bad is set after the j-th query the adversary makes $\mathsf{BAD}_{>j}^\mathcal{A} = \bigvee_{i=j+1}^\infty$. Clearly, $\Pr[\mathsf{BAD}^\mathcal{A}] = \Pr[\mathsf{BAD}_{\leqslant j}^\mathcal{A}] + \Pr[\mathsf{BAD}_{>j}^\mathcal{A}]$. Again we can equivalently think of these events as occurring in either game. When the

---

[4] We emphasize that these algorithms are not allowed any randomness beyond the use of these coins.

adversary is clear from context we may choose to omit it from the superscript in our notation.

The fact that both games behave identically until bad is set true allows us to make several nice observations. If BAD does not hold, then $Q_0 = Q_1$ must hold. If BAD_t holds for some t, then both Q_0 and Q_1 must be at least t. One implication of this is that if $Q_1 = q$ holds for some q, then BAD is equivalent to $\mathsf{BAD}_{\leqslant q}$. Additionally, we can see that $\Pr[\mathsf{BAD}_{>q}] \leqslant \Pr[Q_b > q]$ must hold.

Defining our events and random variables in this single experiment will later allow to consider the expectation $\mathsf{E}[Q_0^d | Q_1 = q]$ for some $d, q \in \mathbb{N}$. In words, that is the expected value of Q_0 raised to the d-th power conditioned on $c_0, c_1, c_{\mathcal{A}}$ having been chosen so that $Q_1 = q$ held. Since Q_0 and Q_1 can only differ if BAD occurs we will be able to use $\Pr[\mathsf{BAD} | Q_1 = q]$ to bound how far $\mathsf{E}[Q_0^d | Q_1 = q]$ can be from $\mathsf{E}[Q_1^d | Q_1 = q] = q^d$.

δ-BOUNDEDNESS. Existing analysis of identical-until-bad games is done by assuming a worst-case bound $q_{\mathcal{A}}$ on the number of oracle queries that $\mathcal{A}$ makes (in either game). Given such a bound, one shows that $\Pr[\mathsf{BAD}^{\mathcal{A}}] \leqslant \delta(q_{\mathcal{A}})$ for some function δ. We will say that a game specification (G, G') is δ-bounded if for all $\mathcal{A}$ and $q \in \mathbb{N}$ we have that

$$\Pr[\mathsf{BAD}^{\mathcal{A}} | Q_1 = q] \leqslant \delta(q).$$

As observed earlier, if $Q_1 = q$ holds then bad_t cannot be set for any $t > q$. Hence $\Pr[\mathsf{BAD}^{\mathcal{A}} | Q_1 = q] = \Pr[\mathsf{BAD}^{\mathcal{A}}_{\leqslant q} | Q_1 = q]$.

We will, in particular, be interested in that case that $\delta(q) = \Delta \cdot q^d / N$ for some $\Delta, d, N \geqslant 1$[5]. We think of Δ and d as "small" and of N as "large". The main result of this section bounds the probability that an adversary sets bad by $O\left(\sqrt[d]{\delta(\mathsf{E}[Q_b])} \right)$ for either b if (G, G') is δ-bounded for such a δ.

While δ-boundedness may seem to be a strange condition, we show in Sect. 3.3 that the existing techniques for proving results of the form $\Pr[\mathsf{BAD}^{\mathcal{A}}] \leqslant \delta(q_{\mathcal{A}})$ for $\mathcal{A}$ making at most $q_{\mathcal{A}}$ queries can often be easily extended to show the δ-boundedness of a game (G, G'). The examples we consider are the collision-resistance and PRF security of a random oracle and the security of discrete log in the generic group model. In particular, these examples all possess a common form. First, we note that the output of $G(1, \dots)$ is independent of c_0. Consequently, the view of $\mathcal{A}$ when $b = 1$ is independent of c_0 and hence Q_1 is independent of c_0. To analyze $\Pr[\mathsf{BAD} | Q_1 = q]$ we can then think of c' and c_1 being fixed (fixing the transcript of interaction between $\mathcal{A}$ and its oracle in G_1^G) and argue that for any such length q interaction the probability of BAD is bounded by $\delta(q)$ over a random choice of c_0.

We note that this general form seems to typically be implicit in the existing analysis of bad flags for the statistical problems one comes across in ideal model analysis, but would not extend readily to examples where the probability of the

---

[5] We could simply let $\varepsilon = \Delta/N$ and instead say $\delta(q) = \varepsilon q^d$, but for our examples we found it more evocative to write these terms separately.

bad flag being set is reduced to the probability of an adversary breaking some computational assumption.

3.2   Expected-Time Bound from δ-boundedness

We can now state our result lifting δ-boundedness to a bound on the probability that an adversary sets bad given only its expected number of oracle queries.

Theorem 1. *Let* $\delta(q) = \Delta \cdot q^d / N$ *for* $\Delta, d, N \geqslant 1$. *Let* (G, G') *be a* δ-*bounded game specification. If* $N \geqslant \Delta \cdot 6^d$, *then for any* $\mathcal{A}$,

$$\Pr[\mathsf{BAD}^{\mathcal{A}}] \leqslant 5 \sqrt[d]{\frac{\Delta \cdot \mathsf{E}[Q_0^{\mathcal{A}}]^d}{N}} = 5 \sqrt[d]{\delta\left(\mathsf{E}[Q_0^{\mathcal{A}}]\right)}.$$

If $N \geqslant \Delta \cdot 2^d$, *then for any* $\mathcal{A}$,

$$\Pr[\mathsf{BAD}^{\mathcal{A}}] \leqslant 3 \sqrt[d]{\frac{\Delta \cdot \mathsf{E}[Q_1^{\mathcal{A}}]^d}{N}} = 3 \sqrt[d]{\delta\left(\mathsf{E}[Q_1^{\mathcal{A}}]\right)}.$$

We provide bounds based on the expected runtime in either of the two games since they are not necessarily the same. Typically, one of the two games will correspond to a "real" world and it will be natural to desire a bound in terms of the expected runtime in that game. The proof for Q_0 is slightly more complex and is given in this section. The proof for Q_1 is simpler and deferred to the full version of this paper [13]. In the full version we show via a simple attack that the d-th root in these bounds is necessary.

Proof (of Theorem 1). Let $u = 2^{-d}$ and $U = \left\lfloor \sqrt[d]{Nu/\Delta} \right\rfloor$. Note that $\delta(U) \leqslant u$. Now let $\mathcal{B}$ be an adversary that runs exactly like $\mathcal{A}$, except that it counts the number of oracle queries made by $\mathcal{A}$ and halts execution if $\mathcal{A}$ attempts to make a $U + 1$-th query. We start our proof by bounding the probability of $\mathsf{BAD}^{\mathcal{A}}$ by the probability of $\mathsf{BAD}^{\mathcal{B}}$ and an $O\left(\sqrt[d]{\delta\left(\mathsf{E}[Q_0^{\mathcal{A}}]\right)}\right)$ term by applying Markov's inequality. In particular we perform the calculations

$$\Pr[\mathsf{BAD}^{\mathcal{A}}] = \Pr[\mathsf{BAD}_{\leqslant U}^{\mathcal{A}}] + \Pr[\mathsf{BAD}_{>U}^{\mathcal{A}}] \tag{3}$$

$$= \Pr[\mathsf{BAD}_{\leqslant U}^{\mathcal{B}}] + \Pr[\mathsf{BAD}_{>U}^{\mathcal{A}}] \tag{4}$$

$$\leqslant \Pr[\mathsf{BAD}^{\mathcal{B}}] + \Pr\left[Q_0^{\mathcal{A}} > U\right] \tag{5}$$

$$\leqslant \Pr[\mathsf{BAD}^{\mathcal{B}}] + \mathsf{E}[Q_0^{\mathcal{A}}]/U \tag{6}$$

$$\leqslant \Pr[\mathsf{BAD}^{\mathcal{B}}] + 3\mathsf{E}[Q_0^{\mathcal{A}}] \sqrt[d]{\Delta/N}. \tag{7}$$

Step 4 follows because for all queries up to the U-th, adversary $\mathcal{B}$ behaves identically to $\mathcal{A}$ (and thus $\mathsf{BAD}_i^{\mathcal{A}} = \mathsf{BAD}_i^{\mathcal{B}}$ for $i \leqslant U$). Step 5 follows because $\mathsf{BAD}_{>U}^{\mathcal{B}}$ cannot occur (because $\mathcal{B}$ never makes more than U queries) and $\mathsf{BAD}_{>U}^{\mathcal{A}}$ can only occur if $Q_0^{\mathcal{A}}$ is at greater than U. Step 6 follows from Markov's inequality.

Step 7 follows from the following calculation which uses the assumption that $N \geqslant \Delta \cdot 6^d$ and that $u = 2^{-d}$,

$$U = \left\lfloor \sqrt[d]{Nu/\Delta} \right\rfloor \geqslant \sqrt[d]{Nu/\Delta} - 1 = \sqrt[d]{N/\Delta} \left(\sqrt[d]{u} - \sqrt[d]{\Delta/N} \right)$$

$$\geqslant \sqrt[d]{N/\Delta} \left(\sqrt[d]{2^{-d}} - \sqrt[d]{\Delta/(\Delta \cdot 6^d)} \right) = \sqrt[d]{N/\Delta} \left(1/2 - 1/6 \right).$$

In the rest of the proof we need to establish that $\Pr[\mathsf{BAD}^{\mathcal{B}}] \leqslant 2\mathsf{E}[Q_0^{\mathcal{A}}] \sqrt[d]{\Delta/N}$. We show this with $\mathsf{E}[Q_0^{\mathcal{B}}]$, which is clearly upper bounded by $\mathsf{E}[Q_0^{\mathcal{A}}]$. We will do this by first bounding $\Pr[\mathsf{BAD}^{\mathcal{B}}]$ in terms of $\mathsf{E}[(Q_1^{\mathcal{B}})^d]$, then bounding $\mathsf{E}[(Q_1^{\mathcal{B}})^d]$ in terms of $\mathsf{E}[(Q_0^{\mathcal{B}})^d]$, and then concluding by bounding this in terms of $\mathsf{E}[Q_0^{\mathcal{B}}]$. For the first of these steps we expand $\Pr[\mathsf{BAD}^{\mathcal{B}}]$ by conditioning on all possible values of $Q_1^{\mathcal{B}}$ and applying our assumption that (G, G') is δ-bounded to get

$$\Pr[\mathsf{BAD}^{\mathcal{B}}] = \sum_{q=1}^{U} \Pr[\mathsf{BAD}^{\mathcal{B}} | Q_1^{\mathcal{B}} = q] \Pr[Q_1^{\mathcal{B}} = q] \leqslant \sum_{q=1}^{U} (\Delta \cdot q^d / N) \Pr[Q_1^{\mathcal{B}} = q]$$

$$= \Delta/N \sum_{q=1}^{U} q^d \Pr[Q_1^{\mathcal{B}} = q] = \Delta \mathsf{E}[(Q_1^{\mathcal{B}})^d]/N.$$

So next we will bound $\mathsf{E}[(Q_1^{\mathcal{B}})^d]$ in terms of $\mathsf{E}[(Q_0^{\mathcal{B}})^d]$. To start, we will give a lower bound for $\mathsf{E}[(Q_0^{\mathcal{B}})^d | Q_1^{\mathcal{B}} = q]$ (when $q \leqslant U$) by using our assumption that (G, G') is δ-bounded. Let R_0 be a random variable which equals $Q_0^{\mathcal{B}}$ if $\mathsf{BAD}^{\mathcal{B}}$ does not occur and equals 0 otherwise. Clearly $R_0 \leqslant Q_0^{\mathcal{B}}$ always. Recall that if $\mathsf{BAD}^{\mathcal{B}}$ does not occur, then $Q_0^{\mathcal{B}} = Q_1^{\mathcal{B}}$ (and hence $R_0 = Q_1^{\mathcal{B}}$) must hold. We obtain

$$\mathsf{E}[(Q_0^{\mathcal{B}})^d | Q_1^{\mathcal{B}} = q] \geqslant \mathsf{E}[R_0^d | Q_1^{\mathcal{B}} = q]$$

$$= q^d \Pr[\neg \mathsf{BAD}^{\mathcal{B}} | Q_1^{\mathcal{B}} = q] + 0^d \Pr[\mathsf{BAD}^{\mathcal{B}} | Q_1^{\mathcal{B}} = q]$$

$$= q^d (1 - \Pr[\mathsf{BAD}^{\mathcal{B}} | Q_1^{\mathcal{B}} = q])$$

$$\geqslant q^d (1 - \delta(q)) \geqslant q^d (1 - u).$$

The last step used that $\delta(q) \leqslant \delta(U) \leqslant u$ because $q \leqslant U$.

Now we proceed by expanding $\mathsf{E}[(Q_1^{\mathcal{B}})^d]$ by conditioning on the possible value of $Q_1^{\mathcal{B}}$ and using the above bound to switch $\mathsf{E}[(Q_0^{\mathcal{B}})^d | Q_1^{\mathcal{B}} = q]$ in for q^d. This gives,

$$\mathsf{E}[(Q_1^{\mathcal{B}})^d] = \sum_{q=1}^{U} q^d \cdot \Pr[Q_1^{\mathcal{B}} = q]$$

$$= \sum_{q=1}^{U} \mathsf{E}[(Q_0^{\mathcal{B}})^d | Q_1^{\mathcal{B}} = q] \cdot \frac{q^d}{\mathsf{E}[(Q_0^{\mathcal{B}})^d | Q_1^{\mathcal{B}} = q]} \cdot \Pr[Q_1^{\mathcal{B}} = q]$$

$$\leqslant \sum_{q=1}^{U} \mathsf{E}[(Q_0^{\mathcal{B}})^d | Q_1^{\mathcal{B}} = q] \cdot \frac{q^d}{q^d (1 - u)} \cdot \Pr[Q_1^{\mathcal{B}} = q]$$

$$= (1 - u)^{-1} \mathsf{E}[(Q_0^{\mathcal{B}})^d]$$

Our calculations so far give us that $\Pr[\mathrm{BAD}^{\mathcal{B}}] \leqslant (1-u)^{-1}\mathsf{E}[(Q_0^{\mathcal{B}})^d] \cdot \Delta/N$. We need to show that this is bounded by $2\mathsf{E}[Q_0^{\mathcal{B}}]\sqrt[d]{\Delta/N}$. First note that $Q_0^{\mathcal{B}} \leqslant U$ always holds by the definition of $\mathcal{B}$, so

$$(1-u)^{-1}\mathsf{E}[(Q_0^{\mathcal{B}})^d] \cdot \Delta/N \leqslant (1-u)^{-1}\mathsf{E}[Q_0^{\mathcal{B}}] \cdot U^{d-1} \cdot \Delta/N.$$

Now since $U = \left\lfloor \sqrt[d]{Nu/\Delta} \right\rfloor$, we have $U^{d-1} \leqslant (Nu/\Delta)^{(d-1)/d}$ which gives

$$(1-u)^{-1}\mathsf{E}[Q_0^{\mathcal{B}}] \cdot U^{d-1} \cdot \Delta/N \leqslant (1-u)^{-1}(u^{(d-1)/d})\mathsf{E}[Q_0^{\mathcal{B}}]\sqrt[d]{\Delta/N}.$$

Finally, recall that we set $u = 2^{-d}$ and so

$$(1-u)^{-1}(u^{(d-1)/d}) = \frac{2^{-d\cdot(d-1)/d}}{1-2^{-d}} = \frac{2^{1-d}}{1-2^{-d}} \leqslant \frac{2^{1-1}}{1-2^{-1}} = 2.$$

Bounding $\mathsf{E}[Q_0^{\mathcal{B}}] \leqslant \mathsf{E}[Q_0^{\mathcal{A}}]$ and combining with our original bound on $\Pr[\mathrm{BAD}^{\mathcal{A}}]$ completes the proof.   □

3.3   Example Applications of Bad Flag Analysis

In this section we walk through some basic examples to show how a bound of $\Pr[\mathsf{bad}|Q_1 = q] \leqslant \Delta \cdot q^d/N$ can be proven using essentially the same techniques as typical bad flag analysis for worst-case runtime, allowing Theorem 1 to be applied. All of our examples follow the basic structure discussed earlier in this section. We write the analysis in terms of two games which are identical-until-bad and parameterized by a bit b. In the $b = 1$ game, the output of its oracles will depend on some coins we identify as c_1, while in the $b = 0$ case the output will depend on both c_1 and independent coins we identify as c_0. Then we think of fixing coins c_1 and the coins used by the adversary, which together fix Q_1 (the number of queries $\mathcal{A}$ would make in the $b = 1$ case), and argue a bound on the probability that bad is set over a random choice of c_0.

We write the necessary games in convenient pseudocode and leave the mapping to a game specification (G, G') to apply Theorem 1 implicit. We will abuse notation and use the name of our pseudocode game to refer to the corresponding game specification.

COLLISION-RESISTANCE OF A RANDOM ORACLE. Our first example is the collision resistance of a random oracle. Here an adversary is given access to a random function $h : \{0,1\}^* \to [N]$. It wins if it can find $x \neq y$ for which $h(x) = h(y)$, i.e., a collision in the random oracle. One way to express this is by the game $\mathsf{H}_0^{\mathrm{cr}}$ shown in Fig. 3. The random oracle is represented by the oracle Ro and the oracle FIN allows the adversary to submit supposed collisions.

In it, we have written Ro in a somewhat atypical way to allow comparison to $\mathsf{H}_1^{\mathrm{cr}}$ with which it is identical-until-bad. The coins used by these games determine a permutation π sampled at the beginning of the game and a value X chosen

Game $H_b^{cr}(\mathcal{A})$	Ro(x)
$t \leftarrow 0$	If $T[x] \neq \perp$ then return $T[x]$
$\pi \leftarrow^s \text{Perm}([N])$	$t \leftarrow t + 1$
For $i > N$ do $\pi[i] \leftarrow i$	$T[x] \leftarrow \pi[t]$
win $\leftarrow$ false	$X \leftarrow^s [N]$
Run $\mathcal{A}^{\text{Ro,Fin}}$	If $X \in \{\pi[i] : i < t\}$ then
Return win	bad $\leftarrow$ true
	If $b = 0$ then
Fin(x, y)	$T[x] \leftarrow X$
If $x \neq y$ and Ro$(x) =$ Ro(y) then	$t \leftarrow t - 1$
win $\leftarrow$ true	Return $T[x]$
Return win

Fig. 3. Game capturing collision-resistance of a random oracle (when $b = 0$).

Game $H_b^{prf}(\mathcal{A})$	Ro(k, x)
$T[\cdot, \cdot] \leftarrow^s \text{Fcs}([N] \times \mathcal{D}, \mathcal{R})$	If $k = K$ then
$F[\cdot] \leftarrow^s \text{Fcs}(\mathcal{D}, \mathcal{R})$	bad $\leftarrow$ true
$K \leftarrow^s [N]$	If $b = 0$ then return $F[x]$
$b' \leftarrow^s \mathcal{A}^{\text{Ror,Ro}}$	Return $T[k, x]$
Return $b' = 1$	Ror(x)
	Return $F[x]$

Fig. 4. Games capturing PRF security of a random oracle.

at random from $[N]$ during each Ro query[6]. We think of the former as c_1 and the latter as c_0. Ignoring repeat queries, when in H_1^{cr} the output of Ro is simply $\pi[1], \pi[2], \ldots$ in order. Thus clearly, $\Pr[H_1^{cr}(\mathcal{A})] = 0$ since there are no collisions in Ro. In H_0^{cr} the variable X modifies the output of Ro to provide colliding outputs with the correct distribution.

These games are identical-until-bad, so the fundamental lemma of game playing [4] gives us,

$$\Pr[H_0^{cr}(\mathcal{A})] \leqslant \Pr[H_0^{cr}(\mathcal{A}) \text{ sets bad}] + \Pr[H_1^{cr}(\mathcal{A})] = \Pr[H_0^{cr}(\mathcal{A}) \text{ sets bad}].$$

Now think of the adversary's coins and the choice of π as fixed. This fixes a value of Q_1 and a length Q_1 transcript of $\mathcal{A}$'s queries in $H_1^{cr}(\mathcal{A})$. If $\mathcal{A}$ made all of its queries to Fin, then Ro will have been executed $2Q_1$ times. On the i-th query to Ro, there is at most an $(i-1)/N$ probability that the choice of X will cause bad to be set. By a simple union bound we can get,

$$\Pr[\text{BAD}|Q_1 = q] \leqslant q(2q - 1)/N.$$

---

[6] We define $\pi[i] = i$ for $i > N$ just so the game H_1^{cr} is well-defined if $\mathcal{A}$ makes more than N queries.

Setting $\delta(q) = 2q^2/N$ we have that H^{cr} is δ-bounded, so Theorem 1 gives

$$\Pr[\mathsf{H}^{\mathsf{cr}}_0(\mathcal{A})] \leqslant 5\sqrt[2]{\frac{2 \cdot \mathsf{E}[Q^{\mathcal{A}}_0]^2}{N}}.$$

PSEUDORANDOMNESS OF A RANDOM ORACLE. Now consider using a random oracle with domain $[N] \times \mathcal{D}$ and range $\mathcal{R}$ as a pseudorandom function. The games for this are shown in Fig. 4. The real world is captured by $b = 0$ (because to output of the random oracle RO is made to be consistent with output of the real-or-random oracle ROR) and the ideal world by $b = 1$.

The coins of the game are random tables T and F as well as a random key K. We think of the key as c_0 and the tables as c_1. Because we have written the games so that the consistency check occurs in RO, we can clearly see the output of the oracles in $\mathsf{H}^{\mathsf{prf}}_1$ are independent of $c_0 = K$.

These games are identical-until-bad so from the fundamental lemma of game playing we have,

$$\Pr[\mathsf{H}^{\mathsf{prf}}_0(\mathcal{A})] - \Pr[\mathsf{H}^{\mathsf{prf}}_1(\mathcal{A})] \leqslant \Pr[\mathsf{H}^{\mathsf{prf}}_0(\mathcal{A}) \text{ sets bad}].$$

Now we think of c_1 and the coins of $\mathcal{A}$ as fixed. Over a random choice of K, each RO query has a $1/N$ change of setting bad. By a simple union bound we get,

$$\Pr[\mathsf{BAD}|Q_1 = q] \leqslant q/N.$$

Defining $\delta(q) = q/N$ we have that $\mathsf{H}^{\mathsf{prf}}$ is δ-bounded, so Theorem 1 gives

$$\Pr[\mathsf{H}^{\mathsf{prf}}_0(\mathcal{A})] - \Pr[\mathsf{H}^{\mathsf{prf}}_1(\mathcal{A})] \leqslant 5 \cdot \mathsf{E}[Q^{\mathcal{A}}_0]/N.$$

DISCRETE LOGARITHM SECURITY IN THE GENERIC GROUP MODEL. Next we consider discrete logarithm security in the generic group model for a prime order group $\mathbb{G}$ with generator g. One way to express this is by the game $\mathsf{H}^{\mathsf{dl}}_0$ shown in Fig. 5. In this expression, the adversary is given labels for the group elements it handles based on the time that this group element was generated by the adversary. The more general framing of the generic group model where $g^x \in \mathbb{G}$ is labeled by $\sigma(x)$ for a randomly chosen $\sigma : \mathbb{Z}_{|\mathbb{G}|} \to \{0,1\}^l$ for some $l \geqslant \lceil \log |\mathbb{G}| \rceil$ can easily be reduced to this version of the game.

At the beginning of the game polynomials $p_0(\cdot) = 0$, $p_1(\cdot) = 1$, and $p_2(\cdot) = X$ are defined. These are polynomials of the symbolic variable X, defined over $\mathbb{Z}_{|\mathbb{G}|}$. Then a random x is sampled and the goal of the adversary is to find this x. Throughout the game, a polynomial p_i represents the group element $g^{p_i(x)}$. Hence p_0 represents the identity element of the group, p_1 represents the generator g, and p_2 represents g^x. We think of the subscript of a polynomial as the adversary's label for the corresponding group element. The variable t tracks the highest label the adversary has used so far.

We let $\mathcal{P}^i$ denote the set of the first i polynomials that have been generated and $\mathcal{P}^i_x$ be the set of their outputs when evaluated on x. The oracle INIT tells the adversary if x happened to be 0 or 1 by returning the appropriate value

Game $H_b^{dl}(\mathcal{A})$	$\text{OP}(\boldsymbol{j}, \boldsymbol{\alpha})$
$p_0(\cdot) \leftarrow 0;\ p_1(\cdot) \leftarrow 1$	Require $\boldsymbol{j}[i] \leqslant t$ for $i = 1, \ldots, |\boldsymbol{j}|$
$p_2(\cdot) \leftarrow X$	Require $\boldsymbol{\alpha} \in \mathbb{Z}_{|\mathbb{G}|}^{|\boldsymbol{j}|}$
$t \leftarrow 2;\ x \leftarrow\!\!\$\ \mathbb{Z}_{|\mathbb{G}|}$	$t \leftarrow t + 1$
$x' \leftarrow\!\!\$\ \mathcal{A}^{\text{INIT}, \text{OP}}$	$p_t(\cdot) \leftarrow \sum_{i=1}^{|\boldsymbol{j}|} \boldsymbol{\alpha}[i] \cdot p_{\boldsymbol{j}[i]}(\cdot)$
Return $x = x'$	$\ell \leftarrow t$
	If $p_t(\cdot) \in \mathcal{P}^{t-1}$ then
$\underline{\text{INIT}()}$	$\quad \ell \leftarrow \min\{k < t : p_t(\cdot) = p_k(\cdot)\}$
$\ell \leftarrow 2$	If $p_t(x) \in \mathcal{P}_x^{t-1}$ and $p_t(\cdot) \notin \mathcal{P}^{t-1}$ then
If $p_2(x) \in \mathcal{P}_x^1$ then	$\quad$ bad $\leftarrow$ true
$\quad$ bad $\leftarrow$ true	$\quad$ If $b = 0$ then $\ell \leftarrow \min\{k < t : p_t(x) = p_k(x)\}$
$\quad$ If $b = 0$ then $\ell \leftarrow x$	Return ℓ
Return ℓ	

Fig. 5. Game capturing discrete logarithm security of a generic group (when $b = 0$). For $i \in \mathbb{N}$ and $x \in \mathbb{Z}_{|\mathbb{G}|}$, we use the notation $\mathcal{P}^i = \{p_0, \ldots, p_i\} \subset \mathbb{Z}_{|\mathbb{G}|}[X]$ and $\mathcal{P}_x^i = \{p(x) : p \in \mathcal{P}^i\} \subset \mathbb{Z}_{|\mathbb{G}|}$.

of ℓ. The oracle OP allows the adversary to perform multi-exponentiations. It specifies a vector $\boldsymbol{j}$ of labels for group elements and a vector $\boldsymbol{\alpha}$ of coefficients. The variable t is incremented and its new value serves as the label for the group element $\prod_i g_{\boldsymbol{j}[i]}^{\boldsymbol{\alpha}[i]}$ where $g_{\boldsymbol{j}[i]}$ is the group element with label $\boldsymbol{j}[i]$, i.e., $g^{p_{\boldsymbol{j}[i]}(x)}$. The returned value ℓ is set equal to the prior label of a group element which equals this new group element (if $\ell = t$, then no prior labels represented the same group element).

The only coins of this game are the choice of x which we think of as c_0. In H_1^{dl}, the adversary is never told when two labels it handles non-trivially represent the same group element so the view of $\mathcal{A}$ is independent of c_0, as desired[7]. Because the view of $\mathcal{A}$ is independent of x when $b = 1$ we have that $\Pr[H_1^{dl}(\mathcal{A})] = 1/|\mathbb{G}|$.

From the fundamental lemma of game playing,

$$\Pr[H_0^{dl}(\mathcal{A})] \leqslant \Pr[H_0^{dl}(\mathcal{A}) \text{ sets bad}] + \Pr[H_1^{dl}(\mathcal{A})] = \Pr[H_0^{cr}(\mathcal{A}) \text{ sets bad}] + 1/|\mathbb{G}|$$

Now thinking of the coins of $\mathcal{A}$ as fixed, this fixes a value of Q_1 and a length Q_1 transcript of queries that would occur in $H_1^{dl}(\mathcal{A})$. This in turn fixes the set of polynomials $\mathcal{P}^{Q_1+2}$. The flag bad will be set iff any of polynomials in the set

$$\{p(\cdot) - r(\cdot) | p \neq r \in \mathcal{P}^{Q_1+2}\}$$

have the value 0 when evaluated on x. Note these polynomials are non-zero and have degree at most 1. Thus, applying the Schwartz-Zippel lemma and a union bound we get,

$$\Pr[\text{BAD}|Q_1 = q] \leqslant \binom{q+3}{2} \cdot (1/|\mathbb{G}|) \leqslant 6q^2/|\mathbb{G}|.$$

---

[7] Two labels trivially represent the same group element if they correspond to identical polynomials.

Note the bound trivially holds when $q = 0$, since $\Pr[\mathsf{bad}|Q_1 = q] = 0$, so we have assumed $q \geqslant 1$ for the second bound. Defining $\delta(q) = 6q^2/|\mathbb{G}|$ we have that H^{dl} is δ-bounded, so Theorem 1 gives

$$\Pr[\mathsf{H}_0^{\mathsf{dl}}(\mathcal{A})] \leqslant 5\sqrt[2]{\frac{6 \cdot \mathsf{E}[Q_0^{\mathcal{A}}]^2}{|\mathbb{G}|}} + \frac{1}{|\mathbb{G}|}.$$

4 Concrete Security for a Forking Lemma

In this section we apply our techniques to obtaining concrete bounds on the soundness of proof systems. Of particular interest to us will be proof systems that can be proven to achieve a security notion known as witness-extended emulation via a very general "Forking Lemma" introduced by Bootle, Cerulli, Chaidos, Groth, and Petit (BCCGP) [6]. Some examples include Bulletproofs [7], Hyrax [24], and Supersonic [8]. Our expected-time techniques arise naturally for these proof systems because witness-extended emulation requires the existence of an expected-time *emulator* E for a proof system which is given oracle access to a cheating prover and produces transcripts with the same distribution as the cheating prover, but additionally provides a witness w for the statement being proven whenever it outputs an accepting transcript.

In this section we use a new way of expressing witness-extended emulation as a special case of a more general notion we call *predicate-extended emulation*. The more general notion will serve as a clean, modular way to provide a concrete security version of the BCCGP forking lemma. This modularity allows us to hone in on the steps where our expected time analysis can be applied to give concrete bounds and avoid some technical issues with the original BCCGP formulation of the lemma.

In the BCCGP blueprint, the task of witness-extended emulation is divided into a generic *tree-extended emulator* which for any public coin proof system produces transcripts with the same distribution as a cheating prover together with a set of accepting transcripts satisfying a certain tree structure and an *extractor* for the particular proof system under consideration which can extract a witness from such a tree of transcripts. The original forking lemma of BCCGP technically only applied for extractors that always output a witness given a valid tree with no collisions. However, typical applications of the lemma require that the extractor be allowed to fail when the cheating prover has (implicitly) broken some presumed hard computational problem. Several works subsequent to BCCGP noticed this gap in the formalism [7,8,24] and stated slight variants of the BCCGP forking lemma. However, these variants are still unsatisfactory. The variant lemmas in [7,24] technically only allows extractors which fail in extracting a witness with at most negligible probability *for every tree* (rather than negligible probably with respect to some efficiently samplable distribution over trees, as is needed). The more recent variant lemma in [8] is stated in such a way that the rewinding analysis at the core of the BCCGP lemma is *omitted* from the variant lemma and (technically) must be shown separately anytime it

Π	$\Pi(\pi, u, \text{aux})$ returns true iff	Name
Π_{wit}	$(u, \text{aux}) \in R_\pi$	Valid Witness
$\Pi_{\text{dl}}^{G,n}$	$\prod_{i=0}^{n} \pi_i^{\text{aux}_i} = 1_G$	Discrete Log Relation
Π_{val}^{n}	aux is a valid n-tree for u	Valid Tree
Π_{nocol}^{n}	aux has no challenge collisions	Collision-Free Tree

Fig. 6. Predicates we use. Other predicates Π_{bind} and Π_{rsa} are only discussed informally.

is to be applied to a proof system. None of these issues represent issues with the security of the protocols analyzed in these works. The intended meaning of each of their proofs is clear from context and sound, these issues are just technical bugs with the formalism of the proofs. However, to accurately capture concrete security it will be important that we have a precise and accurate formalism of this. Our notion of predicate-extended emulation helps to enable this.

In Sect. 4.1, we provide the syntax of proof systems as well as defining our security goals of predicate-extended emulation (a generalization of witness-extended emulation) and generator soundness (a generalization of the standard notion of soundness). Then in Sect. 4.2, we provide a sequence of simple lemmas and show how they can be combined to give our concrete security version on the forking lemma. Finally in Sect. 4.3, we discuss how our forking lemma can easily be applied to provide concrete bounds on the soundness of various existing proof systems. As a concrete example we give the first concrete security bound on the soundness of the Bulletproof zero-knowledge proof system for arithmetic circuits by Bünz et al. [7].

4.1 Syntax and Security of Proof Systems

PROOF SYSTEM. A proof system PS is a tuple $\text{PS} = (S, R, P, V, \mu)$ specifying a setup algorithm S, a relation R, a prover P, verifier V, and $\mu \in \mathbb{N}$. The setup algorithm outputs public parameters π. We say w is a witness for the statement u if $(u, w) \in R_\pi$. The prover (with input (u, w)) and the verifier (with input u) interact via $2\mu + 1$ moves as shown in Fig. 7.

Here tr is the *transcript* of the interaction and $d \in \{0, 1\}$ is the *decision* of V (with $d = 1$ representing acceptance and $d = 0$ representing rejection). *Perfect completeness* requires that for all π and $(u, w) \in R_\pi$, $\Pr[d = 1 : (\cdot, d) \leftarrow_\$ \langle P_\pi(u, w), V_\pi(u) \rangle] = 1$. If PS is public-coin, then m_{2i-1} output by V each round is set equal to its random coins. In this case, we let

$$
\begin{aligned}
&\underline{\langle P_\pi(u, w), V_\pi(u) \rangle} \\
&\sigma_P \leftarrow \bot; \ \sigma_V \leftarrow \bot; \ m_{-1} \leftarrow \bot \\
&(m_0, \sigma_P) \leftarrow_\$ P_\pi(u, w, m_{-1}, \sigma_P) \\
&\text{For } i = 1, \ldots, \mu \text{ do} \\
&\quad (m_{2i-1}, \sigma_V) \leftarrow_\$ V_\pi(u, m_{2i-2}, \sigma_V) \\
&\quad (m_{2i}, \sigma_P) \leftarrow_\$ P_\pi(u, w, m_{2i-1}, \sigma_P) \\
&tr \leftarrow (m_{-1}, m_0, m_1, \ldots, m_{2\mu}) \\
&d \leftarrow V_\pi(m_{2\mu}, u, \sigma_V) \\
&\text{Return } (tr, d)
\end{aligned}
$$

Fig. 7. Interaction between (honest) prover P and verifier V with public parameters π. Here tr is the transcript and $d \in \{0, 1\}$ is the decision.

$V_\pi(u, tr) \in \{0, 1\}$ denote V's decision after an interaction that produced transcript tr[8]. Throughout this section we will implicitly assume that any proof systems under discussion is public-coin. We sometimes refer to the verifier's outputs as challenges.

PREDICATE-EXTENDED EMULATION. The proof systems we consider were all analyzed with the notion of *witness-extended emulation* [11, 16]. This requires that for any efficient cheating prover P* there exists an efficient emulator E which (given oracle access to P* interacting with V and the ability to rewind them) produces transcripts with the same distribution as P* and almost always provides a witness for the statement when the transcript it produces is accepting. We will capture witness-extended emulation as a special case of what we refer to as *predicate-extended emulation*. We cast the definition as two separate security properties. The first (emulation security) requires that E produces transcripts with the same distribution as P*. The second (predicate extension) is parameterized by a predicate Π and requires that whenever E produces an accepting transcript, its auxiliary output must satisfy Π. As we will see, this treatment will allow a clean, modular treatment of how BCCGP and follow-up work [6–8, 24] analyze witness-extended emulation.

We start by considering game H^{emu} defined in Fig. 8. It is parameterized by a public-coin proof system PS, emulator E, and bit b. The adversary consists of a cheating prover P* and an attacker $\mathcal{A}$. This game measures $\mathcal{A}$'s ability to distinguish between a transcript generated by $\langle \mathsf{P}^*_\pi(u, s), \mathsf{V}_\pi(u) \rangle$ and one generated by E. The emulator E is given access to oracles NEXT and REW. The former has P* and V perform a round of interaction and returns the messages exchanged. The latter rewinds the interaction to the prior round. We define the advantage function $\mathsf{Adv}^{emu}_{\mathsf{PS},\mathsf{E}}(\mathsf{P}^*, \mathcal{A}) = \Pr[\mathsf{H}^{emu}_{\mathsf{PS},\mathsf{E},1}(\mathsf{P}^*, \mathcal{A})] - \Pr[\mathsf{H}^{emu}_{\mathsf{PS},\mathsf{E},0}(\mathsf{P}^*, \mathcal{A})]$. For the examples we consider there will be an E which (in expectation) performs a small number of oracle queries and does a small amount of local computation such that for any P* and $\mathcal{A}$ we have $\mathsf{Adv}^{emu}_{\mathsf{PS},\mathsf{E}}(\mathsf{P}^*, \mathcal{A}) = 0$.

Note that creating a perfect emulator is trivial in isolation; E can just make $\mu + 1$ calls to NEXT to obtain a tr with the exactly correct distribution. Where it gets interesting is that we will consider a second, auxiliary output of E and insist that it satisfies some predicate Π whenever tr is an accepting transcript. The adversary wins whenever tr is accepting, but the predicate is not satisfied. This is captured by the game $\mathsf{H}^{predext}$ shown in Fig. 8. We define $\mathsf{Adv}^{predext}_{\mathsf{PS},\mathsf{E},\Pi}(\mathsf{P}^*, \mathcal{A}) = \Pr[\mathsf{H}^{predext}_{\mathsf{PS},\mathsf{E},\Pi}(\mathsf{P}^*, \mathcal{A})]$. Again this notion is trivial in isolation; E can just output rejecting transcripts. Hence, both security notions need to be considered together with respect to the same E.

The standard notion of witness-extended emulating is captured by the predicate Π_{wit} which checks if aux is a witness for u, that is, $\Pi_{\mathsf{wit}}(\pi, u, \mathsf{aux}) = ((u, \mathsf{aux}) \in \mathsf{R}_\pi)$. Later we will define some other predicates. All the predicates we will make use of are summarized in Fig. 6. A proof system with a good witness-

---

[8] We include $m_{-1} = \perp$ in tr as a notational convenience.

Game $\mathsf{H}^{\mathsf{emu}}_{\mathsf{PS},\mathsf{E},b}(\mathsf{P}^*,\mathcal{A})$

$i \leftarrow 0;\ (\mathsf{S},\cdot,\cdot,\mathsf{V},\mu) \leftarrow \mathsf{PS}$
$\pi \leftarrow_{\$} \mathsf{S}$
$(u,s,\sigma_{\mathcal{A}}) \leftarrow_{\$} \mathcal{A}(\pi)$
$(tr_1,\cdot) \leftarrow_{\$} \langle \mathsf{P}^*_{\pi}(u,s), \mathsf{V}_{\pi}(u)\rangle$
$(tr_0,\cdot) \leftarrow_{\$} \mathsf{E}^{\mathrm{NEXT,REW}}(\pi,u)$
$b' \leftarrow_{\$} \mathcal{A}(tr_b,\sigma_{\mathcal{A}})$
Return $b' = 1$

Game $\mathsf{H}^{\mathsf{predext}}_{\mathsf{PS},\mathsf{E},\Pi}(\mathsf{P}^*,\mathcal{A})$

$i \leftarrow 0;\ (\mathsf{S},\cdot,\cdot,\mathsf{V},\mu) \leftarrow \mathsf{PS}$
$\pi \leftarrow_{\$} \mathsf{S}$
$(u,s,\cdot) \leftarrow_{\$} \mathcal{A}(\pi)$
$(tr,\mathrm{aux}) \leftarrow_{\$} \mathsf{E}^{\mathrm{NEXT,REW}}(\pi,u)$
Return $(\mathsf{V}_{\pi}(u,tr) \wedge \neg\Pi(\pi,u,\mathrm{aux}))$

NEXT()

Require $i \leqslant \mu$
If $i = 0$ then
$\quad \sigma^0_{\mathsf{P}} \leftarrow \bot;\ \sigma^1_{\mathsf{V}} \leftarrow \bot;\ m_{-1} \leftarrow \bot$
Else
$\quad (m_{2i-1}, \sigma^{i+1}_{\mathsf{V}}) \leftarrow_{\$} \mathsf{V}_{\pi}(u, m_{2i-2}, \sigma^i_{\mathsf{V}})$
$\quad (m_{2i}, \sigma^{i+1}_{\mathsf{P}}) \leftarrow_{\$} \mathsf{P}^*_{\pi}(u, s, m_{2i-1}, \sigma^i_{\mathsf{P}})$
$\quad m \leftarrow (m_{2i-1}, m_{2i})$
$i \leftarrow i + 1$
Return m

REW()

Require $i > 0$
$i \leftarrow i - 1$
Return ε

Fig. 8. Games defining predicate-extended emulation security of proof system PS.

extended emulator under some computational assumption may be said to be an *argument of knowledge*.

HARD PREDICATES. One class of predicates to consider are those which embed some computational problem about the public parameter π that is assumed to be hard to solve. We will say that Π is *witness-independent* if its output does not depend on its second input u. For example, if S outputs of length n vector of elements from a group $\mathbb{G}$ (we will denote this setup algorithm by $\mathsf{S}^n_{\mathbb{G}}$) we can consider the predicate $\Pi^{\mathbb{G},n}_{\mathsf{dl}}$ which checks if aux specifies a non-trivial discrete log relation. This predicate is useful for the analysis of a variety of proof systems [6,7,24]. Other useful examples include: (i) if S output parameters for a commitment scheme with Π_{bind} that checks if aux specifies a commitment and two different opening for it [6,8,24] and (ii) if S outputs a group of unknown order together with an element of that group and Π_{rsa} checks if aux specifies a non-trivial root of that element [8].

Whether a witness-independent predicate Π is hard to satisfy given the output of S is captured by the game $\mathsf{H}^{\mathsf{pred}}$ shown on the left side of Fig. 9. We define $\mathsf{Adv}^{\mathsf{pred}}_{\mathsf{S},\Pi}(\mathcal{A}) = \Pr[\mathsf{H}^{\mathsf{pred}}_{\mathsf{S},\Pi}(\mathcal{A})]$. Note, for example, that if $\mathsf{S}^n_{\mathbb{G}}$ and $\Pi^{\mathbb{G},n}_{\mathsf{dl}}$ is used, then this game is identical to discrete log relation security, i.e., $\mathsf{Adv}^{\mathsf{pred}}_{\mathsf{S}^n_{\mathbb{G}},\Pi^{\mathbb{G},n}_{\mathsf{dl}}}(\mathcal{A}) = \mathsf{Adv}^{\mathsf{dl\text{-}rel}}_{\mathbb{G},n}(\mathcal{A})$ for any adversary $\mathcal{A}$.

GENERATOR SOUNDNESS. Consider the games shown on the right side of Fig. 9. Both are parameterized by a *statement generator* G which (given the parameters π) outputs a statement u and some auxiliary information s about the statement. The first game $\mathsf{H}^{\mathsf{sound}}$ measure how well a (potentially cheating) prover P^* can use s to convince V that u is true. The second game $\mathsf{H}^{\mathsf{wit}}$ measures how well

Game $H^{pred}_{S,\Pi}(\mathcal{A})$	Game $H^{sound}_{PS,G}(P^*)$	Game $H^{wit}_{PS,G}(\mathcal{B})$
$\pi \leftarrow_{\$} S$	$(S,\cdot,\cdot,V,\cdot) \leftarrow PS$	$(S,\cdot,\cdot,V,\cdot) \leftarrow PS$
$aux \leftarrow_{\$} \mathcal{A}(\pi)$	$\pi \leftarrow_{\$} S$	$\pi \leftarrow_{\$} S$
Return $\Pi(\pi, \varepsilon, aux)$	$(u,s) \leftarrow_{\$} G(\pi)$	$(u,s) \leftarrow_{\$} G(\pi)$
	$(\cdot, d) \leftarrow_{\$} \langle P^*_\pi(u,s), V_\pi(u) \rangle$	$w \leftarrow \mathcal{B}(\pi, u, s)$
	Return $d = 1$	Return $(u,w) \in R_\pi$

Fig. 9. Left. Game defining hardness of satisfying predicate Π. **Right.** Games defining soundness of proof system PS with respect to instance generator G and difficulty of finding witness for statements produced by G.

an adversary $\mathcal{B}$ can produce a witness for u given s. We define $Adv^{sound}_{PS,G}(P^*) = Pr[H^{sound}_{PS,G}(P^*)]$ and $Adv^{wit}_{PS,G}(\mathcal{B}) = Pr[H^{wit}_{PS,G}(\mathcal{B})]$.

Note that the standard notion of soundness (that proving false statements is difficult) is captured by considering G which always outputs false statements. In this case, $Adv^{wit}_{PS,G}(\mathcal{A}) = 0$ for all $\mathcal{A}$. In other contexts, it may be assumed that it is computationally difficult to find a witness for G's statement.

4.2 Concrete Security Forking Lemma

Now we will work towards proving our concrete security version of the BCCGP forking lemma. This lemma provides a general framework for how to provide a good witness-extended emulator for a proof system. First, BCCGP showed how to construct a tree-extended emulator T which has perfect emulation security and (with high probability) outputs a set of transcripts satisfying a tree-like structure (defined later) whenever it outputs an accepting transcript. Then one constructs, for the particular proof system under consideration, an "extractor" X which given such a tree of transcripts can always produce a witness for the statement or break some other computational problem assumed to be difficult. Combining T and X appropriately gives a good witness-extended emulator.

Before proceeding to our forking lemma we will provide the necessary definitions of a tree-extended emulator and extractor, then state some simple lemmas that help build toward our forking lemma.

TRANSCRIPT TREE. Fix a proof system $PS = (S, R, P, V, \mu)$ and let the vector $\boldsymbol{n} = (n_1, \ldots, n_\mu) \in \mathbb{N}^\mu_{>0}$ be given. Let π be an output of S and u be a statement. For $h = 0, \ldots, \mu$ we will inductively define an $(n_{\mu-h+1}, \ldots, n_\mu)$-tree of transcripts for (PS, π, u). We will often leave some of (PS, π, u) implicit when they are clear from context.

First when $h = 0$, a ()-tree is specified by a tuple $(m_{2\mu-1}, m_{2\mu}, \ell)$ where $m_{2\mu-1}, m_{2\mu} \in \{0,1\}^*$ and ℓ is an empty list. Now an $(n_{\mu-(h+1)}, \ldots, n_\mu)$-tree is specified by a tuple $(m_{2(\mu-h)-1}, m_{2(\mu-h)}, \ell)$ where $m_{2(\mu-h)-1}, m_{2(\mu-h)} \in \{0,1\}^*$ and ℓ is a length $n_{\mu-(h+1)}$ list of $(n_{\mu-h}, \ldots, n_\mu)$-trees for (PS, π, u, tr).

When discussing such trees we say their height is h. When $h < \mu$ we will sometimes refer to it as a *partial tree*. We use the traditional terminology of *nodes, children, parent, root,* and *leaf.* We say the root node is at height h, its children are at height $h-1$, and so on. The leaf nodes are thus each at height 0. If a node is at height h, then we say it is at depth $\mu - h$.

Every path from the root to a leaf in a height h tree gives a sequence $(m_{2(\mu-h)-1}, m_{2(\mu-h)}, \ldots, m_{2\mu-1}, m_{2\mu})$ where $(m_{2(\mu-i)-1}, m_{2(\mu-i)})$ are the pair from the node at height i. Now if we fix a transcript prefix $tr' = (m_{-1}, m_0, \ldots, m_{2(\mu-h-1)-1}, m_{2(\mu-h-1)})$, then we can think of tr' and the tree as inducing $\prod_{i=1}^{\mu} n_i$ different transcripts $tr = (m_0, \ldots, m_{2\mu-1}, m_{2\mu})$, one for each path. We will say that the tree is *valid* for tr' if $V_\pi(u, tr) = 1$ for each transcript tr induced by the tree. Note that tr' is an empty list when $h = \mu$ so we can omit reference to tr' and simply refer to the tree as valid.

Suppose V's coins are drawn from $S \times \mathbb{Z}_p$ for some set S and $p \in \mathbb{N}$. We will refer to the second component of its coins are the integer component. Let node be a parent node at height $i > 0$. If any two of its children have $m_{2(\mu-i+1)-1}$ with identical integer components, then we say that node has a challenge collision. A tree has a *challenge collision* if any of its nodes have a challenge collision.

A tree-extractor emulator should return trees which are valid and have no challenge collision. We capture this with the predicates Π_{val}^n and Π_{nocol}^n defined by:

- $\Pi_{\mathsf{val}}^n(\pi, u, \mathrm{aux})$ returns true iff aux is a valid n-tree.
- $\Pi_{\mathsf{nocol}}^n(\pi, u, \mathrm{aux})$ returns true iff aux is an n-tree that does not have a challenge collision.

TREE-EXTENDED EMULATOR. Let a proof system $\mathsf{PS} = (\mathsf{S}, \mathsf{R}, \mathsf{P}, \mathsf{V}, \mu)$ and let $(n_1, \ldots, n_\mu) \in \mathbb{N}_{>2}^\mu$ be given. Then consider the tree-extended emulator T given in Fig. 10 which comes from BCCGP. The sub-algorithms T_i are given a partial transcript tr. They call NEXT to obtain the next messages of a longer partial transcript and attempt to create a partial tree with is valid for it. This is done by repeatedly calling T_{i+1} to construct each branch of the tree. Should the first such call fail, then T_i will abort. Otherwise, it will continue calling T_{i+1} as many times as necessary to have n_{i+1} branches. The base case of this process is T_μ which does not need children branches and instead just checks if its transcript is accepting, returning $\perp$ to its calling procedure if not. The following result shows that T emulates any cheating prover perfectly and almost always outputs a valid tree whenever it outputs an accepting transcript. The technical core of the lemma is in the bound on the expected efficiency of T.

Lemma 4. *Let* $\mathsf{PS} = (\mathsf{S}, \mathsf{R}, \mathsf{P}, \mathsf{V}, \mu)$ *be a public coin proof system. Suppose* V's *challenges are uniformly drawn from* $S \times \mathbb{Z}_p$ *for set* S *and* $p \in \mathbb{N}$. *Let* $\boldsymbol{n} = (n_1, \ldots, n_\mu) \in \mathbb{N}_{>0}^\mu$ *be given. Let* $N = \prod_{i=1}^{\mu} n_i$. *Let* P^* *be a cheating prover and* $\mathcal{A}$ *be an adversary. Define* T *as shown in Fig. 10. Then the following all hold:*

1. $\mathsf{Adv}_{\mathsf{PS}, \mathsf{T}}^{\mathsf{emu}}(\mathsf{P}^*, \mathcal{A}) = 0$
2. $\mathsf{Adv}_{\mathsf{PS}, \mathsf{T}, \Pi_{\mathsf{val}}^n}^{\mathsf{predext}}(\mathsf{P}^*, \mathcal{A}) = 0$
3. $\mathsf{Adv}_{\mathsf{PS}, \mathsf{T}, \Pi_{\mathsf{nocol}}^n}^{\mathsf{predext}}(\mathsf{P}^*, \mathcal{A}) \leqslant 5\mu N / \sqrt{2p}$
4. *The expected number of times* T *executes* $V_\pi(u, \cdot)$ *is* N.

Algorithm $\mathsf{T}^{\text{NEXT},\text{REW}}(\pi, u)$	$\mathsf{T}_i^{\text{NEXT},\text{REW}}(\pi, u, tr)$ $//0 \leqslant i < \mu$
$(tr, \text{tree}) \leftarrow_{\$} \mathsf{T}_0^{\text{NEXT},\text{REW}}(\pi, u, ())$	$(m_{2i-1}, m_{2i}) \leftarrow \text{NEXT}()$
Return (tr, tree)	$tr.\text{add}(m_{2i-1}, m_{2i})$
	$(tr', \text{tree}') \leftarrow_{\$} \mathsf{T}_{i+1}^{\text{NEXT},\text{REW}}(\pi, u, tr)$
$\mathsf{T}_\mu^{\text{NEXT},\text{REW}}(\pi, u, tr)$	If $\text{tree}' \neq \bot$ then
$(m_{2\mu-1}, m_{2\mu}) \leftarrow \text{NEXT}()$	$\quad \ell \leftarrow (\text{tree}')$
$tr.\text{add}(m_{2\mu-1}, m_{2\mu})$	$\quad$ While $|\ell| < n_{i+1}$ do
If $\mathsf{V}_\pi(u, tr) = 1$ then	$\qquad (\cdot, \text{tree}') \leftarrow_{\$} \mathsf{T}_{i+1}^{\text{NEXT},\text{REW}}(\pi, u, tr)$
$\quad \ell \leftarrow ()$	$\qquad$ If $\text{tree}' \neq \bot$ then $\ell.\text{add}(\text{tree}')$
$\quad \text{tree} \leftarrow (m_{2\mu-1}, m_{2\mu}, \ell)$	$\quad \text{tree} \leftarrow (m_{2i-1}, m_{2i}, \ell)$
Else $\text{tree} \leftarrow \bot$	Call $\text{REW}()$
Call $\text{REW}()$	Return (tr', tree)
Return (tr, tree)	

Fig. 10. The BCCGP tree-extended emulator.

5. *The expected number of queries that* T *makes to* NEXT *is less than* $\mu N + 1$[9]. *Exactly one of these queries is made while* $i = 1$ *in* NEXT.

For comparison, in the full version of this paper [13] we analyze a natural tree-extended emulator with a small bounded worst-case runtime. Its ability to produce valid trees is significantly reduced by its need to work within a small worst-case runtime, motivating the need for T to only be efficient in expected runtime.

Proof (of Lemma 4). All of the claims except the third follow from BCCGP's analysis of T. The advantage $\mathsf{Adv}_{\mathsf{PS},\mathsf{T},\Pi_{\text{nocol}}^n}^{\text{predext}}(\mathsf{P}^*, \mathcal{A})$ can be upper-bounded by the probability that the integer component of V's output is repeated across *any* of T's queries to NEXT. BCCGP bounded this probability by applying Markov's inequality to obtain an upper bound on T's running time and then applying the birthday bound to get an $O(\mu N/\sqrt[3]{p})$ bound. We can instead apply our switching lemma analysis from the full version of this paper [13] (or the techniques from our analysis of the collision resistance of a random oracle in Sect. 3.3) to obtain the stated bound because V will sample μN challenges in expectation. $\qquad \square$

EXTRACTORS. Let X be an algorithm and Π_1, Π_2 be predicates. We say that X is a (Π_1, Π_2)-extractor if $\Pi_1(\pi, u, \text{aux}) \Rightarrow \Pi_2(\pi, u, \mathsf{X}(\pi, u, \text{aux}))$. Let T be an emulator. Then we define $\mathsf{E}^\dagger[\mathsf{T}, \mathsf{X}]$ to be the emulator that on input (π, u) with oracle access to NEXT and REW will first compute $(tr, \text{aux}) \leftarrow_{\$} \mathsf{T}^{\text{NEXT},\text{REW}}(\pi, u)$ and then returns $(tr, \mathsf{X}(\pi, u, \text{aux}))$. The following straightforward lemma relates the security of T and $\mathsf{E}^\dagger$.

Lemma 5. *Let* PS *be a proof system,* T *be an emulator,* Π_1 *and* Π_2 *be predicates,* P^* *be a cheating prover, and* $\mathcal{A}$ *be an adversary. Let* X *be a* (Π_1, Π_2)-*extractor. Then the following hold:*

---

[9] More precisely, the expected number of queries that T makes to NEXT is the number of nodes in a $(n_1, \ldots, n_\mu)$-tree. This is $\sum_{i=0}^{\mu} \prod_{j=1}^{i} n_j$, where $\prod_{j=1}^{0} n_j = 1$.

$$
\boxed{
\begin{array}{l}
\underline{\text{Adversary } \mathcal{B}_{\mathsf{E}}(\pi)} \\
i \leftarrow 0 \\
(u, s, \cdot) \leftarrow_{\$} \mathcal{A}(\pi) \\
(\cdot, \text{aux}) \leftarrow_{\$} \mathsf{E}^{\text{Next},\text{Rew}}(\pi, u) \\
\text{Return aux} \\
\hline
\underline{\text{Next},\text{Rew}} \\
//\text{Defined as in Fig. 8}
\end{array}
}
$$

Fig. 11. Reduction adversary for Theorem 2.

- $\mathsf{Adv}^{\text{emu}}_{\mathsf{PS},\mathsf{E}^\dagger[\mathsf{T},\mathsf{X}]}(\mathsf{P}^*, \mathcal{A}) = \mathsf{Adv}^{\text{emu}}_{\mathsf{PS},\mathsf{T}}(\mathsf{P}^*, \mathcal{A})$
- $\mathsf{Adv}^{\text{predext}}_{\mathsf{PS},\mathsf{E}^\dagger[\mathsf{T},\mathsf{X}],\Pi_2}(\mathsf{P}^*, \mathcal{A}) \leqslant \mathsf{Adv}^{\text{predext}}_{\mathsf{PS},\mathsf{T},\Pi_1}(\mathsf{P}^*, \mathcal{A})$

FORKING LEMMA. Finally, we can state and prove our concrete security version of the BCCGP forking lemma. It captures the fact that any protocol with a $(\Pi^n_{\text{val}} \wedge \Pi^n_{\text{nocol}}, \Pi_{\text{wit}} \vee \Pi^*)$-extractor has a good witness-extended emulator (assuming Π^* is computationally difficult to satisfy)[10].

Theorem 2 (Forking Lemma). *Let* $\mathsf{PS} = (\mathsf{S}, \mathsf{R}, \mathsf{P}, \mathsf{V}, \mu)$ *be a public coin proof system. Suppose* V*'s challenges are uniformly drawn from* $S \times \mathbb{Z}_p$ *for set* S *and* $p \in \mathbb{N}$. *Let* $\boldsymbol{n} = (n_1, \ldots, n_\mu) \in \mathbb{N}^\mu_{>0}$ *be given. Let* $N = \prod^\mu_{i=1} n_i$. *Let* P^* *be a cheating prover and* $\mathcal{A}$ *be an adversary. Define* T *as shown in Fig. 10. Let* Π^* *be a witness-independent predicate. Let* X *be a* $(\Pi^n_{\text{val}} \wedge \Pi^n_{\text{nocol}}, \Pi_{\text{wit}} \vee \Pi^*)$-extractor. *Let* $\mathsf{E} = \mathsf{E}^\dagger[\mathsf{T}, \mathsf{X}]$. *Let* $\mathcal{B}_{\mathsf{E}}$ *be as defined in Fig. 11. Then the following all hold:*

1. $\mathsf{Adv}^{\text{emu}}_{\mathsf{PS},\mathsf{E}}(\mathsf{P}^*, \mathcal{A}) = 0$
2. $\mathsf{Adv}^{\text{predext}}_{\mathsf{PS},\mathsf{E},\Pi_{\text{wit}}}(\mathsf{P}^*, \mathcal{A}) \leqslant \mathsf{Adv}^{\text{pred}}_{\mathsf{PS},\Pi^*}(\mathcal{B}_{\mathsf{E}}) + 5\mu N/\sqrt{2p}$
3. *The expected number of times* T *executes* $\mathsf{V}_\pi(u, \cdot)$ *(inside of* E*) is* N.
4. *The expected number of queries that* E *makes to* NEXT *is less than* $\mu N + 1$. *Exactly one of these queries is made while* $i = 1$ *in* NEXT.
5. *The expected runtime of* $\mathcal{B}_{\mathsf{E}}$ *is approximately* $T_{\mathcal{A}} + Q_{\mathsf{E}} \cdot T_{\mathsf{P}^*} + T_{\mathsf{E}}$ *where* T_x *is the worst-case runtime of* $x \in \{\mathcal{A}, \mathsf{P}^*, \mathsf{E}\}$ *and* $Q_{\mathsf{E}} < \mu N + 1$ *is the expected number of queries that* E *makes to* NEXT *in* $\mathsf{H}^{\text{predext}}_{\mathsf{PS},\mathsf{E},\Pi^*}(\mathsf{P}^*, \mathcal{A})$.

It will be useful to have the following simple lemma for comparing $\mathsf{Adv}^{\text{predext}}$ with different choices of predicate that are related by logical operators. It can be derived from basic probability calculations.

Lemma 6. *Let* PS *be a proof system,* E *be an emulator,* Π_1 *and* Π_2 *be predicates,* P^* *be a cheating prover, and* $\mathcal{A}$ *be an adversary. Then,*

$$
\mathsf{Adv}^{\text{predext}}_{\mathsf{PS},\mathsf{E},\Pi_1 \vee \Pi_2}(\mathsf{P}^*, \mathcal{A}) + \mathsf{Adv}^{\text{predext}}_{\mathsf{PS},\mathsf{E},\Pi_1 \wedge \Pi_2}(\mathsf{P}^*, \mathcal{A})
$$

$$
=
$$

$$
\mathsf{Adv}^{\text{predext}}_{\mathsf{PS},\mathsf{E},\Pi_1}(\mathsf{P}^*, \mathcal{A}) + \mathsf{Adv}^{\text{predext}}_{\mathsf{PS},\mathsf{E},\Pi_2}(\mathsf{P}^*, \mathcal{A}).
$$

---

[10] The existence a $(\Pi^n_{\text{val}} \wedge \Pi^n_{\text{nocol}}, \Pi_{\text{wit}} \vee \Pi^*)$-extractor is a natural generalization of special soundness.

and

$$\mathsf{Adv}^{\mathsf{predext}}_{\mathsf{PS,E,\Pi_1}}(\mathsf{P}^*,\mathcal{A}) \leqslant \mathsf{Adv}^{\mathsf{predext}}_{\mathsf{PS,E,\Pi_1\vee\Pi_2}}(\mathsf{P}^*,\mathcal{A}) + \mathsf{Adv}^{\mathsf{predext}}_{\mathsf{PS,E,\neg\Pi_2}}(\mathsf{P}^*,\mathcal{A}).$$

Proof (of Theorem 2). Applying Lemmas 4 and 5, and observing how E is constructed give us the first, third, and fourth claim. For the other claims we need to consider the adversary $\mathcal{B}_\mathsf{E}$. Note that it runs E just it would be run in $\mathsf{H}^{\mathsf{predext}}_{\mathsf{PS,E,\Pi^*}}(\mathsf{P}^*,\mathcal{A})$, so the distribution over (π,aux) is identical in $\mathsf{H}^{\mathsf{pred}}_{\mathsf{S,\Pi}}(\mathcal{B}_\mathsf{E})$ as in that game. Furthermore, recall that Π^* is witness-independent, so it ignores its second input. It follows that,

$$\mathsf{Adv}^{\mathsf{predext}}_{\mathsf{PS,E,\neg\Pi^*}}(\mathsf{P}^*,\mathcal{A}) = \Pr[V_\pi(u,tr) \wedge \neg(\neg\Pi^*(\pi,u,\mathsf{aux})) \text{ in } \mathsf{H}^{\mathsf{predext}}]$$

$$\leqslant \Pr[\Pi^*(\pi,u,\mathsf{aux}) \text{ in } \mathsf{H}^{\mathsf{predext}}]$$

$$= \Pr[\Pi^*(\pi,\varepsilon,\mathsf{aux}) \text{ in } \mathsf{H}^{\mathsf{pred}}] = \mathsf{Adv}^{\mathsf{pred}}_{\mathsf{S,\Pi}}(\mathcal{B}_\mathsf{E}).$$

The claimed runtime of $\mathcal{B}$ is clear from its pseudocode (noting that the view of E is distributed identically to its view in $\mathsf{H}^{\mathsf{predext}}$ so its expected number of NEXT queries is unchanged).

For the second claim, we perform the calculations

$$\mathsf{Adv}^{\mathsf{predext}}_{\mathsf{PS,E,\Pi_{wit}}}(\mathsf{P}^*,\mathcal{A}) \leqslant \mathsf{Adv}^{\mathsf{predext}}_{\mathsf{PS,E,\Pi_{wit}\vee\Pi^*}}(\mathsf{P}^*,\mathcal{A}) + \mathsf{Adv}^{\mathsf{predext}}_{\mathsf{PS,E,\neg\Pi^*}}(\mathsf{P}^*,\mathcal{A})$$

$$= \mathsf{Adv}^{\mathsf{predext}}_{\mathsf{PS,E,\Pi^n_{val}\wedge\Pi^n_{nocol}}}(\mathsf{P}^*,\mathcal{A}) + \mathsf{Adv}^{\mathsf{pred}}_{\mathsf{PS,\Pi^*}}(\mathcal{B})$$

$$= \mathsf{Adv}^{\mathsf{predext}}_{\mathsf{PS,E,\Pi^n_{val}}}(\mathsf{P}^*,\mathcal{A}) + \mathsf{Adv}^{\mathsf{predext}}_{\mathsf{PS,E,\Pi^n_{nocol}}}(\mathsf{P}^*,\mathcal{A}) + \mathsf{Adv}^{\mathsf{pred}}_{\mathsf{PS,\Pi^*}}(\mathcal{B})$$

$$\leqslant 5\mu N/\sqrt{2p} + \mathsf{Adv}^{\mathsf{pred}}_{\mathsf{PS,\Pi^*}}(\mathcal{B}).$$

This sequence of calculation uses (in order) Lemma 6, Lemma 5 and the bound we just derived, Lemma 6 (again), and Lemma 4.

4.3 Concrete Bounds on Soundness

Now we discuss how the forking lemma we just derived can be used to provide concrete bounds on soundness. First we make the generic observation that witness-extended emulation implies soundness. Then we discuss how we can use these results together with our expected-time generic group model bound on discrete log security to give concrete bounds on the soundness of various proof systems based on discrete log security, in particular giving the first concrete bound on the soundness of the Bulletproofs proof system for arithmetic circuits.

WITNESS-EXTENDED EMULATION IMPLIES SOUNDNESS. The following theorem observes that finding a witness for u cannot be much more difficult that convincing a verifier u if an efficient witness-extended extractor exists.

Theorem 3. *Let* $\mathsf{PS} = (\mathsf{S,R,P,V},\mu)$ *be a proof system,* G *be a statement generator,* E *be an emulator, and* P^* *be a cheating prover. Define* $\mathcal{A}$ *and* $\mathcal{B}$ *as shown in Fig. 12. Then,*

$$\mathsf{Adv}^{\mathsf{sound}}_{\mathsf{PS},G}(\mathsf{P}^*) \leqslant \mathsf{Adv}^{\mathsf{wit}}_{\mathsf{PS},G}(\mathcal{B}) + \mathsf{Adv}^{\mathsf{emu}}_{\mathsf{PS,E}}(\mathsf{P}^*,\mathcal{A}) + \mathsf{Adv}^{\mathsf{predext}}_{\mathsf{PS,E,\Pi_{wit}}}(\mathsf{P}^*,\mathcal{A}).$$

Adversary $\mathcal{A}(\pi)$	Adversary $\mathcal{B}(\pi, u, s)$
$(u, s) \leftarrow_\$ G(\pi)$	$i \leftarrow 0$
Return $(u, s, (\pi, u))$	$(\cdot, w) \leftarrow_\$ \mathsf{E}^{\text{NEXT,REW}}(\pi, u)$
	Return w
$\mathcal{A}(tr, \sigma_A)$	
$(\pi, u) \leftarrow \sigma_A$	NEXT,REW
$b' \leftarrow \mathsf{V}_\pi(u, tr)$	//Defined as in Fig. 8
Return b'	

Fig. 12. Adversaries used in Theorem 3.

The runtime of that $\mathcal{A}$ is roughly that of G plus that of V. The runtime of $\mathcal{B}$ is roughly that of E when given oracle access to P^* and V interacting.

Proof (Sketch). The use of V in $\mathcal{A}$ ensures that the probability E outputs an accepting transcript must be roughly the same as the probability that P^* convinces V to accept. The difference between these probabilities is bounded by $\mathsf{Adv}_{\mathsf{PS,E}}^{\mathsf{emu}}(\mathsf{P}^*, \mathcal{A})$. Then the Π_{wit} security of E ensures that the probability it outputs a valid witness cannot be much less than the probability it outputs an accepting transcript. The difference between these probabilities is bounded by $\mathsf{Adv}_{\mathsf{PS,E},\Pi_{\mathsf{wit}}}^{\mathsf{predext}}(\mathsf{P}^*, \mathcal{A})$. Adversary $\mathcal{B}$ just runs E to obtain a witness, so $\mathsf{Adv}_{\mathsf{PS},G}^{\mathsf{wit}}(\mathcal{B})$ is the probability that E would output a valid witness.

DISCRETE LOG PROOF SYSTEMS. A number of the proof systems in [6,7,24] were shown to have a $(\Pi_{\mathsf{val}}^n \wedge \Pi_{\mathsf{nocol}}^n, \Pi_{\mathsf{wit}} \vee \Pi_{\mathsf{dl}}^{G,n})$-extractor X. For any such proof system PS, Theorem 3 and Theorem 2 bound the soundness of PS by the discrete log relation security of $\mathbb{G}$ against an expected-time adversary $\mathcal{B}_{\mathsf{E}^\dagger[\mathsf{T,X}]}$. Moreover, we can then apply Lemma 3 to tightly bound this adversary's advantage by the advantage of an expected-time adversary against normal discrete log security. *We know* how to bound the advantage of such an adversary in the generic group model from Sect. 3.3.

So to obtain a bound on the soundness of these proof systems in the generic group model we can just apply these results to the proof system. To obtain our final concrete security bound in the generic group model we need only to read the existing analysis of the proof system and extract the following parameters,

- p: the size of the set V draws the integer component of its challenges from
- $|\mathbb{G}|$: the size of the group used
- $N = \prod_{i=1}^{\mu} n_i$: the size of the tree that X requires
- $n \geqslant 1$: the number of group elements in the discrete log relation instance
- q_{V}: the number of multi-exponentiations V performs[11]
- q_{X}: the number of multi-exponentiations that X performs

We say such a proof system $\mathsf{PS} = (\mathsf{S}, \mathsf{R}, \mathsf{P}, \mathsf{V}, \mu)$ and extractor X *have parameters* $(p, |\mathbb{G}|, N, n, q_{\mathsf{V}}, q_{\mathsf{X}})$. We obtain the following theorem for such a system, bounding its soundness in the generic group model.

---

[11] Note that the size of these multi-exponentiations does not matter.

Theorem 4. *Let* $\mathsf{PS} = (\mathsf{S}, \mathsf{R}, \mathsf{P}, \mathsf{V}, \mu)$ *be a proof system and* X *be an extractor that has parameters* $(p, |\mathbb{G}|, N, n, q_{\mathsf{V}}, q_{\mathsf{X}})$. *Let* G *be a statement generator performing at most* q_G *multi-exponentiations and* P^* *be a cheating prover that performs at most* q_{P^*} *multi-exponentiations each time it is run. Define* $\mathcal{B}$ *as shown in Fig. 12. Then in the generic group model we have,*

$$\mathsf{Adv}^{\mathsf{sound}}_{\mathsf{PS},G}(\mathsf{P}^*) \leqslant \mathsf{Adv}^{\mathsf{wit}}_{\mathsf{PS},G}(\mathcal{B}) + 5\sqrt{\frac{6 \cdot Q_{\mathcal{C}}^2}{|\mathbb{G}|}} + \frac{2}{|\mathbb{G}|} + \frac{5\mu N}{\sqrt{2p}}$$

where $Q_{\mathcal{C}} = q_G + (\mu N + 1)q_{\mathsf{P}^*} + q_{\mathsf{X}} + Nq_{\mathsf{V}} + n + 1$. *The runtime of* $\mathcal{B}$ *is roughly that of* $\mathsf{E}^\dagger[\mathsf{T}, \mathsf{X}]$ *when given oracle access to* P^* *and* V *interacting.*

Proof. The result follows by applying Theorem 3, Theorem 2, Lemma 3, and the generic group model bound from Sect. 3.3 as discussed above. □

CONCRETE SECURITY OF BULLETPROOFS. Finally, we can use the above to obtain a concrete security bound on the soundness of the Bulletproofs proof system for arithmetic circuits of Bünz et al. [7][12]. To do so we only need to figure out the parameters discussed above. Suppose the proof system is being used for an arithmetic circuit with M multiplication gates. Using techniques of BCCGP [6] this is represented by a size M Hadamard product and $L \leqslant 2M$ linear constraints. Then per Bünz et al. the proof system has the following parameters:

- $p = (|\mathbb{G}| - 1)/2^{13}$
- $|\mathbb{G}|$ is the size of group $\mathbb{G}$ in which discrete logs are assumed to be hard
- $N = 7(L + 1)M^3$
- $n = 2M + 2$
- $q_{\mathsf{V}} = 3M + \log_2(M) + 4$
- $q_{\mathsf{X}} = 0$

Having proven our discrete log bound in a generic group model allowing multi-exponentiations is helpful here; it makes our bound not depend on the size of V's multi-exponentiations.

Corollary 1. *Let* PS *be the Bulletproofs proof system for arithmetic circuits define in Sect. 5.2 of [7] using a group of size* $|\mathbb{G}|$. *Let* M *denote the number of multiplication gates in the circuit and* $L \leqslant 2M$ *the number of linear constraints. Let* G *be a statement generator performing at most* q_G *multi-exponentiations and* P^* *be a cheating prover that performs at most* q_{P^*} *multi-exponentiations*

---

[12] In particular, throughout this section we refer to the logarithmic-sized arithmetic circuit protocol described in Section 5.2 of their paper.

[13] As described in [7], the challenges are drawn from $\mathbb{Z}^*_{|\mathbb{G}|}$. For some rounds of the protocol $x, y \in \mathbb{Z}^*_{|\mathbb{G}|}$ would be considered colliding if $x \equiv_{|\mathbb{G}|} \pm y$. We capture this by thinking of coins drawn from $\{+, -\} \times \mathbb{Z}_p$. Then $(+, x)$ represents $x + 1 \in \mathbb{Z}^*_{|\mathbb{G}|}$ and $(-, x)$ represents $-x - 1 \bmod |\mathbb{G}| = |\mathbb{G}| - x - 1 \in \mathbb{Z}^*_{|\mathbb{G}|}$. Hence the collision condition corresponds to equality in the $\mathbb{Z}_p$ component.

each time it is run. Define $\mathcal{B}$ as shown in Fig. 12. Assume $|\mathbb{G}| \geqslant 2$, $L \geqslant 1$, and $M \geqslant 16$. Then in the generic group model,

$$\mathsf{Adv}^{\mathsf{sound}}_{\mathsf{PS},G}(\mathsf{P}^*) < \mathsf{Adv}^{\mathsf{wit}}_{\mathsf{PS},G}(\mathcal{B}) + \frac{13q_G + 258q_{\mathsf{P}^*} \cdot LM^3 \log_2(M) + 644 \cdot LM^4}{\sqrt{|\mathbb{G}|}}.$$

The runtime of $\mathcal{B}$ is roughly that of $\mathsf{E}^{\dagger}[\mathsf{T}, \mathsf{X}_B]$ when given oracle access to P^* and V interacting, where X_B is the Bulletproofs extractor.

We expect q_{P^*} to be the largest of the parameters, so the bound is dominated by the $O\left(q_{\mathsf{P}^*} \cdot LM^3 \log_2(M)/\sqrt{|\mathbb{G}|}\right)$ term.

Proof. The bound was obtained by plugging our parameters (and $\mu = 3 + \log_2(M)$) into Theorem 4, then simplifying the expression using that $|\mathbb{G}| \geqslant 2$, $L \geqslant 1$, and $M \geqslant 16$. The (straightforward) details of this are provided in the full version of this paper [13]. □

Acknowledgments. We thank Ahsrujit Ghoshal for extensive discussions and his involvement in the earlier stages of this work. We also thank Benedikt Bünz for some clarification regarding [7].

This work was partially supported by NSF grants CNS-1930117 (CAREER), CNS-1926324, CNS-2026774, a Sloan Research Fellowship, and a JP Morgan Faculty Award.

References

1. Barak, B., Lindell, Y.: Strict polynomial-time in simulation and extraction. In: 34th ACM STOC, pp. 484–493. ACM Press (2002)
2. Bellare, M., Neven, G.: Multi-signatures in the plain public-key model and a general forking lemma. In: Juels, A., Wright, R.N., De Capitani, S., di Vimercati, (eds.) ACM CCS 2006, pp. 390–399. ACM Press (2006)
3. Bellare, M., Rogaway, P.: Random oracles are practical: a paradigm for designing efficient protocols. In: Denning, D.E., Pyle, R., Ganesan, R., Sandhu, R.S., Ashby, V. (eds.) ACM CCS 93, pp. 62–73. ACM Press (1993)
4. Bellare, M., Rogaway, P.: The security of triple encryption and a framework for code-based game-playing proofs. In: Vaudenay, S. (ed.) EUROCRYPT 2006. LNCS, vol. 4004, pp. 409–426. Springer, Heidelberg (2006). https://doi.org/10.1007/11761679_25
5. Bernstein, D.J.: How to stretch random functions: the security of protected counter sums. J. Cryptol. **12**(3), 185–192 (1999)
6. Bootle, J., Cerulli, A., Chaidos, P., Groth, J., Petit, C.: Efficient zero-knowledge arguments for arithmetic circuits in the discrete log setting. In: Fischlin, M., Coron, J.-S. (eds.) EUROCRYPT 2016. LNCS, vol. 9666, pp. 327–357. Springer, Heidelberg (2016). https://doi.org/10.1007/978-3-662-49896-5_12
7. Bünz, B., Bootle, J., Boneh, D., Poelstra, A., Wuille, P., Maxwell, G.: Bulletproofs: short proofs for confidential transactions and more. In: 2018 IEEE Symposium on Security and Privacy, pp. 315–334. IEEE Computer Society Press (2018)
8. Bünz, B., Fisch, B., Szepieniec, A.: Transparent SNARKs from DARK compilers. In: Canteaut, A., Ishai, Y. (eds.) EUROCRYPT 2020. LNCS, vol. 12105, pp. 677–706. Springer, Cham (2020). https://doi.org/10.1007/978-3-030-45721-1_24

9. Chen, S., Steinberger, J.: Tight security bounds for key-alternating ciphers. In: Nguyen, P.Q., Oswald, E. (eds.) EUROCRYPT 2014. LNCS, vol. 8441, pp. 327–350. Springer, Heidelberg (2014). https://doi.org/10.1007/978-3-642-55220-5_19

10. Goldreich, O.: On expected probabilistic polynomial-time adversaries: a suggestion for restricted definitions and their benefits. J. Cryptol. **23**(1), 1–36 (2010)

11. Groth, J., Ishai, Y.: Sub-linear zero-knowledge argument for correctness of a shuffle. In: Smart, N. (ed.) EUROCRYPT 2008. LNCS, vol. 4965, pp. 379–396. Springer, Heidelberg (2008). https://doi.org/10.1007/978-3-540-78967-3_22

12. Hoang, V.T., Tessaro, S.: Key-alternating ciphers and key-length extension: exact bounds and multi-user security. In: Robshaw, M., Katz, J. (eds.) CRYPTO 2016. LNCS, vol. 9814, pp. 3–32. Springer, Heidelberg (2016). https://doi.org/10.1007/978-3-662-53018-4_1

13. Jaeger, J., Tessaro, S.: Expected-time cryptography: generic techniques and applications to concrete soundness. Cryptology ePrint Archive (2020). http://eprint.iacr.org/2020/

14. Katz, J., Lindell, Y.: Handling expected polynomial-time strategies in simulation-based security proofs. In: Kilian, J. (ed.) TCC 2005. LNCS, vol. 3378, pp. 128–149. Springer, Heidelberg (2005). https://doi.org/10.1007/978-3-540-30576-7_8

15. Katz, J., Lindell, Y.: Handling expected polynomial-time strategies in simulation-based security proofs. J. Cryptol. **21**(3), 303–349 (2008)

16. Lindell, Y.: Parallel coin-tossing and constant-round secure two-party computation. J. Cryptol. **16**(3), 143–184 (2003)

17. Maurer, U.: Indistinguishability of random systems. In: Knudsen, L.R. (ed.) EUROCRYPT 2002. LNCS, vol. 2332, pp. 110–132. Springer, Heidelberg (2002). https://doi.org/10.1007/3-540-46035-7_8

18. Maurer, U.: Abstract models of computation in cryptography. In: Smart, N.P. (ed.) Cryptography and Coding 2005. LNCS, vol. 3796, pp. 1–12. Springer, Heidelberg (2005). https://doi.org/10.1007/11586821_1

19. Maurer, U., Pietrzak, K., Renner, R.: Indistinguishability amplification. In: Menezes, A. (ed.) CRYPTO 2007. LNCS, vol. 4622, pp. 130–149. Springer, Heidelberg (2007). https://doi.org/10.1007/978-3-540-74143-5_8

20. Patarin, J.: The "coefficients H" technique (invited talk). In: Avanzi, R.M., Keliher, L., Sica, F. (eds.) SAC 2008. LNCS, vol. 5381, pp. 328–345. Springer, Heidelberg (2009). https://doi.org/10.1007/978-3-642-04159-4_21

21. Pointcheval, D., Stern, J.: Security arguments for digital signatures and blind signatures. J. Cryptol. **13**(3), 361–396 (2000)

22. Shoup, V.: Lower bounds for discrete logarithms and related problems. In: Fumy, W. (ed.) EUROCRYPT 1997. LNCS, vol. 1233, pp. 256–266. Springer, Heidelberg (1997). https://doi.org/10.1007/3-540-69053-0_18

23. Shoup, V.: Sequences of games: a tool for taming complexity in security proofs. Cryptology ePrint Archive, Report 2004/332 (2004). http://eprint.iacr.org/2004/332

24. Wahby, R.S., Tzialla, I., Shelat, A., Thaler, J., Walfish, M.: Doubly-efficient zkSNARKs without trusted setup. In: 2018 IEEE Symposium on Security and Privacy, pp. 926–943. IEEE Computer Society Press (2018)

On the Complexity of Arithmetic Secret Sharing

Ronald Cramer[1,2], Chaoping Xing[3], and Chen Yuan[1(✉)]

[1] CWI, Amsterdam, The Netherlands
{cramer,chen.yuan}@cwi.nl
[2] Mathematical Institute, Leiden University, Leiden, The Netherlands
[3] School of Electronic Information and Electric Engineering, Shanghai Jiao Tong
University, Shanghai, People's Republic of China
xingcp@sjtu.edu.cn

Abstract. Since the mid 2000s, asymptotically-good strongly-multiplicative linear (ramp) secret sharing schemes over a fixed finite field have turned out as a central theoretical primitive in numerous constant-communication-rate results in multi-party cryptographic scenarios, and, surprisingly, in two-party cryptography as well.

Known constructions of this most powerful class of arithmetic secret sharing schemes all rely heavily on algebraic geometry (AG), i.e., on dedicated AG codes based on asymptotically good towers of algebraic function fields defined over finite fields. It is a well-known open question since the first (explicit) constructions of such schemes appeared in CRYPTO 2006 whether the use of "heavy machinery" can be avoided here. i.e., the question is whether the mere existence of such schemes can also be proved by "elementary" techniques only (say, from classical algebraic coding theory), even disregarding effective construction. So far, there is no progress.

In this paper we show the theoretical result that, (1) *no matter whether this open question has an affirmative answer or not*, these schemes *can* be constructed explicitly by *elementary algorithms* defined in terms of basic algebraic coding theory. This pertains to all relevant operations associated to such schemes, including, notably, the generation of an instance for a given number of players n, as well as error correction in the presence of corrupt shares. We further show that (2) the algorithms are *quasi-linear time* (in n); this is (asymptotically) significantly more efficient than the known constructions. That said, the *analysis* of the mere termination of these algorithms *does* still rely on algebraic geometry, in the sense that it requires "blackbox application" of suitable *existence* results for these schemes.

Our method employs a nontrivial, novel adaptation of a classical (and ubiquitous) paradigm from coding theory that enables transformation of *existence* results on asymptotically good codes into *explicit construction* of such codes via *concatenation*, at some constant loss in parameters achieved. In a nutshell, our generating idea is to combine a cascade of explicit but "asymptotically-bad-yet-good-enough schemes" with an asymptotically good one in such a judicious way that the latter can be

R. Pass and K. Pietrzak (Eds.): TCC 2020, LNCS 12552, pp. 444–469, 2020.
https://doi.org/10.1007/978-3-030-64381-2_16

selected with exponentially small number of players in that of the compound scheme. This opens the door to efficient, elementary exhaustive search.

In order to make this work, we overcome a number of nontrivial technical hurdles. Our main handles include a novel application of the recently introduced notion of Reverse Multiplication-Friendly Embeddings (RMFE) from CRYPTO 2018, as well as a novel application of a natural variant in arithmetic secret sharing from EUROCRYPT 2008.

1 Introduction

Background

This paper deals with linear secret sharing schemes (LSSS for short) defined over a finite field $\mathbb{F}_q$, with the *additional* property of being *strongly-multiplicative* [12]. We first briefly recall these (well-known) notions below (for precise definitions, see Sect. 2). We consider LSSS with share-space dimension 1, i.e., each of the n players is assigned a single $\mathbb{F}_q$-element as a share. The dimension of the secret-space or the size of the secret, however, is not restricted, i.e., the secret is generally a vector in $\mathbb{F}_q^k$ (for some given positive integer k) instead of an element of $\mathbb{F}_q$. As a matter of terminology, we speak of an *LSSS for $\mathbb{F}_q^k$ over $\mathbb{F}_q$* (on n players).[1]

The *linearity property* means that an $\mathbb{F}_q$-linear combination of "input" sharings, adding shares "player-wise" (similar for scalar multiplication), results in a correct "output" sharing where the corresponding secret is defined by taking the same combination over the secrets of the input sharings. There is *t-privacy* if the shares of any t out of n players jointly give no information about the secret and there is *r-reconstruction* if the shares of any r out of n players jointly always determine the secret uniquely, as follows: for each set of r-players, there is an $\mathbb{F}_q$-linear map that, when applied to the vector consisting of their shares, always gives the secret,

An LSSS Σ for $\mathbb{F}_q^k$ over $\mathbb{F}_q$ on n players is *t-strong-multiplicative*[2] if there is t-privacy ($t \geq 1$) and if "the square of the LSSS" has $(n-t)$-reconstruction. For a vector $(s_0, s_1, \ldots, s_n) \in \Sigma$, $(s_1, \ldots, s_n) \in \mathbb{F}_q^n$ is said to be a full share-vector with secret $s_0 \in \mathbb{F}_q^k$. The latter is equivalent to the statement that, if $\mathbf{x}, \mathbf{x}' \in \mathbb{F}_q^n$ are full share-vectors with respective secrets $s_0, s_0' \in \mathbb{F}_q^k$, then, for each set A of $n - t$ players, the "player-wise" product $\mathbf{x}_A * \mathbf{x}_A' \in \mathbb{F}_q^{n-t}$ of the respective share-vectors $\mathbf{x}_A, \mathbf{x}_A'$ held by A determines the coordinate-wise product $s_0 * s_0' \in \mathbb{F}_q^k$ of the secrets uniquely in that, for each such A, there exists an $\mathbb{F}_q$-linear map $\phi^{(A)}$ such that $\phi^{(A)}(\mathbf{x}_A * \mathbf{x}_A') = s_0 * s_0'$ always holds.[3] We may also refer to the t as

---

[1] Secret space can be easily adapted to $\mathbb{F}_Q^k$ where $\mathbb{F}_Q$ is an extension field of $\mathbb{F}_q$ [6].

[2] In [13]. A t-strongly multiplicative LSSS on n players for $\mathbb{F}_q^k$ over $\mathbb{F}_q$ is also called an $(n, t, 2, t)$-arithmetic secret sharing scheme with secret space $\mathbb{F}_q^k$ and share space $\mathbb{F}_q$.

[3] The coordinate-wise product of the secrets being thus uniquely determined *does not* imply that corresponding maps are *linear*. (See [7]) As linearity is essential in many applications, it is not sufficient to simply require this uniqueness.

the *adversary-parameter*. We note that t-strong-multiplicativity trivially implies $(n - t)$-reconstruction. Also, it implies an effective algorithm for recovering the secret from n shares even if at most t of them are corrupted, by a generalization of the Berlekamp-Welch algorithm (see [13]).

We note that the classical application of these schemes is in information-theoretic multiparty computation (MPC) perfectly secure against an active adversary (in [1] and follow-up work based on Shamir's secret sharing scheme, abstracted and generalized in [12] for linear secret sharing). Although the Shamir secret sharing scheme satisfies the t-strong-multiplicativity mentioned above, the share size grows with the number of players, i.e., the share size of the Shamir secret sharing scheme on n players is $n \log n$. On the other hand, there does exist secret sharing scheme that the share size does not grow with the number of players. We call it asymptotically good secret sharing scheme.

For an infinite family of such schemes, *with $\mathbb{F}_q$ fixed and n tending to infinity*, we say it is *asymptotically good* if $k, t \in \Omega(n)$. We emphasize that, in this asymptotic context, there is yet another parameter of importance to some (theoretical) applications, namely the *density* (within the set of positive integers) of the infinite sequence of player-numbers $n_1, n_2, \ldots$ realized by the successive instances. Concretely, we equate this density to $\limsup_{i \to \infty} n_{i+1}/n_i$. If this is bounded by a constant (as is the case for known constructions), i.e., not infinity, then we may as well assume that the family realizes *any given player-number* n if it is large enough. Briefly, this is by *folding* the schemes and by slightly generalizing the definitions as follows. For $n \in (n_i, n_{i+1})$ we simply give each player an appropriate constant number of shares in the n_{i+1}-st scheme, thereby shrinking the length to its desired magnitude. Effectively, the share-space is now a product over a constant number of copies of $\mathbb{F}_q$, endowed with coordinate-wise multiplication (and-addition). This will affect the adversary parameter t only by a constant multiplicative factor (and will not affect the secret-space dimension k). The definitions are trivially adapted to this situation. Finally, note that if the density equals 1, then there is essentially no such loss.[4]

This asymptotic notion was first considered and realized in [3] in 2006, thereby enabling an "asymptotic version" of the general MPC theorem from [1]. Since 2007, with the advent of the so-called "MPC-in-the-head paradigm" [19], these asymptotically-good schemes have been further exposed as a central theoretical primitive in numerous constant communication-rate results in multi-party cryptographic scenarios, and, surprisingly, in two-party cryptography as well.

As to the construction of these schemes, all known results [3,5,9] rely heavily on algebraic geometry, more precisely, on dedicated algebraic geometric codes based on good towers of algebraic function fields defined over finite fields. It is a well-known open question since 2006 whether the use of "heavy machinery" can be avoided here. I.e., the question is whether the mere existence of such schemes can also be proved by "elementary" techniques only (say, from classical algebraic

---

[4] Whenever it is deemed convenient, one may even drop the condition that n is large enough, by inserting into the family a finite number of schemes for small player-numbers consistent with asymptotic parameters.

coding theory), even disregarding effective construction. So far, no progress on this question has been reported. For a full account on history, constructions and applications, see [13].

Our Results

In this paper we show the theoretical result that, no matter *whether this open question has an affirmative answer or not*, these schemes *can* be constructed explicitly by elementary algorithms defined in terms of basic algebra. This pertains to all relevant operations associated to such schemes: the generation of an instance for a given number of players n, the generation of shares, the computation of the linear maps associated to the strongly-multiplicative property, as well as error correction in the presence of corrupt shares. In fact, we show the algorithms are *quasi-linear time* (in n). To the best of our knowledge, the asymptotically-good strongly-multiplicative LSSS based on algebraic geometry code has time complexity at least quadratic [22]. The density in our construction is *minimal*, i.e., it equals 1. As a contrast, the best explicit algebraic geometry codes lead to an strongly-multiplicative LSSS over $\mathbb{F}_q$ with density $\sqrt{q}$. On the other hand, the algebraic geometry code derived from Shimura curve achieves density 1 but is non-constructive.

In spite of the elementary nature of the algorithms, the *analysis* of their mere termination *does* currently rely on algebraic geometry, in that it is founded, in part, on "blackbox use" of suitable existence results on asymptotically good schemes. Thus. in particular, there is no paradox here. In some sense, we may conclude that, even though algebraic geometry may be essential to the *existence* of these schemes (as the state-of-the-art may seem to suggest), it is not essential to their *explicit construction*.

We do note, however, that the positive adversary rate t/n we achieve is smaller than the optimal rate achieved by known results. Namely, here we achieve rate $1/27$ instead of getting arbitrarily close to $1/3$. Also, we do not achieve t-uniformity of the shares (i.e., the additional property that, besides t-privacy, the shares of any t players are uniformly random in $\mathbb{F}_q^t$, But, for (almost) all theoretical applications, this does not matter.

Finally, though this is somewhat besides the theoretical point we are making here, our quasi-linear time algorithms may perhaps help to show that some of the theoretical applications enjoy overall quasi-linear time complexity as well. This could be interesting in its own right, but it still remains to be seen.

Overview of Our Method

A naive hope for elementary, effective (Monte-Carlo) construction would be the following. At the core of all known constructions is the observation that it suffices to find linear codes C over $\mathbb{F}_q$ such that *each of the codes C, $C^\perp$ (its dual)* and C^{*2} (its *square*[5]) is asymptotically-good.[6] If such codes could be shown to be "sufficiently dense", then an approach by selecting random codes could potentially work. However, using the theory of quadratic forms over finite fields, it has been shown in [8] that, over a fixed finite field $\mathbb{F}_q$, a random linear code C of length n and dimension $\sqrt{n}+\lambda$, has the property that $C^{*2} = \mathbb{F}_q^n$ with probability exponentially (in λ) close to 1. Thus, although C and $C^\perp$ can be rendered asymptotically good in this way (by Gilbert-Varshamov arguments), the code C^{*2} would be "maximally-bad" almost certainly; the powering operation on codes is very destructive, almost always.

Instead, our method employs a nontrivial, novel adaptation of a classical paradigm from coding theory that enables transformation of *existence* results on asymptotically good codes into *explicit construction* of such codes via *concatenation*, at some constant loss in parameters achieved. In a nutshell, the idea is to combine an effective construction of "asymptotically-bad-yet-good-enough codes" with asymptotically good ones in such a judicious way that the latter can be selected with exponentially small length in that of the compound code. This opens the door to efficient, elementary exhaustive search. That said, the *analysis* of the time-complexity of these algorithms (in fact, that there exists correct such algorithms at all, even disregarding their actual complexity) continues to rely on algebraic geometry. We note that this complexity is superior to that of previous schemes. On the other hand, the adversary-rate is some small factor below the optimal rate of $1/3$ achieved by previous schemes.

The approach taken in this paper is inspired by a classical idea from coding theory, going back to the 1960s [14]: results on the *existence* of asymptotically good linear codes may be transformed into *effective construction* of such codes via *concatenation*, incurring just a constant loss in the parameters achieved.

On a high level, this works as follows. One can take a "sufficiently good" code defined over an extension of the target "base field" as the *outer code*. This code needs not to be *asymptotically* good. Viewing the extension field as a vector space over the base field, one then encodes each coordinate to a vector over the base field through an asymptotically good code defined over the base field, the inner code. This compound scheme is linear over the base field and its length is the product of the lengths of the outer and inner codes.

The point is now that, if the outer code has constant rate and relative minimum distance as a function of its length and the degree of the extension grows very slowly with respect to its length, say logarithmically (which could be achieved e.g. with Reed-Solomon codes), then, in order for the compound code to be asymptotically good, it suffices that the inner code has exponentially small length as a function of the length of the outer code. This makes it possible to derandomize the random argument for Gilbert-Varshamov bound so as to find a linear inner code attaining this bound in polynomial time with respect to the

---

[5] The $\mathbb{F}_q$-linear code generated by all terms of the form $x * y$, where $x, y \in C$ and where $x * y$ is the coordinate-wise product of two vectors.

[6] I.e., The finite field $\mathbb{F}_q$ is fixed, the length of the codes tends to infinity, and the relative dimension and relative minimum distance are positive.

length of the outer code [17].[7] The concatenation idea that reduces the dimension of the searching space also enlightens us to look for a similar result in linear secret sharing scheme with strong multiplication.

In order to make such a paradigm work for us here, we overcome a number of nontrivial obstacles.

1. How to define a proper and useful concatenation for linear secret sharing schemes with strong multiplication. The purpose of concatenation is to bring down the field size so as to make our exhaustive search run in quasi-linear time. Let Σ_1 be an LSSS on n_1 players for $\mathbb{F}_{Q^m}$ over $\mathbb{F}_Q$ and Σ_2 be an LSSS on n_2 players for $\mathbb{F}_Q$ over $\mathbb{F}_q$ where $\mathbb{F}_Q$ is an extension field of $\mathbb{F}_q$. Let us call Σ_1 an *outer* LSSS and Σ_2 an *inner* LSSS. The concatenation $\Sigma_1 \circ \Sigma_2$ of Σ_1 with Σ_2 is an LSSS on $n_1 n_2$ players defined as follows: $(s_0, \mathbf{z}_1, \ldots, \mathbf{z}_{n_1}) \in \Sigma_1 \circ \Sigma_2 \subseteq \mathbb{F}_{Q^m} \times (\mathbb{F}_q^{n_2})^{n_1}$ if $(s_i, \mathbf{z}_i) \in \Sigma_2 \subseteq \mathbb{F}_Q \times \mathbb{F}_q^{n_2}$ for $i = 1, \ldots, n_1$ and $(s_0, s_1, \ldots, s_{n_1}) \in \Sigma_1 \subseteq \mathbb{F}_{Q^m} \times \mathbb{F}_Q^{n_1}$.[8] As an analogy to concatenated codes, we show that if Σ_1 is a t_1-strongly-multiplicative LSSS on n_1 players and Σ_2 is a t_2-strongly-multiplicative LSSS on n_2 players, then $\Sigma_1 \circ \Sigma_2$ is a $t_1 t_2$-strongly-multiplicative LSSS on $n_1 n_2$ players.

2. The exhaustive search space should be small. We first describe what we can achieve for one concatenation. We set our outer LSSS Σ_1 to be a Shamir secret sharing scheme. The encoding and decoding time of this LSSS is quasi-linear. Since our compound scheme is defined over a constant field, we set $q = O(1)$ and $n_2 = \log Q$ in Σ_2 defined above. Now, the search space has dimension $\log Q$. Since the Shamir secret sharing scheme is asymptotically-bad, the compound scheme $\Sigma_1 \circ \Sigma_2$ is not asymptotically-good strongly-multiplicative LSSS unless Σ_2 is asymptotically-good strongly-multiplicative LSSS. The existence of asymptotically-good strongly-multiplicative LSSS is ensured by algebraic geometry codes. However, to meet our elementary algorithm claim, we have to replace the explicit construction with an exhaustive search algorithm which enumerates every linear subspace. This can only be done in time $\exp(\Omega(\log^2 Q))$. Clearly, the search space is not small enough to meet our quasi-linear time claim. We resolve this issue by concatenating *twice*. Let Σ_1 be an Shamir secret sharing scheme Σ_1 on $O(Q)$ players for $\mathbb{F}_{Q^m}$ over $\mathbb{F}_Q$ and Σ_2 be *another Shamir secret sharing scheme* on $O(q)$ players for $\mathbb{F}_Q$ over $\mathbb{F}_q$ with $q = O(\log Q)$. The compound scheme $\Sigma := \Sigma_1 \circ \Sigma_2$ is a strongly-multiplicative LSSS for $\mathbb{F}_{Q^m}$ over $\mathbb{F}_q$. Let Σ_3 be an asymptotically-good strongly-multiplicative LSSS on $O(\log \log Q)$ players for $\mathbb{F}_q$ over $\mathbb{F}_p$ with $p = O(1)$ which is found by an exhaustive search and ensured by algebraic geometry codes. The final scheme $\Sigma \circ \Sigma_3$ turns out to be an asymptotically-good strongly-multiplicative LSSS on $O(Q \log Q \log \log Q)$ players for $\mathbb{F}_{Q^m}$ over $\mathbb{F}_p$ with $p = O(1)$. We can see that this two-rounds

---

[7] More precisely, this random argument is applied to the Toeplitz matrix which only has $O(n)$ independent entries, i.e., a random linear code whose generator matrix is a Toeplitz matrix reaches Gilbert-Varshamov bound with high probability.

[8] This can be viewed as a twist of re-sharing the share in MPC protocols.

concatenation brings down the field size so small that an exhaustive search only runs in time complexity polynomial in $\log Q$.

3. The dimension of secret space should be linear in the number of players. When we overcome the above two obstacles, we already obtain an asymptotically-good strongly-multiplicative LSSS $\Sigma \circ \Sigma_3$ for $\mathbb{F}_{Q^m}$ over $\mathbb{F}_p$ that runs in quasi-linear time. Note that the secret space is still $\mathbb{F}_{Q^m}$. We are not done yet since we claim that our LSSS has secret space $\mathbb{F}_p^k$ with $k = \Omega(Q)$. We resort to a recent developed tool called reverse multiplication friendly embedding (RMFE) [10] to overcome this obstacle. An RMFE is a pair of maps (ϕ, ψ) with $\phi : \mathbb{F}_q^k \to \mathbb{F}_{q^m}$ and $\psi : \mathbb{F}_{q^m} \to \mathbb{F}_q^k$ such that for any $\mathbf{x}, \mathbf{y} \in \mathbb{F}_q^k$, $\mathbf{x} * \mathbf{y} = \psi(\phi(\mathbf{x}) \cdot \phi(\mathbf{y}))$. This RMFE keeps multiplication property and bring down the field size at a price of constant loss in rate, i.e., the component-wise product of two secrets $\mathbf{x}, \mathbf{y} \in \mathbb{F}_q^k$ are mapped to the product of two elements $\phi(\mathbf{x}), \phi(\mathbf{y}) \in \mathbb{F}_{q^m}$ with $m = O(k)$. By applying RMFE to our secret space, we are able to obtain an strongly-multiplicative LSSS with a linear-dimensional secret space. The original paper [5] about RMFE does not take quasi-linear time and elementary algorithm into account. To meet quasi-linear time and elementary algorithm claim, we apply above paradigm to our RMFE as well.

4. The last obstacle is the density issue. The density issue affects the performance of LSSS in the following way. Assume that we have a class of LSSSs on the number of players $n_1, \ldots$, such that $\liminf_{i \to \infty} \frac{n_{i+1}}{n_i} = \tau$. Then, we have to use the same LSSS on the number of players between $n_i + 1$ to n_{i+1}. The density issue implies that the LSSS on $n_i + 1$ players is only $\frac{1}{\tau}$-fractionally as good as arithmetic secret sharing schemes on n_{i+1}. Thus, we prefer LSSS with density 1. We observe that our compound scheme $\Sigma \circ \Sigma_3$ can be made to satisfy density 1 even if Σ_3 has any constant density larger than 1. This is because Σ is a concatenation of two Shamir secret sharing scheme which yields a secret sharing scheme on any desired number of players. By exploiting this property and carefully tuning the length of Σ so as to cope with the length of Σ_3, we manage to produce an LSSS with density 1. It is worth emphasizing that LSSS based on algebraic geometry codes has density either significantly bigger than 1 or density 1 but non-explicit. To see this, let us first take a look at the best constructive algebraic geometry codes derived from Garcia-Stichtenoth function field tower. Unfortunately, the density of these algebraic geometry codes over $\mathbb{F}_q$ is merely $\sqrt{q}$. On the other hand, there does exist families of algebraic geometry codes with density 1, e.g. the Shimura curve. To our best knowledge, none of them is explicit. In conclusion, our strongly-multiplicative LSSS is explicit and has density 1 both of which can not be simultaneously satisfied by previous constructions.

The paper is organized as follows. In Sect. 2, we briefly recall linear secret sharing schemes, then introduce the concatenation of linear secret sharing schemes. In Sect. 3, we present a quasi-linear time elementary algorithm to generate an asymptotically-good strongly-multiplicative linear secret sharing schemes. To convert the secret space from the extension field $\mathbb{F}_{q^m}$ to $\mathbb{F}_q^k$, we resort to reverse multiplication friendly embedding that was recently developed in [10].

In the appendix, we include linear secret sharing from algebraic curves and the decoding of concatenated codes.

2   Linear Secret Sharing Schemes and Concatenation

The relation between linear secret sharing schemes and linear codes has been well understood since the work of [20]. Further details on this relation can be found in [5,9]. In this section, we briefly introduce strongly-multiplicative LSSS and some related notational convention that will be used throughout this paper.

Denote by $[n]$ the set $\{1, 2, \ldots, n\}$ and denote by $2^{[n]}$ the set of all subsets of $[n]$. Let q be a prime power and denote by $\mathbb{F}_q$ the finite field of q elements. For vectors $\mathbf{u} = (u_0, u_1, \ldots, u_n)$ and $\mathbf{v} = (u_0, v_1, \ldots, v_n)$ in $\mathbb{F}_{q^{k_0}} \times \mathbb{F}_{q^{k_1}} \times \cdots \times \mathbb{F}_{q^{k_n}}$ with integers $k_i \geqslant 1$, we define the *Schur product* $\mathbf{u} * \mathbf{v}$ to be the componentwise product of $\mathbf{u}$ and $\mathbf{v}$, i.e., $\mathbf{u} * \mathbf{v} = (u_0 v_0, u_1 v_1, \ldots, u_n v_n)$. The notion Schur product plays a crucial role in multiplicative LSSS. Although the secret space $\mathbb{F}_{q^{k_0}}$ and share spaces $\mathbb{F}_{q^i}$ can be different, both of them are $\mathbb{F}_q$-linear.

For an subset A of $\{0\} \cup [n]$, define the projection $\text{proj}_A(\mathbf{u})$ of $\mathbf{u}$ at A by $(u_i)_{i \in A}$. For an $\mathbb{F}_q$-subspace C of $\mathbb{F}_{q^{k_0}}^s \times \mathbb{F}_{q^{k_1}} \times \cdots \times \mathbb{F}_{q^{k_n}}$, we denote by C^{*2} the $\mathbb{F}_q$-linear span of $\{\mathbf{b} * \mathbf{c} : \mathbf{b}, \mathbf{c} \in C\}$. Motivated by multiplicative secret sharing schemes, the square codes C^{*2} have been extensively studied [8,21,23,24]. To have a good multiplicative secret sharing scheme from an $\mathbb{F}_q$-linear code C, we require that the square code C^{*2} and its dual code $C^{\perp}$ should have large minimum distance. That means, we need a special class of linear codes so that we can control the dimension and minimum distance of C^{*2}. There are some candidates satisfying this requirement, e.g. Reed-Solomon codes and algebraic geometry codes.

For convenience, we require that all-one vector $\mathbf{1}$ belongs to C. If this happens, then C becomes an $\mathbb{F}_q$-linear subspace of C^{*2}. C is said to be *unitary* if C contains the all-one vector $\mathbf{1}$.

Definition 1. A q-ary *linear secret sharing scheme* on n players with secret space $\mathbb{F}_{q^\ell}^s$, share space $\mathbb{F}_{q^k}$ is an $\mathbb{F}_q$-subspace C of $\mathbb{F}_{q^\ell}^s \times \mathbb{F}_{q^k}^n$ such that (i) $\text{proj}_{\{0\}}(C) = \mathbb{F}_{q^\ell}^s$; and (ii) the map $C \to \text{proj}_{[n]}(C)$; $(\mathbf{c}_0, c_1, c_2, \ldots, c_n) \mapsto (c_1, c_2, \ldots, c_n)$ is a bijection, i.e., for any $\mathbf{c} \in C$, $\text{proj}_{[n]}(\mathbf{c}) = \mathbf{0}$ if and only if $\mathbf{c} = \mathbf{0}$. Thus, for a codeword $(\mathbf{c}_0, c_1, c_2, \ldots, c_n) \in C$, the map ρ sending $(c_1, c_2, \ldots, c_n)$ to $\mathbf{c}_0$ is well defined. We call ρ the share-to-secret map. Furthermore, c_i is called the i-th share and $\mathbf{c}_0$ is called the secret.

It can be easily shown that (i) a subset A of $[n]$ is authorized[9] if $\text{proj}_A(\mathbf{c}) = \mathbf{0}$ implies $\text{proj}_{A \cup \{0\}}(\mathbf{c}) = \mathbf{0}$; and (ii) a subset B of $[n]$ is unauthorized[10] if for any $\mathbf{c}_0 \in \text{proj}_0(C)$, there is a codeword $\mathbf{c} \in C$ such that $\text{proj}_B(\mathbf{c}) = \mathbf{0}$ and $\text{proj}_{\{0\}}(\mathbf{c}) = \mathbf{c}_0$. The proj_A plays the same role as the map π_A in Definition 1 [5].

---

[9] The shares hold by players in A can recover the secret.
[10] The shares hold by players in B imply nothing about the secret.

Definition 2. Let $C \subseteq \mathbb{F}_{q^\ell}^s \times \mathbb{F}_{q^k}^n$ be an LSSS.

(i) C is said to have r-reconstruction if for any subset A of $[n]$ of size at least r and $\mathbf{c} \in C$, one has that $\text{proj}_A(\mathbf{c}) = \mathbf{0}$ if and only if $\text{proj}_{A \cup \{0\}}(\mathbf{c}) = \mathbf{0}$ (note that an LSSS on n players always has n-reconstruction).

(ii) We say that C has t-privacy if for any subset A of $[n]$ of size at most t and $\mathbf{u} \in \mathbb{F}_{q^\ell}^s$, there is a codeword $\mathbf{c} \in C$ such that $\text{proj}_A(\mathbf{c}) = \mathbf{0}$ and $\text{proj}_{\{0\}}(\mathbf{c}) = \mathbf{u}$.

(iii) We say that C is a t-strongly multiplicative LSSS if C has t-privacy and C^{*2} has r-reconstruction for any $r \leqslant n - t$ (note that C is 0-strongly multiplicative if and only if C^{*2} is an LSSS). In this case, t is called corruption tolerance of C.

(iv) Let $\mathcal{C} = \{C_i\}_{i=1}^\infty$ be a family of LSSS. Suppose that each C_i is a t_i-strongly multiplicative LSSS on n_i players. If $\lim_{i \to \infty} n_i = \infty$ and $\lim_{i \to \infty} \frac{t_i}{n_i} = \tau$, we say that $\mathcal{C}$ is τ-strongly multiplicative.

(v) Let $\mathcal{C} = \{C_i\}_{i=1}^\infty$ be a family of LSSS. Suppose that each C_i has n_i players. We say $\mathcal{C}$ has density θ if $\lim_{i \to \infty} n_i = \infty$ and $\limsup_{i \to \infty} \frac{n_i}{n_{i-1}} \leqslant \theta$.

Lemma 1. *Let $C \subseteq \mathbb{F}_{q^\ell}^s \times \mathbb{F}_{q^k}^n$ be an LSSS. Then C^{*2} has t-privacy as long as C has t-privacy.*

Proof. Let $\mathbf{c}_0 \in \text{proj}_0(C^{*2})$. Let B be a subset of $[n]$ of size at most t. Let $\mathbf{c} = \sum \lambda_i \mathbf{b}_i * \mathbf{c}_i \in C^{*2}$ with $\text{proj}_0(\mathbf{c}) = \mathbf{c}_0$ for some $\lambda_i \in \mathbb{F}_q$ and $\mathbf{b}_i, \mathbf{c}_i \in C$. Then there exist $\mathbf{u}_i, \mathbf{v}_i \in C$ such that $\text{proj}_B(\mathbf{u}_i) = \text{proj}_B(\mathbf{v}_i) = \mathbf{0}$ and $\text{proj}_0(\mathbf{u}_i) = \text{proj}_0(\mathbf{b}_i)$, $\text{proj}_0(\mathbf{v}_i) = \text{proj}_0(\mathbf{c}_i)$. Put $\mathbf{w} = \sum \lambda_i \mathbf{u}_i * \mathbf{v}_i \in C^{*2}$. Then $\text{proj}_B(\mathbf{w}) = \mathbf{0}$ and $\text{proj}_0(\mathbf{w}) = \sum \lambda_i \text{proj}_0(\mathbf{u}_i) * \text{proj}_0(\mathbf{v}_i) = \sum \lambda_i \text{proj}_0(\mathbf{b}_i) * \text{proj}_0(\mathbf{c}_i) = \mathbf{c}_0$. The proof is completed.

One of the key ideas of this paper is to exploit concatenation techniques which have been widely used in coding theory. We resort to this concatenation technique to achieve quasi-linear time strongly-multiplicative LSSS. Let us briefly describe the concatenation technique in coding theory. Let $C_0 \subseteq \mathbb{F}_q^{n_0}$ be a linear code over $\mathbb{F}_q$ of dimension k_0 and let $C_1 \subseteq \mathbb{F}_{q^{k_0}}^{n_1}$ be an $\mathbb{F}_q$-linear code of dimension k_1. Fix an $\mathbb{F}_q$-linear isomorphism ϕ from $\mathbb{F}_{q^{k_0}}$ to C_0. Then the concatenated code $C = \{(\phi(c_1), \phi(c_2), \dots, \phi(c_{n_1})) : (c_1, c_2, \dots, c_{n_1}) \in C_1\}$ is an $\mathbb{F}_q$-linear code of length $n_0 n_1$ and dimension k_1. There are various purposes in coding theory for concatenation. For instance, one can construct long codes over small field through long codes over large field. As for secret sharing scheme, we can also apply this concatenation technique accordingly with some variation. One can view this technique as re-sharing the share. The formal definition is given below.

Definition 3. Let C_0 be a q-ary linear secret sharing scheme on n_0 players with secret space $\mathbb{F}_{q^k}$, share space $\mathbb{F}_q$. Let C_1 be a q-ary linear secret sharing scheme on n_1 players with secret space $\mathbb{F}_{q^\ell}$, share space $\mathbb{F}_{q^k}$. Then the concatenated LSSS is a q-ary linear secret sharing scheme on $n_0 n_1$ players with secret space $\mathbb{F}_{q^\ell}$, share space given by

$$C = \{(c_0, \mathbf{c}_1, \dots, \mathbf{c}_{n_1}) \in \mathbb{F}_{q^\ell} \times (\text{proj}_{[n_0]}(C_0))^{n_1} : (c_0, \rho(\mathbf{c}_1), \dots, \rho(\mathbf{c}_{n_1})) \in C_1\},$$

where ρ is the share-to-secret map for the LSSS C_0. Then C is a subset of $\mathbb{F}_{q^\ell} \times \mathbb{F}_q^{n_0 n_1}$.

Remark 1. (i) Let us verify that this concatenated scheme is an LSSS with secret space $\mathbb{F}_{q^\ell}$. Suppose $(c_0, \mathbf{c}_1, \ldots, \mathbf{c}_{n_1}) \in C$ with $\mathbf{c}_i = \mathbf{0}$ for all $1 \leqslant i \leqslant n_1$. Then we have $\rho(\mathbf{c}_i) = 0$. This forces $c_0 = 0$ as C_1 is an LSSS. To prove that $\mathrm{proj}_{\{0\}}(C) = \mathbb{F}_{q^\ell}$, we pick an arbitrary element $c_0 \in \mathbb{F}_{q^\ell}$. Then there exists a vector $(c_0, a_1, a_2, \ldots, a_n) \in C_1 \subseteq \mathbb{F}_{q^\ell} \times \mathbb{F}_{q^k}^{n_1}$. As $\mathrm{proj}_{\{0\}}(C_0) = \mathbb{F}_{q^k}$, there exists $\mathbf{c}_i \in \mathrm{proj}_{[n_0]}(C_0)$ such that $(a_i, \mathbf{c}_i) \in C_0$ for all $1 \leqslant i \leqslant n_1$. This implies that $(c_0, \mathbf{c}_1, \ldots, \mathbf{c}_{n_1}) \in C$. Hence, $\mathrm{proj}_{\{0\}}(C) = \mathbb{F}_{q^\ell}$.

(ii) It is clear that the concatenated LSSS is still $\mathbb{F}_q$-linear. The $\mathbb{F}_q$-dimension of C is $\dim(C_1) + n_1(\dim(C_0) - k)$. To see this, each secret $\alpha \in \mathbb{F}_{q^k}$, there are $q^{\dim(C_0)-k}$ possible ways of re-sharing. Thus, for a given a $(n+1)$-tuple $(c_0, c_1, \ldots, c_{n_1})$, there are $q^{n_1(\dim(C_0)-k)}$ ways of re-sharing. Hence, the total number of elements in C is $q^{\dim(C_1)+n_1(\dim(C_0)-k)}$.

Let C be a unitary LSSS and assume that C^{*2} is an LSSS. Let ρ be the share-to-secret map of C. Then ρ can be extended to the share-to-secret map of C^{*2}, i.e., the share-to-secret map ρ' of C^{*2} satisfies $\rho'|_C = \rho$.

Definition 4. Let C be a unitary LSSS and ρ be the share-to-secret map of C. We say ρ is multiplicative if $\rho(\mathbf{u} * \mathbf{v}) = \rho(\mathbf{u})\rho(\mathbf{v})$ for any $\mathbf{u}, \mathbf{v} \in \mathrm{proj}_{[n]}(C)$. C is said to be multiplicative if C^{*2} is an LSSS and ρ is multiplicative.

Remark 2. Whenever we say that the share-to-secret map ρ of a q-ary LSSS C is multiplicative, the conditions that C is unitary and ρ can be extended to the share-to-secret map of C^{*2} are satisfied.

Lemma 2. *Let C_0 be a q-ary linear secret sharing scheme on n_0 players with secret space $\mathbb{F}_{q^k}$, share space $\mathbb{F}_q$. Let C_1 be a q-ary linear secret sharing scheme on n_1 players with secret space $\mathbb{F}_{q^\ell}$, share space $\mathbb{F}_{q^k}$. Let ρ_i be the share-to-secret map of C_i for $i = 0, 1$. If C_i is multiplicative for $i = 0, 1$, then*

(i) C^{*2} *is an $\mathbb{F}_q$-subspace of the concatenated LSSS Σ of C_0^{*2} with C_1^{*2}, where C is the concatenated LSSS C_0 with C_1, i.e., $C = \{(c_0, \mathbf{c}_1, \ldots, \mathbf{c}_{n_1}) \in \mathbb{F}_{q^\ell} \times (\mathrm{proj}_{[n_0]}(C_0))^{n_1} : (c_0, \rho_0(\mathbf{c}_1), \ldots, \rho_0(\mathbf{c}_{n_1})) \in C_1\}$.*
(ii) C *is also multiplicative.*

Proof. To prove Part (i), we have to show that $(b_0, \mathbf{b}) * (c_0, \mathbf{c}) = (b_0 c_0, \mathbf{b} * \mathbf{c}) \in \Sigma$ for any $(b_0, \mathbf{b}), (c_0, \mathbf{c}) \in C$. This is true since

$$(b_0 c_0, \rho_0(\mathbf{b}_1 * \mathbf{c}_1), \ldots, \rho_0(\mathbf{b}_{n_1} * \mathbf{c}_{n_1}))$$
$$= (b_0 c_0, \rho_0(\mathbf{b}_1)\rho_0(\mathbf{c}_1), \ldots, \rho_0(\mathbf{b}_{n_1})\rho_0(\mathbf{c}_{n_1})) \in C_1^{*2},$$

and $(\rho_0(\mathbf{b}_i)\rho_0(\mathbf{c}_i), \mathbf{b}_i * \mathbf{c}_i) \in C_0^{*2}$. We conclude C^{*2} is an $\mathbb{F}_q$-subspace of Σ.

It remains to check that C is multiplicative. By the definition of share-to-secret map ρ of C, for any $(c_0, \mathbf{c}_1, \ldots, \mathbf{c}_{n_1}) \in C$, we have

$\rho_1(\rho_0(\mathbf{c}_1), \ldots, \rho_0(\mathbf{c}_{n_1})) = c_0 = \rho(\mathbf{c}_1, \ldots, \mathbf{c}_{n_1})$. Then, for any $(b_0, \mathbf{b}), (c_0, \mathbf{c}) \in C$ with $\mathbf{b} = (\mathbf{b}_1, \ldots, \mathbf{b}_{n_1})$ and $\mathbf{c} = (\mathbf{c}_1, \ldots, \mathbf{c}_{n_1})$, we have

$$
\begin{aligned}
\rho(\mathbf{b} * \mathbf{c}) &= \rho_1(\rho_0(\mathbf{b}_1 * \mathbf{c}_1), \ldots, \rho_0(\mathbf{b}_{n_1} * \mathbf{c}_{n_1})) \\
&= \rho_1(\rho_0(\mathbf{b}_1)\rho_0(\mathbf{c}_1), \ldots, \rho_0(\mathbf{b}_{n_1})\rho_0(\mathbf{c}_{n_1})) \\
&= \rho_1((\rho_0(\mathbf{b}_1), \ldots, \rho_0(\mathbf{b}_{n_1})) * (\rho_0(\mathbf{c}_1), \ldots, \rho_0(\mathbf{c}_{n_1}))) \\
&= \rho_1(\rho_0(\mathbf{b}_1), \ldots, \rho_0(\mathbf{b}_{n_1}))\rho_1(\rho_0(\mathbf{c}_1), \ldots, \rho_0(\mathbf{c}_{n_1})) = \rho(\mathbf{b})\rho(\mathbf{c})
\end{aligned}
$$

This completes the proof.

The above lemma shows that a concatenated LSSS is multiplicative as long as both C_0 and C_1 are multiplicative. In fact we can further show that this concatenated LSSS is strongly-multiplicative as long as both C_0 and C_1 are strongly-multiplicative.

Lemma 3. *Let C_0 be a q-ary LSSS on n_0 players with secret space $\mathbb{F}_{q^k}$, share space $\mathbb{F}_q$. Let C_1 be a q-ary LSSS on n_1 players with secret space $\mathbb{F}_{q^\ell}$, share space $\mathbb{F}_{q^k}$. If C_i has r_i-reconstruction and t_i-privacy for $i = 0, 1$. Then the concatenated LSSS C defined in Definition 3 has $n_0 n_1 - (n_0 - r_0 + 1)(n_1 - r_1 + 1)$-reconstruction and has $(t_0 + 1)t_1$-privacy.*

Furthermore, if C_1^{*2} (and C_0^{*2}, respectively) has r_1' (and r_0', respectively)-reconstruction and the share-to-secret maps ρ_i of C_i are multiplicative for $i = 0, 1$, then C is a t-strongly multiplicative LSSS with $t = \min\{(t_0 + 1)t_1, (n_0 - r_0' + 1)(n_1 - r_1' + 1)\}$.

Proof. Given a codeword $\mathbf{c}$ in C, we can write $\mathbf{c} = (c_0, c_{1,1}, \ldots, c_{1,n_0}, c_{2,1}, \ldots, c_{2,n_0}, \ldots, c_{n_1,n_0})$ where $\mathbf{c}_i = (c_{i,1}, \ldots, c_{i,n_0})$ is a share-vector of C_0. Let S be the collection of indices of C, i.e., $S := \{0, (1,1), \ldots, (1,n_0), (2,1), \ldots, (2,n_0), \cdots, (n_1, 1), \ldots, (n_1, n_0)\}$. Let A be a subset of $S \backslash \{0\}$ and $A_i = A \cap \{(i,1), \ldots, (i,n_0)\}$ for $i = 1, 2, \ldots, n_1$. Then A is partitioned into $\cup_{i=1}^{n} A_i$. Let $B_i = \{j : (i,j) \in A_i\}$. It is clear that $|B_i| = |A_i|$ and B_i is a subset of $[n_0]$. This gives $\sum_{i=1}^{n_1} |B_i| = |A|$.

If $|A| \geq n_0 n_1 - (n_0 - r_0 + 1)(n_1 - r_1 + 1)$, then there exists a subset $I \subseteq [n_1]$ with $|I| \geq r_1$ such that $|B_i| \geq r_0$ for all $i \in I$. Otherwise, we have $|A| \leq n_1(r_0 - 1) + (n_0 - r_0 + 1)(r_1 - 1) < n_0 n_1 - (n_0 - r_0 + 1)(n_1 - r_1 + 1)$. If $\mathbf{c} = (c_0, \mathbf{c}_1, \ldots, \mathbf{c}_{n_1}) \in C$ such that $\mathrm{proj}_A(\mathbf{c}) = \mathbf{0}$, then $\mathrm{proj}_{B_i}(\mathbf{c}_i) = \mathbf{0}$ for all $i \in I$. As $|B_i| \geq r_0$ and C_0 has r_0-reconstruction, we must have $\rho_0(\mathrm{proj}_{B_i}(\mathbf{c}_i)) = 0$. Thus, $\mathrm{proj}_I(\rho_0(\mathbf{c}_1), \ldots, \rho_0(\mathbf{c}_{n_1})) = \mathbf{0}$. This implies that $c_0 = 0$ since $|I| \geq r_1$.

Now we consider the case where $|A| \leq (t_0 + 1)t_1$. Let J be the subset of $[n_1]$ such that $|B_j| \geq t_0 + 1$ if and only if $j \in J$. Then $|J| \leq t_1$. Let $\alpha \in \mathbb{F}_{q^\ell}$. We choose a vector $\mathbf{c} = (c_0, c_1, \ldots, c_{n_1}) \in C_1$ such that $\mathrm{proj}_J(\mathbf{c}) = 0$ and $\mathrm{proj}_{\{0\}}(\mathbf{c}) = \alpha$. For $j \in J$, let $\mathbf{u}_j = \mathbf{0}$. For $j \notin J$, choose $\mathbf{u}_j \in C_0$ such that $\rho_0(\mathbf{u}_j) = c_j$ and $\mathrm{proj}_{B_j}(\mathbf{u}_j) = \mathbf{0}$. This implies that $\mathbf{u} := (\alpha, \mathbf{u}_1, \ldots, \mathbf{u}_{n_1}) \in C$ and $\mathrm{proj}_A(\mathbf{u}) = \mathbf{0}$.

Now, we turn to furthermore part of the claim. The assumption says that C_1^{*2} and C_0^{*2} has r_1' and r_0'-reconstruction respectively. By Lemma 2, C^{*2} is an $\mathbb{F}_q$-subspace of the concatenated LSSS Σ of C_0^{*2} with C_1^{*2}. By the first part of the proof, Σ has $(n_0 n_1 - (n_0 - r_0' + 1)(n_1 - r_1' + 1))$-reconstruction and hence C^{*2} also has $(n_0 n_1 - (n_0 - r_0' + 1)(n_1 - r_1' + 1))$-reconstruction. The desired result follows.

Remark 3. To the best of our knowledge, no prior work considered concatenation of two strongly-multiplicative LSSSs. Perhaps the most relevant reference is the multiplication friendly embedding in [5]. Multiplication friendly embedding can be viewed as a multiplicative LSSS without privacy.

3   Quasi-linear Time LSSS with Strong Multiplication

3.1   Secret Space Is the Extension Field $\mathbb{F}_{q^m}$

The parameters of LSSS based on Reed-Solomon codes and algebraic geometry codes can be found in appendix. In general, those codes derived from algebraic curves can be converted into a LSSS with strong multiplication. This becomes the building block of our quasi-linear time LSSS. Our LSSS is obtained via the concatenation of two LSSS, one based on Reed-Solomon codes and another one based on algebraic geometry codes. The following theorem shows that the density of our LSSS can be 1 as long as we pick an asymptotically good algebraic geometry code as an inner code.

Theorem 1. *Let q be an even power of a prime. Then for any positive real $\varepsilon \in \left(0, \frac{1}{2} - \frac{2}{\sqrt{q}-1}\right)$ and $\eta \in (0, \frac{1}{2})$, there exists a family $\mathcal{C} = \{\Gamma_i\}_{i=1}^{\infty}$ of τ_q-strongly multiplicative q-ary LSSS with density 1, each Γ_i has N_i players, secret space $\mathbb{F}_{q^{s_i}}$ and quasi-linear time (depending on ε) for share generation and secret reconstruction, where*

$$\tau_q = \frac{1}{9}(1 - 2\eta)\left(1 - 2\varepsilon - \frac{4}{\sqrt{q}-1}\right), \quad \frac{s_i}{N_i} \to \varepsilon\eta.$$

Proof. Let $\{C_i\}_{i=1}^{\infty}$ be the family of q-ary LSSS with the same ε and γ given in Theorem 6. We can set $\gamma = \frac{1}{3}(1 + \varepsilon + \frac{2}{\sqrt{q}-1})$. Note that we have $\frac{k_i}{k_{i-1}} \to \sqrt{q}$ and $\frac{n_i}{n_{i-1}} \to \sqrt{q}$. Put $t_i = n_i - 2\lfloor \gamma n_i \rfloor$, $r_i = \lfloor \gamma n_i \rfloor$ and $\alpha = \frac{1}{\sqrt{q}}$, $\lambda = \frac{1}{3}(1 + \eta)$.

Consider $\Sigma_{ij} := \mathsf{RS}_{k_i, R_{ij}}[N_{ij}, K_{ij}]_q$ with $N_{ij} = \alpha q^{k_{i-1}} + j$ and $K_{ij} = \lfloor \lambda N_{ij} \rfloor$, $R_{ij} = \lfloor \eta N_{ij} \rfloor$ for $j = 0, 1, 2, \ldots, q^{k_i} - \alpha q^{k_{i-1}}$ and $i \geqslant 2$. Then by Lemma 2, the concatenated LSSS of C_i with Σ_{ij} is a q-ary LSSS Γ_{ij} on $n_i N_{ij}$ players of secret space $\mathbb{F}_{q^{k_i R_{ij}}}$, share space $\mathbb{F}_q$. By Lemmas 2, 3 and Theorem 6, it has t_{ij}-privacy with $t_{ij} = (t_i + 1)(K_{ij} - R_{ij} - 1)$. Furthermore, Γ_{ij}^{*2} has r_{ij}-reconstruction with

$$r_{ij} = N_{ij} n_i - (N_{ij} - 2K_{ij} + 1)(n_i - 2r_i + 1).$$

where $r_i = \lfloor \gamma n_i \rfloor$. Put $\tau_{ij} = \min\{(t_i + 1)(K_{ij} - R_{ij} - 1), (N_{ij} - 2K_{ij} + 1)(n_i - 2r_i + 1)\}$. Due to the setting of our parameters, $t_i \approx n_i - 2r_i$ and $K_{ij} - R_{ij} \approx N_{ij} - 2K_{ij}$, we come to the conclusion that

$$r_{ij} = (N_{ij} - 2K_{ij} + 1)(n_i - 2r_i + 1), \quad \frac{\tau_{ij}}{N_{\Gamma_{ij}}} = \frac{\tau_{ij}}{n_i N_{ij}} \to \tau_q.$$

As the secret space of Γ_{ij} is $\mathbb{F}_{q^{k_i R_{ij}}}$ and the number of players is $n_i N_{ij}$, we have $\frac{k_i R_{ij}}{n_i N_{ij}} \to \eta\varepsilon$.

Now we arrange the order of Γ_{ij} in the following way

$$\Gamma_{1,0}, \Gamma_{2,0}, \ldots, \Gamma_{2,q^{k_2}-\alpha q^{k_1}}, \Gamma_{3,0}, \ldots, \Gamma_{3,q^{k_3}-\alpha q^{k_2}}, \Gamma_{4,0}, \ldots, \Gamma_{4,q^{k_4}-\alpha q^{k_3}}, \ldots. \quad (1)$$

The number of players $N_{\Gamma_{ij}}$ of Γ_{ij} is $n_i(\alpha q^{k_{i-1}} + j)$. Thus we have, (i) for $1 \leqslant j \leqslant q^{k_i} - \alpha q^{k_{i-1}}$

$$\frac{N_{\Gamma_{i,j}}}{N_{\Gamma_{i,j-1}}} = \frac{n_i(\alpha q^{k_{i-1}} + j)}{n_i(\alpha q^{k_{i-1}} + j - 1)} = 1 + \frac{1}{\alpha q^{k_{i-1}} + j - 1} \to 1,$$

and (ii) for $i \geqslant 2$

$$\frac{N_{\Gamma_{(i+1),0}}}{N_{\Gamma_{i,q^{k_i}-\alpha q^{k_i-1}}}} = \frac{n_{i+1}\alpha q^{k_i}}{n_i q^{k_i}} = \frac{\alpha n_{i+1}}{n_i} \to 1.$$

By abuse of notation, we denote the ith LSSS in (1) by Γ_i. Let N_i be the number of players of Γ_i. Then we have $\frac{N_i}{N_{i-1}} \to 1$ as i tends to ∞.

Finally, we analyze time complexity for share generation and secret reconstruction. Note that $N_{ij} \geqslant n_i q^{k_{i-1}}$. As $k_i = \Omega_\varepsilon(n_i)$, we have $n_i = O_\varepsilon(\log_q N_{ij})$. The share generation consists of encoding of Σ_{ij} which is quasi-linear in q^{k_i}, and share generation of LSSS in Theorem 6 which is polynomial in n_i. Hence, the total time complexity of share generation is quasi-linear in the number of players. As for secret reconstruction, by Lemma 15, a similar analysis shows that the time complexity is also quasi-linear in the number of players. This completes the proof.

Our concatenation idea can greatly reduce the complexity of construction, sharing secret and reconstructing secret by letting this algebraic geometry code to be an inner LSSS. If the number of players of this inner LSSS is small enough, we do not even need an explicit construction of it. In fact, we can brute force all possible generator matrix of algebraic geometry code C such that C, its dual code $C^\perp$ and its square code C^{*2} are all asymptotically good. All we have to acknowledge is the existence of such code. This could allow us to present an explicit construction of strongly multiplicative LSSS based on a quasi-linear time searching algorithm without any prior knowledge of algebraic geometry codes.

Theorem 2. *Let q be an even power of a prime. Then for any positive real $\varepsilon \in \left(0, \frac{1}{2} - \frac{2}{\sqrt{q}-1}\right)$, $\lambda \in (0, \frac{1}{2})$ and $\eta \in (0, \frac{1}{2})$, there exists an quasi-linear time elementary algorithm to generate a family C of τ_q-strongly multiplicative q-ary LSSS on N_i players with density 1, secret space $\mathbb{F}_{q^{s_i}}$ and quasi-linear time (depending on ε) for share generation and secret reconstruction, where*

$$\tau_q = \frac{1}{27}(1 - 2\eta)(1 - 2\lambda)\left(1 - 2\varepsilon - \frac{4}{\sqrt{q}-1}\right), \qquad \frac{s_i}{N_i} \to \eta\lambda\varepsilon.$$

Proof. We notice that it takes $q^{O(n^2)}$ times to enumerate generator matrices of all linear codes in $\mathbb{F}_q^n$. For each linear code C, we check its multiplicative property by checking minimum distance, dual distance and the distance of C^{*2}. We know the existence of this linear code by algebraic geometry codes given in Sect. 3. This algorithm must find at least one such a code. The question is now reduced to how to make our exhaustive search algorithm run in quasi-linear time. It turns out that if $n = \log \log N$, the running time is then sublinear in N. Moreover, the encoding and reconstructing time is bounded by $\exp(O(n)) = O(\log N)$.

To let our exhaustive search to be quasi-linear, we have to concatenate twice instead of once. Theorem 1 says there exists a class of $\frac{1}{9}(1 - 2\eta)(1 - 2\varepsilon - \frac{4}{\sqrt{q}-1})$-strongly multiplicative q-ary LSSS C_i on n_i players with secret space $\mathbb{F}_{q^{s_i}}$ and share space $\mathbb{F}_q$ such that $\lim_{i \to \infty} \frac{n_{i+1}}{n_i} = 1$ and $\frac{s_i}{n_i} = \eta\varepsilon$. We use this C_i to be our new inner LSSS. Our outer LSSS is a Shamir secret sharing scheme defined as follows. Let D_{ij} be a Shamir secret sharing scheme on N_{ij} players with secret space $\mathbb{F}_{q^{\lambda N_{ij} s_i}}$ and share space $\mathbb{F}_{q^{s_i}}$ such that $N_{ij} = q^{s_i - 1} + j$ for $j = 1, \ldots, q^{s_i} - q^{s_i - 1}$. By Lemma 13, D_{ij} is a class of $(1 - 2\lambda)$-strongly multiplicative LSSS with density 1. Then by Lemma 2 and Lemma 3, the concatenation Σ_{ij} of D_{ij} with C_i yields a $\tau_q N_{ij} n_i$-strongly LSSS on $N_{ij} n_i$ players with secret space $\mathbb{F}_{q^{\lambda N_{ij} s_i}}$ and share space $\mathbb{F}_q$ where $\frac{\lambda N_{ij} s_i}{N_{ij} n_i} = \frac{\lambda s_i}{n_i} = \lambda \eta \varepsilon$. Moreover, Σ_{ij} has density 1 as both of the inner LSSS C_i and the outer LSSS D_{ij} have density 1. Note that the inner LSSS in C_i is derived from algebraic geometry code. We want to construct it via exhaustive search instead of exploiting its mathematical structure. By Theorem 1, the number of players in C_i is $O(\log_q s_i) = O(\log_q \log_q N_{ij})$. Our desired result follows.

Remark 4. (i) Reducing time complexity via concatenation is not a new technique for coding theorists and it can be dated back to 1966 [14]. They discovered that the concatenation of codes yields a large constructive family of asymptotically good codes. To show the existence of codes with some special property, we usually resort to randomness argument. The concatenation idea allows us to reduce the space of our inner code and make it possible to find it in polynomial time. Different from the traditional randomness argument, our existence argument depends on the result from algebraic geometry codes, i.e., showing the existence of asymptotically-good code C, its dual $C^\perp$ and its square code C^{*2}. This extra multiplicative property creates some difficulties in finding the desirable codes by concatenating only once. Instead, we concatenate twice so as to further narrowing down the searching space.

(ii) If we abandon either quasi-linear time construction claim or elementary algorithm claim, we only need to concatenate once. As a result, this concatenated LSSS is $\frac{1}{9}(1 - 2\lambda)(1 - 2\varepsilon - \frac{4}{\sqrt{q}-1})$-strongly multiplicative.

3.2   Reverse Multiplication Friendly Embedding

As we have seen, the secret space of LSSS in the previous subsection is an extension field $\mathbb{F}_{q^m}$. In order to convert $\mathbb{F}_{q^m}$ to a secret space $\mathbb{F}_q^k$, we need reverse multiplication friendly embeddings (RMFE for short).

Before introducing RMFEs, let us recall multiplication friendly embedding that have found various applications such as complexity of multiplication in extension fields [4], hitting set construction [18] and concatenation of LSSS [5].

Definition 5. *Let q be a power of a prime and let $\mathbb{F}_q$ be a field of q elements, let $k, m \geqslant 1$ be integers. A pair (σ, π) is called a $(k, m)_q$-multiplication friendly embedding (MFE for short) if $\sigma : \mathbb{F}_{q^k} \to \mathbb{F}_q^m$ and $\pi : \mathbb{F}_q^m \to \mathbb{F}_{q^k}$ are two $\mathbb{F}_q$-linear maps satisfying*

$$\alpha\beta = \pi(\sigma(\alpha) * \sigma(\beta))$$

for all $\alpha, \beta \in \mathbb{F}_{q^k}$. A multiplication friendly embedding (σ, π) is called unitary if $\sigma(1) = \mathbf{1}$.

It is easy to verify that the map σ must be injective and $\sigma(\mathbb{F}_{q^k})$ is a q-ary $[m, k]$-linear code with minimum distance at least k. So far, the only way to construct $(k, m)_q$-multiplication friendly embedding with $m = O(k)$ is via algebraic curves over finite fields [4]. Now we explain how multiplication friendly embeddings are used to concatenate LSSS.

Assume that $C \subset \mathbb{F}_{q^m} \times \mathbb{F}_{q^k}^n$ is an LSSS and let (σ, π) be a $(k, m)_q$-multiplication friendly embedding. Consider the concatenation:

$$\sigma(C) = \{(c_0, \sigma(c_1), \sigma(c_2), \ldots, \sigma(c_n)) : (c_0, c_1, c_2, \ldots, c_n) \in C\}.$$

Then $\sigma(C) \subseteq \mathbb{F}_q^{m(n+1)}$.

Lemma 4. *Let (σ, π) be a unitary multiplication friendly embedding. Then $\sigma(C)$ is a multiplicative LSSS as long as C is a multiplicative LSSS.*

Proof. Assume that C is a multiplicative LSSS. If $(c_0, c_1, c_2, \ldots, c_n) \in C$ and $(\sigma(c_1), \ldots, \sigma(c_n)) = \mathbf{0}$, then $\sigma(c_i) = \mathbf{0}$ for all $1 \leqslant i \leqslant n$. As σ is injective, we have $c_i = 0$. Hence, $c_0 = 0$. This means that $\sigma(c_0) = \mathbf{0}$. Thus, $\sigma(C)$ is an LSSS.

Next we show that $\sigma(C)^{*2}$ is an LSSS. Let $(b_0, b_1, b_2, \ldots, b_n), (c_0, c_1, c_2, \ldots, c_n) \in C$ and $\sigma(b_1, b_2, \ldots, b_n) * \sigma(c_1, c_2, \ldots, c_n) = \mathbf{0}$, i.e., $\sigma(b_i) * \sigma(c_i) = \mathbf{0}$ for all $1 \leqslant i \leqslant n$. Then we have $0 = \pi(\sigma(b_i) * \sigma(c_i)) = b_i c_i$. This implies that $b_0 c_0 = 0$ since C^{*2} is an LSSS.

To prove multiplicativity, let ρ and ρ' be the share-to-secret maps of C and $\sigma(C)$, respectively. Let $(b_0, b_1, b_2, \ldots, b_n), (c_0, c_1, c_2, \ldots, c_n) \in C$. Since C is multiplicative,

$$\rho((b_1, b_2, \ldots, b_n) * (c_1, c_2, \ldots, c_n)) = b_0 c_0.$$

On the other hand, we have

$$\rho'(\sigma(b_1, b_2, \ldots, b_n) * \sigma(c_1, c_2, \ldots, c_n)) = b_0 c_0 = \rho'(\sigma(b_1, b_2, \ldots, b_n))\rho'(\sigma(c_1, c_2, \ldots, c_n)).$$

This completes the proof.

Remark 5. Concatenation of an LSSS via a unitary multiplication friendly embedding does not maintain privacy although it maintains multiplitivity because dual distance of $\sigma(C)$ is destroyed. That is why we introduce our concatenation of LSSS given in this paper to maintains both privacy and multiplitivity as shown in Lemmas 2 and 3.

By applying the concatenation techniques given in this paper, we are able to bring down share size to a constant at a constant fractional loss in privacy and reconstruction (see Lemma 3). However, our secret is still defined over the extension field of the share space. For most applications of multiplicative secret sharing schemes, the share space is a fixed finite field $\mathbb{F}_q$ and the secret space is desirably $\mathbb{F}_q^k$ for some integer $k \geqslant 1$. We make use of reverse multiplication friendly embedding to convert the secret space from the extension field $\mathbb{F}_{q^m}$ to $\mathbb{F}_q^k$ while still maintaining strong multiplitivity.

Let us first give a formal definition of RMFE.

Definition 6. *Let q be a power of a prime and let $\mathbb{F}_q$ be a field of q elements, let $k, m \geqslant 1$ be integers. A pair (ϕ, ψ) is called an $(k, m)_q$-reverse multiplication friendly embedding if $\phi : \mathbb{F}_q^k \to \mathbb{F}_{q^m}$ and $\psi : \mathbb{F}_{q^m} \to \mathbb{F}_q^k$ are two $\mathbb{F}_q$-linear maps satisfying*

$$\mathbf{x} * \mathbf{y} = \psi(\phi(\mathbf{x}) \cdot \phi(\mathbf{y}))$$

for all $\mathbf{x}, \mathbf{y} \in \mathbb{F}_q^k$.

The definition of RMFE was first proposed in [10]. Thanks to this technique, the authors managed to bring down the amortized complexity of communication complexity from $O(n \log n)$ to $O(n)$ for Shamir-based MPC protocols over any finite field. The key observation is that the classic threshold MPC protocols requires large field to implement the hyper-invertible matrix technique and the threshold secret sharing scheme. Therefore, even faced with MPC protocol over binary field, one has to choose an extension field for its share while the secret is still restricted to the binary field, a subfield of its secret space. This causes another $\Omega(\log n)$ overhead. In fact, the authors in [10] noticed that such overhead can be amortized away if one can convert the extension field of the secret space into a vector space so that it is possible to implement several multiplication in parallel via RMFE.

In this work, we need RMFE for a different purpose, namely, we convert the extension field $\mathbb{F}_{q^m}$ of the secret space into a vector space $\mathbb{F}_q^k$ via RMFE while maintaining strong multiplicitivity.

Lemma 5. *If (ϕ, ψ) is a $(k, m)_q$-RMFE, then ϕ is injective and $m \geqslant 2k - 1$.*

Proof. Let $\mathbf{x}, \mathbf{y} \in \mathbb{F}_q^k$ such that $\phi(\mathbf{x}) = \phi(\mathbf{y})$. Let $\mathbf{1} \in \mathbb{F}_q^k$ be the all-one vector. Then we have

$$\mathbf{x} = \mathbf{1} * \mathbf{x} = \psi(\phi(\mathbf{1})\phi(\mathbf{x})) = \psi(\phi(\mathbf{1})\phi(\mathbf{y})) = \mathbf{1} * \mathbf{y} = \mathbf{y}.$$

This shows the injectivity of ϕ.

To show the second claim, let us show that ψ is surjective. For any $\mathbf{x} \in \mathbb{F}_q^k$, we have $\psi(\phi(\mathbf{1})\phi(\mathbf{x})) = \mathbf{1} * \mathbf{x} = \mathbf{x}$. This means that ψ is surjective. Let $\mathbf{u} \in \mathbb{F}_q^k$ be the vector $(1, 0, 0, \ldots, 0)$. Consider the set $A := \{\mathbf{x} \in \mathbb{F}_q^k : \psi(\phi(\mathbf{u})\phi(\mathbf{x})) = 0\}$. As $\psi(\phi(\mathbf{u})\phi(\mathbf{x})) = \mathbf{u} * \mathbf{x} = (x_1, 0, 0, \ldots, 0)$, we have $A = \{(0, \mathbf{c}) : \mathbf{c} \in \mathbb{F}_q^{k-1}\}$. It is clear that $\phi(\mathbf{u})\phi(A)$ is a subspace of the kernel of ψ. As the dimension of $\phi(\mathbf{u})\phi(A)$ is $k - 1$, we have that $m = \dim(\ker(\psi)) + \dim(\text{Im}(\psi)) \geqslant \dim(\phi(\mathbf{u})\phi(A)) + k = k - 1 + k = 2k - 1$.

Though we have the inequality $m \geqslant 2k - 1$, it was shown in [10] that, via construction of algebraic function fields, one has $m = O(k)$ with a small hidden constant.

Lemma 6 (see [10]). *Let $F/\mathbb{F}_q$ be a function field of genus $\mathfrak{g}$ with k distinct rational places $P_1, P_2, \ldots, P_k$. Let G be a divisor of F such that $\text{supp}(G) \cap \{P_1, \ldots, P_k\} = \emptyset$ and $\deg(G) \geqslant 2\mathfrak{g} - 1 + k$. If there is a place R of degree m with $m > 2\deg(G)$, then there exists an $(k, m)_q$-RMFE.*

Let us briefly recall construction of the RMFE given in Lemma 6. Consider the map

$$\pi : \mathcal{L}(G) \to \mathbb{F}_q^k; \quad f \mapsto (f(P_1), \ldots, f(P_k)).$$

Then π is surjective. Thus, we can choose a subspace V of $\mathcal{L}(G)$ of dimension k such that $\pi(V) = \mathbb{F}_q^k$. We write by $\mathbf{c}_f$ the vector $(f(P_1), \ldots, f(P_k))$, and by $f(R)$ the evaluation of f in the higher degree place R, for a function $f \in \mathcal{L}(2G)$. We now define

$$\phi : \pi(V) = \mathbb{F}_q^k \to \mathbb{F}_{q^m}; \quad \mathbf{c}_f \mapsto f(R) \in \mathbb{F}_{q^m}.$$

Note that the above $f \in V$ is uniquely determined by $\mathbf{c}_f$. The map ψ can then be defined (see the detail in [10, Lemma 6]). Thus, the time complexity of constructing such a RMFE consists of finding a basis of $\mathcal{L}(G)$ and evaluation of functions of $\mathcal{L}(G)$ at the place R and the rational places $P_1, P_2, \ldots, P_k$.

As the algebraic geometry code associated with this function field tower can not run in quasi-linear time, we need to apply our concatenation idea again so as to give rise to a quasi-linear time RMFE.

Lemma 7 (see [10]). *Assume that (ϕ_1, ψ_1) is an $(n_1, k_1)_{q^{k_2}}$-RMFE and (ϕ_2, ψ_2) is an $(n_2, k_2)_q$-RMFE. Then $\phi : \mathbb{F}_q^{n_1 n_2} \to \mathbb{F}_{q^{k_1 k_2}}$*

$$(\mathbf{x}_1, \ldots, \mathbf{x}_{n_1}) \mapsto (\phi_2(\mathbf{x}_1), \ldots, \phi_2(\mathbf{x}_{n_1})) \in \mathbb{F}_{q^{k_2}}^{n_1} \mapsto \phi_1(\phi_2(\mathbf{x}_1), \ldots, \phi_2(\mathbf{x}_{n_1}))$$

and $\psi : \mathbb{F}_{q^{k_1 k_2}} \to \mathbb{F}_q^{n_1 n_2}$

$$\alpha \mapsto \psi_1(\alpha) = (\mathbf{u}_1, \ldots, \mathbf{u}_{n_1}) \in \mathbb{F}_{q^{k_2}}^{n_1} \mapsto (\psi_2(\mathbf{u}_1), \ldots, \psi_2(\mathbf{u}_{n_1}))$$

give an $(n_1 n_2, k_1 k_2)_q$-RMFE.

Lemma 8. *The Reed-Solomon code leads to a $(k,r)_q$-RMFE (ϕ, ψ) for all $2 \leq r \leq 2q$ and $k \leqslant r/2$. Furthermore, the pair (ϕ, ψ) can be computed in quasi-linear time.*

Proof. Apply the rational function field $\mathbb{F}_q(x)$ to the construction of RMFE given in Lemma 6. Choose an irreducible polynomial R of $\mathbb{F}_q[x]$ of degree r and k distinct elements $\alpha_1, \alpha_2, \ldots, \alpha_k$ of $\mathbb{F}_q$. Then it turns out that the codes are Reed-Solomon codes and hence (ϕ, ψ) can be computed in time $O(k \log^2 k \log \log k)$ (see [2]).

By applying the Garcia-Stichtenoth tower to the construction of the RMFE given in Lemma 6, we obtain the following result.

Lemma 9. *For any integer $a > 1$, there exists a family of $(k,a)_q$-RMFEs with $k \to \infty$ and $\lim_{k \to \infty} \frac{a}{k} \to 2 + \frac{4}{\sqrt{q}-1}$ that can be computed in time $O(a^3)$.*

Lemma 10. *For any integers $a > 1$ and r with $2r \leqslant q^a$, there exists a family of $(k, ar)_q$-RMFEs with $k \to \infty$ and $\lim_{k \to \infty} \frac{ar}{k} = 4 + \frac{8}{\sqrt{q}-1}$ that can be computed in time $O(a^3 + r \log^2 r \log \log r)$.*

Proof. Let (ϕ_1, ψ_1) be a $(k_1, r)_{q^a}$-RMFE with $k_1 = \lfloor r/2 \rfloor$ given in Lemma 8 and let (ϕ_2, ψ_2) be a $(k_2, a)_q$-RMFE with $\frac{a}{k_2} \to 2 + \frac{4}{\sqrt{q}-1}$ given in Lemma 9. By Lemma 7, concatenation of these two RMFEs gives an $(k_1 k_2, ar)_q$-RMFE (ϕ, ψ) with $\frac{ar}{k_1 k_2} \to 4 + \frac{8}{\sqrt{q}-1}$. Moreover, since (ϕ_1, ψ_1) is associated with Reed-Solomon codes, it can be computed in time $O(r \log^2 r \log \log r)$. As (ϕ_2, ψ_2) is constructed via the Garcia-Stichtenoth tower, it can be computed in time $O(a^3)$. The overall running time for (ϕ, ψ) is then upper bounded by $O(a^3 + r \log^2 r \log \log r)$.

Recall that we claim that our LSSS is generated by an elementary algorithm. In this sense, This RMFE should also be produced by an elementary algorithm. We again resort to exhaustive search instead of using Garcia-Stichtenoth tower to find this RMFE. As we argue in Theorem 2, we need to concatenate twice instead of once. The first two RMFEs are associated with Reed-Solomon codes and the third one is found by exhaustive search and guaranteed by Lemma 9. The exhaustive search consists of enumerating all linear subspaces $C \subseteq \mathbb{F}_q^{\log \log n}$ and determining the distance, dual distance of C and the distance of its square code C^{*2}. The first step takes time $2^{\Omega(\log \log n)^2}$ and the second step takes time $2^{\Omega(\log \log n)}$. Therefore, this exhaustive search will find the desired linear subspaces in less than $O(n)$ time. Emulating the proof of Lemma 10 gives the following result.

Lemma 11. *There exists an quasi-linear time* **elementary** *algorithm to generate a family of $(k_i, m_i)_q$-RMFEs with $k_i \to \infty$ and $\lim_{i \to \infty} \frac{m_i}{k_i} = 8 + \frac{16}{\sqrt{q}-1}$ that can be computed in time $O(m_i \log^2 m_i \log \log m_i)$.*

Given a LSSS Σ with secret space $\mathbb{F}_{q^m}$, the following theorem shows how to obtain a LSSS with secret space $\mathbb{F}_q^k$ by applying RMFE to the secret space of Σ.

Theorem 3. *Assume that there is a t-strongly multiplicative linear secret sharing scheme C with secret space $\mathbb{F}_{q^m}$ and share space $\mathbb{F}_q$. If there exists a $(k, m)_q$-RMFE (ϕ, ψ), then there exists a t-strongly multiplicative linear secret sharing scheme Σ with secret space $\mathbb{F}_q^k$. Moreover, the time complexity of share generation and secret reconstruction of Σ is bounded by that of C and (ϕ, ψ).*

Proof. Note that for any $\mathbf{s} \in \mathbb{F}_q^k$, $\phi(\mathbf{s}) \in \mathbb{F}_{q^m}$. Let

$$C_1 = \{(\mathbf{s}, c_1, \ldots, c_n) : \mathbf{s} \in \mathbb{F}_q^k, (\phi(\mathbf{s}), c_1, \ldots, c_n) \in C\}$$

where $\mathbf{s}$ is the secret and c_i is the i-th share. Let us show that C_1 is indeed a LSSS with the secret space $\mathbb{F}_q^k$. If $(\mathbf{s}, c_1, \ldots, c_n) \in C_1$ with $(c_1, \ldots, c_n) = \mathbf{0}$, then we must have $\phi(\mathbf{s}) = 0$ since $(\phi(\mathbf{s}), c_1, \ldots, c_n) \in C$. As ϕ is injective, this forces that $\mathbf{s} = \mathbf{0}$. Hence, C_1 is a LSSS. To show that the secret space is $\mathbb{F}_q^k$, we choose an arbitrary $\mathbf{s} \in \mathbb{F}_q^k$. Then $\phi(\mathbf{s}) \in \mathbb{F}_{q^m}$. As the secret space of C is $\mathbb{F}_{q^m}$, there exists a vector $(c_1, \ldots, c_n) \in \mathbb{F}_q^n$ such that $(\phi(\mathbf{s}), c_1, \ldots, c_n) \in C$. Thus, $(\mathbf{s}, c_1, \ldots, c_n)$ belongs to C_1.

It is clear that C_1 is an $\mathbb{F}_q$-LSSS as ϕ is a linear map and C is an $\mathbb{F}_q$-LSSS. We next show that C_1 has t-privacy and C_1^{*2} has $(n-t)$-reconstruction. The t-privacy argument follows from the fact that C has t-privacy and $\{(\phi(\mathbf{s}), c_1, \ldots, c_n) \in C : \mathbf{s} \in \mathbb{F}_q^k\}$ is a subset of C. As C is multiplicative, we can find the secret-to-share map ρ such that for $(b_0, \mathbf{b}), (c_0, \mathbf{c}) \in C$ with $\mathbf{b} = (b_1, \ldots, b_n)$ and $\mathbf{c} = (c_1, \ldots, c_n)$,

$$\rho(\mathbf{b} * \mathbf{c}) = \rho(\mathbf{b})\rho(\mathbf{c}) = b_0 c_0.$$

For any $(\mathbf{s}, c_1, \ldots, c_n) \in C_1$, we define the share-to-secret map

$$\rho_1(c_1, \ldots, c_n) = \psi \circ \rho(c_1, \ldots, c_n) = \psi(\phi(\mathbf{s}) \cdot \phi(\mathbf{1})) = \mathbf{s}.$$

The second step is due to the fact that C is unitary. To see that C_1 is multiplicative, for any $(\mathbf{x}, x_1, \ldots, x_n), (\mathbf{y}, y_1, \ldots, y_n) \in C_1$, we have

$$\rho_1(x_1 y_1, \ldots, x_n y_n) = \psi \circ \rho(x_1 y_1, \ldots, x_n y_n) = \psi(\phi(\mathbf{x}) \cdot \phi(\mathbf{y})) = \mathbf{x} * \mathbf{y}.$$

The last step comes from the definition of RMFE. It remains to prove the $(n - t)$-reconstruction of C_1^{*2}. We note that $(\mathbf{s}, c_1, \ldots, c_n) \in C_1^{*2}$ indicates that $(\phi(\mathbf{s}), c_1, \ldots, c_n) \in C^{*2}$. That means we can reconstruct $\phi(\mathbf{s})$ from any $(n - t)$ shares in $(c_1, \ldots, c_n)$ due to the $(n - t)$-reconstruction property of C^{*2}. The desired result follows as $\mathbf{s} = \psi \circ \phi(\mathbf{s})$.

3.3 Make the Secret Space to Be $\mathbb{F}_q^k$

Putting Theorems 1, 3 and Lemma 10 together leads to our main results.

Theorem 4. *Let q be any even power of prime. Then for any positive real $\varepsilon \in (0, \frac{1}{2} - \frac{2}{\sqrt{q}-1})$ and $\eta \in (0, \frac{1}{2})$, there exists a family $\mathcal{C}$ of τ_q-strongly multiplicative*

q-ary LSSS on N_i players with density 1, secret space $\mathbb{F}_q^{s_i}$ and quasi-linear time for share generation and secret reconstruction, where

$$\tau_q = \frac{1}{9}(1 - 2\eta)\left(1 - 2\varepsilon - \frac{4}{\sqrt{q} - 1}\right), \qquad \frac{s_i}{N_i} \to \varepsilon\eta\left(\frac{1}{4 + \frac{8}{\sqrt{q}-1}}\right).$$

Proof. Note that the secret space of Γ_i in Theorem 1 is $\mathbb{F}_{q^{k_i R_{ij}}}$. By Lemma 10, there exists a $(s_i, k_i R_{ij})_q$-RMFE (ϕ, ψ) with $\frac{k_i R_{ij}}{s_i} \to \frac{1}{4 + \frac{8}{\sqrt{q}-1}}$ that can be computed in time $O(k_i^3 + R_{ij}\log^2 R_{ij}\log\log R_{ij}) = O(N_i \log^2 N_i \log\log N_i)$ as $k_i = O(\log R_{ij})$. The desired result follows from Theorem 3.

By emulating the proof of Theorem 2 and referring to RMFE in Lemma 11, we can also obtain a similar result without resorting to the Garcia-Stichtenoth tower at a cost of slightly worse strong multiplicative property.

Theorem 5 (Elementary construction of LSSS with strong multiplicative property). *Let q be any even power of prime. Then for any positive real $\varepsilon \in (0, \frac{1}{2} - \frac{2}{\sqrt{q}-1})$ and $\eta \in (0, \frac{1}{2})$, there exists a quasi-linear time **elementary** algorithm to generate a family $\mathcal{C}$ of τ_q-strongly multiplicative q-ary LSSS on N_i players with density 1, secret space $\mathbb{F}_q^{s_i}$ and quasi-linear time (depending on ε) for share generation and secret reconstruction, where*

$$\tau_q = \frac{1}{27}(1 - 2\eta)(1 - 2\lambda)\left(1 - 2\varepsilon - \frac{4}{\sqrt{q} - 1}\right), \qquad \frac{s_i}{N_i} \to \frac{\varepsilon\eta\lambda}{8 + \frac{16}{\sqrt{q}-1}}.$$

Acknowledgments. Ronald Cramer and Chen Yuan have been funded by the ERC-ADG-ALGSTRONGCRYPTO project. (no. 740972). The research of Chaoping Xing was partially supported by the Huawei-SJTU joint project.

A   LSSS from Algebraic Curves

As we have seen, a concatenated LSSS consists of two LSSSs, one used as an inner LSSS and another one used as an outer LSSS. In this section, we provide a construction of LSSS via algebraic function fields. This gives us LSSSs with desired property. Let us briefly recall some background on algebraic function fields. The reader may refer to [27] for the details.

A function field $F/\mathbb{F}_q$ is an algebraic extension of the rational function field $\mathbb{F}_q(x)$, that contains all fractions of polynomials in $\mathbb{F}_q[x]$. Associated to a function field, there is a non-negative integer $\mathfrak{g}$ called the genus, and an infinite set of "places" P, each having a degree $\deg P \in \mathbb{N}$. The number of places of a given degree is finite. The places of degree 1 are called rational places. Given a function $f \in F$ and a place P, two things can happen: either f has a pole in P, or f can be evaluated in P and the evaluation $f(P)$ can be seen as an element of the field $\mathbb{F}_{q^{\deg P}}$. If f and g do not have a pole in P then the evaluations satisfy the rules $\lambda(f(P)) = (\lambda f)(P)$ (for every $\lambda \in \mathbb{F}_q$), $f(P) + g(P) = (f + g)(P)$ and

$f(P) \cdot g(P) = (f \cdot g)(P)$. Note that if P is a rational place (and f does not have a pole in P) then $f(P) \in \mathbb{F}_q$. The functions in F always have the same zeros and poles up to multiplicity (called order). An important fact of the theory of algebraic function fields is as follows: call $N_1(F)$ the number of rational places of F. Then over every finite field $\mathbb{F}_q$, there exists an infinite family of function fields $\{F_n\}$ such that their genus $\mathfrak{g}_n$ grow with n and $\lim_{n \to \infty} N_1(F_n)/\mathfrak{g}_n = c_q$ with $c_q \in \mathbb{R}$, $c_q > 0$. The largest constant c_q satisfying the property above is called Ihara's constant $A(q)$ of $\mathbb{F}_q$. It is known that $0 < A(q) \leq \sqrt{q} - 1$ for every finite field $\mathbb{F}_q$. Moreover, $A(q) = \sqrt{q} - 1$ for a square q. The result is constructive, since explicit families of function fields attaining these values are known and given in [15, 16].

A divisor G is a formal sum of places, $G = \sum c_P P$, such that $c_P \in \mathbb{Z}$ and $c_P = 0$ except for a finite number of P. We call this set of places where $c_P \neq 0$ the support of G, denoted by $\mathrm{supp}(G)$. The degree of G is $\deg G := \sum c_P \deg P \in \mathbb{Z}$.

The Riemann-Roch space $\mathcal{L}(G)$ is the set of all functions in F with certain prescribed poles and zeros depending on G (together with the zero function). More precisely if $G = \sum c_P P$, every function $f \in \mathcal{L}(G)$ must have a zero of order at least $|c_P|$ in the places P with $c_P < 0$, and f can have a pole of order at most c_P in the places with $c_P > 0$. The space $\mathcal{L}(G)$ is a vector space over $\mathbb{F}_q$. Its dimension is governed by certain laws (given by the so-called Riemann-Roch theorem). A weaker version of that theorem called Riemann's theorem states that if $\deg G \geq 2\mathfrak{g} - 1$ then $\dim \mathcal{L}(G) = \deg(G) - \mathfrak{g} + 1$. On the other hand, if $\deg G < 0$, then $\dim \mathcal{L}(G) = 0$.

Lastly, we note that, given $f, g \in \mathcal{L}(G)$, its product $f \cdot g$ is in the space $\mathcal{L}(2G)$.

Lemma 12. *Let $F/\mathbb{F}_q$ be a function field of genus $\mathfrak{g}$ with $n + 1$ distinct rational places $P_\infty, P_1, P_2, \ldots, P_n$. If there is a place P_0 of degree $k > 1$ and $n/2 > m \geqslant k + 2\mathfrak{g} - 1$, then there exists a q-ary LSSS C satisfying*

(i) *C has $(m + 1)$-reconstruction and $(m - k - 2\mathfrak{g} + 1)$-privacy.*
(ii) *The share-to-secret map ρ of C is multiplicative.*
(iii) *C^{*2} has $(2m + 1)$-reconstruction.*

Proof. Denote by F_{P_0} the residue class field of place P_0. Then we know that $F_{P_0} \simeq \mathbb{F}_{q^k}$. For a function f that is regular at P_0, we denote by $f(P_0)$ the residue class of f in F_{P_0}. Consider the map $\pi : f \in \mathcal{L}(G) \mapsto (f(P_0), f(P_1), \ldots, f(P_n)) \in F_{P_0} \times \mathbb{F}_q^n \simeq \mathbb{F}_{q^k} \times \mathbb{F}_q^n$ and define

$$C := \mathrm{Im}(\pi) = \{(f(P_0), f(P_1), \ldots, f(P_n)) : f \in \mathcal{L}(mP_\infty)\} \subseteq F_{P_0} \times \mathbb{F}_q^n.$$

For a subset A of $\{0\} \cup [n]$, we denote by π_A the map

$$f \in \mathcal{L}(G) \mapsto \mathrm{proj}_A(f(P_0), f(P_1), \ldots, f(P_n)).$$

Since the kernel of $\pi_{\{0\}}$ is $\mathcal{L}(mP_\infty - P_0)$ and $\dim \mathcal{L}(mP_\infty) - \dim \mathcal{L}(mP_\infty - P_0) = k$, $\pi_{\{0\}}$ is surjective. Hence, we have $\mathrm{proj}_0(C) = \mathbb{F}_{q^k}$.

Let A be a subset of $[n]$. If $|A| \geqslant m+1$ and $\text{proj}_A(f(P_0), f(P_1), \ldots, f(P_n)) = 0$. Then $f \in \mathcal{L}(mP_\infty - \sum_{i \in A} P_i)$. This implies that $f = 0$ as $\deg(mP_\infty - \sum_{i \in A} P_i) < 0$. Therefore, $f(P_0) = 0$.

If $|A| \leqslant m - k - 2\mathfrak{g} + 1$, then $\dim \mathcal{L}(mP_\infty) - \dim \mathcal{L}\left(mP_\infty - \sum_{i \in A} P_i - P_0\right) = k + |A|$. This implies that $\pi_{\{0\} \cup A}$ is surjective. Hence, for any $\alpha \in F_{P_0}$, there is a function f such that $\text{proj}_A(f(P_0), f(P_1), \ldots, f(P_n)) = 0$ and $f(P_0) = \alpha$.

Next we will prove that the share-to-secret map of C is multiplicative. First, we note that C is unitary as $1 \in \mathcal{L}(mP_\infty)$. Consider the $\mathbb{F}_q$-linear space

$$\Sigma = \{(f(P_0), f(P_1), \ldots, f(P_n)) : f \in \mathcal{L}(2mP_\infty)\} \subseteq F_{P_0} \times \mathbb{F}_q^n.$$

Then Σ contains C^{*2}. As $2m + 1 \leqslant n$, the vector $(f(P_1), \ldots, f(P_n))$ determines the function $f \in \mathcal{L}(2mP_\infty)$ uniquely, and hence $f(P_0)$. Therefore, Σ has n-reconstruction. Thus, we can define the share-to-secret map ρ: $\rho(f(P_1), \ldots, f(P_n)) = f(P_0)$. It is clear that ρ is an extension of the share-to-secret map of C. Furthermore, for any two functions $f, g \in \mathcal{L}(mP_\infty)$, we have $fg \in \mathcal{L}(2mP_\infty)$. Hence, we have

$$\rho((f(P_1), \ldots, f(P_n)) * (g(P_1), \ldots, g(P_n))) = \rho((fg)(P_1), \ldots, (fg)(P_n))$$
$$= (fg)(P_0) = f(P_0)g(P_0).$$

Since Σ has $(2m + 1)$-reconstruction, so does C^{*2}.

A.1   Construction via Reed-Solomon Codes

Let $\alpha_1, \ldots, \alpha_N \in \mathbb{F}_{q^k}$ be N pairwise distinct nonzero elements. Let α_0 be a root of an irreducible polynomial over $\mathbb{F}_{q^k}$ of degree ℓ. Denote by $\mathbb{F}_{q^k}[x]_{<K}$ the set of polynomials over $\mathbb{F}_{q^k}$ of degree less than K. The Reed-Solomon code is defined by

$$\mathsf{RS}_{k,\ell}[N, K]_q := \{(f(\alpha_0), f(\alpha_1), \ldots, f(\alpha_N)) : f \in \mathbb{F}_{q^k}[x]_{<K}\} \subset \mathbb{F}_{q^{k\ell}} \times \mathbb{F}_{q^k}^N.$$

Applying Lemma 12 to the rational function fields gives the following result.

Lemma 13. *Let $\mathsf{RS}_{k,\ell}[N, K]_q$ be the Reed-Solomon code defined above. If $N/2 > K - 1 \geqslant \ell - 1$, then it is a q^k-ary LSSS on N players with secret space $\mathbb{F}_{q^{k\ell}}$, share space $\mathbb{F}_{q^k}$. Moreover, we have the following properties*

(i) *It has K-reconstruction and $(K - \ell)$-privacy.*
(ii) *The share-to-secret of $\mathsf{RS}_{k,\ell}[N, K]_q$ is multiplicative.*
(iii) *$\mathsf{RS}_{k,\ell}[N, K]_q^{*2}$ has $(2K - 1)$-reconstruction.*
(iv) *If $N = \Omega(q^k)$, then the share generation and secret reconstruction can be computed in time $O(N \log^2 N \log \log N)$.*

Proof. The first three parts follows from Lemma 12 when applying the rational function field $\mathbb{F}_{q^k}(x)$. As the encoding and decoding of a Reed-Solomon code can be run in time $O(N \log^2 N \log \log N)$ (see [2]), the last claim follows.

A.2   Garcia-Stichtenoth Tower

In the Garcia-Stichtenoth tower $\{E_i\}$ over $\mathbb{F}_q$, each extension E_i/E_{i-1} has degree $\sqrt{q}$. The detailed result is given below.

Lemma 14 (via Garcia-Stichtenoth tower). *Let q be an even power of a prime. Then there exists a family $\{F_i/\mathbb{F}_q\}$ function fields such that*

(i) *The number $N(F_i)$ of $\mathbb{F}_q$-rational places is strictly increasing as i increases.*

(ii) $\lim_{i\to\infty} \frac{N(F_i)}{\mathfrak{g}(F_i)} = \sqrt{q} - 1$, *where $\mathfrak{g}(F_i)$ denotes the genus of F_i.*

(iii) $\lim_{i\to\infty} \frac{N(F_i)}{N(F_{i-1})} = \sqrt{q}$.

Furthermore, algebraic-geometry codes of length n based on this family can be encoded and decoded in time $O(n^3 \log^2 q)$ (see [26]).

A.3   Construction via Garcia-Stichtenoth Tower

By applying the Garcia-Stichtenoth tower given in Lemma 14 and the construction of LSSS given in Lemma 12, we obtain the following result.

Theorem 6 (via Garcia-Stichtenoth tower). *Assume q is an even power of a prime. Let $\varepsilon \in \left(0, \frac{1}{2} - \frac{2}{\sqrt{q}-1}\right)$ and $\gamma \in \left(0, \frac{1}{2}\right)$ be two reals with $\gamma \geqslant \varepsilon + \frac{2}{\sqrt{q}-1}$. Then there exists a sequence $\{C_i\}$ of q-ary LSSS on n_i players with the secret space $\mathbb{F}_{q^{k_i}}$, the share space $\mathbb{F}_q$ such that*

(i) $\frac{k_i}{k_{i-1}} \to \sqrt{q}$.

(ii) $\lim_{i\to\infty} \frac{k_i}{n_i} = \varepsilon$.

(iii) C_i *has $\lfloor \gamma n_i \rfloor$-reconstruction and t_i-privacy satisfying $\frac{t_i}{n_i} \to \gamma - \frac{2}{\sqrt{q}-1} - \varepsilon$.*

(iv) C_i^{*2} *has $2\lfloor \gamma n_i \rfloor$-reconstruction.*

(v) *the share-to-secret map ρ_i of C_i is multiplicative.*

(vi) C_i *can be constructed and computed in time $O(n_i^3)$.*

Proof. Let $\{F_i/\mathbb{F}_q\}$ be the family of the function fields given in Lemma 14. Put $n_i = N(F_i) - 1$, $m_i = \lfloor \gamma n_i \rfloor - 1$ and $k_i = \lfloor \varepsilon n_i \rfloor$. Then $n_i/2 > m_i \geqslant k_i + 2\mathfrak{g}(F_i) - 1$ and

$$\frac{k_i}{k_{i-1}} = \frac{\lfloor \varepsilon n_i \rfloor}{\lfloor \varepsilon n_{i-1} \rfloor} \to \sqrt{q}.$$

The desired results on Parts (i)–(v) follow from Lemma 12. $\qquad\blacksquare$

B   Decode Concatenated Codes up to Its Unique Decoding Radius

A naive decoding algorithm for concatenated code can not correct errors up to its unique decoding radius. Let us explain why a naive algorithm fails to achieve this goal. Let C be a concatenated code with an inner code C_1 and outer code C_0. Let En_0 and En_1 be the encoding algorithm of C_0 and C_1 respectively. Let Dec_0 and Dec_1 be the decoding algorithm of C_0 and C_1 respectively. Given a codeword $\mathbf{c} \in C$, we can write $\mathbf{c} = (\mathbf{c}_1, \ldots, \mathbf{c}_n)$ with $\mathbf{c}_i \in C_1$. Let $\mathbf{y} = (\mathbf{y}_1, \ldots, \mathbf{y}_n)$ be a corrupted codeword. The naive decoding algorithm goes as follows: we first decode each substring $\mathbf{y}_i$ by running the unique decoding algorithm $Dec_1(\mathbf{y}_i)$. Let $\mathbf{c}_i = Dec_1(\mathbf{y}_i)$ and x_i be the message encoded to $\mathbf{c}_i$, i.e., $En_1(x_i) = \mathbf{c}_i$. The second step of our decoding algorithm is to decode $(x_1, \ldots, x_n)$ by running Dec_0. Since the decoding algorithm of inner code and outer code can correct errors up to half of its minimum distance, this decoding strategy can correct errors up to one-fourth of its minimum distance.

Forney [14] proposed a randomized algorithm to decoding concatenated code up to its unique decoding radius provided that the decoding algorithms of inner code and outer code are available. The time complexity of this random decoding algorithm is the same as that of the naive decoding algorithm. Let us briefly introduce this algorithm. This randomized algorithm first runs the decoding algorithm of inner code on each $\mathbf{y}_i$ of $\mathbf{y} = (\mathbf{y}_1, \ldots, \mathbf{y}_n)$, i.e., $\mathbf{c}_i := Dec_1(\mathbf{y}_i)$. Let $\mathbf{e}_i = \mathbf{c}_i - \mathbf{y}_i$ be the error vector. This randomized algorithm labels coordinate i an erasure error with probability $\frac{2wt(\mathbf{e}_i)}{d}$. Then, we run the erasure and error decoding algorithm of the outer code on $(x_1, \ldots, x_n)$ with $En_1(x_i) = \mathbf{c}_i$ or $x_i = \perp$. This randomized algorithm can be further derandomized at the cost of $\log n$ factor increase in the time complexity [17] by setting a threshold w such that an erasure error happens when $\frac{2wt(\mathbf{e}_i)}{d} \geq w$. We summarize the result in the following lemma and refer interested readers to Chap. 12 in [17] for details.

Lemma 15. *Let C be a concatenated code whose inner code C_1 is a linear code of length N and minimum distance D and outer code C_0 is a linear code of length n and minimum distance d. Assume that the decoding algorithm of C_0 can correct e errors and r erasures with $2e + r \leq D - 1$ in time $T_0(N)$ and the decoding algorithm of C_1 can correct errors up to its unique decoding radius $\frac{d-1}{2}$ in time $T_1(n)$. Then, there exists a deterministic decoding algorithm for C that can correct errors up to its unique decoding radius $\frac{Dd-1}{2}$ and run in time $O((T_1(n)N + T_0(N))n)$.*

Remark 6. If we let $n = O(\log N)$, $T_0(N)$ be quasi-linear in N and $T_1(n)$ is a polynomial in n. Then, the total running time is quasi-linear in N and thus quasi-linear in the code length of C. We will see that our concatenated LSSS meets this condition. Thus, we can assume that our concatenated LSSS can be decoded up to its unique decoding radius.

References

1. Ben-Or, M., Goldwasser, S., Wigderson, A.: Completeness Theorems for non-cryptographic fault-tolerant distributed computation. In: STOC, pp. 1–10 (1988)
2. Alekhnovich, M.: Linear Diophantine equations over polynomials and soft decoding of Reed-Solomon codes. In: Proceedings of the FOCS 2002, Vancouver, BC, pp. 439-448 (2002)

3. Chen, H., Cramer, R.: Algebraic geometric secret sharing schemes and secure multi-party computations over small fields. In: Dwork, C. (ed.) CRYPTO 2006. LNCS, vol. 4117, pp. 521–536. Springer, Heidelberg (2006). https://doi.org/10.1007/11818175_31

4. Chudnovsky, D.V., Chudnovsky, G.V.: Algebraic complexities and algebraic curves over finite fields. Proc. Nat. Acad. Sci. U.S.A. **84**(7), 1739–1743 (1987)

5. Cascudo, I., Chen, H., Cramer, R., Xing, C.: Asymptotically good ideal linear secret sharing with strong multiplication over *any* fixed finite field. In: Halevi, S. (ed.) CRYPTO 2009. LNCS, vol. 5677, pp. 466–486. Springer, Heidelberg (2009). https://doi.org/10.1007/978-3-642-03356-8_28

6. Chen, H., Cramer, R., de Haan, R., Pueyo, I.C.: Strongly multiplicative ramp schemes from high degree rational points on curves. In: Smart, N. (ed.) EUROCRYPT 2008. LNCS, vol. 4965, pp. 451–470. Springer, Heidelberg (2008). https://doi.org/10.1007/978-3-540-78967-3_26

7. Cascudo, I., Cramer, R., Mirandola, D., Padró, C., Xing, C.: On secret sharing with nonlinear product reconstruction. SIAM J. Discrete Math. **29**(2), 1114–1131 (2015)

8. Cascudo, I., Cramer, R., Mirandola, D., Zémor, G.: Squares of random linear codes. IEEE Trans. Inf. Theory **61**(3), 1159–1173 (2015)

9. Cascudo, I., Cramer, R., Xing, C.: The torsion-limit for algebraic function fields and its application to arithmetic secret sharing. In: Rogaway, P. (ed.) CRYPTO 2011. LNCS, vol. 6841, pp. 685–705. Springer, Heidelberg (2011). https://doi.org/10.1007/978-3-642-22792-9_39

10. Cascudo, I., Cramer, R., Xing, C., Yuan, C.: Amortized complexity of information-theoretically secure MPC revisited. In: Shacham, H., Boldyreva, A. (eds.) CRYPTO 2018. LNCS, vol. 10993, pp. 395–426. Springer, Cham (2018). https://doi.org/10.1007/978-3-319-96878-0_14

11. Cramer, R., Damgård, I., Dziembowski, S.: On the complexity of verifiable secret sharing and multi-party computation. In: STOC 2000, pp. 325–334 (2000)

12. Cramer, R., Damgård, I., Maurer, U.: General secure multi-party computation from any linear secret-sharing scheme. In: Preneel, B. (ed.) EUROCRYPT 2000. LNCS, vol. 1807, pp. 316–334. Springer, Heidelberg (2000). https://doi.org/10.1007/3-540-45539-6_22

13. Cramer, R., Damgard, I., Nielsen, J.: Secure Multiparty Computation and Secret Sharing. Cambridge University Press, Cambridge (2015)

14. Forney, G.D.: Generalized minimum distance decoding. IEEE Trans. Inf. Theory **12**(2), 125–131 (1966)

15. Garcia, A., Stichtenoth, H.: A tower of Artin-Schreier extensions of function fields attaining the Drinfeld-Vlăduţ bound. Invent. Math. **121**, 211–222 (1995)

16. Garcia, A., Stichtenoth, H.: On the asymptotic behaviour of some towers of function fields over finite fields. J. Number Theory **61**(2), 248–273 (1996)

17. Guruswami, V., Rudra, A., Sudan, M.: Essential Coding Theory. https://cse.buffalo.edu/faculty/atri/courses/coding-theory/book/web-coding-book.pdf

18. Guruswami, V., Xing, C.: Hitting sets for low-degree polynomials with optimal density. In: CCC, pp. 161–168 (2014)

19. Ishai, Y., Kushilevitz, E., Ostrovsky, R., Sahai, A.: Zero-knowledge from secure multiparty computation. In: STOC, pp. 21–30 (2007)

20. Massey, L., Farrell, P.G.: Some applications of coding theory in cryptography. In: Codes and Ciphers Cryptography and Coding IV, pp. 33–47. Formara Lt, Esses, England (1995)

21. Mirandola, D., Zémor, G.: Critical pairs for the product singleton bound. IEEE Trans. Inf. Theory **61**(7), 4928–4937 (2015)
22. Narayanan, A.K., Weidner, M.: Subquadratic time encodable codes beating the Gilbert-Varshamov bound. IEEE Trans. Inf. Theory **65**(10), 6010–6021 (2019)
23. Randriambololona, H.: An upper bound of singleton type for componentwise products of linear codes. IEEE Trans. Inform. Theor. **59**(12), 7936–7939 (2013)
24. Randriambololona, H.: On products and powers of linear codes under componentwise multiplication, In: Contemporary Mathematics, vol. 637. AMS, Providence (2015)
25. Shparlinski, I.E., Tsfasman, M.A., Vladut, S.G.: Curves with many points and multiplication in finite fileds. In: Stichtenoth, H., Tsfasman, M.A. (eds.) Coding Theory and Algebraic Geometry. LNM, vol. 1518, pp. 145–169. Springer, Heidelberg (1992). https://doi.org/10.1007/BFb0087999
26. Shum, K., Aleshnikov, I., Kumar, P.V., Stichtenoth, H., Deolalikar, V.: A low-complexity algorithm for the construction of algebraic-geometric codes better than the Gilbert-Varshamov bound. IEEE Trans. Inf. Theory **47**, 2225–2241 (2001)
27. Stichtenoth, H.: Algebraic Function Fields and Codes, 2nd edn. Springer, Berlin (2009). https://doi.org/10.1007/978-3-540-76878-4

Robust Secret Sharing with Almost Optimal Share Size and Security Against Rushing Adversaries

Serge Fehr[1,2] and Chen Yuan[1(✉)]

[1] CWI, Amsterdam, The Netherlands
{serge.fehr,chen.yuan}@cwi.nl
[2] Mathematical Institute, Leiden University, Leiden, The Netherlands

Abstract. We show a robust secret sharing scheme for a maximal threshold $t < n/2$ that features an optimal overhead in share size, offers security against a rushing adversary, and runs in polynomial time. Previous robust secret sharing schemes for $t < n/2$ either suffered from a suboptimal overhead, offered no (provable) security against a rushing adversary, or ran in superpolynomial time.

1   Introduction

Background. Robust secret sharing is a version of secret sharing that enables the reconstruction of the shared secret s in the presence of *incorrect* shares: given all n shares but with t of them possibly incorrect, and of course without knowing which ones are incorrect, it should still be possible to recover s. If $t < n/3$ then this can be achieved by standard error-correction techniques, while for $t \geq n/2$ the task is impossible. When $n/3 \leq t < n/2$, robust secret sharing is possible, but only if one accepts a small failure probability and an overhead in the share size, i.e., shares of bit size *larger* than the bit size of s. The goal then is to minimize the overhead in the share size for a given (negligible) failure probability 2^{-k}. Following up on earlier work on the topic [2,4–7,10], Bishop et al. proposed a scheme with optimal overhead $O(k)$ in the share size, neglecting polylogarithmic terms (in n and k and the bit size of s) [3]. In particular, their scheme was the first robust secret sharing with an overhead that is *independent* of n (neglecting $polylog(n)$ terms). However, as pointed out by Fehr and Yuan [8], the Bishop et al. scheme does not (appear to) offer security in the presence of a *rushing* adversary that may choose the incorrect shares depending on the shares of the honest parties. This is in contrast to most of the earlier schemes, which do offer security against such rushing attacks (but are less efficient in terms of

© International Association for Cryptologic Research 2020
R. Pass and K. Pietrzak (Eds.): TCC 2020, LNCS 12552, pp. 470–498, 2020.
https://doi.org/10.1007/978-3-030-64381-2_17

share size).[1] Towards recovering security against a rushing adversary, Fehr and Yuan [8] proposed a new robust secret sharing scheme that features security against a rushing adversary *and* an overhead "almost independent" of n, i.e., $O(n^\epsilon)$ for an arbitrary $\epsilon > 0$. Furthermore, a variation of their scheme offers security against a rushing adversary and an overhead that is *truly independent* of n (neglecting polylogarithmic terms), but this version of the scheme has a running time that is superpolynomial.

Our Result. In this work, we close the final gap left open in [8]: we propose and analyze a new robust secret sharing scheme that is secure against a rushing adversary, has an overhead independent of n as in [3] (i.e., independent up to the same poly-logarithmic $O(\log^4 n + \log n \log m)$ term as in [3], where m is the bit size of the secret), and has a polynomial running time.

Our new scheme recycles several of the ideas and techniques of [8]. The basic idea, which goes back to [3], is to have each share s_i be authenticated by a *small randomly chosen subset* of the other parties. Following [8], our approach here differs from [3] in that the keys for the authentication are not authenticated. Indeed, this "circularity" of having the authentication keys authenticated causes the solution in [3] to not allow a rushing adversary; on the other hand, by not authenticating the authentication keys, we give the dishonest parties more flexibility in lying, making the reconstruction harder.

The reconstruction is in terms of a careful (and rather involved) inspection of the resulting consistency graph, exploiting that every honest party can verify the correctness of the shares of a small but *random* subset of parties, and that these choices of random "neighborhoods" become known to the adversary only *after* having decided about which shares s_i to lie about. As a matter of fact, in our scheme, every honest party can verify the correctness of the shares of *several* randomly chosen small neighborhoods, giving rise to several global verification graphs. Furthermore, to ensure "freshness" of each such neighborhood conditioned on the adversary's behavior so far, these neighborhoods are revealed *sequentially* in subsequent rounds of communication during the reconstruction phase.

As in [8], in our scheme the reconstructor first learns from the consistency graph whether the number p of "passive" parties, i.e., dishonest parties that did not lie about the actual share s_i (but possibly about other pieces of information), is "large" or "small". For p small, we can recycle the solution from [8], which happens to also work for the tighter parameter setting we consider here. When p is large though, the solution in [8] is to exploit the given redundancy in the shares s_i by means of applying list decoding, and then to find the right candidate from the list by again resorting to the consistency graph. However, this list decoding

---

[1] In order to achieve security against a rushing adversary when $n/3 \le t < n/2$, it is necessary that the shares are disclosed part-by-part in subsequent rounds of communication; for the adversary to be *rushing* then means that he can choose his messages in each communication round depending on the parts of the shares of the honest parties that are communicated in this round (and earlier ones), but not depending on what the honest parties will communicate in the upcoming rounds.

technique only works in a parameter regime that then gives rise to the $O(n^\epsilon)$ overhead obtained in [8]. To overcome this in our solution, we invoke a new technique for dealing with the case of a large p.

We quickly explain this new part on a very high level. The idea is to design a procedure that works *assuming* the exact value of p is known. This procedure is then repeated for every possible choice of p, leading to a list of possible candidates; similarly to how the scheme in [8] finds the right candidate from the list produced by the list decoding, we can then find the right one from the list. As for the procedure assuming p is known, exploiting the fact that p is large and known, we can find subsets V and V_1 so that either we can recover the shared secret from the shares of the parties in $V \cup V_1$ by standard error correction (since it happens that there is more redundancy than errors in this collection of shares), or we can argue that the complement of V is a set for which the small-p case applies and thus we can again resort to the corresponding technique in [8].

One technical novelty in our approach is that we also invoke one layer of random neighborhoods that are publicly known. In this case, the adversary can corrupt parties *depending* on who can verify whose share, but the topology of the global verification graph is fixed and cannot be modified by dishonest parties that lie about their neighborhoods.

Following [3,8], we point out that it is good enough to have a robust secret sharing scheme with a constant failure probability and a (quasi-)constant overhead; a scheme with 2^{-k} failure probability and a (quasi-) $O(k)$ overhead can then be obtained by means of parallel repetition. This is what we do here as well: at the core is a scheme where each party is given a *quasi-constant* number of bits on top of the actual share s_i (i.e., the size of the authentication keys and the size of the random neighborhoods are chosen to be quasi-constant), and we show that this scheme has a constant failure probability.

Concurrent Work. In concurrent and independent work [9], a very similar result as ours was obtained (using rather different techniques though). They also show an optimal (up to poly-logarithmic terms) robust secret sharing scheme with security against a rushing adversary. Compared to our scheme, their scheme has a slightly better poly-logarithmic dependency on n: $O(\log^2 n + \log m \log n)$. On the other hand, in a setting where the reconstruction is towards an external reconstructor R, our scheme works simply by revealing the shares to R (over multiple rounds) and R doing some local computation, whereas their scheme requires interaction *among* the shareholders and, as far as we can see, the shareholders will then learn the shared secret as well. For instance in the context of robust storage, the latter is undesirable.

2   Preliminaries

2.1   Graph Notation

We follow the graph notation in [8], which we briefly recall. Let $G = ([n], E)$ be a graph with vertex set $[n] := \{1, \ldots, n\}$ and edge set E. By convention, $(v, w) \in E$

represents an edge directed from v to w is . We let $G|_S$ be the restriction of G to S for any $S \subseteq [n]$, i.e., $G|_S = (S, E|_S)$ with $E|_S = \{(u, v) \in E : u, v \in S\}$.

For vertex $v \in [n]$, we set

$$N^{\text{out}}(v) = \{w \in [n] : (v, w) \in E\} \quad \text{and} \quad N^{\text{in}}(v) = \{w \in [n] : (w, v) \in E\}.$$

We use E_v as a short hand for $N^{\text{out}}(v)$, the *neighborhood* of v. For $S \subseteq [n]$, we set

$$N_S^{\text{out}}(v) = N^{\text{out}}(v) \cap S \quad \text{and} \quad N_S^{\text{in}}(v) = N^{\text{in}}(v) \cap S.$$

This notation is extended to a *labeled* graph, i.e., when G comes with a function $L : E \to \{\text{good}, \text{bad}\}$ that labels each edge. Namely, for $v \in [n]$ we set

$$N^{\text{out}}(v, \text{good}) = \{w \in N^{\text{out}}(v) : L(v, w) = \text{good}\},$$
$$N^{\text{in}}(v, \text{good}) = \{w \in N^{\text{in}}(v) : L(w, v) = \text{good}\},$$

and similarly $N^{\text{out}}(v, \text{bad})$ and $N^{\text{in}}(v, \text{bad})$. Also, $N_S^{\text{out}}(v, \text{good})$, $N_S^{\text{in}}(v, \text{good})$, $N_S^{\text{out}}(v, \text{bad})$ and $N_S^{\text{in}}(v, \text{bad})$ are defined accordingly for $S \subseteq [n]$. Finally, we set

$$n^{\text{out}}(v) = |N^{\text{out}}(v)| \quad \text{and} \quad n_S^{\text{in}}(v, \text{bad}) = |N_S^{\text{in}}(v, \text{bad})|$$

and similarly for all other variations.

2.2 Random Graphs

We call a graph $G = ([n], E)$ a *randomized* graph if each edge in E is actually a random variable. We are particularly interested in randomized graphs where (some or all of) the E_v's are uniformly random and independent subsets $E_v \subset [n] \setminus \{v\}$ of a given size d. For easier terminology, we refer to such neighborhoods E_v as being *random and independent*. G is called a *random degree-d graph* if E_v is a random subset of size d in the above sense *for all* $v \in [n]$. The following properties are direct corollaries of the Chernoff-Hoeffding bound: the first follows from Chernoff-Hoeffding with independent random variables, and the latter from Chernoff-Hoeffding with negatively correlated random variables (see Appendix A).[2]

Corollary 1. *Let* $G = ([n], E)$ *be a randomized graph with the property that, for some fixed* $v \in [n]$, *the neighborhood* E_v *is a random subset of* $[n] \setminus \{v\}$ *of size d. Then, for any fixed subset* $T \subset [n]$, *we have*

$$\Pr\left[n_T^{\text{out}}(v) \geq \mu + \Delta\right] \leq 2^{-\frac{\Delta^2}{3\mu}} \quad \text{and} \quad \Pr\left[n_T^{\text{out}}(v) \leq \mu - \Delta\right] \leq 2^{-\frac{\Delta^2}{2\mu}},$$

where $\mu := \frac{|T|d}{n}$.

---

[2] We refer to [1] for more details, e.g., for showing that the random variables $X_j = 1$ if $j \in E_v$ and 0 otherwise are negatively correlated for E_v as in Corollary 1.

Corollary 2. *Let $G = ([n], E)$ be a randomized graph with the property that, for some fixed $T \subset [n]$, the neighborhoods E_v for $v \in T$ are random and independent of size d (in the sense as explained above). Then, for any $v \notin T$, we have*

$$\Pr\left[n_T^{\text{in}}(v) \geq \mu + \Delta\right] \leq 2^{-\frac{\Delta^2}{3\mu}} \quad and \quad \Pr\left[n_T^{\text{in}}(v) \leq \mu - \Delta\right] \leq 2^{-\frac{\Delta^2}{2\mu}},$$

where $\mu := \frac{|T|d}{n}$.

We will also encounter a situation where the set T may *depend* on the graph G; this will be in the context of a random but publicly known verification graph, where the adversary can then influence T dependent on G. The technical issue then is that *conditioned* on the set T, the neighborhood E_v may *not* be random anymore, so that we cannot apply the above two corollaries. Instead, we will then use the following properties, which require some more work to prove.

Lemma 1. *Let $G = ([n], E)$ be a random degree-d graph. Then, there exists no $\gamma \in \frac{1}{n}\mathbb{Z} \cap \left[0, \frac{1}{2}\right]$ and $T \subset [n]$ of size $|T| \geq (\gamma - \alpha)n$ for $\alpha^2 d = 24 \log n$ with the property that*

$$\left|\{v \in [n] : n_T^{\text{in}}(v) < d(\gamma - 2\alpha)\}\right| \geq \frac{\gamma n}{2},$$

except with probability n^{1-5n}.[3]

Proof. See appendix.

Lemma 2. *Let $G = ([n], E)$ be a random degree-d graph. Then, there exists no $\gamma \in \frac{1}{n}\mathbb{Z} \cap \left[\frac{1}{\log n}, \frac{1}{2}\right]$ and $T \subset [n]$ of size $|T| \leq (\gamma - 3\alpha)n$ for $\alpha^2 d = 24 \log n$ with the property that*

$$\left|\{v \in [n] : n_T^{\text{in}}(v) \geq d(\gamma - 2\alpha)\}\right| \geq \frac{\gamma n}{2},$$

except with probability n^{1-3n}.

The proof goes along the very same lines as for Lemma 1.

2.3 Robust Secret Sharing

A robust secret sharing scheme consists of two interactive protocols: the *sharing* protocol **Share** and the *reconstruction* protocol **Rec**. There are three different roles in this scheme, a *dealer* D, a *receiver* R and n parties labeled $1, \ldots, n$. The sharing protocol is executed by D and n parties: D takes as input a message **msg**, and each party $i \in \{1, \ldots, n\}$ obtains as output a *share*. Typically, D generates these shares locally and then sends to each party the corresponding share. The reconstruction protocol is executed by R and the n parties: each party is supposed to use its share as input, and the goal is that R obtains **msg**

---

[3] We emphasize that γ and T are allowed to depend on G.

as output. Ideally, the n parties simply send their shares to R—possibly using multiple communication rounds—and R then performs some local computation to reconstruct the message.[4]

We want a robust secret sharing scheme to be secure in the presence of an active adversary who can corrupt up to t of n parties. Once a party is corrupted, the adversary can see the share of this party. In addition, in the reconstruction protocol, the corrupt parties can arbitrarily deviate from the protocol. The following captures the formal security requirements of a robust secret sharing scheme.

Definition 1 (Robust Secret Sharing). *A pair* (**Share, Rec**) *of protocols is called a* (t, δ)-*robust secret sharing scheme if the following properties hold for any distribution of* **msg** *(from a given domain).*

- Privacy: *Before* **Rec** *is started, the adversary has no more information on the shared secret* **msg** *than he had before the execution of* **Share**.
- Robust reconstructability: *At the end of* **Rec**, *the reconstructor R outputs* **msg′** = **msg** *except with probability at most δ.*

As for the precise corruption model, we consider an adversary that can corrupt up to t of the n parties (but not the dealer and receiver). We consider the adversary to be *rushing*, meaning that the messages sent by the corrupt parties during any communication round in the reconstruction phase may depend on the messages of the honest parties sent in that round. Also, we consider the adversary to be *adaptive*, meaning that the adversary can corrupt parties *one by one* (each one depending on the adversary's current view) and *between any two rounds of communication*, as long as the total number of corrupt parties is at most t. We point out that we do not allow the adversary to be "*corruption-rushing*", i.e., to corrupt parties *during* a communication round, depending on the messages of (some of) the honest parties in this round, and to then "rush" and modify this round's messages of the freshly corrupt parties.[5]

2.4 Additional Building Blocks

We briefly recall a couple of techniques that we use in our construction. For more details, see Appendix B.

Message Authentication Codes. The construction uses unconditionally secure message authentication codes (MAC) that satisfy the usual authentication security, but which also feature a few additional properties: (1) an authentication tag σ is computed in a *randomized* way as a function $MAC_{key}(m, r)$ of the message m, the key key, and freshly chosen randomness r, (2) it is ensured that for any ℓ keys $key_1, \ldots, key_\ell$ (with ℓ a parameter), the list of

---

[4] This is not the case in [9]; see our discussion at the very end of Sect. 1.

[5] It is not fully clear to us what the impact would be of such a "corruption-rushing" adversary to our scheme.

tags $MAC_{key_1}(m,r), \ldots, MAC_{key_\ell}(m,r)$ is independent of m over the choice of random string r, and (3) for any message m and fixed randomness r, the tag $MAC_{key}(m,r)$ is uniformly distributed (over the random choice of the key). The specific construction we use is polynomial-evaluation construction

$$MAC_{(x,y)} : \mathbb{F}^a \times \mathbb{F}^\ell \to \mathbb{F}, (m,r) \mapsto \sum_{i=1}^{a} m_i x^{i+\ell} + \sum_{i=1}^{\ell} r_i x^i + y,$$

with $\mathbb{F}$ a finite field of appropriate size and the key being $key = (x,y) \in \mathbb{F}^2$.

Robust Distributed Storage. Following [3,8], the tags in the construction of our robust secret sharing scheme will be stored *robustly* yet *non-privately*; the latter is the reason why the extra privacy property (2) for the MAC is necessary. This design ensures that cheaters cannot lie about the tags that authenticate their shares to, say, provoke disagreement among honest parties about the correctness of the share of a dishonest party.

Formally, a *robust distributed storage scheme* is a robust secret sharing scheme but without the privacy requirement, and it can be achieved using a list-decodable code (see Appendix B or [8] for more details). Important for us will be that the share of each party i consists of two parts, p_i and q_i, and robustness against a rushing adversary is achieved by first revealing p_i and only then, in a second communication round, q_i. Furthermore, we can do with p_i and q_i that are (asymptotically) smaller than the message by a fraction $1/n$, and with correct reconstruction except with probability $2^{-\Omega(\log^2 n)}$.

3   The Robust Secret Sharing Scheme

3.1   The Sharing Protocol

Let t be an arbitrary positive integer and $n = 2t + 1$. Let $d = 600\log^3 n$.[6] We consider the message **msg** to be shared to be m bits long. We let $\mathbb{F}$ be a field with $\log |\mathbb{F}| = \log m + 3\log n$, and we set $a := \frac{m}{\log m + 3\log n}$ so that **msg** $\in \mathbb{F}^a$. Our robust secret sharing scheme uses the following three building blocks. A linear secret sharing scheme **Sh** that corresponds to a Reed-Solomon code of length n and dimension $t + 1$ over an extension field $\mathbb{K}$ over $\mathbb{F}$ with $[\mathbb{K} : \mathbb{F}] = a$,[7] together with its corresponding error-correcting decoding algorithm **Dec**, the MAC construction from Theorem 6 with $\ell = 10d$, and the robust distributed storage scheme from Theorem 7. On input **msg** $\in \mathbb{F}^a$, our sharing protocol **Share(msg)** works as follows.

1. Let $(s_1, \ldots, s_n) \leftarrow \mathbf{Sh}(\mathbf{msg})$ to be the non-robust secret sharing of **msg**.
2. Sample MAC randomness $r_1, \ldots, r_n \leftarrow \mathbb{F}^{10d}$ and repeat the following 5 times.

---

[6] We are not trying to optimize this constant. We specify the constant 600 for the convenience of probability estimate.

[7] So that we can identify **msg** $\in \mathbb{F}^a$ with **msg** $\in \mathbb{K}$.

(a) For each $i \in [n]$, choose a random set $E_i \subseteq [n] \setminus \{i\}$ of size d. If there exists $j \in [n]$ with in-degree more than $2d$, do it again.[8]

(b) For each $i \in [n]$, sample a random MAC keys $key_{i,j} \in \mathbb{F}^2$ for each $j \in E_i$, and set $\mathcal{K}_i = (key_{i,j})_{j \in E_i}$.

(c) Compute the MACs[9]

$$\sigma_{i \to j} = MAC_{key_{i,j}}(s_j, r_j) \in \mathbb{F} \quad \forall j \in E_i$$

and set $\mathbf{tag}_i = (\sigma_{i \to j})_{j \in E_i} \in \mathbb{F}^d$.

Let $E_i^{(m)}$, $\mathcal{K}_i^{(m)}$ and $\mathbf{tag}_i^{(m)}$ be the resulting choices in the m-th repetition.

3. Set $\mathbf{tag} = (\mathbf{tag}_i^{(m)})_{m \in [5], i \in [n]} \in \mathbb{F}^{5nd}$, and use the robust distributed storage scheme to store $\mathbf{tag}$ *together with* $E^{(2)}$. Party i gets p_i and q_i.

4. For $i \in [n]$, define $\mathbf{s}_i = (s_i, E_i^{(1)}, E_i^{(3)}, E_i^{(4)}, E_i^{(5)}, \mathcal{K}_i^{(1)}, \ldots, \mathcal{K}_i^{(5)}, r_i, p_i, q_i)$ to be the share of party i. Output $(\mathbf{s}_1, \ldots, \mathbf{s}_n)$.

We emphasize that the topology of the graph G_2, determined by the random neighborhoods $E_i^{(2)}$, is stored robustly (yet non-private). This means that the adversary will know $G^{(2)}$ but dishonest parties cannot lie about it. For G_1, G_3, G_4, G_5 it is the other way round: they remain private until revealed (see below), but a dishonest party i can then lie about $E_i^{(m)}$.

3.2 The Reconstruction Protocol

The reconstruction protocol **Rec** works as follows. First, using 5 rounds of communication, the different parts of the shares $(\mathbf{s}_1, \ldots, \mathbf{s}_n)$ are gradually revealed to the reconstructor R:

Round 1: Every party i sends (s_i, r_i, p_i) to the reconstructor R.
Round 2: Every party i sends $(q_i, E_i^{(1)}, \mathcal{K}_i^{(1)}, \mathcal{K}_i^{(2)})$ to the reconstructor R.
Round 3: Every party i sends $(E_i^{(3)}, \mathcal{K}_i^{(3)})$ to the reconstructor R.
Round 4: Every party i sends $(E_i^{(4)}, \mathcal{K}_i^{(4)})$ to the reconstructor R.
Round 5: Every party i sends $(E_i^{(5)}, \mathcal{K}_i^{(5)})$ to the reconstructor R.

Remark 1. We emphasize that since the keys for the authentication tags are announced *after* the Shamir/Reed-Solomon shares s_i, it is ensured that the MAC does its job also in the case of a rushing adversary. Furthermore, it will be crucial that also the $E_i^{(1)}$'s are revealed in the second round only, so as to ensure that once the (correct and incorrect) Shamir shares are "on the table", the $E_i^{(1)}$'s for the honest parties are still random and independent. Similarly for the $E_i^{(m)}$'s in the m-th round for $m = 3, 4, 5$. The graph G_2 is stored robustly; hence, the adversary knows all of it but cannot lie about it.

Then, second, having received the shares of n parties, the reconstructor R locally runs the reconstruction algorithm given in the box below.

---

[8] This is for privacy purposes.

[9] The same randomness r_j is used for the different i's and the 5 repetitions.

Local reconstruction algorithm

Collecting the data:

1. R collects $\mathbf{s} := (s_1, \ldots, s_n)$ and $(r_1, \ldots, r_n)$, and, round by round, all the authentication keys $key_{i,j}^{(m)}$ and the graphs G_1, G_3, G_4, G_5.

2. R reconstructs all the tags $\sigma_{i \to j}^{(m)}$ and the graph G_2 from $(p_i, q_i)_{i \in [n]}$.

3. R turns $G_1, \ldots, G_5$ into *labeled* "consistency" graphs by marking any edge $(i,j) \in E^{(m)}$ as **good** for which $\sigma_{i \to j}^{(m)} = MAC_{key_{i,j}^{(m)}}(s_j, r_j)$.

Exploring the consistency graphs:

1. Estimate the number p of "passive parties" by running $\mathrm{Check}(G_1, \frac{n}{\log n})$.

2. If the output is **yes** (indicating a "large" p) then compute

$$\mathbf{c}_\gamma := \mathrm{BigP}(G_1, G_2, G_3, G_4, \gamma, \mathbf{s})$$

   for every $\gamma \in \Gamma := [\frac{1}{\log n}, \frac{1}{4}] \cap \frac{1}{n}\mathbb{Z}$, set $\mathbf{c}_1 = \mathbf{Dec}(\mathbf{s})$, and output

$$\mathbf{c} := \mathrm{Cand}(\{\mathbf{c}_\gamma\}_{\gamma \in \Gamma} \cup \{\mathbf{c}_1\}, G_5, \mathbf{s}).$$

3. Otherwise, i.e., if the output is **no** (indicating a "small" p), compute

$$\mathbf{c}_i = \mathrm{GraphB}(G_3, G_4, \tfrac{4n}{\log n}, i, \mathbf{s})$$

   for every $i \in [n]$, and output $\mathbf{c} := \mathrm{maj}(\mathbf{c}_1, \ldots, \mathbf{c}_n)$, the majority.

In a first step, this reconstruction algorithm considers the graphs G_1, G_2, G_3, G_4 and all the authentication information, and turns there graphs into *labeled* graphs by marking edges as **good** or **bad** depending on whether the corresponding authentication verification works out. Then, makes calls to various subroutines; we will describe and analyze them at a time. As indicated in the description of the reconstruction algorithm, the overall approach is to first find out if the number p of passive parties[10] is small or large, i.e., if there is either lots of redundancy or many errors in the Shamir shares, and then use a procedure that is tailored to that case. Basically speaking, there are three subroutines to handle p in three different ranges. The unique decoding algorithm $\mathbf{Dec}(\mathbf{s})$ handles the case $p \geq \frac{n}{4}$ where there is sufficient redundancy in the shares to *uniquely* decode (this is the trivial case, which we do not discuss any further below but assume for the remainder that $p \leq \frac{n}{4}$). The graph algorithm GraphB handles the case $p \leq \frac{4n}{\log n}$, and the algorithm BigP deals with $p \in [\frac{n}{\log n}, \frac{n}{4}]$; there is some overlap in those two ranges as will not be able to pinpoint the range precisely.

---

[10] Formally, p is defined as t minus the number of active parties; thus, we implicitly assume that t parties are corrupt (but some of them may behave honestly).

In order to complete the description of the reconstruction procedure and to show that it does its job (except with at most constant probability), we will show the following in the upcoming sections.

1. An algorithm Check that distinguishes "small" from "large" p.
2. An algorithm BigP that, when run with $\gamma = p/n$ and given that p is "large", outputs a valid codeword $\mathbf{c}$ for which $c_i = s_i$ for all honest i, and thus which decodes to s. Given the p is not know, this algorithm is run with all possible choices for p, and all the candidates for $\mathbf{c}$ are collected.
3. An algorithm Cand that finds the right $\mathbf{c}$ in the above list of candidates.
4. An algorithm GraphB that, when run with an *honest* party i and given that p is "small", outputs the codeword corresponding to the correct secret s. This algorithm very much coincides with the algorithm used in [8] to deal with the case of a "small" p, except for an adjustment of the parameters. We defer description of this algorithm to our appendix as the security analysis is quite similar to the graph algorithm in BigP.

3.3   "Active" and "Passive" Dishonest Parties

As in previous work on the topic, for the analysis of our scheme, it will be convenient to distinguish between corrupt parties that announce the correct Shamir share s_i and the correct randomness r_i in the first round of the reconstruction phase (but may lie about other pieces of information) and between corrupt parties that announce an incorrect s_i or r_i. Following the terminology of previous work on the topic, the former parties are called *passive* and the latter are called *active* parties, and we write P and A for the respective sets of passive and active parties, and we write H for the set of honest parties.

A subtle issue is the following. While the set A of active parties is determined and fixed after the first round of communication, the set of passive parties P may increase over time, since the adversary may keep corrupting parties as long as $|A \cup P| \le t$, and make them lie in later rounds. Often, this change in P is no concern since many of the statements are in terms of $H \cup P$, which is fixed like A. In the other cases, we have to be explicit about the communication round we consider, and P is then understood to be the set of passive parties *during* this communication round.

3.4   The Consistency Graphs

As in [8], using a lazy sampling argument, it is not hard to see that after every communication round (including the subsequent "corruption round") in the reconstruction procedure, the following holds. Conditioned on anything that can be computed from the information announced up to that point, the neighbourhoods $E_i^{(m)}$ of the currently honest parties that are then announced in the *next* round are still random and independent. For example, conditioned on the set A of active parties and the set P of passive parties after the first round, the $E_i^{(1)}$'s announced in the second round are random and independent for all

$i \in H = [n] \setminus (A \cup P)$. Whenever we make probabilistic arguments, the randomness is drawn from these random neighbourhoods. The only exception is the graph G_2, which is robustly but non-privately stored, and which thus has the property that the $E_i^{(2)}$'s are random and independent for *all* parties, but not necessarily anymore when conditioned on, say, A and/or P.

Furthermore, by the security of the robust distributed storage of **tag** (Theorem 7) and the MAC (Theorem 6) with our choice of parameters, it is ensured that all of the labeled graphs $G_1, \ldots, G_5$ satisfy the following property except with probability $O\big(\log^3(n)/n^2\big)$. For any edge (i, j) in any of these graphs G_m, if i is honest at the time it announces $E_i^{(m)}$ then (i, j) is labled **good** whenever j is honest or passive.[11] Also, (i, j) is labeled **bad** whenever j is active.

These observations give rise to the following definition, given a partition $[n] = H \cup P \cup A$ into disjoint subsets with $|H| \geq t + 1$.

Definition 2. *A randomized labeled graph $G = ([n], E)$ is called a degree-d consistency graph (w.r.t. the given partition) if the following two properties hold.*

(Randomness) *The neighborhoods $E_i = \{j \mid (i, j) \in E\}$ of the vertices $i \in H$ are uniformly random and independent subsets of $[n] \setminus \{i\}$ of size d.*

(Labelling) *For any edge $(i, j) \in E$ with $i \in H$, if $j \in H \cup P$ then $L(i, j) = $ good and if $j \in A$ then $L(i, j) = $ bad.*

In order to emphasize the randomness of the neighborhoods E_i *given* the partition $[n] = H \cup P \cup A$ (and possibly of some other information X considered at a time), we also speak of a *fresh* consistency graph (w.r.t. to the partition and X). When we consider a variant of a consistency graph that is a random degree-d graph, i.e., the randomness property holds for *all* $i \in [n]$, while the partition $[n] = H \cup P \cup A$ (and possibly of some other information X considered at a time) may *depend* on the choice of the random edges, we speak of a *random but non-fresh* consistency graph.

Using this terminology, we can now capture the above remarks as follows:

Proposition 1. *The graphs G_1, G_3, G_4, G_5, as announced in the respective communication rounds, are fresh consistency graphs w.r.t. the partition $[n] = H \cup P \cup A$ given by the active and (at that time) passive parties and w.r.t. any information available to R or the adversary prior to the respective communication round, except that the labeling property may fail with probability $O\big(\log^3(n)/n^2\big)$ (independent of the randomness of the edges). On the other hand, G_2 is a random but non-fresh consistency graph (where, again, the labeling property may fail with probability $O\big(\log^3(n)/n^2\big)$).*

In the following analysis we will suppress the $O\big(\log^3(n)/n^2\big)$ failure probability for the labeling property; we will incorporate it again in the end. Also, we take it as understood that the partition $[n] = H \cup P \cup A$ always refers to the honest, the passive and the active parties, respectively.

---

[11] Note that we are exploiting here the fact that the authentication tags are *robustly* stored; thus, passive parties cannot lie about them.

3.5   The Check Subroutine

Let A be the set of active parties (well defined after the first communication round), and let $p := t - |A|$, the number of (potential) passive parties. The following subroutine distinguishes between $p \geq \frac{n}{\log n}$ and $p \leq \frac{4n}{\log n}$. This very subroutine was already considered and analyzed in [8]; thus, we omit the proof. The intuition is simply that the number of good outgoing edges of the honest parties reflects the number of active parties.

Check(G, ϵ)

Output **yes** if

$$|\{i \in [n] \ : \ n^{\mathsf{out}}(i, \mathsf{good}) \geq \frac{d}{2}(1 + \epsilon)\}| \geq t + 1\,;$$

otherwise, output **no**.

Proposition 2 [8]. *Except with probability $\epsilon_{check} \leq 2^{-\Omega(\epsilon d)}$, Check$(G, \epsilon)$ outputs* **yes** *if $p \geq \epsilon n$ and* **no** *if $p \leq \epsilon n/4$ (and either of the two otherwise).*

3.6   The Cand Subroutine

For simplicity, we next discuss the algorithm Cand. Recall that the set of correct Shamir sharings form a (Reed-Solomon) code with minimal distance t, and $\mathbf{s}$ collected by R is such a codeword, but with the coordinates in A (possibly) altered. The task of Cand is to find "the right" codeword $\mathbf{c}$, i.e., the one with $c_i = s_i$ for all $i \notin A$, out of a given list $\mathcal{L}$ of codewords. The algorithm is given access to a "fresh" consistency graph, i.e., one that is still random when conditioned on the list $\mathcal{L}$, and it is assumed that p is not too small.

Cand$(\mathcal{L}, G, \mathbf{s})$

For each codeword $\mathbf{c} \in \mathcal{L}$, set

$$S := \{i \in [n] \,|\, c_i = s_i\} \quad \text{and} \quad T := \{v \in S : n^{\mathsf{out}}_{[n] \backslash S}(v, \mathsf{good}) = 0\}$$

until $|T| \geq t + 1$, and output $\mathbf{c}$ then.

Proposition 3. *If $p \geq \frac{n}{\log n}$, $\mathcal{L}$ is a set of codewords of cardinality $O(n^2)$ for which there exists $\mathbf{c} \in \mathcal{L}$ with $c_i = s_i$ for all $i \in H \cup P$, and G is a fresh consistency graph, then Cand$(\mathcal{L}, G, \mathbf{s})$ outputs this $\mathbf{c} \in \mathcal{L}$ except with probability $\epsilon_{cand} \leq e^{-\Omega(\log^2 n)}$.*

Proof. Consider first a codeword $\mathbf{c} \in \mathcal{L}$ for which $c_i \neq s_i$ for some $i \in H \cup P$. Then, due to the minimal distance of the code, $|(H \cup P) \cap S| \leq t$. Therefore,

$$|(H \cup P) \setminus S| \geq |H \cup P| - t > p \geq \frac{n}{\log n}.$$

By the properties of G and using Corollary 1, this implies that for any $v \in H$

$$\Pr[n_{[n] \setminus S}^{\mathsf{out}}(v, \mathsf{good}) = 0] \leq \Pr[n_{(H \cup P) \setminus S}^{\mathsf{out}}(v, \mathsf{good}) = 0] \leq 2^{-\Omega(\frac{d}{\log n})},$$

which is $2^{-\Omega(\log^2 n)}$ by the choice of d. Taking a union bound over all such $\mathbf{c} \in \mathcal{L}$ does not affect this asymptotic bound.

Next, if $\mathbf{c} \in \mathcal{L}$ with $c_i = s_i$ for all $i \in H \cup P$, i.e., $[n] \setminus S \subseteq A$, then, by the properties of G,

$$n_{[n] \setminus S}^{\mathsf{out}}(v, \mathsf{good}) \leq n_A^{\mathsf{out}}(v, \mathsf{good}) = 0$$

for any $v \in H \subseteq S$. This proves the claim. $\square$

4   The Algorithm for Big p

We describe and discuss here the algorithm BigP, which is invoked when p is large. We show that BigP works, i.e., outputs a codeword $\mathbf{c}$ for which $c_i = s_i$ for all $i \in H \cup P$, and thus which decodes to the correct secret s, *if* it is given p as input. Since, p is not known, in the local reconstruction procedure BigP is run with all possible choices for p, producing a list of codewords, from which the correct one can be found by means of Cand, as shown above.

BigP$(G_1, G_2, G_3, G_4, \gamma, \mathbf{s})$

1. *Find V with no active parties and many honest parties:*

$$V := \mathrm{Filter}(G_1, \gamma).$$

2. *Find a correct codeword assuming $V \cap P$ to be small or V to be large:*

$$\mathbf{c} := \mathrm{Find}(G_2, V, \gamma, \mathbf{s}).$$

3. *Find a list of candidate codewords otherwise:* Let $W := [n] \setminus V$ and

$$\mathbf{c}_i := \mathrm{Graph}(G_3, G_4, W, \gamma, i) \text{ for } i \in W.$$

4. Output $\{\mathbf{c}\} \cup \{\mathbf{c}_1, \ldots, \mathbf{c}_{|W|}\}$.

Below, we describe the different subroutines of BigP and show that they do what they are supposed to do. Formally, we will prove the following.

Theorem 1. *If the number $p := t - |A|$ of passive parties satisfies $\frac{n}{\log n} \leq p \leq \frac{n}{4}$, and $\gamma := \frac{p}{n}$, then BigP will output a list that contains the correct codeword except with probability $\epsilon_{bigp} \leq O(n^{-3})$. Moreover, it runs in time $poly(n, m)$.*

For the upcoming description of the subroutines of BigP, we define the global constant

$$\alpha := \frac{1}{5 \log n} \qquad \text{so that} \qquad \alpha^2 d = \frac{600 \log^3 n}{25 \log^2 n} = 24 \log n.$$

Also, recall that $\frac{1}{\log n} \leq \gamma = \frac{p}{n} \leq \frac{1}{4}$.

4.1 Filter Out Active Parties

The goal of the algorithm Filter is to find a set V with no active parties and many honest parties. It has access to γ and to a fresh consistency graph.

Filter(G, γ)

Compute

$$T := \left\{ v \in [n] : n_{[n]}^{\text{out}}(v, \text{bad}) \leq \frac{d(1 - 2\gamma + \alpha)}{2} \right\}$$

and

$$V := \left\{ v \in T : n_T^{\text{in}}(v, \text{bad}) \leq \frac{d(1 - \alpha)}{2} \right\}$$

and output V.

Proposition 4. *If $\gamma = (t - |A|)/n$ and G is a fresh consistency graph then Filter(G, γ) outputs a set V that satisfies*

$$|V \cap H| \geq |H| - t + (\gamma - \alpha)n \geq (\gamma - \alpha)n \qquad \text{and} \qquad V \cap A = \emptyset \qquad (1)$$

except with probability $O(n^{-3})$.

We point out that the statement holds for the set of honest parties H as it is *before* Round 2 of the reconstruction procedure, but lower bound $(\gamma - \alpha)n$ will still hold *after* Round 2, since $|H|$ remains larger than t.

Proof. By the property of G and using Corollary 1, recalling that $\frac{|A|}{n} \leq \frac{1 - 2\gamma}{2}$, we have

$$\Pr\left[n^{\text{out}}(v, \text{bad}) \geq \frac{d(1 - 2\gamma + \alpha)}{2}\right] = \Pr\left[n_A^{\text{out}}(v, \text{bad}) \geq \frac{d(1 - 2\gamma + \alpha)}{2}\right] \leq 2^{-\alpha^2 d/6} = n^{-4}$$

for all $v \in H$. Taking a union bound over all honest parties, we conclude that all $v \in H$ are contained in T, except with probability n^{-3}.

In order for an honest party $v \in H$ to fail the test for being included in V, there must be $d(1 - \alpha)/2$ bad incoming edges, coming from dishonest parties in T. However, there are at most t dishonest parties in T, each one contributing at most $d(1 - 2\gamma + \alpha)/2$ bad outgoing edges; thus, there are at most

$$\frac{td(1 - 2\gamma + \alpha)}{d(1 - \alpha)} \leq t(1 - 2\gamma + 2\alpha) = t - (\gamma - \alpha)n$$

honest parties excluded from V, where the inequality holds because

$$\frac{1 - 2\gamma + \alpha}{1 - 2\gamma + 2\alpha} \leq \frac{(1 - 2\gamma + \alpha) + 2(\gamma - \alpha)}{(1 - 2\gamma + 2\alpha) + 2(\gamma - \alpha)} = 1 - \alpha,$$

using $\gamma - \alpha \geq 0$. This proves the claim on the number of honest parties in V.

For an active party $v \in A$, again by the properties of G but using Corollary 2 now, it follows that

$$\Pr\left[n_T^{\mathsf{in}}(v, \mathsf{bad}) \leq \tfrac{d(1-\alpha)}{2}\right] \leq \Pr\left[n_H^{\mathsf{in}}(v, \mathsf{bad}) \leq \tfrac{d(1-\alpha)}{2}\right] \leq 2^{-\alpha^2 d/4} = n^{-6},$$

recalling that $\frac{|H|}{n} \geq \frac{1}{2}$ and $H \subseteq T$. Taking the union bound, we conclude that V contains no active party, except with probability $O(n^{-5})$.

4.2 Find the Correct Codeword—In Some Cases

On input the set V as produced by Filter above, the goal of Find is to find the correct decoding of $\mathbf{s}$. Find is given access to γ and to a modified version of a consistency graph G. Here, the consistency graph has uniformly random neighbourhoods E_i for *all* parties, but the set V as well as the partition of $[n]$ into honest, passive and active parties may *depend* on the topology of G. Indeed, this is the property of the graph G_2, on which Find is eventually run.

Find$(G, V, \gamma, \mathbf{s})$

If $|V| < (2\gamma + 2\alpha)n$ then set

$$V_1 := \{v \in [n] \setminus V : n_V^{\mathsf{in}}(v, \mathsf{good}) \geq d(\gamma - 2\alpha)\},$$

while

$$V_1 := \{v \in [n] \setminus V : n_V^{\mathsf{in}}(v, \mathsf{good}) \geq d(\gamma + 2\alpha)\}$$

otherwise. Then, run the unique decoding algorithm on the shares s_i for $i \in V_1 \cup V$, and output the resulting codeword $\mathbf{c}$.

We will show that the algorithm Find succeeds as long as

$$|V \cap P| \leq (\gamma - 3\alpha)n \qquad \text{or} \qquad |V| \geq (2\gamma + 2\alpha)n. \tag{2}$$

This condition implies that honest parties outnumber passive parties by at least $2\alpha n$ in V. We notice that $2\alpha n$ is a very narrow margin which may become useless if passive parties in V can lie about their neighbours by directing all their outgoing edges to active parties. This behaviour may result in many active parties admitted to V_1. To prevent passive parties in V from lying about their neighbours, we introduce a non-fresh consistency graph G whose topology is publicly known but can not be modified. With the help of this graph G, we first prove that under condition (2), $V \cup V_1$ contains many honest and passive parties with high probability. Then, we further prove that under the same condition, $V \cup V_1$ contains very few active parties with high probability.

We stress that in the following statement, the partition $[n] = H \cup P \cup A$ (and thus γ) and the set V may depend on the choice of the (random) edges in G.

Lemma 3. *For $\gamma = (t - |A|)/n$, $V \subseteq [n]$ and G a random but non-fresh consistency graph, the following holds except with probability $2^{-\Omega(n)}$. If*

$$|V \cap H| \geq (\gamma - \alpha)n \qquad and \qquad |V| < (2\gamma + 2\alpha)n,$$

or

$$|V| \geq (2\gamma + 2\alpha)n,$$

then V_1 produced by $Find(G, V, \gamma)$ satisfies $|(H \cup P) \setminus (V \cup V_1)| \leq \frac{\gamma n}{2}$.

Proof. Consider $T := V \cap H$. Note that for $v \in H \cup P$

$$n_T^{in}(v) = n_{V \cap H}^{in}(v) = n_{V \cap H}^{in}(v, \mathsf{good}) \leq n_V^{in}(v, \mathsf{good}),$$

and thus

$$B := \{v \in H \cup P : n_V^{in}(v, \mathsf{good}) < d(\gamma - 3\alpha)\} \subseteq \{v \in H \cup P : n_T^{in}(v) < d(\gamma - 3\alpha)\}.$$

By Lemma 1 the following holds, except with probability $2^{-\Omega(n)}$. If $|V \cap H| \geq (\gamma - \alpha)n$ then $|B| < \frac{\gamma n}{2}$. But also, by definition of V_1 in case $|V| < (2\gamma + 2\alpha)n$, $(H \cup P) \setminus (V \cup V_1) \subseteq B$. This proves the claim under the first assumption on V.

The proof under the second assumption goes along the same lines, noting that the lower bound on $|V|$ then implies that $|V \cap H| \geq |V| - |P| \geq (\gamma + 2\alpha)n$, offering a similar gap to the condition $n_V^{in}(v, \mathsf{good}) < d(\gamma + \alpha)$ in the definition of V_1 then.

We proceed to our second claim.

Lemma 4. *For $\gamma = (t - |A|)/n$, $V \subseteq [n]$ and G a random but non-fresh consistency graph, the following holds except with probability $2^{-\Omega(n)}$. If $V \cap A = \emptyset$, as well as*

$$|V \cap P| \leq (\gamma - 3\alpha)n \qquad and \qquad |V| < (2\gamma + 2\alpha)n$$

or

$$|V| \geq (2\gamma + 2\alpha)n,$$

then V_1 produced by $Find(G, V, \gamma)$ satisfies $|V_1 \cap A| \leq \frac{\gamma n}{2}$.

Proof. Consider $T := V \cap P$. Note that for $v \in A$

$$n_T^{\text{in}}(v) = n_{V \cap P}^{\text{in}}(v) \geq n_{V \cap P}^{\text{in}}(v, \text{good}) = n_V^{\text{in}}(v, \text{good}),$$

and thus

$$C := \left\{ v \in A : n_V^{\text{in}}(v, \text{good}) \geq d(\gamma - 2\alpha) \right\} \subseteq \left\{ v \in A : n_T^{\text{in}}(v) \geq d(\gamma - 2\alpha) \right\}.$$

By Lemma 2 the following holds, except with probability $2^{-\Omega(n)}$. If $|V \cap P| \leq (\gamma - 3\alpha)n$ then $|C| < \frac{\gamma n}{2}$. But also, by definition of V_1 in case $|V| < (2\gamma + 2\alpha)n$, $V_1 \cap A \subseteq C$. This proves the claim under the first assumption on V.

The proof under the second assumption goes along the same lines, noting that $|V \cap P| \leq |P| \leq \gamma n$ offers a similar gap to the condition $n_V^{\text{in}}(v, \text{good}) < d(\gamma + \alpha)$ in the definition of V_1 then.

The following theorem is a consequence of Lemma 3 and Lemma 4. The statement holds for P and H after Round 2 in the reconstruction procedure.

Proposition 5. *The following holds except with probability* $2^{-\Omega(n)}$*. If (1) is satisfied, i.e.,* $|V \cap H| \geq (\gamma - \alpha)n$ *and* $V \cap A = \emptyset$*, and additionally*

$$|V \cap P| \leq (\gamma - 3\alpha)n \qquad \text{or} \qquad |V| \geq (2\gamma + 2\alpha)n$$

holds, and if G is a non-fresh consistency graph, then $\text{Find}(G, V, \gamma, \mathbf{s})$ will output the correct codeword (determined by the s_i for $i \in H$).

Proof. It follows from Lemma 3 and Lemma 4 that, except with the claimed probability, $|(V \cup V_1) \cap A| \leq \frac{\gamma n}{2}$ and $|(V \cup V_1) \cap (P \cup H)| \geq t + 1 + \frac{\gamma n}{2}$. Therefore, the punctured codeword, obtained by restricting to the coordinates in $V \cup V_1$, has more redundancy than errors, thus unique decoding works and produces the correct codeword.

Remark 2. Given that (1), i.e., $|V \cap H| \geq (\gamma - \alpha)n$ and $V \cap A = \emptyset$, is promised to be satisfied (except with small probability), the only case when Find fails is $|V| < (2\gamma + 2\alpha)n$ yet $|V \cap P| > (\gamma - 3\alpha)n$, where P is the set of passive parties before the third communication round. These conditions together with (1) imply that

$$|V| = |V \cap H| + |V \cap P| \geq (\gamma - \alpha)n + (\gamma - 3\alpha)n = (2\gamma - 4\alpha)n$$

and

$$|V \cap H| = |V| - |V \cap P| \le |V| - |V \cap P| \le (2\gamma + 2\alpha)n - (\gamma - 3\alpha)n \le (\gamma + 5\alpha)n$$

This holds for set of honest parties H even before Round 4 as the set of honest parties before Round 4 is a subset of that before Round 3. Combine this observation with Proposition 4, we come to conclusion that $|V \cap H| \in [(\gamma - \alpha)n, (\gamma + 5\alpha)n]$ holds for the set of honest parties H before Round 4, i.e., the number of honest parties within V is in the above range.

We can thus conclude that if Find fails then the set $W := [n] \setminus V$ satisfies

$$(1 - 2\gamma - 2\alpha)n \le |W| \le (1 - 2\gamma + 4\alpha)n$$

and, given that $|W \cap H| = t + 1 - |V \cap H|$,

$$(\frac{1}{2} - \gamma - 5\alpha)n \le |W \cap H| \le (\frac{1}{2} - \gamma + \alpha)n + 1.$$

As we mention before, this holds for the set of honest parties H before Round 4. Moreover,

$$|W \cap P| = |P| - |V \cap P| = |P \cup H| - |H| - |V \cap P| \le \gamma n - (\gamma n - 3\alpha n) \le 3\gamma n.$$

as $|P| \le \gamma n$. We point out that the statement $|W \cap P| \le 3\gamma n$ holds even for the set of passive parties P before Round 4 as $|P \cup H| = t + 1 + \gamma n$, $|H|$ remains bigger than $t + 1$ and $|V \cap P|$ remains bigger than $\gamma - 3\alpha n$. In the following section we show that if W satisfies the above constraints then the algorithm Graph finds the correct decoding of $\mathbf{s}$ (when initiated with an honest party v and two fresh consistency graphs).

4.3   Graph Algorithm

Recall that n'^{out}_W refers to n^{out}_W but for the graph G' rather than G, and similarly for n'^{in}_W. This graph algorithm resembles the one in [8], due to that they share the same goal of finding a subset of parties that contains all honest parties and a few dishonest parties whose majority are the passive parties. The differences lie in the range of parameters due to that the graph algorithm in this paper takes the subset of n parties as an input instead of n parties and honest parties may not be a majority in this subset.

The algorithm $\mathbf{Graph}(G, G', W, \gamma, v)$

i. Set $X := \{v\}$.

ii. *Expand X to include more honest parties:*

$$\text{While } |X| \leq \frac{\alpha t}{2d} \text{ do } X := \text{Expan}(G, W, X, \tfrac{1}{2} - \gamma).$$

iii. *Include all honest parties into V:*

$$V := V \cup \{v \in W \setminus X : n_X^{\text{in}}(v, \text{good}) \geq \tfrac{d|X|}{2n}\}.$$

iv. *Remove all active parties from V (and maybe few honest parties):*

$$U := \{v \in X : n_X^{\text{in}}(v, \text{bad}) \geq \tfrac{d}{10}\} \quad \text{and} \quad X := X \setminus U.$$

v. 1. *Bound the degree of parties in X:*

$$V := V \setminus \{v \in X : n_U'^{\text{out}}(v) \geq \tfrac{d}{8}\}.$$

2. *Include the honest parties from U (and perhaps few active parties):*

$$X := X \cup \{v \in U : n_V'^{\text{in}}(v, \text{good}) \geq \tfrac{d}{6}\}.$$

3. *Error correction:*
   Run the unique decoding algorithm algorithm on the shares of parties in $X \cup ([n] \setminus W)$ and output the result.

In this section, we assume that the graph algorithm $\text{Graph}(G, G', W, \epsilon, v)$ starts with an honest party v. Set $c = \tfrac{1}{2} - \gamma$ and we have $c \in [\tfrac{1}{4}, \tfrac{1}{2}]$ as $\gamma \leq \tfrac{1}{4}$. Note that P and H now become the set of passive parties and honest parties before Round 3. According to Remark 2, it suffices to prove the correctness of this graph algorithm under the condition that

$$|W| \in [(2c - 2\alpha)n, (2c + 4\alpha)], \quad |W \cap H| \in [c - 5\alpha, c + \alpha], \quad |W \cap P| \leq 3\alpha n. \quad (3)$$

Recall that $\alpha = \frac{1}{5 \log n}$ and $\alpha^2 d = 24 \log n$. We also note that by Remark 2, the above condition also holds for the set of passive parties and honest parties before Round 4. In what follows, when we claim that some event happens with high probability, we mean this holds for all set W, P and H in above range.

Let $H_W = H \cap W$ and $P_W = P \cap W$. The subset of active parties in W is still A. The out-degree of vertices in $G|_W$ and $G'|_W$ is expected to be $d\frac{|W|}{n} \in [(2c - 2\alpha)d, (2c + 4\alpha)d]$ and that (due to the MAC's) the edges from honest parties to active parties are labeled bad, and the edges from honest parties to honest or passive parties are labeled good.

We also recall that whether a corrupt party i is *passive* or *active*, i.e., in P or in A, depends on s_i and r_i only, as announced in the first communication round in the reconstruction phase. Note that a passive party may well lie about, say, his neighborhood E_i. Our reasoning only relies on the neighborhoods of the honest parties, which are random and independent conditioned on the adversary's view, as explained in Proposition 1.

Theorem 2. *Under the claim of Proposition 1, and assuming that v is honest and W satisfies (3), the algorithm will output a correct codeword except with probability $\epsilon_{graph} \leq n^{-15}$. Moreover, it runs in time $poly(m, n)$.*

The proof follows almost literally the one of [8] adjusted to the parameter regime considered here. For completeness, we provide the proof of this theorem. The proof of Theorem 2 consists of the analysis of Step ii to Step v and the Graph expansion algorithm. The analysis of Step ii to Step v is deferred to the Appendix.

4.4   Graph Expansion

We start by analyzing the expansion property of $G|_{H_W}$, the subgraph of G restricted to the set of honest parties H_W.

Lemma 5 (Expansion property of $G|_{H_W}$). *If $H' \subset H_W$ is so that $|H'| \leq \frac{\alpha |H_W|}{2d}$ and the E_v's for $v \in H'$ are still random and independent in G when given H' and H, then*

$$n_H^{out}(H') := \left| \bigcup_{v \in H'} N_H^{out}(v) \right| \geq (c - 7\alpha)d|H'|$$

except with probability $O(n^{-23})$.

Graph expansion algorithm Expan(G, W, X, c)

Set $X' = \emptyset$. For each vertex $v \in X$ do the following:

   if $n_W^{out}(v, \text{good}) \leq d(c + 5\alpha)$ then $X' := X' \cup N_W^{out}(v, \text{good})$.

Then, output $X' \cup X$.

Proof. By Remark 2, we know that the size of H_W is at least $(c - 5\alpha)n$. By assumption on the E_i's and by Corollary 1, for any vertex $v \in H'$, $\Pr[n_{H_W}^{out}(v) < (c - 6\alpha)d] \leq 2^{-\alpha^2 d/2c} = O(n^{-24})$ as $\alpha^2 d = 24 \log n$ and $c \leq 1/2$. Taking the union bound, this hold for all $v \in H'$ except with probability $O(n^{-23})$. In the remainder of the proof, we may thus assume that $N_{H_W}^{out}(v)$ consist of $d' := (c - 6\alpha)d$ random outgoing edges.

   Let $N := |H_W|$, $N' := |H'|$, and let $v_1, \ldots, v_{d'N'}$ denote the list of neighbours of all $v \in H'$, with repetition. To prove the conclusion, it suffices to bound the probability p_f that more than $\alpha dN'$ of these $d'N'$ vertices are repeated.

The probability that a vertex v_i is equal to one of $v_1, \ldots, v_{i-1}$ is at most

$$\frac{i}{N-1} \le \frac{d'N'}{N-1} = (c-6\alpha)d \cdot \frac{\alpha|N|}{2d} \cdot \frac{1}{N-1} \le \frac{\alpha}{4}.$$

as $c \le \frac{1}{2}$.

Taking over all vertex sets of size $\alpha dN'$ in these $d'N'$ neighbours, the union bound shows that p_f is at most

$$\binom{d'N'}{\alpha dN'}\left(\frac{\alpha}{4}\right)^{\alpha dN'} \le \binom{dN'}{\alpha dN'}\left(\frac{\alpha}{4}\right)^{\alpha dN'} \le 2^{dN'H(\alpha)+\alpha dN'(\log\alpha-2)}$$

$$\le 2^{\alpha dN'(\frac{1}{\ln 2}-2+O(\alpha))} \le 2^{-\Omega(\alpha dN')} \le 2^{-\Omega(\log^2 n)}.$$

The first inequality is due to that $\binom{n}{k} \le 2^{nH(\frac{k}{n})}$ and the second due to

$$H(\alpha) = -\alpha\log\alpha - (1-\alpha)\log(1-\alpha) = -\alpha\log\alpha + \frac{\alpha}{\ln 2} + O(\alpha^2)$$

for $\alpha = \frac{1}{5\log n}$ and the Taylor series $\ln(1-\alpha) = \alpha + O(\alpha^2)$.

5   Parallel Repetition

The failure probability δ of our local reconstruction scheme includes the failure probability of recovering tag ϵ_{tag}, the failure probability of labelling of consistency graph ϵ_{mac}, the failure probability of algorithm GraphB ϵ_{graph}, the failure probability of algorithm BigP ϵ_{bigP}, the failure probability of algorithm Cand ϵ_{Cand} and the failure probability of Check ϵ_{check}. Therefore, we have

$$\delta = \epsilon_{mac} + \epsilon_{tag} + \epsilon_{check} + (t+1)\epsilon_{graph} + \epsilon_{bigP} + \epsilon_{cand} = O(\frac{\log^3 n}{n^2}).$$

Note that our graph has degree $d = \Omega(\log^3 n)$ and $\mathbb{F}$ is a finite field with mn^3 elements. The total share size is $m + O(d(\log n + \log m)) = m + O(\log^4 n + \log m \log^3 n)$. We summarize our result as follows.

Theorem 3. *The scheme* (**Share, Rec**) *is a* $2t+1$-*party* $(t, O(\frac{\log^3 n}{n^2}))$-*robust secret sharing scheme with running time* $poly(m, n)$ *and share size* $m + O(\log^4 n + \log m \log^3 n)$.

The error probability can be made arbitrarily small by several independent executions of (**Share, Rec**), except that the same Shamir shares s_i would be used in all the instances. This could be done in a same manner in [8] or [3]. We skip the details but refer interested reader to [8] or [3]. In conclusion, we obtain the following main result.

Theorem 4. *For any set of positive integers t, n, κ, m with $t < n/2$, there exists a n-party $(t, 2^{-\kappa})$-robust secret sharing scheme against rushing adversary with secret size m, share size $m + O(\kappa(\log^4 n + \log^3 n \log m))$, and running time $poly(m, n)$.*

Acknowledgments. Chen Yuan has been funded by the ERC-ADG-ALGSTRONG CRYPTO project. (no. 740972)

A   Chernoff Bound

Like for [3], much of our analysis relies on the Chernoff-Hoeffding bound, and its variation to "sampling without replacement". Here and throughout, $[n]$ is a short hand for $\{1, 2, \ldots, n\}$.

Definition 3 (Negative Correlation [1]). *Let $X_1, \ldots, X_n$ be binary random variables. We say that they are negatively correlated if for all $I \subset [n]$:*

$$\Pr[X_i = 1 \; \forall i \in I] \le \prod_{i \in I} \Pr[X_i = 1] \quad and \quad \Pr[X_i = 0 \; \forall i \in I] \le \prod_{i \in I} \Pr[X_i = 0].$$

Theorem 5 (Chernoff-Hoeffding Bound). *Let $X_1, \ldots, X_n$ be random variables that are independent and in the range $0 \le X_i \le 1$, or binary and negatively correlated, and let $u = E\left[\sum_{i=1}^n X_i\right]$. Then, for any $0 < \delta < 1$:*

$$\Pr\left[\sum_{i=1}^n X_i \le (1 - \delta)u\right] \le 2^{-\delta^2 u/2} \quad and \quad \Pr\left[\sum_{i=1}^n X_i \ge (1 + \delta)u\right] \le 2^{-\delta^2 u/3}.$$

B   Building Blocks

B.1   MAC Construction

We adopt the definition as well as the construction of message authentication codes (MAC) from [8].

Definition 4. *A message authentication code (MAC) for a finite message space $\mathcal{M}$ consists of a family of functions $\{MAC_{key} : \mathcal{M} \times \mathcal{R} \to \mathcal{T}\}_{key \in \mathcal{K}}$. This MAC is said to be (ℓ, ϵ)-secure if the following three conditions hold.*

1. Authentication security: *For all $(m, r) \neq (m', r') \in \mathcal{M} \times \mathcal{R}$ and all $\sigma, \sigma' \in \mathcal{T}$,*

$$\Pr_{key \leftarrow \mathcal{K}}[MAC_{key}(m', r') = \sigma' | MAC_{key}(m, r) = \sigma] \le \epsilon.$$

2. Privacy over Randomness: *For all $m \in \mathcal{M}$ and $key_1, \ldots, key_\ell \in \mathcal{K}$, the distribution of ℓ values $\sigma_i = MAC_{key_i}(m, r)$ is independent of m over the choice of random string $r \in \mathcal{R}$, i.e.,*

$$\Pr_{r \leftarrow \mathcal{R}}[(\sigma_1, \ldots, \sigma_\ell) = \mathbf{c} | m] = \Pr_{r \leftarrow \mathcal{R}}[(\sigma_1, \ldots, \sigma_\ell) = \mathbf{c}]$$

for any $\mathbf{c} \in \mathcal{T}^\ell$.

3. Uniformity: *For all* $(m, r) \in \mathcal{M} \times \mathcal{R}$, *the distribution of* $\sigma = MAC_{key}(m, r)$ *is uniform at random over the random element* $key \in \mathcal{K}$.

The following variation of the standard polynomial-evaluation MAC construction meets the requirements.

Theorem 6 (Polynomial Evaluation [8]). *Let* $\mathbb{F}$ *be a finite field. Let* $\mathcal{M} = \mathbb{F}^a$, $\mathcal{R} = \mathbb{F}^\ell$ *and* $\mathcal{T} = \mathbb{F}$ *such that* $\frac{a+\ell}{|\mathbb{F}|} \le \epsilon$. *Define the family of MAC functions* $\{MAC_{(x,y)} : \mathbb{F}^a \times \mathbb{F}^\ell \to \mathbb{F}\}_{(x,y) \in \mathbb{F}^2}$ *such that*

$$MAC_{(x,y)}(\mathbf{m}, \mathbf{r}) = \sum_{i=1}^{a} m_i x^{i+\ell} + \sum_{i=1}^{\ell} r_i x^i + y$$

for all $\mathbf{m} = (m_1, \dots, m_a) \in \mathbb{F}^a$, $\mathbf{r} = (r_1, \dots, r_\ell) \in \mathbb{F}^\ell$ *and* $(x, y) \in \mathbb{F}^2$. *Then, this family of MAC functions is* (ℓ, ϵ)*-secure.*

B.2 Robust Distributed Storage

Following [3] and [8], the authentication tags in the construction of our robust secret sharing scheme will be stored *robustly* yet *non-privately*; indeed, the latter is the reason why the extra privacy property 2 in Definition 4 is necessary. The purpose of this design is to make sure that dishonest parties can not lie about the tags that authenticate their share e.g., to provoke disagreement among honest parties about the correctness of the share of a dishonest party.

Formally, a *robust distributed storage scheme* is a robust secret sharing scheme as in Definition 1 but without the privacy requirement. Such a scheme can easily be obtained as follows; we refer the interested readers to [3] or [8] for details. First of all, a list-decodable code is used to store the messages robustly. Then, the share of each party i consists of p_i and q_i, where p_i is the i-th component of list-decodable encoding of the message, and q_i is a hash-key and the hash of the message. Reconstruction works in the obvious way: a list of candidate messages is obtained by applying list decoding, and the correct message is then filtered out by means of checking the hashes. The robustness against a rushing adversary is achieved by first revealing p_i and only then, in a second communication round, q_i.

The following summarizes the result obtained by adapting the scheme in [8] to our parameter setting.

Theorem 7. *For any* $n = 2t + 1$ *and* $u = O(\log^3 n)$, *there exists a robust distributed storage against rushing adversary with messages of length* $m = \Omega(nu)$, *shares of length* $O(u)$ *that can recover the message with probability* $1 - 2^{-\Omega(\log^2 n)}$ *up to* t *corruptions.*

C   Graph Algorithm for Small p

The graph algorithm GraphB that is invoked for small p is exactly the same as that in [8] (for completeness, we recall it below); GraphB is also very similar to the graph algorithm Graph appearing inside the algorithm BigP. Thus, we omit the analysis of GraphB and rely on Theorem 8 from [8], re-stated below using our terminology and instantiated with our choice of parameters. Note that n'^{out}_W refers to n^{out}_W but for the graph G' rather than G, and similarly for n'^{in}_W.

Theorem 8 (Theorem 8, [8]). *If G is a fresh consistency graph, and G' is a fresh consistency graphy w.r.t. G', and if $|P| \leq \frac{4 \log n}{n}$ and v is an honest party, then GraphB$(G, G', \epsilon, v, \mathbf{s})$ will output the correct secret except with probability $\epsilon_{graph} \leq 2^{-\Omega(d/\log^2 n)} = O(n^{-3})$. Moreover, it runs in time poly(n, m).*

The algorithm GraphB$(G, G', \epsilon, v, \mathbf{s})$ for small p

i.   Input $G = ([n], E, L), G' = ([n], E', L'), d, \epsilon$ and $v \in [n]$.

ii.   Expand set $V = \{v\}$ to include more honest parties:

$$\text{While } |V| \leq \frac{\epsilon t}{d} \text{ do } T = \{v \in V : n^{\text{out}}(v, \mathbf{good}) \leq \frac{d}{2}(1 + 3\epsilon)\}$$

$$\text{and } V := V \cup \bigcup_{v \in T} N^{\text{out}}(v, \mathbf{good}).$$

iii. Include all honest parties into V:

$$V := V \cup \{v \notin V : n^{\text{in}}_V(v, \mathbf{good}) \geq \tfrac{d|V|}{2n}\}.$$

iv.   Remove all active parties from V (and maybe few honest parties as well):

$$W := \{v \in V : n^{\text{in}}_V(v, \mathbf{bad}) \geq \tfrac{d}{4}\} \quad \text{and} \quad V := V \setminus W.$$

v.   1. Bound the degree of parties in V:

$$V := V \setminus \{v \in V : n'^{\text{out}}_W(v) \geq \tfrac{d}{8}\}.$$

   2. Include the honest parties from W (and perhaps few active parties):

$$V := V \cup \{v \in W : n'^{\text{in}}_V(v, \mathbf{good}) \geq \tfrac{d}{4}\}.$$

   3. Error correction: run the unique decoding algorithm algorithm on the shares s_i of parties in V and output the result.

D   Proof of Lemma 1

For *fixed* $\gamma \in \frac{1}{n}\mathbb{Z} \cap [0, \frac{1}{2}]$ and $T \subseteq [n]$ with $|T| = (\gamma - \alpha)n$, by Corollary 2,

$$\Pr[n_T^{\text{in}}(v) < d(\gamma - 2\alpha)] \leq 2^{-\frac{\alpha^2 d}{27}}.$$

Thus, setting $\Sigma(T) := \{v \in [n] : n_T^{\text{in}}(v) < d(\gamma - 2\alpha)\}$ and considering another arbitrary but fixed subset $S \subseteq [n]$, we have (by negative correlation)

$$\Pr[S \subseteq \Sigma(T)] = \Pr[n_T^{\text{in}}(v) < d(\gamma - 2\alpha) \, \forall v \in S] \leq 2^{-\frac{\alpha^2 d}{27}|S|}.$$

Therefore, noting that $\Sigma(T) \subseteq \Sigma(T')$ for $T' \subseteq T$,

$$\Pr\big[\exists \gamma, T : |T| \geq (\gamma - \alpha)n \wedge |\Sigma(T)| \geq \frac{\gamma n}{2}\big]$$
$$= \Pr\big[\exists \gamma, T : |T| = (\gamma - \alpha)n \wedge |\Sigma(T)| \geq \frac{\gamma n}{2}\big]$$
$$= \Pr\big[\exists \gamma, T, S : |T| = (\gamma - \alpha)n \wedge |S| = \frac{\gamma n}{2} \wedge S \subseteq \Sigma(T)\big].$$

Taking union bound by summing over all $\gamma \in \frac{1}{n}\mathbb{Z} \cap [0, \frac{1}{2}]$ and $T, S \subseteq [n]$ with $|T| = (\gamma - \alpha)n \wedge |S| = \frac{\gamma n}{2}$, this is bounded by

$$\leq \sum_{\gamma} \sum_{S, T} \Pr[S \subseteq \Sigma(T)] \leq \sum_{\gamma} \binom{n}{\frac{\gamma n}{2}} \binom{n}{(\gamma - \alpha)n} 2^{-\frac{\alpha^2 d}{4}n}$$
$$\leq \sum_{\gamma} n^{\frac{\gamma n}{2}} \cdot n^{\gamma n} \cdot n^{-6n} \leq n^{1-5n},$$

proving the claim.   □

E   Analysis of Step ii to Step v

E.1   Analysis of Step ii

Set $\epsilon = \frac{1}{\log \log n}$ and recall that $\alpha = \frac{1}{5 \log n}$. The following shows that after Step ii, at most an $O(\epsilon)$-fraction of the parties in X is dishonest.

Proposition 6. *At the end of Step ii, with probability at least $1 - O(n^{-15})$, X is a set of size $\Omega(\epsilon n)$ with $|H_W \cap X| \geq (1 - O(\epsilon))|X|$ and $|(P \cup A) \cap X| \leq O(\epsilon|X|).$*

Proof. First of all, we observe that for every honest party v, the number of its good outgoing edges is expected to be $\frac{|P_W \cup H_W|d}{n} \leq (c + 4\alpha)d$ since only honest parties and passive parties can pass the verification of v. By assumption on the E_v's and by Corollary 1, we have

$$\Pr[n_W^{\text{out}}(v, \text{good}) \geq d(c + 5\alpha)] \leq 2^{\alpha^2 d/3c} = O(n^{-16}).$$

Taking an union bound over all $v \in H_W$ leads to the claim that except with probability $O(n^{-15})$, all honest parties in X will be included in the expansion of $\text{Expan}(G, W, X, c)$.

Recall that $\text{Expan}(G, W, X, c)$ has been invoked multiple times. Let X_i be the set X after Expan has been invoked i times, $X_0 = \{v\}$, $X_1 = \text{Expan}(G, W, X_0, c)$ etc., and let $H_0 = \{v\}$ and $H_1 = \text{Expan}(G, W, H_0, c) \cap H$, etc. be the corresponding sets when we include only honest parties into the sets.

Using a similar lazy-sampling argument as for Proposition 1, it follows that conditioned on $H_0, H_1, \ldots, H_i$, the E_v's for $v \in H_i \setminus H_{i-1}$ are random and independent for any i. Therefore, we can apply Lemma 5 to $H_i' = H_i \setminus H_{i-1}$ to obtain that $|H_{i+1}| \geq |H_i'| d(c - 7\alpha)$. It follows that $|H_i| \geq (d(1 - 7\alpha))^i$ except with probability $O(n^{-23})$. Our algorithm jumps out of Step ii when X is of size $\Omega(\alpha n)$. We next bound the number of rounds in this step. For $i = \frac{\log n}{\log \log n}$, noting that $d \geq \log^3 n$ and $c \geq \frac{1}{4}$, it thus follows that

$$|X_i| \geq |H_i| \geq \left(d(c - 7\alpha)\right)^i \geq (\log^3 n)^{\frac{\log n}{\log \log n}} (c - 7\alpha)^{\frac{\log n}{\log \log n}}$$

$$\geq n^3 \cdot c^{\frac{\log n}{\log \log n}} \geq \Omega(n^3).$$

This means $\text{Expan}(G, W, X, c)$ is invoked $r \leq \frac{\log n}{\log \log n}$ times assuming n is large enough.

On the other hand, we trivially have $|X_r| \leq (d(c + 5\alpha))^r$ by specification of Expan. Thus,

$$|X_r| - |H_r| \leq \left(d(c + 5\alpha)\right)^r - \left(d(c - 7\alpha)\right)^r$$

$$= 12\alpha d \left(\sum_{i=0}^{r-1} \left((d(c + 5\alpha))\right)^i \left(d(c - 7\alpha)\right)^{r-1-i}\right) \leq 12\alpha r d \left((d(c + 5\alpha))\right)^{r-1}$$

$$= O\left(\frac{1}{\log \log n} |X_r|\right) = O(\epsilon |X_r|),$$

as $\epsilon = \frac{1}{\log \log n}$. The first equality is due to $a^n - b^n = (a - b)(\sum_{i=0}^{n-1} a^i b^{n-1-i})$ and the last one is due to $r \leq \frac{\log n}{\log \log n}$ and $\alpha = \frac{1}{5 \log n}$.

This upper bound implies that there are at least $|X_r|(1 - O(\epsilon))$ honest parties in X_r while the number of dishonest parties is at most $O(\epsilon |X_r|)$.

E.2   Analysis of Step iii

The analysis of Step iii is based on the intuition that every honest party v outside $H_W \setminus X$ will get sufficient support from parties in X as X consists almost entirely of honest parties in H_W. In particular, any such v is expected have have close to $\frac{d}{n} |X|$ good incoming edges from the parties in X.

Proposition 7. *At the end of Step iii, with probability at least $1 - 2^{-\Omega(\alpha d)}$, X contains all honest parties in H_W and $O(\epsilon n)$ dishonest parties.*

Proof. Recall that conditioned on H_r, the E_v's for $v \in H_r \setminus H_{r-1}$ are random and independent.

Set $\tilde{H} := H_r \setminus H_{r-1}$ and $d_1 := \frac{|X|d}{n} = \Omega(\alpha d)$. This implies $|\tilde{H}| = (1 - o(1))|H_r| = (1 - o(1))|X|$ as $H_{r-1} = o(H_r)$ and X contains at most $O(\epsilon|X|) = O(\frac{|X|}{\log\log n})$ dishonest parties. Using Corollary 2 for the final bound, it follows that for a given honest party $v \in H_W/\tilde{H}$,

$$\Pr\left[n_X^{\text{in}}(v, \text{good}) < \frac{d_1}{2}\right] \leq \Pr\left[n_{\tilde{H}}^{\text{in}}(v, \text{good}) < \frac{d_1}{2}\right]$$
$$= \Pr\left[n_{\tilde{H}}^{\text{in}}(v) < \frac{d_1}{2}\right] \leq 2^{-\Omega(\alpha d)}.$$

By union bound over all honest parties in $H_W \setminus \tilde{H}$, all these honest parties are added to X except with probability at most $2^{-\Omega(\alpha d)}$.

On the other hand, Admitting any active party w outside X requires at least $\frac{d_1}{2}$ good incoming edges. Recall that only dishonest party can verify active party. Therefore, these edges must be directed from dishonest parties in X. Since there are at most $O(\epsilon)|X|$ dishonest parties in X and each of them contributes to at most d good incoming edges, the number of active parties admitted to X is at most $\frac{O(\epsilon)|X|d}{d_1/2} = O(\epsilon n) = O(\frac{n}{\log\log n})$.

E.3   Analysis of Step iv

The goal of Step iv is to remove all active parties from X. This can be done by exploiting the fact that the vast majority of X are honest parties.

Proposition 8. *At the end of Step iv, with probability at least* $1 - 2^{-\Omega(d)}$, X *consists of* $|H_W| - O(\epsilon n)$ *honest parties and no active parties, and* U *consists of the rest of honest parties in* H_W *and* $O(\epsilon n)$ *dishonest parties.*

Proof. Observe that $\frac{|H_W|d}{n} \geq (c - 5\alpha)d \geq \frac{d}{5}$ as $c \geq \frac{1}{4}$ and $\alpha = \frac{1}{5\log n}$. It follows, again using Corollary 2, that for an active party v in X, we have

$$\Pr\left[n_X^{\text{in}}(v, \text{bad}) < \frac{d}{10}\right] \leq \Pr\left[n_{H_W}^{\text{in}}(v, \text{bad}) < \frac{d}{10}\right] = \Pr\left[n_{H_W}^{\text{in}}(v) < \frac{d}{10}\right] \leq 2^{-\Omega(d)}.$$

By union bound over all active parties in X, all of them are removed from X with probability at least $1 - t2^{-\Omega(d)} = 1 - 2^{-\Omega(d)}$.

On the other hand, if the honest party v is removed from X, v must receive at least $\frac{d}{10}$ bad incoming edges from dishonest parties in X. Since the number of dishonest parties is at most $a := O(\epsilon n)$, there are at most $\frac{ad}{d/10} = O(\epsilon n)$ honest parties removed from X.

E.4   Analysis of Step v

From the analysis of Step iv, we learn that $|U| = O(\epsilon n)$ and X has size $|H_W| - O(\epsilon n) = cn - O(\epsilon n)$. In order to analyze this step, we introduce the following notation. Let P and H be the set of passive parties and honest parties before the fourth communication round respectively. According to Remark 2, the condition (3) still holds. Then, $H_W = H \cap W$ has size $cn - O(\alpha n)$ and $H_P = P \cap W$ has size at most $3\alpha n$. By Proposition 8, this implies that X consists of $cn - O(\epsilon n)$ honest parties and a few passive parties and U is as set of size $O(\epsilon)$ which contains all honest parties in $H_W \setminus X$. Let $X = X_H \cup X_P$ where X_H is a of honest parties and X_P is a set of passive parties. Let $U = U_H \cup U_C$ where U_H is a set of honest parties and U_C is a set of dishonest parties. Then, we have $X_H \cup U_H = H_W$ and $|U_H| \leq |U| = O(\epsilon n)$ as U and X together contains all honest parties in H_W.

Note that in Step v, we introduce a new fresh consistency graph G'. Given the adversary's strategy, all the previous steps of the graph algorithm are determined by the graph G and thus independent of the new fresh consistency graph G'. Therefore, by Proposition 1, at this point in the algorithm the E_v''s for $v \in H_W$ are still random and independent conditioned on X_H, X_P, U_C, U_H.

Proposition 9. *Except with probability $2^{-\Omega(d)}$, after Step v the set X will contain all honest parties in H_W and at least as many passive parties as active ones. Therefore, Step v will output the correct codeword with probability at least $1 - 2^{-\Omega(d)}$.*

Proof. **Step v.1.** For any $i \in X_H$, $n_U'^{\text{out}}(i)$ is expected to be $\frac{|U|d}{n} = O(\epsilon d)$. By Corollary 1 we thus have

$$\Pr\left[n_U'^{\text{out}}(i) \geq \frac{d}{8}\right] \leq 2^{-\Omega(d)}.$$

Hence, by union bound, all honest parties in X remain in X except with probability $2^{-\Omega(d)}$.

Let X_P' be the set of passive parties left in X after this step, and set $p := |X_P'|$. Note that $n_U^{\text{out}}(v) \leq d/8$ for every $v \in X$.

Step v.2. Observe that $\frac{d|X_H|}{n} = (c - O(\epsilon))d \geq (\frac{1}{4} - O(\epsilon))d$ as $d \leq \frac{1}{4}$. It follows from Corollary 2 that for any honest party $i \in U_H$,

$$\Pr\left[n_X'^{\text{in}}(i, \text{good}) \leq \frac{d}{6}\right] \leq \Pr\left[n_{X_H}'^{\text{in}}(i, \text{good}) \leq \frac{d}{6}\right] = \Pr\left[n_{X_H}'^{\text{in}}(i) \leq \frac{d}{6}\right] \leq 2^{-\Omega(d)}.$$

Thus, all honest parties in U are added to X, except with probability $2^{-\Omega(d)}$.

On the other hand, the good incoming edges of the active parties must be directed from passive parties in X_P'. Observe that each party in X is allowed to have at most $\frac{d}{8}$ outgoing neighbours in U. This implies there are at most $\frac{|X_P|d/8}{d/6} = \frac{3|X_P|}{4}$ active parties admitted to X in this step, proving the first part of the statement.

Step v.3. Observe that the set $[n] \setminus W$ consists of the rest of honest parties and passive parties. This implies that $([n] \setminus W) \cup X$ contains all honest parties and is a set where the number of active parties is less than the number of passive parties. The shares of the parties in $([n] \setminus W) \cup X$ form a Reed-Solomon code. Since the number of errors is less than the redundancy of this code, the unique decoding algorithm will output a correct codeword.

References

1. Auger, A., Doerr, B.: Theory of Randomized Search Heuristics. World Scientific, Singapore (2011)
2. Bishop, A., Pastro, V.: Robust secret sharing schemes against local adversaries. In: Cheng, C.-M., Chung, K.-M., Persiano, G., Yang, B.-Y. (eds.) PKC 2016. LNCS, vol. 9615, pp. 327–356. Springer, Heidelberg (2016). https://doi.org/10.1007/978-3-662-49387-8_13
3. Bishop, A., Pastro, V., Rajaraman, R., Wichs, D.: Essentially optimal robust secret sharing with maximal corruptions. In: Fischlin, M., Coron, J.-S. (eds.) EURO-CRYPT 2016. LNCS, vol. 9665, pp. 58–86. Springer, Heidelberg (2016). https://doi.org/10.1007/978-3-662-49890-3_3
4. Carpentieri, M., De Santis, A., Vaccaro, U.: Size of shares and probability of cheating in threshold schemes. In: Helleseth, T. (ed.) EUROCRYPT 1993. LNCS, vol. 765, pp. 118–125. Springer, Heidelberg (1994). https://doi.org/10.1007/3-540-48285-7_10
5. Cevallos, A., Fehr, S., Ostrovsky, R., Rabani, Y.: Unconditionally-secure robust secret sharing with compact shares. In: Pointcheval, D., Johansson, T. (eds.) EUROCRYPT 2012. LNCS, vol. 7237, pp. 195–208. Springer, Heidelberg (2012). https://doi.org/10.1007/978-3-642-29011-4_13
6. Cramer, R., Damgård, I., Fehr, S.: On the cost of reconstructing a secret, or VSS with optimal reconstruction phase. In: Kilian, J. (ed.) CRYPTO 2001. LNCS, vol. 2139, pp. 503–523. Springer, Heidelberg (2001). https://doi.org/10.1007/3-540-44647-8_30
7. Cramer, R., Damgård, I.B., Döttling, N., Fehr, S., Spini, G.: Linear secret sharing schemes from error correcting codes and universal hash functions. In: Oswald, E., Fischlin, M. (eds.) EUROCRYPT 2015. LNCS, vol. 9057, pp. 313–336. Springer, Heidelberg (2015). https://doi.org/10.1007/978-3-662-46803-6_11
8. Fehr, S., Yuan, C.: Towards optimal robust secret sharing with security against a rushing adversary. In: Ishai, Y., Rijmen, V. (eds.) EUROCRYPT 2019. LNCS, vol. 11478, pp. 472–499. Springer, Cham (2019). https://doi.org/10.1007/978-3-030-17659-4_16
9. Manurangsi, P., Srinivasan, A., Vasudevan, P.N.: Nearly optimal robust secret sharing against rushing adversaries. In: Micciancio, D., Ristenpart, T. (eds.) CRYPTO 2020. LNCS, vol. 12172, pp. 156–185. Springer, Cham (2020). https://doi.org/10.1007/978-3-030-56877-1_6
10. Rabin, T., Ben-Or, M.: Verifiable secret sharing and multiparty protocols with honest majority (extended abstract). In: Proceedings of the 21st Annual ACM Symposium on Theory of Computing, 14–17 May 1989, Seattle, Washigton, USA, pp. 73–85 (1989)

The Share Size of Secret-Sharing Schemes for Almost All Access Structures and Graphs

Amos Beimel[1] and Oriol Farràs[2]([⊠])

[1] Ben-Gurion University of the Negev, Be'er-Sheva, Israel
amos.beimel@gmail.com
[2] Universitat Rovira i Virgili, Tarragona, Catalonia, Spain
oriol.farras@urv.cat

Abstract. The share size of general secret-sharing schemes is poorly understood. The gap between the best known upper bound on the total share size per party of $2^{0.64n}$ (Applebaum et al., STOC 2020) and the best known lower bound of $\Omega(n/\log n)$ (Csirmaz, J. of Cryptology 1997) is huge (where n is the number of parties in the scheme). To gain some understanding on this problem, we study the share size of secret-sharing schemes of almost all access structures, i.e., of almost all collections of authorized sets. This is motivated by the fact that in complexity, many times almost all objects are hardest (e.g., most Boolean functions require exponential size circuits). All previous constructions of secret-sharing schemes were for the worst access structures (i.e., all access structures) or for specific families of access structures.

We prove upper bounds on the share size for almost all access structures. We combine results on almost all monotone Boolean functions (Korshunov, Probl. Kibern. 1981) and a construction of (Liu and Vaikuntanathan, STOC 2018) and conclude that almost all access structures have a secret-sharing scheme with share size $2^{\tilde{O}(\sqrt{n})}$.

We also study graph secret-sharing schemes. In these schemes, the parties are vertices of a graph and a set can reconstruct the secret if and only if it contains an edge. Again, for this family there is a huge gap between the upper bounds – $O(n/\log n)$ (Erdös and Pyber, Discrete Mathematics 1997) – and the lower bounds – $\Omega(\log n)$ (van Dijk, Des. Codes Crypto. 1995). We show that for almost all graphs, the share size of each party is $n^{o(1)}$. This result is achieved by using robust 2-server conditional disclosure of secrets protocols, a new primitive introduced and

A. Beimel—This work was done while visiting Georgetown University, supported by NSF grant no. 1565387, TWC: Large: Collaborative: Computing Over Distributed Sensitive Data and also supported by ERC grant 742754 (project NTSC), by ISF grant 152/17, and by a grant from the Cyber Security Research Center at Ben-Gurion University of the Negev.

O. Farràs—This work is supported by grant 2017 SGR 705 from the Government of Catalonia and grant RTI2018-095094-B-C21 "CONSENT" from the Spanish Government.

R. Pass and K. Pietrzak (Eds.): TCC 2020, LNCS 12552, pp. 499–529, 2020.
https://doi.org/10.1007/978-3-030-64381-2_18

constructed in (Applebaum et al., STOC 2020), and the fact that the size of the maximal independent set in a random graph is small. Finally, using robust conditional disclosure of secrets protocols, we improve the total share size for all very dense graphs.

1   Introduction

A dealer wants to store a string of secret information (a.k.a. a secret) on a set of computers such that only some pre-defined subsets of the computers can reconstruct the information. We will refer to the computers as the parties, their number as n, and the collection of authorized sets that can reconstruct the secret as an access structure. To achieve this goal the dealer uses a secret-sharing scheme – a randomized function that is applied to the secret and produces n strings, called shares. The dealer gives the i-th share to the i-th party, and any authorized set of parties can reconstruct the secret from its shares. Nowadays, secret-sharing schemes are used as a building box in many cryptographic tasks (see, e.g., [10,13]). We consider schemes where unauthorized sets of parties gain absolutely no information on the secret from their shares, i.e., the security is information theoretic. We will mainly try to reduce the sizes of the shares given to the parties. To understand why minimizing the share size is important, let us consider the original secret-sharing schemes of [44] for an arbitrary access structure; in these schemes the size of each share is greater than 2^n, making them impractical when, for example, $n = 100$. Even in the most efficient scheme known today, the share size is $2^{0.64n}$ [5] (improving on [4,48]).

We ask the question if the above share size can be reduced for almost all access structures. One motivation for this question is that in complexity theory, almost all Boolean functions are often the hardest functions. For example, Shannon [58] showed that almost all Boolean functions require circuits of size $2^{\Omega(n)}$, this lower bound applies also to other models, e.g., formulas. Furthermore, almost all *monotone* Boolean functions require monotone circuits and monotone formulas of size $2^{\Omega(n)}$. Dealing with properties of almost all objects is a common theme in combinatorics, e.g., properties of almost all graphs. A famous example states that the size of the maximum independent set (and clique) of almost all n-vertex graphs is approximately $2 \log n$ [43]; we use this property in our constructions. Using a result on almost all monotone Boolean functions [47], we show that almost all access structures can be realized by a secret-sharing scheme with maximum share size $2^{\tilde{O}(\sqrt{n})}$.

In this paper, we also study graph secret-sharing schemes. In a secret-sharing scheme realizing a graph G, the parties are vertices of the graph G and a set can reconstruct the secret if and only if it contains an edge. The naive scheme to realize a graph is to share the secret independently for each edge; this result implies a share of size $O(n)$ per party. A better scheme with share size $O(n/\log n)$ per party is implied by a result of Erdös and Pyber [38]. Graph secret-sharing schemes were studied in many previous works. One motivation for studying graph secret-sharing schemes is that they are simpler than secret-sharing schemes for general access structures and phenomena proved for graph secret-sharing schemes were later generalized to general access structures (e.g., Blundo et al. [26] proved that in any non-ideal access structure the share size of at least one party is at least 1.5 times the size of the secret, a result that was later proved for every access structure [51]). Another motivation is that, by [54, Section 6.3.1], for every $0 < c < 1/2$ any graph secret-sharing scheme with share size $O(n^c)$ per party implies a secret-sharing scheme for any access structure with share size $2^{(0.5+c/2+o(1))n}$; thus, major improvement in the share size for all graphs will result in improved schemes for all access structures. However, in spite of the recent improvements in the share size for general access structures [4,5,48] and for specific families of access structures (e.g., forbidden graphs [18,41,49] and uniform access structures [2,4,19]), no such improvement was achieved for schemes for graphs. We show that almost all graphs can be realized by a secret-sharing scheme with share size $n^{o(1)}$ per party.

1.1 Previous Results

We next describe the most relevant previous results. We refer the reader to Fig. 1 for a description of the maximum share size in previous constructions and our constructions.

	Share size (one bit secret)	Share size of linear schemes over $\mathbb{F}_q$ (log q-bit secret)	Inf. ratio multi-linear schemes (long secrets)
Forbidden graphs	$n^{o(1)}$ [49] $\Omega(1)$	$\tilde{O}(\sqrt{n}\log q)$ [41] $\Omega(\sqrt{n})$ [15]	$O(\log n)$ [2] $\Omega(1)$
Almost all graphs	$n^{o(1)}$ Th. 5.1 $\Omega(\log\log n)$ [35]	$\tilde{O}(\sqrt{n}\log q)$ Th. 5.1 $\Omega(\sqrt{n})$ [15]	$\tilde{O}(\log n)$ Th. 5.1 $\Omega(\log^{1/2} n)$ Th. 5.5
All graphs	$O(n/\log n)$ [38] $\Omega(\log n)$ [37,36]	$O(\frac{n}{\log n}\log q)$ [38] $\Omega(\sqrt{n}\log q)$ [17]	$O(n/\log n)$ [38] $\Omega(\sqrt{n})$ [11,17]
Almost all access structures	$2^{O(\sqrt{n}\log n)}$ Th. 3.3 $\Omega(1)$	$2^{0.5n+o(n)}\log q$ Th. 3.3 $\Omega(2^{n/2-o(n)})$ [9], Th. 3.11 $\Omega(2^{n/3-o(n)}\log q)$ [56], Th. 3.10	$2^{O(\sqrt{n\log n})}$ Th. 3.3 $\Omega(1)$
All access structures	$2^{0.64n}$ [5] $\Omega(n/\log n)$ [34]	$2^{0.76n}\log q$ [5] $2^{\Omega(n)}\log q$ [55]	$2^{0.64n}$ [5] $n^{\Omega(\log n)}$ [11,17]

Fig. 1. A summary of the upper and lower bounds on the maximum share size for secret-sharing schemes for forbidden graph access structures, almost all graph access structures, graph access structures, almost all access structures, and all access structures. The results proved in this paper are in **boldface**.

Measures of Share Size. The size of a share is simply the length of the string representing it. For a secret-sharing scheme, two measures of for the share size were considered: (1) the maximum share size, i.e., the maximum over all parties in the scheme of the size of the share of the party, (2) the total share size, i.e., the sum over all parties in the scheme of the size of the share of the party. For a given scheme, the maximum share size is bounded from above by the total share size, which is bounded from above by n times the maximum share size. The distinction between these two measures is important for graph secret-sharing schemes, and there might be trade-offs between optimizing one measure and optimizing the other. On the other hand, the share size in the secret-sharing schemes considered in this paper for general access structures is larger than $2^{\sqrt{n}}$, thus for these schemes the distinction between the measures is less important.

We will also consider the normalized total (respectively, maximum) share size, i.e., the ratio between the sum of the share sizes (respectively, maximum share size) and the size of the secret. This normalized maximum share size (also known as information ratio) is similar in spirit to measures considered in information theory and it is interesting since the length of each share is at least the length of the secret [46]. In this work, we will consider the normalized share size for two regimes: (1) Moderately short secrets of size $\tilde{O}(n)$, and (2) Following [2,3], we also consider exponentially long secrets of size 2^{n^2}. The latter size is not reasonable, however, these schemes may lead to schemes with the same share size for shorter secrets and they provide barriers for proving lower bounds via information inequalities.

Bounds on the Share Size. Secret-sharing schemes were introduced by Blakely [24] and Shamir [57] for the threshold case and by Ito, Saito, and Nishizeki [44] for the general case. In the original secret-sharing schemes for arbitrary access structures of Ito et al. [44] the maximum share size is 2^{n-1}. Additional constructions of secret-sharing schemes followed, e.g., [22,23,29,45,59]. For specific access structures, the share size in these schemes is less than the share size in the scheme of [44]; however, the share size in the above schemes for arbitrary access structures is $2^{n-o(n)}$. In a recent breakthrough work, Liu, and Vaikuntanathan [48] (using results of [50]) constructed a secret-sharing scheme for arbitrary access structures with share size $2^{0.944n}$ and a linear secret-sharing scheme with share size $2^{0.999n}$. Applebaum et al. [5] (using results of [4,50]) improved these results, constructing a secret-sharing schemes for arbitrary access structures with share size $2^{0.637n}$ and a linear secret-sharing scheme with share size $2^{0.762n}$. It is an important open problem if the share size can be improved to $2^{o(n)}$ (or even smaller). Lower bounds for secret-sharing were proven in, e.g., [25,30,33,34,37]. These lower bounds are very far from the upper bounds – the best lower bound is $\Omega(n^2/\log n)$ for the normalized *total* share size for an explicit access structure (proven by Csirmaz [33]).

For graph secret-sharing schemes there is also a big gap between the upper bounds and lower bounds. Erdös and Pyber [38] have proved that every graph can be partitioned into complete bipartite graphs such that each vertex is contained in at most $O(n/\log n)$ complete bipartite graphs. Blundo et al. [25] observed that this implies that the normalized maximum share size of realizing every n-vertex graph is $O(n/\log n)$ (for secrets of size $\log n$). Van Dijk [37] proved a lower bound of $\Omega(\log n)$ on the normalized maximum share size of realizing an explicit n-vertex graph. Csirmaz [35] extended this lower bound to the n-vertex Boolean cube. He observed that a lower bound of $\Omega(\log n)$ on a specific graph implies a lower bound of $\Omega(\log\log n)$ for almost all graphs (as almost all n-vertex graphs contain a copy of every $\log n$-vertex graph [28]). Furthermore, Csirmaz asked if for almost every graph there is a scheme with normalized maximum share size $o(n/\log n)$. We answer this question affirmatively by showing for almost all graphs a secret-sharing scheme with maximum share size $n^{o(1)}$.

Linear Secret-Sharing Schemes. Linear secret-sharing schemes, introduced by [29,45], are schemes in which the random string is a vector of elements over some finite field $\mathbb{F}_q$, the domain of secrets is also $\mathbb{F}_q$, and the shares are computed as a linear map over $\mathbb{F}_q$. Many known schemes are linear, e.g., [22,24,57] and the schemes for graphs implied by [38]. They are equivalent to a linear-algebraic model of computation called monotone span programs [45]. Linear secret-sharing schemes are useful as they are homomorphic: given shares of two secrets s, s', each party can locally add its shares and obtain a share of $s + s'$. For many applications of secret sharing, linearity is essential, e.g., [8,32,61], hence, constructing linear secret-sharing schemes is important. The size of the shares in the best known linear secret-sharing scheme is $2^{0.76n}$ [5] (improving upon [48]). Pitassi and Robere [55] proved an exponential lower bound of $2^{cn}\log q$ on the share in linear secret-sharing schemes over $\mathbb{F}_q$ for an explicit access structure of (where $0 < c < 1/2$ is a constant). Babai et al. [9] proved a lower bound of $2^{n/2-o(n)}\sqrt{\log q}$ on the share in linear secret-sharing schemes over $\mathbb{F}_q$ for almost all access structures.

Multi-linear secret-sharing schemes, introduced by [23], are a generalization of linear secret-sharing schemes in which the domain of secrets is $\mathbb{F}_q^\ell$ for some integer ℓ. In [2,5], such schemes improve the normalized maximum share size compared to the linear secret-sharing schemes constructed in those papers (i.e., the multi-linear schemes share a longer secret while using the same share size as the linear schemes). Beimel et al. [11] proved that every lower bound proved for linear secret-sharing schemes using the Gal-Pudlák criteria [40] also applies to multi-linear secret-sharing schemes. In particular, this implies that the $n^{\Omega(\log n)}$ lower bound of [9] for the normalized maximum share size for an explicit access structure and the $\Omega(\sqrt{n})$ lower bound of [17] for the normalized maximum share size for an explicit graph access structure hold also for multi-linear secret-sharing schemes. We note that it is not clear if multi-linear secret-sharing schemes can replace linear secret-sharing schemes in many applications, e.g., in the MPC protocols of [32] that are secure against general adversarial structures.

Conditional Disclosure of Secrets (CDS) Protocols [42]. A CDS protocol for a Boolean function f involves k servers and a referee. Each server holds a common secret s, a common random string r, and a private input x_i; using these r, s, and x_i the i-th server computes one message (without seeing any other input or message) and sends it to the referee. The referee, knowing the inputs $x_1, \ldots, x_k$

and the messages, should be able to compute s iff $f(x_1, \ldots, x_k) = 1$. CDS protocols were used in many cryptographic applications, such as symmetric private information retrieval protocols [42], attribute based encryption [8,41,61], priced oblivious transfer [1], and secret-sharing schemes [4,5,48]. Applebaum et al. [5] defined *robust* CDS protocols (see Definition 2.10) and used them to construct secret-sharing schemes for arbitrary access structures. We use robust CDS protocols to construct schemes for almost all graphs and for all very dense graphs.

The original construction of k-server CDS protocols for general k-input functions, presented in [42], has message size $O(N^k)$ (where N is the input domain size of each server). This construction is linear. Recently, better constructions of CDS protocols for general functions have been presented. Beimel et al. [18] have shown a non-linear 2-server CDS protocol with message size $O(N^{1/2})$ and Gay et al. [41] constructed a linear 2-server CDS protocol with the same message size. Then, Liu et al. [49] have designed a 2-server non-linear CDS protocol with message size $2^{O(\sqrt{\log N \log \log N})}$ and Liu et al. [50] have constructed a k-server CDS protocol with message size $2^{\tilde{O}(\sqrt{k \log N})}$. Beimel and Peter [20] and Liu et al. [50] have constructed a linear CDS protocol with message size $O(N^{(k-1)/2})$; by [20], this bound is optimal for linear CDS protocols (up to a factor of k). Applebaum and Arkis [2] (improving on Applebaum et al. [3]) have showed that there is a CDS protocol with long secrets – of size $\Theta(2^{N^k})$ – in which the message size is 4 times the secret size. Lower bounds on the message size in CDS protocols and in linear CDS protocols have been proven in [3,6,7,41].

Forbidden Graph Access Structures. In a forbidden-graph secret-sharing scheme for a graph G, introduced by Sun and Shieh [60], the parties are the vertices of the graph G and a set is authorized if it is an edge or its size is at least 3. A forbidden-graph secret-sharing scheme for a graph G is not harder than a graph secret-sharing realizing G: Given a secret-sharing scheme realizing a graph, one can construct a forbidden-graph secret-sharing scheme for G by giving a share of the graph secret-sharing scheme and a share of a 3-out-of-n threshold secret-sharing schemes. Furthermore, forbidden graph secret-sharing schemes are closely related to 2-server CDS protocols: Beimel et al. [18] have described a transformation from a CDS protocol for a function describing the graph G to a forbidden graph secret-sharing scheme for G in which the maximum share size of the scheme is $O(\log n)$ times the message size of the CDS protocol. Furthermore, by [2,18], if we consider secrets of size at least $O(\log^2 n)$, then there is a transformation in which the normalized maximum share size is a constant times the message size of the CDS protocol. As a result, we get that every forbidden graph G can be realized by a secret-sharing with maximum share size $n^{o(1)}$ (using the CDS protocol of [49]), by a linear secret-sharing scheme over $\mathbb{F}_q$ with maximum share size $\tilde{O}(\sqrt{n} \log q)$ for every prime power q (using the CDS protocol of [41]), and a multi-linear secret-sharing scheme with normalized maximum share size $O(1)$ for secrets of length 2^{n^2} [2]. We nearly match these bounds for graph access structures for almost all graphs.

1.2   Our Results and Techniques

We next describe the results we achieve in this paper. We again refer the reader to Fig. 1 for a description of the maximum share size in previous constructions and our constructions.

Almost All Access Structures. We prove upper bounds on the share size for almost all access structures, namely almost all access structures have a secret-sharing scheme with share size $2^{\tilde{O}(\sqrt{n})}$, a linear secret-sharing scheme with share size $2^{n/2+o(n)}$, and a multi-linear secret-sharing scheme with maximum share size $\tilde{O}(\log n)$ for secrets of size 2^{n^2}. Our linear secret-sharing scheme for almost all access structures are optimal (up to a factor of $2^{o(n)}$) for a one-bit secret (by a lower bound of Babai et al. [9]).

The construction for almost all access structures is a simple combination of previous results. The first result, proved by Korshunov [47] in 1981, is that in almost all access structures with n parties all minimum authorized sets are of size between $n/2-1$ and $n/2+2$, i.e., all sets of size at most $n/2-2$ are unauthorized and all sets of size at least $n/2+3$ are authorized. The second result we use, proved by Liu and Vaikuntanathan [48], is that such access structures can be realized by secret-sharing schemes with share size as above. These results are presented in Sect. 3.

We also prove lower bounds on the normalized share size in linear secret-sharing schemes for almost all access structures. Rónyai et al. [56] proved that for every finite field $\mathbb{F}_q$ for almost all access structures the normalized share size of linear secret-sharing schemes over $\mathbb{F}_q$ realizing the access structure is at least $\Omega(2^{n/3-o(n)})$. The result of Rónyai et al. [56] does not rule-out the possibility that for every access structures there exists some finite field $\mathbb{F}_q$ (possibly with a large q) such that the access structure can be realized by a linear secret-sharing schemes over $\mathbb{F}_q$ with small normalized share size. This could be plausible since we know that there are access structures that can be realized by an efficient linear secret-sharing scheme over one field, but require large shares in any linear secret-sharing scheme over fields with a different characteristic [21,55]. Pitassi and Robere [55] proved that there exists an explicit access structure for which this is not true, i.e., there exists a constant $c > 0$ such that in any linear secret-sharing scheme realizing it the normalized share size is 2^{cn}. In Theorem 3.10, we prove that this is not true for almost all access structures, namely, for almost every access structure the normalized share size in any linear secret-sharing scheme realizing the access structure is $\Omega(2^{n/3-o(n)})$. Our proof uses a fairly recent result on the number of representable matroids [53].

(G,t)-Graph Secret-Sharing Schemes and Robust CDS. We define a hierarchy of access structures between forbidden graph access structures and graph access structures. In a (G,t)-secret-sharing scheme, every set containing an edge is authorized and, in addition, every set of size $t+1$ is authorized. In other words, the unauthorized sets are independent sets in G of size at most t. We show that (G,t)-secret-sharing schemes are equivalent to 2-server t-robust CDS protocols. As a result, using the robust CDS protocols of [5], we get efficient (G,t)-secret-

sharing schemes, e.g., schemes with maximum share size $n^{o(1)}t$. These results are presented in Sect. 4. We note that, for an arbitrary graph G, our (G,n)-secret-sharing scheme, which is a graph secret-sharing scheme realizing G, the share size does not improve upon the scheme of [38].

Almost All Graph Secret-Sharing Schemes. We show that for almost all graphs, there exists a secret-sharing scheme with maximum share size $n^{o(1)}$, a linear secret-sharing scheme with normalized maximum share size $\tilde{O}(\sqrt{n})$ (for moderately short secrets), and a multi-linear secret-sharing scheme with normalized maximum share size $\tilde{O}(\log n)$ for exponentially long secrets. By [11,17], there exists a graph such that in every multi-linear secret-sharing scheme realizing the graph the normalized maximum share size is $\Omega(\sqrt{n})$, thus, we get a separation for multi-linear secret-sharing schemes between the normalized maximum share size for almost all graphs and the maximum share size of the worst graph. These results are presented in Sect. 5.

To construct our scheme for almost all graphs, we use the fact that if the size of every independent set in a graph G is at most t, then a (G,t)-secret-sharing scheme is a graph secret-sharing scheme realizing G. Our construction follows from the fact that for almost every graph, the size of the maximal independent set in a random graph is $O(\log n)$ [43].

We also consider the maximum share size of random n-vertex graphs drawn from the Erdös-Rényi [39] distribution $\mathscr{G}(n,p)$, that is, each pair of vertices is independently connected by an edge with probability p. For example, $\mathscr{G}(n,1/2)$ is the uniform distribution over the n-vertex graphs. On one hand, with probability nearly 1 the size of the maximum independent set in a graph drawn from $\mathscr{G}(n,p)$ is at most $O(\frac{1}{p}\log n)$, thus, using (G,t)-secret-sharing schemes with $t = O(\frac{1}{p}\log n)$, we realize a graph in $\mathscr{G}(n,p)$ with normalized maximum share size $n^{o(1)}/p$. On the other hand, with probability nearly 1 the degree of all vertices in the graph drawn from $\mathscr{G}(n,p)$ is $O(pn)$, thus, it can be realized by the trivial secret-sharing scheme with maximum share size $O(pn)$. Combining these two schemes, the hardest distribution in our construction is $\mathscr{G}(n,1/\sqrt{n})$ for which the normalized maximum share size is $\sqrt{n}$. We do not know if there is a better secret-sharing scheme for graphs drawn from $\mathscr{G}(n,1/\sqrt{n})$ or this distribution really requires shares of size $n^{\Omega(1)}$.

Dense Graph Secret-Sharing Schemes. Following [14], we study graph secret-sharing schemes for very dense graphs, i.e., graphs with at least $\binom{n}{2} - n^{1+\beta}$ edges for some constant β. For these graphs, Beimel et al. [14] have constructed a linear secret-sharing scheme with maximum share size $\tilde{O}(n^{1/2+\beta/2})$ and another linear secret-sharing scheme with total share size $\tilde{O}(n^{5/4+3\beta/4})$. We improve on the latter result and show that all very dense graphs can be realized by a secret-sharing scheme with normalized total share size of $n^{1+\beta+o(1)}$ for moderately short secrets of size $\tilde{O}(n)$. To put this result in perspective, this total share size matches (up to a factor of $n^{o(1)}$) to the total share size of the naive secret-sharing scheme for sparse graphs with $n^{1+\beta}$ edges. These schemes are presented in Sect. 6.

We next describe the high-level ideas of our construction realizing a graph G with at least $\binom{n}{2} - n^{1+\beta}$ edges. If every vertex in G has degree at least $n - n^{\beta}$, then the size of every independent set in G is at most $n^{\beta} + 1$, and we can use a $(G, n^{\beta} + 1)$-secret-sharing schemes, resulting in normalized total share size $O(n^{1+\beta+o(1)})$. While in a graph with at least $\binom{n}{2} - n^{1+\beta}$ edges the average degree is at least $n - O(n^{\beta})$, the graph can contain vertices whose degree is small. To overcome this problem, we use an idea of [14]. We consider the set of vertices A whose degree is smallest in G and execute a secret-sharing scheme realizing the graph restricted to this set (denoted G'). We choose the size of this set such that: (1) the size of the set is small, thus, the total share size in realizing G' is small, and (2) the degree of the each vertex not in A is big, thus, we can realize the graph without the edges between vertices in A by a (G, t)-secret-sharing scheme for a relatively small t. We apply the above construction iteratively to get our scheme.

Hypergraph Secret-Sharing Schemes. A secret-sharing realizes a hypergraph H if the parties of the scheme are the vertices of H and a set of parties can reconstruct the secret if and only if it contains a hyperedge. In this work, we construct schemes for k-hypergraphs, that is, hypergraphs whose hyperedges are all of size k. The access structures of these schemes are also called k-homogeneous. The best secret-sharing scheme for k-hypergraphs known to date is the original scheme of [44], which have maximum share size $O(\binom{n}{k-1})$. Extending the results explained above, we show a connection between k-hypergraph secret-sharing schemes and k-server t-robust CDS protocols. For any constant k, we show that for almost every k-hypergraph there exists a secret-sharing scheme with maximum share size is $n^{o(1)}$, a linear secret-sharing scheme with normalized maximum share size $\tilde{O}(n^{(k-1)/2})$, and a multi-linear secret-sharing scheme with normalized maximum share size $\tilde{O}(\log^{k-1} n)$ for exponentially long secrets. These schemes are presented in the full version of this paper [13].

Interpretation of Our Results. In this work we have shown that for almost all access structures there exist secret-sharing schemes that are more efficient than the *known* secret-sharing schemes for the worst access structures. Similarly, we have constructed for almost every graph G a secret-sharing schemes realizing G that are more efficient than the *known* secret-sharing schemes realizing the worst graph. One possible conclusion from this result is that in secret-sharing schemes almost all access structures might not be the hardest access structures. Another possible interpretation is that our results may be generalized to all access structures. We note that in one case we know that the former interpretation is true: there is a graph for which the normalized maximum share size for multi-linear schemes is at least $\Omega(\sqrt{n})$ (for every size of secrets) [11,17], while we show an upper bound for almost all graphs of $\tilde{O}(\log n)$ (for long secrets).

Open Problems. Can the normalized share size of almost all access structures can be improved? We do not have any non-trivial lower-bound on the normalized share size for them. Recall that an access structure is $n/2$-uniform if all sets of size less than $n/2$ are unauthorized, all sets of size greater than $n/2$ are authorized, and sets of size exactly $n/2$ can be either authorized or unauthorized. By [4] (using results of [2]), every $n/2$-uniform access structure can be realized by a scheme with normalized maximum share size $O(n^2)$ (with exponentially long secrets). Since almost all access structures somewhat resemble uniform access structures (see Theorem 3.2), one can hope that almost every access structure can be realized by a scheme with polynomial normalized share size.

Another research problem is to study the complexity of almost all functions for other primitives with information-theoretic security, for example, private simultaneous messages (PSM) protocols, MPC protocols, MPC protocols with constant number of rounds, and private information retrieval (PIR) protocols for almost all databases. For all these primitives there is a huge gap between the known upper bounds and lower bounds on the message size. Are there more efficient protocols for any of these primitives for almost all functions than the protocols for all functions?

2   Preliminaries

In the section, we present the preliminary results needed for this work. First, we define secret-sharing schemes, linear secret-sharing schemes, graph secret-sharing schemes, and homogeneous access structures. Second, we define conditional disclosure of secrets (CDS) protocols, and robust CDS protocols. We also present several CDS and robust CDS protocols from [2,20,49,50] that are used in this work. Finally, we present a short introduction to random graphs and random access structures.

Secret-Sharing Schemes. We present the definition of secret-sharing scheme as given in [12,31]. For more information about this definition and secret-sharing in general, see [10].

Definition 2.1 (Access Structures). *Let $P = \{P_1, \ldots, P_n\}$ be a set of parties. A collection $\Gamma \subseteq 2^P$ is monotone if $B \in \Gamma$ and $B \subseteq C$ imply that $C \in \Gamma$. An access structure is a monotone collection $\Gamma \subseteq 2^P$ of non-empty subsets of P. Sets in Γ are called authorized, and sets not in Γ are called forbidden.*

Definition 2.2 (Secret-Sharing Schemes). *A secret-sharing scheme Π with domain of secrets S, such that $|S| \geq 2$, is a mapping from $S \times R$, where R is some finite set called the set of random strings, to a set of n-tuples $S_1 \times S_2 \times \cdots \times S_n$, where S_j is called the domain of shares of P_j. A dealer distributes a secret $s \in S$ according to Π by first sampling a random string $r \in R$ with uniform distribution, computing a vector of shares $\Pi(s, r) = (s_1, \ldots, s_n)$, and privately communicating each share s_j to party P_j. For a set $A \subseteq P$, we denote $\Pi_A(s, r)$ as the restriction of $\Pi(s, r)$ to its A-entries (i.e., the shares of the parties in A).*

A secret-sharing scheme Π with domain of secrets S realizes an access structure Γ if the following two requirements hold:

CORRECTNESS. *The secret s can be reconstructed by any authorized set of parties. That is, for any set $B = \{P_{i_1}, \ldots, P_{i_{|B|}}\} \in \Gamma$ there exists a reconstruction function $\mathrm{Recon}_B : S_{i_1} \times \cdots \times S_{i_{|B|}} \to S$ such that $\mathrm{Recon}_B(\Pi_B(s,r)) = s$ for every secret $s \in S$ and every random string $r \in R$.*

PRIVACY. *Any forbidden set cannot learn anything about the secret from its shares. Formally, for any set $T = \{P_{i_1}, \ldots, P_{i_{|T|}}\} \notin \Gamma$ and every pair of secrets $s, s' \in S$, the distributions $\Pi_T(s,r)$ and $\Pi_T(s',r)$ are identical, where the distributions are over the choice of r from R at random with uniform distribution.*

Given a secret-sharing scheme Π, define the size *of the secret as $\log|S|$, the* share size *of party P_j as $\log|S_j|$, the* maximum share size *as $\max_{1 \le j \le n}\{\log|S_j|\}$, and the* total share size *as $\sum_{j=1}^{n} \log|S_j|$.*

A secret-sharing scheme is multi-linear if the mapping that the dealer uses to generate the shares given to the parties is linear, as we formalize at the following definition.

Definition 2.3 (Multi-linear and Linear Secret-Sharing Schemes). *Let Π be a secret-sharing scheme with domain of secrets S. We say that Π is a* multi-linear *secret-sharing scheme over a finite field $\mathbb{F}$ if there are integers $\ell_d, \ell_r, \ell_1, \ldots, \ell_n$ such that $S = \mathbb{F}^{\ell_d}$, $R = \mathbb{F}^{\ell_r}$, $S_1 = \mathbb{F}^{\ell_1}, \ldots, S_n = \mathbb{F}^{\ell_n}$, and the mapping Π is a linear mapping over $\mathbb{F}$ from $\mathbb{F}^{\ell_d + \ell_r}$ to $\mathbb{F}^{\ell_1 + \cdots + \ell_n}$. We say that a scheme is* linear *over $\mathbb{F}$ if $S = \mathbb{F}$ (i.e., when $\ell_d = 1$).*

Definition 2.4 (Graph secret-sharing schemes). *Let $G = (V, E)$ be an undirected graph with $|V| = n$; for simplicity we assume that $E \ne \emptyset$. We define Γ_G as the access structure whose minimal authorized subsets are the edges in G, that is, the unauthorized sets are independent sets in the graph. A secret-sharing scheme realizing an access structure Γ_G is said to be a secret-sharing scheme realizing the graph G and is called a* graph secret-sharing schemes.

These schemes are one of the main topics in this work. In this paper, we study very dense graphs, graphs with at least $\binom{n}{2} - n^{1+\beta}$ edges for some $0 \le \beta < 1$.

We also study k-*homogeneous access structures*, which are access structures whose minimal authorized subsets are of the size k. For example, graph access structures are 2-homogeneous access structures. For $k > 2$, it is convenient to define k-homogeneous access structures from hypergraphs. A *hypergraph* is a pair $H = (V, E)$ where V is a set of vertices and $E \subseteq 2^V \setminus \{\emptyset\}$ is the set of *hyperedges*. A hypergraph is k-*uniform* if $|e| = k$ for every $e \in E$. A k-uniform hypergraph is *complete* if $E = \binom{V}{k} = \{e \subseteq V : |e| = k\}$. Observe that there is a one-to-one correspondence between uniform hypergraphs and homogeneous access structures, and that complete uniform hypergraphs correspond to threshold access structures. Given a hypergraph $H = (V, E)$, we define Γ_H as the access structure whose minimal authorized sets are the hyperedges of H.

We contrast homogeneous access structures with *uniform* access structures (studied, e.g., in [2,4,19,60]). A k-uniform access structures is also described by a k-uniform hyper-graph and its authorized sets are all the hyper-edges and all sets of size at least $k + 1$. Thus, k-homogeneous access structures are harder to realize as they might contain forbidden sets of size much larger than k.[1]

Conditional Disclosure of Secrets. We define k-server conditional disclosure of secrets protocols, originally defined in [42].

Definition 2.5 (Conditional Disclosure of Secrets Protocols). *Let* $f :$ $X_1 \times \cdots \times X_k \to \{0, 1\}$ *be a* k-*input function. A* k-*server CDS protocol* $\mathcal{P}$ *for* f *with domain of secrets* S *consists of:*

1. *A finite domain of common random strings* R, *and* k *finite message domains* $M_1, \ldots, M_k$,
2. *Deterministic message computation functions* $\mathrm{ENC}_1, \ldots, \mathrm{ENC}_k$, *where* $\mathrm{ENC}_i :$ $X_i \times S \times R \to M_i$ *for every* $i \in [k]$ *(we also say that* $\mathrm{ENC}_i(x_i, s, r)$ *is the message sent by the* i-*th server to the referee), and*
3. *A deterministic reconstruction function* $\mathrm{DEC} : X_1 \times \cdots \times X_k \times M_1 \times \cdots \times M_k \to$ $\{0\}, 1$.

We denote $\mathrm{ENC}(x, s, r) = (\mathrm{ENC}_1(x_1, s, r), \ldots, \mathrm{ENC}_k(x_k, s, r))$. *We say that a CDS protocol* $\mathcal{P}$ *is a CDS protocol for a function* f *if the following two requirements hold:*

CORRECTNESS. *For any input* $(x_1, \ldots, x_k) \in X_1 \times \cdots \times X_k$ *for which* $f(x_1, \ldots, x_k) = 1$, *every secret* $s \in S$, *and every common random string* $r \in R$,

$$\mathrm{DEC}(x_1, \ldots, x_k, \mathrm{ENC}_1(x_1, s, r), \ldots, \mathrm{ENC}_k(x_k, s, r)) = s.$$

PRIVACY. *For any input* $x = (x_1, \ldots, x_k) \in X_1 \times \cdots \times X_k$ *for which* $f(x_1, \ldots, x_k) = 0$ *and for every pair of secrets* s, s', *the distributions* $\mathrm{ENC}(x, s, r)$ *and* $\mathrm{ENC}(x, s', r)$ *are identical, where the distributions are over the choice of* r *from* R *at random with uniform distribution.*

The message size of a CDS protocol $\mathcal{P}$ *is defined as the size of largest message sent by the servers, i.e.,* $\max_{1 \leq i \leq k} \{\log |M_i|\}$.

Next, we present the properties of three CDS protocols that are used in this work. The CDS protocol presented in Theorem 2.6 has linear properties: the messages are generated from the secret and the randomness with linear mappings. Theorem 2.6 is a particular case of Theorem 6 of [2], while Theorem 2.7 is from [49].

Theorem 2.6 ([2]). *For any 2-input function* $f : [n] \times [n] \to \{0, 1\}$ *there is a 2-server CDS protocol in which, for sufficiently large secrets, i.e., secrets of size* 2^{n^2}, *each server communicates at most 3 bits per each bit of the secret.*

---

[1] For example, given a secret-sharing realizing the k-homogeneous access structures of a hyper-graph H, we can realize the k-uniform access structures of H by additionally sharing the secret in a $(k + 1)$-out-of-k secret-sharing scheme.

Theorem 2.7 ([49]). *For any 2-input function $f : [n] \times [n] \to \{0, 1\}$ there is a 2-server CDS protocol with a one bit secret and message size $n^{O(\sqrt{\log \log n / \log n})} = n^{o(1)}$.*

Theorem 2.8 ([50]). *For any k-input functions $f : [n]^k \to \{0, 1\}$ there is a k-server CDS protocol with a one bit secret and message size $n^{O(\sqrt{k / \log n} \log(k \log n))}$.*

Robust Conditional Disclosure of Secrets. In a recent work [5], Applebaum et al. define a stronger notion of CDS protocols that is useful for constructing secret-sharing schemes. In a k-server CDS protocol, we assume that each server sends one message to the referee. Therefore, the referee only has access to k messages. In a *robust* k-server CDS protocol, we consider the case that the referee can have access to more than one message from some servers (generated with the same common random string), and privacy is guaranteed even if an adversary sees a bounded number of messages from each server.

Definition 2.9 (Zero sets). *Let $f : X_1 \times \cdots \times X_k \to \{0, 1\}$ be a k-input function. We say that a set of inputs $Z \subseteq X_1 \times \cdots \times X_k$ is a zero set of f if $f(x) = 0$ for every $x \in Z$. For sets $Z_1, \ldots, Z_k$, we denote $\mathrm{ENC}_i(Z_i, s, r) = (\mathrm{ENC}_i(x_i, s, r))_{x_i \in Z_i}$, and*

$$\mathrm{ENC}(Z_1 \times \cdots \times Z_k, s, r) = (\mathrm{ENC}_1(Z_1, s, r), \ldots, \mathrm{ENC}_k(Z_k, s, r)).$$

Definition 2.10 (Robust conditional disclosure of secrets (RCDS) protocols). *Let $\mathcal{P}$ be a k-server CDS protocol for a k-input function $f : X_1 \times \cdots \times X_k \to \{0, 1\}$ and $Z = Z_1 \times \cdots \times Z_k \subseteq X_1 \times \cdots \times X_k$ be a zero set of f. We say that $\mathcal{P}$ is robust for the set Z if for every pair of secrets $s, s' \in S$, it holds that $\mathrm{ENC}(Z, s, r)$ and $\mathrm{ENC}(Z, s', r)$ are identically distributed. Let $t_1, \ldots, t_k$ be integers. We say that $\mathcal{P}$ is a $(t_1, \ldots, t_k)$-robust CDS protocol if it is robust for every zero set $Z_1 \times \cdots \times Z_k$ such that $|Z_i| \leq t_i$ for every $i \in [k]$ and it is a t-robust CDS protocol if it is $(t, \ldots, t)$-robust.*

In this work we use several constructions of robust CDS protocols presented in [4], which are based on non-robust CDS protocols. Theorem 2.11 presents linear and multi-linear robust CDS protocols in which the underlying CDS protocol is from [41]. Then, Theorem 2.12 presents a generic transformation from non-robust CDS protocols to robust CDS protocols. In this transformation, if the original CDS is linear, then the resulting robust CDS is multi-linear.

Theorem 2.11 ([5, Theorem D.5]). *Let $f : [N] \times [N] \to \{0, 1\}$ be a function. Then, for every finite field $\mathbb{F}_q$ and every integer $t \leq N/(2 \log^2 N)$, there is a linear 2-server (t, N)-robust CDS protocol for f with one element secrets in which the message size is $O((t \log^2 t + \sqrt{N}) t \log t \log^2 N \log q)$. Furthermore, there is p_0 such that for every prime-power $q > p_0$ there is a multi-linear 2-server (t, N)-robust CDS protocol for f over $\mathbb{F}_q$ with secrets of size $\Theta(t^2 \log q \log t \log^3 N)$ in which the normalized message size is $O(t \log^2 t + \sqrt{N})$.*

Theorem 2.12 ([5, **Theorem E.2**]). *Let* $f : [N]^k \to \{0,1\}$ *be a* k-*input function, for some integer* $k > 1$, *and* $t \leq \min\{kN/2, 2\sqrt{N/k}\}$ *be an integer. Assume that for some integer* $m \geq 1$, *there is a* k-*server CDS protocol* $\mathcal{P}$ *for* f *with secrets of size* m *in which the message size is* $c(N,m)$. *Then, there is a* k-*server* t-*robust CDS protocol for* f *with secrets of size* m *in which the message size is* $O\left(c(N,m)k^{3k-1}2^k t^k \log^{2k-1} t \log^2(N)\right)$. *If* $\mathcal{P}$ *is a linear protocol over* $\mathbb{F}_{2^m}$, *then the resulting protocol is also linear. Furthermore, there is a* k-*server* t-*robust CDS protocol for* f *with secrets of size* $\Theta(mk^2 t \log t \log^2(N))$ *in which the normalized message size is* $O\left(\frac{c(N,m)}{m}k^{3k-3}2^k t^{k-1} \cdot \log^{2k-2} t\right)$.

Random Graphs and Access Structures. In this work, we use several results on random graphs to construct secret-sharing schemes for almost all graphs with improved share size. First, we present the Erdös-Rényi model for random graphs [39]. For an introduction to this topic see, e.g., [27].

Let $\mathscr{G}_n$ be the family of graphs with the vertex set $V = \{1, \ldots, n\}$. Given $0 < p < 1$, the model $\mathscr{G}(n,p)$ is a probability distribution over $\mathscr{G}_n$ in which each edge is chosen independently with probability p, that is, if G is a graph with m edges, then $\Pr[\{G\}] = p^m (1-p)^{\binom{n}{2}-m}$. Note that when $p = 1/2$, any two graphs are equiprobable.

We say that *almost every graph in* $\mathscr{G}(n,p)$ *has a certain property* Q if $\Pr[Q] \to 1$ as $n \to \infty$. For $p = 1/2$, saying that almost every graph in $\mathscr{G}(n,p)$ has a certain property Q is equivalent to saying that the number of graphs in $\mathscr{G}_n$ satisfying Q divided by $|\mathscr{G}_n|$ tends to 1 as $n \to \infty$. In this case, we will say that *almost all graphs satisfy* Q.

Analogously, we will use the same expression for any family of access structures F_n. We say that *almost all* access structures in F_n satisfy Q if the number of access structures in F_n satisfying Q divided by $|F_n|$ tends to 1 as $n \to \infty$. In particular, we study the family of homogeneous access structures and the family of all access structures.

Next, we present some properties of the maximum independent sets of graphs in $\mathscr{G}(n,p)$. Lemma 2.13 was presented by Grimmett and McDiarmid in [43]. Several subsequent results gave more accurate bound on the size of maximum independent sets, but it is enough for our purposes. In Lemma 2.14 we give bounds to the maximum independent sets in $\mathscr{G}(n,p)$ for non-constant p. In Lemma 2.15 and Theorem 2.16 we present further properties of almost all graphs. The proofs of Lemmas 2.14 and 2.15 are in the full version of this paper [13].

Lemma 2.13 ([43]). *Let* $0 < p < 1$ *be a constant. Then the size of a maximum independent set in almost every graph in* $\mathscr{G}(n,p)$ *is smaller than* $2 \log n / \log(\frac{1}{1-p}) + o(\log n)$.

As a consequence of Lemma 2.13, the size of a maximum independent set in almost every graph in $\mathscr{G}_n$ is smaller than $(2 + o(1)) \log n$.

Lemma 2.14. *The size of a maximum independent set in almost every graph in $\mathscr{G}(n,p)$ is $O(\frac{\log n}{p})$ if $1/n \leq p \leq 1/2$, and $1 + \frac{2+o(1)}{\alpha}$ if $p = 1 - n^{-\alpha}$ for some $1/\log n \leq \alpha \leq 1$.*

With a similar proof, we can also show that for every $0 \leq \beta \leq 1 - \frac{1}{\log n}$, almost all graph with $n^{1+\beta}$ edges have maximal independent sets of size at most $O(n^{1-\beta}\log n)$, and almost all graphs with $\binom{n}{2} - n^{1+\beta}$ have maximal independent sets of size at most $1 + \frac{2+o(1)}{1-\beta}$.

Lemma 2.15. *Almost all graphs in $\mathscr{G}(n,p)$ with $p = \omega(\log n/n)$ have degree at most $2pn$.*

Lemma 2.16 ([28, Theorem 1]). *Almost every graph with $n = \lceil r^2 2^{r/2} \rceil$ vertices contains every graph of r vertices as an induced subgraph.*

3 Secret-Sharing Schemes for Almost All Access Structures

This section is dedicated to the study of general access structures. Combining results on monotone Boolean functions by Korshunov [47] and secret-sharing schemes from [2,48], we obtain secret-sharing schemes for almost all access structures. Then, we present lower bounds on the maximum share size for almost all access structures.

3.1 Upper Bounds for Almost All Access Structures

First, we define the family of slice access structures. These access structures have a special role in the general constructions presented in [4,5,48]. In Theorem 3.2, we present a family of slice access structures that contains almost all access structures. It is direct consequence of the results in [47] for monotone Boolean functions (also presented in [62, p. 99]).

Definition 3.1. *Let a,b be two integers satisfying $1 \leq a < b \leq n$. We define $S_{a,b}$ as the family of access structures Γ satisfying that, for every $A \subseteq P$: if $|A| > b$, then $A \in \Gamma$, and if $|A| < a$, then $A \notin \Gamma$.*

Theorem 3.2 ([47]). *Let $\ell = \lfloor n/2 \rfloor$. Almost all access structures (i.e., monotone collections of sets) are in $S_{\ell-1,\ell+1}$ if n is even, and in $S_{\ell-1,\ell+2}$ if n is odd.*

Theorem 3.3. *Almost all access structures can be realized by the following secret-sharing schemes.*

1. *A secret-sharing scheme with maximum share size $2^{O(\sqrt{n}\log n)}$.*
2. *A linear secret-sharing scheme with maximum share size $2^{n/2+o(n)}$.*
3. *A multi-linear secret-sharing scheme with normalized maximum share size $2^{O(\sqrt{n}\log n)}$ for secrets of size 2^{n^2}.*

Proof. By Theorem 3.2, constructing secret-sharing schemes for access structures in $S_{\ell-1,\ell+2}$ suffices for constructing secret-sharing schemes for almost all access structures.

Assume that for every k-input function $f : [N]^k \to \{0,1\}$ and secret of size m there is a k-server CDS protocol for f in which the message size is $c(N, m)$. By [48], for every k there is a secret-sharing scheme for $\Gamma \in S_{a,b}$ with maximum share size at most

$$c(N, m)2^{(b-a+1)n/k}O(n)\binom{n}{a}\bigg/\left(\frac{n/k}{a/k}\right)^k$$

for $N = \binom{n/k}{a/k}$. In our case, $a = \lfloor \frac{n}{2} \rfloor - 1$ and $b = \lfloor \frac{n}{2} \rfloor + 2$. Choosing $k = \sqrt{\frac{n}{\log n}}$, we have

$$c(N, m)2^{4n/k}O(n)\binom{n}{n/2-1}\bigg/\left(\frac{n/k}{(n-2)/2k}\right)^k =$$

$$= c(N, m)2^{4\sqrt{n\log n}}O(\text{poly}(n))\left(\frac{n}{k}\right)^{\frac{k}{2}} = c(N, m)2^{O(\sqrt{n\log n})}.$$

Taking the k-server CDS protocol with message size $c(N, m) = 2^{O(\sqrt{\log N}\log\log N)} \leq 2^{O(\sqrt{n}\log n)}$ from [50], we get the first secret-sharing scheme. If we take the linear k-server CDS protocol from [20,50] with message size $O(N^{(k-1)/2}) \leq 2^{n/2+o(n)}$, we get the second secret-sharing scheme. The third secret-sharing scheme is obtained by using the k-server CDS protocol with message size $c(N, m) \leq 4m$ from [2].   □

As a consequence of this result, Hypotheses 1 and 3 in [2] are true for almost all access structures:

Hypothesis 3.4 (SS is short). *Every access structure over n parties is realizable with small information ratio (say $2^{o(n)}$).*

Hypothesis 3.5 (SS is amortizable). *For every access structure over n parties, and every sufficiently long secret s, there exists a secret-sharing scheme with small information ratio (e.g., sub-exponential in n).*

3.2 Almost All Access Structures Require Long Shares in Linear Secret-Sharing Schemes

Rónyai et al. [56] proved that for every finite field $\mathbb{F}_q$ for almost every access structure Γ the normalized total share size of linear secret-sharing schemes over $\mathbb{F}_q$ realizing Γ is at least $2^{n/3-o(n)}$. We reverse the order of quantifiers and prove that for almost every access structure Γ, for every finite field $\mathbb{F}_q$ the normalized total share size of linear secret-sharing schemes over $\mathbb{F}_q$ realizing Γ is at least $2^{n/3-o(n)}$.

The rest of the section is organized as follows. We start by defining monotone span program and representable matroids; these notions are used to prove the lower bounds. Thereafter, we prove our new lower bound on the normalized total share size of linear secret-sharing schemes. More details about these results can be found in [13].

Definitions. A linear secret-sharing scheme with total share size m can be described by a matrix M with m rows such that the shares are computed by multiplying M by a vector whose first coordinate is the secret s and the other coordinates are random field elements. It is convenient to describe a linear secret-sharing scheme by a monotone span program, a computational model introduced by Karchmer and Wigderson [45]. The reader is referred to [10] for more background on monotone span programs and their connections to secret sharing.

Definition 3.6 (Monotone Span Program [45]). *A monotone span program is a triple $\mathcal{M} = (\mathbb{F}, M, \rho)$, where $\mathbb{F}$ is a field, M is an $d \times b$ matrix over $\mathbb{F}$, and $\rho : \{1, \ldots, d\} \to \{p_1, \ldots, p_n\}$ labels each row of M by a party.[2] The size of $\mathcal{M}$ is the number of rows of M (i.e., d). For any set $A \subseteq \{p_1, \ldots, p_n\}$, let M_A denote the sub-matrix obtained by restricting M to the rows labeled by parties in A. We say that $\mathcal{M}$ accepts B if the rows of M_B span the vector $e_1 = (1, 0, \ldots, 0)$. We say that $\mathcal{M}$ accepts an access structure Γ if $\mathcal{M}$ accepts a set B if and only if $B \in \Gamma$.*

Theorem 3.7 ([45]). *There exists a linear secret-sharing scheme over $\mathbb{F}_q$ realizing an access structure Γ with secrets of size $\log q$ and total share size $d \log q$ if and only if there exists a monotone span program $\mathcal{M} = (\mathbb{F}_q, M, \rho)$ accepting the access structure Γ such that M is an $d \times d$ matrix.*

We next define representable matroids and quote the result of [53]. For our proof, we do not need the definition of matroids; we note that they are an axiomatic abstraction of linear independency.

Definition 3.8. *A matroid representable over a field $\mathbb{F}$ is a pair (A, r), where A is a finite set, called a ground set, and $r : 2^A \to \{0, 1, \ldots, |A|\}$ is a function, called a rank function, such that there are vectors $\{v_a\}_{a \in A}$ in $\mathbb{F}^{|A|}$ for which for every $B \subseteq A$*

$$r(B) = \mathrm{rank}(\{v_a\}_{a \in B}),$$

where $\mathrm{rank}(V)$ is the linear-algebraic rank of vectors, i.e., the maximum number of linearly independent vectors in V. A representable matroid is a matroid representable over some field.

Theorem 3.9 ([53]). *For every $d \geq 12$, there are at most $2^{d^3/4}$ representable matroids with ground set $[d]$.*

The following theorem generalize the lower bounds of [9, 56].

Theorem 3.10. *For almost every access structure Γ with n parties the following property holds: For every prime-power q, the normalized total share size in every linear secret-sharing scheme realizing Γ over the field $\mathbb{F}_q$ is at least $2^{n/3 - o(n)}$.*

---

[2] For simplicity, in this paper we label a row by a party p_j rather than by a variable x_j as done in [45].

Proof. The proof is similar to the proof of [9], with a more complex upper bound on the number of access structure that can be realized with a monotone span program of size d.

Fix some labeling function $\rho_0 : [d] \to \{p_1, \ldots, p_n\}$ and assume that there is a monotone span program $\mathcal{M} = (\mathbb{F}_q, M, \rho_0)$ accepting an access structure Γ where M is matrix over some field $\mathbb{F}_q$ of size $d \times d$. Let M_i be the i-th row of M and $M_0 = e_1$ and define a representable matroid with a ground set $A = \{0, \ldots, d\}$ and a rank function $r(B) = \text{rank}\{M_i : i \in B\}$. We next show that the rank function r together with ρ_0 determines the access structure Γ accepted by $\mathcal{M}$. Indeed, $B \in \Gamma$ if and only if $e_1 \in \text{span}\{M_i : p_{\rho_0(i)} \in B\}$ if and only if

$$\text{rank}(\{M_i : p_{\rho_0(i)} \in B\}) = \text{rank}(\{M_i : p_{\rho_0(i)} \in B\} \cup \{e_1\})$$

if and only if $r(\{i : p_{\rho_0(i)} \in B\}) = r(\{i : p_{\rho_0(i)} \in B\} \cup \{0\})$. Thus, the number of access structures that can be realized by a linear scheme with normalized total share size is upper-bounded by the number of labeling functions ρ times the number of representable matroids with ground set $\{0, \ldots, d\}$, i.e., by $n^d \times 2^{(d+1)^3/4} \leq 2^{d^3/2}$. To conclude, for $d = 2^{n/3}/n^{1/6}$, almost all access structures do not have a linear secret-sharing scheme with normalized total share size smaller than d. $\square$

A Lower Bound on the Share Size in Linear Secret-Sharing Schemes with a One Bit Secret. Finally, for a one-bit secret, we obtain in Theorem 3.11 a lower bound of $2^{n/2-o(n)}$ on the total share size of linear secret-sharing schemes over any field realizing almost all access structures, even if the secret is a bit. Notice that this lower bound is on the total share size (and not on the normalized total share size). When we share a bit using a linear secret-sharing scheme over $\mathbb{F}_q$ for $q > 2$, we only use the scheme to share the secrets $0, 1 \in \mathbb{F}_q$. Since we are proving a lower bound the total share size, assuming that the secret is a bit only makes the result stronger.

The constant in the exponent in Theorem 3.11 is $1/2$ (compared to a constant $1/3$ in Theorem 3.10), matching the construction of linear secret-sharing schemes for almost all access structures in Theorem 3.3 (up to lower order terms). This theorem is a special case of [4, Theorem 5.5], however, the proof of this special case is simpler.

Theorem 3.11. *For almost every access structure Γ with n parties the following property holds: For every prime-power q, the total share size in every linear secret-sharing scheme over $\mathbb{F}_q$ realizing Γ with a one bit secret is at least $2^{n/2-o(n)}$.*

Proof. There are at most $n^d q^{d^2}$ monotone span programs of size d over $\mathbb{F}_q$ (as there are q^{d^2} matrices and n ways to label each row by a party). For $d > \log n$, $n^d q^{d^2} < q^{2d^2}$. The total share size in the linear secret-sharing scheme constructed from such monotone span program is $D = d \log q$. Thus, the number of linear secret-sharing schemes over $\mathbb{F}_q$ with total share size D is at most $q^{2(D/\log q)^2} <$

2^{2D^2}. Furthermore, when $q > 2^D$, the share size of each party is at least $\log q > D$ as each share contains at least on element from $\mathbb{F}_q$. Thus, the number of linear secret-sharing schemes with total share size D is at most

$$\sum_{q \, : \, q \leq 2^D, q \text{ is a prime power}} 2^{2D^2} \leq 2^D \cdot 2^{2D^2} \leq 2^{3D^2}.$$

Taking $D = 0.4 \cdot 2^{n/2 - 0.25 \log n}$, the number of access structures that have a linear secret-sharing scheme over any field with total share size at most D is less than $2^{3 \cdot 0.16 \cdot 2^n / \sqrt{n}}$, i.e., almost all access structures require total share size larger than D in all linear secret-sharing schemes. □

4 (G, t)-Secret-Sharing Schemes

In this section, we present a new family of schemes that we call (G, t)-secret-sharing schemes. We show that there is a close bi-directional connection between these schemes and 2-server robust CDS protocols, generalizing the connection between (non-robust) CDS protocols and forbidden graphs secret-sharing schemes. These schemes will be later used to construct graph secret-sharing schemes.

4.1 The Definition of (G, t)-Secret-Sharing Schemes

Definition 4.1. *Let $G = (V, E)$ be an undirected graph with $|V| = n$ such that $E \neq \emptyset$ and let Γ_G be the graph access structure determined by G (that is, each edge is a minimal authorized set and each independent set is forbidden). For any $0 \leq t \leq n - 1$, define Γ_t as the t-out-of-n threshold access structure on V (that is, $\Gamma_t = \{A \subseteq X : |A| \geq t\}$) and define the access structure $\Gamma_{G,t}$ on V as $\Gamma_{G,t} = \Gamma_G \cup \Gamma_{t+1}$. We say a secret-sharing scheme is a (G, t)-secret-sharing scheme if it realizes the access structure $\Gamma_{G,t}$.*

Next, we present some properties of these schemes. If Π is a (G, t)-secret-sharing scheme, then all subsets containing edges are authorized, independent subsets of G of size at most t are forbidden, and subsets of size greater than t are authorized. If $t = 2$, then $\Gamma_{G,t}$ is a *forbidden graph* access structure determined by a graph G (for an introduction to these access structures, see [16], for example). If the size of a largest independent set of G is μ, then every subset of size $\mu + 1$ is authorized in Γ_G. Therefore, $\Gamma_{G,t} = \Gamma_G$ for every $t \geq \mu$. In particular, $\Gamma_{G,n-1} = \Gamma_G$ for every graph G.

4.2 (G, t)-Secret-Sharing Schemes from Robust CDS Protocols

We now present constructions of (G, t)-secret-sharing schemes. First, we present a transformation from robust CDS protocols to (G, t)-secret-sharing schemes. Then, using the robust CDS schemes presented in Sect. 2, we provide explicit (G, t)-secret-sharing schemes.

Lemma 4.2. *Let $G = (V, E)$ be a graph with $|V| = n$, and let $0 < t < n$. If there exists a 2-server t-robust CDS protocol with secrets of size m and messages of size $c(N, m)$ for functions $f : [n]^2 \to \{0, 1\}$, then there is a (G, t)-secret-sharing scheme with secrets of size m and shares of size $2 \cdot c(N, m) + \max\{m, O(\log n)\}$. Moreover, if CDS protocol is linear, then the secret-sharing scheme is also linear.*

Proof. We construct the (G, t)-secret-sharing scheme using the scheme in Fig. 2. Next we prove the correctness and privacy properties.

CORRECTNESS: Let $A \subseteq [n]$ be a minimal authorized subset in $\Gamma_{G,t}$. Then A is either in E or A is of size $t + 1$. If $A = \{i, j\}$ is in E, then $f(i, j) = 1$, i.e., the message of Alice (the first server) on i and the message of Bob (the second server) on j determines s, so the pair $\{i, j\}$ can recover s. If $|A| = t + 1$, then A can recover s using the $(t + 1)$-out-of-n secret-sharing scheme.

PRIVACY: Let A be a maximal forbidden subset. Then A does not contain any edge in E and $|A| \leq t$. The shares received from the threshold secret-sharing scheme do not provide any information about s. Now we analyze the information provided by the messages of $\mathcal{P}$. The parties in A receive Alice's messages for A and Bob's messages for A. Observe that the set $A \times A$ does not contain edges of G, thus, $A \times A$ is a zero-set of f and the t-robustness of $\mathcal{P}$ guarantees the privacy of the scheme.

The maximum share size of the resulting scheme is twice the message size of $\mathcal{P}$ plus the share size of the $(t + 1)$-out-of-n secret-sharing scheme.

If $\mathcal{P}$ is a linear protocol over $\mathbb{F}_q$, we can choose a Shamir $(t + 1)$-out-of-n secret-sharing scheme over a finite field $\mathbb{F}_{q^\ell}$ with $q^\ell > n$. Since this scheme is also linear over $\mathbb{F}_q$, the resulting secret-sharing scheme is also linear over $\mathbb{F}_q$. $\square$

In Lemma 4.2, we showed a way to construct (G, t)-secret-sharing schemes from t-robust CDS protocols. Conversely, we can also construct robust CDS protocols from (G, t)-secret-sharing schemes, as shown in Lemma 4.3.

Lemma 4.3. *Let $f : [n] \times [n] \to \{0, 1\}$ be a function and let $0 < t < n$. Define $G = (([n] \times \{1\}) \cup ([n] \times \{2\}), E)$ as the bipartite graph with $E = \{((i, 1), (j, 2)) : i \in [n], j \in [n], f(i, j) = 1\}$. If there exists a $(G, 2t)$-secret-sharing scheme with secrets of size m and maximum share size $c(2n, m)$, then there exists a 2-server t-robust CDS protocol for f with message size $c(2n, m)$.*

Proof. Let Π be a $(G, 2t)$-secret-sharing scheme. We define a 2-server t-robust CDS protocol $\mathcal{P}$ for f as follows. The message spaces M_1 and M_2 of the servers are the spaces of shares of parties $[n] \times \{1\}$ and $[n] \times \{2\}$, respectively. The common randomness r is the randomness of the dealer in Π. The function $\text{ENC}_i(j, s, r)$ for $i \in \{1, 2\}$ outputs the share of party (j, i) with the secret s and randomness r, and DEC is the reconstruction function of Π.

The correctness of $\mathcal{P}$ is guaranteed because every pair in E is authorized in Π. The t-robustness of $\mathcal{P}$ is guaranteed because every zero-set $Z_1 \times Z_2$ where $|Z_1|, |Z_2| \leq t$ corresponds to an independent set $(Z_1 \times \{1\}) \cup (Z_2 \times \{2\})$ of size at most $2t$ in G, thus the messages of the inputs in $Z_1 \cup Z_2$ are shares of a forbidden set in Π. $\square$

The secret: An element $s \in S$.
The parties: $V = \{1, \ldots, n\}$.
The access structure: $\Gamma_{G,t}$ for some graph $G = (V, E)$ and $0 \le t \le n-1$.
The scheme:

- Let $f : [n] \times [n] \to \{0, 1\}$ be the function defined as $f(i, j) = 1$ if and only if $(i, j) \in E$.
- Let $\mathcal{P}$ be a 2-server t-robust CDS protocol with secrets from $\{0, 1\}^m$ for the function f; denote its servers by Alice and Bob.

Then,

1. Execute the protocol $\mathcal{P}$ for the secret s.
2. Share s independently among V with a $(t+1)$-out-of-n secret-sharing scheme.
3. The share of party $i \in V$ is the message of Alice on the input i, the message of Bob on the input i, and the share of i in the $(t+1)$-out-of-n secret-sharing scheme.

Fig. 2. A (G, t)-secret-sharing scheme Π for a graph $G = (V, E)$.

Now that we showed the connection between (G, t)-secret-sharing schemes from t-robust CDS protocols, we present (G, t)-secret-sharing schemes that use Theorems 2.12 and 2.11.

Lemma 4.4. *Let $G = (V, E)$ be a graph with $|V| = n$, and let $1 \le t < n/2$. If there exist a 2-server CDS protocol with message size $c(N, m)$ for functions with domain size n and secrets of size m, then there exists a (G, t)-secret-sharing scheme with maximum share size $O(t^2 \log^3 t \log^2 n \cdot c(N, m))$, and a (G, t)-secret-sharing scheme with secrets of size $\Theta(mt \log t \log^2 n)$ and normalized maximum share size $O(t \log^2 t \cdot c(N, m)/m)$.*

Proof. Theorem 2.12 guarantees that there exists a 2-server t-robust CDS protocol with message size $\ell(n) = O(t^2 c(N, m) \log^3 t \log^2 n)$, and a 2-server t-robust CDS protocol with secrets of size $m' = \Theta(mt \log t \log^2 n)$ with normalized message size $\ell(n)/m' = O(t \log^2 t \cdot c(N, m)/m)$. Using these 2-server t-robust CDS protocols and Lemma 4.2 we obtain the lemma. □

We conclude this section presenting different (G, t)-secret-sharing schemes that are obtained from robust CDS schemes applying Lemma 4.2 and Theorem 4.4.

Theorem 4.5. *Let $G = (V, E)$ be a graph with $|V| = n$ and let $1 < t < n$.*

1. *There exists a (G, t)-secret-sharing scheme with moderately-short secrets of size $O(t \log^3 n)$, normalized maximum share size*

$$n^{O(\sqrt{\log \log n / \log n})} t \log^2 n = n^{o(1)} t \log^2 n,$$

and normalized total share size $n^{1 + O(\sqrt{\log \log n / \log n})} t \log^2 n = n^{1 + o(1)} t \log^2 n;$

2. *For every prime power q, there exists a linear (G, t)-secret-sharing scheme over $\mathbb{F}_q$ with and maximum share size $O\left((t \log^2 t + \sqrt{n}) t \log t \log^2 n \log q\right)$;*
3. *There exists an integer p_0 such that for every prime power $q > p_0$, there exists a multi-linear (G, t)-secret-sharing scheme over $\mathbb{F}_q$ with moderately-short secrets of size $\Theta(t^2 \log t \log^2 n \log n \log q)$ and normalized maximum share size $O(t \log^2 t + \sqrt{n})$;*
4. *There exists a multi-linear (G, t)-secret-sharing scheme over $\mathbb{F}_2$ with secrets of size 2^{n^2} and normalized maximum share size $O(t \log^2 t)$.*

Proof. Scheme 1: By Theorem 2.7, for any function $f : [n]^2 \rightarrow \{0, 1\}$ there exists a 2-server CDS protocol with secret of size $m = 1$ and messages size $c(n, 1) = n^{O(\sqrt{\log \log n / \log n})}$. Applying Theorem 2.12 with the CDS protocol from Theorem 2.7 results in a 2-server t-robust CDS protocol with secrets of size $O(t \log t \log^2 n) = O(t \log^3 n)$, message size $O(n^{O(\sqrt{\log \log n / \log n})} t^2 \log^5 t)$, and normalized message size $O(n^{O(\sqrt{\log \log n / \log n})} t \log^2 t)$. By Lemma 4.2, there is a (G, t)-secret-sharing with secrets of size $O(t \log^3 n)$ and maximum share size $O(n^{O(\sqrt{\log \log n / \log n})} t^2 \log^5 t)$, thus with normalized maximum share size $O(n^{O(\sqrt{\log \log n / \log n})} t \log^2 n)$ and with normalized total share size $O(n^{1 + O(\sqrt{\log \log n / \log n})} t \log^2 n)$.

Scheme 2: Theorem 2.11 guarantees that for $t \leq n/(2 \log^2 n)$ there exists a linear 2-server t-robust CDS protocol over $\mathbb{F}_q$ with message size $O\left((t \log^2 t + \sqrt{n}) t \log t \log^2 n \log q\right)$. Thus, by Lemma 4.2 there is a (G, t)-secret-sharing scheme where the maximum share size is the above message size. For $t > n/(2 \log^2 n)$, the upper bound also holds because there is always a linear (G, t)-secret-sharing with maximum share size $O(n/\log n)$ [38].

Scheme 3: Theorem 2.11 also guarantees, for a large enough q, a 2-server (t, n)-robust CDS protocol with secrets of size $\Theta(t^2 \log t \log^2 n \log q)$ and normalized message size $O(t \log^2 t + \sqrt{n})$. Again, we construct the desired (G, t)-secret-sharing with from the robust CDS protocol applying Lemma 4.2.

Scheme 4: By Theorem 2.6, there exists a multi-linear CDS protocol over $\mathbb{F}_2$ with normalized message size $c(N, m)/m = 3$ for secrets of size 2^{n^2}. Applying Theorem 4.4, we obtain a multi-linear (G, t)-secret-sharing over $\mathbb{F}_2$ with normalized maximum share size $O(t \log^2 t \cdot c(N, m)/m) = O(t \log^2 t)$.   □

5   Secret-Sharing Schemes for Almost All Graphs

In this section we study the maximum share size of secret-sharing schemes for almost all graphs and for almost all graphs in $\mathscr{G}(n, p)$ for different values of p. The previous and new results for almost all graphs are summarized in Fig. 1, while the results for $\mathscr{G}(n, p)$ are summarized in Fig. 4.

Schemes presented in this section rely on the properties of almost all graphs shown in the end of Sect. 2, and use the (G, t)-secret-sharing schemes presented in Sect. 4. In order to understand the share size of secret-sharing schemes for almost all graphs, we provide lower bounds for them in Theorems 5.5 and 5.7.

5.1   Schemes for Almost All Graphs

As a consequence of Lemma 2.13, the size of every independent set in almost every graph in $\mathscr{G}_n$ is $O(\log n)$. We observed in Sect. 4 that a (G, t)-secret-sharing scheme is also a secret-sharing scheme realizing G when t is bigger than the size of a largest independent set of G. Hence, we consider the four constructions presented in Theorem 4.5 for $t = O(\log n)$. In Theorem 5.1 we present the resulting schemes.

Theorem 5.1. *Almost all graphs with n vertices can be realized by the following schemes.*

1. *A secret-sharing scheme with maximum share size $n^{O(\sqrt{\log\log n/\log n})} = n^{o(1)}$,*
2. *A linear secret-sharing scheme over $\mathbb{F}_q$ with maximum share size $\tilde{O}(\sqrt{n}\log q)$ for every prime power q,*
3. *A multi-linear secret-sharing scheme over $\mathbb{F}_q$ with normalized maximum share size $O(\sqrt{n})$ and moderately-short secrets of size $\Theta(\log q \log^3 n \log\log n)$ for a large enough q, and*
4. *A multi-linear secret-sharing scheme over $\mathbb{F}_2$ with normalized maximum share size $O\left(\log n(\log\log n)^2\right)$ for secrets of size 2^{n^2}.*

5.2   Secret-Sharing Schemes for $\mathscr{G}(n, p)$

In order to study properties of sparse graphs, we study $\mathscr{G}(n, n^{-\alpha})$ for a constant $0 < \alpha < 1$. Almost all graphs in $G(n, n^{-\alpha})$ have maximal independent sets of size at most $t = O(n^\alpha \log n)$. Following the procedure we developed in the previous section, we can construct secret-sharing schemes for almost all graphs in $G(n, n^{-\alpha})$ using Theorem 4.5. Similar bounds can be obtained for linear schemes and multi-linear schemes. They are presented in Fig. 4.

Theorem 5.2. *Let $0 < \alpha < 1$ be a constant. Almost every graph in $\mathscr{G}(n, n^{-\alpha})$ can be realized by a secret-sharing scheme with normalized maximum share size $n^{\min(\alpha, 1-\alpha)+o(1)}$ and secret of size $\tilde{O}(\sqrt{n})$.*

Proof. We present two schemes Π_1 and Π_2 for almost all graphs in $\mathscr{G}(n, n^{-\alpha})$. The scheme Π_1 consists on sharing the secret for each edge independently. By Lemma 2.15, almost every graph in $\mathscr{G}(n, n^{-\alpha})$ has maximum degree of at most $2n^{1-\alpha}$. Therefore, the maximum share size of Π_1 is $2n^{1-\alpha}$ for almost all graphs in $\mathscr{G}(n, n^{-\alpha})$.

The second scheme Π_2 is obtained from Theorem 4.5. For almost every graph in $\mathscr{G}(n, n^{-\alpha})$ the size of a maximum independent set is $O(n^\alpha \log n)$ (by Lemma 2.14). Thus, we let Π_2 be the $(G, O(n^\alpha \log n))$-secret-sharing scheme of Theorem 4.5 with secret of size $\Theta(t \log^3 n) = \Theta(n^\alpha \log^4 n)$ and normalized maximum share size $O(n^{o(1)} t \log^2 n) = O(n^{\alpha+o(1)} \log^3 n) = n^{\alpha+o(1)}$.

Therefore, almost every graph in $\mathscr{G}(n, n^{-\alpha})$ can be realized by a secret-sharing scheme with normalized maximum share size $\min(2n^{1-\alpha}, n^{\alpha+o(1)}) \leq n^{\min(1-\alpha, \alpha)+o(1)}$. $\qquad\square$

For $\alpha \leq 1/2$, the best choice is Π_1, and for $\alpha > 1/2$, the best choice is Π_2. For $\alpha = 1/2$, the normalized maximum share size of almost all graphs in $\mathscr{G}(n, n^{-\alpha})$ in our scheme is $O(\sqrt{n})$. This is the constant α that gives the worst upper bound on the normalized maximum share size of secret-sharing schemes for $\mathscr{G}(n, n^{-\alpha})$.

Finally, we study properties of very dense graphs by analyzing $\mathscr{G}(n, 1 - n^{-\alpha})$ for a constant $0 < \alpha < 1$. By Lemma 2.14, the size of a maximum independent set for almost all graphs in $\mathscr{G}(n, 1 - n^{-\alpha})$ is constant. As we saw above, graphs with small independent sets admit more efficient schemes. In Theorem 5.4 we present secret-sharing schemes for almost all graphs in $\mathscr{G}(n, 1 - n^{-\alpha})$. Two of the schemes we present in Theorem 5.4 follow quite easily from our previous results. In contrast, the linear scheme we construct in Theorem 5.4 does not follow from previous results on robust CDS protocols. Rather, it follows from the following theorem of [16] on the total share size for forbidden graph secret sharing schemes and the techniques of [5].

Theorem 5.3 ([16, Theorem 6]). *Let $G = (V, E)$ graph with n vertices and at least $\binom{n}{2} - n^{1+\beta}$ edges, for some $0 \leq \beta < 1$. Then for every prime-power $q > n$ there is a linear $(G, 2)$-secret-sharing scheme over $\mathbb{F}_q$ that with total share size $\tilde{O}(n^{1+\beta/2} \log q)$.*

Theorem 5.4. *Let $0 \leq \beta < 1$ be a constant. Almost all graphs in $\mathscr{G}(n, 1 - n^{\beta-1})$ can be realized by a secret-sharing scheme with maximum share size $n^{o(1)}$, a linear secret-sharing scheme over $\mathbb{F}_q$ with total share size $\tilde{O}(n^{1+\beta/2} \log q)$ for every prime-power $q > n$, and a multi-linear secret-sharing scheme over $\mathbb{F}_2$ with exponentially long secrets of size 2^{n^2} and normalized maximum share size $O(1)$.*

Proof. By Lemma 2.14, the size of a maximum independent set for almost all graphs in $\mathscr{G}(n, 1 - n^{-\alpha})$ is some constant c. The non-linear secret-sharing scheme and the secret-sharing scheme with long secrets are obtained by applying Theorem 4.5 with $t = O(1)$.

To construct the linear secret-sharing scheme we note that the maximum degree of almost every graph G in $\mathscr{G}(n, 1 - n^{\beta-1})$ is at least $n - 2n^\beta$ (by Lemma 2.15 applied to $\overline{G}$), thus the number of edges in G is at least $\binom{n}{2} - n^{1+\beta}$. The linear scheme is derived by using the technique of [5] to transform the $(G, 2)$-secret-sharing scheme from Theorem 5.3 to a (G, c)-secret-sharing scheme: Let $\mathcal{H} = \{h_i : [n] \rightarrow [c^2] : 1 \leq i \leq \ell\}$ be a family of perfect hash functions,[3] where $|\mathcal{H}| = \ell = O(\log n)$. The (G, c)-secret-sharing scheme, denoted Π, is as follows:

– Input: a secret $s \in \mathbb{F}_q$.
– Choose $\ell - 1$ random elements $s_1, \ldots, s_{\ell-1}$ from $\mathbb{F}_q$ and let $s_\ell = s - (s_1 + \cdots + s_{\ell-1})$.

---

[3] A family $\mathcal{H}$ is a family of perfect hash functions for sets of size at most c if for every $B \subset \{1, \ldots, n\}$ such that $|B| \leq c$, there exists a function $h \in \mathcal{H}$ such that h is one-to-one on B, that is, $h(u) \neq h(v)$ for every distinct $u, v \in B$. By a standard probabilistic argument, such family of size $O(c \log n)$ exists. For a constant c, the size of the family is $O(\log n)$.

– For every $i \in \{1, \ldots, \ell\}$ and every $a, b \in \{1, \ldots, c^2\}$, independently share s_i using the $(G, 2)$-secret-sharing scheme and give the share of vertex v to v if and only if $h_i(v) \in \{a, b\}$.

For the correctness of the scheme Π, let (u, v) be an edge in G (i.e., an authorized set). For every i, the parties u, v can reconstruct s_i from the scheme for $a = h(u), b = h(v)$. For the privacy of Π, let B be an independent set in G (i.e., a forbidden set). By Lemma 2.14, we can assume that the size of B is at most c, thus, there exists a hash function $h_i \in \mathcal{H}$ such that $h_i(u) \neq h_i(v)$ for every distinct $u, v \in B$. Therefore, in any sharing of s_i for some values a, b the parties in B hold at most 2 shares, and these shares are of a forbidden set. The privacy of the $(G, 2)$-secret-sharing scheme implies that the parties in B do not get any information on s_i from this execution. Since all executions of the $(G, 2)$-secret-sharing scheme are executed with an independent random string, the parties in B do not get any information on s_i from the shares of Π, hence they get no information on s. Note that the total share size in Π is $O(\log n)$ times the total share size of the $(G, 2)$-secret-sharing scheme.   □

5.3 Lower Bounds for the Share Size for Almost All Graphs

Next, we present lower bounds for the maximum share size of secret-sharing schemes for almost all graphs. This question was first addressed by Csirmaz in [35], where he proved a lower bound which we include in Theorem 5.5.

Theorem 5.5. *For almost every graph G, the normalized maximum share size of every secret-sharing scheme realizing G is $\Omega(\log \log n)$, and the normalized maximum share size of every multi-linear secret-sharing scheme realizing G is $\Omega(\log^{1/2} n)$.*

Proof (Sketch). Both bounds are a consequence of Theorem 2.16 (which says that almost all n-vertex graphs contain all graphs of size $\log n$ as an induced graph), taking different graphs with $\log n$ vertices. The first bound was proved by Csirmaz in [35], taking the family of hypercube graphs (or the graphs of [37]). The second bound is a consequence of the results in [11, 17]. The complete proof is in the full version of this paper [13].   □

Remark 5.6. Theorem 2.16 provides a connection between the maximum share size of schemes for *every* graph access structure with $r = \log n$ vertices and the maximum share size of schemes for almost all graph access structures with n vertices. In Theorem 5.5 we used it in one direction, but it could also be used in the converse direction. For instance: if there exist secret-sharing schemes for almost all n-vertex graphs with (normalized) maximum share size $\ll \frac{\log n}{\log \log n}$, then there exist secret-sharing schemes realizing every r-vertex graph with (normalized) maximum share size $\ll r/\log r$, which is currently the best upper bound [38].

In Theorem 5.7, we quote a lower bound on the maximum share size for linear graph secret-sharing schemes, proved in [15, 52]. Notice, however, that this bound does not grow as a function of the size of the secrets.

Theorem 5.7 ([15,52]). *For almost every graph G, the maximum share size of every linear secret-sharing scheme realizing G is $\Omega(\sqrt{n})$.*

6   Secret-Sharing Schemes for Very Dense Graphs

In this section we study secret-sharing schemes for very dense graphs, i.e., graphs with n vertices and at least $\binom{n}{2} - n^{1+\beta}$ edges for some $0 \leq \beta < 1$. This problem was originally studied in [14], and the best previously known upper bounds on the maximum share size and the total share size are presented in Theorems 6.1 and 6.2.

Theorem 6.1 ([14]). *Let $G = (V, E)$ be a graph with $|V| = n$ and $|E| \geq \binom{n}{2} - n^{1+\beta}$ for some $0 \leq \beta < 1$. Then, there exists a linear secret-sharing scheme realizing G with maximum share size $\tilde{O}(n^{1/2+\beta/2})$, total share size $\tilde{O}(n^{3/2+\beta/2})$, and secret of size $O(\log n)$.*

The above theorem hides poly-logarithmic factors in the share size. It was also shown in [14] that these poly-logarithmic factors can be avoided if we consider multi-linear secret-sharing schemes and normalized share size: for the graphs considered in Theorem 6.1, there exists a multi-linear secret-sharing scheme with normalized maximum share size $O(n^{1/2+\beta/2})$ and secret of size $O(\log^2 n)$.

In [14], there is another secret-sharing construction for very dense graphs, presented in Theorem 6.2. The total share size of this scheme is smaller than the one in Theorem 6.1, but the maximum share size may be larger.

Theorem 6.2 ([14]). *Let $G = (V, E)$ be a graph with $|V| = n$ and $|E| \geq \binom{n}{2} - n^{1+\beta}$ for some $0 \leq \beta < 1$. There exists a linear secret-sharing scheme realizing G with total share size $\tilde{O}(n^{5/4+3\beta/4})$.*

As an observation, notice that as a direct implication of the results in previous sections we can construct a scheme whose maximum share size is similar to the maximum share size as in the scheme of Theorem 6.2 (see the full version of this paper [13]).

We use (G, t)-secret-sharing schemes, described in the Sect. 4, to construct secret-sharing schemes for *all* very dense graphs. Our main result for dense graphs is Theorem 6.4, where we show that graphs with at least $\binom{n}{2} - n^{1+\beta}$ edges admit secret-sharing schemes with normalized total share size $n^{1+\beta+o(1)}$. This result nearly matches the best total share size for sparse graphs with at most $n^{1+\beta}$ edges (for which we share the secret independently for each edge). The construction follows the ideas described in the introduction.

In Fig. 3, we present a secret-sharing scheme Π_{dense} realizing very dense graphs. In Theorem 6.4, we use Π_{dense} recursively to obtain our improved secret-sharing scheme for dense graphs. The proofs of Lemma 6.3 and Theorem 6.4 are presented in the full version of this paper [13].

Lemma 6.3. *Let $G = (V, E)$ be a graph with $|V| = n$ and $|E| \geq \binom{n}{2} - n^{1+\beta}$ for some $0 \leq \beta < 1$. The scheme described in Fig. 3 is a secret-sharing scheme realizing G.*

> **The secret:** An element $s \in S$.
> **The parties:** $V = \{1, \ldots, n\}$
> **The scheme:**
>
> 1. Let $\beta < \alpha < (1 + \beta)/2$ and $n' = n^{1+\beta-\alpha}$.
> 2. Let $A \subseteq V$ be a subset of n' vertices of lowest degree and $G' = (A, E \cap (A \times A))$.
> 3. Share s among A using Π_1, a secret-sharing scheme realizing G'.
> 4. Choose $r \in S$ uniformly at random.
> 5. Share r using Π_2, a $(G, 2n^\alpha + 1)$-secret-sharing scheme.
> 6. Share $r + s$ using Π_3, a secret-sharing scheme where A is the only maximal forbidden subset (that is, give $r + s$ to every party not in A).

Fig. 3. A secret-sharing scheme Π_{dense} realizing a graph $G = (V, E)$ with $|E| \geq \binom{n}{2} - n^{1+\beta}$ for some $0 \leq \beta < 1$.

	total inf. ratio (moderate short secrets)	total share size of linear schemes over $\mathbb{F}_q$	total inf. ratio multi-linear schemes
$n^{1+\beta}$ edges	$n^{1+\beta}$ [44] $\Omega(n \log n)$ [36]	$n^{1+\beta} \log q$ [44] $\Omega(n^{\min(1+\beta,3/2)} \log q)$ [17]	$n^{1+\beta}$ [44] $\Omega(n^{\min(1+\beta,3/2)})$ [17,11]
$\mathscr{G}(n, n^{\beta-1})$	$n^{\min(1+\beta,2-\beta)+o(1)}$ Th. 5.2	$n^{\min(1+\beta,3-2\beta)+o(1)} \log q$ Th. 5.2	$n^{\min(1+\beta,2-\beta)}$ Th. 5.2
$\binom{n}{2} - n^{1+\beta}$ edges	$n^{1+\beta+o(1)}$ Th. 6.4 $\Omega(n \log n)$ [14]	$\tilde{O}(n^{5/4+\beta/4} \log q)$ [14] $\Omega(n^{1+\beta/2} \log q)$ [14]	$\tilde{O}(n^{1+\beta})$ Rem. 6.5 $\Omega(n^{1+\beta/2})$ [14,11]
$\mathscr{G}(n, 1 - n^{\beta-1})$	$n^{1+o(1)}$ Th. 5.4	$O(n^{1+\beta/2}) \log q$ Th. 5.4	$O(1)$ Th. 5.4

Fig. 4. Total share size for different families of graphs and constant $0 < \beta < 1$. Note that almost all graphs in $\mathscr{G}(n, n^{\beta-1})$ and in $\mathscr{G}(n, 1 - n^{\beta-1})$ have $\Theta(n^{1+\beta})$ and $\binom{n}{2} - \Theta(n^{1+\beta})$ edges, respectively.

Theorem 6.4. *Let $G = (V, E)$ be a graph with $|V| = n$ and $|E| \geq \binom{n}{2} - n^{1+\beta}$ for some $0 \leq \beta < 1$. Then G can be realized by a secret-sharing schemes with secrets of size $O(n \log^3 n)$ and normalized total share size $n^{1+\beta+o(1)}$.*

Remark 6.5. In Theorem 6.4, we combine the secret-sharing scheme for very dense graphs in Theorem 6.1 with several instances of the first scheme of Theorem 4.5. Instead, if we replace the former by the fourth scheme of Theorem 4.5, we obtain a multi-linear secret-sharing scheme with secrets of exponential size and normalized total share size $\tilde{O}(n^{1+\beta})$ for exponentially long secrets.

In Fig. 4, we summarize the current bounds on the total share size for graphs with at most $n^{1+\beta}$ edges, graphs with at least $\binom{n}{2} - n^{1+\beta}$ edges, $\mathscr{G}(n, n^{\beta-1})$, and $\mathscr{G}(n, 1 - n^{\beta-1})$, for constant $0 < \beta < 1$. Additional remarks and observations are presented in the full version of this paper [13].

References

1. Aiello, B., Ishai, Y., Reingold, O.: Priced oblivious transfer: how to sell digital goods. In: Pfitzmann, B. (ed.) EUROCRYPT 2001. LNCS, vol. 2045, pp. 119–135. Springer, Heidelberg (2001). https://doi.org/10.1007/3-540-44987-6_8

2. Applebaum, B., Arkis, B.: On the power of amortization in secret sharing: d-uniform secret sharing and CDS with constant information rate. In: Beimel, A., Dziembowski, S. (eds.) TCC 2018. LNCS, vol. 11239, pp. 317–344. Springer, Cham (2018). https://doi.org/10.1007/978-3-030-03807-6_12

3. Applebaum, B., Arkis, B., Raykov, P., Vasudevan, P.N.: Conditional disclosure of secrets: amplification, closure, amortization, lower-bounds, and separations. In: Katz, J., Shacham, H. (eds.) CRYPTO 2017. LNCS, vol. 10401, pp. 727–757. Springer, Cham (2017). https://doi.org/10.1007/978-3-319-63688-7_24

4. Applebaum, B., Beimel, A., Farràs, O., Nir, O., Peter, N.: Secret-sharing schemes for general and uniform access structures. In: Ishai, Y., Rijmen, V. (eds.) EURO-CRYPT 2019. LNCS, vol. 11478, pp. 441–471. Springer, Cham (2019). https://doi.org/10.1007/978-3-030-17659-4_15

5. Applebaum, B., Beimel, A., Nir, O., Peter, N.: Better secret sharing via robust conditional disclosure of secrets. In: Proceedings of the 52th ACM Symposium on the Theory of Computing, pp. 280–293 (2020)

6. Applebaum, B., Holenstein, T., Mishra, M., Shayevitz, O.: The communication complexity of private simultaneous messages, revisited. In: Nielsen, J.B., Rijmen, V. (eds.) EUROCRYPT 2018. LNCS, vol. 10821, pp. 261–286. Springer, Cham (2018). https://doi.org/10.1007/978-3-319-78375-8_9

7. Applebaum, B., Vasudevan, P.N.: Placing conditional disclosure of secrets in the communication complexity universe. In: 10th ITCS, pp. 4:1–4:14 (2019)

8. Attrapadung, N.: Dual system encryption via doubly selective security: framework, fully secure functional encryption for regular languages, and more. In: Nguyen, P.Q., Oswald, E. (eds.) EUROCRYPT 2014. LNCS, vol. 8441, pp. 557–577. Springer, Heidelberg (2014). https://doi.org/10.1007/978-3-642-55220-5_31

9. Babai, L., Gál, A., Wigderson, A.: Superpolynomial lower bounds for monotone span programs. Combinatorica **19**(3), 301–319 (1999)

10. Beimel, A.: Secret-sharing schemes: a survey. In: Chee, Y.W., et al. (eds.) IWCC 2011. LNCS, vol. 6639, pp. 11–46. Springer, Heidelberg (2011). https://doi.org/10.1007/978-3-642-20901-7_2

11. Beimel, A., Ben-Efraim, A., Padró, C., Tyomkin, I.: Multi-linear secret-sharing schemes. In: Lindell, Y. (ed.) TCC 2014. LNCS, vol. 8349, pp. 394–418. Springer, Heidelberg (2014). https://doi.org/10.1007/978-3-642-54242-8_17

12. Beimel, A., Chor, B.: Universally ideal secret sharing schemes. IEEE Trans. Inf. Theory **40**(3), 786–794 (1994)

13. Beimel, A., Farràs, O.: The share size of secret-sharing schemes for almost all access structures and graphs. IACR Cryptology ePrint Archive 2020, 664 (2020)

14. Beimel, A., Farràs, O., Mintz, Y.: Secret-sharing schemes for very dense graphs. J. Cryptol. **29**(2), 336–362 (2016)

15. Beimel, A., Farràs, O., Mintz, Y., Peter, N.: Linear secret-sharing schemes for forbidden graph access structures. Technical report 2017/940, IACR Cryptology ePrint Archive (2017). Full version of [16]

16. Beimel, A., Farràs, O., Mintz, Y., Peter, N.: Linear secret-sharing schemes for forbidden graph access structures. In: Kalai, Y., Reyzin, L. (eds.) TCC 2017. LNCS, vol. 10678, pp. 394–423. Springer, Cham (2017). https://doi.org/10.1007/978-3-319-70503-3_13

17. Beimel, A., Gál, A., Paterson, M.: Lower bounds for monotone span programs. Comput. Complex. **6**(1), 29–45 (1997)

18. Beimel, A., Ishai, Y., Kumaresan, R., Kushilevitz, E.: On the cryptographic complexity of the worst functions. In: Lindell, Y. (ed.) TCC 2014. LNCS, vol. 8349, pp. 317–342. Springer, Heidelberg (2014). https://doi.org/10.1007/978-3-642-54242-8_14

19. Beimel, A., Kushilevitz, E., Nissim, P.: The complexity of multiparty PSM protocols and related models. In: Nielsen, J.B., Rijmen, V. (eds.) EUROCRYPT 2018. LNCS, vol. 10821, pp. 287–318. Springer, Cham (2018). https://doi.org/10.1007/978-3-319-78375-8_10

20. Beimel, A., Peter, N.: Optimal linear multiparty conditional disclosure of secrets protocols. In: Peyrin, T., Galbraith, S. (eds.) ASIACRYPT 2018. LNCS, vol. 11274, pp. 332–362. Springer, Cham (2018). https://doi.org/10.1007/978-3-030-03332-3_13

21. Beimel, A., Weinreb, E.: Separating the power of monotone span programs over different fields. SIAM J. Comput. **34**(5), 1196–1215 (2005)

22. Benaloh, J., Leichter, J.: Generalized secret sharing and monotone functions. In: Goldwasser, S. (ed.) CRYPTO 1988. LNCS, vol. 403, pp. 27–35. Springer, New York (1990). https://doi.org/10.1007/0-387-34799-2_3

23. Bertilsson, M., Ingemarsson, I.: A construction of practical secret sharing schemes using linear block codes. In: Seberry, J., Zheng, Y. (eds.) AUSCRYPT 1992. LNCS, vol. 718, pp. 67–79. Springer, Heidelberg (1993). https://doi.org/10.1007/3-540-57220-1_53

24. Blakley, G.R.: Safeguarding cryptographic keys. In: Proceedings of the 1979 AFIPS National Computer Conference. AFIPS Conference Proceedings, vol. 48, pp. 313–317 (1979)

25. Blundo, C., De Santis, A., Gargano, L., Vaccaro, U.: On the information rate of secret sharing schemes. Theoret. Comput. Sci. **154**(2), 283–306 (1996)

26. Blundo, C., Santis, A.D., Gaggia, A.G., Vaccaro, U.: New bounds on the information rate of secret sharing schemes. IEEE Trans. Inf. Theory **41**(2), 549–553 (1995)

27. Bollobás, B.: Random Graphs, 2nd edn. Cambridge University Press, Cambridge (2001)

28. Bollobás, B., Thomason, A.: Graphs which contain all small graphs. Eur. J. Combin. **2**(1), 13–15 (1981)

29. Brickell, E.F.: Some ideal secret sharing schemes. J. Combin. Math. Combin. Comput. **6**, 105–113 (1989)

30. Capocelli, R.M., De Santis, A., Gargano, L., Vaccaro, U.: On the size of shares for secret sharing schemes. J. Cryptol. **6**(3), 157–168 (1993)

31. Chor, B., Kushilevitz, E.: Secret sharing over infinite domains. J. Cryptol. **6**(2), 87–96 (1993)

32. Cramer, R., Damgård, I., Maurer, U.: General secure multi-party computation from any linear secret-sharing scheme. In: Preneel, B. (ed.) EUROCRYPT 2000. LNCS, vol. 1807, pp. 316–334. Springer, Heidelberg (2000). https://doi.org/10.1007/3-540-45539-6_22

33. Csirmaz, L.: The dealer's random bits in perfect secret sharing schemes. Studia Sci. Math. Hungar. **32**(3–4), 429–437 (1996)

34. Csirmaz, L.: The size of a share must be large. J. Cryptol. **10**(4), 223–231 (1997)

35. Csirmaz, L.: Secret sharing schemes on graphs. Technical report 2005/059, Cryptology ePrint Archive (2005). eprint.iacr.org/

36. Csirmaz, L.: An impossibility result on graph secret sharing. Des. Codes Cryptogr. **53**(3), 195–209 (2009)

37. van Dijk, M.: On the information rate of perfect secret sharing schemes. Des. Codes Cryptogr. **6**(2), 143–169 (1995)

38. Erdös, P., Pyber, L.: Covering a graph by complete bipartite graphs. Discrete Math. **170**(1–3), 249–251 (1997)

39. Erdös, P., Rényi, A.: On random graphs. I. Publ. Math. Debrecen **6**, 290–297 (1959)

40. Gál, A., Pudlák, P.: Monotone complexity and the rank of matrices. Inf. Process. Lett. **87**, 321–326 (2003)

41. Gay, R., Kerenidis, I., Wee, H.: Communication complexity of conditional disclosure of secrets and attribute-based encryption. In: Gennaro, R., Robshaw, M. (eds.) CRYPTO 2015. LNCS, vol. 9216, pp. 485–502. Springer, Heidelberg (2015). https://doi.org/10.1007/978-3-662-48000-7_24

42. Gertner, Y., Ishai, Y., Kushilevitz, E., Malkin, T.: Protecting data privacy in private information retrieval schemes. J. Comput. Syst. Sci. **60**(3), 592–629 (2000)

43. Grimmett, G.R., McDiarmid, C.J.H.: On colouring random graphs. Math. Proc. Cambridge Philos. Soc. **77**(2), 313–324 (1975)

44. Ito, M., Saito, A., Nishizeki, T.: Secret sharing schemes realizing general access structure. In: GLOBECOM 1987, pp. 99–102 (1987). Journal version: Multiple assignment scheme for sharing secret. J. Cryptol. **6**(1), 15–20 (1993)

45. Karchmer, M., Wigderson, A.: On span programs. In: 8th Structure in Complexity Theory, pp. 102–111 (1993)

46. Karnin, E.D., Greene, J.W., Hellman, M.E.: On secret sharing systems. IEEE Trans. Inf. Theory **29**(1), 35–41 (1983)

47. Korshunov, A.D.: On the number of monotone Boolean functions. Probl. Kibern. **38**, 5–108 (1981)

48. Liu, T., Vaikuntanathan, V.: Breaking the circuit-size barrier in secret sharing. In: 50th STOC, pp. 699–708 (2018)

49. Liu, T., Vaikuntanathan, V., Wee, H.: Conditional disclosure of secrets via non-linear reconstruction. In: Katz, J., Shacham, H. (eds.) CRYPTO 2017. LNCS, vol. 10401, pp. 758–790. Springer, Cham (2017). https://doi.org/10.1007/978-3-319-63688-7_25

50. Liu, T., Vaikuntanathan, V., Wee, H.: Towards breaking the exponential barrier for general secret sharing. In: Nielsen, J.B., Rijmen, V. (eds.) EUROCRYPT 2018. LNCS, vol. 10820, pp. 567–596. Springer, Cham (2018). https://doi.org/10.1007/978-3-319-78381-9_21

51. Martí-Farré, J., Padró, C.: On secret sharing schemes, matroids and polymatroids. J. Math. Cryptol. **4**(2), 95–120 (2010)

52. Mintz, Y.: Information ratios of graph secret-sharing schemes. Master's thesis, Department of Computer Science, Ben Gurion University (2012)

53. Nelson, P.: Almost all matroids are non-representable. Bull. Lond. Math. Soc. **50**(2), 245–248 (2018)
54. Peter, N.: Secret-sharing schemes and conditional disclosure of secrets protocols. Ph.D. thesis, Ben-Gurion University of the Negev (2020). http://aranne5.bgu.ac.il/others/PeterNaty19903.pdf
55. Pitassi, T., Robere, R.: Lifting Nullstellensatz to monotone span programs over any field. In: 50th STOC, pp. 1207–1219 (2018)
56. Rónyai, L., Babai, L., Ganapathy, M.K.: On the number of zero-patterns of a sequence of polynomials. J. AMS **14**(3), 717–735 (2001)
57. Shamir, A.: How to share a secret. Commun. ACM **22**, 612–613 (1979)
58. Shannon, C.E.: The synthesis of two-terminal switching circuits. Bell Syst. Tech. J. **28**(1), 59–98 (1949)
59. Simmons, G.J.: How to (really) share a secret. In: Goldwasser, S. (ed.) CRYPTO 1988. LNCS, vol. 403, pp. 390–448. Springer, New York (1990). https://doi.org/10.1007/0-387-34799-2_30
60. Sun, H.M., Shieh, S.P.: Secret sharing in graph-based prohibited structures. In: INFOCOM 1997, pp. 718–724 (1997)
61. Wee, H.: Dual system encryption via predicate encodings. In: Lindell, Y. (ed.) TCC 2014. LNCS, vol. 8349, pp. 616–637. Springer, Heidelberg (2014). https://doi.org/10.1007/978-3-642-54242-8_26
62. Wegener, I.: The Complexity of Boolean Functions. Wiley-Teubner Series in Computer Science. B. G. Teubner and John Wiley, Chichester (1987)

Transparent Error Correcting in a Computationally Bounded World

Ofer Grossman[1], Justin Holmgren[2], and Eylon Yogev[3(✉)]

[1] MIT, Cambridge, USA
[2] NTT Research, Silicon Valley, USA
[3] Tel Aviv University, Tel Aviv, Israel
eylony@gmail.com

Abstract. We construct uniquely decodable codes against channels which are computationally bounded. Our construction requires only a public-coin (transparent) setup. All prior work for such channels either required a setup with secret keys and states, could not achieve unique decoding, or got worse rates (for a given bound on codeword corruptions). On the other hand, our construction relies on a strong cryptographic hash function with security properties that we only instantiate in the random oracle model.

1 Introduction

Error correcting codes (ECCs) are a tool for handling errors when transmitting messages over an unreliable communication channel. They work by first encoding the message with additional redundant information, which is then sent over the channel. This allows the recipient to recover the original encoded message, even in the presence of a limited number of errors that might occur during transmission.

Since their introduction in the 1950s, error correcting codes [Ham50] have been a thriving research area due to their role both in practical applications and in theoretical computer science. One of the central open questions concerns the exact tradeoff between a code's *rate* (message length divided by codeword length) and the code's *error tolerance* (the number of errors that its decoding algorithm can tolerate). There are several known fundamental bounds (e.g. the Hamming, Singleton, and Plotkin bounds) on the maximum rate of a code in terms of its distance, and state of the art codes (especially over small alphabets) often only achieve significantly lower rates.

To achieve better rates, two major relaxations of error correction have been proposed. In the first, called *list decoding* [Eli57, Woz58], a decoding algorithm is no longer required to output the originally encoded message, but may instead output a short *list* of messages which is required to *contain* the original message. In this work, we will focus on standard (unique) decoding, but we will use list-decodable codes as a central building block.

© International Association for Cryptologic Research 2020
R. Pass and K. Pietrzak (Eds.): TCC 2020, LNCS 12552, pp. 530–549, 2020.
https://doi.org/10.1007/978-3-030-64381-2_19

In the second relaxation, the communication channel between the sender and receiver is assumed to be restricted in some way. In other words, the code is no longer required to handle fully worst-case errors. The most relevant model for us is the *computationally bounded channel* [Lip94], which loosely speaking, models codeword errors as generated by a *polynomial-time* process.

Lipton [Lip94] and Micali et al. [MPSW10] construct codes for the computationally bounded channel with better rates than are achievable by codes for worst-case errors, but their codes require a trusted setup. Specifically, the encoding algorithms for their codes (and in the case of [Lip94], also the decoding algorithm) require a secret key that, if leaked, allows an efficient channel to thwart the decoding algorithm with a relatively small number of corruptions. Secret randomness is much more difficult to instantiate than public randomness (also known as transparent), which leads us to ask:

Are there "good" uniquely decodable codes for the computationally bounded channel with transparent setup?

An additional drawback of the constructions of [Lip94] and [MPSW10] is that they require a *stateful* encoder, which may render them unsuitable for use in data storage or in applications requiring concurrent transmission of multiple messages. In [Lip94], it is essential for security that the encoder's state never repeats, and essential for correctness that the decoder's state is synchronized with the encoder's state. In [MPSW10], the decoder is stateless, but it is essential for security that errors are chosen in an online fashion. In other words, there are no guarantees if a codeword c is corrupted after seeing a codeword c' that was encoded after c. This exemplifies the undesirable dependence, induced by the encoder's statefulness, of the code's error tolerance on the precise environment in which it is used. Thus we ask:

Are there "good" uniquely decodable codes for the computationally bounded channel with a stateless encoder?

1.1   Our Contributions

We answer both questions affirmatively, constructing a code for computationally bounded channels (with transparent setup *and* stateless encoding) that outperforms codes for worst-case errors. As a contribution that may be of independent interest, we also construct codes with high "pseudodistance", i.e., codes for which it is hard to find two codewords that are close in Hamming distance.

Pseudounique Decoding. The main goal of an error correcting code C is to facilitate the recovery of a transmitted message given a partially corrupted copy of $C(m)$. To formalize this (in the information-theoretic setting), a polynomial-time algorithm D is said to be a *unique decoding algorithm for C against ρ errors* if for all messages m and all strings c' that are ρ-close in Hamming distance to $C(m)$, we have $D(c') = m$.

In reality, messages and noise are created by nature, which can be conservatively modeled as a computationally bounded adversary. We thus relax the above *for all* quantification and only require efficient decoding when *both m* and *c'* are chosen by a computationally bounded process. Our codes will be described by a randomly generated seed that is used in the encoding and decoding procedures. In other words, we will work with a *seeded family* of codes $\{C_{pp}\}$, where pp is the seed, which we will also refer to as the *public parameters* for the code. In our constructions, the public parameters are merely unstructured uniformly random strings of a certain length.

More formally, we say that a polynomial-time algorithm D is a *pseudounique decoding algorithm for* $\{C_{pp}\}$ *against* ρ *errors* if no polynomial-time adversary A can win the following game with noticeable probability. The public parameters pp are first sampled uniformly at random and given to A. The adversary then produces a message m and a string c', and is said to win if c' is ρ-close to $C_{pp}(m)$ and $D(pp, c') \neq m$.

Under cryptographic assumptions (or in the random oracle model), we construct codes with pseudounique decoding algorithms for a larger fraction of errors than is possible in the standard setting. Our main theorem requires a "good" cryptographic hash function (which is used as a black box), where we defer the formalization of the necessary security requirements to Sect. 3. For now, we simply mention that it is a *multi-input* generalization of correlation intractability, and in Section 3 we show that it can be instantiated by a (non-programmable) random oracle. The precise statement and details about the construction appear in Sect. 4.

Informal Theorem 1. *For any* $r \in (0,1)$ *and any* $\rho < \min(1 - r, \frac{1}{2})$ *there exist rate-r codes, over large (polynomial-sized) alphabets, that are efficiently pseudouniquely decodable against up to a ρ fraction of errors, assuming good hash functions exist (or in the random oracle model).*

This should be contrasted with the Singleton bound, which rules out (standard) unique decoding for more than $\min(\frac{1-r}{2}, \frac{1}{2})$ errors. Our positive result is a corollary of a more general connection to efficient list-decodability, which we prove in Sect. 4. This connection also implies results over binary alphabets, albeit with bounds that are harder to state (see Corollary 3) because known binary codes do not achieve list-decoding capacity and instead have messy rate vs. error correction tradeoffs.

Pseudodistance. Our second notion is an analogue of distance. Recall that a code C is said to have distance d if for all pairs of distinct messages m_0, m_1, their encodings $C(m_0)$ and $C(m_1)$ have Hamming distance d. We can similarly replace this *for all* quantifier and only require $C_{pp}(m_0)$ and $C_{pp}(m_1)$ to be far for pairs m_0, m_1 that are computed from pp by a computationally bounded adversary.

We note that a code's pseudodistance may be arbitrarily high without implying anything about its decodability, even by an inefficient algorithm. It is instructive to imagine a rate-1 code whose encoding algorithm is given by a (sufficiently obfuscated) random permutation mapping $\{0,1\}^n \to \{0,1\}^n$. The pseudodistance of this code will be roughly $n/2$, but it is information theoretically impossible to decode in the presence of even a single error.

Still, pseudodistance is a useful intermediate notion for us in the construction of pseudouniquely decodable codes, and the notion may be of independent interest.

1.2   Main Definitions and Main Theorem Statement

The preceding discussion is formalized in the following definitions.

Definition 1. *A* seeded code *with alphabet size $q(\cdot)$ is a pair $\mathcal{C} = (\mathsf{Setup}, \mathsf{Enc})$ of polynomial-time algorithms with the following syntax:*

- Setup *is probabilistic, takes a domain length $k \in \mathbb{Z}^+$ (in unary), and outputs public parameters pp.*
- Enc *is deterministic, takes parameters pp and a message $m \in \{0,1\}^k$, and outputs a codeword $c \in [q(k)]^{n(k)}$, where $n(\cdot)$ is called the* length *of $\mathcal{C}$.*

When $\lim_{k \to \infty} \frac{k}{n(k) \log_2 q(k)} \in [0,1]$ is well-defined it is called the rate *of $\mathcal{C}$. If Setup simply outputs a uniformly random binary string of some length that depends on k, then we say that $\mathcal{C}$ is* public-coin.

Definition 2. *A seeded code $\mathcal{C} = (\mathsf{Setup}, \mathsf{Enc})$ is said to have $(s(\cdot), \epsilon(\cdot))$ - pseudodistance $d(\cdot)$ if for all size-$s(\cdot)$ circuit ensembles $\{\mathcal{A}_k\}_{k \in \mathbb{Z}^+}$, we have*

$$\Pr_{\substack{\mathsf{pp} \leftarrow \mathsf{Setup}(1^k) \\ (m_0, m_1) \leftarrow \mathcal{A}_k(\mathsf{pp})}} \left[\Delta\big(\mathsf{Enc}(\mathsf{pp}, m_0), \mathsf{Enc}(\mathsf{pp}, m_1)\big) < d \right] \le \epsilon(k),$$

where $\Delta(\cdot, \cdot)$ denotes the (absolute) Hamming distance.

$\mathcal{C}$ is said simply to have pseudodistance *$d(\cdot)$ if for all $s(k) \le k^{O(1)}$, there exists $\epsilon(k) \le k^{-\omega(1)}$ such that $\mathcal{C}$ has (s, ϵ)-pseudodistance d.*

Definition 3. *An algorithm Dec is said to be an $(s(\cdot), \epsilon(\cdot))$-pseudounique decoder for $\mathcal{C} = (\mathsf{Setup}, \mathsf{Enc})$ against $d(\cdot)$ errors if for all size-$s(\cdot)$ circuit ensembles $\{\mathcal{A}_k\}_{k \in \mathbb{Z}^+}$*

$$\Pr_{\substack{\mathsf{pp} \leftarrow \mathsf{Setup}(1^k) \\ (m,c) \leftarrow \mathcal{A}_k(\mathsf{pp})}} \left[\Delta\big(c, \mathsf{Enc}(\mathsf{pp}, m)\big) \le d(k) \ \wedge \ \mathsf{Dec}(\mathsf{pp}, c) \ne m \right] \le \epsilon(k).$$

We say that $\mathcal{C}$ is efficiently *$(s(\cdot), \epsilon(\cdot))$-pseudouniquely decodable against $d(\cdot)$ errors if there is a polynomial-time algorithm Dec that is an $(s(\cdot), \epsilon(\cdot))$-pseudounique decoder for $\mathcal{C}$. We omit s and ϵ in usage of the above definitions when for all $s(k) \le k^{O(1)}$, there exists $\epsilon(k) \le k^{-\omega(1)}$ such that the definition is satisfied.*

We sometimes say a "ρ fraction of errors" to refer to some $d(k)$ such that $\lim_{k \to \infty} \frac{d(k)}{n(k)} = \rho$, where $n(\cdot)$ is the length of $\mathcal{C}$.

As in the previous theorem, we assume the existence of random-like hash functions to obtain our result. These hash functions can be instantiated in the random oracle model.

Informal Theorem 2. *If $\{C : \{0,1\}^k \to [q]^{n_k}\}$ is a rate-r ensemble of codes that is efficiently list-decodable against a ρ fraction of errors, and if good hash functions exist, then there exists a rate-r seeded code that is efficiently pseudouniquely decodable against a* $\min\left(\rho, \dfrac{H_q^{-1}\left(r + H_q(\rho)\right)}{2}\right)$ *fraction of errors.*

The above bound has a nice interpretation when C approaches capacity, i.e. when $r + H_q(\rho) \approx 1$. Then $\frac{H_q^{-1}(r + H_q(\rho))}{2} \approx \frac{1}{2} \cdot \left(1 - \frac{1}{q}\right)$, which upper bounds the pseudo-unique decodability of any positive-rate code (implied by the proof of the Plotkin bound, and made explicit in [MPSW10]). So if C achieves capacity, Theorem 2 says that one can uniquely decode up to the (efficient) list-decoding radius of C, as long as that doesn't exceed $\frac{1}{2} \cdot \left(1 - \frac{1}{q}\right)$.

1.3 Related Work

The notion of a computationally bounded channel was first studied by Lipton [Lip94], and has subsequently been studied in a variety of coding theory settings including local decodability, local correctability, and list decoding, with channels that are bounded either in time complexity or space complexity [DGL04, GS16, BGGZ19, MPSW10, SS16, HOSW11, HO08, OPS07]. We compare some of these works in Table 1. Focusing on unique decoding against polynomial-time computationally bounded errors, the work most relevant to us is [MPSW10], improving on [Lip94].

Lipton [Lip94] showed that assuming one-way functions, any code that is (efficiently) uniquely decodable against ρ *random* errors can be upgraded to a "secret-key, stateful code" that is (efficiently) uniquely decodable against any ρ errors that are computed in polynomial time. Using known results on codes for random errors, this gives rate-r (large alphabet) codes that are uniquely decodable against a $1 - r$ fraction of errors. However, these codes require the sender and receiver to share a secret key, and to be stateful (incrementing a counter for each message sent/received).

Micali et al. [MPSW10] improve on this result, obtaining a coding scheme where only the sender needs a secret key (the receiver only needs a corresponding public key), and only the sender needs to maintain a counter. They show that these limitations are inherent in the high-error regime; namely, it is impossible to uniquely decode beyond error rates $1/4$ (in the binary case) and more generally $\frac{1}{2} \cdot \left(1 - \frac{1}{q}\right)$ over q-ary alphabets, even if the errors are computationally bounded. Compared to [Lip94], [MPSW10] starts with codes that are efficiently list decodable, rather than codes that are uniquely decodable against random errors. The crux of their technique is using cryptographic signatures to "sieve" out all but one of the candidate messages returned by a list-decoding algorithm. Our construction also uses list decodability in a similar way. The key difference is that we use a different sieving mechanism that is stateless and transparent (i.e., the only setup is a public uniformly random string), but is only applicable for error rates below $\frac{1}{2} \cdot (1 - \frac{1}{q})$.

Our work improves over [MPSW10] in the amount of setup required for the code. In [MPSW10], the sender must initially create a secret key and share the corresponding public key with the receiver (and the adversarial channel is also allowed to depend on the public key). In contrast, our code allows anyone to send messages—no secret key is needed. This property may be useful in applications such as Wi-Fi and cellular networks, where many parties need to communicate.

Another important difference between [MPSW10] and our work is that in [MPSW10], the sender is stateful. That is, whenever the sender sends a message, he updates some internal state which affects the way the next message will be encoded. We do not make such an assumption. Note that in some situations, maintaining a state may not be possible. For example, if there are multiple senders (or a single sender who is operating several servers in different locations), it is unclear how to collectively maintain state. Whenever one of the senders sends a message, he must inform all the other senders so they can update their state accordingly, which may not be possible, or significantly slow down communication. Moreover, the guarantees of [MPSW10] only apply to adversaries that operate in a totally "online" fashion. The error tolerance guarantees break down if an adversary is able to corrupt a codeword after seeing a subsequently encoded message. In our construction, the sender and receiver are both stateless, so these issues do not arise.

One drawback of our construction compared to [MPSW10] is that our construction is not applicable in the high-error regime (error rates above $1/4$ for binary codes or $1/2$ for large alphabet codes). However, over large alphabets we match the performance of [MPSW10] for all error rates below $1/2$.

2 Preliminaries

2.1 Combinatorics

Definition 4. *The ith falling factorial of $n \in \mathbb{R}$ is $(n)_i \stackrel{\text{def}}{=} n \cdot (n-1) \cdots (n-i+1)$.*

Definition 5. *The q-ary entropy function $H_q : [0, 1] \to [0, 1]$ is defined as*

$$H_q(x) \stackrel{\text{def}}{=} x \log_q(q - 1) - x \log_q x - (1 - x) \log_q(1 - x).$$

We write $H_\infty(x)$ to denote $\lim_{q \to \infty} H_q(x)$, which is equal to x. If we write $H(x)$, omitting the subscript, we mean $H_2(x)$ by default.

Definition 6. *For any alphabet Σ, any n, and any $u, v \in \Sigma^n$, the Hamming distance between u and v, denoted $\Delta(u, v)$, is*

$$\Delta(u, v) \stackrel{\text{def}}{=} \left| \{i \in [n] : u_i \neq v_i\} \right|.$$

When $\Delta(u, v) \leq \delta n$, we write $u \approx_\delta v$. If S is a set, we write $\Delta(u, S)$ to denote $\min_{v \in S} \Delta(u, v)$.

Table 1. Summary of related work. The column "message" refers to how the message are generated. The column "noise" describes the computational power of the adversary adding noise. URS stands for uniform random string (shared publicly between the sender, receiver, and adversary), BSC for binary symmetric channel, and PRG for pseudorandom generator.

Work	Setup	Noise	Decoding	Rate	Assumptions
This paper	URS	P/poly	unique	arbitrarily close to $1-p$ for large alphabets	two-input correlation intractablility
[GS16]	URS	SIZE(n^c)	list	arbitrarily close to $1-H(p)$	no assumptions
[SS16]	none	SIZE(n^c)	list	arbitrarily close to $1-H(p)$	PRGs for small circuits
[SS20]	none	SPACE(n^δ)	unique	arbitrarily close to $1-H(p)$	none
[MPSW10]	public key	P/poly	unique	matches list decoding radius	stateful sender and one-way functions
[OPS07]	private shared randomness	P/poly	local	$\Omega(1)$ (for error rate $\Omega(1)$)	one-way functions
[HOSW11]	public key	P/poly	local	$\Omega(1)$ (for error rate $\Omega(1)$)	public-key encryption
[BGGZ19]	URS	P/poly	local correction	$\Omega(1)$ (for error rate $\Omega(1)$)	collision-resistant hash function
[Lip94]	private shared randomness	P/poly	unique	matches BSC channel	stateful sender and one-way functions

2.2   Codes

Definition 7. *A deterministic q-ary code is a function $C : [K] \to [q]^n$, where n is called the* block length *of C, $[K]$ is called the* message space, *and $[q]$ is called the* alphabet. *The* distance *of C is the minimum Hamming distance between $C(m)$ and $C(m')$ for distinct $m, m' \in [K]$. A* probabilistic q-ary code *of block length n and message space $[K]$ is a randomized function $C : [K] \xrightarrow{\$} [q]^n$.*

When discussing the asymptotic performance of (deterministic or probabilistic) codes, it makes sense to consider ensembles of codes $\{C_i : [K_i] \to [q_i]^{n_i}\}$ with varying message spaces, block lengths, and alphabet sizes. We will assume several restrictions on K_i, n_i, and q_i that rule out various pathologies. Specifically, we will assume that:

- K_i, q_i, and n_i increase weakly monotonically with i and are computable from i in polynomial time (i.e. in time polylog(i)).
- q_i is at most polylog(K_i).
- There is a polynomial-time algorithm E that given (i, x) for $x \in [K_i]$ outputs $C_i(x)$.

- The limit $r = \lim_{i \to \infty} \frac{\log K_i}{n_i \cdot \log q_i}$ exists with $r \in (0, 1)$. We call r the rate of the ensemble.
- $\limsup_{i \to \infty} \frac{\log K_{i+1}}{\log K_i} = 1$. This is important so that the cost of padding (to encode arbitrary-length messages) is insignificant.

One implication of these restrictions is that without loss of generality we can assume that $\{K_i\}_{i \in \mathbb{Z}^+} = \{2^k\}_{k \in \mathbb{Z}^+}$ and we can index our codes by k rather than by i.

Definition 8. *We say that an ensemble of codes $\{C_k : \{0,1\}^k \to [q_k]^{n_k}\}_{k \in \mathbb{Z}^+}$ is* combinatorially ρ-list decodable *if for any $y \in [q_k]^{n_k}$, there are at most* $\mathrm{poly}(k)$ *values of $m \in \{0,1\}^k$ for which $C_k(m) \approx_\rho y$. If there is a polynomial-time algorithm that outputs all such m given y (and 1^k), we say that $\{C_k\}$ is* efficiently ρ-list decodable.

2.3 Pseudorandomness

Definition 9. *Random variables $X_1, \ldots, X_n$ are said to be* t-wise independent *if for any set $S \subseteq [n]$ with size $|S| = t$, the random variables $\{X_i\}_{i \in S}$ are mutually independent.*

Definition 10. *Discrete random variables $X_1, \ldots, X_n$ are said to be* t-wise β-dependent *in Rényi∞-divergence if for all sets $S \subseteq [n]$ of size $|S| = t$, it holds for all $(x_i)_{i \in S}$ that*

$$\Pr\left[\bigwedge_{i \in S} X_i = x_i\right] \leq \beta \cdot \prod_{i \in S} \Pr[X_i = x_i].$$

Permutations. If X is a finite set, we write S_X to denote the set of all permutations of X.

Definition 11. *A family of permutations $\Pi \subseteq S_X$ is said to be* t-wise ϵ-dependent *if for all distinct $x_1, \ldots, x_t \in X$, the distribution of $(\pi(x_1), \ldots, \pi(x_t))$ for uniformly random $\pi \leftarrow \Pi$ is ϵ-close in statistical distance to uniform on $\{(y_1, \ldots, y_t) : y_1, \ldots, y_t$ are distinct$\}$.*

To avoid pathological issues regarding the domains of permutation families (e.g. their sampleability, decidability, and compressability), we will restrict our attention to permutations on sets of the form $\{0,1\}^k$ for $k \in \mathbb{Z}^+$.

Definition 12. *We say that an ensemble $\{\Pi_k \subseteq S_{\{0,1\}^k}\}_{k \in \mathbb{Z}^+}$ of permutation families is* fully explicit *if there are $\mathrm{poly}(k)$-time algorithms for:*

- *sampling a description of $\pi \leftarrow \Pi_k$; and*
- *computing $\pi(x)$ and $\pi^{-1}(x)$ given x and a description of $\pi \in \Pi_k$.*

Imported Theorem 3 ([KNR09]). *For any $t = t(k) \leq k^{O(1)}$, and any $\epsilon = \epsilon(k) \geq 2^{-k^{O(1)}}$, there is a fully explicit t-wise ϵ-dependent ensemble $\{\Pi_k \subseteq S_{\{0,1\}^k}\}_{k \in \mathbb{Z}^+}$ of permutation families.*

The following non-standard variation on the notion of t-wise almost-independence will prove to be more convenient for us.

Definition 13. *A probability distribution P is said to be β-close in Rényi∞-divergence to a distribution Q if for all x, $P(x) \leq \beta \cdot Q(x)$.*

Definition 14. *We say that a family $\Pi \subseteq S_X$ is t-wise β-dependent in Rényi∞-divergence if for all distinct $x_1, \ldots, x_t \in X$, the distribution of $\big(\pi(x_1), \ldots, \pi(x_t)\big)$ is β-close in Rényi∞-divergence to the uniform distribution on X^t.*

It is easily verified that any family of permutations $\Pi \subseteq S_{[K]}$ that is t-wise ϵ-dependent as in Definition 11 is also t-wise β-dependent in Rényi∞-divergence with $\beta = \epsilon \cdot K^t + \frac{K^t}{(K)_t}$. Thus Theorem 3 gives us the following.

Corollary 1. *For any $t = t(k) \leq k^{O(1)}$, there is a fully explicit t-wise $O(1)$-dependent (in Rényi∞-divergence) ensemble $\{\Pi_k \subseteq S_{\{0,1\}^k}\}_{k \in \mathbb{Z}^+}$ of permutation families.*

3   Multi-input Correlation Intractability

Correlation intractability was introduced by Canetti Goldreich and Halevi [CGH04] as a way to model a large class of random oracle-like security properties of hash functions. Roughly speaking, H is said to be correlation intractable if for any sparse relation R it is hard to find x such that $(x, H(x)) \in R$. In recent years, CI hash functions have been under the spotlight with surprising results on instantiating CI hash families from concrete computational assumptions (e.g., [CCR16,KRR17,CCRR18,CCH+18,PS19]).

In this work, we need a stronger *multi-input* variant of correlation intractability. We formulate a notion of multi-input sparsity such that a hash function can plausibly be correlation intractable for all sparse multi-input relations. Indeed, we prove that a random oracle has this property.

Definition 15 (Multi-input Relations). *For sets $\mathcal{X}$ and $\mathcal{Y}$, an ℓ-input relation on $(\mathcal{X}, \mathcal{Y})$ is a subset $R \subseteq \mathcal{X}^\ell \times \mathcal{Y}^\ell$.*

We say that R is p-sparse if for all $i \in [\ell]$, all distinct $x_1, \ldots, x_\ell \in \mathcal{X}$, and all $y_1, \ldots, y_{i-1}, y_{i+1}, \ldots, y_\ell \in \mathcal{Y}$, we have

$$\Pr_{y_i \leftarrow \mathcal{Y}}[(x_1, \ldots, x_\ell, y_1, \ldots, y_\ell) \in R] \leq p.$$

An ensemble of ℓ-input relations $\{R_\lambda\}_{\lambda \in \mathbb{Z}^+}$ is said simply to be sparse if there is a negligible function $p \colon \mathbb{Z}^+ \to \mathbb{R}$ such that each R_λ is $p(\lambda)$-sparse.

Remark 1. A natural but flawed generalization of single-input sparsity for an ℓ-input relation R might instead require that for all $x_1, \ldots, x_\ell$, it holds with overwhelming probability over a uniform choice of $y_1, \ldots, y_\ell$ that $(x_1, \ldots, x_\ell, y_1, \ldots, y_\ell) \notin R$. Unfortunately this definition does not account for an adversary's ability to choose some x_i adaptively. Indeed, even a random oracle would not be 2-input correlation intractable under this definition for the relation $\{(x_1, x_2, y_1, y_2) : x_2 = y_1\}$, which does satisfy the aforementioned "sparsity" property.

Definition 16 (Multi-Input Correlation Intractability). *An ensemble* $\mathcal{H} = \{\mathcal{H}_\lambda\}_{\lambda \in \mathbb{Z}^+}$ *of function families* $\mathcal{H}_\lambda = \{H_k : \mathcal{X}_\lambda \to \mathcal{Y}_\lambda\}_{k \in \mathcal{K}_\lambda}$ *is* ℓ-input $(s(\cdot), \epsilon(\cdot))$-correlation intractable for a relation ensemble $\{R_\lambda \subseteq \mathcal{X}_\lambda^\ell \times \mathcal{Y}_\lambda^\ell\}$ *if for every size-$s(\lambda)$ adversary* $\mathcal{A}$:

$$\Pr_{\substack{k \leftarrow \mathcal{K}_\lambda \\ (x_1,\ldots,x_\ell) \leftarrow \mathcal{A}(k)}} \left[(x_1, \ldots, x_\ell, H_k(x_1), \ldots, H_k(x_\ell)) \in R_\lambda \right] \leq \epsilon(\lambda).$$

3.1 Multi-input Correlation Intractability of Random Oracles

We show that a random oracle is ℓ-input correlation intractable as in Definition 16.

Theorem 4. *Let F be a uniformly random function mapping $\mathcal{X} \to \mathcal{Y}$, and let $\ell \in \mathbb{Z}^+$ be a constant. Then, for any p-sparse ℓ-distinct-input relation R on $(\mathcal{X}, \mathcal{Y})$, and any T-query oracle algorithm $\mathcal{A}^{(\cdot)}$, we have*

$$\Pr \left[\mathcal{A}^F \text{ outputs } (x_1, \ldots, x_\ell) \in \mathcal{X}^\ell \text{ s.t. } (x_1, \ldots, x_\ell, F(x_1), \ldots, F(x_\ell)) \in R \right]$$
$$\leq p \cdot (T)_\ell \leq p \cdot T^\ell.$$

Proof Overview. We give an overview of the proof which should give some intuition as to why get the expression $p \cdot T^\ell$. Fix a set of elements $x_1, \ldots, x_\ell$ then the probability, over the random oracle, that these elements will be in the relation with respect with the random oracle is at most p, which follows from the definition of sparsity. However, for a longer list of elements of length, we would need to take into account all the possible tuples of size ℓ in that list, and apply a union bound. Since the number of queries is bounded by T, we get that the probability is at most $p \cdot T^\ell$.

The above arguments work for a *fixed* list of elements, and gives intuition for the probability expression achieved in the theorem. However, an oracle algorithm is allowed to perform *adaptive* queries where the next query might depend on the result of the random oracle for previous queries. This makes the proof more challenging and, in particular, much more technical.

Proof. We begin the proof by stating a few assumptions about the algorithm $\mathcal{A}$, and observe that these assumption hold without loss of generality:

- $\mathcal{A}$ is deterministic;
- $\mathcal{A}$ never makes repeated queries to F nor does $\mathcal{A}$ output non-distinct $x_1, \ldots, x_\ell$; and
- If at any point $\mathcal{A}$ has made queries $q_1, \ldots, q_j$ and received answers $a_1, \ldots, a_j$ such that for some $i_1, \ldots, i_k \in [j]^\ell$ the tuple $(q_{i_1}, \ldots, q_{i_\ell}, a_{i_1}, \ldots, a_{i_\ell})$ is in R, then $\mathcal{A}$ immediately outputs one such tuple (without making any further queries).

We denote the random variables representing the various queries of the algorithm $\mathcal{A}$, and their responses from the oracle. Let M be a random variable denoting the number of queries made by $\mathcal{A}$, let $Q_1, \ldots, Q_M$ denote the queries made by $\mathcal{A}$ to F, let $A_1, \ldots, A_M$ denote the corresponding evaluations of F, let $\mathcal{Q}$ denote $\{Q_1, \ldots, Q_M\}$, let $X_1, \ldots, X_\ell$ denote the output of $\mathcal{A}^F$, and let $Y_1, \ldots, Y_\ell$ denote the corresponding evaluations of F.

We split our analysis into two cases: either $(X_1, \ldots, X_\ell) \in \mathcal{Q}^k$, or not, meaning that the algorithm did not query all of the ℓ elements it outputs. We argue about each case separately and at the end combine to the two to a single argument. We begin with the second case.

Claim. For any algorithm $\mathcal{A}$ it holds that

$$\Pr\left[(X_1, \ldots, X_\ell, Y_1, \ldots, Y_\ell) \in R \mid (X_1, \ldots, X_\ell) \notin \mathcal{Q}^\ell\right] \leq p \cdot \ell.$$

where the probability is over the random oracle.

Proof Sketch. There exists some component of $\mathcal{A}$'s output whose image under F is independent of $\mathcal{A}$'s view, and thus is uniformly random. Since R is p-sparse, this ensures that $(X_1, \ldots, X_\ell, Y_1, \ldots, Y_\ell)$ is in R with probability at most p.

Proof. Fix any $i \in [\ell]$ and any $(q_1, \ldots, q_\ell, a_1, \ldots, a_{i-1}, a_{i+1}, \ldots, a_\ell)$. Since the relation is p-sparse, we know that

$$\Pr[(q_1, \ldots, q_\ell, a_1, \ldots, a_{i-1}, Y_i, a_{i+1}, \ldots, a_\ell) \in R] \leq p.$$

Thus, we can write:

$$\Pr\left[(X_1, \ldots, X_\ell, Y_1, \ldots, Y_\ell) \in R \mid (X_1, \ldots, X_\ell) \notin \mathcal{Q}^\ell\right]$$
$$\leq \sum_{i \in [\ell]} \Pr\left[(X_1, \ldots, X_\ell, Y_1, \ldots, Y_\ell) \in R \mid X_i \in \mathcal{Q}\right] \cdot \Pr[X_i \notin \mathcal{Q}]$$
$$\leq \sum_{i \in [\ell]} \sum_{\substack{q_1, \ldots, q_\ell \\ a_1, \ldots, a_{i-1}, a_{i+1}, \ldots, a_\ell}} \Pr\left[(q_1, \ldots, q_\ell, a_1, \ldots, a_{i-1}, Y_i, a_{i+1}, \ldots, a_\ell) \in R\right] \cdot$$
$$\Pr[\forall j \neq i : X_j = q_j, Y_j = a_j, X_i = a_i] \cdot \Pr[X_i \notin \mathcal{Q}]$$
$$\leq p \cdot \sum_{i \in [\ell]} \Pr[X_i \notin \mathcal{Q}] \cdot \sum_{\substack{q_1, \ldots, q_\ell \\ a_1, \ldots, a_{i-1}, a_{i+1}, \ldots, a_\ell}} \Pr[\forall j \neq i : X_j = q_j, Y_j = a_j, X_i = a_i]$$
$$\leq p \cdot \sum_{i \in [\ell]} \Pr[X_i \notin \mathcal{Q}] \leq p \cdot \ell.$$

We turn to prove the first case, where all the elements in the algorithm's output where queried. This case is where we pay the $p \cdot T^k$ in the probability.

Claim. For any T-query algorithm $\mathcal{A}$ it holds that:

$$\Pr\left[(X_1, \ldots, X_\ell, Y_1, \ldots, Y_\ell) \in R \mid (X_1, \ldots, X_\ell) \in \mathcal{Q}^\ell\right] \leq p \cdot T^k.$$

Proof. For any $m \in [T]$, let Z_m be an indicator random variable to the event that the mth query of the algorithm $\mathcal{A}$ along with some $\ell - 1$ previous queries form an instance in the relation. Formally, we define:

$$Z_m = \begin{cases} 1 \text{ if } \exists i_1, \ldots, i_\ell \in [m] \text{ s.t. } (Q_{i_1}, \ldots, Q_{i_\ell}, A_{i_1}, \ldots, A_{i_{\ell-1}}, A_m) \in R \text{ and } m \in \{i_1, \ldots, i_\ell\} \\ 0 \text{ otherwise} \end{cases}$$

Observe that using this notation, we have that if the event $(X_1, \ldots, X_\ell, Y_1, \ldots, Y_\ell) \in R$ implies that there exist an $m \in [T]$ such that $Z_m = 1$. Using the fact that R is p-sparse, we bound $\Pr[Z_m = 1]$, for any $m \in [T]$ as follows:

$$\Pr[Z_m] = 1$$
$$\Pr[\exists i_1, \ldots, i_\ell \in [m] \text{ such that } (Q_{i_1}, \ldots, Q_{i_\ell}, A_{i_1}, \ldots, A_{i_\ell}) \in R \text{ and } m \in \{i_1, \ldots, i_\ell\}]$$
$$\leq \sum_{i_1, \ldots, i_\ell \in [m], \, m \in \{i_1, \ldots, i_\ell\}} \Pr[(Q_{i_1}, \ldots, Q_{i_\ell}, A_{i_1}, \ldots, A_{i_\ell}) \in R]$$
$$\leq \sum_{i_1, \ldots, i_\ell \in [m], \, m \in \{i_1, \ldots, i_\ell\}} p \leq p \cdot \ell \cdot (m-1)_{\ell-1}.$$

Then, we union bound over all z_m for $m \in [T]$ and get that

$$\Pr\left[(X_1, \ldots, X_\ell, Y_1, \ldots, Y_\ell) \in R \mid (X_1, \ldots, X_\ell) \in \mathcal{Q}^\ell\right] \leq \Pr[\exists m \in [T] : Z_m = 1]$$
$$\leq \sum_{m=1}^T \Pr[Z_m = 1] \leq \sum_{m=1}^T p \cdot \ell \cdot (m-1)_{\ell-1} \leq p \cdot (T)_\ell.$$

Finally, using the two claims we get that

$$\Pr[(X_1, \ldots, X_\ell, Y_1, \ldots, Y_\ell) \in R]$$
$$= \Pr\left[(X_1, \ldots, X_\ell, Y_1, \ldots, Y_\ell) \in R \mid (X_1, \ldots, X_\ell) \in \mathcal{Q}^\ell\right] \cdot \Pr[(X_1, \ldots, X_\ell) \in \mathcal{Q}^\ell]$$
$$+ \Pr\left[(X_1, \ldots, X_\ell, Y_1, \ldots, Y_\ell) \in R \mid (X_1, \ldots, X_\ell) \notin \mathcal{Q}^\ell\right] \cdot \Pr[(X_1, \ldots, X_\ell) \notin \mathcal{Q}^\ell]$$
$$\leq p \cdot (T)_\ell \cdot \Pr[(X_1, \ldots, X_\ell) \in \mathcal{Q}^\ell] + p \cdot \ell \cdot \Pr[(X_1, \ldots, X_\ell) \notin \mathcal{Q}^\ell]$$
$$\leq p \cdot (T)_\ell \cdot \Pr[(X_1, \ldots, X_\ell) \in \mathcal{Q}^\ell] + p \cdot (T)_\ell \cdot \Pr[(X_1, \ldots, X_\ell) \notin \mathcal{Q}^\ell]$$
$$= p \cdot (T)_\ell \leq p \cdot T^\ell.$$

4   Our Construction

We have defined the notion of a multi-input correlation intractable hash, and showed that they can be constructed in the random oracle model. We now construct a seeded family of codes that is pseudouniquely decodable against a large fraction of errors, using 2-input correlation intractable hash functions as a central tool (in a black-box way). Loosely speaking, our construction starts with any efficiently list-decodable code $C\colon \{0,1\}^k \to [q]^n$, and modifies it in several steps.

1. We first apply a decodability- and rate-preserving seeded transformation to C to obtain (a seeded family of) *stochastic* codes in which with all pairs of messages are mapped to far apart codewords with overwhelmingly probability.

   Specifically, the seed is (loosely speaking) a pseudorandom permutation $\pi\colon \{0,1\}^k \to \{0,1\}^k$, and the stochastic code maps $m' \in \{0,1\}^{k-\ell}$ to $C\big(\pi(m'\|r)\big)$ for uniformly random $r \leftarrow \{0,1\}^\ell$, where ℓ satisfies $\omega(k) \leq \ell \leq o(k)$.

2. We derandomize these codes by generating randomness deterministically as a hash of the message.

More formally, we will consider the following parameterized construction of a seeded code family.

Construction 5. *Suppose that*

- $C = \{C_k : \{0,1\}^k \to [q_k]^{n_k}\}_{k \in \mathbb{Z}^+}$ *is a fully explicit ensemble of codes,*
- $\Pi = \{\Pi_k \subseteq S_{\{0,1\}^k}\}_{k \in \mathbb{Z}^+}$ *is a fully explicit ensemble of permutation families, and*
- $\mathcal{H} = \{\mathcal{H}_k\}$ *is a fully explicit ensemble of hash function families, where functions in $\mathcal{H}_k$ map $\{0,1\}^{k-\ell_k}$ to $\{0,1\}^{\ell_k}$ for some $\ell = \ell_k$ satisfying $\omega(\log k) \leq \ell_k \leq o(k)$.*

Then we define a seeded family of codes $SC[C, \Pi, \mathcal{H}]$ by the following algorithms (Setup, Enc)*:*

- Setup *takes 1^k as input, samples $\pi \leftarrow \Pi_k$ and $h \leftarrow \mathcal{H}_k$, and outputs (π, h).*
- Enc *takes (π, h) as input, as well as a message $m \in \{0,1\}^{k-\ell}$, and outputs $C_k\big(\pi(m, h(m))\big)$.*

$SC[C, \Pi, \mathcal{H}]$ inherits several basic properties from C, including alphabet size and block length. We only consider hash family ensembles $\{\mathcal{H}_k\}$ in which the output length ℓ_k of functions in $\mathcal{H}_k$ satisfies $\ell_k \leq o(k)$. With such parameters, the resulting coding scheme $SC[C, \Pi, \mathcal{H}]$ has the same rate as C.

4.1　From 2-Input Correlation Intractability to Pseudodistance

In this section, we show that if C is a sufficiently good ensemble of codes, $\mathcal{H}$ is a two-input correlation intractable hash with an appropriate output length, and Π is pseudorandom, then $SC[C, \Pi, \mathcal{H}]$ has high pseudodistance.

Proposition 1. *For any:*

- *rate-r (combinatorially) ρ-list decodable ensemble of codes $\{C_k : \{0,1\}^k \to [q_k]^{n_k}\}_{k \in \mathbb{Z}^+}$;*
- *ensemble $\Pi = \{\Pi_k \subseteq S_{\{0,1\}^k}\}_{k \in \mathbb{Z}^+}$ of $\omega(1)$-wise $O(1)$-dependent (in Rényi∞-divergence) permutation families;*
- *$\delta \in (0,1)$ satisfying $H_q(\delta) - H_q(\rho) < r$, where $q = \lim_{k \to \infty} q_k$*

$SC[\mathcal{C}, \Pi, \mathcal{H}]$ has relative pseudodistance δ as long as $\mathcal{H}$ is 2-input correlation intractable for a specific family of sparse relations.

Proof. By construction, $SC[\mathcal{C}, \Pi, \mathcal{H}]$ has relative pseudodistance δ if and only if given $\pi \leftarrow \Pi_k$ and $h \leftarrow \mathcal{H}_k$, it is hard to find $m_0, m_1 \in \{0,1\}^{k-\ell_k}$ such that $C_k\Big(\pi\big(m_0, h(m_0)\big)\Big) \approx_\delta C_k\Big(\pi\big(m_1, h(m_1)\big)\Big)$, i.e. if $\big(m_0, m_1, h(m_0), h(m_1)\big)$ is in the relation:

$$\mathcal{R}^{\text{close}}_{\mathcal{C}, \pi, \delta, \ell_k} \subseteq \big(\{0,1\}^{k-\ell_k}\big)^2 \times \big(\{0,1\}^{\ell_k}\big)^2$$

$$\mathcal{R}^{\text{close}}_{\mathcal{C}, \pi, \delta, \ell_k} \overset{\text{def}}{=} \Big\{(m_0, m_1, r_0, r_1) : C_k\big(\pi(m_0, r_0)\big) \approx_\delta C_k\big(\pi(m_1, r_1)\big)\Big\}.$$

To finish the proof of Proposition 1, it suffices to show that this relation is sparse with high probability (over the choice of $\pi \leftarrow \Pi_k$), which is established by the following claim.

Claim. For any:

- *rate-r combinatorially ρ-list decodable ensemble of codes $\{C_k : \{0,1\}^k \to [q_k]^{n_k}\}_{k \in \mathbb{Z}^+}$;*
- *$\delta \in (0,1)$ satisfying $\lim_k \big(H_{q_k}(\delta) - H_{q_k}(\rho)\big) < r$;*

for $t_k \geq \omega(1)$ and all t_k-wise $O(1)$-dependent (in Rényi∞-divergence) permutation families $\{\Pi_k \subseteq S_{\{0,1\}^k}\}$ and all $\ell_k \leq o(k)$, it holds for random $\pi \leftarrow \Pi_k$ that the relation $\mathcal{R}^{\text{close}}_{C_k, \pi, \delta, \ell_k}$ is $t_k \cdot 2^{-\ell_k}$-sparse with all but $2^{-\Omega(k \cdot t_k)}$ probability.

Proof (Proof of Section 4.1). For simplicity of presentation, we omit the explicit dependencies of C_k, Π_k, q_k, n_k, t_k, and ℓ_k on k, simply writing C, q, n, t, and ℓ respectively in statements that are to be interpreted as holding for all sufficiently large k.

Fix any $(x_1, y_1) \in \{0,1\}^{k-\ell} \times \{0,1\}^\ell$ and consider the Hamming ball $B \subseteq [q]^n$ of relative radius δ around $C(x_1, y_1)$. Using Theorem 12, we get that B can be covered by $q^{n \cdot (H_q(\delta) - H_q(\rho))} \cdot \text{poly}(n)$ balls of relative radius ρ. By C's combinatorial ρ-list decodability, each such ball contains at most $\text{poly}(k)$ codewords of C. The total number of codewords in C is at most $2^k \approx q^{rn}$ which lets us write:

$$\Pr_{c \leftarrow C} [c \approx_\delta C(x_1, y_1)] \leq \text{poly}(k) \cdot \text{poly}(n) \cdot q^{n \cdot \big(H_q(\delta) - H_q(\rho)\big)} \cdot q^{-nr} \leq q^{-\Omega(n)} \leq 2^{-\Omega(k)}.$$

Now, observe that as long as $t \geq 2$, by the t-wise $O(1)$-dependence of Π, there exists a constant c such that for any x_1, x_2, y_1, y_2 with $x_1 \neq x_2$ it holds that:

$$\Pr_\pi[(x_1, x_2, y_1, y_2) \in \mathcal{R}^{\text{close}}_{\mathcal{C}, \pi, \delta, \ell}] \leq c \cdot \Pr_{c \leftarrow C} [c \approx_\delta C(x_1, y_1)] \leq 2^{-\Omega(k)}.$$

Thus, the expected number μ of y_2' for which $(x_1, x_2, y_1, y_2') \in \mathcal{R}_{\mathcal{C},\pi,\delta,\ell}^{\text{close}}$ satisfies $\mu \leq 2^{\ell - \Omega(k)}$. Applying a concentration bound for t-wise almost-dependent random variables (Theorem 10), we see that for any fixed x_1, x_2, y_1 with $x_1 \neq x_2$ it holds that

$$\Pr_{\pi}\left[\Pr_{y_2 \leftarrow \{0,1\}^\ell}\left[(x_1, x_2, y_1, y_2) \in \mathcal{R}_{\mathcal{C},\pi,\delta,\ell}^{\text{close}}\right] \geq \frac{t+1}{2^\ell} \right] \leq O\left(\frac{\mu^t}{(t+1)!}\right) \leq O\left(\mu^t\right).$$

Thus, by a union bound over x_1, x_2, y_1, it holds that, with all but $O\left(2^{2k-\ell} \cdot \mu^t\right)$ probability, for *all* x_1, x_2, y_1,

$$\Pr_{y_2 \leftarrow \{0,1\}^\ell}\left[(x_1, x_2, y_1, y_2) \in \mathcal{R}_{\mathcal{C},\pi,\delta,\ell}^{\text{close}}\right] \leq \frac{t}{2^\ell}. \tag{1}$$

By a symmetric argument, it holds with all but $O\left(2^{2k-\ell} \cdot \mu^t\right)$ probability that for all x_1, x_2, y_2,

$$\Pr_{y_1 \leftarrow \{0,1\}^\ell}\left[(x_1, x_2, y_1, y_2) \in \mathcal{R}_{\mathcal{C},\pi,\delta,\ell}^{\text{close}}\right] \leq \frac{t}{2^\ell}. \tag{2}$$

Applying one last union bound, Eqs. (1) and (2) hold simultaneously with probability all but

$$O\left(2^{2k-\ell} \cdot \mu^t\right) \leq 2^{2k-\ell} \cdot 2^{t\left(\ell - \Omega(k)\right)}$$
$$\leq 2^{-\Omega(tk)},$$

where the last inequality is because $\ell \leq o(k)$ and $t \geq \omega(1)$.

This concludes the proof of Proposition 1.

4.2   From Efficient List Decodability to Pseudounique Decodability

We next observe that if $\mathcal{C}$ is *efficiently ρ-list decodable* then so is $\mathcal{C}' = \mathcal{SC}[\mathcal{C}, \Pi, \mathcal{H}]$ (as long as Π and $\mathcal{H}$ are fully explicit). We show that this, combined with the high pseudodistance that we have already established, implies that $\mathcal{C}'$ has a pseudounique decoding algorithm against a large fraction of errors.

We first define the straight-forward adaptation of list decoding for seeded families of codes.

Definition 17. *We say that* Dec *is an* $(L(\cdot), \rho)$-*list decoding algorithm for a seeded family of codes* (Setup, Enc) *if for all* pp *in the support of* Setup(1^k), *all* $m \in \{0,1\}^k$, *and all* $y \approx_\rho$ Enc(pp, m), Dec(pp, y) *is an* $L(k)$-*sized set that contains* m. *We say that* Dec *is simply a ρ-list decoding algorithm if it is an* $(L(\cdot), \rho)$-*list decoding algorithm for some* $L(k) \leq k^{O(1)}$.

We say that $\mathcal{C} =$ (Setup, Enc) *is efficiently ρ-list decodable if there exists a polynomial-time ρ-list decoding algorithm for $\mathcal{C}$.*

Proposition 2. *If $C = \{C_k\}$ is efficiently ρ-list decodable and Π and $\mathcal{H}$ are fully explicit, then so is $\mathcal{SC}[C, \Pi, \mathcal{H}]$.*

Proof. Given public parameters $(\pi, h) \leftarrow \mathsf{Setup}(1^k)$ and a noisy codeword c', we can list-decode by:

1. Running the list-decoding algorithm for C_k to obtain strings $y_1, \ldots, y_L \in \{0,1\}^k$,
2. Inverting each y_i under π to obtain pairs $(m_1, r_1), \ldots, (m_L, r_L)$,
3. Outputting the set $\{m_i : r_i = h(m_i) \wedge C_k(\pi(m_i, r_i)) \approx_\rho c'\}$.

Proposition 3. *If $C = (\mathsf{Setup}, \mathsf{Enc})$ is a seeded family of codes that:*

- *is efficiently list-decodable against a ρ fraction of errors; and*
- *has relative pseudodistance $\tilde{\delta}$,*

then C is efficiently pseudouniquely decodable against a ρ' fraction of errors for any $\rho' < \min(\rho, \frac{\tilde{\delta}}{2})$.

Proof. Let $q = q(k)$ and $n = n(k)$ denote the alphabet and block length of C, respectively. The efficient pseudounique decoding algorithm Dec operates as follows, given public parameters pp and corrupted codeword $y \in [q]^n$ as input:

1. Run the list-decoding algorithm for C on (pp, y) to obtain a list of messages $m_1, \ldots, m_L$ (and corresponding codewords $c_1, \ldots, c_L$).
2. Output m_i for the $i \in [L]$ minimizing $\Delta(c_i, y)$.

This algorithm clearly runs in polynomial-time, so it suffices to analyze correctness. Suppose we have $(m, y) \leftarrow \mathcal{A}(\mathsf{pp})$, where $\mathcal{A}$ is a polynomial-size adversary and $\Delta(y, \mathsf{Enc}(\mathsf{pp}, m)) \leq \rho'n$. We first observe that some $m_i = m$ by the list-decodability of C. No other m_j can also have $\Delta(y, \mathsf{Enc}(\mathsf{pp}, m)) \leq \rho'n$, because otherwise we would have $\Delta(m_i, m_j) \leq 2\rho'n < \tilde{\delta}n$ by the triangle inequality. This contradicts the C's pseudodistance since the above process for generating $\{m_1, \ldots, m_L\}$ is efficient.

In other words, c_i is the closest codeword to y, and the decoding algorithm outputs $m_i = m$ as desired.

4.3 Main Theorem

We are now ready to state our main theorem:

Theorem 6. *For any:*

- *rate-r (efficiently) ρ-list decodable fully explicit ensemble C of codes $\{C_k : \{0,1\}^k \rightarrow [q_k]^{n_k}\}_{k \in \mathbb{Z}^+}$;*
- *ensemble $\Pi = \{\Pi_k \subseteq S_{\{0,1\}^k}\}_{k \in \mathbb{Z}^+}$ of $\omega(1)$-wise $O(1)$-dependent (in Rényi∞-divergence) permutation families;*
- *ensemble $\mathcal{H} = \{\mathcal{H}_k\}$ of 2-input correlation intractable hash families, where functions in $\mathcal{H}_k$ map $\{0,1\}^k$ to $\{0,1\}^{k-\ell_k}$ for $\omega(\log k) \leq \ell_k \leq o(k)$;*

$$- \rho' < \min\left(\rho, \frac{H_q^{-1}\left(r + H_q(\rho)\right)}{2}\right) \text{ where } q = \lim_{k \to \infty} q_k,$$

$\mathcal{SC}[\mathcal{C}, \Pi, \mathcal{H}]$ is efficiently pseudouniquely decodable against a ρ' fraction of errors.

Proof. Follows immediately by combining Propositions 1 to 3.

4.4   Instantiations with Known Codes

Finally, we apply Theorem 6 with some known codes, first recalling applicable results from coding theory. We focus on large alphabets ($q_k \to \infty$) and binary alphabets ($q_k = 2$).

Imported Theorem 7 ([GR08]). *For all $r, \rho \in (0, 1)$ satisfying $r + \rho < 1$, there is a rate-r, efficiently ρ-list decodable, fully explicit ensemble of codes $\{C_k : \{0, 1\}^k \to [q_k]^{n_k}\}_{k \in \mathbb{Z}^+}$ with $q_k \leq \text{poly}(k)$.*

Imported Theorem 8 ([GR09]). *For all r, ρ satisfying $0 < \rho < 1/2$ and*

$$0 < r < R_{\mathsf{BZ}}(\rho) \stackrel{\text{def}}{=} 1 - H(\rho) - \rho \cdot \int_0^{1 - H(\rho)} \frac{dx}{H^{-1}(1 - x)}, \tag{3}$$

there is a rate-r, efficiently ρ-list decodable, fully explicit ensemble of codes $\{C_k : \{0, 1\}^k \to \{0, 1\}^{n_k}\}_{k \in \mathbb{Z}^+}$. The bound of Eq. (3) is called the Blokh-Zyablov bound.

Plugging these codes into Theorem 6, we get

Corollary 2. *For all r, ρ with $r + \rho < 1$, there is a rate-r seeded family of codes (with alphabet size $q_k \leq \text{poly}(k)$), that is efficiently pseudouniquely decodable against a ρ fraction of errors.*

This result should be contrasted with the Singleton bound, which states that if rate-r code is uniquely decodable against a ρ fraction of errors, then $r + 2\rho \leq 1$.

Corollary 3. *For all $0 < \rho < 1/2$ and all $0 < r < R_{\mathsf{BZ}}(\rho)$, there is a rate-$r$ seeded family of binary codes that is efficiently pseudouniquely decodable against a $\min\left(\rho, \frac{H^{-1}\left(r + H(\rho)\right)}{2}\right)$ fraction of errors.*

Acknowledgments. This work was done (in part) while the authors were visiting the Simons Institute for the Theory of Computing. Eylon Yogev is funded by the ISF grants 484/18, 1789/19, Len Blavatnik and the Blavatnik Foundation, and The Blavatnik Interdisciplinary Cyber Research Center at Tel Aviv University.

A Limited Independence Tail Bound

We rely on the following:

Imported Theorem 9 ([LL14]). *Let* $X_1, \ldots, X_N$ *be* $\{0,1\}$-*valued random variables, let* $t, \tau \in \mathbb{Z}^+$ *satisfy* $0 < t < \tau < N$. *Then*

$$\Pr\left[\sum_{i=1}^{N} X_i \geq \tau\right] \leq \frac{1}{\binom{\tau}{t}} \cdot \sum_{A \in \binom{[N]}{t}} \mathbb{E}\left[\prod_{i \in A} X_i\right].$$

We apply this theorem to obtain a concentration bound on t-wise almost-dependent random variables.

Theorem 10. *Let* $X_1, \ldots, X_n$ *be* $\{0,1\}$-*valued random variables that are* t-*wise* β-*dependent in Rényi∞-divergence with* $\mathbb{E}\left[\sum_i X_i\right] = \mu$.
  Then for any $\tau \in \mathbb{Z}^+$ *with* $\tau > \mu$,

$$\Pr\left[\sum_i X_i \geq \tau\right] \leq \beta \cdot \frac{\mu^k}{(\tau)_k},$$

where $k = \min(t, \lfloor \tau - \mu \rfloor)$ *and* $(\tau)_k = \tau \cdot (\tau - 1) \cdots (\tau - k + 1)$ *denotes the* k^{th} *falling factorial of* τ.

Proof. We invoke Theorem 9. For any $k < \tau$ and $k \leq t$, we have

$$\Pr\left[\sum_{i=1}^{N} X_i \geq \tau\right] \leq \binom{\tau}{k}^{-1} \cdot \sum_{A \in \binom{[n]}{k}} \mathbb{E}\left[\prod_{i \in A} X_i\right]$$

$$\leq \beta \cdot \binom{\tau}{k}^{-1} \cdot \sum_{A \in \binom{[n]}{k}} \prod_{i \in A} \mathbb{E}[X_i] \qquad \text{(by k-wise β-dependence)}$$

$$= \beta \cdot \binom{\tau}{k}^{-1} \cdot \sum_{1 \leq i_1 < \cdots < i_k \leq [n]} \prod_{j \in [k]} \mathbb{E}[X_{i_j}]$$

$$\leq \frac{\beta}{k!} \cdot \binom{\tau}{k}^{-1} \cdot \sum_{\text{distinct } i_1, \ldots, i_k} \prod_{j \in [k]} \mathbb{E}[X_{i_j}]$$

$$\leq \frac{\beta}{k!} \cdot \binom{\tau}{k}^{-1} \cdot \sum_{i_1, \ldots, i_k} \prod_{j \in [k]} \mathbb{E}[X_{i_j}]$$

$$= \frac{\beta}{k!} \cdot \binom{\tau}{k}^{-1} \cdot \mu^k$$

$$= \beta \cdot \frac{\mu^k}{(\tau)_k}.$$

This is minimized by picking $k \leq t$ as large as possible subject to $\tau - k + 1 \geq \mu$, i.e. $k = \min(t, \lfloor \tau - \mu + 1 \rfloor)$.

B Covering Number Bounds

Definition 18. *q-ary n-dimensional Hamming space is the metric space* $([q]^n, \Delta)$, *where* $\Delta(x,y) = |\{i : x_i \neq y_i\}|$.

Definition 19. *In a metric space* (X, d), *the ball of radius r centered at x, which we denote by* $B_r(x)$, *is the set* $\{y : d(x,y) \leq r\}$. *The sphere of radius r centered at x, which we denote by* $S_r(x)$, *is* $\{y : d(x,y) = r\}$.

Definition 20. *The q-ary entropy function is* $H_q(x) \overset{\text{def}}{=} x \log_q(q-1) - x \log_q(x) - (1-x) \log_q(1-x)$.

The following bounds are well-known.

Fact 11. *In q-ary n-dimensional Hamming space, we have* $q^{n \cdot H_q(r/n)} \cdot n^{-O(1)} \leq |B_r(x)| \leq q^{n \cdot H_q(r/n)}$ *for all* $r \leq n \cdot (1 - 1/q)$.

Fact 12. *In q-ary n-dimensional Hamming space, any ball of radius* $r_1 \leq n \cdot (1 - 1/q)$ *can be covered by* $\text{poly}(n) \cdot \ln(q) \cdot q^{n \cdot \left(H_q(r_1/n) - H_q(r_0/n)\right)}$ *balls of radius* r_0 *for any* $r_0 \leq r_1$.

References

[BGGZ19] Blocki, J., Gandikota, V., Grigorescu, E., Zhou, S.: Relaxed locally correctable codes in computationally bounded channels. In: 2019 IEEE International Symposium on Information Theory (ISIT), pp. 2414–2418. IEEE (2019)

[CCH+18] Canetti, R., Chen, Y., Holmgren, J., Lombardi, A., Rothblum, G.N., Rothblum, R.D.: Fiat-Shamir from simpler assumptions. IACR Cryptology ePrint Archive 2018:1004 (2018)

[CCR16] Canetti, R., Chen, Y., Reyzin, L.: On the correlation intractability of obfuscated pseudorandom functions. In: Kushilevitz, E., Malkin, T. (eds.) TCC 2016. LNCS, vol. 9562, pp. 389–415. Springer, Heidelberg (2016). https://doi.org/10.1007/978-3-662-49096-9_17

[CCRR18] Canetti, R., Chen, Y., Reyzin, L., Rothblum, R.D.: Fiat-Shamir and correlation intractability from strong KDM-secure encryption. In: Nielsen, J.B., Rijmen, V. (eds.) EUROCRYPT 2018. LNCS, vol. 10820, pp. 91–122. Springer, Cham (2018). https://doi.org/10.1007/978-3-319-78381-9_4

[CGH04] Canetti, R., Goldreich, O., Halevi, S.: The random oracle methodology, revisited. J. ACM **51**(4), 557–594 (2004)

[DGL04] Ding, Y.Z., Gopalan, P., Lipton, R.J.: Error correction against computationally bounded adversaries. Manuscript. Appeared initially as [Lip94] (2004)

[Eli57] Elias, P.: List decoding for noisy channels. Technical report 335, Research Laboratory of Electronics, MIT (1957)

[GR08] Guruswami, V., Rudra, A.: Explicit codes achieving list decoding capacity: error-correction with optimal redundancy. IEEE Trans. Inf. Theory **54**(1), 135–150 (2008)

[GR09]   Guruswami, V., Rudra, A.: Better binary list decodable codes via multi-level concatenation. IEEE Trans. Inf. Theory **55**(1), 19–26 (2009)

[GS16]   Guruswami, V., Smith, A.: Optimal rate code constructions for computationally simple channels. J. ACM (JACM) **63**(4), 1–37 (2016)

[Ham50] Hamming, R.W.: Error detecting and error correcting codes. Bell Syst. Tech. J. **29**(2), 147–160 (1950)

[HO08]   Hemenway, B., Ostrovsky, R.: Public-key locally-decodable codes. In: Wagner, D. (ed.) CRYPTO 2008. LNCS, vol. 5157, pp. 126–143. Springer, Heidelberg (2008). https://doi.org/10.1007/978-3-540-85174-5_8

[HOSW11] Hemenway, B., Ostrovsky, R., Strauss, M.J., Wootters, M.: Public key locally decodable codes with short keys. In: Goldberg, L.A., Jansen, K., Ravi, R., Rolim, J.D.P. (eds.) APPROX/RANDOM -2011. LNCS, vol. 6845, pp. 605–615. Springer, Heidelberg (2011). https://doi.org/10.1007/978-3-642-22935-0_51

[KNR09] Kaplan, E., Naor, M., Reingold, O.: Derandomized constructions of k-wise (almost) independent permutations. Algorithmica **55**(1), 113–133 (2009)

[KRR17] Kalai, Y.T., Rothblum, G.N., Rothblum, R.D.: From obfuscation to the security of Fiat-Shamir for proofs. In: Katz, J., Shacham, H. (eds.) CRYPTO 2017. LNCS, vol. 10402, pp. 224–251. Springer, Cham (2017). https://doi.org/10.1007/978-3-319-63715-0_8

[Lip94] Lipton, R.J.: A new approach to information theory. In: Enjalbert, P., Mayr, E.W., Wagner, K.W. (eds.) STACS 1994. LNCS, vol. 775, pp. 699–708. Springer, Heidelberg (1994). https://doi.org/10.1007/3-540-57785-8_183

[LL14]   Linial, N., Luria, Z.: Chernoff's inequality - a very elementary proof (2014)

[MPSW10] Micali, S., Peikert, C., Sudan, M., Wilson, D.A.: Optimal error correction for computationally bounded noise. IEEE Trans. Inf. Theory **56**(11), 5673–5680 (2010)

[OPS07] Ostrovsky, R., Pandey, O., Sahai, A.: Private locally decodable codes. In: Arge, L., Cachin, C., Jurdziński, T., Tarlecki, A. (eds.) ICALP 2007. LNCS, vol. 4596, pp. 387–398. Springer, Heidelberg (2007). https://doi.org/10.1007/978-3-540-73420-8_35

[PS19]   Peikert, C., Shiehian, S.: Noninteractive Zero knowledge for np from (plain) learning with errors. In: Boldyreva, A., Micciancio, D. (eds.) CRYPTO 2019. LNCS, vol. 11692, pp. 89–114. Springer, Cham (2019). https://doi.org/10.1007/978-3-030-26948-7_4

[SS16]   Shaltiel, R., Silbak, J.: Explicit list-decodable codes with optimal rate for computationally bounded channels. In: Approximation, Randomization, and Combinatorial Optimization. Algorithms and Techniques (APPROX/RANDOM 2016). Schloss Dagstuhl-Leibniz-Zentrum fuer Informatik (2016)

[SS20]   Shaltiel, R., Silbak, J.: Explicit uniquely decodable codes for space bounded channels that achieve list-decoding capacity. Electron. Colloq. Comput. Complex. (ECCC) **27**, 47 (2020)

[Woz58] Wozencraft, J.M.: List decoding. Q. Progr. Rep. **48**, 90–95 (1958)

New Techniques in Replica Encodings
with Client Setup

Rachit Garg[1(✉)], George Lu[1], and Brent Waters[1,2]

[1] University of Texas at Austin, Austin, USA
rachit0596@gmail.com, {gclu,bwaters}@cs.utexas.edu
[2] NTT Research, Palo Alto, USA

Abstract. A proof of replication system is a cryptographic primitive that allows a server (or group of servers) to prove to a client that it is dedicated to storing multiple copies or replicas of a file. Until recently, all such protocols required fine-grained timing assumptions on the amount of time it takes for a server to produce such replicas.

Damgård, Ganesh, and Orlandi (CRYPTO' 19) [11] proposed a novel notion that we will call proof of replication with client setup. Here, a client first operates with secret coins to generate the replicas for a file. Such systems do not inherently have to require fine-grained timing assumptions. At the core of their solution to building proofs of replication with client setup is an abstraction called replica encodings. Briefly, these comprise a private coin scheme where a client algorithm given a file m can produce an encoding σ. The encodings have the property that, given any encoding σ, one can decode and retrieve the original file m. Secondly, if a server has significantly less than $n \cdot |m|$ bit of storage, it cannot reproduce n encodings. The authors give a construction of encodings from ideal permutations and trapdoor functions.

In this work, we make three central contributions.

- Our first contribution is that we discover and demonstrate that the security argument put forth by [11] is fundamentally flawed. Briefly, the security argument makes assumptions on the attacker's storage behavior that does not capture general attacker strategies. We demonstrate this issue by constructing a trapdoor permutation which is secure assuming indistinguishability obfuscation, serves as a counterexample to their claim (for the parameterization stated).
- In our second contribution we show that the DGO construction is actually secure in the ideal permutation model (or ideal cipher model) and the random oracle (or random function) model from any trapdoor permutation when parameterized correctly. In particular, when the number of rounds in the construction is equal to $\lambda \cdot n \cdot b$ where λ is the security parameter, n is the number of replicas and b is the number of blocks. To do so we build up a proof approach from the ground up that accounts for general attacker storage behavior where we create an analysis technique that we call "sequence-then-switch".

R. Garg and G. Lu—Supported by NSF CNS-1908611, CNS-1414082, Packard Foundation Fellowship, and Simons Investigator Award.

R. Pass and K. Pietrzak (Eds.): TCC 2020, LNCS 12552, pp. 550–583, 2020.
https://doi.org/10.1007/978-3-030-64381-2_20

– Finally, we show a new construction that is provably secure in the random oracle model. Thus requiring less structure on the ideal function.

1 Introduction

In a proof of replication system [5,6], a user wants to distribute a file m and ensure that a server or group of servers will dedicate the resources to storing multiple copies or replicas of it. That is, the server should either receive or generate n replicas $\sigma_1, \ldots, \sigma_n$ where the file m can be efficiently decoded from any single replica. In the original notion of proofs of replication, a server could take a file m as input and independently generate all the replicas $\sigma_1, \ldots, \sigma_n$. Later it could prove possession if challenged. Since the introduction of this concept, several such solutions [7,9,16,17,25] have emerged.

However, in these solutions, there exist a tension that stems from the following attack. Consider a non-compliant server that stores just a single copy of m. When challenged to prove possession of replicas, it on the fly, generates $\sigma_1, \ldots, \sigma_n$ using the legitimate generation algorithm and proceeds to prove replication using the ephemeral values as though it were storing these replicas all along.

It is easy to see that achieving meaningful security against such an attack is impossible without imposing a concrete time-bound between when a server is challenged and when it must answer. The setting of this time-bound must be coupled with an understanding of how long it takes an honest system to retrieve the replicas and produce a proof and balanced against how fast a highly provisioned server might take to produce the replicas from scratch. This balancing act creates a certain tension in that more costly replica generation will help security, but also imposes a higher burden on initiation. Moreover, other issues can arise in the context of a more extensive system. For example, if audit challenges come out at a predictable time (e.g., daily), then a cheating server could start generating the response ahead of time.

To address these issues, Damgård, Ganesh, and Orlandi [11] proposed a novel notion that we will call proof of replication with client setup. In this notion, a client that wishes to store a file m will generate replicas $\sigma_1, \ldots, \sigma_n$, along with a (short) public verification key vk. The system will have the properties that (1) one can reconstruct the file from any replica along with the verification key, and (2) a server can prove possession of the replicas to any client that holds the verification key. Unlike the previous systems, proof of replication with client setup need not require fine-grained timing assumptions as a server will not be able to regenerate the replicas from only the message m and vk. Indeed the security definition says (informally) that any poly-time server that devotes significantly fewer resources than n times message length will not be able to pass the possession test.

The solution proposed in [11] combines two high-level ingredients. The first is a proof of retrievability system as proposed in prior work [8,12,29]. Roughly, if a server executes a proof of retrievability for data d with a client, this means that now, the server was capable of reconstructing d. However, a proof of retrievability in and of itself gives no guarantee about the amount of resources required to store d.

Second, the authors introduce a notion of a replica encoding. A replica encoding system consists of three algorithms: $(\mathsf{rSetup}, \mathsf{rEnc}, \mathsf{rDec})$. The setup algorithm on input, a security parameter κ and the maximum number of replicas n of a scheme, outputs a public and secret key pair as $(\mathsf{pk}, \mathsf{sk}) \leftarrow \mathsf{rSetup}(1^\kappa, 1^n)$. The encoding algorithm takes as input the secret key and a message m to produce an encoding as $y \leftarrow \mathsf{rEnc}(\mathsf{sk}, m)$. Finally, the decoding algorithm takes as input an encoding y and the public key to retrieve the message as $m \leftarrow \mathsf{rDec}(\mathsf{pk}, y)$ or outputs $\bot$ to indicate failure. The algorithms are randomized, and the encoding procedure can be run multiple times to produce multiple encodings. The correctness of the scheme dictates that if one encodes any message m under a secret key and then decodes it under the corresponding public key, m will be decoded.

To capture security, we will consider a soundness game which uses a two-stage attacker $(\mathcal{A}_1, \mathcal{A}_2)$. In the first stage, $\mathcal{A}_1$ will be given a challenger-generated public key pk and reply with a message m. It is then given n encodings generated by the challenger as $y_1, \ldots, y_n$. The attacker outputs a state variable state, which we will generally think of as being smaller than $|m| \cdot n$. At the second phase, the algorithm $\mathcal{A}_2$ is given the input state and is tasked with outputting guesses $\tilde{y}_1, \ldots, \tilde{y}_n$. The security property intuitively states that if the size of the storage $|\mathsf{state}|$ is significantly less than $v \cdot |m|$, then the number of i where $y_i = \tilde{y}_i$ will be less than v. That is, the attacker cannot do much better than simply storing a set of values y_i.

Damgård, Ganesh, and Orlandi showed how a natural compilation of existing proof of retrievability schemes along with replica encodings gave way to proofs of storage with client setup. Also, they provided a candidate construction for replica encodings from trapdoor permutations under the ideal cipher model and the random oracle model. We turn our attention to these.

The DGO Construction: We now outline (a slight variant of the) construction for [11], which is given in the ideal permutation and the random oracle model. We remark that the DGO construction itself is an adaptation of one of the "hourglass" schemes of van Dijk et al. [30]. The building blocks will consists of a trapdoor permutation $\mathsf{f}, \mathsf{f}^{-1}$, along with the ideal cipher $\mathsf{T}, \mathsf{T}^{-1}$, and a random oracle H. We again let κ be the security parameter and let $\lambda = \lambda(\kappa)$ be the output length of the trapdoor permutation as well as the block length of an ideal permutation $\mathsf{T} : \{0, 1\}^\lambda \to \{0, 1\}^\lambda$. For pedagogical purposes, we will assume for the sketch below that messages consist of λ bits, but in our main body, we consider the more realistic case of many block messages.

The setup algorithm simply chooses a TDP public/secret key pair as $\mathsf{KeyGen}(1^\kappa)$ outputs $(\mathsf{pk}, \mathsf{sk})$ where KeyGen is the trapdoor permutation key generation algorithm. The public and secret key pair of the TDP serve as the keypair of the replicated encoding scheme.

The encoding algorithm $\mathsf{rEnc}(\mathsf{sk}, m)$ takes as input the TDP secret key and message m. It first chooses a string $\rho \xleftarrow{R} \{0, 1\}^\kappa$. It then initializes a value

$Y_0 = m \oplus H(\rho)$ where H is modeled as a random oracle function. Then for $j = 1$ to r rounds it computes $Y_j = f^{-1}(sk, T(Y_{j-1}))$ where r is the number of rounds, which grows linearly with the number of replicas. The encoding is output as (Y_r, ρ).

Finally, the decoding algorithm $rDec(pk, y = (Y_r, \rho))$ recovers a message as follows. For setting j from $r - 1$ down to 0 compute $Y_j = T^{-1}(f(pk, Y_{j+1}))$. Then output $m = Y_0 \oplus H(\rho)$.

The fact that the decoding step recovers the message follows straightforwardly from the correctness of the trapdoor permutation and ideal permutation. We also observe that it is publicly computable since it uses the public key and forward direction of the trapdoor permutation.

1.1 Our Contributions

We make three core contributions to this area:

1. Our first contribution is that we discover and demonstrate that the security argument put forth by [11] is fundamentally flawed. The security argument makes implicit assumptions about an attacker's behavior which are not generally true. More specifically, in the security game applied to the DGO construction (in the ideal permutation and random oracle model) an attacker works in two phases. The first stage attacker $\mathcal{A}_1$ receives the replicas, can make several queries to the ideal permutation and then records some state state of limited size. This state state is passed to a stage two attacker $\mathcal{A}_2$ which can make further permutation queries and attempts to reconstruct the queries. In general a first stage attacker can apply arbitrary strategies to breaking the scheme so long as it poly-time and state state is sufficiently small. However, the proof argument of [11] assume that the ideal permutation queries made by the attacker will be "uniquely stored". Roughly, they will argue that a query output bit will either be stored explicitly or not at all. This discounts the possibility of an attacker strategy such as making several oracle queries and storing the XOR of all the outputs together.

   We demonstrate that the above error manifests in a false theorem statement in [11]. The authors claim that the scheme is secure for *any* trapdoor permutation (TDP) if $r = \lambda \cdot n$ rounds are applied when doing n encodings of b blocks with security parameter λ. (I.e. Claim the number of rounds does not need to scale with b.) We provide an explicit counterexample to this claim in Sect. 7. We give a TDP that is secure assuming indistinguishability obfuscation, but for which the scheme is attackable using these parameters. The attacker strategy actually works by XORing several query values together and is thus directly tied to the flaw in the security proof. There does not appear to be any simple "fix" to the security argument of [11] as we will see that addressing general attacker storage strategies comprises the core difficulty of proving security.

We also note that an explicit "partitioning assumption" appears in the security definition of [30] for "hourglass schemes" where the authors conjecture (but do not prove) that it seems implausible that mixing together two representations can give an advantage to an attacker. Although we do not do so formally, we believe that our counterexample can be adapted to the work of [30] as well (at least if one considered the scheme for general trapdoor permutations) and demonstrates the danger of making assumptions that restrict adversarial strategies.

2. For our second contribution we show that the DGO construction is actually secure when parameterized correctly. In particular, when the number of rounds is equal to $\lambda \cdot n \cdot b$. To do so we need to build up a proof approach from the ground up that accounts for general attacker storage behavior. We first develop an analysis technique that we call "sequence-then-switch". We show how in this framework, we can prove security against an attacker that arbitrarily assigns state. In particular, we show how to analyze the security of a close variant of the [11] construction in the ideal permutation and random oracle model. In addition, we give an explicit construction of a trapdoor permutation using indistinguishability obfuscation which allows for an attack strategy not covered by their restricted model, showing the [11] construction as given is in fact explicitly *insecure* against general adversaries.

3. The prior construction and proof relies on the ideal permutation model. A perhaps better goal would be to have a construction secure in the random oracle or random function model as this assumes less structure on the ideal object. Typically, this is dealt with by building a random permutation from a function using a Feistel network and showing that this is "indifferentiable" in the indifferentiability framework of Mauer et al. [22]. Prior works have shown this for 14 [20] and then 8 round Feistel [10]. However, Ristenpart, Shacham, and Shrimpton [27] show that the framework does not compose for multi-round games. Since the above construction relies on a multi-round game, proof from an ideal permutation cannot be reduced to a proof to an ideal function.

We give a new construction that relies only on the ideal function model and analyze its security. Our construction uses the random function to embed a Feistel like structure into the construction. However, instead of arguing in the indifferentiablity framework, we provide direct proof of security, which bypasses any composability issues. In both proofs, we allow the attacker to assign its storage arbitrarily.

1.2   Our Techniques

We begin by describing our analysis for the first construction using a TDP and ideal permutation. We focus on the construction producing many replicas on a single block, as described in the introduction for simplicity. Also, for simplicity, we consider the particular case where an attacker that asks for n replicas in the first stage and wants to produce all n of these replicas, but we significantly less than $n \cdot \lambda$ storage. In particular consider an adversary with state of length

$n \cdot \lambda - n \cdot \omega(\log \kappa)$ bits of storage for security parameter κ and block length λ. Our central idea is to organize the proof into two parts where we first show that any storage bounded $\mathcal{A}_2$ must make "sequential" oracle queries on at least one replica. Then we show that on this particular replica, how one can swap out permutation output for another.

1. **Sequentiality:** In our security game, the challenger first creates n replicas of m. To create the i-th replica by choosing ρ_i randomly. It sets $Y_0^{(i)} = m \oplus H(\rho_i)$. Then for $j = 1$ to r rounds it computes $Y_j^{(i)} = f^{-1}(sk, T(Y_{j-1}^{(i)}))$. The encoding is output to $\mathcal{A}_1$ as $(Y_r^{(i)}, \rho_i)$ for $i \in [n]$. The attacker $\mathcal{A}_1$ receives the encodings, makes some more oracles queries before producing state of $n \cdot \lambda - n \cdot \omega(\log \kappa)$ bits and passing it to $\mathcal{A}_2$.

   Let's examine the behavior of $\mathcal{A}_2$ whose job it is to output the encodings using the state plus oracle queries. We say that $\mathcal{A}_2$ "queries sequentially" on replica i if for all $j \in [0, r-1]$ it queries the oracle T on $Y_j^{(i)}$ before it queries the oracle on $Y_{j+1}^{(i)}$. (We will think of outputting the encoding $Y_r^{(i)}$ at the end as implicitly querying on the final value.) That is for $\mathcal{A}_2$ to query sequentially on replica i it must both make all $r + 1$ oracle queries and make them in (relative) order. However, there could be many other queries outside the replica chain interspersed between $Y_j^{(i)}$ and $Y_{j+1}^{(i)}$.

   We will first argue that except with negligible probability whenever $\mathcal{A}_2$ produces all the encodings, it queries sequentially on at least one replica. Observe that we cannot hope to say that it queried sequentially on all replicas as state could directly store several of the replica encodings, which allows the algorithm to bypass any additional queries related to that replica.

   To prove this, we first define and prove a useful matching pairs lemma. Consider an algorithm $\mathcal{B}$ that takes as input a string advice of length $n \cdot \lambda - n \cdot \omega(\log \kappa)$ and gets access to a string oracle access to a randomly chosen permutation $T(\cdot), T^{-1}$ of block length λ. The goal of $\mathcal{B}$ is to provide n *distinct* pairs (x_i, y_i) such that $T(x_i) = y_i$, but *without* querying the oracle a either x_i nor y_i. Thus $\mathcal{B}$ can make several oracle queries on many values; however, once a query is made on some x, it spoils using x as a value from one of the pairs. Note that to win in this game, $\mathcal{B}$ needs to produce the pairs— not just distinguish them from random. Also observe that $\mathcal{B}$ can use advice to help it win this game. For example, advice might encode the several pairs. We prove that no attacker $\mathcal{B}$ that makes a polynomially bounded number of queries can win in this game by a simple application of the union bound. Consider a fixed value of an advice string a—that is a is fixed before the permutation is chosen. We show that the probability of $\mathcal{B}(a)$ winning is at most $\frac{\text{poly}(\lambda)}{2^{n\lambda}}$. Then by the union bound the probability that there exists *any* string a which it could win with is at most $2^{n \cdot \lambda - n \cdot \omega(\log \kappa)} \cdot \frac{\text{poly}(\lambda)}{2^{n\lambda}}$ which is negligible in λ.

   Now we need to show that an attacker that wins but is not sequentially querying on any replica will break our matching pairs game. We consider $(\mathcal{A}_1, \mathcal{A}_2)$ that does this. Let's think of the algorithm pair as deterministic. (If they are randomized for each security parameter, we can fix their coins that maximize success probability.) We construct an algorithm $\mathcal{B}$ along with the process of determining an advice string that does this. Conceptually we can think of a preprocessing algorithm $\mathcal{B}'$ that generates the advice. $\mathcal{B}'$ will first run $\mathcal{A}_1$, which makes several queries and then produce state. It then runs $\mathcal{A}_2$ on state. If $\mathcal{A}_2$ either did not produce all the replica encodings or it did sequentially query on some replica i, then abort. However, if it did not make sequential queries on all replicas, then there must be values $j_1, \ldots, j_n$ where $\mathcal{A}_2$ made an oracle query on $Y_{j_i}^{(i)}$ (or $f(\mathsf{pk}, Y_{j_i}^{(i)})$), but had not yet made a query on $Y_{j_i-1}^{(i)}$. Let $q_1, \ldots, q_n$ be the indices of the queries (ordered chronologically) for which this occurs. Note the number of queries $\mathcal{A}_2$ can make is polynomial in κ, but in general, it could be much more than $r \cdot n \cdot \lambda$. The preprocessing algorithm will package its advice string as state along with $j_1, \ldots, j_n$ and $q_1, \ldots, q_n$. Importantly, the size of this information is bounded by $\lg(\mathsf{poly}(\kappa))$ for some polynomial poly since n, r, and the number of replicas is polynomially bounded. This means that if state is of size $n \cdot \lambda - n \cdot \omega(\log \kappa)$, then the advice string will be within $n \cdot \lambda - \omega(\log \kappa)$.

We now consider algorithm $\mathcal{B}$, which receives the advice string. $\mathcal{B}$ will run $\mathcal{A}_2$ with the following modifications. Suppose $\mathcal{A}_2$ makes its q-th query where $q = q_i$ for some i. This means that $\mathcal{A}_2$ is querying on $Y_{j_i}^{(i)}$, but had not yet made a query on $Y_{j_i-1}^{(i)}$. At this point $\mathcal{B}$ determines $Y_{j_i-1}^{(i)}$ by querying $Y_1^{(i)} = f^{-1}(\mathsf{sk}, \mathsf{T}(Y_0^{(i)}))$ up to $Y_{j_i-1}^{(i)} = f^{-1}(\mathsf{sk}, \mathsf{T}(Y_{j_i-2}^{(i)}))$. It then submits $(Y_{j_i-1}^{(i)}, f(\mathsf{pk}, Y_{j_i}^{(i)}))$ as one of its matching pairs noting that neither $\mathsf{T}(Y_{j_i-1}^{(i)})$ nor $\mathsf{T}^{-1}(f(\mathsf{pk}, Y_{j_i}^{(i)}))$ were made before. It can also continue to run $\mathcal{A}_2$ without making either of these queries to the oracles since it already knows the answers to them. As this process proceeds, $\mathcal{B}$ will eventually recover n such pairs which breaks our matching pairs lemma and arrives at a contradiction.

2. **Switching:**

   Once sequentiality is established, we will proceed to argue that the adversary must still be sequential with good probability even when we "switch" the random oracle output of some $Y_j^{(\gamma)}$ to a random value only for $\mathcal{A}_2$, allowing us to embed a trapdoor permutation challenge.

   In more detail, we now consider a new switched game that is almost equivalent to the prior one. In the switched game the challenger first chooses r random values $A_{i,b} \in \{0, 1\}^\lambda$ for $j \in [1, r], b \in \{0, 1\}$ along with a bit string $x \in \{0, 1\}$. It programs the oracle T such that $Y_j^{(\gamma)} = A_{i,b}$. This game can be shown to be almost equivalent to the previous one.

   Next, we consider a game where the challenger answers queries according to a string x with $\mathcal{A}_1$, but switches to using a string x' (and keeps everything else the same) when responding to $\mathcal{A}_2$. The challenger chooses the string x' such that the output state given by $\mathcal{A}_1$ is the same as if the queries are answered according to x' in the first phase. The attacker is considered to win only if it would produce sequential queries *both* for when x was used with $\mathcal{A}_2$ and when x' was used with $\mathcal{A}_2$.

With high probability, such an x' will exist from the fact that $|\text{state}| \leq n \cdot \lambda - \omega(\log \kappa)$ and r is set to be $n \cdot \lambda$. We emphasize that to make this argument we do not make any further assumptions on how $\mathcal{A}_1$ assigns state other than the bound on the size. We can then use the heavy row lemma [24] to argue that if an attacker wins with probability ϵ in the previous game, it wins with probability $\approx \epsilon$ in this game. We note that the game takes exponential time to find such an x', but this is not an issue as the closeness lemma is information-theoretic.

Finally, in order to embed a TDP challenge, we need to move to a security game that can be efficiently simulated. While it might take exponential time to find x' from x above, we observe that this is not necessary. Instead, we can embed the challenge from just knowing the shortest common prefix of x and x'. Moreover, given x, we can simply guess what the prefix is with a $\frac{1}{r}$ loss. Thus we move to a final game where the challenger simply chooses a random value j and a random permutation T in the first phase and then replaces the oracle output of $Y_j^{(i)}$ with a random R in the second phase. The attacker wins if it queries $\mathsf{f}^{-1}(\mathsf{sk}, R)$. A simple reduction then shows that any attacker that wins in this game breaks the TDP security.

Extending to the Ideal Function Model. We can now return to our goal of building a secure construction by replacing the ideal permutation model with a random oracle model. As argued earlier, doing so is desirable as an ideal function imposes less structure and appears to be a less risky heuristic. Our solution will build upon the analysis principles established above, but proving security involves more complications.

We begin by sketching out the encoding construction. In this setting, we will have a TDP in the domain λ bits and use a random oracle T' that outputs λ bits. We will use blocks of length 2λ, and for this sketch, focus on the particular case where each replica consists of a single block message.

The setup algorithm again chooses a TDP public/secret key pair as $\mathsf{KeyGen}(1^\kappa) \to (\mathsf{pk}, \mathsf{sk})$ as before. The encoding algorithm $\mathsf{rEnc}(\mathsf{sk}, m)$ takes as input the TDP secret key and message $m \in \{0,1\}^{2\lambda}$. It first chooses a string $\rho \xleftarrow{R} \{0,1\}^\kappa$. It then initializes values $Y_0 = L(m \oplus \mathsf{H}(\rho))$ and $Y_1 = R(m \oplus \mathsf{H}(\rho))$ where H is a random oracle that produces an 2λ bit output and L, R are functions that take the left and right halves. Then on rounds j from 2 to r compute Y_j from Y_{j-1} and Y_{j-2} as

$$Y_j = \mathsf{f}^{-1}(\mathsf{sk}, Y_{j-2} \oplus \mathsf{T}'(Y_{j-1})).$$

The replica encoding value is 2λ bits long and consists of the last two values as $Y_{r-1}||Y_r$. The decoding algorithm rDec works backward down the Feistel structure to recover the message.

In this setting, we want to prove that in the security game, an attacker with $n \cdot 2\lambda - n \cdot \omega(\log \kappa)$ cannot produce n replica encodings. (The extra factor of two is solely due to blocks being 2λ bits here.)

Our proof will follow in the same theme of showing that there must be a form of sequential querying made on at least one replica. However, the new structure of the construction presents additional complications. For example, we could imagine an attacker $\mathcal{A}_1$, which stores all the values Y_j^i for some j. This is possible since storing these only take $n\lambda$ bits, and our assumption is only that the storage is less than $2n\lambda$ bits. On the one hand, it is unclear how the attacker can leverage storing all these values because one needs consecutive values (e.g., $Y_j^{(i)}$, $Y_{j+1}^{(i)}$) to propagate further. And, storing n different consecutive pairs requires $2n\lambda$ bits of storage. On the other hand, the attacker can store these means at the very least we need a new notion of sequentiality.

For our new notion of sequentiality, we say that the queries to replica i meet our requirements if the longest common subsequence of the queries made and $Y_1^{(i)}, Y_2^{(i)}, \ldots, Y_r^{(i)}$ is of length at least $r-3$. Intuitively, this is close to our original notion but allows for a little skipping. To prove this form of sequentiality, we invoke a random function analog of our matching pairs lemma from before. The reduction to matching pairs follows in a similar spirit to before but requires a more nuanced case analysis.

Once that is in place, our proof proceeds analogously, but again with more nuances and complications arising from the fact that we only can guarantee the weaker form of longest common subsequence.

The Proposed Construction Is Round Optimal. We now consider the general case of a message having b blocks and give intuition that our construction is round optimal up to constant factors. We construct a secure trapdoor permutation scheme from indistinguishability obfuscation which gives an insecure replica encoding scheme for any number of rounds $\notin \Omega(b \cdot n)$ (i.e. $\in o(b \cdot n)$). Incidentally, this also shows that the construction provided by [11], which claims to only requires $O(n)$ rounds, is insecure against general adversaries.

We provide the intuition for our construction by considering the ideal VBB notion of obfuscation. The overall idea is to construct a trapdoor permutation family where we can amortize the 'state' space required to invert multiple independent instances. We will consider our permutations to be on domain $\{0,1\}^\lambda$. If we assume we have VBB obfuscation, then consider a program that takes in b many inputs $\{y_i\}_{i\in b}$ where $y_i \in \{0,1\}^\lambda$ and an advice string also in $\{0,1\}^\lambda$ and outputs the preimages of the messages $\{x_i = \mathsf{f}^{-1}(\mathsf{sk}, y_i)\}_{i\in b}$ iff the advice string that was input was equal to $\bigoplus_{i\in b} x_i$. The program has the secret key hardcorded and simply computes x_i and makes the check against the advice string and outputs $\{x_i\}_{i\in b}$ if the check succeeds. The VBB obfuscation of this program is then posted in the public parameters and provides a way for the adversary to compress $b \cdot \lambda$ bits to λ bits and still preserve information. Thus an adversary with outputting $r \cdot \lambda$ bits can recompute the replica from storing $o(b \cdot n\lambda)$ information. This would violate the security if we proved soundness for the same parameters as our scheme. A formal treatment is presented in Sect. 7.

1.3   Additional Prior Work

Proofs of Retrievability:
Proofs of retrievability guarantee to a verifier that a server is storing all of client's data. The notion was formalized in [21], where, in an audit protocol the verifier stores a (short) verification key locally and interacts with the server to enforce accountability of the storage provider. If the server can pass an audit, then there exists an extractor algorithm, that must be able to extract the file on interaction with the server. There are different constructions for this primitive, [8,12,29]. The construction of [29] showed how to do this in the random oracle model that allow public verifiability.

Proofs of Space: Proof of space are interactive protocols between a prover (server) and a verifier (client) that guarantee that a prover has dedicated a specific amount of space. It guarantees that it would be more expensive for a dishonest prover to deviate from the honest protocol. They were introduced in [14] and have been further studied in [1,26]. Compared to a proof of replicated storage, they have an additional requirement of communication being succinct between a prover and verifier and are usually studied in the public-key setting.

Other examples of works which are different from proofs of space but enforce storage requirements similar to our soundness game on the prover are storage-enforcing commitments [19], hourglass scheme [30] and the model of computation considered by [15].

Proofs of Replicated Storage:
The formal treatment of proofs of replicated storage was given by [9,11,16]. The idea was introduced in [5,6] where they proposed Filecoin, a decentralized storage network that performs consensus using proofs of replication. Recently, [7,9,16,17,25] have given constructions for proof of replication using timing assumptions (encoding process is much slower so that a server cannot replicate data on demand). On the other hand, the scheme of [11] is not based on timing assumptions and considers the protocol with a client setup. They introduce the notion of a replica encoding that can be combined with a public verifiable proof of retrievability [29] to give a proof of replicated storage. Please see [11] for other related works such as proof of data replication.

Hourglass Scheme:
Our constructions and the construction from [11] are reminiscent of the hourglass scheme of [30]. Our construction in the ideal permutation model differs from the RSA based hourglass function of [30] in explicitly ensuring that the encoding blocks are uniformly distributed by applying a random oracle H and increasing the number of rounds suggested by their scheme. Because of our explicit encoding function, we do not need to make a partitioning assumption in our security proof. The brief analysis of their scheme gives a similar intuition to the security as used by [11] and gives a construction for the number of rounds independent of the number of blocks. But as we see in Sect. 7, this intuition does not hold true for general adversaries.

Technique Similarities in Literature:
Some of our techniques have a flavor that appears in the study of pebbling strategies on random oracle graphs and the memory hardness literature [2–4, 13, 15]. Pebbling strategies on random oracle graphs look at the amount of resources (the list of random-oracle calls) made by the adversary and help in proving complexity lower-bounds on the resources. Our notion of "sequentiality" is similar to the notion of a legal "ex-post-facto pebbling" on a directed acyclic graph (see [4] for details). The reductions there are proven using a core lemma which looks at a legal ex-post-facto pebbling given hints; Lemma 1 of [4, 13, 15] which is similar to our core lemmas for proving sequentiality Lemma 1. Interestingly, [2] considered adversaries that can store secret shares of the random oracle queries (such as a xor) and introduced the notion of an entangled pebbling game. They look at the resource of "Cumulative Memory Complexity (CMC)" and constructed an example to show that such strategies can help the adversary reduce it's resource requirement. The followup work of [3] improved on their lower bounds results for any general adversarial strategy.

1.4   Concurrent Work

After completing our work we learned of a concurrent and independent work of Moran and Wichs [23]. They introduce a variant of replica encodings which they call incompressible encodings, and proceed to provide constructions in the random-oracle model (and the common random string model) using the Decisional Composite Residuosity or Learning with Errors assumptions. Their construction utilizes some new techniques to apply lossiness to construct said encodings. In addition, they introduce an additional "big-key" application for intrusion resilience which applies to our constructions and proofs as well.

At a very high level, our work depends on the general assumption of trapdoor permutations, whereas they use the specific number theoretic assumptions of Decisional Composite Residuosity and Learning with Errors. Comparing our construction instantiated with RSA trapdoor permutation to their DCR construction, their construction appears to be more practically efficient from a computational perspective due to the round complexity required for our construction, however, ours makes tighter use of space for small "s" values used in the DCR construction. An interesting future direction could be to explore concrete space and computational efficiency tradeoffs for increasing the s parameter in their DCR construction.

Similar to us, Moran and Wichs discovered foundational issues in the proof arguments of [11]. In a personal communication Wichs noted that there is a simple heuristic counterexample to the claim of [11] if one uses the heuristic of ideal obfuscation. We subsequently developed a counterexample based on the concrete assumption of indistinguishability obfuscation that we added as Sect. 7 of our work.

2   Preliminaries

Notation. These notations are used consistently throughout the text.
We use κ to denote the security parameter. $y \leftarrow \mathcal{B}(x)$ denotes the output of the algorithm $\mathcal{B}$ when we run x on it. A negligible function $\mathsf{negl}(x)$ is a function such that for every positive integer c, there exists an integer N_c such that for all $x > N_c$, $\mathsf{negl}(x) < \frac{1}{x^c}$. $[n]$ denotes the set $\{1, 2, \ldots, n\}$ and $[a, b]$ denotes the interval between a and b inclusive. $y \xleftarrow{R} \mathcal{D}$ implies that we are uniformly sampling y from a domain set $\mathcal{D}$. We say an adversary or an algorithm $\mathcal{A}$ is probabilistic poly time (PPT) if there is a polynomial $\mathsf{poly}(\cdot)$ such that for all κ, $\mathcal{A}$ will halt in $\leq \mathsf{poly}(\kappa)$ time in expectation on any input of length κ.

A trapdoor permutation is defined as a collection of three PPT algorithms $\mathsf{KeyGen}(.), \mathsf{f}(.,.), \mathsf{f}^{-1}(.,.)$. $i\mathcal{O}(\kappa, C)$ is an indistinguishability obfuscator for a circuit class $\{\mathcal{C}_\kappa\}$ and security parameter κ. A puncturable pseudorandom function family (PPRF) on domain $\mathcal{D}_\kappa$ and range $\mathcal{R}_\kappa$ is defined using a set of algorithms $(\mathsf{PPRF.KeyGen}, \mathsf{PPRF.Eval}, \mathsf{PPRF.Puncture})$. Due to space limitations, please find the complete definitions in the full version of the paper [18].

3   Defining Replica Encoding

A Replica Encoding scheme - ReplicaEncoding is defined as a tuple of algorithms $(\mathsf{rSetup}, \mathsf{rEnc}, \mathsf{rDec})$, where rSetup takes in the security parameter denoted by 1^κ and the maximum number of replicas a client wishes to replicate denoted by 1^n and outputs a public key secret key pair $(\mathsf{pk}, \mathsf{sk})$, rEnc is a randomized algorithm which takes a message $m \in \{0, 1\}^*$, a secret key sk and outputs a replica encoding. rDec is a deterministic algorithm that takes as input a public key pk, a replica encoding and outputs a message m. Formally,

$$(\mathsf{pk}, \mathsf{sk}) \leftarrow \mathsf{rSetup}(1^\kappa, 1^n), \quad y \leftarrow \mathsf{rEnc}(\mathsf{sk}, m), \quad m \leftarrow \mathsf{rDec}(\mathsf{pk}, y).$$

Definition 1. *A tuple (rSetup,rEnc,rDec) is a replica encoding if the following holds:*

- *Correctness: For any choice of coins of* rSetup*, the probability of incorrect decoding is*

$$\forall n, m, \quad \Pr\left[\begin{array}{l} (\mathsf{pk}, \mathsf{sk}) \leftarrow \mathsf{rSetup}(1^\kappa, 1^n) \\ \mathsf{rDec}(\mathsf{pk}, \mathsf{rEnc}(\mathsf{sk}, m)) \neq m \end{array} \right] \leq \mathsf{negl}(\kappa)$$

where the probability is over the coins of rEnc [1].

---

[1] There exists a generic method for converting a scheme with negligible correctness error into a perfectly correct scheme. To do so augment the rEnc algorithm so that it first produces the encoding. Then the new rEnc algorithm run the deterministic rDec algorithm on the encoding to check that the message was recovered. If not, output the message in the clear and a flag bit indicating that the message is output in plain instead of the encoding. This adds a negligible hit in the security as opposed to the correctness.

- *Length of the encoding scheme is denoted by a function* $\mathsf{len}(\cdot, \cdot) : \mathbb{N} \times \mathbb{N} \to \mathbb{N}$ *that takes in the security parameter and the length of the message and outputs the length of the encoding, formally for any* κ, m, *choice of coins of* rSetup,

$$\forall \kappa, m, \quad \Pr \left[\begin{array}{l} (\mathsf{pk}, \mathsf{sk}) \leftarrow \mathsf{rSetup}(1^\kappa, 1^n) \\ \mathsf{len}(\kappa, |m|) \neq |\mathsf{rEnc}(\mathsf{sk}, m)| \end{array} \right] \leq \mathsf{negl}(\kappa)$$

  where the probability is over the coins of rEnc.
- s-*Sound: Consider the game* $\mathsf{Sound}_{\mathcal{A}_1, \mathcal{A}_2}(\kappa, n)$ *between an adversary pair* $(\mathcal{A}_1, \mathcal{A}_2)$ *and a challenger defined in Fig. 1. A replica encoding scheme is* s-*sound (*s : $\mathbb{N} \times \mathbb{N} \to [0, 1]$*), if for any probabilistic poly-time adversaries* $(\mathcal{A}_1, \mathcal{A}_2)$, *for all* $n \in \mathbb{N}$, *there exists a function* negl *such that the following holds.*

$$\Pr \left[\begin{array}{l} (v, \mathsf{state}, m) \leftarrow \mathsf{Sound}_{\mathcal{A}_1, \mathcal{A}_2}(\kappa, n), s.t. \\ |\mathsf{state}| < v \cdot \mathsf{s}(\kappa, |m|) \cdot \mathsf{len}(\kappa, |m|) \end{array} \right] \leq \mathsf{negl}(\kappa).$$

  where the probability is over the coins with the challenger and the two adversaries $\mathcal{A}_1, \mathcal{A}_2$.

A Remark on the Efficiency. We remark that there can exist trivial constructions of replica encoding by simply concatenating a string m with the randomness ρ i.e. let $\mathsf{rEnc}(\mathsf{sk}, m) = m || \rho$. These schemes are secure for $\mathsf{s} \in \frac{|\rho|}{|m|+|\rho|} - \frac{\omega(\log \kappa)}{|m|+|\rho|}$. If we consider long ρ, we can construct a sound replica encoding scheme for arbitrary $\mathsf{s}(\kappa, |m|)$. As a specific example, imagine $\mathsf{rEnc}(\mathsf{sk}, m) = m || \rho$ where $\rho \xleftarrow{R} \{0, 1\}^{99|m|}$. This scheme is trivially correct as m is output in the clear and $\mathsf{len}(\kappa, |m|) = 100|m|$. For all functions s such that $\mathsf{s}(\kappa, |m|) \in \frac{99}{100} - \frac{\omega(\log \kappa)}{100\,m\rceil}$, the proposed scheme is s sound. Intuitively, for each encoding $\mathcal{A}_2$ has $99|m| - \omega(\log \kappa)$ information in state and is supposed to output $99|m|$ random bits. Even if they randomly guess the remaining bits the probability of success will be negligible in κ. For this reason we are interested in schemes that do better than the soundness efficiency tradeoffs of this trivial solution.

Definitions in Prior Work. The formal definition of proof of replica encoding was given by Damgård et al. [11]. The soundness game can also be defined from the proof of space literature where the input message to be stored is generated through a private key setup (not revealed to the prover and the verifier) and the time bound for the prover is polynomial. We simply clean up the definitions proposed by [11] and highlight a few differences.

The earlier soundness definition is stated in terms of a constant c,

$$\Pr \left[|\mathsf{state}| < c \cdot v \cdot \mathsf{len}(\kappa, |m|) \mid (v, \mathsf{state}, m) \leftarrow \mathsf{Sound}_{\mathcal{A}_1, \mathcal{A}_2}(\kappa, n) \right] \leq \mathsf{negl}(\kappa).$$

We make 2 changes to this definition. First, rather than using a constant c, our soundness is stated in terms of a function $\mathsf{s}(\kappa, |m|)$. This change is purely for increasing the flexibility of the definition, as we can always take $\mathsf{s}(\kappa, |m|)$ to be a constant function. It also highlights our theorem statement (Theorems 1 and 2) parameters: s soundness for a larger class of functions. Next, we consider

---

Game Sound$_{\mathcal{A}_1,\mathcal{A}_2}(\kappa,n)$

- **Setup:** The challenger(denoted by $\mathcal{C}$) runs $(\mathsf{pk},\mathsf{sk}) \leftarrow \mathsf{rSetup}(1^\kappa,1^n)$ and sends pk to $\mathcal{A}_1$. It keeps the secret key sk for itself.
- **File Challenge:** The adversary $\mathcal{A}_1$, on input $(1^\kappa,\mathsf{pk})$, chooses a file $m \in \{0,1\}^*$. It sends m to $\mathcal{C}$.
- The challenger outputs n encodings of m by calling rEnc n times.

$$\forall i \in [n],\ y^{(i)} \leftarrow \mathsf{rEnc}(\mathsf{sk},m)$$

  and returns $y^{(1)},\ldots,y^{(n)}$ to $\mathcal{A}_1$.
- **State Sharing:** $\mathcal{A}_1$ outputs $\mathsf{state} \leftarrow \mathcal{A}_1(1^\kappa,\mathsf{pk},y^{(1)},\ldots,y^{(n)})$ and sends state, the number of replicas 1^n and message m to $\mathcal{A}_2$.
- **Guess:** $\mathcal{A}_2$ on receiving state state, outputs the replica guess to $\mathcal{C}$,

$$(\tilde{y}^{(1)},\ldots,\tilde{y}^{(n)}) \leftarrow \mathcal{A}_2(1^\kappa,1^n,\mathsf{pk},m,\mathsf{state})$$

- **Verify:** Let $v_i = 1$ if $\tilde{y}^{(i)} = y^{(i)}$ and 0 otherwise. Output $(v = \sum_{i=1}^n v_i,\mathsf{state},m)$.

Fig. 1. The soundness game for the replica encoding scheme.

the total probability of the adversary winning the soundness game with any number v replicas rather than the conditional probability per fixed v value. In the original definition, the security can trivially be broken. Consider an attack algorithm that tries to guess the secret information used by $\mathcal{C}$ when constructing the challenge (e.g. it tries to guess the TDP secret key and the randomness used during the encryption algorithms). If its guess is correct, it can recover the replica encodings by running rEnc in the forward direction and outputs the n replicas; otherwise, it simply gives up and outputs all 0's. Clearly such an adversary should not be viewed as successful since it only succeeds a negligible fraction of the time. However, if its guess is correct (which happens only with negligible probability) it wins the game with $v = n$ and no state bits used. Otherwise, if the guess is incorrect even for some encoding then $v < n$. Even though the winning probability of winning is negligible, when conditioned on $v = n$, this adversary succeeds with probability 1.

Tweaking their definition to include v,state as output of the game and not conditioning on events where the correct replica is output solves the issue.

Other minor differences between our definitions include a rSetup algorithm that sets up the parameters for the scheme. We do this to formalize the alignment and use the KeyGen environment of the underlying trapdoor permutation. The formal definition of replica encoding in DGO includes an efficiency condition defined as exactly $|m| + O(\kappa)$. We do not restrict the efficiency in the formal definition in our work and state it as a desired property that should be required for a practical replica encoding scheme.

4   Lemmas on Random Functions and Permutations

This section contains useful information theoretic lemmas on analyzing random permutations. The first is a result on the hardness of outputting relations on the required ideal primitive given limited advice and restricted behavior. We will use this later in showing adversaries capable in distinguishing between certain games will be able to do the following with noticeable probability. Due to space constraints, we defer the proofs of these lemmas to the full version [18]. Additionally, in the full version we discuss and prove the random function analogues of these lemmas.

Lemma 1. *Let* $\mathsf{T}, \mathsf{T}^{-1} : \{0,1\}^\lambda \to \{0,1\}^\lambda$ *be oracles to a random permutation and its inverse. Consider any computationally unbounded adversary* $\mathcal{B}$ *that makes polynomially bounded (in* λ*) queries to* $\mathsf{T}, \mathsf{T}^{-1}$ *on input a bounded* advice *and outputs* n *pairs* (x_i, y_i) *without querying them explicitly. If* advice *is bounded by* $n \cdot \lambda - \omega(\log \lambda)$ *bits where* n *is polynomial in* λ*, the probability that it succeeds is negligible in* λ*.*

More formally, let the inputs and outputs by $\mathcal{B}$ *to oracle* $\mathcal{O}$ *be denoted by lists* $\mathsf{s}_\mathcal{B}^\mathcal{O}$, $\mathsf{S}_\mathcal{B}^\mathcal{O}$ *respectively. Then,*

$$\Pr \left[\begin{array}{l} \exists\, \mathsf{advice} \in \{0,1\}^* \ s.t. \ |\mathsf{advice}| \leq n \cdot \lambda - \omega(\log \lambda), \\ \{(x_i, y_i)\}_{i=1}^n \leftarrow \mathcal{B}^{\mathsf{T}(\cdot), \mathsf{T}^{-1}(\cdot)}(\mathsf{advice}) \ where \\ \forall i \neq j \in [n], x_i \neq x_j, \ \mathsf{T}(x_i) = y_i, \ x_i \notin \mathsf{s}_\mathcal{B}^\mathsf{T} \ and \ y_i \notin \mathsf{s}_\mathcal{B}^{\mathsf{T}^{-1}} \end{array} \right] \leq \mathsf{negl}(\lambda),$$

the probability is over the choice of the permutation T*.*

Definition 2. *Let* π *be a permutation or permutation oracle with domain* $\mathcal{D}$*, and let* $x_1, x_2 \in \mathcal{D}$*. We define the notation* $\pi' = \pi[\mathsf{swap}(x_1, x_2)]]$ *to imply* π' *to be same as* π *but swapped on points* $x_1, \pi^{-1}(x_2)$*. Concretely,*

$$\pi'(x) = \begin{cases} x_2 & x = x_1 \\ \pi(x_1) & x = \pi^{-1}(x_2) \\ \pi(x) & otherwise. \end{cases}$$

Lemma 2. *Let* $S_\mathcal{D}$ *denote the symmetric group on* $\mathcal{D}$*. Let* $x, r \xleftarrow{R} \mathcal{D}$*, and* $\pi \xleftarrow{R} S_\mathcal{D}$*. Then* $(x, \pi[\mathsf{swap}(x, r)])$ *is uniform on* $\mathcal{D} \times S_\mathcal{D}$ *- i.e.* x *is independent of* $\pi[\mathsf{swap}(x, r)]$*.*

Definition 3. *Multiple invocations of the swap notation are defined as following* $\pi[\mathsf{swap}(x_1, y_1), \dots, \mathsf{swap}(x_k, y_k)]$:

- *Let* $\pi_0 = \pi$*.*
- *Iterate from* $i = 1$ *to* k*,*
  - *Perform* i^{th} *swap,* $\pi_i = \pi_{i-1}[\mathsf{swap}(x_i, y_i)]$*.*
- *Output* π_k*.*

Lemma 3. *Let* $\{r_0, r_1, \ldots r_k\} \overset{R}{\leftarrow} \mathcal{D}$ *and* π *be a random permutation. Let* $S_{\mathcal{D}}$ *be the set of all permutations. Let* τ *be a fixed permutation on* $\mathcal{D}$. *Then*

$$(r_k, \pi[\text{swap}(r_0, \tau(r_1)), \ldots, \text{swap}(r_{k-1}, \tau(r_k))])$$

is uniform on $\mathcal{D} \times S_{\mathcal{D}}$.

We introduce another useful result on the probability of finding collisions on a deterministic function h.

Lemma 4. *Let* $\mathcal{D}(\kappa), \mathcal{R}(\kappa)$ *represent domain,range respectively dependent on the security parameter. Let* h *be any deterministic function that maps values in domain* $\mathcal{D}(\kappa)$ *to range* $\mathcal{R}(\kappa)$. *Then,*

$$\Pr_a[\exists b \neq a \in \mathcal{D}(\kappa), \text{h}(a) = \text{h}(b)] \geq \frac{|\mathcal{D}(\kappa)| - |\mathcal{R}(\kappa)| + 1}{|\mathcal{D}(\kappa)|}.$$

5   Replica Encoding in the Ideal Permutation Model

We now give the construction and proof of our replica encoding scheme from trapdoor permutations in the ideal permutation model and the random oracle model. As stated in the introduction, the construction itself is a close variant of [11]. However, our proof will introduce new analysis techniques that account for an attacker that stores state in an arbitrary manner.

Let κ denote the security parameter. Let $\lambda(\kappa)$ (denoted by λ) be a function polynomial in κ and represents block length in our construction. We use a trapdoor permutation $(\text{KeyGen}, \text{f}(.,,)\text{f}^{-1}(.,.))$ where the domain for the family of trapdoor functions is $\mathcal{D}_{\text{pk}} = \{0,1\}^\lambda$ where KeyGen is setup with security parameter κ. Let T, T^{-1} be random permutation oracles on the same domain $\{0,1\}^\lambda$ and H be a random oracle on the range $\{0,1\}^\lambda$.

5.1   Construction

Let $r(\kappa, n, |m|)$ (denoted by r) be the number of rounds in our scheme. For our construction, it depends on the security parameter, maximum number of replicas chosen during setup and the message length.

rSetup($1^\kappa, 1^n$):
    Run KeyGen(1^κ) $\to$ (pk, sk). Output (pk$'$ = (pk, n), sk$'$ = (sk, n)).

rEnc(sk$'$, m):

– Parse sk$'$ = (sk, n).
– Choose a string $\rho \overset{R}{\leftarrow} \{0,1\}^\kappa$.
– Divide m into b blocks of length λ i.e. $m = m_1 || m_2 || \ldots || m_b$, $b = \lceil |m|/\lambda \rceil$.
– Set $r = n \cdot b \cdot \lambda$.

- Compute $\forall t \in [b]$,

$$Y_{t,0} = m_t \oplus \mathsf{H}(\rho||t).$$

- For rounds j from 1 to r, compute:

$$Y_{t,j} = \mathsf{f}^{-1}(\mathsf{sk}, \mathsf{T}(Y_{t,j-1})).$$

- Let $y_r = Y_{1,r}||\ldots||Y_{b,r}$ and output (y_r, ρ).

rDec(pk$'$, y):

- Parse pk$'$ = (pk, n).
- Parse y as (y_r, ρ). Parse y_r as $Y_{1,r}||\ldots||Y_{b,r}$, where $b = \lceil |y_r|/\lambda \rceil$ and $r = n \cdot b \cdot \lambda$.
- For rounds j from $r - 1$ to 0:

- Compute $\forall t \in [b]$,

$$Y_{t,j} = \mathsf{T}^{-1}(\mathsf{f}(\mathsf{pk}, Y_{t,j+1})).$$

- $\forall t \in [b]$ compute,

$$m_t = Y_{t,0} \oplus \mathsf{H}(\rho||t)$$

Output $m = m_1||\ldots||m_b$.

The encoding length for our scheme is $\mathsf{len}(\kappa, |m|) = |m| + O(\kappa).$[2]

5.2 Security of Replica Encoding Scheme

Theorem 1. *Assuming* $(\mathsf{KeyGen}(1^\kappa), \mathsf{f}(\cdot,\cdot), \mathsf{f}^{-1}(\cdot,\cdot))$ *is a secure trapdoor permutation and* $\mathsf{T}, \mathsf{T}^{-1}$ *are oracles to a random permutation on domain and range* $\{0,1\}^\lambda$ *and* H *is a random oracle on the same range. Then our construction for* ReplicaEncoding *described above is* s-*sound according to Definition 1 for all* $\kappa, n \in \mathbb{N}$ *and* $\mathsf{s} \in 1 - \frac{\omega(\log \kappa)}{\lambda}$.

Sequence of Games. Our proof proceeds via a sequence of games as described below. We assume that adversaries have their randomness non-uniformly fixed in each game to maximize their success. The changes in each game in comparison to the previous one are indicated with red. Details of the previous game are copied without explicit rewriting. We defer the formal proof of indistinguishability between successive games to the full version [18].

Game 0: This is the original Sound$_{\mathcal{A}_1, \mathcal{A}_2}(\kappa, n)$ security game where we record the queries made by the adversaries in lists. We also assume that any list is ordered and stores distinct elements. More concretely, when in Phase 1 a query x is made on $\mathcal{O}$, $\mathcal{C}$ checks if $x \notin \mathbf{u}^{\mathcal{O}}$ and updates the list $\mathbf{u}^{\mathcal{O}}$ if the condition is true. It performs this operation of maintaining the list for each Phase and

---

[2] Upto additional rounding factors.

oracle separately. Denote $q_1{}^{\mathcal{O}}, q_2{}^{\mathcal{O}}, q_3{}^{\mathcal{O}}$ as the functions that take in the security parameter and output the total distinct queries made by the adversaries to oracle $\mathcal{O}$ during the three phases respectively. Note that the functionality of the oracles is still the same, we just record queries.

- **Setup:** The challenger(denoted by $\mathcal{C}$) runs $(\mathsf{pk}', \mathsf{sk}') \leftarrow \mathsf{rSetup}(1^\kappa, 1^n)$ and sends public key pk' to $\mathcal{A}_1$. It keeps the secret key sk' for itself.
- **Phase 1:** The adversary $\mathcal{A}_1$ issues queries on $\mathsf{T}, \mathsf{T}^{-1}, \mathsf{H}, \mathcal{C}$ responds the query back to $\mathcal{A}_1$. Let the queries on oracle $\mathcal{O}$ be denoted by an ordered and distinct list $\mathbf{u}^{\mathcal{O}} = (u_1^{\mathcal{O}}, \dots, u_{q_1}^{\mathcal{O}})$ and their outputs be denoted by an ordered and distinct list $\mathbf{U}^{\mathcal{O}} = (U_1^{\mathcal{O}}, \dots, U_{q_1}^{\mathcal{O}})$.
- **File Challenge:** $m \in \{0,1\}^* \leftarrow \mathcal{A}_1^{\mathsf{H}(\cdot), \mathsf{T}(\cdot), \mathsf{T}^{-1}(\cdot)}(1^\kappa, \mathsf{pk}')$. It sends m to $\mathcal{C}$ who parses pk' as (pk, n); sk' as (sk, n) and does the following:

  • Divide m into b blocks of length λ i.e. $m = m_1 || m_2 || \dots || m_b$, $b = \lceil |m|/\lambda \rceil$.
  • For $i \in [n]$,

  * Choose a string $\rho_i \xleftarrow{R} \{0,1\}^\kappa$.
  * Compute $\forall t \in [b]$,
  $$Y_{t,0}^{(i)} = m_t \oplus \mathsf{H}(\rho_i || t).$$
  * For rounds j from 1 to r and $\forall t \in [b]$,

  · Compute $Y_{t,j}^{(i)}$ from $Y_{t,j-1}^{(i)}$ as
  $$Y_{t,j}^{(i)} = \mathsf{f}^{-1}(\mathsf{sk}, \mathsf{T}(Y_{t,j-1}^{(i)})).$$

  - * Let $y_r^{(i)} = Y_{1,r}^{(i)} || \dots || Y_{b,r}^{(i)}$ and set $y^{(i)} = (y_r^{(i)}, \rho_i)$.
  $\mathcal{C}$ returns $y^{(1)}, y^{(2)}, \dots y^{(n)}$ to $\mathcal{A}_1$.

- **Phase 2:** $\mathcal{A}_1$ issues additional queries on $\mathsf{T}, \mathsf{T}^{-1}, \mathsf{H}, \mathcal{C}$ responds the query back to $\mathcal{A}_1$. Let the queries on oracle $\mathcal{O}$ be denoted by an ordered and distinct list $\mathbf{v}^{\mathcal{O}} = (v_1^{\mathcal{O}}, \dots, v_{q_2}^{\mathcal{O}})$ and their outputs be denoted by an ordered and distinct list $\mathbf{V}^{\mathcal{O}} = (V_1^{\mathcal{O}}, \dots, V_{q_2}^{\mathcal{O}})$.
- **State Sharing:** $\mathcal{A}_1$ outputs state $\mathsf{state} \leftarrow \mathcal{A}_1^{\mathsf{H}(\cdot), \mathsf{T}(\cdot), \mathsf{T}^{-1}(\cdot)}(1^\kappa, \mathsf{pk}', y)$ and sends state to $\mathcal{A}_2$.
- **Phase 3:** The adversary $\mathcal{A}_2$ queries on $\mathsf{T}, \mathsf{T}^{-1}, \mathsf{H}, \mathcal{C}$ responds the query back to $\mathcal{A}_2$. Let the queries on oracle $\mathcal{O}$ be denoted by an ordered and distinct list $\mathbf{w}^{\mathcal{O}} = (w_1^{\mathcal{O}}, \dots, w_{q_3}^{\mathcal{O}})$ and their outputs be denoted by an ordered and distinct list $\mathbf{W}^{\mathcal{O}} = (W_1^{\mathcal{O}}, \dots, W_{q_3}^{\mathcal{O}})$.
- **Guess:** $\mathcal{A}_2$ outputs the replica guesses to $\mathcal{C}$.
  $$\{\tilde{y}^{(i)}\} \leftarrow \mathcal{A}_2(1^\kappa, \mathsf{pk}', m, \mathsf{state}).$$

- **Verify:** Let $v_i = 1$ if $\tilde{y}^{(i)} = y^{(i)}$ and 0 otherwise. Adversary wins if $|\mathsf{state}| < \sum v_i \cdot \mathsf{s}(\kappa, |m|) \cdot \mathsf{len}(\kappa, |m|)$.

Game 1: In this game we remove the sk and rely on the public key with an additional reprogramming step at oracle H. This helps us further down the road in showing a reduction to the security of the trapdoor permutation.

- **Setup:** The challenger(denoted by $\mathcal{C}$) runs $(\mathsf{pk}', \mathsf{sk}') \leftarrow \mathsf{rSetup}(1^\kappa, 1^n)$ and sends public key pk' to $\mathcal{A}_1$. It keeps the secret key sk' for itself. Set flag $= 0$.
- **Phase 1:** ...
- **File Challenge:** $m \in \{0,1\}^* \leftarrow \mathcal{A}_1^{\mathsf{H}(\cdot),\mathsf{T}(\cdot),\mathsf{T}^{-1}(\cdot)}(1^\kappa, \mathsf{pk}')$. It sends m to $\mathcal{C}$ who parses pk' as (pk, n); sk' as (sk, n) and does the following:

  • Divide m into b blocks of length λ i.e. $m = m_1 || m_2 || \ldots || m_b$, $b = \lceil |m|/\lambda \rceil$.
  • For $i \in [n]$,

  * Choose a string $\rho_i \xleftarrow{R} \{0,1\}^\kappa$.
  Prequery Check H If $\exists t \in [b]: \rho_i || t \in u^{\mathsf{H}}$, set flag $= 1$.
  * Sample $\{Y_{t,r}^{(i)}\}_{t \in [b]} \xleftarrow{R} \{0,1\}^\lambda$
  * For rounds j from r to 1 and $\forall t \in [b]$,

    · Compute $Y_{t,j-1}^{(i)}$ from $Y_{t,j}^{(i)}$ as

    $$Y_{t,j-1}^{(i)} = \mathsf{T}^{-1}(\mathsf{f}(\mathsf{pk}, Y_{t,j-1}^{(i)})).$$

  * For each block $\forall t \in [b]$, reprogram H

    $$H(\rho_i || t) = m_t \oplus Y_{t,0}^{(i)}$$

  * Let $y_r^{(i)} = Y_{1,r}^{(i)} || \ldots || Y_{b,r}^{(i)}$ and set $y^{(i)} = (y_r^{(i)}, \rho_i)$.

  $\mathcal{C}$ returns $y^{(1)}, y^{(2)}, \ldots y^{(n)}$ to $\mathcal{A}_1$.

- **Phase 2, State Sharing, Phase 3, Guess:** ...
- **Verify:** Let $v_i = 1$ if $\tilde{y}^{(i)} = y^{(i)}$ and 0 otherwise. Adversary wins if flag $= 0$ and $|\mathsf{state}| < \sum v_i \cdot \mathsf{s}(\kappa, |m|) \cdot \mathsf{len}(\kappa, |m|)$.

Game 2: In this game an adversary wins if they query on the oracle rather than outputting the replica. This helps us ease the notation by only focussing at the oracle query lists.

- **Setup, Phase 1, File Challenge, Phase 2, State Sharing, Phase 3:**
  ....
- **Guess:** ....
  $\mathcal{C}$ adds the guess to $\mathcal{A}_2$'s lists of queries to T in Phase 3, i.e. $\forall i \in [n]$, let $\tilde{y}^{(i)} = (\tilde{Y}_{0,r}^{(i)} || \ldots || \tilde{Y}_{b,r}^{(i)}, \tilde{\rho}_i)$. $\forall t \in [b]$ add $\tilde{Y}_{t,r}^{(i)}$ to list of queries to T by $\mathcal{A}_2$ in Phase 3.
- **Verify:** Let $v_i = 1$ if $\forall t \in [b]$, T is queried on $Y_{t,r}^{(i)}$ and 0 otherwise. Adversary wins if flag $= 0$ and $|\mathsf{state}| < \sum v_i \cdot \mathsf{s}(\kappa, |m|) \cdot \mathsf{len}(\kappa, |m|)$.

Game 3: In this game, we look at the queries made by the adversary and require that it traverses atleast one block in some replica sequentially.

– **Setup, Phase 1, File Challenge, Phase 2, State Sharing, Phase 3, Guess:** ....

– **Sequentiality:** We consider going through $\mathcal{A}_2's$ ordered list of queries to T and T^{-1}. If $\forall i \in [n]\ \forall t \in [b]$, there is a point in time such that some $Y_{t,j+1}^{(i)}$ was queried on T or $\mathsf{f}(\mathsf{pk}, Y_{t,j+1}^{(i)})$ was queried on T^{-1} when $\mathcal{A}_2$ has not made a query to T for $Y_{t,j}^{(i)}$), then set $\mathsf{flag} = 1$.

– **Verify:** Let $v_i = 1$ if $\forall t \in [b]$, T is queried on $Y_{t,r}^{(i)}$ and 0 otherwise. Adversary wins if $\mathsf{flag} = 0$ and $|\mathsf{state}| < \sum v_i \cdot \mathsf{s}(\kappa, |m|) \cdot \mathsf{len}(\kappa, |m|)$.

Game 4: In this game, we guess the block which the adversary traversed sequentially. We concentrate on one randomly chosen block and replica and the adversary wins if it outputs the correct encoding for this block. We lose a multiplicative factor of $b \cdot n$ in the reduction due to this change.

– **Setup:** The challenger(denoted by $\mathcal{C}$) runs $(\mathsf{pk}', \mathsf{sk}') \leftarrow \mathsf{rSetup}(1^\kappa, 1^n)$ and sends public key pk' to $\mathcal{A}_1$. It keeps the secret key sk' for itself. Set $\mathsf{flag} = 0$. Choose a random $\beta \in [b]$ and $\gamma \in [n]$.

– **Phase 1, File Challenge, Phase 2, State Sharing, Phase 3, Guess:** ....

– **Sequentiality:**
We consider going through $\mathcal{A}_2's$ list of queries to T and T^{-1}. If there is a point in time such that some $Y_{\beta,j+1}^{(\gamma)}$ was queried on T or $\mathsf{f}(\mathsf{pk}, Y_{\beta,j+1}^{(\gamma)})$ was queried on T^{-1} when $\mathcal{A}_2$ has not made a query to T for $Y_{\beta,j}^{(\gamma)}$, then set $\mathsf{flag} = 1$.

– **Verify:** ~~Let $v_i = 1$ if $\forall t \in [b]$, T is queried on $Y_{t,r}^{(i)}$ and 0 otherwise.~~ Adversary wins if T is queried on $Y_{\beta,r}^{(\gamma)}$, $\mathsf{flag} = 0$, and $|\mathsf{state}| < n \cdot \mathsf{s}(\kappa, |m|) \cdot \mathsf{len}(\kappa, |m|)$.

Game 5: In this game, we reprogram the oracles H, T to have a permutation which we can analyze cleanly. The primary idea behind this game is that there will exist two sequences of values on the chosen block and replica for which any adversary $\mathcal{A}_1$ produces the same state. These possibilities for a "switch" are set up in this game. H is programmed to output $Y_{\beta,0}^{(\gamma)}$ and for $i \in [r]$, the values $A_{i,0}, A_{i,1}$ have a choice to be mapped to either of the two $A_{i+1,0}, A_{i+1,1}$ depending on the sampled index x. The collision check makes sure that the reprogramming preserves the permutation property of T and the prequery check is done to make sure that none of the values were queried in the oracle lists in the previous phase. The oracle T_x is then reprogrammed according to the swap operation defined in Definition 3 where for $i \in [r]$, x_i is now mapped to $\mathsf{f}(\mathsf{pk}, \mathsf{x}_{i+1})$ where x_i is used to indicate the notation for $A_{i,\mathsf{x}[i]}$.

– **Setup, Phase 1:** ....
– **Sampling a new permutation:**

- Sample, $Y_{\beta,0}^{(\gamma)}, A_{1,0}, \ldots, A_{r,0}, A_{1,1}, \ldots, A_{r,1} \xleftarrow{R} \{0,1\}^{\lambda}$.

  Let $\mathcal{Z}_1 = \{Y_{\beta,0}^{(\gamma)}, A_{1,0} \ldots, A_{r,0}, A_{1,1}, \ldots, A_{r,1}\}$.

  Let $\mathcal{Z}_2 = \{f(\mathsf{pk}, A_{1,0}) \ldots, f(\mathsf{pk}, A_{r,0}), f(\mathsf{pk}, A_{1,1}), \ldots, f(\mathsf{pk}, A_{r,1})\}$.

  Collision Check: If $|\mathcal{Z}_1| \neq 2r + 1$, set flag $= 1$.

  Prequery Check T: If $(\mathcal{Z}_1 \cup \mathcal{Z}_2) \cap \left(\mathbf{u}^\mathsf{T} \cup \mathbf{u}^{\mathsf{T}^{-1}} \cup \mathbf{U}^\mathsf{T} \cup \mathbf{U}^{\mathsf{T}^{-1}}\right) \neq \emptyset$, set flag $= 1$.

- Sample a random setting $\mathsf{x} \xleftarrow{R} \{0,1\}^r$. Let $\mathsf{x}[k]$ denote the kth bit of x. We will write x_j to refer to $A_{j,\mathsf{x}[j-1]}$ and denote $A_{j,\bar{\mathsf{x}}[j-1]}$ with $\bar{\mathsf{x}}_j$. Set x_0 to denote $Y_{\beta,0}^{(\gamma)}$.

- Define T_x using swap (Definition 3):

$$\mathsf{T}_\mathsf{x} = \mathsf{T}[\mathsf{swap}(\mathsf{x}_0, f(\mathsf{pk}, \mathsf{x}_1)), \ldots, \mathsf{swap}(\mathsf{x}_{r-1}, f(\mathsf{pk}, \mathsf{x}_r))].$$

- Let $\mathsf{T}_\mathsf{x}^{-1}$ be the inverse of T_x.

– **File Challenge:** $m \in \{0,1\}^* \leftarrow \mathcal{A}_1^{\mathsf{H}(\cdot), \mathsf{T}(\cdot), \mathsf{T}^{-1}(\cdot)}(1^\kappa, \mathsf{pk}')$. It sends m to $\mathcal{C}$ who parses pk' as (pk, n); sk' as (sk, n) and does the following:

- Divide m into b blocks of length λ i.e. $m = m_1 || m_2 || \ldots || m_b$, $b = \lceil |m|/\lambda \rceil$.
- For $i \in [n]$,

* Choose a string $\rho_i \xleftarrow{R} \{0,1\}^\kappa$.
  Prequery Check H If $\exists t \in [b] : \rho_i || t \in \mathbf{u}^\mathsf{H}$, set flag $= 1$.
* Sample $\{Y_{t,r}^{(i)}\}_{t \in [b]} \xleftarrow{R} \{0,1\}^\lambda$
* For rounds j from r to 1 and $\forall t \in [b]$, continue if $t \neq \beta$ or $i \neq \gamma$,

  · Compute $Y_{t,j-1}^{(i)}$ from $Y_{t,j}^{(i)}$ as

$$Y_{t,j-1}^{(i)} = \mathsf{T}^{-1}(f(\mathsf{pk}, Y_{t,j-1}^{(i)})).$$

* For each block $\forall t \in [b]$, reprogram H

$$\mathsf{H}(\rho_i || t) = m_t \oplus Y_{t,0}^{(i)}.$$

* Let $y_r^{(i)} = Y_{1,r}^{(i)} || \ldots || Y_{b,r}^{(i)}$ and set $y^{(i)} = (y_r^{(i)}, \rho_i)$.

$\mathcal{C}$ returns $y^{(1)}, y^{(2)}, \ldots y^{(n)}$ to $\mathcal{A}_1$.

– **Phase 2:** Use $\mathsf{T}_\mathsf{x}, \mathsf{T}_\mathsf{x}^{-1}$ to answer queries for $\mathsf{T}, \mathsf{T}^{-1}$ respectively.
– **State Sharing:** ....
– **Phase 3:** Use $\mathsf{T}_\mathsf{x}, \mathsf{T}_\mathsf{x}^{-1}$ to answer queries for $\mathsf{T}, \mathsf{T}^{-1}$ respectively.

- **Guess, Sequentiality:** ....
- **Verify:** Adversary wins if T is queried on $Y_{\beta,r}^{(\gamma)}$, flag $= 0$, and $|\mathsf{state}| <$ $n \cdot \mathsf{s}(\kappa, |m|) \cdot \mathsf{len}(\kappa, |m|)$.

Game 6: In this game, $\mathcal{C}$ has unbounded computation time and calls $\mathcal{A}_1, \mathcal{A}_2$ exponentially many times to find a collision to state through the procedure search. The setting y' for which the procedure search outputs a collision in state is stored in a set which is outputted at the end of the procedure. $\mathsf{search}(1^\kappa, \mathsf{y}, \mathsf{state}; \zeta)$ takes input $\mathsf{y} \in \{0,1\}^r, \mathsf{state}$ and runs algorithms $\mathcal{A}_1, \mathcal{A}_2$ on Game 5. Let ζ be the randomness used by the procedure and denotes all the random coins (except those used to sample x) used by $\mathcal{C}$. The procedure is described in Fig. 2.

$$\mathsf{search}(1^\kappa, \mathsf{y}, \mathsf{state}; \zeta)$$

Inputs: Security parameter - 1^κ

Oracle Settings on T - $\mathsf{y} \in \{0,1\}^r$

State - state

Randomness used in the game - ζ

Output: Set containing all oracle settings with collision in state - $\mathcal{S}$

- Set $\mathcal{S} = \emptyset$.
- $\forall \mathsf{y}' \neq \mathsf{y} \in \{0,1\}^r$,
  - Run $\mathcal{A}_1, \mathcal{A}_2$ on Game 5 with randomness defined by ζ and using y' instead of x in the game.
  - Let state' be the state shared between $\mathcal{A}_1, \mathcal{A}_2$.
  - If $\mathsf{state}' = \mathsf{state}$ and $\mathcal{A}_2$ wins Game 5, then $\mathcal{S} = \mathcal{S} \cup \{\mathsf{y}'\}$.
- Output $\mathcal{S}$.

Fig. 2. Routine search

- **Setup, Phase 1, Sampling a New Permutation, File Challenge, Phase 2, State Sharing:** ....
  - **Running search:** Let ζ be all the random coins (except those used to sample x) used by $\mathcal{C}$. Let $\mathcal{S} \leftarrow \mathsf{search}(1^\kappa, \mathsf{x}, \mathsf{state}; \zeta)$.

  If $\mathcal{S} = \emptyset$ set flag $= 1$ and $\mathsf{x}' = \mathsf{x}$, otherwise sample $\mathsf{x}' \xleftarrow{R} \mathcal{S}$.
  - **Setting switched oracle:**

    - Let $\mathsf{x}'[k]$ denote the kth bit of x'. We will write x'_j to refer to $A_{j,\mathsf{x}'[j-1]}$ and denote $A_{j,\bar{\mathsf{x}}'[j-1]}$ with $\bar{\mathsf{x}}'_j$. Set x'_0 to denote $Y_{\beta,0}^{(\gamma)}$.
    - Define $\mathsf{T}_{\mathsf{x}'}$ to be:

    $$\mathsf{T}_{\mathsf{x}'} = \mathsf{T}[\mathsf{swap}(\mathsf{x}'_0, \mathsf{f}(\mathsf{pk}, \mathsf{x}'_1)), \ldots, \mathsf{swap}(\mathsf{x}'_{r-1}, \mathsf{f}(\mathsf{pk}, \mathsf{x}'_r))].$$

    - Let $\mathsf{T}_{\mathsf{x}'}^{-1}$ be the inverse of $\mathsf{T}_{\mathsf{x}'}$.

- **Phase 3:** Use $T_{x'}, T_{x'}^{-1}$ to answer queries for T, T^{-1} respectively.
- **Guess:** ....
- **Sequentiality:**
  If $\exists j \in [0, r] : (x'_{j+1}$ was queried on T or $f(pk, x'_{j+1})$ was queried on T^{-1} while T had not been queried on $x'_j)$, set flag $= 1$.
- **Verify:** Adversary wins if T is queried on x'_r, flag $= 0$, and $|state| < n \cdot s(\kappa, |m|) \cdot len(\kappa, |m|)$.

Game 7: In this game we modify the verification step for which an adversary can win this game. We increase it's winning probability so that the adversary can win if it doesn't query the full sequence, but queries at the point where the sequences x, x' diverge. Notice that we define another oracle $T_{x'}^{\delta}$ here that doesn't reprogram the complete sequence. This change is statistically indistinguishable to the adversary.

- **Setup, Phase 1, Sampling a New Permutation, File Challenge, Phase 2, State Sharing, Running search:** ....
- **Setting switched oracle:**

  • Let $x'[k]$ denote the kth bit of x'. We will write x'_j to refer to $A_{j, x'[j-1]}$ and denote $A_{j, \bar{x}'[j-1]}$ with $\bar{x}'_j$. Set x'_0 to denote $Y_{\beta, 0}^{(\gamma)}$.
  • Let δ be the first index for which $x_\delta \neq x'_\delta$.
  • Define $T_{x'}^{\delta}$ to be:

  $$T_{x'}^{\delta} = T[swap(x'_0, f(pk, x'_1)), \ldots, swap(x'_{\delta-1}, f(pk, x'_\delta))]$$
  $$= T[swap(x_0, f(pk, x_1)), \ldots, swap(x_{\delta-1}, f(pk, \bar{x}_\delta))].$$

  • Let $T_{x'}^{-1}$ be the inverse of $T_{x'}$.

  - **Phase 3, Guess:** ....
  - ~~**Sequentiality:**~~
  - **Verify:** Adversary wins of T is queried on $\bar{x}_\delta$, flag $= 0$ ~~and $|state| < n \cdot s(\kappa, |m|) \cdot len(\kappa, |m|)$.~~

Game 8: In this game we observe that $\mathcal{C}$ need not be unbounded computation time and only needs to the guess the first prefix at which x, x' differ to successfully output one sequential query.

- **Setup, Phase 1, Sampling a New Permutation, File Challenge, Phase 2, State Sharing:** ....
- ~~**Running search:** ....~~
- **Setting switched oracle:**

  • ~~Let $x'[k]$ denote the kth bit of x'. We will write x'_j to refer to $A_{j, x'[j-1]}$ and denote $A_{j, \bar{x}'[j-1]}$ with $\bar{x}'_j$. Set x'_0 to denote $Y_{\beta, 0}^{(\gamma)}$.~~
  • Let $\delta \xleftarrow{R} [r]$

- Define $\mathsf{T}_{\mathsf{x}'}^{\delta}$ to be:

$$\mathsf{T}_{\mathsf{x}'}^{\delta} = \mathsf{T}[\mathsf{swap}(\mathsf{x}_0, \mathsf{f}(\mathsf{pk}, \mathsf{x}_1)), \ldots, \mathsf{swap}(\mathsf{x}_{\delta-1}, \mathsf{f}(\mathsf{pk}, \bar{\mathsf{x}}_{\delta}))].$$

- Let $\mathsf{T}_{\mathsf{x}'}^{-1}$ be the inverse of $\mathsf{T}_{\mathsf{x}'}$.

- **Phase 3, Guess:** ....
- **Verify:** Adversary wins of T is queried on $\bar{\mathsf{x}}_{\delta}$ and $\mathsf{flag} = 0$.

6   Replica Encodings in the Random Function Model

We now turn toward building Replica Encodings from trapdoor permutations in the ideal function model. Our construction will embed a Feistel like structure into the replica encoding construction. We will directly prove security of this construction. Our construction makes use of the $\mathsf{KeyGen}, \mathsf{f}$, and f^{-1} defined for a trapdoor permutation on domain $\{0,1\}^{\lambda}$ and a random function T' on the same domain. Let H be a random oracle on the range $\{0,1\}^{\lambda}$.

Define functions $\mathsf{L}, \mathsf{R} : \{0,1\}^* \to \{0,1\}^*$ on even length inputs as follows. If $x = y\|z$, where $x, y, z \in \{0,1\}^*$, $|y| = |z|$, then the function $\mathsf{L}(.)$ denotes the left half of x i.e. $\mathsf{L}(x) = y$ and the function $\mathsf{R}(.)$ denotes the right half of x i.e. $\mathsf{R}(x) = z$.

6.1   Construction

$\underline{\mathsf{rSetup}(1^{\kappa}, 1^n)}$:

Run $\mathsf{KeyGen}(1^{\kappa}) \to (\mathsf{pk}, \mathsf{sk})$. Output $(\mathsf{pk}' = (\mathsf{pk}, n), \mathsf{sk}' = (\mathsf{sk}, n))$.

$\underline{\mathsf{rEnc}(\mathsf{sk}', m)}$:

- Parse $\mathsf{sk}' = (\mathsf{sk}, n)$.
- Choose a string $\rho \xleftarrow{R} \{0,1\}^{\kappa}$.
- Divide m into b blocks of length 2λ i.e. $m = m_1\|m_2\|\ldots\|m_b$, $b = \lceil|m|/2\lambda\rceil$.
- Set $r = n \cdot b \cdot \lambda$.
- Compute $\forall t \in [b]$,

$$Y_{t,0} = L(m_t \oplus \mathsf{H}(\rho\|t)).$$

$$Y_{t,1} = R(m_t \oplus \mathsf{H}(\rho\|t)).$$

- For rounds j from 2 to r compute:
- Compute $Y_{t,j}$ from $Y_{t,j-1}$ and $Y_{t,j-2}$ as

$$Y_{t,j} = \mathsf{f}^{-1}(\mathsf{sk}, Y_{t,j-2} \oplus \mathsf{T}'(Y_{t,j-1}))$$

- Let $Z_t = Y_{t,r-1}\|Y_{t,r}$
- Let $y_r = Z_1\|\ldots\|Z_b$ and output (y_r, ρ).

rDec(pk', y):

- Parse pk' = (pk, n).
- Parse y as (y_r, ρ). Parse y_r as $Z_1||Z_2||\ldots||Z_b$, where $b = \lceil |y_r|/2\lambda \rceil$ and $r = n \cdot b \cdot \lambda$.
- For each $Z_t = Y_{t,r-1}||Y_{t,r}$ and for rounds j from $r - 2$ to 0 compute:
- Compute $Y_{t,j}$ from $Y_{t,j+1}$ and $Y_{t,j+2}$ as

$$Y_{t,j} = f(\mathsf{pk}, Y_{t,j+2}) \oplus \mathsf{T}'(Y_{t,j+1})$$

- $\forall t \in [b]$ compute,
$$m_t = Y_{t,0}||Y_{t,1} \oplus \mathsf{H}(\rho||t)$$

Output $m = m_1||\ldots||m_b$.

The encoding length for our scheme is $\mathsf{len}(\kappa, |m|) = |m| + O(\kappa)$.[3]

6.2   Proof of Security

Theorem 2. *Assuming* $(\mathsf{KeyGen}(1^\kappa), f(\cdot, \cdot), f^{-1}(\cdot, \cdot))$ *is a secure trapdoor permutation on domain and range* $\{0, 1\}^\lambda$ *and* T' *is an oracle to a random function on the same domain and range, and* H *is a random oracle with range* $\{0, 1\}^{2\lambda}$. *Then our construction for* ReplicaEncoding *described above is* s-*sound according to Definition 1 for all* $\kappa, n \in \mathbb{N}$ *and* $\mathsf{s} \in 1 - \frac{\omega(\log \kappa)}{2\lambda}$.

Due to space constraints, we defer the sequence of games and the proof of this theorem to the full version of our paper, [18].

7   Counterexample for Round Function Independent of Blocks

We gave intuition in Sect. 1.2 using VBB obfuscation that our construction is round optimal up to constant factors i.e. is insecure for any number of rounds $\in o(b \cdot n)$. Below we formalize the notion by giving a construction from $i\mathcal{O}$ that captures this intuition formally and constructs a scheme in the end that breaks soundness security.

We assume the existence of a trapdoor permutation $(\mathsf{KeyGen}, f(\cdot, \cdot), f^{-1}(\cdot, \cdot))$ with domain $\{0, 1\}^\lambda$ for $\lambda \in \omega(\kappa)^4$, a puncturable PRF family (PPRF.KeyGen, PPRF.Eval, PPRF.Puncture), indistinguishability obfuscation $i\mathcal{O}$ for all polynomial sized circuits.

---

[3] Upto additional rounding factors.

[4] Note it suffices to have some trapdoor permutation with domain $\lambda \in \omega(\kappa^\epsilon)$ for $\epsilon > 0$, and we can generically transform this by taking said TDP on security parameter $\kappa' = \kappa^{1/\epsilon}$.

7.1   Construction

Let $(\mathsf{KeyGen}, \mathsf{f}(\cdot, \cdot), \mathsf{f}^{-1}(\cdot, \cdot))$ be a trapdoor permutation on $\{0,1\}^{\kappa}$, where KeyGen uses some $r(\kappa)$ bits of randomness. Let $(\mathsf{PPRF.KeyGen}, \mathsf{PPRF.Eval}, \mathsf{PPRF.Puncture})$ be a puncturable PRF on domain $\{0,1\}^{\kappa}$ and range $\{0,1\}^{r(\kappa)}$. We will construct a trapdoor permutation $(\mathsf{keygen}'_n, \mathsf{f}'_n(\cdot, \cdot), \mathsf{f}'_n{}^{-1}(\cdot, \cdot))$ on domain $\{0,1\}^{2\kappa}$ parameterized by a quantity $n \in \mathsf{poly}(\kappa)$ (Figs. 3 and 4).

Program $\mathsf{f}(z, x)$

Inputs: Index $z \in \{0,1\}^{\kappa}$

Input $x \in \{0,1\}^{\kappa}$

Constants: Punctured PRF key K

Output: $y \in \{0,1\}^n$

1. Let $r \leftarrow \mathsf{PPRF.Eval}(K, z)$
2. Let $(\mathsf{pk}', \mathsf{sk}') \leftarrow \mathsf{KeyGen}(1^{\kappa}; r)$
3. Output $\mathsf{f}(\mathsf{pk}', x)$

Fig. 3. Routine Program f

Program $\mathsf{f}^{-1}((z_1, y_1), \dots, (z_n, y_n) \in \{0,1\}^{2\kappa}, x \in \{0,1\}^{\kappa})$

Inputs: Images $(z_1, y_1), \dots, (z_n, y_n) \in \{0,1\}^{2\kappa}$

Advice $x \in \{0,1\}^{\kappa}$

Constants: Punctured PRF key K

Output: Preimages $\{x_i \in \{0,1\}^{\kappa}\}_{i \in [n]}$

1. If $\exists i, j \in [n] : i \neq j \wedge z_i = z_j$ output $\perp$.
2. For $i \in [n]$
   (a) Let $r_i \leftarrow \mathsf{PPRF.Eval}(K, z_i)$
   (b) Let $(\mathsf{pk}_i, \mathsf{sk}_i) \leftarrow \mathsf{KeyGen}(1^{\kappa}; r_i)$
   (c) Let $x_i = \mathsf{f}^{-1}(\mathsf{sk}_i, y_i)$
3. If $\bigoplus_{i \in [n]} x_i \neq x$ output $\perp$.
4. If the above checks pass, output $\{x_i\}_{i \in [n]}$.

Fig. 4. Routine Program f^{-1}

$\mathsf{keygen}'_n(1^{\kappa})$

1. Sample $K \leftarrow \mathsf{PPRF.KeyGen}(1^{\kappa})$
2. Let $\mathcal{O}\mathsf{Program\ f} = i\mathcal{O}(\kappa, \mathsf{Program\ f})$ and $\mathcal{O}\mathsf{Program\ f}^{-1} = i\mathcal{O}(\kappa, \mathsf{Program\ f}^{-1})$.

   3. Output $(\mathsf{pk} = (\mathcal{O}\mathsf{Program}\ \mathsf{f}, \mathcal{O}\mathsf{Program}\ \mathsf{f}^{-1}), \mathsf{sk} = K)$
$\mathsf{f}'_n(\mathsf{pk} = (\mathcal{O}\mathsf{Program}\ \mathsf{f}, \mathcal{O}\mathsf{Program}\ \mathsf{f}^{-1}), (z, x))$
   1. Let $y \leftarrow \mathcal{O}\mathsf{Program}\ \mathsf{f}(z, x)$ and output (z, y).
$\mathsf{f}'^{-1}_n(\mathsf{sk} = K, (z, y))$
   1. Let $r \leftarrow \mathsf{PPRF.Eval}(K, z)$.
   2. Let $(\mathsf{pk}_0, \mathsf{sk}_0) \leftarrow \mathsf{KeyGen}(1^\kappa; r)$.
   3. Output $(z, \mathsf{f}^{-1}(\mathsf{sk}_0, y))$.

7.2   Proofs

Efficiency

Claim. $(\mathsf{keygen}'_n, \mathsf{f}'_n(\cdot, \cdot), \mathsf{f}'^{-1}_n(\cdot, \cdot))$ are polynomial time algorithms

Proof. keygen'_n simply calls $i\mathcal{O}$ twice. The programs $\mathsf{Program}\ \mathsf{f}$ and $\mathsf{Program}\ \mathsf{f}^{-1}$ simply call the underlying PRF and trapdoor primitives at most $n \in \mathsf{poly}(\kappa)$ times. By the efficiency of the underlying PRF and trapdoor permutation, $\mathsf{Program}\ \mathsf{f}$ and $\mathsf{Program}\ \mathsf{f}^{-1}$ are poly-sized circuits and $i\mathcal{O}$ runs in poly time, thus keygen'_n runs in polynomial time.
f'_n simply evaluates a polynomial sized circuit, which is polynomial time.
f'^{-1}_n does a single call to $\mathsf{PPRF.Eval}, \mathsf{KeyGen}, \mathsf{f}^{-1}(\cdot, \cdot)$, which are all polynomial time algorithms by definition.

Correctness

Claim. The correctness of $i\mathcal{O}$ and correctness of $\mathsf{f}^{-1}(\mathsf{sk}', \cdot)$ computing inverse of $\mathsf{f}(\mathsf{pk}', \cdot)$ implies $\mathsf{f}'^{-1}_n(\mathsf{sk}, \cdot)$ computes the inverse of $\mathsf{f}'_n(\mathsf{pk}, \cdot)$, i.e.

$$\forall \kappa, (\mathsf{pk}, \mathsf{sk}) \leftarrow \mathsf{keygen}'_n(1^\kappa), \forall x' \in \{0, 1\}^{2\kappa}, \mathsf{f}'^{-1}_n(\mathsf{sk}, \mathsf{f}'_n(\mathsf{pk}, x')) = x'.$$

Proof. Let $x' = (z, x) \in \{0, 1\}^{2\kappa}$ be an arbitrary input to function f'_n. Recall that f'_n simply runs $\mathcal{O}\mathsf{Program}\ \mathsf{f}$ on (z, x) and is same as the result of outputting $\mathsf{Program}\ \mathsf{f}$ on (z, x) from correctness of $i\mathcal{O}$. The output produced is $(z, \mathsf{f}(\mathsf{pk}', x))$ where $(\mathsf{pk}', \mathsf{sk}') = \mathsf{KeyGen}(1^\kappa, F(K, z))$. f'^{-1}_n when run on $(z, \mathsf{f}(\mathsf{pk}', x))$ produces the same $(\mathsf{pk}', \mathsf{sk}')$ pair as $\mathcal{O}\mathsf{Program}\ \mathsf{f}$. Since,

$$\forall \kappa, (\mathsf{pk}', \mathsf{sk}') \leftarrow \mathsf{KeyGen}(1^\kappa), \forall x \in \{0, 1\}^\kappa, \mathsf{f}^{-1}(\mathsf{sk}', \mathsf{f}(\mathsf{pk}', x)) = x.$$

f'^{-1}_n returns $(z, \mathsf{f}^{-1}(\mathsf{sk}', \mathsf{f}(\mathsf{pk}', x))) = (z, x)$.

Security

Theorem 3. *Assuming* $(\mathsf{KeyGen}, \mathsf{f}(\cdot, \cdot), \mathsf{f}^{-1}(\cdot, \cdot))$ *is a secure one way permutation, indistinguishability of* $i\mathcal{O}$ *and a puncturable PRF family* $(\mathsf{PPRF.KeyGen},$

PPRF.Eval, PPRF.Puncture) *secure*, $(\mathsf{keygen}'_n, \mathsf{f}'_n, \mathsf{f}'_n{}^{-1})$ *is a secure one way permutation - i.e., that for all PPT algorithms* $\mathcal{A}$

$$\Pr\left[\begin{array}{c} \mathsf{f}'_n(\mathsf{pk}, (z_0, x_0)) = (z, y) \ s.t. \\ (\mathsf{pk}, \mathsf{sk}) \leftarrow \mathsf{keygen}'_n(1^\kappa), (z_0, x_0) \xleftarrow{R} \{0,1\}^{2\kappa}, \\ (z, y) = \mathsf{f}'_n(\mathsf{pk}, (z_0, x_0)), (z', x') \leftarrow \mathcal{A}(\mathsf{pk}, (z, y)) \end{array}\right] \le \mathsf{negl}(\kappa),$$

over the random coins of keygen'_n *and sampling of* (z_0, x_0).

We will show this via a sequence of games, where the view of the adversary between successive games is indistinguishable. Due to space constraints, the formal proof is deferred to the full version [18]. The proof follows the punctured programming technique of [28].

Game 0 This is the original security game.

1. Challenger samples a random $(z_0, x_0) \xleftarrow{R} \{0,1\}^{2\kappa}$
   (a) Sample $K \leftarrow \mathsf{PPRF.KeyGen}(1^\kappa)$
   (b) Let $\mathcal{O}\mathsf{Program\ f} = i\mathcal{O}(\kappa, \mathsf{Program\ f})$ and $\mathcal{O}\mathsf{Program\ f}^{-1} = i\mathcal{O}(\kappa, \mathsf{Program\ f}^{-1}).$[5]
   (c) Output $(\mathsf{pk} = (\mathcal{O}\mathsf{Program\ f}, \mathcal{O}\mathsf{Program\ f}^{-1}), \mathsf{sk} = K)$
2. Challenger runs $\mathsf{f}'_n(\mathsf{pk}, (z_0, x_0))$
   (a) Let $y_0 \leftarrow \mathcal{O}\mathsf{Program\ f}(z_0, x_0)$.
3. Adversary is given $(\mathsf{pk}, (z_0, y_0))$.
4. Adversary outputs (z', x')
5. If $\mathsf{f}'_n(\mathsf{pk}, (z', x')) = (z_0, y_0)$ then output 1 else output 0

Game 1

In this game, we change the way Program f is programmed (Fig. 5).

1. Challenger samples a random $(z_0, x_0) \xleftarrow{R} \{0,1\}^{2\kappa}$
   (a) Sample $K \leftarrow \mathsf{PPRF.KeyGen}(1^\kappa)$
   (b) Compute $(\mathsf{pk}_0, \mathsf{sk}_0) \leftarrow \mathsf{KeyGen}(1^\kappa, F(K, z_0))$
   (c) Compute punctured key $K(\{z_0\})$
   (d) Let $\underline{\mathcal{O}\mathsf{Program\ f}^* = i\mathcal{O}(\kappa, \mathsf{Program\ f}^*)}$ and $\mathcal{O}\mathsf{Program\ f}^{-1} = i\mathcal{O}(\kappa, \mathsf{Program\ f}^{-1}).$
   (e) Output $(\mathsf{pk} = (\mathcal{O}\mathsf{Program\ f}^*, \mathcal{O}\mathsf{Program\ f}^{-1}), \mathsf{sk} = K)$
2. Challenger runs $\mathsf{f}'_n(\mathsf{pk}, (z_0, x_0))$
   (a) Let $y_0 \leftarrow \mathcal{O}\mathsf{Program\ f}^*(z_0, x_0)$.
3. Adversary is given $(\mathsf{pk}, (z_0, y_0))$.
4. Adversary outputs (z', x')
5. If $\mathsf{f}'_n(\mathsf{pk}, (z', x')) = (z_0, y_0)$ then output 1 else output 0

Game 2

In this game, we change the way Program f^{-1} is programmed (Fig. 6).

---

[5] The security parameter in the input to $i\mathcal{O}$ algorithm is the smallest λ for which Program f, Program f* are in $\mathcal{C}_\lambda$ which will be polynomial in κ as the circuits are polynomial. We denote this by κ here for notation clarity.

Program $f^*(z, x)$

Inputs: Index $z \in \{0,1\}^\kappa$

Input $x \in \{0,1\}^\kappa$

Constants: Punctured PRF key $K(\{z_0\})$

Public Key pk_0

Output: $y \in \{0,1\}^n$

1. If $z = z_0$, output $\mathsf{f}(\mathsf{pk}_0, x)$.
2. Let $r \leftarrow \mathsf{PPRF.Eval}(K(\{z_0\}), z)$
3. Let $(\mathsf{pk}', \mathsf{sk}') \leftarrow \mathsf{KeyGen}(1^\kappa; r)$
4. Output $\mathsf{f}(\mathsf{pk}', x)$

Fig. 5. Routine Program f^*

Program $f^{-1^*}((z_1, y_1), \ldots, (z_n, y_n) \in \{0,1\}^{2\kappa}, x \in \{0,1\}^\kappa)$

Inputs: Images $(z_1, y_1), \ldots, (z_n, y_n) \in \{0,1\}^{2\kappa}$

Advice $x \in \{0,1\}^\kappa$

Constants: Punctured PRF key $K(\{z_0\})$

Public Key pk_0

Output: Preimages $\{x_i \in \{0,1\}^\kappa\}_{i \in [n]}$

1. If $\exists i, j \in [n] : i \neq j \wedge z_i = z_j$ output $\perp$.
2. For $i \in [n]$ when $z_i \neq z_0$
   (a) Let $r_i \leftarrow \mathsf{PPRF.Eval}(K(\{z_0\}), z_i)$
   (b) Let $(\mathsf{pk}_i, \mathsf{sk}_i) \leftarrow \mathsf{KeyGen}(1^\kappa; r_i)$
   (c) Let $x_i = \mathsf{f}^{-1}(\mathsf{sk}_i, y_i)$
3. If $\exists i' : z_{i'} = z_0$
   (a) Let $x_{i'} = x \oplus (\bigoplus_{i \in [n] \setminus \{i'\}} x_i)$.
   (b) If $\mathsf{f}(\mathsf{pk}_0, x_{i'}) \neq y_i$, output $\perp$.
4. If $\bigoplus_{i \in [n]} x_i \neq x$ output $\perp$.
5. If the above checks pass, output $\{x_i\}_{i \in [n]}$.

Fig. 6. Routine Program f^{-1^*}

---

1. Challenger samples a random $(z_0, x_0) \xleftarrow{R} \{0,1\}^{2\kappa}$
   (a) Sample $K \leftarrow \mathsf{PPRF.KeyGen}(1^\kappa)$
   (b) Compute $(\mathsf{pk}_0, \mathsf{sk}_0) \leftarrow \mathsf{KeyGen}(1^\kappa, F(K, z_0))$
   (c) Compute punctured key $K(\{z_0\})$
   (d) Let $\mathcal{O}\mathsf{Program\ f}^* = i\mathcal{O}(\kappa, \mathsf{Program\ f}^*)$ and $\mathcal{O}\mathsf{Program\ f}^{-1^*} = i\mathcal{O}(\kappa, \mathsf{Program\ f}^{-1^*})$.
   (e) Output $(\mathsf{pk} = (\mathcal{O}\mathsf{Program\ f}^*, \mathcal{O}\mathsf{Program\ f}^{-1^*}), \mathsf{sk} = K)$
2. Challenger runs $\mathsf{f}'_n(\mathsf{pk}, (z_0, x_0))$
   (a) Let $y_0 \leftarrow \mathcal{O}\mathsf{Program\ f}^*(z_0, x_0)$.

3. Adversary is given $(\mathsf{pk}, (z_0, y_0))$.
4. Adversary outputs (z', x')
5. If $\mathsf{f}'_n(\mathsf{pk}, (z', x')) = (z_0, y_0)$ then output 1 else output 0

Game 3
In this game, we compute $(\mathsf{pk}_0, \mathsf{sk}_0) \leftarrow \mathsf{KeyGen}(1^\kappa, r_0)$ using true randomness r_0.

1. Challenger samples a random $(z_0, x_0) \xleftarrow{R} \{0, 1\}^{2\kappa}$
   (a) Sample $K \leftarrow \mathsf{PPRF.KeyGen}(1^\kappa)$
   (b) Sample $r_0 \xleftarrow{R} \{0, 1\}^{r(\kappa)}$
   (c) $\overline{\text{Compute } (\mathsf{pk}_0, \mathsf{sk}_0) \leftarrow \mathsf{KeyGen}(1^\kappa, r_0)}$
   (d) Compute punctured key $K(\{z_0\})$
   (e) Let $\mathcal{O}\mathsf{Program}\ \mathsf{f}^* = i\mathcal{O}(\kappa, \mathsf{Program}\ \mathsf{f}^*)$ and $\mathcal{O}\mathsf{Program}\ \mathsf{f}^{-1*} = i\mathcal{O}(\kappa, \mathsf{Program}\ \mathsf{f}^{-1*})$.
   (f) Output $(\mathsf{pk} = (\mathcal{O}\mathsf{Program}\ \mathsf{f}^*, \mathcal{O}\mathsf{Program}\ \mathsf{f}^{-1*}), \mathsf{sk} = K)$
2. Challenger runs $\mathsf{f}'_n(\mathsf{pk}, (z_0, x_0))$
   (a) Let $y_0 \leftarrow \mathcal{O}\mathsf{Program}\ \mathsf{f}^*(z_0, x_0)$.
3. Adversary is given $(\mathsf{pk}, (z_0, y_0))$.
4. Adversary outputs (z', x')
5. If $\mathsf{f}'_n(\mathsf{pk}, (z', x')) = (z_0, y_0)$ then output 1 else output 0

7.3 Attack on Replica Encoding Scheme

First, we restate the security game in the context of the above TDP. We consider a variation of our construction in Sect. 5 with $r \in o(b \cdot n)$ instantiated with the above trapdoor permutation and present a concrete attack adversary which breaks the s-soundness of our replica encoding scheme for any constant $\mathsf{s} \in (0, 1)$. We remark that this attack also applies to the construction in Sect. 6.

Game 0: $\mathsf{Sound}_{\mathcal{A}_1, \mathcal{A}_2}(\kappa, n)$

- **Setup:** The challenger(denoted by $\mathcal{C}$) runs $(\mathsf{pk}', \mathsf{sk}') \leftarrow \mathsf{rSetup}(1^\kappa, 1^n)$ and sends public key $\mathsf{pk}' = (C'_0, C'_1, n)$ to $\mathcal{A}_1$. It keeps the secret key $\mathsf{sk}' = (K, n)$ for itself.
- **Phase 1:** The adversary $\mathcal{A}_1$ issues queries on $\mathsf{T}, \mathsf{T}^{-1}, \mathsf{H}, \mathcal{C}$ responds the query back to $\mathcal{A}_1$.
- **File Challenge:** $m \in \{0, 1\}^* \leftarrow \mathcal{A}_1^{\mathsf{H}(\cdot), \mathsf{T}(\cdot), \mathsf{T}^{-1}(\cdot)}(1^\kappa, \mathsf{pk}')$. It sends m to $\mathcal{C}$ who parses pk' as (C'_0, C'_1, n); sk' as (K, n) and does the following:

  - Divide m into b blocks of length λ i.e. $m = m_1 || m_2 || \ldots || m_b$, $b = \lceil |m|/\lambda \rceil$.
  - For $i \in [n]$,

    * Choose a string $\rho_i \xleftarrow{R} \{0, 1\}^\kappa$.
    * Compute $\forall t \in [b]$,
    $$Y_{t,0}^{(i)} = m_t \oplus \mathsf{H}(\rho_i || t).$$
    * For rounds j from 1 to r and $\forall t \in [b]$,

· Let $z_{t,j}^{(i)}, x_{t,j}^{(i)} \in \{0,1\}^{\lambda/2}$
· Let $z_{t,j}^{(i)} || x_{t,j}^{(i)} = \mathsf{T}(Y_{t,j}^{(i)})$
· Compute $Y_{t,j}^{(i)}$ from $Y_{t,j}^{(i)}$ as

$$(\mathsf{pk}_{t,j}^{(i)}, \mathsf{sk}_{t,j}^{(i)}) = \mathsf{KeyGen}(1^\kappa; \mathsf{PPRF.Eval}(K, z_{t,j}^{(i)})).$$

$$Y_{t,j}^{(i)} = z_{t,j}^{(i)} || \mathsf{f}^{-1}(\mathsf{sk}_{t,j}^{(i)}, x_{t,j}^{(i)})$$

* Let $y_r^{(i)} = Y_{1,r}^{(i)} || \ldots || Y_{b,r}^{(i)}$ and set $y^{(i)} = (y_r^{(i)}, \rho_i)$.
$\mathcal{C}$ returns $y^{(1)}, y^{(2)}, \ldots y^{(n)}$ to $\mathcal{A}_1$.

- **Phase 2:** $\mathcal{A}_1$ issues additional queries on $\mathsf{T}, \mathsf{T}^{-1}, \mathsf{H}, \mathcal{C}$ responds the query back to $\mathcal{A}_1$.
- **State Sharing:** $\mathcal{A}_1$ outputs state state $\leftarrow \mathcal{A}_1^{\mathsf{H}(\cdot),\mathsf{T}(\cdot),\mathsf{T}^{-1}(\cdot)}(1^\kappa, \mathsf{pk}', y)$ and sends state to $\mathcal{A}_2$.
- **Phase 3:** The adversary $\mathcal{A}_2$ queries on $\mathsf{T}, \mathsf{T}^{-1}, \mathsf{H}, \mathcal{C}$ responds the query back to $\mathcal{A}_2$.
- **Guess:** $\mathcal{A}_2$ outputs the replica guesses to $\mathcal{C}$.

$$\{\tilde{y}^{(i)}\} \leftarrow \mathcal{A}_2(1^\kappa, \mathsf{pk}', m, \mathsf{state}).$$

- **Verify:** Let $v_i = 1$ if $\tilde{y}^{(i)} = y^{(i)}$ and 0 otherwise. Adversary wins if $|\mathsf{state}| < \sum v_i \cdot \mathsf{s}(\kappa, |m|) \cdot \mathsf{len}(\kappa, |m|)$.

Now below, we present out construction of adversaries $\mathcal{A}_1, \mathcal{A}_2$.

$\mathcal{A}_1(1^\kappa, \mathsf{pk}' = (\mathsf{pk}, n))$

- Choose any message $m \in \{0,1\}^{b \cdot \lambda}$ where $b \geq 1$.
- Send m to challenger.
- Receive $\{y^{(i)} = \{Y_{t,r}^{(i)}\}_{t \in [b]}, \rho_i\}_{i \in [n]}$.
- For each $j \in [r]$, set $x_j = \bigoplus_{t \in [b], i \in [n]} Y_{t,j}^{(i)}$.
- Send $\{x_j\}, \{\rho_i\}$ as state.

$\mathcal{A}_2(1^\kappa, \mathsf{pk}' = (C_0', C_1', n), m, (\{x_j\}, \rho_i))$

- Divide m into b blocks of length λ, $m = m_1 || \ldots || m_b$
- For $i \in [r], t \in [b]$

  • Compute $Y_{t,0}^{(i)} = H(\rho_i || t) \oplus m_t$

- For $j \in [r]$

  • Set $\{Y_{t,j}^{(i)}\}_{i \in [r], t \in [b]} = C_1'(\{\mathsf{T}(Y_{t,j-1}^{(i)})\}, x_j)$

– For $i \in [r]$

• Let $y_r^{(i)} = Y_{1,r}^{(i)} || \dots || Y_{b,r}^{(i)}$ and output $(y_r^{(i)}, \rho_i)$

Lemma 5. $(\mathcal{A}_1, \mathcal{A}_2)$ *use* $\lambda \cdot o(b \cdot n) + n \cdot o(\lambda)$ *space.*

Proof. We observe that the state output is $\{x_j\}, \{\rho_i\}$, which use $r \cdot \lambda$, and $\kappa \cdot n$ space respectively. We use the fact that $r \in o(b \cdot n)$ and $\lambda \in \omega(\kappa)$ to give us our result. $\qquad\square$

Lemma 6. $\forall n \geq 1$, *there exists a negligible function* negl *such that the probability that* $\sum_i v_i = n$ *in the verification stage of* $\mathsf{Sound}_{\mathcal{A}_1, \mathcal{A}_2}(\kappa, n)$ *for adversaries* $(\mathcal{A}_1, \mathcal{A}_2)$ *is* $1 - \mathsf{negl}(\kappa)$.

Proof. We recall that C_1' is simply an obfuscation of program $\mathsf{Program}\ f^{-1}$. Thus, as long as the collection $\{z_{t,j}^{(i)}\}_{t \in [b], i \in [n]}$ is unique for every $j \in [r]$ and x_j is the $\oplus$ of $\{x_{t,j}^{(i)}\}_{t \in [b], i \in [n]}$, then C_1' will successfully invert. By the fact that H is a random oracle, and that T and f are permutations, we use the fact that a uniform random variable under a permutation is uniformly random to get that $\{z_{t,j}^{(i)}\}_{t \in [b], i \in [n]}$ is a uniform and independently random set. Thus, we can union bound the probability that any of them collide with $\binom{b \cdot n}{2} \cdot 2^{-\lambda/2} \in \mathsf{negl}(\kappa)$. In addition, we know that x_j is the aforementioned value by construction. Thus, we can inductively reason that our adversary computes $\{Y_{t,j}^{(i)}\}_{i \in [r], t \in [b]}$ correctly, and thus can recover the original encodings. $\qquad\square$

Lemma 7. *When instantiated with a round function* $r \in o(b \cdot n)$, *the construction in Sect. 5 is not* s*-sound for any constant functions* $\mathsf{s}(\kappa, |m|) = c \in (0, 1)$.

Proof. Recall the definition of s-soundness as

$$\Pr\left[\begin{array}{l} (v, \mathsf{state}, m) \leftarrow \mathsf{Sound}_{\mathcal{A}_1, \mathcal{A}_2}(\kappa, n), s.t. \\ |\mathsf{state}| < v \cdot \mathsf{s}(\kappa, |m|) \cdot \mathsf{len}(\kappa, |m|) \end{array} \right] \leq \mathsf{negl}(\kappa).$$

We know by Lemma 6 that $v = n$ with all but negligible probability, and from Lemma 5 that $|\mathsf{state}| \in \lambda \cdot o(b \cdot n) + n \cdot o(\lambda)$. We recall that $\mathsf{len}(\kappa, |m|) = |m| + O(\kappa) > \lambda \cdot b$. From this, we can conclude that for sufficiently large $\kappa, |m|$, we know

$$\lambda \cdot o(b \cdot n) + n \cdot o(\lambda) < n \cdot c \cdot \lambda \cdot b < v \cdot \mathsf{s}(\kappa, |m|) \cdot \mathsf{len}(\kappa, |m|)$$

with all but negligible probability, and so this scheme is not s-sound. $\qquad\square$

References

1. Abusalah, H., Alwen, J., Cohen, B., Khilko, D., Pietrzak, K., Reyzin, L.: Beyond Hellman's time-memory trade-offs with applications to proofs of space. In: Takagi, T., Peyrin, T. (eds.) ASIACRYPT 2017. LNCS, vol. 10625, pp. 357–379. Springer, Cham (2017). https://doi.org/10.1007/978-3-319-70697-9_13

2. Alwen, J., Chen, B., Kamath, C., Kolmogorov, V., Pietrzak, K., Tessaro, S.: On the complexity of scrypt and proofs of space in the parallel random oracle model. In: Fischlin, M., Coron, J.-S. (eds.) EUROCRYPT 2016. LNCS, vol. 9666, pp. 358–387. Springer, Heidelberg (2016). https://doi.org/10.1007/978-3-662-49896-5_13

3. Alwen, J., Chen, B., Pietrzak, K., Reyzin, L., Tessaro, S.: Scrypt is maximally memory-hard. In: Coron, J.-S., Nielsen, J.B. (eds.) EUROCRYPT 2017. LNCS, vol. 10212, pp. 33–62. Springer, Cham (2017). https://doi.org/10.1007/978-3-319-56617-7_2

4. Alwen, J., Serbinenko, V.: High parallel complexity graphs and memory-hard functions. In: Proceedings of the 47th Annual ACM Symposium on Theory of Computing, pp. 595–603 (2015)

5. Benet, J., Greco, N.: Filecoin: A decentralized storage network. Protocol Labs (2018)

6. Benet, J., Dalrymple, D., Greco, N.: Proof of replication. Protocol Labs (2017)

7. Boneh, D., Bonneau, J., Bünz, B., Fisch, B.: Verifiable delay functions. In: Shacham, H., Boldyreva, A. (eds.) CRYPTO 2018. LNCS, vol. 10991, pp. 757–788. Springer, Cham (2018). https://doi.org/10.1007/978-3-319-96884-1_25

8. Bowers, K.D., Juels, A., Oprea, A.: Proofs of retrievability: theory and implementation. In: Proceedings of the 2009 ACM Workshop on Cloud Computing Security, pp. 43–54 (2009)

9. Cecchetti, E., Fisch, B., Miers, I., Juels, A.: PIEs: public incompressible encodings for decentralized storage. In: Proceedings of the 2019 ACM SIGSAC Conference on Computer and Communications Security, pp. 1351–1367 (2019)

10. Dai, Y., Steinberger, J.: Indifferentiability of 8-round Feistel networks. In: Robshaw, M., Katz, J. (eds.) CRYPTO 2016. LNCS, vol. 9814, pp. 95–120. Springer, Heidelberg (2016). https://doi.org/10.1007/978-3-662-53018-4_4

11. Damgård, I., Ganesh, C., Orlandi, C.: Proofs of replicated storage without timing assumptions. In: Boldyreva, A., Micciancio, D. (eds.) CRYPTO 2019. LNCS, vol. 11692, pp. 355–380. Springer, Cham (2019). https://doi.org/10.1007/978-3-030-26948-7_13

12. Dodis, Y., Vadhan, S., Wichs, D.: Proofs of retrievability via hardness amplification. In: Reingold, O. (ed.) TCC 2009. LNCS, vol. 5444, pp. 109–127. Springer, Heidelberg (2009). https://doi.org/10.1007/978-3-642-00457-5_8

13. Dwork, C., Naor, M., Wee, H.: Pebbling and proofs of work. In: Shoup, V. (ed.) CRYPTO 2005. LNCS, vol. 3621, pp. 37–54. Springer, Heidelberg (2005). https://doi.org/10.1007/11535218_3

14. Dziembowski, S., Faust, S., Kolmogorov, V., Pietrzak, K.: Proofs of space. In: Gennaro, R., Robshaw, M. (eds.) CRYPTO 2015. LNCS, vol. 9216, pp. 585–605. Springer, Heidelberg (2015). https://doi.org/10.1007/978-3-662-48000-7_29

15. Dziembowski, S., Kazana, T., Wichs, D.: One-time computable self-erasing functions. In: Ishai, Y. (ed.) TCC 2011. LNCS, vol. 6597, pp. 125–143. Springer, Heidelberg (2011). https://doi.org/10.1007/978-3-642-19571-6_9

16. Fisch, B.: Tight proofs of space and replication. Cryptology ePrint Archive, Report 2018/702 (2018). https://eprint.iacr.org/2018/702

17. Fisch, B., Bonneau, J., Benet, J., Greco, N.: Proofs of replication using depth robust graphs. In: Blockchain Protocol Analysis and Security Engineering 2018 (2018)

18. Garg, R., Lu, G., Waters, B.: New techniques in replica encodings with client setup (2020)

19. Golle, P., Jarecki, S., Mironov, I.: Cryptographic primitives enforcing communi-
    cation and storage complexity. In: Blaze, M. (ed.) FC 2002. LNCS, vol. 2357, pp.
    120–135. Springer, Heidelberg (2003). https://doi.org/10.1007/3-540-36504-4_9
20. Holenstein, T., Künzler, R., Tessaro, S.: The equivalence of the random oracle
    model and the ideal cipher model, revisited. In: Fortnow, L., Vadhan, S.P. (eds.)
    Proceedings of the 43rd ACM Symposium on Theory of Computing, STOC 2011,
    San Jose, CA, USA, 6–8 June 2011, pp. 89–98. ACM (2011)
21. Juels, A., Kaliski Jr., B.S.: Pors: proofs of retrievability for large files. In: Proceed-
    ings of the 14th ACM Conference on Computer and Communications Security, pp.
    584–597 (2007)
22. Maurer, U., Renner, R., Holenstein, C.: Indifferentiability, impossibility results on
    reductions, and applications to the random oracle methodology. In: Naor, M. (ed.)
    TCC 2004. LNCS, vol. 2951, pp. 21–39. Springer, Heidelberg (2004). https://doi.
    org/10.1007/978-3-540-24638-1_2
23. Moran, T., Wichs, D.: Incompressible encodings. Manuscript (2020)
24. Ohta, K., Okamoto, T.: On concrete security treatment of signatures derived from
    identification. In: Krawczyk, H. (ed.) CRYPTO 1998. LNCS, vol. 1462, pp. 354–
    369. Springer, Heidelberg (1998). https://doi.org/10.1007/BFb0055741
25. Pietrzak, K.: Proofs of catalytic space. Cryptology ePrint Archive, Report
    2018/194 (2018). https://eprint.iacr.org/2018/194
26. Ren, L., Devadas, S.: Proof of space from stacked expanders. In: Hirt, M., Smith,
    A. (eds.) TCC 2016. LNCS, vol. 9985, pp. 262–285. Springer, Heidelberg (2016).
    https://doi.org/10.1007/978-3-662-53641-4_11
27. Ristenpart, T., Shacham, H., Shrimpton, T.: Careful with composition: limitations
    of the indifferentiability framework. In: Paterson, K.G. (ed.) EUROCRYPT 2011.
    LNCS, vol. 6632, pp. 487–506. Springer, Heidelberg (2011). https://doi.org/10.
    1007/978-3-642-20465-4_27
28. Sahai, A., Waters, B.: How to use indistinguishability obfuscation: deniable encryp-
    tion, and more. In: Proceedings of the 46th Annual ACM Symposium on Theory
    of Computing, pp. 475–484 (2014)
29. Shacham, H., Waters, B.: Compact proofs of retrievability. In: Pieprzyk, J. (ed.)
    ASIACRYPT 2008. LNCS, vol. 5350, pp. 90–107. Springer, Heidelberg (2008).
    https://doi.org/10.1007/978-3-540-89255-7_7
30. Van Dijk, M., Juels, A., Oprea, A., Rivest, R.L., Stefanov, E., Triandopoulos, N.:
    Hourglass schemes: how to prove that cloud files are encrypted. In: Proceedings
    of the 2012 ACM Conference on Computer and Communications Security, pp.
    265–280 (2012)

Non-malleable Codes, Extractors and Secret Sharing for Interleaved Tampering and Composition of Tampering

Eshan Chattopadhyay[1][✉] and Xin Li[2]

[1] Cornell University, Ithaca, NY 14853, USA
eshan@cs.cornell.edu
[2] Johns Hopkins University, Baltimore, MD 21218, USA
lixints@cs.jhu.edu

Abstract. Non-malleable codes were introduced by Dziembowski, Pietrzak, and Wichs (JACM 2018) as a generalization of standard error correcting codes to handle severe forms of tampering on codewords. This notion has attracted a lot of recent research, resulting in various explicit constructions, which have found applications in tamper-resilient cryptography and connections to other pseudorandom objects in theoretical computer science. We continue the line of investigation on explicit constructions of non-malleable codes in the information theoretic setting, and give explicit constructions for several new classes of tampering functions. These classes strictly generalize several previously studied classes of tampering functions, and in particular extend the well studied split-state model which is a "compartmentalized" model in the sense that the codeword is partitioned *a prior* into disjoint intervals for tampering. Specifically, we give explicit non-malleable codes for the following classes of tampering functions.

- Interleaved split-state tampering: Here the codeword is partitioned in an unknown way by an adversary, and then tampered with by a split-state tampering function.
- Affine tampering composed with split-state tampering: In this model, the codeword is first tampered with by a split-state adversary, and then the whole tampered codeword is further tampered with by an affine function. In fact our results are stronger, and we can handle affine tampering composed with interleaved split-state tampering.

Our results are the first explicit constructions of non-malleable codes in any of these tampering models. As applications, they also directly give non-malleable secret-sharing schemes with *binary shares* in the split-state joint tampering model and the stronger model of affine tampering composed with split-state joint tampering. We derive all these results from explicit constructions of seedless non-malleable extractors, which we believe are of independent interest.

Using our techniques, we also give an improved seedless extractor for an unknown interleaving of two independent sources.

© International Association for Cryptologic Research 2020
R. Pass and K. Pietrzak (Eds.): TCC 2020, LNCS 12552, pp. 584–613, 2020.
https://doi.org/10.1007/978-3-030-64381-2_21

Keywords: Non-malleable code · Tamper-resilient cryptography · Extractor

1 Introduction

1.1 Non-malleable Codes

Non-malleable codes were introduced by Dziembowski, Pietrzak, and Wichs [36] as an elegant relaxation and generalization of standard error correcting codes, where the motivation is to handle much larger classes of tampering functions on the codeword. Traditionally, error correcting codes only provide meaningful guarantees (e.g., unique decoding or list-decoding) when *part* of the codeword is modified (i.e., the modified codeword is close in Hamming distance to an actual codeword), whereas in practice an adversary can possibly use much more complicated functions to modify the entire codeword. In the latter case, it is easy to see that error correction or even error detection becomes generally impossible, for example an adversary can simply change all codewords into a fixed string. On the other hand, non-malleable codes can still provide useful guarantees here, and thus partially bridge this gap. Informally, a non-malleable code guarantees that after tampering, the decoding either correctly gives the original message or gives a message that is completely unrelated and independent of the original message. This captures the notion of non-malleability: that an adversary cannot modify the codeword in a way such that the tampered codeword decodes back to a related but different message.

The original intended application of non-malleable codes is in tamper-resilient cryptography [36], where they can be used generally to prevent an adversary from learning secret information by observing the input/output behavior of modified ciphertexts. Subsequently, non-malleable codes have found applications in non-malleable commitments [40], non-malleable encryption [30], public-key encryptions [31], non-malleable secret-sharing schemes [38], and privacy amplification protocols [19]. Furthermore, interesting connections were found to non-malleable extractors [27], and very recently to spectral expanders [54]. Along the way, the constructions of non-malleable codes used various components and sophisticated ideas from additive combinatorics [5,22] and randomness extraction [18], and some of these techniques have also found applications in constructing extractors for independent sources [46]. As such, non-malleable codes have become fundamental objects at the intersection of coding theory and cryptography. They are well deserved to be studied in more depth in their own right, as well as to find more connections to other well studied objects in theoretical computer science.

We first introduce some notation before formally defining non-malleable codes. For a function $f : S \to S$, we say $s \in S$ is a fixed point (of f) if $f(s) = s$.

Definition 1 (Tampering functions). *For any $n > 0$, let $\mathcal{F}_n$ denote the set of all functions $f : \{0,1\}^n \to \{0,1\}^n$. Any subset of $\mathcal{F}_n$ is a family of tampering functions.*

We use the statistical distance to measure the distance between distributions.

Definition 2. *The statistical distance between two distributions $\mathcal{D}_1$ and $\mathcal{D}_2$ over some universal set Ω is defined as $|\mathcal{D}_1 - \mathcal{D}_2| = \frac{1}{2}\sum_{d\in\Omega} |\mathbf{Pr}[\mathcal{D}_1 = d] - \mathbf{Pr}[\mathcal{D}_2 = d]|$. We say $\mathcal{D}_1$ is ϵ-close to $\mathcal{D}_2$ if $|\mathcal{D}_1 - \mathcal{D}_2| \leq \epsilon$ and denote it by $\mathcal{D}_1 \approx_\epsilon \mathcal{D}_2$.*

To introduce non-malleable codes, we need to define a function called copy that takes in two inputs. If the first input is the special symbol "same*", the copy function just outputs its second input. Else it outputs its first input. This is useful in defining non-malleable codes where one wants to model the situation that the decoding of the tampered codeword is either the original message or a distribution independent of the message. Thus, we define a distribution on the message space and the special symbol same*, where the probability that the distribution takes on the value same* corresponds to the probability that the tampered codeword is decoded back to the original message. More formally, we have

$$\text{copy}(x, y) = \begin{cases} x & \text{if } x \neq \text{same}^\star \\ y & \text{if } x = \text{same}^\star \end{cases}$$

Following the treatment in [36], we first define coding schemes.

Definition 3 (Coding schemes). *Let $\text{Enc} : \{0,1\}^k \rightarrow \{0,1\}^n$ and $\text{Dec} : \{0,1\}^n \rightarrow \{0,1\}^k \cup \{\perp\}$ be functions such that Enc is a randomized function (i.e., it has access to private randomness) and Dec is a deterministic function. We say that (Enc, Dec) is a coding scheme with block length n and message length k if for all $s \in \{0,1\}^k$, $\Pr[\text{Dec}(Enc(s)) = s] = 1$, where the probability is taken over the randomness in Enc.*

We can now define non-malleable codes.

Definition 4 (Non-malleable codes). *A coding scheme $\mathcal{C} = (\text{Enc}, \text{Dec})$ with block length n and message length k is a non-malleable code with respect to a family of tampering functions $\mathcal{F} \subset \mathcal{F}_n$ and error ϵ if for every $f \in \mathcal{F}$ there exists a random variable D_f on $\{0,1\}^k \cup \{\text{same}^\star\}$ which is independent of the randomness in Enc and is efficiently samplable given oracle access to $f(.)$, such that for all messages $s \in \{0,1\}^k$, it holds that*

$$|\text{Dec}(f(\text{Enc}(s))) - \text{copy}(D_f, s)| \leq \epsilon.$$

We say the code is explicit if both the encoding and decoding can be done in polynomial time. The rate of $\mathcal{C}$ is given by k/n.

Relevant Prior Work on Non-malleable Codes in the Information Theoretic Setting. There has been a lot of exciting research on non-malleable codes, and it is beyond the scope of this paper to provide a comprehensive survey of them. Instead we focus on relevant explicit (unconditional) constructions in the information theoretic setting, which is also the focus of this paper. One of the most studied classes of tampering functions is the so called *split-state* tampering, where the codeword is divided into (at least two) disjoint intervals and the adversary can tamper with each interval arbitrarily but independently. This model arises naturally in situations where the codeword may be stored in different parts of memory or different devices. Following a very successful line of work [1,2,4,5,7,18,22,27,34,41,43,44,46,47], we now have explicit constructions of non-malleable codes in the 2-split state model with constant rate and negligible error.

The split state model is a "compartmentalized" model, where the codeword is partitioned *a priori* into disjoint intervals for tampering. Recently, there has been progress towards handling non-compartmentalized tampering functions. A work of Agrawal, Gupta, Maji, Pandey and Prabhakaran [8] gave explicit constructions of non-malleable codes with respect to tampering functions that permute or flip the bits of the codeword. Ball, Dachman-Soled, Kulkarni and Malkin [12] gave explicit constructions of non-malleable codes against t-local functions for $t \leq n^{1-\epsilon}$. However in all these models, each bit of the tampering function only depends on part of the codeword. A recent work of Chattopadhyay and Li [21] gave the first explicit constructions of non-malleable codes where each bit of the tampering function may depend on all bits of the codeword. Specifically, they gave constructions for the classes of affine functions and small-depth (unbounded fain-in) circuits. The rate of the non-malleable code with respect to small-depth circuits was exponentially improved by a subsequent work of Ball, Dachman-Soled, Guo, Malkin, and Tan [11]. In a recent work, Ball, Guo and Wichs [13] constructed non-malleable codes with respect to bounded depth decision trees.

Given all these exciting results, a major goal of the research on non-malleable codes remains to give explicit constructions for broader classes of tampering functions, as one can use the probabilistic method to show the existence of non-malleable codes with rate close to $1 - \delta$ for any class $\mathcal{F}$ of tampering functions with $|\mathcal{F}| \leq 2^{2^{\delta n}}$ [26].

Our Results. We continue the line of investigation on explicit constructions of non-malleable codes, and give explicit constructions for several new classes of non-compartmentalized tampering functions, where in some classes each bit of the tampering function can depend on all the bits of the codeword. In Sect. 1.2, we discuss motivations and applications of our new non-malleable codes in cryptography. The new classes strictly generalize several previous studied classes of tampering functions. In particular, we consider the following classes.

1. *Interleaved 2-split-state tampering*, where the adversary can divide the codeword into two arbitrary disjoint intervals and tamper with each interval arbitrarily but independently. This model generalizes the split-state model and captures the situation where the codeword is partitioned into two blocks (not necessarily of the same length) in an unknown way by the adversary before applying a 2-split-state tampering function. Constructing non-malleable codes for this class of tampering functions was left as an open problem by Cheraghchi and Guruswami [27].

2. *Composition of tampering*, where the adversary takes two tampering functions and composes them together to get a new tampering function. We note

that function composition is a natural strategy for an adversary to achieve more powerful tampering, and it has been studied widely in other fields (e.g., computational complexity and communication complexity). We believe that studying non-malleable codes for the composition of different classes of tampering functions is also a natural and important direction.

We now formally define these classes and some related classes below. For notation, given any permutation $\pi : [n] \to [n]$ and any string x of length n, we let $y = x_\pi$ denote the length n string such that $y_{\pi(i)} = x_i$.

- The family of 2-split-state functions $2SS \subset \mathcal{F}_{2n}$: Any $f \in 2SS$ comprises of two functions $f_1 : \{0,1\}^n \to \{0,1\}^n$ and $f_2 : \{0,1\}^n \to \{0,1\}^n$, and for any $x, y \in \{0,1\}^n$, $f(x,y) = (f_1(x), f_2(y))$. This family of tampering functions has been extensively studied, with a long line of work achieving near optimal explicit constructions of non-malleable codes.
- The family of affine functions $\text{Lin} \subset \mathcal{F}_n$: Any $f \in \text{Lin}$ is an affine function from $\{0,1\}^n$ to $\{0,1\}^n$ (viewing $\{0,1\}^n$ as $\mathbb{F}_2^n$), i.e., $f(x) = Mx + v$, for some $n \times n$ matrix M on $\mathbb{F}_2$ and $v \in \mathbb{F}_2^n$.
- The family of interleaved 2-split-state functions $(2,t)\text{-ISS} \subset \mathcal{F}_n$: Any $f \in (2,t)\text{-ISS}$ comprises of two functions $f_1 : \{0,1\}^{n_1} \to \{0,1\}^{n_1}$, $f_2 : \{0,1\}^{n_2} \to \{0,1\}^{n_2}$ such that $n_1 + n_2 = n$ and $\min\{n_1, n_2\} \geq t$ (i.e both partitions are of length at least t), and a permutation $\pi : [n] \to [n]$. For any $z = (x,y)_\pi \in \{0,1\}^n$, where $x \in \{0,1\}^{n_1}, y \in \{0,1\}^{n_2}$, let $f(z) = (f_1(x), f_2(y))_\pi$. In this paper we require that $t \geq n^\beta$ for some fixed constant $0 < \beta < 1$. Note this includes as a special case the situation where the two states have the same size, which we denote by 2ISS, and in particular 2SS.
- For any tampering function families $\mathcal{F}, \mathcal{G} \subset \mathcal{F}_n$, define the family $\mathcal{F} \circ \mathcal{G} \subset \mathcal{F}_n$ to be the set of all functions of the form $f \circ g$, where $f \in \mathcal{F}$, $g \in \mathcal{G}$ and $\circ$ denotes function composition.

We now formally state our results. Our most general result is an explicit non-malleable code with respect to the tampering class of $\text{Lin} \circ (2, n^\beta)\text{-ISS}$, i.e, an affine function composed with an interleaved 2-split-state tampering function. Specifically, we have the following theorem.

Theorem 5. *There exist constants* $\beta, \delta > 0$ *such that for all integers* $n > 0$ *there exists an explicit non-malleable code with respect to* $\text{Lin} \circ (2, n^\beta)\text{-ISS}$ *with rate* $1/n^\delta$ *and error* 2^{-n^δ}.

We immediately have the following corollary, which records the classes of functions for which no explicit non-malleable codes were known (for any rate) prior to this work.

Corollary 1. *There exist constants* $\beta, \delta > 0$ *such that for all integers* $n > 0$ *there exists an explicit non-malleable code with respect to the following classes of functions with rate* $1/n^\delta$ *and error* 2^{-n^δ}:

- 2ISS, $(2, n^\beta)\text{-ISS}$, $\text{Lin} \circ 2\text{ISS}$ *and* $\text{Lin} \circ 2\text{SS}$.

1.2   Motivations and Applications in Cryptography

Just as standard non-malleable codes for split-state tampering arise from natural cryptographic applications, our non-malleable codes for interleaved 2-split-state tampering and affine tampering composed with interleaved split-state tampering also have natural cryptographic motivations and applications.

It is known that any non-malleable code in the 2-split-state model gives a 2 out of 2 secret-sharing scheme, if one views the two split states as two shares [6]. We show that any non-malleable code in the interleaved 2-split state model gives a *non-malleable secret-sharing* scheme with *binary shares*. Secret-sharing schemes [14,58] are fundamental objects in cryptography, and building blocks for many other more advanced applications such as secure multiparty computation. In short, a secret-sharing scheme shares a message secretly among n parties, such that any qualified subset can reconstruct the message, while any unqualified subset reveals nothing (or almost nothing) about the message. Equivalently, one can view this as saying that any leakage function which leaks the shares in an unqualified subset reveals nothing. In the standard threshold or t out of n secret-sharing, any subset of size at most t is an unqualified subset while any subset of size larger than t is a qualified subset. However, it is known that in such a scheme, the share size has to be at least as large as the message size. Thus, a natural and interesting question is whether the share size can be smaller under some relaxed notion of secret-sharing. This is indeed possible when one considers the notion of (r,t)-*ramp* secret-sharing, where $r > t + 1$. In this setting, any subset of size at most t reveals nothing about the message, while any subset of size at least r can reconstruct message. Thus t is called the privacy threshold and r is called the reconstruction threshold. Subsets of size between $t + 1$ and $r - 1$ may reveal some partial information about the message. Again, it is not hard to see that the share size in this case has to be at least as large as $m/(r - t)$, where m is the message length. Thus, if one allows a sufficiently large gap between r and t, then it is possible to achieve a secret-sharing scheme even with binary shares.

Secret-sharing schemes are also closely related to error correcting codes. For example, the celebrated Shamir's scheme [58] is based on Reed-Solomon codes. Similarly, binary secret-sharing schemes are largely based on binary error correcting codes, and they are studied in a series of recent works [15,16,25,48] in terms of the tradeoff between the message length, the privacy threshold t, the reconstruction threshold r, and the complexity of the sharing and reconstruction functions.

However, standard secret-sharing schemes only allow an adversary to passively observe some shares, thus one can ask the natural question of whether it is possible to protect against even active adversaries who can tamper with the shares. In this context, the notion of *robust* secret-sharing schemes (e.g., [17,51]) allows qualified subsets to recover the message even if the adversary can modify *part* of the shares. More recently, by generalizing non-malleable codes, Goyal and Kumar [38] introduced non-malleable secret-sharing schemes, where the adversary can tamper with *all* shares in some restricted manner. Naturally, the guarantee is that if tampering happens, then the reconstructed message is either the original message or something completely unrelated. In particular, they constructed t out of n non-malleable secret-sharing schemes in the following two tampering models. In the independent tampering model, the adversary can tamper with each share independently. In the joint tampering model, the adversary can divide any subset of $t+1$ shares arbitrarily into two sets of *different size*, and tamper with the shares in each set jointly, but independently across the two sets. Note that the adversary in the second model is strictly stronger than the adversary in the first one, since for reconstruction one only considers subsets of size $t + 1$. Several follow up works [3,9,39] studied different models such as non-malleable secret-sharing schemes for general access structures, and achieved improvements in various parameters.

However, in all known constructions of non-malleable secret-sharing schemes the share size is always larger than 1 bit. In other words, no known non-malleable secret-sharing scheme can achieve binary shares. This is an obstacle that results from the techniques in all known constructions. Indeed, even if one allows (r,t)-*ramp* non-malleable secret-sharing with an arbitrarily large gap between r and t, no known constructions can achieve binary shares, because they all need to put at least *two* shares of some standard secret-sharing schemes together to form a single share in the non-malleable scheme. Thus it is a natural question to see if one can construct non-malleable secret-sharing schemes with binary shares using different techniques.

Our non-malleable codes for interleaved 2-split-state tampering directly give non-malleable secret-sharing schemes with binary shares that protect against joint tampering. We have the following theorem.

Theorem 6. *There exist constants $0 < \alpha < \beta < 1$ such that for all integers $n > 0$ there exists an explicit (r,t)-ramp non-malleable secret-sharing scheme with binary shares, where $r = n$, $t = n-n^{\beta}$ and the message length is n^{α}. The scheme has statistical privacy with error $2^{-n^{\Omega(1)}}$, and is resilient with error $2^{-n^{\Omega(1)}}$ to joint tampering where the adversary arbitrarily partitions the r shares into two blocks, each with at most t shares, and tampers with each block independently using an arbitrary function.*

Intuitively, any n-bit non-malleable code for interleaved 2-split-state tampering gives a ramp non-malleable secret-sharing scheme with reconstruction threshold $r = n$, as follows. If the code protects against an adversary who can partition the codeword into two disjoint sets and tamper with each set arbitrarily but independently, then each set must reveal (almost) nothing about the secret message. Otherwise, the adversary can simply look at one set and use the leaked information to modify the shares in this set, and make the reconstructed message become a different but related message. In particular, the same proof in [6] for the standard 2-split state model also works for the interleaved 2-split state model. Since our code works for interleaved 2-split-state tampering and the size of one set can be as large as $n - n^{\beta}$, this implies privacy threshold at least $n - n^{\beta}$, with the small error in privacy coming from the error of the non-malleable code. We refer the reader to the full version of our paper for more details.

It is an interesting open question to construct explicit non-malleable secret-sharing schemes with binary shares where the reconstruction threshold $r < n$. We note that this question is closely related to constructing non-malleable codes for the tampering class 2SS∘Lin or 2ISS∘Lin (i.e., reverse the order of composition). This is because to get such a scheme, one natural idea is to apply another secret-sharing scheme on top of our non-malleable code. If one uses a linear secret-sharing scheme as in many standard schemes, then the tampering function on the codeword becomes 2SS ∘ Lin or 2ISS ∘ Lin.

We also note that in an (r, t)-ramp secret-sharing scheme with binary shares, unless the message has only one bit, we must have $r > t + 1$. Thus in the joint tampering model, instead of allowing the adversary to divide r shares arbitrarily into two sets, one must put an upper bound t on the size of each set as in our theorem. For example, one cannot allow an adversary to look at a set of shares with size $r - 1$, because $r - 1 > t$ and this set of shares may already leak some information about the secret message.

In both standard secret-sharing and non-malleable secret-sharing, in addition to looking at sets of shares, researchers have also studied other classes of leakage function or tampering function. For example, the work of Goyal et al. [37] studied secret-sharing schemes that are resilient to affine leakage functions on all shares, and used them to construct parity resilient circuits and bounded communication leakage resilient protocols. A recent work of Lin et al. [49] also studied non-malleable secret-sharing schemes where the adversary can tamper with *all* shares jointly using some restricted classes of functions. Specifically, [49] considered the model of "adaptive" affine tampering, where the adversary is allowed to first observe the shares in some unqualified subset, and then choose an affine function based on this to tamper with all shares. In this sense, our non-malleable codes for affine tampering composed with interleaved 2-split-state tampering also directly give non-malleable secret-sharing schemes with binary shares that protect against affine tampering composed with joint tampering, which is strictly stronger than both the joint tampering model and the affine tampering model (although our affine tampering is non-adaptive compared to [49]). Specifically, we have the following theorem (which strictly generalizes Theorem 6).

Theorem 7. *There exist constants $0 < \alpha < \beta < 1$ such that for all integers $n > 0$ there exists an explicit (r, t)-ramp non-malleable secret-sharing scheme with binary shares, where $r = n$, $t = n - n^\beta$ and the message length is n^α. The scheme has statistical privacy with error $2^{-n^{\Omega(1)}}$, and is resilient with error $2^{-n^{\Omega(1)}}$ to an adversary that tampers in two stages: In the first stage, the adversary partitions the r shares arbitrarily into two blocks, each with at most t shares, and tampers with each block independently using an arbitrary function. In the second stage, the adversary applies an arbitrary affine tampering function jointly on all the already tampered (from the first stage) r shares.*

We provide a formal proof of the above theorem in the full version of our paper.

Again, it is an interesting open question to construct explicit non-malleable secret-sharing schemes where the order of tampering is reversed.

1.3   Seedless Non-malleable Extractors

Our results on non-malleable codes are based on new constructions of seedless non-malleable extractors, which we believe are of independent interest. Before defining seedless non-malleable extractors formally, we first recall some basic notation from the area of randomness extraction.

Randomness extraction is motivated by the problem of purifying imperfect (or defective) sources of randomness. The concern stems from the fact that natural random sources often have poor quality, while most applications require high quality (e.g., uniform) random bits. We use the standard notion of min-entropy to measure the amount of randomness in a distribution.

Definition 8. *The min-entropy $H_\infty(\mathbf{X})$ of a probability distribution $\mathbf{X}$ on $\{0,1\}^n$ is defined to be $\min_x(-\log(\Pr[\mathbf{X} = x]))$. We say $\mathbf{X}$ is an $(n, H_\infty(\mathbf{X}))$-source and the min-entropy rate is $H_\infty(\mathbf{X})/n$.*

It turns out that it is impossible to extract from a single general weak random source even for min-entropy $n - 1$. There are two possible ways to bypass this barrier. The first one is to relax the extractor to be a *seeded extractor*, which takes an additional independent short random seed to extract from a weak random source. The second one is to construct deterministic extractors for special classes of weak random sources.

Both kinds of extractors have been studied extensively. Recently, they have also been generalized to stronger notions where the inputs to the extractor can be tampered with by an adversary. Specifically, Dodis and Wichs [33] introduced the notion of *seeded non-malleable extractor* in the context of privacy amplification against an active adversary. Informally, such an extractor satisfies the stronger property that the output of the extractor is independent of the output of the extractor on a tampered seed. Similarly, and more relevant to this paper, a seedless variant of non-malleable extractors was introduced by Cheraghchi and Guruswami [27] as a way to construct non-malleable codes. Apart from their original applications, both kinds of non-malleable extractors are of independent interest. They are also related to each other and have applications in constructions of extractors for independent sources [46].

We now define seedless non-malleable extractors.

Definition 9 (Seedless non-malleable extractors). *Let $\mathcal{F} \subset \mathcal{F}_n$ be a family of tampering functions such that no function in $\mathcal{F}$ has any fixed points. A function $\mathrm{nmExt} : \{0,1\}^n \to \{0,1\}^m$ is a seedless (n, m, ϵ)-non-malleable extractor with respect to $\mathcal{F}$ and a class of sources $\mathcal{X}$ if for every distribution $\mathbf{X} \in \mathcal{X}$ and every tampering function $f \in \mathcal{F}$, there exists a random variable that is $D_{f,X}$ on $\{0,1\}^m \cup \{\mathrm{same}^\star\}$ that is independent of $\mathbf{X}$, such that*

$$|\mathrm{nmExt}(\mathbf{X}), \mathrm{nmExt}(f(\mathbf{X})) - \mathbf{U}_m, \mathrm{copy}(D_{f,X}, \mathbf{U}_m)| \leq \epsilon.$$

Further, we say that nmExt is ϵ'-invertible, if there exists a polynomial time sampling algorithm $\mathcal{A}$ that takes as input $y \in \{0,1\}^m$, and outputs a sample from a distribution that is ϵ'-close to the uniform distribution on the set $\mathrm{nmExt}^{-1}(y)$.

In the above definition, when the class of sources $\mathcal{X}$ is the distribution $\mathbf{U}_n$, we simply say that nmExt is a seedless (n, m, ϵ)-non-malleable extractor with respect to $\mathcal{F}$.

Relevant Prior Work on Seedless Non-malleable Extractors. The first construction of seedless non-malleable extractors was given by Chattopadhyay and Zuckerman [22] with respect to the class of 10-split-state tampering. Subsequently, a series of works starting with the work of Chattopadhyay, Goyal and Li [18] gave explicit seedless non-malleable extractors for 2-split-state tampering. The only known constructions with respect to a class of tampering functions different from split state tampering is from the work of Chattopadhyay and Li [21], which gave explicit seedless non-malleable extractors with respect to the tampering class Lin and small depth circuits, and a subsequent follow-up work of Ball et al. [10] where they constructed non-malleable extractors against tampering functions that are low-degree polynomials over large fields. We note that constructing explicit seedless non-malleable extractors with respect to 2ISS was also posed as an open problem in [27].

Our Results. As our most general result, we give the first explicit constructions of seedless non-malleable extractors with respect to the tampering class Lin ○ $(2, n^\beta)$-ISS.

Theorem 10. *There exists a constant $\beta > 0$ such that for all $n > 0$ there exists an efficiently computable seedless $(n, n^{\Omega(1)}, 2^{-n^{\Omega(1)}})$-non-malleable extractor with respect to* Lin ○ $(2, n^\beta)$*-ISS, that is $2^{-n^{\Omega(1)}}$-invertible.*

This immediately yields the first explicit non-malleable extractors against the following classes of tampering functions.

Corollary 2. *For all $n > 0$ there exists an efficiently computable seedless $(n, n^{\Omega(1)}, 2^{-n^{\Omega(1)}})$-non-malleable extractor with respect to the following classes of tampering functions:*

– 2ISS, $(2, n^\beta)$-ISS, Lin ○ 2ISS, *and* Lin ○ 2SS.

We derive our results on non-malleable codes using the above explicit constructions of non-malleable extractors based on a beautiful connection discovered by Cheraghchi and Gurswami [27] (see Theorem 25 for more details).

1.4 Extractors for Interleaved Sources

Our techniques also yield improved explicit constructions of extractors for interleaved sources, which generalize extractors for independent sources in the following way: the inputs to the extractor are samples from a few independent sources mixed (interleaved) in an unknown (but fixed) way. Raz and Yehudayoff [57] showed that such extractors have applications in communication complexity and proving lower bounds for arithmetic circuits. In a subsequent work, Chattopadhyay and Zuckerman [24] showed that such extractors can also be used to construct extractors for certain samplable sources, extending a line of work initiated by Trevisan and Vadhan [60]. We now define interleaved sources formally.

Definition 11 (Interleaved Sources). *Let* $\mathbf{X}_1, \ldots, \mathbf{X}_r$ *be arbitrary independent sources on* $\{0,1\}^n$ *and let* $\pi : [rn] \to [rn]$ *be any permutation. Then* $\mathbf{Z} = (\mathbf{X}_1, \ldots, \mathbf{X}_r)_\pi$ *is an r-interleaved source.*

Relevant Prior Work on Interleaved Extractors. Raz and Yehudayoff [57] gave explicit extractors for 2-interleaved sources when both the sources have min-entropy at least $(1 - \delta)n$ for a tiny constant $\delta > 0$. Their construction is based on techniques from additive combinatorics and can output $\Omega(n)$ bits with exponentially small error. Subsequently, Chattopadhyay and Zuckerman [24] constructed extractors for 2-interleaved sources where one source has entropy $(1 - \gamma)n$ for a small constant $\gamma > 0$ and the other source has entropy $\Omega(\log n)$. They achieve output length $O(\log n)$ bits with error $n^{-\Omega(1)}$.

A much better result (in terms of the min-entropy) is known if the extractor has access to an interleaving of more sources. For a large enough constant C, Chattopadhyay and Li [20] gave an explicit extractor for C-interleaved sources where each source has entropy $k \geq \text{poly}(\log n)$. They achieve output length $k^{\Omega(1)}$ and error $n^{-\Omega(1)}$.

Our Results. Our main result is an explicit extractor for 2-interleaved sources where each source has min-entropy at least $2n/3$. The extractor outputs $\Omega(n)$ bits with error $2^{-n^{\Omega(1)}}$.

Theorem 12. *For any constant* $\delta > 0$ *and all integers* $n > 0$, *there exists an efficiently computable function* $i\ell\text{Ext} : \{0,1\}^{2n} \to \{0,1\}^m$, $m = \Omega(n)$, *such that for any two independent sources* $\mathbf{X}$ *and* $\mathbf{Y}$, *each on* n *bits with min-entropy at least* $(2/3 + \delta)n$, *and any permutation* $\pi : [2n] \to [2n]$,

$$|i\ell\text{Ext}((\mathbf{X}, \mathbf{Y})_\pi) - \mathbf{U}_m| \leq 2^{-n^{\Omega(1)}}.$$

2   Overview of Constructions and Techniques

Our results on non-malleable codes are derived from explicit constructions of invertible seedless non-malleable extractors (see Theorem 25). In this section, we illustrate our main ideas used to give explicit constructions of seedless non-malleable extractors with respect to the relevant classes of tampering functions, and explicit extractors for interleaved sources.

We first focus on the main ideas involved in constructing non-malleable extractors against 2-split-state adversaries when the partition are of equal length (we denote this by 2ISS). This serves to illustrate the important ideas that go into all our explicit non-malleable extractor constructions. We refer the reader to the full version of our paper for complete details of our non-malleable extractor and code constructions.

2.1   Seedless Non-malleable Extractors with Respect to Interleaved 2-split-state Tampering

We discuss the construction of a non-malleable extractor with respect to 2ISS. In such settings, it was shown in [27] that it is enough to construct non-malleable extractors assuming that at least one of f and g does not have any fixed points, assuming that the sources $\mathbf{X}$ and $\mathbf{Y}$ have entropy at least $n - n^\delta$. Thus, we construct a seedless non-malleable extractor $\mathrm{nmExt} : \{0,1\}^n \times \{0,1\}^n \to \{0,1\}^m$, $m = n^{\Omega(1)}$ such that the following hold: let $\mathbf{X}$ and $\mathbf{Y}$ be independent $(n, n - n^\delta)$-sources, for some small $\delta > 0$. Let $f : \{0,1\}^n \to \{0,1\}^n$, $g : \{0,1\}^n \to \{0,1\}^n$ be arbitrary functions such that at least one of them has not fixed points, and $\pi : [2n] \to [2n]$ be an arbitrary permutation. Then,

$$\mathrm{nmExt}((\mathbf{X}, \mathbf{Y})_\pi), \mathrm{nmExt}((f(\mathbf{X}), g(\mathbf{Y}))_\pi)) \approx_\epsilon \mathbf{U}_m, \mathrm{nmExt}((f(\mathbf{X}), g(\mathbf{Y}))_\pi) \quad (1)$$

where $\epsilon = 2^{-n^{\Omega(1)}}$.

Our construction is based on the framework of advice generators and correlation breakers set up in the work [18], and used in various follow-up works on non-malleable extractors and codes. Before explaining this framework, we introduce some notation for ease of presentation. Let $\mathbf{Z} = (\mathbf{X}, \mathbf{Y})_\pi$. We use the notation that if $\mathbf{W} = h((\mathbf{X}, \mathbf{Y})_\pi)$ (for some function h), then $\mathbf{W}'$ or $(\mathbf{W})'$ stands for the corresponding random variable $h((f(\mathbf{X}), g(\mathbf{Y}))_\pi)$. Thus, $\mathbf{Z}' = (f(\mathbf{X}), g(\mathbf{Y}))_\pi$.

On a very high level, the task of constructing a non-malleable extractor can be broken down into the following two steps:

1. Generating advice: the task here is to construct a function advGen : $\{0,1\}^{2n} \to \{0,1\}^a$, $a \le n^\delta$, such that $\mathrm{advGen}(\mathbf{Z}) \ne \mathrm{advGen}(\mathbf{Z}')$ with high probability.
2. Breaking correlation: here we construct an object that can be seen as a relaxation of a non-malleable extractor, in the sense that we supply the non-malleable extractor with a short advice string. This object is called an advice correlation breaker. We require that for all distinct strings $s, s' \in \{0,1\}^a$,

$$\mathrm{ACB}(\mathbf{Z}, s), \mathrm{ACB}(\mathbf{Z}', s') \approx \mathbf{U}_m, \mathrm{ACB}(\mathbf{Z}', s').$$

Given the above components, the non-malleable extractor is defined as:

$$\mathrm{nmExt}(\mathbf{Z}) = \mathrm{ACB}(\mathbf{Z}, \mathrm{advGen}(\mathbf{Z})).$$

The fact that the above satisfies (1) is not direct, but relies on further properties of the function advGen. In particular, we require that with high probability over the fixings of the random variables $\mathrm{advGen}(\mathbf{Z})$ and $\mathrm{advGen}(\mathbf{Z}')$, $\mathbf{X}$ and $\mathbf{Y}$ remain independent high min-entropy sources.

An Explicit Advice Generator. A natural first idea to construct an advice generator can be as follows: Take a slice (prefix) of $\mathbf{Z}$, say $\mathbf{Z}_1$, and use this to sample some coordinates from an encoding (using a good error correcting code) of $\mathbf{Z}$. A similar high level strategy has for example been used in [18], and other follow-up works. The intuition behind such a strategy is that since we assume $\mathbf{Z} \neq \mathbf{Z}'$, encoding it will ensure that they differ on a lot of coordinates. Thus, sampling a random set of coordinates will include one such coordinate with high probability. However, in the present case, it is not clear why this should work since it could be that $\mathbf{Z}_1$ contains all bits from say $\mathbf{X}$, and the set of coordinates where the encoding of $\mathbf{Z}$ and $\mathbf{Z}'$ differ may be a function of $\mathbf{X}$, which leads to unwanted correlations.

The next natural idea could be the following: First use the slice $\mathbf{Z}_1$ to sample a few coordinates from $\mathbf{Z}$. Let $\mathbf{Z}_2$ indicate $\mathbf{Z}$ projected onto the sampled coordinates. Now, it is not hard to prove that $\mathbf{Z}_2$ contains roughly equal number of bits from both the sources $\mathbf{X}$ and $\mathbf{Y}$. A strategy could be to now use $\mathbf{Z}_2$ to sample coordinates from an encoding of $\mathbf{Z}$. However, in this case, we run into similar problems as before: there may be unwanted correlations between the randomness used for sampling, and the random variable corresponding to the set of coordinates where the encoding of $\mathbf{Z}$ and $\mathbf{Z}'$ differ.

It turns out that the following subtler construction works:

Let $n_0 = n^{\delta'}$ for some small constant $\delta' > 0$. We take two slices from $\mathbf{Z}$, say $\mathbf{Z}_1$ and $\mathbf{Z}_2$ of lengths $n_1 = n_0^{c_0}$ and $n_2 = 10n_0$, for some constant $c_0 > 1$. Next, we use a good linear error correcting code (let the encoder of this code be E) to encode $\mathbf{Z}$ and sample n^γ coordinates (let $\mathbf{S}$ denote this set) from this encoding using $\mathbf{Z}_1$ (the sampler is based on seeded extractors [61]). Let $\mathbf{W}_1 = E(\mathbf{Z})_{\mathbf{S}}$. Next, using $\mathbf{Z}_2$, we sample a random set of indices $\mathbf{T} \subset [2n]$, and let $\mathbf{Z}_3 = \mathbf{Z}_{\mathbf{T}}$. We now use an extractor for interleaved sources, i.e., an extractor that takes as input an unknown interleaving of two independent sources and outputs uniform bits (see Sect. 1.4). Let $i\ell\mathrm{Ext}$ be this extractor (say from Theorem 12), and we apply it to $\mathbf{Z}_3$ to get $\mathbf{R} = i\ell\mathrm{Ext}(\mathbf{Z}_3)$. Finally, let $\mathbf{W}_2$ be the output of a linear seeded extractor[1] LExt on $\mathbf{Z}$ with $\mathbf{R}$ as the seed. The output of the advice generator is $\mathbf{Z}_1, \mathbf{Z}_2, \mathbf{Z}_3, \mathbf{W}_1, \mathbf{W}_2$.

Notation: Define $\overline{x} = (x, 0^n)_\pi$ and $\overline{y} = (0^n, y)_\pi$. Similarly, define $\overline{f(x)} = (f(x), 0^n)_\pi$ and $\overline{g(y)} = (0^n, g(y))_\pi$. Thus, $(x, y)_\pi = \overline{x} + \overline{y}$ and $(f(x), g(y))_\pi = \overline{f(x)} + \overline{g(y)}$. Let $\mathbf{X}_i$ be the bits of $\mathbf{X}$ in $\mathbf{Z}_i$ for $i = 1, 2, 3$ and $\mathbf{X}_4$ be the remaining bits of $\mathbf{X}$. Similarly define $\mathbf{Y}_i$'s, $i = 1, 2, 3, 4$.

We now proceed to argue the correctness of the above construction. Note that the correctness of advGen is direct if $\mathbf{Z}_i \neq \mathbf{Z}'_i$ for some $i \in \{1, 2, 3\}$. Thus, assume $\mathbf{Z}_i = \mathbf{Z}'_i$ for $i = 1, 2, 3$. It follows that $\mathbf{S} = \mathbf{S}', \mathbf{T} = \mathbf{T}'$ and $\mathbf{R} = \mathbf{R}'$. Recall that $(\mathbf{X}, \mathbf{Y})_\pi = \overline{\mathbf{X}} + \overline{\mathbf{Y}}$ and $(f(\mathbf{X}), g(\mathbf{Y})_\pi) = \overline{f(\mathbf{X})} + \overline{g(\mathbf{Y})}$. Since E is a linear code and LExt is a linear seeded extractor, the following hold:

$$\mathbf{W}_1 - \mathbf{W}'_1 = (E(\overline{\mathbf{X}} + \overline{\mathbf{Y}} - \overline{f(\mathbf{X})} - \overline{g(\mathbf{Y})}))_{\mathbf{S}},$$
$$\mathbf{W}_2 - \mathbf{W}'_2 = \mathrm{LExt}(\overline{\mathbf{X}} + \overline{\mathbf{Y}} - \overline{f(\mathbf{X})} - \overline{g(\mathbf{Y})}, \mathbf{R}).$$

---

[1] A linear seeded extractor is a seeded extractor where for any fixing of the seed, the output is a linear function of the source.

Suppose that $\mathbf{Z}_1$ contains more bits from $\mathbf{X}$ than $\mathbf{Y}$, i.e., $|\mathbf{X}_1| \geq |\mathbf{Y}_1|$ (where $|\alpha|$ denotes the length of the string α).

Now the idea is the following: Either (i) we can fix $\overline{\mathbf{X}} - \overline{f(\mathbf{X})}$ and claim that $\mathbf{X}_1$ still has enough min-entropy, or (ii) we can claim that $\overline{\mathbf{X}} - \overline{f(\mathbf{X})}$ has enough min-entropy conditioned on the fixing of $(\mathbf{X}_2, \mathbf{X}_3)$. Let us first discuss why this is enough. Suppose we are in the first case. Then, we can fix $\overline{\mathbf{X}} - \overline{f(\mathbf{X})}$ and $\mathbf{Y}$ and argue that $\mathbf{Z}_1$ is a deterministic function of $\mathbf{X}$ and contains enough entropy. Note that $\overline{\mathbf{X}} + \overline{\mathbf{Y}} - \overline{f(\mathbf{X})} - \overline{g(\mathbf{Y})}$ is now fixed, and in fact it is fixed to a non-zero string (using the assumption that at least one of f or g has no fixed points). Thus, $E(\overline{\mathbf{X}} + \overline{\mathbf{Y}} - \overline{f(\mathbf{X})} - \overline{g(\mathbf{Y})})$ is a string with a constant fraction of the coordinates set to 1 (since E is an encoder of a linear error correcting code with constant relative distance), and it follows that with high probability $(E(\overline{\mathbf{X}} + \overline{\mathbf{Y}} - \overline{f(\mathbf{X})} - \overline{g(\mathbf{Y})}))_{\mathbf{S}}$ contains a non-zero entry (using the fact that $\mathbf{S}$ is sampled using $\mathbf{Z}_1$, which has enough entropy). This finishes the proof in this case since it implies $\mathbf{W}_1 \neq \mathbf{W}_1'$ with high probability.

Now suppose we are in case (ii). We use the fact that $\mathbf{Z}_2$ contains entropy to conclude that the sampled bits $\mathbf{Z}_3$ contain almost equal number of bits from $\mathbf{X}$ and $\mathbf{Y}$ (with high probability over $\mathbf{Z}_2$). Now we can fix $\mathbf{Z}_2$ without loosing too much entropy from $\mathbf{Z}_3$ (by making the size of $\mathbf{Z}_3$ to be significantly larger than $\mathbf{Z}_2$). Next, we observe that $\mathbf{Z}_3$ is an interleaved source, and hence $\mathbf{R}$ is close to uniform. We now fix $\mathbf{X}_3$, and argue that $\mathbf{R}$ continues to be uniform. This follows roughly from the fact that any extractor for an interleaving of 2-sources is strong. Thus, $\mathbf{R}$ now becomes a deterministic function of $\mathbf{Y}$ while at the same time, $\overline{\mathbf{X}} - \overline{f(\mathbf{X})}$ still has enough min-entropy. Hence, $\text{LExt}(\overline{\mathbf{X}} - \overline{f(\mathbf{X})}, \mathbf{R})$ is close to uniform even conditioned on $\mathbf{R}$. We can now fix $\mathbf{R}$ and $\text{LExt}(\overline{\mathbf{Y}} - \overline{g(\mathbf{Y})}, \mathbf{R})$ without affecting the distribution $\text{LExt}(\overline{\mathbf{X}} - \overline{f(\mathbf{X})}, \mathbf{R})$, since $\text{LExt}(\overline{\mathbf{Y}} - \overline{g(\mathbf{Y})}, \mathbf{R})$ is a deterministic function of $\mathbf{Y}$ while $\text{LExt}(\overline{\mathbf{X}} - \overline{f(\mathbf{X})}, \mathbf{R})$ is a deterministic function of $\mathbf{X}$ conditioned on the previous fixing of $\mathbf{R}$. It follows that after these fixings, $\mathbf{W}_2 - \mathbf{W}_2'$ is close to a uniform string and hence $\mathbf{W}_2 - \mathbf{W}_2' \neq 0$ with probability $1 - 2^{-n^{\Omega(1)}}$, which completes the proof.

The fact that it is enough to consider case (i) and case (ii) relies on a careful convex combination analysis based on the pre-image size of the function $f(x) - x$. In addition, for the above argument to work we need to carefully adjust the sizes of $\mathbf{Z}_1$, $\mathbf{Z}_2$ and $\mathbf{Z}_3$. We skip the details here, and refer the interested reader to later parts of the paper for more details.

An Explicit Advice Correlation Breaker. We now discuss the other crucial component in the construction, the advice correlation breaker $\text{ACB} : \{0, 1\}^{2n} \times \{0, 1\}^a \rightarrow \{0, 1\}^m$. Informally, the advice correlation breaker we construct takes 2 inputs, the interleaved source $\mathbf{Z}$ (that contains some min-entropy) and an advice string $s \in \{0, 1\}^a$, and outputs a distribution on $\{0, 1\}^m$ with the following guarantee. If $s' \in \{0, 1\}^a$ is another advice such that $s \neq s'$, then

$$\text{ACB}(\mathbf{Z}, s), \text{ACB}(\mathbf{Z}', s') \approx \mathbf{U}_m, \text{ACB}(\mathbf{Z}', s') \tag{2}$$

Our construction crucially relies on an explict advice correlation breaker constructed in [21] that satisfies the following property: Let $\mathbf{A}$ be an (n, k)-source, and $\mathbf{A}' = f(\mathbf{A})$ be a tampered version of $\mathbf{A}$. Further let $\mathbf{B}$ be a uniform random variable, and $\mathbf{B}' = g(\mathbf{B})$. Finally, let $\mathbf{C}, \mathbf{C}'$ be arbitrary random variables such that $\{\mathbf{A}, \mathbf{A}'\}$ is independent of $\{\mathbf{B}, \mathbf{B}', \mathbf{C}, \mathbf{C}'\}$. Then [21] constructed an advice correlation breaker ACB_1 such that for advice strings $s \neq s'$,

$$\mathrm{ACB}_1(\mathbf{B}, \mathbf{A} + \mathbf{C}, s), \mathrm{ACB}_1(\mathbf{B}', \mathbf{A}' + \mathbf{C}', s') \approx U_m, \mathrm{ACB}_1(\mathbf{B}', \mathbf{A}' + \mathbf{C}', s'). \quad (3)$$

The construction of ACB_1 is based on the powerful technique of alternating extraction introduced by Dziembowski and Pietrzak [35], and later used in almost all recent works on non-malleable extractors. In particular, the construction in [21] relies on linear seeded extractors and an elegant primitive known as the *flip-flop* alternating extraction, which was introduced by Cohen [29].

Recall that since $\mathbf{Z} = \overline{\mathbf{X}} + \overline{\mathbf{Y}}$ and $\mathbf{Z}' = \overline{f(\mathbf{X})} + \overline{g(\mathbf{Y})}$, (2) can be stated as

$$\mathrm{ACB}(\overline{\mathbf{X}} + \overline{\mathbf{Y}}, s), \mathrm{ACB}(\overline{f(\mathbf{X})} + \overline{g(\mathbf{Y})}, s') \approx_\epsilon \mathbf{U}_m, \mathrm{ACB}(\overline{f(\mathbf{X})} + \overline{g(\mathbf{Y})}, s')$$

Our main idea of reducing (2) to (3) is as follows: we again take a short slice from $\mathbf{Z}$, say $\mathbf{Z}_4$ (larger than the size of $\{\mathbf{Z}_1, \mathbf{Z}_2, \mathbf{Z}_3\}$), and use a linear seeded extractor LExt to convert $\mathbf{Z}_4$ into a somewhere random source (i.e, a matrix, where some rows are uniform). This can be done by defining row i of the matrix to be $\mathbf{W}_i = \mathrm{LExt}(\mathbf{Z}_4, i)$. The idea now is to simply apply ACB_1 on each row $\mathbf{W}_i$, using the source $\mathbf{Z}$, and the concatenation of s and the index of the row as the new advice string, i.e., compute $\mathrm{ACB}_1(\mathbf{W}_i, \mathbf{Z}, s, i)$. By appealing to a slightly more general version of (3), where we allow multiple tampering, it follows that the output of ACB_1 corresponding to some uniform row is now independent of the output of ACB_1 on all other rows (including tampered rows). Thus, we can simply output $\oplus_i(\mathrm{ACB}_1(\mathbf{W}_i, \mathbf{Z}, s, i))$.

This almost works, modulo a technical caveat–the somewhere random source constructed out of $\mathbf{Z}_4$ is a tall matrix, with more rows than columns, but the parameters of ACB_1 require us to work with a fat matrix, with more columns that rows. This is roughly because, we want the uniform row to have more entropy than the total size of all tampered random variables. To fix this, we use another linear seeded extractor on the source $\mathbf{Z}$ with each row $\mathbf{W}_i$ as the seed to obtain another somewhere random source of the right shape.

2.2   From Non-malleable Extractors to Non-malleable Codes

To obtain our non-malleable codes, the decoding function corresponds to computing the extractor, which is already efficient. On the other hand, the encoding function corresponds to sampling from the pre-image of any given output of the non-malleable extractor. Thus we need to find an efficient way to do this, which is quite non-trivial. We suitably modify our extractor to support efficient sampling. Here we briefly sketch some high level ideas involved and refer the reader to the full version of our paper for more details.

Recall $\mathbf{Z} = (\mathbf{X}, \mathbf{Y})_\pi$. The first modification is that in all applications of seeded extractors in our construction, we specifically use linear seeded extractors. This allows us to argue that the pre-image we are trying to sample from is in fact a convex combination of distributions supported on subspaces. The next crucial observation is the fact that we can use smaller disjoint slices of $\mathbf{Z}$ to carry out various steps outlined in the construction. This is to ensure that the dimensions of the subspaces that we need to sample from, do not depend on the values of the random variables that we fix. For the steps where we use the entire source $\mathbf{Z}$ (in the construction of the advice correlation breaker), we replace $\mathbf{Z}$ by a large enough slice of $\mathbf{Z}$. However this is problematic if we choose the slice deterministically, since in an arbitrary interleaving of two sources, a slice of length less than n might have bits only from one source. We get around this by pseudorandomly sampling enough coordinates from $\mathbf{Z}$ (by first taking a small slice of $\mathbf{Z}$ and using a sampler that works for weak sources [61]).

We now use an elegant trick introduced by Li [46] where the output of the non-malleable extractor described above (with the modifications that we have specified) is now used as a seed in a linear seeded extractor applied to an even larger pseudorandom slice of $\mathbf{Z}$. The linear seeded extractor that we use has the property that for any fixing of the seed, the rank of the linear map corresponding to the extractor is the same, and furthermore one can efficiently sample from the pre-image of any output of the extractor. The final modification needed is a careful choice of the error correcting code used in the advice generator. For this we use a dual BCH code, which allows us to argue that we can discard some output bits of the advice generator without affecting its correctness (based on the dual distance of the code). This is crucial in order to argue that the rank of the linear restriction imposed on the free variables of $\mathbf{Z}$ does not depend on the values of the bits fixed so far. We refer the reader to the full version of our paper where we provide more intuition and complete details of the modified non-malleable extractor and sampling procedure.

2.3 Extractors for Interleaved Sources

Here we give a sketch of our improved extractor for interleaved sources $\mathbf{Z} = (\mathbf{X}, \mathbf{Y})_\pi$. We refer the reader to the full version of our paper for more details. We present our construction and also explain the proof along the way, as this gives more intuition to the different steps of the construction. The high level idea is the following: transform $\mathbf{Z}$ into a matrix of random variables (called a somewhere random source) such that at least one of the random variables is uniform, and the matrix is of the right shape, i.e, a fat matrix with more columns than rows. Once we have such a matrix, the idea is to use the advice correlation breaker from [21] mentioned above to break the correlation among the rows of the matrix. The final output will just be a bit-wise XOR of the output of the advice correlation breaker on each row of the matrix. We now give some more details on how to make this approach work.

Let $\mathbf{Z} = (\mathbf{X}, \mathbf{Y})_\pi$. We start by taking a large enough slice $\mathbf{Z}_1$ from $\mathbf{Z}$ (say, of length $(2/3 + \delta/2)n$). Let $\mathbf{X}$ have more bits in this slice than $\mathbf{Y}$. Let $\mathbf{X}_1$ be the bits of $\mathbf{X}$ in $\mathbf{Z}_1$ and $\mathbf{X}_2$ be the remaining bits of $\mathbf{X}$. Similarly define $\mathbf{Y}_1$ and $\mathbf{Y}_2$. Notice that $\mathbf{X}_1$ has linear entropy and also that $\mathbf{X}_2$ has linear entropy conditioned on $\mathbf{X}_1$. We fix $\mathbf{Y}_1$ and use a condenser (from work of Raz [55]) to condense $\mathbf{Z}_1$ into a matrix with a constant number of rows such that at least one row is close to a distribution with entropy rate at least 0.9. Notice that this matrix is a deterministic function of $\mathbf{X}$. The next step is to use $\mathbf{Z}$ and each row of the matrix as a seed to a linear seeded extractor to get longer rows. This requires some care for the choice of the linear seeded extractor since the seed has some deficiency in entropy. After this step, we use the advice correlation breaker from [21] on $\mathbf{Z}$ and each row of the somewhere random source, with the row index as the advice (similar to what is done in the construction of non-malleable extractors sketched above). Finally we compute the bit-wise XOR of the different outputs that we obtain. Let $\mathbf{V}$ denote this random variable. To output $\Omega(n)$ bits, we use a linear seeded extractor on $\mathbf{Z}$ with $\mathbf{V}$ as the seed. The correctness of various steps in the proof exploits the fact that $\mathbf{Z}$ can be written as the bit-wise sum of two independent sources, and the fact that we use linear seeded extractors.

2.4   Organization

We use Sect. 3 to introduce some background and notation. We present our seed-less non-malleable extractors with respect to interleaved split-state tampering in Sect. 4. We conclude with some open problems in Sect. 5.

3   Background and Notation

We use $\mathbf{U}_m$ to denote the uniform distribution on $\{0,1\}^m$.

For any integer $t > 0$, $[t]$ denotes the set $\{1, \ldots, t\}$.

For a string y of length n, and any subset $S \subseteq [n]$, we use y_S to denote the projection of y to the coordinates indexed by S.

We use bold capital letters for random variables and samples as the corresponding small letter, e.g., $\mathbf{X}$ is a random variable, with x being a sample of $\mathbf{X}$.

For strings $x, y \in \{0,1\}^n$, we use $x + y$ (or equivalently $x - y$) to denote the bit-wise xor of the two strings.

3.1   Probability Lemmas

The following result on min-entropy was proved by Maurer and Wolf [50].

Lemma 1. *Let* $\mathbf{X}, \mathbf{Y}$ *be random variables such that the random variable* $\mathbf{Y}$ *takes at most* ℓ *values. Then*

$$\mathbf{Pr}_{y \sim \mathbf{Y}}[H_\infty(\mathbf{X}|\mathbf{Y} = y) \geq H_\infty(\mathbf{X}) - \log \ell - \log(1/\epsilon)] > 1 - \epsilon.$$

The following lemma is useful in bounding statistical distance of distributions after conditionings.

Lemma 2. *Let D_1 and D_2 be distributions on some universe Ω such that $|X - Y| \leq \epsilon$. Let $\mathcal{E}$ be some event some that $\Pr[D_1 \in \mathcal{E}] \geq \delta$. Then, $|(D_1|\mathcal{E}) - (D_2|\mathcal{E})| \leq \epsilon/\delta$.*

3.2   Conditional Min-Entropy

Definition 13. *The average conditional min-entropy of a source $\mathbf{X}$ given a random variable $\mathbf{W}$ is defined as*

$$\widetilde{H}_\infty(\mathbf{X}|\mathbf{W}) = -\log\left(\mathbf{E}_{w \sim W}\left[\max_x \Pr[\mathbf{X} = x|\mathbf{W} = w]\right]\right) = -\log\left(\mathbf{E}\left[2^{-H_\infty(\mathbf{X}|\mathbf{W}=w)}\right]\right).$$

We recall some results on conditional min-entropy from the work of Dodis et al. [32].

Lemma 3. *([32]). For any $\epsilon > 0$,*

$$\mathbf{Pr}_{w \sim \mathbf{W}}\left[H_\infty(\mathbf{X}|\mathbf{W} = w) \geq \widetilde{H}_\infty(\mathbf{X}|\mathbf{W}) - \log(1/\epsilon)\right] \geq 1 - \epsilon.$$

Lemma 4 ([32]). *If a random variable $\mathbf{Y}$ has support of size 2^ℓ, then $\widetilde{H}_\infty(\mathbf{X}|\mathbf{Y}) \geq H_\infty(\mathbf{X}) - \ell$.*

3.3   Seeded Extractors

Definition 14. *A function $\mathrm{Ext} : \{0,1\}^n \times \{0,1\}^d \to \{0,1\}^m$ is a (k, ϵ)-seeded extractor if for any source $\mathbf{X}$ of min-entropy k, $|\mathrm{Ext}(\mathbf{X}, \mathbf{U}_d) - \mathbf{U}_m| \leq \epsilon$. Ext is called a strong seeded extractor if $|(\mathrm{Ext}(\mathbf{X}, \mathbf{U}_d), \mathbf{U}_d) - (\mathbf{U}_m, \mathbf{U}_d)| \leq \epsilon$, where $\mathbf{U}_m$ and $\mathbf{U}_d$ are independent.*

Further, if for each $s \in \mathbf{U}_d$, $\mathrm{Ext}(\cdot, s) : \{0,1\}^n \to \{0,1\}^m$ is a linear function, then Ext is called a linear seeded extractor.

We require extractors that can extract uniform bits when the source only has sufficient conditional min-entropy.

Definition 15. *A (k, ϵ)-seeded average case seeded extractor $\mathrm{Ext} : \{0,1\}^n \times \{0,1\}^d \to \{0,1\}^m$ for min-entropy k and error ϵ satisfies the following property: For any source $\mathbf{X}$ and any arbitrary random variable $\mathbf{Z}$ with $\widetilde{H}_\infty(\mathbf{X}|\mathbf{Z}) \geq k$,*

$$\mathrm{Ext}(\mathbf{X}, \mathbf{U}_d), \mathbf{Z} \approx_\epsilon \mathbf{U}_m, \mathbf{Z}.$$

It was shown in [32] that any seeded extractor is also an average case extractor.

Lemma 5. *([32]). For any $\delta > 0$, if Ext is a (k, ϵ)-seeded extractor, then it is also a $(k + \log(1/\delta), \epsilon + \delta)$-seeded average case extractor.*

We record a folklore lemma, and include a proof for completeness.

Lemma 6. *Let* $\mathrm{Ext} : \{0,1\}^n \times \{0,1\}^d \to \{0,1\}^m$ *be a* (k,ϵ) *strong seeded. Then, for any source* (n,k)-*source* $\mathbf{X}$ *and any independent* $(d, d - \lambda)$-*source* $\mathbf{Y}$,

$$|\mathrm{Ext}(\mathbf{X}, \mathbf{Y}), \mathbf{Y} - \mathbf{U}_m, \mathbf{Y}| \leq 2^\lambda \epsilon.$$

Proof. Suppose $\mathbf{Y}$ is uniform over a set $A \subset \{0,1\}^d$ of size $2^{d-\lambda}$. We have,

$$
\begin{aligned}
|\mathrm{Ext}(\mathbf{X}, \mathbf{Y}), \mathbf{Y} - \mathbf{U}_m, \mathbf{Y}| &= \frac{1}{2^{d-\lambda}} \cdot \sum_{y \in A} |\mathrm{Ext}(\mathbf{X}, y) - \mathbf{U}_m| \\
&\leq \frac{1}{2^{d-\lambda}} \cdot \sum_{y \in \{0,1\}^d} |\mathrm{Ext}(\mathbf{X}, y) - \mathbf{U}_m| \\
&= \frac{1}{2^{d-\lambda}} \cdot 2^d \cdot |\mathrm{Ext}(\mathbf{X}, \mathbf{U}_d), \mathbf{U}_d - \mathbf{U}_m, \mathbf{U}_d| \\
&= 2^\lambda \cdot \epsilon,
\end{aligned}
$$

where the last inequality follows from the fact that Ext is a (k, ϵ) strong seeded extractor. $\qquad\square$

3.4   Samplers and Extractors

Zuckerman [61] showed that seeded extractors can be used as samplers given access to weak sources. This connection is best presented by a graph theoretic representation of seeded extractors. A seeded extractor $\mathrm{Ext} : \{0,1\}^n \times \{0,1\}^d \to \{0,1\}^m$ can be viewed as an unbalanced bipartite graph G_{Ext} with 2^n left vertices (each of degree 2^d) and 2^m right vertices. Let $\mathcal{N}(x)$ denote the set of neighbors of x in G_{Ext}.

Theorem 16 ([61]). *Let* $\mathrm{Ext} : \{0,1\}^n \times \{0,1\}^d \to \{0,1\}^m$ *be a seeded extractor for min-entropy* k *and error* ϵ. *Let* $D = 2^d$. *Then for any set* $R \subseteq \{0,1\}^m$,

$$|\{x \in \{0,1\}^n : ||\mathcal{N}(x) \cap R| - \mu_R D| > \epsilon D\}| < 2^k,$$

where $\mu_R = |R|/2^m$.

Theorem 17 ([61]). *Let* $\mathrm{Ext} : \{0,1\}^n \times \{0,1\}^d \to \{0,1\}^m$ *be a seeded extractor for min-entropy* k *and error* ϵ. *Let* $\{0,1\}^d = \{r_1, \ldots, r_D\}$, $D = 2^d$. *Define* $\mathrm{Samp}(x) = \{\mathrm{Ext}(x, r_1), \ldots, \mathrm{Ext}(x, r_D)\}$. *Let* $\mathbf{X}$ *be an* $(n, 2k)$-*source. Then for any set* $R \subseteq \{0,1\}^m$,

$$\mathbf{Pr}_{x \sim \mathbf{X}}[||\mathrm{Samp}(x) \cap R| - \mu_R D] > \epsilon D] < 2^{-k},$$

where $\mu_R = |R|/2^m$.

3.5   Explicit Extractors from Prior Work

We recall an optimal construction of strong-seeded extractors.

Theorem 18 ([42]). *For any constant $\alpha > 0$, and all integers $n, k > 0$ there exists a polynomial time computable strong-seeded extractor* Ext $: \{0,1\}^n \times \{0,1\}^d \to \{0,1\}^m$ *with* $d = O(\log n + \log(1/\epsilon))$ *and* $m = (1 - \alpha)k$.

The following are explicit constructions of linear seeded extractors.

Theorem 19 ([56,59]). *For every* $n, k, m \in \mathbb{N}$ *and* $\epsilon > 0$, *with* $m \leq k \leq n$, *there exists an explicit strong linear seeded extractor* LExt $: \{0,1\}^n \times \{0,1\}^d \to \{0,1\}^m$ *for min-entropy k and error ϵ, where* $d = O\left(\log^2(n/\epsilon)/\log(k/m)\right)$.

A drawback of the above construction is that the seeded length is $\omega(\log n)$ for sub-linear min-entropy. A construction of Li [45] achieves $O(\log n)$ seed length for even polylogarithmic min-entropy.

Theorem 20 ([45]). *There exists a constant $c > 1$ such that for every* $n, k \in \mathbb{N}$ *with* $c\log^8 n \leq k \leq n$ *and any* $\epsilon \geq 1/n^2$, *there exists a polynomial time computable linear seeded extractor* LExt $: \{0,1\}^n \times \{0,1\}^d \to \{0,1\}^m$ *for min-entropy k and error ϵ, where* $d = O(\log n)$ *and* $m \leq \sqrt{k}$.

A different construction achieves seed length $O(\log(n/\epsilon))$ for high entropy sources.

Theorem 21 ([18,46]). *For all $\delta > 0$ there exist $\alpha, \gamma > 0$ such that for all integers* $n > 0$, $\epsilon \geq 2^{-\gamma n}$, *there exists an efficiently computable linear strong seeded extractor* LExt $: \{0,1\}^n \times \{0,1\}^d \to \{0,1\}^{\alpha d}$, $d = O(\log(n/\epsilon))$ *for min-entropy δn. Further, for any $y \in \{0,1\}^d$, the linear map* LExt$(\cdot, y)$ *has rank* αd.

The above theorem is stated in [46] for $\delta = 0.9$, but it is straightforward to see that the proof extends for any constant $\delta > 0$.

We use a property of linear seeded extractors proved by Rao [53].

Lemma 7 ([53]). *Let* Ext $: \{0,1\}^n \times \{0,1\}^d \to \{0,1\}^m$ *be a linear seeded extractor for min-entropy k with error $\epsilon < \frac{1}{2}$. Let X be an affine (n, k)-source. Then*

$$\Pr_{u \sim U_d}\left[|\text{Ext}(X, u) - U_m| > 0\right] \leq 2\epsilon.$$

We recall a two-source extractor construction for high entropy sources based on the inner product function.

Theorem 22 ([28]). *For all* $m, r > 0$, *with* $q = 2^m$, $n = rm$, *let* $\mathbf{X}, \mathbf{Y}$ *be independent sources on $\mathbb{F}_q^r$ with min-entropy k_1, k_2 respectively. Let* IP *be the inner product function over the field $\mathbb{F}_q$. Then, we have:*

$$|\text{IP}(\mathbf{X}, \mathbf{Y}), \mathbf{X} - \mathbf{U}_m, \mathbf{X}| \leq \epsilon, \qquad |\text{IP}(\mathbf{X}, \mathbf{Y}), \mathbf{Y} - \mathbf{U}_m, \mathbf{Y}| \leq \epsilon$$

where $\epsilon = 2^{-(k_1 + k_2 - n - m)/2}$.

Rao [52] (based on an argument by Boaz Barak) proved that every two-source extractor is strong. It is easy to observe that the proof generalizes to the case of interleaved two-source extractors. We record this below in a slightly more general setting of unequal length sources.

Theorem 23 ([52]). *Suppose* $i\ell\text{Ext} : \{0,1\}^{n_1+n_2} \to \{0,1\}^m$ *be an interleaved source extractor that satisfies the following: if* $\mathbf{X}$ *is a* (n_1, k_1)-*source,* $\mathbf{Y}$ *is an independent* (n_2, k_2)-*source, and* $\pi : [n_1 + n_2] \to [n_1 + n_2]$ *is an arbitrary permutation, then*

$$|i\ell\text{Ext}((\mathbf{X}, \mathbf{Y})_\pi) - \mathbf{U}_m| \leq \epsilon.$$

Then, in fact $i\ell\text{Ext}$ *satisfies the following stronger properties:*

- *Let* $\mathbf{X}$ *be a* (n_1, k)-*source,* $\mathbf{Y}$ *be an independent* (n_2, k_2)-*source, and* $\pi : [n_1 + n_2] \to [n_1 + n_2]$ *be an arbitrary permutation. Then,*

$$|i\ell\text{Ext}((\mathbf{X}, \mathbf{Y})_\pi), \mathbf{X} - \mathbf{U}_m, \mathbf{X}| \leq 2^m \cdot (2^{k-k_1} + \epsilon).$$

- *Let* $\mathbf{X}$ *be a* (n_1, k_1)-*source,* $\mathbf{Y}$ *be an independent* (n_2, k)-*source, and* $\pi : [n_1 + n_2] \to [n_1 + n_2]$ *be an arbitrary permutation. Then,*

$$|2i\ell\text{Ext}(\mathbf{X}, \mathbf{Y}), \mathbf{Y} - \mathbf{U}_m, \mathbf{Y}| \leq 2^m \cdot (2^{k-k_2} + \epsilon).$$

3.6   Advice Correlation Breakers

We use a primitive called 'correlation breaker' in our construction. Consider a situation where we have arbitrarily correlated random variables $\mathbf{Y}^1, \ldots, \mathbf{Y}^r$, where each $\mathbf{Y}^i$ is on ℓ bits. Further suppose $\mathbf{Y}^1$ is a 'good' random variable (typically, we assume $\mathbf{Y}^1$ is uniform or has almost full min-entropy). A correlation breaker CB is an explicit function that takes some additional resource $\mathbf{X}$, where $\mathbf{X}$ is typically additional randomness (an (n, k)-source) that is independent of $\{\mathbf{Y}^1, \ldots, \mathbf{Y}^r\}$. Thus using $\mathbf{X}$, the task is to break the correlation between $\mathbf{Y}^1$ and the random variables $\mathbf{Y}^2, \ldots, \mathbf{Y}^r$, i.e., $\text{CB}(\mathbf{Y}^1, \mathbf{X})$ is independent of $\{\text{CB}(\mathbf{Y}^2, \mathbf{X}), \ldots, \text{CB}(\mathbf{Y}^r, \mathbf{X})\}$. A weaker notion is that of an advice correlation breaker that takes in some advice for each of the $\mathbf{Y}^i$'s as an additional resource in breaking the correlations. This primitive was implicitly constructed in [18] and used in explicit constructions of non-malleable extractors, and has subsequently found many applications in explicit constructions of extractors for independent sources and non-malleable extractors.

We recall an explicit advice correlation breaker constructed in [20]. This correlation breaker works even with the weaker guarantee that the 'helper source' $\mathbf{X}$ is now allowed to be correlated to the sources random variables $\mathbf{Y}^1, \ldots, \mathbf{Y}^r$ in a structured way. Concretely, we assume the source to be of the form $\mathbf{X} + \mathbf{Z}$, where $\mathbf{X}$ is assumed to be an (n, k)-source that is uncorrelated with $\mathbf{Y}^1, \ldots, \mathbf{Y}^r, \mathbf{Z}$. We now state the result more precisely.

Theorem 24 ([20]). *For all integers* $n, n_1, n_2, k, k_1, k_2, t, d, h, \lambda$ *and any* $\epsilon > 0$, *such that* $d = O(\log^2(n/\epsilon))$, $k_1 \geq 2d + 8tdh + \log(1/\epsilon)$, $n_1 \geq 2d + 10tdh + (4ht + 1)n_2^2 + \log(1/\epsilon)$, *and* $n_2 \geq 2d + 3td + \log(1/\epsilon)$, *let*

- $\mathbf{X}$ *be an* (n, k_1)-*source,* $\mathbf{X}'$ *a r.v on* n *bits,* $\mathbf{Y}^1$ *be an* $(n_1, n_1 - \lambda)$-*source,* $\mathbf{Z}, \mathbf{Z}'$ *are r.v's on* n *bits, and* $\mathbf{Y}^2, \ldots, \mathbf{Y}^t$ *be r.v's on* n_1 *bits each, such that* $\{\mathbf{X}, \mathbf{X}'\}$ *is independent of* $\{\mathbf{Z}, \mathbf{Z}', \mathbf{Y}^1, \ldots, \mathbf{Y}^t\}$,

– $id^1, \ldots, id^t$ be bit-strings of length h such that for each $i \in \{2, t\}$, $id^1 \neq id^i$.

Then there exists an efficient algorithm ACB : $\{0,1\}^{n_1} \times \{0,1\}^n \times \{0,1\}^h \rightarrow \{0,1\}^{n_2}$ which satisfies the following: let

– $\mathbf{Y}_h^1 = \mathrm{ACB}(\mathbf{Y}^1, \mathbf{X} + \mathbf{Z}, id^1)$,
– $\mathbf{Y}_h^i = \mathrm{ACB}(\mathbf{Y}^i, \mathbf{X}' + \mathbf{Z}', id^i)$, $i \in [2, t]$

Then,

$$\mathbf{Y}_h^1, \mathbf{Y}_h^2, \ldots, \mathbf{Y}_h^t, \mathbf{X}, \mathbf{X}' \approx_{O((h+2^\lambda)\epsilon)} \mathbf{U}_{n_2}, \mathbf{Y}_h^2, \ldots, \mathbf{Y}_h^t, \mathbf{X}, \mathbf{X}'.$$

3.7   A Connection Between Non-malleable Codes and Extractors

The following theorem proved by Cheraghchi and Guruswami [27] that connects non-malleable extractors and codes.

Theorem 25 ([27]). *Let* $\mathrm{nmExt} : \{0,1\}^n \rightarrow \{0,1\}^m$ *be an efficient seedless* (n, m, ϵ)-*non-malleable extractor with respect to a class of tampering functions* $\mathcal{F}$ *acting on* $\{0,1\}^n$. *Further suppose* nmExt *is* ϵ'-*invertible. Then there exists an efficient construction of a non-malleable code with respect to the tampering family* $\mathcal{F}$ *with block length* $= n$, *relative rate* $\frac{m}{n}$ *and error* $2^m \epsilon + \epsilon'$.

4   NM Extractors for Interleaved Split-State Adversaries

The main result of this section is an explicit non-malleable extractor for interleaved 2-split-state tampering families with equal length partitions, which we denote by $2\mathrm{ISS} \subset \mathcal{F}_{2n}$.

Theorem 26. *For all integers* $n > 0$ *there exists an explicit function* $\mathrm{nmExt} : \{0,1\}^{2n} \rightarrow \{0,1\}^m$, $m = n^{\Omega(1)}$, *such that the following holds: for arbitrary tampering functions* $f, g \in \mathcal{F}_n$, *any permutation* $\pi : [2n] \rightarrow [2n]$ *and independent uniform sources* $\mathbf{X}$ *and* $\mathbf{Y}$ *each on* n *bits, there exists a distribution* $\mathcal{D}_{f,g,\pi}$ *on* $\{0,1\}^m \cup \{\mathrm{same}^\star\}$, *such that*

$$|\mathrm{nmExt}((\mathbf{X}, \mathbf{Y})_\pi), \mathrm{nmExt}((f(\mathbf{X}), g(\mathbf{Y}))_\pi)) - \mathbf{U}_m, \mathrm{copy}(\mathcal{D}_{f,g,\pi}, \mathbf{U}_m)| \leq 2^{-n^{\Omega(1)}}.$$

In such settings, it was shown in [27] that it is enough to construct non-malleable extractors assuming that at least one of f and g does not have any fixed points, assuming that the sources $\mathbf{X}$ and $\mathbf{Y}$ have entropy at least $n - n^\delta$. We thus prove the following theorem, from which Theorem 26 is direct.

Theorem 27. *There exists a* $\delta > 0$ *such that for all integers* $n, k > 0$ *with* $n \geq k \geq n - n^\delta$, *there exists an explicit function* $\mathrm{nmExt} : \{0,1\}^{2n} \rightarrow \{0,1\}^m$, $m = n^{\Omega(1)}$, *such that the following holds: for arbitrary tampering functions* $f, g \in \mathcal{F}_n$, *any permutation* $\pi : [2n] \rightarrow [2n]$ *and independent* (n, k)-*sources* $\mathbf{X}$ *and* $\mathbf{Y}$, *the following holds:*

$$|\mathrm{nmExt}((\mathbf{X}, \mathbf{Y})_\pi), \mathrm{nmExt}((f(\mathbf{X}), g(\mathbf{Y}))_\pi)) - \mathbf{U}_m, \mathrm{nmExt}((f(\mathbf{X}), g(\mathbf{Y}))_\pi)| \leq 2^{-n^{\Omega(1)}}.$$

We will prove a slightly more general result which is a direct by-product of our proof technique for proving the above theorem, and lets us re-use this non-malleable extractor for the class of linear adversaries composed with split-state adversaries. We prove the following theorem.

Theorem 28. *There exists a $\delta > 0$ such that for all integers $n, k > 0$ with $n \geq k \geq n - n^\delta$, there exists an explicit function $\mathrm{nmExt} : \{0,1\}^{2n} \to \{0,1\}^m$, $m = n^{\Omega(1)}$, such that the following holds: Let $\mathbf{X}$ and $\mathbf{Y}$ be independent $(n, n-n^\delta)$-sources, $\pi : [2n] \to [2n]$ any arbitrary permutation and arbitrary tampering functions $f_1, f_2, g_1, g_2 \in \mathcal{F}_n$ that satisfy the following condition:*

- *$\forall x \in support(\mathbf{X})$ and $y \in support(\mathbf{Y})$, $f_1(x) + g_1(y) \neq x$ or*
- *$\forall x \in support(\mathbf{X})$ and $y \in support(\mathbf{Y})$, $f_2(x) + g_2(y) \neq y$.*

Then,

$$|\mathrm{nmExt}((\mathbf{X}, \mathbf{Y})_\pi), \mathrm{nmExt}(((f_1(\mathbf{X}) + g_1(\mathbf{Y})), (f_2(\mathbf{X}) + g_2(\mathbf{Y})))_\pi) -$$
$$\mathbf{U}_m, \mathrm{nmExt}(((f_1(\mathbf{X}) + g_1(\mathbf{Y})), (f_2(\mathbf{X}) + g_2(\mathbf{Y})))_\pi)| \leq 2^{-n^{\Omega(1)}}.$$

Clearly, Theorem 27 follows directly from the above theorem by setting $g_1(y) = 0$ for all y and $f_2(x) = 0$ for all x. We use the rest of the section to prove Theorem 28.

Our high level ideas in constructing the non-malleable extractor is via the framework set up in [18] of using advice generators and correlation breakers. We give intuition behind our construction in Sect. 2. We use Sect. 4.1 to construct an advice generator and Sect. 4.2 to construct an advice correlation breaker. Finally, we present the non-malleable extractor construction in Sect. 4.3.

Notation:

- If $\mathbf{W} = h((\mathbf{X}, \mathbf{Y})_\pi)$ (for some function h), then we use $\mathbf{W}'$ or $(\mathbf{W})'$ to denote the random variable $h(((f_1(\mathbf{X}) + g_1(\mathbf{Y})), (f_2(\mathbf{X}) + g_2(\mathbf{Y}))_\pi)$.
- Define $\overline{\mathbf{X}} = (\mathbf{X}, 0^n)_\pi$, $\overline{\mathbf{Y}} = (0^n, \mathbf{Y})_\pi$, $\overline{f_1(\mathbf{X})} = (f_1(\mathbf{X}), 0^n)_\pi$, $\overline{f_2(\mathbf{X})} = (0^n, f_2(\mathbf{X}))_\pi$, $\overline{g_1(\mathbf{Y})} = (g_1(\mathbf{Y}), 0^n)_\pi$ and $\overline{g_2(\mathbf{Y})} = (0^n, g_2(\mathbf{Y}))_\pi$.
- Finally, define $\mathbf{Z} = \overline{\mathbf{X}} + \overline{\mathbf{Y}}$ and $\mathbf{Z}' = \overline{f_1(\mathbf{X})} + \overline{g_1(\mathbf{Y})} + \overline{f_2(\mathbf{X})} + \overline{g_2(\mathbf{Y})}$.

4.1   An Advice Generator

Lemma 8. *There exists an efficiently computable function $\mathrm{advGen} : \{0,1\}^n \times \{0,1\}^n \to \{0,1\}^{n_4}$, $n_4 = n^\delta$, such that with probability at least $1 - 2^{-n^{\Omega(1)}}$ over the fixing of the random variables $\mathrm{advGen}((\mathbf{X}, \mathbf{Y})_\pi), \mathrm{advGen}(((f_1(\mathbf{X}) + g_1(\mathbf{Y})), (f_2(\mathbf{X}) + g_2(\mathbf{Y})))_\pi)$, the following hold:*

- *$\{\mathrm{advGen}((\mathbf{X}, \mathbf{Y})_\pi) \neq \mathrm{advGen}(((f_1(\mathbf{X}) + g_1(\mathbf{Y})), (f_2(\mathbf{X}) + g_2(\mathbf{Y})))_\pi)\}$,*
- *$\mathbf{X}$ and $\mathbf{Y}$ are independent,*
- *$H_\infty(\mathbf{X}) \geq k - 2n^\delta$, $H_\infty(\mathbf{Y}) \geq k - 2n^\delta$.*

We present the construction of our advice generator and refer the reader to the full version of our paper for the proof. We claim that the function advGen computed by Algorithm 1 satisfies the above lemma. We first set up some parameters and ingredients.

- Let C be a large enough constant and $\delta' = \delta/C$.
- Let $n_0 = n^{\delta'}, n_1 = n_0^{c_0}, n_2 = 10n_0$, for some constant c_0 that we set below.
- Let $E : \{0,1\}^{2n} \to \{0,1\}^{n_3}$ be the encoding function of a linear error correcting code $\mathcal{C}$ with constant rate α and constant distance β.
- Let $\text{Ext}_1 : \{0,1\}^{n_1} \times \{0,1\}^{d_1} \to \{0,1\}^{\log(n_3)}$ be a $(n_1/20, \beta/10)$-seeded extractor instantiated using Theorem 18. Thus $d_1 = c_1 \log n_1$, for some constant c_1. Let $D_1 = 2^{d_1} = n_1^{c_1}$.
- Let $\text{Samp}_1 : \{0,1\}^{n_1} \to [n_3]^{D_1}$ be the sampler obtained from Theorem 17 using Ext_1.
- Let $\text{Ext}_2 : \{0,1\}^{n_2} \times \{0,1\}^{d_2} \to \{0,1\}^{\log(2n)}$ be a $(n_2/20, 1/n_0)$-seeded extractor instantiated using Theorem 18. Thus $d_2 = c_2 \log n_2$, for some constant c_2. Let $D_2 = 2^{d_2}$. Thus $D_2 = 2^{d_2} = n_2^{c_2}$.
- Let $\text{Samp}_2 : \{0,1\}^{n_2} \to [2n]^{D_2}$ be the sampler obtained from Theorem 17 using Ext_2.
- Set $c_0 = 2c_2$.
- Let $i\ell\text{Ext} : \{0,1\}^{D_2} \to \{0,1\}^{n_0}$ be the extractor from Theorem 12.
- Let $\text{LExt} : \{0,1\}^{2n} \times \{0,1\}^{n_0} \to \{0,1\}^{n_0}$ be a linear seeded extractor instantiated from Theorem 22 set to extract from min-entropy $n_1/100$ and error $2^{-\Omega(\sqrt{n_0})}$.

Algorithm 1: advGen(z)

Input: Bit-string $z = (x,y)_\pi$ of length $2n$, where x and y are each n bit-strings and $\pi : [2n] \to [2n]$ is a permutation.

Output: Bit string v of length n_4.

1 Let $z_1 = \text{Slice}(z, n_1), z_2 = \text{Slice}(z, n_2)$.
2 Let $S = \text{Samp}_1(z_1)$.
3 Let $T = \text{Samp}_2(z_2)$ and $z_3 = z_T$.
4 Let $r = i\ell\text{Ext}(z_3)$.
5 Let $w_1 = (E(z))_S$.
6 Let $w_2 = \text{LExt}(z, r)$.
7 Output $v = z_1, z_2, z_3, w_1, w_2$.

4.2   An Advice Correlation Breaker

We recall the setup of Theorem 28. $\mathbf{X}$ and $\mathbf{Y}$ are independent (n, k)-sources, $k \geq n - n^\delta$, $\pi : [2n] \to [2n]$ is an arbitrary permutation and $f_1, f_2, g_1, g_2 \in \mathcal{F}_n$ satisfy the following conditions:

- $\forall x \in support(\mathbf{X})$ and $y \in support(\mathbf{Y})$, $f_1(x) + g_1(y) \neq x$ or
- $\forall x \in support(\mathbf{X})$ and $y \in support(\mathbf{Y})$, $f_2(x) + g_2(y) \neq y$.

Further, we defined the following: $\overline{\mathbf{X}} = (\mathbf{X}, 0^n)_\pi$, $\overline{\mathbf{Y}} = (0^n \circ \mathbf{Y})_\pi$, $\overline{f_1(\mathbf{X})} = (f_1(\mathbf{X}), 0^n)_\pi$, $\overline{f_2(\mathbf{X})} = (0^n, f_2(\mathbf{X}))_\pi$, $\overline{g_1(\mathbf{Y})} = (g_1(\mathbf{Y}), 0^n)_\pi$ and $\overline{g_2(\mathbf{Y})} = (0^n, g_2(\mathbf{Y}))_\pi$. It follows that $\mathbf{Z} = \overline{\mathbf{X}} + \overline{\mathbf{Y}}$ and $\mathbf{Z}' = \overline{f_1(\mathbf{X})} + \overline{g_1(\mathbf{Y})} + \overline{f_2(\mathbf{X})} + \overline{g_2(\mathbf{Y})}$. Thus, for some functions $f, g \in \mathcal{F}_{2n}$, $\mathbf{Z}' = f(\overline{\mathbf{X}}) + g(\overline{\mathbf{Y}})$. Let $\overline{\mathbf{X}'} = f(\overline{\mathbf{X}})$ and $\overline{\mathbf{Y}'} = g(\overline{\mathbf{Y}})$.

The following is the main result of this section. Assume that we have some random variables such that $\mathbf{X}$ and $\mathbf{Y}$ continue to be independent, and $H_\infty(\mathbf{X}), H_\infty(\mathbf{Y}) \geq k - 2n^\delta$.

Lemma 9. *There exists an efficiently computable function* ACB $: \{0,1\}^{2n} \times \{0,1\}^{n_1} \to \{0,1\}^m$, $n_1 = n^\delta$ *and* $m = n^{\Omega(1)}$, *such that*

$$\mathrm{ACB}(\overline{\mathbf{X}} + \overline{\mathbf{Y}}, w), \mathrm{ACB}(\overline{f(\mathbf{X})} + \overline{g(\mathbf{Y})}, w') \approx_\epsilon \mathbf{U}_m, \mathrm{ACB}(\overline{f(\mathbf{X})} + \overline{g(\mathbf{Y})}, w'),$$

for any fixed strings $w, w' \in \{0,1\}^{n_1}$ *with* $w \neq w'$.

We present the construction of our advice correlation breaker, and refer the reader to the full version of our paper for the proof. We prove that the function ACB computed by Algorithm 2 satisfies the conclusion of Lemma 9.

We start by setting up some ingredients and parameters.

- Let $\delta > 0$ be a small enough constant.
- Let $n_2 = n^{\delta_1}$, where $\delta_1 = 2\delta$.
- Let $\mathrm{LExt}_1 : \{0,1\}^{n_2} \times \{0,1\}^d \to \{0,1\}^{d_1}$, $d_1 = \sqrt{n_2}$, be a linear-seeded extractor instantiated from Theorem 19 set to extract from entropy $k_1 = n_2/10$ with error $\epsilon_1 = 1/10$. Thus $d = C_1 \log n_2$, for some constant C_1. Let $D = 2^d = n^{\delta_2}$, $\delta_2 = 2C_1\delta$.
- Set $\delta' = 20C_1\delta$.
- Let $\mathrm{LExt}_2 : \{0,1\}^{2n} \times \{0,1\}^{d_1} \to \{0,1\}^{n_4}$, $n_4 = n^{8\delta_3}$ be a linear-seeded extractor instantiated from Theorem 19 set to extract from entropy $k_2 = 0.9k$ with error $\epsilon_2 = 2^{-\Omega(\sqrt{d_1})} = 2^{-n^{\Omega(1)}}$, such that the seed length of the extractor LExt_2 (by Theorem 19) is d_1.
- Let $\mathrm{ACB}' : \{0,1\}^{n_{1,acb'}} \times \{0,1\}^{n_{acb'}} \times \{0,1\}^{h_{acb'}} \to \{0,1\}^{n_{2,acb'}}$, be the advice correlation breaker from Theorem 24 set with the following parameters: $n_{acb'} = 2n, n_{1,acb'} = n_4, n_{2,acb'} = m = O(n^{2\delta_2}), t_{acb'} = 2D, h_{acb'} = n_1 + d, \epsilon_{acb'} = 2^{-n^\delta}, d_{acb'} = O(\log^2(n/\epsilon_{acb'})), \lambda_{acb'} = 0$. It can be checked that by our choice of parameters, the conditions required for Theorem 24 indeed hold for $k_{1,acb'} \geq n^{2\delta_2}$.

4.3   The Non-malleable Extractor

We are now ready to present the construction of iℓNM that satisfies the requirements of Theorem 28.

- Let $\delta > 0$ be a small enough constant, $n_1 = n^\delta$ and $m = n^{\Omega(1)}$.

Algorithm 2: $\mathrm{ACB}(z, w)$

Input: Bit-strings $z = (x, y)_\pi$ of length $2n$ and bit string w of length n_1, where x and y are each n bit-strings and $\pi : [2n] \to [2n]$ is a permutation.
Output: Bit string of length m.

1 Let $z_1 = \mathrm{Slice}(z, n_2)$.
2 Let v be a $D \times n_3$ matrix, with its i'th row $v_i = \mathrm{LExt}_1(z_1, i)$.
3 Let r be a $D \times n_4$ matrix, with its i'th row $r_i = \mathrm{LExt}_2(z, v_i)$.
4 Let s be a $D \times m$ matrix, with its i'th row $s_i = \mathrm{ACB}'(r_i, z, w, i)$.
5 Output $\oplus_{i=1}^{D} s_i$.

- Let $\mathrm{advGen} : \{0,1\}^{2n} \to \{0,1\}^{n_1}$, $n_1 = n^\delta$, be the advice generator from Lemma 8.
- Let $\mathrm{ACB} : \{0,1\}^{2n} \times \{0,1\}^{n_1} \to \{0,1\}^m$ be the advice correlation breaker from Lemma 9.

Algorithm 3: $i\ell\mathrm{NM}(z)$

Input: Bit-string $z = (x, y)_\pi$ of length $2n$, where x and y are each n bit-strings, and $\pi : [2n] \to [2n]$ is a permutation.
Output: Bit string of length m.

1 Let $w = \mathrm{advGen}(z)$.
2 Output $\mathrm{ACB}(z, w)$

The function $i\ell\mathrm{NM}$ computed by Algorithm 3 satisfies the conclusion of Theorem 28 as follows: Fix the random variables $\mathbf{W}, \mathbf{W}'$. By Lemma 8, it follows that $\mathbf{X}$ remains independent of $\mathbf{Y}$, and with probability at least $1 - 2^{-n^{\Omega(1)}}$, $H_\infty(\mathbf{X}) \geq k - 2n_1$ and $H_\infty(\mathbf{Y}) \geq k - 2n_1$ (recall $k \geq n - n^\delta$). Theorem 28 is now direct using Lemma 9.

5 Open Questions

Non-malleable Codes for Composition of Functions. Here we give efficient constructions of non-malleable codes for the tampering class Lin ∘ 2ISS. Many natural questions remain to be answered. For instance, one open problem is to efficiently construct non-malleable codes for the tampering class 2SS ∘ Lin or 2ISS ∘ Lin, which as explained before is closely related to the question of constructing explicit (r, t)-ramp non-malleable secret-sharing schemes with binary shares, where $t < r$. It looks like one needs substantially new ideas to give such constructions. More generally, for what other interesting classes of functions $\mathcal{F}$ and $\mathcal{G}$ can we construct non-malleable codes for the composed class $\mathcal{F} \circ \mathcal{G}$? Is it possible to efficiently construct non-malleable codes for any tampering class $\mathcal{F} \circ \mathcal{G}$ as long as we have efficient non-malleable codes for the classes $\mathcal{F}$ and $\mathcal{G}$?

Other Applications of Seedless Non-malleable Extractors. The explicit seedless non-malleable extractors that we construct satisfy strong pseudorandom properties. A natural question is to find more applications of these non-malleable extractors in explicit constructions of other interesting objects.

Improved Seedless Extractors. We construct an extractor for 2-interleaved sources that works for min-entropy rate 2/3. It is easy to verify that there exists extractors for sources with min-entropy as low as $C \log n$, and a natural question here is to come up with such explicit constructions. Given the success in constructing 2-source extractors for low min-entropy [23,47], we are optimistic that more progress can be made on this problem.

Acknowledgments. We are grateful for useful comments from anonymous referees.

References

1. Aggarwal, D.: Affine-evasive sets modulo a prime. Inf. Process. Lett. **115**(2), 382–385 (2015)
2. Aggarwal, D., Briët, J.: Revisiting the sanders-Bogolyubov-Ruzsa theorem in Fpn and its application to non-malleable codes. In: 2016 IEEE International Symposium on Information Theory (ISIT), pp. 1322–1326. IEEE (2016)
3. Aggarwal, D., et al.: Stronger leakage-resilient and non-malleable secret-sharing schemes for general access structures. IACR Crypt. ePrint Arch. **2018**, 1147 (2018)
4. Aggarwal, D., Dodis, Y., Kazana, T., Obremski, M.: Non-malleable reductions and applications. In: Proceedings of the Forty-Seventh Annual ACM Symposium on Theory of Computing, pp. 459–468. ACM (2015)
5. Aggarwal, D., Dodis, Y., Lovett, S.: Non-malleable codes from additive combinatorics. SIAM J. Comput. **47**(2), 524–546 (2018)
6. Aggarwal, D., Dziembowski, S., Kazana, T., Obremski, M.: Leakage resilient non-malleable codes. In: Theory of Cryptography Conference, TCC 2015, pp. 398–426 (2015)
7. Aggarwal, D., Obremski, M.: A constant-rate non-malleable code in the split-state model. IACR Crypt. ePrint Arch. **2019**, 1299 (2019)
8. Agrawal, S., Gupta, D., Maji, H.K., Pandey, O., Prabhakaran, M.: A rate-optimizing compiler for non-malleable codes against bit-wise tampering and permutations. In: Theory of Cryptography - 12th Theory of Cryptography Conference, TCC 2015, Warsaw, Poland, 23–25 March 2015, Proceedings, Part I, pp. 375–397 (2015)
9. Badrinarayanan, S., Srinivasan, A.: Revisiting non-malleable secret sharing. IACR Crypt. ePrint Arch. **2018**, 1144 (2018)
10. Ball, M., Chattopadhyay, E., Liao, J.J., Malkin, T., Tan, L.Y.: Non-malleability against polynomial tampering. In: Crypto (2020), to appear
11. Ball, M., Dachman-Soled, D., Guo, S., Malkin, T., Tan, L.Y.: Non-malleable codes for small-depth circuits. In: 2018 IEEE 59th Annual Symposium on Foundations of Computer Science (FOCS) pp. 826–837. IEEE (2018)
12. Ball, M., Dachman-Soled, D., Kulkarni, M., Malkin, T.: Non-malleable codes for bounded depth, bounded fan-in circuits. In: TCC (2016)

13. Ball, M., Guo, S., Wichs, D.: Non-malleable codes for decision trees. IACR Crypt. ePrint Arch. **2019**, 379 (2019)
14. Blakley, G.R.: Safeguarding cryptographic keys. In: Proceedings of the 1979 AFIPS National Computer Conference, pp. 313–317 (1979)
15. Bogdanov, A., Ishai, Y., Viola, E., Williamson, C.: Bounded indistinguishability and the complexity of recovering secrets. In: Robshaw, M., Katz, J. (eds.) CRYPTO 2016. LNCS, vol. 9816, pp. 593–618. Springer, Heidelberg (2016). https://doi.org/10.1007/978-3-662-53015-3_21
16. Bogdanov, A., Williamson, C.: Approximate bounded indistinguishability. In: International Colloquium on Automata, Languages, and Programming (2017)
17. Carpentieri, M., Santis, A.D., Vaccaro, U.: Size of shares and probability of cheating in threshold schemes. In: EUROCRYPT 1993, 12th Annual International Conference on the Theory and Applications of Cryptographic Techniques (1993)
18. Chattopadhyay, E., Goyal, V., Li, X.: Non-malleable extractors and codes, with their many tampered extensions. In: STOC (2016)
19. Chattopadhyay, E., Kanukurthi, B., Obbattu, S.L.B., Sekar, S.: Privacy amplification from non-malleable codes. IACR Crypt. ePrint Arch. **2018**, 293 (2018)
20. Chattopadhyay, E., Li, X.: Extractors for sumset sources. In: STOC (2016)
21. Chattopadhyay, E., Li, X.: Non-malleable codes and extractors for small-depth circuits, and affine functions. In: Proceedings of the 49th Annual ACM SIGACT Symposium on Theory of Computing pp. 1171–1184. ACM (2017)
22. Chattopadhyay, E., Zuckerman, D.: Non-malleable codes against constant split-state tampering. In: Proceedings of the 55th Annual IEEE Symposium on Foundations of Computer Science, pp. 306–315 (2014)
23. Chattopadhyay, E., Zuckerman, D.: Explicit two-source extractors and resilient functions. In: STOC (2016)
24. Chattopadhyay, E., Zuckerman, D.: New extractors for interleaved sources. In: CCC (2016)
25. Cheng, K., Ishai, Y., Li, X.: Near-optimal secret sharing and error correcting codes in AC0. In: TCC, pp. 424–458 (2017)
26. Cheraghchi, M., Guruswami, V.: Capacity of non-malleable codes. IEEE Trans. Inf. Theor. **62**(3), 1097–1118 (2016). https://doi.org/10.1109/TIT.2015.2511784
27. Cheraghchi, M., Guruswami, V.: Non-malleable coding against bit-wise and split-state tampering. J. Crypt. **30**(1), 191–241 (2017)
28. Chor, B., Goldreich, O.: Unbiased bits from sources of weak randomness and probabilistic communication complexity. SIAM J. Comput. **17**(2), 230–261 (1988)
29. Cohen, G.: Local correlation breakers and applications to three-source extractors and mergers. SIAM J. Comput. **45**(4), 1297–1338 (2016)
30. Coretti, S., Dodis, Y., Tackmann, B., Venturi, D.: Non-malleable encryption: simpler, shorter, stronger. In: Kushilevitz, E., Malkin, T. (eds.) TCC 2016. LNCS, vol. 9562, pp. 306–335. Springer, Heidelberg (2016). https://doi.org/10.1007/978-3-662-49096-9_13
31. Coretti, S., Maurer, U., Tackmann, B., Venturi, D.: From single-bit to multi-bit public-key encryption via non-malleable codes. In: Dodis, Y., Nielsen, J.B. (eds.) TCC 2015. LNCS, vol. 9014, pp. 532–560. Springer, Heidelberg (2015). https://doi.org/10.1007/978-3-662-46494-6_22
32. Dodis, Y., Ostrovsky, R., Reyzin, L., Smith, A.: Fuzzy extractors: how to generate strong keys from biometrics and other noisy data. SIAM J. Comput. **38**, 97–139 (2008)
33. Dodis, Y., Wichs, D.: Non-malleable extractors and symmetric key cryptography from weak secrets. In: STOC, pp. 601–610 (2009)

34. Dziembowski, S., Kazana, T., Obremski, M.: Non-malleable codes from two-source extractors. In: Canetti, R., Garay, J.A. (eds.) CRYPTO 2013. LNCS, vol. 8043, pp. 239–257. Springer, Heidelberg (2013). https://doi.org/10.1007/978-3-642-40084-1_14

35. Dziembowski, S., Pietrzak, K.: Intrusion-resilient secret sharing. In: Proceedings of the 48th Annual IEEE Symposium on Foundations of Computer Science, FOCS 2007, pp. 227–237. IEEE Computer Society, Washington, DC, USA (2007). https://doi.org/10.1109/FOCS.2007.35

36. Dziembowski, S., Pietrzak, K., Wichs, D.: Non-malleable codes. J. ACM **65**(4), 20:1–20:32 (2018). https://doi.org/10.1145/3178432

37. Goyal, V., Ishai, Y., Maji, H.K., Sahai, A., Sherstov, A.A.: Bounded-communication leakage resilience via parity-resilient circuits. In: Proceedings of the 57th Annual IEEE Symposium on Foundations of Computer Science (2016)

38. Goyal, V., Kumar, A.: Non-malleable secret sharing. In: Proceedings of the 50th Annual ACM SIGACT Symposium on Theory of Computing, pp. 685–698. ACM (2018)

39. Goyal, V., Kumar, A.: Non-malleable secret sharing for general access structures. In: Advances in Cryptology - CRYPTO 2018–38th Annual International Cryptology Conference, Santa Barbara, CA, USA, 19–23 August 2018, Proceedings, Part I, pp. 501–530 (2018)

40. Goyal, V., Pandey, O., Richelson, S.: Textbook non-malleable commitments. In: Proceedings of the forty-eighth annual ACM symposium on Theory of Computing pp. 1128–1141. ACM (2016)

41. Gupta, D., Maji, H.K., Wang, M.: Constant-rate non-malleable codes in the split-state model. Technical Report Report 2017/1048, Cryptology ePrint Archive (2018)

42. Guruswami, V., Umans, C., Vadhan, S.P.: Unbalanced expanders and randomness extractors from Parvaresh-Vardy codes. J. ACM **56**(4) (2009)

43. Kanukurthi, B., Obbattu, S.L.B., Sekar, S.: Four-state non-malleable codes with explicit constant rate. In: Kalai, Y., Reyzin, L. (eds.) TCC 2017. LNCS, vol. 10678, pp. 344–375. Springer, Cham (2017). https://doi.org/10.1007/978-3-319-70503-3_11

44. Kanukurthi, B., Obbattu, S.L.B., Sekar, S.: Non-malleable randomness encoders and their applications. In: Nielsen, J.B., Rijmen, V. (eds.) EUROCRYPT 2018. LNCS, vol. 10822, pp. 589–617. Springer, Cham (2018). https://doi.org/10.1007/978-3-319-78372-7_19

45. Li, X.: Improved two-source extractors, and affine extractors for polylogarithmic entropy. In: 2016 IEEE 57th Annual Symposium on Foundations of Computer Science (FOCS), pp. 168–177. IEEE (2016)

46. Li, X.: Improved non-malleable extractors, non-malleable codes and independent source extractors. In: Proceedings of the 49th Annual ACM SIGACT Symposium on Theory of Computing, STOC 2017, pp. 1144–1156 (2017)

47. Li, X.: Non-malleable extractors and non-malleable codes: Partially optimal constructions. In: Electronic Colloquium on Computational Complexity (ECCC) (2018)

48. Lin, F., Cheraghchi, M., Guruswami, V., Safavi-Naini, R., Wang, H.: Secret sharing with binary shares. CoRR arXiv:cs/1808.02974 (2018)

49. Lin, F., Cheraghchi, M., Guruswami, V., Safavi-Naini, R., Wang, H.: Non-malleable secret sharing against affine tampering. CoRR arXiv:cs/1902.06195 (2019)

50. Maurer, U., Wolf, S.: Privacy amplification secure against active adversaries. In: Kaliski, B.S. (ed.) CRYPTO 1997. LNCS, vol. 1294, pp. 307–321. Springer, Heidelberg (1997). https://doi.org/10.1007/BFb0052244

51. Rabin, T., Ben-Or, M.: Verifiable secret sharing and multiparty protocols with honest majority (extended abstract). In: Proceedings of the 21st Annual ACM Symposium on Theory of Computing, pp. 73–85 (1989)

52. Rao, A.: An exposition of Bourgain's 2-source extractor. In: Electronic Colloquium on Computational Complexity (ECCC) 14(034) (2007)

53. Rao, A.: Extractors for low-weight affine sources. In: Proceedings of the 24th Annual IEEE Conference on Computational Complexity (2009)

54. Rasmussen, P.M.R., Sahai, A.: Expander graphs are non-malleable codes. CoRR (2018). https://arxiv.org/abs/1810.00106

55. Raz, R.: Extractors with weak random seeds. In: Proceedings of the 37th Annual ACM Symposium on Theory of Computing, pp. 11–20 (2005)

56. Raz, R., Reingold, O., Vadhan, S.: Extracting all the randomness and reducing the error in Trevisan's extractors. JCSS 65(1), 97–128 (2002)

57. Raz, R., Yehudayoff, A.: Multilinear formulas, maximal-partition discrepancy and mixed-sources extractors. J. Comput. Syst. Sci. 77, 167–190 (2011). https://doi.org/10.1016/j.jcss.2010.06.013

58. Shamir, A.: How to share a secret. Commun. ACM 22(11), 612–613 (1979)

59. Trevisan, L.: Extractors and pseudorandom generators. J. ACM 48, 860–879 (2001)

60. Trevisan, L., Vadhan, S.P.: Extracting randomness from samplable distributions. In: IEEE Symposium on Foundations of Computer Science, pp. 32–42 (2000). https://doi.org/10.1109/SFCS.2000.892063

61. Zuckerman, D.: Randomness-optimal oblivious sampling. Random Struct. Algorithms 11, 345–367 (1997)

On Average-Case Hardness in **TFNP**
from One-Way Functions

Pavel Hubáček[1]([✉]) [ID], Chethan Kamath[2], Karel Král[1] [ID],
and Veronika Slívová[1] [ID]

[1] Charles University, Prague, Czech Republic
{hubacek,kralka,slivova}@iuuk.mff.cuni.cz
[2] Northeastern University, Boston, USA
ckamath@protonmail.com

Abstract. The complexity class **TFNP** consists of all **NP** *search* problems that are *total* in the sense that a solution is guaranteed to exist for all instances. Over the years, this class has proved to illuminate surprising connections among several diverse subfields of mathematics like combinatorics, computational topology, and algorithmic game theory. More recently, we are starting to better understand its interplay with cryptography.

We know that certain cryptographic primitives (e.g. one-way permutations, collision-resistant hash functions, or indistinguishability obfuscation) imply average-case hardness in **TFNP** and its important subclasses. However, its relationship with the most basic cryptographic primitive – i.e., one-way functions (OWFs) – still remains unresolved. Under an additional complexity theoretic assumption, OWFs imply hardness in **TFNP** (Hubáček, Naor, and Yogev, ITCS 2017). It is also known that average-case hardness in most structured subclasses of **TFNP** does not imply any form of cryptographic hardness in a black-box way (Rosen, Segev, and Shahaf, TCC 2017) and, thus, one-way functions might be sufficient. Specifically, no negative result which would rule out basing average-case hardness in **TFNP** *solely* on OWFs is currently known. In this work, we further explore the interplay between **TFNP** and OWFs and give the first negative results.

As our main result, we show that there cannot exist constructions of average-case (and, in fact, even worst-case) hard **TFNP** problem from OWFs with a certain type of *simple* black-box security reductions. The class of reductions we rule out is, however, rich enough to capture many of the currently known cryptographic hardness results for **TFNP**. Our results are established using the framework of black-box separations (Impagliazzo and Rudich, STOC 1989) and involve a novel application of the reconstruction paradigm (Gennaro and Trevisan, FOCS 2000).

This research was supported in part by the Grant Agency of the Czech Republic under the grant agreement no. 19-27871X, by the Charles University projects PRIMUS/17/SCI/9, UNCE/SCI/004, and GAUK 1568819, and by the Charles University grant SVV-2017-260452. The second author is supported by the IARPA grant IARPA/2019-19-020700009.

R. Pass and K. Pietrzak (Eds.): TCC 2020, LNCS 12552, pp. 614–638, 2020.
https://doi.org/10.1007/978-3-030-64381-2_22

Keywords: TFNP · PPAD · Average-case hardness · One-way functions · Black-box separations.

1   Introduction

The complexity class TFNP ofi *total* search problems [41], i.e., with syntactically guaranteed existence of a solution for all instances, holds a perplexing place in the hierarchy of computational complexity classes. The standard method for arguing computational hardness in TFNP is via clustering these problems into subclasses characterised by the existential argument guaranteeing their totality [42]. This approach was particularly successful in illuminating the connections between search problems in seemingly distant domains such as combinatorics, computational topology, and algorithmic game theory (see, for example, [14,17,18,23,37] and the references therein). However, all results of this type ultimately leave open the possibility of the existence of polynomial time algorithms for all of TFNP.

An orthogonal line of work, which can be traced to Papadimitriou [42], shows the existence of hard problems in subclasses of TFNP under cryptographic assumptions. Such conditional lower bounds for structured subclasses of TFNP were recently given under increasingly more plausible cryptographic assumptions [6,7,11,12,16,20,28,33,38]. The end of the line in this sequence of results would correspond to a "dream theorem" establishing average-case hardness in one of the lower classes in the TFNP hierarchy (e.g. CLS [15]) under some weak general cryptographic assumptions (e.g. the existence of one-way functions).

An informative parallel for the limits of this methodology can be drawn by considering average-case hardness of *decision* problems (i.e., languages) in NP ∩ coNP. The existence of a hard-on-average decision problem in NP∩coNP follows from the existence of hard-core predicates for any one-way permutation [24]. However, the existence of injective one-way functions is insufficient for black-box constructions of hard-on-average distributions for languages in NP ∩ coNP even assuming indistinguishability obfuscation [5] (in fact, [5] ruled out even black-box constructions of worst-case hardness in NP∩coNP using these cryptographic primitives).

For total *search* problems, the existence of hard-on-average TFNP distributions is straightforward either from one-way permutations or collision-resistant hash functions. Moreover, there exist constructions of hard-on-average TFNP distributions either assuming indistinguishability obfuscation and one-way functions [7,20] or under derandomization-style assumptions and one-way functions [27]. On the other hand, no analogue of the impossibility result for basing average-case hardness in NP ∩ coNP on (injective) one-way functions [5] is currently known for TFNP. Rosen, Segev, and Shahaf [47] showed that most of the known structured subclasses of TFNP do not imply (in a black-box way) any form of cryptographic hardness; thus, it is plausible that hard-on-average distributions in TFNP can be based *solely* on the existence of one-way functions.

Rosen et al. [47] also provided some insight into the structure of hard-on-average distributions in TFNP. They showed that any hard-on-average distribution of a TFNP problem from any primitive which exists relative to a random injective trapdoor function oracle (e.g. one-way functions, injective trapdoor functions, or collision-resistant hash functions) must result in instances with a nearly exponential number of solutions. Even though the [47] result restricts the structure of hard-on-average distributions in TFNP constructed from these cryptographic primitives, it certainly does not rule out their existence. Indeed, a collision-resistant hash function constitutes a hard-on-average TFNP distribution, albeit with an exponential number of solutions.

Motivated by the significant gap between negative and positive results, we revisit the problem of existence of average-case hardness in TFNP under weak general cryptographic assumptions and address the following question:

Are (injective) one-way functions sufficiently structured to imply hard-on-average total search problems?

Towards answering this question, we provide negative results and show that *simple* fully black-box constructions of hard-on-average TFNP distributions from injective one-way functions do not exist.

1.1   Our Results

We recall the details of the construction of a hard-on-average distribution in TFNP from one-way permutations to highlight the restrictions on the type of reductions considered in our results.

Consider the total search problem PIGEON, in which you are given a length-preserving n-bit function represented by a Boolean circuit C and are asked to find either a preimage of the all-zero string (i.e., $x \in \{0,1\}^n : C(x) = 0^n$) or a non-trivial collision (i.e., $x \neq x' \in \{0,1\}^n : C(x) = C(x')$). PIGEON is complete for a subclass of TFNP known as PPP, and Papadimitriou [42] gave the following construction of a hard PIGEON problem from one-way permutations. Given a (one-way) permutation $f \colon \{0,1\}^n \to \{0,1\}^n$ and a challenge $y \in \{0,1\}^n$ for inversion under f, the reduction algorithm defines an instance of PIGEON by the oracle-aided circuit C_y^f computing the function $C_y^f(x) = f(x) \oplus y$. It is not hard to see that the instance of PIGEON C_y^f has a unique solution corresponding to the preimage of y under f and, therefore, any algorithm solving it breaks the one-wayness of f.

Note that the above construction of a hard (on average) TFNP problem is extremely simple in various aspects:

- The construction is *fully black-box*, i.e., the PIGEON instance can be implemented via an oracle-aided circuit treating the one-way permutation as a black-box and the reduction inverts when given oracle access to an arbitrary solver for PIGEON.
- The reduction is *many-one*, i.e., a single call to a PIGEON-solving oracle suffices for finding the preimage of y.

- The reduction is *f-oblivious*, i.e., the oracle-aided circuit C_y^f defining the PIGEON instance depends only on the challenge y and does not depend on the one-way permutation f in the sense that C_y^f itself can be fully specified without querying f. In other words, given the challenge y, the instance C_y^f submitted to the PIGEON oracle by the reduction is, as an oracle-aided circuit, identical for all permutations f.
- The reduction is *deterministic*, i.e., it simply passes y to specify the PIGEON instance.

Such a fully black-box construction of PIGEON with a deterministic f-oblivious many-one reduction exists also assuming collision-resistant hash functions exist (folklore). Specifically, for any hash function $h\colon \{0,1\}^n \to \{0,1\}^{n-1}$ from the collision-resistant family, the PIGEON instance is defined as $C^h(x) = h(x) \parallel 1$, where $\parallel$ represents the operation of string concatenation. Since C^h concatenates the value $h(x)$ with 1 for any input x, it never maps to the all-zero string and, therefore, has the same collisions as h. Note that, unlike in the above construction from one-way permutations, the instances resulting from collision-resistant hash functions do not have a unique solution. In fact, there are always at least 2^{n-1} nontrivial collisions (even in two-to-one functions where each $y \in \{0,1\}^{n-1}$ has exactly two preimages) and this structural property is inherent as shown by Rosen et al. [47]. Importantly, the property of having nearly exponentially many solutions is not in contradiction with the resulting distribution being hard-on-average. Currently, there is no actual evidence suggesting that average-case hardness in TFNP cannot be based on the existence of injective one-way functions.

The above constructions motivate us to study whether there exist such "simple" constructions of an average-case hard TFNP problem under weaker cryptographic assumptions such as the existence of injective one-way functions, and we answer this question in negative (see Sect. 3.2 for the formal statement of Theorem 1).

Theorem 1. (Main Theorem - Informal). *There is no efficient fully black-box construction of a worst-case hard TFNP problem from injective one-way functions with a randomized f-oblivious non-adaptive reduction.*

Thus, we actually rule out a larger class of fully black-box constructions with reductions to injective one-way functions than the *deterministic f*-oblivious *many-one* reductions from the motivating examples of *average-case hardness* of PIGEON from one-way permutations, respectively collision-resistant hash functions. We rule out even constructions of *worst-case hard* TFNP problems using *randomized f*-oblivious *non-adaptive*[1] reductions. The formal definitions of fully black-box constructions with *f*-oblivious non-adaptive reductions are given in Sect. 3.1 (see Definition 2 and Definition 3).

Even though restricted, our results are the first step towards the full-fledged black-box separation of TFNP and (injective) one-way functions. We note that

---

[1] Reductions which can ask *multiple* queries *in parallel* to the TFNP oracle.

the full-fledged separation would necessarily subsume the known separation of collision-resistant hash functions and injective one-way functions [49], for which, despite the recent progress, there are only non-trivial proofs [4, 25, 40].

1.2 Our Techniques

Our results employ the framework of black-box separations [19, 30, 45]. The approach suggested in [30] for demonstrating that there is no fully black-box construction of a primitive P from another primitive Q is to come up with an oracle O relative to which Q exists, but every black-box implementation C^Q of P is broken. However, as explained in [40, 45], this approach actually rules out a larger class of constructions (so-called "relativized" constructions), and to rule out just fully black-box constructions it suffices to use the so-called two-oracle technique [26]. Here, the oracle O usually consists of two parts: an idealised implementation of the primitive Q and a "breaker" oracle for primitive P. In our context, P corresponds to a TFNP problem and the oracle O comprises of a random injective function (which yields an injective one-way function) and a procedure SOLVE which provides a solution for any instance of a TFNP problem. To rule out the existence of fully black-box constructions of hard-on-average TFNP problems from injective one-way functions, one then has to argue that access to such a "breaker" oracle SOLVE for TFNP does not help any reduction R in inverting injective one-way functions. Designing such a SOLVE oracle and then arguing that it does not help inverting injective one-way function, which we carry out using the reconstruction paradigm of Gennaro ond Trevisan [21], constitute the main technical challenges. Before giving an overview of these two steps, we explain the structural insight that is key to our separation, and guided us in the design of the two steps.

The Existence of a "Useless" Solution. At the core of our negative result is a new structural insight about TFNP instances constructed from (injective) one-way functions. Observe that any one-way function gives rise to a search problem with a hard-on-average distribution which is total over its support (but all instances outside its support have no solution). Specifically, for any one-way function $f : \{0,1\}^n \to \{0,1\}^{n+1}$, an instance is any $y \in \{0,1\}^{n+1}$ and the solution for y is any $x \in \{0,1\}^n$ such that $f(x) = y$. The hard-on-average distribution then corresponds to sampling x uniformly from $\{0,1\}^n$ and outputting the instance $y = f(x)$ (as in the standard security experiment for one-way functions). When attempting to construct a hard search problem which is truly total and has a solution for all instances (not only for the support of the hard distribution), one has to face the frustrating obstacle in the form of "useless" solutions which do not help the reduction in inverting its challenge y. Note that, as the resulting TFNP problem must be total for all oracles f, there must exist a solution even for oracles with no preimage for the challenge y. By a simple probabilistic argument, it follows that for a random oracle f and a random challenge y, with overwhelming probability, there exists a solution to any TFNP instance which does not query a preimage of y, i.e., a "useless" solution from the perspective of the reduction.[2] Thus, demonstrating a black-box separation would be straightforward if the TFNP solver knew which challenge y is the reduction attempting to invert. Our solver would simply output such a "useless" solution and we could argue via the reconstruction paradigm that no reduction can succeed in inverting y given access to our solver. In this work, we show that it is possible to construct a TFNP solver which returns such a "useless" solution with overwhelming probability even though the solver *does not know* the input challenge of the reduction.

Reduction-Specific SOLVE. Note that a reduction in a fully black-box construction must succeed in breaking the primitive P when given access to *any* oracle SOLVE (see Definition 2). In other words, to rule out the existence of constructions with a fully black-box reduction, it is sufficient to show that for every reduction there exists a SOLVE which is not helpful in inverting; in particular, SOLVE may depend on the reduction. To enable SOLVE to answer the reduction's query with a "useless" solution with overwhelming probability, we take exactly this approach and construct a reduction-specific SOLVE for any construction of a TFNP problem from injective one-way functions. We significantly differ in this respect from the previous works which relied on the reconstruction paradigm of Gennaro and Trevisan [21], e.g., the works which employed the collision-finding oracle of Simon [8,25,43,46,49]. We note that the possibility of designing a breaker oracle which depends on the fully black-box construction was exploited already by Gertner, Malkin, and Reingold [22], who considered SOLVE which depends on the implementation rather than the reduction algorithm (as in our case). That is, to rule out the construction of a primitive P from a primitive Q, they considered an oracle SOLVE that depends on the implementation C^Q of the primitive P, whereas in our case SOLVE depends on the reduction algorithm R that is supposed to break Q given access to an algorithm that breaks C^Q. The possibility of proving black-box separations via reduction-specific oracles was also observed in the work of Hsiao and Reyzin [26] who, nevertheless, did not have to leverage this observation in their proofs.

On a high level, given that SOLVE can use the code of the reduction R, SOLVE can simulate R on all possible challenges y to identify the set of challenges on which R outputs the present instance that SOLVE needs to solve. As we show, the solution then can be chosen adversarially so that it avoids such solutions of interest to the reduction. To turn this intuition into a formal proof, one needs to show that our SOLVE indeed does not help in inverting injective one-way functions and we do so along the lines of the reconstruction paradigm of [21].

---

[2] Note that the above argument fails in the case of one-way permutations, where the challenge $y \in \{0,1\}^n$ is in the image for any permutation $f \colon \{0,1\}^n \to \{0,1\}^n$. The construction of a TFNP problem then simply does not have to deal with the case when the challenge y is not in the image of f, and it can ensure that every solution is useful for inverting the challenge y. Indeed, the hard instances C_y^f of PIGEON from one-way permutations described in Sect. 1.1 have a unique solution on which C_y^f always queries a preimage of y under any f.

Applying the Compression Argument. Two important subtleties arise in the proof when we try to turn the reduction into a pair of compression and decompression algorithms, which we explain next. First, the reconstruction paradigm is conventionally applied to random permutations [21,25], whereas the reduction R and the algorithm SOLVE are designed for random injective functions. The natural approach is to simply proceed with the same style of proof even in our setting. Specifically, one would presume that a similar incompressibility argument can be leveraged if we manage to somehow encode the image of the random injective function. While this intuition is correct in the sense that it allows *correct* compression and reconstruction, it turns out that the space required to encode the image is too prohibitive for reaching the desired contradiction with known information-theoretic lower bounds on the expected length of encoding for a random injective function. To resolve this issue, we construct compressor and decompressor algorithms for a random permutation, but we equip the algorithms with *shared randomness* in the form of a random injective function $h: \{0,1\}^n \rightarrow \{0,1\}^{n+1}$ independent of the random permutation $\pi: \{0,1\}^n \rightarrow \{0,1\}^n$ to be compressed. Whenever the compressor and decompressor need to provide the reduction or SOLVE with access to the injective function $f: \{0,1\}^n \rightarrow \{0,1\}^{n+1}$, they compose the permutation π with the shared injective function h and then pass off the composed injective function $f = h \circ \pi$ to the reduction. With this modification, we are able to show that any reduction which succeeds in inverting injective one-way functions given access to our SOLVE can be used to compress a random permutation on $\{0,1\}^n$ below a standard information-theoretic lower bound on the size of a prefix-free encoding of such random variable. We note that this is reminiscent of the approach used in [40] for separating *injective* one-way functions from one-way permutations.

Second, we cannot employ the actual oracle SOLVE in our compression and decompression algorithms: even though we can use the reduction when compressing and decompressing the random permutation, we must be able to *consistently* simulate SOLVE without accessing the whole permutation. In general, the choice of the "breaker" oracle that can be simulated efficiently without too many queries to the permutation (e.g., the collision finding oracle of Simon [2,49]) is a crucial part of the whole proof, and, a priori, it is unclear how to design a TFNP solver which also has such a property. Nevertheless, we show that there exists a SOLVE which can be efficiently simulated given only (sufficiently small) partial information about the permutation.

f-Oblivious Reductions. As our SOLVE simulates the reduction on possible challenges y, we need for technical reasons that the reduction is f-oblivious (namely, for correctness of our encoding and decoding algorithms). However, we believe that f-obliviousness is not overly restrictive as it is a natural property of security reductions. Besides the two fully black-box constructions of PIGEON with f-oblivious reductions described in Sect. 1.1, f-oblivious security reductions appear also in the cryptographic literature – see for example the standard security reduction in the Goldreich-Levin theorem establishing the existence of hard-core predicate for any one-way function (note that this particular security reduction is also non-adaptive). An orthogonal notion of a π-oblivious construction appears in the work of Wee [50]. However, it is the implementation of the constructed primitive which is "oblivious" to the one-way permutation π in his work.

1.3 Related Work

TFNP *and its Subclasses.* The systematic study of total search problems was initiated by Megiddo and Papadimitriou [41] with the definition of complexity class TFNP. They observed that a "semantic" class such as TFNP is unlikely to have complete problems, unless NP = coNP. As a resolution, Papadimitriou [42] defined "syntactic" subclasses of TFNP with the goal of clustering search problems based on the various *existence theorems* used to argue their totality. Perhaps the best known such class is PPAD [42], which captures the computational complexity of finding Nash equilibria in bimatrix games [10,14]. Other subclasses of TFNP include:

- PPA [42], which captures computational problems related to the *parity argument* like Borsuk-Ulam theorem or fair division [18];
- PLS [34], defined to capture the computational complexity of problems amenable to *local search* and its "continuous" counterpart CLS $\subseteq$ PLS [15] (in fact CLS $\subseteq$ PLS $\cap$ PPAD), which captures finding the computational complexity of finding (approximate) local optima of continuous functions and contains interesting problems from game theory (e.g., solving the simple stochastic games of Condon or Shapley); and
- PPP [42] and PWPP $\subseteq$ PPP [33], motivated by the *pigeonhole principle* and contain important problems related to finding collisions in functions.

The relative complexity of some of these classes was studied in [3] as it was shown using (worst-case) oracle separations that many of these classes are distinct.

Cryptographic hardness in TFNP. Hardness from standard cryptographic primitives was long known for the "higher" classes in TFNP like PPP and PPA. We have already mentioned that one-way permutations imply average-case hardness in PPP [42] and existence of collision-resistant hashing (e.g. hardness of integer factoring or discrete-logarithm problem in prime-order groups) implies average-case hardness in PPP (as well as in PWPP). In addition, Jeřábek [33], building on the work of Buresh-Oppenheim [9], showed that PPA is no easier than integer factoring.

However, it is only recently that we are better understanding the cryptographic hardness of the lower classes in TFNP. This was catalysed by the result of Bitansky et al. [7] who reduced hardness in PPAD to indistinguishability obfuscation (and injective OWFs) expanding on Abbot, Kane, and Valiant [1]; Hubáček and Yogev [28] extended this result to CLS $\subseteq$ PLS $\cap$ PPAD. The underlying assumption was relaxed further to cryptographic assumptions that are more plausible than indistinguishability obfuscation in [11,12,16]. Using similar ideas, Bitansky and Gerichter [6] presented a construction for hard-on-average distributions in the complexity class PLS in the random oracle model. Building on these results, a flurry of recent works [31,32,35,36,39] further weakened the assumptions required for proving average-case hardness in CLS to sub-exponential hardness of learning with errors, bringing us closer to proving average-case hardness in CLS under a standard *concrete* cryptographic assumption.

One-Way Functions and TFNP. Hubáček et al. [27] showed that average-case hardness in NP (which is implied by OWFs) implies average-case hardness in TFNP under complexity theoretical assumptions related to derandomization. Pass and Venkitasubramaniam [44] recently complemented the [27] result by showing that when OWFs *do not exist*, average-case hardness in NP implies average-case hardness in TFNP. However, a definitive relationship between OWFs and TFNP has remained elusive. This prompted Rosen et al. [47] to explore impossibility of reducing TFNP hardness to OWFs. They gave a partial answer by showing that there do not exist hard-on-average distributions of TFNP instances over $\{0,1\}^n$ with $2^{n^{o(1)}}$ solutions from any primitive which exists relative to a random injective trapdoor function oracle (e.g. one-way functions). Their main observation was that the argument in [48], which separates one-way functions from one-way permutations, can be strengthened to separate other unstructured primitives from structured primitives (such as problems in TFNP). However, it seems that the [48] argument has been exploited to its limits in [47], and, therefore, it is not clear whether their approach can be extended to fully separate one-way functions and TFNP. Thus, the situation is contrasting to NP∩coNP, the decision counterpart of TFNP, whose relationship with (injective) OWFs is much better studied. In particular, we know that hardness is implied by one way permutations but injective OWFs, even with indistinguishability obfuscation, (and, therefore, public-key encryption) cannot imply hardness in NP ∩ coNP in a black-box way [5].

2   Preliminaries

Unless stated otherwise, all logarithms are base two. For $X \subseteq \{0,1\}^*$, we use $\overline{X}$ to denote the set $\{0,1\}^* \setminus X$. For strings $x, y \in \{0,1\}^*$, we use $x <_{\text{lex}} y$ or $y >_{\text{lex}} x$ to denote that x is lexicographically strictly smaller than y.

Notation 2. (Functions) *Let $X, Y \subseteq \{0,1\}^*$, $f \colon X \to Y$ be a function and $X' \subseteq X$ be a set.*

1. *$f \upharpoonright X'$ denotes the restriction of f on X', i.e., the function $f' \colon X' \to Y$ such that $\forall x \in X' \colon f'(x) = f(x)$.*
2. *$\text{Dom}(f)$ denotes the domain of f, i.e., the set X.*
3. *$\text{Im}(f)$ denotes the image of f, i.e., the set $\{f(x) \mid x \in X\} \subseteq Y$.*
4. *$f[X']$ denotes the image of the restriction of f on X', i.e., the set $\text{Im}(f \upharpoonright X')$.*

Notation 3. (Injective functions) *We denote by Inj_n^m the set of all injective functions from $\{0,1\}^n$ to $\{0,1\}^m$. For the special case when $n = m$ we get the set of all permutations on $\{0,1\}^n$.*

The set Inj is the set of all functions $f\colon \{0,1\}^* \to \{0,1\}^*$, such that f can be interpreted as a sequence $f = \left\{ f_n \mid f_n \in Inj_n^{m(n)} \right\}_{n \in \mathbb{N}}$ of injective functions, where $m\colon \mathbb{N} \to \mathbb{N}$ is an injective function such that for all $n \in \mathbb{N}\colon m(n) > n$ and $m(n) \leq 100n^{\log n}$.

We say that the function m is the type *of f and we define the corresponding type operator $\tau\colon Inj \to (\mathbb{N} \to \mathbb{N})$ such that $\tau(f) = m$.*

We denote the set of all possible types by T, *i.e.,*

$$\mathrm{T} = \{\mu\colon \mathbb{N} \to \mathbb{N} \mid \exists f \in Inj \text{ such that } \tau(f) = \mu\}.$$

Through the paper f_n denotes the function $f \upharpoonright \{0,1\}^n$ (i.e., restriction of f to the domain $\{0,1\}^n$.), where $f \in Inj$.

In our proofs, we often compose a function defined on all binary strings with a function defined only for binary strings of certain length; namely, we often want to compose a function from Inj with a permutation of n-bit strings. The desired resulting function should always be a function from all binary strings. For the ease of exposition, we extend the standard notation for function composition as follows.

Notation 4. (Function composition). *Let X, Y, Z be any sets such that $X \subseteq Y$ and let $f\colon X \to Y$ and $g\colon Y \to Z$. We define the function $g \circ f\colon Y \to Z$ as:*

$$(g \circ f)(x) = \begin{cases} g(f(x)) & \text{if } x \in X, \\ g(x) & \text{if } x \in Y \setminus X. \end{cases}$$

Finally, we recall some basic information-theoretic results about prefix-free codes.

Definition 1. (Prefix-free code). *A set of code-words $C \subseteq \{0,1\}^*$ is a prefix-free code if there are no two distinct $c_1, c_2 \in C$ such that c_1 is a prefix (initial segment) of c_2, i.e., for any two distinct $c_1, c_2 \in C$ there exists $0 \leq j < \min(|c_1|, |c_2|)$ such that $(c_1)_j \neq (c_2)_j$.*

Proposition 1. (Theorem 5.3.1 in [13]). *The expected length L of any prefix-free binary code for a random variable X is greater than or equal to the entropy $H(X)$.*

Corollary 1. *To encode a uniformly random permutation $\pi \in Inj_n^n$ using prefix-free encoding it takes at least $\log(2^n!)$ bits in expectation.*

Proof. The entropy of a uniformly randomly chosen permutation from Inj_n^n is $\log(2^n!)$ as we choose uniformly at random from $2^n!$ distinct permutations. By Theorem 1, we get that the expected size of the encoding is at least $\log(2^n!)$. $\square$

3   Separating **TFNP** and Injective One-Way Functions

3.1   Fully Black-Box Construction of Hard **TFNP** Problem from iOWF

Below, we give a definition of fully black-box construction of a (worst-case) hard TFNP problem from an injective one-way function.

Definition 2. (Fully black-box construction of a worst-case hard TFNPproblem from $iOWF$**).** *A fully black-box construction of a worst-case hard TFNP problem from injective one-way function is a tuple* (R, T_R, C, T_C, p) *of oracle-aided algorithms* R, C*, functions* T_R, T_C*, and a polynomial* p *satisfying the following properties:*

1. ***R and C halt on all inputs:*** *For all* $f \in Inj$, $n \in \mathbb{N}$*, and* $y, i, s \in \{0,1\}^*$*, the algorithm* $R^f(1^n, y)$ *halts in time* $T_R(|y|)$*, and the algorithm* $C^f(i, s)$ *halts in time* $T_C(|i| + |s|)$.
2. ***Correctness:*** *For all* $f \in Inj$ *and for all* $i \in \{0,1\}^*$*, there exists* $s \in \{0,1\}^*$ *such that* $|s| \le p(|i|)$ *and* $C^f(i, s) = 1$*, i.e., for any instance of the* TFNP *problem there exists a solution of polynomial length.*
3. ***Fully black-box proof of security:*** *There exists a polynomial* p' *such that for all* $f \in Inj$ *and any oracle-aided algorithm* SOLVE*, if*

$$\forall i \in \{0,1\}^* : \text{SOLVE}^f(i) \text{ returns } s \text{ such that } C^f(i, s) = 1$$

then for infinitely many $n \in \mathbb{N}$*,*

$$\Pr_{x \leftarrow \{0,1\}^n, R} \left[R^{f, \text{SOLVE}}(1^n, f(x)) = x \right] \ge \frac{1}{p'(n)} .$$

Definition 2 has the following semantics. The deterministic algorithm C specifies the TFNP problem and the algorithm R is the (security) reduction which, given access to any TFNP solver, breaks the security of any injective one-way function. For example in the case of the hard PIGEON problem from one-way permutations discussed in Sect. 1.1, C would be an algorithm which on input (C_y^f, x), respectively (C_y^f, x, x'), outputs 1 if and only if $\mathsf{C}_y^f(x) = 0^n$, respectively $\mathsf{C}_y^f(x) = \mathsf{C}_y^f(x')$. The reduction algorithm $R(1^n, y)$ simply queries the TFNP solver SOLVE with the instance $i = \mathsf{C}_y^f$, i.e., a circuit computing the function $\mathsf{C}_y^f(x) = f(x) \oplus y$, and outputs the solution s returned by SOLVE for which, by construction, $f(s) = y$.

Below, we provide some additional remarks on important points in the above definition.

Reduction-Specific SOLVE. Let us emphasize the order of quantifiers restricting the security reduction in Definition 2:

$$\exists (R, T_R, C, T_C, p) \; \forall f \; \forall \text{SOLVE}:$$

$$\text{SOLVE}^f \text{ solves the TFNP problem } C \implies R^{f, \text{SOLVE}} \text{ inverts } f .$$

Importantly, the reduction must invert when given access to *any* oracle SOLVE. As a consequence, in order to establish a separation, the above statement is negated and it suffices to show that for every reduction there exists a solver (see proof of [26, Proposition 1] for more details). Thus, in the proof an oracle separation, the oracle SOLVE may even depend on the behaviour of the reduction R, and, in particular, SOLVE can simulate the security reduction R on an arbitrary input. We exploit these properties in establishing our results.

Constructions of Worst-Case vs. Average-Case Hardness in TFNP. Our Definition 2 considers constructions of a *worst-case* hard TFNP problem – the reduction has access to SOLVE which is promised to return a solution to *any* instance of the TFNP problem. To capture constructions of *average-case* hardness in TFNP, we would need to extend the construction with an efficiently sampleable distribution D of instances of the TFNP problem and require the reduction to invert when given access to any SOLVE that returns solutions for instances coming from the specific distribution D (see Definition 5.1 in [47]). However, given that we are proving a black-box separation, showing impossibility for worst-case hardness is a stronger result.

The Quality of SOLVE. Note that we consider security reductions which invert given access to SOLVE which outputs a solution with probability 1, whereas some definitions in the literature allow the reduction to work only with some non-negligible probability. This also makes our negative result stronger – it is potentially easier to give a reduction when given access to SOLVE which is guaranteed to always return a solution.

Direct and Indirect Queries to f. The security reduction R can learn something about f in various ways. It may query f directly or the information might be deduced from the solution of some queried instance of the TFNP problem returned by SOLVE. We introduce the following notation in order to distinguish where queries originate, which allows us to reason about the view the security reduction has over the function f in our proof of Theorem 1.

Notation 5. (Query sets Q) *We distinguish the following sets of queries to oracles depending on where these queries originated and which oracle is queried.*

- *Let $Q(C^f(i,s))$ denote the set of all preimages $x \in \{0,1\}^*$ on which the oracle f has been queried by C running on an input (i,s).*
- *Let $Q_{\text{SOLVE}}(R^{f,\text{SOLVE}}(1^n, y))$ denote the set of all instances $i \in \{0,1\}^*$ on which the oracle SOLVE has been queried by R running on a security parameter n and challenge y.*
- *Let $Q_f^{dir}(R^{f,\text{SOLVE}}(1^n, y))$ denote the set of preimages $x \in \{0,1\}^*$ on which the oracle f has been queried by R running on an input y and security parameter n.*
- *Let $Q_f^{indir}(R^{f,\text{SOLVE}}(1^n, y))$ denote the set of all preimages $x \in \{0,1\}^*$ on which the oracle f has been queried indirectly, i.e., it has been queried by C running on an input (i,s) where $i \in Q_{\text{SOLVE}}(R^{f,\text{SOLVE}}(1^n, y))$ and $s = \text{SOLVE}^f(i)$.*
- *Let $Q_f(R^{f,\text{SOLVE}}(1^n, y)) = Q_f^{dir}(R^{f,\text{SOLVE}}(1^n, y)) \cup Q_f^{indir}(R^{f,\text{SOLVE}}(1^n, y))$.*

Note that these sets may not be disjoint. When f is a partial function (i.e., when f is not defined on all inputs) the query set contains all queries queried up to the point of the first undefined answer and the query with the undefined answer is included as well.

Restrictions on the power of the reduction. We consider various restricted classes of security reductions as defined below.

Definition 3. (Deterministic/randomized, many-one/non-adaptive, f-oblivious reductions) *Let (R, T_R, C, T_C, p) be a fully black-box construction of a hard TFNP problem from injective one-way functions.*

We distinguish deterministic / randomized reductions. For a randomized security reduction, we extend the input of R to a triple $(1^n, y; r)$, where the meaning of n, resp. y, remains unchanged (i.e., n is the security parameter, y is the challenge), and $r \in \{0,1\}^*$ is the randomness of the security reduction.

The security reduction R is many-one if for all $f \in Inj$, for any oracle SOLVE and for all $y \in \{0,1\}^*$, $R^{f,\text{SOLVE}}(1^n, y)$ makes a single query to the oracle SOLVE.

The security reduction R is non-adaptive if for all $f \in Inj$, for any oracle SOLVE and for all $y \in \{0,1\}^*$, all the queries of $R^{f,\text{SOLVE}}(1^n, y)$ to the oracle SOLVE are submitted in parallel (i.e., the queries to SOLVE do not depend on the answers received from SOLVE).

The security reduction R is f-oblivious if for all $y \in \{0,1\}^*$, for any oracle SOLVE, and any pair of functions $f, f' \in Inj$, the distributions of queries $Q_{\text{SOLVE}}(R^{f,\text{SOLVE}}(1^n, y))$ and $Q_{\text{SOLVE}}(R^{f',\text{SOLVE}}(1^n, y))$ are identical (i.e., the queries to SOLVE depend only on the input y and are independent of the oracle f).

3.2 Impossibility for a Deterministic f-Oblivious Many-One Reduction

In this section, we show that there is no fully black-box construction of a hard TFNP problem from injective one-way functions with a deterministic f-oblivious many-one reduction. The proof of this result is already non-trivial and highlights our main technical contributions. In Sect. 3.3, we explain how to extend this result to rule out fully black-box constructions even with a *randomized f-oblivious non-adaptive* reduction. For lack of space, we omit the proofs of the technical lemmata and instead, for interested readers, provide pointers to the appropriate part of full version [29].

Theorem 1. *There is no fully black-box construction (R, T_R, C, T_C, p) of a worst-case hard TFNP problem from injective one-way functions with deterministic f-oblivious many-one reduction with success probability at least $2^{-0.1n}$ such that both running times $T_R, T_C \in O(n^{polylog(n)})$.*

In the above theorem, the running time of both R and C is restricted to quasi-polynomial. Note that the standard notion of cryptographic constructions

---

Algorithm 1: The oracle SOLVE.

Hardwired : a fully black-box construction (R, T_R, C, T_C, p) of a hard TFNP problem from iOWF

Oracle access: an injective function $f = \{f_n\}_{n \in \mathbb{N}} \in \mathrm{Inj}$

Input : an instance $i \in \{0,1\}^*$

Output : a solution $s \in \{0,1\}^*$ such that $C^f(i, s) = 1$

1   Compute $Y_i = \bigcup_{n=1}^{T_C(|i|+p(|i|))} \{y \in \mathrm{Im}(f_n) \mid i \in Q_{\mathrm{SOLVE}}(R^{f,\mathrm{SOLVE}}(1^n, y))\}$

2   Compute $N_i = \{n \in \mathbb{N} \mid Y_i \cap \mathrm{Im}(f_n) \neq \emptyset\}$

3   **for** $n \in N_i$ **do**

4 | Compute $Y_{i,n} = Y_i \cap \mathrm{Im}(f_n)$

5   **end**

6   Compute $S_{i,f} = \{s \in \{0,1\}^* \mid |s| \leq p(|i|) \text{ and } C^f(i,s) = 1\}$

7   **while** *True* **do**

8 | $B_{i,f} = \{s \in S_{i,f} \mid f[Q(C^f(i,s))] \cap Y_i = \emptyset\}$

9 | **if** $B_{i,f} \neq \emptyset$ **then**

10 | | **return** lexicographically smallest $s \in B_{i,f}$

11 | **end**

12 | Choose $n \in N_i$ such that $\frac{|Y_{i,n}|}{2^n}$ is maximized.

13 | Set $N_i = N_i \setminus \{n\}$

14 | Set $Y_i = Y_i \setminus Y_{i,n}$

15   **end**

---

requires R, C to run in polynomial time in order to be considered efficient. We are ruling out a broader class of potentially less efficient reductions.

The proof of Theorem 1 uses, on a high level, a similar template as other black-box separations in the literature. That is, we design an oracle O relative to which (injective) one-way functions exist but TFNP is broken (even in the worst case). We follow the two-oracle approach [26], and, therefore, our oracle $O = (f, \mathrm{SOLVE})$ consist of:

1. $f \in \mathrm{Inj}$: a sequence of random injective functions which implements injective one-way functions; and
2. SOLVE: a reduction-specific oracle that solves TFNP instances.

That a random injective function is one-way is a well-established result (see, e.g., Claim 5.3 in [47] for the more general case of random functions). The bulk of technical work revolves around showing that f remains one-way even in the presence of SOLVE. For any fully black-box construction with a deterministic f-oblivious many-one reduction, we provide an oracle SOLVE which finds a solution for any TFNP instance (i.e., TFNP is easy in the presence of SOLVE) and argue that it does not help the reduction in inverting injective one-way functions. The description of our oracle SOLVE is given in Algorithm 1 and it is explained below.

Oracle SOLVE: Let (R, T_R, C, T_C, p) be the construction of a hard TFNP problem from injective one-way function with a deterministic f-oblivious many-one security reduction which is hardwired in the oracle SOLVE. Ideally, SOLVE should output a solution i which gives the reduction R no information about the inversion of its challenge y. Unfortunately, SOLVE is unaware of the particular challenge y on which $R^f(1^n, y)$ queried SOLVE with the instance i. Nevertheless, SOLVE can compute the set Y_i of all challenges y on which the reduction would query the instance i.[3] The challenges in Y_i become "protected" and SOLVE will attempt to provide a solution which does not reveal a preimage of any $y \in Y_i$, i.e., s such that $C^f(i, s)$ does not make an f-query on a preimage of any $y \in Y_i$.

Note that we could run into a potential technical issue when defining Y_i, as the set of *all* challenges y on which R queries the instance i might be infinite. However when the instance i is queried by the security reduction R on some very long challenge y then C contributes no indirect query to $f^{-1}(y)$ as the running time of C depends only on the length of the instance i. More formally: the running time of C is bounded by $T_C(|i| + p(|i|))$ thus C cannot query f on longer inputs. Therefore, we can consider only possible challenges y from $\text{Im}(f_n)$ for $n \le T_C(|i| + p(|i|))$.

On lines 2–6, SOLVE computes the following auxiliary sets N_i, $Y_{i,n}$, and $S_{i,f}$. The set N_i contains all the input lengths for the preimages x such that the reduction $R^{f,\text{SOLVE}}(1^n, f(x))$ queries the instance i. SOLVE then splits Y_i into subsets $Y_{i,n}$ using the input lengths of interest in N_i. Finally, SOLVE computes the set $S_{i,f}$ which is the set of *all* possible solutions for the instance i.

The strategy of SOLVE is to return a solution from the set of "benign" solutions $B_{i,f}$, which do not induce any query to preimages of the protected challenges in Y_i. If there is any such benign solution then SOLVE simply halts and returns the lexicographically smallest one. Unfortunately, it might be the case that every solution queries a preimage of some $y \in Y_i$, e.g., if the instance i is queried for all challenges y of a given preimage length n and on each solution s at least one x of length n is queried (i.e., $B_{i,f} = \emptyset$ unless we remove $Y_{i,n}$ from Y_i). Since SOLVE in general cannot output a solution while protecting the whole set Y_i, it will proceed to gradually relax the condition on the set of protected challenges.

Note that we might allow SOLVE to return a solution even though it induces queries to preimages of protected challenges, as long as the reduction queries the instance i on the corresponding image length often enough, as any fixed solution induces only a bounded number of queries to f (bounded by T_C). Therefore, if the set of challenges on which R queries i is dense enough w.r.t. some image length then, with overwhelming probability, an arbitrary solution will be benign for the random challenge y given to the reduction. Thus, we allow SOLVE to return a solution revealing preimages of challenges from the auxiliary set $Y_{i,n}$ maximizing $\frac{|Y_{i,n}|}{2^n}$. If the fraction $\frac{|Y_{i,n}|}{2^n}$ is small then SOLVE is able to find a benign solution which protects the preimages of length n (see [29, Claim 13]). Whereas, if the fraction $\frac{|Y_{i,n}|}{2^n}$ is large enough then any fixed solution will be benign w.r.t. the actual challenge of R with overwhelming probability as each

---

[3] Here we crucially rely on f-obliviousness of the reduction algorithm R which ensures that Y_i depends only on the image of f, which allows SOLVESIM to simulate SOLVE without querying f on too many inputs.

Algorithm 2: The algorithm $\textsc{Encode}_n$.

Hardwired   : a fully black-box construction (R, T_R, C, T_C, p) of a hard TFNP problem from iOWF

Common Input: an injective function $h \in \mathrm{Inj}$ shared with $\textsc{Decode}_n$

Input   : a permutation $\pi \in \mathrm{Inj}_n^n$ on $\{0,1\}^n$

Output   : an encoding $\mathcal{M}$ of π

1 $f = h \circ \pi$, i.e., $f(x) = \begin{cases} h(\pi(x)) & \text{for all } x \text{ of length } n \\ h(x) & \text{otherwise} \end{cases}$

2 $\mathrm{INV}_f = \{ y \in \mathrm{Im}(h_n) \mid R^{\textsc{Solve},f}(1^n, y) = f^{-1}(y) \}$

3 $G_f = \{ y \in \mathrm{INV}_f \mid f^{-1}(y) \notin Q_f^{\mathrm{indir}}(R^{f,\textsc{Solve}}(1^n, y)) \}$

4 $Y_f = \emptyset$ and $X_f = \emptyset$

5 **while** $G_f \neq \emptyset$ **do**

6 | Pick lexicographically smallest $y \in G_f$

7 | $G_f = G_f \setminus \big(f[Q_f(R^{f,\textsc{Solve}}(1^n, y))] \cup \{y\} \big)$

8 | $Y_f = Y_f \cup \{y\}$ and $X_f = X_f \cup \{f^{-1}(y)\}$

9 **end**

10 **if** $|X_f| < 2^{0.6n}$ **then**

11 | **return** $\mathcal{M} = (0, \pi)$

12 **end**

13 **else**

14 | **return** $\mathcal{M} = (1, |X_f|, Y_f, X_f, \sigma = f \restriction (\{0,1\}^n \setminus X_f)) \in$
    | $\{0,1\}^{1 + n + \left\lceil \log \binom{2^n}{|Y_f|} \right\rceil + \left\lceil \log \binom{2^n}{|X_f|} \right\rceil + \left\lceil \log (|\{0,1\}^n \setminus X_f|!) \right\rceil}$

15 **end**

---

solution can induce queries to only a small number of preimages of challenges from the set $Y_{i,n}$ (see [29, Claim 12]).

In order to show formally that $\textsc{Solve}$ does not help in inverting the injective one-way function, we employ an incompressibility argument similar to [21]. Specifically, we present algorithms $\textsc{Encode}_n$ (given in Algorithm 2) and $\textsc{Decode}_n$ (given in Algorithm 3) which utilize the reduction R to allow compression of a random permutation more succinctly than what is information-theoretically possible. When compressing the random permutation by $\textsc{Encode}_n$, we have access to the whole permutation and we can effectively provide the reduction with access to $\textsc{Solve}$. However, to be able to use the reduction also in the $\textsc{Decode}_n$, we have to be able to simulate access to our $\textsc{Solve}$ oracle given access only to a partially defined oracle f (as we are reconstructing f). For the description of the algorithm $\textsc{SolveSim}$, which simulates the $\textsc{Solve}$ oracle for the purpose of decoding in $\textsc{Decode}_n$, see Algorithm 4.

$\textsc{Encode}_n$ *Algorithm:* The algorithm $\textsc{Encode}_n$ (Algorithm 2) uses the reduction R to compress a random permutation π on bit strings of length n. Note that even though R succeeds in inverting an injective function, for technical reasons, we leverage its power in order to compress a permutation. One particular issue we would run into when trying to compress an injective function f which is not surjective is that the encoding would have to comprise also of the encoding of the image of f which might render the encoding inefficient.

Nevertheless, in order to use the reduction for compressing, we must provide it with oracle access to an injective function which is *not a bijection*. Thus, we equip ENCODE_n (as well as DECODE_n) with an injective function h. ENCODE_n then computes the function f as a composition of the functions $h \circ \pi$ and uses the reduction with respect to the composed oracle f. We emphasize that h is independent of π, therefore it cannot be used in order to compress π on its own.

First, ENCODE_n computes the set INV_f which is the set of all challenges y on which the reduction successfully inverts (i.e., the reduction returns $f^{-1}(y)$). Then ENCODE_n computes the set G_f, which is the set of "good" challenges y, on which the reduction successfully inverts even though SOLVE returns a solution which does not induce a query to any preimage of y. This set is used to reduce the size of the trivial encoding of f – the part of f corresponding to the challenges in G_f will be algorithmically reconstructed by DECODE_n using the security reduction R.

Specifically, ENCODE_n computes Y_f, the subset of G_f for which the preimages will be algorithmically reconstructed, as follows: ENCODE_n processes the challenges y in G_f one by one in lexicographically increasing order and stores all f-queries needed for reconstruction by R (i.e, for any x such that there was an f-query x, the element $f(x)$ is removed from the "good" set G_f as we cannot reconstruct the preimage of y using R without knowing the image of x under f).

ENCODE_n outputs an encoding $\mathcal{M}$ which describes the size of X_f, the sets Y_f and X_f (where X_f is the set of preimages corresponding to Y_f), and the partial function representing the function f on inputs of length n outside of X_f. Thus, the encoding saves bits by not revealing the bijection between X_f and Y_f which is algorithmically reconstructed instead (Lemma 4). Specifically, the size of X_f (equal to the size of Y_f) can be encoded using $\log 2^n = n$ bits. Y_f is a subset of $\text{Im}(f_n) = \text{Im}(h_n)$ and it is encoded using $\lceil \log \binom{2^n}{|Y_f|} \rceil$ bits as the index of the corresponding subset of size $|Y_f|$ (the set X_f is encoded in a similar manner). Finally, the bijection between $\{0,1\}^n \setminus X_f$ and $\text{Im}(f) \setminus Y_f$ is encoded as the index of the corresponding permutation on a set of size $|\{0,1\}^n \setminus X_f|$ using $\lceil \log (|\{0,1\}^n \setminus X_f|!) \rceil$ bits.

A small technicality arises when the set X_f, respectively the set Y_f, is not large enough, the above mentioned encoding would be inefficient as the trivial encoding outputting the whole description of the permutation π would use fewer bits. Thus, ENCODE_n simply outputs the trivial encoding when X_f is too small. The first bit of the encoding distinguishes between the two cases.

DECODE_n *Algorithm:* The encoding returned by ENCODE_n is uniquely decodable by DECODE_n given in Algorithm 3 (see [29, Section 4.2]). When the output of ENCODE_n starts with 0, the rest of the encoding is an explicit encoding of π and we are immediately done with its reconstruction. If the output starts with bit 1, the following n bits represent $|X_f| = |Y_f|$. DECODE_n then reads the following $\lceil \log \binom{2^n}{|X_f|} \rceil$ bits of the encoding to reconstruct the set Y_f (as the j-th subset of

---

Algorithm 3: The algorithm $\textsc{Decode}_n$.

Hardwired	: a fully black-box construction (R, T_R, C, T_C, p) of a hard TFNP problem from iOWF
Common Input	: an injective function $h \in \text{Inj}$ shared with $\textsc{Encode}_n$
Input	: an encoding $\mathcal{M}$
Output	: a permutation $\pi \in \text{Inj}_n^n$

1 Parse $\mathcal{M} = (b, \mathcal{M}')$, where $b \in \{0, 1\}$
2 if $b = 0$ **then**
3   Decode π from $\mathcal{M}'$
4   **return** π
5 end
6 Parse $\mathcal{M}' = (|X_f|, Y_f, X_f, \sigma)$
7 Set partial function $f' = \begin{cases} \sigma & \text{for inputs of length } n \\ h & \text{otherwise} \end{cases}$ // f' is defined only

      outside X_f
8 while $Y_f \neq \emptyset$ **do**
9   Pick lexicographically smallest $y \in Y_f$
10   Let $f''(x) = \begin{cases} y & \text{for all } x \in \text{Dom}(h) \setminus \text{Dom}(f') \\ f'(x) & \text{otherwise} \end{cases}$
11 $x = R^{f'', \textsc{SolveSim}(h, f', \cdot)}(1^n, y)$
12   Let $f'(x) = y$
13   Set $Y_f = Y_f \setminus \{y\}$
14 end
15 return $\pi = (h^{-1} \circ f') \upharpoonright \{0, 1\}^n$

2^n of size $|X_f|$). Similarly, $\textsc{Decode}_n$ reconstructs the set X_f using the following $\left\lceil \log \binom{2^n}{|X_f|} \right\rceil$ bits. The remaining bits represent σ, a restriction of f on all the n-bit inputs outside of X_f, given by the index of the corresponding bijection between $\{0, 1\}^n \setminus X_f$ and $\text{Im}(f) \setminus Y_f$. Note that such encoding of σ does preserve the structure of the restriction but it looses the information about the domain and image of σ. However, both are easy to reconstruct. The domain is simply $\{0, 1\}^n \setminus X_f$ and the image of σ can be computed from Y_f and the common input h as $\text{Im}(\sigma) = \text{Im}(f) \setminus Y_f = \text{Im}(h \circ \pi) \setminus Y_f = \text{Im}(h) \setminus Y_f$.

$\textsc{Decode}_n$ then computes the remaining preimages one by one in lexicographic order using the security reduction R, adding the reconstructed mapping into a partial function f'. Note that during the computation of the preimage of y, the reduction might make an f-query on x which has no defined output. But as $\textsc{Decode}_n$ takes $y \in Y_f$ in the same order as $\textsc{Encode}_n$ added them to the set Y_f, this happens if and only if the preimage of y is being queried. Thus, we answer any such query by y (it is crucial that this happens only for f-queries made directly by R) which is captured in the definition of the auxiliary function f'' defined by $\textsc{Decode}_n$ and used as the oracle for the security reduction R.

Once ENCODE$_n$ finds the preimages of all challenges y from Y_f, the function f' is defined everywhere. To reconstruct the permutation π on $\{0,1\}^n$, DECODE$_n$ can simply compose the inverse of h with the reconstructed function f'.

SOLVESIM *Algorithm:* For the ease of presentation we usually do not explicitly mention the oracle h as it is given by context (we run DECODE$_n$ and SOLVESIM) with respect to only one h at a time.

The computation of the algorithm SOLVESIM (Algorithm 4) is similar to the computation of SOLVE (Algorithm 1). First, SOLVESIM computes the sets Y_i. There is one big difference between SOLVE and SOLVESIM. As SOLVESIM does not have access to the whole f it uses h or the partial knowledge of f, namely the partial function f' everywhere f is used in the SOLVE algorithm.

- We use h whenever we need to determine the image of f_n for some n. As $\forall n \in \mathbb{N} \colon \mathrm{Im}(h_n) = \mathrm{Im}(f_n)$ using $\mathrm{Im}(h_n)$ instead of $\mathrm{Im}(f_n)$ makes no difference to the computation.
- The second place where h is used instead of f is when SOLVESIM computes the set Y_i. Specifically, when determining images y for which the security reduction R queries the given instance i, the algorithm SOLVESIM computes the same Y_i as if it used f by the f-obliviousness of the security reduction.
- In all other places, SOLVESIM uses the partial knowledge of f (i.e., the partial function f'). This causes a real difference in the computation. In particular, the set $S_{i,f'}$ (as computed by SOLVESIM) may differ a lot from $S_{i,f}$ (as computed by SOLVE) as some solutions from $S_{i,f}$ potentially query some unknown parts of f. Thus, the set $S_{i,f'}$ computed by SOLVESIM is just a subset of the whole $S_{i,f}$. The set $S_{i,f'}$ contains only the solutions SOLVESIM is "aware of" (f' is defined for all queries and thus SOLVESIM may verify the solution). The rest of the computation is practically the same, except that SOLVESIM is restricted just to the set of solutions $S_{i,f'}$. The main trick is that we make sure that SOLVESIM is aware of the solution which should be returned and it does not matter that it ignores other solutions of the instance.

Structure of the Proof of Theorem 1. For ease of presentation and understanding, we divide the proof into four lemmata, Lemma 1 through 4. Lemma 1 shows that given an instance i of the TFNP problem represented by the algorithm C^f, our SOLVE always returns a solution, i.e., an s such that $C^f(i,s) = 1$ (formal proof is given in [29, Section 4.1]). Thus, any distribution of instances of the TFNP problem is easy in the presence of SOLVE.

Lemma 1. *For any instance $i \in \{0,1\}^*$ and any $f \in Inj$, the algorithm* SOLVE$^f(i)$ *halts and returns a solution, i.e., it returns a string $s \in \{0,1\}^*$ such that $|s| \leq p(|i|)$ and $C^f(i,s) = 1$.*

To argue that SOLVE does not help in inverting injective functions, we analyze the joint properties of the algorithms ENCODE$_n$ and DECODE$_n$. First, we show that DECODE$_n$ always returns the correct permutation encoded by ENCODE$_n$ (see [29, Section 4.2] for the formal proof).

Algorithm 4: The algorithm SOLVESIM.

Hardwired : a fully black-box construction (R, T_R, C, T_C, p) of a hard TFNP problem from iOWF

Input : A function $h \in \text{Inj}$, partial injective function $f' \in \text{Inj}$, and an instance $i \in \{0, 1\}^*$

Output : Solution, i.e., $s \in \{0, 1\}^*$ such that $C^{f'}(i, s) = 1$

1 Compute $Y_i = \bigcup_{n=1}^{T_C(|i| + p(|i|))} \{ y \in \text{Im}(h_n) \mid i \in Q_{\text{SOLVE}}(R^{h, \text{SOLVE}}(1^n, y)) \}$

2 Compute $N_i = \{ n \in \mathbb{N} \mid Y_i \cap \text{Im}(h_n) \neq \emptyset \}$

3 **for** $n \in N_i$ **do**

4 $\quad$ Compute $Y_{i,n} = Y_i \cap \text{Im}(h_n)$

5 **end**

6 Compute

$$S_{i,f'} = \left\{ s \in \{0, 1\}^* \;\middle|\; |s| \le p(|i|) \text{ and } Q(C^{f'}(i, s)) \subseteq \text{Dom}(f') \text{ and } C^{f'}(i, s) = 1 \right\}$$

7 **while** *True* **do**

8 $\quad$ $B_{i,f'} = \{ s \in S_{i,f'} \mid f[Q(C^{f'}(i, s))] \cap Y_i = \emptyset \}$ // "benign" solutions

9 $\quad$ **if** $B_{i,f'} \neq \emptyset$ **then**

10 $\quad\quad$ **return** lexicographically smallest $s \in B_{i,f'}$

11 $\quad$ **end**

12 $\quad$ Choose $n \in N_i$ such that $\frac{|Y_{i,n}|}{2^n}$ is maximized.

13 $\quad$ Set $N_i = N_i \setminus \{n\}$

14 $\quad$ Set $Y_i = Y_i \setminus Y_{i,n}$

15 **end**

Lemma 2. *For all* $n \in \mathbb{N}$, $\pi \in \text{Inj}_n^n$, *and* $h \in \text{Inj}$,

$$\text{DECODE}_n^h(\text{ENCODE}_n^h(\pi)) = \pi,$$

where ENCODE_n, *respectively* DECODE_n, *is given in Algorithm 2, respectively Algorithm 3.*

We crutialy rely on f-obliviousness of the reduction for the proof of Lemma 2. It is the property which allows us to simulate the algorithm SOLVE during the decoding phase, as SOLVESIM needs to be able to compute the same set Y_i as SOLVE does. Moreover, SOLVESIM cannot query f on all preimages as SOLVE does when computing Y_i. Due to f-obliviousness of the reduction, we may substitute f by h in the computation of Y_i in SOLVESIM as the resulting set depends only on the image of the function given to R as an oracle (and $\text{Im}(f) = \text{Im}(h)$).

Second, we show that the encoding output by ENCODE_n is prefix-free (see [29, Section 4.3]).

Lemma 3. *Let* $h \in \text{Inj}$ *be any injective function and* $n \in \mathbb{N}$, *then the encoding given by the algorithm* ENCODE_n *(Algorithm 2) is prefix-free, i.e.,*

$$\forall \pi, \pi' \in \text{Inj}_n^n \text{ such that } \pi \neq \pi': \text{ENCODE}_n^h(\pi) \text{ is not a prefix of } \text{ENCODE}_n^h(\pi').$$

Finally, we bound the expected size of the encoding given by ENCODE_n (see [29, Section 4.4]) which contradicts the information-theoretic bound implied by Corollary 1.

Lemma 4. *Let (R, T_R, C, T_C, p) be a fully black-box construction of a hard TFNP problem from an injective one-way function. Assume $n \in \mathbb{N}$ is large enough so that $n \geq 50$ and $2q(n) + 1 \leq 2^{0.2n}$, where $q(n)$ is the maximal number of f-queries made by C on the queried instance Let the success probability of R be $\beta \geq 2^{-0.1n}$, i.e., for any f we have*

$$\Pr_{x \leftarrow \{0,1\}^n} [R^{f,\text{SOLVE}}(1^n, f(x)) = x] = \beta \geq 2^{-0.1n}.$$

Then

$$\exists h \in Inj \colon \mathbb{E}_{\pi \leftarrow Inj_n^n, h \leftarrow Inj}[|\text{ENCODE}_n^h(\pi)|] \leq \log 2^n! - \frac{8}{10} n 2^{0.1n}.$$

We claim (see [29, Claim 10]) that the upper bound $2q(n) + 1 \leq 2^{0.2n}$ used in the statement of the lemma is without loss of generality for large enough n and for all quasi-polynomial (and, hence, also for efficient) algorithms R, C. We use this fact again in the proof of the main theorem (Theorem 1), and refer the readers to [29, Section 4.4] for the precise statement and its proof.

Equipped with the above lemmata, we next prove Theorem 1.

Proof. (of Theorem 1). Suppose to the contrary that there is such a reduction (R, T_R, C, T_C, p). By Lemma 1, the algorithm SOLVE (Algorithm 1) returns a valid solution with probability one. Thus, the reduction R must invert f with high probability when given access to any oracle $f \in Inj$ and our oracle SOLVE, i.e.,

$$\Pr_{x \leftarrow \{0,1\}^n} [R^{f,\text{SOLVE}}(1^n, f(x)) = x] \geq \frac{1}{p'(n)}$$

for some polynomial p' and infinitely many $n \in \mathbb{N}$.

Let $n \in \mathbb{N}$ be large enough such that

1. $2q(n) + 1 \leq 2^{0.2n}$,
2. $\Pr_{x \leftarrow \{0,1\}^n} [R^{f,\text{SOLVE}}(1^n, f(x)) \in f^{-1}(f(x))] \geq \frac{1}{p'(n)}$,

where $q(n)$ is the maximal number of f-queries made by C on the queried instance As already pointed out, the quasi-polynomial bounds on running times $T_C, T_R \in O(n^{\text{polylog}(n)})$ imply that $q(n) \in o(2^{0.2n})$ (see [29, Claim 10]). Thus, for large enough n, the upper bound $2q(n) + 1 \leq 2^{0.2n}$ holds without loss of generality.

For any $h \in Inj$, we can use the algorithm ENCODE_n^h (Algorithm 2) to encode a given permutation $\pi \in Inj_n^n$. Decodability of the encoding follows from Lemma 2. Moreover, by Lemma 3, the encoding is a prefix-free code. By Lemma 4, there is a function $h \in Inj$ such that the pair of algorithms ENCODE_n^h and DECODE_n^h defines an encoding of $\pi \leftarrow Inj_n^n$ with expected length at most $\log(2^n!) - \frac{8}{10} n 2^{0.1n}$. This contradicts the information-theoretic bound on the expected length of any prefix-free encoding of a random permutation on $\{0,1\}^n$ given by Corollary 1. $\qquad\qquad\square$

3.3   Extensions

In this section, we state some extensions to the result in the previous section. We refrain from providing the details and refer the readers to [29, Section 5].

First, it is possible to extend our proof from Sect. 3.2 to rule out even *non-adaptive* security reductions which submit multiple queries to the oracle SOLVE in parallel, though still f-obliviously, as defined in Definition 3. The description of the algorithms SOLVE, ENCODE$_n$, DECODE$_n$, and SOLVESIM remain unchanged, but we require a slightly different analysis tailored for non-adaptive reductions. We refer the readers to [29, Section 5.2] for the details.

Second, we can extend our results to randomised reductions with additional changes to our algorithm SOLVE. One could imagine that the construction has some instance i created for a concrete challenge y, on which R queries i with high probability. But R might also query the instance i for many other challenges y' (on each of them with small probability) to hide the real challenge y. Thus we need to take the probability of querying the instance i into account. Roughly speaking, the SOLVE for randomised reductions is an extension of the SOLVE given in Algorithm 1 taking this probability into account. SOLVESIM is designed accordingly and thanks to f-obliviousness we are still able to show that the simulation is faithful. The rest of the changes involve modifying the existing argument taking into account the changes to SOLVE and SOLVESIM. We refer the readers to [29, Section 5.3] for the details.

4   Conclusions

In this work, we have shown that there are intrinsic barriers preventing *simple* fully black-box constructions of hard TFNP problems from injective one-way functions. The main technical contribution of our work is the technique of designing a "TFNP-breaker" oracle SOLVE which depends on the reduction.

The natural direction towards extending our results would be attempting to lift the restriction to f-oblivious and non-adaptive reductions. One reason for why this might be challenging is that a black-box separation of TFNP and injective one-way functions would subsume the separation of collision-resistant hash functions and one-way functions [49], for which, despite the recent progress, there are only non-trivial proofs [4,25,40].

Acknowledgments. We wish to thank the anonymous reviewers for their comments which helped us to clarify the presentations of our results.

References

1. Abbot, T., Kane, D., Valiant, P.: On algorithms for Nash equilibria. Unpublished manuscript (2004). http://web.mit.edu/tabbott/Public/final.pdf
2. Baecher, P.: Simon's circuit. IACR Cryptol. ePrint Arch. **2014**, 476 (2014)
3. Beame, P., Cook, S.A., Edmonds, J., Impagliazzo, R., Pitassi, T.: The relative complexity of NP search problems. J. Comput. Syst. Sci. **57**(1), 3–19 (1998)

4. Bitansky, N., Degwekar, A.: On the Complexity of Collision Resistant Hash Functions: New and Old Black-Box Separations. In: Hofheinz, D., Rosen, A. (eds.) TCC 2019. LNCS, vol. 11891, pp. 422–450. Springer, Cham (2019). https://doi.org/10.1007/978-3-030-36030-6_17

5. Bitansky, N., Degwekar, A., Vaikuntanathan, V.: Structure vs. Hardness Through the Obfuscation Lens. In: Katz, J., Shacham, H. (eds.) CRYPTO 2017. LNCS, vol. 10401, pp. 696–723. Springer, Cham (2017). https://doi.org/10.1007/978-3-319-63688-7_23

6. Bitansky, N., Gerichter, I.: On the cryptographic hardness of local search. In: 11th Innovations in Theoretical Computer Science Conference, ITCS 2020, January 12–14, 2020, Seattle, Washington, USA, pp. 6:1–6:29 (2020)

7. Bitansky, N., Paneth, O., Rosen, A.: On the cryptographic hardness of finding a Nash equilibrium. In: IEEE 56th Annual Symposium on Foundations of Computer Science, FOCS 2015, Berkeley, CA, USA, 17–20 October, 2015, pp. 1480–1498 (2015)

8. Brakerski, Z., Katz, J., Segev, G., Yerukhimovich, A.: Limits on the Power of Zero-Knowledge Proofs in Cryptographic Constructions. In: Ishai, Y. (ed.) TCC 2011. LNCS, vol. 6597, pp. 559–578. Springer, Heidelberg (2011). https://doi.org/10.1007/978-3-642-19571-6_34

9. Buresh-Oppenheim, J.: On the TFNP complexity of factoring (2006). http://www.cs.toronto.edu/~bureshop/factor.pdf (unpublished)

10. Chen, X., Deng, X., Teng, S.: Settling the complexity of computing two-player Nash equilibria. J. ACM 56(3) (2009)

11. Choudhuri, A.R., Hubáček, P., Kamath, C., Pietrzak, K., Rosen, A., Rothblum, G.N.: Finding a Nash equilibrium is no easier than breaking Fiat-Shamir. In: Proceedings of the 51st Annual ACM SIGACT Symposium on Theory of Computing, STOC 2019, Phoenix, AZ, USA, June 23–26, 2019. pp. 1103–1114. ACM (2019)

12. Choudhuri, A.R., Hubáček, P., Kamath, C., Pietrzak, K., Rosen, A., Rothblum, G.N.: PPAD-hardness via iterated squaring modulo a composite. IACR Cryptol. ePrint Arch. 2019, 667 (2019)

13. Cover, T.M., Thomas, J.A.: Elements of Information Theory. John Wiley & Sons, New Jersey (2012)

14. Daskalakis, C., Goldberg, P.W., Papadimitriou, C.H.: The complexity of computing a Nash equilibrium. SIAM J. Comput. 39(1), 195–259 (2009)

15. Daskalakis, C., Papadimitriou, C.H.: Continuous local search. In: Proceedings of the Twenty-Second Annual ACM-SIAM Symposium on Discrete Algorithms, SODA 2011, San Francisco, California, USA, January 23–25, 2011, pp. 790–804 (2011)

16. Ephraim, N., Freitag, C., Komargodski, I., Pass, R.: Continuous Verifiable Delay Functions. In: Canteaut, A., Ishai, Y. (eds.) EUROCRYPT 2020. LNCS, vol. 12107, pp. 125–154. Springer, Cham (2020). https://doi.org/10.1007/978-3-030-45727-3_5

17. Filos-Ratsikas, A., Goldberg, P.W.: Consensus halving is PPA-complete. In: Proceedings of the 50th Annual ACM SIGACT Symposium on Theory of Computing, STOC 2018, Los Angeles, CA, USA, June 25–29, 2018, pp. 51–64 (2018)

18. Filos-Ratsikas, A., Goldberg, P.W.: The complexity of splitting necklaces and bisecting ham sandwiches. In: Proceedings of the 51st Annual ACM SIGACT Symposium on Theory of Computing, STOC 2019, Phoenix, AZ, USA, June 23–26, 2019, pp. 638–649 (2019)

19. Fischlin, M.: Black-Box Reductions and Separations in Cryptography. In: Mitrokotsa, A., Vaudenay, S. (eds.) AFRICACRYPT 2012. LNCS, vol. 7374, pp. 413–422. Springer, Heidelberg (2012). https://doi.org/10.1007/978-3-642-31410-0_26

20. Garg, S., Pandey, O., Srinivasan, A.: Revisiting the Cryptographic Hardness of Finding a Nash Equilibrium. In: Robshaw, M., Katz, J. (eds.) CRYPTO 2016. LNCS, vol. 9815, pp. 579–604. Springer, Heidelberg (2016). https://doi.org/10.1007/978-3-662-53008-5_20

21. Gennaro, R., Trevisan, L.: Lower bounds on the efficiency of generic cryptographic constructions. In: FOCS. pp. 305–313. IEEE Computer Society (2000)

22. Gertner, Y., Malkin, T., Reingold, O.: On the impossibility of basing trapdoor functions on trapdoor predicates. In: 42nd Annual Symposium on Foundations of Computer Science, FOCS 2001, 14–17 October 2001, Las Vegas, Nevada, USA, pp. 126–135. IEEE Computer Society (2001)

23. Goldberg, P.W., Hollender, A.: The hairy ball problem is PPAD-complete. In: 46th International Colloquium on Automata, Languages, and Programming, ICALP 2019, July 9–12, 2019, Patras, Greece, pp. 65:1–65:14 (2019)

24. Goldreich, O., Levin, L.A.: A hard-core predicate for all one-way functions. In: Proceedings of the 21st Annual ACM Symposium on Theory of Computing, May 14–17, 1989, Seattle, Washigton, USA, pp. 25–32 (1989)

25. Haitner, I., Hoch, J.J., Reingold, O., Segev, G.: Finding collisions in interactive protocols - tight lower bounds on the round and communication complexities of statistically hiding commitments. SIAM J. Comput. **44**(1), 193–242 (2015)

26. Hsiao, C.-Y., Reyzin, L.: Finding Collisions on a Public Road, or Do Secure Hash Functions Need Secret Coins? In: Franklin, M. (ed.) CRYPTO 2004. LNCS, vol. 3152, pp. 92–105. Springer, Heidelberg (2004). https://doi.org/10.1007/978-3-540-28628-8_6

27. Hubáček, P., Naor, M., Yogev, E.: The journey from NP to TFNP hardness. In: 8th Innovations in Theoretical Computer Science Conference, ITCS 2017, January 9–11, 2017, Berkeley, CA, USA, pp. 60:1–60:21 (2017)

28. Hubáček, P., Yogev, E.: Hardness of continuous local search: Query complexity and cryptographic lower bounds. In: Proceedings of the Twenty-Eighth Annual ACM-SIAM Symposium on Discrete Algorithms, SODA 2017, Barcelona, Spain, Hotel Porta Fira, January 16–19, pp. 1352–1371 (2017)

29. Hubáček, P., Kamath, C., Král, K., Slívová, V.: On average-case hardness in TFNP from one-way functions. IACR Cryptol. ePrint Arch. **2020**, 1162 (2020)

30. Impagliazzo, R., Rudich, S.: Limits on the provable consequences of one-way permutations. In: Proceedings of the 21st Annual ACM Symposium on Theory of Computing, May 14–17, 1989, Seattle, Washigton, USA, pp. 44–61. ACM (1989)

31. Jawale, R., Kalai, Y.T., Khurana, D., Zhang, R.: SNARGs for bounded depth computations and PPAD hardness from sub-exponential LWE. IACR Cryptol. ePrint Arch. **2020**, 980 (2020)

32. Jawale, R., Khurana, D.: Lossy correlation intractability and PPAD hardness from sub-exponential LWE. IACR Cryptol. ePrint Arch. **2020**, 911 (2020)

33. Jeřábek, E.: Integer factoring and modular square roots. J. Comput. Syst. Sci. **82**(2), 380–394 (2016)

34. Johnson, D.S., Papadimitriou, C.H., Yannakakis, M.: How easy is local search? J. Comput. Syst. Sci. **37**(1), 79–100 (1988)

35. Kalai, Y.T., Paneth, O., Yang, L.: Delegation with Updatable Unambiguous Proofs and PPAD-Hardness. In: Micciancio, D., Ristenpart, T. (eds.) CRYPTO 2020. LNCS, vol. 12172, pp. 652–673. Springer, Cham (2020). https://doi.org/10.1007/978-3-030-56877-1_23

36. Kalai, Y.T., Zhang, R.: SNARGs for bounded depth computations from sub-exponential LWE. IACR Cryptol. ePrint Arch. **2020**, 860 (2020)

37. Kintali, S., Poplawski, L.J., Rajaraman, R., Sundaram, R., Teng, S.: Reducibility among fractional stability problems. SIAM J. Comput. **42**(6), 2063–2113 (2013)

38. Komargodski, I., Segev, G.: From Minicrypt to Obfustopia via Private-Key Functional Encryption. In: Coron, J.-S., Nielsen, J.B. (eds.) EUROCRYPT 2017. LNCS, vol. 10210, pp. 122–151. Springer, Cham (2017). https://doi.org/10.1007/978-3-319-56620-7_5

39. Lombardi, A., Vaikuntanathan, V.: Fiat-Shamir for Repeated Squaring with Applications to PPAD-Hardness and VDFs. In: Micciancio, D., Ristenpart, T. (eds.) CRYPTO 2020. LNCS, vol. 12172, pp. 632–651. Springer, Cham (2020). https://doi.org/10.1007/978-3-030-56877-1_22

40. Matsuda, T., Matsuura, K.: On Black-Box Separations among Injective One-Way Functions. In: Ishai, Y. (ed.) TCC 2011. LNCS, vol. 6597, pp. 597–614. Springer, Heidelberg (2011). https://doi.org/10.1007/978-3-642-19571-6_36

41. Megiddo, N., Papadimitriou, C.H.: On total functions, existence theorems and computational complexity. Theor. Comput. Sci. **81**(2), 317–324 (1991)

42. Papadimitriou, C.H.: On the complexity of the parity argument and other inefficient proofs of existence. J. Comput. Syst. Sci. **48**(3), 498–532 (1994)

43. Pass, R., Venkitasubramaniam, M.: Private Coins versus Public Coins in Zero-Knowledge Proof Systems. In: Micciancio, D. (ed.) TCC 2010. LNCS, vol. 5978, pp. 588–605. Springer, Heidelberg (2010). https://doi.org/10.1007/978-3-642-11799-2_35

44. Pass, R., Venkitasubramaniam, M.: A round-collapse theorem for computationally-sound protocols; or, TFNP is hard (on average) in Pessiland (2019). CoRR abs/1906.10837

45. Reingold, O., Trevisan, L., Vadhan, S.: Notions of Reducibility between Cryptographic Primitives. In: Naor, M. (ed.) TCC 2004. LNCS, vol. 2951, pp. 1–20. Springer, Heidelberg (2004). https://doi.org/10.1007/978-3-540-24638-1_1

46. Rosen, A., Segev, G.: Chosen-ciphertext security via correlated products. SIAM J. Comput. **39**(7), 3058–3088 (2010)

47. Rosen, A., Segev, G., Shahaf, I.: Can PPAD Hardness be Based on Standard Cryptographic Assumptions? In: Kalai, Y., Reyzin, L. (eds.) TCC 2017. LNCS, vol. 10678, pp. 747–776. Springer, Cham (2017). https://doi.org/10.1007/978-3-319-70503-3_25

48. Rudich, S.: Limits on the Provable Consequences of One-way Functions. Ph.D. thesis, EECS Department, University of California, Berkeley, Dec 1988. http://www2.eecs.berkeley.edu/Pubs/TechRpts/1988/6060.html

49. Simon, D.R.: Finding collisions on a one-way street: Can secure hash functions be based on general assumptions? In: Nyberg, K. (ed.) EUROCRYPT 1998. LNCS, vol. 1403, pp. 334–345. Springer, Heidelberg (1998). https://doi.org/10.1007/BFb0054137

50. Wee, H.: Lower Bounds for Non-interactive Zero-Knowledge. In: Vadhan, S.P. (ed.) TCC 2007. LNCS, vol. 4392, pp. 103–117. Springer, Heidelberg (2007). https://doi.org/10.1007/978-3-540-70936-7_6

On Pseudorandom Encodings

Thomas Agrikola[1]($\boxtimes$), Geoffroy Couteau[2], Yuval Ishai[3], Stanisław Jarecki[4], and Amit Sahai[5]

[1] Karlsruhe Institute of Technology, Karlsruhe, Germany
thomas.agrikola@kit.edu
[2] IRIF, Paris-Diderot University, CNRS, Paris, France
couteau@irif.fr
[3] Technion, Haifa, Israel
yuvali@cs.technion.ac.il
[4] UC Irvine, Irvine, USA
stasio@ics.uci.edu
[5] UCLA, Los Angeles, USA
sahai@cs.ucla.edu

Abstract. We initiate a study of *pseudorandom encodings*: efficiently computable and decodable encoding functions that map messages from a given distribution to a random-looking distribution. For instance, every distribution that can be perfectly and efficiently compressed admits such a pseudorandom encoding. Pseudorandom encodings are motivated by a variety of cryptographic applications, including password-authenticated key exchange, "honey encryption" and steganography.

The main question we ask is whether *every* efficiently samplable distribution admits a pseudorandom encoding. Under different cryptographic assumptions, we obtain positive and negative answers for different flavors of pseudorandom encodings, and relate this question to problems in other areas of cryptography. In particular, by establishing a two-way

T. Agrikola—Supported by ERC Project PREP-CRYPTO 724307 and by the German Federal Ministry of Education and Research within the framework of the project KASTEL_SKI in the Competence Center for Applied Security Technology (KASTEL).
G. Couteau—Supported by ERC Projects PREP-CRYPTO 724307 and CryptoCloud 339563. Work done in part while visiting UCLA and the Technion.
Y. Ishai—Supported by ERC Project NTSC (742754), NSF-BSF grant 2015782, BSF grant 2018393, ISF grant 2774/20, and a grant from the Ministry of Science and Technology, Israel and Department of Science and Technology, Government of India. Work done in part while visiting UCLA.
S. Jarecki—Supported by the NSF SaTC award 1817143.
A. Sahai—Supported in part by DARPA SAFEWARE and SIEVE awards, NTT Research, NSF Frontier Award 1413955, and NSF grant 1619348, BSF grant 2012378, a Xerox Faculty Research Award, a Google Faculty Research Award, an equipment grant from Intel, and an Okawa Foundation Research Grant. This material is based upon work supported by the Defense Advanced Research Projects Agency through the ARL under Contract W911NF-15-C-0205. The views expressed are those of the authors and do not reflect the official policy or position of the Department of Defense, the National Science Foundation, NTT Research, or the U.S. Government.

R. Pass and K. Pietrzak (Eds.): TCC 2020, LNCS 12552, pp. 639–669, 2020.
https://doi.org/10.1007/978-3-030-64381-2_23

relation between pseudorandom encoding schemes and efficient invertible sampling algorithms, we reveal a connection between adaptively secure multiparty computation for randomized functionalities and questions in the domain of steganography.

1   Introduction

The problem of *compression* has been extensively studied in the field of information theory and, more recently, in computational complexity and cryptography [23, 27, 40, 42]. Informally, given a distribution X, compression aims to efficiently encode samples from X as short strings while at the same time being able to efficiently recover these samples. While the typical information-theoretic study of compression considers the case of compressing multiple independent samples from the same source X, its study in computer science, and in particular in this work, considers the "single-shot" case. Compression in this setting is closely related to *randomness condensers* [18, 34, 38, 39] and *resource-bounded Kolmogorov complexity* [32, 33] – two well-studied problems in computational complexity. Randomness condensers, which relax randomness extractors, are functions that efficiently map an input distribution into an output distribution with a higher entropy rate. A randomness condenser can be viewed as an efficient compression algorithm, without a corresponding efficient decompression algorithm. The resource-bounded Kolmogorov complexity of a string is the smallest description length of an efficient program that outputs this string. This program description can be viewed as a compressed string, such that decoding is efficiently possible, while finding the compressed string may be inefficient.

An important property of efficient compression algorithms, which combines the efficiency features of randomness condensers and resource-bounded Kolmogorov complexity, is their ability to efficiently produce "random-looking" outputs while allowing the original input to be efficiently recovered. Despite the large body of work on compression and its computational variants, this fundamental property has, to our knowledge, never been the subject of a dedicated study. In this work, we fill this gap by initiating such a study. Before formalizing the problem, we give a simple motivating example.

Consider the goal of encrypting a sample x from a distribution X (say, a random 5-letter English word from the Merriam-Webster Dictionary) using a low-entropy secret key k. Applying a standard symmetric-key encryption scheme with a key derived from k gives rise to the following brute-force attack: Try to decrypt with different keys until obtaining x' in the support of X. In the typical case that wrong keys always lead to x' outside the support of X, this attack successfully recovers x. Variants of this attack arise in different scenarios, including password-authenticated key exchange [4], honey encryption [30], subliminal communication and steganography [26], and more. A natural solution is to use perfect compression: if x can be compressed to a *uniformly random* string $\hat{x} \in \{0,1\}^n$ before being encrypted, it cannot be distinguished from another random string $\hat{x}' \in \{0,1\}^n$ obtained by trying the wrong key. Note, however, that compression may be an overkill for this application. Instead, it suffices to efficiently encode x into a (possibly longer) *pseudorandom* string from which x can be efficiently decoded. This more general solution motivates the question we consider in this work.

Encoding into the Uniform Distribution. We initiate the study of encoding distributions into a random-looking distribution. Informally, we say that a distribution ensemble X_λ admits a *pseudorandom encoding* if there exist efficient encoding and decoding algorithms $(\mathsf{E}_X, \mathsf{D}_X)$, where D_X is deterministic, such that

$$\Pr\left[y \leftarrow X_\lambda : \mathsf{D}_X(\mathsf{E}_X(y)) = y\right] \text{ is overwhelming and} \qquad (1)$$

$$\left\{y \leftarrow X_\lambda : \mathsf{E}_X(y)\right\} \approx U_{n(\lambda)}. \qquad (2)$$

Here, "$\approx$" denotes some notion of indistinguishability (we will consider both computational and statistical indistinguishability), and the probability is over the randomness of both E_X and X_λ. The polynomial $n(\lambda)$ denotes the output length of the encoding algorithm E_X. We refer to Eq. (1) as *correctness* and to Eq. (2) as *pseudorandomness*. It will also be useful to consider distribution ensembles parameterized by an input m from a language L. We say that such a distribution ensemble $(X_m)_{m \in L}$ admits a pseudorandom encoding if there exist efficient algorithms $(\mathsf{E}_X, \mathsf{D}_X)$ as above satisfying correctness and pseudorandomness for all $m \in L$, where E_X and D_X both additionally receive m as input. Note that we insist on the decoding algorithm being efficient. This is required for our motivating applications.[1] Note also that encoding and decoding above are *keyless*; that is, we want encoded samples to be close to uniform *even though anyone can decode them*. This is a crucial distinction from, for instance, encryption schemes with pseudorandom ciphertexts, which look uniformly distributed to everyone except the owner of the decryption key, and cannot be efficiently decrypted except by the owner of the decryption key. Here, we seek to simultaneously achieve pseudorandomness and correctness for all parties.

Our motivation for studying pseudorandom encodings stems from the fact that this very natural problem appears in a wide variety of – sometimes seemingly unrelated – problems in cryptography. We already mentioned steganography, honey encryption, and password-authenticated key exchange; we will cover more such connections in this work. Yet, this notion of encoding has to our knowledge never been studied systematically. In this work we study several natural flavors of this notion, obtain positive and negative results about realizing them, and map their connections with other problems in cryptography.

The main focus of this work is on the hypothesis that *all* efficiently samplable distributions admit a pseudorandom encoding. Henceforth, we refer to this hypothesis the *pseudorandom encoding hypothesis* (PREH).

For describing our results, it will be convenient to use the following general notion of efficiently samplable distributions. A distribution family ensemble

---

[1] Without this requirement, the problem can be solved using non-interactive commitment schemes with the additional property that commitments are pseudorandom (which exist under standard cryptographic assumptions).

$(X_m)_{m \in L}$ (for some language $L \subseteq \{0,1\}^*$) is efficiently samplable if there exists a probabilistic polynomial time (PPT) algorithm S such that $S(m)$ is distributed according to X_m for every $m \in L$. In case the distribution does not depend on additional inputs, L can be considered equal to $\mathbb{N}$.

Overview of Contributions. Following is a brief summary of our main contributions. We will give an expanded overview of the contributions and the underlying techniques in the rest of this section.

- We provide a unified study of different flavors of pseudorandom encodings (PRE) and identify computational, randomized PRE in the CRS model as a useful and achievable notion.
- We establish a two-way relation between PRE and the previously studied notion of invertible sampling This reveals unexpected connections between seemingly unrelated problems in cryptography (e.g., between adaptively secure computation for general functionalities and "honey encryption").
- We bootstrap "adaptive PRE" from "static PRE" As a consequence, one can base succinct adaptively secure computation on standard iO as opposed to subexponential iO [15].
- We use PRE to obtain a compiler from standard secure multiparty computation (MPC) protocols to *covert* MPC protocols.

1.1 Flavors of Pseudorandom Encoding

The notion of pseudorandom encoding has several natural flavors, depending on whether the encoding algorithm is allowed to use randomness or not, and whether the pseudorandomness property satisfies a computational or information-theoretic notion of indistinguishability. We denote the corresponding hypotheses that every efficiently samplable distribution can be pseudorandomly encoded according to the above variants as $\mathsf{PREH}^{\mathsf{rand}}_{\approx_c}$, $\mathsf{PREH}^{\mathsf{rand}}_{\equiv_s}$, $\mathsf{PREH}^{\mathsf{det}}_{\approx_c}$ and $\mathsf{PREH}^{\mathsf{det}}_{\equiv_s}$.[2]

Further, we explore relaxations which rely on a trusted setup assumption: we consider the pseudorandom encoding hypothesis in the *common reference string model*, in which a common string sampled in a trusted way from some distribution is made available to the parties. This is the most common setup assumption in cryptography and it is standard to consider the feasibility of cryptographic primitives in this model to overcome limitations in the plain model. That is, we ask whether for every efficiently samplable distribution X, there exists an

---

[2] We note that not all efficiently samplable distributions can be pseudorandomly encoded with a deterministic encoding algorithm. For instance, a distribution which has one very likely event and many less likely ones requires one specific encoding to appear with high probability. Thus, we formally restrict the deterministic variants of the pseudorandom encoding hypothesis to only hold for "compatible" samplers, which still results in interesting connections. In this overview, however, we ignore this restriction.

efficiently samplable CRS distribution and efficient encoding and decoding algorithms (E_X, D_X) as above, such that correctness and pseudorandomness hold, where the encoding and decoding algorithm as well as the distinguisher receive the CRS as input, and the distributions in Eqs. (1) and (2) are additionally over the choice of the CRS.

Considering distributions which may depend on an input $m \in L$ further entails two different flavors. On the one hand, we consider the notion where inputs m are chosen adversarially but *statically* (that is, independent of the CRS) and, on the other hand, we consider the stronger notion where inputs m are chosen adversarially and *adaptively* depending on the CRS. We henceforth denote these variants by the prefix "c" and "ac", respectively.

Static-to-Adaptive Transformation. The adaptive notion, where inputs may be chosen depending on the CRS, is clearly stronger than the static notion. However, surprisingly, the very nature of pseudorandom encodings allows one to apply an indirection argument similar to the one used in [11, 12, 25], which yields a static-to-adaptive transformation.

Theorem (informal). *If all efficiently samplable distributions can be pseudorandomly encoded in the CRS model with a* static *choice of inputs, then all efficiently samplable distributions can be pseudorandomly encoded in the CRS model with an* adaptive *choice of inputs.*

Static-to-adaptive transformations in cryptography are generally non-trivial, and often come at a big cost in security when they rely on a "complexity leveraging" technique. This connection and its application we will discuss below are a good demonstration of the usefulness of the notion of pseudorandom encodings.

Relaxing Compression. The notion of statistical deterministic pseudorandom encodings recovers the notion of optimal compression. Hence, this conflicts with the existence of one-way functions.[3] In our systematic study of pseudorandom encodings, we gradually relax perfect compression in several dimensions, while maintaining one crucial property – the indistinguishability of the encoded distribution from true randomness.

Example. To illustrate the importance of this property, we elaborate on the example we outline at the beginning of the introduction, focusing more specifically on password-authenticated key exchange (PAKE). A PAKE protocol allows two parties holding a (low entropy) common password to jointly and confidentially generate a (high entropy) secret key, such that the protocol is resilient against offline dictionary attacks, and no adversary can establish a shared key with a party if he does not know the matching password. A widely used PAKE protocol due to Bellovin and Merritt [4] has a very simple structure: the parties use their low-entropy password to encrypt the flows of a key-exchange protocol

---

[3] If perfect compression exists, pseudorandom generators cannot exist (observation attributed to Levin in [23]).

using a block cipher. When the block cipher is modeled as a random cipher, it has the property that decrypting a ciphertext (of an arbitrary plaintext) under an incorrect secret key yields a fresh random plaintext. Thus, Bellovin and Merritt point out that the security of their PAKE protocol requires that "the message to be encrypted by the password must be indistinguishable from a random number." This is easy to achieve for Diffie-Hellman key exchange over the multiplicative group of integers modulo a prime p. However, for elliptic curve groups this is no longer the case, and one needs to resort to alternative techniques including nontrivial *point compression* algorithms that compress the representation of a random group element into a nearly uniform bitstring [6].

Clearly, our relaxation of compression does not preserve the useful property of obtaining outputs that are *shorter* than the inputs. However, the remaining pseudorandomness property is good enough for many applications.

In the following, we elaborate on our weakest notion of pseudorandom encodings, that is, pseudorandom encodings allowing the encoding algorithm to be randomized and providing a computational pseudorandomness guarantee. We defer the discussion on the stronger statistical or deterministic variants to Sect. 1.3, where we derive negative results for most of these stronger notions, which leaves computational randomized pseudorandom encodings as the "best possible" notion that can be realized for general distributions.

Randomized, Computational Pseudorandom Encodings. Computational randomized pseudorandom encodings allow the encoding algorithm to be randomized and require only computational pseudorandomness.

Relation to Invertible Sampling. We show a simple but unexpected connection with the notion of *invertible sampling* [9,17,22]. Informally, invertible sampling refers to the task of finding, given samples from a distribution, random coins that *explain* the sample. Invertible sampling allows to *obliviously* sample from distributions, that is, sampling from distributions *without knowing the corresponding secrets*. This can be useful for, e.g., sampling common reference strings without knowing the random coins or public keys without knowing the corresponding secret keys. A natural relaxation of this notion was systematically studied by Ishai, Kumarasubramanian, Orlandi and Sahai [29]. Concretely, a PPT sampler S is *inverse samplable* if there exists an alternative PPT sampler $\overline{S}$ and a PPT inverse sampler $\overline{S}^{-1}$ such that

$$\{y \leftarrow S(1^\lambda) : y\} \approx_c \{y \leftarrow \overline{S}(1^\lambda) : y\},$$
$$\{y \leftarrow \overline{S}(1^\lambda; r) : (r, y)\} \approx_c \{y \leftarrow \overline{S}(1^\lambda) : (\overline{S}^{-1}(1^\lambda, y), y)\}.$$

Note that the inverse sampling algorithm is only required to efficiently inverse-sample from another distribution $\overline{S}$, but this distribution must be computationally close to the distribution induced by S. The main question studied in [29] is whether *every* efficient sampler admits such an invertible sampler. They refer to this hypothesis as the *invertible sampling hypothesis* (ISH), and show that

ISH is equivalent to adaptive MPC for general randomized functionalities that may hide their internal randomness. In this work, we show the following two-way relation with pseudorandom encoding.

Theorem (informal). *A distribution admits a pseudorandom encoding if and only if it admits invertible sampling.*

Intuitively, the efficient encoding algorithm corresponds to the inverse sampling algorithm, and decoding an encoded string corresponds to sampling with the de-randomized alternative sampler $\overline{S}$. This equivalence immediately extends to all variants of pseudorandom encodings and corresponding variants of invertible sampling we introduce in this work. Invertible sampling is itself connected to other useful cryptographic notions, such as oblivious sampling, trusted common reference string generations, and adaptively secure computation (which we will elaborate upon below).

Building on this connection, the impossibility result of [29] translates to our setting. On a high level, extractable one-way functions (EOWFs) conflict with invertible sampling because they allow to extract a "secret" (in this case a pre-image) from an image, independently of how it was computed. This conflicts with invertible sampling because invertible sampling is about sampling without knowing the secrets.

Theorem (informal, [29]). *Assuming the existence of extractable one-way functions (EOWF) and a non-interactive zero-knowledge proof system, $\mathsf{PREH}^{\mathsf{rand}}_{\approx_c}$ does not hold.*

This suggests that towards a realizable notion of pseudorandom encodings, a further relaxation is due. Thus, we ask whether the above impossibility result extends to the CRS model. In the CRS model, the above intuition why ISH conflicts with EOWFs fails, because the CRS can contain an obfuscated program that samples an image using some secret, but does not output this secret.

Dachman-Soled, Katz, and Rao [16] (building on the universal deniable encryption construction of Sahai and Waters [35]) construct a so-called "explainability compiler" that implies $\mathsf{cISH}^{\mathsf{rand}}_{\approx_c}$ based on indistinguishability obfuscation[4] (iO). By our equivalence theorem above, this implies pseudorandom encodings for all efficiently samplable distributions in the CRS model, with static choice of inputs, from iO. Invoking the static-to-adaptive transformation detailed above, this also applies to the adaptive variant.

Theorem (informal). *Assuming the existence of (polynomially secure) indistinguishability obfuscation and one-way functions, $\mathsf{acPREH}^{\mathsf{rand}}_{\approx_c}$ holds.*

---

[4] Informally, an iO scheme is a PPT algorithm that takes as input a circuit C and produces another circuit $\mathsf{iO}(C)$ such that C and $\mathsf{iO}(C)$ compute the same function, but $\mathsf{iO}(C)$ is unintelligible in the following sense. If two circuits C_1 and C_2 compute the same function, then $\mathsf{iO}(C_1)$ and $\mathsf{iO}(C_2)$ are computationally indistinguishable. The notion of iO was introduced in [2] and first instantiated in [21].

Note that [29] claim that their impossibility result extends to the CRS model, whereas the above theorem seems to suggest the opposite. We show that technically the result of [29] does extend to the CRS model at the cost of assuming *unbounded auxiliary-input* extractable one-way functions, a strong flavor of EOWFs that seems very unlikely to exist but cannot be unconditionally ruled out.

Theorem (informal). *Assuming the existence of extractable one-way functions with* unbounded *common auxiliary input and a non-interactive zero-knowledge proof system,* cPREH$_{\approx_c}^{rand}$ *does not hold.*

In fact, this apparent contradiction has been the source of some confusion in previous works: the work of [29] makes an informal claim that their impossibility result for ISH extends to the CRS model. However, due to the connection between ISH and adaptively secure MPC (which we will discuss in more details later on), this claim was challenged in [16]: the authors achieve a construction of adaptively secure MPC for all functionalities assuming iO, which seemingly contradicts the claim of [29]. The authors of [16] therefore stated that the "impossibility result of Ishai et al. [...] does not hold in the CRS model." Our extension clarifies that the distinction is in fact more subtle: the result of [29] *does* extend to the CRS model, but at the cost of assuming EOWF with *unbounded auxiliary inputs*. This does not contradict the constructions based on iO, because iO and EOWF with unbounded auxiliary inputs are known to be contradictory [5].

Overview. In Fig. 1, we provide a general summary of the many flavors of the pseudorandom encoding hypothesis, and how they relate to a wide variety of other primitives.

Further Relaxation. We further study an additional relaxation of pseudorandom encodings, where we allow the encoding algorithm to run in super-polynomial time. We show that this relaxed variant can be achieved from cryptographic primitives similar to *extremely lossy functions* [45], which can be based on the exponential hardness of the decisional Diffie-Hellman problem – a strong assumption, but (still) more standard than indistinguishability obfuscation. However, the applicability of the resulting notion turns out to be rather restricted.

1.2   Implications and Applications of Our Results

In this section, we elaborate on the implications of the techniques we develop and the results we obtain for a variety of other cryptographic primitives.

New Results for Adaptively Secure Computation. As mentioned above, a sampler admits invertible sampling if and only if it can be pseudorandomly encoded. A two-way connection between invertible sampling and *adaptively secure MPC for general randomized functionalities* was established in [29]. An

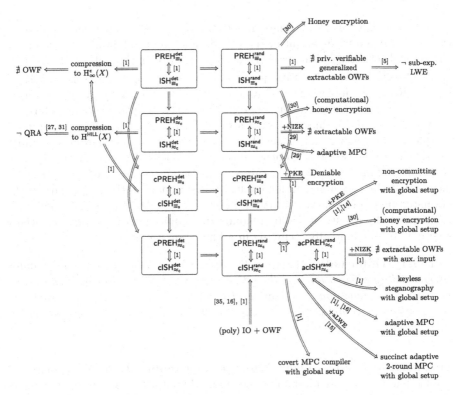

Fig. 1. An overview of the relations between the pseudorandom encoding hypothesis and other fields of cryptography and computational complexity theory. For simplicity, our static-to-adaptive transformation only appears in the computational, randomized setting in this overview, but also applies to the other settings. (Since the deterministic variants of the pseudorandom encoding hypothesis are impossible for some pathologic samplers, the arrows between deterministic and randomized variants of the pseudorandom encoding hypothesis are to be read as if the deterministic variant is true *for some sampler*, then the corresponding randomized variant is true *for that sampler*.)

MPC protocol allows two or more parties to jointly evaluate a (possibly randomized) functionality $\mathcal{F}$ on their inputs without revealing anything to each other except what follows from their inputs and outputs. This should hold even in the presence of an adversary who can corrupt *any* number of parties in an adaptive (sequential) fashion. When we write "adaptive MPC", we mean adaptive MPC for *all* randomized functionalities. This should be contrasted with weaker notions of adaptive MPC for strict subsets of corrupted parties [3,9,20] or for adaptively well-formed functionalities[5] [10] which can both be done from mild assumptions. The connection from [29] shows that adaptive MPC for all randomized functions is possible if and only if every PPT sampler admits invertible sampling, i.e., the invertible sampling hypothesis is true.

---

[5] Adaptively well-formed functionalities do not hide internal randomness.

We show that this result generalizes to the global CRS model. More precisely, we prove the adaptive variant of the pseudorandom encoding hypothesis in the CRS model acPREH$^{\text{rand}}_{\approx_c}$ is equivalent to adaptive MPC in the global CRS model.[6]

As detailed above, the static pseudorandom encoding hypothesis cPREH$^{\text{rand}}_{\approx_c}$ in the CRS model follows from iO (and one-way functions). Applying our static-to-adaptive transformation, the same holds for the adaptive variant. Thus, we obtain the first instantiation of an adaptive explainability compiler [16] without complexity leveraging and, hence, based only on polynomial hardness assumptions. The recent work of Cohen, shelat, and Wichs [15] uses such an adaptive explainability compiler to obtain succinct adaptive MPC, where "succinct" means that the communication complexity is sublinear in the complexity of the evaluated function. Due to our instantiation of acPREH$^{\text{rand}}_{\approx_c}$ from polynomial iO, we improve the results of [15] by relaxing the requirement for subexponentially secure iO to polynomially secure iO in a black-box way.

Corollary (informal). *Assuming the existence of polynomially secure indistinguishability obfuscation and the adaptive hardness of the learning with errors problem, then malicious, two-round, UC-secure adaptive MPC and sublinear communication complexity is possible (in the local CRS model, for all deterministic functionalities).*

Steganography and Covert Multi-party Computation. We explore the connection of the pseudorandom encoding hypothesis to various flavors of steganography. The goal of steganography, informally, is to embed secret messages in distributions of natural-looking messages, in order to hide them from external observers. While the standard setting for steganography relies on shared secret keys to encode the messages, we show that pseudorandom encodings naturally give rise to a strong form of *keyless steganography*. Namely, one can rely on pseudorandom encodings to encode any message into an innocent-looking distribution, without truly hiding the message (since anyone can decode the stream), but providing *plausible deniability*, in the sense that, even with the decoded message, it is impossible to tell apart whether this message was indeed encoded by the sender, or whether it is simply the result of decoding the innocent distribution.

Corollary (informal). *Assuming pseudorandom encodings, then there exists a keyless steganographic protocol which provides plausible deniability.*

Plausible deniability is an important security notion; in particular, an important cryptographic primitive in this area is the notion of (sender-)deniable encryption [8], which is known to exist assuming indistinguishability obfuscation [35]. Deniable encryption enables to "explain" ciphertexts produced for

---

[6] Together with the conflict between cPREH$^{\text{rand}}_{\approx_c}$ and EOWFs with unbounded auxiliary input, this corrects a claim made in [16] that the impossibility result of adaptive MPC from [29] would not extend to the CRS model.

some message to any arbitrary other message by providing corresponding random coins for a faked encryption process. We view it as an interesting open problem to build deniable encryption under the pseudorandom encoding hypothesis together with more standard cryptographic primitives; we make a first step in this direction and show the following: the *statistical* variant of pseudorandom encodings, together with the existence of public-key encryption, implies deniable encryption. Interestingly, we also show that the computational randomized pseudorandom encoding hypothesis suffices to imply non-committing encryption, a weaker form of deniable encryption allowing to explain only *simulated* ciphertexts to arbitrary messages [9].

Covert Secure Computation. Covert MPC [13,41] is an intriguing flavor of MPC that aims at achieving the following strong security guarantee: if the output of the protocol is not "favorable," the transcript of the interaction should not leak any information to the parties parties, including whether any given party was *actually taking part in the protocol.* This strong form of MPC aims at providing security guarantees when the very act of starting a computation with other parties should remain hidden. As an example [41], suppose that a CIA agent who infiltrated a terrorist group wants to make a handshake with another individual to find out whether she is also a CIA agent. Here, we show that pseudorandom encodings give rise to a general compiler transforming a standard MPC protocol into a covert one, in a round-preserving way. The idea is to encode each round of the protocol such that encoded messages look random. Together with the equivalence between adaptively secure MPC and pseudorandom encodings, this gives a connection between two seemingly unrelated notions of secure computation.

Corollary (informal). *Assuming adaptively secure MPC for all functionalities, there exists a round-preserving compiler that transforms a large class of "natural" MPC protocols into covert MPC protocols (in the static, semi-honest setting).*

Other Results. Due to our infeasibility results of $\mathsf{PREH}^{\mathrm{rand}}_{\equiv_s}$, distribution transforming encoders (DTEs) for all efficiently samplable distributions are infeasible. Even the computational relaxation of DTEs is infeasible assuming extractable one-way functions. Since all currently known constructions of honey encryption rely on DTEs, we conditionally refute the existence of honey encryption based on the DTE-then-encrypt framework from [30]. On the positive side, due to our feasibility result of $\mathsf{acPREH}^{\mathrm{rand}}_{\approx_c}$, computational honey encryption is feasible in the CRS model.

Theorem (informal). *Assuming* $\mathsf{acPREH}^{\mathrm{rand}}_{\approx_c}$ *and a suitable symmetric-key encryption scheme (modeled as a random cipher), computational honey encryption for all efficiently samplable distributions exists in the CRS model.*

1.3   Negative Results for Stronger Notions of Pseudorandom Encodings

Below we describe how we gradually relax optimal compression via different notions of pseudorandom encodings and derive infeasibility results for all variants of pseudorandom encodings which restrict the encoding algorithm to be deterministic or require an information-theoretic pseudorandomness guarantee. This leaves computational randomized pseudorandom encodings as the best possible achievable notion.

Deterministic, Statistical Pseudorandom Encodings. The notion of pseudorandom encodings with a deterministic encoding algorithm and information-theoretic indistinguishability is perhaps the simplest notion one can consider. As we will prove in this paper, this notion recovers the notion of optimal compression: since the encoding algorithm for some source X is deterministic, it can be seen with an entropy argument that the output size of E_X must be at most $\mathsf{H}_\infty(X)$, the min-entropy of X; otherwise, the distribution $\{\mathsf{E}_X(X)\}$ can necessarily be distinguished from random with some statistically non-negligible advantage. Therefore, E_X is an optimal and efficient compression algorithm for X, with decompression algorithm D_X; this is true even for the relaxation in the CRS model. The existence of efficient compression algorithms for various categories of samplers was thoroughly studied [40]. In particular, the existence of compression algorithms for all efficiently samplable sources implies the inexistence of one-way functions (this is an observation attributed to Levin in [23]) since compressing the output of a pseudorandom generator to its entropy would distinguish it from a random string, and the existence of one-way functions implies the existence of pseudorandom generators [24]).

Theorem (informal). *Assuming the existence of one-way functions, neither* $\mathsf{PREH}^{\mathsf{det}}_{\equiv_\mathsf{s}}$ *nor* $\mathsf{cPREH}^{\mathsf{det}}_{\equiv_\mathsf{s}}$ *hold.*

This is a strong impossibility result, as one-way functions dwell among the weakest assumptions in cryptography, [28]. One can circumvent this impossibility by studying whether compression can be achieved for more restricted classes of distributions, as was done e.g. in [40]. Our work can be seen as pursuing an orthogonal direction. We seek to determine whether a relaxed notion of compression can be achieved for *all* efficiently samplable distributions. The relaxations we consider comprise the possibility to use randomness in the encoding algorithm, and weakening the requirement on the encoded distribution to being only computationally indistinguishable from random. Clearly, these relaxations remove one of the most important features of compression algorithms, which is that their outputs are smaller than their inputs (i.e., they compress). Nevertheless, the indistinguishability of the encoded distribution from the uniform distribution is another crucial feature of optimal compression algorithms, which has independent applications.

Deterministic, Computational Pseudorandom Encodings. We now turn towards a relaxation where the encoded distribution is only required to be computationally indistinguishable from random, but the encoding algorithm is still required to be deterministic. This flavor is strongly connected to an important problem in cryptography: the problem of separating HILL entropy [24] from Yao entropy [44]. HILL and Yao entropy are different approaches of formalizing computational entropy, i.e., the amount of entropy a distribution appears to have from the viewpoint of a computationally bounded entity. Informally, a distribution has high HILL entropy if it is computationally close to a distribution with high min-entropy; a distribution has high Yao entropy if it cannot be compressed efficiently. Finding a distribution which, under standard cryptographic assumptions, has high Yao entropy, but low HILL entropy constitutes a long standing open problem in cryptography. Currently, only an oracle separation [42] and a separation for conditional distributions [27] are known. To establish the connection between $\mathsf{PREH}^{\mathsf{det}}_{\approx_c}$ and this problem, we proceed as follows: informally, a deterministic pseudorandom encoding must necessarily *compress its input to the HILL entropy of the distribution*. That is, the output size of the encoding cannot be much larger than the HILL entropy of the distribution. This, in turn, implies that a distribution which admits such a pseudorandom encoding cannot have high Yao entropy.

In this work, we formalize the above argument, and show that the *conditional* separation of HILL and Yao entropy from [27] suffices to refute $\mathsf{PREH}^{\mathsf{det}}_{\approx_c}$. This separation holds under the assumption that non-interactive zero-knowledge proofs with some appropriate structural properties exist (which in turn can be based on standard assumptions such as the quadratic residuosity assumption). Thus, we obtain the following infeasibility result:

Theorem (informal). *If the quadratic residuosity assumption holds, then $\mathsf{PREH}^{\mathsf{det}}_{\approx_c}$ does not hold.*

Hence, we may conclude that towards a feasible variant of pseudorandom encodings for all efficiently samplable distributions, requiring the encoding algorithm to be deterministic poses a strong restriction.

Randomized, Statistical Pseudorandom Encodings. We now consider the relaxation of perfect compression by allowing the encoding algorithm to be randomized while still requiring information-theoretic indistinguishability from randomness. This flavor of pseudorandom encoding was used in the context of *honey encryption* [30]. Honey encryption is a cryptographic primitive which has been introduced to mitigate attacks on encryption schemes resulting from the use of low-entropy passwords. Honey encryption has the property that decrypting a ciphertext with an incorrect key always yields a valid-looking plaintext which seems to come from the expected distribution, thereby mitigating brute-force attacks. This is the same property that was useful in the previous PAKE example.

The study of honey encryption was initiated in [30], where it was shown that honey encryption can naturally be constructed by composing a block cipher (modeled as a random cipher) with a *distribution transforming encoder* (DTE), a notion which is equivalent to our notion of pseudorandom encoding with randomized encoding and statistical pseudorandomness. The focus of [30] was on obtaining such DTEs for simple and useful distributions. In contrast, we seek to understand the feasibility of this notion for *arbitrary* distributions. Intuitively, it is not straightforward to encode any efficient distribution into the uniform distribution; consider for example the distribution over RSA moduli, i.e., products of two random n-bit primes. Since no efficient algorithm is known to test membership in the support of this distribution, natural approaches seem to break down. In fact, we show in this work that this difficulty is inherent: building on techniques from [5, 29], we demonstrate the impossibility of (randomized, statistical) pseudorandom encodings for all efficiently samplable distributions, under a relatively standard cryptographic assumption.

Theorem (informal). *Assuming the sub-exponential hardness of the learning with errors (LWE) problem,* $\mathsf{PREH}^{\mathsf{rand}}_{\equiv_s}$ *does not hold.*

This result directly implies that under the same assumption, there exist efficiently samplable distributions (with input) for which no distribution transforming encoder exists. We view it as an interesting open problem whether this result can be extended to rule out the existence of honey encryption for arbitrary distributions under the same assumption.

1.4   Open Questions and Subsequent Work

The most intriguing question left open by our work is whether the weakest variant of the pseudorandom encoding hypothesis $\mathsf{cPREH}^{\mathsf{rand}}_{\approx_c}$, which is implied by iO, also *implies* iO. Very recently, this question was settled in the affirmative by Wee and Wichs [43] under the LWE assumption. More concretely, by modifying a heuristic iO construction of Brakerski et al. [7], they show that iO is implied by LWE if one is additionally given an *oblivious LWE-sampler* in the CRS model. Such a sampler, given a matrix $\boldsymbol{A} \in \mathbb{Z}_q^{m \times n}$, generates outputs that are indistinguishable from LWE samples $\boldsymbol{A} \cdot \boldsymbol{s} + \boldsymbol{e}$ without knowing the secrets $\boldsymbol{s}$ or the noise $\boldsymbol{e}$. The existence of an oblivious LWE sampler is nontrivial even under the LWE assumption, because $\boldsymbol{A}$ can be such that $\boldsymbol{A} \cdot \boldsymbol{s} + \boldsymbol{e}$ is not pseudorandom; however, such a sampler still follows from the invertible sampling hypothesis [29], which we show to be equivalent to the pseudorandom encoding hypothesis. By proposing an explicit heuristic construction of (a relaxed flavor of) an oblivious LWE sampler, the end result of [43] is a construction of iO from a new "falsifiable" assumption.

Whether $\mathsf{cPREH}^{\mathsf{rand}}_{\approx_c}$ implies iO under weaker or different assumptions than LWE remains open. A potentially easier goal is using $\mathsf{cPREH}^{\mathsf{rand}}_{\approx_c}$ to construct public-key encryption from one-way functions. This is related to the possibility of constructing oblivious transfer from any public-key encryption in which public keys and ciphertexts are obliviously samplable [19,22], which is implied by public-key encryption and $\mathsf{cPREH}^{\mathsf{rand}}_{\approx_c}$. Here $\mathsf{cPREH}^{\mathsf{rand}}_{\approx_c}$ is used to bypass the black-box separation between public-key encryption and oblivious transfer [22].

Finally, there is a lot of room for relaxing the intractability assumptions we use to rule out the statistical ($\mathsf{cPREH}^{\mathsf{rand}}_{\equiv_s}$) and deterministic ($\mathsf{cPREH}^{\mathsf{det}}_{\approx_c}$) flavors of pseudorandom encodings.

Organization. In Sect. 2, we provide a technical overview of a selection of our results. In Sect. 3, we provide condensed definitions of pseudorandom encodings and invertible sampling and a formal proof of their equivalence and in Sect. 4 we describe the static-to-adaptive transformation. We refer the reader to the full version [1] for more details and for the other results we described.

2   Overview of Techniques

In this section, we elaborate on some of our technical results in more detail. In the following, we identify a PPT sampler S with the distribution (family) ensemble it induces.

The Relation to Invertible Sampling. A PPT sampler S is *inverse samplable* [17,29], if there exists an alternative sampler $\overline{S}$ inducing a distribution which is computationally indistinguishable to the distribution induced by S such that the computations of $\overline{S}$ can be efficiently inverted. Efficiently inverting the computation of $\overline{S}$ means that there exists an efficient inverse sampler $\overline{S}^{-1}$ which, given an output of $\overline{S}$, recovers a well-distributed random tape for $\overline{S}$ to compute the given output in the following sense. The inverse sampled random tape is required to be computationally indistinguishable from the actually used random tape. More formally, a PPT sampler S is inverse samplable if there exists an efficient alternative sampler $\overline{S}$ and an efficient inverse sampler $\overline{S}^{-1}$ such that

$$\{y \leftarrow S(1^\lambda): y\} \approx_c \{y \leftarrow \overline{S}(1^\lambda): y\}, \tag{3}$$

$$\{y \leftarrow \overline{S}(1^\lambda; r): (r, y)\} \approx_c \{y \leftarrow \overline{S}(1^\lambda): (\overline{S}^{-1}(1^\lambda, y), y)\}. \tag{4}$$

We refer to Eq. (3) as *closeness* and to Eq. (4) as *invertibility*. If the sampler S admits an input m, the above is required to hold for all inputs m in the input space L, where $\overline{S}$ and $\overline{S}^{-1}$ both additionally receive m as input. In accordance with [29], we refer to the hypothesis that all PPT algorithms with input are inverse samplable as the *invertible sampling hypothesis*. Restricting the invertible sampling hypothesis to algorithms which do not admit inputs is denoted the *weak invertible sampling hypothesis*.

The concepts of inverse samplability and pseudorandom encodings are tightly connected. Suppose a PPT algorithm S is inverse samplable. Then, there exists an alternative and an inverse sampler $(\overline{S}, \overline{S}^{-1})$ satisfying closeness and invertibility. Invertibility guarantees that the inverse sampler $\overline{S}^{-1}$ on input of a sample y from $\overline{S}(1^\lambda)$, outputs a computationally well-distributed random tape r. Hence, with overwhelming probability over the choice of $y \leftarrow \overline{S}(1^\lambda)$ and $r \leftarrow \overline{S}^{-1}(y)$, the alternative sampler on input of r, recovers y. In other words, the inverse sampler $\overline{S}^{-1}$ can be seen as encoding a given sample y, whereas the *de-randomized* alternative sampler $\overline{S}$ given this encoding *as random tape*, is able to recover y. Looking through the lens of pseudorandom encoding, this almost proves correctness except that y is sampled according to $\overline{S}(1^\lambda)$ instead of $S(1^\lambda)$. This difference can be bridged due to closeness. We now turn towards showing pseudorandomness of the encoded distribution. Due to closeness, the distributions $\{y \leftarrow \overline{S}(1^\lambda): (\overline{S}^{-1}(1^\lambda, y), y)\}$ and $\{y \leftarrow S(1^\lambda): (\overline{S}^{-1}(1^\lambda, y), y)\}$ are computationally indistinguishable. Invertibility guarantees that, given a sample y from $\overline{S}(1^\lambda)$, an encoding of y is indistinguishable to uniformly chosen randomness conditioned on the fact that decoding yields y. Removing y from this distribution, almost corresponds to pseudorandomness, except that y is sampled according to $\overline{S}(1^\lambda)$ instead of $S(1^\lambda)$. Again, we are able to bridge this gap due to closeness. Note that we crucially use the fact that the initial randomness used by $\overline{S}$ resides outside of the view of an adversary. Summing up, if a PPT sampler S is inverse samplable, then it can be pseudorandomly encoded.

Interestingly, this connection turns out to be bidirectional. Suppose a PPT algorithm S can be pseudorandomly encoded. Then, there exists an efficient encoding algorithm E_S and an efficient deterministic decoding algorithm D_S satisfying correctness and pseudorandomness. Looking through the lens of invertible sampling, we identify the decoding algorithm to correspond to the alternative sampler (viewing the random tape of the alternative sampler as explicit input to D_S) and the encoding algorithm to correspond to the inverse sampler. Pseudorandomness guarantees that $\mathsf{E}_S(S(1^\lambda))$ is indistinguishable from uniform randomness. Hence, applying the decode algorithm D_S on uniform randomness is indistinguishable from applying D_S to outputs of $\mathsf{E}_S(S(1^\lambda))$. Correctness guarantees that $\mathsf{D}_S(\mathsf{E}_S(y))$ for y sampled according to $S(1^\lambda)$ recovers y with overwhelming probability. Thus, the distribution induced by applying D_S on uniform randomness is computationally close to the distribution induced by $S(1^\lambda)$. This shows closeness. For the purpose of arguing about invertibility, consider the distribution $A := \{y \leftarrow \mathsf{D}_S(r): (r, y)\}$. Due to pseudorandomness r can be considered an encoded sample from $S(1^\lambda)$. Hence, A is indistinguishable to the distribution, where r is produced by $\mathsf{E}_S(y')$ for some *independent* $y' \leftarrow S(1^\lambda)$, i.e.

$$\{y \leftarrow \mathsf{D}_S(r): (r, y)\} \approx_c \{y' \leftarrow S(1^\lambda), r \leftarrow \mathsf{E}_S(y'), y \leftarrow \mathsf{D}_S(r): (r, y)\}.$$

Note that by correctness, y and y' are identical with overwhelming probability. Therefore, A is indistinguishable to $\{y' \leftarrow S(1^\lambda), r \leftarrow \mathsf{E}_S(y'): (r, y')\}$. Since sampling y' via D_S applied on uniform randomness is computationally close to the above distribution due to closeness, invertibility follows. Summing up, a sampler S can be pseudorandomly encoded *if and only if* it is inverse samplable.

Likewise to the variations and relaxations described for pseudorandom encodings, we vary and relax the notion of invertible sampling. The inverse sampler can be required to be deterministic or allowed to be randomized. Further, closeness and invertibility can be required to hold information theoretically or computationally. We denote these variants as $\mathsf{ISH}^{\mathsf{rand}}_{\approx_c}$, $\mathsf{ISH}^{\mathsf{rand}}_{\equiv_s}$, $\mathsf{ISH}^{\mathsf{det}}_{\approx_c}$ and $\mathsf{ISH}^{\mathsf{det}}_{\equiv_s}$. To circumvent impossibilities in the plain model, we also define the relaxations in the common reference string model in static and adaptive flavors, denoted the prefix "c" and "ac", respectively. The above equivalence extends to all introduced variations of the pseudorandom encoding and invertible sampling hypotheses.

The Static-to-Adaptive Transformation. The static variant of pseudorandom encodings in the CRS model only guarantees correctness and pseudorandomness as long as the input m for the sampler S is chosen independently of the CRS. The adaptive variant, on the other hand, provides correctness and pseudorandomness even for adaptive choices of inputs. Adaptive notions always imply their static analogues. Interestingly, for pseudorandom encodings, the opposite direction is true as well. The core idea is to use an *indirection* argument (similar to [11,12,25]) to delay CRS generation until during the actual encoding process. Thus, the advantage stemming from adaptively choosing the input is eliminated.

Suppose that the static variant of the pseudorandom encoding hypothesis in the CRS model is true and let S be some PPT sampler. Since S can be pseudorandomly encoded in the CRS model with static choice of inputs, there exist algorithms (Setup', E', D') such that static correctness and pseudorandomness hold. Further, the algorithm Setup' can also be pseudorandomly encoded as above. Let (Setup'', E'', D'') be the corresponding algorithms such that static correctness and pseudorandomness hold. Note that since the sampler Setup' does not expect an input, static and adaptive guarantees are equivalent.

Then, the sampler S can be pseudorandomly encoded in the CRS model with *adaptive* choice of inputs as follows. Initially, we sample a common reference string crs'' via Setup''(1^λ) and make it available to the parties. Given crs'' and a sample y from $S(m)$, adaptive encoding works in two phases. First, a fresh CRS crs' is sampled via Setup'(1^λ) and pseudorandomly encoded via $r_1 \leftarrow$ E''(crs'', crs'). Second, the given sample y is pseudorandomly encoded via $r_2 \leftarrow$ E'(crs', m, y). The encoding of y then consists of (r_1, r_2). To decode, the CRS crs' is restored via D''(crs'', r_1). Then, using crs', the original sample y is recovered via D'(crs', m, r_2).

Since crs' is chosen freshly during the encoding process, the input m which may depend on crs'', cannot depend on crs'. Further, the distribution Setup'' does not expect an input. Hence, static guarantees suffice.

To realize that adaptive pseudorandomness holds, consider the encoding of $S(m)$ for some adaptively chosen message m. Since the view of $\mathcal{A}$ when choosing the message m is independent of crs', static pseudorandomness can be applied to replace the distribution E'$(crs', m, S(m))$ with uniform randomness. Further, since the sampler Setup' does not expect any input, static pseudorandomness suffices to replace the distribution E''$(crs'', $ Setup'$(1^\lambda))$ with uniform randomness. This proves adaptive pseudorandomness.

The adaptive variant of correctness follows similarly from the static variant of correctness. Consider the distribution of decoding an encoded sample of $S(m)$, where m is adaptively chosen. Since the sampler Setup' does not expect an input, static correctness can be applied to replace decoding $\mathsf{D}''(crs'', r_1)$ with the crs' sampled during encoding. Again, since crs' does not lie in the view of the adversary when choosing the message m, static correctness guarantees that decoding succeeds with overwhelming probability. This proves adaptive correctness.

On Deterministic Pseudorandom Encoding and Compression. The notion of pseudorandom encoding is inspired by the notion of compression. A tuple of deterministic functions $(\mathsf{E}_X, \mathsf{D}_X)$ is said to compress a source X_λ to length $m(\lambda)$ with decoding error $\epsilon(\lambda)$, if (i) $\Pr[\mathsf{D}_X(\mathsf{E}_X(X_\lambda)) \neq X_\lambda] \leq \epsilon(\lambda)$ and (ii) $\mathbb{E}[|\mathsf{E}_X(X_\lambda)|] \leq m(\lambda)$, see [40,42]. Pseudorandom encoding partially recovers the notion of compression if we require the encoding algorithm to be deterministic. If a source X_λ can be pseudorandomly encoded with a deterministic encoding algorithm having output length $n(\lambda)$, then X_λ is compressible to length $n(\lambda)$. Note, however, that the converse direction is not true. Compression and decompression algorithms for a compressible source do not necessarily encode that source pseudorandomly. The output of a compression algorithm is not required to look pseudorandom and, in some cases, admits a specific structure which makes it easily distinguishable from uniform randomness, e.g. instances using Levin search, [40].

Clearly, the requirement for correctness, poses a lower bound on the encoding length $n(\lambda)$, [36]. Conversely, requiring the encoding algorithm E_X to be deterministic means that the only source of entropy in the distribution $\mathsf{E}_X(X_\lambda)$ originates from the source X_λ itself. Hence, for the distributions $\mathsf{E}_X(X_\lambda)$ and the uniform distribution over $\{0,1\}^{n(\lambda)}$ to be indistinguishable, the encoding length $n(\lambda)$ must be "sufficiently small". We observe that correctness together with the fact that E_X is deterministic implies that the event $\mathsf{E}_X(\mathsf{D}_X(\mathsf{E}_X(X_\lambda))) = \mathsf{E}_X(X_\lambda)$ occurs with overwhelming probability. Applying pseudorandomness yields that $\mathsf{E}_X(\mathsf{D}_X(U_{n(\lambda)})) = U_{n(\lambda)}$ holds with overwhelming probability, wherefore we can conclude that D_X operates almost injectively on the set $\{0,1\}^{n(\lambda)}$. Hence, the (smooth) min-entropy of $\mathsf{D}_X(U_{n(\lambda)})$ is at least $n(\lambda)$.

Considering information theoretical pseudorandomness, the distributions $\mathsf{D}_X(U_{n(\lambda)})$ and X_λ are statistically close. Hence, by the reasoning above, the encoding length $n(\lambda)$ is upper bounded by the (smooth) min-entropy of the source X_λ. In conclusion, if a distribution can be pseudorandomly encoded such that the encoding algorithm is deterministic satisfying statistical pseudorandomness, then this distribution is compressible to its (smooth) min-entropy. Using a technical "Splitting Lemma", this extends to the relaxed variant of the pseudorandom encoding hypothesis in the CRS model.

Considering computational pseudorandomness, by a similar argument as above, we obtain that X_λ is computationally close to a distribution with min-entropy $n(\lambda)$. This does not yield a relation between the encoding length and the min-entropy of the source. However, we do obtain relations to computational analogues of entropy. Computational entropy is the amount of entropy a distribution appears to have from the perspective of a computationally bounded entity. The notion of HILL entropy [24] is defined via the computational indistinguishability from a truly random distribution. More formally, a distribution

X_λ has HILL entropy at least k, if there exists a distribution with min-entropy k which is computationally indistinguishable from X_λ. Hence, the encoding length $n(\lambda)$ is upper bounded by the HILL entropy of the source X_λ. Another important notion of computational entropy is the notion of Yao entropy [44]. Yao entropy is defined via the incompressibility of a distribution. More precisely, a distribution X_λ has Yao entropy at least k if X_λ cannot be efficiently compressed to length less than k (and successfully decompressed). If a distribution can be pseudorandomly encoded with deterministic encoding, then it can be compressed to the encoding length $n(\lambda)$. This poses an upper bound on the Yao entropy of the source. In summary, this yields

$$n(\lambda) \leq \mathrm{H}^{\mathsf{HILL}}(X_\lambda) \quad \text{and} \quad \mathrm{H}^{\mathsf{Yao}}(X_\lambda) \leq n(\lambda). \tag{5}$$

However, due to [27,31], if the Quadratic Residuosity Assumption (QRA) is true, then there exist distributions which have low *conditional* HILL entropy while being *conditionally* incompressible, i.e. have high conditional Yao entropy.[7] The above observations, particularly Eq. (5), can be extended to conditional HILL and conditional Yao entropy, by considering $\mathsf{PREH}^{\mathsf{det}}_{\approx_c}$ for PPT algorithms with input. Therefore, if the Quadratic Residuosity Assumption is true, $\mathsf{PREH}^{\mathsf{det}}_{\approx_c}$ cannot be true for those distributions.

Unfortunately, we do not know whether this extends to the relaxed variants of the pseudorandom encoding hypothesis admitting access to a CRS. On a high level, the problem is that the HILL entropy, in contrast to the min-entropy, does not remain untouched when additionally conditioning on some common reference string distribution, even though the initial distribution is independent of the CRS. Hence, the splitting technique can not be applied here.

3   Pseudorandom Encodings and Invertible Sampling

In this section, we formally define pseudorandom encodings and invertible sampling. We will work with the hypothesis that every efficiently samplable distribution can be pseudorandomly encoded and invertible sampled and we refer to these hypotheses as the pseudorandom encoding hypothesis and the invertible sampling hypothesis, respectively. This section is a condensed and much less detailed version of [1].

Definition 1 (Pseudorandom encoding hypothesis, $\mathsf{PREH}^{\mathsf{rand}}_{\approx_c}$). *For every PPT algorithm S, there exist efficient algorithms E_S (the encoding algorithm) with output length $n(\lambda)$ and D_S (the decoding algorithm), where D_S is deterministic and E_S is randomized satisfying the following two properties.*

Correctness. For all inputs $m \in L$, $\epsilon_{\mathsf{dec-error}}(\lambda) := \Pr\left[y \leftarrow S(m) \colon \mathsf{D}_S(m, \mathsf{E}_S(m, y)) \neq y\right]$ is negligible.

---

[7] Let (X, Z) be a joint distribution. The conditional computational entropy is the entropy X appears to have to a bounded adversary when additionally given Z.

Pseudorandomness. *For all PPT adversaries $\mathcal{A}$ and all inputs $m \in L$,*

$$Adv^{\text{pre}}_{\mathcal{A},m}(\lambda) := \left| \Pr[Exp^{\text{pre}}_{\mathcal{A},m,0}(\lambda) = 1] - \Pr[Exp^{\text{pre}}_{\mathcal{A},m,1}(\lambda) = 1] \right| \leq \text{negl}(\lambda),$$

where $Exp^{\text{pre}}_{\mathcal{A},m,0}$ and $Exp^{\text{pre}}_{\mathcal{A},m,1}$ are defined below.

$Exp^{\text{pre}}_{\mathcal{A},m,0}(\lambda)$	$Exp^{\text{pre}}_{\mathcal{A},m,1}(\lambda)$
$r \leftarrow \{0,1\}^{p(\lambda)}$	$u \leftarrow \{0,1\}^{n(\lambda)}$
$y := S(m;r)$	**return** $\mathcal{A}(m,u)$
return $\mathcal{A}(m, \mathsf{E}_S(m,y))$	

Definition 2 (Invertible sampling hypothesis, $\mathsf{ISH}^{\text{rand}}_{\approx_c}$, [29]). *For every PPT algorithm S, there exists a PPT algorithm $\overline{S}$ (the alternate sampler) with randomness space $\{0,1\}^{n(\lambda)}$ and an efficient randomized algorithm $\overline{S}^{-1}$ (the inverse sampler), satisfying the following two properties.*

Closeness. *For all PPT adversaries $\mathcal{A}$ and all inputs $m \in L$,*

$$Adv^{\text{close}}_{\mathcal{A},m}(\lambda) := \left| \Pr[Exp^{\text{close}}_{\mathcal{A},m,0}(\lambda) = 1] - \Pr[Exp^{\text{close}}_{\mathcal{A},m,1}(\lambda) = 1] \right| \leq \text{negl}(\lambda),$$

where $Exp^{\text{close}}_{\mathcal{A},m,0}$ and $Exp^{\text{close}}_{\mathcal{A},m,1}$ are defined below.

Invertibility. *For all PPT adversaries $\mathcal{A}$ and all inputs $m \in L$,*

$$Adv^{\text{inv}}_{\mathcal{A},m}(\lambda) := \left| \Pr[Exp^{\text{inv}}_{\mathcal{A},m,0}(\lambda) = 1] - \Pr[Exp^{\text{inv}}_{\mathcal{A},m,1}(\lambda) = 1] \right| \leq \text{negl}(\lambda),$$

where $Exp^{\text{inv}}_{\mathcal{A},m,0}$ and $Exp^{\text{inv}}_{\mathcal{A},m,1}$ are defined below.

$Exp^{\text{close}}_{\mathcal{A},m,0}(\lambda)$	$Exp^{\text{close}}_{\mathcal{A},m,1}(\lambda)$	$Exp^{\text{inv}}_{\mathcal{A},m,0}(\lambda)$	$Exp^{\text{inv}}_{\mathcal{A},m,1}(\lambda)$
$r \leftarrow \{0,1\}^{p(\lambda)}$	$r \leftarrow \{0,1\}^{n(\lambda)}$	$r \leftarrow \{0,1\}^{n(\lambda)}$	$r \leftarrow \{0,1\}^{n(\lambda)}$
$y := S(m;r)$	$y := \overline{S}(m;r)$	$y := \overline{S}(m;r)$	$y := \overline{S}(m;r)$
return $\mathcal{A}(m,y)$	**return** $\mathcal{A}(m,y)$	**return** $\mathcal{A}(m,r,y)$	$\overline{r} \leftarrow \overline{S}^{-1}(m,y)$
			return $\mathcal{A}(m,\overline{r},y)$

Theorem 1. *$\mathsf{PREH}^{\text{rand}}_{\approx_c}$ is true if and only if $\mathsf{ISH}^{\text{rand}}_{\approx_c}$ is true.*

Lemma 1. *If $\mathsf{ISH}^{\text{rand}}_{\approx_c}$ holds, then $\mathsf{PREH}^{\text{rand}}_{\approx_c}$ holds.*

Proof. Assume $\mathsf{ISH}^{\text{rand}}_{\approx_c}$ holds. Let S be a PPT algorithm. $\mathsf{ISH}^{\text{rand}}_{\approx_c}$ implies that there exists an alternative sampler $\overline{S}$ (with randomness space $\{0,1\}^{n(\lambda)}$) and a corresponding inverse sampler $\overline{S}^{-1}$ satisfying closeness and invertibility.

For $m \in L, y \in \{0,1\}^*, r \in \{0,1\}^{n(\lambda)}$, we define the algorithms $\mathsf{E}_S(m,y) := \overline{S}^{-1}(m,y)$ (potentially randomized) and $\mathsf{D}_S(m,r) := \overline{S}(m;r)$ (deterministic).

$\mathbf{G_0}$	$\mathbf{G_1}$	$\mathbf{G_2}$
$r \leftarrow \{0,1\}^{n(\lambda)}$	$r \leftarrow \{0,1\}^{n(\lambda)}$	$r \leftarrow \{0,1\}^{p(\lambda)}$
$y := \overline{S}(m;r)$	$y := \overline{S}(m;r)$	$y := S(m;r)$
$\mathbf{return}\ \mathcal{A}(m,r,y)$	$\overline{r} \leftarrow \overline{S}^{-1}(m,y)$	$\overline{r} \leftarrow \overline{S}^{-1}(m,y)$
	$\mathbf{return}\ \mathcal{A}(m,\overline{r},y)$	$\mathbf{return}\ \mathcal{A}(m,\overline{r},y)$

Fig. 2. Hybrids used in the proof of correctness.

Correctness. We consider a series of hybrids, see Fig. 2.

Game $\mathbf{G_0}$ is identical to $Exp^{inv}_{\mathcal{A},m,0}$ and game $\mathbf{G_1}$ is identical to $Exp^{inv}_{\mathcal{A},m,1}$. Hence, $|\Pr[out_1 = 1] - \Pr[out_0 = 1]| \leq Adv^{inv}_{\mathcal{A},m}(\lambda)$.

Claim. For all PPT adversaries $\mathcal{A}$, for all $m \in L$, there exists a PPT adversary $\overline{\mathcal{A}}$, such that $|\Pr[out_2 = 1] - \Pr[out_1 = 1]| \leq Adv^{close}_{\overline{\mathcal{A}},m}(\lambda)$.

Proof. Construct an adversary $\overline{\mathcal{A}}$ on closeness. On input of (m,y), $\overline{\mathcal{A}}$ computes $\overline{r} \leftarrow \overline{S}^{-1}(m,y)$, calls $\mathcal{A}$ on input of $(m,\overline{r},y)$ and outputs the resulting output. If y is sampled using $\overline{S}(m;r)$ (for $r \leftarrow \{0,1\}^{n(\lambda)}$), $\overline{\mathcal{A}}$ perfectly simulates game $\mathbf{G_1}$ for $\mathcal{A}$. If y is sampled using $S(m;r)$ (for $f \leftarrow \{0,1\}^{p(\lambda)}$), $\overline{\mathcal{A}}$ perfectly simulates game $\mathbf{G_2}$ for $\mathcal{A}$. Therefore, $\Pr[out_1 = 1] = \Pr[Exp^{close}_{\overline{\mathcal{A}},m,1}(\lambda) = 1]$ and $\Pr[out_2 = 1] = \Pr[Exp^{close}_{\overline{\mathcal{A}},m,0}(\lambda) = 1]$. $\square$

Thus, we have that $|\Pr[out_2 = 1] - \Pr[out_0 = 1]| \leq Adv^{close}_{\overline{\mathcal{A}},m}(\lambda) + Adv^{inv}_{\overline{\mathcal{A}}',m}(\lambda)$ for some PPT adversaries $\overline{\mathcal{A}}, \overline{\mathcal{A}}'$.

Consider the adversary $\mathcal{A}$ distinguishing between game $\mathbf{G_0}$ and game $\mathbf{G_2}$ that on input of (m,r,y), outputs 0 if $\overline{S}(m;r) = y$ and outputs 1 otherwise. By definition, $\mathcal{A}$ always outputs 0 in $\mathbf{G_0}$. Hence, $\epsilon_{dec-error}(\lambda) = \Pr[y \leftarrow S(m): \overline{S}(m, \overline{S}^{-1}(m,y)) \neq y] = \Pr[out_{2,\mathcal{A}} = 1] = |\Pr[out_{2,\mathcal{A}} = 1] - \Pr[out_{0,\mathcal{A}} = 1]|$.

Pseudorandomness. We consider a sequence of hybrids starting from $Exp^{pre}_{\mathcal{A},m,0}$ and concluding in $Exp^{pre}_{\mathcal{A},m,1}$, see Fig. 3.

$\mathbf{G_0}$	$\mathbf{G_1}$	$\mathbf{G_2}$
$r \leftarrow \{0,1\}^{p(\lambda)}$	$r \leftarrow \{0,1\}^{n(\lambda)}$	$r \leftarrow \{0,1\}^{n(\lambda)}$
$y := S(m;r)$	$y := \overline{S}(m;r)$	$\mathbf{return}\ \mathcal{A}(m,r)$
$u \leftarrow \overline{S}^{-1}(m,y)$	$u \leftarrow \overline{S}^{-1}(m,y)$	
$\mathbf{return}\ \mathcal{A}(m,u)$	$\mathbf{return}\ \mathcal{A}(m,u)$	

Fig. 3. Hybrids used in the proof of pseudorandomness.

Claim. For all PPT adversaries $\mathcal{A}$, for all $m \in L$, there exists a PPT adversary $\overline{\mathcal{A}}$, such that $|\Pr[out_1 = 1] - \Pr[out_0 = 1]| \leq Adv^{\mathsf{close}}_{\overline{\mathcal{A}},m}(\lambda)$.

Proof. Construct a PPT adversary $\overline{\mathcal{A}}$ on the closeness property as follows. On input of (m, y), $\overline{\mathcal{A}}$ calls $\mathcal{A}$ on input of $(m, \overline{S}^{-1}(m, y))$ and outputs the resulting output.

If $y \leftarrow S(m)$, $\overline{\mathcal{A}}$ simulates game $\mathbf{G}_0$ for $\mathcal{A}$, and if $y \leftarrow \overline{S}(m)$, $\overline{\mathcal{A}}$ simulates game $\mathbf{G}_1$ for $\mathcal{A}$. Hence, $\Pr[out_0 = 1] = \Pr[Exp^{\mathsf{close}}_{\overline{\mathcal{A}},m,0}(\lambda) = 1]$ and $\Pr[out_1 = 1] = \Pr[Exp^{\mathsf{close}}_{\overline{\mathcal{A}},m,1}(\lambda) = 1]$. $\qquad\square$

Claim. For all PPT adversaries $\mathcal{A}$, for all $m \in L$, there exists a PPT adversary $\overline{\mathcal{A}}$, such that $|\Pr[out_2 = 1] - \Pr[out_1 = 1]| \leq Adv^{\mathsf{inv}}_{\overline{\mathcal{A}},m}(\lambda)$.

Proof. We construct a PPT adversary $\overline{\mathcal{A}}$ on the invertibility property. On input of (m, r, y), $\overline{\mathcal{A}}$ calls $\mathcal{A}$ on input of (m, r) and outputs its output.

If $r \leftarrow \overline{S}^{-1}(m, y)$ for $y \leftarrow \overline{S}(m)$, $\overline{\mathcal{A}}$ simulates game $\mathbf{G}_1$ for $\mathcal{A}$. If $r \leftarrow \{0,1\}^{n(\lambda)}$, $\overline{\mathcal{A}}$ simulates game $\mathbf{G}_2$ for $\mathcal{A}$. Therefore, $\Pr[out_1 = 1] = \Pr[Exp^{\mathsf{inv}}_{\overline{\mathcal{A}},m,0}(\lambda) = 1]$ and $\Pr[out_2 = 1] = \Pr[Exp^{\mathsf{inv}}_{\overline{\mathcal{A}},m,1}(\lambda) = 1]$. $\qquad\square$

Hence, $Adv^{\mathsf{pre}}_{\mathcal{A},m}(\lambda) = |\Pr[out_2 = 1] - \Pr[out_0 = 1]| \leq Adv^{\mathsf{close}}_{\overline{\mathcal{A}},m}(\lambda) + Adv^{\mathsf{inv}}_{\overline{\mathcal{A}}',m}(\lambda)$ for some PPT adversaries $\overline{\mathcal{A}}$ and $\overline{\mathcal{A}}'$. $\qquad\square$

Lemma 2. *If* $\mathsf{PREH}^{\mathsf{rand}}_{\approx_c}$ *holds, then* $\mathsf{ISH}^{\mathsf{rand}}_{\approx_c}$ *holds.*

Proof. We prove the statement for the computational randomized case. The remaining cases are similar.

Assume $\mathsf{PREH}^{\mathsf{rand}}_{\approx_c}$ holds. Let S be a PPT algorithm. $\mathsf{PREH}^{\mathsf{rand}}_{\approx_c}$ implies that for S there exist efficient algorithms E_S (potentially randomized) with output length $n(\lambda)$ and D_S (deterministic) satisfying correctness and pseudorandomness.

For $m \in L, r \in \{0,1\}^{n(\lambda)}, y \in \{0,1\}^*$, we define the alternative sampler as $\overline{S}(m; r) := \mathsf{D}_S(m, r)$ (randomized) and the corresponding inverse sampler $\overline{S}^{-1}(m, y) := \mathsf{E}_S(m, y)$ (potentially randomized).

Closeness. Let $\mathcal{A}$ be an adversary on closeness. We consider a sequence of games starting from $Exp^{\mathsf{close}}_{\mathcal{A},m,0}$ and concluding in $Exp^{\mathsf{close}}_{\mathcal{A},m,1}$, see Fig. 4.

$\mathbf{G}_0$	$\mathbf{G}_1$	$\mathbf{G}_2$	$\mathbf{G}_3$
$r_S \leftarrow \{0,1\}^{p(\lambda)}$	$r_S \leftarrow \{0,1\}^{p(\lambda)}$	$r_S \leftarrow \{0,1\}^{p(\lambda)}$	$r_S \leftarrow \{0,1\}^{p(\lambda)}$
$y_S := S(m; r_S)$	$y_S := S(m; r_S)$	$y_S := S(m; r_S)$	$y_S := S(m; r_S)$
return $\mathcal{A}(m, y_S)$	$r_D \leftarrow \mathsf{E}_S(m, y_S)$	$r_D \leftarrow \mathsf{E}_S(m, y_S)$	$r_D \leftarrow \{0,1\}^{n(\lambda)}$
	$y_D := \mathsf{D}_S(m, r_D)$	$y_D := \mathsf{D}_S(m, r_D)$	$y_D := \mathsf{D}_S(m, r_D)$
	return $\mathcal{A}(m, y_S)$	**return** $\mathcal{A}(m, y_D)$	**return** $\mathcal{A}(m, y_D)$

Fig. 4. Hybrids used in the proof of closeness.

The difference between game $\mathbf{G}_0$ and game $\mathbf{G}_1$ is only conceptional, hence, $\Pr[out_0 = 1] = \Pr[out_1 = 1]$.

$\mathbf{G}_1$ and $\mathbf{G}_2$ proceed exactly identical if $y_S = y_D$. More formally, let F be the event that $y_S \neq y_D$. We have that $out_1 = 1 \wedge \neg F \Leftrightarrow out_2 \wedge \neg F$. Hence, the Difference Lemma (due to Shoup, [37]) bounds $|\Pr[out_2 = 1] - \Pr[out_1 = 1]| \leq \Pr[F]$. Correctness guarantees that for all $m \in L$, $\Pr[F] = \Pr[y_S \leftarrow S(m) \colon \mathsf{D}_S(m, \mathsf{E}_S(m, y_S)) \neq y_S] = \epsilon_{\mathsf{dec-error}}(\lambda)$ is negligible.

Claim. For all PPT adversaries $\mathcal{A}$, for all $m \in L$, there exists a PPT adversary $\overline{\mathcal{A}}$, such that $|\Pr[out_3 = 1] - \Pr[out_2 = 1]| \leq Adv_{\overline{\mathcal{A}},m}^{\mathsf{pre}}(\lambda)$.

Proof. Construct an adversary $\overline{\mathcal{A}}$ on pseudorandomness as follows. On input of $(m, u =: r_D)$, $\overline{\mathcal{A}}$ calls $\mathcal{A}$ on input $(m, \mathsf{D}_S(m, r_D))$ and outputs the resulting output. If $u \leftarrow \mathsf{E}_S(m, y)$ for $y \leftarrow S(m)$, $\overline{\mathcal{A}}$ perfectly simulates game $\mathbf{G}_2$ for $\mathcal{A}$. Otherwise, if u is uniformly random over $\{0,1\}^{n(\lambda)}$, $\overline{\mathcal{A}}$ perfectly simulates game $\mathbf{G}_3$ for $\mathcal{A}$. Hence, $\Pr[out_3 = 1] = \Pr[Exp_{\overline{\mathcal{A}},m,1}^{\mathsf{pre}}(\lambda) = 1]$ and $\Pr[out_2 = 1] = \Pr[Exp_{\overline{\mathcal{A}},m,0}^{\mathsf{pre}}(\lambda) = 1]$. $\square$

Hence, $Adv_{\mathcal{A},m}^{\mathsf{close}}(\lambda) = |\Pr[out_3 = 1] - \Pr[out_0 = 1]| \leq Adv_{\overline{\mathcal{A}},m}^{\mathsf{pre}}(\lambda) + \epsilon_{\mathsf{dec-error}}(\lambda)$ for some PPT adversary $\overline{\mathcal{A}}$.

Invertibility. We consider a sequence of hybrids, see Fig. 5.

$\mathbf{G}_0$	$\mathbf{G}_1$	$\mathbf{G}_2$
$r \leftarrow \{0,1\}^{n(\lambda)}$	$r_S \leftarrow \{0,1\}^{p(\lambda)}$	$r_S \leftarrow \{0,1\}^{p(\lambda)}$
$y := \mathsf{D}_S(m, r)$	$y_S := S(m; r_S)$	$y_S := S(m; r_S)$
$\bar{r} \leftarrow \mathsf{E}_S(m, y)$	$r_D \leftarrow \mathsf{E}_S(m, y_S)$	$r_D \leftarrow \mathsf{E}_S(m, y_S)$
return $\mathcal{A}(m, \bar{r}, y)$	**return** $\mathcal{A}(m, r_D, y_S)$	$y_D := \mathsf{D}_S(m, r_D)$
		return $\mathcal{A}(m, r_D, y_S)$

$\mathbf{G}_3$	$\mathbf{G}_4$	$\mathbf{G}_5$
$r_S \leftarrow \{0,1\}^{p(\lambda)}$	$r_S \leftarrow \{0,1\}^{p(\lambda)}$	$r_D \leftarrow \{0,1\}^{n(\lambda)}$
$y_S := S(m; r_S)$	$y_S := S(m; r_S)$	$y_D := \mathsf{D}_S(m, r)$
$r_D \leftarrow \mathsf{E}_S(m, y_S)$	$r_D \leftarrow \{0,1\}^{n(\lambda)}$	**return** $\mathcal{A}(m, r_D, y_D)$
$y_D := \mathsf{D}_S(m, r_D)$	$y_D := \mathsf{D}_S(m, r_D)$	
return $\mathcal{A}(m, r_D, y_D)$	**return** $\mathcal{A}(m, r_D, y_D)$	

Fig. 5. Hybrids used in the proof of invertibility.

Claim. For all PPT adversaries $\mathcal{A}$, for all $m \in L$, there exists a PPT adversary $\overline{\mathcal{A}}$, such that $|\Pr[out_1 = 1] - \Pr[out_0 = 1]| \leq Adv_{\overline{\mathcal{A}},m}^{\mathsf{pre}}(\lambda) + \epsilon_{\mathsf{dec-error}}(\lambda)$.

Proof. Let $\mathcal{A}$ be an adversary distinguishing $\mathbf{G}_0$ and $\mathbf{G}_1$. Construct an adversary $\overline{\mathcal{A}}$ on the closeness property. On input of (m, y), $\overline{\mathcal{A}}$ computes $\overline{r} \leftarrow \mathsf{E}_S(m, y)$ and calls $\mathcal{A}$ on input $(m, \overline{r}, y)$. If $y \leftarrow \overline{S}(m)$, $\overline{\mathcal{A}}$ simulates game $\mathbf{G}_0$ for $\mathcal{A}$. Else, if $y \leftarrow S(m)$, $\overline{\mathcal{A}}$ simulates game $\mathbf{G}_1$ for $\mathcal{A}$. Hence, $|\Pr[out_1 = 1] - \Pr[out_0 = 1]| = Adv_{\overline{\mathcal{A}}, m}^{\mathsf{close}}(\lambda)$. $\qquad\square$

The difference between $\mathbf{G}_1$ and $\mathbf{G}_2$ is purely conceptional. Hence, $\Pr[out_1 = 1] = \Pr[out_2 = 1]$. $\mathbf{G}_2$ and $\mathbf{G}_3$ behave identical if $y_D = y_S$. Let F denote the failure event $y_D \neq y_S$. We have that $out_2 = 1 \wedge \neg \Leftrightarrow out_3 \wedge \neg F$. The Difference Lemma (due to Shoup, [37]) bounds $|\Pr[out_3 = 1] - \Pr[out_2 = 1]| \leq \Pr[F]$. Due to correctness, for all $m \in L$, $\Pr[F] = \Pr[y_S \leftarrow S(m) \colon \mathsf{D}_S(m, \mathsf{E}_S(m, y_S)) \neq y_S] = \epsilon_{\mathsf{dec-error}}(\lambda)$ is negligible.

Claim. For all PPT adversaries $\mathcal{A}$, for all $m \in L$, there exists a PPT adversary $\overline{\mathcal{A}}$, such that $|\Pr[out_4 = 1] - \Pr[out_3 = 1]| \leq Adv_{\overline{\mathcal{A}}, m}^{\mathsf{pre}}(\lambda)$.

Proof. Construct a PPT adversary $\overline{\mathcal{A}}$ on the pseudorandomness property. On input of (m, u), $\overline{\mathcal{A}}$ calls $\mathcal{A}$ on input $(m, u =: r_D, \mathsf{D}_S(m, u) =: y_D)$ and outputs the resulting output. If $u \leftarrow \mathsf{E}_S(m, y)$ for $y \leftarrow S(m)$, $\overline{\mathcal{A}}$ perfectly simulates game $\mathbf{G}_3$ for $\mathcal{A}$. Otherwise, if u is uniformly random over $\{0,1\}^{n(\lambda)}$, $\overline{\mathcal{A}}$ perfectly simulates game $\mathbf{G}_4$ for $\mathcal{A}$. Hence, $\Pr[out_3 = 1] = \Pr[Exp_{\overline{\mathcal{A}}, m, 0}^{\mathsf{pre}}(\lambda) = 1]$ and $\Pr[out_4 = 1] = \Pr[Exp_{\overline{\mathcal{A}}, m, 1}^{\mathsf{pre}}(\lambda) = 1]$. $\qquad\square$

The difference between $\mathbf{G}_4$ and $\mathbf{G}_5$ is again only conceptional and $\Pr[out_4 = 1] = \Pr[out_5 = 1]$. Hence, $|\Pr[out_5 = 1] - \Pr[out_0 = 1]| \leq 2 \cdot Adv_{\overline{\mathcal{A}}, m}^{\mathsf{pre}}(\lambda) + 2 \cdot \epsilon_{\mathsf{dec-error}}(\lambda)$ for some PPT adversary $\overline{\mathcal{A}}$. $\qquad\square$

4   Static-to-Adaptive Transformation

We obtain a natural relaxation of the pseudorandom encoding hypothesis by introducing public parameters. That is, a distribution defined via S can be pseudorandomly encoded in this relaxed sense, if there exists a probabilistic setup algorithm Setup_S and encode and decode algorithms as before such that for all $m \in L$, the event $\mathsf{D}_S(crs, \mathsf{E}_S(crs, S(m))) = S(m)$ occurs with overwhelming probability, where the probability is also over the choice of crs, and the distribution $(\mathsf{Setup}_S(1^\lambda), \mathsf{E}_S(\mathsf{Setup}_S(1^\lambda), S(m)))$ is indistinguishable from the distribution $(\mathsf{Setup}_S(1^\lambda), U_{n(\lambda)})$. See the full version [1] for more details.

There are two variants of this definition. The input m can be required to be chosen independently of crs or allowed to be chosen depending on crs. Clearly, the adaptive variant implies the non-adaptive (or static) variant. Interestingly, the opposite direction is true as well by an "indirection" argument similar to the one from the work on universal samplers [25]. A similar technique was used in the context of non-committing encryption [11] and adaptively secure MPC [12].

Theorem 2. *Let $\alpha \in \{\approx_c, \equiv_s\}$ and $\beta \in \{\mathsf{rand}, \mathsf{det}\}$. If $\mathsf{cPREH}_\alpha^\beta$ is true, then $\mathsf{acPREH}_\alpha^\beta$ is true.*

Proof. We prove the statement for the computational randomized case. A very similar proof applies to the remaining cases.

Let S be a PPT sampler with input space L. Since $\mathsf{cPREH}^{\mathrm{rand}}_{\approx_c}$ is true, for the PPT sampler S, there exist $(\mathsf{Setup}'_S, \mathsf{E}'_S, \mathsf{D}'_S)$ with output length $n'(\lambda)$ such that correctness and pseudorandomness hold (statically). Again, since $\mathsf{cPREH}^{\mathrm{rand}}_{\approx_c}$ is true, for the PPT sampler Setup'_S, there exist $(\mathsf{Setup}'', \mathsf{E}'', \mathsf{D}'')$ with output length $n''(\lambda)$ such that correctness and pseudorandomness hold (statically). [8] Note that Setup'_S does not expect an input.

In Fig. 6, we define algorithms $(\mathsf{Setup}_S, \mathsf{E}_S, \mathsf{D}_S)$ satisfying *adaptive* correctness and pseudorandomness.

$\mathsf{Setup}_S(1^\lambda)$	$\mathsf{E}_S(crs, m, y)$	$\mathsf{D}_S(crs, m, r)$
$crs'' \leftarrow \mathsf{Setup}''(1^\lambda)$	$crs' \leftarrow \mathsf{Setup}'_S(1^\lambda)$	**parse** $r =: r_1 \parallel r_2$
$crs := crs''$	$r_1 \leftarrow \mathsf{E}''(crs'', crs')$	$crs' := \mathsf{D}''(crs'', r_1)$
return crs	$r_2 \leftarrow \mathsf{E}'_S(crs', m, y)$	$y := \mathsf{D}'_S(crs', m, r_2)$
	return $r_1 \parallel r_2$	**return** y

Fig. 6. Adaptive pseudorandom encodings.

On a high level, since crs' is chosen freshly and independently after the adversary fixes the message m, selective security suffices. Furthermore, since the distribution of crs' has no input, selective security is sufficient.

Adaptive correctness. We define a series of hybrid games to prove correctness, see Fig. 7. Game $\mathbf{G_0}$ corresponds to encoding and subsequently decoding a sample y (for adaptively chosen input m) and game $\mathbf{G_1}$ is simply a reordering

$\mathbf{G_1}$	$\mathbf{G_2}$	$\mathbf{G_3}$
$crs'' \leftarrow \mathsf{Setup}''(1^\lambda)$	$crs'' \leftarrow \mathsf{Setup}''(1^\lambda)$	$crs'' \leftarrow \mathsf{Setup}''(1^\lambda)$
$crs' \leftarrow \mathsf{Setup}'_S(1^\lambda)$	$crs' \leftarrow \mathsf{Setup}'_S(1^\lambda)$	$m \leftarrow \mathcal{A}(crs'')$
$r_1 \leftarrow \mathsf{E}''(crs'', crs')$	$r_1 \leftarrow \mathsf{E}''(crs'', crs')$	$crs' \leftarrow \mathsf{Setup}'_S(1^\lambda)$
$crs'_D := \mathsf{D}''(crs'', r_1)$	$crs'_D := \mathsf{D}''(crs'', r_1)$	$y \leftarrow S(m)$
$m \leftarrow \mathcal{A}(crs'')$	$m \leftarrow \mathcal{A}(crs'')$	$r_2 \leftarrow \mathsf{E}'_S(crs', m, y)$
$y \leftarrow S(m)$	$y \leftarrow S(m)$	$y_D := \mathsf{D}'_S(crs', m, r_2)$
$r_2 \leftarrow \mathsf{E}'_S(crs', m, y)$	$r_2 \leftarrow \mathsf{E}'_S(crs', m, y)$	**return** $y_D = y$
$y_D := \mathsf{D}'_S(crs'_D, m, r_2)$	$y_D := \mathsf{D}'_S(crs', m, r_2)$	
return $y_D = y$	**return** $y_D = y$	

Fig. 7. Hybrid games for the proof of adaptive correctness.

---

[8] For notational convenience, we do not write the sampler Setup'_S as index.

of the commands of $\mathbf{G}_0$. The game hop from $\mathbf{G}_0$ to $\mathbf{G}_1$ only conceptional and $\Pr[out_0 = 1] = \Pr[out_1 = 1]$.

Claim. For all PPT adversaries $\mathcal{A}$, there exists a PPT adversary $\overline{\mathcal{A}}$, such that $|\Pr[out_2 = 1] - \Pr[out_1 = 1]| \leq \epsilon^{\mathsf{c-dec-error}}_{(\mathsf{Setup''},\mathsf{E''},\mathsf{D''}),\overline{\mathcal{A}}}(\lambda)$.

Proof. The games $\mathbf{G}_1$ and $\mathbf{G}_2$ proceed exactly identically if $crs'_D = crs'$. Let E be the event that $crs' \neq crs'_D$. We have that $out_1 = 1 \wedge \neg E \Leftrightarrow out_2 \wedge \neg E$. Due to correctness of $(\mathsf{Setup''}, \mathsf{E''}, \mathsf{D''})$,

$$\Pr \begin{bmatrix} crs'' \leftarrow \mathsf{Setup}(1^\lambda) \\ crs' \leftarrow \mathsf{Setup}'_S(1^\lambda) \\ r_1 \leftarrow \mathsf{E''}(crs'', crs') \\ crs'_D := \mathsf{D''}(crs'', r_1) \end{bmatrix} : crs'_D \neq crs'$$

is negligible. Hence, the Difference Lemma (due to Shoup, [37]) upper bounds

$$|\Pr[out_2 = 1] - \Pr[out_1 = 1]| \leq \Pr[E]. \qquad \square$$

The game hop from $\mathbf{G}_2$ to $\mathbf{G}_3$ only conceptional and $\Pr[out_2 = 1] = \Pr[out_3 = 1]$.

Claim. For all PPT adversaries $\mathcal{A}$, there exists a PPT adversary $\overline{\mathcal{A}}$, such that $\Pr[out_3 = 1] \geq 1 - \epsilon^{\mathsf{c-dec-error}}_{(\mathsf{Setup}'_S,\mathsf{E}'_S,\mathsf{D}'_S),\overline{\mathcal{A}}}(\lambda)$.

Proof. Due to correctness of $(\mathsf{Setup}'_S, \mathsf{E}'_S, \mathsf{D}'_S)$, we have that for all PPT adversaries $\overline{\mathcal{A}}$,

$$\Pr \begin{bmatrix} m \leftarrow \overline{\mathcal{A}}(1^\lambda) \\ crs' \leftarrow \mathsf{Setup}'_S(1^\lambda) \\ y \leftarrow S(m) \\ r \leftarrow \mathsf{E}'_S(crs', m, y) \\ y_D := \mathsf{D}'_S(crs', m, r) \end{bmatrix} : y = y_D$$

is overwhelming. Therefore, for all PPT adversaries $\mathcal{A}$, $\Pr[out_3 = 1]$ is overwhelming. $\qquad \square$

Adaptive Pseudorandomness. We define a series of hybrid games to prove pseudorandomness, see Fig. 8.

Game $\mathbf{G}_0$ corresponds to the adaptive pseudorandomness game. That is, $\mathbf{G}_0$ first samples crs'', the adversary $\mathcal{A}$ chooses the message m adaptively depending on crs'', and $\mathbf{G}_0$ then samples y using $S(m)$, encodes that sample and gives the encoding to $\mathcal{A}$.

Claim. For all PPT adversaries $\mathcal{A}$, there exists a PPT adversary $\overline{\mathcal{A}}$, such that $|\Pr[out_1 = 1] - \Pr[out_0 = 1]| \leq Adv^{\mathsf{crs-pre}}_{(\mathsf{Setup}'_S,\mathsf{E}'_S,\mathsf{D}'_S),\overline{\mathcal{A}}}(\lambda)$.

G_1	G_2	G_3
$crs'' \leftarrow \mathsf{Setup}''(1^\lambda)$	$crs'' \leftarrow \mathsf{Setup}''(1^\lambda)$	$crs'' \leftarrow \mathsf{Setup}''(1^\lambda)$
$m \leftarrow \mathcal{A}(crs'')$	$crs' \leftarrow \mathsf{Setup}'_S(1^\lambda)$	$r_1 \leftarrow \{0,1\}^{n''(\lambda)}$
$y \leftarrow S(m)$	$r_1 \leftarrow \mathsf{E}''(crs'', crs')$	$m \leftarrow \mathcal{A}(crs'')$
$crs' \leftarrow \mathsf{Setup}'_S(1^\lambda)$	$m \leftarrow \mathcal{A}(crs'')$	$r_2 \leftarrow \{0,1\}^{n'(\lambda)}$
$r_1 \leftarrow \mathsf{E}''(crs'', crs')$	$r_2 \leftarrow \{0,1\}^{n'(\lambda)}$	$\mathbf{return}\ \mathcal{A}(crs'', m, r_1 \parallel r_2)$
$r_2 \leftarrow \{0,1\}^{n'(\lambda)}$	$\mathbf{return}\ \mathcal{A}(crs'', m, r_1 \parallel r_2)$	
$\mathbf{return}\ \mathcal{A}(crs'', m, r_1 \parallel r_2)$		

Fig. 8. Hybrid games for the proof of adaptive pseudorandomness.

Proof. Construct an adversary $\overline{\mathcal{A}}$ on *static* pseudorandomness relative to $(\mathsf{Setup}'_S, \mathsf{E}'_S, \mathsf{D}'_S)$ as follows. On input of 1^λ, $\overline{\mathcal{A}}$ samples $crs'' \leftarrow \mathsf{Setup}''(1^\lambda)$ calls $\mathcal{A}$ on input of crs'', and outputs the message m produced by $\mathcal{A}$. In return, $\overline{\mathcal{A}}$ receives $crs' \leftarrow \mathsf{Setup}'_S(1^\lambda)$ and either $u := \mathsf{E}'_S(crs', m, S(m))$ or a uniform random string $u \leftarrow \{0,1\}^{n'(\lambda)}$ from $Exp^{\mathsf{crs-pre}}_{(\mathsf{Setup}'_S, \mathsf{E}'_S, \mathsf{D}'_S), \mathcal{A}, b}(\lambda)$. $\overline{\mathcal{A}}$ computes $r_1 \leftarrow \mathsf{E}''(crs'', crs')$, calls $\mathcal{A}$ on input of $(crs'', m, r_1 \parallel u)$ and returns $\mathcal{A}$'s output.

If $\overline{\mathcal{A}}$ plays $Exp^{\mathsf{crs-pre}}_{(\mathsf{Setup}'_S, \mathsf{E}'_S, \mathsf{D}'_S), \overline{\mathcal{A}}, 0}(\lambda)$, then it perfectly simulates $\mathbf{G}_0$. On the other hand, if $\overline{\mathcal{A}}$ plays $Exp^{\mathsf{crs-pre}}_{(\mathsf{Setup}'_S, \mathsf{E}'_S, \mathsf{D}'_S), \overline{\mathcal{A}}, 1}(\lambda)$, then it perfectly simulates $\mathbf{G}_1$. □

The game hop from $\mathbf{G}_1$ to $\mathbf{G}_2$ is only conceptional and $\Pr[out_2 = 1] = \Pr[out_1 = 1]$.

Claim. For all PPT adversaries $\mathcal{A}$, there exists a PPT adversary $\overline{\mathcal{A}}$, such that $|\Pr[out_3 = 1] - \Pr[out_2 = 1]| \leq Adv^{\mathsf{crs-pre}}_{(\mathsf{Setup}'', \mathsf{E}'', \mathsf{D}''), \overline{\mathcal{A}}}(\lambda)$.

Proof. Construct an adversary $\overline{\mathcal{A}}$ on *static* pseudorandomness relative to $(\mathsf{Setup}'', \mathsf{E}'', \mathsf{D}'')$ as follows. On input of 1^λ, $\overline{\mathcal{A}}$ returns $\perp$ since the input space L of the sampler $\mathsf{Setup}'_S(1^\lambda)$ is empty. In return, $\overline{\mathcal{A}}$ receives crs'' sampled via $\mathsf{Setup}''(1^\lambda)$ and u which is either produced via $\mathsf{E}''(crs'', \mathsf{Setup}'(1^\lambda))$ or via uniform sampling from $\{0,1\}^{n''(\lambda)}$. $\overline{\mathcal{A}}$ calls $\mathcal{A}$ on input of crs'' and receives a message m from $\mathcal{A}$. Finally, $\overline{\mathcal{A}}$ samples $r_2 \leftarrow \{0,1\}^{n'(\lambda)}$, calls $\mathcal{A}$ on input of $(crs'', m, u \parallel r_2)$ and outputs his output.

If $\overline{\mathcal{A}}$ plays $Exp^{\mathsf{crs-pre}}_{(\mathsf{Setup}'', \mathsf{E}'', \mathsf{D}''), \overline{\mathcal{A}}, 0}(\lambda)$, then it perfectly simulates $\mathbf{G}_2$. On the other hand, if $\overline{\mathcal{A}}$ plays $Exp^{\mathsf{crs-pre}}_{(\mathsf{Setup}'', \mathsf{E}'', \mathsf{D}''), \overline{\mathcal{A}}, 1}(\lambda)$, then it perfectly simulates $\mathbf{G}_3$. □

□

Acknowledgments. We thank Daniel Wichs for suggesting the unconditional static-to-adaptive transformation, as well as anonymous reviewers for extremely useful feedback.

References

1. Agrikola, T., Couteau, G., Ishai, Y., Jarecki, S., Sahai, A.: On pseudorandom encodings. Cryptology ePrint Archive, report 2020/445 (2020). https://eprint.iacr.org/2020/445
2. Barak, B., Goldreich, O., Impagliazzo, R., Rudich, S., Sahai, A., Vadhan, S., Yang, K.: On the (Im)possibility of Obfuscating Programs. In: Kilian, J. (ed.) CRYPTO 2001. LNCS, vol. 2139, pp. 1–18. Springer, Heidelberg (2001). https://doi.org/10.1007/3-540-44647-8_1
3. Beaver, D., Haber, S.: Cryptographic Protocols Provably Secure Against Dynamic Adversaries. In: Rueppel, R.A. (ed.) EUROCRYPT 1992. LNCS, vol. 658, pp. 307–323. Springer, Heidelberg (1993). https://doi.org/10.1007/3-540-47555-9_26
4. Bellovin, S.M., Merritt, M.: Encrypted key exchange: password-based protocols secure against dictionary attacks. In: 1992 IEEE Symposium on Security and Privacy, pp. 72–84. IEEE Computer Society Press, (1992). doi: 10.1109/RISP.1992.213269
5. Bitansky, N., Canetti, R., Paneth, O., Rosen, A.: On the existence of extractable one-way functions. In: Shmoys, D.B., ed., 46th ACM STOC, pp. 505–514. ACM Press, May/June 2014. doi: 10.1145/2591796.2591859
6. Boyd, C., Montague, P., Nguyen, K.: Elliptic Curve Based Password Authenticated Key Exchange Protocols. In: Varadharajan, V., Mu, Y. (eds.) ACISP 2001. LNCS, vol. 2119, pp. 487–501. Springer, Heidelberg (2001). https://doi.org/10.1007/3-540-47719-5_38
7. Brakerski, Z., Döttling, N., Garg, S., Malavolta, G.: Candidate iO from Homomorphic Encryption Schemes. In: Canteaut, A., Ishai, Y. (eds.) EUROCRYPT 2020. LNCS, vol. 12105, pp. 79–109. Springer, Cham (2020). https://doi.org/10.1007/978-3-030-45721-1_4
8. Canetti, R., Dwork, C., Naor, M., Ostrovsky, R.: Deniable Encryption. In: Kaliski, B.S. (ed.) CRYPTO 1997. LNCS, vol. 1294, pp. 90–104. Springer, Heidelberg (1997). https://doi.org/10.1007/BFb0052229
9. Canetti, R., Feige, U., Goldreich, O., Naor, M.: Adaptively secure multi-party computation. In: 28th ACM STOC, pp. 639–648. ACM Press, May 1996. doi: https://doi.org/10.1145/237814.238015
10. Canetti, R., Lindell, Y., Ostrovsky, R., Sahai, A.: Universally composable two-party and multi-party secure computation. In: 34th ACM STOC, pp. 494–503. ACM Press, May 2002. doi: 10.1145/509907.509980
11. Canetti, R., Poburinnaya, O., Raykova, M.: Optimal-Rate Non-Committing Encryption. In: Takagi, T., Peyrin, T. (eds.) ASIACRYPT 2017. LNCS, vol. 10626, pp. 212–241. Springer, Cham (2017). https://doi.org/10.1007/978-3-319-70700-6_8
12. Canetti, R., Poburinnaya, O., Venkitasubramaniam, M.: Better Two-Round Adaptive Multi-party Computation. In: Fehr, S. (ed.) PKC 2017. LNCS, vol. 10175, pp. 396–427. Springer, Heidelberg (2017). https://doi.org/10.1007/978-3-662-54388-7_14
13. Chandran, N., Goyal, V., Ostrovsky, R., Sahai, A.: Covert multi-party computation. In: 48th FOCS, pp. 238–248. IEEE Computer Society Press, October 2007. doi: 10.1109/FOCS.2007.21
14. Choi, S.G., Dachman-Soled, D., Malkin, T., Wee, H.: Improved Non-committing Encryption with Applications to Adaptively Secure Protocols. In: Matsui, M. (ed.) ASIACRYPT 2009. LNCS, vol. 5912, pp. 287–302. Springer, Heidelberg (2009). https://doi.org/10.1007/978-3-642-10366-7_17

15. Cohen, R., Shelat, A., Wichs, D.: Adaptively Secure MPC with Sublinear Communication Complexity. In: Boldyreva, A., Micciancio, D. (eds.) CRYPTO 2019. LNCS, vol. 11693, pp. 30–60. Springer, Cham (2019). https://doi.org/10.1007/978-3-030-26951-7_2

16. Dachman-Soled, D., Katz, J., Rao, V.: Adaptively Secure, Universally Composable, Multiparty Computation in Constant Rounds. In: Dodis, Y., Nielsen, J.B. (eds.) TCC 2015. LNCS, vol. 9015, pp. 586–613. Springer, Heidelberg (2015). https://doi.org/10.1007/978-3-662-46497-7_23

17. Damgård, I., Nielsen, J.B.: Improved Non-committing Encryption Schemes Based on a General Complexity Assumption. In: Bellare, M. (ed.) CRYPTO 2000. LNCS, vol. 1880, pp. 432–450. Springer, Heidelberg (2000). https://doi.org/10.1007/3-540-44598-6_27

18. Dodis, Y., Ristenpart, T., Vadhan, S.: Randomness Condensers for Efficiently Samplable, Seed-Dependent Sources. In: Cramer, R. (ed.) TCC 2012. LNCS, vol. 7194, pp. 618–635. Springer, Heidelberg (2012). https://doi.org/10.1007/978-3-642-28914-9_35

19. Even, S., Goldreich, O., Lempel, A.: A randomized protocol for signing contracts. Commun. ACM **28**(6), 637–647 (1985). https://doi.org/10.1145/3812.3818

20. Garg, S., Sahai, A.: Adaptively Secure Multi-Party Computation with Dishonest Majority. In: Safavi-Naini, R., Canetti, R. (eds.) CRYPTO 2012. LNCS, vol. 7417, pp. 105–123. Springer, Heidelberg (2012). https://doi.org/10.1007/978-3-642-32009-5_8

21. Garg, S., Gentry, C., Halevi, S., Raykova, M., Sahai, A., Waters, B.: Candidate indistinguishability obfuscation and functional encryption for all circuits. In: 54th FOCS, pp. 40–49. IEEE Computer Society Press, October 2013. doi: 10.1109/FOCS.2013.13

22. Gertner, Y., Kannan, S., Malkin, T., Reingold, O., Viswanathan, M.: The relationship between public key encryption and oblivious transfer. FOCS **2000**, 325–335 (2000). https://doi.org/10.1109/SFCS.2000.892121

23. Goldberg, A.V., Sipser, M.: Compression and ranking. In: 17th ACM STOC, pp. 440–448. ACM Press, May 1985. doi: 10.1145/22145.22194

24. Håstad, J., Impagliazzo, R., Levin, L.A., Luby, M.: A pseudorandom generator from any one-way function. SIAM J. Comput. **28**(4), 1364–1396 (1999). https://doi.org/10.1137/S0097539793244708

25. Hofheinz, D., Jager, T., Khurana, D., Sahai, A., Waters, B., Zhandry, M.: How to Generate and Use Universal Samplers. In: Cheon, J.H., Takagi, T. (eds.) ASIACRYPT 2016. LNCS, vol. 10032, pp. 715–744. Springer, Heidelberg (2016). https://doi.org/10.1007/978-3-662-53890-6_24

26. Wei, F., Li, Y., Roy, S., Ou, X., Zhou, W.: Deep Ground Truth Analysis of Current Android Malware. In: Polychronakis, M., Meier, M. (eds.) DIMVA 2017. LNCS, vol. 10327, pp. 252–276. Springer, Cham (2017). https://doi.org/10.1007/978-3-319-60876-1_12

27. Hsiao, C.-Y., Lu, C.-J., Reyzin, L.: Conditional Computational Entropy, or Toward Separating Pseudoentropy from Compressibility. In: Naor, M. (ed.) EUROCRYPT 2007. LNCS, vol. 4515, pp. 169–186. Springer, Heidelberg (2007). https://doi.org/10.1007/978-3-540-72540-4_10

28. Impagliazzo, R.: A personal view of average-case complexity. In: Proceedings of the Tenth Annual Structure in Complexity Theory Conference, Minneapolis, Minnesota, USA, 19–22 June 1995, pp. 134–147 (1995). https://doi.org/10.1109/SCT.1995.514853

29. Ishai, Y., Kumarasubramanian, A., Orlandi, C., Sahai, A.: On Invertible Sampling and Adaptive Security. In: Abe, M. (ed.) ASIACRYPT 2010. LNCS, vol. 6477, pp. 466–482. Springer, Heidelberg (2010). https://doi.org/10.1007/978-3-642-17373-8_27

30. Juels, A., Ristenpart, T.: Honey Encryption: Security Beyond the Brute-Force Bound. In: Nguyen, P.Q., Oswald, E. (eds.) EUROCRYPT 2014. LNCS, vol. 8441, pp. 293–310. Springer, Heidelberg (2014). https://doi.org/10.1007/978-3-642-55220-5_17

31. Lepinski, M., Micali, S., Shelat, A.: Fair-Zero Knowledge. In: Kilian, J. (ed.) TCC 2005. LNCS, vol. 3378, pp. 245–263. Springer, Heidelberg (2005). https://doi.org/10.1007/978-3-540-30576-7_14

32. Li, M., Vitányi, P.M.B.: Handbook of theoretical computer science, vol. a, chapter Kolmogorov Complexity and Its Applications, pp. 187–254. MIT Press, Cambridge, MA, USA (1990). ISBN 0-444-88071-2. http://dl.acm.org/citation.cfm?id=114872.114876

33. Li, M., Vitányi, P.M.B.: An Introduction to Kolmogorov Complexity and Its Applications. Texts in Computer Science, 4th edn. Springer, New York (2019). https://doi.org/10.1007/978-3-030-11298-1. ISBN 978-3-030-11297-4

34. Raz, R., Reingold, O.: On recycling the randomness of states in space bounded computation. In: 31st ACM STOC, pp. 159–168. ACM Press, May 1999. doi: 10.1145/301250.301294

35. Sahai, A., Waters, B.: How to use indistinguishability obfuscation: deniable encryption, and more. In: Shmoys, D.B. (ed.) 46th ACM STOC, pp. 475–484. ACM Press, May/June 2014. https://doi.org/10.1145/2591796.2591825

36. Shannon, C.E.: A mathematical theory of communication. Bell Syst. Tech. J. **27**(3), 379–423 (1948)

37. Shoup, V.: Sequences of games: a tool for taming complexity in security proofs. Cryptology ePrint Archive, report 2004/332 (2004). http://eprint.iacr.org/2004/332

38. Ta-Shma, A., Umans, C., Zuckerman, D.: Loss-less condensers, unbalanced expanders, and extractors. In: 33rd ACM STOC, pp. 143–152. ACM Press, July 2001. doi: 10.1145/380752.380790

39. Trevisan, L., Vadhan, S.P.: Extracting randomness from samplable distributions. In: 41st FOCS, pp. 32–42. IEEE Computer Society Press, November 2000. doi: 10.1109/SFCS.2000.892063

40. Trevisan, L., Vadhan, S.P., Zuckerman, D.: Compression of samplable sources. Comput. Compl. **14**(3), 186–227 (2005). https://doi.org/10.1007/s00037-005-0198-6

41. von Ahn, L., Hopper, N.J., Langford, J.: Covert two-party computation. In: Gabow, H.N., Fagin, R. (eds.) 37th ACM STOC, pp. 513–522. ACM Press, May 2005. https://doi.org/10.1145/1060590.1060668

42. Wee, H.: On pseudoentropy versus compressibility. In: 19th Annual IEEE Conference on Computational Complexity (CCC 2004), 21–24 June 2004, Amherst, MA, USA, pp. 29–41. IEEE Computer Society (2004). ISBN 0-7695-2120-7. doi: 10.1109/CCC.2004.1313782

43. Wee, H., Wichs, D.: Candidate obfuscation via oblivious LWE sampling. Cryptology ePrint Archive, report 2020/1042 (2020). https://eprint.iacr.org/2020/1042

44. Yao, A.C.-C.: Theory and applications of trapdoor functions (extended abstract). In: 23rd Annual Symposium on Foundations of Computer Science, Chicago, Illinois, USA, 3–5 November 1982, pp. 80–91. IEEE Computer Society (1982). doi: 10.1109/SFCS.1982.45

45. Zhandry, M.: The Magic of ELFs. In: Robshaw, M., Katz, J. (eds.) CRYPTO 2016. LNCS, vol. 9814, pp. 479–508. Springer, Heidelberg (2016). https://doi.org/10.1007/978-3-662-53018-4_18

Author Index

Printed in the United States
By Bookmasters